Criminal Law

Criminal Law

Cases and Materials

FOURTH EDITION

Stephen A. Saltzburg
PROFESSOR OF LAW
THE GEORGE WASHINGTON UNIVERSITY LAW SCHOOL

John L. Diamond
PROFESSOR OF LAW
UNIVERSITY OF CALIFORNIA
HASTINGS COLLEGE OF THE LAW

Kit Kinports
POLISHER DISTINGUISHED FACULTY SCHOLAR AND
PROFESSOR OF LAW
PENNSYLVANIA STATE UNIVERSITY
DICKINSON SCHOOL OF LAW

Thomas H. Morawetz
TAPPING REEVE PROFESSOR OF LAW AND ETHICS
UNIVERSITY OF CONNECTICUT SCHOOL OF LAW

Rory K. Little
JOSEPH W. COTCHETT PROFESSOR OF LAW
UNIVERSITY OF CALIFORNIA
HASTINGS COLLEGE OF THE LAW

CAROLINA ACADEMIC PRESS
Durham, North Carolina

ISBN 978-1-53100-418-7
eISBN 978-1-53100-419-4
Looseleaf ISBN 978-1-53100-517-7
LCCN 2017942690

Carolina Academic Press, LLC
700 Kent Street
Durham, North Carolina 27701
Telephone (919) 489-7486
Fax (919) 493-5668
www.cap-press.com

Printed in the United States of America
2018 Printing

In gratitude to our families and our students.

Summary of Contents

Contents

Preface

This casebook is our attempt to freshen and vivify the study of criminal law in several ways. We use theoretical perspectives and questions as a framework for prompting students to reflect on the general purposes of law and government. In doing so, we hope to acquaint them with a spectrum of controversial and stimulating contemporary approaches, from liberalism to critical theory. At the same time, the book is unusually rich and varied in its presentation of substantive material. These features allow unprecedented flexibility in tailoring an introductory course in criminal law to your interests and those of your students.

We bring a variety of insights and points of view to criminal law. In addition to our backgrounds in criminal law, our publications and teaching experiences extend to many related areas, such as criminal procedure, trial advocacy, analytical jurisprudence, feminist theory, critical legal studies, and evidence. Insights from all these areas are pervasive throughout this book.

While most casebooks focus primarily on homicide as the illustrative crime, this book offers an exciting menu of opportunities to teach substantive criminal law in different ways. In addition to its comprehensive coverage of homicide, it also features a long section on rape that draws extensively on new scholarship about current controversies. Our treatment of property crimes includes stimulating chapters on theft and other "advanced" property crimes.

The book also provides the reader an opportunity to consider in depth the theoretical and practical issues posed in cases involving white-collar crimes. Several chapters and sections of chapters ask students to focus on the increasing interaction between civil and criminal law. (This is particularly relevant since most students will not end up practicing criminal law.) The interaction is explored in such questions as: When is a breach of contract criminal false pretenses? When is a negotiating threat extortion? When is a company's contribution a bribe? When does misuse of a computer or trade information constitute criminal theft?

Moreover, this book introduces students to a variety of theoretical perspectives in a clear and accessible way. Throughout the book, we explain and employ such perspectives as moralism, liberalism, economics and law, critical legal theory, feminist theory, and critical race theory, and we focus attention on their practical implications.

The first chapter asks students to consider controversial applications of criminal law and invites them to formulate the purposes and boundaries of criminal law. It also offers a brief introduction to different ways of looking at the criminal sanction's origins and justifications. Chapter 2 provides an array of perspectives on punishment that differs markedly in scope and depth from the treatments available in other casebooks. It includes materials on the history, the psychology, and the economics of punishment—with comprehensive coverage of capital punishment, the pros and cons of incarceration, alternative sentencing, the Federal Sentencing Guidelines, and the proposed revisions to the Model Penal Code's sentencing provisions.

The substantive and doctrinal chapters that follow incorporate the perspectives of the introductory chapters. Finally, Chapter 16 describes a variety of theoretical perspectives in greater depth. Depending on time constraints and preference, the instructor can use this chapter in the introductory weeks or as background to enrich discussion of substantive topics throughout the course.

The cases are selected to excite students and provoke their interest. Many raise questions about such contemporary concerns as civil rights, issues affecting women and people of color, economic rights and relations, and public policy. In many instances, the cases stress evolving and controversial questions concerning the role of law and politics. Other cases touch on political scandals from Watergate to Irangate to the Clinton impeachment hearings.

Some of the cases directly implicate the interests of students. They involve, for example, defendants who used university computers without authorization, stole examination questions, or referred police informants to campus drug dealers.

The book is designed to provide an unprecedented range of options. The theoretical and substantive materials are presented in such a manner that the instructor can choose the coverage most appropriate for his or her class and can vary and tailor the format from year to year.

————————

We are greatly indebted to our student research assistants for their exemplary, imaginative, and significant contributions to all phases of the creation of this casebook. We wish to express our gratitude to the following individuals: at the University of California, Hastings College of the Law, Bret C. Birdsong, Michael A. Cox, Benjamin P. Fay, David J. Huffaker, Stefan P. Kennedy, Geoffrey H. Simon, Lucia M. Walters, and Kathryn P. Wilke; at the University of Connecticut School of Law, Christopher Kelland, James Scrimgeour, and Kevin Shay; at George Washington University Law School, Elisa D'Andrea and Rubin M. Sinins; at the University of Illinois College of Law, Orete Jonas, Bates McIntyre, Mike McMorrow, Michael Schafler, Aylon Schulte, Dawn Weber, and Mary Beth Welch.

In addition, this book could not have been published without the extraordinary help of Terri MacFarlane Hovde of the staff of the University of Illinois College of Law; and Stephen R. Lothrop, supervisor of faculty support, and Margaret G. Arnold of the library staff at the University of California, Hastings College of the Law. We would also like to thank Dean Jack Friedenthal and Dean Michael Young for providing equipment, resources, and support for both the first and second editions.

For the second edition, we are additionally very indebted for the helpful suggestions of Professors Kate Bloch, Evan Tsen Lee, and Rory K. Little of the University of California, Hastings College of the Law; the excellent research assistance of Paul J. Myslin; the very generous assistance of librarians John Borden, Charles Marcus, Vincent Moyer, Jenni Parrish, and Linda Weir of the University of California, Hastings College of the Law, and the exceptional assistance of Stephen R. Lothrop, Beverly Taylor, and Barbara Topchov of Faculty Support at the University of California, Hastings College of the Law.

For the third edition, we are grateful for the very able research assistance of Michael Cummings, Dennis Griffin, and Meredith Long of the University of Connecticut School of Law, and Edward Ahn, Todd Daloz, and Morgan Weibel of the University of California, Hastings College of the Law, and for the very helpful assistance of Divina Morgan of Faculty Support at the University of California, Hastings College of the Law.

For the fourth edition, we are grateful for the industrious and imaginative research assistance of Martha Adams, Benjamin Cantor, Stephanie O'Loughlin, and Michael Rondon of the University of Connecticut School of Law, and Amy Dunitz, Arash Razavi, Matthew Reneris, Anthony Rodregous, Philip Tacason, and Karim Troost of the University of California, Hastings College of the Law, and for the very helpful assistance of Divina Morgan of Faculty Support at the University of California, Hastings College of the Law.

Criminal Law

Chapter 1

The Nature and Structure of Criminal Law

[A] The Core and Periphery of Criminal Law

[1] The Familiarity of Criminal Law

Articles, shows, and books about crime fill newspapers, television, the best-seller list, and the movie multiplex. Crime is one of the main preoccupations of news and culture, and it has played this role throughout human history. Even those who are lucky enough to avoid direct involvement in crime experience it vicariously.

With whom do we identify when we think and fantasize about crime? Many of us see ourselves as potential victims. Crime embodies our most serious fears. Criminal law and the institutions behind it safeguard us against disruption, even termination, of our lives. Other identifications are also at work. We want not only protection from harm but an active role in protecting ourselves. In our imagination we are the police, private investigators, prosecutors, or judges. We defend order against those who threaten it.

Even this oversimplifies our interest. Do we not play out, in our imagination if not in our actions, the roles of law-breakers? To understand crime is to understand what moves persons to commit crime, to stand in the shoes of criminals. According to many accounts of the natural world in philosophy and myth, disorder and mutual predation are the norm, while order and mutual respect are artificial. Criminal law, paradigmatically among the branches of law, imposes a regime of responsibility, judgment, and control. Yet we are all witnesses to the temptation to act irrationally or irresponsibly.

Thus, crime is psychologically important both as fact and symbol. Symbolically it represents the essence of law in general, the imposition of order and reason over impulse and arbitrary action.

[2] The Capacity to Obey

Let's assume that most of us never commit crimes. The most flattering explanation is that we generally act out of moral principle and respect for others. A less flattering explanation is that we obey because we fear punishment. No doubt the motivation to commit crime is affected by economic, sociological, and psychological factors.

In drafting any criminal code, legislators must consider the capacity of persons to obey. Should laws be formulated in such a way that the average person finds it easy to obey? Or should laws set an ideal of conduct, one that may present a superhuman challenge in some circumstances? Of course, it would be self-defeating to set a standard that most persons most of the time cannot satisfy. But perhaps society *may* justifiably set a standard that demands superhuman sacrifice in identifiable but *rare* circumstances. For example, we generally excuse persons acting under duress, namely those who cause harm because they were coerced to do so by serious threats. ("We have kidnapped your family. You will never see them again unless you commit the following terrorist act . . . .") Should we allow the duress defense — or should we demand resistance and resilience from those unlucky enough to fall into such circumstances?

In posing these dilemmas, we take for granted the idea of the average person with normal capacities for self-control. But do we agree about what this means? The following case considers whether we have a clear idea about the capacities of the average person and how the demands of the criminal law are affected by that understanding.

The Queen v. Dudley & Stephens
Queens Bench Division
14 Q.B.D. 273 (1884)

Indictment for the murder of Richard Parker on the high seas within the jurisdiction of the Admiralty.

At the trial before Huddleston, B., at the Devon and Cornwall Winter Assizes, November 7, 1884, the jury, at the suggestion of the learned judge, found the facts of the case in a special verdict which stated

"that on July 5, 1884, the prisoners, Thomas Dudley and Edward Stephens, with one Brooks, all able-bodied English seamen, and the deceased also an English boy, between seventeen and eighteen years of age, the crew of an English yacht, a registered English vessel, were cast away in a storm on the high seas 1600 miles from the Cape of Good Hope, and were compelled to put into an open boat belonging to the said yacht. That in this boat they had no supply of water and no supply of food, except two 1lb. tins of turnips, and for three days they had nothing else to subsist upon. That on the fourth day they caught a small turtle, upon which they subsisted for a few days, and this was the only food they had up to the twentieth day when the act now in question was committed. That on the twelfth day the remains of the turtle were entirely consumed, and for the next eight days they had nothing to eat. That they had no fresh water, except such rain as they from time to time caught in their oilskin capes. That the boat was drifting on the ocean, and was probably more than 1000 miles away from land. That on the eighteenth day, when they had been seven days without food and five without water, the prisoners spoke to Brooks as to what should be done if no succour came, and suggested that some one should be sacrificed to save the rest, but Brooks dissented, and the boy, to whom they were understood to refer, was not consulted. That on the 24th of July, the day before the act now in question, the prisoner Dudley proposed to Stephens and Brooks that lots should be cast who should be put to death to save the rest, but Brooks refused to consent, and it was not put to the boy, and in point of fact there was no drawing of lots. That on that day the prisoners spoke of their having families, and suggested it would be better to kill the boy that their lives should be saved, and Dudley proposed that if there was no vessel in sight by the morrow morning the boy should be killed. The next day, the 25th of July, no vessel appearing, Dudley told Brooks that he had better go and have a sleep, and made signs to Stephens and Brooks that the boy had better be killed. The prisoner Stephens agreed to the act, but Brooks dissented from it. That the boy was then lying at the bottom of the boat quite helpless, and extremely weakened by famine and by drinking sea water, and unable to make any resistance, nor did he ever assent to his being killed. The prisoner Dudley offered a prayer asking forgiveness for them all if either of them should be tempted to commit a rash act, and that their souls might be saved. That Dudley, with the assent of Stephens, went to the boy, and telling him that his time was come, put a knife into his throat and killed him then and there; that the three men fed upon the body and blood of the boy for four days; that on the fourth day after the act had been committed the boat was picked up by a passing vessel, and the prisoners were rescued, still alive, but in the lowest state of prostration. That they were carried to the port of Falmouth, and committed for trial at Exeter. That if the men had not fed upon the body of the boy they would probably not have survived to be so picked up and rescued, but would within the four days have died of famine. That the boy, being in a much weaker condition, was likely to have died before them. That at the time of the act in question there was no sail in sight, nor any reasonable prospect of relief. That under these circumstances there appeared to the prisoners every probability that unless they then fed or very soon fed upon the boy or one of themselves they would die of starvation. That there was no appreciable chance of saving life except by killing some one for the others to eat. That assuming any necessity to kill anybody, there was no greater necessity for killing the boy than any of the other three men. But whether upon the whole matter by the jurors found the killing of Richard Parker by Dudley and Stephens be felony and murder the jurors are ignorant, and pray the advice of the Court thereupon, and if upon the whole matter the Court shall be of opinion that the killing of Richard Parker be felony and murder, then the jurors say that Dudley and Stephens were each guilty of felony and murder as alleged in the indictment."

LORD COLERIDGE, CHIEF JUSTICE.

. . . [I]t appears sufficiently that the prisoners were subject to terrible temptation, to sufferings which might break down the bodily power of the strongest man, and try the conscience of the best. Other details yet more harrowing, facts still more loathsome and appalling, were presented to the jury, and are to be found recorded in my learned Brother's notes. But nevertheless this is clear, that the prisoners put to death a weak and unoffending boy upon the chance of preserving their own lives by feeding upon his flesh and blood after he was killed, and with a certainty of depriving him of any possible chance of survival. The verdict finds in terms that: "if the men had not fed upon the body of the boy, they would probably have not survived . . ." and that "the boy, being in a much weaker condition, was likely to have died before them." They might possibly have been picked up next day by a passing ship; they might not have been picked up at all; in either case it is obvious that the killing of the boy would have been an unnecessary and profitless act. It is found by the verdict that the boy was incapable of resistance, and, in fact, made none; and it is not even suggested that his death was due to any violence on his part attempted against, or even so much as feared by, those who killed him. Under these circumstances the jury say that they are ignorant whether those who killed him were guilty of murder, and have referred it to this Court to determine what is the legal consequence which follows from the facts which they have found. . . .

[T]he real question in the case [is] whether killing under the circumstances set forth in the verdict be or not be murder. The contention that it could be anything else was, to the minds of us all, both new and strange, . . . a proposition which appeared to us to be at once dangerous, immoral, and opposed to all legal principle and analogy. . . . [I]t is said that it follows from various definitions of murder in books of authority . . . that in order to save your own life you may lawfully take away the life of another, when that other is neither attempting nor threatening yours, nor is guilty of any illegal act whatever towards you or anyone else. But if these definitions be looked at they will not be found to sustain this contention. . . .

[I]t is admitted that the deliberate killing of this unoffending and unresisting boy was clearly murder, unless the killing can be justified by some well recognised excuse admitted by the law. It is further admitted that there was in this case no such excuse, unless the killing was justified by what has been called "necessity." But the temptation to the act which existed here was not what the law has ever called necessity. Nor is this to be regretted. Though law and morality are not the same, and though many things may be immoral which are not necessarily illegal, yet the absolute divorce of law from morality would be of fatal consequence, and such divorce would follow if the temptation to murder in this case were to be held by law an absolute defence of it. It is not so. To preserve one's life is generally speaking, a duty, but it may be the plainest and the highest duty to sacrifice it. War is full of instances in which it is a man's duty not to live, but to die. The duty, in case of shipwreck, of a captain to his crew, of the crew to the passengers, or soldiers to women and children . . . ; these duties impose on men the moral necessity, not of the preservation, but of the sacrifice of their lives for others, from which in no country, least of all, it is to be hoped, in England, will men ever shrink, as indeed, they have not shrunk. It is not correct, therefore, to say that there is any absolute or unqualified necessity to preserve one's life. . . . It is not needful to point out the awful danger of admitting the principle which has been contended for. Who is to be the judge of this sort of necessity? By what measure is the comparative value of lives to be measured? Is it to be strength, or intellect, or what? It is plain that the principle leaves to him who is to profit by it to determine the necessity which will justify him in deliberately taking another's life to save his own. In this case the weakest, the youngest, the most unresisting was chosen. Was it more necessary to kill him than one of the grown men? The answer must be, "No." . . .

It must not be supposed that, in refusing to admit temptation to be an excuse for crime, it is forgotten how terrible the temptation was; how awful the suffering; how hard in such trials to keep the judgment straight and the conduct pure. We are often compelled to set up standards we cannot reach ourselves, and to lay down rules which we could not ourselves satisfy. But a man has no right to declare temptation to be an excuse, though he might himself have yielded to it, nor allow compassion for the criminal to change or weaken in any manner the legal definition of the crime. It is therefore our duty to declare that the prisoners' act in this case was wilful murder.

Judgment for the Crown. [Sentence of death, commuted a week later by Queen Victoria's Home Secretary to six months' imprisonment.]

Notes and Questions

1. **The Necessity Defense.** The modern term for the kind of defense Dudley and Stephens sought to offer is necessity, the claim that they intended to prevent a greater evil (the death of all occupants of the lifeboat) by committing a lesser evil (the killing of the cabin boy). Obviously such extreme situations arise rarely. But when they do, they may receive world-wide attention. The plight of the survivors of a crash in the Andes, who were also faced with the alternatives of cannibalism or death, is the subject of the book ALIVE by Piers Paul Read (1979) and the movie made from it.

2. **Modern Law.** Would Dudley and Stephens prevail under modern law? Should they prevail? The modern law on necessity is considered in detail in Chapter 14, Section D.

A question that is relevant to modern law no more and no less than it is to Dudley and Stephens is whether punishing them achieves any of the goals of punishment. The purpose of specific deterrence, preventing the cannibals from repeating their act, seems irrelevant since the circumstances of the shipwreck are unlikely to recur. The same can be said for general deterrence. Very few persons will, one hopes, find themselves in such a situation—and, if in fact they do, the imperative to save their lives may trump their legal obligations. The purpose of reform or rehabilitation is similarly oblique to the case. It is hardly clear that Dudley and Stephens need rehabilitation. It remains to consider retribution. Does their act constitute an evil that calls for retribution in a verdict that amplifies society's values? Lord Coleridge certainly thought so. Do you?

3. Pardons and Commutations. The commutation of Dudley's and Stephens' death sentence presumably reflects appreciation of special moral circumstances. Is it generally desirable to dispose of unusually difficult cases in this way, by applying the law in all its harshness and then allowing the processes of pardon or commutation to respond to special facts? What are the drawbacks of such an approach? Is it likely to be applied fairly in the sense of providing similar dispositions for similar offenders?

4. Law and the Ability to Comply. Compare Lord Coleridge's view that "we are often compelled to set up standards we cannot reach ourselves" with the following statement taken from the Model Penal Code commentaries on the subject of duress:

> Though . . . the submission that the actor lacked the fortitude to make the moral choice should not be entertained as a defense, a different situation is presented if the claimed excuse is based upon the incapacity of men in general to resist the coercive pressures to which the individual has succumbed. . . . Law is ineffective in the deepest sense, indeed . . . it is hypocritical, if it imposes on the actor who has the misfortune to confront a dilemmatic choice, a standard that his judges are not prepared to affirm that they should and could comply with if their turn to face the problem should arise. Condemnation in such a case is bound to be an ineffective threat; what is, however, more significant is that it is divorced from any moral base. . . .

Model Penal Code § 2.09 Comment at 374–75.

Can this view be reconciled with that of Lord Coleridge? If not, which position do you find more compelling?

Keep in mind that both views reflect deep philosophical positions about law. Lord Coleridge's view is motivated by the sense that law should tell us how to behave. It should set the highest standard for mutual respect and deference. He maintains the Victorian notion that our institutions should make us better than we are naturally, that they should require us to transcend our natures. The modern view reflected in the Model Penal Code is much less idealistic and much more skeptical. It implies that the law can do little to make us better or worse morally, and it insists on a minimal standard of conduct that allows us to live with one another with all our flaws.

5. More on Cannibalism. An elegant historical study of most aspects of the *Dudley & Stephens* case is Cannibalism and the Common Law, by A.W. Brian Simpson (1984). *See also* Allen Boyer, *Crime, Cannibalism and Joseph Conrad*, 20 Loyola L.A. L. Rev. 9 (1986).

Another interesting and detailed study of *The Queen v. Dudley & Stephens* is The Custom of the Sea by Neil Hanson (1999). Hanson discusses the trial in detail using personal letters and diaries, court records, and first person narratives. Barry Collins' play, *Judgment* (1991), is a three-hour monologue on the subject of cannibalism. It was hugely successful as a theater piece in Britain. It explores cannibalism among Russian soldiers trapped by retreating foreign troops near the end of World War II.

In 1838, a half-century before the *Dudley & Stephens* case, Edgar Allen Poe published his only complete novel, a story about a marooned whaling boat that coincidentally featured a character named Richard Parker. In the book, THE NARRATIVE OF ARTHUR GORDON PYM OF NANTUCKET, Parker drew the "short straw" and was promptly cannibalized. Less coincidental, the tiger stranded on a lifeboat with the title character in LIFE OF PI, the 2002 novel that became an award-winning film in 2012, was also called Richard Parker.

[3] The Use and Abuse of Freedom

The legitimacy of criminal law rests on distinguishing between the use and abuse of freedom. The most flagrant abuse of freedom occurs when one acts unjustifiably with the intention of harming others or creates unjustifiably a high risk that they will be harmed.

In this sense, criminal law rests on a shared conception of what kinds of harm are most serious and what kinds of limits on freedom are justified. In other words, we can define a sphere of liberty—a sphere in which government is not justified in interfering with the freedom of individuals—by restricting the role of legal prohibitions to demonstrable harms. This view of the restricted reach and role of formal criminal prohibitions lies at the heart of the work of the nineteenth-century philosopher John Stuart Mill, the father of classical liberalism. In the following selection, he tries to define the distinction between two spheres, two ways of addressing the conduct of others. On the one hand, we have conduct of which we may disapprove, but that we recognize as within the actor's rights. On the other hand, we have conduct that should be punished by the state under law. Every system of criminal law must first develop a way of making this principled distinction. (Further implications of classical liberalism for criminal law are discussed in Chapter 16.)

JOHN STUART MILL, ON LIBERTY (1859)

The distinction between the loss of consideration which a person may rightly incur by defect of prudence or of personal dignity, and the reprobation which is due to him for an offence against the rights of others, is not a merely nominal distinction. It makes a vast difference both in our feelings and in our conduct towards him whether he displeases us in things in which we think we have a right to control him, or in things in which we know that we have not. If he displeases us, we may express our distaste, and we may stand aloof from a person as well as from a thing that displeases us; but we shall not therefore feel called on to make his life uncomfortable. We shall reflect that he already bears, or will bear, the whole penalty of his error; if he spoils his life by mismanagement, we shall not, for that reason, desire to spoil it still further; instead of wishing to punish him, we shall rather endeavour to alleviate his punishment, by showing him how he may avoid or cure the evils his conduct tends to bring upon him. He may be to us an object of pity, perhaps of dislike, but not of anger or resentment; we shall not treat him like an enemy of society; the worst we shall think ourselves justified in doing is leaving him to himself, if we do not interfere benevolently by showing interest or concern for him. It is far otherwise if he has infringed the rules necessary for the protection of his fellow-creatures, individually or collectively. The evil consequences of his acts do not then fall on himself, but on others; and society, as the protector of all its members, must retaliate on him, must inflict pain on him for the express purpose of punishment, and must take care that it be sufficiently severe. In the one case, he is an offender at our bar, and we are called on not only to sit in judgment on him, but, in one shape or another, to execute our own sentence; in the other case, it is not our part to inflict any suffering on him, except what may incidentally follow from our using the same liberty in the regulation of our own affairs, which we allow to him in his.

It seems hard to reject the insight that some acts have obvious "evil consequences" and that no organized society can tolerate them. For the most part, these actions stand at the broad intersection between law and morality. They are the most destructive and unjustifiable ways in which persons can encroach upon and harm the interests of others.

Joel Feinberg explores this intersection between law and morality to uncover the uncontroversial core of criminal law in the "harm to others" principle:

JOEL FEINBERG, HARM TO OTHERS 10–12 (1984)

. . . About the propriety of one class of crimes there can be no controversy. Willful homicide, forcible rape, aggravated assault, and battery are crimes (under one name or another) everywhere in the civilized world, and no reasonable person could advocate their "decriminalization." Almost as noncontroversial as these serious "crimes against the person" are various serious "crimes against property": burglary, grand larceny, and various offenses involving fraud and misrepresentation. The common element in crimes of these two categories is the direct production of serious harm to individual persons and groups. Other kinds of properly prohibited behavior, like reckless driving and the reckless discharging of lethal weapons, are banned not because they necessarily cause harm in every case, but rather because they create unreasonable risks of harm to other persons.

Still other crimes that have an unquestioned place in our penal codes are kinds of conduct that rarely cause clear and substantial harm to any specific person or group, but are said to cause harm to "the public," "society," "the state," public institutions or practices, the general ambience of neighborhoods, the economy, the climate, or the environment. Typical of crimes in this general category are counterfeiting, smuggling, income tax evasion, contempt of court, and violation of zoning and antipollution ordinances. The harms produced by such crimes can be labeled "public" as opposed to "private" harms provided it is kept in mind that the public is composed of private individuals standing in complex social and legal relations to one another.

In some cases of public harm—for example the poisoning of a city's water supply or the undermining of a government's currency—the harm to many or all private citizens is direct and serious. In other cases—for example, a single instance of tax evasion—the harm to any given individual is highly dilute and unnoticeable. . . .

Generalizing then from the clearest cases of legitimate or proper criminalization, we can assert tentatively that it is legitimate for the state to prohibit conduct that causes serious private harm, or the unreasonable risk of such harm, or harm to important public institutions and practices. . . . More concisely, the need to prevent harm (private or public) to parties other than the actor is always an appropriate *reason* for legal coercion.

Notes and Questions

1. **Justifying Criminal Law.** Feinberg cautiously echoes Mill in observing that "the harm principle is a valid legislative principle." In his influential four-volume treatise, The Moral Limits of the Criminal Law (1984–1988), Feinberg considers three other bases on which criminal laws may be justified: offense to others, harm to self, and harmless wrongdoing. He raises the questions of how to distinguish harmful behavior from merely offensive behavior and whether offensiveness is an appropriate justification for criminal prohibitions. In considering "harm to self," he addresses the question of paternalism—whether governments are justified in prohibiting conduct because it may harm the actor. As you consider (in the next Section) some of the unusual or controversial ways in which criminal law has been used, ask yourself what kinds of harm criminal law should be concerned with, when and whether it should be concerned with offensive conduct, and whether it should be used paternalistically.

2. **Applying the "Harm to Others" Justification.** Even if the "harm to others" principle clearly fits our intuitions about the core of criminal law, its applications are by no means clear. Should we hold persons criminally liable *only* when they cause harm? Or should they be liable whenever they *try* to cause harm, whether or not they succeed? If they should be held liable for attempts, should they be punished with equal severity whether or not they succeed?

Should punishment be measured by the amount of harm actually caused, or by what the actor *intends* to cause? Suppose Jones steals stock certificates intending to deprive Smith of his fortune. However, Jones discovers that the stock certificates are nearly worthless and that Smith has vast hidden resources. How serious is Jones' crime?

3. **History and Consistency of Criminal Law.** George Fletcher, in his 1978 book Rethinking Criminal Law, suggests that modern criminal law has evolved from several different, and not necessarily compatible, general patterns of criminality. According to one pattern, guilt and punishment should depend on the extent to which the actor caused harm. This is an objective test (assuming there are objective measures for actual harm). According to a different and conflicting pattern, guilt and punishment are determined by the intentions of the actor whether or not they were

accomplished. This latter pattern reflects a subjective test. Fletcher concludes that the attempt to generalize about criminal law as a harmonious conceptual structure may have limits.

Historically, criminal law begins with situations of actual harm. Society cannot survive if individuals kill, harm, and steal from others with impunity. The convention that such acts must be punished, and punished consistently in the light of shared rules, developed early as a mandate of social order. Over time, such primitive systems came to address two kinds of complications, situations in which harm was caused accidentally rather than intentionally and situations in which persons acted with the intention to cause harm, but for some reason or other failed to achieve their goal. The first complication revealed the need to address a "state of mind" component to criminal liability. The second one involved a more basic question: in developing a system of criminal law, are we more concerned with rectifying actual harm or with identifying and punishing those who act with the *intention* of causing harm regardless of the result?

One of Fletcher's main points is that this question has never been answered decisively. Both purposes coexist in criminal law. On one hand, criminal law is based on the requirement of a criminal state of mind and a criminal act that flows from it; this way of stating the basic mandate of criminal law seems to dispense with any requirement that the act *actually* cause harm. On the other hand, we generally punish completed crimes more severely than we punish attempts and for the most part (reckless endangerment notwithstanding) we do not punish reckless behavior unless it results in actual harm. This suggests that the *actual harm* requirement continues to play a significant role.

4. The Elastic Notion of Harm. Over the last 40 to 50 years, the notion of harm as a fundamental basis for criminal law has undergone constant revision. Our basic conception of harm and the examples that come most immediately to mind involve physical harm and financial harm. But it is hard to avoid the awareness and importance of psychological harm, even if it is harder to determine and measure.

Our conception of harm now extends beyond harm-to-individuals in all sorts of ways. When we draft statutes denoting "hate" crimes, we are acknowledging harm to racial, religious, and ethnic groups that extends beyond harm to individuals. When we criminalize terrorism, we sanction acts intended to do harm to the fabric of community, to society itself. When we recognize the existence of environmental crimes, we make clear that not only humans but other entities on the planet can be harmed and merit legal protection. And, by the same token, we take account of harm not just to our contemporaries but to future generations of non-individuated persons.

[4] Controversial Crimes

Most crimes that are familiar from both fact and fiction are ones that clearly involve (in Feinberg's phrase) harm to others, crimes such as homicide, assault, rape, theft, and burglary. But the scope of criminal law is continually under revision.

Criminal law can be seen as defining the boundary between private and public matters. It is an attempt to answer the question of when someone's conduct is of such concern that public institutions must set boundaries to private choice and private action. One answer to the question is obviously that the law must intervene, that public concern trumps privacy, when one chooses to inflict harm. This answer is clear in principle, but it raises many other questions in turn.

Keep in mind how much our sense of what is a matter of such public concern that conduct must be criminalized has changed in the last 50 years. Fifty years ago there was a consensus that spousal abuse, child abuse, sexual harassment, and spousal and date rape were private matters with private solutions. At the same time, in some parts of this country, interracial dating, not to speak of interracial marriage, was criminally prohibited, as was homosexual activity.

Before we focus on the general contours of criminal law, it is useful to consider how it defines and monitors the border between public and private, and to consider as well how controversial those borders are. Some of the following considerations arise in most of these controversies.

(1) Does the prohibited conduct involve genuine harm to others, or does it merely offend some opinions about how others should conduct themselves? Is there a shared social morality—or are these merely diverse moral opinions of various subgroups, some of which may end up in the majority some of the time?

(2) How does the public-private distinction affect conduct that involves harm to one's self rather than to others? Is part of the function of criminal law paternalistic? What infringements on personal freedom may be justified by the sense that we sometimes need to be protected from ourselves?

(3) Does criminal law ever reflect ethnic, racial, or gender biases with regard to the seriousness of harm and the right to personal freedom?

[a] Unprotected Sex as Assault

State v. Stark

832 P.2d 109 (Wash. Ct. App. 1992)

PETRICH, CHIEF JUDGE.

On March 25, 1988, Calvin Stark tested positive for HIV, which was confirmed by further tests on June 25 and on June 30, 1988. From June 30, 1988, to October 3, 1989, the staff of the Clallam County Health Department had five meetings with Stark during which Stark went through extensive counseling about his infection. He was taught about "safe sex," the risk of spreading the infection, and the necessity of informing his partners before engaging in sexual activity with them. On October 3, 1989, Dr. Locke, the Clallam County Health Officer, after learning that Stark had disregarded this advice and was engaging in unprotected sexual activity, issued a cease and desist order as authorized by RCW 70.24.024(3)(b). [This statute authorizes the state to intervene when someone is found to have a sexually transmitted disease and is also found to be endangering the public health.]

Stark did not cease and desist, and, consequently, on March 1, 1990, Dr. Locke went to the county prosecutor's office intending to seek the prosecutor's assistance, pursuant to RCW 70.24.034(1), in obtaining judicial enforcement of the cease and desist order. The prosecutor instead had Dr. Locke complete a police report. The State then charged Stark with three counts of assault in the second degree under RCW 9A.36.021(1)(e).[1] Each count involved a different victim. . . .

Stark contends that his convictions should be dismissed because the State failed to present sufficient evidence of an intent to inflict bodily harm. In determining whether sufficient evidence supports a conviction, "[the] standard of review is whether, after viewing the evidence in a light most favorable to the State, any rational trier of fact could have found the essential elements of the charged crime beyond a reasonable doubt." Stark contends that there is insufficient evidence to prove that he "exposed" anyone to HIV or that he acted with intent to inflict bodily harm. Since Stark is undisputedly HIV positive, he necessarily exposed his sexual partners to the virus by engaging in unprotected sexual intercourse. The testimony of the three victims supports this conclusion.

The testimony supporting the element of intent to inflict bodily harm includes Dr. Locke's statements detailing his counseling sessions with Stark. With regard to the first victim, we know that Stark knew he was HIV positive, that he had been counseled to use "safe sex" methods, and that it had been explained to Stark that coitus interruptus will not prevent the spread of the virus. While there is evidence to support Stark's position, all the evidence viewed in a light most favorable to the State supports a finding of intent beyond a reasonable doubt. The existence of noncriminal explanations does not preclude a finding that a defendant intended to harm his sexual partners. With regard to the later victims, we have, in addition to this same evidence, Stark's neighbor's testimony that Stark, when confronted about his sexual practices, said, "I don't care. If I'm going to die, everybody's going to die." We also have the testimony of the victim in count 2 that Stark attempted to have anal intercourse with her and did have oral sex, both methods the counselors told Stark he needed to avoid.

. . . Stark contends that this court should dismiss his convictions because RCW 9A.36.021(1)(e) is unconstitutionally vague. He contends that the statute does not define the prohibited conduct with sufficient specificity to put an ordinary citizen on notice as to what conduct he or she must avoid. Statutes that are susceptible to arbitrary and discriminatory enforcement are invalid. Criminal statutes must contain ascertainable standards for consistent adjudication.

To succeed on his claim, Stark must prove . . . that the statute is unconstitutionally vague, thereby defeating the presumption of constitutionality. If persons of

---

1. [n.1] RCW 9A.36.021(1)(e) provides: "(1) A person is guilty of assault in the second degree if he or she, under circumstances not amounting to assault in the first degree: . . . (e) With intent to inflict bodily harm, exposes or transmits human immunodeficiency virus as defined in chapter 70.24 RCW. . . ."

common intelligence must necessarily guess at a statute's meaning and differ as to its application, the statute is unconstitutionally vague.

When a defendant asserts that a statute is unconstitutionally vague on its face, as opposed to vague as applied, the reviewing court must still look to the facts of the case before looking for hypothetically constitutional situations. If the defendant's conduct fits within the proscribed conduct of the statute, the defendant cannot assert other hypothetical applications of the law. . . .

Stark complains that the statute "nowhere defines the term expose, nor does it state that it is a crime to transmit the HIV virus to another human being." No reasonably intelligent person would think the statute criminalizes the transmission of HIV to nonhumans. Stark's argument regarding the term "expose" is also unpersuasive. Any reasonably intelligent person would understand from reading the statute that the term refers to engaging in conduct that can cause another person to become infected with the virus. Stark engaged in unprotected sexual intercourse with other human beings after being counseled on several occasions that such conduct would expose his partners to the virus he carries. He was not forced to guess at what conduct was criminal . . . .

We affirm the convictions.

Notes and Questions

1. AIDS and the Law. The AIDS crisis forced many legal scholars and judges to reconsider the boundaries of privacy and personal responsibility. Cases such as *Stark* remain controversial and are the harbingers of many similar legal dilemmas to come with regard to medical privacy.

2. Stark's Criminal Act. What was the basis of Stark's criminality—the act of having unprotected sex while aware that he was HIV-positive or the failure to tell his partners of his condition? If it is the former, may the law criminalize sexual activity by persons with other transmittable conditions? If it is the latter, may the law require persons to convey other kinds of information in the course of consensual activity? Is this an appropriate situation for the use of criminal sanctions?

If so, is the Washington statute too narrowly drawn in that it requires "intent to inflict bodily harm" as opposed to a likelihood of inflicting such harm? Does the statute punish only the defendant who wanted to expose a sex partner to the risks associated with HIV and not the defendant who simply did not like condoms and feared that a partner who knew the defendant was HIV-positive would refuse to have unprotected sex?

3. Cease and Desist Orders. What is the proper role of cease and desist orders of the kind to which Stark was subject? May they be used generally to limit the activity of persons whose conditions may expose others to risk? How might such orders be abused? Does a cease and desist order at least make absolutely clear to the target that certain activity is prohibited, thus making it easier to justify imposing a criminal sanction if the person ignores the order?

4. The Law of Warning and Transmission. A majority of states have enacted HIV-specific laws criminalizing the intentional or knowing transmission (or risk of transmission) of the HIV virus. The laws vary widely in content and specificity. Florida, for example, prohibits sexual intercourse by HIV-positive persons unless the partner gives informed consent expressly. Fla. Stat. Ann. § 384.24. Idaho criminalizes the intentional "transfer of bodily fluid which may contain the HIV virus." Idaho Code § 39-608. Missouri simply criminalizes any reckless conduct that exposes another person to the risk of HIV infection. Mo. Ann. Stat. § 191.677.

Needless to say, many of these provisions have been criticized as vague and of dubious constitutionality. Critics sometimes cite the California law, Cal. Health & Safety Code § 120291, which requires specific intent to transmit the HIV virus, as imposing a desirably stringent standard. But others argue that it creates a burden of proof that prosecutors will rarely be able to meet. *See* Dee McAree, *The Debate over HIV Exposure Laws*, Nat'l L.J., Sept. 29, 2003, at 4.

Challenges to recent statutes of this kind have generally failed to establish vagueness. In most such cases the defendants knew they were HIV positive and failed to inform their partners in consensual sex. The relevant statutes clearly established that such knowledge in the light of such actions satisfied the conditions for liability, such that the criteria for neither the relevant state of mind nor for the criminal act were vague. *See, e.g., State v. Gamberella*, 633 So. 2d 595 (La. 1993); *People v. Jensen*, 586 N.W.2d 748 (Mich. Ct. App. 1998).

[b] Prenatal Delivery of Drugs

Johnson v. State
578 So. 2d 419 (Fla. Dist. Ct. App. 1991)

Dauksch, Judge.

This is an appeal from two convictions for delivery of a controlled substance to minors. It was established by the evidence that appellant consumed cocaine knowing that the cocaine would pass to her soon-to-be-born fetus. Upon the birth of her children it was medically determined that each of them had received some of the cocaine into their bodies. A qualified witness testified that some of the cocaine left the mother and was received by the child after birth but before the umbilical cord was cut. Under Florida law a person comes into being upon birth. . . .

Section 893.13(1)(c), Florida Statutes (1989) says:

(c) Except as authorized by this chapter, it is unlawful for any person 18 years of age or older to deliver any controlled substance to a person under the age of 18 years, or to use or hire a person under the age of 18 years as an agent or employee in the sale or delivery of such a substance, or to use such person to assist in avoiding detection or apprehension for a violation of this chapter.

The question is whether the acts of appellant violate the statute. Logic leads us to say that appellant violated the statute.

Appellant voluntarily took cocaine into her body, knowing it would pass to her fetus and knowing (or should have known) that birth was imminent. She is deemed to know that an infant at birth is a person, and a minor, and that delivery of cocaine to the infant is illegal. We can reach no other conclusion logically.

We have spent the necessary time and effort considering the many arguments of appellant and her supporters who argue the mother's rights to her body and the analogies to the abortion cases. We have also considered appellant's assertion that the Florida legislature declined to pass a child abuse statute which forbade similar conduct. We have considered other arguments, such as what pregnant mothers might resort to if they know they may be charged with this crime; we were singularly unimpressed with those latter arguments.

This appellant on two occasions took cocaine into her pregnant body and caused the passage of that cocaine to each of her children through the umbilical cord after birth of the child, then an infant person. The statute was twice violated.

We certify to the Supreme Court of Florida that the question resolved by this opinion is of great public importance and suggest that court answer:

> whether the ingestion of a controlled substance by a mother who knows the substance will pass to her child after birth is a violation of Florida law?

Convictions Affirmed.

Johnson v. State
602 So. 2d 1288 (Fla. 1992)

HARDING, JUSTICE.

. . . I conclude that the Legislature never intended for the general drug delivery statute to authorize prosecutions of those mothers who take illegal drugs close enough in time to childbirth that a doctor could testify that a tiny amount passed from mother to child in the few seconds before the umbilical cord was cut. Criminal prosecution of mothers like Johnson will undermine Florida's express policy of "keeping families intact" and could destroy the family by incarcerating the child's mother when alternative measures could protect the child and stabilize the family.

In similar cases in which charges have been brought against mothers after delivery of drug-affected newborns, those charges have been dismissed. In *People v. Bremer*, No. 90-32227-FH (Mich. Cir. Ct. January 31, 1991), the defendant was charged with delivery of cocaine to her newborn daughter after urine samples from the defendant and child following birth tested positive for benzoylecgonine. The circuit court concluded that the Michigan Legislature never intended to include the action of the defendant under the delivery statute:

> To interpret this section to cover ingestion of cocaine by a pregnant woman would be a radical incursion upon existing law. A person may not

be punished for a crime unless her acts fall clearly within the language of the statute. The specific language of this act does not allow the strained construction advanced by the prosecution.

Neither judges nor prosecutors can make criminal laws. This is the purview of the Legislature. If the Legislature wanted to punish the uterine transfer of cocaine from a mother to her fetus, it would be up to the Legislature to consider the attending public policy and constitutional arguments and then pass its legislation. The Legislature has not done so and the court has no power to make such a law.

. . . The Court declines the State's invitation to walk down a path that the law, public policy, reason and common sense forbid it to tread. Therefore, we quash the decision below, answer the certified question in the negative, and remand with directions that Johnson's two convictions be reversed.

Notes and Questions

1. **Policy Issues.** What goals do you think the lower courts were trying to achieve by convicting Johnson of violating § 893.13(1)(c)? What values do you think the Supreme Court of Florida had in mind in reversing Johnson's conviction? Which court is using § 893.13(1)(c) in the way the legislature intended or would have anticipated? Is it appropriate for a court to use a criminal statute in a way that the legislature never intended?

What assumptions and attitudes toward women who are addicts are reflected in these uses of criminal law? Are they based on stereotypes?

Should the legislature pass a statute that criminalizes this kind of conduct? What general arguments should control the legislature's decision?

The strategists of the "war on drugs" have sometimes been accused of insensitivity to privacy. Is this a case in which the defendant's privacy has been infringed? Does the kind of dilemma represented by this situation suggest that the use of drugs should or should not be decriminalized?

2. **The Facts of *Johnson*.** Technically, *Johnson* is not about *prenatal* delivery of drugs since "it was medically determined that [the infants] received [cocaine] after birth but before the umbilical cord was cut." Why does it make a possible difference in the legal disposition of such cases that cocaine was not passed (or not only passed) to the child while it was still in the mother's body, i.e., before birth, but rather after the child emerged from the womb and before the cord was cut? Does the legal difference reflect a moral difference?

In *Whitner v. State*, 492 S.E.2d 777 (S.C. 1997), *cert. denied*, 523 U.S. 1145 (1998), the defendant gave birth to a baby who was born with cocaine in its system. She pleaded guilty to criminal child neglect and was sentenced to eight years. Whitner later appealed, and the South Carolina Supreme Court held that its criminal child neglect statute covered viable fetuses. The court also rejected the argument that the statute thus interpreted violated Whitner's right of privacy.

Whitner is not unique in allowing a woman to be convicted under a general criminal statute for conduct she committed during pregnancy that affected her fetus. *See Ex parte Ankrom*, 152 So. 3d 397 (Ala. 2013) (holding that statute prohibiting chemical endangerment of a child applies to viable fetuses), *cert. denied sub nom. Kimbrough v. Alabama*, 135 S. Ct. 50 (2014). But *Johnson* follows the prevailing view. *See, e.g., Arms v. State*, 471 S.W.3d 637, 642 (Ark. 2015) (refusing to interpret drug statute as "criminaliz[ing] the passive bodily processes that result[] in a mother's use of a drug entering her unborn, or newborn child's system"); *State v. Stegall*, 828 N.W.2d 526, 533 (N.D. 2013) (dismissing child endangerment charges based on "prenatal conduct that ultimately harms a child born alive").

3. An excellent summary of legal developments, both statutory and in the case law, with regard to the issues in *Johnson* is Ellen Marrus, *Crack Babies and the Constitution: Ruminations About Addicted Pregnant Women after* Ferguson v. City of Charleston, 47 VILL. L. REV. 299 (2002). *See also* Michele Goodwin, *Fetal Protection Laws: Moral Panic and the New Constitutional Battlefront*, 102 CALIF. L. REV. 781 (2014). For a discussion of homicide charges brought in this context, see Note 7(c) in Chapter 6, Section C.2.

[c] General Discussion

The shape of criminal law changes because society changes. The moral, psychological, and technological parameters of society are constantly changing. And these changes affect our sense of when and how criminal law should be used to single out and punish those who break the shared rules of communal living.

The core of criminal law is more or less impervious to these changes. Through fact and fiction we are familiar with most destructive and dramatic ways in which persons prey upon others. The kinds of acts that constitute the universal core of criminal law involve serious harm to important interests. Changes in moral and psychological thinking and changes in technology will not affect our responses to those who deliberately choose to take the lives or property of others with no excusing or mitigating circumstances. And there always have been and will be such persons.

[i] Moral and Psychological Flux

[A] Prostitution

There are many ways in which changes in public morality are reflected by changes and uncertainties in the law. Prostitution is one example. Most societies have condemned prostitution and many have criminalized it. There is wide agreement, however, that it involves a consensual activity, and most commentators call it a victimless crime. That is to say, it seems that the legal response of criminalization is triggered not by the fact that one party harms another but rather by the fact that many people are offended by the practice. It remains arguable, of course, that some people are indeed harmed, but there is little agreement about the nature of the harm or its scope.

In *People v. James & McCray*, 415 N.Y.S.2d 342 (N.Y. Crim. Ct. 1979), Judge Stanley Gartenstein dismissed prostitution charges "in the interests of justice" after the District Attorney's office reversed its traditional practice of not pressing prostitution charges against first-time offenders. In the course of his opinion, the judge said the following:

> Prostitution is a victimless crime in which two equal contracting parties negotiate for the performance of an act proscribed by law, usually performed in private by consenting adults. . . . An object lesson that morality cannot be legislated might properly be coupled with a realization that the real victim of prostitution is the prostitute herself and the real criminal, her pimp, who keeps her virtually enslaved by threats of cutting her up and by fostering ignorance of the fact that she can make it in life without him.

The judge went to say that "the public interest is not served by intransigence on an issue whose irrelevance to the real problem of violent crime is recognized almost universally." In other words, prosecution of prostitutes does not conform with the purposes of criminal law.

In 2013, the Supreme Court of Canada struck down that country's prostitution laws as a violation of the right to "security of the person" guaranteed by the Charter of Rights and Freedoms. *See Canada (Attorney General) v. Bedford*, [2013] 3 S.C.R. 1101 (Can.). In the court's unanimous decision, the Chief Justice wrote: "Parliament has the power to regulate against nuisances, but not at the cost of the health, safety and lives of prostitutes." In response, the Canadian legislature enacted The Protection of Communities and Exploited Persons Act, which prohibits buying (but not selling) sexual services and also limits advertising of sexual services. *See* Julie Kaye, *Canada's Flawed Sex Trade Law*, N.Y. TIMES, Jan. 21, 2015.

One form of criminal activity that has raised enormous concern in recent years and has been the target of national and international enforcement efforts is sex trafficking, which often involves forced prostitution. Prosecutors and law enforcement agencies have come to recognize that both males and females engaged in prostitution are often themselves victims. Their customers might be seeking consensual sexual activity, but they may have no way of knowing in many cases whether those performing the sexual acts are victims of coercion.

[B] Homosexuality

An extreme recent example of criminal law responding to a change in public morality is the decriminalization of homosexual activity and the widespread acknowledgment that homosexual couples should stand, morally and legally, on the same ground as other couples. *See Lawrence v. Texas*, 539 U.S. 558 (2003) (striking down Texas statute criminalizing same-sex sodomy); *Obergefell v. Hodges*, 135 S. Ct. 2584 (2015) (interpreting the Fourteenth Amendment to guarantee same-sex couples the right to marry).

[C] Suicide

It can be difficult and perhaps pointless to distinguish moral changes from psychological changes as causes of changing legal attitudes. For example, suicide has historically been associated with irrationality and mental illness, although there have been many societies in which suicide has been considered a respectable and even honorable response to some of life's circumstances. Current thinking is more nuanced and less doctrinaire. Can ending one's life be a rational decision, even when one is not in the late stages of a terminal illness? Do we have the tools to answer this question—or do we simply have newfound appreciation for its difficulty?

In legal terms, the question has most often been addressed in terms of the permissibility of physician-assisted suicide. Several states have enacted statutes with broad criminal prohibitions on such assistance by doctors. See, for example, *Vacco v. Quill*, 521 U.S. 793 (1997), and *Washington v. Glucksberg*, 521 U.S. 702 (1997), in which the Supreme Court upheld the constitutionality of such statutes.

In the 1990s, Dr. Jack Kevorkian, the controversial "suicide doctor," made a career out of supplying the means for terminally ill patients to end their lives. At his trial, Kevorkian argued unsuccessfully that death was a lesser evil than continued suffering for the terminally ill and that they had the right to choose the former, enlisting his help. When Kevorkian was released from prison in 2007 having served eight years for second-degree murder, the legal status of physician-assisted suicide remained largely unchanged.

In 1997, Oregon became the first state to pass a "Death with Dignity" statute, which recognizes the right of terminally ill patients to request a lethal amount of medication from their physicians under certain circumstances. Four other states (Washington, Vermont, California, and Colorado) have since followed suit. *See also Baxter v. State*, 224 P.3d 1211 (Mont. 2009) (interpreting the state statute making consent a defense to homicide to apply to doctors who assist their patients to die).

[D] Addiction

Criminal law has been slow to reflect any recognition of the suggestion that addiction can compromise personal responsibility. And yet psychologists and laypersons have little doubt that addiction to drugs and alcohol, and other addictions as well, can have drastic effects on an individual's motivation, self-control, priorities, and general cognition. In general, criminal law works by holding all persons equally responsible and, more important, by assuming that all persons are, except in extreme cases, equally capable of forming and carrying out intentions, equally capable of taking account of the likely effects of their actions. Not only is this demonstrably a fiction when it comes to addicts, it is also highly implausible as an expectation and description of any random collection of persons. Should the criminal law account for such differences?

[ii] Changes in Technology

Many of the dilemmas that appear at the periphery of criminal law involve the effects of technological progress on social conditions. For recent examples where the U.S. Supreme Court had addressed technological change, see *Riley v. California*, 134 S. Ct. 2473 (2014) (refusing to allow the warrantless inspection of cellphone data as part of a search incident to arrest); *Maryland v. King*, 133 S. Ct. 1958 (2013) (upholding the constitutionality of a statute requiring that DNA samples be taken from all persons arrested for serious crimes); and *United States v. Jones*, 132 S. Ct. 945 (2012) (holding that the installation and use of a GPS tracing device on a car constitutes a Fourth Amendment "search"). In criminal law, as in many other areas of law, legislators and theorists are constantly playing catch-up in dealing with changes that have no precedent and no obvious guidelines. As new technologies reshape how we share information and communicate, law must address what ways of transmitting data (music, movies, books, inventions, ideas) are permissible given the evolving notions of intellectual property and what ways demand limitations, protection, and sanctions. As medical technology affects our ability to heal and change our bodies and minds and even affects how we conceive our nature as physical and mental beings, law must confront and redefine our rights to draw benefits from medical progress and to control our destiny. As we draw upon technology to form new communities that do not depend on geography or genealogy, we need to set the rules by which we may assume roles in each other's lives. In these areas certain kinds of conduct will be allowed and perhaps even seen as desirable, and other kinds will be seen as harmful and subject to prohibition.

[B] The Functional and Procedural Bases of Criminal Law

[1] The Function of Criminal Law

The materials in Section A suggest an explanation of the central place of crime in our social and cultural awareness. If social institutions exist to allow us to pursue our goals in ordered and predictable ways, we must be prepared to deal with persons who refuse to play by the rules and seek their own advantage by violating others' interests. Special blame attaches to those who knowingly harm other persons. Their blameworthiness consists in the conjunction of two factors. Not only do they act to cause harm—or at least with the *likely* result of causing harm—but also they act with an *attitude* of disregard for the interests of others.

In its simplicity, the term "outlaw," from the lore of the old West, captures the essence of criminal responsibility. We blame those who deliberately put themselves outside the law and in opposition to society's interests. As we have seen, interest in criminal law has many elements: fascination with the outlaw's psychology, fear of the danger posed by outlaws, identification with their freedom, and awareness of the fragility of the social order.

Criminal law differs from other basic law subjects. These subjects—contracts, tort law, and property law—are mainly concerned with facilitating order and cooperation, not with handling disorder and opposition. Contract law is a response to the fact that even the most rudimentary society requires a system of enforceable agreements. It needs rules for the creation, enforcement, and interpretation of agreements. It also needs tort law because, among the members of any group, accidents will occur and the costs of those accidents will have to be allocated. Furthermore, it needs property law because persons will tend to compete to possess, occupy, and use the goods available in any society. Property law supplies rules to define and coordinate the interests involved in acquisition, transfer, and use of land and objects. Each of these three basic subject areas of the common law—contracts, tort law, and property law—thus addresses a fundamental and unavoidable social need to coordinate activity.

By contrast, the function of criminal law is not coordination, but prohibition, since it defines the kinds of conduct that disrupt social bonds. This distinctive character of criminal law has important conceptual and practical implications. Some of the differences between criminal and civil law are generic and appear in many legal systems. Others are tied to the American constitutional and legal framework. The next Section explores a number of these differences.

[2] Procedural Aspects of Criminal Law

[a] The State as Plaintiff: Civil Versus Criminal Liability

The most obvious formal distinction between criminal law and civil law is, in the words of Professor Joshua Dressler, that "because crimes violate the public interest they are prosecuted by public attorneys representing the community at large and not by privately retained counsel. The plaintiff—the injured party—is society." Joshua Dressler, Understanding Criminal Law 1 (original edition, 1987). The plaintiff in American cases is the state or, in federal crimes, the United States. In the United Kingdom, the plaintiff is the Crown, represented as "rex" or "regina."

The underlying distinction is between public interests and private interests. The criminal, unlike the civil defendant, is said to violate interests shared by the community. Since the criminal is blameworthy in acting harmfully with unjustifiable disregard for others' interests, the state is justified in using its legal resources to punish.

How clear and convincing is this distinction? Some leading commentators have emphasized its purely procedural or formal character. Formally it is easy to see which volumes of statutes are labeled criminal codes; formally we can tell which cases are litigated in the name of the state. But can we, substantively, always distinguish those who disregard the interests of society at large, the public interests, from those who disregard the rights or interests of particular individuals? We have already seen that in many cases particular questions about what should be criminalized are often highly controversial. In this light consider the following.

Henry M. Hart, Jr., *The Aims of the Criminal Law,* 23 Law & Contemp. Probs. 401 (1958)[2]

Can crimes be distinguished from civil wrongs on the ground that they constitute injuries to society generally which society is interested in preventing? The difficulty is that society is interested also in the due fulfillment of contracts and the avoidance of traffic accidents and most of the other stuff of civil litigation. The civil law is framed and interpreted and enforced with a constant eye to these social interests. Does the distinction lie in the fact that proceedings to enforce the criminal law are instituted by public officials rather than private complainants? The difficulty is that public officers may also bring many kinds of "civil" enforcement actions—for an injunction, for the recovery of a "civil" penalty, or even for the detention of the defendant by public authority. Is the distinction, then, in the peculiar character of what is done to people who are adjudged to be criminals? The difficulty is that, with the possible exception of death, exactly the same kinds of unpleasant consequences, objectively considered, can be and are visited upon unsuccessful defendants in civil proceedings.

If one were to judge from the notions apparently underlying many judicial opinions, and the overt language even of some of them, the solution of the puzzle is simply that a crime is anything which is *called* a crime, and a criminal penalty is simply the penalty provided for doing anything which has been given that name. So vacant a concept is a betrayal of intellectual bankruptcy. Certainly, it poses no intelligible issue for a constitution-maker concerned to decide whether to make use of "the method of the criminal law." Moreover, it is false to popular understanding, and false also to the understanding embodied in existing constitutions[.] By implicit assumptions that are more impressive than any explicit assertions, these constitutions proclaim that a conviction for crime is a distinctive and serious matter—a something, and not a nothing. What is that something?

What distinguishes a criminal from a civil sanction and all that distinguishes it, it is ventured, is the judgment of community condemnation which accompanies and justifies its imposition. As Professor Gardner wrote not long ago, in a distinct but cognate connection:

> The essence of punishment for moral delinquency lies in the criminal conviction itself. One may lose more money on the stock market than in a courtroom; a prisoner of war camp may well provide a harsher environment than a state prison; death on the field of battle has the same physical characteristics as death by sentence of law. It is the expression of the community's hatred, fear, or contempt for the convict which alone characterizes physical hardship as punishment.

If this is what a "criminal" penalty is, then we can say readily enough what a "crime" is. It is not simply anything which a legislature chooses to call a "crime." It is not simply antisocial conduct which public officers are given a responsibility to suppress. It is not simply any conduct to which a legislature chooses to attach a "criminal" penalty. It is conduct which, if duly shown to have taken place, will incur a formal and solemn pronouncement of the moral condemnation of the community.

Notes and Questions

1. Can One Identify Society's Interests? Hart rejects the idea that we have a litmus test for society's interests and can use that test to decide what should be criminalized. He implies that the search for such a test is simplistic and illusory. Rather, the only distinction between society's interests and individual interests is an ex post facto test: whether in fact criminal penalties, with their accompanying moral stigma, are imposed.

In a recent article, *How Feminist Theory Became (Criminal) Law: Tracing the Path to Mandatory Criminal Intervention in Domestic Violence Cases* (21 Mich. J. Gender & L. 217 (2014)), Claire Houston traces the evolution, over the last 40 years, of domestic violence from a "private relationship problem" to a public crime with mandatory intervention policies. Houston discusses two pivotal class action cases, *Bruno v. Codd* and *Scott v. Hart,* in which it was argued successfully that "the protections and remedies afforded by the civil law cannot substitute for effective enforcement of protections and remedies under the criminal justice system." Both spousal and child abuse came to be perceived and understood as implicating not just victims and perpetrators but the public interest. The assumption of these concerns into criminal law made clear newly evolved public attitudes toward responsibility and blame and toward the need for deterrence.

2. Comparing Civil and Criminal Remedies. In comparing criminal law with civil law, keep in mind that criminal law is not the only tool by which society's interests can be defined and protected. We can also use civil law or non-legal tools. Examples of the latter include health warnings on cigarette packages and public service ads urging conservation and protection of the environment.

Civil law might respond to the problem of drug use by legalizing drugs and licensing their sale. Similarly, civil law might alleviate the problems associated with prostitution by public control and administration of the service. In general, taxes can be used to affect the market for various goods and services. Thus, each of the controversial cases considered previously in this Chapter raises two distinct questions. Is this an appropriate concern for legal intervention? If so, should criminal law or civil law be used?

An excellent survey of the punitive as opposed to the regulatory use of civil sanctions is Kenneth Mann, *Punitive Civil Sanctions: The Middle Ground Between Criminal and Civil Law*, 101 Yale L.J. 1795 (1995).

3. Crime and Blameworthiness. Some writers have suggested that because criminal conviction carries a distinct stigma, it should be reserved for those cases and situations in which persons choose to cause clear and significant harm to others and in which there is general agreement that the kind of harm at stake cannot be tolerated. In other words, it focuses on blameworthy conduct.

4. The Gap between Legislation and Enforcement. Many areas of law involve both civil proceedings and criminal prosecutions. While tax penalties most often are imposed under civil law, more serious violations of tax law are crimes. In other words, the legislation that sets the rules for tax makes clear that some breaches of tax law are civil and others are criminal. But the line is not always indelible. The language spelling out the distinction may be elastic enough so that it becomes a matter of prosecutorial discretion whether to proceed with a criminal charge in a given situation or leave the matter to the civil courts.

Copyright is another area of law in which violations can be civil or criminal. In *The Criminal Copyright Gap* (18 Stan. Tech. L. Rev. 247 (2015)), Eldar Habler points out that, from a legislative standpoint, copyright has been increasingly criminalized over the last several decades. At the same time, criminal copyright prosecutions remain rare. His explanation is that different motives may control the decisions of legislators and those of prosecutors and the police. Interest groups and international organizations may demand legislation as a statement of principle, but have relatively little interest in its enforcement. Deterrence may be achieved by the existence of legislation, whether or not it is seriously enforced. Moreover, legislation may be easy to draft but very hard and expensive to enforce when, as with copyright infringement, it involves changing technology, overlapping jurisdictions, and great difficulty in identifying offenders and the specific nature of their offense.

Some legislators and some writers see criminal law as a way of defining the scope of personal culpability and responsibility, with constant reference to moral underpinnings. Others more simply see it as a general method of social control and argue that one may criminalize behavior that one wants to discourage even when it is not morally reprehensible.

Your own position on these questions will color your response to many controversial cases, including the ones discussed above. Professor Abraham Goldstein explores this distinction in the following excerpt.

Abraham S. Goldstein, *White-Collar Crime and Civil Sanctions*, 101 Yale L.J. 1895, 1895–97 (1992)[3]

The central concepts of what we now regard as a distinctive body of criminal law emerged from cases involving crimes of passion, violence, and theft. These concepts

---

3. Reprinted by permission of the author and The Yale Law Journal Company and Fred B. Rothman & Company.

take as their model the genuinely culpable individual who "deserves" to be used for the criminal law's purposes—whose condemnation will assuage retributive impulses, deter potential offenders, reinforce legal norms, and lead to incarceration of the demonstrably dangerous. Much of contemporary scholarly writing embraces this model and treats it as fundamental, as inherent in the very concept of crime. To lack culpability (blameworthiness), it is said, is not to be a criminal at all. The underlying assumptions are that criminal law is less concerned with social control of deviant behavior than with defining *who* should be used in that effort, and that criminal law is a technique of social control which is to be used sparingly—with a wholesome regard for its stigmatizing power and the extraordinary pains imposed by imprisonment. . . .

Those who embrace [this] dominant theory have treated as virtually illegitimate the older lines of cases that reflected an entirely different theory—one that focused more on achieving social control than on assessing personal culpability. This secondary theory is exemplified in the opinions of English and American courts dealing with offenses like bigamy and adultery—older versions of what we now tend to call public welfare offenses. Those opinions reflected a willingness on the part of courts and legislatures to abandon, or at least to limit sharply, a subjective theory of liability when necessary to achieve important social objectives. As Holmes pointed out in his famous essay *The Criminal Law*, from the beginnings of our criminal law, courts have not hesitated to impose criminal liability on those who are only objectively liable. And that perspective has endured to the present day. Our Supreme Court has upheld the imposition of strict liability, or liability for negligence or vicarious liability, for offenses carrying very heavy prison sentences. Those cases, like the earlier ones, assume that to achieve social control it may be necessary to abandon the mens rea requirement or to keep notions of subjective culpability to a minimum.

The two theories of criminal liability—one emphasizing social control and the other stressing personal culpability—have long been competing for primacy, most conspicuously in the law of traditional crimes. Doctrines based on objective theories of liability (like the felony murder rule or vicarious responsibility) have met fierce criticism. For the most part, the advocates of personal culpability and strict procedures have won the contest. But in doing so, they have tended to carry their critique beyond the traditional crimes to which it had been addressed—the crimes of passion and violence and theft. These crimes are indeed "personal" and are easy targets for a subjective theory. It is less clear that the subjectivist critique has equal application to the new types of crimes. These are usually characterized by vague definitions and by the abandonment or reduction of the mens rea requirement, as legislatures try to respond to the pressures of the Industrial Revolution and the regulatory state. Nevertheless, the academic community and the [American Law Institute] have tended to describe the law on the books as if it had already accepted the subjective theory of liability across the board.

This apparent consensus has made legislatures, courts, and prosecutors reluctant to use criminal law to achieve the kind of social control that is the *raison d'etre* of many of the new regulatory crimes. Thus, by narrowing the boundaries of the area that may or should be reached by criminal law, the reformers have created strong pressures on the courts either (1) to stretch criminal law beyond the newly proper ("subjectivist") boundaries, or (2) to avoid the constraints associated with criminal law and criminal procedure by abandoning the criminal law as a regulatory tool. The latter course, abandonment, would obviously be easier if civil measures were available that could do better, and more efficiently, the work of criminal law in the specialized areas associated with white-collar crime.

Notes

1. **Product Liability as White-Collar Crime.** In recent years, products liability cases have given rise to legislative proposals to extend criminal procedures and sanctions to certain kinds of corporate malfeasance. Litigation in 2000 and 2001 over Firestone's manufacture and marketing of defective SUV tires led to proposals that would make it a felony to withhold information about dangerous products from consumers and regulatory agencies, that would eliminate the cap on damages for defendants who withhold such information, and that would prohibit settlement agreements with secrecy provisions. Texas House Bill 3125 included the first two conditions, but it was not enacted. Consider whether you would regard criminal penalties and criminal discovery rules as appropriate for such cases.

2. **Sarbanes-Oxley.** The Sarbanes-Oxley Act of 2002, 15 U.S.C. §7201, was a response to corporate scandals involving dubious transactions that led to some of the largest bankruptcies in American history, notably those of Enron and WorldCom. Sarbanes-Oxley imposes criminal penalties for (a) willful lapses by accountants of requirements to retain and review work papers for at least seven years; (b) any attempts by corporate officers to influence or coerce accountants to issue misleading financial statements; (c) any retaliatory acts by corporate officers against whistle-blowers; and (d) any attempts to alter, destroy, or falsify documents in certain cases before bankruptcy courts and other federal courts. The act strengthened existing securities laws by enhancing criminal penalties as well as creating new corporate crimes.

Even if the line between civil law and criminal law is in flux and is controversial, the formal distinction between criminal and civil actions marks a significant fault line in any legal system. The concept of litigation between two private parties is, intuitively, the concept of conflict (or combat) between equals. In fact, the parties may hardly be equal in power, wealth, or resources. Consider suits between large corporations and ordinary plaintiffs.

Nonetheless, special safeguards seem needed when the individual confronts the power and resources of the state. The state is both a party to the conflict and the decision-maker in the conflict. Although the doctrine of separation of powers is designed to ensure that the accuser and the trier work independently of each other, many of the most egregious atrocities in history have been carried out by the state under the rubric of criminal law.

Modern democratic societies have devised a number of safeguards under the assumption (or illusion) that they equalize the power of accused and accuser, or more plausibly that they restrain the worst excesses of which state power is capable. Critics sometimes question whether these safeguards are justified and whether they frustrate efficient crime detection and prevention.

[b] Constitutional Safeguards

Some of these safeguards are rooted in the Bill of Rights of the Constitution. For the most part, the Fourth, Fifth, Sixth, and Eighth Amendments are concerned with constraints on criminal procedure, with the rights of persons accused of crime.

The Fourth Amendment guarantees the right of persons to be secure against unreasonable searches and seizures; it also limits the issuance of warrants by setting relevant conditions. The Fifth Amendment prohibits double jeopardy and says that an individual in "a criminal case" shall not be forced to be a "witness against himself." It also requires grand jury indictments for "infamous" crimes. The Sixth Amendment lists rights that are mandated for "all criminal prosecutions"—the rights to a speedy trial, a public trial, an impartial jury in the state and district where the crime was committed, notice of the "nature and cause of the accusation," confrontation of adverse witnesses, compulsory process for finding favorable witnesses, and assistance of counsel. The Eighth Amendment prohibits excessive bail, excessive fines, and cruel and unusual punishment. In addition, the Fifth and Fourteenth Amendment due process clauses have consistently been understood to include the criminal justice process in the prohibition against the "deprivat[ion] of life, liberty or property" (that is, imposing capital sentencing, incarceration, and criminal fines) without "due process of law."

Keep in mind that the Bill of Rights applies on its face to the federal government, and federal criminal jurisdiction extends to only one percent of criminal prosecutions. For these rights to be effective in state proceedings, these provisions had to be held applicable to the states as well the federal government. The conceptual and interpretative strategy that made this possible, most significantly in the decisions of the Warren Court in the 1960s, was the "due process" clause of the Fourteenth Amendment, a post-civil war amendment adopted in 1868. The process of bringing these rights to the states under the umbrella of the Fourteenth Amendment was called "incorporation."

Courts have also been aware that individual guarantees can be read narrowly or expansively. Familiar examples are the provisions determining the scope of lawful searches and determining what counts as being compelled to incriminate oneself.

Notes and Questions

1. Understanding Criminal Procedure. A substantial part of the agenda of the Supreme Court is concerned with criminal procedure, with the important constitutional topics outlined above. As you examine various aspects of criminal law, keep in mind the context of criminal investigation and adjudication that is defined by these constraints.

2. Two Models: Due Process and Crime Control. In his book, THE LIMITS OF THE CRIMINAL SANCTION (1968), Professor Herbert Packer identified two distinctive ways to think about the constitutional constraints on criminal procedure, the due process model and the crime control model. The due process model stresses the ways in which the state can abuse its power over individuals accused of crime. It puts great emphasis on the constitutional presumption of innocence and the moral commitment that, until they are convicted, criminal defendants are entitled to the same dignity and respect as all other citizens. This model also takes note of the potential unreliability of evidence, for example the testimony of witnesses, and therefore warns against the danger of the appearance of guilt.

The crime control model, on the other hand, is profoundly concerned with the preservation of public order and with the efficient enforcement of criminal law. It stresses the need for public certainty that the system work to apprehend and convict criminals with a high degree of reliability. Professor Packer associated these models respectively with those who are preoccupied with the rights of the accused and those who are concerned with efficiency in enforcing the law.

In what practical ways are the values underlying the crime control and the due process models—efficiency in enforcement of laws and fairness to those who are accused—at odds with each other? Can you imagine devising a system that achieves both goals to a significant degree?

(a) How is the process of reconciling these goals constrained by available resources? What economic and political conditions make such reconciliation difficult?

(b) What are the psychological assumptions behind Packer's two models? In particular, what assumptions do they make about the behavior and attitudes of the police and of persons accused of crime?

(c) How would you characterize the present situation with regard to the relevance of the two models? Which values are most effectively safeguarded? Is the situation satisfactory?

3. Packer's Models in the New Millennium. The advent of terrorism in the twenty-first century has given new urgency and new dimensions to Packer's distinction. In proposing and imposing indefinite detention without conviction, along with such other measures as limited access to legal representation and constraints on such representation, the Bush Administration reinterpreted the "crime control" model. It no longer meant interpreting the rights of defendants narrowly in the light of exigent circumstances implicating community safety; it instead meant the indefinite suspension and curtailment of constitutional rights under special circumstances such as those defined by the "war on terror." And the circumstances themselves are not clearly bounded by time and space; criteria for the re-establishment of and eligibility for constitutional rights involving detention and counsel are at best vague and open.

In addition, it had long been assumed that all persons tried under the American system of criminal justice could avail themselves of the procedural rights listed in the Constitution. Laws passed in the wake of the 9/11 terrorist acts have cast substantial doubt on this assumption. See Note 11 in Section 2.e below on the status of the so-called "unlawful enemy combatants" and the putative use of military tribunals.

The constitutionality of these new crime control (and terror control) strategies is being tested in the courts. Both the law on these matters and the relevant scholarship will continue to develop in the coming years. Among the academic contributions to these debates is Ken Roach & Gary Trotter, *Miscarriages of Justice in the War Against Terror*, 109 Penn. St. L. Rev. 967 (2005).

4. Learning Criminal Procedure. Students and others are often confused by the ambiguity of the phrase "criminal procedure." As a subject for a law school course and for academic study, it is the study of the constitutional parameters of criminal law. Its subject matter is primarily the Fourth, Fifth, Sixth, Eighth, and Fourteenth Amendments to the Constitution, along with some of the analogous constraints in state constitutions. The term also refers to a different subject, one that readily comes to mind. This is the process whereby criminal charges are brought, pleas are entered, preliminary steps leading to trial go forward, and finally the defendant is tried or the matter is settled without a trial (through a guilty plea—often the result of a plea negotiation—or through a successful motion by the defense, e.g., a motion to dismiss charges). These matters are covered in courses such as criminal clinics and trial practice.

It is highly advisable to familiarize yourself with some of these rules and processes by looking at the introductory sections of a first-rate criminal procedure casebook or hornbook. *See, e.g.,* Yale Kamisar et al., Modern Criminal Procedure: Cases, Comments and Questions (14th ed. 2015); Stephen A. Saltzburg & Daniel J. Capra, American Criminal Procedure: Cases and Commentary (10th ed. 2014).

[c] Standard of Proof

The Due Process Clause of the Constitution has been held to require "proof beyond a reasonable doubt of every fact necessary to constitute the crime charged." *In re Winship*, 397 U.S. 358, 364 (1970). This contrasts with the standard of proof in civil litigation, proof by a preponderance of the evidence. The proof-beyond-a-reasonable-doubt standard applies to conviction at criminal trials. Obviously it is not the standard that applies to other decisions by officials in the criminal process, for example the decision of the police to arrest a suspect, the decision of a prosecutor to charge, or the decision of a grand jury to indict.

The significance of the requirement of proof beyond a reasonable doubt is, as we have already considered, to restrain the power of the state when it seeks to impose blame and punish individuals. It is a way of safeguarding liberty. The assumptions and implications of the standard are explained in the following passages from *In re Winship*:

The requirement that guilt of a criminal charge be established by proof beyond a reasonable doubt dates at least from our early years as a Nation. The "demand for a higher degree of persuasion in criminal cases was recurrently expressed from ancient times, [though] its crystallization into the formula 'beyond a reasonable doubt' seems to have occurred as late as 1798. It is now accepted in common law jurisdictions as the measure of persuasion by which the prosecution must convince the trier of all the essential elements of guilt." . . .

The reasonable doubt standard plays a vital role in the American scheme of criminal procedure. It is a prime instrument for reducing the risk of convictions resting on factual error. The standard provides concrete substance for the presumption of innocence—that bedrock "axiomatic and elementary" principle whose "enforcement lies at the foundation of the administration of our criminal law." . . . [A] person accused of a crime . . . would be at a severe disadvantage, a disadvantage amounting to a lack of fundamental fairness, if he could be adjudged guilty and imprisoned for years on the strength of the same evidence as would suffice in a civil case. . . .

Moreover, use of the reasonable-doubt standard is indispensable to command the respect and confidence of the community in applications of the criminal law. It is critical that the moral force of the criminal law not be diluted by a standard of proof that leaves people in doubt whether innocent men are being condemned. It is also important in our free society that every individual going about his ordinary affairs have confidence that his government cannot adjudge him guilty of a criminal offense without convincing a proper factfinder of his guilt with utmost certainty.

Id. at 361, 363–64.

Justice Harlan's concurrence in *Winship* discusses the "beyond a reasonable doubt" standard and explores its implications:

. . . [E]ven though the labels used for alternative standards of proof are vague and not a very sure guide to decisionmaking, the choice of the standard for a particular variety of adjudication does, I think, reflect a very fundamental assessment of the comparative social costs of erroneous factual determinations.

To explain why I think this so, I begin by stating two propositions, neither of which I believe can be fairly disputed. First, in a judicial proceeding in which there is a dispute about the facts of some earlier event, the factfinder cannot acquire unassailably accurate knowledge of what happened. Instead, all the factfinder can acquire is a belief of what *probably* happened. The intensity of this belief—the degree to which a factfinder is convinced that a given act actually occurred—can, of course, vary. In this regard, a standard of proof represents an attempt to instruct the factfinder concerning the degree of confidence our society thinks he should have in the correctness of factual conclusions for a particular type of adjudication. Although the phrases "preponderance of the evidence" and "proof beyond a reasonable doubt" are quantitatively imprecise, they do communicate to the finder of fact different notions concerning the degree of confidence he is expected to have in the correctness of his factual conclusions.

A second proposition, which is really nothing more than a corollary of the first, is that the trier of fact will sometimes, despite his best efforts, be wrong in his factual conclusions. In a lawsuit between two parties, a factual error can make a difference in one of two ways. First, it can result in a judgment in favor of the plaintiff when the true facts warrant a judgment for the defendant. The analogue in a criminal case would be the conviction of an innocent man. On the other hand, an erroneous factual determination can result in a judgment for the defendant when the true facts justify a judgment in plaintiff's favor. The criminal analogue would be the acquittal of a guilty man.

The standard of proof influences the relative frequency of these two types of erroneous outcomes. If, for example, the standard of proof for a criminal trial were a preponderance of the evidence rather than proof beyond a reasonable doubt, there would be a smaller risk of factual errors that result in freeing guilty persons, but a far greater risk of factual errors that result in convicting the innocent. Because the standard of proof affects the comparative frequency of these two types of erroneous outcomes, the choice of the standard to be applied in a particular kind of litigation should, in a rational world, reflect an assessment of the comparative social disutility of each.

When one makes such an assessment, the reason for different standards of proof in civil as opposed to criminal litigation becomes apparent. In a civil suit between two private parties for money damages, for example, we view it as no more serious in general for there to be an erroneous verdict in the defendant's favor than for there to be an erroneous verdict in the plaintiff's favor. A preponderance of the evidence standard therefore seems peculiarly appropriate for, as explained most sensibly, it simply requires the trier of fact "to believe that the existence of a fact is more probable than its nonexistence before [he] may find in favor of the party who has the burden to persuade the [judge] of the fact's existence."

In a criminal case, on the other hand, we do not view the social disutility of convicting an innocent man as equivalent to the disutility of acquitting someone who is guilty. . . .

In this context, I view the requirement of proof beyond a reasonable doubt in a criminal case as bottomed on a fundamental value determination of our society that it is far worse to convict an innocent man than to let a guilty man go free.

Id. at 370–72 (Harlan, J., concurring).

Notes and Questions

1. Defining the Standard. The beyond-a-reasonable-doubt standard raises logical questions. Does it mean that the jury must be convinced there is no *logical* possibility that the defendant is innocent? Is this the same thing as complete certainty?

One widely cited definition of reasonable doubt notes that "everything relating to human affairs and depending on moral evidence is open to some possible or imaginary doubt. . . . [Reasonable doubt] leaves the minds of the jurors in that condition that they cannot say they feel an abiding conviction, to a moral certainty, of the truth of the charge." California Jury Instructions, Criminal, No. 2.90 (1979).

The model California jury instruction defining reasonable doubt has been amended, and the concept of "moral certainty" has been eliminated. The current model instruction defines reasonable doubt as follows:

> . . . not a mere possible doubt, because everything relating to human affairs is open to some possible or imaginary doubt. It is that state of the case which, after the entire comparison and consideration of all the evidence, leaves the minds of the jurors in that condition that they cannot say they feel an abiding conviction of the truth of the charge.

California Jury Instructions, Criminal, No. 2.90 (2005).

In *People v. Johnson*, 14 Cal. Rptr. 3d 780 (Cal. Ct. App. 2004), the trial judge, while using this instruction, also told jurors that reasonable doubt was the basis for "everyday decisionmaking." In addition, he observed that anyone who believed that having "no doubt" was possible was "brain dead"; there is always "some doubt," he said. The appellate court reversed, noting that well over a century ago, in *People v. Brannon*, 47 Cal. 96 (1873), the California Supreme Court had rejected a standard of proof for criminal trials resting merely upon the "judgment of a reasonable man in the ordinary affairs of life." The appellate court in *Johnson* ruled that judges should not deviate from the model jury instruction, and also held that error in defining "reasonable doubt" is fundamental "structural" error, requiring reversal even if the defendant did not object. The U.S. Supreme Court ruled similarly that a constitutionally deficient reasonable doubt instruction cannot be harmless error in *Sullivan v. Louisiana*, 508 U.S. 275 (1993).

2. Reasonable Doubt and Probability. Can the absence of reasonable doubt be expressed quantitatively, as a probability?

In *McCullough v. State*, 657 P.2d 1157 (Nev. 1983), a Nevada trial court instructed the jury that, whereas the standard for civil cases was around "five" on a scale of one to ten, the requirement of an absence of reasonable doubt shifted the requirement to "seven and a half." The Nevada Supreme Court reversed the lower court, noting that reasonable doubt is "inherently qualitative. Any attempt to quantify it . . . is likely to confuse rather than clarify."

Do you find this comment useful or confusing? Is the distinction between quantitative and qualitative matters clear in this context?

3. Standard of Proof and Burden of Proof. Be careful to distinguish questions about standard of proof from questions about burden of proof, which in turn involve burden of production and burden of persuasion. The burden of production is the burden of coming forward with sufficient evidence to put a certain fact into consideration. For example, defendants may wish to claim that their actions were justified as self-defense, that their actions were prompted by duress, or that a disability undercuts their legal responsibility. In these situations the defendants alone may have access to evidence supporting their claims, and therefore it is appropriate for them to have the burden of producing such evidence. The prosecution cannot disprove claims of which it is unaware. But to say that defendants have the burden of production does not mean that they also have the burden of persuasion. The prosecution may still have to prove beyond a reasonable doubt that the alleged justification or excuse is not sufficient to exculpate a defendant. (Jurisdictions vary with regard to which party has the burden of persuasion for affirmative defenses. *See* Chapter 14, end of Section B; Chapter 15, end of Sections A and C.2.)

4. Scholarship on the Standard of Proof. Several scholars have examined the scope and adequacy of the notion of proof beyond a reasonable doubt. Melissa Corwin, in *Defining "Proof Beyond a Reasonable Doubt" for the Criminal Jury*, 46 Vill. L. Rev. 829 (2001), argues that the Third Circuit Court of Appeals has defined the standard so expansively that "criminal defendants will have an extremely difficult time establishing due process violations." Lawrence Solan, in *Refocusing the Burden of Proof in Criminal Cases: Some Doubt About Reasonable Doubt*, 78 Tex. L. Rev. 105 (1999), proposes that the reasonable doubt standard may not be "the best way to promote the values our system of criminal law claims to venerate." Echoing suggestions made by Justice Ruth Bader Ginsburg, he gives several reasons for favoring an instruction that requires juries to be "firmly convinced" of the defendant's guilt. In a slightly different vein, Rory Little, in *Guilt, Reasonable Doubt, and the Reasonable Woman*, 6 Hastings Women's L.J. 275 (1995), has pointed out that definitions of "reasonable doubt" fail to explain whether jurors evaluating the "reasonableness" of a doubt are to apply an "objective" or a more individualistic, subjective perspective. Finally, in his article, *Reasonable Doubt: How in the World Is It Defined?*, 12 Amer. U. J. Int'l L. & Pol'y 195 (1997), Thomas Mulrine addresses the vagueness of the idea of reasonable doubt. He concludes that the criterion of being firmly convinced is too weak and too easily satisfied. Instead, he recommends that the standard be explained as different from absolute certainty and as satisfied when careful consideration of the evidence presented leaves no reasonable doubt of guilt.

5. Judicial Review After *Winship*. Once *In re Winship* established "proof beyond a reasonable doubt" as a constitutional requirement for valid criminal convictions, state court defendants could style claims of evidentiary insufficiency as claims of constitutional error. This greatly expanded the number of criminal convictions that, theoretically at least, could be pursued all the way to the United States Supreme Court as presenting a "federal question."

In *Jackson v. Virginia*, 443 U.S. 307, 319 (1979), the Supreme Court articulated the constitutionally required standard of review appellate courts should use in evaluating the sufficiency of the evidence in criminal cases: "the relevant question is whether, after viewing the evidence in the light most favorable to the prosecution, *any* rational trier of fact could have found the essential elements of the crime beyond a reasonable doubt." Note that this standard is in some sense the reverse of the trial court perspective: on appeal, the evidence, and "all reasonable inferences therefrom," must be viewed in the light most favorable to the prosecution, not the defendant. This means that on appeal, all of the defendant's evidence, and argued inferences, may be ignored (unless they actually help the government). It effectively makes an appellate reversal for evidentiary insufficiency very difficult to achieve. This change in perspective is important to keep in mind as you read cases in this book that often represent *appellate* decisions about criminal convictions.

6. *Apprendi* and Its Aftermath. In *Apprendi v. New Jersey*, 530 U.S. 466, 490 (2000), the Supreme Court extended *In re Winship* to require that the prosecution prove beyond a reasonable doubt any fact "[o]ther than the fact of a prior conviction . . . that increases the penalty for a crime beyond the prescribed statutory maximum." Such facts are equivalent, the Court held, to elements of the crime and thus must be proved by the government. For further information about *Apprendi* and the line of cases applying it, see Chapter 2, Section D.2.

[d] The Claims and Rights of Victims

In civil law, we tend to talk about persons who have been injured or wronged, but not about victims. "Victim" connotes someone who has been harmed through the kind of disregard with which criminal law is concerned.

At the beginning of this Section, we contrasted the functions of civil and criminal law. The object of a civil proceeding is rectification, while the object of a criminal proceeding is punishment. Because a crime is considered an offense against the public at large, a criminal prosecution seeks to vindicate the interests of society as a whole and not to rectify the results of criminal conduct for the individual.

But criminal law seems to trade on a myth when it contrasts damage to the interests of society with harm to particular individuals. Surely crimes usually affect some individuals dramatically and leave the rest of us relatively unscathed.

Although it is often impossible to restore victims to the condition they were in before the crime, it may be possible in many cases to compensate victims. This consideration has given rise to the "victims' rights" movement, which, since the 1960s, has drawn attention to the plight of victims and convinced several state legislatures to recognize victims' rights. Advocates of victims' rights have pursued at least four goals: (a) finding resources and processes to compensate victims, (b) imposing punishments that compel offenders to correct or undo the harm they have caused, (c) ensuring that victims be allowed to participate in the process of litigation, and (d) giving victims a voice in determination of punishment.

Each goal is controversial and difficult. An obvious problem with victim compensation is cost. State budgets, straining to meet basic welfare needs, cannot give priority to compensating victims. The rationale for alternative punishments has led to creative sentencing by some judges, but rectification is possible only in relatively few situations. (Other aspects of alternative sentencing are discussed in Chapter 2.)

Victim participation is the area in which the movement has had its greatest success. Giving victims a role in determining penalties is, however, particularly controversial because it implies that the treatment of the offender will depend on the degree of forgiveness or, alternatively, vindictiveness that the victim feels.

Notes and Questions

1. Defining Victims' Rights. Statutes like the Crime Victims Protection Act, 18 U.S.C. § 3771, are designed to assure victims the opportunity to be heard by providing, *inter alia*, the following:

(1) The right to be reasonably protected from the accused.

(2) The right to reasonable, accurate, and timely notice of any public court proceeding, or any parole proceeding, involving the crime or of any release or escape of the accused.

(3) The right not to be excluded from any such public court proceeding, unless the court, after receiving clear and convincing evidence, determines that testimony by the victim would be materially altered if the victim heard other testimony at that proceeding.

(4) The right to be reasonably heard at any public proceeding in the district court involving release, plea, sentencing, or any parole proceeding.

(5) The reasonable right to confer with the attorney for the Government in the case.

(6) The right to full and timely restitution as provided in law.

(7) The right to proceedings free from unreasonable delay.

(8) The right to be treated with fairness and with respect for the victim's dignity and privacy.

(9) The right to be informed in a timely manner of any plea bargain or deferred prosecution agreement.

(10) The right to be informed of the rights under this section and the services described in section 503(c) of the Victims' Rights and Restitution Act of 1990 (42 U.S.C. 10607(c)) and provided contact information for the Office of the Victims' Rights Ombudsman of the Department of Justice.

Which of these provisions are most likely to make a difference in victims' lives and welfare? Which, if any, are impractical? What provisions would you add to this list?

2. Victim Impact Statements. Victim impact statements describe the physical, economic, social, and emotional consequences of the offender's acts. Justice Stevens has criticized their use in sentencing as "hav[ing] strong political appeal but no proper place in a reasoned judicial opinion." *Payne v. Tennessee*, 501 U.S. 808, 859 (1991) (Stevens, J., dissenting). Do you agree?

The Victim and Witness Protection Act of 1982 amended Rule 32 of the Federal Rules of Criminal Procedure, requiring that sentencing judges be given victim impact statements before making sentencing decisions. Many states have since used this provision as a model for their own reforms. These various statutes differ widely both with regard to the manner in which victim impact evidence may be presented and the content of such evidence.

The record of the U.S. Supreme Court in considering this issue in light of the Eighth Amendment's prohibition of cruel and unusual punishment is one of inconsistency. In *Booth v. Maryland*, 482 U.S. 496 (1987), the Court held that the Eighth Amendment prohibited a capital sentencing jury from considering victim impact evidence because it created a risk that the death penalty would be imposed in an arbitrary and capricious manner. In *Payne v. Tennessee*, 501 U.S. 808 (1991), the Court reversed itself on this question, holding that the Eighth Amendment did not impose a per se bar of such evidence. The disagreement within the Court on the underlying issue appeared to turn on the permissibility of using evidence related not to the defendant's overall blameworthiness but merely to the harm caused by the crime, which is arguably only one ingredient in a determination of blameworthiness. Accordingly, two equally blameworthy defendants may cause different amounts of harm, may in other words have different impact on their victims. The decision in *Booth* rested on the assumption that the Eighth Amendment limits the relevant evidence to matters of blameworthiness; *Payne* rejects that limitation. It should be noted that the difference between *Booth* and *Payne* is partially explainable by a change of personnel on the Court in the intervening years.

In *Victim Impact Evidence in Capital Sentencing: A History of Incompatibility*, 23 Am. J. Crim. L. 375 (1996), Ashley Paige Dugger discusses the history of victim impact evidence in capital sentencing and evaluates the result. Echoing the reasoning in *Booth*, Dugger concludes that "[v]ictim impact evidence in capital sentencing prejudices both the defendant and the victim. Victim impact evidence brings about disparity in sentencing based on the perceived 'worth' of the victim. The attributes of the victim often have no real connection to the commission of the crime itself because [he is often] unknown to the defendant at the time of the crime. . . . [I]t is an unfair comparison to bring in the worth of the victim at this stage of the process. . . . The sentencing phase is not designed to be a contest between the victim and the defendant as to whose life is worth more." *Id*. at 403–04.

In recent years, victims' rights have remained controversial. Senators, including Jon Kyl and Dianne Feinstein, have promulgated and supported a victims' rights amendment to the Constitution that would guarantee victims a right to be notified about procedures and trials relevant to their victimization and to be heard at such hearings. Several states, including Utah, Oregon, Alaska, and California, have entertained such amendments to their state constitutions as well. Such a provision has been upheld in Utah and declared unenforceable in Rhode Island. None of these proposals and procedures allow victims to challenge the results of trials or judges' motions. Observers continue to debate the impact of such laws, along with their effects on the right to a fair trial for defendants. The scholarly literature is expansive. *See, e.g., Symposium: Crime Victim Law: Theory and Practice*, 9 Lewis & Clark L. Rev. 481 (2005); Victoria Schwartz, *Recent Development: The Victims' Rights Amendment*, 42 Harv. J. on Legis. 525 (2005); David Friedman, *Should the Characteristics of Victims and Criminals Count?*, 34 B.C. L. Rev. 731 (1993).

[e] Due Process and Fair Warning

Criminal law is concerned with various kinds of power. First, it addresses the power of individuals to harm other persons and disrupt their lives. Second, it is concerned with the power of government to articulate laws forbidding certain kinds of conduct and to punish violations of those rules. Third, it attempts to limit the process of applying those rules in order to prevent the institutions of government from abusing their power. We have already considered a number of procedural limitations on the government's power, many of which are incorporated into federal and state constitutions.

Among the most important limitations is the principle of fair warning. It refers to the formulation and interpretation of rules and mandates that their content and scope be clear and specific. The principle of fair warning itself is understood by courts to be part of the constitutional requirement that criminal defendants be accorded "due process of law." Under the incorporation doctrine, the due process requirement extends to state as well as federal practice.

It is useful to think of due process as an umbrella concept for many kinds of safeguards. One of those safeguards is that all citizens, all of whom are *potential* offenders, should be able to anticipate what kinds of acts are permitted and what kinds are prohibited. Scholars have long talked about the principle of *nulla peona sine lege*, Latin for "no punishment without law," which is sometimes called the "principle of legality." This means that a judge does not have free rein to declare some kinds of conduct illegal just by saying so. A judge who disapproves of an attorney wearing red socks in court cannot fine the attorney for a legal infraction (unless there is a relevant legal prohibition).

The implication of this convention is not only that laws must exist before they are enforced but also that the laws that *do in fact* exist must be clear and specific — at least specific enough for most persons most of the time to know what they specify. Thus, a law that says the judges and the police must insure public order and punish conduct that disrupts public order would be impermissibly vague. It would give judges and the police too free a hand to decide what to regard as criminal.

Vagueness is only one of several aspects of fair warning. A law may be clear but inadequately promulgated. Suppose a state decides to prohibit anyone entering that state from carrying explosives without registering them. Notice of this law must be published and made accessible to make sure that those affected are likely to be aware of it. Or a law may be clear in most of its applications, but there may be a sharply defined area of uncertainty. In the *Keeler* case, below, the homicide statute is generally clear, but it is unclear whether it applies to fetuses. The convention for judges is to interpret such laws narrowly, restricting them to their clear intent. This convention is followed often but not always.

––––––––––

In reading the following case, keep in mind (a) the various contexts and situations in which fair warning questions are likely to arise, (b) the criteria by which the fair warning test is applied, and (c) the scope of fair warning.

Keeler v. Superior Court

470 P.2d 617 (Cal. 1970)

Mosk, Justice.

In this proceeding for writ of prohibition we are called upon to decide whether an unborn but viable fetus is a "human being" within the meaning of the California statute defining murder (Pen. Code, § 187). We conclude that the Legislature did not intend such a meaning, and that for us to construe the statute to the contrary and apply it to this petitioner would exceed our judicial power and deny petitioner due process of law.

The evidence received at the preliminary examination may be summarized as follows: Petitioner and Teresa Keeler obtained [an] interlocutory decree of divorce on September 27, 1968. They had been married for 16 years. Unknown to petitioner, Mrs. Keeler was then pregnant by one Ernest Vogt, whom she had met earlier that summer. She subsequently began living with Vogt in Stockton, but concealed the fact from petitioner. Petitioner was given custody of their two daughters, aged 12 and 13 years, and under the decree Mrs. Keeler had the right to take the girls on alternate weekends.

On February 23, 1969, Mrs. Keeler was driving on a narrow mountain road in Amador County after delivering the girls to their home. She met petitioner driving in the opposite direction; he blocked the road with his car, and she pulled over to the side. He walked to her vehicle and began speaking to her. He seemed calm, and she rolled down her window to hear him. He said, "I hear you're pregnant. If you are you had better stay away from the girls and from here." She did not reply, and he opened the car door; as she later testified, "He assisted me out of the car. . . . [I]t wasn't roughly at this time." Petitioner then looked at her abdomen and became "extremely upset." He said, "You sure are. I'm going to stomp it out of you." He pushed her against the car, shoved his knee into her abdomen, and struck her in the face with several blows. She fainted, and when she regained consciousness petitioner had departed.

Mrs. Keeler drove back to Stockton, and the police and medical assistance were summoned. She had suffered substantial facial injuries, as well as extensive bruising of the abdominal wall. A Caesarian section was performed and the fetus was examined in utero. Its head was found to be severely fractured, and it was delivered stillborn. The pathologist gave as his opinion that the cause of death was skull fracture with consequent cerebral hemorrhaging, that death would have been immediate, and that the injury could have been the result of force applied to the mother's abdomen. There was no air in the fetus' lungs, and the umbilical cord was intact.

. . . [T]he expert testimony on the point concluded "with reasonable medical certainty" that the fetus had developed to the stage of viability, i.e., that in the event of premature birth on the date in question it would have had a 75 percent to 96 percent chance of survival.

An information was filed charging petitioner, in count I, with committing the crime of murder (Pen. Code, § 187) in that he did "unlawfully kill a human being, to wit Baby Girl Vogt, with malice aforethought." . . . His motion to set aside the information for lack of probable cause (Pen. Code, § 995) was denied, and he now seeks a writ of prohibition; as will appear, only the murder count is actually in issue. Pending our disposition of the matter, petitioner is free on bail. . . .

Penal Code section 187 provides: "Murder is the unlawful killing of a human being, with malice aforethought." The dispositive question is whether the fetus which petitioner is accused of killing was, on February 23, 1969, a "human being" within the meaning of the statute. If it was not, petitioner cannot be charged with its "murder" and prohibition will lie.

Section 187 was enacted as part of the Penal Code of 1872. Inasmuch as the provision has not been amended since that date, we must determine the intent of the Legislature at the time of its enactment. But section 187 was, in turn, taken verbatim from the first California statute defining murder, part of the Crimes and Punishments Act of 1850. (Stats. 1850, ch. 99, § 19, p. 231.)[4] Penal Code section 5 (also enacted in 1872) declares: "The provisions of this code, so far as they are substantially the same as existing statutes, must be construed as continuations thereof, and not as new enactments." We begin, accordingly, by inquiring into the intent of the Legislature in 1850 when it first defined murder as the unlawful and malicious killing of a "human being."

It will be presumed, of course, that in enacting a statute the Legislature was familiar with the relevant rules of the common law, and, when it couches its enactment in common law language, that its intent was to continue those rules in statutory form. This is particularly appropriate in considering the work of the first session of our

---

4. [n.2] "Murder is the unlawful killing of a human being, with malice aforethought, either express or implied. The unlawful killing may be effected by any of the various means by which death may be occasioned."

Legislature: its precedents were necessarily drawn from the common law, as modified in certain respects by the Constitution and by legislation of our sister states.

We conclude that in declaring murder to be the unlawful and malicious killing of a "human being" the Legislature of 1850 intended that term to have the settled common law meaning of a person who had been born alive, and did not intend the act of feticide — as distinguished from abortion — to be an offense under the laws of California.

Nothing occurred between the years 1850 and 1872 to suggest that in adopting the new Penal Code on the latter date the Legislature entertained any different intent. . . .

The People urge, however, that the sciences of obstetrics and pediatrics have greatly progressed since 1872, to the point where with proper medical care a normally developed fetus prematurely born at 28 weeks or more has an excellent chance of survival, i.e., is "viable"; that the common law requirement of live birth to prove the fetus had become a "human being" who may be the victim of murder is no longer in accord with scientific fact, since an unborn but viable fetus is now fully capable of independent life; and that one who unlawfully and maliciously terminates such a life should therefore be liable to prosecution for murder under section 187. We may grant the premises of this argument; indeed, we neither deny nor denigrate the vast progress of medicine in the century since the enactment of the Penal Code. But we cannot join in the conclusion sought to be deduced: we cannot hold this petitioner to answer for murder by reason of his alleged act of killing an unborn — even though viable — fetus. To such a charge there are two insuperable obstacles, one "jurisdictional" and the other constitutional.

Penal Code section 6 declares in relevant part that "No act or omission" accomplished after the code has taken effect "is criminal or punishable, except as prescribed or authorized by this code, or by some of the statutes which it specifies as continuing in force and as not affected by its provisions, or by some ordinance, municipal, county, or township regulation. . . ." This section embodies a fundamental principle of our tripartite form of government, i.e., that subject to the constitutional prohibition against cruel and unusual punishment, the power to define crimes and fix penalties is vested exclusively in the legislative branch. Stated differently, "there are no common law crimes in California. . . . In order that a public offense be committed, some statute, ordinance or regulation prior in time to the commission of the act, must denounce it; likewise with excuses or justifications — if no statutory excuse or justification apply as to the commission of the particular offense, neither the common law nor the so-called 'unwritten law' may legally supply it." (*People v. Whipple* (1929) 100 Cal. App. 261, 262 [279 P. 1008].)

Settled rules of construction implement this principle. Although the Penal Code commands us to construe its provisions "according to the fair import of their terms, with a view to effect its objects and to promote justice" (Pen. Code, § 4), it is clear the courts cannot go so far as to create an offense by enlarging a statute, by inserting or deleting words, or by giving the terms used false or unusual meanings. Penal statutes will not be made to reach beyond their plain intent; they include only those offenses coming clearly within the import of their language. Indeed, "constructive crimes—crimes built up by courts with the aid of inference, implication, and strained interpretation—are repugnant to the spirit and letter of English and American criminal law." (*Ex parte McNulty* (1888) 77 Cal. 164, 168 [19 P. 237].)

Applying these rules to the case at bar, we would undoubtedly act in excess of the judicial power if we were to adopt the People's proposed construction of section 187. As we have shown, the Legislature has defined the crime of murder in California to apply only to the unlawful and malicious killing of one who has been born alive. We recognize that the killing of an unborn but viable fetus may be deemed by some to be an offense of similar nature and gravity; but as Chief Justice Marshall warned long ago, "It would be dangerous, indeed, to carry the principle, that a case which is within the reason or mischief of a statute, is within its provisions, so far as to punish a crime not enumerated in the statute, because it is of equal atrocity, or of kindred character, with those which are enumerated." (*United States v. Wiltberger* (1820) 18 U.S. (5 Wheat.) 76, 96.) Whether to thus extend liability for murder in California is a determination solely within the province of the Legislature. For a court to simply declare, by judicial fiat, that the time has now come to prosecute under section 187 one who kills an unborn but viable fetus would indeed be to rewrite the statute under the guise of construing it. Nor does a need to fill an asserted "gap" in the law between abortion and homicide—as will appear, no such gap in fact exists—justify judicial legislation of this nature: to make it "a judicial function 'to explore such new fields of crime as they may appear from time to time' is wholly foreign to the American concept of criminal justice" and "raises very serious questions concerning the principle of separation of powers." (*In re Davis* (1966) 242 Cal. App. 2d 645, 655–656 & fn. 12.)

The second obstacle to the proposed judicial enlargement of section 187 is the guarantee of due process of law. Assuming arguendo that we have the power to adopt the new construction of this statute as the law of California, such a ruling, by constitutional command, could operate only prospectively, and thus could not in any event reach the conduct of petitioner on February 23, 1969.

The first essential of due process is fair warning of the act which is made punishable as a crime. "That the terms of a penal statute creating a new offense must be sufficiently explicit to inform those who are subject to it what conduct on their part will render them liable to its penalties, is a well recognized requirement, consonant alike with ordinary notions of fair play and the settled rules of law." (*Connally v. General Constr. Co.* (1926) 269 U.S. 385, 391). "No one may be required at peril of life, liberty or property to speculate as to the meaning of penal statutes. All are entitled to be informed as to what the State commands or forbids." (*Lanzetta v. New Jersey* (1939) 306 U.S. 451, 453.)

This requirement of fair warning is reflected in the constitutional prohibition against the enactment of ex post facto laws (U.S. Const., art. I, §§ 9, 10; Cal.

Const., art. I, §16). When a new penal statute is applied retrospectively to make punishable an act which was not criminal at the time it was performed, the defendant has been given no advance notice consistent with due process. And precisely the same effect occurs when such an act is made punishable under a preexisting statute but by means of an unforeseeable *judicial* enlargement thereof. (*Bouie v. City of Columbia* (1964) 378 U.S. 347.)

. . . In the case at bar the conduct with which petitioner is charged is certainly "improper" and "immoral," and it is not contended he was exercising a constitutionally favored right. But the matter is simply one of degree, and it cannot be denied that the guarantee of due process extends to violent as well as peaceful men. The issue remains, would the judicial enlargement of section 187 now proposed have been foreseeable to this petitioner? . . .

We conclude that the judicial enlargement of section 187 now urged upon us by the People would not have been foreseeable to this petitioner, and hence that its adoption at this time would deny him due process of law.

Notes and Questions

1. **Obsolete and Unused Statutes.** In *New Jersey v. Palendrano*, 293 A.2d 747 (N.J. Super. Ct. 1972), the defendant was charged with being a "common scold" under an old statute which defined a common scold as someone who through "an habitual course of conduct . . . breaks the public peace, increases discord, and becomes a nuisance in the neighborhood." The court noted that being a common scold was widely recognized as criminal conduct in some common-law jurisdictions until as late as 1890. Similar provisions had, however, long fallen into disuse in England. The Superior Court of New Jersey concluded that the significant provisions of the statute have been superseded by the disorderly persons prohibition and that otherwise the statute was void for vagueness. The judges observed that "[o]ne can scarcely conceive of anything more vague and indefinite. To know the criminal risks he might run, the average citizen would be obliged to carry a pocket edition of Blackstone with him."

2. **Vagueness in General and Vagueness in Application.** Compare the principal case with *Kolender v. Lawson*, 461 U.S. 352 (1983), in which appellant challenged as unconstitutionally vague a criminal statute that required persons found loitering or wandering on the streets to provide a "credible and reliable" identification and to account for their presence when requested to do so by the police. Justice O'Connor, speaking for the majority, found the statute unconstitutionally vague because it "vest[ed] virtually complete discretion in the hands of the police to determine whether the suspect has satisfied the statute and must be permitted to go on his way in the absence of probable cause to arrest." She concluded that the statute failed "constitutional standards for definiteness and clarity."

Dissenting in *Kolender*, Justice White argued that under established practice a statute "should not be held unconstitutionally vague on its face unless it is vague in all of its possible applications." Does this criterion make sense? Can you think of a statute that satisfies this criterion? Does the "common scold" notion come close to being vague "in all of its possible applications"? Can the same be said about the homicide statute in *Keeler*?

Keep in mind the distinction between two arguments exemplified by *Palendrano* and *Keeler*. A constitutional challenge based on fair warning may argue (*Palendrano*) that the relevant statute is generally vague, or it may argue (*Keeler*) that it is vague as applied to the particular defendant. A finding that the law is generally vague, as in *Kolender*, means that the law is fatally flawed and cannot be enforced. A finding of the latter kind implies that the law can continue to be applied in its domain of clear application. As in *Keeler*, such a determination puts a burden on the legislature to clarify and amend the law.

In *Johnson v. Athens-Clarke County*, 529 S.E.2d 613 (Ga. 2000), the Georgia Supreme Court found unconstitutionally vague a loitering statute that prohibited lingering in a public place "under circumstances which cause a justifiable and reasonable alarm or immediate concern that such person is involved in unlawful drug activity." Building on the U.S. Supreme Court's decision in *City of Chicago v. Morales*, 527 U.S. 41 (1999), which struck down a Chicago ordinance that banned loitering by "criminal street gang members," the state supreme court concluded that the Georgia statute failed to "give sufficient notice" of what conduct is forbidden: "an innocent person unfamiliar with the drug culture could stand or sit in a 'known drug area' without knowing the area had such a designation, and could return to the area for a legitimate reason, or for no reason at all, . . . and be subject to arrest and conviction." The court also held that the Georgia statute might "encourage arbitrary and discriminatory enforcement" because it "leaves speculative the tests for ascertaining the line separating guilty from innocent acts."

3. Interpretive Strategies: *Original Intention and Evolved Meaning.* In deciding *Keeler*, Justice Mosk looks to the way the California legislature of 1850 would have defined "human being." Is this the appropriate criterion? Did the California legislature of 1850 contemplate persons who might be kept alive by life-support systems? If not, does it follow that such persons are not human beings under the homicide statute?

Consider a different interpretive method that looks not only at the meanings a statute's words had at the time of enactment but also at the evolution of their meaning over time. Some constitutional scholars, for example Ronald Dworkin and Michael Perry, have suggested that because language evolves, constitutional and statutory language should be read in the light of changing usages. Accordingly, if the term "human being" now refers unequivocally and uncontroversially to persons on life support, then even old homicide statutes may be taken to refer to them. Of course, since the use of the term "human being" to include fetuses is still controversial, the Dworkin-Perry approach might yield the same conclusion as *Keeler* but by a different route.

4. Specificity and Fairness. What is unfair about holding Keeler liable for murder? Is it unfair because we can assume that he reasonably considered and rejected the possibility that he would be liable for murder before he attacked Ms. Keeler? Or are we concerned with a different notion of fairness, one that has nothing to do with the actual course of his thinking but is concerned rather with the possible abuse of power by the state?

5. Vagueness and Matters of Reasonable Judgment. Is a statute always impermissibly vague when it makes liability depend on matters of judgment? In *Nash v. United States*, 229 U.S. 373 (1913), the defendants, charged with violating the Sherman Act, argued that the Act was unconstitutionally vague because it criminalized conspiracies "in restraint of trade" and conspiracies "to monopolize trade." Their claim was that these notions "contain in their definition an element of degree as to which estimates may differ, with the result that a man might find himself in prison because his honest judgment does not anticipate that of a jury of less competent men."

Speaking for the Court, Justice Holmes rejected the appeal, noting that "the law is full of instances where a man's fate depends on his estimating rightly, that is, as the jury subsequently estimates it, some matter of degree. If his judgment is wrong, not only may he incur a fine or a short imprisonment, as here; he may incur the penalty of death."

6. Vagueness and Reasonable Judgment: The Limits of the Doctrine. Justice Holmes had an opportunity to define the limits of the *Nash* dictum in *International Harvester Co. v. Kentucky*, 234 U.S. 216 (1914), when the Court concluded that a price-fixing statute that prohibited charging prices above or below the product's "real value" was unconstitutionally vague.

Holmes remarked that determining a product's "real value" wholly apart from its "market value" involved "a problem that no human ingenuity could solve." He distinguished *Nash* as holding merely that "between the two extremes of the obviously illegal and the plainly lawful there is a gradual approach, and that the complexity of life makes it impossible to draw a line in advance without an artificial simplification that would be unjust." On the other hand, the *International Harvester* statute "exacted gifts that mankind does not possess."

Note the degree of vagueness that Holmes says is inevitable in the drafting and application of statutes. Are his observations consistent with the letter and spirit of *Keeler* and *Palendrano*?

7. Ex Post Facto Laws. Are ex post facto laws ever permissible? Wholly apart from the requirement of due process and fair warning, the Constitution explicitly prohibits ex post facto laws in Article 1, Sections 9 and 10. The typical ex post facto law criminalizes conduct that occurred before the effective date of the law, acts that were not criminal when they took place.

Ex post facto laws are so clearly inconsistent with fairness that writers usually discuss them in the context of discontinuities of government. They are generally not contemplated as part of the normal operation of constitutional government. For an intriguing hypothetical situation in which ex post facto laws seem to be called for, see Lon Fuller, *The Problem of the Grudge Informer*, in THE MORALITY OF LAW 187–95 (1969).

A complete discussion of ex post facto laws would require us to consider the constitutional status of the following issues:

(a) Are states (and the federal government) prohibited from retroactively applying an increase in the penalty for a crime (that was already prohibited at the time it occurred)?

(b) If evidence or procedure rules have been changed in a way that is disadvantageous to a defendant, is the defendant's trial governed by the old or new rules of evidence?

(c) What is the date of an offense for purposes of determining whether application of the law is ex post facto? In the case of a continuing offense, is it the date of the initial act or the date of completion of the offense?

8. Scholarship on Vagueness. One of the most detailed and exhaustive examinations of the concepts of vagueness and fair warning as constitutional mandates is John Decker's survey, *Addressing Vagueness, Ambiguity, and Other Uncertainty in American Criminal Laws*, 80 DENV. U. L. REV. 241 (2002). Decker concludes unsurprisingly that there are no clear statutory guidelines and that no wholly consistent rules of application emerge from the case law. The article is particularly useful as an encyclopedic review of the case law.

9. Subsequent Developments in Fetal Homicide. Since the California Supreme Court's decision in *Keeler*, a number of state legislatures have amended their homicide statutes to include the killing of an unborn child. *See, e.g.*, Cal. Penal Code § 187 (defining murder as "the unlawful killing of a human being, or a fetus, with malice aforethought"); N.Y. Penal Law § 125.00 (defining homicide to include "the death of a person or an unborn child with which a female has been pregnant for more than twenty-four weeks").

In *People v. Davis*, 872 P.2d 591 (Cal. 1994), the California Supreme Court refused to require proof of viability in order to sustain a fetal homicide conviction under the murder statute amended in response to *Keeler*. The court did, however, require the prosecution to show that "the fetus has progressed beyond the embryonic stage of seven to eight weeks." *Id.* at 602. More recently, in *People v. Taylor*, 86 P.3d 881 (Cal. 2004), the California Supreme Court held that a defendant could be convicted of second-degree murder in connection with the death of an approximately 12-week-old fetus even though he did not know the woman he shot was pregnant. The defendant "acted with knowledge of the danger to and conscious disregard for life in general," the court explained, and "[t]hat is all that is required for implied malice murder. He did not need to be specifically aware how many potential victims his conscious disregard for life endangered." *Id.* at 884–85.

In 2004, President Bush signed into law the Unborn Victims of Violence Act, 18 U.S.C. § 1841, which makes it a separate federal offense for one who is committing a federal crime of violence to kill or injure "a child, who is in utero at the time the conduct takes place." The Act does not require proof that the defendant "had knowledge or should have had knowledge that the victim of the underlying offense was pregnant," and a crime committed under this statute is punishable by the same penalty that would have been imposed had the "injury or death occurred to the unborn child's mother." *Id.* § 1841(a)(2).

10. Vagueness and Sentencing. In *Johnson v. United States*, 135 S. Ct. 2551 (2015), the Supreme Court struck down as unconstitutionally vague the so-called "residual clause" of the Armed Career Criminal Act (ACCA), the federal statute that increases the penalties for various weapons offenses if the defendant had three or more prior convictions for a "serious drug offense" or a "violent felony." 18 U.S.C. § 924(e). The residual clause provided that the ACCA's definition of a "violent felony" included any felony that "otherwise involves conduct that presents a serious potential risk of physical injury to another." *Id.* § 924(e)(2)(B). In finding this language impermissibly vague, Justice Scalia's opinion for the Court reasoned that "[t]wo features of the residual clause conspire to make it unconstitutionally vague": it "leaves grave uncertainty" both "about how to estimate the risk posed by a crime" and "about how much risk it takes for a crime to qualify as a violent felony." *Johnson*, 135 S. Ct. at 2557–58.

11. Vagueness and Jurisdiction. In the wake of the terrorist acts of 9/11, the courts have had to face a new kind of vagueness question. As we have seen, vagueness is typically raised as a defense and involves claims about the definition of crime and criminal activity; it takes the form of an argument that the definition lacks sufficient specificity to afford fair warning to actors and to circumscribe the actions of those who enforce the law. The new kind of question was one of jurisdiction and standing. It concerned the question of who is entitled to be tried in civilian criminal courts and to take advantage of the procedural guarantees of the Constitution.

Just one week after 9/11, Congress passed the Authorization for Use of Military Force Against Terrorists, which drew upon Congress' preexisting War Powers Resolution. On November 13, 2001, President Bush issued a presidential military order under these powers to authorize the indefinite detention at Guantanamo of "enemy combatants," defined as members or supporters of the Taliban or al-Qaida forces engaged in hostilities against the United States. The Military Commissions Act of 2006, passed by Congress in response to *Hamdan v. Rumsfeld*, 548 U.S. 557 (2006), distinguished between lawful and unlawful enemy combatants. The latter, according to the Act, were in a legal limbo, entitled to access neither the U.S. civil justice system nor the procedures granted to prisoners of war by the Geneva Conventions. In *Boumediene v. Bush*, 553 U.S. 723 (2008), the Supreme Court held that Congress was not empowered to deny such individuals the right to use the U.S. federal courts system. Thus, habeas corpus petitions of these individuals were reinstated.

The Obama administration followed the Bush administration's policy and sought to bar "unlawful" enemy combatants from the civil courts. The Obama Department of Justice, however, phased out the term "enemy combatant," referring instead to "person[s] engaged in hostilities against the United Sates or its coalition partners during an armed conflict." (Department of Defense Dictionary.)

The indefiniteness of a term such as "unlawful enemy combatant" in the current use lies in the fact that it was invented for political reasons to circumscribe a category that had not existed previously—individuals who were detained under the American criminal justice system but could not avail themselves of the rights associated with such detention; at the same time, these individuals were not prisoners of war and therefore not protected by international rules of war. The term was invented not simply as a description of an independently identifiable category of actors, but as embodying the conclusion that certain actors lacked particular legal rights. The term embodied the postulate that unlawful enemy combatants could not avail themselves of these procedural rights; it did not leave it an open question. The courts, on the other hand, persist in regarding the question as open and determinable. Thus, the term is fatally ambiguous.

[C] Specificity and Discretion in Criminal Law

The discussion of due process and fair warning above is part of a larger historical and political story. The historical story is the gradual evolution in English common law from judge-made, ad hoc law to legislative (parliamentary) exclusivity in law-creation, in making law statutory. The American story begins after the shift to a stable legislature with law-making responsibility has largely been made. The *Shaw* case, below, reflects on these changes.

The political aspect concerns power and discretion. Formally, the power of courts lies in interpreting and applying law, not making it. Formally, the power of the police and other parts of the executive branch of government lies in carrying out the law, rather than in interpreting or making it. This reinforces a system of checks and balances. But it is never completely clear how these roles are distinguished one from another. In other words, questions remain about the degree of discretion that each branch of government has in defining the scope of its formal role.

[1] From Common Law to Statute

Modern criminal law is, for the most part, statutory. Although every state now has a penal code, most did not adopt systematic codes until the latter part of the twentieth century.

Criminal law as we know it is derived from the common law of England. English common law has two components. Its earliest and strongest roots are found in judicial decisions in response to individual controversies. Although most historians regard laws passed by Parliament as the main source of law from the Tudor period on, judges long claimed to retain the power to invent new crimes when faced with situations Parliament had not addressed.

In the modern era, judges in England and America are generally said to have lost this power. Nonetheless, cases and statutes remain coordinate sources of the law. Even where the law has been codified, judges look to case law to situate and interpret modern statutes.

The question of judicial power to make new law arises when the underlying statutory mandate is broad and vague. The previous section on vagueness and fair warning considered the constitutional limits of legislative power. The present section considers the limits of discretion in the criminal process more broadly.

The following English case exemplifies such a context.

Shaw v. Director of Public Prosecutions

[1962] A.C. 220 (House of Lords)

[The defendant published a magazine which was called the Ladies Directory in which names, addresses, telephone numbers, photographs, and salient details of prostitutes appeared. He was convicted of conspiracy to corrupt public morals (and two other counts) and appealed.]

Viscount Simonds.

My Lords, as I have already said, the first count in the indictment is "Conspiracy to corrupt public morals," and the particulars of offence will have sufficiently appeared. I am concerned only to assert what was vigorously denied by counsel for the appellant, that such an offence is known to the common law, and that it was open to the jury on the facts of this case that the appellant was guilty of such an offence. I must say categorically that, if it were not so, Her Majesty's courts would strangely have failed in their duty as servants and guardians of the common law. Need I say, My Lords, that I am no advocate of the right of the judges to create new criminal offences? . . . But I am at a loss to understand how it can be said either that the law does not recognise a conspiracy to corrupt public morals or that, though there may not be an exact precedent for such a conspiracy as this case reveals, it does not fall fairly within the general words by which it is described. . . . The fallacy in the argument that was addressed to us lay in the attempt to exclude from the scope of general words acts well calculated to corrupt public morals just because they had not been committed or had not been brought to the notice of the court before. It is not thus that the common law has developed. We are perhaps more accustomed to hear this matter discussed upon the question whether such a transaction is contrary to public policy. At once the controversy arises. On the one hand it is said that it is not possible in the twentieth century for the court to create a new head of public policy, on the other it is said that this is but a new example of a well-established head. In the sphere of criminal law I entertain no doubt that there remains in the courts of law a residual power to enforce the supreme and fundamental purpose of the law, to conserve not only the safety and order but also the moral welfare of the State, and that it is their duty to guard it against attacks which may be the more insidious because they are novel and unprepared for. That is the broad head (call it public policy if you wish) within which the present indictment falls. It matters little what label is given to the offending act. To one of your Lordships it may appear an affront to public decency, to another considering that it may succeed in its obvious intention of provoking libidinous desires it will seem a corruption of public morals. Yet others may deem it aptly described as the creation of a public mischief or the undermining of moral conduct. The same act will not in all ages be regarded in the same way. The law must be related to the changing standards of life, not yielding to every shifting impulse of the popular will but having regard to fundamental assessments of human values and the purpose of society. Today a denial of the fundamental Christian doctrine, which in past centuries would have been regarded by the ecclesiastical courts as heresy and by the common law as blasphemy, will no longer be an offence if the decencies of controversy are observed. When Lord Mansfield, speaking long after the Star Chamber had been abolished, said that the Court of King's Bench was the *custos morum* of the people and had the superintendency of offences *contra bonos mores*, he was asserting, as I now assert, that there is in that court a residual power, where no statute has yet intervened to supersede the common law, to superintend those offences which are prejudicial to the public welfare. Such occasions will be rare, for Parliament has not been slow to legislate when attention has been sufficiently aroused. But gaps remain and will always remain since no one can foresee every way in which the wickedness of man may disrupt the order of society. Let me take a single instance. . . . Let it be supposed that at some future, perhaps early, date homosexual practices between adult consenting males are no longer a crime. Would it not be an offence if even without obscenity, such practices were publicly advocated and encouraged by pamphlet and advertisement? Or must we wait until Parliament finds time to deal with such conduct? I say, my Lords, that if the common law is powerless in such an event, then we should no longer do her reverence. But I say that her hand is still powerful and that it is for Her Majesty's judges to play the part which Lord Mansfield pointed out to them. . . .

Appeal dismissed.

Lord Reid.

I think, or at least I hope, that it is now established, that the courts cannot create new offences by individuals. So far at least I have the authority of Lord Goddard, C.J., in delivering the opinion of the court in *Newland* [[1954] 1 Q.B. 158]: "The dictum in *Rex v. Higgins* was that all offences of a public nature, that is, all such acts or attempts as tend to the prejudice of the public are indictable, but no other member of the court stated the law in such wide terms. It is the breadth of that dictum that was so strongly criticised by Sir Fitzjames Stephen in the passage in his History of the Criminal Law (vol. 3, p. 359). . . . In effect it would leave it to the judges to declare new crimes and enable them to hold anything which they considered prejudicial to the community to be a misdemeanor. However beneficial that might have been in days when Parliament met seldom or at least only at long intervals it surely is now the province of the legislature and not of the judiciary to create new criminal offenses." Every argument against creating new offences by any individual appears to me to be equally valid against creating new offences by a combination of individuals. . . .

Even if there is still a vestigial power of this kind it ought not, in my view, to be used unless there appears to be general agreement that the offence to which it is applied ought to be criminal if committed by an individual. Notoriously, there are wide differences of opinion today as to how far the law ought to punish immoral acts which are not done in the face of the public. Some think that the law already goes too far, some that it does not go far enough. Parliament is the proper place, and I am firmly of opinion the only proper place, to settle that. When there is sufficient support from public opinion, Parliament does not hesitate to intervene. Where Parliament fears to tread it is not for the courts to rush in. . . .

In my judgment this House is in no way bound and ought not to sanction the extension of "public mischief" to any new field, and certainly not if such extension would be in any way controversial. . . .

Finally I must advert to the consequences of holding that this very general offence exists. It has always been thought to be of primary importance that our law, and particularly our criminal law, should be certain: that a man should be able to know what conduct is and what is not criminal, particularly when heavy penalties are involved.

Notes and Questions

1. **The English Consensus.** More recent English cases firmly reject Lord Simonds' argument that judges have residual power to make law in cases where morality makes it appropriate to do so. *See, e.g., Rex v. Knuller* [1973] AC 435 (opinion by Lord Reid, elaborating upon his opinion in *Shaw*).

2. **The European Tradition.** In FREEDOM UNDER THE LAW (1949), at 40–42, Lord Denning points out that European countries with a long tradition of adhering to a written code reject the general principle defended by Lord Simonds in *Shaw*. They regard the idea that "no one shall be punished for anything that is not expressly forbidden by law" as an essential requirement of justice. Denning goes on to criticize the suggestion that "all offences of a public nature, that such acts or attempts as tend to the prejudice of the community, are indictable." He notes that this claim of authority is similar to the reasoning used by Soviet judges to punish any acts that could be labeled "socially dangerous."

3. **Vagueness and Moral Discretion.** Are such epithets as "socially dangerous" or "tending to corrupt public morals" necessarily so vague that they allow judges to do whatever they want and fail to give potential offenders fair warning? Are they problematic because they presuppose that there is a consensus about public morals in a pluralistic society?

4. **Relevance of the American Concept of Democracy.** Consider the claim that American democratic government makes it appropriate for legislators but not judges to create new crimes. *Shaw* can be criticized on three grounds: (a) as an instance of

judge-invented crime, (b) as an ex post facto application of criminal law, and (c) as a situation in which the law fails to give fair warning and allows the police and prosecutors unlimited discretion.

———————

In the United States, the definition and enforcement of criminal law is primarily in the hands of the states. States have regulatory (police) power over public safety and public welfare. The federal government may prohibit acts only when there is express or implied authority under the Constitution. Examples of federal crimes are treason, fraudulent use of the mail, and racketeering.

The first half of the twentieth century was an era of legal reform. Many jurists, scholars, and politicians argued that law must be shaped by the external goal of progressive improvement of society and by the internal goals of clarifying, modernizing, and systematizing the law. The language of criminal law, in some instances, dated back to the fourteenth century and reflected the psychological and social assumptions of that period.

Founded in 1923, the American Law Institute is an organization of scholars, judges, and lawyers formed with the purpose of bringing the law in each subject matter area to a state of coherence and contemporary relevance. In its first 30 years, it promulgated so-called restatements of law in such areas as contracts, torts, property, etc. These well-structured compilations of law were widely influential and formed a basis for law reform in countless instances. By the 1950s, the ALI turned its attention to criminal law, having initially faced and then dropped a similar project in 1931. It was widely appreciated that, in the words of Herbert Wechsler, who became the main voice of the Model Penal Code, there was serious need "for a guide to long-delayed reform" of criminal law rather than simply a "description and reaffirmation of existing law."

The Model Penal Code (MPC) in its Proposed Official Draft was published in 1962. It affirmed and tried to achieve conceptual clarity and transparent structure. Over time, the MPC has had enormous influence in guiding the rethinking and reformulation of criminal law in virtually every state. Pedagogically, a strong argument can be made that if one assimilates and becomes comfortable with the distinctions in the MPC and the arguments supporting them, one has the tools to quickly and easily master the specific criminal law of any of the 50 states. And the MPC makes it possible to understand the complexities and confusions remaining in those aspects of law that have not been reformed. At the same time, not all of the MPC's recommendations have been equally persuasive, and some, both for conceptual and political reasons, have remained matters of theory rather than practice. The MPC treatment of felony murder is one example.

Among the most significant reforms in the MPC was its re-framing of the mental aspect of culpability, *mens rea*. It suggested that blameworthiness be determined by the extent to which an individual acted purposely, knowingly, recklessly, or negligently with regard to the material elements of the particular crime. The

MPC also led to a re-thinking of inchoate crimes and of the appropriate scope of strict liability. Aside from these general provisions, the authors of the MPC re-drafted the nature and elements of many particular crimes.

While no state has adopted the MPC is its entirety, its influence continues to be great more than 50 years after its promulgation. Arguably it remains the single best representation of an internally coherent and morally defensible model of criminal law.

Notes and Questions

1. The Model Penal Code and Neutrality. The Model Penal Code is an attempt to formulate principles of criminal responsibility that are politically neutral, that reflect a consensus in society about what kinds of conduct are dangerous and blameworthy. It is surely not a coincidence that Herbert Wechsler, the principal drafter of the MPC, is also the author of an influential article in legal theory, *Toward Neutral Principles of Constitutional Law*, 73 HARV. L. REV. 1 (1959).

The assumption that some principles of law are politically neutral is challenged by the critical legal studies movement. These arguments are discussed in Chapter 16.

2. Revising the Model Penal Code. Lawyers and academics have long criticized aspects of the Model Penal Code and long debated the merits of a radical revision, a Model Penal Code Second. No such document is imminent, although the American Law Institute's ongoing efforts to revise the provisions relating to sentencing and rape are discussed below in Chapter 2 and Chapter 7. Three interesting symposia on the strengths and weaknesses of the MPC are the following: *Symposium: Model Penal Code*, 7 BUFF. CRIM. L. REV. 1 (2003); *Symposium: The Model Penal Code Revisited*, 4 BUFF. CRIM. L. REV. 1 (2000); *Symposium: Model Penal Code Second: Good or Bad Idea?*, 1 OHIO ST. J. CRIM. L. 7 (2003).

[2] Points of Discretion

Our discussion of fair warning in Section B flags one limitation on the discretion and power of legislators and judges. Our constitutional commitment to fair warning has a historical dimension in the shift from judge-made law to statute, and from common law to code, because adopting a code can be a definitive way of limiting the creative discretion of judges.

To speak of discretion in the criminal process by referring only to the limits on the roles of legislators and judges in defining what is a crime gives an incomplete picture. The criminal process is rife with discretionary decision-making at many levels. Sociologists and criminologists are often concerned with the use and misuse of discretion throughout the criminal process. A course in criminal law, however, typically focuses on what the rules are to the exclusion of considering how they are in fact applied.

Some discretionary decisions are compelled by circumstances. Our resources do not allow complete enforcement of criminal law. Other exercises of discretion are not compelled: the police, prosecutors, and parole boards often make decisions for personal or political reasons.

To consider a decision discretionary is not necessarily to criticize or condemn it, since discretionary decisions can be made for laudable reasons. But there is inevitably a danger in the use of discretion, especially when it is exercised invisibly, without public oversight or awareness. The risk of unfairness and even corruption is always present.

Police officers, prosecutors, judges, prison guards and wardens, parole boards, and probation officers must make discretionary calls at every turn. Three focal points of particular interest to scholars are decisions by police to arrest, decisions by prosecutors to file charges, and decisions by judges and prosecutors made in the context of plea bargaining.

[a] Police Discretion

Police may abuse discretion by being overzealous (and thus infringing the rights of suspects) or by enforcing the law selectively. Selective enforcement may occur for defensible and indefensible reasons. One can defend a decision not to charge a suspect who helps the police in making a case against more dangerous or serious offenders, but not a decision based on racial bias.

It is generally acknowledged that full enforcement of law puts an impossible demand on the police. No department has adequate resources. Therefore, every department develops tacit policies about the kinds of cases that need to be pursued most vigorously. Such policies should be impartial and reviewable at a high level of responsibility, and they should reflect widely-shared intuitions about which crimes are most dangerous and disruptive. Legislatures can help by criminalizing only those actions that threaten public order and by giving clear indications of intended priorities.

[b] Prosecutorial Discretion

The decision to charge an individual with a crime, in other words the decision to prosecute, is momentous. For the individual charged, it may mean loss of freedom until and during the trial or release under serious financial constraints. It means that the process will be resolved by a guilty plea, often the result of a plea negotiation (plea bargaining), or by a verdict. The reputational effects of being charged can be significant. Obviously the effects of a charge can go well beyond the individual to family members, associates, and the community at large.

In their treatise, Criminal Procedure (4th edition 2004), Wayne LaFave, Jerold Israel, and Nancy King point out the factors that are most likely to determine the decision to prosecute:

> (1) whether there is sufficient evidence to support a prosecution; (2) if so, whether there are nonetheless reasons for not subjecting the defendant to

the criminal process; (3) if so, whether nonprosecution should be conditioned upon the defendant's participation in a diversion program; and (4) if prosecution is to be undertaken, with what offense or offenses the defendant should be charged.

LaFave and his colleagues also point out that the work of the police often determines the feasibility of bringing a charge. The majority of cases are brought to the attention of prosecutors by the police. The police must initially determine whether to make an arrest, and this will be affected by "whether the evidence is sufficient or whether any good purpose would be served by invoking the criminal process." The role of the victim is also often crucial. "In many locales certain crimes such as nonsupport and the passing of bad checks are unlikely to come to public attention" unless raised by victims or other concerned parties.

The authors identify a range of factors that may lead to a decision not to prosecute and that are therefore important in the exercise of prosecutorial discretion. Among these factors are the following:

(i) When the victim has expressed a desire that the offender not be prosecuted. Particularly in assault cases involving a dispute between spouses or prior acquaintances, the victim's disinterest in prosecution usually is determinative. . . .

(ii) When the costs of prosecution would be excessive, considering the nature of the violation. . . .

(iii) When the mere fact of prosecution would, in the prosecutor's judgment, cause undue harm to the offender. For example, when it was learned that a married woman had filed a false report of rape with the police and that she had done so to conceal her indiscretion from her husband, it was decided that prosecution for filing a false crime report would be unwise because it would jeopardize her marriage.

(iv) When the offender, if not prosecuted, will likely aid in achieving other enforcement goals. . . .

(v) When the "harm" done by the offender can be corrected without prosecution. The best example is the frequent decision not to prosecute persons who have committed minor property crimes, such as writing bad checks, if full restitution is made to the victim.

These factors weigh in favor of leniency, of a decision not to prosecute. But the authors also point out that "[a] particular individual may be selected out for prosecution notwithstanding the fact that the case is one which ordinarily would not result in an affirmative charging decision. Such selection may occur in response to press and public pressure . . . [or] to rid society of certain 'bad actors' who are thought to have committed more serious crimes."

[c] Plea Bargaining

About 90 percent of criminal cases do not go to trial but are resolved by guilty pleas. Of those, the majority are the result of plea bargains. Most observers concede that, absent the safety valve of settlement through bargained pleas, courts would be gridlocked beyond hope of repair. There is no agreement, however, about whether the system of plea bargaining works justly. Does it flout the principle of equal treatment for similar crimes? Does it encourage innocent persons to plead guilty to low-grade offenses? Does it allow serious offenders to evade appropriate sanctions? Does it give prosecutors unbridled and unprincipled discretion? The following brief comments reflect the diversity of views. The system of plea bargaining is both praised for embodying private "autonomous" dispute resolution and condemned for its relative amorality. As you consider in the Chapters that follow the ways in which various crimes are defined by legislatures and criminal statutes are interpreted by courts, you might develop a sense of why both prosecutors and defendants are so willing to resolve cases by agreement rather than trial.

Roland Acevedo, Note, *Is a Ban on Plea Bargaining an Ethical Abuse of Discretion?*, 64 Fordham L. Rev. 987, 991–92 (1995)

Plea bargaining allows defendants, in exchange for the surrender of certain constitutional rights, to gain prompt and final disposition of their cases, avoid the uncertainties and anxieties of a trial, and escape the maximum penalties authorized by law. Prosecutors, by agreeing to reduce charges or to recommend lower sentences, avoid costly time-consuming trials, and thus, conserve vital and scarce prosecutorial resources. Defense counsel, most of whom are court appointed public defenders, dispose of cases quickly and reduce overwhelming caseloads.... Judges ameliorate congested court calendars and conserve judicial resources.... Victims may benefit by avoiding the rigors of a trial.... Finally, the public is protected from the risks posed by defendants who are free on bail.

Peter Arenella, *Rethinking The Functions of Criminal Procedure: The Warren and Burger Courts' Competing Ideologies*, 72 Geo. L.J. 185, 219 (1983)

Plea bargaining undercuts [the] distinctive moral aspects of the criminal law. First, negotiated dispute resolution "privatizes" the dispute by empowering the parties themselves to resolve it without any significant involvement by either the public or the courts. Second, negotiated settlements permit the parties to resolve questions concerning the appropriate degree of liability that should attach to the defendant's acts. Such party compromises destroy any notion that an objective societal determination of moral guilt has been made. Worse, negotiation dilutes the moral force of the criminal sanction by treating questions concerning the offender's just deserts as a negotiating chip whose value lies primarily in how it affects the parties' rational adjustment of litigation risks. Consequently, plea bargaining may distort the legislature's labeling of offenses and frustrate its sentencing objectives. Finally, the negotiation process undermines the moral legitimacy of the system in both the defendant's and public's eyes.

In contrast, an adjudicatory process reflects the values that the substantive criminal law is trying to promote. It reinforces the moral content of substantive guilt by forcing the state to offer compelling proof of the defendant's guilt to a disinterested third party in a public forum. Regardless of whether the adjudicatory mechanism uses inquisitorial or adversarial procedures, it provides a process that has its own moral-educative effect on both defendants and the public. A public trial, if fairly conducted, sends its own message about dignity, fairness, and justice that contributes to the moral force of the criminal sanction. Finally, independent adjudication promotes the criminal law's punishment goals by assuring that an objective social determination of the actor's just deserts will be made by either a community body or by a judicial official before the state is given the right to use the defendant as a means to promote society's future welfare.

———

Commentators distinguish three forms of plea negotiation. In one form, the defendant is allowed to plead guilty to a less serious charge than the one supported by evidence. In a second form, the defendant pleads guilty to the original charge in exchange for some promise of leniency in sentencing. A third form is a guilty plea to one of several charges in exchange for dismissal of the rest.

The system of plea bargaining, which goes back more than 100 years, plays a much greater role in American criminal procedure than in other countries. While the expense and difficulty of trying cases in courts with unmanageably crowded dockets is often cited as the main reason, the popularity of plea bargaining may be explained by the following reasons as well: (1) relatively few cases involve genuine disputes about guilt and innocence, (2) broadening of the right to counsel and the rights of defendants generally has given defense attorneys new roles in the period before trial, and (3) prosecutors and defense attorneys feel the process allows them to shape penalties to individual offenders by taking more considerations into account than would be permitted at trial.

Some important cases have considered when and whether plea bargaining is coercive. In *Scott v. United States*, Chief Judge Bazelon of the District of Columbia Circuit considered the implications of differentiating between those who pled guilty and those who did not when imposing sentence.

Scott v. United States

419 F.2d 264 (D.C. Cir. 1969)

Bazelon, Chief Judge.

. . . The trial judge . . . stated at the sentencing hearing, "If you had pleaded guilty to this offense, I might have been more lenient with you." The stark import of this comment is that the defendant paid a price for demanding a trial. In view of the prohibitions the Supreme Court has laid down against making the exercise of Fourth, Fifth, and Sixth Amendment rights costly, the pricetag thus placed on the right to a fair trial which these amendments guarantee would, on first impression, seem clearly impermissible. And yet, despite the startling incongruity, empirical evidence supports the proposition that judges do sentence defendants who have demanded a trial more severely. At least one Court of Appeals has taken approving "judicial notice of the fact that trial courts quite generally impose a lighter sentence on pleas of guilty than in cases where the accused pleaded not guilty but has been found guilty by a jury." An advisory committee of the American Bar Association has concluded that "it is proper for the court to grant charge and sentence concessions to defendants who enter a plea of guilty . . . when the interest of the public in the effective administration of criminal justice would thereby be served."

Much of this adulation for differential sentencing has been rationalized without frank recognition of the fact that whatever its advantages, the practice does exact a price from those who insist upon a trial. But the arguments in favor of differential sentencing cannot be dismissed by a wooden insistence that the exercise of constitutional rights can never be made costly. Some rights may be so vital that no deterrence to their free exercise can be tolerated. The Supreme Court has accorded such preeminent status to the self-incrimination privilege. But in other areas the Court has suggested the need for a less truncated analysis. In *United States v. Jackson* [390 U.S. 570 (1968)], the Court held that Congress could not provide for a death penalty "applicable only to those defendants who assert the right to contest their guilt before a jury." But in doing so the majority did not rely upon the summary argument that the exercise of such a right could in no way be made costly. The Court rather asked "whether that effect is unnecessary and therefore excessive."

The Supreme Court has offered little guidance concerning which constitutional rights can tolerate some chilling effect and which cannot. Perhaps the right to a trial, like the self-incrimination privilege but apparently unlike the right to a jury, belongs in the latter camp. But until the Supreme Court speaks, the practice of differential sentencing should be evaluated with some attention paid to the nature of the price exacted from those who plead innocent and why it is exacted.

Two arguments inevitably appear whenever differential sentencing is discussed. The first is that the defendant's choice of plea shows whether he recognizes and repents his crime. One difficulty with this argument is that no court or commentator has explained why a defendant's insistence upon his self-incrimination privilege is not also evidence of a lack of repentance. Or his insistence that evidence unconstitutionally seized should not be admitted.

Repentance has a role in penology. But the premise of our criminal jurisprudence has always been that the time for repentance comes after trial. The adversary process is a fact-finding engine, not a drama of contrition in which a prejudged defendant is expected to knit up his lacerated bonds to society.

There is a tension between the right of the accused to assert his innocence and the interest of society in his repentance. But we could consider resolving this conflict in favor of the latter interest only if the trial offered an unparalleled opportunity to test the repentance of the accused. It does not. There is other, and better, evidence of such repentance. The sort of information collected in presentence reports provides a far more finely brushed portrait of the man than do a few hours or days at trial. And the offender while on probation or in prison after trial can demonstrate his insight into his problems far better than at trial.

If the defendant were unaware that a proper display of remorse might affect his sentence, his willingness to admit the crime might offer the sentencing judge some guidance. But with the inducement of a lighter sentence dangled before him, the sincerity of any cries of *mea culpa* becomes questionable. Moreover, the refusal of a defendant to plead guilty is not necessarily indicative of a lack of repentance. A man may regret his crime but wish desperately to avoid the stigma of a criminal conviction. . . .

The second argument for differential sentencing is necessity. Most convictions, perhaps as many as 90 per cent in some jurisdictions, are the product of guilty pleas. Unless a large proportion of defendants plead guilty, the argument runs, the already crowded dockets in many jurisdictions would collapse into chaos. Since most defendants are indigent, the only price they can be forced to pay for pleading innocent is time in jail. Ergo, differential sentences are justified for those who plead guilty and those who plead innocent.

When approached from this perspective, the problem inevitably becomes entwined with that of plea bargaining. And the difficulties that practice presents are exceeded only by its pervasiveness. In many areas such bargaining dominates the criminal process. Its format may vary. The prosecutor may agree to reduce the charge in exchange for a guilty plea, or he may agree to recommend a lighter sentence. The judge may be aware of the agreement or he may not. If aware that a bargain has been struck, the court may or may not ratify the agreement before a plea is offered and accepted.

When a defendant pleads guilty in exchange for the promise of the prosecutor or court, a subsequent challenge to the voluntariness of his plea raises a recognized constitutional issue. When the accused refuses to plead guilty and subsequently receives a heavier sentence, the invisibility with which the system operates in individual cases too often conceals the constitutional issue. But the problem is the same in both contexts. Whether the defendant surrenders his right to a trial because of a bargain with court or prosecutor, or exercises his right at the cost of a stiffer sentence, a price has been put on the right.

The two sides of this coin are related in a practical sense as well. At least when only a single charge is involved, the effectiveness of plea bargaining depends upon the willingness of the court to impose a lighter sentence when a defendant pleads guilty. If such is the custom within a jurisdiction, the prosecutor enjoys credibility. Indeed, if the custom is sufficiently well known, actual bargaining may be unnecessary: enough defendants will be cowed into guilty pleas simply by the force of their lawyers' warnings that defendants convicted after demanding a trial receive long sentences.

Thus, to the extent that the appellant here received a longer sentence because he pleaded innocent, he was a pawn sacrificed to induce other defendants to plead guilty. . . .

Notes and Questions

1. **Plea Bargains: The Role of Judges.** One of the issues facing Judge Bazelon in *Scott* is whether judges should be parties to plea bargains. Courts often pay lip service to the charade that a guilty plea was spontaneous and not made on the basis of promises. What dangers are involved in making judges parties to plea bargains? What purposes are served by pretending that the plea was not made in response to promises (of leniency, etc.)?

2. **Plea Bargains and Coercion.** In what ways is the process of plea bargaining coercive? Does it corrupt the process of achieving just results?

3. **Plea Bargains and Justice.** Does the process of plea bargaining have an egalitarian effect, providing a semblance of justice even for those without the ability to pay high-priced attorneys? Or does it have the opposite effect, favoring those who can afford attorneys who are especially effective in manipulating the bargaining process?

In general, does the wide use of plea bargaining put too much power in the hands of prosecutors?

4. *Scott* **and Controversy.** Many courts have disagreed with the reasoning and conclusions of the *Scott* case. For example, the U.S. Court of Appeals for the District of Columbia Circuit, in its subsequent decision in *United States v. Jones*, 973 F.2d 928, 936 (D.C. Cir. 1992), *aff'd on other grounds*, 997 F.2d 1475 (D.C. Cir. 1993) (en banc), challenged the reasoning behind *Scott*'s suggestion that "although a prosecutor may engage in plea bargaining, a trial judge may neither involve himself in the process nor even express a policy of differential sentencing." Judge Stephen Williams, writing for the panel in *Jones*, said that "[a]lthough clearly the prosecutor's proper role is quite different from the judge's, *Scott*'s apparent ban on *any* judicial consideration of the defendant's choice between plea and trial is hard to reconcile with *Blackledge* [*v. Perry*, 417 U.S. 21 (1974)], which suggested that a prosecutor is at least as likely a source of vindictiveness as a judge, or with *Roberts v. United States*, 445 U.S. 552

(1980), which upheld judicial consideration of the defendant's failure to cooperate with the government, a failure that is typically (though not invariably) linked with the decision to stand trial."

5. Scholarship on Plea Bargains. In *Plea Bargaining and Convicting the Innocent: The Role of the Prosecutor, the Defense Counsel and the Judge* (16 BYU J. Pub. L. 189 (2002)), F. Andrew Hessick III and Reshma Saujani examine the role of the judge in plea bargaining. The authors argue, among other things, that the structural incentives on judges to allow plea bargaining increase the possibility that innocent defendants will be incarcerated. They offer suggestions to reduce that likelihood, including increased availability of discovery for the defense. In *Reconcilable Differences: The Supreme Court Should Allow the Marriage of* Brady *and Plea Bargaining* (78 Ind. L.J. 899 (2003)), Andrew P. O'Brien seeks to demonstrate that the holding in *Brady v. Maryland*, 373 U.S. 83 (1963), which bars prosecutors from withholding evidence favorable to the defendant and material to guilt or punishment after the defense has requested it, should be made relevant to the plea bargaining process as well as to trial preparation. His main concern is also safeguarding the innocent from punishment.

[D] Structuring the Study of Criminal Law

[1] Basic Elements

What kinds of questions and problems are bound to come up in any course on criminal law? What issues are bound to be addressed by legislators and judges in defining and developing a system of criminal law? This section offers a brief structured preview of the main issues.

We saw above that instances of criminal conduct have two aspects: (a) an act that causes or is likely to cause harm to the interests of others and (b) an accompanying state of mind that displays culpable disregard for those interests. The terms for these aspects of crime are *actus reus* and *mens rea*. (This principle is relaxed for a limited class of crimes, called strict liability crimes, in which *mens rea* is not a relevant factor.)

[a] Acts

The notion of an act generates much philosophical anguish. Writers contrast *acts* with *mere behavior*: amoebas, blips on computer screens, and butterflies all behave (predictably or erratically), but they are not capable of acting. Some writers suggest that only beings who are capable of thought can act — but they may act, out of habit for example, even when they are not thinking. Not everything that a being-capable-of-thought does is action; one's movements may be the product of an automatic reflex or may occur during sleepwalking.

If we are responsible, legally and morally, for our acts and only our acts, then it is important to clarify the notion of an act. The notion may be broader than one first thinks: we sometimes act by refraining from carrying out some movement rather than by moving. For example, deliberately withholding life-sustaining medicine from a patient in need may be as effective a way of killing as direct action.

[b] States of Mind

There are many ways of describing states of mind that accompany action. One may act carefully or carelessly, meanly or generously, self-interestedly or altruistically, foolishly or wisely, and so on. Criminal law is not interested in most characterizations of an individual's state of mind. It is concerned only with one's attitude toward the interests of others — specifically with whether one acted with the purpose or at least with the awareness of harming others.

For the most part crimes involve purposive conduct. (This will be true, in fact, of most instances of criminal conduct even if the relevant legal requirement for the prosecutor may be to prove that the defendants *knew* the nature of their conduct.) Acts of theft, rape, arson, and kidnapping typically have a well-defined purpose. But sometimes, acting notwithstanding a known and unjustifiable risk of harm will be the basis for criminal liability. This state of mind is generally called recklessness. Reckless conduct is most likely to be criminalized when the consequences are especially serious — loss of life, for example.

Some writers distinguish between a criminal state of mind in general — a culpable and unjustifiable disregard for the interests of others — and particular specific criminal states of mind legally required for specific offenses. In other words, there are many particular ways in which one can express a general disregard and many particular interests that can be injured. Although the particular interests at stake in a particular kind of crime may be intuitively obvious, the description of the relevant state of mind may be complex. For example, to be guilty of stealing your neighbor's goldfish, you must (a) intentionally take the goldfish, (b) know that the goldfish is not yours, and (c) intend to deprive your neighbor of his or her pet permanently.

It is possible, of course, to impose criminal liability on the basis of harm-causing acts alone without consideration of the actor's state of mind. For the most part, to do so runs against the grain of the moral and practical bases of most legal systems. Fairness seems to require punishing only those who deserve blame for acts they have chosen to perform. Moreover, the practical constraint of deterrence seems to require punishing those who were in a position to avoid causing harm but chose otherwise.

Nonetheless, some crimes seem to be exceptions to this rule. We will see that such crimes as statutory rape and bigamy have sometimes been treated as strict liability crimes (with liability based solely on harm-causing acts). Moreover, modern legal systems extend strict liability to *public welfare* offenses, situations in which the operation of a business or activity endangers the community at large and in which it is very hard to find agents with culpable states of mind.

[2] A Basic Model of Liability and Its Permutations

[a] The Basic Model

The simplest instance of criminal activity has three aspects, an actor, an act, and a victim. Human circumstances being what they are, the basic model of an actor harming a victim can be elaborated with a series of complications. The meat and potatoes of any course on criminal law is (a) to show how the actor-act-victim triad is defined with regard to various crimes and (b) to introduce those complications of the basic model and explain how they are handled by law.

Two complications are (a) situations in which the actor and the victim are the same person (paternalistic uses of law), and (b) situations in which the act does not harm and is not intended to harm the victim, but merely has some lesser consequence, such as offense. These controversial uses of criminal law are not the main focus of our inquiry. They remain important, however, especially for legislators. *See* Section A.4 of this Chapter.

[b] Causation

A sniper on the roof of a building aims a rifle at a pedestrian and fires. The sniper misses the target, but the pedestrian, seeking cover, runs in front of a car and is killed. Is the sniper responsible for the pedestrian's death?

A poisoner intends to cause the victim's death, but the poison merely induces a coma. In their efforts to reverse the coma, doctors administer a commonly used medication to which the victim is allergic. The victim has a severe allergic reaction and dies. Can the poisoner be held liable for homicide?

These situations illustrate an intriguing complication of the basic model. In each case, the actor sets out with a criminal purpose and that purpose is achieved. Moreover, the actor plays an essential causal role in bringing about the result. But death is caused in a *different way* than was intended or foreseen by the responsible actor. It is important to see what consequences, if any, this has for liability.

[c] Attempt

Let's alter these two examples slightly. Suppose the sniper misses the pedestrian, who proceeds unscathed. Suppose the poisoning victim emerges from the coma and leaves the hospital. In what way is this relevant to criminal liability? On the one hand, we have assumed that crime involves causing harm, and in these cases the intended harm, loss of life, did not occur. On the other hand, the acts and states of mind of the sniper and the poisoner were exactly the same as they would have been had the intended result been achieved.

Does it seem that there should be liability in these cases and that achieving the intended harm is not essential? But is success irrelevant? Should the sniper and the poisoner be punished *in exactly the same way* whether or not they succeed?

Thus, one way of complicating the basic model is by assuming that the would-be victim is not victimized, or at least not victimized with the intended result. The law of attempts addresses such situations.

[d] Accomplice Liability

Crime is often a joint enterprise. The law of accomplice, or accessorial, liability sorts out the circumstances of joint participation in crime. How much of a role must one play to be liable as an accessory? Suppose you send a timing mechanism for a bomb to someone intending to commit a terrorist bombing. The package is lost in the mail and the mechanism is never used. The terrorist carries out the bombing with other means. Are you an accomplice? Does it matter whether the terrorist knew of your intention to help?

Should a getaway driver be punished as severely as the bank robber? In the previous example, should the person who merely wishes to help an offender be punished at all? Is the person who tries to help as culpable as the person who actually helps?

[e] Conspiracy

When we suppose that there are several actors, rather than one, we introduce two kinds of complications. Not only must we consider the acts that implicate one as an accomplice, but we must also consider the acts that may give rise to conspiracy liability. A mere agreement to commit crime is itself a crime. Such an agreement shows sufficient disregard for the interests of society and presents a sufficient threat for criminal punishment to be thought appropriate.

Thus someone who neither helps nor intends nor promises to help others to commit a crime may nonetheless have criminal liability — as long as the individual agrees with the others that one or more of them will commit a crime. Many questions follow. When is a co-conspirator liable for the substantive crimes of the conspiracy? Can one be punished both for the crime of conspiracy and the substantive crime? If one enters a single agreement to commit a series of crimes, how many counts of conspiracy may result?

In large part, the crime of conspiracy is a tool used against organized crime. Recently, the federal racketeering law (RICO) has given authorities even more leverage over such criminal activity by positing criteria for crimes that are even wider than those of conspiracy.

[3] Defenses

In addition to examining the elements of culpability, the legally relevant aspects of the criminal situation that constitute the case the prosecutor must prove, we will also consider defenses, arguments that the defense can present to rebut culpability.

These sorts of arguments can have two forms, justifications and excuses. A justification is an argument that concedes the actors carried out a proscribed kind of harm but argues that they did so under circumstances that are recognized as justificatory. Examples are self-defense, necessity (acting to minimize harm in choosing the lesser of evils), and privilege (e.g., police entitlement to stop dangerous offenders from effecting harm). An excuse, on the other hand, involves an admission that the actors carried out regrettable acts involving harm but asserts that they did so in a state of mind that excuses the conduct (e.g., that they were acting in a relevantly mistaken belief, that they were acting under duress or threat of harm, and so on).

Chapter 2

Punishment

[A] Punishment and Blame

Let's assume that criminal law does reflect values generally shared in our society, values represented by judgments about harmful and blameworthy conduct. Let's assume, in other words, that the rules of criminal law describe conduct generally seen as threatening to the security and freedom of persons within our society. Most of the rest of this book is given over to an account of what those rules are, of what kinds of conduct criminal law generally prohibits.

This chapter is concerned not with explaining and justifying the prohibitory rules themselves but with justifying punishment of offenders. Before we proceed, consider the following points as background.

(1) It is conceivable that we could set out prohibitions without having an organized system of punishment. We already have such a system in what we call "morality." These sanctions, such as they are, are informal, the responses of private individuals. Most people take for granted that, for various psychological and sociological reasons, criminal law would be impotent without a system of punishment. Do you agree? If so, why is this the case? How would society or human nature have to change for there to be sanctionless compliance with criminal rules? Is such change conceivable?

(2) The very term *punishment* connotes a moral dimension of responsibility and blame. Punishing a person is not like responding to one force of nature by creating a counterforce — by creating a dam to prevent floods, or spraying insecticide to fight beetles. Such a simple mechanistic model will not do.

A simple learning (behaviorist) model of stimulus and response will not explain the effects of punishment either. It leaves out the "internal aspect," the way in which punishment is understood by authorities, citizens, and offenders. Punishing a person is not like disciplining a dog for failing to heel. Rather, punishment sends two messages: that society holds the actor responsible and blameworthy for the prohibited conduct, *and* that moral condemnation by the community, with whatever stigma is attached, is appropriate.

Philosophers have considered what it is about the circumstances of life and human nature that require us to have a legal system that necessarily involves punishment. The legal philosopher, H.L.A. Hart, in his book, THE CONCEPT OF LAW, argues that from the minimal shared purpose of mutual survival, we can infer the need for a system of rules along with the hope that most persons would cooperate under those rules voluntarily and that those unwilling to cooperate would be subject to coercion and sanctions (punishment). The circumstances, which Hart argues are universal across societies, are (1) that persons are vulnerable to being killed or injured, (2) that they are approximately equal as individuals in their ability to inflict harm on others and to have harm inflicted on themselves, (3) that their altruism is limited, i.e., that they are neither angels nor demons, (4) that their resources are limited and that they have to compete with each other for the resources they need, and (5) that they have limited understanding of their circumstances and limited strength of will. Given all of these factors, a system of rules backed by sanctions is appropriate and necessary for long-term perpetuation and success of any society. *See* H.L.A. Hart, The Concept of Law 189–94 (1961).

Notes and Questions

1. **Necessary and Sufficient Conditions.** Note that some of the items on Hart's list make punishment *necessary* (e.g., limited altruism and understanding) and others make it *possible* (e.g., approximate equality of strength). Which of his observations fall into each category?

2. **Universality.** Are the characteristics on Hart's list equally relevant to all societies at all times? To what extent does the availability of resources or the distribution of altruistic attitudes vary from one society to another? What implications does this have for the goals and content of criminal law?

3. **Social Diversity and Social Choice.** Notwithstanding the characteristics on Hart's list, diversity among societies should not be underestimated. For example, the fact of limited resources is compatible with a socialistic or a capitalistic mode of distribution. Whatever mode is chosen will impinge significantly on the content of criminal law. Similarly, an overpopulated society with constrained resources may take a different position on the criminalization of suicide or on mercy killing than a society in which needs are more easily met.

4. **Volition and Punishment.** Does Hart's analysis have any implications for modes of punishment? Which items on his list would have to be different for us to be able to dispense with punishment and rely on voluntary compliance? Which facts about human nature make imprisonment effective? Which facts might lead us to favor or disfavor capital punishment?

[B] General Justifications of Punishment

Is punishment an inevitable adjunct of criminal law? How close is the relationship between legal punishment and the moral categories of blame and responsibility?

In this section we assume that punishment is necessary and that moral responsibility plays some necessary role in the institutions of criminal law. Nonetheless, there is room for wide disagreement about the goals and justification of punishment. The debate has the following aspects.

(1) To the extent that the offender appears to be a danger to others, the function of punishment is to restrain and deter the offender from causing further harm. This can be achieved by punishment in two ways. Punishment as incarceration (or execution) physically removes the offender, thus limiting the offender's ability to affect others. Second, punishment of any form *except* execution is, it is hoped, likely to affect (psychologically) the offender's inclination to commit other crimes, since such acts may lead to unpleasant consequences for the offender.

Obviously, this first dimension of punishment is relevant only when the offender in fact constitutes a risk to society—and that is not true of all offenders. When the offender is dangerous, it seems logical that punishment should be measured by its effectiveness in eliminating the danger at least cost to society (and the offender). Of course, making this determination can be very difficult.

(2) A second dimension of punishment is closely related to the first and involves hope about the effects of punishment on the offender. As we will see below when we consider the invention of prisons, they were intended to reform offenders, to redirect their lives in ways that reflected the values and aims of society.

Unlike restraint, the goal of reform is logically relevant even when offenders do not present a continuing danger. One can always hope that the process of punishment will make their lives and prospects better. Obviously, the optimistic goal of reform depends on two easily questioned assumptions. The first is that we generally know how to reform offenders and can do so without compromising their legal rights and autonomy. The second is that we have and are willing to use the economic resources to bring about these results.

(3) A different dimension of punishment considers its effects on society in general rather than its effects on offenders or their victims. The argument is that the community, seeing and knowing that others are punished for committing crimes, will be deterred from committing such offenses themselves.

The basic reasoning behind general deterrence is impeccable. It doesn't take much psychology or observation to know that people are deterred from actions likely to have painful consequences. The English philosopher Jeremy Bentham (Introduction to the Principles of Morals and Legislation, 1780) left us common-sense guidelines for administering a system of this kind. For example, he suggested that there is an inverse relationship between the severity of punishment and its certainty: the more certain it is that a potential offender will be punished, the less severe the punishment has to be (to achieve the same deterrent effect). Similarly, the more closely the punishment follows the offense, the more effective it will be as a deterrent.

But does the theory of general deterrence take too seriously the notion that we are all rational calculators and that we all make our calculations in more or less the same way? Those who commit crimes on impulse or who are excessive risk-takers may not be deterrable. Those who calculate odds in ways that do not echo the thinking of legislators may also not be deterrable. Thus, in a society where rational calculation does not universally determine action, general deterrence may be a theory in vain quest of reality.

(4) In addition to general deterrence, punishment is said to be justified by its moral impact on society in general. By showing that they take criminal prohibitions seriously, courts reinforce the values that those prohibitions represent. Thus, literally and symbolically, punishment is a way in which society expresses its sense that the offender did something blameworthy, that the offender's act was inexcusable, and that the offended values deserve allegiance and protection.

This last justification of punishment presupposes that criminal prohibitions truly represent a moral consensus. Otherwise, as critical theorists (*see* Chapter 16) remind us, the expression and reinforcement of such values merely coerce one class or group to adopt the standards of another.

The expressive role of punishment in reinforcing values can be described as the blaming function of punishment. Adherence to values is expressed by "casting out" or disadvantaging the offender with deserved punishment. To describe punishment in this way is to emphasize both its backward-looking and forward-looking aspects: to say it expresses values is to look backward to values that have come to define society, while to say it *reinforces* values is to anticipate the survival of those values in the future.

This interpretation of the idea of blame is a way of seeing how society uses criminal law to demand retribution. This way of explaining retribution avoids some familiar criticisms of the idea of retribution. Thus some writers such as Bentham have supposed that retribution has no place in a system of governance because it involves irrational feelings of vengeance and hatred toward offenders. Others, such as the philosopher Hegel, have pointed out that some forms of retribution set unintelligible goals because they involve inflicting on offenders the same harm they have caused ("an eye for an eye") when the results of doing so would be morally incoherent and practically incalculable. (For example, a rich man embezzles $200,000. Does one merely deprive him of the same amount? If not, then what counts as equal treatment? Suppose a reckless driver runs over and cripples a pedestrian. Should the driver's spine also be severed?)

The following readings explore several aspects of punishment. Keep in mind that in traditional discussions of punishment the question of the justification of punishment is posed as a question about what aspects are *sufficient* to justify punishment. Thus, so-called retributivists argue that the moral sense that punishment is deserved and appropriate is enough to justify punishment even if there are no positive effects. The discussion above implies that this is virtually inconceivable in practice, since the administration of deserved punishment is *bound* to have expressing and reinforcing effects. So-called utilitarians on the other hand argue that punishment is not justified *unless* it has positive consequences (restraint, general deterrence, reform).

This debate is part of a more substantial debate among philosophers about the nature of moral justification. Is the nature of justification such that it involves intuitions of rightness and wrongness of acts? If so, then blameworthiness (wrongness) may be enough to justify punishment. Or is the nature of justification such that it involves appeal to positive future consequences? If so, then some kind of utilitarian argument for punishment is required.

[1] Retribution

The writings of Immanuel Kant are universally regarded as the most influential and uncompromising statement of a kind of retributivist position. Responses to Kant are many and varied. In reading the following excerpts, consider what the role of punishment is for Kant, and whether his argument is coherent, practicable, and persuasive.

Immanuel Kant, From The Metaphysical Elements of Justice (1797)

Judicial punishment (*poena forensis*) is entirely distinct from natural punishment (*poena naturalis*). In natural punishment, vice punishes itself, and this fact is not taken into consideration by the legislator. Judicial punishment can never be used merely as a means to promote some other good for the criminal himself or for civil society, but instead it must in all cases be imposed on him only on the ground that he has committed a crime; for a human being can never be manipulated merely as a means to the purposes of someone else and can never be confused with the objects of the Law of things [*Sachenrecht*]. His innate personality [that is, his right as a person] protects him against such treatment, even though he may indeed be condemned to lose his civil personality. . . .

What kind and what degree of punishment does public legal justice adopt as its principle and standard? None other than the principle of equality (illustrated by the pointer on the scales of justice), that is, the principle of not treating one side more favorably than the other. Accordingly, any undeserved evil that you inflict on someone else among the people is one that you do to yourself. If you vilify him, you vilify yourself; if you steal from him, you steal from yourself; if you kill him, you kill yourself. Only the Law of retribution (*jus talionis*) can determine exactly the kind and degree of punishment; it must be well understood, however, that this determination [must be made] in the chambers of a court of justice (and not in your private judgment). All other standards fluctuate back and forth and, because extraneous considerations are mixed with them, they cannot be compatible, with the principle of pure and strict legal justice. . . .

But what is meant by the statement: "If you steal from him, you steal from yourself"? Inasmuch as someone steals, he makes the ownership of everyone else insecure, and hence he robs himself (in accordance with the Law of retribution) of the security of any possible ownership. He has nothing and can also acquire nothing, but he still wants to live, and this is not possible unless others provide him with nourishment. But, because the state will not support him gratis, he must let the state have his labor at any kind of work it may wish to use him for (convict labor), and so he becomes a slave, either for a certain period of time or indefinitely, as the case may be.

If, however, he has committed a murder, he must die. In this case, there is no substitute that will satisfy the requirements of legal justice. There is no sameness of kind between death and remaining alive even under the most miserable conditions, and consequently there is also no equality between the crime and the retribution unless the criminal is judicially condemned and put to death. But the death of the criminal must be kept entirely free of any maltreatment that would make an abomination of the humanity residing in the person suffering it. Even if a civil society were to dissolve itself by common agreement of all its members (for example, if the people inhabiting an island decided to separate and disperse themselves around the world), the last murderer remaining in prison must first be executed, so that everyone will duly receive what his actions are worth and so that the bloodguilt thereof will not be fixed on the people because they failed to insist on carrying out the punishment; for if they fail to do so, they may be regarded as accomplices in this public violation of legal justice.

In the following selection, the legal philosopher Jeffrie Murphy summarizes the most common and the most persuasive criticisms of Kant's position.

Jeffrie Murphy, Retribution, Justice and Therapy 82–90 (1979)[1]

Kant maintains that guilt is a necessary condition for the legitimate infliction of punishment. . . .

That guilt is a necessary condition for the legitimate infliction of punishment will be accepted by most people—even, I suppose, by all but the most simple-minded utilitarians. What will not be so readily accepted, however, is Kant's belief that guilt is a *sufficient* condition for justifying punishment, regardless of utility. . . . Kant . . . offers a theory of punishment which is based on his general view that political obligation is to be analyzed, quasi-contractually, in terms of *reciprocity*. In order to enjoy the benefits that a legal system makes possible, each man must make certain sacrifices—e.g. the sacrifice of obeying the law even when he does not desire to do so. Each man calls on others to do this, and it is only just or fair that he bear a comparable burden when his turn comes. Now if the system is to remain just, it is important to guarantee that those who disobey will not gain an unfair advantage over those who obey voluntarily. Criminal punishment thus attempts to maintain the

1. Copyright © 1979 by D. Reidel Publishing Company, Dordrecht, Holland. Reprinted by permission of Kluwer Academic Publishers.

proper balance between benefit and obedience by insuring that there is no profit in wrongdoing. The criminal himself has no complaint, because he has rationally willed or consented to his own punishment. That is, those very rules which he has broken work, when they are obeyed by others, to his own advantage as *citizen*. He would have chosen such rules for himself in an antecedent position of choice—what John Rawls calls "the original position." And since he derives benefit from them, he owes obedience as a *debt* to his fellow-citizens for their sacrifices in maintaining them. If he chooses not to sacrifice by exercising self-restraint and obedience, this is tantamount to his choosing to sacrifice in another way—namely, by paying the prescribed penalty....

Now it is essential to see that Kant's theory is not a disguised form of utilitarianism. His principle is that no man should profit from his own wrongdoing, and retribution attempts to keep this from happening. If a man does profit from his own wrongdoing, from his disobedience, this is *unfair* or *unjust*, not just to his victim, but to all those who have been obedient. Now it may be, as the utilitarian might argue, that such unfairness—if widespread—would have undesirable consequences. But this is not Kant's argument. His argument is that *justice or fairness itself*, regardless of consequences, demands retribution. As H.L.A. Hart has argued, "A theory of punishment which disregarded these moral convictions [about justice] or viewed them simply as factors, frustration of which made for socially undesirable excitement is a different kind of theory from one which *out of deference to those convictions themselves* [justifies] punishment." ... Kant's theory is clearly of the latter sort.

... I should now like to sketch five of the most interesting objections to it. Some of these are anticipated by Kant himself in his correspondence and other writings (e.g. the *Religion*). Some of them, I think, can be met. Others remain deeply troublesome.

(1) *The Inapplicability of Jus Talionis.* Perhaps the most common criticism of Kant's theory is the claim that the principle *jus talionis* (return like for like) cannot with sense be taken literally. As Hegel observes, "It is easy enough ... to exhibit the retributive character of punishment as an absurdity (theft for theft, robbery for robbery, an eye for an eye, a tooth for a tooth—and then you can go on to suppose that the criminal has only one eye or no teeth)."

But this objection, as Hegel rightly sees, is superficial. Surely the principle *jus talionis*, though requiring likeness of punishment, does not require *exact* likeness in all respects. There is no reason in *principle* (though there are practical difficulties) against trying to specify in a general way what the costs in life and labor of certain kinds of crime might be, and how the costs of punishments might be calculated, so that retribution could be understood as preventing criminal profit.

There are still more remaining difficulties here, however—the chief being that, once a literal reading of *jus talionis* is abandoned, its application "in spirit" seems to be merely a matter of intuition unguided by any systematic theory. Kant's favorite example of *jus talionis* is the penalty of death for the crime of murder—this in spite of the fact that the punishment for *almost everything else* is imprisonment, a punishment which can literally satisfy "like for like" only for the offenses of false imprisonment or kidnapping. And even he is prepared to admit that there are some things which we should not do to the criminal even if he has done them to others. The state should never, he argues, do anything to a criminal that humiliates and degrades his dignity as a man. (So Kant presumably should oppose punishing the torturer and mutilator with torture and mutilation).

The problem here seems to be the following: Though a conception of reciprocity explains why the guilty should be punished, it is not clear that this same principle will explain why like should be returned for like or even why the evil inflicted on the criminal should be of equal gravity with that which the criminal has inflicted on others. . . .

(2) *The Gap Between Theory and Practice.* Another common criticism of Kant's theory may be regarded as Marxist in character. Kant's theory, it may be argued, involves an ideal model of society which is in fact so utterly different from the actual character of society as to render it useless in understanding or evaluating any existing practice of criminal punishment. Indeed, the theory is dangerous. For it allows us to hide from ourselves the vicious character of actual social arrangements and thereby perpetuate gross injustice.

Let me elaborate: Punishment as retribution (paying a debt to one's fellow-citizens) makes good sense with respect to a community of responsible individuals, of approximate equality, bound together by freely adopted and commonly accepted rules which benefit everyone. This is an ideal community, approximating what Kant would call a kingdom of ends. In such a community, punishment would be justly retributive in that it would flow as an accepted consequence of accepted rules which benefited everyone (including, as citizen, the criminal). But surely existing human societies are not in *fact* like this at all. Many people neither benefit nor participate but rather operate at a built-in economic or racial disadvantage which is in fact, if not in theory, permanent. The majority of criminals who are in fact punished are drawn from these classes, and they utterly fail to correspond to the model which underlies the retributive theory. . . .

(3) *Good Reasons and Sufficient Reasons.* Retribution (paying a debt) thus explains why there is a good reason, or a good *prima facie* case, for punishing the guilty. But this analysis cannot establish, in a non question-begging way, the sufficiency of the case. Why not? For the following reason: When considerations of justice or fairness compete with utilitarian considerations (presenting, let us suppose, a good case against punishment in a particular case) one cannot decide this conflict by an appeal to justice. One cannot evaluate some value system S by the very same values definitive of S. Now it may be that considerations of justice should always override considerations of utility; but if this claim is correct, its correctness will have to be established by some principle *independent* of either justice or utility.

(4) *Let Him Who Is without Sin Cast the First Stone.* Let us grant that Kant has established that the criminal deserves his punishment. A question that still must be

considered is the following: Do the other members of the community (given their moral failings) have a *moral right* to administer the punishment through their representatives? If they have no right to do this, then they surely can have no duty to do it.

Kant believes that he can meet this worry in the following way: First, he draws a distinction between *juridical* duties or duties of justice and *ethical* duties or duties of virtue. No man is without ethical failings, without failings of virtue. But society typically does not punish for such failings, does not punish for such things as omissions or bad motives. Society only punishes for injustice, for the active violation of the rights of others, for the breach of juridical duty. Most of us are without these failings (failings of justice) and thus we can, without hypocrisy, demand punishment for these failings in others. Bad though our motives may be, most of us do not actively harm others. Regardless, then, of our failings of virtue, we are the moral superiors of the criminal in at least one sense: we are *just* and he is not.

But are we? Can motives be so easily disregarded? According to Kant's official theory, the unjust man is morally less than the rest of us because we have exercised restraint whereas he has not—regardless of his or our motives in the respective cases. . . . The point here (for our purpose) is the following: The criminal has not restrained himself and thus appears to manifest a moral failing sufficient for excluding him from the community of the just, those who have restrained themselves. But the lurking question is the following: *Why* have the so-called just restrained themselves? Suppose they have not restrained themselves from any morally creditable motive (respect for duty, say) but only self-interest—e.g. fear of punishment. In what sense are they more *deserving* of citizenship than the criminal? . . . The criminal is, of course, *eligible* for his punishment in a way that most of us are not. But this does not show that he *deserves* punishment any more than the rest of us. Consider the following analogy: Jones, a superior athlete, has a cramp and loses his race to Smith, an inferior runner. Given the rules, Smith is eligible for the award and gets it. But surely Jones deserved it; Smith would surely have no right to regard himself as superior to Jones.

(5) *Shared Guilt*. Suppose that Jones commits a criminal act. Our initial temptation is to regard his guilt as individual for this and to regard ourselves as acting rightly in demanding his punishment alone. But even in the law there are inroads against stopping here. Those who counsel Jones, aid him, and profit from his act may be criminally prosecuted. It would be unfair to make Jones bear the burden for what has been a collective endeavor.

Some writers have sought to extrapolate from the legal notion of complicity and argue that our collective responsibilities are wider than we might at first imagine. Though not many would follow Dostoevsky in believing that we are all responsible for everything, we have in recent times heard such charges as that most law-abiding Germans were responsible for Nazi crimes and that most white Americans are responsible for black violence. Though these claims go against the grain, they are by no means clearly silly. Consider the following sort of case: If preventing a crime (through befriending a homeless and alienated child, say) would have caused me less personal sacrifice than the sacrifice that was later required of the child (when adult) to refrain from crime, can I really judge myself his superior or claim that he is more guilty of the crime than I? Surely I and my fellow citizens have some share in the pathology. . . .

Such a door, once opened, is hard to close. And once we begin to look at the moral world in this way, we will perhaps be hesitant in being too certain in our judgments as to just what punishment we can in justice demand for others. Once again, here is an insight which leads to moral humility and which is thus in tension with the smug tone of the official theory.

In conclusion, I should note (as I suppose has been obvious) that my reaction to Kant's theory of criminal punishment is one of deeply mixed feelings. On the one hand, it is a theory which respects human dignity, regards human beings as responsible agents and not merely as things or resources to be manipulated for the social good. On the other hand, it tends perhaps to encourage blindness to the way things really are and to give rise to smugness and self-righteousness. It is a theory built on tension — tension between justice and utility, tension between ideal states and actual states, tension between righteousness and humility. This, I suspect, accounts for its eternal fascination.

Notes and Questions

1. **Kant and Equality.** How do you interpret what Kant calls the principle of equality? Does it mean taking an amount from the thief that is equal to that which was stolen? If not, and if the fact that the thief puts the entire system of property in jeopardy must be taken into account, how is that factor to be measured? How would the principle of equality apply, for example, in crimes of rape, kidnapping, or terrorism?

2. **Implications for Capital Punishment.** Is it possible to preserve the concept of legal justice and reject capital punishment? Is there some way of punishing the person who commits homicide that is equal to the fatal act insofar as it shows a degree of respect for life that compensates for the disrespect shown by the offender? How would Kant's stance on homicide apply to those who kill in circumstances of recklessness or provocation?

3. **Applying Kant's Principles.** Many writers influenced by Kant argue that his main points are: (1) that punishment must never be administered unless it is seen as deserved and (2) that the amount of punishment must be measured by the amount that the offender is seen as deserving. Do you agree with these principles? Are there problems in applying them? Are these principles compatible or incompatible with using punishment for restraint and deterrence?

4. **Retribution and Juvenile Offenders.** To what extent is retribution a relevant justification for punishing juvenile offenders? Does it play the same role in juvenile

justice as in adult justice? Or does youth present a special claim on mercy and indulgence as well as a special problem for the attribution of responsibility? Writers and scholars on criminal justice have increasingly focused on these issues as the media have increasingly brought atrocious criminal conduct by juveniles to public attention. Jarod Hofacker, in *Justice or Vengeance: How Young Is Too Young for a Child to Be Tried as an Adult?*, 34 Tex. Tech L. Rev. 159 (2002), argues for a continued focus on rehabilitation and on the limited capacities of underage defendants.

In *Is Lowering the Age at Which Juveniles Can Be Transferred to Adult Criminal Court the Answer to Juvenile Crime? A State-by-State Assessment*, 37 San Diego L. Rev. 783 (2000), Lisa Beresford concludes that "[t]he answer to juvenile crime is not as simple as getting tougher and stricter. The best results in the long run will be through community involvement and treatment to learn why younger children are committing such crimes." She recommends that the decisions of judges and judicial officers be informed to a much greater degree by training in "child development, cultural factors, resources for families, . . . and research findings regarding rehabilitative interventions." She urges juvenile court personnel to "appreciate the stages of child development, the educational needs of children at various stages in their development, and child behavioral issues." And she argues that "delinquency is . . . a symptom of more fundamental problems—social, psychological, economic, educational, vocational, physical, and even philosophical."

Although the United States stood "alone in the world" in officially sanctioning the death penalty for juveniles and "in convicting young adolescents as adults and sentencing them to live out their lives in prison," the Supreme Court has imposed constitutional limitations on those practices. *See* Adam Liptak, *Lifers as Teenagers, Now Seeking Second Chance*, N.Y. Times, Oct. 17, 2007, at A1 (reporting that 73 prisoners in this country were serving sentences for crimes they committed when they were 13 or 14 years old). *Roper v. Simmons*, 543 U.S. 551 (2005), discussed in Chapter 6, Section E.2, bars the execution of defendants whose crimes were committed when they were under the age of 18. *Graham v. Florida*, 560 U.S. 48 (2010), and *Alabama v. Miller*, 132 S. Ct. 2455 (2012), which are described below in Note 6 in Section D.3, restrict sentencing juveniles to life in prison without parole.

[2] The Antinomy between Retributivism and Utilitarianism

The justification of punishment has long been a common and popular topic among scholars. They tend to divide into two adversarial camps, the retributivists and the utilitarians. The retributivists, claiming to follow Kant, argue that punishment is justified by considerations of moral blame and desert. If an individual deserves blame and punishment for criminal acts, then it is irrelevant whether or not the punishment has good consequences for the community as a whole. Utilitarians, on the other hand, argue that the justification of punishment, like the justification of any action, depends on its good consequences for the community (or the individuals that make up the community).

This debate seems to produce an impasse (while also producing lots of work for scholars). But some of the most prominent writers on the subject claim that the two positions can be reconciled, that there is no "antinomy" or opposition between them. One view is that the retributivist position should be seen not as moral but as definitional. Logically, a decision cannot be called punishment unless those who are punished are thought to be blameworthy, thought to deserve the treatment inflicted on them. Once the threshold of blameworthiness is passed, then the extent and nature of the punishment may be determined in part by utilitarian considerations such as deterrence and rehabilitation.

A complementary view is that every punishment, insofar as it expresses blame and desert, also has utilitarian consequences as an inevitable effect. Thus, punishing and blaming affirm in a visible way the shared rules and values embodied in the law and public morality. Even if benefit to the community is not the purpose and justification of punishment, it is likely for this reason to be a result.

Does this mean that the war between retributivists and utilitarians is over? Not quite. The different positions are most obviously reflected in the weighing of factors to determine the severity of punishment. Consider an offender who has committed homicide under unusual circumstances, ones that may seem to offer mitigation. Suppose a teenager kills his father, who has a long history of abusing all members of his family. The killing does not fit the usual criteria of self-defense; the teenager is not in imminent danger at the moment he kills. A retributivist will tend to emphasize the seriousness of killing regardless of circumstances and will tend to demand a harsh penalty. A utilitarian will argue that there is little to be gained by punishing the teenager and will opt for leniency. In this sense, the retributivist does not merely hold a definitional view whereby blame is a logical condition of punishment, but also has a view about how the seriousness of the offense is to be determined.

In his book, Doing and Deserving, the legal philosopher Joel Feinberg discusses what he calls the expressive function of punishment, the symbolic public disavowal and condemnation that is inherent in the process of finding individuals guilty of crime and imposing punishment. He urges us to consider the role of the expressive function insofar as it complements the more traditional goals of deterrence and reform. Accordingly, he looks at punishment as: (1) authoritative disavowal of certain kinds of conduct, (2) symbolic non-acquiescence in the choices and acts of the offender, (3) vindication of the law, and (4) absolution of those who comply with the law. *See* Joel Feinberg, Doing and Deserving, 101–05, 114–16 (1970).

Notes and Questions

1. **Retribution as Justification and Retribution as Measure.** Throughout the debate over reconciliation, two different questions must be distinguished. The first is whether retributivism or utilitarianism provides the *sole and sufficient* justification for punishment. To this question, retributivism seems to have the better answer, namely that we are justified in punishing someone who deserves punishment whether or not the act of punishing serves deterrence or other utilitarian ends. The theory of

retribution does not simply make the *logical* point that punishment is not punishment unless it is deserved; it also makes the moral point that desert may be a sufficient basis for punishing, that no further justification is needed. This does not mean, however, that we may not decline to punish the guilty in some circumstances. The fact that we are justified in doing so does not preclude us from choosing to refrain. The utilitarian theory, on the other hand, clearly does not seek to give an account of a sufficient justification of punishment.

The second question is what role consideration of retribution (desert) and deterrence (and other forward-looking goals) should play in measuring sentences. Here the retributivist argument is only as clear as our intuitions about what particular offenders deserve. As we will see later in this Chapter, much disagreement haunts any specific discussion of desert. In measuring desert, how much weight should we give to the intentions, to the actual harm caused, to the character of the actor, to mitigating circumstances, etc.? Given disagreements about all such issues, it seems entirely appropriate for other considerations to play a significant role in determining the scope of punishment.

2. Punishment as Expression. What do you see as the relationship of what Feinberg calls "the expressive function of punishment" to retribution (desert) on the one hand and utilitarian considerations on the other? Is Feinberg's account a way of showing how the institutional recognition of desert and blame through punishment achieves forward-looking (utilitarian) results by integrating the community around its laws and reinforcing them? Do you agree that criminal law serves this goal?

3. Limits of Utilitarian Thinking. In discussing utilitarian justifications for criminal law, it is important to keep in mind that criminal law is distinctive insofar as it is not *obviously* a domain for utilitarian thinking. Most other areas of law (contracts, torts, tax, property law) have as their *raison d'etre* the purpose of creating rules to make society better off. The ultimate justification of any law is that the community would be better *with* that law than without it. Criminal law implicates utilitarianism in a more complicated way, as Kant pointed out. Persons are singled out for harm/ punishment on the basis of what they have done. The main calculus involves the consideration that harm has occurred and now more harm must be inflicted by the state in the light of that harmful/criminal act. To the utilitarian, this piling-on of harms is counterintuitive.

[C] Methods of Punishment

[1] Incarceration

[a] *The Invention of Prisons*

The most common and widely accepted sanction in our system, incarceration, is also a questionable one. The French philosopher Michel Foucault examined the significance of the invention of imprisonment as a sanction and of its wide-scale acceptance and use in the eighteenth century. Does it work? What other sanctions (or mix of sanctions) would work as well or better? Does our preference for incarceration demonstrate a collective breakdown of imagination? Would the experiment of trying alternatives to incarceration be too risky, too costly? Is our preference for incarceration fueled by vengeance toward offenders?

In his influential book, DISCIPLINE AND PUNISH: THE BIRTH OF THE PRISON, Foucault explores imprisonment by considering the revolution of technology, politics, and social thought in the eighteenth century that gave rise to a rethinking of criminal law. A significant aspect was the replacement of torture and execution—i.e., public spectacle—as the standard mode of punishment.

> Punishment has gradually ceased to be a spectacle [by the early 1800s]. . . . This has several consequences: it leaves the domain of more or less everyday perception and enters that of abstract consciousness; its effectiveness is seen as resulting from its inevitability, not from its visible intensity; it is the certainty of being punished and not the horrifying spectacle of public punishment that must discourage crime. . . . Th[e] sense of shame is constantly growing.

MICHEL FOUCAULT, DISCIPLINE AND PUNISH: THE BIRTH OF THE PRISON 9–10 (1975; English edition, 1977).

As Foucault observes, the replacement of public spectacle with incarceration in a penitentiary (explicitly for the purpose of penitence) de-emphasizes the role of inflicting harm and pain on the body of the offender. It turns such punishment into a taboo. "Physical pain, the pain of the body itself is no longer the constituent element of the penalty. From being an art of unbearable sensations punishment has become an economy of suspended rights." *Id.* at 11.

Foucault draws the implication that imprisonment became the "'self-evident' penalty *par excellence*" in a world in which liberty and its deprivation were central concerns. This way of thinking was imbued with great confidence that prisons were an ideal "apparatus for transforming individuals." They could be compared to "a rather disciplined barracks, a strict school, a dark workshop." Id. at 232–33. There was enormous confidence that prisons could and would achieve the aim of reform and rehabilitation.

Notes and Questions

1. **Rehabilitation as an Ideal.** Foucault makes the point that optimism and humanism played a large role in motivating the adoption of prisons. Is it still possible to be optimistic and to use prisons to rehabilitate and improve offenders? Did Enlightenment reformers base their optimism on a misguided view of the sources of crime, the changeability of human nature, and the availability of resources? Or must our own more pessimistic view of these matters change?

Has imprisonment lost most of its *raison d'etre*? Or do we have new reasons and justifications for imprisonment that eighteenth-century thinkers never even contemplated?

2. Current Imprisonment Statistics. The United States is the world leader in incarceration, accounting for five percent of the world's population and 25 percent of its prison population. The prison population in this country doubled between 1980 and 1990, and increased by more than 700 percent between 1970 and 2010, before starting to decline in recent years as concerns about mass incarceration grew. State expenditures on corrections rose from $6.7 billion in 1985 to $51.9 billion in 2013. *See* E. Ann Carson, Bureau of Justice Statistics, Prisoners in 2014, at 2 (2015), http://www .bjs.gov/content/pub/pdf/p14.pdf; The Sentencing Project, Trends in U.S. Corrections 1–2 (2015), http://sentencingproject.org/wp-content/uploads/2016/01/Trends -in-US-Corrections.pdf.

As of December 31, 2014, 1,561,525 prisoners were held in federal or state prisons in this country, representing 471 of every 100,000 residents (and 612 of every 100,000 adults). *See* Carson, *supra*, at 2, 7. This qualifies as the highest incarceration rate in the world; by comparison, the incarceration rate per 100,000 residents is 145 in the United Kingdom, 119 in China, 114 in Canada, 99 in France, and 78 in Germany. *See* Peter Wagner & Alison Walsh, *States of Incarceration: The Global Context 2016*, Prison Policy Initiative (June 16, 2016), http://www.prisonpolicy.org/global/2016 .html; The Sentencing Project, *supra*, at 1.

At the end of 2014, the incarceration rate in this country was 2,724 per 100,000 African-American men; the comparable rate for Latino men was 1,091 and 465 for white men. *See* Carson, *supra*, at 15. One in three African-American males born in 2001 can be expected to be incarcerated at some point in their lives, compared to one in six Latino males and one in 17 white males. *See* The Sentencing Project, *supra*, at 5. Overall, the number of African-Americans under the authority of the criminal justice system (in prison, on probation or parole, or awaiting trial) is higher than the number of slaves in this country in 1850, and, as the result of felony disenfranchisement laws, more African-American men are barred from voting today than when the Fifteenth Amendment was ratified. *See* Michelle Alexander, The New Jim Crow: Mass Incarceration in the Age of Colorblindness 271 n.7, 175 (2010).

[b] The Critique of Prisons

By the end of the nineteenth century, much of the optimism cited by Foucault had already evaporated. The playwright and essayist George Bernard Shaw saw prisons as a reflection of the debasement and inhumanity of society. In a pamphlet titled "Imprisonment" (1921), he looks back at the comparison of physical punishments, flogging for example, and asks whether they were indeed more cruel than imprisonment.

> The objection to retrogression [to physical punishments] is not that such punishments are more cruel than imprisonment. They are less cruel, and far less permanently injurious. The decisive objection to them is that they are sports in disguise.... [S]uch exhibitions are degrading and demoralizing; ... the executioner is a wretch whose hand no decent person cares to

take; and . . . the enjoyment of the spectators is fiendish. We have then to find some form of torment which can give no sensual satisfaction to the tormentor, and which is hidden from public view. That is how imprisonment, being just such a torment, became the normal penalty. The fact that it may be worse for the criminal is not taken into account. The public is seeking its own salvation, not that of the lawbreaker. For him it would be far better to suffer in the public eye; for among the crowd of sightseers there might be a Victor Hugo or a Dickens, able and willing to make the sightseers think of what they are doing and ashamed of it. The prisoner has no such chance.

Because of the mental and emotional impact of the deprivation of liberty, Shaw argues that imprisonment is "at once the most cruel of punishments and the one that those who inflict it without having experienced it cannot believe to be cruel." Implicitly he urges us to think hard about how years and decades of isolation from society affect those who are punished in this way. And he is mindful of the fact that we have conflicting and irreconcilable aims when we try to think both retributively and humanely about punishment.

And now comes a further complication. When people are at last compelled to think about what they are doing to our unfortunate convicts, they think so unsuccessfully and confusedly that they only make matters worse. Take, for example, the official list of the results aimed at by the Prison Commissioners. First, imprisonment must be "retributory" (the word vindictive is not in official use). Second, it must be deterrent. Third, it must be reformative.

Now, if you are to punish a man retributively, you must injure him. If you are to reform him, you must improve him. And men are not improved by injuries. To propose to punish and reform people by the same operation is exactly as if you were to take a man suffering from pneumonia, and attempt to combine punitive and curative treatment. . . . We are told that the reformation of the criminal is kept constantly in view; yet the destruction of the prisoner's self-respect by systematic humiliation is deliberately ordered and practiced. . . . [T]he contradictions are obvious here only because I put them on the same page. The Prison Commissioners keep them a few pages apart; and the average reader's memory, it seems, is not long enough to span the gap when his personal interests are not at stake.

Notes and Questions

1. Prisons and Knowledge. Do you agree with Shaw that "blood sports disguised as punishment are less cruel than imprisonment"? In your view, does the general public understand the psychological and emotional aspects of long-term imprisonment? Should such understanding be an essential qualification for legislators or sentencing judges? (The contemporary debate surrounding the revival of shaming punishments is described below in Part 2.)

2. Shaw and the Goals of Punishment. Do you agree with Shaw that the goals of reform and retribution are contradictory and rely on different notions of moral responsibility—that "men are not improved by injuries"?

3. Shaw and CLS. Compare Shaw's analysis with the criticism offered by critical legal studies (discussed below in Chapter 16, Section C.1). Both analyses suggest that criminals are scapegoats for the ills of society. In both cases, one class within society, rulers and administrators, is said to single out another class for coercion in the guise of criminal sanctions. Do you see merit in such arguments?

[c] Prisons through Psychoanalytic Eyes: Rehabilitation and Respect for Persons

One aspect of retributivism that is central to most of the foregoing attempts to examine punishment is respect for persons as morally responsible beings who are held to account for their choices. It is sometimes said that a purely utilitarian theory has no place for responsibility and morality, that it simply considers persons as manipulable for the communal good. The moral dimensions of their conduct are irrelevant as long as they can be exploited to bring about positive consequences.

It is clear that we assume for purposes of criminal liability that offenders are fully responsible for their conduct when the moral examination of those individuals and their conduct would be much less clear and much more nuanced. Thus individuals who are substance-addicted, who have mental and emotional limitations and difficulties, or who have personal histories of abuse and deprivation may be given leeway in our moral judgments about them. No such leeway exists, for the most part, in the determination of guilt and innocence in the processes of criminal law (absent proof of a defense like insanity). Nor are judges generally required to take such factors into account in making decisions about imprisonment.

Psychologists throughout the last century or so have frequently argued that a serious commitment to rehabilitation of those persons who have committed crimes would lead us to reconceive what we do in two ways. First, we would look at the mental element of criminal culpability in a richer and more realistic way, a way more compatible with the descriptions offered by psychologists. Second, we would deal with those who are judged to have committed crimes in a way that would remove their incentives for social disruption and would give them a genuine opportunity to reform their choices and their lives. The renowned psychoanalyst, Karl Menninger, was a prominent defender of this point of view, and his 1959 article, *Therapy, Not Punishment* (HARPER'S MAGAZINE), is a clear statement of it.

> [W]hat do we do with such offenders? After a solemn public ceremony we pronounce them enemies of he people, and then consign them for arbitrary periods to institutional confinement on the basis of laws written many years ago. Here they languish until time has ground out so many weary months and years. Then with a planlessness and stupidity only surpassed by that of their original incarceration they are dumped back upon society, regardless

of whether any change has taken place in them for the better and with every assurance that changes have taken place in them for the worse. Once more they enter the unequal tussle with society. Proscribed for employment by most concerns, they are expected to invent a new way to make a living and to survive without any further help from society.

What Menninger recommends is a drastically different process of disposition of these cases. His suggestions reflect a high degree of optimism about the resources available, the political will to use them in the ways he favors, and a high degree of effectiveness in the work of psychologists and social administrators.

> If we were to follow scientific methods, the convicted offender would be detained indefinitely pending a decision as to whether and how and when to reintroduce him successfully into society. All the skill and knowledge of modern behavioral science would be used to examine his personality assets, his liabilities and potentialities, the environment from which he came, its effects upon him, and his effects upon it. Having arrived at some diagnostic grasp of the offender's personality, those in charge can decide whether there is a chance that he can be redirected into a mutually satisfactory adaption to the world. If so, the most suitable techniques in education, industrial training, group administration, and psychotherapy should be selectively applied. All this may be best done extramurally or intramurally. It may require maximum "security" or only minimum "security." If, in due time, perceptible change occurs, the process should be expedited by finding a suitable spot in society and industry for him, and getting him out of prison control and into civil status (with parole control) as quickly as possible.

Menninger also raises a different concern by defining three categories of offenders, and it is clear that he believes that most offenders fall into his second category. That is obviously the point of his recommended protocols. Accordingly, he laments our "persistent failure . . . to distinguish between crime as an accidental, incidental, explosive event, crime as a behavior pattern expressive of chronic unutterable rage and frustration, and crime as a business or elected way of life." He concludes that, as psychologists, he and his colleagues "don't want anyone excused, but neither do we want anyone stupidly disposed of, futilely detained, or prematurely released. We don't want them tortured, either sensationally with hot irons or quietly by long-continued and forced idleness."

Notes and Questions

1. **Assessing Menninger.** To what extent do you agree with Menninger's general account of how the criminal law system works, his account of who is punished, how they are punished, and the effects of punishment?

Does Menninger's account allow us to distinguish persons who are responsible for their conduct and therefore blameworthy from those who are not? In this respect, you may wish to compare his views with the materials in Chapter 10 on free will and responsibility.

2. Implications of the Therapeutic Point of View. Is the therapeutic and rehabilitative model of punishment a way of demonstrating respect for persons, or is it, as some have argued, necessarily at odds with respect for persons? Is it a way of manipulating them as pawns to serve the overarching interests of society? Or is it a way of bringing them to a level of personal autonomy and responsibility?

3. Constitutional Constraints. Do some of Menninger's suggestions, for example indefinite sentences, conflict with the constraints of the Constitution with regard to due process?

[d] Realizing Deterrence

How much do we know about the deterrent effects of criminal prohibitions? How confident are we that legal rather than social and economic factors are effective levers for controlling crime? One of the most influential studies of deterrence is an article, *Does Punishment Deter Crime?*, 11 Crim. L.Q. 76 (1968), by Johannes Andenaes. In his research for the article, Andenaes identified and tested some of the assumptions that are generally made about both specific deterrence and general deterrence. He concluded that certain naive assumptions and intuitions are as likely to be wrong as right, and, even a half-century since the article appeared, his insights still have significant importance.

Andenaes asks us to distinguish deterrence with regard to those who have been caught, those who have committed offenses but not been caught, and non-offenders. In each case the effect of deterrence will depend on the particular susceptibilities and circumstances of the individual. For those who have been caught and punished, the general assumption is that experiencing punishment will strengthen its deterrent effect. Andenaes points out the alternative possibility, that one may conclude that punishment "was not as bad as he had imagined" and that the overall experience may teach the offender how to offend and not be caught the next time. For offenders who have not been found and punished, self-confidence in the ability to get away with crime may grow and the deterrent effect may diminish. And for non-offenders, a full range of attitudes may exist, from those who are very fearful of punishment and seriously deterred to those who abstain from crime for altogether other reasons and have little fear.

Moreover, Andenaes urges us to consider the effect of punishment, both long- and short-term, on the disposition to commit crime. The experiences one has in prison may deter, but they may also lead to self-identification as a criminal and to absorption in criminal culture, both while imprisoned and after release. He concludes that short-term imprisonment is a more effective deterrent than long-term; "the more lenient the treatment, the better the results." At the same time, "the dominant feature of the results is that the overall differences between various methods of treatment are small or nonexistent" as long as the methods are of comparable leniency. Finally, there is a stark difference between first offenders, who are very effectively deterred from future crime, and others. The recidivism rate increases with the number and seriousness of prior offenses.

Notes and Questions

1. Recidivism Rates. A study of the prisoners released by 30 states in 2005 reported that more than two-thirds of them (67.8%) were arrested for a new crime within three years, and more than three-fourths (76.6%) within five years. *See* Matthew R. Durose et al., Bureau of Justice Statistics, Recidivism of Prisoners Released in 30 States in 2005: Patterns from 2005 to 2010, at 1 (2014), http://www.bjs.gov /content/pub/pdf/rprts05p0510.pdf. Other research, however, suggests that these figures are misleading because they give too much weight to the minority of individuals who are frequently in and out of prison. *See* William Rhodes, *American Prisons Are Not a Revolving Door: Most Released Offenders Never Return*, LSE US Centre (Oct. 17, 2014), http://blogs.lse.ac.uk/usappblog/2014/10/17/american-prisons-are -not-a-revolving-door-most-released-offenders-never-return/ (finding that two-thirds of inmates released between 2000 and 2012 never returned to prison and only 11 percent returned more than once).

2. Habitual Offender Statutes. In *Habitual Offender Statutes and Criminal Deterrence*, 34 Conn. L. Rev. 55 (2001), Linda Beres and Thomas Griffith evaluate the deterrent effect of habitual offender statutes and cast doubt on their efficacy. They seek to show that "[s]entencing repeat offenders to much longer sentences than first time offenders . . . may provide less effective deterrence than punishing all offenders equally." They reason that "[t]he deterrent effect of a sanction depends on its perceived severity. While lengthening a sentence increases its perceived severity, doubling the prison time is unlikely to double the perceived severity of the sanction because offenders are likely to discount time to be served in the future. Potential first-time offenders, moreover, are likely to be more numerous than potential repeat offenders, thus increasing the importance of deterring them." The constitutionality of repeat offender statutes is reviewed below in Note 4 in Section D.3.

3. Scholarship on Deterrence. Professor Andenaes' observations and conclusions are still widely accepted by scholars. A good summary of recent statistics is offered in Andrew Leipold's article, *Recidivism, Incapacitation, and Criminal Sentencing Policy*, 3 U. St. Thomas L.J. 536 (2006). Leipold's thesis is "that the explanations and justifications for punishment focus too much on deterrence and retribution, and not enough on a simple, unglamorous rationale — incapacitation to prevent recidivism." He points out, however, that "[t]he appeal and apparent success of disabling offenders from repeating their crimes presents a significant obstacle to those who seek to reduce current levels of incarceration." *Id.* at 539.

Francis Cullen, Cheryl Johnson, and Daniel Nagin, in *Prisons Do Not Reduce Recidivism: The High Cost of Ignoring Science*, 91 Prison J. 48S (Sept. 2011), suggest that prisons may actually have "a criminogenic effect." They conclude that "beyond crime saved through incapacitation, the use of custodial sanctions may have the unanticipated consequence of making society less safe."

In *Do Harsher Prison Conditions Reduce Recidivism? A Discontinuity-Based Approach*, 9 Am. L. & Econ. Rev. 1 (2007), M. Keith Chan and Jesse M. Shapiro test the hypothesis that harsher prison conditions reduce recidivism. They conclude that their data suggest the opposite, that harsh conditions do not have a negative correlation with recidivism and may in fact encourage it.

[2] Alternative Sentencing

Alleged political cover-ups, both at the federal and state levels, have focused attention on such crimes as perjury, tampering with evidence, and illegally withholding information. Political commentators have debated both the seriousness of such crimes in highly politicized contexts and the appropriate punishment. These debates are part of a larger debate about the purposes and effects of incarceration. The United States has lagged behind European countries, for example, in experimentation with and regular use of alternative sentences.

Of course, some alternative sanctions are very familiar. Fines, community service, a suspended sentence, or mandatory attendance at training programs are all common alternatives to imprisonment. Most often, they are used for less serious offenses and/or for first-time offenders. In many cases, judges retain the discretion to use such sanctions on a case-by-case basis, notwithstanding the general movement over the last 30 years of limiting judicial options in the interest of uniformity and stringency. (*See* Section D.2 below.) Critics contend that alternative sanctions are used much too conservatively and unimaginatively.

One widely discussed topic among criminal law scholars is the revival and refinement of shaming and educative punishments. In his influential article, *What Do Alternative Sanctions Mean?*, 63 U. Chi. L. Rev. 591 (1996), Dan M. Kahan addresses the failure of such alternative sanctions as fines and public service by observing that they do not satisfy the expressive function of punishment, they convey confusing and unsatisfactory public messages, and they are insufficiently condemnatory. Accordingly, they imply that one can purchase exemption from punishment and that community service is an appropriate sanction. Kahan instead proposes a menu of alternative sentences that stigmatize offenders by shaming them — for example, requiring offenders to wear shirts or bracelets publicizing their convictions, to post signs at their homes, or to issue public apologies — sentences that may be expected to deter and perhaps rehabilitate, and that at the same time express blame.

A partial challenge to Kahan is offered by Steven Garvey in *Can Shaming Punishments Educate?*, 65 U. Chi. L. Rev. 733 (1998). Garvey argues that "shame . . . menaces certain ideals that any morally respectable mode of punishment should honor, not the least of which is human dignity." He looks closely at the likely effects of various "creative" punishments on offenders and defends what he calls "the educating model" of punishment. Garvey concludes that if we take seriously the so-called talionic principle, which "requires that the punishment an offender suffers mirrors the harm he inflicted on his victim," we will emphasize guilt over shame. He suggests that certain well-crafted apology rituals and restitution strategies may well serve this educative and therefore reformist function.

In his Note, *Beyond First Blush: The Utility of Shame as a Master Emotion in Criminal Sentencing*, 2015 MICH. ST. L. REV. 415, Dustyn Coontz examines several psychological aspects of the emotion of shame (intensity, ease of recollection, universality, individualization) that arguably enable it to "effectively alter individual behavior and satisfy the traditional justifications for criminal punishment."

Another suggested sentencing reform is a greater focus on "restorative justice," "a process whereby all the parties with a stake in a particular offense come together to resolve collectively how to deal with the aftermath of the offense and its implications for the future." John Braithwaite, *Restorative Justice: Assessing Optimistic and Pessimistic Accounts, in* 25 CRIME AND JUSTICE: A REVIEW OF RESEARCH 1, 5 (Michael Tonry ed., 1999). Restorative justice gives a defendant the opportunity to meet face-to-face with victims and apologize to them, and victims in turn can choose to forgive as well as explain to the defendant the impact the crime has had on their lives.

Supporters of restorative justice argue that this "interactive process teaches moral lessons, brings catharsis, and reconciles and heals offenders, victims, and society." Stephanos Bibas & Richard A. Bierschbach, *Integrating Remorse and Apology into Criminal Procedure*, 114 YALE L.J. 85, 89 (2004).

Critics, on the other hand, are concerned about the "potential disparity in treatment of identical offenders committing identical offenses," given that "the offender's punishment depend[s] not on his personal blameworthiness but rather on the chance collection" of who happens to be involved in the process. Paul H. Robinson, *The Virtues of Restorative Processes, the Vices of "Restorative Justice"*, 2003 UTAH L. REV. 375, 381.

Notes and Questions

1. **The Fairness Issue.** Is the danger in adopting a system of alternative forms of punishment that they will be made available disproportionately to those with advantages of class or wealth? What is an egalitarian and fair way of determining alternative sentences?

The media pay particular attention to this issue when celebrities are involved, whether they are in entertainment (Chris Brown, Lindsay Lohan), business (Martha Stewart), politics (Scooter Libby), or sports (Michael Vick, O.J. Simpson). A tendency to consider alternative sentences can be seen (correctly or not) as leniency, and the appearance of leniency may be shunned because of the awareness and fear of special scrutiny. Public officials can find it difficult to put aside these complicating factors.

2. **Freedom and Alternative Sanctions.** Do you think most alternative forms of punishment involve greater freedom for offenders? Does this mean that control over offenders is compromised? Does adopting a scheme of alternative punishment mean that goals of reform and rehabilitation will clash with goals of control and restraint?

3. **Political Realities.** What are the political obstacles to making alternative sentencing acceptable to legislators and the general public?

4. Making Punishment Fit. What constitutes an appropriate alternative sentence for a given offender? What kinds of information do we have to know about an offender to design an appropriate alternative sentence?

5. Grading Punishment. In grading offenses a legislature has to make both absolute and comparative judgments. Absolute judgments involve such questions as whether capital punishment is to be used, what maximum terms of imprisonment are allowed, whether so-called alternative sentencing is to be used widely. Comparative judgments involve determining which crimes are more serious, which less serious, and by how much.

Some comparative judgments are easy. Damaging property is not as bad as destroying it. Assaulting someone is not as bad as killing. Stealing something of little value is not as bad as stealing something of great value. Once we go beyond these banalities, however, the terrain rapidly grows difficult. Do comparative judgments about seriousness reflect a value consensus? Do they reflect, on the other hand, the preferences of one social or economic class or the preferences of one gender or one race?

[3] Capital Punishment

The death penalty is one of the most controversial topics within criminal law. The topic has three aspects, each of them open to endless and volatile debate: (1) philosophical and moral considerations, (2) constitutional and legal aspects, and (3) empirical and criminological data. In this section we will consider primarily the first aspect, which is closely tied to the justification of punishment in general. However, the philosophical and moral questions rest heavily on empirical assumptions about the effects of punishment. Therefore, we have included criminological materials in this section as well. The constitutional and legal aspects of the death penalty are explored in Chapter 6, Section E.

WALTER BERNS, FOR CAPITAL PUNISHMENT 153–55, 162–63 (1979)[2]

[In *Furman v. Georgia*, 428 U.S. 238, 272–73 (1972),] Justice Brennan . . . says the death penalty does not "comport with human dignity" because it treats "members of the human race as nonhumans, as objects to be toyed with and discarded." On the contrary, it treats them as responsible moral beings. . . . By way of claiming dignity for his own position, Justice Brennan also says that the authors of the cruel and unusual clause of the Eighth Amendment intended to forbid all punishments that do not comport with human dignity, and that the death penalty does not comport with human dignity because it is too severe, and that it is too severe because it causes death. Of course it does. But, as Brennan knows, the authors of the Eighth Amendment were not opposed to it, and, therefore, could not have regarded it as too severe, and, therefore, could not have regarded it as incompatible with human dignity. Brennan

---

concludes by saying that "even the vilest criminal remains a human being possessed of human dignity," which is cited as evidence of Brennan's humanism. But what sort of humanism is it that respects equally the life of Thomas Jefferson and Charles Manson, Abraham Lincoln and Adolf Eichmann, Martin Luther King and James Earl Ray? To say that these men, some great and some unspeakably vile, equally possess human dignity is to demonstrate an inability to make a moral judgment derived from or based on the idea of human dignity. Understood as Brennan understands it, the term should be dropped from the debate; it is meaningless, empty, as empty as the morality he and his abolitionist colleagues espouse.

CHARLES L. BLACK, JR., CAPITAL PUNISHMENT: THE INEVITABILITY OF CAPRICE AND MISTAKE 92–93 (1974)

When we turn from the two usual arguments in *favor of* capital punishment — retribution and deterrence — to the other side, we find, above all, that the *cruelty* of it is what its opponents hate — the cruelty of death, the cruelty of the manner of death, the cruelty of waiting for death, and the cruelty to the innocent persons attached by affection to the condemned — unless, of course, he has no relatives and no friends, a fairly common condition on death row. (I do not intend to broach at this point the question whether, as a matter of *law*, death is a "cruel and unusual punishment" within the meaning of the Eighth Amendment to the national Constitution; whatever the answer to that question may be, no sane person can doubt that the agony of waiting and of execution is cruel in the colloquial sense.) Here again, the connection with the thesis of this book is clear. One might decide (though I never could) that the infliction of this suffering is justified when it is inflicted on the right person — the person selected by the invariant and correct application of clear standards, set up by society through its constitutional forms. It would, I think, take a much hardier mind to conclude that this suffering may legitimately or desirably be inflicted on the basis of *unclear* standards, or no standards, with mistake, in the long run, a certainty. And it must be added that cruelty itself is greater when the arbitrariness or the mistake is visible to the condemned person, as must sometimes be the case. To sum up, if the nature of our institutions — and, indeed, of any institutions we can project — is such that the choice for death must often be standardless or mistaken, then the retribution question, the deterrence question, and the cruelty question all take on a different form and must be rethought. . . .

The trouble is that the system . . . must be viewed, as one in which a few people are selected, without adequately shown or structured reason for their being selected, to die. The inevitable corollary of sparing some people through mere grace or favor is standardless condemnation of others.

Notes and Questions

1. **Empirical Studies.** In his book, Professor Black argues that mistakes are inevitable in any system of criminal litigation and that such mistakes are especially

disturbing (because they are irreversible) in a system that uses capital punishment. This argument is an invitation to empirical criminologists to try to document the incidence of such mistakes.

With the 2000 publication of the book ACTUAL INNOCENCE: FIVE DAYS TO EXECUTION AND OTHER DISPATCHES FROM THE WRONGLY CONVICTED by Barry Scheck, Peter Neufeld, and Jim Dwyer, questions regarding the accuracy of death penalty conviction procedures were raised across the nation. Although advocates differ about the meaning of "actually innocent" (as opposed to merely unconvicted after a remand or retrial), there appears to be no doubt that at least some actually innocent defendants have been found on America's death rows, some within days of execution.

2. Viewing the Issue from Different Perspectives. For a moving discussion of the range of reactions that survivors and victims' family members had to the trial and execution of Timothy McVeigh, who masterminded the 1995 bombing of the federal building in Oklahoma City that left 168 people dead, see JODY LYNEÉ MADEIRA, KILLING MCVEIGH: THE DEATH PENALTY AND THE MYTH OF CLOSURE xxiii (2012). Madeira concludes that "closure is most affirmatively *not* what contemporary culture says it is — absolute finality, in the sense of such colloquial phrases as 'over and done with,' 'dealt with,' 'put behind one's self,' 'let bygones be bygones,' 'forgive and forget.'"

For a perspective from death row, see the five-part illustrated series published by cartoonist Patrick Chappatte based on interviews he and his wife, journalist Anne-Frédérique Widmann, conducted with a dozen inmates awaiting execution. *Inside Death Row*, N.Y. TIMES, May 5, 2016, *available at* http://www.nytimes.com/interactive /2016/05/04/opinion/the-last-phone-call.html.

For the views of a former superintendent of the Oregon State Penitentiary, who "planned and carried out that state's only two executions in the last 54 years" and became an opponent of capital punishment, see Semon Frank Thompson, *What I Learned from Executing Two Men*, N.Y. TIMES, Sept. 18, 2016, at SR3. Thompson describes the "the anxiety [he] felt about the possibility of a botched procedure," and notes that "[t]he state-ordered killing of a person is premeditated and calculated, and . . . [i]t's hard to avoid giving up some of your empathy and humanity to aid in the killing of another human being." *See also* Susan A. Bandes, *What Executioners Can — and Cannot — Teach Us About the Death Penalty*, 35 CRIM. JUST. ETHICS 183 (2016).

An accessible book discussing the current controversies surrounding the death penalty, written by Scott Turow, the well-known author, former prosecutor, and member of the Illinois Commission to Study the Death Penalty, is ULTIMATE PUNISHMENT (2004).

3. The Economics of Capital Punishment. It is widely believed that the death penalty is economically efficient, that it is cheaper to execute prisoners than to warehouse them for the rest of their lives. In fact, a substantial number of studies establish the opposite. Given the cost of litigating a capital case through all possible appeals in our constitutional system, execution is the more expensive alternative. *See, e.g.,* Carol S. Steiker & Jordan M. Steiker, *Cost and Capital Punishment: A New Consideration Transforms an Old Debate*, 2010 U. Chi. Legal F. 117, 118 (noting that cost is an "argument for abolition" that was "virtually nonexistent in the debates of prior generations" but has become "extraordinarily powerful in current public policy debates"); Ronald J. Tabak, *How Empirical Studies Can Affect Positively the Politics of the Death Penalty*, 83 Cornell L. Rev. 1431 (1998). For statistical studies showing the death penalty's economic impact in particular states, see Death Penalty Information Center, *Costs of the Death Penalty*, http://www.deathpenaltyinfo.org /costs-death-penalty.

4. The Debate on Deterrence. Empirical studies attempting to measure the death penalty's deterrent effect have reached conflicting results. In the book excerpted above, Charles Black notes that "the 'deterrence' question is wide open and will, as far as anyone can see, remain wide open indefinitely." Black concludes, "I think the answer has to be that, after all possible inquiry, including the probing of all possible methods of inquiry, we do not know, and for systematic and easily visible reasons cannot know, what the truth about th[e] 'deterrent' effect [of capital punishment] may be." Charles L. Black, Jr., Capital Punishment: The Inevitability of Caprice and Mistake 25–27 (1974).

In *The Ethics and Empirics of Capital Punishment: Is Capital Punishment Morally Required? Acts, Omissions, and Life-Life Tradeoffs*, 58 Stan. L. Rev. 703 (2005), Cass Sunstein and Adrian Vermeule draw on "a significant body of recent evidence that capital punishment may well have a deterrent effect, possibly a quite powerful one," and observe that "[i]f it is stipulated that substantial deterrence exists, both consequentialist and deontological accounts of morality will or should converge upon the view that capital punishment is morally obligatory."

Charles Keckler, in *Life v. Death: Whom Should Capital Punishment Marginally Deter?*, 2 J.L. Econ. & Pol'y 51 (2006), notes that while "[e]conometric measures of the effect of capital punishment have increasingly provided evidence that it deters homicide," "most researchers on both sides of the death penalty debate continue to rely on rather simple assumptions about criminal behavior." Keckler offers "a more nuanced and predictive rational choice model of incentives and disincentives to kill," and concludes that, "[a]t least for some offenders, the death penalty should induce greater caution in their use of lethal violence" when compared to life imprisonment without parole.

Thomas Kleven, by comparison, in *Is Capital Punishment Immoral Even If It Deters Murder?*, 46 Santa Clara L. Rev. 599 (2006), concludes that "at low levels of execution there is no deterrent effect and even a brutalizing effect that increases murder," but "beyond some threshold level of executions capital punishment is an effective deterrent."

The death penalty's deterrent effect is also the main concern of Allan Johnson in his Note, *The Illusory Death Penalty: Why America's Death Penalty Process Fails to*

Support the Economic Theories of Criminal Sanctions and Deterrence, 52 HASTINGS L.J. 1101 (2001). His unusual argument for abolition of the death penalty is not its putative unfairness or the risk of mistake, but rather its economic inefficiency and the unlikelihood of making it efficient.

5. **Constitutional Limitations.** Although the U.S. Supreme Court has rejected the argument that the death penalty falls within the Eighth Amendment's ban on "cruel and unusual punishments," the Court has held that the Amendment forecloses the execution of various categories of murder defendants. Thus, defendants who are mentally incompetent (*Ford v. Wainwright*, 477 U.S. 399 (1986)) or intellectually disabled (*Atkins v. Virginia*, 536 U.S. 304 (2002)), and those who were under 18 years of age at the time of their crimes (*Roper v. Simmons*, 543 U.S. 551 (2005)), are ineligible for the death penalty. For further discussion of these cases, see the materials below in Chapter 6, Section E.2.

[D] Severity of Punishment

Questions of punishment involve questions of degree. The question whether to punish involves the question how much to punish. Thus, any justification of punishment must account not only for the distinction between those we decide to punish and stigmatize and those we do not, but also for distinctions of severity in punishing.

Questions about severity are of two kinds. At the first level, the demand may be to justify a particular sentence for a particular offender. At the second level, the question is comparative: Why do we punish one *kind* of offense more than another kind? The first-level question is primarily a question for judges (subject to constitutional limitations) and comes up in sentencing. The second-level question is for legislators and comes up in drafting criminal statutes.

[1] On Sentencing

One of the main dilemmas of sentencing is, simply put, whether one punishes the criminal or the crime. Criminal codes define crimes, and the jury's job is to determine whether the accused's conduct fits one or another (or several) of these defined categories. But once the jury makes the decision about guilt or innocence, the disposition of the offender does not follow automatically. We could punish *every* instance of voluntary homicide, or aggravated assault, or arson, in exactly the same way—but we do not. Instead, we determine punishment by considering the nature of the criminal and the relevant circumstances. Ordinarily, that task belongs to the judge.

Consider two problems. How does the decisionmaker decide what sentence is appropriate? What are the ramifications of such decisions for parties other than the defendant, i.e., for general attitudes toward law, for compliance with law, etc.?

In many instances relevant sentencing considerations point in opposite ways. Thus, an offender may have caused very serious and irreversible harm — may have committed homicide — but may not present a future public danger. Or an offender may have done something minor — may have shoplifted an item of little value — but may be very likely to repeat the offense over and over again. In these cases the seriousness of the harm points toward one kind of sentence, while the likelihood that the offender presents a continuing danger to the community points toward a different decision. And a third factor in each case is the message that the sentence conveys to other potential offenders and the general public.

The need to balance all of these conflicting factors in coming up with a particular sentence led one judge to call sentencing "the most difficult thing we do." Benjamin Weiser, *Madoff Judge Recalls Rationale for Imposing 150-Year Sentence*, N.Y. TIMES, June 29, 2011, at A1 (quoting federal district judge Denny Chin).

United States v. Bergman
416 F. Supp. 496 (S.D.N.Y. 1976)

FRANKEL, DISTRICT JUDGE.

Defendant is being sentenced upon his plea of guilty to two counts of an 11-count indictment. The sentencing proceeding is unusual in some respects. It has been the subject of more extensive submissions, written and oral, than this court has ever received upon such an occasion. The court has studied some hundreds of pages of memoranda and exhibits, plus scores of volunteered letters. A broad array of issues has been addressed. Imaginative suggestions of law and penology have been tendered. A preliminary conversation with counsel, on the record, preceded the usual sentencing hearing. Having heard counsel again and the defendant speaking for himself, the court postponed the pronouncement of sentence for further reconsideration of thoughts generated during the days of studying the briefs and oral pleas. It seems fitting now to report in writing the reasons upon which the court concludes that defendant must be sentenced to a term of four months in prison.

Defendant and His Crimes

Defendant appeared until the last couple of years to be a man of unimpeachably high character, attainments, and distinction. A doctor of divinity and an ordained rabbi, he has been acclaimed by people around the world for his works of public philanthropy, private charity, and leadership in educational enterprises. Scores of letters have come to the court from across this and other countries reporting debts of personal gratitude to him for numerous acts of extraordinary generosity. (The court has also received a kind of petition, with fifty-odd signatures, in which the signers, based upon learning acquired as newspaper readers, denounce the defendant and urge a severe sentence. Unlike the pleas for mercy, which appear to reflect unquestioned facts inviting compassion, this document should and will be disregarded.) In addition to his good works, defendant has managed to amass considerable wealth in the ownership and operation of nursing homes, in real estate ventures, and in a course of substantial investments.

Beginning about two years ago, investigations of nursing homes in this area, including questions of fraudulent claims for Medicaid funds, drew to a focus upon this defendant among several others. The results that concern us were the present indictment and two state indictments. After extensive pretrial proceedings, defendant embarked upon elaborate plea negotiations with both state and federal prosecutors. A state guilty plea and the instant plea were entered in March of this year. (Another state indictment is expected to be dismissed after defendant is sentenced on those to which he has pled guilty.) As part of the detailed plea arrangements, it is expected that the prison sentence imposed by this court will comprise the total covering the state as well as the federal convictions.[3]

For purposes of the sentence now imposed, the precise details of the charges, and of defendant's carefully phrased admissions of guilt, are not matters of prime importance. Suffice it to say that the plea on Count One (carrying a maximum of five years in prison and a $10,000 fine) confesses defendant's knowing and wilful participation in a scheme to defraud the United States in various ways, including the presentation of wrongfully padded claims for payments under the Medicaid program to defendant's nursing homes. Count Three, for which the guilty plea carries a theoretical maximum of three more years in prison and another $5,000 fine, is a somewhat more "technical" charge. Here, defendant admits to having participated in the filing of a partnership return which was false and fraudulent in failing to list people who had bought partnership interests from him in one of his nursing homes, had paid for such interests, and had made certain capital withdrawals.

The conspiracy to defraud, as defendant has admitted it, is by no means the worst of its kind; it is by no means as flagrant or extensive as has been portrayed in the press; it is evidently less grave than other nursing-home wrongs for which others have been convicted or publicized. At the same time, the sentence, as defendant has acknowledged, is imposed for two federal felonies including, as the more important, a knowing and purposeful conspiracy to mislead and defraud the Federal Government.

The Guiding Principle of Sentencing

. . . The court agrees that this defendant should not be sent to prison for "rehabilitation." Apart from the patent inappositeness of the concept to this individual, this court shares the growing understanding that no one should ever be sent to prison *for rehabilitation*. That is to say, nobody who would not otherwise be locked up should suffer that fate on the incongruous premise that it will be good for him or her.

---

3. [n.2] This is not absolutely certain. Defendant has been told, however, that the imposition of any additional prison sentence by the state court will be an occasion for reconsidering today's judgment. [In fact, one of the state court indictments later led to an additional one-year sentence to be served consecutively with the sentence imposed by Judge Frankel. *See Bergman v. Lefkowitz*, 569 F.2d 705 (2d Cir. 1977).]

Imprisonment is punishment. Facing the simple reality should help us to be civilized. It is less agreeable to confine someone when we deem it an affliction rather than a benefaction. If someone must be imprisoned—for other, valid reasons—we should seek to make rehabilitative resources available to him or her. But the goal of rehabilitation cannot fairly serve in itself as grounds for the sentence to confinement.

Equally clearly, this defendant should not be confined to incapacitate him. He is not dangerous. It is most improbable that he will commit similar, or any, offenses in the future. There is no need for "specific deterrence."

Contrary to counsel's submissions, however, two sentencing considerations demand a prison sentence in this case:

> *First*, the aim of *general deterrence*, the effort to discourage similar wrongdoing by others through a reminder that the law's warnings are real and that the grim consequence of imprisonment is likely to follow from crimes of deception for gain like those defendant has admitted.

> *Second*, the related, but not identical, concern that any lesser penalty would, in the words of the Model Penal Code, § 7.01(1)(c), "depreciate the seriousness of the defendant's crime."

. . . [W]e are driven regularly in our ultimate interests as members of the community to use ourselves and each other, in war and in peace, for social ends. One who has transgressed against the criminal laws is certainly among the more fitting candidates for a role of this nature. This is no arbitrary selection. Warned in advance of the prospect, the transgressor has chosen, in the law's premises, "between keeping the law required for society's protection or paying the penalty."

But the whole business, defendant argues further, is guesswork; we are by no means certain that deterrence "works." The position is somewhat overstated; there is, in fact, some reasonably "scientific" evidence for the efficacy of criminal sanctions as deterrents, at least as against some kinds of crimes. Moreover, the time is not yet here when all we can "know" must be quantifiable and digestible by computers. The shared wisdom of generations teaches meaningfully, if somewhat amorphously, that the utilitarians have a point; we do, indeed, lapse often into rationality and act to seek pleasure and avoid pain. It would be better, to be sure, if we had more certainty and precision. Lacking these comforts, we continue to include among our working hypotheses a belief (with some concrete evidence in its support) that crimes like those in this case—deliberate, purposeful, continuing, non-impulsive, and committed for profit—are among those most likely to be generally deterrable by sanctions most shunned by those exposed to temptation.

The idea of avoiding depreciation of the seriousness of the offense implicates two or three thoughts, not always perfectly clear or universally agreed upon, beyond the idea of deterrence. It should be proclaimed by the court's judgment that the offenses are grave, not minor or purely technical. Some attention must be paid to the demand for equal justice; it will not do to leave the penalty of imprisonment a dead letter as against "privileged" violators while it is employed regularly, and with vigor, against others. There probably is in these conceptions an element of retributiveness, as counsel urge. And retribution, so denominated, is in some disfavor as a reason for punishment. It remains a factor, however, as Holmes perceived, and as is known to anyone who talks to judges, lawyers, defendants, or people generally. It may become more palatable, and probably more humanely understood, under the rubric of "deserts" or "just deserts." However the concept is formulated, we have not yet reached a state, supposing we ever should, in which the infliction of punishments for crime may be divorced generally from ideas of blameworthiness, recompense, and proportionality.

An Alternative "Behavioral Sanction"

Resisting prison above all else, defense counsel included in their thorough memorandum on sentencing two proposals for what they call a "constructive," and therefore a "preferable" form of "behavioral sanction." One is a plan for Dr. Bergman to create and run a program of Jewish vocational and religious high school training. The other is for him to take charge of a "Committee on Holocaust Studies," again concerned with education at the secondary school level.

A third suggestion was made orally at yesterday's sentencing hearing. It was proposed that Dr. Bergman might be ordered to work as a volunteer in some established agency as a visitor and aide to the sick and the otherwise incapacitated. The proposal was that he could read, provide various forms of physical assistance, and otherwise give comfort to afflicted people.

No one can doubt either the worthiness of these proposals or Dr. Bergman's ability to make successes of them. But both of the carefully formulated "sanctions" in the memorandum involve work of an honorific nature, not unlike that done in other projects to which the defendant has devoted himself in the past. It is difficult to conceive of them as "punishments" at all. . . .

Measuring the Sentence

. . . [T]he setting of a term remains to be accomplished. And in some respects it is a subject even more perplexing, unregulated, and unprincipled.

Days and months and years are countable with a sound of exactitude. But there can be no exactitude in the deliberations from which a number emerges. Without pretending to a nonexistent precision, the court notes at least the major factors.

The criminal behavior, as has been noted, is blatant in character and unmitigated by any suggestion of necessitous circumstance or other pressures difficult to resist. However metaphysicians may conjure with issues about free will, it is a fundamental premise of our efforts to do criminal justice that competent people, possessed of their faculties, make choices and are accountable for them. In this sometimes harsh light, the case of the present defendant is among the clearest and least relieved. Viewed against the maxima Congress ordained, and against the run of sentences in other federal criminal cases, it calls for more than a token sentence.

On the other side are factors that take longer to enumerate. Defendant's illustri-
ous public life and works are in his favor, though diminished, of course, by what this
case discloses. This is a first, probably a last, conviction. Defendant is 64 years old
and in imperfect health, though by no means so ill, from what the court is told, that
he could be expected to suffer inordinately more than many others of advanced years
who go to prison. . . .

. . . Much of defendant's sentencing memorandum is devoted to the extensive bar-
rage of hostile publicity to which he has been subjected during the years before and
since his indictment. He argues, and it appears to be undisputed, that the media (and
people desiring to be featured in the media) have vilified him for many kinds of evil-
doing of which he has in fact been innocent. Two main points are made on this
score with respect to the problem of sentencing.

First, as has been mentioned, counsel express the concern that the court may be
pressured toward severity by the force of the seeming public outcry. That the court
should not allow itself to be affected in this way is clear beyond discussion. . . .

Defendant's second point about his public humiliation is the frequently heard contention that he should not be incarcerated because he "has been punished enough."
The thought is not without some initial appeal. If punishment were wholly or mainly
retributive, it might be a weighty factor. In the end, however, it must be a matter of
little or no force. Defendant's notoriety should not in the last analysis serve to lighten,
any more than it may be permitted to aggravate, his sentence.

Notes and Questions

1. **Punishment and Desert.** This case presents a unique sentencing dilemma, but
it casts light on conflicts that judges face often. How does one measure desert? How
does one use intuitions about desert to determine a penalty?

On one hand, Bergman committed several serious offenses intentionally. Retributive reasoning suggests, whether one looks at the harm he intended or the harm he
caused, a substantial punishment is deserved. Moreover, the so-called "expressive
function of law" is served by such a punishment. In other words, utilitarian considerations of general deterrence require significant punishment. All of these considerations point harmoniously in the same direction. And yet the defendant's background
and character suggest that these acts were aberrations and that he was a man of notable achievement in both public and private matters. In the end the judge cannot
separate punishing the crime from punishing the man. And no formula is likely to
resolve the dilemmas of fairness and justice.

A recurrent criticism is that legislators, in setting penalties, and judges, in applying them, treat white-collar criminals more leniently than others. They are readier
to impose fines or alternative service instead of imprisonment, and to mitigate
terms of imprisonment. Critics argue that a class bias underlies this tendency, that
legislators and judges identify with white-collar criminals as persons with similar
backgrounds and similar attitudes to themselves. "There but for the grace of God go I."

These critics add that, because of their own economic circumstances, judges under-estimate the havoc that economic loss can cause among those with marginal resources. Defenders of leniency argue that white-collar criminals do not present the same risks to security and inspire the same kind of terror as those who commit robbery, arson, homicide, and rape. Which side of this controversy does *Bergman* support? Note that, in addition to serving a year in prison — the four-month sentence imposed by Judge Frankel and then eight months on a state court indictment) — Bergman paid resti-tution in the amount of $2.5 million.

Following high-profile corporate criminal scandals in recent years, some courts have taken a more severe approach to sentencing white-collar offenders than that reflected in *Bergman*. After the collapse of Enron and WorldCom in 2002, Jeffrey Skilling, the chief executive officer at Enron, was sentenced to 24 years in prison for fraud and conspiracy (reduced after appeal to 14 years). Bernard Ebbers, the chief executive at WorldCom, is serving a 25-year sentence, also for fraud and conspiracy. In 2009, investment advisor Bernie Madoff received the maximum sentence of 150 years after he pled guilty to 11 counts of fraud, money laundering, perjury, and theft in connection with a $65 billion Ponzi scheme that defrauded thousands of investors. For additional information on the Skilling case, see Chapter 8, Section D. For an interesting interview with the federal judge who sentenced Madoff, see Benjamin Weiser, *Madoff Judge Recalls Rationale for Imposing 150-Year Sentence*, N.Y. Times, June 29, 2011, at A1.

2. The Harris Case. The Bergman case can be compared with that of Jean Harris, the headmistress of a prestigious New York private school. In 1980, Harris, in a suicidal depression, shot to death Dr. Herman Tarnower (the Scarsdale Diet doctor), with whom she was having a sexual relationship and who was treating her with humili-ation and duplicity. By all accounts, Harris had led an exemplary life. What punish-ment did Harris deserve? She was convicted of second-degree murder and served 12 years of a 15-year prison term before her sentence was commuted in 1992.

Since the Harris case involved violence, should she have been punished more severely than Bergman? Or were his crimes more serious because acts of fraud and deceit cannot be called spontaneous, emotional, and uncharacteristic of the actor's nature?

Both the Bergman and Harris cases drew much public attention. What effect do you think media coverage might have had on the ultimate result? Are sentences likely to be more severe than in cases in which defendants are not celebrities? Does noto-riety prevent fairness? Does it create a distorted lens through which it is impossible to see the defendants for what they are? Or does *any* trial lead us to see defendants through the equivalent of a funhouse mirror?

3. Alternative Sentences. Should alternative sentencing have been considered more seriously than it was in these cases? Should a fine have been considered more seri-ously, with the amount of the fine "set at whatever level imposes the same disutility on the defendant, and thus yield[s] the same deterrence," as a prison sentence?

Richard A. Posner, *Optimal Sentences for White-Collar Criminals*, 17 Am. Crim. L. Rev. 409, 410 (1980).

4. Old Crimes. A different kind of issue is raised by the sentencing of offenders who committed crimes in the distant past and who, while evading capture and prosecution, led exemplary lives for years. In the late 1960s and early 1970s, many self-styled social revolutionaries from middle- and upper-class families joined such organizations as the Weather Underground, the Symbionese Liberation Army (SLA), and the New World Liberation Front. Among other activities of civil (and criminal) disobedience, they staged violent protests and carried out bombings that cost lives. Many of these revolutionaries were later identified and charged with serious crimes committed decades earlier.

It can be argued that their unexceptionable conduct over more than 25 years showed that these individuals were no longer dangerous. The circumstances under which they acted were distinctive, a period of unrest and social dislocation. Nonetheless, the retributive argument that the seriousness of their crimes did not diminish over time and the argument from deterrence, that society should continue to express its intolerance of such conduct, were powerful. How should such cases have been resolved?

The case of Sara Jane Olson, who was charged with conspiring with members of the SLA, illustrates these issues. In 2001 Olson was charged with having conspired with members of the SLA in the early 1970s to murder and bomb various individuals. She initially announced plans to challenge the charges, which were based on circumstantial evidence. But after the events of September 11, 2001, the changed national attitude toward all forms of terrorism convinced her to plead guilty to conspiracy and possession of bombing materials. She was sentenced to 10 years on these charges and two years later received an additional five-year sentence after pleading guilty to second-degree murder for her role in the death of a bystander during a robbery committed by the SLA. Her habeas corpus petition challenging the length of her sentence was denied, *see In re* Olson, 57 Cal. Rptr. 3d 284 (Cal. Ct. App. 2007), and she ultimately spent seven years in prison before being released in 2009.

[2] Sentencing Discretion

[a] *The Traditional Approach to Sentencing: Before Guidelines*

Traditional criminal statutes allowed wide discretion in sentencing by prescribing a broad range of possible sentences for a given category and degree of offense. The arguments in favor of broad discretion are obvious. Offenders convicted of the same offense may differ in infinitely many ways. The circumstances of their actions are always unique, and so are their natures—their attitudes, personal histories, experiences, vulnerability, reformability, and so on. Allowing the court to adapt the punishment to the offender serves to take account of considerations of desert, deterrence, and reform that are idiosyncratic to the particular case.

On the other hand, the argument for discretion presupposes great skill and rationality on the part of the judge (or other decisionmaker). In the absence of such characteristics, and in the face of time constraints and other practical considerations, the system's discretion can generate arbitrariness and chaos. In the following selections, Professor Zimring describes the points of discretion under the traditional approach to sentencing, and Judge Frankel, who presided over the Bergman trial, shows their limitations.

Franklin Zimring, *Making the Punishment Fit the Crime: A Consumer's Guide to Sentencing Reform,* Hastings Center Report, Dec. 1976, at 13–14[4]

The best single phrase to describe the allocation of sentencing power in state and federal criminal justice is "multiple discretion." Putting aside the enormous power of the police to decide whether to arrest, and to select initial charges, there are four separate institutions that have the power to determine criminal sentences—the legislature, the prosecutor, the judge, and the parole board or its equivalent.

The *legislature* sets the range of sentences legally authorized after conviction for a particular criminal charge. Criminal law in the United States is noted for extremely wide ranges of sentencing power, delegated by legislation to discretionary agents, with extremely high maximum penalties and very few limits on how much less than the maximum can be imposed. In practice, then, most legislatures delegate their sentencing powers to other institutions. . . .

The *prosecutor* is not normally thought of as an official who has, or exercises, the power to determine punishment. In practice, however, the prosecutor is the most important institutional determinant of a criminal sentence. He has the legal authority to drop criminal charges, thus ending the possibility of punishment. He has the legal authority in most systems to determine the specific offense for which a person is to be prosecuted, and this ability to select a charge can also broaden or narrow the range of sentences that can be imposed upon conviction. In congested urban court systems (and elsewhere) he has the absolute power to reduce charges in exchange for guilty pleas and to recommend particular sentences to the court as part of a "plea bargain"; rarely will his recommendation for a lenient sentence be refused in an adversary system in which he is supposed to represent the punitive interests of the state.

The *judge* has the power to select a sentence from the wide range made available by the legislature for any charge that produces a conviction. His powers are discretionary—within this range of legally authorized sanctions his selection cannot be appealed, and is not reviewed. . . . On occasion, the legislature will provide a mandatory minimum sentence, such as life imprisonment for first-degree murder, that reduces the judge's options once a defendant has been convicted of that particular

---

4. Copyright © by The Hastings Center. Reprinted with permission.

offense. In such cases the prosecutor and judge retain the option to charge or convict a defendant for a lesser offense in order to retain their discretionary power. More often the judge has a wide range of sentencing choices and, influenced by the prosecutor's recommendation, will select either a single sentence (such as two years) or a minimum and maximum sentence (not less than two nor more than five years) for a particular offender.

The *parole* or *correctional authority* normally has the power to modify judicial sentences to a considerable degree. When the judge pronounces a single sentence, such as two years, usually legislation authorizes release from prison to parole after a specified proportion of the sentence has been served. When the judge has provided for a minimum and maximum sentence, such as two to five years, the relative power of the correctional or parole authority is increased, because it has the responsibility to determine at what point in a prison sentence the offender is to be released. The parole board's decision is a discretionary one, traditionally made without guidelines or principles of decision.

This outline of our present sentencing system necessarily misses the range of variation among jurisdictions in the fifty states and the federal system, and oversimplifies the complex interplay among institutions in each system. It is useful, however, as a context in which to consider specific proposed reforms; it also helps to explain why the labyrinthine status quo has few articulate defenders. . . .

Marvin Frankel, Criminal Sentences: Law without Order 5, 9–11, 17–23 (1973)[5]

. . . The judges simply are not good enough — nobody could be — to redress the fundamental absurdities of the system. . . .

[S]weeping penalty statutes allow sentences to be "individualized" not so much in terms of defendants but mainly in terms of the wide spectrums of character, bias, neurosis, and daily vagary encountered among occupants of the trial bench. It is no wonder that wherever supposed professionals in the field — criminologists, penologists, probation officers, and, yes, lawyers and judges — discuss sentencing, the talk inevitably dwells upon the problem of "disparity." Some writers have quibbled about the definitiveness of the evidence showing disparity. It is among the least substantial of quibbles. The evidence is conclusive that judges of widely varying attitudes on sentencing, administering statutes that confer huge measures of discretion, mete out widely divergent sentences where the divergences are explainable only by the variations among the judges, not by material differences in the defendants or their crimes. Even in our age of science and skepticism, the conclusion would seem to be among those still acceptable as self-evident. What would require proof of a weighty kind, and something astonishing in the way of theoretical explanation, would be the

_____

5. Copyright © 1973 by Marvin E. Frankel. Reprinted with permission.

suggestion that assorted judges, subject to little more than their own unfettered wills, could be expected to impose consistent sentences. In any event, if proof were needed that sentences vary simply because judges vary, there is plenty of it.

. . . [T]he tragic state of disorder in our sentencing practices is not attributable to any unique endowments of sadism or bestiality among judges as a species. Without claiming absolute detachment, I am prepared to hypothesize that judges in general, if only because of occupational conditioning, may be somewhat calmer, more dispassionate, and more humane than the average of people across the board. But nobody has the experience of being sentenced by "judges in general." The particular defendant on some existential day confronts a specific judge. The occupant of the bench on that day may be punitive, patriotic, self-righteous, guilt-ridden, and more than customarily dyspeptic. The vice in our system is that all such qualities have free rein as well as potentially fatal impact upon the defendant's finite life.

Such individual, personal powers are not evil only, or mainly, because evil people may come to hold positions of authority. The more pervasive wrong is that a regime of substantially limitless discretion is by definition arbitrary, capricious, and antithetical to the rule of law.

[b] Sentencing Guidelines and Beyond

The Federal Sentencing Guidelines. In response to the discretionary sentencing model and its perceived arbitrariness and leniency, many state and federal legislators in the 1970s and 1980s began to support mandatory or determinate sentencing, whereby sentences would be prescribed by statute with little room for discretion. In addition to abolishing parole for federal prisoners, the Crime Control Act of 1984 put in place sentencing procedures for federal prosecutions and charged a U.S. Sentencing Commission with the responsibility for creating sentencing guidelines for judges. The Federal Sentencing Guidelines that came out of that process went into effect in 1987. Although the federal guidelines were "mandatory" for federal judges, they were upheld in the face of challenges that they violated the separation of powers doctrine. *See Mistretta v. United States*, 488 U.S. 361 (1989).

The Federal Sentencing Guidelines present a table or grid of presumptive sentences, which can be found in Appendix B. Although these sentences were "presumptive," federal judges were required to follow them in determining sentences and to justify any decision to deviate from them. In this sense, the guidelines were intended to be mandatory rather than discretionary.

The Sentencing Table divides the facts relevant in making an individual sentencing decision into two categories: facts about the offense and facts about the offender. One axis of the grid (the vertical, or "y" axis) refers to "offense characteristics," with each federal crime assigned an offense level between 1 and 43, depending on the gravity of the offense. For example, first-degree murder is a level 43 offense; the offense level for less culpable forms of homicide ranges between 12 and 38, and aggravated assault is a level 14 offense.

Once the initial offense level for the defendant's crime is determined, the Sentencing Commission added a number of case-specific upward and downward "adjustments" that can increase or decrease the offense level, thereby moving the potential sentence up or down the "y" axis. For example, an offense level is increased by two if the defendant physically restrained the victim during the crime, or knew (or should have known) that the victim was a vulnerable person. A defendant who was a minor participant in the crime receives a downward adjustment of two offense levels, and the offense level for a minimal participant is reduced by four. Accepting responsibility for the crime also decreases the offense level by two. The higher an "adjusted offense level," the more severe the defendant's presumptive sentence.

The other axis of the Sentencing Table (the horizontal, or "x" axis) refers to the defendant's criminal history. Defendants are assigned to one of six categories depending on their "criminal history points," which are largely calculated based on prior convictions and sentences. Defendants with a criminal history point total of zero or one are placed in Group I, whereas those with 13 points or more are placed in Group VI. The number of points attached to a prior conviction varies from one to three, depending on the sentence the defendant received. Two additional points are added if the defendant was, for example, on probation or parole when the prior crime was committed. As with the offense characteristics, a higher criminal history score yields a more severe presumptive sentence.

Once the judge determines the defendant's adjusted offense level and criminal history points, the Sentencing Table prescribes a presumptive sentence range for each intersecting point on the grid, with no more than a 25 percent spread between the minimum and maximum sentence. For example, the presumptive sentence for a defendant with an adjusted offense level of 15 who falls into Group III based on criminal history points is between 24 and 30 months. The judge was expected to choose a sentence within that range or justify a "departure" by identifying unusual aggravating or mitigating factors not considered by the Sentencing Commission. Controversially, the guidelines explicitly deem a number of factors (such as charitable or public service, drug dependence, "a disadvantaged upbringing," and "family ties and responsibilities") to be "not ordinarily relevant" in determining "whether a sentence should be outside the applicable guideline range." U.S. Sentencing Commission Guidelines Manual § 5H (2016).

The "zones" marked on the Sentencing Table determine whether probation is a permissible sentence. Defendants who fall into Zone A may be sentenced to probation, whereas those who fall into Zones C and D may not. For defendants in Zone B, probation is allowed so long as the judge also "imposes a condition or combination of conditions requiring intermittent confinement, community confinement, or home detention" for the minimum period of time called for by the applicable guidelines range. Id. § 5B1.1.

It is important to distinguish sentencing guidelines from so-called mandatory minimum sentences. Sentencing guidelines prescribe a particular sentence or sentence range for a particular crime and give judges some, if limited, discretion to deviate from the prescription in unusual cases. Mandatory minimums, on the other hand, legislatively mandate minimum sentences for particular crimes and leave no room for leniency. Both sentencing guidelines and mandatory minimums have been criticized for limiting flexibility and producing unfairness in individual cases.

Thus, guided and mandatory sentencing schemes have generated their own problems and critics. While the new federal regime was intended to produce more uniform, and often more severe, sentences, it in fact led to complex and highly formalized sentencing protocols, prison overcrowding, and perceived unfairness in particular cases. Dissatisfaction with the restrictive federal guidelines was widespread, even among federal judges of varying political backgrounds. Just as it seems unfair to treat like cases differently, it seems equally unfair to treat unlike cases the same. But it turns out that identifying which individual cases should fall into which categories may be beyond the competence of regularized rulemaking. The ultimate practical and institutional lessons are harder to determine, controversial, and still under intense study within the executive, legislative, and judicial branches.

Apprendi **and** *Booker.* The constitutionality of mandatory minimums and sentencing guidelines was called into question following the Supreme Court's five-to-four decision in *Apprendi v. New Jersey*, 530 U.S. 466 (2000). In *Apprendi*, the Court held that the Due Process Clause and Sixth Amendment right to jury trial require that any fact "[o]ther than the fact of a prior conviction . . . that increases the penalty for a crime beyond the prescribed statutory maximum must be submitted to a jury, and proved beyond a reasonable doubt." Apprendi pled guilty to possessing a firearm "for an unlawful purpose," a crime that carried a maximum prison sentence of 10 years. But he was sentenced to 12 years under the state's hate crime statute, which allowed an "'extended term' of imprisonment" if the sentencing judge found by a preponderance of the evidence that a defendant "acted with a purpose to intimidate an individual or group of individuals because of race, color, gender, handicap, religion, sexual orientation or ethnicity." Discriminatory purpose was not an "element" included in the language of the weapons possession statute that led to Apprendi's conviction, but because it increased his sentence beyond the 10-year statutory maximum for that crime, the Court ruled that it must be treated as an "element" of his crime and therefore submitted to the jury and found beyond a reasonable doubt (or admitted by the defendant as part of a guilty plea).

The Court's decision in *Apprendi* spawned a great deal of confusion and litigation, and the Supreme Court struggled with a number of cases in its wake. In *Blakely v. Washington*, 542 U.S. 296 (2004), by the same five-to-four vote that decided *Apprendi*, the Supreme Court applied *Apprendi*'s reasoning to a state sentencing guidelines scheme. *Blakely* held that *Apprendi* prohibited a state judge from following legislated state guidelines that allowed a sentence higher than the standard presumptive sentence range (49–53 months) if the judge found that the defendant committed his crime (kidnapping in Blakely's case) with "deliberate cruelty." Deliberate cruelty was a factor specified by the legislature as a permissible "aggravating factor," but it had not been found beyond a reasonable doubt by the jury or admitted by the defendant as part of a guilty plea. Even though the defendant's 90-month sentence was well within the 10-year statutory maximum for the crime of kidnapping, the *Blakely* majority concluded that "the relevant statutory maximum" for *Apprendi* purposes was not 10 years ("the maximum sentence a judge may impose after finding additional facts"), but instead 53 months ("the maximum [the judge] may impose without any additional findings").

Blakely involved state sentencing guidelines, and the Supreme Court quickly granted "certiorari before judgment" in *United States v. Booker*, 543 U.S. 220 (2005), to determine *Blakely*'s impact on the Federal Sentencing Guidelines. After hearing evidence that 92.5 grams of crack cocaine had been found in Booker's duffel bag, a jury convicted him of possessing at least 50 grams of crack with intent to distribute. Booker's presumptive sentence under the Federal Sentencing Guidelines grid was between 210 and 262 months. But he received a 30-year sentence based on the trial judge's finding at the sentencing hearing, applying a preponderance of the evidence standard, that Booker had possessed an additional 566 grams of crack and that his offense level should also be adjusted upward because he had obstructed justice. The same five Justices who formed the majority in *Apprendi* and *Blakely* announced that the mandatory Federal Sentencing Guidelines regime was unconstitutional because it suffered from the same flaw found in the earlier cases: sentences could be increased above the statutory maximum (here, the otherwise mandatory Federal Sentencing Guidelines range) based on facts not found by the jury or proved beyond a reasonable doubt.

In a surprising turn of events, however, Justice Ginsburg (who first voted with the *Booker* majority to hold the Federal Sentencing Guidelines unconstitutional) silently switched to form a different *Booker* majority (with the four *Apprendi/Blakely* dissenters) to address the remedy. Justice Breyer (who, prior to being appointed to the federal judiciary, had been a Federal Sentencing Commissioner and who has been credited with largely writing the federal guidelines) wrote for this "remedial majority" that the section of the Federal Sentencing Reform Act that made the guidelines mandatory could be "severed" from the rest of the statute, thereby leaving the guidelines in place, but only in an "advisory" capacity. Other statutory provisions left standing require that federal judges must still calculate a defendant's offense level and criminal history points and determine what the presumptive sentencing range would be under the guidelines. The sentence ultimately imposed need not be within the guidelines range, however, and federal judges have discretion to impose any sentence they think justified by the facts of the particular case. Finally, the remedial *Booker* majority held, federal appellate courts asked to review sentences are simply to determine whether the final sentence was "reasonable." Thus, the practical effect of *Booker* is to leave the Federal Sentencing Guidelines in place, and require their calculation in every case, although the decision whether or not to follow them in the end is discretionary with the sentencing judge.

Post-*Booker* Developments on the Federal Sentencing Guidelines. Subsequent Supreme Court opinions have addressed the weight to be given the Federal Sentencing

Guidelines in the wake of *Booker*. In *Rita v. United States*, 551 U.S. 338 (2007), the Court held that federal appellate courts, in reviewing sentences for reasonableness, *may* (but need not) presume that sentences falling *within* the sentencing guidelines' presumptive range are reasonable.

In *Gall v. United States*, 552 U.S. 38 (2007), by contrast, the Court ruled that an appellate court *may not* presume that a sentence *outside* the sentencing guidelines' presumptive range is unreasonable. Likewise, the Court held, federal courts of appeals may not require " 'extraordinary' circumstances to justify . . . sentence[s] outside the Guidelines range" and may not adopt "a rigid mathematical formula" to evaluate the reasonableness of such sentences. "[W]hile the extent of the difference between a particular sentence and the recommended Guidelines range is surely relevant," the Court continued, "courts of appeals must review all sentences — whether inside, just outside, or significantly outside the Guidelines range — under a deferential abuse-of-discretion standard."

The Court then went on to describe in detail the sentencing procedures to be used in the post-*Booker* world:

> [A] district court should begin all sentencing proceedings by correctly calculating the applicable Guidelines range. As a matter of administration and to secure nationwide consistency, the Guidelines should be the starting point and the initial benchmark. The Guidelines are not the only consideration, however. Accordingly, after giving both parties an opportunity to argue for whatever sentence they deem appropriate, the district judge should then consider all of the [18 U.S.C.] § 3553(a) factors to determine whether they support the sentence requested by a party.[6] In so doing, he may not presume that the Guidelines range is reasonable. He must make an individualized assessment based on the facts presented. If he decides that an

---

6. [n.6] Section 3553(a) lists seven factors that a sentencing court must consider. The first factor is a broad command to consider "the nature and circumstances of the offense and the history and characteristics of the defendant." The second factor requires the consideration of the general purposes of sentencing, including:

"the need for the sentence imposed —
    (A) to reflect the seriousness of the offense, to promote respect for the law, and to provide just punishment for the offense;
    (B) to afford adequate deterrence to criminal conduct;
    (C) to protect the public from further crimes of the defendant; and
    (D) to provide the defendant with needed educational or vocational training, medical care, or other correctional treatment in the most effective manner."

The third factor pertains to "the kinds of sentences available," the fourth to the Sentencing Guidelines, the fifth to any relevant policy statement issued by the Sentencing Commission, the sixth to "the need to avoid unwarranted sentence disparities," and the seventh to "the need to provide restitution to any victim." Preceding this list is a general directive to "impose a sentence sufficient, but not greater than necessary, to comply with the purposes" of sentencing described in the second factor. The fact that § 3553(a) explicitly directs sentencing courts to consider the Guidelines supports the premise that district courts must begin their analysis with the Guidelines and remain cognizant of them throughout the sentencing process.

outside-Guidelines sentence is warranted, he must consider the extent of the deviation and ensure that the justification is sufficiently compelling to support the degree of the variance. We find it uncontroversial that a major departure should be supported by a more significant justification than a minor one. After settling on the appropriate sentence, he must adequately explain the chosen sentence to allow for meaningful appellate review and to promote the perception of fair sentencing.

Regardless of whether the sentence imposed is inside or outside the Guidelines range, the appellate court must review the sentence under an abuse-of-discretion standard. . . . Assuming that the district court's sentencing decision is procedurally sound, the appellate court should then consider the substantive reasonableness of the sentence imposed under an abuse-of-discretion standard. When conducting this review, the court will, of course, take into account the totality of the circumstances, including the extent of any variance from the Guidelines range. If the sentence is within the Guidelines range, the appellate court may, but is not required to, apply a presumption of reasonableness [under *Rita*]. But if the sentence is outside the Guidelines range, the court may not apply a presumption of unreasonableness. It may consider the extent of the deviation, but must give due deference to the district court's decision that the § 3553(a) factors, on a whole, justify the extent of the variance. The fact that the appellate court might reasonably have concluded that a different sentence was appropriate is insufficient to justify reversal of the district court.

Justices Thomas and Alito dissented in *Gall*. Justice Alito took the position that federal judges should "give the policy decisions . . . embodied in the Sentencing Guidelines at least some significant weight" in making sentencing determinations. Justice Thomas' dissent was more complex. His view, first expressed in separate opinions in *Apprendi* and *Booker*, is that *all* facts relied upon to determine a guidelines sentence should be submitted to a jury and found beyond a reasonable doubt. If, however, *Booker*'s severance remedy is to be accepted, Justice Thomas would simply require federal judges to comply with all aspects of the Federal Sentencing Guidelines, thereby effectively returning to the pre-*Booker* regime of mandatory sentencing guidelines.

Booker and its progeny have not dramatically changed federal sentencing decisions. Although the number of sentences falling outside the presumptive guideline range has gradually increased in the decade since *Booker* was decided, more than half of federal sentences still fall within that presumptive range, prompting one scholar to comment that "[t]he endurance of the Guidelines, but more particularly the degree to which they continue to drive actual sentences, has surprised nearly everyone." Frank O. Bowman, III, *Dead Law Walking: The Surprising Tenacity of the Federal Sentencing Guidelines*, 51 Hous. L. Rev. 1227, 1238, 1268 (2014). Moreover, although both the mean and median lengths of prison sentences in federal cases have decreased since *Booker*, they are "only three to six months lower than they were in the early

2000s, when the outcry against the Guidelines' asserted severity was at fever pitch." *Id.* at 1236–37.

Other Decisions in the *Apprendi* Line of Cases. In addition to the guidelines cases, the Supreme Court has had occasion to apply its ruling in *Apprendi* to other sentencing issues. In *Cunningham v. California*, 549 U.S. 270 (2007), for example, the Court struck down California's determinate sentencing scheme. California's criminal statutes prescribed three different ranges of prison sentences for each offense, and required trial judges to select the middle range unless they found "circumstances in aggravation or mitigation" by a preponderance of the evidence. Finding the case controlled by *Blakely* and *Booker*, the *Cunningham* majority explained that the "relevant statutory maximum" in California was the middle sentence, "the maximum [a judge] may impose *without* any additional findings." The California legislature responded to the Court's decision by making sentencing completely discretionary. Specifically, the legislature amended Cal. Penal Code § 1170(b) to provide that when a criminal statute "specifies three possible [prison] terms, the choice of the appropriate term shall rest within the sound discretion of the court," which is to "select the term which, in the court's discretion, best serves the interests of justice."

In *Alleyne v. United States*, 133 S. Ct. 2151 (2013), the Court held that *Apprendi* requires that the jury, not the judge, find any facts that increase a defendant's mandatory minimum sentence (as opposed to the maximum sentences at issue in *Apprendi*). "Any fact that, by law, increases the penalty for a crime is an 'element' that must be submitted to the jury and found beyond a reasonable doubt," the Court reasoned, and "[i]t is impossible to dissociate the floor of a sentencing range from the penalty affixed to the crime."

For a description of *Ring v. Arizona*, 536 U.S. 584 (2002), where the Court applied *Apprendi* in the context of a capital sentencing hearing, see Note 7 following *Lockett v. Ohio* in Chapter 6, Section E.2. *See also Washington v. Recuenco*, 546 U.S. 1166 (2006) (concluding that an *Apprendi* violation is not a "structural error" and is therefore subject to harmless error analysis); *Oregon v. Ice*, 555 U.S. 160 (2009) (holding that the decision whether to impose a consecutive or concurrent prison sentence may be based on facts found by the judge because juries traditionally had no role in such determinations); *Southern Union Co. v. United States*, 132 S. Ct. 2344 (2012) (extending *Apprendi* to the imposition of criminal fines).

[c] Sentencing under the Model Penal Code and Its Proposed Revisions

The Model Penal Code as originally published in 1985 endorsed a hybrid approach to sentencing. Sections 6.06 through 6.09 resemble a traditional sentencing model, setting minimum and maximum sentences for different grades of offenses that give the trial judge a good deal of discretion in choosing the sentence to be imposed in a particular case. But the MPC then goes on in § 7.01 through § 7.04 to articulate specific criteria for judges to take into account in making sentencing decisions, including factors to be considered in imposing the "extended term[s] of imprisonment" authorized in §§ 7.03–7.04 in cases involving, for example, "persistent offender[s]," "professional criminal[s]," and "dangerous, mentally abnormal person[s]." In addition, § 1.02 describes the drafters' views of the appropriate purposes of punishment.

The MPC sentencing provisions are currently in the process of being revised, and the American Law Institute has already voted in favor of some changes. Under the newly approved provisions, the following considerations are relevant in choosing sentences for particular defendants: to make sentences "proportionate to the gravity of offenses, the harms done to crime victims, and the blameworthiness of offenders"; "when reasonably feasible, to achieve offender rehabilitation, general deterrence, incapacitation of dangerous offenders, restoration of crime victims and communities, and reintegration of offenders into the law-abiding community"; and to impose sentences "no more severe than necessary" to achieve these purposes of punishment. Model Penal Code: Sentencing § 1.02(2)(a) (Tentative Draft No. 4, 2016) (approved May 2016). The overall purposes of "the sentencing system" include "preserv[ing] judicial discretion to individualize sentences"; making sentences uniform; "eliminat[ing] inequities in sentencing across population groups"; and "encourag[ing] the use of intermediate sanctions." *Id.* § 1.02(2)(b).

The new provisions no longer require any minimum sentences (like those currently set out in §§ 6.06–6.09), and they create five instead of three degrees of felonies, which carry the following maximum prison terms: life in prison for a first-degree felony; 20 years for a second-degree felony; 10 years for a third-degree felony; five years for a fourth-degree felony; and three years for a fifth-degree felony. The maximum sentence for a misdemeanor remains at one year and for a petty misdemeanor is increased to six months. The revisions do not authorize any "extended term[s] of imprisonment" like those currently provided for in §§ 7.03–7.04. *See* Model Penal Code: Sentencing § 6.06 (Tentative Draft No. 2, 2011) (approved May 2011).

A new provision that applies specifically to defendants who were under the age of 18 at the time of their crime cautions that sentencing in such cases is to focus on rehabilitation and reintegration into the community unless the defendant committed "a serious violent offense" and "presents a high risk of serious violent offending in the future." This section adds a provision prohibiting sentencing these defendants to a term longer than 25 years "for any offense or combination of offenses," and that maximum is reduced to 20 years for defendants under the age of 16 and to 10 years for those under 14. *Id.* § 6.11A.

In place of the sentencing criteria set out in § 7.01 through § 7.04 of the MPC, the new sentencing provisions envision the creation of state sentencing commissions that would be charged with submitting proposed sentencing guidelines to the legislature and then conducting "an omnibus review of the sentencing system" every 10 years. Model Penal Code: Sentencing §§ 6A.01, 6A.09(1) (Tentative Draft No. 1, 2007) (approved Apr. 2007). In addition to fixing presumptive sentences, the sentencing guidelines would include "nonexclusive lists of aggravating and mitigating factors that may be used as grounds for departure from presumptive sentences" but, unlike the Federal Sentencing Guidelines, would not "quantify the effect given to specific aggravating or mitigating factors." *Id.* §§ 6B.02(1), 6B.04(4). But the MPC creates "a heavy presumption" against any upward departure greater than twice the presumptive sentence, admonishing that such "extraordinary departure[s]" should occur only if "extraordinary and compelling circumstances demonstrate" that the presumptive sentence is "unreasonable" in light of the purposes of punishment. *Id.* § 7.XX(3).

Unlike the Federal Sentencing Guidelines, the new MPC provisions would not necessarily consider a defendant's criminal history, but instead leave to the discretion of each individual sentencing commission whether to take the defendant's prior record into account either in determining the presumptive sentence or as an aggravating factor. *See* Model Penal Code: Sentencing § 6B.07(1) (Tentative Draft No. 4, 2016) (approved May 2016). But the drafters seem somewhat skeptical about criminal history, requiring sentencing commissions "to explain and justify any use of criminal history" and warning that the use of such history "may over-predict" the "risk of reoffending" and have a "disparate impact[] on racial or ethnic minorities, or other disadvantaged groups." *Id.* And the MPC would not allow consideration of prior convictions more than 10 years old, *id.* § 6B.07(3), or of any "alleged criminal conduct" other than an actual conviction or "criminal conduct admitted by the offender at sentencing." Model Penal Code: Sentencing § 6B.06(2)(b) (Tentative Draft No. 1, 2007) (approved Apr. 2007).

The revisions also set the maximum fine that may be assessed for each grade of criminal offense, ranging from $200,000 for a first-degree felony to $1,000 for a petty misdemeanor. In addition, this provision would limit fines to five times "the pecuniary gain" realized by the defendant or five times "the loss or damage" incurred by the victim. Model Penal Code: Sentencing § 6.04B(1) (Tentative Draft No. 3, 2014) (approved May 2014). Fines in excess of these maxima could be imposed if the state opted to create a "means-based fine plan," which would vary fines based on defendants' "wealth and/or income . . . so that the punitive force of financial penalties will be comparable for offenders of varying economic means." *Id.* §§ 6.04B(3), 6.04B(5).

The revisions also discuss alternative sentencing and the collateral consequences of conviction. They would allow a sentence of probation for any felony or misdemeanor conviction, for a maximum period of one year for a misdemeanor and three years for a felony, with the proviso that "ordinarily" a felon will be discharged from probation "after successful completion of a minimum term" of not more than one year. *Id.* § 6.03.

Other sections of the revisions address economic sanctions, asset forfeiture, postrelease supervision, and victim compensation. *See id.* §§ 6.04, 6.04C, 6.09; Model Penal Code: Sentencing § 6.04(A) (Tentative Draft No. 4, 2016) (approved May 2016). The new provisions would also authorize judges to use "restorative justice practices" (described above in Section C.2) either instead of, or in addition to, traditional sentencing procedures if the defendant and participating victims agreed. *Id.* § 6.14.

The provisions on the collateral consequences of conviction would bar denying the right to vote, except to felons while they were incarcerated, and would allow disqualification from jury service only while defendants were serving their sentence, "including any period of community supervision." Model Penal Code: Sentencing § 6x.03 (Tentative Draft No. 3, 2014) (approved May 2014).

Finally, the revisions add a provision that allows prisoners to move to modify their sentences after serving 15 years and then at least every 10 years thereafter. These sentence-modification proceedings are "analogous to a resentencing in light of present circumstances," and a prisoner's sentence may be reduced if the purposes of punishment "would better be served" by a lesser sentence. Model Penal Code: Sentencing § 305.6 (Tentative Draft No. 2, 2011) (approved May 2011). In addition, a prisoner may seek a sentence modification based on "advanced age, physical or mental infirmity, exigent family circumstances, or other compelling reasons." *Id.* § 305.7.

In addition to these approved changes, other modifications of the MPC's sentencing provisions are still under review. The issues remaining to be resolved include sentencing hearing procedures and appeals.

[3] Proportionality

Both state and federal constitutional provisions limit the punishment that legislators can assign for particular crimes. The Eighth Amendment to the U.S. Constitution prohibits "cruel and unusual punishment" and many state constitutions have similar provisions.

Courts have frequently held that punishments that are in themselves acceptable for some offenses—imprisonment for life, execution—may violate the prohibition of cruel and unusual punishment if they are disproportionate in severity to the crime. The following case describes the guidelines the Supreme Court has used in making such judgments.

Solem v. Helm
463 U.S. 277 (1983)

JUSTICE POWELL delivered the opinion of the Court.

The issue presented is whether the Eighth Amendment proscribes a life sentence without possibility of parole for a seventh nonviolent felony.

By 1975 the State of South Dakota had convicted respondent Jerry Helm of six nonviolent felonies. In 1964, 1966, and 1969 Helm was convicted of third-degree burglary. In 1972 he was convicted of obtaining money under false pretenses. In 1973 he was convicted of grand larceny. And in 1975 he was convicted of third-offense driving while intoxicated. The record contains no details about the circumstances of any of these offenses, except that they were all nonviolent, none was a crime against a person, and alcohol was a contributing factor in each case.

In 1979 Helm was charged with uttering a "no account" check for $100. . . . Helm pleaded guilty. Ordinarily the maximum punishment for uttering a "no account" check would have been five years' imprisonment in the state penitentiary and a $5,000 fine. As a result of his criminal record, however, Helm was subject to South Dakota's recidivist statute:

> When a defendant has been convicted of at least three prior [felonies] in addition to the principal felony, the sentence for the principal felony shall be enhanced to the sentence for a Class 1 felony.

The maximum penalty for a "Class 1 felony" was life imprisonment in the state penitentiary and a $25,000 fine. Moreover, South Dakota law explicitly provides that parole is unavailable. . . . The Governor is authorized to pardon prisoners, or to commute their sentences, S.D. Const., Art. IV, § 3, but no other relief from sentence is available even to a rehabilitated prisoner.

Immediately after accepting Helm's guilty plea, the South Dakota Circuit Court sentenced Helm to life imprisonment. . . . The court explained:

> I think you certainly earned this sentence and certainly proven that you're an habitual criminal and the record would indicate that you're beyond rehabilitation and that the only prudent thing to do is to lock you up for the rest of your natural life, so you won't have further victims of your crimes, just be coming back before Courts. You'll have plenty of time to think this one over.

The South Dakota Supreme Court, in a 3–2 decision, affirmed the sentence despite Helm's argument that it violated the Eighth Amendment.

After Helm had served two years in the state penitentiary, he requested the Governor to commute his sentence to a fixed term of years. Such a commutation would have had the effect of making Helm eligible to be considered for parole when he had served three-fourths of his new sentence. The Governor denied Helm's request. . . .

In November 1981, Helm sought habeas relief in the United States District Court for the District of South Dakota. . . . Although the District Court recognized that the sentence was harsh, it . . . denied the writ.

The United States Court of Appeals for the Eighth Circuit reversed. . . .

The Eighth Amendment declares: "Excessive bail shall not be required, nor excessive fines imposed, nor cruel and unusual punishments inflicted." The final clause prohibits not only barbaric punishments, but also sentences that are disproportionate to the crime committed.

The principle that a punishment should be proportionate to the crime is deeply rooted and frequently repeated in common-law jurisprudence. . . .

The constitutional principle of proportionality has been recognized explicitly in this Court for almost a century. . . .

. . . And our prior cases have recognized explicitly that prison sentences are subject to proportionality analysis.

In sum, we hold as a matter of principle that a criminal sentence must be proportionate to the crime for which the defendant has been convicted. Reviewing courts, of course, should grant substantial deference to the broad authority that legislatures necessarily possess in determining the types and limits of punishments for crimes, as well as to the discretion that trial courts possess in sentencing convicted criminals. But no penalty is per se constitutional. As the Court noted in *Robinson v. California*, [370 U.S. 660, 667 (1962),] a single day in prison may be unconstitutional in some circumstances.

When sentences are reviewed under the Eighth Amendment, courts should be guided by objective factors that our cases have recognized. First, we look to the gravity of the offense and the harshness of the penalty. . . .

Second, it may be helpful to compare the sentences imposed on other criminals in the same jurisdiction. If more serious crimes are subject to the same penalty, or to less serious penalties, that is some indication that the punishment at issue may be excessive. . . .

Third, courts may find it useful to compare the sentences imposed for commission of the same crime in other jurisdictions. . . .

Application of these factors assumes that courts are competent to judge the gravity of an offense, at least on a relative scale. In a broad sense this assumption is justified, and courts traditionally have made these judgments—just as legislatures must make them in the first instance. Comparisons can be made in light of the harm caused or threatened to the victim or society, and the culpability of the offender. . . .

. . . The absolute magnitude of the crime may be relevant. Stealing a million dollars is viewed as more serious than stealing a hundred dollars—a point recognized in statutes distinguishing petty theft from grand theft. Few would dispute that a lesser included offense should not be punished more severely than the greater offense. Thus a court is justified in viewing assault with intent to murder as more serious than simple assault. It also is generally recognized that attempts are less serious than completed crimes. Similarly, an accessory after the fact should not be subject to a higher penalty than the principal.

Turning to the culpability of the offender, there are again clear distinctions that courts may recognize and apply. Most would agree that negligent conduct is less serious than intentional conduct. South Dakota, for example, ranks criminal acts in ascending order of seriousness as follows: negligent acts, reckless acts, knowing acts, intentional acts, and malicious acts. A court, of course, is entitled to look at a defendant's motive in committing a crime. Thus a murder may be viewed as more serious when committed pursuant to a contract.

This list is by no means exhaustive. It simply illustrates that there are generally accepted criteria for comparing the severity of different crimes on a broad scale, despite the difficulties courts face in attempting to draw distinctions between similar crimes.

Application of the factors that we identify also assumes that courts are able to compare different sentences. This assumption, too, is justified. The easiest comparison, of course, is between capital punishment and noncapital punishments, for the death penalty is different from other punishments in kind rather than degree. For sentences of imprisonment, the problem is not so much one of ordering, but one of line-drawing. . . .

It remains to apply the analytical framework established by our prior decisions to the case before us. We first consider the relevant criteria, viewing Helm's sentence as life imprisonment without possibility of parole. We then consider the State's argument that the possibility of commutation is sufficient to save an otherwise unconstitutional sentence.

Helm's crime was "one of the most passive felonies a person could commit." *State v. Helm*, 287 N.W.2d at 501 (Henderson, J., dissenting). It involved neither violence nor threat of violence to any person. The $100 face value of Helm's "no account" check was not trivial, but neither was it a large amount. One hundred dollars was less than half the amount South Dakota required for a felonious theft. It is easy to see why such a crime is viewed by society as among the less serious offenses.

Helm, of course, was not charged simply with uttering a "no account" check, but also with being a habitual offender. [7] And a State is justified in punishing a recidivist more severely than it punishes a first offender. Helm's status, however, cannot be considered in the abstract. His prior offenses, although classified as felonies, were all relatively minor. All were nonviolent and none was a crime against a person. Indeed, there was no minimum amount in either the burglary or the false pretenses statutes, and the minimum amount covered by the grand larceny statute was fairly small.

Helm's present sentence is life imprisonment without possibility of parole. Barring executive clemency, Helm will spend the rest of his life in the state penitentiary. . . . Only capital punishment, a penalty not authorized in South Dakota when Helm was sentenced, exceeds it.

We next consider the sentences that could be imposed on other criminals in the same jurisdiction. . . .

[T]here were a handful of crimes that were necessarily punished by life imprisonment: murder, and, on a second or third offense, treason, first-degree manslaughter, first-degree arson, and kidnapping. There was a larger group for which life imprisonment was authorized in the discretion of the sentencing judge, including: treason, first-degree manslaughter, first-degree arson, and kidnapping; attempted murder, placing an explosive device on an aircraft, and first-degree rape on a second or third offense; and any felony after three prior offenses. Finally, there was a

---

7. [n.21] We must focus on the principal felony — the felony that triggers the life sentences — since Helm already has paid the penalty for each of his prior offenses. But we recognize, of course, that Helm's prior convictions are relevant to the sentencing decision.

large group of very serious offenses for which life imprisonment was not authorized, including a third offense of heroin dealing or aggravated assault.

Criminals committing any of these offenses ordinarily would be thought more deserving of punishment than one uttering a "no account" check—even when the bad-check writer had already committed six minor felonies. . . .

Finally, we compare the sentences imposed for commission of the same crime in other jurisdictions. The Court of Appeals found that "Helm could have received a life sentence without parole for his offense in only one other state, Nevada." . . . But even under Nevada law, a life sentence without possibility of parole is merely authorized in these circumstances. We are not advised that any defendant such as Helm, whose prior offenses were so minor, actually has received the maximum penalty in Nevada. . . .

The State argues that the present case is essentially the same as *Rummel v. Estelle*, [445 U.S. 263 (1980),] for the possibility of parole in that case is matched by the possibility of executive clemency here. . . .

As a matter of law, parole and commutation are different concepts, despite some surface similarities. Parole is a regular part of the rehabilitative process. Assuming good behavior, it is the normal expectation in the vast majority of cases. The law generally specifies when a prisoner will be eligible to be considered for parole, and details the standards and procedures applicable at that time. Thus it is possible to predict, at least to some extent, when parole might be granted. Commutation, on the other hand, is an ad hoc exercise of executive clemency. A Governor may commute a sentence at any time for any reason without reference to any standards.

In South Dakota commutation is more difficult to obtain than parole. . . . In fact, no life sentence has been commuted in over eight years, while parole—where authorized—has been granted regularly during that period. . . .

The possibility of commutation is nothing more than a hope for "an ad hoc exercise of clemency." It is little different from the possibility of executive clemency that exists in every case in which a defendant challenges his sentence under the Eighth Amendment. Recognition of such a bare possibility would make judicial review under the Eighth Amendment meaningless.

The Constitution requires us to examine Helm's sentence to determine if it is proportionate to his crime. Applying objective criteria, we find that Helm has received the penultimate sentence for relatively minor criminal conduct. He has been treated more harshly than other criminals in the State who have committed more serious crimes. He has been treated more harshly than he would have been in any other jurisdiction, with the possible exception of a single State. We conclude that his sentence is significantly disproportionate to his crime, and is therefore prohibited by the Eighth Amendment.[8]

---

8. [n.32] Contrary to the suggestion in the dissent, our conclusion today is not inconsistent with *Rummel v. Estelle*. The *Rummel* Court recognized—as does the dissent—that some sentences

Chief Justice Burger, with whom Justice White, Justice Rehnquist, and Justice O'Connor join, dissenting.

The controlling law governing this case is crystal clear, but today the Court blithely discards any concept of stare decisis, trespasses gravely on the authority of the states, and distorts the concept of proportionality of punishment by tearing it from its moorings in capital cases. Only three Terms ago, we held in *Rummel v. Estelle* that a life sentence imposed after only a *third* nonviolent felony conviction did not constitute cruel and unusual punishment under the Eighth Amendment. Today, the Court ignores its recent precedent and holds that a life sentence imposed after a *seventh* felony conviction constitutes cruel and unusual punishment under the Eighth Amendment. Moreover, I reject the fiction that all Helm's crimes were innocuous or nonviolent. Among his felonies were three burglaries and a third conviction for drunken driving. By comparison Rummel was a relatively "model citizen." Although today's holding cannot rationally be reconciled with *Rummel*, the Court does not purport to overrule *Rummel*. I therefore dissent.

The Court's starting premise is that the Eighth Amendment's Cruel and Unusual Punishments Clause "prohibits not only barbaric punishments, but also sentences that are disproportionate to the crime committed." What the Court means is that a sentence is unconstitutional if it is more severe than five Justices think appropriate. In short, all sentences of imprisonment are subject to appellate scrutiny to ensure that they are "proportional" to the crime committed. . . .

The *Rummel* Court categorically rejected the very analysis adopted by the Court today. Rummel had argued that various objective criteria existed by which the Court could determine whether his life sentence was proportional to his crimes. In rejecting Rummel's contentions, the Court explained why each was insufficient to allow it to determine in an *objective* manner whether a given sentence of imprisonment is proportionate to the crime for which it is imposed.

. . . Today's conclusion by five Justices that they are able to say that one offense has less "gravity" than another is nothing other than a bald substitution of individual subjective moral values for those of the legislature. . . .

The simple truth is that "[no] neutral principle of adjudication permits a federal court to hold that in a given situation individual crimes are too trivial in relation to the punishment imposed." . . . Legislatures are far better equipped than we are to balance the competing penal and public interests and to draw the essentially arbitrary lines between appropriate sentences for different crimes.

---

of imprisonment are so disproportionate that they violate the Eighth Amendment. 445 U.S. at 274 n.11. . . . *Rummel* did reject a proportionality challenge to a particular sentence. But since the *Rummel* Court—like the dissent today—offered no standards for determining when an Eighth Amendment violation has occurred, it is controlling only in a similar factual situation. Here the facts are clearly distinguishable. Whereas Rummel was eligible for a reasonably early parole, Helm, at age 36, was sentenced to life with no possibility of parole.

By asserting the power to review sentences of imprisonment for excessiveness the Court launches into uncharted and unchartable waters. Today it holds that a sentence of life imprisonment, without the possibility of parole, is excessive punishment for a seventh allegedly "nonviolent" felony. How about the eighth "nonviolent" felony? The ninth? The twelfth? Suppose one offense was a simple assault? Or selling liquor to a minor? Or statutory rape? Or price fixing? The permutations are endless and the Court's opinion is bankrupt of realistic guiding principles. . . . I can see no limiting principle in the Court's holding.

The differences between this case and *Rummel* are insubstantial. First, Rummel committed three truly nonviolent felonies, while respondent, as noted at the outset, committed seven felonies, four of which cannot fairly be characterized as "nonviolent." At the very least, respondent's burglaries and his third-offense drunken driving posed real risk of serious harm to others. It is sheer fortuity that the places respondent burglarized were unoccupied and that he killed no pedestrians while behind the wheel. What would have happened if a guard had been on duty during the burglaries is a matter of speculation, but the possibilities shatter the notion that respondent's crimes were innocuous, inconsequential, minor, or "nonviolent." Four of respondent's crimes, I repeat, had harsh potentialities for violence. Respondent, far more than Rummel, has demonstrated his inability to bring his conduct into conformity with the minimum standards of civilized society. Clearly, this difference demolishes any semblance of logic in the Court's conclusion that respondent's sentence constitutes cruel and unusual punishment although Rummel's did not.

The Court's opinion necessarily reduces to the proposition that a sentence of life imprisonment with the possibility of commutation, but without possibility of parole, is so much more severe than a life sentence with the possibility of parole that one is excessive while the other is not. This distinction does not withstand scrutiny. . . .

Notes and Questions

1. Comparing *Solem* and *Rummel*. It is not at all obvious that the Court's reasoning in *Solem v. Helm* can be reconciled with its reasoning in the earlier case of *Rummel v. Estelle*, which is discussed in *Solem*. Both cases were decided by five-to-four votes. The apparent inconsistency is the following. *Solem* appears to hold that a statute violates the Eighth Amendment when it prescribes a term of imprisonment that (1) is harsher than is justified by the gravity of the offense, (2) is inconsistent with sentences for other crimes in the same jurisdiction, and (3) is inconsistent with sentences for the same crime in other jurisdictions. *Rummel*, on the other hand, holds that it is improper for the Court to evaluate such statutory prescriptions by these criteria because penalties involve subjective judgments that are appropriately made by state legislatures.

One may respond to this debate in three ways: (1) One may agree that the cases are inconsistent and favor *Solem*, arguing that the Court in *Solem* exercised its power appropriately. (2) One may agree that the cases are inconsistent and favor *Rummel*, arguing that the Court in *Solem* exercised its power improperly. (3) One may claim, as does Justice Powell in *Solem*, that the cases are distinguishable because one involves the possibility of parole and the other involves only the possible relief of a pardon. (One may infer that most members of the Court favored either response (1) or response (2) since most Justices who dissented in one case were in the majority in the other.)

Which response to this constitutional dilemma seems most persuasive to you?

2. *Harmelin*: The Court Remains Divided. In *Harmelin v. Michigan*, 501 U.S. 957 (1991), the petitioner received a mandatory sentence of life imprisonment for possession of more than 650 grams of cocaine, his first offense. Harmelin claimed that the statute under which he was sentenced was unconstitutional because it did not allow the sentencer to take into account mitigating factors. The Court affirmed the sentence. A majority concluded that severe mandatory penalties might be "cruel," but were not necessarily "unusual," having been employed throughout our history.

The Justices arrived at the result in different ways. Speaking only for himself and Chief Justice Rehnquist, Justice Scalia argued that it was incorrect to use the Eighth Amendment for proportionality review, that the Amendment contains no proportionality guarantee, and that the line of cases culminating in *Solem* was based on error. The three other Justices who joined the majority argued that, in accord with *Rummel* and *Solem*, the Court could review proportionality but that its powers were narrow and that such review "should be informed by objective factors to the maximum extent possible." They concluded that Harmelin's sentence was not grossly disproportionate to his crime and that the seriousness of his offense obviated the need to do any "comparative analysis" between his sentence and the sentences imposed for other crimes or in other jurisdictions.

Four Justices dissented. They reaffirmed the methodology of *Solem*, emphasizing the relevance of all three parts of that analysis.

Thus, both *Rummel* and *Solem* are in good standing. The Court remains conspicuously divided with regard to both the standards and the scope of proportionality review.

3. Mandatory Penalties and the Eighth Amendment. Note that *Harmelin* raises two distinguishable but related issues. One, as we have seen, is the issue of proportionality, the *Rummel/Solem* question of when a penalty mandated by statute is disproportionately severe. The more general question, never fully confronted by the Supreme Court, is whether mandatory sentences in general violate due process by requiring courts to treat unlike cases alike and barring them from making important and relevant distinctions.

4. "Three Strikes" Laws and *Ewing v. California*. In *Ewing v. California*, 538 U.S. 11 (2003), the Supreme Court resolved a constitutional challenge to California's so-called "three strikes" law. California's law imposed an indeterminate sentence of life in prison on a defendant convicted of a felony who had previously been convicted of two or more violent or otherwise serious felonies. The crime that triggered the three-strikes law in Ewing's case was grand theft: he was convicted on this charge after he walked out of a pro shop with three golf clubs, which had a total value of about $1,200, hidden in the leg of his pants. Under California law, the judge had discretion to treat this crime as a misdemeanor or a felony. Ewing was sentenced to an indeterminate life sentence, with no possibility of parole for 25 years.[9]

Ewing argued that under the circumstances his punishment was grossly disproportionate to his offense and therefore violated the Eighth Amendment's ban on cruel and unusual punishment under the standard set out in *Solem* and the reasoning applied in *Harmelin*. The Court rejected his argument. There was no majority opinion.

Speaking for a three-Justice plurality consisting of Chief Justice Rehnquist, Justice Kennedy, and herself, Justice O'Connor observed that "federal courts should be reluctant to review legislatively mandated terms of imprisonment, and that successful challenges to the proportionality of particular sentences should be exceedingly rare." Although Justice O'Connor did not view the Eighth Amendment as requiring "strict proportionality between crime and sentence," she did think it barred sentences that were "grossly disproportionate" to the crime. Noting that the California three-strikes law "was intended to be a focused effort to create a sentencing policy that would use the judicial system to reduce serious and violent crime," Justice O'Connor reasoned that "Ewing's sentence [was] justified by the State's public-safety interest in incapacitating and deterring recidivist felons." She concluded that his sentence "reflect[ed] a rational legislative judgment, entitled to deference," and was not grossly disproportionate to his crime.

Justices Scalia and Thomas, providing the two votes necessary for a majority, concurred only in the judgment and wrote separate opinions. Justice Scalia reasserted his conviction that the constitutional prohibition against cruel and unusual punishments was not intended as a guarantee against disproportionate prison sentences but was only intended to ban certain kinds of punishment. He accused the plurality of "not applying law but evaluating policy." Justice Thomas asserted that *Solem*'s proportionality test is "incapable of judicial application" and that the Eighth Amendment "contains no proportionality principle."

Justices Stevens and Breyer wrote separate dissents, joining in each other's views and joined as well by Justices Souter and Ginsburg. Justice Stevens, noting the

---

9. In the 2012 elections, the California electorate voted to narrow the state's three-strikes law to require that the defendant's third crime, like the first two, must be a serious or violent felony. As a result, a substantial number of the prisoners sentenced under the three-strikes law became eligible to seek a reduction in their sentence. By early 2015, California judges had released more than 2,000 prisoners under the new law, refusing to reduce the sentences of only 132 eligible prisoners on the ground that they presented an "unreasonable risk of danger to public safety." The prisoners who have been released have had a relatively low recidivism rate of 4.7 percent. *See* Erik Eckholm, *Out of Prison, and Staying Out, After 3rd Strike in California*, N.Y. TIMES, Feb. 27, 2015, at A1.

continuing viability and usefulness of *Solem*, remarked that it would be "anomalous indeed to suggest that the Eighth Amendment makes proportionality review applicable in the context of bail and fines but not in the context of other forms of punishment, such as imprisonment." Justice Breyer set forth an elaborate scheme of analysis. Inferring from *Harmelin* and other cases, he described a threshold test of gross disproportionality. Looking to the length of Ewing's "real time" sentence, his "sentence-triggering criminal conduct," and his criminal history, Justice Breyer concluded the case could not be significantly distinguished from *Solem*. Having determined that Ewing's claim passed the threshold test, he then applied the three criteria announced in *Solem* to determine that the Eighth Amendment had been violated.

Ewing demonstrates that the Court remains sharply divided on the underlying issue of proportionality. Significantly, the composition of the Court has changed since *Ewing* was decided, and the new Justices have yet to provide their views on these issues.

5. Proportionality and the Crack-Powder Cocaine Debate. Under the federal Anti-Drug Abuse Act of 1986, possession of five grams of crack cocaine with an intent to distribute yielded a five-year mandatory minimum sentence. By comparison, a defendant had to possess 500 grams of powder cocaine in order to receive the same five-year sentence. Proponents of this disparity argued that crack was cheaper than powder, more addictive, and more frequently associated with violence. *See* Christopher Wren, *Study Questions Cost of Shift to Harsh Cocaine Sentences*, N.Y. TIMES, May 13, 1997, at A14. On the other hand, critics of the scheme pointed to its racially disproportionate impact: about 90 percent of defendants in federal crack offense cases were African-American, compared to only 27 percent in federal powder cocaine cases. *See* David A. Sklansky, *Cocaine, Race, and Equal Protection*, 47 STAN. L. REV. 1283 (1995). Sklansky reviewed cases in which the circuit courts had uniformly rejected challenges to this disparity based on equal protection grounds. He concluded that there are "certain important dimensions of racial injustice that law does not see." *Id.* at 1283.

Although the U.S. Sentencing Commission initially adopted this 100-to-1 disparity in the Federal Sentencing Guidelines that went into effect in 1987, the Commission issued a recommendation to Congress in 1995 that the disparity between powder and crack cocaine offenses be completely eliminated. Congress rejected that suggestion and then failed to act on two subsequent Sentencing Commission recommendations: a 1997 proposal to reduce the disparity in the sentencing guidelines to 5-to-1, and a 2002 recommendation that the disparity be decreased to 20-to-1.

In 2007, the Sentencing Commission again urged Congress to reduce the disparity, but given the response to its previous recommendations, the Commission also acted on its own to effect a "partial remedy." Specifically, the Commission reduced the offense level for crack cocaine offenses under the sentencing guidelines by two levels, thus "yield[ing] sentences for crack offenses between two and five times longer than sentences for equal amounts of powder." *Kimbrough v. United States*, 552 U.S. 85 (2007). The Commission then voted unanimously to make this change retroactive, setting the stage for about 19,500 federal prisoners to petition for resentencing in hopes of seeing an estimated average 17 percent reduction in their sentences. *See* David Stout, *Retroactively, Panel Reduces Drug Sentences*, N.Y. Times, Dec. 12, 2007, at A1. *But cf. Dillon v. United States*, 560 U.S. 817 (2010) (holding that *Booker*'s decision to make the Federal Sentencing Guidelines advisory does not apply to the sentence-modification proceedings occasioned by the Sentencing Commission's reduction of the offense level for crack cocaine offenses).

Meanwhile, in *Kimbrough*, the Supreme Court upheld a federal trial judge's decision to consider the "disproportionate and unjust effect" of the sentencing guidelines for crack cocaine in deciding to impose a prison sentence of 180 months, well below the presumptive guidelines range of 228–270 months. The Court thought that the guideline sentences for crack cocaine did not "exemplify the [Sentencing] Commission's exercise of its characteristic institutional role"—both because of the Commission's subsequent criticism of the crack-powder disparity and because, in creating the guidelines sentences for crack offenses, the Commission simply adopted the disparity put into place by the Anti-Drug Abuse Act, rather than "tak[ing] account of 'empirical data and national experience.'" The Court therefore concluded that it was not "an abuse of discretion for a district court to conclude . . . that the crack/powder disparity yields a sentence 'greater than necessary' . . . even in a mine-run case."

Although the Anti-Drug Abuse Act's mandatory minimum sentences, and the 100-to-1 disparity they reflected, were not affected by either the Sentencing Commission's actions or the ruling in *Kimbrough*, Congress acted to decrease the disparity in the Fair Sentencing Act of 2010. The statute increases the amount of crack that triggers a mandatory five-year minimum sentence from five to 28 grams (about one ounce), thus reducing the sentencing disparity between crack and powder cocaine to about 18-to-1. *See Dorsey v. United States*, 132 S. Ct. 2321 (2012) (interpreting the statute's more lenient penalties to apply to those defendants who committed their crimes before, but were sentenced after, the act went into effect).

Dorsey and the Fair Sentencing Act do not help the thousands of federal prisoners sentenced before the 2010 statute took effect, although the Smarter Sentencing Act introduced in Congress would allow those prisoners to seek reductions in their sentences. *See* Linda Greenhouse, *Crack Cocaine Limbo*, N.Y. Times, Jan. 6, 2014, at A19.

In an additional effort to decrease the prison population, the Justice Department in 2014 announced support for the elimination of mandatory minimum sentences for nonviolent drug offenders and encouraged such offenders currently serving lengthy prison sentences to apply for clemency. About 36,000 federal prisoners have filed petitions seeking clemency, which Justice Department guidelines limit to those who have already served at least 10 years, who have no significant criminal history and no link to gangs or organized crime, and who likely would have been given a "substantially lower sentence" today. Although the process for reviewing these applications has been slow and somewhat cumbersome, President Obama commuted the sentences of more than 1,700 nonviolent federal offenders, more than his previous 12 predecessors combined. *See* Sari Horwitz, *Obama Commutes Sentences of 330 Nonviolent Offenders*, Wash. Post, Jan. 20, 2017, at A2; Sari Horwitz, *Obama Push on Clemency Is Stunted by Review Logjam*, Wash. Post, May 8, 2016, at A3; Matt Apuzzo, *Holder Backs Proposal to Reduce Drug Sentences*, N.Y. Times, Mar. 14, 2014, at A1.

6. Proportionality and Crimes Committed by Minors. In *Graham v. Florida*, 560 U.S. 48 (2010), the Supreme Court held that the Eighth Amendment's prohibition on cruel and unusual punishment precludes sentencing defendants to life in prison without parole for nonhomicide crimes committed before they turned 18. In practice, the Court reasoned, only 11 states sentenced juveniles to life without parole in nonhomicide cases and the United States was the only country to do so. Moreover, the Court was skeptical that judges can accurately identify "the few juvenile offenders having sufficient psychological maturity and depravity to merit a life without parole sentence."

In *Alabama v. Miller*, 132 S. Ct. 2455 (2012), the Court extended *Graham* in finding that the Eighth Amendment likewise prohibits sentencing schemes that *mandate* life imprisonment without the possibility of parole for homicides committed by juveniles. The Court concluded that precluding sentencers from considering a homicide defendant's youth "contravenes *Graham*'s . . . foundational principle: that imposition of a State's most severe penalties on juvenile offenders cannot proceed as though they were not children." *See also Montgomery v. Louisiana*, 136 S. Ct. 718 (2016) (holding that *Miller* applies retroactively to cases on collateral review); *Malvo v. Mathena*, 2017 U.S. Dist. Lexis 54886 (D. Md. Apr. 11, 2017) (holding that John Lee Malvo, the 17-year-old who pled guilty to multiple counts of murder in connection with the highly publicized 2002 Washington, D.C., area sniper shootings, is entitled to resentencing under *Miller* and *Montgomery*).

Many of the defendants who have been resentenced in the wake of these Supreme Court decisions have received lengthy prison terms of 50 years or more. *See* Erik Eckholm, *Juveniles Facing Lifelong Terms Despite Rulings*, N.Y. Times, Jan. 20, 2014, at A1. The Supreme Court has thus far refused to resolve a conflict among the lower courts on the question whether sentencing a juvenile to "consecutive, fixed terms resulting in an aggregate sentence that exceeds the defendant's life expectancy" is "a de facto life without parole sentence and therefore violates the spirit, if not the letter, of *Graham*." *Bunch v. Smith*, 685 F.3d 546, 552 (6th Cir. 2012), *cert, denied* 133 S. Ct. 1996 (2013).

Chapter 3

The Act Requirement

[A] Voluntary Acts

Wayne R. LaFave, Criminal Law
§ 6.1, at 321–23 (5th ed. 2010)[1]

One basic premise of Anglo-American criminal law is that no crime can be committed by bad thoughts alone. Something in the way of an act, or of an omission to act where there is a legal duty to act, is required too. To wish an enemy dead, . . . to think about taking another's wallet — such thoughts constitute none of the existing crimes (not murder . . . or larceny) so long as the thoughts produce no action to bring about the wished-for results. But, while it is no crime merely to entertain an intent to commit a crime, an attempt (or an agreement with another person) to commit it may be criminal; but the reason is that an attempt (or a conspiracy) requires some activity beyond the mere entertainment of the intent.

Mere thoughts must be distinguished from speech; an act sufficient for criminal liability may consist of nothing more than the movement of the tongue so as to form spoken words. Some crimes are usually committed by the act of speech, such as perjury and false pretenses and the inchoate crimes of conspiracy and solicitation. Other crimes, usually committed by other forms of activity, may nevertheless be committed by spoken words; thus one person can murder another by maneuvering him into the electric chair by giving perjured testimony at his trial for a capital crime. And, because one is guilty of a crime if he encourages or commands or hires another to commit it, it would seem that practically all crimes may be committed by conduct which includes no voluntary bodily movement other than speaking.

The common law crimes all require an act or omission in addition to a bad state of mind. A statute purporting to make it criminal simply to think bad thoughts would, in the United States, be held unconstitutional. And a statute which is worded vaguely on the question of whether an act (or omission), in addition to a state of mind, is required for criminal liability will be construed to require some act (or omission).

Several reasons have been given in justification for the requirement of an act. One is that a person's thoughts are not susceptible of proof except when demonstrated by outward actions. But, while this is doubtless true in most instances, it fails to take account of the possibility that one might confess or otherwise acknowledge to others

---

1. Copyright © 2010 by West Academic. Reprinted with permission.

the fact that he has entertained a certain intent. Another reason given is the difficulty in distinguishing a fixed intent from mere daydream and fantasy. Most persuasive, however, is the notion that the criminal law should not be so broadly defined to reach those who entertain criminal schemes but never let their thoughts govern their conduct.

. . . .

The word "act" might be defined in a broad sense to include such involuntary actions as bodily movements during sleep or unconsciousness, or in a narrow sense to mean only voluntary bodily movement. At all events, it is clear that criminal liability requires that the activity in question be voluntary. The deterrent function of the criminal law would not be served by imposing sanctions for involuntary action, as such action cannot be deterred. Likewise, assuming revenge or retribution to be a legitimate purpose of punishment, there would appear to be no reason to impose punishment on this basis as to those whose actions were not voluntary. Restraint or rehabilitation might be deemed appropriate, however, where individuals are likely to constitute a continuing threat to others because of their involuntary movements, but it is probably best to deal with this problem outside the criminal law.

Just what is meant by the term "voluntary" has caused the theorists considerable difficulty. Sometimes a voluntary act is said to be an external manifestation of the will. Or, it may be said to be behavior which would have been otherwise if the individual had willed or chosen it to be otherwise. There are those who believe that the term is indefinable, and also those who take the view that a voluntary act must be defined in terms of conditions which render an act involuntary. The Model Penal Code comes closest to the last approach. . . .

Model Penal Code § 2.01

Section 2.01. Requirement of Voluntary Act;
Omission as Basis of Liability; Possession as an Act

(1) A person is not guilty of an offense unless his liability is based on conduct which includes a voluntary act or the omission to perform an act of which he is physically capable.

(2) The following are not voluntary acts within the meaning of this Section:

  (a) a reflex or convulsion;

  (b) a bodily movement during unconsciousness or sleep;

  (c) conduct during hypnosis or resulting from hypnotic suggestion;

  (d) a bodily movement that otherwise is not a product of the effort or determination of the actor, either conscious or habitual.

(3) Liability for the commission of an offense may not be based on an omission unaccompanied by action unless:

  (a) the omission is expressly made sufficient by the law defining the offense;

or

(b) a duty to perform the omitted act is otherwise imposed by law.

(4) Possession is an act, within the meaning of this Section, if the possessor knowingly procured or received the thing possessed or was aware of his control thereof for a sufficient period to have been able to terminate his possession.

Sleepwalker Acquitted in Mother-in-Law Slaying, SAN FRANCISCO EXAMINER, May 28, 1988, at 1[2]

TORONTO—A jury has acquitted a man of second-degree murder in the slaying of his mother-in-law after deciding he was sleepwalking when he drove 14 miles to her home, beat her with a tire iron [that he retrieved from the trunk of his car, used his own key to enter her home,] and stabbed her to death.

An Ontario Supreme Court jury handed down its verdict in favor of Kenneth Parks, 24, late Thursday. He had been charged in the May 1987 slaying of his mother-in-law, Barbara Woods, and still faces an attempted-murder charge for an attack that same night on his father-in-law.

During the trial, doctors testified for the defense that medical literature lists about 30 cases of murder committed by sleepwalkers. They said Parks would have been capable of driving such a distance while asleep, stabbing and trying to strangle his father-in-law and stabbing and beating his mother-in-law with a tire iron.

The attacks were said to be triggered by stress caused by Parks' gambling addiction and his embezzlement of about $28,000 to cover his gambling losses. Witnesses said Parks had a family history of somnambulism and had walked in his sleep on two previous occasions.

A defense lawyer told the jury Parks regained consciousness after the attacks and remembered calling out to the Woods' children, who only heard "animal grunting noises." He fled to a nearby police station and told officials he believed he had just killed two people.

The jury deliberated for nine hours before finding Parks innocent. The judge had instructed the jurors that they could not reach a verdict of not guilty by reason of insanity because sleepwalking was a sleep disorder and not a form of insanity.

State v. Tippetts
43 P.3d 455 (Or. Ct. App. 2000)

KISTLER, JUDGE.

Defendant appeals from a judgment of conviction for supplying contraband. He argues that the trial court should have granted his motion for a judgment of acquittal

---

2. Reprinted with permission of the *San Francisco Examiner.*

because he did not voluntarily introduce marijuana into the Washington County Jail. We agree and reverse.

In October 1998, police officers obtained a warrant to search defendant's house. The officers located the house and, after knocking on the door and announcing their presence, forced the door open. Once inside, the officers saw defendant running towards the back of the house. They followed and subdued him. They placed him in handcuffs, read him his *Miranda* rights, and searched him. The officers found no drugs or other contraband on defendant. The officers then searched defendant's home, where they found methamphetamine and a weapon.

The officers formally placed defendant under arrest and took him to the Washington County Jail, where they turned him over to Officer Morey. Before searching him, Morey asked defendant whether he had any knives, needles, or drugs on him that he was bringing into the jail. Morey then searched defendant and found a small bag of marijuana in his pants pocket. Based on the marijuana Morey found, the state charged defendant with supplying contraband. A person commits the crime of supplying contraband if "the person knowingly introduces any contraband into a correctional facility, youth correction facility or state hospital[.]" ORS 162.185(1)(a).

At trial, defendant moved for a judgment of acquittal on the charge of supplying contraband. Relying on ORS 161.095(1), he argued that he could be found guilty of that crime only if he voluntarily introduced the contraband into the jail. Defendant contended that no reasonable juror could find that he acted voluntarily. He argued that, once he was arrested, he could not avoid taking the marijuana with him into the jail. The trial court denied defendant's motion, reasoning that defendant could have avoided the charge by admitting to possession of the marijuana before the officer discovered it.

On appeal, defendant renews his argument that proof of a voluntary act is a necessary prerequisite to proving criminal liability and that he did not voluntarily introduce marijuana into the jail. Defendant bases his argument on ORS 161.095(1), which provides:

> "The minimal requirement for criminal liability is the performance by a person of conduct which includes a voluntary act or the omission to perform an act which the person is capable of performing."

The state, for its part, does not defend the trial court's ruling on the ground that the court articulated, nor does the state argue that there is evidence in this case from which a reasonable juror could find that defendant chose to take the marijuana into the jail with him. Rather, the state argues that defendant reads ORS 161.095(1) too broadly. It argues initially that the term "voluntary act" is defined by statute and means only that the defendant is conscious or aware of the act. In the state's view, as long as defendant was aware that he possessed the marijuana when the officers took him into the jail, that fact alone provides a sufficient basis for saying that he voluntarily introduced the marijuana into the jail. The state argues alternatively that, even if defendant did not voluntarily introduce the marijuana into the jail, he voluntarily possessed it before his arrest and that act is sufficient to satisfy ORS 161.095(1).

We begin with the text and context of ORS 161.095(1). . . . By its terms, the statute requires (1) that the act that gives rise to criminal liability be performed or initiated by the defendant and (2) that the act be voluntary. ORS 161.085(2), in turn, defines the phrase "voluntary act." It means "a bodily movement performed consciously[.]"

The texts of ORS 161.095(1) and 161.085(2) support defendant's position. Applied to the charge of supplying contraband, they require (1) that defendant either initiate the introduction of contraband into the jail or cause it to be introduced and (2) that he do so consciously. Defendant, however, did not initiate the introduction of the contraband into the jail or cause it to be introduced into the jail. Rather, the contraband was introduced into the jail only because the police took defendant (and the contraband) there against his will.

The state argues, however, that the use of the word "consciously" in the definition of the phrase "voluntary act" somehow changes that conclusion. The state reasons that the word consciously means "aware" and that an act will be voluntary as long as the defendant is aware that it is occurring. In explaining its position at oral argument, the state reasoned that, under its interpretation, if the police forcibly took a minor who was intoxicated out of his or her house and brought the minor into a public area, he or she could be convicted of public intoxication. In the state's view, the police's movement of the person into a public area would be a "voluntary act" that would satisfy ORS 161.095(1), as long as the person was aware that he or she was being moved.

The state's interpretation of ORS 161.095(1) and ORS 161.085(2) is problematic. If its interpretation were correct, the use of the word "consciously" would negate the proposition, explicit in ORS 161.095(1) and implicit in ORS 161.085(2), that the defendant him or herself must perform or initiate the bodily movement that gives rise to criminal liability. Contrary to the state's interpretation, it is possible to read "consciously" in a way that is consistent with the rest of those statutes. The legislature could have added the word "consciously" to make clear that a defendant will be held criminally liable only for those acts that he or she consciously performs. In other words, inclusion of the requirement that acts be performed "consciously" serves to exclude unconscious bodily movements that a defendant performs, such as reflex actions or actions that a defendant takes during an epileptic seizure. It does not suggest, as the state reasons, that a defendant who has been moved against his or her will and is conscious of that fact has acted voluntarily.

. . . .

Having considered the text, context, and legislative history of ORS 161.095(1) and ORS 161.085(2), we hold that, when the legislature defined "voluntary act" as a "bodily movement performed consciously," it intended to require more than awareness. It required some evidence that the defendant had the ability to choose to take a particular action. The state does not argue that there is any evidence from which a reasonable juror could find that defendant had such a choice, and we turn to the alternative basis that the state advances for upholding the trial court's ruling.

As noted, the state argues that, even if the introduction of the drugs into the jail was not itself a "voluntary act," ORS 161.095(1) requires only "the performance by a person of conduct which *includes* a voluntary act[.]" (Emphasis added.) The state reasons that, even if defendant did not voluntarily introduce the marijuana into the jail after the police arrested him, he voluntarily possessed it before he was arrested. The earlier voluntary act of possession, the state concludes, is sufficient to hold defendant criminally liable for the later involuntary act of introducing the marijuana into the jail. Defendant responds that ORS 162.185(1)(a) punishes the act of introducing the contraband into a correctional facility; it does not punish the act of possessing drugs. Defendant reasons that turning the voluntary act of possession into the predicate for holding him liable for involuntarily introducing marijuana into the jail stretches the word "includes" too far.

   . . . .

ORS 161.095(1) derives from the Model Penal Code. The commentary to the analogous section of the Model Penal Code explains:

> "It will be noted that the formulation does not state that liability must be based on the voluntary act or the omission *simpliciter*, but rather upon conduct which *includes* such action or omission. The distinction has some analytical importance. If the driver of an automobile loses consciousness with the result that he runs over a pedestrian, none of the movements or omissions that accompany or follow this loss of consciousness may in themselves give rise to liability. But a prior voluntary act, such as the act of driving, or a prior omission, such as failing to stop as he felt illness approaching, may, under given circumstances, be regarded as sufficiently negligent for liability to be imposed. In that event, however, liability is based on the entire course of conduct, including the specific conduct that resulted in the injury."

American Law Institute, Model Penal Code § 2.01, 120 (Tentative Draft No. 4 1955) (emphasis in original). . . .

The commentary to the Model Penal Code makes clear that the mere fact that defendant voluntarily possessed the drugs before he was arrested is insufficient to hold him criminally liable for the later act of introducing the drugs into the jail. Rather, to satisfy ORS 161.095(1), the involuntary act must, at a minimum, be a reasonably foreseeable or likely consequence of the voluntary act on which the state seeks to base criminal liability. *See* American Law Institute, Model Penal Code § 2.01, 120 (Tentative Draft No. 4 1955); *State v. Gooze*, 14 N.J. Super. 277, 81 A.2d 811, 816 (1951) (cited in the commentary to the Model Penal Code). On these facts, no reasonable juror could find that the introduction of contraband into the jail was a reasonably foreseeable consequence of possessing it. Moreover, the state does not dispute that, in this case, the police's act of arresting defendant and transporting him to the jail was an intervening cause that resulted in the marijuana's being introduced into the jail. The state's alternative argument provides no basis for upholding the trial court's ruling.

Conviction for supplying contraband reversed; otherwise affirmed.

Notes and Questions

1. **Introduction.** Do you agree with LaFave that it would be wrong to punish thoughts? While it is reported that the British monarch at one point criminalized treasonous thoughts, English and American common law has repudiated that approach. Does the current practice simply reflect problems of proof, or is there some substantive reason for not punishing thoughts alone? Suppose the police obtain a reliable confession from *A* indicating that she entertained a serious intent to kill? Suppose advances in science lead to the invention of a reliable mind-reading machine? Under such circumstances, would punishing thoughts be no more objectionable than punishing attempts or conspiracies? (For a discussion of the reasons why we punish those crimes, see Chapter 11, Section A.1 and Chapter 13, Section A.1.)

2. **Sleepwalking.** Should involuntary acts be punished if they are dangerous? Was the jury right to conclude that Parks did not commit a voluntary act? Parks had walked in his sleep as a child, and when he was a teenager, his mother had once stopped him before he walked out a window. But he had not had a serious sleepwalking incident as an adult. He was apparently close to his in-laws (in fact, his father-in-law gave testimony to that effect at Parks' trial), and he had been planning on telling them about his gambling problems. He had not consumed any drugs or alcohol before going to bed on the night of the killing, although he had not slept in the prior two days. Brain scans done on Parks after the incident showed blips commonly found in sleepwalkers that, according to experts, could not have been faked. Parks' acquittal was upheld by the Supreme Court of Canada, *see The Queen v. Parks*, [1992] 2 S.C.R. 871 (Can.), and the trial judge dismissed the charges involving his father-in-law. Following his acquittal, Parks underwent psychotherapy and began taking medication before going to bed. He has had no subsequent history of sleepwalking or violence. *See* Edward Dolnick, *Night Moves*, Chi. Trib., Sept. 23, 1991, at C1; Lawrence Walsh, *When Dreams Turn Deadly!*, Denver Rocky Mountain News, Sept. 22, 1994, at A44. *See generally* Emily Grant, Note, *While You Were Sleeping or Addicted: A Suggested Expansion of the Automatism Doctrine to Include an Addiction Defense*, 2000 U. Ill. L. Rev. 997, 1007 (reporting that sleepwalking affects as many as 40 percent of children and between one percent and six percent of adults).

Although Parks was acquitted, it is generally very difficult to use sleepwalking as a defense. In *Sallee v. State*, 544 P.2d 902 (Okla. Crim. App. 1975), for example, Earl Sallee beat his wife to death with a hammer. Sallee remembered being wakened to take his five-year-old daughter to the bathroom. After that, he lost consciousness. When he regained consciousness, he was standing next to his wife's body and a bloody hammer was lying on the floor. Despite expert testimony that the homicide could have occurred while Sallee was sleepwalking, and evidence that he had a history of sleepwalking, the jury found him guilty of second-degree murder. *But cf. Liao v. Junious*, 817 F.3d 678 (9th Cir. 2016) (granting habeas relief on the grounds that defense attorney provided ineffective assistance of counsel by failing to obtain a sleep study, which would have corroborated expert testimony that defendant was sleepwalking when he assaulted his former girlfriend's son with a hammer).

3. Seizures. Suppose *A* knows he has a tendency to faint, and then, in fainting, knocks someone off a cliff? Compare that situation to *People v. Decina*, 138 N.E.2d 799 (N.Y. 1956). In *Decina*, the defendant knew he was prone to severe epileptic attacks that would occur without warning. The court held that he could be found criminally liable for driving "in a reckless or culpably negligent manner, whereby a human being is killed" when he had an epileptic attack while driving alone in March of 1955 and his car jumped onto a sidewalk, killing four young girls. Decina had experienced his first epileptic convulsion in 1946; he had had four or five attacks in 1954, the last one before the accident occurring in September of 1954. In what sense did Decina commit a voluntary act?

4. Hypnosis. To some extent, the Model Penal Code is a product of its time, and in the 1950s when the Code was under consideration, the country was culturally fascinated with psychological phenomena like hypnosis and "brainwashing." Despite §2.01(2)(c) of the Code, it is very difficult to convince a jury that actions under hypnosis were involuntary. When defendants claim that they did not act voluntarily because they were under hypnosis at the time of the crime, the prosecution may introduce evidence of other similar criminal acts committed when the defendant was not under hypnosis to rebut the defense.

For example, in *United States v. Phillips*, 515 F. Supp. 758 (E.D. Ky. 1981), Marion "Buster" Phillips had seemingly acquired control of the will of his wife Melissa. For three years, he hypnotized her up to 15 times a day. He planted memories in her mind showing him holding her when she was first born and saving her from drowning when she was nine, even though he had not known her at the time. He "made her believe that he was her mother and father, and her Lord and God." *Id.* at 760. When marshals escorted Buster into a federal building to be tried for bank robbery, Melissa was waiting in the foyer. Pulling a revolver out of her purse, she stood hesitantly. Buster yelled, "Shoot 'em, baby, shoot 'em . . . ," and she shot one of the marshals. At trial Melissa claimed that due to Buster's "hypnotic programming . . . she was unable to form the requisite criminal intent." *Id.* at 764. The prosecutor introduced evidence, however, showing that two weeks prior to the incident, Melissa had shot at a neighbor with the same or a similar revolver. This evidence was presented to show that Melissa could have formed the criminal intent on her own, independent of the hypnosis. The jury rejected Melissa's defense.

Consider also *United States v. McCollum*, 732 F.2d 1419 (9th Cir. 1984). McCollum entered a bank in Los Angeles and handed the teller a note demanding $100,000. He was immediately arrested without incident. Once in the police car, he shook suddenly and asked, "What are you doing? Why am I here?" Later, under hypnosis, McCollum claimed that in a prior hypnotic session, he had been commanded to commit the robbery and then to forget everything that had happened in the previous eight hours. At trial a specialist who had examined McCollum testified that McCollum was hypnotized at the time of the robbery. To show that McCollum was capable of forming the intent to commit robbery, however, the prosecution was permitted to introduce evidence that he had been convicted of armed robbery 12 years previously. The jury found him guilty. Should either Phillips or McCollum have had a valid defense?

5. **Brainwashing.** Can people be brainwashed so that, although fully conscious, their actions are involuntary? This issue was raised when Patty Hearst, heiress to the Hearst newspaper fortune, was kidnapped in 1974 by a terrorist group, the Symbionese Liberation Army (SLA). While initially a kidnapping victim, Hearst later appeared to convert to the SLA's cause and participated in a bank robbery. Her defense attorney, F. Lee Bailey, argued that the SLA had brainwashed her and thereby coerced her into helping them rob the bank. The jury rejected this argument and convicted her. For a more complete description of this case, see Tom Mathews & William J. Cook, *Patty's Defense*, Newsweek, Mar. 1, 1976, at 20.

A "brainwashing" defense was also advanced on behalf of Lee Malvo, the 17-year-old defendant convicted in the highly publicized 2002 Washington, D.C., area sniper shootings. As in the Hearst case, the Malvo jury rejected the defense, but it also declined to impose the death penalty sought by the prosecution. *See* James Dao, *Mental Health Experts Call Sniper Defendant Brainwashed*, N.Y. Times, Dec. 11, 2003, at A38. For further discussion of these cases, and of the relationship between brainwashing claims and the duress defense, see Note 9(c) in Chapter 15, Section A.

[B] Omissions

Jones v. United States

308 F.2d 307 (D.C. Cir. 1962)

Wright, Circuit Judge.

Appellant, together with one Shirley Green, was tried on a three-count indictment charging them jointly with (1) abusing and maltreating Robert Lee Green, (2) abusing and maltreating Anthony Lee Green, and (3) involuntary manslaughter through failure to perform their legal duty of care for Anthony Lee Green, which failure resulted in his death. At the close of evidence, after trial to a jury, the first two counts were dismissed as to both defendants. On the third count, appellant was convicted of involuntary manslaughter. Shirley Green was found not guilty.[3]

Appellant urges several grounds for reversal. We need consider but two. First, appellant argues that there was insufficient evidence as a matter of law to warrant a jury finding of breach of duty in the care she rendered Anthony Lee. Alternatively, appellant argues that the trial court committed plain error in failing to instruct the jury that it must first find that appellant was under a legal obligation to provide food and necessities to Anthony Lee before finding her guilty of manslaughter in failing to provide them. The first argument is without merit. Upon the latter we reverse.

A summary of the evidence, which is in conflict upon almost every significant issue, is necessary for the disposition of both arguments. In late 1957, Shirley Green became pregnant, out of wedlock, with a child, Robert Lee, subsequently born August 17, 1958. Apparently to avoid the embarrassment of the presence of the child in the Green home, it was arranged that appellant, a family friend, would take the child to her home after birth. Appellant did so, and the child remained there continuously until removed by the police on August 5, 1960. Initially appellant made some motions toward the adoption of Robert Lee, but these came to nought, and shortly thereafter it was agreed that Shirley Green was to pay appellant $72 a month for his care. According to appellant, these payments were made for only five months. According to Shirley Green, they were made up to July, 1960.

Early in 1959 Shirley Green again became pregnant, this time with the child Anthony Lee, whose death is the basis of appellant's conviction. This child was born October 21, 1959. Soon after birth, Anthony Lee developed a mild jaundice condition, attributed to a blood incompatibility with his mother. The jaundice resulted in his retention in the hospital for three days beyond the usual time, or until October 26, 1959, when, on authorization signed by Shirley Green, Anthony Lee was released by the hospital to appellant's custody. Shirley Green, after a two or three day stay in the hospital, also lived with appellant for three weeks, after which she returned to her parents' home, leaving the children with appellant. She testified she did not see them again, except for one visit in March, until August 5, 1960. Consequently, though there does not seem to have been any specific monetary agreement with Shirley Green covering Anthony Lee's support,[4] appellant had complete custody of both children until they were rescued by the police.

With regard to medical care, the evidence is undisputed. In March, 1960, appellant called a Dr. Turner to her home to treat Anthony Lee for a bronchial condition.

---

3. During its deliberations, the jury sent a note to the trial judge asking, "May the jury find both defendants in this case guilty but also recommend clemency for only one of the two defendants?" The judge responded as follows: "The jury has been instructed it can only bring in a verdict as to either or both defendants of guilty or not guilty."

4. [n.5] It was uncontested that during the entire period the children were in appellant's home, appellant had ample means to provide food and medical care.

Appellant also telephoned the doctor at various times to consult with him concerning Anthony Lee's diet and health. In early July, 1960, appellant took Anthony Lee to Dr. Turner's office where he was treated for "simple diarrhea." At this time the doctor noted the "wizened" appearance of the child and told appellant to tell the mother of the child that he should be taken to a hospital. This was not done.

On August 2, 1960, two collectors for the local gas company had occasion to go to the basement of appellant's home, and there saw the two children. Robert Lee and Anthony Lee at this time were age two years and ten months respectively. [Robert's crib was lined with stained newspaper and covered with roaches, and one collector saw roaches on Anthony.]

On August 5, 1960, the collectors returned to appellant's home in the company of several police officers and personnel of the Women's Bureau. At this time, Anthony Lee was upstairs in the dining room in the bassinet, but Robert Lee was still downstairs in his "crib." The officers removed the children to the D.C. General Hospital where Anthony Lee was diagnosed as suffering from severe malnutrition and lesions over large portions of his body, apparently caused by severe diaper rash. Following admission, he was fed repeatedly, apparently with no difficulty, and was described as being very hungry. His death, 34 hours after admission, was attributed without dispute to malnutrition. At birth, Anthony Lee weighed six pounds, fifteen ounces—at death at age ten months, he weighed seven pounds, thirteen ounces. Normal weight at this age would have been approximately 14 pounds.

Appellant argues that nothing in the evidence establishes that she failed to provide food to Anthony Lee. She cites her own testimony and the testimony of a lodger, Mr. Wills, that she did in fact feed the baby regularly. At trial, the defense made repeated attempts to extract from the medical witnesses opinions that the jaundice, or the condition which caused it, might have prevented the baby from assimilating food. The doctors conceded this was possible but not probable since the autopsy revealed no condition which would support the defense theory. It was also shown by the disinterested medical witnesses that the child had no difficulty in ingesting food immediately after birth, and that Anthony Lee, in the last hours before his death, was able to take several bottles, apparently without difficulty, and seemed very hungry. This evidence, combined with the absence of any physical cause for nonassimilation, taken in the context of the condition in which these children were kept, presents a jury question on the feeding issue.

Moreover, there is substantial evidence from which the jury could have found that appellant failed to obtain proper medical care for the child. Appellant relies upon the evidence showing that on one occasion she summoned a doctor for the child, on another took the child to the doctor's office, and that she telephoned the doctor on several occasions about the baby's formula. However, the last time a doctor saw the child was a month before his death, and appellant admitted that on that occasion the doctor recommended hospitalization. Appellant did not hospitalize the child, nor did she take any other steps to obtain medical care in the last crucial month. Thus there was sufficient evidence to go to the jury on the issue of medical care, as well as failure to feed.

Appellant also takes exception to the failure of the trial court to charge that the jury must find beyond a reasonable doubt, as an element of the crime, that appellant was under a legal duty to supply food and necessities to Anthony Lee.

. . . .

The problem of establishing the duty to take action which would preserve the life of another has not often arisen in the case law of this country. The most commonly cited statement of the rule is found in *People v. Beardsley*, 150 Mich. 206, 113 N.W. 1128, 1129 [(1907)]:

> The law recognizes that under some circumstances the omission of a duty owed by one individual to another, where such omission results in the death of the one to whom the duty is owing, will make the other chargeable with manslaughter. . . . This rule of law is always based upon the proposition that the duty neglected must be a legal duty, and not a mere moral obligation. It must be a duty imposed by law or by contract, and the omission to perform the duty must be the immediate and direct cause of death. . . .

There are at least four situations in which the failure to act may constitute breach of a legal duty. One can be held criminally liable: first, where a statute imposes a duty to care for another; second, where one stands in a certain status relationship to another; third, where one has assumed a contractual duty to care for another; and fourth, where one has voluntarily assumed the care of another and so secluded the helpless person as to prevent others from rendering aid.

It is the contention of the Government that either the third or the fourth ground is applicable here. However, it is obvious that in any of the four situations, there are critical issues of fact which must be passed on by the jury — specifically in this case, whether appellant had entered into a contract with the mother for the care of Anthony Lee or, alternatively, whether she assumed the care of the child and secluded him from the care of his mother, his natural protector. On both of these issues, the evidence is in direct conflict, appellant insisting that the mother was actually living with appellant and Anthony Lee, and hence should have been taking care of the child herself, while Shirley Green testified she was living with her parents and was paying appellant to care for both children.

In spite of this conflict, the instructions given in the case failed even to suggest the necessity for finding a legal duty of care. . . . A finding of legal duty is the critical element of the crime charged and failure to instruct the jury concerning it was plain error. . . .

Reversed and remanded.

Notes and Questions

1. Introduction. Most crimes are defined in terms of specific acts committed. Some crimes, however, are committed by a failure to act, or an omission—for example, the failure to file an income tax return or register for the draft. Even for crimes defined in terms of specific acts, criminal liability may be predicated on an omission if the defendant had a legal duty, not just a moral duty, to act. Such legal duties can be based on: (1) statutes, (2) special relationships, (3) contractual obligations, (4) the voluntary assumption of care, (5) the defendant's status as a landowner, which may trigger a duty to make the premises reasonably safe, (6) a duty to control third parties, such as children or employees, or (7) the defendant's creation of peril. *See* Wayne R. LaFave, Criminal Law §6.2, at 330–35 (5th ed. 2010).

In *State v. Walden*, 293 S.E.2d 780 (N.C. 1982), for example, the Supreme Court of North Carolina affirmed the defendant's conviction for aiding and abetting the assault of her baby. The defendant watched as a friend of hers beat the baby and did not say or do anything to stop the assault. The court reasoned that "the failure of a parent who is present to take all steps reasonably possible to protect the parent's child from an attack by another person constitutes an act of omission by the parent showing the parent's consent and contribution to the crime being committed." *Id.* at 787.

Courts have also held that parents have a duty to provide medical care for their children. *See, e.g., People v. Henson*, 304 N.E.2d 358 (N.Y. 1973) (affirming parents' conviction on negligent homicide charges arising from their failure to get medical help for their child, who was obviously very sick and ultimately died of pneumonia). Such cases touch on the controversial subject of Christian Scientists and their children. Are Christian Scientists or others who oppose medical treatment on religious grounds guilty of homicide if they let their children die of an easily curable disease? Or are they protected by the Constitution's guarantee of religious freedom? In *Commonwealth v. Twitchell*, 617 N.E.2d 609 (Mass. 1993), the Massachusetts Supreme Court held that a parent's failure to provide a child with medical treatment can support an involuntary manslaughter conviction even when it is based on religious principles.

In *People v. Heitzman*, 886 P.2d 1229 (Cal. 1994), however, the court concluded that a woman whose disabled father died while living with her brothers could not be convicted of the felony of "willfully caus[ing] or permit[ting] any elder or dependent adult . . . to suffer . . . unjustifiable physical pain or mental suffering." Although the defendant had regularly visited her father and therefore was aware of the extremely poor conditions in which he lived and which ultimately led to his death, the court held that she could not be convicted in the absence of proof that she had a legal duty to control her brothers.

2. Parental Liability for a Child's Crime. While the *Jones* court notes that the parental relationship creates a duty to care for and protect a child, that relationship can also create a duty to act appropriately to protect society from the child. Should homicide or other criminal charges be brought against parents who recklessly fail to intervene when they find explosives or other signs that their child is planning a violent attack? Consider the following report of the tragic shooting at the Columbine High School in suburban Denver in 1999:

> The two killers in the Columbine High School massacre crafted their plot for at least a year, mapping everything from hallway lighting to the best hiding places in a handwritten timeline detailing the exact minute they would "rock and roll," investigators said Saturday.
>
> Bomb-making materials and the sawed-off barrel of a shotgun were later found "clearly visible" in the bedroom of one of the dead suspects, added Jefferson County Sheriff John Stone, who expressed disgust Saturday that the parents did not intervene.
>
> "I think parents should be accountable for their kids' actions," he said.
>
> . . . .
>
> Eric Harris, 18, and Dylan Klebold, 17, launched the rampage against their high school Tuesday morning during a lunch period, planning the mayhem for the moments when large groups of students would gather in the cafeteria and library. They tossed pipe bombs and fired rifles and a pistol in all directions, slaying 12 students and one teacher before killing themselves.
>
> . . . .
>
> A year-long diary and computer materials seized at Harris' home contain repeated references to Adolf Hitler's birthday, which was the day of the attack, as well as a number of German words and "interaction" with Germany-related Internet sites or sources.
>
> The diary made it clear the two students were targeting "jocks" and other groups or individuals they felt had disrespected or threatened them during their high school days, investigators said. It also offers striking detail about how carefully Harris and Klebold had thought to kill as many students as possible. . . .
>
> "They wanted to do as much damage as they could possibly do, they wanted to destroy as many children as they could, and go out in flames," Stone said. The last part of the attack was to include detonation of a gasoline bomb that would burn down much of the school, a device found hidden but unexploded in the school kitchen two days after the killings.
>
> . . . .
>
> The arsenal brought to the school included three hard-to-conceal large guns, a machine pistol and more than 30 bombs, including one with a 20-pound propane gas tank. . . .
>
> "Just the logistics of getting this stuff in the school," Stone said. . . . "They'd been building bombs for a considerable period of time, and acquiring weaponry for a considerable period of time."

Stone said there were additional weapons found in the search of the homes, as well as the leftover bomb-making materials.

The sheriff indicated his dismay at the suspects' parents being oblivious to the brutal attack, given the evidence found all over at least one of the homes in the wake of the deaths.

"A lot of this stuff was lying visible around the house," he said. "I'd be very concerned if I saw the barrel of a gun sawed off clearly visible in my son's room, and bomb-making (materials) clearly visible."

A neighbor of the Harris home . . . said he heard glass smashing and other loud noises coming from the Harris garage on the Monday before the killings. Friends of the Klebold family described the parents as relatively liberal advocates of gun-control laws, while Wayne Harris, Eric's father, is a recently retired Air Force major.

Harris and Klebold, though, had apparently planned their twisted commando mission so carefully that they might have hidden from their families every detail, including materials, until the attack.

Michael Booth, *Diary Shows Gunmen Mapping Out Massacre*, Denver Post, Apr. 25, 1999, at A1.[5]

3. Omissions by Police Officers. Should the police have a duty to the public such that their failure to act can lead to criminal liability? When Los Angeles police officers were filmed on videotape severely beating Rodney King in the course of an arrest in 1991, the officers without supervisory responsibility who stood by and watched were not even indicted, even though their failure to step in could have led to their dismissal from the police force. *See generally Koon v. United States*, 518 U.S. 81 (1996).

In an earlier tort case, the California Supreme Court ruled that a member of the public who "was a reasonably foreseeable victim . . . [by] that factor alone does not . . . establish a special relationship with the officers imposing upon them a duty to warn or protect." *Davidson v. City of Westminster*, 649 P.2d 894, 900 (Cal. 1982). *See also Town of Castle Rock v. Gonzales*, 545 U.S. 748 (2005) (holding that a woman who had obtained a restraining order against her husband did not have a protected entitlement to enforcement of the order, and therefore her due process rights were not violated when police failed to respond to her requests that they enforce the order against her husband, who took the couple's three children without permission and then killed them).

4. The Model Penal Code. Would §2.01(3) of the Model Penal Code produce a different result in any of these cases? The Comments to that section point out:

Subsection (3) states the conventional position with respect to omissions unaccompanied by action as a basis of liability. Unless the omission is expressly made sufficient by the law defining the offense, a duty to perform

_____

5. Copyright © 1999 by The Denver Post. Reprinted with permission.

the omitted act must have been otherwise imposed by law for the omission to have the same standing as a voluntary act for the purposes of liability.[6] It should, of course, suffice, as the courts now hold, that the duty arise under some branch of the civil law. If it does, this minimal requirement is satisfied.

It is arguable that focus on civil duty should not be the crucial criterion for whether an omission can be the basis of criminal liability, but that standard is the one that best deals with most situations in which criminal liability would clearly be appropriate and also gives adequate warning of what omissions may be the basis of such liability. It is also arguable that affirmative duties to act should be enlarged in scope, especially when action is required to prevent bodily injury. This is a problem to be faced, however, in the definition of particular offenses, not in this section of the Code.

Model Penal Code § 2.01 Comment at 222–23.

5. Good Samaritan Laws. Should the law criminalize any failure to offer assistance, without requiring a special relationship? Suppose *A* sees *B,* a young child, drive a tricycle off a dock and need only drop a life ring to save the child. Why shouldn't *A*'s omission be subject to criminal sanction when *A* could have helped *B* with little risk or inconvenience?

Unlike most states, Vermont specifically criminalizes the failure to aid:

(a) A person who knows that another is exposed to grave physical harm shall, to the extent that the same can be rendered without danger or peril to himself or without interference with important duties owed to others, give reasonable assistance to the exposed person unless that assistance or care is being provided by others.

. . . .

(c) A person who willfully violates subsection (a) of this section shall be fined not more than $100.00.

Vt. Stat. Ann. tit. 12, § 519.

The Vermont Supreme Court ruled, however, that this provision did not impose criminal liability on a bystander who failed to intervene in a fight because offering

---

6. [n.30] The "duty imposed by law" may be a statutory duty, a contractual duty, or a duty arising from tort law. *See Regina v. Curtis*, 15 Cox C.C. 746 (Central Crim. Ct. 1885) (statutory duty: public relief officer charged for the failure to render assistance to destitute person who applied for relief); *People v. Montecino*, 66 Cal. App. 2d 85, 152 P.2d 5 (1944) (contractual duty: manslaughter conviction of employed practical nurse who neglected 72 year old invalid affirmed); *Jones v. United States*, 308 F.2d 307 (D.C. Cir. 1962) (contractual duty: neglect of child defendant had contracted to care for); *Jones v. State*, 220 Ind. 384, 43 N.E.2d 1017 (1942) (tort duty: defendant failed to assist person he had criminally assaulted); *Moreland v. State*, 164 Ga. 467, 139 S.E. 77 (1927) (tort duty: car owner convicted of involuntary manslaughter for failing to order chauffeur to slow down). The great majority of homicidal omission cases involve intra-family relationships; most opinions refer to statutory duties. *See Craig v. State*, 220 Md. 590, 155 A.2d 684 (1959) (parent-child); *State v. Clark*, 5 Conn. Cir. Ct. 699, 261 A.2d 294 (1969) (parent-child).

assistance in that context would have involved "danger or peril." *See State v. Joyce*, 433 A.2d 271, 273 (Vt. 1981).

Is the Vermont statute's maximum sentence of $100 too lenient? Should violation of this general duty be sufficient to trigger a homicide conviction?

6. Charging for One's Assistance. Consider the strange incident reported in the *Okanogan (Washington) Chronicle*, October 7, 1992, at 12. The defendant and victim were helping a mutual friend move furniture. The defendant found the victim trapped and severely injured in his overturned pick-up truck, which had fallen into a 100-foot ravine off the road. The defendant offered to seek help and give the victim water and food, but only if he first signed documents transferring his possessions to the defendant. The victim refused to sign the documents (if he had signed, the contract would in all likelihood have been void due to extreme duress), and the defendant left the injured victim stranded in his truck. Two days later a passing motorist discovered the victim, who eventually recovered. The defendant was charged with extortion, but ultimately the charges were dropped. Did the defendant do anything wrong by seeking payment in return for her assistance? Should it be legal to ignore people who are in danger, but criminal to seek compensation for aiding them? (You can reconsider this issue in the discussion of extortion in Chapter 9, Section B.)

7. Failing to Report a Crime. Should it be a crime not to report a crime? In a notorious incident in Queens, New York, in 1964, 38 neighbors reportedly witnessed Kitty Genovese being stabbed to death, but did not call the police or offer any assistance even though Genovese repeatedly cried for help for more than half an hour. The witnesses later explained that they thought they were witnessing a "lovers' quarrel," they were afraid, or they were tired. *See* Maureen Dowd, *20 Years After the Murder of Kitty Genovese, the Question Remains: Why?*, N.Y. TIMES, Mar. 12, 1984, at B1. (*The Witness*, a moving 2016 documentary produced by Genovese's brother Bill, challenges some of the conventional wisdom surrounding this incident.)

Should society tolerate inaction when a person's life is in danger? When police investigating the 2013 Boston Marathon bombing searched the small apartment in which Katherine Russell lived with her husband, Tamerlan Tsarnaev, who masterminded the attacks and died trying to elude police, they found bomb-making materials, such as BBs, nails, and wires. In addition, Russell's computer had been used the previous year to conduct an Internet search on the topic, "If your husband becomes a [martyr], what are the rewards for you?" No charges have been filed against Russell. *See* Patricia Wen & Milton J. Valencia, *Tsarnaev Widow's Lawyer Fears Charges*, BOS. GLOBE, Apr. 30, 2015, at A1. For further information about the case against Tsarnaev's brother Dzhokhar, see Note 9(c) in Chapter 15, Section A.

Consider also the well-publicized incident involving two high school friends traveling together in Nevada in 1997:

> For 19-year-old sophomore David Cash, life at Berkeley consists of going
> to his classes, lying low, and occasionally being yelled at or spat on.

A year and a half ago, Cash chose not to intervene when his high school friend Jeremy Strohmeyer molested and killed a little girl in the bathroom of a Nevada casino. . . .

The murder happened on May 25, 1997 at the Primadonna Casino near Las Vegas. Cash saw Strohmeyer struggling with 7-year old Sherrice Iverson in a restroom stall, but left before Strohmeyer started molesting her. Afterward, Strohmeyer confessed to him that he had strangled the second-grader, but Cash kept quiet until Strohmeyer turned himself in three days later. Cash was questioned about the crime but released, because Nevada doesn't have a "Good Samaritan" law, which would have made his silence a crime. . . .

The legal process has now run its course. Strohmeyer pleaded guilty and has been sentenced to life in prison, and Cash faces no . . . charges. . . .

When he appeared on CBS-TV's September 27 *Sixty Minutes* broadcast called "The Bad Samaritan," Cash seemed strangely disconnected from the crime. Soon after he saw Strohmeyer struggling with the girl, he told interviewer Ed Bradley, he left the bathroom. "Based on what I saw," he said, "this wasn't a situation where I wanted to be around." Why didn't he do anything after Strohmeyer confessed to him? "I knew his day of reckoning would come," said Cash. "I didn't want to be the one to turn him in." Finally, when Bradley asked him what he would do differently, if he could go back and do it all over again, Cash paused, then said, "I don't feel there's much I could have done differently."

William Rodarmor, *The Pariah*, CAL. MONTHLY, Nov. 1998, at 7.

In response to this case, Nevada enacted legislation in 1999 requiring "a person who knows or has reasonable cause to believe another person has committed a violent or sexual offense against a child who is 12 years of age or younger" to report the offense to a law enforcement agency as soon as practical but at least within 24 hours. Failure to comply constitutes a misdemeanor. Nev. Rev. Stat. Ann. § 202.882. An analogous statute was enacted in California in 2000 requiring persons who observe the murder or sexual assault of a child under 14 to report the offense to a police officer. Cal. Penal Code § 52.3.

8. Misprision of Felony. Under the old common law, David Cash and Katherine Russell could have been charged with a misdemeanor called "misprision of felony," defined as the failure to report or prosecute a known felony. Although most modern criminal codes do not include misprision of felony as a crime, *see* WAYNE R. LaFAVE, CRIMINAL LAW § 13.6(b), at 758–59 (5th ed. 2010), the federal criminal code does.

The federal statute, 18 U.S.C. § 4, provides:

Whoever, having knowledge of the actual commission of a felony cognizable by a court of the United States, conceals and does not as soon as possible make known the same to some judge or other person in civil or military authority under the United States, shall be fined . . . or imprisoned not more than three years, or both.

The word "conceals" in the federal statute has been construed to require that the defendant took affirmative steps to conceal the crime. *E.g.*, *Lancey v. United States*, 356 F.2d 407 (9th Cir. 1966). Unlike the common law, then, the federal version of misprision of felony would not punish a mere omission to report a crime and is therefore more akin to the modern obstruction of justice statutes discussed in Chapter 12, Section E.

Although the federal statute is rarely used, misprision of felony charges were brought against Michael Fortier, the principal prosecution witness in the trials of Timothy McVeigh and Terry Nichols, the two men who masterminded the April 1995 bombing of the federal building in Oklahoma City. Fortier, an Army buddy of McVeigh and Nichols, admitted that he became aware of the conspiracy the previous September and helped transport and sell stolen firearms, the proceeds of which were allegedly used to help fund the bombing, which killed 168 people. Fortier pleaded guilty to several charges, including misprision of felony, transporting and conspiring to transport stolen firearms, and making false statements to the FBI, and he received a 12-year prison sentence. *See United States v. Fortier*, 242 F.3d 1224 (10th Cir. 2001).

As the case against Fortier makes clear, the requirement of "affirmative steps" noted above is not a particularly strong one. Fortier's simple failure to respond truthfully to questions regarding his knowledge of the Oklahoma City bombing was considered a sufficient "affirmative act" to support his guilt on misprision charges. Do you see a distinction between these facts and criminal liability for a simple failure to report a crime?

The federal misprision statute has been characterized as a "crime of moral turpitude" that can lead to an undocumented immigrant's deportation. *Itani v. Ashcroft*, 298 F.3d 1213 (11th Cir. 2002). The *Itani* court explained that misprision "has been a federal crime since the First Congress [in 1790], for the common law recognized a duty to raise the 'hue and cry' and report felonies to the authorities." *Id.* at 1216 (citing *Branzburg v. Hayes*, 408 U.S. 665, 696–97 (1972)).

Is there a good argument for reviving the common law's misprision of felony charge for those who fail to report serious crimes?

[C] Possession

Wheeler v. United States

494 A.2d 170 (D.C. 1985)

MACK, ASSOCIATE JUDGE.

The sole issue on this appeal is whether the evidence was sufficient to support appellant Lillian E. Wheeler's conviction for possession of a controlled substance (heroin), D.C. Code § 33-541(d). We find sufficient evidence upon which the trier of fact could determine beyond a reasonable doubt that appellant was guilty of the charged offense, and we therefore affirm.

I

Viewing the evidence in the light most favorable to the government, the facts of this case are as follows. On January 17, 1982, a search warrant was executed for Room 201 of the Logan Inn at 1338 R Street, N.W. In an affidavit in support of the warrant, Detective Alan Penberg stated that a source had informed him that female occupants of Room 201 were selling heroin from that room. The police knocked on the door to Room 201, identifying themselves, but received no response. Instead, they heard what they described as "scurrying" noises behind the door. After at least a minute, they succeeded in breaking down the door. They found appellant and two other women coming out of the bathroom; the toilet had just been flushed. A fourth woman was sitting in a chair next to the bathroom. Two of the women were dressed in street clothes, but appellant and another woman, Mary Sales, were wearing sleeping attire. Luggage and clothes belonging to appellant were found in the room along with other personal effects. Appellant and Sales both gave aliases to the police. Both admitted, however, that they lived in Room 201. There were two beds in the hotel room, at opposite ends of the room. Sales retrieved some slippers from underneath a bed at one end. Under the second bed's pillow, the police found 3,550 milligrams of 2.7% heroin. Sales and appellant were arrested. While the charges against Sales were subsequently dismissed, appellant was found guilty of possession of heroin after a bench trial. This appeal followed. . . .

III

This case was submitted to the trial court on a theory of constructive possession. An individual has constructive possession of an illegal substance when he is knowingly in a position or has the right to exercise dominion and control over it, and has some appreciable ability to guide its destiny. The right to exercise dominion and control may be jointly shared. In evaluating the sufficiency of the evidence submitted by the government, no distinction is made between direct and circumstantial evidence, and the trier may infer knowledge from circumstantial evidence.

Appellant contends that the heroin could have been placed under the pillow by any one of the three other women present in the room at the time the police arrived, and that to hold her responsible for the drug is mere speculation. The case law on the question of who may be held responsible when the police find an illegal item in a location together with more than one individual demonstrates some inconsistency. Several general principles may be extracted from the cases, however. Mere proximity to an illegal substance will be insufficient to uphold a conviction on a theory of constructive possession when an individual is one of several people found by the authorities on the premises together with the substance. *Cook v. United States*, 272 A.2d 444, 447 (D.C. 1971) (conviction for possession of narcotics paraphernalia reversed where the government did not show appellant to be a resident of the premises and the actual tenant and other occupants were also present on the scene at the time of the raid); *United States v. Holland*, 144 U.S. App. D.C. 225, 227, 445 F.2d 701, 703 (1971) (conviction for possession of heroin reversed where drugs were found in codefendant's apartment, and although appellant was present when drugs were found the government did not show that he was residing there); *see United States v. Pardo*, 204 U.S. App. D.C. 263, 277, 636 F.2d 535, 549 (1980) (conviction for possession with intent to distribute narcotics reversed where appellant was merely present while a drug transaction was consummated between other individuals); *United States v. Watkins*, 171 U.S. App. D.C. 158, 162, 519 F.2d 294, 298 (1975) (conviction for possession of narcotics reversed even though police found appellant and narcotics in the same room, where two other individuals were found on the premises and insufficient evidence of appellant's residency at that location was adduced). A common theme running through many of these cases is the courts' reluctance to hold an individual responsible for controlled substances or drug paraphernalia found in a home absent some proof that he is something other than a visitor. In this case, however, the government's evidence showed that appellant admitted that she was living in Room 201.

Even where the government proves that the defendant is a resident of the place where illegal items are seized, the courts are wary of imputing possession to the defendant absent proof of his involvement in some criminal enterprise. *Thompson v. United States*, 293 A.2d 275, 276 (D.C. 1972) (conviction for possession of marijuana reversed where drug was found, along with four individuals, in living room and appellant was found in bedroom); *United States v. Bonham*, 477 F.2d 1137, 1138–40 (3d Cir. 1973) (en banc) (conviction for acquisition of heroin reversed where drugs were found hidden behind a false wall panel in a room appellant shared with his halfbrother; informant's tip did not mention appellant; and half-brother was an addict).

On the other hand, where there are circumstances giving rise to an inference of a concert of illegal action involving drugs by the occupants of the premises where the drugs are found, those circumstances tend to dispel any fear that the "constructive possession" doctrine has cast too wide a net. We have held that proximity may establish a supportable case of constructive possession of narcotics when colored by evidence linking the accused to an ongoing criminal operation of which that possession is a part. Other circumstances that will buttress the "constructive possession" inference include attempts to hide or destroy evidence. *See Logan v. United States*, 489 A.2d 485, 491–92 (D.C. 1985) (joint constructive possession of weapon affirmed where appellants were observed jointly throwing something out of car and gun was thereafter recovered from roadbed); *United States v. Smith*, 171 U.S. App. D.C. 342, 344, 520 F.2d 74, 76 (1975) (constructive possession of phencyclidine found in closet affirmed despite fact that appellant was not sole occupant of apartment, where police had found appellant in bathroom and had discovered bag of marijuana directly below open bathroom window).

While this is a close case, we think that the government's evidence, albeit circumstantial, gives rise to sufficient inferences to support the judgment of conviction. As mentioned previously, appellant admitted to the police that she lived in the room, and the government's proof permitted the inference that appellant occupied the bed from which the heroin was recovered. Appellant failed to open the door or to respond in any way to the knock by the police. The observation by the officers that the toilet was flushed while three of the room's occupants, including appellant, were standing in the bathroom simultaneously, permitted the trier to infer that appellant used the period of time that the police required to break down the door to eliminate evidence. In addition, the fact that appellant identified herself to the police using an alias carries some weight on the question of whether she was involved in a criminal enterprise.

In sum, this is not a case in which the defendant's conduct, other than a shared proximity to the illegal item, is entirely innocent. It is unnecessary for the government either to adduce evidence that would compel a finding of guilt, or to negate every possible inference of innocence. The inference that appellant knew of the presence of the drug is not wholly speculative, and that inference, combined with the other circumstances outlined above, suffice[s] to attribute to appellant a measure of control over the heroin and thus to support a finding of constructive possession.

Affirmed.

People v. Ireland

348 N.E.2d 277 (Ill. App. Ct. 1976)

ALLOY, PRESIDING JUSTICE.

Appellant Steven Ireland was indicted for possession of over 500 grams of cannabis with intent to deliver, and also for possession of less than 200 grams of amphetamines. In a jury trial in Will County he was acquitted on both of the charges referred to but was found guilty of a lesser included offense of possession of over 500 grams of cannabis. [He was sentenced to a prison term of one to three years.] . . .

From the record it appears that on December 15, 1972, law enforcement officers executed a search warrant at the defendant's trailer home near Monee, Illinois. The warrant was directed toward the person of Kathy Szabo (Ireland's wife) and toward the trailer premises insofar as cannabis or controlled substances and related paraphernalia might be found. Ireland was at home when the officers arrived. They discovered over 100 pounds (over 45 kilograms) of marijuana in the trailer, and also paraphernalia and 30 pills containing amphetamines. Most of the cannabis was found in plastic bags in the Ireland bedroom and in the second bedroom which was used for storage. Some was found in the kitchen and the dining room, and the pills were found in the bathroom.

At the trial the defendant testified that he and his wife were married on May 17, 1972, and that they were financially well off at the beginning of the marriage because of a gift from the parents of his wife of $28,500. After they had invested in some land and the trailer, they soon ended up without a cash reserve, although they did make ends meet. Ireland indicated that his wife had come from a wealthy family and was accustomed to having plenty of money. As the financial picture of the couple darkened, defendant's wife told him, in November 1972, she was considering selling marijuana. He told her he was against the idea and she apparently acquiesced in his wishes. Defendant, however, came home from work one day about two weeks before his arrest to find some 200 pounds of marijuana in the trailer. He questioned his wife about it and she became very upset and threatened to go to England alone as she had been planning to do before they met and were married. Ireland then apparently relented and did nothing further. Defendant testified that he did not exercise any control over the marijuana. He said that during the 2-week period following his wife's acquisition of the marijuana, a person named John Benatty visited his wife at the trailer 8 or 10 times. He was also shown State's exhibit 35, which purported to be a list of prices for marijuana, which bore the name "John," and said it was in his wife's handwriting.

. . . At the time the cause was submitted to the jury, the State relied on the fact that marijuana was found in the trailer of defendant and his wife and defendant Ireland relied on the evidence that it was in possession of his wife and not of defendant Ireland. The jury deliberated nine hours before acquitting Ireland on both charges but finding him guilty of the lesser included offense of mere possession.

From an analysis of the evidence and testimony, it appears that the jury's apparent difficulty in reaching a verdict promptly, indicated that this was a very close case from standpoint of liability. It was thus imperative that the jury be correctly instructed as to the applicable law regarding the criminal possession of drugs.

The jury was given Illinois Pattern Instruction (IPI) Criminal No. 4.15, at the request of the State and over defendant's objection. Such instruction read:

> Possession is a voluntary act if the offender knowingly procured or received the thing possessed, or was aware of his control thereof for a sufficient time to have been able to terminate his possession.

While there is no IPI instruction defining "possession" specifically, the defense offered one defining possession as "immediate and exclusive control." Such instruction was rejected by the court as being incomplete. The trial court also refused to give IPI Criminal No. 4.14, when requested by the defendant. That instruction provides that "A material element of every crime is a voluntary act. . . ." The defense insisted that it should be included with No. 4.15 to show that voluntariness is a separate element of the crime.

It, therefore, resulted in having only one relevant instruction concerning possession, IPI Criminal No. 4.15, which simply defines when possession is voluntary. The issue in the cause before us is not whether defendant's possession was voluntary in the first instance but whether he had any possession at all. We agree with the contention of the defendant that the instruction, given alone, could induce the jury to believe that Ireland's mere knowledge of the presence of marijuana in his trailer "for a sufficient time" would make it voluntary and thus possession under the law. . . .

. . . Knowledge alone is not the equivalent of possession. While the law raises an inference of control when narcotics are found on the premises occupied by a defendant, absent facts and circumstances which indicate otherwise, it is only a permissible inference, not an automatic and absolute result. Defendant's presence on the premises does not significantly add to the State's case. One recent case even concludes that the presence of narcotics in premises occupied jointly by a defendant and one or more other persons, and to which even others have access, is insufficient to convict defendant for possession thereof, absent some other evidence tying the defendant to the drugs. (*People v. Wolski* (1st Dist. 1975), 27 Ill. App. 3d 526, 327 N.E.2d 308.) A similar rule is in effect in a number of jurisdictions. In the case before us there was nothing in the way of statements, suspicious behavior, previous sales, or use, which would tie Steven Ireland to the marijuana. In a situation such as we have in the present case, where a very tenuous case is presented by the State on the issue of possession, possession becomes a question of fact to be determined by the jury. As we have noted previously under such circumstances it is essential that the jury be accurately instructed as to the law. . . .

Obviously the jury should have been instructed on the elements of possession. We do not believe the instruction tendered by defendant was sufficient for this test. The doctrine of constructive possession would place narcotics found in a safe deposit box in the possession of the person who had access to the box. Likewise, if the contraband is found in any other location over which the person in question exerts control. "Exclusive" control does not exclude joint control and therefore joint possession. An instruction on possession should be tailored to meet these principles. . . .

Reversed and remanded.

Notes and Questions

1. Introduction. Criminal law characterizes possession as a voluntary act, provided the possessor is conscious of the possession. *See, e.g.,* Model Penal Code § 2.01(4). The concept of possession is not easy to define, however. Most courts define it as having dominion or control over something. *See* WAYNE R. LaFAVE, CRIMINAL LAW § 6.1(e), at 326–29 (5th ed. 2010). Are the views on this question expressed by the courts in *Wheeler* and *Ireland* consistent?

Suppose that Steven Ireland was aware that there were illegal drugs in the house he shared with his wife, that the drugs were in an area to which they both had access, that he had told his wife he did not want the drugs in the house, and that he hoped his wife would eventually remove them. Is he guilty of possession of the drugs? Should a trial judge instruct the jury that a defendant who has joint control over the premises is responsible for everything that the defendant knows another resident possesses, irrespective of the relationship between the two people and any efforts that were made to persuade the other person to remove the contraband?

2. Constructive Possession. Possession crimes do not require proof that the defendant was physically in possession of the item. Rather, the prosecution can make out a case of constructive possession if the defendant exercised control over the item, or in some cases, had an opportunity to control it. Consider the following illustrations:

In *United States v. Borchardt*, 698 F.2d 697 (5th Cir. 1983), Ira Borchardt was charged with possession of marijuana. Borchardt and his accomplices flew $126,000 from Dallas to Mexico in order to purchase 2,600 pounds of marijuana. The marijuana was then to be flown back to Dallas in three planeloads. The first two planes arrived without incident, but the third, which Borchardt had personally helped load, crashed in southern Texas. When Borchardt returned from Mexico, he was arrested for possession of marijuana. He was held to be in constructive possession of the marijuana on the third plane: he was largely responsible for its presence; he had exercised control over it by loading it into the plane; and he was to benefit from the proceeds of its sale.

In *United States v. Zandi*, 769 F.2d 229 (4th Cir. 1985), two brothers, Hadi and Mehdi Zandi, were charged with conspiring to import heroin into the United States. A package containing the heroin was mailed from Pakistan and held at an airport warehouse. At the airport, the defendants paid five dollars for an airway bill receipt and a carrier's certificate. Hadi brought the documents into the warehouse while Mehdi waited outside in the car. Hadi was arrested after the package was handed to him. At trial, the brothers claimed that they never had the package in their possession, but the court held that they possessed the heroin when they acquired the shipping documents, thereby obtaining the power to reduce the heroin to their control.

In *United States v. Lindsey*, 389 F.3d 1334 (10th Cir. 2004), Victor Lindsey was charged with carrying a firearm "during and in relation to" a drug trafficking crime. Lindsey was traveling in tandem with a U-Haul truck and tried to cross the border. Lindsey made it through the checkpoint, but border agents pulled over and searched the U-Haul truck, which was driven by Lindsey's "flunky," Randy Watson. After the agents found 13 handguns, 22 pounds of marijuana, cocaine, and crack cocaine in the truck, Lindsey was apprehended. The evidence showed that Lindsey bought the weapons in Arizona, paid for the U-Haul, and instructed Watson to drive the truck. The court held that even though Lindsey was not physically in the U-Haul, he exercised dominion and control over Watson and the truck and traveled with the truck, which gave him the power and intention to exercise control over the weapons.

3. Awareness of Possession. The crime of possession requires proof that the defendants were aware they possessed the prohibited item. In *Commonwealth v. Juliano*, 490 A.2d 891 (Pa. Super. Ct. 1985), for example, the defendant was charged with possession of a controlled substance when one of his friends, who was a drug dealer, picked up a shipment of drugs at the airport and then picked up the defendant at a hotel. When the car was stopped, the police found the drugs in a satchel on the floor in front of the defendant's seat. The court held that the defendant could not be convicted on possession charges because there was insufficient evidence that he knew the satchel contained drugs.

Likewise, the Supreme Court of Florida has indicated that " 'guilty knowledge' is an element of the offense of possession and must be proven beyond a reasonable doubt." *Garcia v. State*, 901 So. 2d 788 (Fla. 2005). The defendant in that case, Jorge Garcia, was pulled over for erratic driving. When his car was searched, the police found an item wrapped in electrical tape that contained methamphetamine. Garcia testified that his truck had recently been stolen and he had no knowledge of the item. In reversing the conviction, the Florida Supreme Court noted that although the jury may presume knowledge, the trial court must also instruct the jury (when the defendant so requests) that the guilty knowledge element includes "both knowledge of possession and knowledge of the nature of the illegal substance."

Some legislatures have endeavored to lessen the prosecution's burden of proof with respect to possession by creating "presumptions"; for example, that everyone in a car is presumed to be in possession of firearms found in the passenger compartment of the vehicle. *See, e.g., County Court of Ulster v. Allen*, 442 U.S. 140 (1979). As long as the trial judge instructs the jury that it *may* infer possession from such presence, the presumption takes the form of a permissible inference, which does not unconstitutionally diminish the prosecution's burden to prove every element of a crime beyond a reasonable doubt. But if the judge tells the jury that the law "presumes" possession from presence, there is a danger that such an instruction will be taken by the jury as a command and will therefore violate due process under *Sandstrom v. Montana*, 442 U.S. 510 (1979).

[D] Status Crimes

The United States Supreme Court has drawn a constitutional line at criminalizing mere "status" without voluntary conduct.

Robinson v. California
370 U.S. 660 (1962)

Mr. Justice Stewart delivered the opinion of the Court.

A California statute makes it a criminal offense for a person to "be addicted to the use of narcotics." This appeal draws into question the constitutionality of that provision of the state law, [which carries a jail sentence ranging from ninety days to one year].

The appellant was convicted after a jury trial in the Municipal Court of Los Angeles. The evidence against him was given by two Los Angeles police officers. Officer Brown testified that he had had occasion to examine the appellant's arms one evening on a street in Los Angeles some four months before the trial. The officer testified that at that time he had observed "scar tissue and discoloration on the inside" of the appellant's right arm, and "what appeared to be numerous needle marks and a scab which was approximately three inches below the crook of the elbow" on the appellant's left arm. The officer also testified that the appellant under questioning had admitted to the occasional use of narcotics. . . .

It would be possible to construe the statute under which the appellant was convicted as one which is operative only upon proof of the actual use of narcotics within the State's jurisdiction. But the California courts have not so construed this law. Although there was evidence in the present case that the appellant had used narcotics in Los Angeles, the jury were instructed that they could convict him even if they disbelieved that evidence. The appellant could be convicted, they were told, if they found simply that the appellant's "status" or "chronic condition" was that of being "addicted to the use of narcotics." And it is impossible to know from the jury's verdict that the defendant was not convicted upon precisely such a finding.

The instructions of the trial court, implicitly approved on appeal, amounted to "a ruling on a question of state law that is as binding on us as though the precise words had been written" into the statute. *Terminiello v. Chicago*, 337 U.S. 1, 4 [(1949)]. "We can only take the statute as the state courts read it." *Id.* at 6. Indeed, in their brief in this Court counsel for the State have emphasized that it is "the proof of addiction by circumstantial evidence . . . by the tell-tale track of needle marks and scabs over the veins of his arms, that remains the gist of the section."

This statute, therefore, is not one which punishes a person for the use of narcotics, for their purchase, sale or possession, or for antisocial or disorderly behavior resulting from their administration. It is not a law which even purports to provide or require medical treatment. Rather, we deal with a statute which makes the "status" of narcotic addiction a criminal offense, for which the offender may be prosecuted "at any time before he reforms." California has said that a person can be continuously guilty of this offense, whether or not he has ever used or possessed any narcotics within the State, and whether or not he has been guilty of any antisocial behavior there.

It is unlikely that any State at this moment in history would attempt to make it a criminal offense for a person to be mentally ill, or a leper, or to be afflicted with a venereal disease. A State might determine that the general health and welfare require that the victims of these and other human afflictions be dealt with by compulsory treatment, involving quarantine, confinement, or sequestration. But, in the light of contemporary human knowledge, a law which made a criminal offense of such a disease would doubtless be universally thought to be an infliction of cruel and unusual punishment in violation of the Eighth and Fourteenth Amendments.

We cannot but consider the statute before us as of the same category. In this Court counsel for the State recognized that narcotic addiction is an illness. Indeed, it is apparently an illness which may be contracted innocently or involuntarily. We hold that a state law which imprisons a person thus afflicted as a criminal, even though he has never touched any narcotic drug within the State or been guilty of any irregular behavior there, inflicts a cruel and unusual punishment in violation of the Fourteenth Amendment. To be sure, imprisonment for ninety days is not, in the abstract, a punishment which is either cruel or unusual. But the question cannot be considered in the abstract. Even one day in prison would be a cruel and unusual punishment for the "crime" of having a common cold.

We are not unmindful that the vicious evils of the narcotics traffic have occasioned the grave concern of government. There are, as we have said, countless fronts on which those evils may be legitimately attacked. We deal in this case only with an individual provision of a particularized local law as it has so far been interpreted by the California courts.

Reversed.

[Dissenting opinion of Justice White, joined by Justice Clark, omitted.]

Notes and Questions

1. Introduction. Status crimes do not require commission of any specific act. Rather, the prosecution merely has to show that offenders fit within a certain class of people. Offenders can be charged at any time, regardless of any acts they may or may not commit. As *Robinson* makes clear, such crimes are unconstitutional.

2. Public Intoxication. While being a drug addict or an alcoholic cannot itself be made a crime, public intoxication can be criminalized. For example, the Model Penal Code's prohibition of public drunkenness applies to one who "appears in any public place manifestly under the influence of alcohol, narcotics, or other drug, not therapeutically administered, to the degree that he may endanger himself or other persons or property, or annoy persons in his vicinity." Model Penal Code § 250.5. Even alcoholics who are arguably compelled by their disease to become intoxicated can be convicted under such statutes.

In *Powell v. Texas*, 392 U.S. 514 (1968), Leroy Powell was convicted of public intoxication. A psychiatrist testified that once Powell started drinking, he had no control over how much he drank, and that as an alcoholic, his judgment was impaired even before he started drinking. In an attempt to bring public intoxication within the scope of *Robinson*, the trial court found the following facts: (1) alcoholism is a disease that destroys an individual's ability to refrain from consuming excessive amounts of alcohol; (2) alcoholics appear in public as a result of the disease rather than of their own volition; and (3) Powell was an alcoholic. In the Supreme Court, the four Justices in dissent concluded that *Robinson* was controlling, interpreting that opinion as holding that "a person may not be punished if the condition essential to constitute the defined crime is part of the pattern of his disease and is occasioned by a compulsion symptomatic of the disease." *Id.* at 569 (Fortas, J., dissenting).

A majority of the Court declined to accept this interpretation, largely on policy grounds. The plurality opinion reasoned, first, that defining alcoholism is too difficult, and it is unclear whether an alcoholic is completely or only partially compelled to drink. Second, recognizing that public intoxication is a major social problem, the plurality noted that there really is no alternative to brief stints in jail. Finally, the plurality was hesitant to adopt an interpretation of *Robinson* that would make compulsion a defense because doing so might open the door for other compulsions to become defenses (e.g., kleptomania, pedophilia, pyromania). Justice White concurred in the result on the grounds that Powell had not shown that his alcoholism compelled him to appear in public in an intoxicated condition. Because four Justices dissented, Justice White's opinion is viewed as controlling, as he provided the necessary fifth vote for the majority.

3. Loitering. In *Papachristou v. City of Jacksonville*, 405 U.S. 156 (1972), the Supreme Court struck down a loitering ordinance that allowed the police to arrest anyone they suspected of being, among other things, "[r]ogues and vagabonds, or dissolute persons . . . , common night walkers, . . . [or] persons wandering or strolling around from place to place without any lawful purpose or object." The Court found the ordinance unconstitutionally vague because it "fails to give a person of ordinary intelligence fair notice that his contemplated conduct is forbidden by the statute." *Id.* at 162. The Court observed that the ordinance "makes criminal activities which by modern standards are normally innocent. 'Nightwalking' is one. . . . We know . . . from experience that sleepless people often walk at night, perhaps hopeful that sleep-inducing relaxation will result." *Id.* at 163. A second reason the Court gave for striking down the ordinance was "the effect of the unfettered discretion it places in the hands of the Jacksonville police." *Id.* at 168. The Court reasoned: "We allow our police to make arrests only on 'probable cause'. . . . Arresting a person on suspicion, like arresting a person for investigation, is foreign to our system, even when the arrest is for past criminality." *Id.* at 169. The Court feared that this ordinance, and ones like it, allow the police to harass those groups of people they deem undesirable: "poor people, nonconformists, dissenters, idlers." *Id.* at 170.

In a later decision, *City of Chicago v. Morales*, 527 U.S. 41 (1999), the Supreme Court reviewed a Chicago ordinance that prohibited " 'criminal street gang members' from 'loitering' with one another or with other persons in any public place." The Court gave the following description of the ordinance:

> Commission of the offense involves four predicates. First, the police officer must reasonably believe that at least one of the two or more persons present in a "public place" is a "criminal street gang member." Second, the persons must be "loitering," which the ordinance defines as "remaining in any one place with no apparent purpose." Third, the officer must then order "all" of the persons to disperse and remove themselves "from the area." Fourth, a person must disobey the officer's order. If any person, whether a gang member or not, disobeys the officer's order, that person is guilty of violating the ordinance.

Id. at 47.

Writing for the majority, Justice Stevens found the ordinance unconstitutionally vague, concluding that it "reach[es] a substantial amount of innocent conduct" and "provides absolute discretion to police officers to determine what activities constitute loitering." *Id.* at 60. The Court explained:

It is true, as the city argues, that the requirement that the officer reasonably believe that a group of loiterers contains a gang member does place a limit on the authority to order dispersal. That limitation would no doubt be sufficient if the ordinance only applied to loitering that had an apparently harmful purpose or effect, or possibly if it only applied to loitering by persons reasonably believed to be criminal gang members. But this ordinance, for reasons that are not explained in the findings of the city council, requires no harmful purpose and applies to non-gang members as well as suspected gang members. It applies to everyone in the city who may remain in one place with one suspected gang member as long as their purpose is not apparent to an officer observing them. Friends, relatives, teachers, counselors, or even total strangers might unwittingly engage in forbidden loitering if they happen to engage in idle conversation with a gang member.

Ironically, the definition of loitering in the Chicago ordinance not only extends its scope to encompass harmless conduct, but also has the perverse consequence of excluding from its coverage much of the intimidating conduct that motivated its enactment. As the city council's findings demonstrate, the most harmful gang loitering is motivated either by an apparent purpose to publicize the gang's dominance of certain territory, thereby intimidating nonmembers, or by an equally apparent purpose to conceal ongoing commerce in illegal drugs. As the Illinois Supreme Court has not placed any limiting construction on the language in the ordinance, we must assume that the ordinance means what it says and that it has no application to loiterers whose purpose is apparent. The relative importance of its application to harmless loitering is magnified by its inapplicability to loitering that has an obviously threatening or illicit purpose.

Id. at 57.

In a portion of his opinion joined only by Justices Souter and Ginsburg, Stevens continued:

Since the city cannot conceivably have meant to criminalize each instance a citizen stands in public with a gang member, the vagueness that dooms this ordinance is not the product of uncertainty about the normal meaning of "loitering," but rather about what loitering is covered by the ordinance and what is not. The Illinois Supreme Court emphasized the law's failure to distinguish between innocent conduct and conduct threatening harm. Its decision followed the precedent set by a number of state courts that have upheld ordinances that criminalize loitering combined with some other overt act or evidence of criminal intent. However, state courts have uniformly invalidated laws that do not join the term "loitering" with a second specific element of the crime.

Id. at 57–58.

4. The Model Penal Code's Loitering Provision. The Model Penal Code defines "loitering" to encompass cases where one "loiters or prowls in a place, at a time, or in a manner not usual for law-abiding individuals under circumstances that warrant alarm for the safety of persons or property in the vicinity." Model Penal Code § 250.6. The Code gives the following illustrations of "circumstances" that might be relevant in ascertaining whether "alarm is warranted" within the meaning of the ban on loitering: "the fact that the actor takes flight upon appearance of a peace officer, refuses to identify himself, or manifestly endeavors to conceal himself or any object." *Id.* Finally, the Code requires that a police officer, where practicable, give a suspect "an opportunity to dispel any alarm which would otherwise be warranted, by requesting him to identify himself and explain his presence and conduct" before making an arrest for loitering. *Id.*

The Comments accompanying the loitering provision explain:

> All in all, the Model Code provision states an offense vastly different from the traditional crime of loitering or vagrancy. Liability is not based on a status derived from past behavior—e.g., common drunkard—but on present conduct of an unusual sort. Furthermore, the offense is not made out simply by the fact of loitering but requires circumstances such that the actor's behavior justifies alarm for the safety of persons or property. This formulation limits the offense to its essential law enforcement rationale of justifying intervention to prevent incipient crime and avoids the extension of liability to persons who are simply socially undesirable. Finally, Section 250.6 includes a special safeguard in the required opportunity to dispel otherwise warranted alarm by identification and explanation of one's presence and conduct.

Id. § 250.6 Comment at 391. Do the Code's provisions on public drunkenness and loitering make sense?

5. Homelessness. In *Pottinger v. Miami*, 810 F. Supp. 1551 (S.D. Fla. 1992), the district court distinguished the Supreme Court's decision in *Powell v. Texas* (described above in Note 2), and held that it was unconstitutional for the City of Miami to arrest homeless persons for sleeping, sitting, or performing other "life-sustaining activities in public places." The court explained:

> Plaintiffs contend that the City's arrests of class members under various ordinances prohibit them from lying down, sleeping, standing, sitting or performing other essential, life-sustaining activities in any public place at any time. Plaintiffs argue that their status of being homeless is involuntary and beyond their immediate ability to alter and that the conduct for which they are arrested is inseparable from their involuntary homeless status. Consequently, plaintiffs argue, application of these ordinances to them is cruel and unusual in violation of the eighth amendment.

> . . . .

Although the law is well-established that a person may not be punished for involuntary status, it is less settled whether involuntary conduct that is inextricably related to that status may be punished. An initial reading of *Powell* suggests that all conduct is outside the rule of *Robinson*. . . .

However, the *Powell* plurality was not confronted with a critical distinguishing factor that is unique to the plight of the homeless plaintiffs in this case: that they have no realistic choice but to live in public places. . . .

. . . [C]lass members rarely choose to be homeless. They become homeless due to a variety of factors that are beyond their control. In addition, plaintiffs do not have the choice, much less the luxury, of being in the privacy of their own homes. Because of the unavailability of low-income housing or alternative shelter, plaintiffs have no choice but to conduct involuntary, life-sustaining activities in public places. The harmless conduct for which they are arrested is inseparable from their involuntary condition of being homeless. Consequently, arresting homeless people for harmless acts they are forced to perform in public effectively punishes them for being homeless. This effect is no different from the vagrancy ordinances which courts struck because they punished "innocent victims of misfortune" and made a crime of being "unemployed, without funds, and in a public place."

Id. at 1561–64.

In *Joyce v. City & County of San Francisco*, 846 F. Supp. 843 (N.D. Cal. 1994), by contrast, the plaintiffs sued to enjoin San Francisco from implementing a policy that would strictly enforce certain criminal laws violated primarily by homeless persons, including public inebriation, sleeping in public parks, littering, and aggressive panhandling. In denying the plaintiffs' request for a preliminary injunction, the court rejected *Pottinger*'s analysis:

Depicting homelessness as "status" is by no means self-evident. . . . That depiction, made upon serious analysis only in *Pottinger*, is a dubious extension of *Robinson* and *Powell*, and of questionable merit in light of concerns implicating federalism and the proper role of the Court in such adjudications.

Insofar as *Pottinger* attempts to reason from applicable Supreme Court precedent that homelessness equals a "status," and that acts derivative of such status are constitutionally protected, the reasoning of that court cannot be said at this stage of the litigation to be sufficiently persuasive to indicate a likely possibility of success on the merits of the underlying suit. . . .

This Court is unable to conclude at this time that the extension of the Eighth Amendment to the "acts" at issue here is warranted by governing authorities. Plaintiffs argue that the failure of the City to provide sufficient housing compels the conclusion that homelessness on the streets of San

Francisco is cognizable as a status. This argument is unavailing at least for the fundamental reason that status cannot be defined as a function of the discretionary acts of others. . . .

As an analytical matter, more fundamentally, homelessness is not readily classified as a "status." Rather, as expressed for the plurality in *Powell* by Justice Marshall, there is a "substantial definitional distinction between a 'status' . . . and a 'condition' . . . ." While the concept of status might elude perfect definition, certain factors assist in its determination, such as the involuntariness of the acquisition of that quality (including the presence or not of that characteristic at birth), *see Robinson*, 370 U.S. at 665–69 & n.9, and the degree to which an individual has control over that characteristic.

Examples of such "status" characteristics might include age, race, gender, national origin and illness. The reasoning of the [*Robinson*] Court in including drug addiction involved the analogy of drug addiction to a disease or an illness which might be contracted involuntarily. While homelessness can be thrust upon an unwitting recipient, and while a person may be largely incapable of changing that condition, the distinction between the ability to eliminate one's drug addiction as compared to one's homelessness is a distinction in kind as much as in degree. To argue that homelessness is a status and not a condition, moreover, is to deny the efficacy of acts of social intervention to change the condition of those currently homeless.

The Court must approach with hesitation any argument that science or statistics compels a conclusion that a certain condition be defined as a status. The Supreme Court has determined that drug addiction equals a status, and this Court is so bound. But the Supreme Court has not made such a determination with respect to homelessness, and because that situation is not directly analogous to drug addiction, it would be an untoward excursion by this Court into matters of social policy to accord to homelessness the protection of status.

In addition to the fact that homelessness does not analytically fit into a definition of a status under the contours of governing case law, the effects which would ensue from such a determination by this Court would be staggering. Courts seeking analytical consistency with such a holding would be required to provide constitutional protection to any condition over which a showing could be made that the defendant had no control.

846 F. Supp. at 856–58.

Should it make a difference in considering whether homelessness is a status whether or not the city provides facilities for homeless persons? If shelters are available, is it more reasonable to punish the homeless who refuse to avail themselves of the shelters? Should the city be required to provide the homeless with notice of alternative housing before seeking to punish them criminally?

Note that the *Joyce* suit was eventually dismissed as moot after a "sea change" in city policy led San Francisco officials to eliminate the program targeting the homeless and to dismiss all citations and warrants that had been issued under it. *See Joyce v. City & County of San Francisco*, 87 F.3d 1320 (9th Cir. 1996).

Chapter 4

Mens Rea

[A] Introduction

It is commonly said that modern crimes require not only a voluntary act, an *actus reus*, but also a certain state of mind, or *mens rea*, accompanying the act. Although the Latin phrase from which the term "mens rea" is derived—*Actus non facit reum nisi mens sit rea* (an act does not make one guilty, unless the mind be guilty)—speaks of a "guilty" mind, defining the required state of mind in the context of specific crimes historically has been, and continues to be, a difficult and much-debated task.

Before exploring the various ways criminal culpability has been defined, it is useful to consider the requirement of a mental state in the first place. If an act itself causes sufficient harm to society or a protected private interest, why must the criminal sanction depend on proof of a certain state of mind? What societal interest is the mens rea requirement intended to protect? Is the civil law adequate to protect private interests? Might the mens rea requirement actually make it more difficult to protect against the harms that the criminal law is designed to prevent?

Some commentators have suggested eliminating the mens rea requirement and reconstituting the criminal law in terms of the specific harms to be prevented. *See, e.g.*, BARBARA WOOTTON, CRIME AND THE CRIMINAL LAW (1963). Defenders of the mens rea doctrine respond that: (1) the mental state helps to define more precisely the kinds of behavior society wishes to prevent and punish; (2) mens rea requirements protect those who accidently or "innocently" cause harm; and (3) the retributive purposes of criminal law are served by punishing only those who are culpable. *See, e.g.*, Sanford Kadish, *The Decline of Innocence*, 26 CAMBRIDGE L.J. 273 (1968). As Justice Holmes once wrote, "even a dog distinguishes between being stumbled over and being kicked." OLIVER WENDELL HOLMES, THE COMMON LAW 3 (1881).

The history of the role of culpability in criminal law reflects a continual search for adequate definitions, which has resulted in increasingly specific requirements. What began as a vague, generalized concept of "evil" has evolved into specific states of mind applied to specific crimes and acts. Ronald Gainer briefly summarizes the historical development of the concept of culpability:

> Early Anglo-Saxon law is generally understood to have been intended primarily to keep the peace. Although some form of culpability was inherent in the commission of most acts constituting breaches, the law's descriptions were largely untroubled by concepts regarding states of mind. By the twelfth

century, however, the resuscitation of the study of Roman law encouraged the gradual adoption of legal concepts involving moral wrong, and with the concurrent expansion of the influence of canon law the purpose of the criminal law began to be perceived as the curbing of immorality. . . .

Over time, the courts proved to be as inventive as the clerics in describing the moral shortcomings of those who committed criminal acts. The more objective of the terms were tailored to particular offenses, and thus were of limited usefulness. Occasional judicial attempts to draw out generalized standards seemed akin to the apocryphal characterization of an elephant from descriptions produced by the gropings of the blind. In each instance, vision was limited by reach. Thoughtful recitations of necessary mental elements were restricted to those affecting the conduct in the particular cases in which the issues arose.

The general descriptions that did evolve—including "*mens rea*," "general criminal intent," and, less dispassionately, "evil," "viciousness," and "wickedness"—[were] not particularly helpful, yet these terms were employed in holdings as though a single factor were in issue. This gave impetus to the generalization of exceptions to criminal liability based on lack of the requisite mental state. In addition to the generalized defenses, presumptions and other artificial rules emerged as practical substitutes for evidence of the existence or nonexistence of culpable mental states, in part because of the inherent artificiality of some of the legal requirements, and in part because of the preclusion of defendants from the stand where they might supply direct evidence concerning states of mind.

By the mid-nineteenth century, the view again began to predominate that the purpose of the criminal law should be to protect social and public interests, rather than to discourage immoral behavior, and accordingly that proof of a culpable mental state should not be required to convict. The movement toward this view was prodded by recognition that the industrial and commercial revolutions were multiplying means by which serious endangerment of persons and property might arise on a broad scale. Legislatures began prescribing criminal penalties for violations of regulatory provisions governing activities in which the risk of serious injury was high, and the courts upheld them as "*mala prohibita*" offenses requiring no proof of a culpable mental state. This approach eventually expanded beyond bounds that could satisfactorily be explained on the basis of differences between regulated activity and more traditional offense conduct.

The result of this series of events was a chaotic state of the law with regard to the mental elements of offenses. Judges seemed unable to extricate themselves from the morass. Prosecutors found a conveniently amorphous blend of concepts from which they could draw in justifying different exercises of "prosecutorial discretion," but also found frequently distressing challenges in attempting to prove cases to juries. Defense counsel found both a fertile area for exploitation in arguing to juries and in attacking the propriety of jury charges in appellate courts, and a source of potential injustice. Scholars found the subject unrewarding—it was too easy to criticize and too difficult to rationalize. It stood out as the area of the criminal law most obviously in need of reform.

Ronald L. Gainer, *The Culpability Provisions of the Model Penal Code*, 19 RUTGERS L.J. 575, 576–77 (1988).

The Model Penal Code attempts to resolve the confusion Gainer describes. Section 2.02 articulates four levels of mental culpability and instructs that "the question of the kind of culpability required to establish the commission of an offense be faced separately with respect to each material element of the crime." Model Penal Code § 2.02 Comment at 231.

Model Penal Code § 2.02

Section 2.02. General Requirements of Culpability

(1) Minimum Requirements of Culpability. Except as provided in Section 2.05, a person is not guilty of an offense unless he acted purposely, knowingly, recklessly or negligently, as the law may require, with respect to each material element of the offense.

(2) Kinds of Culpability Defined.

(a) Purposely.

A person acts purposely with respect to a material element of an offense when:

(i) if the element involves the nature of his conduct or a result thereof, it is his conscious object to engage in conduct of that nature or to cause such a result; and

(ii) if the element involves the attendant circumstances, he is aware of the existence of such circumstances or he believes or hopes that they exist.

(b) Knowingly.

A person acts knowingly with respect to a material element of an offense when:

(i) if the element involves the nature of his conduct or the attendant circumstances, he is aware that his conduct is of that nature or that such circumstances exist; and

(ii) if the element involves a result of his conduct, he is aware that it is practically certain that his conduct will cause such a result.

(c) Recklessly.

A person acts recklessly with respect to a material element of an offense when he consciously disregards a substantial and unjustifiable risk that the material element exists or will result from his conduct. The risk must be of such a nature and degree that, considering the nature and purpose of the actor's conduct and the circumstances known to him, its disregard involves a gross deviation from the standard of conduct that a law-abiding person would observe in the actor's situation.

(d) Negligently.

A person acts negligently with respect to a material element of an offense when he should be aware of a substantial and unjustifiable risk that the material element exists or will result from his conduct. The risk must be of such a nature and degree that the actor's failure to perceive it, considering the nature and purpose of his conduct and the circumstances known to him, involves a gross deviation from the standard of care that a reasonable person would observe in the actor's situation.

(3) Culpability Required Unless Otherwise Provided. When the culpability sufficient to establish a material element of an offense is not prescribed by law, such element is established if a person acts purposely, knowingly or recklessly with respect thereto.

(4) Prescribed Culpability Requirement Applies to All Material Elements. When the law defining an offense prescribes the kind of culpability that is sufficient for the commission of an offense, without distinguishing among the material elements thereof, such provision shall apply to all the material elements of the offense, unless a contrary purpose plainly appears.

(5) Substitutes for Negligence, Recklessness and Knowledge. When the law provides that negligence suffices to establish an element of an offense, such element also is established if a person acts purposely, knowingly or recklessly. When recklessness suffices to establish an element, such element also is established if a person acts purposely or knowingly. When acting knowingly suffices to establish an element, such element also is established if a person acts purposely.

(6) Requirement of Purpose Satisfied if Purpose Is Conditional. When a particular purpose is an element of an offense, the element is established although such purpose is conditional, unless the condition negatives the harm or evil sought to be prevented by the law defining the offense.

(7) Requirement of Knowledge Satisfied by Knowledge of High Probability. When knowledge of the existence of a particular fact is an element of an offense, such knowledge is established if a person is aware of a high probability of its existence, unless he actually believes that it does not exist.

(8) Requirement of Wilfulness Satisfied by Acting Knowingly. A requirement that an offense be committed wilfully is satisfied if a person acts knowingly with respect to the material elements of the offense, unless a purpose to impose further requirements appears.

(9) Culpability as to Illegality of Conduct. Neither knowledge nor recklessness or negligence as to whether conduct constitutes an offense or as to the existence, meaning or application of the law determining the elements of an offense is an element of such offense, unless the definition of the offense or the Code so provides.

(10) Culpability as Determinant to Grade of Offense. When the grade or degree of an offense depends on whether the offense is committed purposely, knowingly, recklessly or negligently, its grade or degree shall be the lowest for which the determinative kind of culpability is established with respect to any material element of the offense.

The Comments to § 2.02 reflect the concerns of its drafters:

> The purpose of articulating these distinctions in detail is to advance the clarity of draftsmanship in the delineation of definitions of specific crimes, to provide a distinct framework against which those definitions may be tested, and to dispel the obscurity with which the culpability requirement is often treated when such concepts as "general criminal intent," "mens rea," "presumed intent," "malice," "wilfulness," "scienter" and the like have been employed. What Justice Jackson called "the variety, disparity and confusion" of judicial definitions of "the requisite but elusive mental element" in crime should, insofar as possible, be rationalized by a criminal code.

Model Penal Code § 2.02 Comment at 230.

Do the four types of culpability recognized by the Model Penal Code adequately capture the entire array of criminal states of mind? Would even fewer categories suffice? What other concepts or words might describe kinds of culpability not included in the Code's formulation?

Consider Professor Harold Edgar's reservations about the inflexibility of the Code's approach to culpability:

> The Model Penal Code vastly simplifies the common law of mens rea. It identifies only four kinds of culpability, and then uses these terms consistently throughout the formulations of specific crimes. . . . What the Code does . . . is to deprive the system of the ambiguous terms, such as *intent* and *willful*, that might serve as bridges for the reformulation of defenses. . . . The question is whether the Code, in making its choices, provides adequate flexibility for administrators, given that comprehensive legislative reform of criminal law occurs infrequently and piecemeal legislation imposes new penalties more commonly than it mitigates old ones. . . . The problem . . . is that the Model Penal Code, and the states that follow it, are at risk by employing uniform culpability language if the single standard does not fit the common patterns of various crimes and the defensive settings that the Code encompasses. . . . The Model Penal Code . . . gives precise definitions of purpose, knowledge, and recklessness on the supposition that these are

provable occurrences. The supposition is very questionable. . . . [I]s a body of law seriously flawed if it provides an elaborate set of precise rules whose operability depends upon the jury's willingness to make artificial characterizations?

Harold Edgar, *Mens Rea, in* 3 ENCYCLOPEDIA OF CRIME AND JUSTICE 1036–39 (Sanford H. Kadish ed., 1983).

[B] Levels of Culpability

The four levels of mens rea recognized by § 2.02 of the Model Penal Code represented a significant shift from the common law's distinction between "general" and "specific" intent crimes. Nevertheless, as described below, the common-law concepts remain relevant in various contexts, despite their somewhat antiquated status.

[1] The Common Law: General Versus Specific Intent

State v. Peery
28 N.W.2d 851 (Minn. 1947)

GALLAGHER, JUSTICE.

. . . [On] August 13, 1946, defendant, then a student at Concordia College in St. Paul, was arrested without warrant and held without bail until August 16, 1946, when he was brought to trial in the municipal court of St. Paul on a "tab charge" of "Indecent Exposure." . . . [U]pon arraignment on that date defendant entered a plea of "not guilty," and his trial proceeded forthwith; some six witnesses were then called for the state, while defendant and one other witness testified on defendant's behalf; and the court thereupon found defendant guilty and ordered him imprisoned in the workhouse of the city of St. Paul for a term of 90 days. . . .

The evidence presented at the trial indicates that defendant, 23 years of age, a veteran of four major campaigns of the United States army in the South Pacific and at the time in question a seminar student at Concordia College awaiting the opening of the fall term at the University of Minnesota, occupied a corner ground-floor room in the Men's Dormitory at Concordia. The room has two windows, one opening to the west and the other to the north. About 15 to 20 feet from the west window, a cement sidewalk passes through the college grounds. It is used by the public generally and particularly by employees going to and coming from their work at the Brown & Bigelow plant nearby.

The state's witnesses . . . testified in substance that on several occasions in passing by the Men's Dormitory on their way from work about 5 p.m. they had observed defendant unclothed, standing in front of or near the north window of his room, and that he later walked across and stood in the same condition near the west window; that on one such occasion they had observed him raise the west window shade and stand near this window exposed to view, entirely unclothed. There is no evidence that defendant had signaled or called to these witnesses or otherwise endeavored to direct their attention to himself.

In his defense, defendant testified that he returned to his room in the dormitory about 5 p.m. each evening; that it was his custom then to change his work clothing, take a shower in the basement of the dormitory, return to his room, and dress for his evening meal and classes. He denied that he had intentionally exposed himself. He admitted that on some occasions he may have neglected to draw the shades, but testified that he was not conscious of passers-by on the days in question; that he was careful as to his conduct at all times because of his high regard for his classmates who occupied neighboring dormitories. He stated that on at least one of the dates testified to by the state's witnesses he had not worked or changed his clothing at the time such witnesses had testified that they had passed his quarters and observed him.

Dr. Hugo W. Thompson, professor of Religion and Philosophy at Macalester College in St. Paul, testified that he was in charge of the industrial seminar at Concordia College attended by defendant; that the classes therein were held at night; that the students, including defendant, taking such course had been carefully selected from other colleges and were required, as part of the seminar, to be employed during the daytime; that defendant had always conducted himself as a gentleman, and the records of the project so indicated; that he (Dr. Thompson) had often used the walk in front of the Men's Dormitory at about the same time of day the state's witnesses passed defendant's quarters; that on such occasions he had often looked toward the Men's Dormitory, including defendant's room, but at no time had he witnessed any such incidents as testified to by the state's witnesses; that the walk is on college property and not a public street; that west of the walk is a thick hedge; that it is 40 feet from the west wall of the building to said walk; that defendant's room could be seen from his office across the way, but at no time had he seen any conduct on the part of defendant such as testified to by the state's witnesses. A portion of the settled case which the trial court certified as true and correct stated:

> There was no testimony by any of the witnesses either for the Prosecution or the Defense that defendant had waved or signaled to any of the girl witnesses for the Prosecution who claimed to have seen any of the exposures, or that he had in any way attempted to attract their attention or that he had called to or whistled at them or made any sound or done anything else calculated to attract their attention or the attention of anyone; other than the facts hereinbefore specifically recited.
>
> There was no testimony by any of the witnesses that defendant had committed any lewd or indecent acts other than the claimed exposures.

On appeal, defendant urges ... that the evidence [did not] establish that his exposure was wilful or intentionally lewd, and hence that such evidence is insufficient to sustain his conviction. ...

The principle is well established that . . . before the offense of indecent exposure can be established, the evidence must be sufficient to sustain a finding that the misconduct complained of was committed with the deliberate intent of being indecent or lewd. Ordinary acts or conduct involving exposure of the person as the result of carelessness or thoughtlessness do not in themselves establish the offense of indecent exposure. This would seem to be particularly true where the acts complained of take place within the privacy of a lodging removed from public places and where observation thereof is to some extent an invasion of the rights of privacy ordinarily attached to a home, whether it be a dwelling house or a room in a college dormitory. . . .

. . . In *People v. Ulman*, 258 App. Div. 262, 263, 16 N.Y.S. (2d) 222, 223, the New York court . . . stated:

> . . . .
>
> In order to constitute the crime the exposure of one's person in any public place must be intentional, willful and lewd. . . . The intent with which the act is committed forms a material ingredient of the offense. If it appears that the exposure was not the wanton and lewd conduct which the statute condemns but was unintentional, the crime has not been committed. . . . Here the testimony indicates that if there was any apparent misconduct it was due to accident and not to design. Moreover, it is the law that evidence of good character may of itself create a reasonable doubt when without it none would exist. . . . In this case defendant's character evidence considered with all the other proof, we think, was sufficient to create a reasonable doubt of defendant's guilt of the crime charged.

In the instant case, we are far from satisfied that the evidence is sufficient to sustain the trial court's finding that defendant's conduct was wilful and lewd rather than the result of carelessness or thoughtlessness. Defendant has denied the intent. He is a man without a previous blemish against his record. He is a combat veteran of four major campaigns of the South Pacific, honorably discharged as a staff sergeant, seeking a college education, and working part time to help defray his expenses. He concedes that on occasions he may have been careless. His room is small and fairly close to the sidewalk. His ordinary activity therein at about the times in question, when it was his custom to remove his clothing preparatory to bathing, might easily be misinterpreted by passers-by looking into his room.

There is no evidence whatsoever that he endeavored to attract the attention of passers-by by motioning, signaling, or calling to them, unless his act of raising the shade on one occasion might be thus regarded. This would seem rather flimsy evidence upon which to convict a man of the charge specified and to forever blemish his name and character as a result.

The testimony of Dr. Hugo Thompson, professor of Religion and Philosophy at Macalester College, characterizes defendant as a man of good reputation and high standing in the seminar. All the testimony in the case is consistent with defendant's testimony that he may have been careless or heedless, but that he did not intentionally expose himself. In our opinion, the evidence as submitted is insufficient to sustain a finding that defendant wilfully and intentionally indecently exposed himself. . . .

Reversed with directions to enter judgment discharging defendant.

PETERSON, JUSTICE (dissenting).

Because I think that the evidence was sufficient to justify a finding of intentional indecent exposure, I dissent.

There is no dispute concerning certain facts such as those that defendant was nude in the room in question under such circumstances as to be visible through the windows to casual passers-by on the sidewalk outside; that the room is on the first floor at the northwest corner of the building; that there is a window on the north side opening onto the street lying to the north; that there is a window on the west side opening onto the sidewalk; that the bottom sills of the windows are only knee-high from the floor. . . .

The majority holding simply amounts to saying that it is lawful for a man to stand nude in front of a window knowing that passers-by will see him. I cannot subscribe to such a doctrine, because I think it is not the law.

Notes and Questions

1. Framing the Debate. Precisely what does the *Peery* court find lacking to support the defendant's conviction? Does the argument concerning "intention" focus on whether Peery acted purposefully or knowingly? Or does the debate between the majority and the dissent concern what is often referred to as "specific" intent, what might be called the "extra-special" mental element of certain crimes—in this case, an intent to be lewd? Compare the Model Penal Code's definition of indecent exposure, which appears in § 213.5. (Incidentally, Peery's defense team included Warren Burger, who later became Chief Justice of the United States Supreme Court.)

Similar issues arose in *People v. Tombs*, 697 N.W.2d 494, 497 (Mich. 2005), where the defendant was convicted of "distribut[ing] or promot[ing] . . . child sexually abusive material," knowing or having reason to know that "the sexually abusive material included or appeared to include a child." The charges arose after Tombs returned a laptop computer that belonged to his employer and sexually abusive images of a child which had apparently been downloaded from the Internet were found on the computer. Noting that the words "distribute" and "promote" "contemplate knowing, intentional conduct on the part of the accused," the state supreme court interpreted the statute to require proof that Tombs "distributed or promoted child sexually abusive material with criminal intent." *Id.* at 500, 504. The court reversed the conviction, finding insufficient evidence of "criminal intent":

> There is evidence that defendant intended to distribute the laptop to Comcast, but there is no evidence of a criminal intent on his part to distribute

> child sexually abusive material. In fact, all the evidence points to the con-
> trary conclusion, that defendant did not distribute the material with a
> criminal intent. He returned the laptop to his former employer as required
> and with the expectation that his former employer would not search for
> and find the child sexually abusive material. This is further supported by
> the fact that the material was hidden in subfolders seven directory levels
> down.

Id. at 501 n.8. "Obviously, if defendant distributed the material not intending anybody to discover or view it," the court concluded, "he did not distribute it with a
criminal intent." *Id.* at 502.

Writing separately, one justice thought that Tombs had the requisite mens rea
because he "deliberately returned the computer to Comcast, knowing that it contained child sexually abusive material." *Id.* at 508 (Corrigan, J., concurring in part
and dissenting in part). Justice Corrigan criticized the majority's decision to impose
a "heightened mens rea element" unsupported by the statutory language by requiring that a defendant must "specifically intend his or her recipient to 'discover or view'
the prurient material in order to 'distribute'" it. *Id.* at 508, 509.

2. General and Specific Intent. Before the drafting of the Model Penal Code, and
in the jurisdictions where it has not been adopted, courts have commonly distinguished between "general" intent crimes and "specific" intent crimes. Throughout the
history of criminal law, various definitions of "specific" and "general" intent have
risen and fallen. At early common law, when mens rea meant only that the defendant must have had a generally "wicked" state of mind, "specific" intent denoted any
specific mental element required to commit a particular crime. Any crime that contained a particular state-of-mind requirement was classified as a specific intent crime,
whereas a crime that required only proof of general wickedness or blameworthiness
was a general intent crime.

Today, however, nearly all modern statutory crimes explicitly require a specific mental state as an essential element. As a result, the common-law concept of
"specific" intent has lost much of its power to meaningfully distinguish between
crimes.

Nevertheless, courts that continue to rely on this dichotomy define "specific" intent
crimes as those that require evidence of an extra-special mental element *in addition
to* proof that the defendant had a particular state of mind when committing the acts
constituting the crime. By contrast, "general" intent crimes merely require proof of
a particular state of mind accompanying the acts constituting the crime. *See, e.g.,*
Wayne R. LaFave, Criminal Law § 5.2(e), at 268–70 (5th ed. 2010). For specific
intent crimes, the extra-special mental state may pertain to: (1) an intent to commit
some other act in the future, (2) a special motive or purpose for committing the
crime, or (3) an awareness of a special attendant circumstance surrounding the criminal act. *See* Joshua Dressler, Understanding Criminal Law § 10.06, at 139 (7th
ed. 2015).

For example, consider the following crimes:

(a) Common-Law Burglary. Burglary is universally considered a specific intent crime. In addition to intentionally breaking and entering into a building, the actor must have done so with the "extra-special" intent to commit a felony therein.

(b) Common-Law Larceny. Larceny is likewise a specific intent crime. The actor must not only "intentionally" commit the acts of taking and carrying away the property of another, but must also act with the "extra-special" intent to permanently deprive the owner of that property.

(c) Receipt of Stolen Goods. The crime of "receiving stolen property, knowing that it is stolen" is considered a specific intent crime because it requires proof that the defendant was aware of the attendant circumstance that the property was "stolen."

(d) Battery. Battery, on the other hand, is usually considered to be a general intent crime. The prosecution must prove that the defendant intentionally or recklessly inflicted physical injury on another person, or touched that person in an offensive manner, but no further mental state is required.

3. Questioning the Distinction. Do the definitions of specific intent and general intent set out above adequately distinguish levels of culpability on a principled basis? Consider *People v. Hood*, 462 P.2d 370, 377–78 (Cal. 1969):

Specific and general intent have been notoriously difficult terms to define and apply, and a number of text writers recommend that they be abandoned altogether. Too often the characterization as one of specific or general intent is determined solely by the presence or absence of words describing particular psychological phenomena—"intent" or "malice," for example—in the statutory language defining the crime. When the definition of a crime consists of only the description of a particular act, without reference to intent to do a further act or achieve a future consequence, we ask whether the defendant intended to do the proscribed act. This intention is deemed to be general intent. When the definition refers to the defendant's intent to do some further act or achieve some additional consequence, the crime is deemed to be one of specific intent. There is no real difference, however, only a linguistic one, between an intent to do an act already performed and an intent to do that same act in the future.

Despite the California Supreme Court's criticism of the distinction between specific and general intent, the court continues to utilize the terms. *See* Note 2 in Section C.3 below.

4. General and Specific Intent and the Model Penal Code. As noted above, the Model Penal Code's culpability provision was a response to the analytically confused distinctions evolving from common-law notions of mens rea, including the distinction between general and specific intent. The Code's culpability provisions, which omit any reference to specific and general intent, have been adopted in some form by more than 30 states. *See* Ronald L. Gainer, *The Culpability Provisions of the Model Penal Code*, 19 RUTGERS L.J. 575, 586 (1988). In some states, however, traditional notions of specific and general intent are still relevant in cases raising mistake or intoxication defenses. (These defenses are discussed in Section C below.)

5. Specific Intent and Sentencing. A defendant's specific intent may also have an impact at sentencing. For example, in *Wisconsin v. Mitchell*, 508 U.S. 476 (1993), the Supreme Court upheld the constitutionality of a Wisconsin statute that provided for an enhanced sentence in cases where a defendant intentionally selected a victim based on race. This provision in effect imposed a longer sentence because of the specific intent the defendant possessed at the time of the crime. If the defendant was motivated by a desire to victimize certain individuals because of their race, the existence of this extra-special mental element increased the defendant's sentence.

In *Apprendi v. New Jersey*, 530 U.S. 466, 490 (2000), however, the Supreme Court, by a five-to-four margin, struck down the New Jersey hate crime statute as violative of the constitutional mandate that any fact "[o]ther than the fact of a prior conviction . . . that increases the penalty for a crime beyond the prescribed statutory maximum must be submitted to a jury, and proved beyond a reasonable doubt." For further discussion of *Apprendi* and the line of cases following it, see Chapter 2, Section D.2.b.

6. Transferred Intent. Unlike the law governing some intentional torts, the criminal law is generally unwilling to impose liability by "transferring intent" from one crime to another. (This concept might better be described as "transformed" intent; the common law simply does not allow one type of criminal intent to be "transformed" into another.) In *The Queen v. Faulkner*, 13 Cox Crim. Cas. 550 (1877), for example, a sailor went into the ship's hold intending to steal some rum. When he lit a match to enable him to see, he accidentally ignited the rum, causing a fire that destroyed the ship. Following early common-law notions of mens rea, the trial court thought the sailor had the necessary mens rea for arson because he had been engaged in a wicked act—stealing—at the time the fire started. On appeal, the conviction was reversed, reflecting the modern view that an intent to steal cannot be translated into the intent to start a fire required for an arson conviction.

Suppose *A* enters a store and attempts to steal a magazine. In so doing, she accidentally knocks the magazine rack over onto *B*, injuring him. Can *A*'s intent to steal be transferred to battery? No, but she might be guilty of battery based upon her recklessness or negligence in injuring *B*. *See* WAYNE R. LAFAVE, CRIMINAL LAW § 5.2(c), at 264–66 (5th ed. 2010).

Although generally disfavored in criminal cases, a concept of transferred intent does apply in cases of felony murder and misdemeanor manslaughter (as described in Chapter 6, Section D). In addition, the criminal law is willing to "transfer intent" from one victim to another. Thus, if *A* intends to kill *B*, and fires a shot that misses and kills *C* instead, *A* is still guilty of murder.

7. Mens Rea Issues in Corporate Criminal Trials: *Arthur Andersen v. United States.* Proof of a specific criminal intent is often the critical element in white-collar corporate corruption and fraud cases. For example, in 2005 the Supreme Court unanimously reversed the criminal conviction of accounting firm Arthur Andersen for destroying documents related to the bankruptcy of the energy giant Enron, on the grounds that the trial court's jury instructions "simply failed to convey the requisite consciousness of wrongdoing." *Arthur Andersen LLP v. United States*, 544 U.S. 696 (2005).

The government prosecuted Andersen in 2002 under the Victim and Witness Protection Act, 18 U.S.C. § 1512, which made it a crime to "knowingly . . . corruptly persuad[e] another person . . . with intent to . . . cause or induce" that person to withhold or alter documents for use in an official proceeding. The case focused on memos from Andersen's in-house counsel that advised the firm to follow its usual document-destruction policies regarding information related to Enron, even as investigations by the Securities and Exchange Commission loomed. The trial judge instructed the jury that Andersen could be found guilty "even if [it] honestly and sincerely believed that its conduct was lawful."

The Supreme Court's opinion, written by Chief Justice Rehnquist, strongly rejected that approach, saying, "Indeed, it is striking how little culpability the instructions required." Noting that the term "corruptly" is "normally associated with wrongful, immoral, depraved, or evil," the Court interpreted the statutory phrase "knowingly . . . corruptly persuad[e]" to require proof that Andersen destroyed the documents with "consciousness of wrongdoing." Just destroying documents as part of a normal business practice that resulted in impeding an investigation would not be enough. But the Court stopped short of endorsing Andersen's conduct, and it left unresolved what types of document-destruction policies would fall within the reach of the statute. (The Court also held that the government must show a nexus between the destruction of documents and an impending investigation.)

The Supreme Court's ruling did little to help the once high flying Andersen, which ceased to exist after it lost its licenses to practice amid the indictment and Enron fallout. The long-term impact of the decision will be harder to measure because the Court was interpreting an earlier law that was substantially replaced in 2002 by the Sarbanes-Oxley corporate reform law, which expanded and clarified the criminal penalties for obstructing or interfering with investigations by destroying documents. (Sarbanes-Oxley is described above in Chapter 1, Section B.2.a.)

8. Indecent Exposure Revisited. Questions surround even modern versions of the indecent exposure statute at issue in *Peery*. Consider *State v. Beine*, 162 S.W.3d 483 (Mo. 2005), a case involving an elementary-school counselor who was prosecuted for sexual misconduct involving a child, under the portion of the state statute that criminalizes "[k]nowingly expos[ing] the person's genitals to a child less than fourteen years of age in a manner that would cause a reasonable adult to believe that the conduct is likely to cause affront or alarm to a child less than fourteen years of age." Mo. Rev. Stat. § 566.083.1(1). At trial, two students testified that Beine stood three to four feet away from the urinal in a school bathroom, which enabled them to see his penis. On another occasion, the younger brother of one of those students said Beine turned from the urinal he was using with his pants unzipped and penis exposed to tell some students to "shut up" before turning back and zipping up his pants.

A majority of the Missouri Supreme Court found the statute "patently unconstitutional" because it "leaves adults in a state of uncertainty about how they may take care of their biological needs without danger of prosecution when a child is present in the same public restrooms." Moreover, the court noted that Beine's conduct was "constitutionally protected," given that the prosecution's evidence showed only that he "used a public restroom while boys were present and stood at a little further distance from the urinal than men usually do, and that [he] accidentally turned around without zipping his pants zipper up to discipline some boys that were causing a disturbance in the restroom."

The dissent, by contrast, thought there was no constitutional error because the mens rea term "knowingly" applied to the entire provision, which "informed Mr. Beine that he cannot expose himself in a manner that he knows is likely to cause deliberate offense or a feeling of danger." The majority responded that it was unwilling to "rewrite" the statute by "add[ing] a word that the legislature did not see fit to include." Does the majority misinterpret the statute? Or does the statute as written risk criminalizing innocent conduct?

Consider also the prosecution of Erick Williamson, a 29-year-old Northern Virginia man who was home alone one morning after his roommates left for work. He was making coffee in the nude when a neighbor who was walking her seven-year-old son to school saw Williamson in the house. According to Williamson, he did not realize the woman and her son were there until police appeared at his door later that morning and arrested him at gunpoint on indecent exposure charges. But the woman (a police officer's wife) said that Williamson had exposed himself to her at two different windows in the house, and police thought he was trying to attract attention to himself. The Virginia statutes define indecent exposure as "intentionally mak[ing] an obscene display or exposure of [one's] person, or the private parts thereof, in any public place, or in any place where others are present." Va. Code. Ann. § 18.2-387.

When a second witness testified that she too had seen Williamson standing naked in his home several hours earlier on the same day, a judge convicted him, concluding that "the fact that it went on for so long indicates an obscene display." Williamson challenged the judge's decision in a *de novo* appeal, however, and was tried by a jury. The jury voted to acquit him after deliberating for 20 minutes. *See* Tom Jackman, *Jury Finds 'Naked Guy' Was Clearly Innocent*, WASH. POST, Apr. 8, 2010, at B4.

[2] The Model Penal Code

United States v. Villegas

784 F. Supp. 6 (E.D.N.Y. 1991), *reversed on other grounds*,
3 F.3d 643 (2d Cir. 1993)

KORMAN, DISTRICT JUDGE.

On May 26, 1988, a teacher at the Saint John's Lutheran School took her eighth grade class on a field trip to the Alice Austin House, a museum on Staten Island that overlooks Pebble Beach on the Hudson River. While playing on the beach after touring the museum, the students came upon numerous glass vials containing what appeared to be human blood lying in the sand. The New York City Sanitation Department later collected approximately seventy of these vials scattered along the shoreline and floating in the incoming tide. The broken remains of others were found among clusters of rocks in the shallow water. Tests later revealed that five of the vials contained blood infected with hepatitis B, an infectious virus that causes inflammation of the liver and can lead to chronic illness, including cancer, or to death. [These vials formed the basis for Counts Three and Four of the indictment against Villegas.]

Four months later, a maintenance employee at the Admirals Walk Condominium Association (Admirals Walk), an apartment complex bordering the Hudson River in Edgewater, New Jersey, noticed a plastic bag full of blood vials wedged into the rocks of the river bulkhead. Edgewater Police Officers eventually collected at least one hundred vials floating loosely in the river or packed in containers wedged into the bulkhead. Fifty-five of these vials were tested for disease and at least five were found to be infected with hepatitis B. [These vials formed the basis for Counts One and Two of the indictment.]

State investigators traced the vials by the identifying information on their labels to Plaza Health Laboratories, a facility that tests blood for disease and other medical conditions in Brooklyn, New York. The defendant, Geronimo Villegas, was co-owner of Plaza and lived at the Admirals Walk complex when the vials were found. When questioned by state investigators, Mr. Villegas admitted to placing vials in the bulkhead in June, 1988 to make room in his laboratory for incoming blood samples. Although he did not admit to hiding vials there on an earlier occasion, expert evidence on tides and currents established that the vials found in Staten Island could also have originated from the Admirals Walk bulkhead.

On January 31, 1991, a jury found Mr. Villegas guilty of four counts charging violations of the Clean Water Act (33 U.S.C. § 1319). [Counts Two and Four] are premised on the allegation that the defendant knowingly discharged pollutants into navigable waters from a "point source," a term of art established and defined by the Clean Water Act. *See* 33 U.S.C. § 1362(14). [Counts One and Three] are premised on the so-called "knowing endangerment" provision of this statute that imposes substantially enhanced penalties on polluters who knowingly place others "in imminent danger of death or serious bodily injury." 33 U.S.C. § 1319(c)(3).

In a post-trial motion pursuant to Fed. R. Crim. P. 29(c), Mr. Villegas challenges the sufficiency of the evidence supporting [his conviction]. . . .

The defendant . . . argues that even if he is guilty of discharging pollutants from a "point source," the evidence is insufficient to support his convictions on Counts One and Three of the indictment. These counts charge violations of the knowing endangerment provision of the Clean Water Act that reads as follows:

> Any person who knowingly violates section 1311 . . . of this title [which pro-
> hibits the unauthorized discharge of pollutants], . . . and who knows at that
> time that he thereby places another person in imminent danger of death or
> serious bodily injury, shall, upon conviction, be subject to a fine of not more
> than $250,000 or imprisonment of not more than 15 years, or both.

33 U.S.C. § 1319(c)(3)(A). Under this section, the United States Attorney must prove that the defendant discharged pollutants from a point source, and that in doing so, he knew he was placing another person in imminent danger of death or bodily injury. The defendant argues that there is insufficient evidence to prove that when he placed the vials in the Hudson River he knew that he was thereby placing another person in "imminent danger of death or serious bodily injury."

Under the Clean Water Act's knowing endangerment provision, a person acts with the requisite degree of knowledge if he possesses "actual awareness" or an "actual belief" that he is placing another person in imminent danger. 33 U.S.C. § 1319(c)(3)(B). Circumstantial evidence may be used to prove either mental state. *Id.* . . .

The Senate Environment and Public Works Committee emphasized the deliberate omission from § 1319(c)(3) of the definition of knowledge found in an analogous pro- vision in the Resource Conservation and Recovery Act (RCRA). Under the RCRA, "a person's state of mind is knowing with respect to a result of his conduct, if he is aware or believes that his conduct is *substantially certain* to cause danger of death or serious bodily injury." 42 U.S.C. § 6928(f)(1)(C). According to the Senate Report, this lan- guage was left out of the Clean Water Act because it tended to "discourage prosecu- tions." Instead, the Senate Committee intended that knowledge in the knowing endangerment provision of the Clean Water Act be "measured against the standard established by prevailing case law, as it is for any other Federal crime sharing the same state of mind element."

The omission in the Clean Water Act of the RCRA's "substantial certainty" lan- guage, combined with the reference in the legislative history to the "standard estab- lished by prevailing case law," leaves unclear precisely what evidence is necessary to sustain a conviction under 33 U.S.C. § 1319(c)(3). There does not appear to be any "prevailing [federal] case law," defining knowledge in this particular context. The Model Penal Code, the culpability standards of which have been adopted or used as a guide in numerous jurisdictions, provides that when knowledge of the result of one's conduct is an element of an offense, such knowledge is established if a person "is aware that it is *practically certain* that his conduct will cause such a result." Model Penal Code § 2.02(2)(b)(ii) (1962). . . .

Although the "substantially/practically certain" standard appears to be the predominant definition of knowledge with respect to the result of conduct, some states have opted for a "high probability" standard. In Montana, for example, the criminal code defines knowledge with respect to the result of conduct as being "aware that it is *highly probable* that such result will be caused" by the conduct. Mont. Code Ann. § 45-2-101(33) (1990). A similar definition was adopted in *Armour v. State of Indiana*, 479 N.E.2d 1294 (Ind. 1985), which involved the application of a child neglect statute that made it a crime to knowingly put a "dependent in a situation that may endanger his life or health." The Supreme Court of Indiana held that a defendant could be found guilty of violating the statute only if he was "subjectively aware of a *high probability* that he placed the dependent in a dangerous situation."

Significantly, the "high probability" standard also tracks the language of the Model Penal Code as it defines knowledge of a fact inferred from a person's conscious avoidance of that fact. The Code states that "when knowledge of the existence of a particular fact is an element of an offense, such knowledge is established if a person is aware of a *high probability* of its existence, unless he actually believes it does not exist." Model Penal Code § 2.02(7) (1962). The Supreme Court has expressly approved this language, *see Leary v. United States*, 395 U.S. 6, 46 n.93 (1969),[1] and it has been consistently accepted by the Court of Appeals for the Second Circuit.

The "high probability" standard provides a viable alternative to the "substantial certainty" test that Congress apparently rejected when enacting the Clean Water Act's knowing endangerment provision. It allows for conviction on proof less than knowledge of a substantial certainty of imminent danger, while also setting a sufficiently rigorous standard to justify the stiff criminal penalties that attach pursuant to § 1319(c)(3). . . .

The United States Attorney offered three sources of testimony on the element of the defendant's knowledge. Elena Ramos, a former data entry employee at Plaza, testified that Mr. Villegas had worked in two laboratories that handled blood before becoming co-owner and vice-president of marketing at Plaza. She also testified that Mr. Villegas handled blood samples regularly and took precautions when doing so. Shahid Mustaquim, a former medical technologist at Plaza, testified that between 35–50% of the blood specimens brought there were tested for hepatitis. He further stated that Plaza has set aside a separate area and a separate machine for hepatitis testing. Dr. Sashikale Krishnan, former director of pathology at Plaza, confirmed that

---

1. The defendant in that case, Dr. Timothy Leary, was convicted of "knowingly . . . facilitat[ing] the transportation [or] concealment . . . of . . . marihuana [that had been illegally imported into the country], knowing the same to have been imported . . . contrary to law." In dictum, the Supreme Court observed that the legislative history of that statute shed no light on the meaning of the word "knowingly," and the Court therefore "employed as a general guide" the "high probability" standard contained in § 2.02(7) of the Model Penal Code. 395 U.S. at 46 n.93.

Plaza conducted a great deal of testing for diseases like hepatitis and leukemia. He also stated that Mr. Villegas was one of two people in charge of Plaza, that he co-authored the laboratory's safety manual, which included guidelines for handling blood, and that these guidelines were followed by Plaza employees.

This evidence is sufficient to support a jury finding that the defendant acted with knowledge of the dangers of hepatitis, and that some of the discharged vials contained hepatitis-infected blood. The evidence, however, does not support the conclusion that when he placed the vials in the Hudson River, Mr. Villegas knew there was a high probability that he was thereby placing another person in imminent danger of death or serious bodily injury. Of particular significance is the testimony of Dr. Alfred M. Prince, an expert in virology called by the United States Attorney. Dr. Prince suggested that the principal risk of hepatitis infection as a result of exposure to a vial of contaminated blood would arise "if that vial is broken and if a piece of broken glass were to penetrate the skin." While Dr. Prince testified that the likelihood of contamination in those circumstances was "very high," he also testified that the risk of this happening was "low":

> The Court: Doctor, if three or four or five vials like—of the kinds we have been talking about were dropped in the Hudson River, would you say that that would place any person in imminent danger of death or serious bodily injury?
>
> Dr. Prince: If those vials were to land on the shore and someone were to step on them and puncture their skin, they would be in danger of infection, hepatitis B, yes. Those vials that were infected, of course. They all were not.
>
> The Court: Of course, one would have to know that that was going to happen. Or sooner or later everything floats to shore?
>
> Dr. Prince: The risk of this happening is low but it is a risk.

This testimony was elicited outside the presence of the jury, and the defendant's trial counsel declined an invitation to have it repeated to the jury.[2] Nevertheless, the testimony does suggest the need for caution in inferring that the defendant must have known that he was placing another person in imminent danger of death or serious bodily injury merely because he knew that the vials contained a dangerous virus. Yet this is essentially the theory underlying the prosecution's case. The Assistant United States Attorneys trying the case argued that "from the evidence regarding the currents and tides the jury could infer that the defendant knew or should have known that . . . anything thrown into [the] waters would be swept out into the sea and eventually be lodged on a beach," and that the defendant "knew that people walked on the rocks [at] Edgewater." Consequently, they argued, the defendant should have been aware of the risk to those who walk along Hudson River beaches or climb on the Admirals Walk bulkhead.

---

2. [n.6] Wayne Pizzuti, another prosecution expert, testified in the presence of the jury that it was also unlikely that a person swimming in the area where a vial had broken would contract hepatitis B.

There was, however, no evidence introduced at trial showing that the defendant knew "that people walked on the rocks [at] Edgewater" where the vials were hidden, or that such activity even occurs. Moreover, there was no evidence introduced that showed the defendant's knowledge of the tides and, specifically, that the vials would be swept out into the sea and eventually wash ashore in an area where they could cause the kind of injury Dr. Prince described.[3] Indeed, if Dr. Prince, an expert in virology who has a more sophisticated understanding of these matters than Mr. Villegas, viewed the danger of such serious bodily injury or death as remote, it is hard to know why Mr. Villegas should have known it to be highly probable or even likely.

There is no doubt that the defendant's conduct was irresponsible and that it had the potential to cause serious bodily injury. These factors may provide a basis for an upward adjustment of the [sentencing] guideline range applicable to the offense of discharging pollutants into the water. The evidence, however, is insufficient to justify the enhanced penalties provided for cases where a polluter knows that there is a high probability that he is placing another person in imminent danger of death or serious bodily injury.[4]

Notes and Questions

1. Distinguishing Knowledge from Purpose and Recklessness. Ordinarily the legislature determines what level of culpability must be established to prove the violation of a particular criminal statute. When a statute is silent or ambiguous, the courts must construe the legislature's intent.

As a general rule, defendants act purposefully when they act with the conscious objective of causing a particular result. *See, e.g.,* Model Penal Code § 2.02(2)(a). Acting knowingly generally means that defendants are subjectively aware that there is a substantial certainty (or in the case of the Model Penal Code, a "practical certainty") that

---

3. Note, however, that in n.3 of the opinion, the court rejected Villegas' argument that "the containers and vials found at the Admirals Walk bulkhead in September, 1988, cannot provide the basis for a conviction because the point in the bulkhead at which they were found is above the normal high tide line." The court explained:

> There was sufficient evidence . . . for the jury to conclude that the defendant knew that the vials would ultimately be washed into the water. Moreover, even if valid, this argument would affect only Counts One and Two. There is no evidence as to precisely how the vials that washed ashore on Staten Island in May, 1988 were discharged into the Hudson River. Under these circumstances, the jury could infer that the vials were either placed directly in the water or in the bulkhead below the normal high tide line. Because the defendant's sentence will be the same whether or not the convictions on Counts One and Two stand, there is no need to address the validity of the defendant's argument on this point.

4. The trial court sentenced Villegas on the remaining two counts to one year in prison and one year of supervised release. On appeal, however, the convictions on these two counts were reversed on the ground that Villegas had not discharged the vials from a "point source" in the sense in which that term is used in the Clean Water Act. *See United States v. Plaza Health Laboratories, Inc.,* 3 F.3d 643 (2d Cir. 1993). In addition, separate criminal charges that had been brought against Plaza Health Laboratories were dismissed when it went bankrupt.

their actions will cause a particular result. *Id.* § 2.02(2)(b). As *Villegas* indicates, however, "knowledge" may be established in some jurisdictions if defendants are merely aware that it is "highly probable" their conduct will cause a particular result. Recklessness, by contrast, is generally defined as the conscious disregard of a substantial and unjustifiable risk that a material element of the crime will result. *Id.* § 2.02(2)(c).

According to the trial judge, Villegas did not "knowingly" place anyone in imminent danger of death or serious bodily harm. Do you agree with the court's assessment? The court's adoption of the "high probability" test in lieu of the "substantial certainty/practical certainty" test proved to be insignificant to the outcome of the case. Nevertheless, adoption of a lower threshold for establishing "knowledge" could have powerful ramifications in other cases.

Do you find the court's arguments convincing? Does the court blur the distinction between knowledge and recklessness, or is there a good argument for expanding the concept of "knowledge"? For empirical research suggesting that jurors may have difficulty identifying and distinguishing between the Model Penal Code's definitions of knowledge and recklessness, see Matthew R. Ginther et al., *The Language of Mens Rea*, 67 Vand. L. Rev. 1327 (2014); Francis X. Shen et al., *Sorting Guilty Minds*, 86 N.Y.U. L. Rev. 1306 (2011).

2. Deliberate Ignorance as Knowledge. Suppose a stranger offers to pay a traveler a large sum of money for carrying a suitcase from one city to another. Fearful of discovering illegal drugs, the traveler chooses not to open the suitcase to examine its contents. If it turns out that the suitcase does in fact contain illegal drugs and the traveler is charged with the crime of knowingly transporting a controlled substance, does the absence of actual knowledge of the contents of the suitcase allow the traveler to escape conviction?

A number of federal courts have held that a mens rea of "knowledge" can be demonstrated in such "ostrich" cases. According to these courts, the defendant acted knowingly if she was aware of a high probability that a certain fact existed but deliberately avoided finding out for sure in order to escape criminal liability — unless she actually believed that the fact did not exist. *See United States v. Jewell*, 532 F.2d 697 (9th Cir.) (en banc), *cert. denied*, 426 U.S. 951 (1976); Ira P. Robbins, *The Ostrich Instruction: Deliberate Ignorance as a Criminal Mens Rea*, 81 J. Crim. L. & Criminology 191, 192–93 (1990). *See also Global-Tech Appliances, Inc. v. SEB S.A.*, 563 U.S. 754, 766–70 (2011).

Critical of this line of reasoning, Ira Robbins argues that these cases more closely resemble "recklessness" than "knowledge." According to Robbins, treating deliberate ignorance as "knowledge" risks imposing liability based on a defendant's reckless failure to ascertain certain facts, thereby leading to findings of guilt even when the knowledge required by a criminal statute is not actually proven. In order to alleviate this problem, Robbins offers the following suggestion:

> [S]tatutory revision, specifically the addition of recklessness or specific
> deliberate-ignorance provisions as an alternative basis for conviction, would

correct these abuses and limit the deliberate-ignorance defense. A recklessness standard will retain the subjective component of knowledge and will reach those defendants who consciously disregard a substantial risk that a particular fact exists. Statutory identification of the culpable mental state as recklessness or willful blindness, rather than knowledge, will also ensure that the defendant is convicted of the crime charged, instead of a judicially created alternative. Additionally, clarification of the mens rea requirement will produce more precise jury instructions, thus limiting the risk of conviction for negligence.

Robbins, *supra*, at 195–96. By contrast, the Ninth Circuit has explained that "deliberate ignorance" is a *definition* of "knowledge," not a substitute for it. *See United States v. Jewell*, 532 F.2d at 703–04.

3. The Model Penal Code and the "Ostrich" Defense. The Model Penal Code agrees with those courts that have been willing to infer knowledge in "ostrich" cases where defendants act with willful blindness or deliberate ignorance. Section 2.02(7) of the Code provides that "[w]hen knowledge of the existence of a particular fact is an element of an offense, such knowledge is established if a person is aware of a high probability of its existence, unless he actually believes that it does not exist." The Comments describe this subsection as follows:

Subsection (7) deals with the situation that British commentators have denominated "wilful blindness" or "connivance," the case of the actor who is aware of the probable existence of a material fact but does not determine whether it exists or does not exist. Whether such cases should be viewed as instances of acting recklessly or knowingly presents a subtle but important question.

The Code proposes that the case be viewed as one of acting knowingly when what is involved is a matter of existing fact, but not when what is involved is the result of the defendant's conduct, necessarily a matter of the future at the time of acting. [This] position reflects what was believed to be the normal policy of criminal enactments that rest liability on acting "knowingly." The inference of "knowledge" of an existing fact is usually drawn from proof of notice of high probability of its existence, unless the defendant establishes an honest, contrary belief. Subsection (7) solidifies this usual result. . . .

Model Penal Code § 2.02 Comment at 248. Would the Model Penal Code have applied § 2.02(7)'s "high probability" standard to the crime at issue in *Villegas*—knowingly placing others in imminent danger of death or serious bodily injury—or would it have required awareness of a "practical certainty" under § 2.02(2)(b)(ii)?

4. Distinguishing Motive from Intent. Defendants' motives, or overarching reasons for acting in a particular way, must be distinguished from their intent. As the court explained in *State v. Santino*, 186 S.W. 976, 977 (Mo. 1916), "[m]otive is the moving cause which induces action; it has to do wholly with desire. Intent is the purpose or design with which an act is done, and involves the will." The criminal law generally condemns only acts, not bad motives (such as avarice or revenge), and a good motive by itself is not a defense to criminal charges. *E.g.*, *United States v. Pomponio*, 429 U.S. 10 (1976) (per curiam) (criminal tax violations). Defendants may have had a good reason for acting in violation of the criminal laws, but the prosecution can still prove they had the requisite mens rea — even knowledge or purpose — by showing that they knew what they were doing or that it was their purpose to act in the way they did. Motive may be helpful in establishing a recognized defense, like self-defense, necessity, or duress (which are addressed in Chapters 14 and 15), and a good motive may be considered in mitigation of punishment. But good motive does not normally negate mens rea. *See* Wayne R. LaFave, Criminal Law § 5.3, at 272–76 (5th ed. 2010).

In *United States v. Berrigan*, 283 F. Supp. 336 (D. Md. 1968), for example, three defendants were charged with willfully damaging federal property when they burned their draft cards in protest of the Vietnam War. The district court rejected the argument that the defendants' conduct was prompted by their belief that the United States was acting both illegally and immorally by engaging in the war in Vietnam and, therefore, that they lacked the mens rea to commit the crime. Highlighting the distinction between motive and intent, the court wrote, "in law once the commission of a crime is established — the doing of a prohibited act with the necessary intent — proof of a good motive will not save the accused from conviction." *Id.* at 338.

Claims of good motive are commonly made in cases where a defendant kills in order to relieve a loved one's suffering. In *People v. Roberts*, 178 N.W. 690 (Mich. 1920), for example, the defendant concocted a poisonous mixture and, at his wife's request, placed it near her so that she could ingest the poison and kill herself. Despite the fact that his wife was suffering from a painful and incurable illness that rendered her totally helpless, the defendant was convicted of first-degree murder and sentenced to life imprisonment. The Michigan Supreme Court affirmed the conviction.

Ironically, Michigan is the same state whose courts subsequently gained national attention by disallowing murder prosecutions in cases of physician-aided suicides. Until the Michigan legislature passed a bill in 1998 that permanently criminalized the intentional assistance of suicide, *see* Mich. Comp. Laws § 750.329a, efforts to prosecute Dr. Jack Kevorkian for helping a series of terminally ill patients commit suicide had failed. *See A Prosecutor Drops Kevorkian Charges*, N.Y. Times, Jan. 12, 1997, at A20. Ultimately, Kevorkian was convicted of second-degree murder, not assisted suicide, after he videotaped himself injecting a patient with lethal chemicals. *See* Pam Belluck, *Dr. Kevorkian Is a Murderer, the Jury Finds*, N.Y. Times, Mar. 27, 1999, at A1.

5. Distinguishing Recklessness from Negligence. The Model Penal Code does not limit criminal liability to those who act with purpose or knowledge, but also extends liability to those who act recklessly or negligently. Both "recklessness" and "negligence" under the Model Penal Code's formulation require proof that the actor created "a substantial and unjustifiable risk" that constitutes a "gross deviation" from the standard that an ordinary person would have exercised under the circumstances.

They differ in that recklessness requires evidence that the actor was aware of and consciously disregarded the risk, whereas criminal negligence exists even when the actor was not actually aware of the risk, so long as the actor should have been aware of it. *See* Model Penal Code §§ 2.02(2)(c)–(d). Hence, while both recklessness and negligence depend on the creation of an objectively unreasonable risk, recklessness requires a subjective awareness of that risk, and a decision to disregard it. *See* Jerome Hall, General Principles of Criminal Law 116 (2d ed. 1960); David Treiman, *Recklessness and the Model Penal Code*, 9 Am. J. Crim. L. 281, 299–300 (1981).

In adopting these definitions, the Model Penal Code sides with the majority position and rejects those cases that distinguish recklessness from negligence based merely upon the degree to which the defendant's conduct deviated from reasonable behavior. Under this alternative, minority approach, recklessness does not require proof of the defendant's conscious awareness of risk, but the conduct must be more unreasonable than would suffice for mere criminal negligence. *See* Joshua Dressler, Understanding Criminal Law § 10.04[3], at 135–36 (7th ed. 2015).

The Comments to the Model Penal Code describe the analytical steps the jury must take in order to make a finding of recklessness under the Code:

> Ultimately, . . . the jury is asked to perform two distinct functions. First, it is to examine the risk and the factors that are relevant to how substantial it was and to the justifications for taking it. In each instance, the question is asked from the point of view of the actor's perceptions, i.e., to what extent he was aware of risk, of factors relating to its unjustifiability. Second, the jury is to make the culpability judgment in terms of whether the defendant's conscious disregard of the risk justified condemnation. Considering the nature and purpose of his conduct and the circumstances known to him, the question is whether the defendant's disregard of the risk involved a gross deviation from the standards of conduct that a law-abiding person would have observed in the actor's situation.

Model Penal Code § 2.02 Comment at 238.

A finding of negligence, by contrast, can be made without evidence that defendants were subjectively aware of the risks associated with their behavior. According to one commentator, however, this does not mean that negligence involves "an entirely 'objective' inquiry":

> At bottom, negligence involves a judgment that, based on what the actor knew, he or she should have known something else and should therefore have known enough to have understood the obligation to act more carefully. In spite of its concentration on objective components, the baseline for negligence is the context as the actor perceived it. Negligence, therefore, involves a subjective inquiry (what the actor actually knew about the context) and an objective inquiry (the inferences that should have been drawn from what the actor knew).

Peter W. Low, *The Model Penal Code, the Common Law, and Mistakes of Fact: Reck-lessness, Negligence, or Strict Liability?*, 19 RUTGERS L.J. 539, 549 (1988).

In *Voisine v. United States*, 136 S. Ct. 386 (2016), the Supreme Court expressly adopted the Model Penal Code's definition of recklessness in defining the type of reckless assaults that trigger the federal statute banning anyone convicted of a "misdemeanor crime of domestic violence" from possessing a firearm. The Court characterized the Model Penal Code's mens rea definitions as the "dominant for-mulation" and described the common law as "us[ing] a variety of overlapping and, frankly, confusing phrases to describe culpable mental states." For the observation that the Court "has certainly invoked the MPC in the past" but that adopting its mens rea terms "so bluntly" and "without debate" in *Voisine* was "quite a significant step," see Rory Little, *Opinion Analysis: Federal "Use of Force" Encompasses Reckless Domestic Violence Misdemeanor Offenses*, SCOTUSBLOG (June 27, 2016, 9:08 PM), http://www.scotusblog.com/2016/06/opinion-analysis-federal-use-of-force-encom passes-reckless-domestic-violence-misdemeanor-offenses/.

6. Distinguishing Criminal Negligence from Civil Negligence. Criminal negli-gence is usually said to differ in degree from the type of negligence that gives rise to civil liability in tort, but the distinction can be difficult to perceive in practice. In *People v. Beckles*, 448 N.Y.S.2d 398 (N.Y. Sup. Ct. 1982), the defendant hit a man once with the back of his hand, thus fracturing the man's jaw, causing him to fall and strike his head, and ultimately leading to his death six days later. The court dismissed an indictment for criminally negligent homicide, noting that criminal, as opposed to civil, negligence requires proof that the defendant created a "substantial and unjustifiable" risk and that his "failure to perceive the risk is due to an unusual insensitivity to the potential con-sequences of his conduct." *Id.* at 399. The court then listed three significant factors to be considered in measuring the degree of negligence: the defendant's role in creating the risk, the proximity of the ultimate harm in relation to the defendant's acts, and the extent to which the immediate harm was predictable and apparent.

The distinction between civil and criminal negligence is critical in determining when a doctor's negligence in treating a patient should give rise to criminal liability. In *State v. Warden*, 813 P.2d 1146 (Utah 1991), a doctor was charged with negligent homicide based on his careless treatment of a mother and her baby, who was born prematurely and showed signs of respiratory distress syndrome. The doctor's negli-gence was deemed the legal cause of the infant's death, and he was convicted. In affirming the jury's verdict, the court wrote:

> [E]vidence of civil negligence is insufficient to convict a person of negligent homicide. In situations where it is alleged that a medical doctor was negli-gent in the treatment of a patient, that doctor may be held civilly liable if the evidence establishes that it is more likely than not that the doctor's treat-ment fell below the appropriate standard of care. In contrast, a doctor may be held criminally liable only when the evidence establishes beyond a rea-sonable doubt that the doctor's treatment created a substantial and unjusti-fiable risk that the patient would die, that the doctor should have but failed

to perceive this risk, and that the risk is of such a nature and degree that the failure to perceive it constitutes a gross deviation from that standard of care. Given the high showing required for negligent homicide, doctors' negligence in the treatment of patients will rarely precipitate criminal liability. It is also true, however, that if doctors act with criminal negligence, they should not escape criminal liability merely because the negligence occurred in a professional setting.

Id. at 1151. Is it possible to know whether jurors grasp the distinction between civil and criminal negligence? Can jury instructions adequately explain the difference and ensure that juries use the more demanding standard and do not convict doctors for ordinary negligence?

7. Should Criminal Negligence Be Abolished? The dissenting judge in *State v. Warden*, described in the previous Note, argued that "the criminal law should not be used to punish a physician for a death when he or she makes a decision that turns out to have a fatal consequence, simply because some other physician, acting in more favorable circumstances, would have done differently." 813 P.2d at 1156 (Stewart, J., dissenting). Indeed, is it ever fair to punish people who are doing their best, simply because they did not act like a reasonable person should have acted? Does the criminalization of negligence serve to inform or enculturate the community about certain standards of behavior?

Many scholars object to using negligence as a basis for criminal liability on the ground that criminal punishment serves no purpose, and no moral fault is involved, when defendants were not aware that they were doing anything wrong. For example, Professor Hall has strenuously criticized the Model Penal Code's inclusion of negligent behavior within the scope of penal liability, distinguishing between mere inadvertence on the one hand and what he terms "voluntary harm-doing" on the other. *See* Jerome Hall, Law, Social Science, and Criminal Theory 244–65 (1982).

The drafters of the Model Penal Code offered the following response to these concerns:

> No one has doubted that purpose, knowledge, and recklessness are properly the basis for criminal liability but some critics have opposed any penal consequences for negligent behavior. Since the actor is inadvertent by hypothesis, it has been argued that the "threat of punishment for negligence must pass him by, because he does not realize that it is addressed to him." So too, it has been urged that education or corrective treatment, not punishment, is the proper social method for dealing with persons with inadequate awareness, since what is implied is not a moral defect. This analysis, however, oversimplifies the issue. When people have knowledge that conviction and sentence, not to speak of punishment, may follow conduct that inadvertently creates improper risk, they are supplied with an additional motive to take care before acting, to use their faculties and draw on their experience in

gauging the potentialities of contemplated conduct. To some extent, at least, this motive may promote awareness and thus be effective as a measure of control. Moreover, moral defect can properly be imputed to instances where the defendant acts out of insensitivity to the interests of other people, and not merely out of an intellectual failure to grasp them. In any event legislators act on these assumptions in a host of situations, and it would be dogmatic to assert that they are wholly wrong. Accordingly, negligence, as here defined, should not be wholly rejected as a ground of culpability that may suffice for purposes of penal law. . . .

Model Penal Code § 2.02 Comment at 243 (quoting GLANVILLE L. WILLIAMS, CRIMINAL LAW: THE GENERAL PART 123 (2d ed. 1961)). Do the Comments adequately address Hall's concerns?

8. Mens Rea Default Rules. In an effort to aid courts interpreting mens rea requirements, the Model Penal Code creates two default rules. Section 2.02(3) prescribes recklessness as the default mens rea requirement if "the culpability sufficient to establish a material element of an offense is not prescribed." Section 2.02(4) then provides that when a criminal statute "prescribes the kind of culpability that is sufficient for the commission of an offense, without distinguishing among the material elements thereof," that culpability requirement is deemed to "apply to all the material elements of the offense, unless a contrary purpose plainly appears."

Some state legislatures have endorsed the MPC's default mens rea rules. *See, e.g.,* 18 Pa. Cons. Stat. §§ 302(c)–(d). Other states have adopted somewhat different rules. In *State v. Self*, 155 S.W.3d 756 (Mo. 2005), for example, the defendant was convicted of "failing to cause her child to attend school 'regularly,'" thus violating Missouri's compulsory school attendance law. While the statute did not set forth a culpable mental state, the Missouri Supreme Court interpreted it to require proof that Self acted either knowingly or purposefully in causing her child not to attend school regularly. In so holding, the court applied a Missouri statute that prescribes a mens rea of purpose or knowledge for criminal statutes lacking a mens rea requirement.

In states without such default rules, courts must use other tools of statutory interpretation in determining what mens rea a particular criminal statute requires.

RICHARD M. THOMPSON II, CONG. RESEARCH SERV., 7-5700, *MENS REA* REFORM: A BRIEF OVERVIEW (2016), https://www.fas.org/sgp/crs/misc/R44464.pdf

Currently there is debate in Congress over the appropriate default *mens rea* for federal statutes, including two contradicting legislative proposals. The report below describes the opposing perspectives:

. . . .

Criminal justice reform has played a major role in the congressional agenda over the past several Congresses, with sentencing reform bills making up the majority of the legislative action on this issue. However, some reformers have also highlighted the need to strengthen the *mens rea* requirements in federal law. . . . For instance, some laws require that the prosecution demonstrate that the defendant *intentionally* committed the act in question—that is, committing the act with the conscious desire for the harmful conduct to occur—while others require that the act be done *knowingly* or with *reckless disregard* of the harm it may pose. Some modern statutes require no *mens rea* at all; these are commonly referred to as strict liability offenses.

Unlike the Model Penal Code, which includes four categories of "culpability" or moral blameworthiness, the Federal Criminal Code, found largely in Title 18, does not create uniform *mens rea* standards. Instead, each statute may or may not contain a *mens rea* element depending on the statute. Supplementing the statutory text, the Supreme Court has developed a set of presumptions to apply when a *mens rea* term is omitted. However, the Court has applied these rules in a somewhat ad hoc fashion depending on a variety of factors, including the origin of the offense in question (e.g., common law or statutory); the severity of the penalty imposed; and the purpose behind the law (e.g., penal or regulatory).

In an effort to bring greater clarity to this area of criminal law, Senator Orrin Hatch and Representative James Sensenbrenner have introduced, respectively, the Mens Rea Reform Act of 2015 (S. 2298) and the Criminal Code Improvement Act of 2015 (H.R. 4002). Although they take different approaches, these bills aim to create a uniform *mens rea* standard across federal law. . . .

Some have argued that strengthening federal *mens rea* standards would permit corporate actors to evade prosecution under federal statutes aimed at protecting the health, safety, and welfare of the citizenry—including environmental and workplace laws. At the January 20 Senate Judiciary Committee hearing, Assistant Attorney General Leslie Caldwell argued that "[a]pplying a default mens rea to these statutes might insulate culpable individuals, especially senior corporate executives, who deliberately close their eyes to what otherwise would be obvious to them."

Proponents have countered that the bills are not designed to simply protect corporate wrongdoers, but are intended to ensure that persons are not prosecuted for a crime they did not intend to commit or know they were committing.

. . . .

Mens Rea Reform Act of 2015 (S. 2298)

The Mens Rea Reform Act of 2015, introduced by Senator Orrin Hatch, would provide as follows:

(b) DEFAULT REQUIREMENT.—Except as provided in subsections (c) and (d), a covered offense shall be construed to require the Government to prove beyond a reasonable doubt that the defendant acted—

(1) with the state of mind specified in the text of the covered offense for each element for which the text specifies a state of mind; and

(2) willfully, with respect to any element for which the text of the covered offense does not specify a state of mind.

(c) FAILURE TO DISTINGUISH AMONG ELEMENTS — Except as provided in subsection (d), if the text of a covered offense specifies the state of mind required for commission of the covered offense without specifying the elements of the covered offense to which the state of mind applies, the state of mind specified shall apply to all elements of the covered offense, unless a contrary purpose plainly appears.

(d) [Enumerated exceptions].

. . . .

Criminal Code Improvement Act of 2015 (H.R. 4002)

The Criminal Code Improvement Act of 2015, introduced by Representative James Sensenbrenner, would provide as follows:

§ 11. Default state of mind proof requirements in Federal criminal cases

If no state of mind is required by law for a Federal criminal offense —

(1) the state of mind the Government must prove is knowing; and

(2) if the offense consists of conduct that a reasonable person in the same or similar circumstances would not know, or would not have reason to believe, was unlawful, the Government must prove that the defendant knew, or had reason to believe, the conduct was unlawful.

. . . .

The Mens Rea Reform Act of 2015 (S. 2298) and the Criminal Code Improvement [Act] of 2015 (H.R. 4002) would create a set of default *mens rea* rules that would apply to offenses across the United States Code, largely supplanting *mens rea* presumptions employed by the courts. In some instances, these bills would raise the *mens rea* standard currently required by the law. For example, applying S. 2298 to the mail and wire fraud statutes would appear to require that the government prove the defendant committed the act with the heightened *mens rea* of "willfully," rather than "intentionally and knowingly" as is currently required. Likewise, applying both bills to a provision of the Federal Food, Drug, and Cosmetic Act that outlaws the introduction of adulterated or misbranded food or drugs into interstate commerce would modify this crime from a strict liability offense, in which the government need not prove any *mens rea*, to one in which the government would have to prove either knowledge (H.R. 4002) or willfulness (S. 2298).

. . . .

Conversely, the bills would arguably lower the *mens rea* standard necessary for a conviction under some criminal statutes. For example, applying H.R. 4002 to the mail and wire fraud statute would arguably lower the *mens rea* standard from knowingly and intentionally to simply knowingly engaging in the proscribed conduct. In many instances, however, the resulting construction would remain the same regardless of which bill's *mens rea* framework was employed. For instance, application of both bills to a provision of the Clean Air Act that prohibits persons from "negligently violating" the act would result in the same conclusion: the government would still have to prove that the offender negligently violated the statute.

Notes and Questions

1. Evaluating the Congressional Proposals. Note that default culpability standards come into play only when a statute fails to specify a mens rea. Which of the two bills described above is preferable? Or did the drafters of Model Penal Code § 2.02(3) have the right idea in choosing recklessness as the default mens rea? Do you agree with critics of the proposed legislation that these changes would inappropriately impede corporate prosecutions, or do you think they better protect all criminal defendants? (Neither bill was adopted by the 114th Congress, but many expect similar legislation to be reintroduced in 2017.)

2. Defining Willfulness. Is the Congressional Research Service right in thinking that replacing the mail and wire fraud statutes' requirement of proof that defendants acted "intentionally and knowingly" with a mens rea of willfulness could arguably be viewed as increasing the prosecution's mens rea burden? What does "willfully" require that "intentionally and knowingly" do not? Compare the Model Penal Code's definition of "willfulness" in § 2.02(8). For further discussion of the variety of meanings different courts have attached to the term "willfulness," see Notes 4–5 following *People v. Wendt* in Section C.2 below. Does this lack of consensus support the Model Penal Code's effort to promote uniform definitions of culpability levels?

For further discussion of the interpretive issues that arise when a criminal statute seemingly contains no mens rea requirement, see the discussion of strict liability in Chapter 5, Section A.

[C] Defenses Based on Mens Rea

[1] Mistake of Fact

Gordon v. State

52 Ala. 308 (1875)

BRICKELL, CHIEF JUSTICE.

This indictment is founded on the fortieth section of the statute, approved April 22, 1873, entitled "An act to regulate elections in the State of Alabama," which declares: "That any person voting more than once at any election held in this State, or depositing more than one ballot for the same office at such election, or [who] is guilty of any other kind of illegal or fraudulent voting, shall be deemed guilty of a felony." The [indictment] charges that the appellant, not being of the age of twenty-one years, voted at the last general election in this State. . . . Two witnesses were examined on the behalf of defendant; one, his mother, and the other an acquaintance who had known him from his birth and resided in the same neighborhood, and for a long time a member of the same family with defendant, and they testified the defendant was of the age of twenty-one years, in the August preceding the election. That they had frequently told defendant he would be of full age in that month, and subsequently and before the election told him he was of age. The court refused to charge the jury that if the defendant, in reliance on these statements, honestly believed he was of full age when he voted, he should not be convicted, if the evidence convinced the jury he was not of age.

"All crime exists, primarily, in the mind." A wrongful act and a wrongful intent must concur, to constitute what the law deems a crime. When an act denounced by the law is proved to have been committed, in the absence of countervailing evidence, the criminal intent is inferred from the commission of the act. The inference may be, and often is removed by the attending circumstances, showing the absence of a criminal intent. Ignorance of law is never an excuse, whether a party is charged civilly or criminally. Ignorance of fact may often be received to absolve a party from civil or criminal responsibility. On the presumption that every one capable of acting for himself knows the law, courts are compelled to proceed. If it should be abandoned, the administration of justice would be impossible, as every cause would be embarrassed with the collateral inquiry of the extent of legal knowledge of the parties seeking to enforce or avoid liability and responsibility.

The criminal intention being of the essence of crime, if the intent is dependent on a knowledge of particular facts, a want of such knowledge, not the result of carelessness or negligence, relieves the act of criminality. An illustration may be found in the vending of obscene or immoral publications. A knowledge of the character of such publications is an indispensable ingredient of the offence. From the vending it would be inferable; but if it appeared the vendor was blind, and in the course of his trade happened innocently to make the sale, a want of knowledge of the character of the publication would relieve him from criminal responsibility. A man having in his possession counterfeit coin, or forged bank bills, with intent to put them in circulation, could not be convicted of crime, if he was ignorant of their spuriousness. . . .

. . . Illegal voting, when it is supposed to arise from the want of legal qualifications, is dependent on the voter's knowledge of the particular facts which make up the qualification. Every man is bound to know the law requires that every voter shall be a native born or naturalized citizen of the United States, of the age of twenty-one years, and have resided in the State six months, and the county in which he offers to vote, three months next preceding the election, and must not have been convicted of the offences mentioned in the Constitution as the disqualification of an elector. He is bound to exercise reasonable diligence to ascertain the facts which enter into and form these qualifications. Having exercised this diligence, if he resided near the boundary line of a county, and should be informed by those having the means of knowledge that his residence was within the county, and he, without a knowledge of the real facts, honestly acting on this information, should vote, he could not fairly be charged with illegal voting, though on a subsequent survey, or on some other evidence, it should be ascertained his residence was not within the county. The precise time when a man arrives at the age of twenty-one years is a fact, knowledge of which he derives necessarily from his parents, or other relatives or acquaintances having knowledge of the time of his birth. If acting in good faith, on information fairly obtained from them under an honest belief that he had reached the age, he votes, having the other necessary qualifications, illegal voting should not be imputed to him. The intent which makes up the crime cannot be affirmed. Whether he had the belief that he was a qualified voter, and the information was fairly obtained, should be referred to, and determined by the jury. The whole inquiry should be directed to the voter's knowledge of facts, and to his diligence in acquiring the requisite knowledge. If he votes recklessly or carelessly, when the facts are doubtful or uncertain, his ignorance should not excuse him, if the real facts show he was not qualified. If ignorant of the disqualifying fact, and without a want of diligence, under an honest belief of his right to vote, he should be excused, though he had not the right.

The charge given by the circuit court, and several of the refusals to charge, were according to these views erroneous, and the judgment must be reversed, and the cause remanded. The appellant must remain in custody until discharged by due course of law.

Notes and Questions

1. Introduction. A mistake of fact is a defense if it negates the mens rea required to commit the crime. *See* WAYNE R. LaFAVE, CRIMINAL LAW § 5.6(a)-(c), at 298–306 (5th ed. 2010).

Thus, in *People v. Rypinski*, 555 N.Y.S.2d 500 (N.Y. App. Div. 1990), the appellate court reversed a reckless assault conviction where the defendant shot the victim in the leg with a hunting rifle. The defendant claimed that the rifle always contained exactly three rounds of ammunition and that he remembered emptying three rounds before approaching the victim. The court ruled that the jury should have been instructed that the defendant's mistake of fact—as to how many rounds the rifle actually contained—could be a defense if it negated the requisite mens rea of recklessness.

2. Mistake of Fact as a Defense to Specific and General Intent Crimes. In jurisdictions that separate offenses into specific intent and general intent crimes, a mistake of fact must be both honest (sincere) and reasonable in order to afford a defense to a general intent crime. But even an unreasonable mistake of fact can be a defense to a specific intent crime so long as it was sincere.

For example, in *People v. Navarro*, 160 Cal. Rptr. 692 (Cal. App. Dep't Super. Ct. 1979), the defendant was charged with grand theft when he took four wooden beams from a construction site. The trial court instructed the jury that he would have a defense if he honestly and reasonably believed that the beams were abandoned or that he had the owner's permission to take them. The appellate court reversed, noting that a mistake of fact need not be reasonable in order to constitute a defense to the specific intent crime at issue there, which required proof that the defendant took another person's property with the intent to keep it permanently.

3. Mistake of Fact Under the Model Penal Code. Section 2.04(1)(a) of the Model Penal Code provides that "[i]gnorance or mistake as to a matter of fact" constitutes a defense if it "negatives the purpose, knowledge, belief, recklessness or negligence required to establish a material element of the offense." For crimes that require purpose or knowledge, therefore, an honest mistake of fact is a defense, even if the mistake was reckless. For crimes requiring recklessness, a mistake of fact is a defense so long as it was not reckless. And for crimes requiring negligence, a mistake of fact is a defense provided the mistake was not negligent—in other words, it must have been a reasonable mistake. Would Gordon have had a valid mistake of fact defense under the Model Penal Code? In answering this question, consider what impact § 2.02(3) and § 2.02(4) have on this issue. (These provisions are described above in Note 8 following *Villegas* in Section B.2.)

[2] Mistake of Law

People v. Wendt

539 N.E.2d 768 (Ill. App. Ct.), *appeal denied*, 545 N.E.2d 128 (Ill. 1989)

JUSTICE LINDBERG delivered the opinion of the court.

Defendant, Donald D. Wendt, was charged with . . . willfully failing to file an income tax return for the taxable year 1984. . . . A jury found defendant guilty of this offense, and he was sentenced by the court to 2½ years of probation conditioned on payment of a $2,500 fine; performance of 400 hours of community service; payment of all income taxes, interest, and penalties due the State; and service of six months of work release. Defendant has appealed from his conviction.

Defendant . . . argues that his conviction should be reversed because . . . the evidence was insufficient to prove beyond a reasonable doubt that defendant had willfully failed to file a 1984 income tax return. . . .

In 1984, Chrysler Corporation paid $33,131.95 in wages to defendant for his work at Chrysler's Belvidere assembly plant. No money was withheld to pay the Illinois income tax because defendant, who was an Illinois resident, had filed an Illinois W-4 form claiming to be exempt from withholding. Defendant testified that he filed an Illinois 1040 form for 1984 but that it was returned with a letter from the Illinois Department of Revenue (DOR) telling him to sign it and to send the DOR a copy of his W-2 form. Defendant responded with a letter stating that he would sign the Illinois 1040 form if Chrysler signed the W-2 form. The records of the DOR indicated defendant did not file an Illinois 1040 form for the taxable year 1984. Defendant's primary defense was that the State failed to prove beyond a reasonable doubt that he acted willfully. In support of this defense, defendant presented evidence tending to show that, in reliance upon certain court opinions he read, articles interpreting the law and the United States Constitution he read, and speeches at certain seminars he attended, he had in good faith come to believe that he was not subject to the Illinois (and United States) income tax [because only corporate profits, not individual wages, qualified as income and because the method by which the Sixteenth Amendment to the U.S. Constitution had been ratified was fatally flawed].

. . . Defendant contends:

> There was no evidence from which the jury could infer Wendt acted with a bad purpose or without grounds for believing his actions were lawful or with careless disregard for whether or not he had the right to act as he did. In short, they could not infer willfulness from the evidence adduced at trial. . . . The most the jury could reasonably infer from the evidence was that Wendt had a bona fide misunderstanding of the law. They could not infer a voluntary intentional violation of a known legal duty; that is the definition the [United States] Supreme Court has given to willfulness in the context of the tax statutes. A bona fide misunderstanding negates willfulness. The evidence at trial showed Wendt honestly and sincerely believed that he was not subject to the income tax. . . . There was no evidence from which the jury could reasonably infer a voluntary, intentional violation of any known legal duty. The subjective state of mind of Wendt during 1984 was what was at issue. So long as he subjectively believed he was not subject to the tax, and so long as such belief was held in good faith, he was not willful and therefore not guilty. . . .

This argument displays a profound misunderstanding of both the mental state of willfulness and the mistake-of-law defense under Illinois law.

The offense of which defendant was convicted is defined in these terms:

> Any person who is subject to the provisions of this Act and who willfully fails to file a return . . . shall, in addition to other penalties, be guilty of a Class 4 felony for the first offense and a Class 3 felony for each subsequent offense. (Ill. Rev. Stat. 1985, ch. 120, par. 13-1301.)

The Criminal Code provides:

> Conduct performed knowingly or with knowledge is performed willfully, within the meaning of a statute using the latter term, unless the statute clearly requires another meaning. [Criminal Code § 4-5.]

Section 13-1301 of the Act does not clearly require another meaning, so defendant willfully failed to file his income tax return if he knowingly failed to file it.

The statute defining the applicable mental state provides:

A person knows, or acts knowingly or with knowledge of:

> . . . .

The result of his conduct, described by the statute defining the offense, when he is consciously aware that such result is practically certain to be caused by his conduct. [Criminal Code § 4-5(b).]

Thus, to prove the mental element of the offense at bar, it was only necessary to prove that defendant was consciously aware that a failure to file his income tax return was practically certain to be caused by his conduct.

Section [4-3(c)] of the Criminal Code provides:

Knowledge that certain conduct constitutes an offense, or knowledge of the existence, meaning, or application of the statute defining an offense, is not an element of the offense unless the statute clearly defines it as such.

Section 4-8 of the Criminal Code provides:

(a) A person's ignorance or mistake as to a matter of either fact or law, except as provided in Section 4-3(c) above, is a defense if it negatives the existence of the mental state which the statute prescribes with respect to an element of the offense.

(b) A person's reasonable belief that his conduct does not constitute an offense is a defense if: (1) The offense is defined by an administrative regulation or order which is not known to him and has not been published or otherwise made reasonably available to him, and he could not have acquired such knowledge by the exercise of due diligence pursuant to facts known to him; or (2) He acts in reliance upon a statute which later is determined to be invalid; or (3) He acts in reliance upon an order or opinion of an Illinois Appellate or Supreme Court, or a United States appellate court later overruled or reversed; [or] (4) He acts in reliance upon an official interpretation of the statute, regulation or order defining the offense, made by a public officer or agency legally authorized to interpret such statute.

Under these statutes, defendant's contentions with regard to the sufficiency of the evidence of willfulness are meritless.

Section 13-1301 of the Act does not clearly define the offense of willful failure to file a return as including as an element "[knowledge] that certain conduct constitutes an offense, or knowledge of the existence, meaning, or application of" section 13-1301, so such knowledge is not an element of the offense of willful failure to file a return. All of defendant's contentions regarding the deficiencies of the evidence of willfulness really come down to one claim: that defendant believed he was complying with the law. Such a mistake is not a defense under section 4-8(a) of the Criminal Code for two separate reasons. First, such a belief falls squarely within the provisions of section 4-3(c) and so is not a defense under section 4-8(a). Second, such a belief does not negative the existence of the mental state of the offense at bar, i.e., conscious awareness by defendant that a failure to file his return was practically certain to be caused by his conduct. Such a mistake is also not a defense under section 4-8(b), since none of the four alternative conditions listed there existed.

Thus, defendant's contentions . . . that the evidence of willfulness was insufficient because it established that he believed he was not committing any offense are without merit. The ignorance or mistake of law claimed would not constitute a defense under section 4-8 of the Criminal Code. Knowledge that his conduct constituted an offense or knowledge of the existence, meaning, or application of section 13-1301 of the Act was not an element of the offense defined in section 13-1301. Accordingly, all the State was required to prove to establish the willfulness of defendant's failure to file his return was that defendant was consciously aware that a failure to file his return was practically certain to be caused by his conduct. Defendant's contentions regarding his beliefs, even if true, would not affect the propriety of his conviction.

. . . .

The judgment of the circuit court is affirmed.

Notes and Questions

1. Introduction. What explains the well-known maxim "ignorance of the law is no excuse"? The Alabama Supreme Court's opinion in *Gordon*, excerpted above in Part 1, articulates the conventional rationale—that everyone is presumed to know the law and that a contrary assumption would inject into every criminal trial collateral state-of-mind inquiries that are not easily resolved. Do these arguments make sense?

What about a defendant who was raised in another culture that has different laws and customs? For example, Kong Moua, a Hmong tribesman from Laos charged with kidnapping and rape, was ultimately allowed to plead guilty to the lesser charge of false imprisonment and sentenced to four months in jail and a $1000 fine ($900 of which was given to his victim) when he argued that "marriage by capture" was "an accepted form of matrimony akin to elopement" in his culture. Myrna Oliver, *Immigrant Crimes*, L.A. Times, July 15, 1988, at A1 (also describing a case involving a woman from Mexico who beat her teenage son with a wooden spoon, was accused of child abuse, and was ordered to undergo counseling when she explained that that was an acceptable form of discipline in her country). *But see* Livingston Hall & Selig J. Seligman, *Mistake of Law and Mens Rea*, 8 U. Chi. L. Rev. 641, 656 (1941) (pointing out that mistakes of law generally afford no defense even to defendants who are new to a community and come from a culture with different rules). *See generally* Doriane L. Coleman, *Individualizing Justice Through Multiculturalism: The Liberals' Dilemma*, 96 Colum. L. Rev. 1093 (1996).

For an analysis of how the traditional approach to mistake of law illustrates that the criminal laws are aimed primarily at defining social morality rather than condemning blameworthy behavior, see John L. Diamond, *The Myth of Morality and Fault in Criminal Law*, 34 Am. Crim. L. Rev. 111 (1996); John L. Diamond, *The Crisis in the Ideology of Crime*, 31 Ind. L. Rev. 291 (1998).

2. Critics of the Maxim. The venerable mistake of law doctrine has recently come under attack from some academics. *See, e.g.,* Stephen P. Garvey, *When Should Mistake of Fact Excuse?*, 42 Tex. Tech L. Rev. 359, 366 (2009) (supporting a defense for even unreasonable mistakes of law so long as they do not reflect the defendant's "defiance of the law's demands"); Kenneth W. Simons, *Ignorance and Mistake of Criminal Law, Noncriminal Law, and Fact*, 9 Ohio St. J. Crim. L. 487, 523 (2012) (advocating a defense at least for reasonable mistakes of law). See also an article by former United States Attorney General Edwin Meese and former Assistant to the Solicitor General Paul J. Larkin Jr. titled *Reconsidering the Mistake of Law Defense*, 102 J. Crim L. & Criminology 725 (2012).

Do you agree with these commentators that the mistake of law doctrine should be relaxed? Are jurors better equipped to evaluate mistake of fact claims than mistake of law defenses? Does one need legal training to be able to distinguish between reasonable and unreasonable mistakes of law given that statutory and regulatory language and the structure of laws and regulations often will be unfamiliar to lay jurors? If so, would it make sense to ask judges to resolve any mistake of law defense?

3. Mistakes of Law That Negate Mens Rea. Despite the well-known maxim, ignorance of the law is a defense if it negates the mens rea required to commit a crime. Thus, for example, § 2.04(1)(a) of the Model Penal Code does not distinguish between a mistake of fact and a mistake of law, providing that either gives rise to a defense if it "negatives the purpose, knowledge, belief, recklessness or negligence required to establish a material element of the offense." *Cf.* Joshua Dressler, Understanding Criminal Law § 13.02[D], at 177–78 (7th ed. 2015) (pointing out that mistakes of law are likewise a defense if they negate the mens rea for a specific intent crime but are no defense to a general intent crime).

The familiar maxim nevertheless continues to have a great deal of force because, as reflected in *Wendt* and § 2.02(9) of the Model Penal Code, most crimes do not require proof that the defendant was aware of the law. As a result, a mistake of law typically does not negate the mens rea required by the crime.

There are some notable exceptions, however, where a defendant's mistake about a legal rule did negate the mens rea required to commit the crime. For example, in *The Queen v. Smith (David)*, [1974] Q.B. 354, the court reversed a tenant's conviction for the crime of damaging another's property, "intending to damage such property or being reckless as to whether such property would be damaged." In the process of moving out of his apartment, Smith damaged some wall panels and floor boards (which he himself had built with the landlord's permission) in order to gain access to and retrieve some stereo wiring he had installed. The court ruled that the trial judge should have instructed the jury that Smith had a defense if he was unaware that the law deemed any improvements made by a tenant to be the property of the landlord and if, as a result of this mistake, he believed he was destroying his own property. In some cases, it can be difficult to distinguish between mistakes of fact and law. Do you understand why Smith's mistake was one of law and not of fact?

Likewise, in *People v. Weiss*, 12 N.E.2d 514, 514 (N.Y. 1938), the court held that the crime of kidnapping—defined by statute as "wilfully . . . [s]eiz[ing], confin[ing], inveigl[ing], or kidnap[ping] another, with intent to cause him, without authority of law, to be secretly confined or imprisoned against his will"—required proof of "willful intent to seize a person without authority of law." The court concluded that the trial judge had erred in preventing the defendants from arguing that they thought they had officially been deputized by a New Jersey detective and therefore believed they were acting lawfully when they helped seize someone suspected (erroneously, as it turned out) of kidnapping and murdering the Lindbergh baby.

Finally, consider *United States v. Klotz*, 500 F.2d 580 (8th Cir. 1974), and *United States v. Boucher*, 509 F.2d 991 (8th Cir. 1975), where the Eighth Circuit held that defendants who had failed to register for the draft could not be convicted on charges that they "knowingly evade[d] or refuse[d] registration or service in the armed services" unless the prosecution proved that they were aware of their obligation to register. The court explained in *Klotz*: "To knowingly fail to perform a duty a person must be aware of the duty and deliberately or wilfully neglect to perform it." 500 F.2d at 581. Are the two draft cases consistent with *Wendt*? Is the difference in outcome attributable to differences in wording between the Illinois tax statute and the federal draft statute? Or is the Eighth Circuit in essence applying the approach taken in *Cheek v. United States*, which is described in the following Note? *See generally* Steve Kelly, Comment, *Presumption of Notice: Mens Rea and Draft Registration—Ignorance of the Law Is an Excuse*, 1982 Wis. L. Rev. 234.

4. *Cheek v. United States*. Compare *Wendt* with the Supreme Court's decision in *Cheek v. United States*, 498 U.S. 192 (1991). In that case, the Court held that the federal criminal statutes penalizing the "willful" attempt to evade the tax laws and the "willful" failure to file a federal tax return require the prosecution to prove "that the law imposed a duty on the defendant, that the defendant knew of this duty, and that he voluntarily and intentionally violated that duty." *Id*. at 201. The Court thought that "the complexity of the tax laws" justified "carving out an exception to the traditional rule" that mistakes of law afford no defense and instead interpreted the word "willfully" in the federal tax statute to require a "specific intent to violate the law." *Id*. at 200. Accordingly, the Court ruled that the defendant in that case—a pilot who stopped filing federal income tax returns in 1979 and indicated on W-4 forms that he was exempt from the federal income tax—could not be said to be acting "willfully" if he "truly believed that the Internal Revenue Code did not purport to treat wages as income, and the jury believed him, . . . however unreasonable a court might deem such a belief." *Id*. at 202.

The Supreme Court also held in *Cheek*, however, that a defendant's honest belief that the income tax is unconstitutional would not provide a defense:

> Claims that some of the provisions of the tax code are unconstitutional are submissions of a different order. They do not arise from innocent mistakes caused by the complexity of the Internal Revenue Code. Rather, they reveal full knowledge of the provisions at issue and a studied conclusion, however wrong, that those provisions are invalid and unenforceable.

Id. at 205–06.

In another prominent federal tax case, Wesley Snipes, the star of the *Blade* movie trilogy, was acquitted of the most serious charges brought in connection with his failure to pay federal income taxes (and his request for a $7 million refund for taxes he did pay one year). Snipes claimed that, based on advice he received, he believed the federal tax laws applied only to federal officials, residents of Washington, D.C., and those involved in a business or trade. Although Snipes' attorneys conceded his tax theories were "kooky" and "crazy," they argued that he sincerely believed them and therefore lacked criminal intent. The jury acquitted Snipes of fraud and conspiracy charges, but he was convicted on three misdemeanor counts of willfully failing to file a tax return and was sentenced to one year in prison on each count. His conviction was affirmed on appeal, and the Supreme Court denied certiorari. *See United States v. Snipes*, 611 F.3d 855 (11th Cir. 2010), *cert. denied*, 563 U.S. 1032 (2011).

5. Other Federal Statutes. The federal courts have refused to apply the decision in *Cheek* broadly to other non-tax federal statutes, "read[ing] the element of 'actual knowledge of the law' [only] into complex statutes that punish[] 'willful' failures to perform statutory duties." *United States v. Hancock*, 231 F.3d 557 (9th Cir. 2000) (finding that knowledge of the law is not required when Congress uses the mens rea term "knowingly" as opposed to "willfully").

Nevertheless, *Cheek* is not entirely isolated. In *Ratzlaf v. United States*, 510 U.S. 135 (1994), the Supreme Court held that the term "willfully" in the federal money-laundering statutes required actual knowledge of the law. Citing *Cheek*, the five Justices in the majority concluded that "the jury had to find [that the defendant] knew the structuring in which he was engaged was unlawful." (Just months after this decision, Congress amended the statute, removing the word "willfully" and thereby nullifying the effect of the ruling, just as Justice Blackmun had suggested in his *Ratzlaf* dissent.)

The Supreme Court again construed the word "willfully" in 1998, this time in a federal criminal statute prohibiting dealing in firearms without a license, 18 U.S.C. § 924(a)(1)(D). Parsing the concept of "knowledge of the law" more closely, the Court ruled that the government must prove that defendants knew their conduct was "unlawful" in order to convict under this statute, but need not prove that they knew of the precise federal law prohibiting their conduct. *Bryan v. United States*, 524 U.S. 184 (1998). *See also Screws v. United States*, 325 U.S. 91 (1945) (holding that government officials can be convicted of "willfully" violating constitutional rights only if they had "an intent to deprive a person of a [constitutional] right," but that the defendants need not be "thinking in constitutional terms" so long as they "at least act[ed] in reckless disregard of constitutional prohibitions or guarantees"). In addition, see the discussion of *Arthur Andersen LLP v. United States* in Note 7 in Section B.1 above.

Compare, however, the Court's decision in *McFadden v. United States*, 135 S. Ct. 2298 (2015), which held that the mens rea necessary to convict a defendant of "knowingly or intentionally" distributing a controlled substance (or a controlled substance analogue, such as bath salts) can be established in one of two ways. First, the prosecution can prove that the defendant "knew he possessed a substance listed on the schedules" of controlled substances (or treated as such by virtue of the federal Controlled Substance Analogue Enforcement Act), "even if he did not know . . . precisely what substance it [was]." Alternatively, the mens rea requirement is satisfied if the defendant "knew the identity of the substance he possessed." In the latter case, the Court continued, the defendant need not realize the substance is listed as a controlled substance (or considered a controlled substance analogue) "[b]ecause ignorance of the law is typically no defense." Writing separately, Chief Justice Roberts disagreed with the majority's second alternative. Although the Chief Justice acknowledged that ignorance of the law is generally no defense, he noted that an absence of knowledge about a "legal element [of a criminal statute] can be a defense" and here the requirement that the substance be "controlled" is "arguably a legal element."

At least two general points emerge from these cases. First, as § 2.04(1) of the Model Penal Code makes clear, the language of a criminal statute can make "ignorance of the law" a defense where it otherwise might not be. The proper interpretation to be given to statutory mens rea terms can be a fertile ground for litigation; the meaning, for example, of the word "willfully" is neither plain nor uniform. Second (and perhaps just a corollary of the first point), the common-law maxim that "ignorance of the law is no defense" may be less universally true today than it was 300, or even 50, years ago.

6. Mistakes of Law That Do Not Negate Mens Rea. There are four situations in which an erroneous belief that one's conduct is lawful generally constitutes a defense even though the criminal statute does not require knowledge of unlawfulness and the mistake therefore does not negate the mens rea required to commit the crime: (A) when the law is not published; (B) when the mistake arises from reasonable reliance on a statute that is later determined to be invalid; (C) when the mistake is based on reasonable reliance on a court decision that is subsequently overturned; and (D) when the mistake arises from reasonable reliance on a public official who is in a position to interpret the relevant statute. *See* Model Penal Code § 2.04(3); WAYNE R. LAFAVE, CRIMINAL LAW § 5.6(a), at 298–300 (5th ed. 2010). Given that all criminal statutes are published, the first category has no real practical significance today and the Notes that follow therefore deal with the remaining categories.

(a) *Reasonable Reliance on a Statute.* In *State v. Godwin*, 31 S.E. 221 (N.C. 1898), a number of public officials were charged with failing to carry out certain of their duties. In their defense, the defendants pointed out that they had been relieved of those duties by statute. The prosecution responded that because the act was later found to be unconstitutional, the defendants had never actually been released from their responsibilities. In accepting the defendants' argument and affirming the lower court's special verdict of not guilty, the North Carolina Supreme Court commented:

> The defendants here cannot be punished under the criminal law for failing and refusing to perform the duties of an office, which office, and the duties pertaining to it, had been sought to be repealed by a subsequent act of the legislature, afterwards declared by the courts to be unconstitutional. Until

the subsequent statute was declared to be unconstitutional by competent authority, the defendants, under every idea of justice and under our theory of government, had a right to presume that the lawmaking power had acted within the bounds of the Constitution, and their highest duty was to obey.

Id. at 222.

(b) *Reasonable Reliance on a Court Decision.* Reasonable reliance on judicial decisions can also afford a mistake of law defense. Consider, for example, *Ostrosky v. State*, 704 P.2d 786 (Alaska Ct. App. 1985). Harold Ostrosky was convicted of fishing without a license, but the trial judge vacated his conviction on the grounds that the law requiring a fishing license was unconstitutional. While the state appealed that decision, Ostrosky continued fishing without a license. Once again, he was arrested. Two weeks later, the Alaska Supreme Court reversed the trial judge's earlier ruling and upheld the constitutionality of the fishing license laws. When Ostrosky was convicted on the charges stemming from the second arrest, the court of appeals reversed, reasoning that he should have been allowed to argue that he had reasonably relied on the trial judge's ruling. The appellate court emphasized, however, that Ostrosky had a valid defense only if his reliance was reasonable, and it left open the question whether it was reasonable for him to rely on a trial court ruling once he knew it had been appealed.

Ultimately, the courts determined that Ostrosky's reliance on the trial judge's decision was not reasonable: he knew that the decision might be reversed on appeal; two previous trial judges had rejected his constitutional challenges to the license requirement; and his attorney had warned him that he might face further prosecution by continuing to fish without a license. *See Ostrosky v. State*, 725 P.2d 1087 (Alaska Ct. App. 1986). Note that some statutes, like the Illinois provision quoted in *Wendt*, expressly limit this defense to opinions issued by appellate courts. *See* WAYNE R. LAFAVE, CRIMINAL LAW § 5.6(e)(2), at 312–14 (5th ed. 2010).

(c) *Reasonable Reliance on a Public Official Responsible for Interpreting or Administering the Statute.* In *People v. Ferguson*, 24 P.2d 965 (Cal. Ct. App. 1933), the defendant was convicted of violating the Corporate Securities Act when he sold interests in a trust without obtaining the required permit from the corporation commissioner. The Court of Appeal reversed the conviction, concluding that the defendant should have been allowed to present evidence showing that he acted in reliance on the corporation commissioner's advice that a permit was not legally necessary. *But see State v. Foster*, 46 A. 833, 834–35 (R.I. 1900) (reaching the opposite conclusion in a similar case on the grounds that ignorance of the law is no defense).

Moreover, in *Commonwealth v. Twitchell*, 617 N.E.2d 609 (Mass. 1993), a Christian Scientist couple whose child died from a perforated bowel was convicted of involuntary manslaughter. The court found that the couple's failure to obtain medical treatment for the child was an omission contrary to legal duty, thus satisfying the voluntary act requirement (*see* Chapter 3, Section B). Nevertheless, it reversed the conviction on the grounds that the parents should have been allowed to argue that they had reasonably relied on an opinion issued by the state attorney general that "[a] reasonable person not trained in the law might fairly read" to suggest that parents could not be prosecuted if they were acting on their religious beliefs in failing to provide medical treatment to their children. *Id.* at 618. In issuing this opinion, the state attorney general was "acting in an area of his official responsibility," the court concluded, because he was "statutorily empowered to 'give his opinion upon questions of law submitted to him.'" *Id.* at 619. The prosecutor ultimately decided not to retry the couple.

Some jurisdictions limit the reach of this defense. In certain states, only written interpretations suffice to make out a defense. *See* WAYNE R. LaFAVE, CRIMINAL LAW §6(e)(3), at 314–16 (5th ed. 2010). Moreover, the identity of the public official issuing the interpretation can be important. The Illinois statute cited in *Wendt*, for example, restricted the defense to officials authorized to interpret the statute. In *United States v. Achter*, 52 F.3d 753 (8th Cir. 1995), the court ruled that the defendant could not rely on representations made by *state or local* officials in interpreting a *federal* firearms statute.

In addition, at least one court has seemingly refused to recognize any defense in these cases. In *Hopkins v. State*, 69 A.2d 456 (Md. 1949), *appeal dismissed*, 339 U.S. 940 (1950), the defendant put up signs at the entrance to his home and along a highway that read "Rev. W.F. Hopkins" and "W.F. Hopkins, Notary Public, Information." He was charged with violating a statute that made it a crime "to erect or maintain any sign intended to aid in the solicitation or performance of marriages." The defendant contended that he had sought the State's Attorney's advice before putting up the signs, and that the State's Attorney had assured him his signs would not violate the law. Nevertheless, the Maryland Court of Appeals affirmed the defendant's conviction, concluding that "advice given by a public official, even a State's Attorney, that a contemplated act is not criminal will not excuse an offender if, as a matter of law, the act performed did amount to a violation of the law." *Id.* at 460.

7. Attorney's Legal Advice Usually Not a Defense. Suppose a client consults an attorney about the lawfulness of certain conduct, and the lawyer erroneously tells the client that the conduct is legal. Would the client's reasonable reliance on the advice of an attorney afford a defense? Most courts say no. In *Hopkins v. State*, 69 A.2d 456, 460 (Md. 1950), for example, the court noted:

> It is generally held that the advice of counsel, even though followed in good faith, furnishes no excuse to a person for violating the law and cannot be relied upon as a defense in a criminal action. . . . These rules are founded upon the maxim that ignorance of the law will not excuse its violation. If an accused could be exempted from punishment for crime by reason of the advice of counsel, such advice would become paramount to the law.

See also People v. Honig, 55 Cal. Rptr. 2d 555, 590 (Cal. Ct. App. 1996) (expressing the view that recognizing such a defense "would place the advice of counsel above the law, and would also place a premium on counsel's ignorance or indifference to the law").

By contrast, federal courts more commonly recognize "advice of counsel" as a defense, at least with regard to federal tax cases or other specific complex statutes requiring a "willful" violation. Nevertheless, as Judge Posner has clarified, "[t]here is no such thing as an 'advice of counsel' defense [per se]. What is true . . . is that if a criminal statute requires proof that the defendant knew he was violating the statute in order to be criminally liable for the violation, and it is unclear whether the statute forbade his conduct, the fact that he was acting on the advice of counsel is relevant because it bears on whether he knew that he was violating the statute." *United States v. Sprong*, 287 F.3d 663, 665–66 (7th Cir. 2002).

8. New Jersey's Broader Mistake of Law Defense. New Jersey departs from the majority rule and allows a broader mistake of law defense. Specifically, New Jersey law provides that an erroneous belief in the legality of one's conduct is a defense not only in the situations described in § 2.04(3) of the Model Penal Code, but also if "[t]he actor otherwise diligently pursues all means available to ascertain the meaning and application of the offense to his conduct and honestly and in good faith concludes his conduct is not an offense in circumstances in which a law-abiding and prudent person would also so conclude." N.J. Stat. Ann. § 2C:2-4(c)(3).

In *State v. Guice*, 621 A.2d 553 (N.J. Super. Ct. Law Div. 1993), the court refused to extend this statute to cover two defendants who mistakenly concluded, based on their own legal research, that they had a First Amendment right to distribute pamphlets on a private college campus. The court ruled that the defendants had not conducted a "diligent investigation of the law" because "some knowledge of the law, verified by an independent and typically competent source, is required" and the defendants had not consulted an attorney. *Id.* at 558.

United States v. Barker

546 F.2d 940 (D.C. Cir. 1976)

Per Curiam.

The mandate of the court is that the Judgment of the District Court is reversed and the case is remanded for a new trial. Judges Wilkey and Merhige have filed separate opinions. Judge Leventhal dissents.

Wilkey, Circuit Judge.

Two of the "footsoldiers" of the Watergate affair, Bernard Barker and Eugenio Martinez, are with us again. They haven't been promoted, they are still footsoldiers. They come before us this time to challenge their convictions under 18 U.S.C. § 241, for their parts in the 1971 burglary of the office of Dr. Lewis J. Fielding.

I. FACTS

During the summer of 1971, following the publication of the now famous "Pentagon Papers," a decision was made to establish a unit within the White House to investigate the leaks of classified information. This "Room 16" unit, composed of Egil Krogh, David Young, G. Gordon Liddy, and E. Howard Hunt — and under the general supervision of John Ehrlichman—determined, or was instructed, to obtain all possible information on Daniel Ellsberg, the source of the Pentagon Papers leak. After Ellsberg's psychiatrist, Dr. Fielding, refused to be interviewed by FBI agents, the unit decided to obtain copies of Ellsberg's medical records through a covert operation.

Hunt had been a career agent in the CIA before his employment in the White House. One of his assignments was as a supervising agent for the CIA in connection with the Bay of Pigs invasion, and, as "Eduardo," he was well known and respected in Miami's Cuban-American community. A fact destined to be of considerable importance later, he had been Bernard Barker's immediate supervisor in that operation. When the "Room 16" unit determined that it would be best if the actual entry into Dr. Fielding's office were made by individuals not in the employ of the White House, Hunt recommended enlisting the assistance of some of his former associates in Miami. Hunt had previously reestablished contact with Barker in Miami in late April 1971, and he met Martinez at the same time. He gave Barker an unlisted White House number where he could be reached by phone and wrote to Barker on White House stationery. On one occasion Barker met with Hunt in the Executive Office Building. By August 1971 Hunt returned to Miami and informed Barker that he was working for an organization at the White House level with greater jurisdiction than the FBI and the CIA. He asked Barker if he would become "operational" again and help conduct a surreptitious entry to obtain national security information on "a traitor to this country who was passing . . . classified information to the Soviet Embassy." He stated further that "the man in question . . . was being considered as a possible Soviet agent himself."

Barker agreed to take part in the operation and to recruit two additional people. He contacted Martinez and Felipe deDiego. Barker conveyed to Martinez the same information Hunt had given him, and Martinez agreed to participate. Like Barker, Martinez had begun working as a covert agent for the CIA after Castro came to power in Cuba. Although Barker's formal relationship with the CIA had ended in 1966, Martinez was still on CIA retainer when he was contacted.

Both testified at trial that they had no reason to question Hunt's credentials. He clearly worked for the White House and had a well known background with the CIA. During the entire time they worked for the CIA, neither Barker nor Martinez was ever shown any credentials by their superiors. Not once did they receive written instructions to engage in the operations they were ordered to perform. Nevertheless, they testified, their understanding was always that those operations had been authorized by the Government of the United States. That they did not receive more detail on the purpose of the Fielding operation or its target was not surprising to them; Hunt's instructions and actions were in complete accord with what their previous experience had taught them to expect. They were trained agents, accustomed to rely on the discretion of their superiors and to operate entirely on a "need-to-know" basis.

On 2 September 1971 Hunt and Liddy met Barker, Martinez, and deDiego at a hotel in Beverly Hills, California. Hunt informed the defendants that they were to enter an office, search for a particular file, photograph it, and replace it. The following day the group met again. Hunt showed Barker and Martinez identification papers and disguises he had obtained from the CIA. That evening the defendants entered Dr. Fielding's office. Contrary to plan, it was necessary for them to use force to effect the break-in. As instructed in this event, the defendants spilled pills on the floor to make it appear the break-in had been a search for drugs. No file with the name Ellsberg was found.

The next day Barker and Martinez returned to Miami. The only funds they received from Hunt in connection with the entry of Dr. Fielding's office were reimbursement for their living expenses, the cost of travel, and $100.00 for lost income.

On 7 March 1974 the defendants were indicted under 18 U.S.C. § 241, along with Ehrlichman, Liddy, and deDiego for conspiring to violate the Fourth Amendment rights of Dr. Fielding by unlawfully entering and searching his office.[5]

. . . .

IV. THE DEFENSE OF GOOD FAITH, REASONABLE RELIANCE ON APPARENT AUTHORITY

A.

The primary ground upon which defendants Barker and Martinez rest their appeal is the refusal of the District Court to allow them a defense based on their good faith, reasonable reliance on Hunt's apparent authority. They characterize this defense as a mistake of fact "coupled with" a mistake of law which negated the mens rea required for a violation of section 241. "The mistake of fact was the belief that Hunt was a duly authorized government agent; the mistake of law was that Hunt possessed the legal prerequisites to conduct a search—either probable cause or a warrant."

It is a fundamental tenet of criminal law that an honest mistake of fact negates criminal intent, when a defendant's acts would be lawful if the facts were as he supposed them to be. A mistake of law, on the other hand, generally will not excuse the commission of an offense. A defendant's error as to his *authority* to engage in particular activity, if based upon a mistaken view of legal requirements (or ignorance thereof), is a mistake of *law*. Typically, the fact that he relied upon the erroneous advice of another is not an exculpatory circumstance. He is still deemed to have acted with a culpable state of mind.

Thus, at first blush the trial judge's rejection of the defense proffered by the defendants—both in his pre-trial order and in his instruction to the jury—seems legally sound. He advised the jury that if the defendants honestly believed a *valid warrant* had been obtained, this would constitute a mistake of *fact* which would render them innocent of a conspiracy to conduct a search in violation of the Fourth Amendment.

---

5. Section 241 makes it a crime for "two or more persons [to] conspire to injure, oppress, threaten, or intimidate" anyone "in the free exercise or enjoyment of any right or privilege secured to him by the Constitution or laws of the United States."

If, in contrast, they simply believed, despite the absence of a warrant, that for reasons of national security or superior authority the break-in was legal, such a mistake of *law* would not excuse their acts.

B.

With all due deference to the trial judge, I must conclude that both charges were in fact incorrect. . . . The technical difficulty with the first instruction points up the deeper problem with the second.

A governmental search and seizure is not rendered lawful under the Fourth Amendment by the simple fact that a warrant has been obtained. The search is constitutionally proper only if the accompanying warrant is based upon legally sufficient probable cause. A factual mistake as to whether a warrant has been obtained, therefore, would not necessarily excuse an unlawful search — because that search would not necessarily have been legal under the facts as the defendant believed them to be. As the District Court instructed the jury, only a mistake as to whether a *valid* warrant has been obtained would excuse the defendant's action, and that is a mistake of law. That the recipient of the warrant may have relied upon the opinion of a judge in determining that he had legally adequate probable cause to make a search does not, under traditional analysis, alter the situation. His mistake remains one of law, and, under a strict construction of the rule, will not excuse his unlawful act.

It is readily apparent that few courts would countenance an instruction to a jury — even assuming a criminal prosecution were brought against the government agents in such a situation — which advised that since the mistake in acting on an invalid warrant was one of *law*, it would not excuse the agent's unlawful search. It is neither fair nor practical to hold such officials to a standard of care exceeding that exercised by a judge. Moreover, although the basic policy behind the mistake of law doctrine is that, at their peril, all men should know and obey the law, in certain situations there is an overriding societal interest in having individuals rely on the authoritative pronouncements of officials whose decisions we wish to see respected.

For this reason, a number of exceptions to the mistake of law doctrine have developed where its application would be peculiarly unjust or counterproductive. Their recognition in a particular case should give the defendant a defense similar to one based upon mistake of fact, I submit, with one important difference. His mistake should avail him only if it is *objectively reasonable* under the circumstances. The mistake of a government agent in relying on a magistrate's approval of a search can be considered virtually *per se* reasonable. The first instruction of the District Court, therefore, was incorrect only in characterizing a defense based on the belief that a valid warrant had been obtained as one of fact, rather than as an exception to the mistake of law doctrine. Similarly, if a private person is summoned by a police officer to assist in effecting an unlawful arrest, his reliance on the officer's authority to make the arrest may be considered reasonable as a matter of law. The citizen is under a legal obligation to respond to a proper summons and is in no position to second-guess the officer's determination that an arrest is proper. Indeed, it is society's hope in recognizing the reasonableness of a citizen's mistake in this situation to encourage unhesitating compliance with a police officer's call.[6]

Other situations in which a government official enlists the aid of a private citizen to help him perform a governmental task are not so obviously reasonable on their face. If the official does not *order* the citizen to assist him, but simply asks for such assistance, the citizen is not under a legal compulsion to comply.[7] Also, if the circumstances do not require immediate action, the citizen may have time to question the lawfulness of the planned endeavor. Nevertheless, the public policy of encouraging citizens to respond ungrudgingly to the request of officials for help in the performance of their duties remains quite strong. Moreover, the gap (both real and perceived) between a private citizen and a government official with regard to their ability and authority to judge the lawfulness of a particular governmental activity is great. It would appear to serve both justice and public policy in a situation where an individual acted at the behest of a government official to allow the individual a defense based upon his reliance on the official's authority — *if* he can show that his reliance was *objectively reasonable* under the particular circumstances of his case.

. . . .

It is clear from the above discussion . . . that the court's instruction did not state the law, and [can be justified] *if and only if* Barker and Martinez could not show *both* (1) *facts* justifying their reasonable reliance on Hunt's apparent authority and (2) *a legal theory* on which to base a reasonable belief that Hunt possessed such authority.

Barker and Martinez meet the test as to *facts*. There was abundant evidence in the case from which the jury could have found that the defendants honestly and reasonably believed that they were engaged in a top-secret national security operation lawfully authorized by a government intelligence agency. They were enlisted for the break-in by a White House official, E. Howard Hunt, whom they knew as a long time government agent with the CIA. They were told that the operation concerned national security involving "a traitor to this country who was passing . . . classified information to the Soviet Embassy." Further, their long experience with the CIA had taught the defendants the importance of complete reliance on, and obedience to, their

---

6. [n.25] This common law exception to the mistake of law doctrine is codified in section 3.07(4)(a) of the Model Penal Code. . . .

7. [n.27] The Special Prosecutor argues in the instant case that since the defendants were not ordered to aid in the Fielding break-in, they can draw no support from the common law "call to aid" rule. He cites section 3.07(4)(b) of the Model Penal Code for the position that when one is "not summoned" but nevertheless aids a police officer in making an unlawful arrest, only a mistake of fact is a valid defense. It would appear, however, that a citizen who is "asked" or "entreated" to assist a police officer bears a heavy civic responsibility to comply. He is effectively, if not technically, "summoned." In such a situation, although we might hesitate to presume the reasonableness of his action as a matter of law, if the citizen can show that his mistake as to the officer's lawful authority was in fact reasonable under the circumstances, I submit he makes out a valid defense.

supervisor. That they should be expected to operate on a "need-to-know" basis was neither unusual nor cause for inquiry.

Barker and Martinez likewise meet the test as to the *legal theory* on which Hunt could have possessed such authority. That the President had the authority to confer upon a group of aides in the White House "more authority than the FBI or CIA," was in 1971 and is now by no means inconceivable as a matter of law. I certainly do not assert that the President here actually did so act (see the court's opinion in *Ehrlichman* [546 F.2d 910 (D.C. Cir. 1976)]), nor do we in this case need to decide the question of Executive authority to conduct warrantless searches pertaining to foreign agents, which issue was left open by the Supreme Court in *United States v. United States District Court (Keith)* [407 U.S. 297 (1972)]. . . .

MERHIGE, DISTRICT JUDGE (concurring).

. . . I am not, despite my concurrence with the results reached by Judge Wilkey, willing to fully subscribe to the views expressed by him in his analysis of the mistake of law issue. Our differences arise from my inability to acquiesce in the broad framework inherent in his analysis. . . .

. . . [T]he district judge [here] was applying the general rule on mistake of law that has long been an integral part of our system of jurisprudence. . . . Exceptions to the rule, however, have developed in situations where its policy foundations have failed to apply with strength, and alternative policy consideration[s] strongly favor a different result. The exceptions have been both statutory and judicial. The instant case fits the pattern of a set of circumstances that has been recognized by some, and that in my view should be endorsed by this Court as an exception to the general rule. Defendants Barker and Martinez contend that they were affirmatively misled by an official interpretation of the relevant law, and are entitled to an instruction to that effect, permitting the jury to assess the reasonableness and sincerity of their alleged reliance.

The Model Penal Code states the defense [in § 2.04(3)(b)]. . . .

[That] defense has been most commonly accepted when an individual acts in reliance on a statute later held to be unconstitutional, or on an express decision of unconstitutionality of a statute by a competent court of general jurisdiction that is subsequently overruled. Most jurisdictions will not permit a defense based on reliance upon the advice of counsel. The defense, however, . . . has been extended to cases of reliance on official advisory opinions. In *State v. Davis*, 63 Wisc. 2d 75, 216 N.W.2d 31 (1974), the defendant was exonerated on the basis of reliance on erroneous advice of a county corporation counsel and assistant district attorney. In *People v. Ferguson*, 134 Cal. 41, 24 P.2d 965 (1933), reliance on the advice of the state corporation commissioner and deputy commissioners was held to excuse a violation of the state's blue sky laws.

Arguments against extending the defense to reliance on the advice of government officials take a form of the following proposition: Minor government officials will have the ability to effectively "immunize" individuals from prosecution. In response, it must be noted that with the respect to a particular statement, a government official is himself culpable if he knowingly mistakes the law. Hence he may proffer mistaken advice without retribution only until he discovers its invalidity. To argue further, that incompetent or dishonest minor officials may exist in numbers serious enough to question reliance on their decisions or interpretations, inherently characterizes those public servants upon whom we must depend for the ultimate success of the operation of our government, as suspect. I, for one, am not willing to assume that the incidence of incompetent, insensitive or dishonest public officials is significant enough to dispute the premise that in general, public officials merit the respect of the public. . . .

. . . Finally, it should be noted that the strength of the arguments premised upon the potential extent of the defense is mitigated by the requirement of objective reasonableness. If a public official's opinion of the law is fairly outrageous, the jury may conclude that a reasonable man would take appropriate steps to verify it prior to reliance thereon.

Applying the defense to the facts of this case, the record discloses sufficient evidence of reliance on an official interpretation of the law for the matter to have been submitted to the jury. Barker and Martinez assert that they relied on Hunt's authority as delegated from an intelligence superstructure controlled by the White House, and firmly believed that they were acting in a legal capacity. The Executive Branch of the United States Government is vested with substantive responsibilities in the field of national security, and decisions of its officials on the extent of their legal authority deserve some deference from the public. A jury may well find that John Ehrlichman, then assistant to the President for Domestic Affairs, expressed or implied that the break-in of Dr. Fielding's office was legal under a national security rationale, and that Hunt, as an executive official in a go-between capacity, passed the position on to the defendants, which they, acting as reasonable men, relied upon in performing the break-in.

Accordingly, while I concur with Judge Wilkey that the jury should have been instructed on a limited mistake of law defense, I believe any such instruction should, in the event of a retrial[8] be couched consistent with the views herein expressed.

LEVENTHAL, CIRCUIT JUDGE (dissenting).

. . . .

Exceptions to the Mistake of Law Doctrine

I do not discount defendants' claims that their background, and particularly their previous relations with the CIA and Hunt explain their good faith reliance on Hunt's apparent authority and their consequent failure to inquire about the legality of the activities they were to undertake on his request. I feel compassion for men who were

---

8. The government ultimately decided not to retry this case.

simultaneously offenders and victims, and so did the trial judge when it came to sentencing.[9] But testing their special circumstances against analogies they rely on to project a mistake of law defense, leads me to reject their claim to be relieved of personal accountability for their acts.

1. *Claim of Good Faith Reliance on an Official's Authority*

Appellants invoke the acceptance of good faith reliance defenses in the Model Penal Code. However, the American Law Institute carefully limited the sections cited to persons responding to a call for aid from a police officer making an unlawful arrest [§ 3.07(4)], and to obeying unlawful military orders [§ 2.10], and specifically rejected the defense for other mistake of law contexts. In both instances, the A.L.I. recognizes limited curtailment of the doctrine excluding a mistake of law defense on the ground that the actor is under a duty to act — to help a police officer in distress to make an arrest when called upon, or to obey military orders. In each case, society has no alternative means available to protect its interest short of imposing a duty to act without a correlative duty to inquire about the legality of the act. Punishing an individual for failure to inquire as to the lawful basis for the officer's request would frustrate the effective functioning of the duly constituted police (and military) force and in its operation on the individual would compel a choice between the whirlpool and the rock.

There is no similar incapacity of the government to act to protect its ends when a citizen takes action when he is under no duty to do so. Thus under the Model Penal Code, a citizen who volunteers to assist another citizen, or volunteers to assist a police officer in making an unlawful arrest, cannot avail himself of the defense — available to a person responding to an officer's call — that he participated without making an inquiry as to whether the arrest was lawful. The volunteer is exculpated only if he believed that the arrest was lawful *and* believed in the "existence of facts which, if they existed, would render the arrest valid" [quoting Model Penal Code § 3.07(4)(b)]. Thus, even if private citizen intervention appears socially desirable in a particular case, the citizen's scope of action and protection in the event of mistakes are narrow, because, overall, forceful citizen enforcement of the law is susceptible of abuse and mischief.

Barker and Martinez were under no tension of conflicting duties comparable to that experienced by a soldier or citizen responding to orders. They had and claim no obligation to aid Hunt. . . . Nor is there a compelling social interest to be served in allowing private citizens to undertake extra-legal activities, acting simply on the word of a government official. The purposes of the law in rejecting such a defense are underscored by the very kinds of extra-governmental, outside-normal-channels conduct that Barker and Martinez engaged in here. Government officials who claim to be seeking to implement the ends of government by bypassing the agencies and

---

9. Earlier in his opinion, Judge Leventhal noted that the defendants were sentenced to "a modest probation" of three years.

personnel normally responsible and accountable to the public transmit a danger signal. Barker and Martinez acted to help Hunt on his explanation that he sought their recruitment because the FBI's "hands were tied by Supreme Court decisions and the Central Intelligence Agency didn't have jurisdiction in certain matters." There is reason for the law to carve out limited exceptions to the doctrine negating defenses rooted in mistake of law, but the pertinent reasons have minimal weight, and face countervailing policies, when they are invoked for situations that on their face are outside the basic channels of law and government—in this case, requests for surreptitious or, if necessary, forcible entry and clandestine file search. These are plainly crimes, *malum in se*, unless there is legal authority. Citizens may take action in such circumstances out of emotions and motives that they deem lofty, but they must take the risk that their trust was misplaced, and that they will have no absolution when there was no authority for the request and their response. If they are later to avoid the consequences of criminal responsibility, it must be as a matter of discretion. To make the defense a matter of right would enhance the resources available to individual officials bent on extra-legal government behavior. The purpose of the criminal law is to serve and not to distort the fundamental values of the society.

2. *Exception for Official Misstatements of Law*

Although defendants relied on the analogy to a police officer's request for assistance, Judge Merhige votes to reverse on the ground that appellants could claim as a defense that a citizen has a right to take action in reliance on a government official's assurance that such action is permissible. The Model Penal Code has addressed itself to that broad problem, and has approved a defense that is narrowly confined in order to protect social interests. Its provision yields no excuse for defendants' conduct. . . . Mainly directed to the *mala prohibita* offenses, the categories protected [by § 2.04(3)] "involve situations where the act charged is consistent with entire law-abidingness of the actor, where the possibility of collusion is minimal. . . ."

The section contemplates both accountability and responsible action on the part of the government official giving advice about the law. But defendants do not claim they received any advice, either express or implied, from Ehrlichman, and Hunt had only an *ad hoc*, undefined position in the White House. He had no on-line enforcement or interpretive powers or responsibilities. His undifferentiated power stemmed solely from membership in a large White House bureaucracy. The potential for official abuse of power would be greatly magnified if such a government official can recruit assistance from the general public, constrained neither by accountability guidelines guiding agency action under statutorily mandated powers, nor by the recruited citizen who, under the defendants' formulation, would be under no duty to inquire about the legality of the official's request.

To stretch the official misstatement of law exception for the facts of this case is to undercut the entire rationale for its recognition as an exception. The Model Penal Code hedges in the defense to permit reliance only on an "*official interpretation* of the public officer . . . *charged by law* with responsibility for the interpretation, administration or enforcement of the *law defining the offense*." Certainly Hunt cannot sensibly be described as having been charged by law with responsibility for interpreting or enforcing either § 241, or the Constitution from which the violations of § 241 in this case sprang. Nor can it be said in any meaningful sense that he had the power to provide an official interpretation of the law. These restrictions on the applicability of the official statement exception did not arise haphazardly; they were deliberately drafted to allow, and indeed to promote, good faith reliance on official pronouncements with objective indicia of reliability—those made by officials specifically charged with interpreting or enforcing the specific law defining the specific offense charged against the defendant. A defense so confined has values for the law: It avoids punishing those who rely on a crystallized position taken by the officer or body charged by statute with interpreting the law in a particular area. The officer's position in a channel of authority is readily identifiable; any mistakes he makes can be remedied by readily perceived and structured avenues of relief. There is no opening the door to justification for serious offenses based on unrecorded discourse from someone who has an undefined but high-sounding berth in the government.

. . . .

Notes and Questions

1. *Barker I.* Barker and Martinez were also convicted on charges arising from the burglary of the Democratic Party's headquarters at the Watergate office and condominium complex, and they ultimately served more than a year in prison on those charges. Two crime beat reporters for the Washington Post, Bob Woodward and Carl Bernstein, investigated the Watergate burglary, which ultimately led to the impeachment and resignation of President Richard Nixon. *See generally* Bob Woodward & Carl Bernstein, All the President's Men (1974). When the burglary case reached the court of appeals, the defendants tried to assert a mistake of law defense, but a majority of the court refused to consider the issue because the defendants had already pleaded guilty and it was within the trial judge's discretion not to allow them to withdraw their guilty pleas. *See United States v. Barker (Barker I)*, 514 F.2d 208 (D.C. Cir. 1975) (en banc). The three judges who wrote separately in *Barker I* were, however, somewhat sympathetic to the defendants' mistake of law defense. If the Watergate burglars had not been so quick to plead guilty or if the court had allowed them to withdraw their pleas, perhaps the scenario leading to President Nixon's resignation would have been altered.

2. **Reactions to *Barker*.** Which of the two opinions voting to reverse the defendants' § 241 conviction is most convincing? Is the dissent persuasive? It is unclear how many courts would accept either Judge Wilkey's opinion analogizing the *Barker* defendants to individuals who made a mistake of law when "summoned" to aid a police officer or Judge Merhige's broad interpretation of the mistake of law defense arising from a public official's interpretation of the law.

Consider the views of one commentator, who argues against expanding the mistake of law exceptions to include a case like *Barker*:

> [T]he values promoted by the general mistake of law rule do not obtain when the actor honestly and reasonably relies on what seems to be an authoritative statement of law. By seeking to inform himself of the law and then relying on it, the individual demonstrates his law-abiding nature; this exception to the rule advances, rather than hinders, the social value of making individuals know and obey the law.
>
> Allowing the defense in the circumstances of the *Barker* cases does not serve to advance these policy interests. Reliance on a government official's apparent status as carrying with it all the legal authorization necessary for the operation is inconsistent with an affirmative effort to know the law. The burglars did not seek from Hunt an interpretation as to the legality of the break-in. Their reliance demonstrated not a law-abiding nature, but rather a failure to inquire into the law.
>
> ... [T]he defense should be rejected on policy grounds: because of the societal interest in deterring conduct by government officials that infringes the civil rights of citizens, a person who purports to act on behalf of the government should be held to a high standard of knowledge of the important restrictions imposed by the law on governmental action. Only where such a person has made a reasonable effort to know the basis of legality of his actions, should he be granted a defense. An uninformed subjective belief in the legality of one's actions, unsupported by a reasonable basis for that belief, should not provide a defense.

Thomas A. White, Note, *Reliance on Apparent Authority as a Defense to Criminal Prosecutions*, 77 Colum. L. Rev. 775, 799, 801 (1977).

By contrast, Professor Louis Schwartz has argued for a broad mistake of law defense where a governmental employee is following a superior's orders:

> There are hundreds of thousands of public servants whose duties involve arrest and search behavior ordinarily prohibited by law: customs officials, revenue agents, building guards, policemen, firemen, investigating officials and so on. The line between what is lawful for them to do and what is unlawful is notoriously vague, yet they are under pressure zealously to do all that is lawful in carrying out their responsibilities. Excesses of zeal must be corrected, and in cases of gross and willful abuse of official authority, they must be prosecuted as crimes. But surely in a civilized society the correction of nonculpable transgressions of vaguely defined authority should not be accomplished by criminal prosecution where the servant acted in good faith obedience to seemingly lawful directions of high authorities. It is the errant high authorities who are shown to be at fault, and such correction as is required for too-obedient subordinates should take the form of better training and of civil disciplinary measures such as suspension or discharge from

employment. . . . [I]t would amount to entrapment for society to train and arm men for law enforcement duties, place them in quasi-military subordination to superiors, and then prosecute them for conforming to plausible commands. Even if the mistake of law defense were narrowly defined for ordinary applications, it would have to be broadened for people placed in such circumstances. The ordinary citizen acts on his own initiative in complying or not complying with the law. He is not placed in a crossfire between official demand that he act aggressively and official threat of punishment if the aggressive act, though conforming to a plausible particularization of society's demand through superior orders, is subsequently held to be unlawful.

Louis B. Schwartz, *Reform of the Federal Criminal Laws: Issues, Tactics, and Prospects*, 1977 Duke L.J. 171, 216.

Would providing a broader defense to government officials invite abuse of power and provide excessive protection whenever an official legal opinion provided cover? Should, for example, an official who is told by a government supervisor that waterboarding is legal be immune from prosecution if such conduct is criminal? Or do you agree with Professor Schwartz that government employees should be protected from punishment if they reasonably rely on a superior's advice that their conduct is legal?

Lambert v. California

355 U.S. 225 (1957)

Mr. Justice Douglas delivered the opinion of the Court.

Section 52.38 (a) of the Los Angeles Municipal Code defines "convicted person" as follows:

> Any person who, subsequent to January 1, 1921, has been or hereafter is convicted of an offense punishable as a felony in the State of California, or who has been or who is hereafter convicted of any offense in any place other than the State of California, which offense, if committed in the State of California, would have been punishable as a felony.

Section 52.39 provides that it shall be unlawful for "any convicted person" to be or remain in Los Angeles for a period of more than five days without registering; it requires any person having a place of abode outside the city to register if he comes into the city on five occasions or more during a 30-day period; and it prescribes the information to be furnished the Chief of Police on registering.

Section 52.43(b) makes the failure to register a continuing offense, each day's failure constituting a separate offense.

Appellant, arrested on suspicion of another offense, was charged with a violation of this registration law. The evidence showed that she had been at the time of her arrest a resident of Los Angeles for over seven years. Within that period she had been convicted in Los Angeles of the crime of forgery, an offense which California punishes as a felony. Though convicted of a crime punishable as a felony, she had not at the time of her arrest registered under the Municipal Code. At the trial, appellant asserted that § 52.39 of the Code denies her due process of law and other rights under the Federal Constitution, unnecessary to enumerate. The trial court denied this objection. The case was tried to a jury which found appellant guilty. The court fined her $250 and placed her on probation for three years. . . .

. . . The case having been argued and reargued, we now hold that the registration provisions of the Code as sought to be applied here violate the Due Process requirement of the Fourteenth Amendment.

. . . No element of willfulness is by terms included in the ordinance nor read into it by the California court as a condition necessary for a conviction.

We must assume that appellant had no actual knowledge of the requirement that she register under this ordinance, as she offered proof of this defense which was refused. The question is whether a registration act of this character violates due process where it is applied to a person who has no actual knowledge of his duty to register, and where no showing is made of the probability of such knowledge.

. . . There is wide latitude in the lawmakers to declare an offense and to exclude elements of knowledge and diligence from its definition. But we deal here with conduct that is wholly passive — mere failure to register. It is unlike the commission of acts, or the failure to act under circumstances that should alert the doer to the consequences of his deed. The rule that "ignorance of the law will not excuse" is deep in our law, as is the principle that of all the powers of local government, the police power is "one of the least limitable." On the other hand, due process places some limits on its exercise. Ingrained in our concept of due process is the requirement of notice. Notice is sometimes essential so that the citizen has the chance to defend charges. Notice is required before property interests are disturbed, before assessments are made, before penalties are assessed. Notice is required in a myriad of situations where a penalty or forfeiture might be suffered for mere failure to act. . . . [T]he principle is equally appropriate where a person, wholly passive and unaware of any wrongdoing, is brought to the bar of justice for condemnation in a criminal case.

Registration laws are common and their range is wide. Many such laws are akin to licensing statutes in that they pertain to the regulation of business activities. But the present ordinance is entirely different. Violation of its provisions is unaccompanied by any activity whatever, mere presence in the city being the test. Moreover, circumstances which might move one to inquire as to the necessity of registration are completely lacking. At most the ordinance is but a law enforcement technique designed for the convenience of law enforcement agencies through which a list of the names and addresses of felons then residing in a given community is compiled. The disclosure is merely a compilation of former convictions already publicly recorded in the jurisdiction where obtained. Nevertheless, this appellant on first becoming aware of her duty to register was given no opportunity to comply with the law and avoid its penalty, even though her default was entirely innocent. She could but suffer the consequences of the ordinance, namely, conviction with the imposition of heavy criminal penalties thereunder. We believe that actual knowledge of the duty to register or proof of the probability of such knowledge and subsequent failure to comply are necessary before a conviction under the ordinance can stand. As Holmes wrote in The Common Law, "A law which punished conduct which would not be blameworthy in the average member of the community would be too severe for that community to bear." Its severity lies in the absence of an opportunity either to avoid the consequences of the law or to defend any prosecution brought under it. Where a person did not know of the duty to register and where there was no proof of the probability of such knowledge, he may not be convicted consistently with due process. Were it otherwise, the evil would be as great as it is when the law is written in print too fine to read or in a language foreign to the community.

Mr. Justice Frankfurter, whom Mr. Justice Harlan and Mr. Justice Whittaker join, dissenting.

The present laws of the United States and of the forty-eight States are thick with provisions that command that some things not be done and others be done, although persons convicted under such provisions may have had no awareness of what the law required or that what they did was wrongdoing. The body of decisions sustaining such legislation, including innumerable registration laws, is almost as voluminous as the legislation itself.

. . . But what the Court here does is to draw a constitutional line between a State's requirement of doing and not doing. What is this but a return to Year Book distinctions between feasance and nonfeasance — a distinction that may have significance in the evolution of common-law notions of liability, but is inadmissible as a line between constitutionality and unconstitutionality. One can be confident that Mr. Justice Holmes would have been the last to draw such a line. What he wrote about "blameworthiness" is worth quoting in its context:

> "It is not intended to deny that criminal liability, as well as civil, is founded on blameworthiness. Such a denial would shock the moral sense of any civilized community; or, to put it another way, a law which punished conduct which would not be blameworthy in the average member of the community would be too severe for that community to bear." (This passage must be read in the setting of the broader discussion of which it is an essential part. Holmes, The Common Law, at 49–50.)

If the generalization that underlies, and alone can justify, this decision were to be given its relevant scope, a whole volume of the United States Reports would be required to document in detail the legislation in this country that would fall or be impaired. I abstain from entering upon a consideration of such legislation, and adjudications upon it, because I feel confident that the present decision will turn out to be an isolated deviation from the strong current of precedents—a derelict on the waters of the law. Accordingly, I content myself with dissenting.

Notes and Questions

1. **Questioning Lambert's Innocence.** The Supreme Court bases its decision in *Lambert* on the assumption that the defendant was never told of her obligation to register. Interestingly, the record before the Court provided strong factual evidence that she was informed of her duty to register. *See* Brief for Appellant as Amicus Curiae submitted by Warren M. Christopher [who was later appointed Secretary of State under President Clinton].

2. **Applying Lambert.** *Lambert*'s recognition of a due process defense in circumstances where a mistake of law generally affords no defense has been narrowly construed. In *Reyes v. United States*, 258 F.2d 774 (9th Cir. 1958), for example, the defendant was charged with violating a statute requiring drug users, addicts, and anyone convicted of violating a felony drug law to register before departing or entering the United States. Like Lambert, the defendant claimed that he was unaware of the registration requirement. The court of appeals affirmed his conviction, distinguishing *Lambert* on three grounds. First, while *Lambert* dealt with a mere nonfeasance, here there was a misfeasance, the crossing of the border. Second, while *Lambert* dealt with a common act, living in the community of Los Angeles, here the defendant's act of leaving the country was sufficient to put him on notice that he should find out whether he was required by law to do anything upon crossing the border. Third, the sole purpose of the statute in *Lambert* was to help the police keep an eye on likely criminals, while the statute here served the purpose of protecting the United States from the dangers caused by the illegal importation of drugs.

Likewise, in *McNeely v. United States*, 874 A.2d 371 (D.C. 2005), Robert McNeely unsuccessfully invoked *Lambert* as a defense to charges that he violated a law making it a crime to own a pit bull that causes injury to a person. Rejecting his argument, the D.C. Court of Appeals reasoned that the dangerous temperament of pit bulls is well known, and therefore, McNeely, unlike Lambert, should have been on notice that the law would impose heightened obligations on him. The court held that as long as McNeely knew his animals were pit bulls, there was no constitutional impediment to creating a strict liability crime:

> We think that the Pit Bull Act falls within that class of statutes the purpose of which would be obstructed by a requirement of proof of culpable intent. Once the legislature has determined that a particular breed poses a heightened danger that justifies a special regime, to require proof that a dog owner purposefully, recklessly, or negligently set his dog upon another would undermine the balance struck by the legislature in the statute.

Nevertheless, the Ninth Circuit relied on *Lambert* in reversing the conviction in *Bartlett v. Alameida*, 366 F.3d 1020 (9th Cir. 2004). The defendant in that case received a prison sentence of 25 years to life for willfully "failing to re-register as a sex offender pursuant to California's sex offender registration statute." The defendant claimed that "he was unaware that his duty to register was lifelong" and instead thought the "obligation to register as a sex offender ended when his parole for that offense expired." At trial, the court instructed the jury that "it is not an element of the offense that the convicted sex offender have actual or probable knowledge of his duty to register"; rather, "[t]he convicted sex offender 'need only have been given actual notice of the requirement to register as a sex offender.'" Bartlett's habeas petition was rejected by the federal district court on the grounds that "any federal due process requirement is satisfied by 'proof of the probability' of actual knowledge—supplied in this instance by Bartlett's 'repeated actual notice of the registration requirement.'" The Ninth Circuit reversed based on *Lambert*:

> *Lambert* requires proof that a defendant knew of the duty to register. The state may, of course, prove knowledge through circumstantial evidence such as signed registration forms and prior registration. Such circumstantial evidence may constitute "proof of the probability of such knowledge." *Lambert*, 355 U.S. at 229. But Bartlett is also entitled to present evidence that he did not read the forms, or did not comprehend them, or misinterpreted the requirements. If the jurors believed Bartlett's testimony that he was thus unaware that his duty to register was lifelong, they were required, consistent with *Lambert*, to acquit him. . . .
>
> . . . Both the state court of appeal and the federal district court reasoned that there was ample evidence that Bartlett received actual notice, thereby supplying the requisite actual knowledge sufficient to satisfy the due process requirements of *Lambert*. We disagree. . . . [T]he jurors, during deliberation, sent a note to the court declaring they were deadlocked. In an effort to break the deadlock, the jury asked the court to elaborate on the meaning of "willfully" as it was used in the jury instructions. In response to this inquiry and to an earlier request by the jury to see Bartlett's mandatory release card (apparently to see if the card "had any instructions on the back"), the trial judge thrice instructed the jury that "[a]ctual knowledge is not an element of the crime." The court then reiterated that the state did not have to prove actual knowledge. After this elaboration, the jury returned a guilty verdict. We conclude that the court's repeated misstatement of an element of the crime "had substantial and injurious effect or influence in determining the jury's verdict" because it was apparently the one factor that turned a deadlocked jury—concerned in particular about the actual knowledge/actual notice distinction—into a convicting jury. Therefore, the error was not harmless. . . .
>
> . . . *Lambert* required the state to prove that Bartlett knew or probably knew of his lifelong duty to register as a sex offender. The trial court erroneously instructed the jury that actual knowledge was not an element of the crime. Because this error was not harmless, and because the state court of appeal unreasonably determined that no *Lambert* error occurred, the

district court erred by not granting Bartlett's petition for writ of habeas corpus.

Id. at 1024–25.

3. Recapitulating the Complexities of the Mistake of Law Doctrine. At this point, it may be useful to reconceptualize and distinguish the various circumstances in which the maxim "ignorance of the law is no excuse" cannot simply be taken at face value. As pointed out above in Note 3 following *People v. Wendt*, as a general matter a mistake of law is a defense when it negates the mens rea required by the statute. But what are the kinds of situations in which that *may* be the case, i.e., in which close scrutiny of the maxim is warranted?

The cases and situations examined in this section allow us to identify the following categories:

(a) *Situations in which the word "knowingly" or "willfully" is strategically placed so as to require knowledge and understanding of the law as a condition of culpability.* Examples of opinions that have interpreted statutes so as to fall into this category are *Weiss* (the kidnapping case), *Klotz* and *Boucher* (the draft registration cases), and *Cheek* (the federal tax case), which are described in Notes 3 and 4 following *People v. Wendt*. Statutes are often drafted ambiguously in this respect, leaving it open to dispute whether the "knowing" requirement includes knowledge and understanding of the law. Consider for example a hypothetical statute that criminalizes "knowingly transporting nuclear waste to an unlicensed storage facility in contravention of the requirements of this statute."

(b) *Situations in which defendants had no reason to know of the existence and applicability of the relevant legal requirement, and in which there was therefore no genuine opportunity to comply with the law's mandate.* A clear example of this kind of situation, and the leading case on the subject, is *Lambert*. In light of more recent cases such as *Reyes* (described in the prior Note), the *Lambert* doctrine may refer only to wholly passive conduct.

(c) *Situations in which defendants did indeed have reason to know of the relevant legal requirement, but also had reason to believe that their actions fell outside the ambit of the prohibition.* This is the situation in which mistakes about law are nevertheless typically viewed as *not* providing a defense. As a general matter, even a good faith and reasonable misunderstanding of the law on the part of the defendant (or the defendant's attorney) provides no shield from liability. As discussed in Note 6 following *Wendt*, however, reliance on an "official statement" of the law that is later invalidated (a court decision that is overturned, a statute that is invalidated, or an erroneous interpretation by an official responsible for interpreting the law) is a defense in many jurisdictions. As the cases demonstrate, the "official statement" standard is not always easy to apply.

(d) *Situations in which the defendants' ignorance or mistake is not about the existence or meaning of the criminal prohibition, but about an element of the crime that turns on a legal distinction.* In these situations the mistake undercuts mens rea and thus provides a defense. An example is *Smith* (described in Note 3 after *People v. Wendt*), where the defendant understood all the relevant facts and presumably knew that theft was prohibited and involved taking the property of another. But he believed in good faith that the property in question was his own; his underlying mistake was not about the criminal prohibition but about the legal definition of property found in landlord/tenant law. Another illustration is *State v. Woods*, 179 A. 1 (Vt. 1935), which involved a prosecution for the crime of adultery. The defendant believed that her second husband had obtained a valid divorce from his first wife in Nevada, but the Nevada decree was not recognized in Vermont. The defendant was not mistaken about the adultery statute she was charged with violating, but about the legal effect of the Nevada divorce decree in Vermont. (Although the Vermont Supreme Court rejected her defense, a modern court would presumably analyze whether her mistake negated the mens rea required by the adultery statute, rather than woodenly applying the maxim "ignorance of the law is no excuse.")

(e) *Situations in which the defendants' ignorance or mistake is not about the existence or meaning of the criminal prohibition, but about their entitlement to a special exemption from the reach of that prohibition.* This defense is the subject of *Barker.* It raises vexing questions that have never been adequately resolved. As the various opinions in *Barker* demonstrate, courts will turn themselves inside out to analogize this situation to other kinds of mistakes of law or fact.

[3] Intoxication

United States v. Williams

332 F. Supp. 1 (D. Md. 1971)

MURRAY, DISTRICT JUDGE.

In this case the defendant was charged in a two count indictment under title 18, U.S.C.A. Sections 2113(a) and (b) with robbery of a branch of the Maryland National Bank in Cambridge, Maryland on December 4, 1970. . . .

The basic facts are not in dispute. In a stipulation signed by government counsel, the defendant and his counsel, it was agreed that on the date set out in the indictment, the defendant went into the bank in Cambridge, Maryland and requested a loan from a branch officer of the bank. The officer declined to grant the defendant a loan. Thereafter the defendant walked up to Mrs. Martina Bennett, a teller, and handed to her a note stating "This is a stickup". Mrs. Bennett gave him all her cash, and defendant then left the bank with the money. It was also stipulated that Mrs. Bennett was intimidated by defendant giving her the note and for that reason turned over to defendant the funds in her drawer. An audit made immediately after the robbery showed the defendant had taken $4,727 of the bank's money.

While defendant thus does not contest the fact that a robbery occurred and he committed it, his counsel urges upon the Court that an essential element of the crime is lacking. It is contended that . . . the bank robbery statute . . . require[s] a specific intent to steal, and that at the time of the robbery defendant was so intoxicated from alcohol and drugs that he was incapable of forming such specific intent.

The threshold legal questions thus are whether voluntary intoxication can negative specific intent as an element of crime and, if so, whether the offense[] require[s] proof of specific intent. If specific intent is an element of the offense . . . , the factual question then arises as to whether on all the evidence the degree of defendant's intoxication was such as to create a reasonable doubt that defendant had a specific intent to steal when the robbery took place.

It is clear from the cases that while voluntary intoxication is ordinarily no defense to crime, it may have that effect if specific intent is an element of the crime. *Edwards v. United States*, 84 U.S. App. D.C. 310, 172 F.2d 884 (1949) (housebreaking and larceny—specific intent required); *Proctor v. United States*, 85 U.S. App. D.C. 341, 177 F.2d 656 (1949) (unauthorized use of vehicle—specific intent not required). . . .

The teaching of these cases is embodied in the recommended instruction on voluntary intoxication in Devitt and Blackmar, Federal Jury Practice and Instructions, Sec. 13.18 of Vol. 1, 2nd Edition which reads:

Voluntary Intoxication

Although intoxication or drunkenness alone will never provide a legal excuse for the commission of a crime, the fact that a person may have been intoxicated at the time of the commission of a crime may negate the existence of a specific intent.

So, evidence that a defendant acted or failed to act while in a state of intoxication is to be considered in determining whether or not the defendant acted, or failed to act, with specific intent, as charged.

. . . Thus in the area of criminal responsibility as affected by voluntary intoxication, a distinction must be drawn between so-called "general intent" to commit a crime and a "specific intent" to do a particular criminal act.

. . . Did Congress in the several subsections of the bank robbery statute create "general intent" crimes or "specific intent" crimes? Some cases uncritically lump all subsections of the statute under the "specific intent" label. Other cases ascribe more careful draftsmanship to the Congress, and find a specific intent an element of the crime only in those subsections of the statute where the language "with intent" is used.

Thus, in *United States v. DeLeo*, 422 F.2d 487 (1st Cir. 1970), . . . the defendant contended that the crime was of the common law larceny genus requiring allegation and proof of specific intent. The Court rejected this argument, stating . . . :

Six specific crimes are set out in Section 2113. Felonious intent is specifically incorporated in the definition of two of them: entering a federally insured institution with intent to commit a felony (a—second paragraph), and taking property with intent to steal or purloin (b). However, it is not made part of the crimes of taking by force and violence or by intimidation (a—first paragraph); knowingly receiving stolen property (c); assaulting or putting in jeopardy the life of a person by a dangerous weapon (d); or killing a person, or forcing a person to accompany him, while in the course of committing one of the other offenses or avoiding apprehension or confinement for any of them (e).

. . . The Court in the present case concludes as a matter of law that the distinction made by the 1st Circuit in *DeLeo* . . . is a valid one, and that the act of the defendant, which he admits of taking by intimidation from the presence of another money belonging to the bank, constitutes a violation of subsection (a) of the statute as charged in Count I of the indictment. The Court rejects as a defense to the crime charged in Count I of the indictment any voluntary intoxication of the defendant.

As to Count II of the indictment, [which is based on subsection (b) of the statute,] the Court feels that historically and legally the contention of the defendant is correct, and that a specific intent to steal is an element of the crime. The Court on a review of all the evidence in the case is satisfied beyond a reasonable doubt that defendant when he took and carried away money belonging to the bank exceeding $100 in value did so with the intent to steal or purloin.

The Court in finding as a fact that defendant had the intent to steal is not unmindful of the fact that there was substantial evidence to show that defendant had imbibed significant quantities of alcohol and drugs, but the Court from all the evidence finds beyond a reasonable doubt that he both had the capacity to and did intend to steal when he took the bank's money. The basis for the Court's finding in this regard requires some reference to the evidence of defendant's taking of alcohol and drugs and his condition at the time of the robbery.

In testifying on his own behalf, defendant claimed that as a result of an argument with his wife he started drinking with a companion around 9:00 A.M. on December 3, 1970, the day before the robbery and over the next fourteen hours the two consumed three fifths of whiskey, of which defendant had about half. During this period defendant also took 6 or 7 "yellow jackets" or barbiturate pills. Between midnight on December 3 and the occurrence of the robbery around 1:00 P.M. on December 4, defendant claims that he and a companion drank an additional one or one and a half fifths of whiskey, of which defendant had all but half a pint. In addition, sometime in this latter period defendant took some LSD pills, with the result that he had only "spotty" recollection of events the morning of the robbery. Defendant does recall going into the bank and talking with the branch officer, and leaving the bank stuffing money under his jacket, but disclaims any recollection of confronting the teller, presenting her with a "stickup" note and actually receiving from her over $4,000 in cash.

The witnesses who actually observed the defendant on the day of the robbery indicate he had been drinking but not that he was drunk. A cab driver named Hopkins who drove the defendant at 6:00 A.M. to redeem his watch and then to a drive-in said his eyes were red and he had been drinking. His speech was "heavy" and he did not seem to walk normally.

Mrs. Florence Brannock, a teller in the bank, spoke briefly with defendant when he asked for the loan department and directed him to the branch officer. She felt he smelled strongly of cheap wine or alcohol and that his speech while understandable was not normal—it was a little "slurred" or "thick."

Branch Officer John Bramble testified that the defendant came into his office seeking a $400 loan for Christmas. In their conversation defendant gave his place of employment, said he owned a 1969 Chevrolet and had an account in the Farmer's and Merchant's bank across the street. The witness said he could smell a strong odor of alcohol on the defendant's breath and felt he was under the influence of liquor and that he also appeared somewhat nervous. After declining to grant the defendant a loan, the witness watched the defendant walk towards the lobby of the bank and could not remember anything unusual about the defendant's walk.

Mrs. Martina Bennett, a cash teller, recalled that a little after 1:00 P.M. a man approached from the side aisle of the bank. She recalled having seen him previously at Mrs. Brannock's desk. He put a note on her counter and said nothing. At first she thought he might be deaf and read the note. It was printed in pencil on a torn piece of paper and read "This is a stickup". She noticed that he had his right hand in his jacket pocket which was thrust forward pointing at her as though he had a gun. She was terrified and afraid he was going to shoot her. She put all her money on the counter, but she did not see what he did with it, although she believes he dropped some and then picked it up. She noticed nothing unusual about the defendant's appearance and did not smell any alcohol. When he was standing before her he did not appear to waver, but his eyes did appear sleepy. She watched him walk away from her counter and down a flight of four steps leading to the lobby entrance.

. . . .

The testimony as to acts of the defendant closest in time to the robbery was given by the owner of a small store in Cambridge, George Heist. His store is located about two blocks from the bank. He recalled that the defendant came into his store about noon and asked for a piece of paper to figure a bill. The defendant reached for a sales pad but the witness did not want the defendant to use the pad and gave him a piece of paper instead. The defendant turned around with his back to the witness and put the piece of paper on top of some stocking boxes and started to write. Apparently dissatisfied, he balled up the piece of paper and threw it on the floor. Defendant reached again for the witness' sales pad, which the witness again refused to give him, tearing off a piece of old calendar paper instead. Defendant again turned around and wrote some more, and then left the store.

The witness said that the defendant while in his store seemed coherent, didn't stagger, and acted normally except for trying to take his sales pad twice. However, because the defendant "seemed a little high on something" he decided, after the defendant left the store, to read what was on the balled up piece of paper. It read "This is a stick". Although defendant on leaving the store walked away from and not towards the bank, the witness appropriately concluded a robbery might be in prospect and got a policeman to whom he gave a description of the defendant. Later he heard the fire whistle blow about 1:00 P.M., which was a signal that the bank had been robbed.

. . . .

The Court believes that the defendant had taken alcohol and drugs to the point of being "under the influence" but that he was not so intoxicated as not to understand what he was doing or to not have the intention to steal from the bank. There is a marked difference between the accounts of the persons who observed defendant and defendant's own account as to his condition. It appears . . . that he was able to write a "stickup" note shortly before the robbery, to go into the bank, hold a coherent conversation about a loan, present the note, obtain over $4,000 in cash, none of which has been returned, and make good his escape. The Court concludes beyond a reasonable doubt that defendant had the intent to steal from the bank as required for conviction. . . .

Notes and Questions

1. **Voluntary Intoxication as a Defense to Specific Intent Crimes.** While voluntary intoxication alone never constitutes a legal excuse for committing a crime, the fact that a defendant was intoxicated may be a defense if it negates the mens rea required by the crime. *See* Wayne R. LaFave, Criminal Law § 9.5, at 497–511 (5th ed. 2010).

Hence, in *State v. Burkley*, 804 S.W.2d 458 (Tenn. Crim. App. 1990), despite acknowledging that the evidence supported a finding of guilt, a Tennessee appellate court vacated the defendant's burglary conviction because the trial judge failed to instruct the jury that voluntary intoxication could negate the specific intent required for burglary — i.e., entry with the intent to commit a felony. Similarly, in *People v. Crittle*, 212 N.W.2d 196 (Mich. 1973), the Michigan Supreme Court reversed an armed robbery conviction where the defendant walked into a grocery store and announced, "this is a hold up," only to return later with the money he had stolen, claim it was an April Fool's joke, and pay for a bottle of beer with his own money. Because armed robbery was a specific intent crime and Crittle raised an intoxication defense, he was entitled to an instruction informing the jury that he could not be convicted if he did not have the requisite intent — i.e., to permanently deprive the victim of his property. As the opinion in *Williams* illustrates, however, courts are often reluctant to find that a defendant's voluntary intoxication actually negated specific intent.

2. **Voluntary Intoxication as a Defense to General Intent Crimes.** Although some jurisdictions allow voluntary intoxication to negate specific intent, the courts are virtually unanimous in rejecting voluntary intoxication as a defense to general intent crimes. In *People v. Kelley*, 446 N.W.2d 821 (Mich. 1989), for example, the Michigan Supreme Court held that voluntary intoxication is no defense to the crime of child

torture because it is not a specific intent crime. Likewise, although assault had traditionally been deemed a specific intent crime, the California Supreme Court broke with that precedent in *People v. Hood*, 462 P.2d 370 (Cal. 1969), and declared assault to be a general intent crime. Reclassifying the offense enabled the court to hold that the defendant could not raise intoxication as a defense to the charge that he was guilty of assault with a deadly weapon when he shot a police officer twice in the leg. *But cf. People v. Whitfield*, 868 P.2d 272 (Cal. 1994) (allowing evidence of intoxication to be introduced to negate the malice necessary for depraved heart murder on the grounds that murder is a specific intent crime for purposes of the intoxication defense whether the prosecution is presenting a case of express or implied malice).

Moreover, half of American jurisdictions have now abandoned the specific intent/general intent dichotomy in ruling on intoxication claims. *See* Mitchell Keiter, *Just Say No Excuse: The Rise and Fall of the Intoxication Defense*, 87 J. Crim. L. & Criminology 482, 518–20 (1997); Joshua Dressler, Understanding Criminal Law § 24.03[B][2], at 324 n.29 (7th ed. 2015). Is it logical to continue recognizing voluntary intoxication as a defense only to specific intent crimes? Why shouldn't intoxication be a defense if it negates the mens rea for a general intent crime? According to one commentator, there is "a higher goal than logic to be vindicated: the preservation of law and order, which would be substantially undermined if voluntarily intoxicated offenders could be acquitted of criminal offenses such as assault, which intoxicated persons are particularly prone to commit." David McCord, *The English and American History of Voluntary Intoxication to Negate Mens Rea*, 11 J. Legal Hist. 372, 388 (1990). *See also Director of Public Prosecutions v. Majewski*, [1977] App. Cas. 443 (H.L.). Or, at the other extreme, why should voluntary intoxication *ever* be recognized as a defense to harmful criminal conduct? (This issue is discussed further below in Note 4.)

3. The Model Penal Code. Like the common law, § 2.08(1) of the Model Penal Code refuses to recognize voluntary intoxication as a defense unless "it negatives an element of the offense." The Code goes on, however, in § 2.08(2) to provide: "When recklessness establishes an element of the offense, if the actor, due to self-induced intoxication, is unaware of a risk of which he would have been aware had he been sober, such unawareness is immaterial." Thus, while the Model Penal Code envisions that intoxication can negate a mens rea of purpose or knowledge, it cannot negate recklessness. Even those who are too intoxicated to realize the risks associated with their actions can still be considered reckless.

In *Hendershott v. People*, 653 P.2d 385 (Colo. 1982), the Colorado Supreme Court shed light on the rationale underlying the Model Penal Code and similar approaches:

> The concept of self-induced intoxication, by definition, requires that the defendant be aware at the outset that the substance he is about to ingest may affect his mental faculties. It is a matter of common knowledge that the excessive use of liquor or drugs impairs the perceptual, judgmental and

volitional faculties of the user. Also, because the intoxication must be "self-induced," the defendant necessarily must have had the conscious ability to prevent this temporary incapacity from coming into being at all. Self-induced intoxication, therefore, by its very nature involves a degree of moral culpability. The moral blameworthiness lies in the voluntary impairment of one's mental faculties with knowledge that the resulting condition is a source of potential danger to others. . . . Thus, when a defendant chooses to knowingly introduce intoxicants into his body to the point of becoming temporarily impaired in his powers of perception, judgment and control, [he is prohibited] from utilizing his intoxication as a defense to crimes requiring the mens rea of "knowingly," "willfully," "recklessly," or "with criminal negligence."

Id. at 396.

Do you agree with the view that voluntarily becoming intoxicated is sufficiently culpable in and of itself?

4. Rejecting Voluntary Intoxication as a Defense. As the Colorado Supreme Court's opinion in *Hendershott* suggests, some jurisdictions have gone further in restricting the situations in which voluntary intoxication constitutes a defense. In *Lee v. State*, 403 So. 2d 132 (Miss. 1981), the Mississippi Supreme Court refused to recognize voluntary intoxication as a defense even to specific intent crimes. Affirming the defendant's conviction on burglary charges, the court held that "a defendant, capable of distinguishing between right and wrong when sober, is not entitled to an instruction submitting to the jury his inability to form the specific intent to commit an offense because of his voluntary intoxication at the time the offense was committed." *Id.* at 134. Likewise, in *State v. Stasio*, 396 A.2d 1129, 1132 (N.J. 1979), the New Jersey Supreme Court relied on the policies of "protect[ing] the public" and minimizing false claims by defendants in holding that "voluntary intoxication [does] not excuse criminal conduct" unless the defendant was too intoxicated to engage in the premeditation required for first-degree murder. Is there any justification for denying a voluntary intoxication defense even when it negates the requisite mens rea, or do you believe that this view is "clearly wrong"? Wayne R. LaFave, Criminal Law § 9.5(f), at 504–05 (5th ed. 2010).

In *Montana v. Egelhoff*, 518 U.S. 37 (1996) (plurality opinion), the Supreme Court upheld the constitutionality of a Montana statute that precluded consideration of the defendant's "intoxicated condition in determining the existence of a mental state which is an element of the offense." The defendant had been convicted of deliberate homicide, which required proof that he purposefully or knowingly caused another's death. The plurality noted that the Due Process Clause does not guarantee a criminal defendant the right to introduce all relevant evidence, but only evidence that would be required under a "fundamental principle of justice." *Id.* at 43. In determining that the right to present evidence of intoxication could not be considered a "fundamental principle of justice," the plurality relied on the common law's traditional rejection of the intoxication defense. Although the plurality acknowledged that more recently the criminal law has allowed voluntary intoxication to negate specific intent, it observed that "fully one-fifth of the States either never adopted [this] 'new common-law' rule . . . or have recently abandoned it." *Id.* at 48. The plurality concluded that this trend was "not surprising" given the "considerable justification" underlying the traditional common-law approach:

> A large number of crimes, especially violent crimes, are committed by intoxicated offenders; modern studies put the numbers as high as half of all homicides, for example. Disallowing consideration of voluntary intoxication has the effect of increasing the punishment for all unlawful acts committed in that state, and thereby deters drunkenness or irresponsible behavior while drunk. The rule also serves as a specific deterrent, ensuring that those who prove incapable of controlling violent impulses while voluntarily intoxicated go to prison. And finally, the rule comports with and implements society's moral perception that one who has voluntarily impaired his own faculties should be responsible for the consequences.

Id. at 49–50. For discussion of similar issues that have recently arisen in rape cases, see Note 9 in Chapter 7, Section B.2.

5. Involuntary Intoxication. Involuntary intoxication occurs when defendants are unaware that they are consuming an intoxicating substance, consume it under force or duress, or do so in accord with medical advice. Unlike voluntary intoxication, involuntary intoxication is universally recognized as a defense if it negates the mens rea required for the crime. In addition, in many states involuntary intoxication also affords a defense if it creates a state of mind that would satisfy the state's definition of insanity (discussed in Chapter 15, Section C), even though an insanity defense would otherwise be unavailable because the condition was temporary and was not triggered by a mental disease. *See* WAYNE R. LAFAVE, CRIMINAL LAW § 9.5(g), at 505–08 (5th ed. 2010).

In *People v. Scott*, 194 Cal. Rptr. 633 (Cal. Ct. App. 1983), for example, the defendant unknowingly ingested a PCP-like hallucinogen at a family party. The next day, mistakenly thinking that he was a government agent acting to protect his own life or possibly that of the President, he attempted to commandeer two vehicles. In reversing his conviction for the crime of attempted unlawful driving or taking of a vehicle, the court held that "[a]lthough defendant's mistake of fact was undoubtedly irrational, it was also undoubtedly reasonable under the circumstances, because the circumstances include that the mistake emanated from a delusion caused by defendant's involuntary intoxication." *Id.* at 639.

Likewise, in *People v. Garcia*, 113 P.3d 775 (Colo. 2005), the Colorado Supreme Court held that insulin-induced hypoglycemia could constitute the affirmative defense of involuntary intoxication. The defendant in that case maintained that his alleged hypoglycemic condition excused his attack on his wife. The trial court did not permit him to raise an involuntary intoxication defense, and was willing to allow him to introduce the evidence of hypoglycemia only if he pled not guilty by reason of insanity. The state supreme court rejected this assessment, holding that because insulin is a drug that can cause intoxication, the defendant should have been allowed to present a defense of involuntary intoxication.

6. **Alcoholism and Narcotics Addiction.** Neither narcotics addiction nor chronic alcoholism is usually sufficient to make out a defense of involuntary intoxication. *See* Wayne R. LaFave, Criminal Law §9.5(i), at 509–11 (5th ed. 2010). In *Tacorante v. People*, 624 P.2d 1324 (Colo. 1981), for example, the defendant held up a liquor store about an hour after injecting himself with three bags of heroin. Although a psychiatrist testified that the defendant had been addicted to heroin for approximately 10 years and that addiction greatly diminishes a person's capacity to refrain from using the drug, the trial court refused to instruct the jury on the involuntary intoxication defense. In affirming the defendant's conviction for aggravated robbery, the Colorado Supreme Court held that "[m]ere addiction is not sufficient to render the injection of heroin involuntary or unknowing." *Id.* at 1327. Was the court right in thinking that "the consumption of heroin by an addict causes self-induced, not involuntary, intoxication"? *Id.* Does the court's decision leave any room for the widespread belief that drug addiction is a disease? (For discussion of the question whether addiction constitutes a mental disease for purposes of the insanity defense, see Note 6(e) in Chapter 15, Section C.2. For discussion of the constitutional implications of punishing the status of addiction or the acts associated with it, see Chapter 3, Section D.)

Chapter 5

"Strict Liability" and Public Welfare Offenses; Vicarious and Corporate Liability

Although the general rule, as laid out in Chapter 4, is that some level of mens rea is required for criminal offenses, there are exceptions. Some crimes are said to be "strict liability" offenses, imposing liability for commission of a bad act even without mens rea. At least in theory, not even a low level of criminal negligence is required to convict for such offenses. The concept of "public welfare" regulatory offenses was developed starting in the early twentieth century, and legislatures began to statutorily endorse such "no mens rea" crimes. These crimes were created in response to widespread societal dangers emerging from, for example, environmental pollutants and the unregulated mass marketing of food and drugs. *See* Joshua Dressler, Understanding Criminal Law § 11.01[C], at 149 (7th ed. 2015) (noting that "a single violation of [a public welfare] offense can simultaneously injure a great number of people"). Strict liability offenses are sometimes said to be *malum prohibitum* (wrong because they are prohibited by law) rather than *malum in se* (obviously wrong in themselves) as were the acts condemned as crimes at common law.

Similarly, concepts of vicarious as well as corporate criminal liability were developed over the past century as well. These doctrines typically impose criminal liability on actors who did not directly cause, or intend to cause, harm and yet were in some sense responsible for the conduct that caused it. It is sometimes said that the United States does not recognize the sort of pure "vicarious" liability that some other countries do (for example, Israel sometimes permits the demolition of houses belonging to family members of suicide bombers). However, "parental responsibility" laws, holding parents responsible for bad conduct by their children, have been in existence in the United States for many years. *See, e.g., Williams v. Garcetti*, 853 P.2d 507 (Cal. 1993) (upholding an amendment to the statute making it a misdemeanor to contribute to the delinquency of a minor, which asserted that parents "have the duty to exercise reasonable care, supervision, protection, and control over their minor child").

As you review this Chapter's materials, ask yourself whether, and when, imposing criminal liability for the conduct of others makes sense or is "fair." Also, ask whether so-called strict liability crimes really impose criminal sanctions with no blameworthy mens rea at all. Or is the common-law mens rea requirement just reduced, but not entirely eliminated? Is there really such a thing as "pure" strict liability in the criminal law? Consider again the utility, versus the fairness, of imposing criminal liability on actors who truly lack any culpable mens rea regarding the conduct at issue.

[A] "Public Welfare" Crimes and Vicarious Liability

Commonwealth v. Koczwara

155 A.2d 825 (Pa. 1959)

COHEN, JUSTICE.

This is an appeal from the judgment of the Court of Quarter Sessions of Lackawanna County sentencing the defendant to three months in the Lackawanna County Jail, a fine of five hundred dollars and the costs of prosecution, in a case involving violations of the Pennsylvania Liquor Code.

John Koczwara, the defendant, is the licensee and operator of an establishment on Jackson Street in the City of Scranton known as J.K.'s Tavern. At that place he had a restaurant liquor license issued by the Pennsylvania Liquor Control Board. The Lackawanna County Grand Jury indicted the defendant . . . for violations of the Liquor Code. The first and second counts averred that the defendant permitted minors, unaccompanied by parents, guardians or other supervisors, to frequent the tavern on February 1st and 8th, 1958; the third count charged the defendant with selling beer to minors on February 8th, 1958; the fourth charged the defendant with permitting beer to be sold to minors on February 8th, 1958. . . .

At the conclusion of the Commonwealth's evidence, count three of the indictment, charging the sale by the defendant personally to the minors, was removed from the jury's consideration by the trial judge on the ground that there was no evidence that the defendant had personally participated in the sale or was present in the tavern when sales to the minors took place. Defense counsel then demurred to the evidence as to the other three counts. The demurrer was overruled. Defendant thereupon rested without introducing any evidence and moved for a directed verdict of acquittal. The motion was denied, the case went to the jury and the jury returned a verdict of guilty as to each of the remaining three counts: two counts of permitting minors to frequent the licensed premises without parental or other supervision, and the count of permitting sales to minors.

. . . The defendant took an appeal to the Superior Court, which, in an opinion by Judge Hirt, affirmed the judgment and sentence of the lower court. A petition for an allowance of an appeal was filed by the defendant. Because of the importance of the issues raised, the petition was allowed and an appeal granted.

Defendant raises two contentions, both of which, in effect, question whether the undisputed facts of this case support the judgment and sentence imposed by the Quarter Sessions Court. Judge Hoban found as fact that "in every instance the purchase [by minors] was made from a bartender, not identified by name, and service to the boys was made by the bartender. There was no evidence that the defendant was present on any one of the occasions testified to by these witnesses, nor that he had any personal knowledge of the sales to them or to other persons on the premises." We, therefore, must determine the criminal responsibility of a licensee of the Liquor Control Board for acts committed by his employees upon his premises, without his personal knowledge, participation, or presence, which acts violate a valid regulatory statute passed under the Commonwealth's police power.

While an employer in almost all cases is not criminally responsible for the unlawful acts of his employees, unless he consents to, approves, or participates in such acts, courts all over the nation have struggled for years in applying this rule within the framework of "controlling the sale of intoxicating liquor." At common law, any attempt to invoke the doctrine of *respondeat superior* in a criminal case would have run afoul of our deeply ingrained notions of criminal jurisprudence that guilt must be personal and individual.[1] In recent decades, however, many states have enacted detailed regulatory provisions in fields which are essentially non-criminal, e.g., pure food and drug acts, speeding ordinances, building regulations, and child labor, minimum wage and maximum hour legislation. Such statutes are generally enforceable by light penalties, and although violations are labeled crimes, the considerations applicable to them are totally different from those applicable to true crimes, which involve moral delinquency and which are punishable by imprisonment or another serious penalty. Such so-called statutory crimes are in reality an attempt to utilize the machinery of criminal administration as an enforcing arm for social regulations of a purely civil nature, with the punishment totally unrelated to questions of moral wrongdoing or guilt. It is here that the social interest in the general well-being and security of the populace has been held to outweigh the individual interest of the particular defendant. The penalty is imposed despite the defendant's lack of a criminal intent or mens rea.

Not the least of the legitimate police power areas of the legislature is the control of intoxicating liquor. As Mr. Justice Benjamin R. Jones recently stated in *In re Tahiti Bar, Inc.*, 150 A.2d 112, 115 (Pa. 1959), "There is perhaps no other area of permissible state action within which the exercise of the police power of a state is more plenary than in the regulation and control of the use and sale of alcoholic beverages." It is abundantly clear that the conduct of the liquor business is lawful only to the extent and manner permitted by statute. Individuals who embark on such an

---

1. [n.1] The distinction between *respondeat superior* in tort law and its application to the criminal law is obvious. In tort law, the doctrine is employed for the purpose of settling the incidence of loss upon the party who can best bear such loss. But the criminal law is supported by totally different concepts. We impose penal treatment upon those who injure or menace social interests, partly in order to reform, partly to prevent the continuation of the anti-social activity and partly to deter others. If a defendant has personally lived up to the social standards of the criminal law and has not menaced or injured anyone, why impose penal treatment?

enterprise do so with knowledge of considerable peril, since their actions are rigidly circumscribed by the Liquor Code.

Because of the peculiar nature of this business, one who applies for and receives permission from the Commonwealth to carry on the liquor trade assumes the highest degree of responsibility to his fellow citizens. As the licensee of the Board, he is under a duty not only to regulate his own personal conduct in a manner consistent with the permit he has received, but also to control the acts and conduct of any employee to whom he entrusts the sale of liquor. Such fealty is the *quid pro quo* which the Commonwealth demands in return for the privilege of entering the highly restricted and, what is more important, the highly *dangerous* business of selling intoxicating liquor.

In the instant case, the defendant has sought to surround himself with all the safeguards provided to those within the pale of criminal sanctions. He has argued that a statute imposing criminal responsibility should be construed strictly, with all doubts resolved in his favor. While the defendant's position is entirely correct, we must remember that we are dealing with a statutory crime within the state's plenary police power. In the field of liquor regulation, the legislature has enacted a comprehensive Code aimed at regulating and controlling the use and sale of alcoholic beverages. The question here raised is whether the legislature *intended* to impose vicarious criminal liability on the licensee principal for acts committed on his premises without his presence, participation or knowledge.

This Court has stated, as long ago as *Commonwealth v. Weiss*, 21 Atl. 10 (Pa. 1891), that "whether a criminal intent, or a guilty knowledge, is a necessary ingredient of a statutory offense . . . is a matter of construction. It is for the legislature to determine whether the public injury, threatened in any particular matter, is such and so great as to justify an absolute and indiscriminate prohibition." In the *Weiss* case, and in *Commonwealth v. Miller*, 18 Atl. 938 (Pa. 1890), this Court construed the statute in question in the light of its letter and spirit and its manifest purpose.[2]

In the Liquor Code, Section 493, the legislature has set forth twenty-five specific acts which are condemned as unlawful, and for which penalties are provided in Section 494. Subsections (1) and (14) of Section 493 contain the two offenses charged here. In neither of these subsections is there any language which would require the

---

2. [n.3] This case is not governed by *Carlson's License*, 18 Atl. 8 (Pa. 1889); *Commonwealth v. Sellers*, 18 Atl. 541 (Pa. 1889); *Commonwealth v. Holstine*, 19 Atl. 273 (Pa. 1890); or *Commonwealth v. Zelt*, 21 Atl. 7 (Pa. 1891). Those cases hold persons answerable for sales made by *themselves*, and prevent them from pleading ignorance of the nonage or intemperate habits of those to whom they sell. Nor is this case governed by *Commonwealth v. Junkin et al.*, 32 Atl. 617 (Pa. 1895), which refused to hold a principal criminally liable for the wrongful act of his agent, where the act was in positive disobedience of the principal's instructions. The *Junkin* case did not involve a comprehensive regulatory scheme which clearly evidenced a legislative purpose to hold a licensee responsible for all illegal acts conducted on the licensed premises. The Liquor Code of Pennsylvania in effect makes the act of the employee the act of the licensee for the purpose of enforcing the rigid restrictions on the sale of liquor.

prohibited acts to have been done either knowingly, wilfully or intentionally, there being a significant absence of such words as "knowingly, wilfully, etc." That the legislature intended such a requirement in other related sections of the same Code is shown by examining Section 492(15), wherein it is made unlawful to *knowingly* sell any malt beverages to a person engaged in the business of illegally selling such beverages. The omission of any such word in the subsections of Section 494 is highly significant. It indicates a legislative intent to eliminate both knowledge and criminal intent as necessary ingredients of such offenses. To bolster this conclusion, we refer back to Section 491 wherein the Code states, "It shall be unlawful (1) For any person, by himself, *or by an employe[e] or agent*, to expose or keep for sale, or directly or *indirectly* . . . to sell or offer to sell any liquor within this Commonwealth, except in accordance with the provisions of this act and the regulations of the board." The Superior Court has long placed such an interpretation on the statute.[3]

As the defendant has pointed out, there is a distinction between the requirement of a mens rea and the imposition of vicarious absolute liability for the acts of another. It may be that the courts below, in relying on prior authority, have failed to make such a distinction.[4] In any case, we fully recognize it. Moreover, we find that the intent of the legislature in enacting this Code was not only to eliminate the common law requirement of a mens rea, but also to place a very high degree of responsibility upon the holder of a liquor license to make certain that neither he nor anyone in his employ commit any of the prohibited acts upon the licensed premises. Such a burden of care is imposed upon the licensee in order to protect the public from the potentially noxious effects of an inherently dangerous business. We, of course, express no opinion as to the *wisdom* of the legislature's imposing vicarious responsibility under certain sections of the Liquor Code. There may or may not be an economic-sociological justification for such liability on a theory of deterrence. Such determination is for the legislature to make, so long as the constitutional requirements are met.

Can the legislature, consistent with the requirements of due process, thus establish absolute criminal liability? Were this the defendant's first violation of the Code, and the penalty solely a minor fine of from $100–$300, we would have no hesitation in upholding such a judgment. Defendant, by accepting a liquor license, must bear this financial risk. Because of a prior conviction for violations of the Code, however, the trial judge felt compelled under the mandatory language of the statute, Section 494(a), to impose not only an increased fine of five hundred dollars, but also a three month sentence of imprisonment. Such sentence of imprisonment in a case where liability is imposed vicariously cannot be sanctioned by this Court consistently

---

3. [n.4] It is established that a liquor license may be legally suspended or revoked for violations of the Code committed by employees of the licensee even though there is no evidence that the licensee knew of such violations.

4. [n.5] We must also be extremely careful to distinguish the present situation from the question of corporate criminal liability, such as was involved in *Commonwealth v. Liberty Products Company*, 84 Pa. Super. Ct. 473 (1925). . . . [See Section B below for a discussion of corporate liability.]

with the law of the land clause of Section 9, Article I of the Constitution of the Commonwealth of Pennsylvania.[5]

The Courts of the Commonwealth have already strained to permit the legislature to carry over the civil doctrine of *respondeat superior* and to apply it as a means of enforcing the regulatory scheme that covers the liquor trade. We have done so on the theory that the Code established petty misdemeanors involving only light monetary fines. It would be unthinkable to impose vicarious criminal responsibility in cases involving true crimes. Although to hold a principal criminally liable might possibly be an effective means of enforcing law and order, it would do violence to our more sophisticated modern day concepts of justice. Liability for all true crimes, wherein an offense carries with it a jail sentence, must be based exclusively upon personal causation. It can be readily imagined that even a licensee who is meticulously careful in the choice of his employees cannot supervise every single act of the subordinates. A man's liberty cannot rest on so frail a reed as whether his employee will commit a mistake in judgment.

This Court is ever mindful of its duty to maintain and establish the proper safeguards in a criminal trial. To sanction the imposition of imprisonment here would make a serious change in the substantive criminal law of the Commonwealth, one for which we find no justification. We have found *no* case in any jurisdiction which has permitted a *prison term* for a vicarious offense. . . .

In holding that the punishment of imprisonment deprives the defendant of due process of law under these facts, we are not declaring that Koczwara must be treated as a first offender under the Code. He has clearly violated the law for a second time and must be punished accordingly. Therefore, we are only holding that so much of the judgment as calls for imprisonment is invalid, and we are leaving intact the five hundred dollar fine imposed by Judge Hoban under the subsequent offense section. . . .

BELL, JUSTICE (concurring and dissenting).

Although the question is close, this case is ruled in principle by *Commonwealth v. Sellers, Commonwealth v. Holstine*, [and] *Commonwealth v. Zelt*. . . . I believe that the distinction which is drawn by the majority is of insufficient weight to distinguish and govern the instant case. I would affirm the judgment and sentence on the opinion of Judge Hirt, speaking for a unanimous Superior Court.

MUSMANNO, JUSTICE (dissenting).

The Court in this case is doing what it has absolutely no right to do. It is laying aside its judicial robes and officiating as members of the General Assembly. It is declaring a crime which has no existence in the statute books, it is imposing a penalty which is not authorized by the criminal code.

---

5. [n.7] Sec. 9. ". . . nor can he be deprived of his life, liberty or property, unless by the judgment of his peers or the law of the land." [This is similar to the U.S. Constitution's Due Process Clauses.]

. . . The Majority of this Court is doing something which can find no justification in all the law books which ornament the libraries and enlighten the judges and lawyers in this Commonwealth. It sustains the conviction of a person for acts admittedly not committed by him, not performed in his presence, not accomplished at his direction, and not even done within his knowledge. It is stigmatizing him with a conviction for an act which, in point of personal responsibility, is as far removed from him as if it took place across the seas. The Majority's decision is so novel, so unique, and so bizarre that one must put on his spectacles, remove them to wipe the lenses, and then put them on again in order to assure himself that what he reads is a judicial decision proclaimed in Philadelphia, the home of the Liberty Bell, the locale of Independence Hall, and the place where the fathers of our country met to draft the Constitution of the United States, the Magna Carta of the liberties of Americans and the beacon of hope of mankind seeking justice everywhere.

The decision handed down in this case throws a shadow over that Constitution, applies an eraser to the Bill of Rights, and muffles the Liberty Bell which many decades ago sang its song of liberation from monarchical domination over man's inalienable right to life, liberty, and the pursuit of happiness. Our legal system is based on precedent. The decision of today will become a precedent on which future Dracos may feed to their absolutist and tyrannical content.

. . . The Majority introduces into its discussion a proposition which is shocking to contemplate. It speaks of "vicarious criminal liability." Such a concept is as alien to American soil as the upas tree. There was a time in China when a convicted felon sentenced to death could offer his brother or other close relative in his stead for decapitation. The Chinese law allowed such "vicarious criminal liability." I never thought that Pennsylvania would look with favor on anything approaching so revolting a barbarity.

The Majority Opinion attempts to give authority to its legislative usurpation by referring to twenty-five specific acts which are designated as unlawful in Section 494 of the Liquor Code. It is true that the General Assembly has enumerated certain proscribed situations, but nowhere has the Legislature said that a person may be tried and convicted for a personal act committed in the darkness of his absence and in the night of his utter lack of knowledge thereof.

Battling for some solid terrain upon which to stand to uphold its unstable position, the Majority points to an invisible phantom. It seeks to fortify its argument not by what it finds in the Code, but by what it does not find in the Code. It asserts that the *omission* of the word "knowingly" from Section 494 "indicates a legislative intent to eliminate both knowledge and criminal intent as necessary ingredients of such offenses." But a person's liberties should not hang on so thin a thread as "indicates." Where the sovereign body of the Commonwealth, the General Assembly, decides that a citizen is to be deprived of his life, liberty, or good name upon the commission of a certain act, it does not merely "indicate" the drastic penalty awaiting the person who violates the specific legislative provision. It specifically and in mandatory language orders the penalty. If the Legislature intended to punish a person for acts committed by another (assuming it had the constitutional power to do so), it would have declared that for certain acts committed within a liquor-dispensing establishment the proprietor will be criminally responsible "whether present or not." But the Legislature did not see fit to add such words. This Court is now adding those words and, in doing so, it is usurping the functions of the Legislature which, I repeat, it has no authority to do.

. . . If it is wrong to send a person to jail for acts committed by another, is it not wrong to convict him at all? There are those who value their good names to the extent that they see as much harm in a degrading criminal conviction as in a jail sentence. The laceration of a man's reputation, the blemishing of his good name, the wrecking of his prestige by a criminal court conviction may blast a person's chances for honorable success in life to such an extent that a jail sentence can hardly add much to the ruin already wrought to him by the conviction alone. . . .

McBride, Justice (dissenting).

I would agree that a man who sells liquor to a minor may be punished even if he did not know that the person to whom he sold was a minor. But in my opinion, the statute does not and cannot validly create an indictable misdemeanor under which a liquor licensee is punished by a fine or imprisonment, or both, for the act of an employee in selling to a minor, where, as here, the act itself is done without the licensee's knowledge, consent, or acquiescence. I would reverse the judgment and discharge the defendant.

United States v. Freed

401 U.S. 601 (1971)

Mr. Justice Douglas delivered the opinion of the Court.

. . . .

[The National Firearms Act makes it] unlawful for any person "to receive or possess a firearm which is not registered to him in the National Firearms Registration and Transfer Record." [The defendants here were charged under the Act with possessing and conspiring to possess unregistered "destructive devices"—a type of "firearm" defined in the statute to include the hand grenades at issue here. The crime carried a maximum sentence of ten years.]

. . . The District Court . . . granted the [defendants'] motion to dismiss [on the ground that] . . . the conspiracy "to possess destructive devices" and the possession charged do not allege the element of scienter.

. . . We . . . conclude that the District Court erred in dismissing the indictment for absence of an allegation of scienter. The Act requires no specific intent or knowledge that the hand grenades were unregistered. It makes it unlawful for any person "to receive or possess a firearm which is not registered to him." By the lower court decisions at the time that requirement was written into the Act the only knowledge required to be proved was knowledge that the instrument possessed was a firearm. *See Sipes v. United States*, 321 F.2d 174, 179 [(8th Cir. 1963)], and cases cited.

The presence of a "vicious will" or mens rea (*Morissette v. United States*, 342 U.S. 246 [(1952) (interpreting a statute making it a crime to "embezzle[], steal[], purloin[], or knowingly convert[]" government property)]) was long a requirement of criminal responsibility. But the list of exceptions grew, especially in the expanding regulatory area involving activities affecting public health, safety, and welfare. The statutory offense of embezzlement, borrowed from the common law where scienter was historically required, was in a different category.[6]

"Where Congress borrows terms of art in which are accumulated the legal tradition and meaning of centuries of practice, it presumably knows and adopts the cluster of ideas that were attached to each borrowed word in the body of learning from which it was taken and the meaning its use will convey to the judicial mind unless otherwise instructed." *Id.* at 263.

At the other extreme is *Lambert v. California*, 355 U.S. 225 [(1957)], in which a municipal code made it a crime to remain in Los Angeles for more than five days without registering if a person had been convicted of a felony. Being in Los Angeles is not per se blameworthy. The mere failure to register, we held, was quite "unlike the commission of acts, or the failure to act under circumstances that should alert the doer to the consequences of his deed." *Id.* at 228. The fact that the ordinance was a convenient law enforcement technique did not save it.[7]

"Where a person did not know of the duty to register and where there was no proof of the probability of such knowledge, he may not be convicted consistently with due process. Were it otherwise, the evil would be as great as it is when the law is written in print too fine to read or in a language foreign to the community." *Id.* at 229–30.

In *United States v. Dotterweich*, 320 U.S. 277, 284 [(1943)], a case dealing with the imposition of a penalty on a corporate officer whose firm shipped adulterated and

---

6. [n.13] As respects the *Morissette* case, J. Marshall, Intention — In Law and Society 138 (1968), says:

> "The defendant wished to take government property [rusted bomb casings] from a government bombing range, he had the capacity to take it, he had the opportunity, he tried and succeeded in taking it (his wish was fulfilled, his act accomplished). For recovery in a tort action no more would have to be shown to establish liability, but the court held that to make his action criminal 'a felonious intent,' mens rea, had to be established. This could not be presumed from his actions, which were open, without concealment, and in the belief — according to his statement — that the property had been abandoned. In other words, for the happening to be criminal, the wish had to be to accomplish something criminal. So in discussing intent we may have wishes of two different characters: one giving a basis for civil liability (the wish to take property not one's own), and another which would support criminal liability as well as civil (taking property with criminal intent)."

7. *Lambert* is excerpted above in Chapter 4, Section C.2.

misbranded drugs in violation of the Food and Drug Act, we approved the penalty "though consciousness of wrongdoing be totally wanting."[8]

The present case is in the category neither of *Lambert* nor *Morissette*, but is closer to *Dotterweich*. This is a regulatory measure in the interest of the public safety, which may well be premised on the theory that one would hardly be surprised to learn that possession of hand grenades is not an innocent act.[9] They are highly dangerous offensive weapons, no less dangerous than the narcotics involved in *United States v. Balint*, 258 U.S. 250, 254 [(1922)], where a defendant was convicted of sale of narcotics against his claim that he did not know the drugs were covered by a federal act. We say with Chief Justice Taft in that case:

> "It is very evident from a reading of it that the emphasis of the section is in securing a close supervision of the business of dealing in these dangerous drugs by the taxing officers of the Government and that it merely uses a criminal penalty to secure recorded evidence of the disposition of such drugs as a means of taxing and restraining the traffic. Its manifest purpose is to require every person dealing in drugs to ascertain at his peril whether that which he sells comes within the inhibition of the statute, and if he sells the inhibited drug in ignorance of its character, to penalize him. Congress weighed the possible injustice of subjecting an innocent seller to a penalty against the evil of exposing innocent purchasers to danger from the drug, and concluded that the latter was the result preferably to be avoided." *Id.* at 253–54.

MR. JUSTICE BRENNAN, concurring in the judgment of reversal.

. . . [A]lthough I reach the same result as the Court on the intent the Government must prove to convict, I do so by another route. . . .

. . . The Court's discussion of the intent the Government must prove to convict appellees . . . does not dispel the confusion surrounding a difficult, but vitally important, area of the law. This case does not raise questions of "consciousness of wrongdoing" or "blameworthiness." If the ancient maxim that "ignorance of the law is no excuse" has any residual validity, it indicates that the ordinary intent requirement — mens rea — of the criminal law does not require knowledge that an act is illegal, wrong, or blameworthy. Nor is it possible to decide this case by a simple process of classifying the statute involved as a "regulatory" or a "public welfare" measure. To convict appellees of possession of unregistered hand grenades, the Government must prove three material elements: (1) that appellees possessed certain items; (2) that the

---

8. *Dotterweich* is discussed in the *Park* case, which is excerpted below in Section B.2.

9. [n.14] We need not decide whether a criminal conspiracy to do an act "innocent in itself" and not known by the alleged conspirators to be prohibited must be actuated by some corrupt motive other than the intention to do the act which is prohibited and which is the object of the conspiracy. An agreement to acquire hand grenades is hardly an agreement innocent in itself. Therefore what we have said of the substantive offense satisfies on these special facts the requirements for a conspiracy. *Cf. United States v. Mack*, 112 F.2d 290. [The question whether a "corrupt motive" is an element of conspiracy is discussed below in Chapter 13, Section A.3, Note 4.]

items possessed were hand grenades; and (3) that the hand grenades were not registered. The Government and the Court agree that the prosecutor must prove knowing possession of the items and also knowledge that the items possessed were hand grenades. Thus, while the Court does hold that no intent at all need be proved in regard to one element of the offense — the unregistered status of the grenades — knowledge must still be proved as to the other two elements. Consequently, the National Firearms Act does not create a crime of strict liability as to all its elements. It is no help in deciding what level of intent must be proved as to the third element to declare that the offense falls within the "regulatory" category.

Following the analysis of the Model Penal Code, I think we must recognize, first, that "the existence of a mens rea is the rule of, rather than the exception to, the principles of Anglo-American criminal jurisprudence." *Dennis v. United States*, 341 U.S. 494, 500 (1951) (Vinson, C.J., announcing judgment); *Smith v. California*, 361 U.S. 147, 150 (1959);[10] second, that mens rea is not a unitary concept, but may vary as to each element of a crime; and third, that Anglo-American law has developed several identifiable and analytically distinct levels of intent, e.g., negligence, recklessness, knowledge, and purpose.[11] To determine the mental element required for conviction, each material element of the offense must be examined and the determination made what level of intent Congress intended the Government to prove, taking into account constitutional considerations, *see Screws v. United States*, 325 U.S. 91 (1945), as well as the common law background, if any, of the crime involved. *See Morissette v. United States*, 342 U.S. 246 (1952).

Although the legislative history of the amendments to the National Firearms Act is silent on the level of intent to be proved in connection with each element of the offense, we are not without some guideposts. I begin with the proposition stated in *Morissette v. United States*, that the requirement of mens rea "is no provincial or transient notion. It is as universal and persistent in mature systems of law as belief in freedom of the human will and a consequent ability and duty of the normal individual to choose between good and evil." In regard to the first two elements of the offense, (1) possession of items that (2) are hand grenades, the general rule in favor

---

10. [n.4] "Still, it is doubtless competent for the [government] to create strict criminal liabilities by defining criminal offenses without any element of scienter — though . . . there is precedent in this Court that this power is not without limitations. *See Lambert v. California*, 355 U.S. 225." *Smith v. California*, 361 U.S. 147, 150 (1959). The situations in which strict liability may be imposed were stated by Judge, now Mr. Justice, Blackmun: "Where a federal criminal statute omits mention of intent and where it seems to involve what is basically a matter of policy, where the standard imposed is, under the circumstances, reasonable and adherence thereto properly expected of a person, where the penalty is relatively small, where conviction does not gravely besmirch, where the statutory crime is not one taken over from the common law, and where congressional purpose is supporting, the statute can be construed as one not requiring criminal intent." *Holdridge v. United States*, 282 F.2d 302, 310 (CA8 1960).

11. [n.5] These different levels of intent are defined in the code. ALI Model Penal Code § 2.02 (Prop. Official Draft 1962). This Court has relied on the code's definitions. *Leary v. United States*, 395 U.S. 6, 46 n.93 (1969); *Turner v. United States*, 396 U.S. 398, 416 n.29 (1970).

of some intent requirement finds confirmation in the case law under the provisions replaced by the present amendments. The cases held that a conviction of an individual of illegal possession of unregistered firearms had to be supported by proof that his possession was "willing and conscious" and that he knew the items possessed were firearms. Congress did not disapprove these cases, and we may therefore properly infer that Congress meant that the Government must prove knowledge with regard to the first two elements of the offense under the amended statute.

The third element — the unregistered status of the grenades — presents more difficulty. Proof of intent with regard to this element would require the Government to show that the appellees knew that the grenades were unregistered or negligently or recklessly failed to ascertain whether the weapons were registered. It is true that such a requirement would involve knowledge of law, but it does not involve "consciousness of wrongdoing" in the sense of knowledge that one's actions were prohibited or illegal.[12] Rather, the definition of the crime, as written by Congress, requires proof of circumstances that involve a legal element, namely whether the grenades were registered in accordance with federal law. The knowledge involved is solely knowledge of the circumstances that the law has defined as material to the offense. The Model Penal Code illustrates the distinction:

> "It should be noted that the general principle that ignorance or mistake of law is no excuse is usually greatly overstated; it has no application when the circumstances made material by the definition of the offense include a legal element. So, for example, it is immaterial in theft, when claim of right is adduced in defense, that the claim involves a legal judgment as to the right of property. It is a defense because knowledge that the property belongs to someone else is a material element of the crime and such knowledge may involve matter of law as well as fact. . . . The law involved is not the law defining the offense; it is some other legal rule that characterizes the attendant circumstances that are material to the offense." Model Penal Code § 2.02, Comment 131 (Tent. Draft No. 4, 1955).

Therefore, as with the first two elements, the question is solely one of congressional intent. And while the question is not an easy one, two factors persuade me that proof of mens rea as to the unregistered status of the grenades is not required. First, as the Court notes, the case law under the provisions replaced by the current law dispensed with proof of intent in connection with this element. *Sipes v. United States, supra.* Second, the firearms covered by the Act are major weapons such as machine guns and sawed off shotguns; deceptive weapons such as flashlight guns and

---

12. [n.6] Proof of some crimes may include a requirement of proof of actual knowledge that the act was prohibited by law, or proof of a purpose to bring about the forbidden result. *See James v. United States*, 366 U.S. 213 (1961); *Boyce Motor Lines v. United States*, 342 U.S. 337 (1952); *United States v. Murdock*, 290 U.S. 389 (1933). *See generally* Note, *Counseling Draft Resistance: The Case for a Good Faith Belief Defense*, 78 YALE L.J. 1008, 1022–37 (1969). *Cf.* Model Penal Code § 2.02(2)(a) (Prop. Official Draft 1962) (definition of "purposely").

fountain pen guns; and major destructive devices such as bombs, grenades, mines, rockets, and large caliber weapons including mortars, antitank guns, and bazookas. Without exception, the likelihood of governmental regulation of the distribution of such weapons is so great that anyone must be presumed to be aware of it. In the context of a taxing and registration scheme, I therefore think it reasonable to conclude that Congress dispensed with the requirement of intent in regard to the unregistered status of the weapon, as necessary to effective administration of the statute.

Notes and Questions

1. Strict Liability. Strict liability crimes are said to require no proof of mens rea, and therefore do not allow a defense for even a "reasonable" mistake of fact. (See Chapter 4, Section C.1 for a discussion of mistake of fact.) Consequently, if serving liquor to minors is truly a strict liability crime in a case like *Koczwara*, it would be no excuse that a reasonable person would have thought the minors were well over the legal drinking age.

Is the offense in *Freed* truly a strict liability crime — i.e., one where no mens rea is required? What does Justice Brennan's concurrence add to the analysis of that question? And why, do you think, did Justice Brennan believe it was necessary for him to write a concurrence?

Finally, apply Justice Brennan's more nuanced "elements" analysis to *Koczwara*. What did Koczwara actually know about his business and the potential for a violation of the laws governing liquor sales to minors? Given Koczwara's state of mind, was this really a case involving no blameworthy mens rea? Based on what he knew, should he be considered entirely innocent merely because he was not on the premises at the time of the criminal acts? By contrast, suppose Koczwara had specifically instructed his employees not to sell to minors, threatened to fire them if they did, and even audited the employees from time to time, but a rogue bartender served minors only when Koczwara was not present. Could it be said that Koczwara had even an iota of blameworthy mens rea?

2. Public Welfare Crimes. As discussed by Justice Douglas in *Freed* (and by Professor Dressler in the introduction to this Chapter), modern-day strict liability crimes are often enacted to regulate what are called "public welfare" health and safety dangers. Serving adulterated food, using incorrect weights in commerce, and violating traffic safety regulations are classic strict liability crimes said to dispense with any mens rea requirement. What do you think is the rationale for imposing criminal liability for such offenses even without blameworthy mens rea? Compare this question to the controversy surrounding statutes that punish criminal negligence, discussed in Chapter 4, Section B.2.

Such "public welfare crimes" are said to normally trigger only short jail sentences or modest fines. Because less severe penalties are imposed in the context of significant public health or other regulatory concerns, many find dispensing with any mens rea requirement a reasonable compromise. But what was the maximum penalty for the weapons possession offense at issue in *Freed*? Does that crime fit the description of a "public welfare" crime? If you think it is an appropriate public welfare crime, then what (if anything) would you say limits the concept of "no mens rea" strict liability public welfare offenses? For discussion of public welfare crimes in the context of corporate officer liability, see Note 1 in Section B.2 below.

Strict liability is sometimes justified as a means of allowing prosecutors to punish negligent or reckless offenders where actual proof of such mental states would be difficult. Under this view, the truly innocent will be spared by prosecutorial discretion. Is declining to prosecute a provable crime an appropriate use of a prosecutor's discretion? Are you comfortable relying on prosecutorial discretion for protection even though it is no guarantee of non-prosecution as long as strict liability crimes exist? Are there alternatives for regulators interested in promoting the public health and welfare? What about civil penalties and license revocations or suspensions?

Does economic analysis justify the creation of public welfare crimes? Is it appropriate to demand more than "reasonable" — that is, absolute — precautions under certain circumstances, or for certain societal dangers? Or is strict liability likely to lead to excessive precautions that are inefficient and ultimately damaging to the economic health of the community?

3. The Model Penal Code Position. Section 2.05 of the Mode Penal Code objects to strict liability "crimes," but allows for strict liability "violations," which do not carry either the potential for a prison sentence or the stigma of criminal conviction:

> This section makes a frontal attack on absolute or strict liability in the penal law, whenever the offense carries the possibility of criminal conviction, for which a sentence of probation or imprisonment may be imposed. The method used is not to abrogate strict liability completely, but to provide that when conviction rests upon that basis the grade of the offense is reduced to a violation, which is not a "crime" and under Sections 1.04(5) and 6.02(4) may result in no sentence other than a fine, or a fine and forfeiture or other authorized civil penalty.

> This position is affirmed not only with respect to offenses defined by the penal code; it is superimposed on the entire corpus of the law so far as penal sanctions are involved. Since most strict liability offenses involve special regulatory legislation, normally found in titles of a code other than the criminal title, this superimposition is essential if the principle of no criminality, probation or imprisonment for strict liability offenses is to be made effective.

> The Institute did not doubt that the principle is one that should be given force. The liabilities involved are indefensible, unless reduced to terms that insulate conviction from the type of moral condemnation that is and ought to be implicit when a sentence of probation or imprisonment may be imposed. It has been argued, and the argument undoubtedly will be repeated, that strict liability is necessary for enforcement in a number of the areas where it

obtains. But if practical enforcement precludes litigation of the culpability of alleged deviation from legal requirements, the enforcers cannot rightly demand the use of penal sanctions for the purpose. Crime does and should mean condemnation and no court should have to pass that judgment unless it can declare that the defendant's act was culpable. This is too fundamental to be compromised. The law goes far enough if it permits the imposition of a monetary penalty in cases where strict liability has been imposed.

Model Penal Code § 2.05 Comment at 282–83. Do you find these Comments persuasive? Why does the Model Penal Code allow "violations" punishable by fines instead of relying on purely civil sanctions to enforce strict liability regulations?

4. Bigamy and Statutory Rape. Strict liability is not a twentieth-century, "public welfare" invention. In fact, bigamy and statutory rape were long recognized as strict liability crimes at common law, even though they could lead to lengthy prison sentences. Thus at common law, even a reasonable mistake of fact would not excuse a defendant charged with bigamy or statutory rape.

In *Staley v. State*, 131 N.W. 1028 (Neb. 1911), for example, the defendant legally married his first cousin in Iowa. The couple moved to Nebraska, where marriages between first cousins were not permitted. The defendant was informed by three lawyers that his marriage was void, and a county attorney threatened to prosecute him if he did not terminate his relationship with his cousin. He left her and married another woman. But it turned out that, under an exception to the Nebraska law, the first marriage was actually valid. The defendant was convicted of bigamy, and the Supreme Court of Nebraska affirmed, concluding that his reasonable, but mistaken, belief that the first marriage was void was no defense.

Today, however, courts generally reject the view that a reasonable mistake of fact is no defense to bigamy charges. The Delaware Supreme Court recognized the availability of a mistake of fact defense in *Long v. State*, 65 A.2d 489 (Del. 1949), citing the "great leading English case" of *The Queen v. Tolson*, 23 Q.B.D. 168 (1889). In *Tolson*, the defendant remarried based on her erroneous, but reasonable, belief that her husband was dead. A closely divided Queen's Bench quashed her conviction. Similarly, in *People v. Vogel*, 299 P.2d 850, 855 (Cal. 1956), Justice Traynor wrote: "[t]he severe penalty imposed for bigamy, the serious loss of reputation conviction entails, the infrequency of the offense, and the fact that it has been regarded for centuries as a crime involving moral turpitude, make it extremely unlikely that the Legislature meant to include the morally innocent to make sure the guilty did not escape." Given these modern views, what do you think the justifications were for treating bigamy as a strict liability crime at common law?

By contrast, statutory rape—sex with an underage victim—continues to be a strict liability crime in a majority of states, although great controversy surrounds the issue and many jurisdictions recognize a "reasonable mistake" defense when the victim is below a certain age (e.g., 14 in California). (Statutory rape is discussed in Chapter 7, Section A.)

5. ***Staples v. United States.*** Staples was convicted of the same offense involved in *Freed*, possessing an unregistered dangerous weapon (here, a "machine gun"), a crime punishable by a maximum 10-year sentence. Staples undisputedly possessed a weapon that had originally been designed as a "semi-automatic" rifle, which despite its capability of firing rapid fire shots, would not have fit the statutory definition of a "machine gun" ("any weapon which shoots . . . automatically more than one shot, without manual reloading, by a single function of the trigger"). But Staples' weapon had apparently been modified internally so that it was capable of fully automatic fire, thereby bringing it within the statutory prohibition. The government argued that it was not necessary to prove that the defendant knew the rifle had been modified so as to fire automatically. *See Staples v. United States*, 511 U.S. 600 (1994).

In an opinion written by Justice Thomas, the Court disagreed, ruling that in the absence of evidence that Congress intended to dispense with a mens rea requirement, the statute should be read to require knowledge that the rifle was capable of fully automatic fire. The fact that the statute was silent on mens rea and did not specifically require knowledge did not overcome the *Morissette* presumption (discussed in *Freed*) in favor of implying a mens rea requirement.

The seven Justices in the *Staples* majority rejected the government's argument that the presumption in favor of mens rea did not apply because statutes regulating dangerous weapons are "public welfare" strict liability crimes. The Court distinguished both *Freed* and *United States v. Balint*, 258 U.S. 250 (1922) (cited in *Freed*). In *Balint*, the Court interpreted a statute prohibiting the sale of certain drugs to require proof that defendants knew they were selling drugs, but not proof that they knew the drugs were the subject of federal criminal restrictions. The *Staples* Court explained:

> In such situations, we have reasoned that as long as a defendant knows that he is dealing with a dangerous device of a character that places him "in responsible relation to a public danger," he should be alerted to the probability of strict regulation, and we have assumed that in such cases Congress intended to place the burden on the defendant to "ascertain at his peril whether [his conduct] comes within the inhibition of the statute." Thus, we essentially have relied on the nature of the statutes and the particular character of the items regulated to determine whether Congressional silence concerning the mental element of the offense should be interpreted as dispensing with conventional mens rea requirements.
>
>   . . . .
>
> . . . [T]here is a long tradition of widespread lawful gun ownership by private individuals in this country. Such a tradition did not apply to the possession of hand grenades in *Freed* or to the selling of dangerous drugs that we considered in *Balint*. In fact, in *Freed*, we construed [the federal statute] under the assumption that "one would hardly be surprised to learn that possession of hand grenades is not an innocent act." Here, the Government essentially suggests that we should interpret the section under the altogether different assumption that "one would hardly be surprised to learn that

owning a gun is not an innocent act." That proposition is simply not supported by common experience. Guns in general are not "deleterious devices or products or obnoxious waste materials" that put their owners on notice that they stand "in responsible relation to a public danger."

511 U.S. at 607, 610–11.

Are the decisions in *Freed* and *Staples* reconcilable? Does applying the "element-by-element" analysis Justice Brennan endorsed in *Freed* help explain the result in *Staples*? Do weapons possession statutes like the one at issue in these two cases protect the "public welfare"? If so, what is the difference between "public welfare" offenses and all other criminal offenses?

6. Other Federal Supreme Court Decisions. The Supreme Court has similarly construed federal statutes to impose a mens rea requirement in several other cases. In *Posters 'N' Things v. United States*, 511 U.S. 513 (1994), for example, the Court interpreted federal legislation making it a crime to offer "drug paraphernalia" for sale in interstate commerce to require proof that the defendant knew the items for sale were likely to be used with illegal drugs.

Likewise, in *United States v. X-Citement Video, Inc.*, 513 U.S. 64 (1994), the Court held that the federal child pornography statute requires proof that the defendant knew the performers in a pornographic video were underage. The Court relied on its analysis in *Staples* in reaching this conclusion:

> Persons do not harbor settled expectations that the contents of magazines and film are generally subject to stringent public regulation. In fact, First Amendment constraints presuppose the opposite view. Rather, the statute is more akin to the common law offenses against the "state, person, property, or public morals" that presume a scienter requirement in the absence of express contrary intent.

Id. at 71–72.

Twenty years later, relying on both *Staples* and *X-Citement Video*, the Court declined to interpret the federal statute making it a crime to "transmit[] in interstate . . . commerce . . . any threat to . . . injure" another person as a strict liability crime. *Elonis v. United States*, 135 S. Ct. 2001 (2015). Given the presumption that mens rea is required for "'each of the statutory elements that criminalize otherwise innocent conduct,'" the majority held that one such element here was "the fact that the communication contains a threat." *Id.* at 2011 (quoting *X-Citement Video*, 513 U.S. at 72). The Court went on to reject the view that the statute's mens rea requirement was satisfied so long as a reasonable person would have perceived the defendant's Facebook postings as threatening, reasoning that while a negligence standard is "a familiar feature" of tort law, it is "inconsistent" with the "'awareness of some wrongdoing'" generally required for a criminal conviction. *Id.* (quoting *Staples*, 511 U.S. at 607).

By contrast, the Court ruled in *United States v. Feola*, 420 U.S. 671 (1975), that defendants accused of assaulting and conspiring to assault a federal officer did not have to know of the victim's "federal" status. The Court explained that the official identity of the victim was a "jurisdictional" element, which Congress did not intend to be "germane" to the crime. *Id.* at 693. (*Feola*'s discussion of comparable mens rea issues that arise in conspiracy prosecutions is described in Chapter 13, Section A.3, Note 3.) *See also Dean v. United States*, 556 U.S. 568, 572 (2009) (reasoning that the "use of the passive voice" in the federal statute imposing an enhanced 10-year sentence on defendants who used or carried a weapon in committing any violent or drug trafficking crime "if the firearm is discharged" signaled Congress' intent "not [to] require proof of intent" and therefore to apply even in cases of accidental discharge).

7. Mens Rea for Federal Offenses. It is something of an understatement to say that the mens rea issues surrounding federal criminal offenses have generated a bit of a doctrinal mess. In contrast to the Model Penal Code, the federal criminal statutes do not "create uniform *mens rea* standards." RICHARD M. THOMPSON II, CONG. RESEARCH SERV., 7-5700, *MENS REA REFORM: A BRIEF OVERVIEW* (2016). As explained in the excerpt from this Congressional Research Service report included in Chapter 4, Section B.2, several bills were introduced in Congress in 2015 designed to address this situation and create a default mens rea of "willfully" or "knowingly" unless some other mens rea was specified in a particular federal statute. These proposals were not adopted in the 114th Congress, and critics objected that they could "allow white collar criminals to escape prosecution" by eliminating "strict liability" regulatory offenses. Greg Dotson & Allison Cassady, Center for American Progress (Mar. 11, 2016).

8. Vicarious Liability. Questions of strict liability must be distinguished from "vicarious liability." Vicarious criminal liability dispenses not just with a "mens rea" requirement, but also with any requirement that a defendant be personally responsible for the voluntary criminal act. In *Koczwara*, for example, an employee's acts of selling liquor were attributed to the employer-defendant.

All the Justices in *Koczwara* appeared troubled by the specter of an expansive use of vicarious liability. What limitation did the majority put on the use of criminal sanctions to punish on a *respondeat superior* basis? What about the dissenters? Was it clear that the state legislature intended to impose vicarious liability on employers? Could the court have read a mens rea requirement into the statute and thereby avoided these larger concerns?

While vicarious liability is common in civil litigation—for example, master-servant liability and employer-employee liability in torts—in the criminal law pure "vicarious" liability is rare, but not unheard of. Consider, for example, *In re Marley*, 175 P.2d 832 (Cal. 1946), where the proprietor of a meat market was convicted (and sentenced to 90 days in jail) when his employee sold meat to an undercover government agent after representing that the meat weighed more than it actually did. Similar to *Koczwara*, the proprietor's conviction was affirmed even though he did not personally participate in the transaction, was not on the premises at the time of the sale, and had at no time instructed his employee to give short weight.

In torts, the well-established doctrine of "*respondeat superior*" is said to provide a "deep pocket" to help compensate for damages caused by business activities. Are there utilitarian or moral justifications for imposing vicarious liability in criminal law as well? Is vicarious liability appropriate in the criminal setting if a principal has acted with all reasonable care? Compare *United States v. Park*, excerpted below in Section B.2, which holds corporate executives liable for criminal acts committed by their subordinates if their "'responsible relationship' to, or . . . 'responsible share' in," the violation "imports some measure of blameworthiness," but then gives these corporate officers an "impossibility" defense if they were "'powerless' to prevent or correct the violation."

9. Distinguishing Vicarious Liability from Other Forms of Liability. The vicarious liability imposed in *Koczwara* should be distinguished from accomplice liability (*see* Chapter 12), where criminal punishment is based on the defendant's own act of aiding or encouraging another person to commit a crime. Under vicarious liability, by contrast, employers may theoretically be convicted even though they did not encourage or aid the employee at all; indeed, at least in theory, the employer may even have discouraged the criminal conduct. The only protection in such cases would be prosecutorial discretion or a jury's refusal to convict.

Under the *Pinkerton* doctrine applied in criminal conspiracy cases in some jurisdictions, liability can be imposed on one conspirator for crimes committed by other co-conspirators. *See* Chapter 13, Section B.1. Is this a version of vicarious liability, or is it a recognition that choosing to enter into combinations with others (like partnerships) can be an acceptance of responsibility for the actions of others?

Finally, vicarious liability imposed on an individual human employer should be distinguished from liability imposed on the corporation itself for the criminal acts of its employees. This concept is discussed in the following Section.

[B] Corporate, and Corporate Officer, Liability

[1] Corporate Liability

A corporation is, of course, an artificial legal entity owned by shareholders, and it can act only through the conduct of its directors, officers, and employees. Until the end of the nineteenth century, the concept of criminal liability for such a purely legal entity was rejected on the theory that a corporation, as a non-human legal fiction, could not form the necessary criminal intent. *See* Model Penal Code § 2.07 Comment at 332. Soon, however, corporations began to be treated as legal "persons" that could be taxed and sued. Today, all jurisdictions permit corporations and other business associations to be criminally charged and convicted under certain circumstances that are usually defined by statute. *See, e.g.,* Model Penal Code § 2.07; Cal. Corp. Code §§ 2200–2260. Corporate criminal liability is premised on the theory of agency: if an employee is acting on behalf of the corporation, the corporation can be held liable as the principal. The difficult question is how far the agency doctrine should go—in what circumstances should an employee's criminal acts be attributed (or not be attributed) to the corporation as a whole? Is it as troublesome to prosecute an entity based on the acts of its agents as it is to impose strict liability on individuals, given that an entity cannot be incarcerated so that any penalty is likely to resemble a civil sanction?

United States v. Deak & Co. of California, Inc.

596 F.2d 871 (9th Cir. 1979)

CARTER, CIRCUIT JUDGE.

Deak & Company of California (Deak), headquartered in San Francisco, is a wholly-owned subsidiary of Deak and Co. of New York, the largest foreign currency exchange dealer in the world. Beusch was Vice-President and the senior corporate officer of Deak located in San Francisco. Deak was convicted of 377 misdemeanor violations of the Bank Secrecy Act, 31 U.S.C. §§ 1058 and 11, [for the willful] failure to report receipt of currency in an amount exceeding $5,000 from outside the United States. Beusch, as responsible corporate officer in the offending transactions, was likewise convicted of the 377 misdemeanors. . . . Deak [argues on appeal] that the evidence was insufficient to sustain a finding of willful violation of § 1101, and . . . that one of the jury instructions given constituted reversible error.

   . . . .

For reasons discussed more fully below, we affirm the convictions of Deak and Beusch . . . .

The facts show that in 1972, Beusch initiated contact between Deak and two Filipinos Gimenez and Lai Man who began sending large amounts of currency to the United States for further disbursal throughout the world. Between 1972 and 1976, approximately $11 million were sent and disbursed. None of the money shipments was reported to the Treasury Department as required by certain provisions of the Bank Secrecy Act.

Sometime in the Spring of 1976, customs agents in Hawaii inadvertently discovered currency in a package sent from the Philippines to Deak's offices in San Francisco. Suspicions were aroused when customs, postal, and courier records revealed that in the recent past, many similar packages had been sent from the same source to the same address, but Treasury records showed no [currency transactions reports, required to be filed by Deak]. A search warrant was issued and executed in May, 1976, at Deak's offices in San Francisco. Incriminating ledgers, files and packages of money were discovered there. Convictions and these appeals followed.

   . . . .

Deak contends that the evidence was insufficient to sustain the finding and conclusion that Beusch acted with the intent to benefit Deak so that the willfulness of his acts as an agent could be imputed to Deak, the principal. The acts of an agent may be imputed to the principal, but only if it is the agent's purpose to benefit the principal, thus bringing his acts within the scope of his employment. If intent to benefit is present, then actual benefit is largely irrelevant. *See Standard Oil Co. of Texas v. United States*, 307 F.2d 120 (5th Cir. 1962).

One of the investigating agents testified at trial that Beusch told him in an interview that he had acted for Deak and not for himself. Beusch himself did not testify, apparently because of Fifth Amendment considerations. Deak argued at trial, and it continues to argue here, that other evidence showed Beusch was trying to protect the two Filipinos and therefore was not trying to benefit Deak. The jury believed otherwise. There is support for its finding in the Record, and we cannot say that it was clearly erroneous. . . .

Deak's final contention is that one of the instructions given to the jury prior to its deliberation was erroneous because, in effect, it imposed strict liability on Deak for Beusch's acts . . . . The challenged instruction reads as follows:

> "A corporation may be responsible for the acts of its agents done or made within the scope of its authority, even though the agent's conduct may be contrary to the corporation's actual instruction or contrary to the corporation's stated policies."

We have examined all of the instructions related to vicarious responsibility and find that, read in context, the challenged instruction does not mean what Deak says it means. It does not impose strict liability on Deak without proof of intent. Rather, it suggests that a corporation may be liable for acts of its employees done contrary to express instructions and policies, but that the existence of such instructions and policies may be considered in determining whether the employee in fact acted to benefit the corporation. Merely stating or publishing such instructions and policies without diligently enforcing them is not enough to place the acts of an employee who violates them outside the scope of his employment. *See United States v. Armour*, 168 F.2d 342 (3d Cir. 1947). It is a question of fact whether measures taken to enforce corporate policy in this area will adequately insulate the corporation against such acts, and we see no reason to disturb the jury's finding in this regard. The instruction given the jury, read in context, is a proper statement of the law.

State v. Adjustment Department Credit Bureau, Inc.

483 P.2d 687 (Idaho 1971)

McFADDEN, JUSTICE.

The defendant, Adjustment Department Credit Bureau, Inc., an Idaho corporation, conducts a bill collection service as a part of its operation. It was charged by an amended information of the crime of extortion alleged to have been committed by and through its agent, Howard Short, in August, 1967. . . .

The case was tried to a jury which returned its verdict of guilty of the crime charged in the information and judgment of conviction was entered and a fine of $1,500.00 imposed against the corporation. . . .

One of the defendant's customers, a pharmacy, assigned an open account owed to the pharmacy by Rodney Price to the defendant for collection. Howard Short, an agent of the defendant, handled this particular claim for the defendant company. Price had executed a promissory note to the defendant on this claim, and when the note was not paid in accord with its terms, suit was instituted in a justice court in Ada County and default judgment entered in July of 1967. Short attempted to collect on this judgment against Price, who was out of work at the time. Subsequently, Short accepted a check with the understanding it would be paid in installments. At the time of execution of this check Price told Short that there were no funds in the bank on which the check was written. After other subsequent conversations Short had Price execute another check on a different bank even though Price had told him that he had no account there, and the first check was torn up. This second check was presented for payment to the bank and returned unpaid.

Later in the summer of 1967 Price secured employment away from Boise and Short contacted Mrs. Price concerning the obligation. Price testified that on an occasion when he was in Boise, Short contacted him and advised him that Short would prosecute him for issuance of a bad check unless Price made a payment on the debt. Price then paid $20.00 to Short, which was evidenced by a receipt.

Later Price stated he believed he was going to be prosecuted for the bad check and went to see Mr. Slayton, who was the head of the collection division of the defendant corporation. Price testified "Mr. Slayton told me it was out of his hands, it was between me and Mr. Short." Mr. Slayton testified that he remembered Mr. Price came in to see him one time and was asking questions about the account. Slayton stated "I told him Mr. Short was handling the account."

On this appeal the defendant has made numerous assignments of error. The crucial issue presented by these assignments of error concerns the instruction given by the trial court to the effect that a corporation (which acts only through its agents) can be held criminally liable "for the acts of its agents who are authorized to act for it in the particular matter out of which the unlawful conduct with which it is charged grows or in the business to which it related." It is the defendant's contention that this instruction by the trial court was in error, arguing that the trial court should have instructed that the defendant corporation could have been found guilty only if the agent committed the prohibited acts, and that the agent's acts were authorized, requested or commanded by another corporate agent having responsibility for formation of corporate policy, or by a managerial agent having supervisory responsibility over the subject matter.

It is our conclusion that there is merit in the defendant's position in regard to these instructions. A corporation, being an artificial being, a creature of statute, can only act through its agents and employees. At the early common law, the fact that a corporation had no tangible, physical existence, was regarded as making it impossible for a corporation to commit a crime. Under the modern view, however, a corporation may be found guilty of a breach of a duty imposed by law, both for acts of nonfeasance and misfeasance.

. . . .

Hornstein, 2 Corporation Law and Practice, 1959, § 566, p. 47, in our opinion correctly states the rule as to criminal liability as follows:

> A corporation may be convicted if (a) legislative purpose plainly appears to impose absolute liability on the corporation for the offense; or (b) the offense consists of an omission to perform an act which the corporation is required by law to perform; or (c) the commission of the offense was authorized, requested, commanded or performed (i) by the board of directors, or (ii) by an agent having responsibility for formation of corporate policy or (iii) by a "high managerial agent" having supervisory responsibility over the subject matter of the offense and acting within the scope of his employment on behalf of the corporation. . . .

Thus the instructions given by the trial court to the effect that the corporation could be found guilty if the jury found that the agent was acting within the scope of his authority was not a correct statement of the law under the circumstances of this case; it was not established that Short was in a managerial capacity, and no issue was submitted to the jury as to whether Short's actions were authorized, requested, or commanded by either an agent of the corporation responsible for formation of corporate policy or by a high managerial agent. This error is of a prejudicial nature and the case must be remanded.

Notes and Questions

1. **Evaluating *Deak* and *Adjustment Department Credit Bureau*.** Are *Deak* and *Adjustment Department Credit Bureau* reconcilable? What are the differences between the legal standards for corporate criminal liability applied in each case? What differences can you imagine these distinctions making in the real world? What standards should be imposed to limit criminal liability for corporations? Or should the potential for such liability be expanded?

2. **Comparing the Model Penal Code's Position.** Many jurisdictions follow the approach taken by the trial judge in *Adjustment Department Credit Bureau*, permitting criminal liability for a corporation if an employee commits a prohibited act "within the scope of his or her authority." Some go even further, as in *Deak*. The Model Penal Code however, like the Idaho Supreme Court, is more cautious in imposing criminal liability on a corporation. For crimes that do not expressly impose specific duties on the corporation itself—that is, for "general" crimes that any person might be charged with—the MPC requires that the criminal acts be "authorized, requested, commanded, performed or recklessly tolerated by the board of directors or by a high managerial agent acting in behalf of the corporation within the scope of his office or employment." Model Penal Code § 2.07(1)(c). The Comments to § 2.07 explain:

> It would seem that the ultimate justification of corporate criminal responsibility must rest in large measure on an evaluation of the deterrent effects of corporate fines on the conduct of corporate agents. Is there a reason for

anticipating a substantially higher degree of deterrence from fines levied on corporate bodies than can fairly be anticipated from proceeding directly against the guilty officer or agent or from other feasible sanctions of a non-criminal character?

It may be assumed that ordinarily a corporate agent is not likely to be deterred from criminal conduct by the prospect of corporate liability when, in any event, he faces the prospect of individually suffering serious criminal penalties for his own act. If the agent cannot be prevented from committing an offense by the prospect of personal liability, he ordinarily will not be prevented by the prospect of corporate liability.

Yet the problem cannot be resolved so simply. For there are probably cases in which the economic pressures within the corporate body are sufficiently potent to tempt individuals to hazard personal liability for the sake of company gain, especially where the penalties threatened are moderate and where the offense does not involve behavior condemned as highly immoral by the individual's associates.

Id. § 2.07 Comment at 336.

Which do you find more persuasive: the common law's rationale that an organization cannot form criminal mens rea or the modern trend, which presumes that for criminal liability, an organization's mens rea is the same as that of the individuals acting on its behalf? Is it fair to make an organization responsible for crimes committed by individuals whom the organization has selected to assume certain duties? Should we be as concerned about imputing an individual's state of mind to an organization as we are about attributing it to another individual? Is there a difference between imposing vicarious liability on individuals for criminal acts committed by their subordinates (acts which the individuals might have chosen to do themselves had they known the subordinates would act illegally) and punishing organizations for the same criminal acts committed by their agents (acts which the organizations might have delegated to other employees had they known how the transgressing employees would act)?

3. Policy Arguments in Favor of Corporate Criminal Liability. One of the co-authors of this book, Professor Saltzburg, has written about the arguments for imposing criminal liability on corporations. *See* Stephen A. Saltzburg, *The Control of Criminal Conduct in Organizations*, 71 B.U. L. Rev. 421 (1991). Do you find these arguments persuasive?

Congress has set forth several factors for the federal courts to consider when sentencing a defendant who has been convicted of a federal crime, including: public denouncement, promotion of respect for the law, just punishment, deterrence, incapacitation, and rehabilitation. These purposes mirror the traditional justifications for punishing criminal acts. . . .

Because prosecutors have limited resources, the underlying objective of charging and prosecuting individuals or organizations generally will be to obtain a conviction and an appropriate sentence. Naturally, an appropriate sentence is one which reflects congressional judgment concerning the purposes of the criminal law. To further those purposes, prosecutors commonly ask the court to restrain the liberty of a convicted defendant, whether by prison term, probation, mandatory schooling, home detention or some other means. These sentences are generally accepted as the means most likely to protect society and to secure treatment for the convicted defendant. An organization, however, cannot be confined or psychologically treated. Prosecutors, therefore, must pursue alternative sentences for convicted organizations.

Prosecuting a corporation can serve at least some of the traditional sentencing purposes. For example, a court can impose a fine that reflects the seriousness of the offense. An appropriate fine may promote corporate respect for the law, and may provide just punishment for the offense. Additionally, prosecuting a corporation may deter future corporate criminal activity.

. . . .

[Moreover, to] convict an individual, the government generally must prove that the individual committed the offense with a culpable mens rea. When the government charges an organization, however, it may not have to demonstrate precisely who committed the offense, or the mental state of individual actors in the organizational hierarchy.

In some instances, for example, the law may require an organization to keep records and may provide that a mere failure to do so constitutes a crime. In these cases, the government need not demonstrate which individual employee was responsible for the omission, but can convict solely on the grounds that the organization did not maintain the required records. Similarly, some statutes prohibit an organization from engaging in certain acts. Here, too, the government can convict merely by proving that someone in the organization committed the prohibited conduct.

. . . .

Prosecuting the organization further benefits the government by allowing it to encourage the organization to impose its own sanctions on the officers or employees who actually committed the criminal offenses. Some organizations, especially complex ones, might be better situated than the government both to allocate blame and to impose sanctions upon their members. Allowing the organization to allocate blame, and to recover penalties assessed against it, relieves the government from the burden of penetrating the organizational framework and proving individual fault.

Moreover, in cases in which individual fault is difficult to assign, this approach allows the organization to offer incentives to modify the objectionable behavior which are less intrusive than directing the entire weight of the criminal sanction against a few individuals. The risk of mistake is also less important because if the organization allocates blame wrongly or unfairly, the punished individuals will not be subject to incarceration or criminal stigmatization.

Id. at 422–28.

4. Recent Corporate Prosecutions: Sears, Exxon, Arthur Andersen, and Enron. In reading the accounts of several high-profile corporate prosecutions, consider the challenges Professor Saltzburg identifies that arise in sentencing corporations, given that they cannot be put in prison or placed in behavioral treatment programs. Can criminal prosecution have a positive impact on corporate culture by deterring criminal conduct that is difficult to trace to specific individuals dispersed within a large organization? Does criminal prosecution make it less acceptable within the corporation for individuals to commit crimes that benefit the company? Or does it merely give the government a convenient scapegoat to prosecute rather than discovering and charging the responsible corporate officers? Compare the "responsible relationship" test for imposing criminal liability on individual corporate officers, which is discussed in the *Park* case excerpted below in Part 2.

(a) *Sears, Roebuck & Co.* In 1992, following an undercover investigation by the California Attorney General's office, Sears, Roebuck & Co. entered into a settlement that avoided potential corporate criminal liability stemming from allegations of massive fraud committed by its auto repair shops. Sears reportedly agreed to pay $8 million to settle civil claims that its repair shops had systematically overcharged for repairs. Customers who allegedly had been overcharged an average of $288 per visit received $50 coupons that could be used at Sears; other settlement proceeds went to various California state government departments. The settlement included a standard clause asserting that Sears admitted no wrongdoing, and Sears' stock price rose 62.5 cents per share the day the settlement was announced. *See* Seth Faison, *Sears Will Pay $8 Million to Settle Repair Complaints*, N.Y. Times, Sept. 3, 1992, at D5. What do you think of resolving a corporation's potential criminal liability by imposing large civil settlements? Would a successful criminal prosecution of Sears have added any significant public benefits?

(b) *Exxon.* In 1989, the oil tanker Exxon Valdez ran aground in Prince William Sound in Alaska. Almost 11 million gallons of oil washed up along 1,244 miles of coastline, wreaking havoc on the ecosystem, the fishing industry, and other local businesses and inhabitants. Exxon was criminally charged with negligently polluting navigable waters, unlawfully discharging refuse matter, killing migratory birds, and employing incompetent personnel. As part of a plea agreement, the company paid a $25 million criminal fine plus $100 million in restitution. Was that a sufficient punishment, given that Exxon also paid almost $3.5 billion in civil penalties and cleanup costs? *See* John Balzar, *Exxon Valdez Settlement Hasn't Settled Very Much*, L.A. Times, Feb. 16, 1993, at A4; Linda Greenhouse, *Justices to Hear Exxon's Challenge to Punitive Damages*, N.Y. Times, Oct. 30, 2007, at C5.

In a federal civil suit filed by affected fishermen, property owners, and businesses, Exxon was found liable for the reckless conduct of the captain of the Valdez. In addition to compensatory damages of some $500 million, the jury awarded punitive damages of $5 billion. The Ninth Circuit reduced the punitive damages to $2.5 billion, which was still "the biggest punitive damages award ever ordered by a federal appeals court." *Id.* On appeal to the Supreme Court, the punitive damages award was further reduced to $500 million, an amount equal to the compensatory damages previously awarded. *See Exxon Shipping Co. v. Baker*, 554 U.S. 471 (2008). What value, if any, do you see in imposing criminal, versus civil, liability on Exxon for the Valdez spill?

(c) *Arthur Andersen.* In March 2002, the U.S. Department of Justice indicted one of the nation's "Big 5" accounting firms for allegedly obstructing justice by destroying documents during the Securities and Exchange Commission's ("SEC") investigation of the Enron Corporation. After months of pretrial litigation and a month-long jury trial that ended after 10 days of deliberation, Arthur Andersen was convicted. Three years later, however, the Supreme Court reversed the company's conviction because the jurors had been incorrectly instructed on the mens rea required for obstruction of justice. *See Arthur Andersen LLP v. United States*, 544 U.S. 696 (2005) (also described in Chapter 4, Section B.1, Note 7).

Reversal of the company's convictions provided little solace for the 85,000 Andersen employees who lost their jobs (28,000 in this country), or the thousands of Arthur Andersen stockholders whose investments were ultimately worth next to nothing. The government did not dispute that the huge majority of Andersen's partners and employees (let alone their stockholders) had known nothing about the allegedly criminal conduct of a relatively few employees. *See* Tom Fowler, *The Case Against Arthur Andersen; Ruling Stirs Emotions*, HOUS. CHRON., June 1, 2005, at 1 ("Even before the trial began, audit clients fled from the firm in droves. . . . All that remains of Andersen today is a few dozen employees."). The government chose not to re-try the case (Arthur Andersen having gone out of business many months earlier). At the same time, some commentators have written that the Arthur Andersen prosecution "sent a clear and unmistakable message to Corporate America in general, and to the accounting profession in particular, that companies that deliberately try to block the government from investigating corporate misconduct will be punished swiftly and severely." Christopher A. Wray & Robert K. Hur, *Corporate Criminal Prosecution in a Post-Enron World: The Thompson Memo in Theory and in Practice*, 43 AM. CRIM. L. REV. 1095, 1097 (2006). What lessons, if any, do you see in the Arthur Andersen saga?

(d) *Individual Prosecutions Related to Enron.* In 1985, Kenneth Lay, a Texas businessman, formed a corporation named Enron. By the 1990s, Enron had been quietly transformed into a large "holding" company described as an "energy conglomerate." Initially, Enron was highly successful, and thousands of individuals and organizations invested in its stock. In 2001, however, a "charge to earnings" (loss) of more than $1 billion was announced by Enron. The SEC opened an investigation, and Enron's CEO, Jeffrey Skilling, abruptly resigned. Enron's stock price plummeted to

$1 per share, and the company filed for the then-largest bankruptcy in U.S. history. In 2006, Skilling and Lay were convicted on federal conspiracy and fraud charges (although Lay's conviction was later vacated when he unexpectedly died a few days before sentencing). After appeals, Skilling was ultimately sentenced to 14 years in prison. *See Skilling v. United States*, 561 U.S. 358 (2010). The Enron Corporation, in financial ruin and out of business, was not prosecuted. For further discussion of the Skilling prosecution, see *United States v. Skilling*, excerpted in Chapter 8, Section D, and the accompanying Notes.

[2] Corporate Officer Liability

United States v. Park

421 U.S. 658 (1975)

Mr. Chief Justice Burger delivered the opinion of the Court.

We granted certiorari to consider whether the jury instructions in the prosecution of a corporate officer under § 301(k) of the Federal Food, Drug, and Cosmetic Act ... were appropriate under *United States v. Dotterweich*, 320 U.S. 277 (1943).

Acme Markets, Inc., is a national retail food chain with approximately 36,000 employees, 874 retail outlets, 12 general warehouses, and four special warehouses. Its headquarters, including the office of the president, respondent Park, who is chief executive officer of the corporation, are located in Philadelphia, Pa. In a five-count information filed in the United States District Court for the District of Maryland, the Government charged Acme and respondent with violations of the Federal Food, Drug, and Cosmetic Act. Each count ... alleged that the defendants had received food that had been shipped in interstate commerce and that, while the food was being held for sale in Acme's Baltimore warehouse following shipment in interstate commerce, they caused it to be held in a building accessible to rodents and to be exposed to contamination by rodents. These acts were alleged to have resulted in the food's being [criminally] adulterated ... , in violation of 21 U.S.C. § 331(k).

Acme pleaded guilty to each count of the information. Respondent pleaded not guilty. The evidence at trial demonstrated that in April 1970 the Food and Drug Administration (FDA) advised respondent by letter of insanitary conditions in Acme's Philadelphia warehouse. In 1971 the FDA found that similar conditions existed in the firm's Baltimore warehouse. An FDA consumer safety officer testified concerning evidence of rodent infestation and other insanitary conditions discovered during a 12-day inspection of the Baltimore warehouse in November and December 1971.[13] He also related that a second inspection of the warehouse had been conducted in March 1972. On that occasion the inspectors found that there had been

---

13. [n.4] The witness testified ... :

  "We found extensive evidence of rodent infestation in the form of rat and mouse pellets throughout the entire perimeter area and along the wall.

improvement in the sanitary conditions, but that "there was still evidence of rodent activity in the building and in the warehouses and we found some rodent-contaminated lots of food items."

The Government also presented testimony by the Chief of Compliance of the FDA's Baltimore office, who informed respondent by letter [in January 1972] of the conditions at the Baltimore warehouse after the first inspection. There was testimony by Acme's Baltimore division vice president, who had responded to the letter on behalf of Acme and respondent and who described the steps taken to remedy the insanitary conditions discovered by both inspections. The Government's final witness, Acme's vice president for legal affairs and assistant secretary, identified respondent as the president and chief executive officer of the company and read a bylaw prescribing the duties of the chief executive officer. He testified that respondent functioned by delegating "normal operating duties," including sanitation, but that he retained "certain things, which are the big, broad, principles of the operation of the company," and had "the responsibility of seeing that they all work together."

At the close of the Government's case in chief, respondent moved for a judgment of acquittal on the ground that "the evidence in chief has shown that Mr. Park is not personally concerned in this Food and Drug violation." The trial judge denied the motion . . . .

Respondent was the only defense witness. He testified that, although all of Acme's employees were in a sense under his general direction, the company had an "organizational structure for responsibilities for certain functions" according to which different phases of its operation were "assigned to individuals who, in turn, have staff and departments under them." He identified those individuals responsible for sanitation, and related that upon receipt of the January 1972 FDA letter, he had conferred with the vice president for legal affairs, who informed him that the Baltimore division vice president "was investigating the situation immediately and would be taking corrective action and would be preparing a summary of the corrective action to reply to the letter." Respondent stated that he did not "believe there was anything [he] could have done more constructively than what [he] found was being done."

[Later in the opinion, the Court further described Park's testimony: "Respondent testified . . . that he had employed a system in which he relied upon his subordinates, and that he was ultimately responsible for this system. He testified further that he had found these subordinates to be 'dependable' and had 'great confidence'

"We also found that the doors leading to the basement area from the rail siding had openings at the bottom or openings beneath part of the door that came down at the bottom large enough to admit rodent entry. There were also roden[t] pellets found on a number of different packages of boxes of various items stored in the basement, and . . . there were also broken windows along the rail siding."
On the first floor of the "old building," the inspectors found:
"Thirty mouse pellets on the floor along walls and on the ledge in the hanging meat room. There were at least twenty mouse pellets beside bales of lime Jello and one of the bales had a chewed rodent hole in the product . . . ."

in them. By this and other testimony respondent evidently sought to persuade the jury that, as the president of a large corporation, he had no choice but to delegate duties to those in whom he reposed confidence, that he had no reason to suspect his subordinates were failing to insure compliance with the Act, and that, once violations were unearthed, acting through those subordinates he did everything possible to correct them."]

On cross-examination, respondent conceded that providing sanitary conditions for food offered for sale to the public was something that he was "responsible for in the entire operation of the company," and he stated that it was one of many phases of the company that he assigned to "dependable subordinates." Respondent . . . admitted receiving . . . the April 1970 letter addressed to him from the FDA regarding insanitary conditions at Acme's Philadelphia warehouse. He acknowledged that, with the exception of the division vice president, the same individuals had responsibility for sanitation in both Baltimore and Philadelphia. Finally, in response to questions concerning the Philadelphia and Baltimore incidents, respondent admitted that the Baltimore problem indicated the system for handling sanitation "wasn't working perfectly" and that as Acme's chief executive officer he was responsible for "any result which occurs in our company."

. . . [After jury instructions, to which Park objected,] the jury found respondent guilty on all counts of the information, and he was subsequently sentenced to pay a fine of $50 on each count.[14] We granted certiorari because of an apparent conflict among the Courts of Appeals with respect to the standard of liability of corporate officers . . . . [We affirm Park's conviction.]

I

The question presented by the Government's petition for certiorari in *United States v. Dotterweich, supra,* was whether "the manager of a corporation, as well as the corporation itself, may be prosecuted under the Federal Food, Drug, and Cosmetic Act of 1938 for the introduction of misbranded and adulterated articles into interstate commerce." . . . In . . . reinstating Dotterweich's conviction, this Court looked to the purposes of the Act and noted that they "touch phases of the lives and health of people which, in the circumstances of modern industrialism, are largely beyond self-protection." It observed that the Act is of "a now familiar type" which "dispenses with the conventional requirement for criminal conduct—awareness of some wrong-doing. In the interest of the larger good it puts the burden of acting at hazard upon a person otherwise innocent but standing in responsible relation to a public danger."

---

14. [n.10] Sections 303(a) and (b) of the Act provide:

"(a) Any person who violates a provision of section 331 of this title shall be imprisoned for not more than one year or fined not more than $1,000, or both.

"(b) Notwithstanding the provisions of subsection (a) of this section, if any person commits such a violation after a conviction of him under this section has become final, or commits such a violation with the intent to defraud or mislead, such person shall be imprisoned for not more than three years or fined not more than $10,000, or both." . . .

Central to the Court's conclusion that individuals other than proprietors are sub-ject to the criminal provisions of the Act was the reality that "the only way in which a corporation can act is through the individuals who act on its behalf." The Court also noted that corporate officers had been subject to criminal liability under the Federal Food and Drugs Act of 1906, and it observed that a contrary result under the 1938 legislation would be incompatible with the expressed intent of Congress to "enlarge and stiffen the penal net" and to discourage a view of the Act's criminal penalties as a "license fee for the conduct of an illegitimate business."

At the same time, however, the Court was aware of the concern . . . that literal enforcement "might operate too harshly by sweeping within its condemnation any person however remotely entangled in the proscribed shipment." A limiting princi-ple, in the form of "settled doctrines of criminal law" defining those who "are respon-sible for the commission of a misdemeanor," was available. In this context, the Court concluded, those doctrines dictated that the offense was committed "by all who . . . have . . . a responsible share in the furtherance of the transaction which the statute outlaws."

The Court recognized that, because the Act dispenses with the need to prove "con-sciousness of wrongdoing," it may result in hardship even as applied to those who share "responsibility in the business process resulting in" a violation. It regarded as "too treacherous" an attempt "to define or even to indicate by way of illustration the class of employees which stands in such a responsible relation." The question of responsibility, the Court said, depends "on the evidence produced at the trial . . . ." "In such matters the good sense of prosecutors, the wise guidance of trial judges, and the ultimate judgment of juries must be trusted."

II

The rule that corporate employees who have "a responsible share in the further-ance of the transaction which the statute outlaws" are subject to the criminal provi-sions of the Act was not formulated in a vacuum. *Cf. Morissette v. United States*, 342 U.S. 246, 258 (1952). Cases under the Federal Food and Drugs Act of 1906 reflected the view both that knowledge or intent were not required to be proved in prosecu-tions under its criminal provisions, and that responsible corporate agents could be subjected to the liability thereby imposed. Moreover, the principle had been recog-nized that a corporate agent, through whose act, default, or omission the corpora-tion committed a crime, was himself guilty individually of that crime. The principle had been applied whether or not the crime required "consciousness of wrong-doing," and it had been applied not only to those corporate agents who themselves committed the criminal act, but also to those who by virtue of their managerial positions or other similar relation to the actor could be deemed responsible for its commission.

In the latter class of cases, the liability of managerial officers did not depend on their knowledge of, or personal participation in, the act made criminal by the stat-ute. Rather, where the statute under which they were prosecuted dispensed with "consciousness of wrongdoing," an omission or failure to act was deemed a suffi-cient basis for a responsible corporate agent's liability. It was enough in such cases that, by virtue of the relationship he bore to the corporation, the agent had the power to prevent the act complained of. *See, e.g.,* ... Sayre, *Criminal Responsibility for the Acts of Another,* 43 HARV. L. REV. 689 (1930).

The rationale of the interpretation given the Act in *Dotterweich,* as holding crimi-nally accountable the persons whose failure to exercise the authority and supervisory responsibility reposed in them by the business organization resulted in the violation complained of, has been confirmed in our subsequent cases. Thus, the Court has reaffirmed the proposition that "the public interest in the purity of its food is so great as to warrant the imposition of the highest standard of care on distributors." *Smith v. California,* 361 U.S. 147, 152 (1959). In order to make "distributors of food the strict-est censors of their merchandise," *ibid.,* the Act punishes "neglect where the law requires care, or inaction where it imposes a duty." *Morissette v. United States, supra,* at 255. "The accused, if he does not will the violation, usually is in a position to prevent it with no more care than society might reasonably expect and no more exer-tion than it might reasonably exact from one who assumed his responsibilities." *Id.* at 256. *Cf.* Hughes, *Criminal Omissions,* 67 YALE L.J. 590 (1958). Similarly, in cases deci-ded after *Dotterweich,* the Courts of Appeals have recognized that those corporate agents vested with the responsibility, and power commensurate with that responsi-bility, to devise whatever measures are necessary to ensure compliance with the Act bear a "responsible relationship" to, or have a "responsible share" in, violations.

Thus *Dotterweich* and the cases which have followed reveal that in providing sanctions which reach and touch the individuals who execute the corporate mission — and this is by no means necessarily confined to a single corporate agent or employee — the Act imposes not only a positive duty to seek out and remedy violations when they occur but also, and primarily, a duty to implement measures that will insure that violations will not occur. The requirements of foresight and vigilance imposed on responsible corporate agents are beyond question demanding, and perhaps onerous, but they are no more stringent than the public has a right to expect of those who voluntarily assume positions of authority in business enterprises whose services and products affect the health and well-being of the public that supports them.

The Act does not, as we observed in *Dotterweich,* make criminal liability turn on "awareness of some wrongdoing" or "conscious fraud." The duty imposed by Con-gress on responsible corporate agents is, we emphasize, one that requires the highest standard of foresight and vigilance, but the Act, in its criminal aspect, does not require that which is objectively impossible. The theory upon which responsible corporate agents are held criminally accountable for "causing" violations of the Act permits a claim that a defendant was "powerless" to prevent or correct the violation to "be raised defensively at a trial on the merits." If such a claim is made, the defendant has the burden of coming forward with evidence, but this does not alter the Government's ultimate burden of proving beyond a reasonable doubt the defendant's guilt, includ-ing his power, in light of the duty imposed by the Act, to prevent or correct the prohibited condition. Congress has seen fit to enforce the accountability of responsible corporate agents dealing with products which may affect the health of consumers by penal sanctions cast in rigorous terms, and the obligation of the courts is to give them effect so long as they do not violate the Constitution.

. . . We cannot agree with the Court of Appeals that it was incumbent upon the District Court to instruct the jury that the Government had the burden of establishing "wrongful action" in the sense in which the Court of Appeals used that phrase. The concept of a "responsible relationship" to, or a "responsible share" in, a violation of the Act indeed imports some measure of blameworthiness; but it is equally clear that the Government establishes a prima facie case when it introduces evidence sufficient to warrant a finding by the trier of the facts that the defendant had, by reason of his position in the corporation, responsibility and authority either to prevent in the first instance, or promptly to correct, the violation complained of, and that he failed to do so. The failure thus to fulfill the duty imposed by the interaction of the corporate agent's authority and the statute furnishes a sufficient causal link. The considerations which prompted the imposition of this duty, and the scope of the duty, provide the measure of culpability.

. . . .

Notes and Questions

1. **Public Welfare Offenses and Corporate Officer Liability.** Coming full circle, consideration of corporate officer liability links back directly to the discussion of strict liability and public welfare offenses with which this Chapter began. *See* Note 2 in Section A. The concept that strict corporate officer liability should be limited to "public welfare" offenses has not produced a coherent definition of that term. How would you define it? Are there any criminal laws that are *not* designed to protect the "public welfare," and, if so, why are they crimes at all?

2. **"Impossibility" as a Defense**. The *Park* majority expressly disavowed Justice Stewart's dissenting view that a standard of "criminal negligence" should apply before a corporate officer can be criminally convicted. At the same time, the majority allowed corporate officers to raise a defense of "impossibility." What protections designed to prevent the public dangers created by the businesses in which corporations engage are truly "impossible"? Is that concept really just a defense of "economically infeasible"? Would permitting an economic feasibility defense allow corporations to tolerate dangers to the public as a "cost of doing business"? Or is a "reasonable cost of doing business" defense actually beneficial in order to allow corporations to compete in a global economy?

3. **What Is the "Right" Standard?** Should the standard for imposing criminal liability on individuals occupying corporate positions be different from the standard applied to non-corporate individuals? What arguments support holding corporate officers criminally liable if their positions put them in a "responsible relationship" to the harms caused by corporate misconduct? Should such liability be imposed even

when the conduct cannot be described (beyond a reasonable doubt) as negligent? The Model Penal Code's position on these issues is set forth in § 2.07(6).

4. Liability for Corporate Employees as Well as Corporations? In response to widespread criticism of prosecutors' decisions not to charge individuals in connection with the economic woes suffered in the United States between late 2007 and 2012, the Deputy Attorney General for the United States Department of Justice, Sally Q. Yates, issued a memo to all federal prosecutors in 2015 stressing that individuals, as well as corporations, should be investigated and held criminally responsible for corporate wrongdoing when possible. The "Yates Memo" (which was actually an addendum to the "Thompson memo" issued in 2003 in response to the Enron scandal discussed above in Note 4(d) in Section B.1) can be accessed online at https://www.justice.gov/dag/file/769036/download. Although such a policy memo does not carry the force of law and cannot be relied upon to create "rights" for potential defendants, it presents six "principles" that can be very important in guiding the exercise of prosecutorial discretion:

(1) in order to qualify for any cooperation credit, corporations must provide to the Department [of Justice] all relevant facts relating to the individuals responsible for the misconduct;

(2) criminal and civil corporate investigations should focus on individuals from the inception of the investigation;

(3) criminal and civil attorneys handling corporate investigations should be in routine communication with one another;

(4) absent extraordinary circumstances or approved departmental policy, the Department will not release culpable individuals from civil or criminal liability when resolving a matter with a corporation;

(5) federal attorneys should not resolve corporate investigations without a clear plan to resolve related individual cases, and should memorialize any declinations as to individuals in such cases; and

(6) civil attorneys should consistently focus on individuals as well as the company and evaluate whether to bring suit against an individual based on considerations beyond that individual's ability to pay.

Now that you have reached the end of the Chapter, what are the pros and cons of prosecuting corporate officials for corporate crimes versus prosecuting the corporation itself? Or prosecuting both?

Chapter 6

Homicide

[A] Introduction

Francis B. Sayre, *Mens Rea*,
45 Harv. L. Rev. 974, 994–98 (1932)[1]

... [A]t the beginning of the thirteenth century criminal responsibility attached to all homicides except those in execution of a warrant or in the pursuit of justice, but men who killed in self-defense or by misadventure were seeking and often obtaining pardon from the king. The line between murder and manslaughter was unknown; there was no legal distinction between voluntary and involuntary homicide. The mental element, in other words, was of minimum importance. The history of homicide during the next few centuries is the story of the emergence of the mental element as a factor of prime importance, the gradual freeing from criminal responsibility of those who killed without guilty intent, and the separation of different kinds of homicide into more and less serious offenses dependent upon the psychical element.

. . . .

During the end of the fifteenth and first half of the sixteenth centuries ... felonious homicide was finally divided into two main divisions—that with and that without malice aforethought, and the first was designated as murder. The two classes of homicide were punished very differently. The first, from which benefit of clergy was excluded, was punishable by death; and the second, which was clergyable, came to be practically punishable only by a year's imprisonment and branding on the brawn of the thumb.

The distinction between the capital crime of murder and the less serious form of felonious homicide, which later came to be called manslaughter, depended therefore upon the presence or absence of "malice aforethought." The subsequent history of homicide is largely the story of the shifting meanings attached to the term "malice aforethought." At the beginning, and at least until the early seventeenth century, the term designated a purely psychical element. "Malice" was construed in its popular sense as meaning general malevolence or cold-blooded desire to injure, and referred to the underlying motive rather than to the immediate intent of the actor. ... [L]ater courts through the fiction of implied malice found an easy way to enlarge the meaning of malice aforethought and thus to widen the actual

---

1. Copyright © 1932 by the Harvard Law Review Association. Reprinted with permission.

boundaries of murder. A term used at the beginning to designate a purely psychical element was thus given a tortured and artificial meaning in order to enable courts to visit with a severe penalty killers who, in the public opinion of the day, ought not to be let off with the comparatively slight punishment attaching to clergyable offenses.

Model Penal Code § 210.2 Comment at 13–16

At common law, murder was defined as the unlawful killing of another human being with "malice aforethought." Whatever the original meaning of that phrase, it became over time an "arbitrary symbol" used by judges to signify any of a number of mental states deemed sufficient to support liability for murder. Successive generations added new content to "malice aforethought" until it encompassed a variety of mental attitudes bearing no predictable relation to the ordinary sense of the two words. . . .

. . . First and foremost, there was intent to kill. Common-law authorities included in the notion of intent to kill awareness that the death of another would result from one's actions, even if the actor had no particular desire to achieve such a consequence. Thus, intentional or knowing homicide was murder unless the actor killed in the heat of passion engendered by adequate provocation, in which case the crime was manslaughter. A second species of murder involved intent to cause grievous bodily harm. Again, knowledge that conduct would cause serious bodily injury was generally assimilated to intent and was deemed sufficient for murder if death of another actually resulted. A third category of murder was sometimes called depraved-heart murder. This label derived from decisions and statutes condemning as murder unintentional homicide under circumstances evincing a "depraved mind" or an "abandoned and malignant heart." Older authorities may have described such circumstances as giving rise to an "implied" or "presumed" intent to kill or injure, but the essential concept was one of extreme recklessness regarding homicidal risk. Thus, a person might be liable for murder absent any actual intent to kill or injure. . . . The fourth kind of murder was based on intent to commit a felony. This is the origin of the felony-murder rule, which assigns strict liability for homicide committed during the commission of a felony. These four states of mind exhausted the meaning of "malice aforethought"; the phrase had no residual content.

. . . Prior to the recodification effort begun by the Model Penal Code, most American jurisdictions maintained a law of murder built around these common-law classifications. The most significant departure was the division of murder into degrees, a change initiated by the Pennsylvania legislation of 1794. . . . The thrust of this reform was to confine the death penalty, which was then mandatory on conviction of any common-law murder, to homicides judged particularly heinous. Other states followed the Pennsylvania practice until at one time the vast majority of American jurisdictions differentiated degrees of murder and the term "first-degree murder" passed into common parlance.

The homicide statutes that follow illustrate the variations found in different states' definitions of the crime. The Pennsylvania and California statutes are based on the common law of homicide, whereas the New York statute is modeled on the Model Penal Code. At times, the statutes reflect pressure to extend the definitions of homicide to encompass acts that are the subject of particular public concern.

Pennsylvania Consolidated Statutes, Title 18

§ 2502. Murder

(a) **Murder of the first degree.** — A criminal homicide constitutes murder of the first degree when it is committed by an intentional killing. [Punishable by death or life imprisonment under § 1102(a)(1) assuming the defendant is an adult.]

(b) **Murder of the second degree.** — A criminal homicide constitutes murder of the second degree when it is committed while defendant was engaged as a principal or an accomplice in the perpetration of a felony. [Punishable by life imprisonment under § 1102(b) assuming the defendant is an adult.]

(c) **Murder of the third degree.** — All other kinds of murder shall be murder of the third degree. Murder of the third degree is a felony of the first degree. [Punishable by a maximum prison term of 40 years under § 1102(d).]

(d) **Definitions.** — As used in this section the following words and phrases shall have the meanings given to them in this subsection:

. . . .

"**Intentional killing.**" Killing by means of poison, or by lying in wait, or by any other kind of willful, deliberate and premeditated killing.

"**Perpetration of a felony.**" The act of the defendant in engaging in or being an accomplice in the commission of, or an attempt to commit, or flight after committing, or attempting to commit robbery, rape, or deviate sexual intercourse by force or threat of force, arson, burglary or kidnapping.

§ 2503. Voluntary manslaughter

(a) **General rule.** — A person who kills an individual without lawful justification commits voluntary manslaughter if at the time of the killing he is acting under a sudden and intense passion resulting from serious provocation by:

(1) the individual killed; or

(2) another whom the actor endeavors to kill, but he negligently or accidentally causes the death of the individual killed.

[Section 2301 defines "serious provocation" as "[c]onduct sufficient to excite an intense passion in a reasonable person."]

(b) **Unreasonable belief killing justifiable.** — A person who intentionally or knowingly kills an individual commits voluntary manslaughter if at the time of the killing he believes the circumstances to be such that, if they existed, would justify the killing under Chapter 5 of this title (relating to general principles of justification), but his belief is unreasonable.

(c) **Grading.** — Voluntary manslaughter is a felony of the first degree. [Punishable by a maximum prison term of 20 years under § 1103.]

§ 2504. Involuntary manslaughter

(a) **General rule.** — A person is guilty of involuntary manslaughter when as a direct result of the doing of an unlawful act in a reckless or grossly negligent manner, or the doing of a lawful act in a reckless or grossly negligent manner, he causes the death of another person.

(b) **Grading.** — Involuntary manslaughter is a misdemeanor of the first degree. Where the victim is under 12 years of age and is in the care, custody or control of the person who caused the death, involuntary manslaughter is a felony of the second degree. [Punishable under §§ 1103–1104 by a maximum prison term of five years, or 10 years if the victim was under 12 years old.]

California Penal Code

§ 187. Murder defined

(a) Murder is the unlawful killing of a human being, or a fetus, with malice aforethought. . . .

§ 188. Malice defined

Such malice may be express or implied. It is express when there is manifested a deliberate intention unlawfully to take away the life of a fellow creature. It is implied, when no considerable provocation appears, or when the circumstances attending the killing show an abandoned and malignant heart.

When it is shown that the killing resulted from the intentional doing of an act with express or implied malice as defined above, no other mental state need be shown to establish the mental state of malice aforethought. Neither an awareness of the obligation to act within the general body of laws regulating society nor acting despite such awareness is included within the definition of malice.

§ 189. Degrees of murder

All murder which is perpetrated by means of a destructive device or explosive, a weapon of mass destruction, knowing use of ammunition designed primarily to penetrate metal or armor, poison, lying in wait, torture, or by any other kind of willful, deliberate, and premeditated killing, or which is committed in the perpetration of, or attempt to perpetrate, arson, rape, carjacking, robbery, burglary, mayhem, kidnapping, train wrecking, or any act punishable under Section 206, 286, 288, 288a or 289 [torture and various sex offenses], or any murder which is perpetrated by means of discharging a firearm from a motor vehicle, intentionally at another person outside of the vehicle with the intent to inflict death, is murder of the first degree. All other kinds of murders are of the second degree.

. . . .

To prove the killing was "deliberate and premeditated," it shall not be necessary to prove the defendant maturely and meaningfully reflected upon the gravity of his or her act. [Pursuant to § 190(a), first-degree murder is subject to a maximum sentence of death or life imprisonment, and second-degree murder is generally subject to a sentence of 15 years to life.]

§ 191.5. Gross vehicular manslaughter and vehicular manslaughter while intoxicated

(a) Gross vehicular manslaughter while intoxicated is the unlawful killing of a human being without malice aforethought, in the driving of a vehicle, where the [defendant was driving while intoxicated] and the killing was either the proximate result of the commission of an unlawful act, not amounting to a felony, and with gross negligence, or the proximate result of the commission of a lawful act that might produce death, in an unlawful manner, and with gross negligence. [First offenses are punishable by a sentence of four, six, or ten years under § 191.5(c)(1).]

(b) Vehicular manslaughter while intoxicated is the unlawful killing of a human being without malice aforethought, in the driving of a vehicle, where the [defendant was driving while intoxicated] and the killing was either the proximate result of the commission of an unlawful act, not amounting to a felony, but without gross negligence, or the proximate result of the commission of a lawful act that might produce death, in an unlawful manner, but without gross negligence. [Subject to a maximum sentence of four years under § 191.5(c)(2).]

. . . .

§ 192. Manslaughter

Manslaughter is the unlawful killing of a human being without malice. It is of three kinds:

(a) Voluntary — upon a sudden quarrel or heat of passion. [Punishable by a sentence of three, six, or eleven years under § 193(a).]

(b) Involuntary — in the commission of an unlawful act, not amounting to felony; or in the commission of a lawful act which might produce death, in an unlawful manner, or without due caution and circumspection. This subdivision shall not apply to acts committed in the driving of a vehicle. [Punishable by a sentence of two, three, or four years under § 193(b).]

(c) Vehicular —

(1) Except as provided in subdivision (a) of Section 191.5, driving a vehicle in the commission of an unlawful act, not amounting to a felony, and with gross negligence; or driving a vehicle in the commission of a lawful act which might produce death, in an unlawful manner, and with gross negligence. [Punishable by a maximum sentence of two, four, or six years under § 193(c)(1).]

(2) Driving a vehicle in the commission of an unlawful act, not amounting to a felony, but without gross negligence; or driving a vehicle in the commission of a lawful act which might produce death, in an unlawful manner, but without gross negligence. [Punishable by a maximum sentence of one year under § 193(c)(2).]

. . . .

(d) This section shall not be construed as making any homicide in the driving of a vehicle punishable that is not a proximate result of the commission of an unlawful act, not amounting to a felony, or of the commission of a lawful act which might produce death, in an unlawful manner.

(e) "Gross negligence," as used in this section, does not prohibit or preclude a charge of murder under Section 188 upon facts exhibiting wantonness and a conscious disregard for life to support a finding of implied malice, or upon facts showing malice . . . .

(f)(1) For purposes of determining sudden quarrel or heat of passion pursuant to subdivision (a), the provocation was not objectively reasonable if it resulted from the discovery of, knowledge about, or potential disclosure of the victim's actual or perceived gender, gender identity, gender expression, or sexual orientation, including under circumstances in which the victim made an unwanted nonforcible romantic or sexual advance towards the defendant, or if the defendant and victim dated or had a romantic or sexual relationship. Nothing in this section shall preclude the jury from considering all relevant facts to determine whether the defendant was in fact provoked for purposes of establishing subjective provocation.

(2) For purposes of this subdivision, "gender" includes a person's gender identity and gender-related appearance and behavior regardless of whether that appearance or behavior is associated with the person's gender as determined at birth.

New York Penal Law

§ 125.00. Homicide defined

Homicide means conduct which causes the death of a person or an unborn child with which a female has been pregnant for more than twenty-four weeks under circumstances constituting murder, manslaughter in the first degree, manslaughter in the second degree, criminally negligent homicide, abortion in the first degree or self-abortion in the first degree.

§ 125.10. Criminally negligent homicide

A person is guilty of criminally negligent homicide when, with criminal negligence, he causes the death of another person.

Criminally negligent homicide is a class E felony. [Ordinarily subject to a maximum sentence of four years under § 70.00.]

§ 125.15. Manslaughter in the second degree

A person is guilty of manslaughter in the second degree when:

1. He recklessly causes the death of another person; or

2. He commits upon a female an abortional act which causes her death, unless such abortional act is justifiable pursuant to subdivision three of section 125.05 [explained below in § 125.45]; or

3. He intentionally causes or aids another person to commit suicide.

Manslaughter in the second degree is a class C felony. [Ordinarily subject to a maximum sentence of 15 years under § 70.00.]

§ 125.20. Manslaughter in the first degree

A person is guilty of manslaughter in the first degree when:

1. With intent to cause serious physical injury to another person, he causes the death of such person or of a third person; or

2. With intent to cause the death of another person, he causes the death of such person or of a third person under circumstances which do not constitute murder because he acts under the influence of extreme emotional disturbance, as defined in paragraph (a) of subdivision one of section 125.25 . . . ; or

3. He commits upon a female pregnant for more than twenty-four weeks an abortional act which causes her death, unless such abortional act is justifiable pursuant to subdivision three of section 125.05 [explained below in § 125.45]; or

4. Being 18 years old or more and with intent to cause physical injury to a person less than 11 years old, the defendant recklessly engages in conduct which creates a grave risk of serious physical injury to such person and thereby causes the death of such person.

Manslaughter in the first degree is a class B felony. [Ordinarily subject to a minimum sentence of five years and a maximum of 25 years under § 70.02.]

§ 125.25. Murder in the second degree

A person is guilty of murder in the second degree when:

1. With intent to cause the death of another person, he causes the death of such person or of a third person; except that in any prosecution under this subdivision, it is an affirmative defense that:

> (a) The defendant acted under the influence of extreme emotional disturbance for which there was a reasonable explanation or excuse, the reasonableness of which is to be determined from the viewpoint of a person in the defendant's situation under the circumstances as the defendant believed them to be. Nothing contained in this paragraph shall constitute a defense to a prosecution for, or preclude a conviction of, manslaughter in the first degree or any other crime . . . .

2. Under circumstances evincing a depraved indifference to human life, he recklessly engages in conduct which creates a grave risk of death to another person, and thereby causes the death of another person; or

3. Acting either alone or with one or more other persons, he commits or attempts to commit robbery, burglary, kidnapping, arson, rape in the first degree, criminal sexual act in the first degree, sexual abuse in the first degree, aggravated sexual abuse, escape in the first degree, or escape in the second degree, and, in the course of and in furtherance of such crime or of immediate flight therefrom, he, or another participant, if there be any, causes the death of a person other than one of the participants;

except that in any prosecution under this subdivision, in which the defendant was not the only participant in the underlying crime, it is an affirmative defense that the defendant:

(a) Did not commit the homicidal act or in any way solicit, request, command, importune, cause or aid the commission thereof; and

(b) Was not armed with a deadly weapon, or any instrument, article or substance readily capable of causing death or serious physical injury and of a sort not ordinarily carried in public places by law-abiding persons; and

(c) Had no reasonable ground to believe that any other participant was armed with such a weapon, instrument, article or substance; and

(d) Had no reasonable ground to believe that any other participant intended to engage in conduct likely to result in death or serious physical injury; or

4. Under circumstances evincing a depraved indifference to human life, and being eighteen years old or more the defendant recklessly engages in conduct which creates a grave risk of serious physical injury or death to another person less than eleven years old and thereby causes the death of such person; or

5. Being eighteen years old or more, while in the course of committing rape [or various other sex offenses] against a person less than fourteen years old, he or she intentionally causes the death of such person.

Murder in the second degree is a class A-I felony. [Ordinarily subject to a minimum sentence of 15 years and a maximum of life in prison under § 70.00.]

§ 125.27. Murder in the first degree

A person is guilty of murder in the first degree when:

1. With intent to cause the death of another person, he causes the death of such person or of a third person; and

(a) Either:

[Here the statute lists thirteen types of killings, including those where the intended victim was a police officer, firefighter, witness, prison employee, or judge; where the defendant had a prior murder conviction or was serving a life sentence at the time of the killing; where the defendant had agreed to kill for financial gain; where the defendant killed more than one person; where the defendant killed someone other than a cofelon while "committing or attempting to commit and in furtherance of" certain serious felonies; and where "the victim was killed in furtherance of an act of terrorism" (added following the September 11, 2001, attacks on the World Trade Center)]; and

(b) The defendant was more than eighteen years old at the time of the commission of the crime.

2. In any prosecution under subdivision one, it is an affirmative defense that:

(a) The defendant acted under the influence of extreme emotional disturbance for which there was a reasonable explanation or excuse, the reasonableness of which is to be determined from the viewpoint of a person in the
defendant's situation under the circumstances as the defendant believed
them to be. Nothing contained in this paragraph shall constitute a defense
to a prosecution for, or preclude a conviction of, manslaughter in the first
degree or any other crime except murder in the second degree . . . .

Murder in the first degree is a class A-I felony. [Ordinarily subject to a minimum
sentence of 20 years and a maximum of life in prison or the death penalty under
§§ 60.06 and 70.00. Note, however, that New York's death penalty was held unconstitutional in *People v. LaValle*, 817 N.E.2d 341 (N.Y. 2004).]

§ 125.45. Abortion in the first degree

A person is guilty of abortion in the first degree when he commits upon a female
pregnant for more than twenty-four weeks an abortional act which causes the miscarriage of such female, unless such abortional act is justifiable pursuant to subdivision three of section 125.05. [Section 125.05(3) provides in relevant part that "[a]n
abortional act is justifiable when committed upon a female with her consent by a
duly licensed physician acting (a) under a reasonable belief that such is necessary to
preserve her life, or, (b) within twenty-four weeks from the commencement of her
pregnancy."]

Abortion in the first degree is a class D felony. [Ordinarily subject to a maximum
sentence of seven years under § 70.00.]

§ 125.55. Self-abortion in the first degree

A female is guilty of self-abortion in the first degree when, being pregnant for more
than twenty-four weeks, she commits or submits to an abortional act upon herself
which causes her miscarriage, unless such abortional act is justifiable pursuant to
subdivision three of section 125.05. [Section 125.05(3) provides in relevant part that
a pregnant woman is justified in performing an abortional act on herself "when she
acts upon the advice of a duly licensed physician (1) that such act is necessary to preserve her life, or, (2) within twenty-four weeks from the commencement of her
pregnancy," and that she is justified in submitting to an abortional act "when she
believes that it is being committed by a duly licensed physician, acting under a reasonable belief that such act is necessary to preserve her life, or, within twenty-four
weeks from the commencement of her pregnancy."]

Self-abortion in the first degree is a class A misdemeanor. [Ordinarily subject to
a maximum sentence of one year under § 70.15.]

Model Penal Code

§ 210.2. Murder

(1) Except as provided in Section 210.3(1)(b), criminal homicide constitutes murder when:

(a) it is committed purposely or knowingly; or

(b) it is committed recklessly under circumstances manifesting extreme indifference to the value of human life. Such recklessness and indifference are presumed if the actor is engaged or is an accomplice in the commission of, or an attempt to commit, or flight after committing or attempting to commit robbery, rape or deviate sexual intercourse by force or threat of force, arson, burglary, kidnapping or felonious escape.

(2) Murder is a felony of the first degree. [Ordinarily subject to a maximum sentence of life imprisonment under § 6.06(1).]

§ 210.3. Manslaughter

(1) Criminal homicide constitutes manslaughter when:

(a) it is committed recklessly; or

(b) a homicide which would otherwise be murder is committed under the influence of extreme mental or emotional disturbance for which there is reasonable explanation or excuse. The reasonableness of such explanation or excuse shall be determined from the viewpoint of a person in the actor's situation under the circumstances as he believes them to be.

(2) Manslaughter is a felony of the second degree. [Ordinarily subject to a maximum sentence of 10 years under § 6.06(2).]

§ 210.4. Negligent Homicide

(1) Criminal homicide constitutes negligent homicide when it is committed negligently.

(2) Negligent homicide is a felony of the third degree. [Ordinarily subject to a maximum sentence of five years under § 6.06(3).]

[B] Intentional Homicide

[1] Distinguishing First- and Second-Degree Murder: Premeditation

Commonwealth v. Carroll

194 A.2d 911 (Pa. 1963)

BELL, CHIEF JUSTICE.

The defendant, Carroll, pleaded guilty generally to an indictment charging him with the murder of his wife, and was tried by a Judge without a jury. . . . That Court found him guilty of first degree murder and sentenced him to life imprisonment. Following argument and denial of motions in arrest of judgment and for a new trial, defendant took this appeal. The only questions involved are thus stated by the appellant:

(1) "Does not the evidence sustain a conviction no higher than murder in the second degree?"

(2) "Does not the evidence of defendant's good character, together with the testimony of medical experts, including the psychiatrist for the Behavior Clinic of Allegheny County, that the homicide was not premeditated or intentional, *require* the Court below to fix the degree of guilt of defendant no higher than murder in the second degree?"

The defendant married the deceased in 1955, when he was serving in the Army in California. Subsequently he was stationed in Alabama, and later in Greenland. During the latter tour of duty, defendant's wife and two children lived with his parents in New Jersey. Because this arrangement proved incompatible, defendant returned to the United States on emergency leave in order to move his family to their own quarters. On his wife's insistence, defendant was forced first to secure a "compassionate transfer" back to the States, and subsequently to resign from the Army in July of 1960, by which time he had attained the rank of Chief Warrant Officer. Defendant was a hard worker, earned a substantial salary and bore a very good reputation among his neighbors.

In 1958, decedent-wife suffered a fractured skull while attempting to leave defendant's car in the course of an argument. Allegedly this contributed to her mental disorder which was later diagnosed as a schizoid personality type. In 1959 she underwent psychiatric treatment at the mental hygiene clinic in Aberdeen, Maryland. She complained of nervousness and told the examining doctor "I feel like hurting my children." This sentiment sometimes took the form of sadistic "discipline" toward their very young children. Nevertheless, upon her discharge from the clinic, the doctors considered her much improved. With this background we come to the immediate events of the crime.

In January, 1962, defendant was selected to attend an electronics school in Winston-Salem, North Carolina, for nine days. His wife greeted this news with violent argument. Immediately prior to his departure for Winston-Salem, at the suggestion and request of his wife, he put a *loaded* .22 calibre pistol on the window sill at the head of their common bed, so that she would feel safe. On the evening of January 16, 1962, defendant returned home and told his wife that he had been temporarily assigned to teach at a school in Chambersburg, which would necessitate his absence from home four nights out of seven for a ten week period. A violent and protracted argument ensued at the dinner table and continued until four o'clock in the morning.

Defendant's own statement after his arrest details the final moments before the crime: "We went into the bedroom a little before 3 o'clock on Wednesday morning where we continued to argue in short bursts. Generally she laid with her back to me facing the wall in bed and would just talk over her shoulder to me. I became angry and more angry especially what she was saying about my kids and myself, and sometime between 3 and 4 o'clock in the morning I remembered the gun on the window sill over my head. I think she had dozed off. *I reached up and grabbed the pistol and brought it down and shot her twice in the back of the head.*"[2]

Defendant's testimony at the trial elaborated this theme. He started to think about the children, "seeing my older son's feet what happened to them. I could see the bruises on him and Michael's chin was split open, four stitches. I didn't know what to do. I wanted to help my boys. Sometime in there she said something in there, she called me some kind of name. I kept thinking of this. *During this time I either thought or felt — I thought of the gun, just thought of the gun.* I am not sure whether I felt my hand move toward the gun — I saw my hand move, the next thing — the only thing I can recollect after that is right after the shots or right during the shots I saw the gun in my hand just pointed at my wife's head. She was still lying on her back — I mean her side. I could smell the gunpowder and I could hear something — it sounded like running water. I didn't know what it was at first, didn't realize what I'd done at first. Then I smelled it. I smelled blood before. . . ."

Q. At the time you shot her, Donald, were you fully aware and intend to do what you did?

A. I don't know positively. All I remember hearing was two shots and feeling myself go cold all of a sudden.

Shortly thereafter defendant wrapped his wife's body in a blanket, spread and sheets, tied them on with a piece of plastic clothesline and took her down to the cellar. He tried to clean up as well as he could. That night he took his wife's body, wrapped in a blanket with a rug over it to a desolate place near a trash dump. He then took the children to his parents' home in Magnolia, New Jersey. He was arrested the next Monday in Chambersburg where he had gone to his teaching assignment.

. . . .

The applicable principles of law are . . . set forth and reaffirmed in *Commonwealth v. Gooslin*, 410 Pa. 285, 189 A.2d 157 [(1963)]:

> . . . *"Murder"* . . . *"is defined as an unlawful killing of another with malice aforethought, express or implied."* The legislature divided murder into two classifications, murder in the first degree and murder in the second degree; and provided that (1) all murder perpetrated by poison or lying in wait; or by any other kind of wilful, deliberate [and] premeditated killing, or any murder which shall be committed in the perpetration of or attempt to perpetrate certain specified felonies [arson, rape, robbery, burglary, or kidnapping], is murder in the first degree and (2) every other kind of murder is murder in the second degree.[3]

---

2. [n.1] When pressed on cross-examination defendant approximated that five minutes elapsed between his wife's last remark and the shooting.

3. The Pennsylvania legislature subsequently split first-degree murder into two separate categories. The current version of the statute is reprinted above in Section A.

"Malice express or implied is [the hallmark] . . . and absolutely essential ingredient of murder. Malice in its legal sense exists not only where there is a particular ill will, but also whenever there is a wickedness of disposition, hardness of heart, wanton conduct, cruelty, recklessness of consequences and a mind regardless of social duty. Legal malice may be inferred and found from the attending circumstances."

. . . .

In *Commonwealth v. Tyrrell*, 405 Pa. 210, 174 A.2d 852 [(1961)], the Court said . . . : "The essential difference in a nonfelony murder-killing between murder in the first degree and murder in the second degree is that murder in the first degree requires a specific intent to take the life of another human being . . . ."

The specific intent to kill . . . necessary to constitute . . . murder in the first degree may be found from a defendant's words or conduct or from the attendant circumstances together with all reasonable inferences therefrom, and may be inferred from the intentional use of a deadly weapon on a vital part of the body of another human being.

. . . .

If we consider only the evidence which is favorable to the Commonwealth, it is without the slightest doubt sufficient in law to prove first degree. However, even if we believe all of defendant's statements and testimony, there is no doubt that this killing constituted murder in the first degree. Defendant first urges that there was insufficient time for premeditation in the light of his good reputation. This is based on an isolated and oft repeated statement that "no time is too short for a wicked man to frame in his mind his scheme of murder." Defendant argues that, conversely, a long time is necessary to find premeditation in a "good man." We find no merit in defendant's analogy or contention. "Whether the intention to kill and the killing, that is, the premeditation and the fatal act, were within a brief space of time or a long space of time is immaterial if the killing was in fact intentional, wilful, deliberate and premeditated. . . . 'The law fixes upon no length of time as necessary to form the intention to kill, but leaves the existence of a fully formed intent as a fact to be determined by the jury, from all the facts and circumstances in the evidence.'"

Defendant further contends that the time and place of the crime, the enormous difficulty of removing and concealing the body, and the obvious lack of an escape plan, militate against and make a finding of premeditation legally impossible. This is a "jury argument"; it is clear as crystal that such circumstances do not negate premeditation. This contention of defendant is likewise clearly devoid of merit.

Defendant's most earnestly pressed contention is that the *psychiatrist's opinion of what defendant's state of mind must have been and was at the time of the crime,* clearly establishes not only the lack but also the legal impossibility of premeditation. Dr. Davis, a psychiatrist of the Allegheny County Behavior Clinic, testified that defendant was "for a number of years . . . passively going along with a situation which he . . . [was] not controlling and he . . . [was] not making any decisions, and finally a decision . . . [was] forced on him. . . . He had left the military to take this assignment, and he was averaging about nine thousand a year; he had a good job. He knew that if he didn't accept this teaching assignment in all probability he would be dismissed from the Government service, and at his age and his special training he didn't know whether he would be able to find employment. More critical to that was the fact that at this point, as we understand it, his wife issued an ultimatum that if he went and gave this training course she would leave him. . . . He was so dependent upon her he didn't want her to leave. He couldn't make up his mind what to do. He was trapped . . . ."

The doctor then gave *his opinion* that "rage," "desperation," and "panic" produced "an impulsive automatic reflex type of homicide, . . . as opposed to an intentional premeditated type of homicide. . . . Our feeling was that if this gun had fallen to the floor he wouldn't have been able to pick it up and consummate that homicide. And I think if he had to load the gun he wouldn't have done it. This is a matter of opinion, but this is our opinion about it."

There are three answers to this contention. First, neither a Judge nor a jury has to believe all or any part of the testimony of the defendant or of any witness. Secondly, the opinion of the psychiatrists was based to a large extent upon statements made to them by the defendant, which need not be believed and which are in some instances opposed by the facts themselves. Thirdly, a psychiatrist's opinion of a defendant's impulse or lack of intent or state of mind is, in this class of case, entitled to very little weight, and this is especially so when defendant's own actions, or his testimony or confession, or the facts themselves, belie the opinion.

. . . .

Defendant's *own statement* after his arrest, upon which his counsel so strongly relies, *as well as his testimony at his trial*, clearly convict him of first degree murder and justify the finding and sentence of the Court below. Defendant himself described his actions at the time he killed his wife. From his own statements and from his own testimony, it is clear that, terribly provoked by his allegedly nagging, belligerent and sadistic wife,[4] *defendant remembered the gun, deliberately took it down, and deliberately fired two shots into the head of his sleeping wife*. There is no doubt that this was a wilful, deliberate and premeditated murder.

. . . .

---

4. [n.5] While this picture of his wife is different from that depicted by her neighbors, if defendant's version is true, the remedy lies in a commutation by the Board of Pardons and not by a disregard of the law by the Courts.

People v. Anderson

447 P.2d 942 (Cal. 1968)

Tobriner, Justice.

Defendant was indicted for the murder of Victoria Hammond, a 10-year-old girl, in 1962. The jury found defendant guilty of first degree murder, found that he was sane, and fixed the penalty at death . . . .

Defendant, a San Jose cab driver, had been living for about eight months with a Mrs. Hammond and her three children, Cynthia, aged 17, Kenneth, aged 13, and the victim, Victoria, aged 10. On the morning of the day of the murder, December 7, 1962, Mrs. Hammond left for work at 7:30 a.m., leaving only Victoria at home with the defendant. Defendant was still in bed. He had been home from work for the previous two days, during which time he had been drinking heavily, and apparently he did not go to work on the day of the murder.

The owner of a nearby liquor store testified that defendant purchased a quart of whiskey from him sometime between 1 and 2 p.m. on December 7, 1962. The only other witness who testified as to defendant's whereabouts that day prior to the discovery of the murder was the victim's 13-year-old brother Kenneth.

Kenneth testified that he arrived home from school at 3:30 p.m. on December 7. He found the front door locked, which was not unusual, so he went around to the back of the house and down to the basement. Kenneth stayed there awhile working with his microscope. In a short time he heard noise coming from upstairs in the house which sounded like boxes and other things being moved around, like someone was cleaning up. He then heard the shower water running . . . .

Kenneth testified further that he then came up from the basement and went to the back porch screen door. The screen door was locked, which also was not unusual, so Kenneth jerked on it so the hook would pop out. Kenneth then went from the back porch directly into his bedroom to change his clothes. He then returned through the back porch to the kitchen door which was also locked. Kenneth knocked on the door and the defendant opened it. Kenneth testified that the defendant was wearing slacks only. Kenneth went into the kitchen and asked defendant for $1.00 for a teen club dance he intended to attend that evening. Defendant obtained a dollar for him out of the pocket of another pair of slacks hanging on the knob of a bedroom door. When Kenneth noticed the blood on the kitchen floor and asked defendant about it, the defendant told Kenneth that he had cut himself. This explanation apparently satisfied Kenneth, as he finished dressing and left the house sometime before 4 p.m.

Kenneth testified that no one else was at his house when he was there between 3:30 and 4 p.m. He further testified that about 6:30 he realized that he had forgotten his wallet and returned home. As he approached the front door, his mother came out and asked to see the cut on his arm, and Kenneth explained that he had no cut. His mother then asked defendant about the blood she had noticed and defendant told her that Victoria had cut herself, but that the mother should not worry, as the cut was not serious. After defendant told her that Victoria was at a friend's for dinner, the mother wanted to take Kenneth with her to get Victoria. Kenneth went back to his room to get a jacket. Because he had a "weird" feeling, he looked into Victoria's room. He found her nude, bloody body under some boxes and blankets on the floor near her bed . . . .

Mrs. Hammond testified that she returned home from work at 4:45 p.m. The front door was locked, she rang the doorbell, and defendant answered. Mrs. Hammond noticed blood on the couch in the living room, and when she asked defendant about it, he told her that Kenneth had cut himself playing with a knife and that he was at a teenage dance. Mrs. Hammond then went to the grocery store and returned about 5:30 p.m. . . .

A classmate of Victoria, who was the last person to see Victoria alive, testified that she left Victoria in front of the Hammond house about 3:45 p.m. after the two of them had walked home from school.

. . . .

The arresting officer found Victoria's body on the floor near her bed. He found defendant's blood-spotted shorts on a chair in the living room, and a knife and defendant's socks, with blood encrusted on the soles, in the master bedroom. The evidence established that the victim's torn and bloodstained dress had been ripped from her, that her clothes, including her panties out of which the crotch had been ripped, were found in various rooms of the house, that there were bloody footprints matching the size of the victim's leading from the master bedroom to Victoria's room, and that there was blood in almost every room including the kitchen, the floor of which appeared to have been mopped.

. . . .

Over 60 wounds, both severe and superficial, were found on Victoria's body. The cuts extended over her entire body, including one extending from the rectum through the vagina, and the partial cutting off of her tongue. Several of the wounds, including the vaginal lacerations, were post mortem. No evidence of spermatozoa was found in the victim, on her panties, or on the bed next to which she was found.

The prosecution contended that the murder was sexually motivated. The defendant, who pleaded not guilty and not guilty by reason of insanity, presented no defense whatsoever. . . .

. . . [T]he only bloodstained clothes of defendant's which were discovered were his socks and his shorts, from which facts the People argue that defendant was almost nude during the attack.

. . . .

[The trial court instructed the jury on two possible theories of first degree murder: (1) a wilful, deliberate, and premeditated killing; and (2) felony murder, specifically, murder committed in the perpetration or attempted perpetration of an act punishable under Penal Code § 288, which prohibits lewd or lascivious acts involving children.[5]]

... [W]e find no indication that the Legislature intended to give the words "deliberate" and "premeditated" other than their ordinary dictionary meanings. Moreover, we have repeatedly pointed out that the legislative classification of murder into two degrees would be meaningless if "deliberation" and "premeditation" were construed as requiring no more reflection than may be involved in the mere formation of a specific intent to kill.

Thus we have held that in order for a killing with malice aforethought to be first rather than second degree murder, "'[t]he intent to kill must be . . . formed upon a *pre-existing* reflection' . . . [and must have] been the subject of actual deliberation or *forethought.* . . ." We have therefore held that "a verdict of murder in the first degree . . . [on a theory of a wilful, deliberate, and premeditated killing] is proper only if the slayer killed 'as a result of careful thought and weighing of considerations; as a *deliberate* judgment or plan; carried on coolly and steadily, [especially] according to a *preconceived design.*'"

The type of evidence which this court has found sufficient to sustain a finding of premeditation and deliberation falls into three basic categories: (1) facts about how and what defendant did *prior* to the actual killing which show that the defendant was engaged in activity directed toward, and explicable as intended to result in, the killing—what may be characterized as "planning" activity; (2) facts about the defendant's *prior* relationship and/or conduct with the victim from which the jury could reasonably infer a "motive" to kill the victim . . . ; (3) facts about the nature of the killing from which the jury could infer that the manner of killing was so particular and exacting that the defendant must have intentionally killed according to a "preconceived design" to take his victim's life. . . .

... [T]his court sustains verdicts of first degree murder typically when there is evidence of all three types and otherwise requires at least extremely strong evidence of (1) or evidence of (2) in conjunction with either (1) or (3). As will become clear from the following analysis of representative cases, the present case lacks evidence of any of the three types.

In *People v. Hillery*, 62 Cal. 2d 692, 401 P.2d 382 [(1965)], the jury could reasonably infer that the defendant engaged in the following "extended course of conduct": defendant parked his car near the victim's (a 15-year-old girl's) house, entered the house surreptitiously, seized the victim while she was sewing and covered her head with a towel and slip to prevent outcry or identification, cut a length of cord in another room to secure her hands behind her, took the victim's scissors, dragged her to a nearby irrigation ditch where her body was subsequently found, engaged in a struggle with the victim, and then plunged the scissors directly into her chest.

---

5. The California murder statute reprinted above in Section A is for all relevant purposes identical to the one in effect at the time of Anderson's trial.

Hillery represents a case of very strong type (1) evidence: the defendant's surreptitious conduct, subjection of his victim to his complete control, and carrying off of his victim to a place where others were unlikely to intrude, can be described as "planning" activity directly related to the killing. Moreover, there is also strong evidence of type (3): directly plunging a lethal weapon into the chest evidences a deliberate intention to kill as opposed to the type of "indiscriminate" multiple attack of both severe and superficial wounds which defendant engaged in in the instant case.

. . . .

. . . [T]he condition of the victim's body in the instant case, *when considered in light of the absence of* any evidence of the defendant's conduct immediately prior to the killing or any "unusual" relationship with the victim, points to a "random" attack which was explosive rather than calculated. . . .

The present case is strikingly similar to *People v. Granados,* 49 Cal. 2d 490, 319 P.2d 346 [(1957)], in which this court reduced a verdict of first degree murder to second degree murder on the ground that the evidence was insufficient to show . . . premeditation and deliberation. . . . The evidence of premeditation and deliberation in *Granados,* while clearly insufficient to sustain the verdict of first degree murder . . . , was stronger than in the present case in which we find no evidence from which the jury could *reasonably* infer that defendant acted "*with a deliberate and clear intent to take life.*"

In *Granados,* defendant lived in a common law relationship with the mother of his victim, a 13-year-old girl. After taking the deceased and her brother to a real estate office, [Granados] gave the brother a note requesting money to take to his mother who worked nearby. When the brother returned home with the requested money he saw [Granados] at the rear of the house. As he started to enter the house, [Granados] came running to him and asked him to get some alcohol for his sister (decedent) who had fainted. The brother noticed blood on one of [Granados'] hands and that [Granados] had the other hand behind his back.

The brother unsuccessfully looked for some alcohol. [Granados] then suggested they get a doctor and an ambulance. The brother then noticed that [Granados'] hand had been washed. [Granados] then drove the brother to a drugstore, gave him 50 cents for some alcohol, and told him he would wait for him. [Granados] drove away and did not return for the brother.

[Granados] then called the mother and told her the victim had poisoned herself. The mother returned to the house with a friend who found the victim's body in the bedroom lying on the floor. Her skirt was pulled up exposing her private parts, there were bloodstains on the wall, floor, and decedent's head, and a machete covered with blood was lying in a corner of the living room behind a small heater.

[Granados] testified that on the day of the killing the girl was helping him clean the house and that he asked her if she was a virgin, to which she replied that it was none of his business. [Granados] said that she had never answered him in that way and that he therefore struck her with his hand, but did not remember striking her with the machete.

Decedent's mother testified that she had warned [Granados] that the next time he bothered her daughter, she would tell the police, and that [Granados] in reply threatened to kill her and both her children if she did.

The prosecution argued that the murder was sexually motivated. This court, per Justice McComb, held that the evidence was insufficient as a matter of law to support a verdict of first degree murder.

Applying the standards developed above to *Granados*, we find that the only evidence of (1) [Granados'] behavior prior to the killing which could be described as "planning" activity related to a killing purpose was . . . sending the victim's brother on an errand and apparently returning home alone with the decedent. Such evidence is highly ambiguous in terms of the various inferences it could support as to [Granados'] purpose in so behaving. The evidence of (2) [Granados'] prior behavior with the victim (alleged sexual molestation and his question as to her virginity) is insufficient to support a reasonable inference that [Granados] had a "motive" to kill the girl, which could in turn support an inference that the striking with the machete was the result of a "preconceived design" and "forethought." Finally, the evidence of (3) the manner of killing (brutal hacking) does not support a reasonable inference of deliberately placed blows, which could in turn support an inference that the act of killing was premeditated rather than "hasty and impetuous."

. . . Here, on the other hand, we do not have any evidence of either (1) any conduct by [Anderson] prior to the killing which would indicate that he was planning anything, felonious or otherwise, or (2) any behavior towards Victoria from which the jury could reasonably infer that [Anderson] had a "motive" or desire to sexually attack and/or kill her. The evidence of (3), the manner of killing and the condition of the body, is the same in both cases: the only inference which the evidence reasonably supports in either case is that the killing resulted from a "random," violent, indiscriminate attack rather than from deliberately placed wounds inflicted according to a preconceived design.

Finally, the defendant in *Granados*, as here, attempted to "cover up" the crime by lying to the brother and the mother of the victim. Although this type of evidence may possibly bear on defendant's state of mind *after* the killing, it is irrelevant to ascertaining defendant's state of mind immediately prior to, or during, the killing. Evasive conduct shows fear: it cannot support the double inference that defendant planned to hide his crime at the time he committed it and that therefore defendant committed the crime with premeditation and deliberation.

. . . .

[Two members of the California Supreme Court dissented and would have affirmed Anderson's conviction on the ground that "the homicide was committed by defendant in his attempted performance or actual performance of lewd or lascivious acts upon the body of the child victim in violation of Penal Code section 288 and there-fore constituted first degree murder under the felony-murder rule." In addition, the dissenting opinion had this comment on the evidence of premeditation:

> Although I believe there is credible evidence from which the jury could find a premeditated homicide, e.g. the locking of the doors (whether before or after the actual killing is a matter of conjecture), the duration of the assault, the pursuit through many rooms with a quantity of blood being left in each room, the extensive stabbings many of which would have sufficed as fatal, the removal of the murder weapon from one room and the apparent repeated use of it in other rooms, it is not necessary to rest the jury's determination of first degree murder on that ground since the evidence is substantial that the homicide was first degree murder under the felony-murder rule.]

Notes and Questions

1. Premeditation in Other Jurisdictions. In defining premeditation, other courts have disagreed with the approach taken in *Carroll*, reasoning that the concept of premeditation should adequately distinguish "ruthless, cold-blooded, calculated" killings from intentional killings that were "spontaneous and nonreflective." *State v. Guthrie*, 461 S.E.2d 163, 182 (W. Va. 1995).

Thus, for example, in *State v. Thompson*, 65 P.3d 420, 427 (Ariz. 2003), the court thought it important to preserve a "meaningful distinction" between first- and second-degree murder and make clear that premeditation is "more than just a snap decision made in the heat of passion." The court therefore "discourage[d] the use of the phrase 'as instantaneous as successive thoughts of the mind'" in instructing juries on first-degree murder and instead approved the following definition:

> "Premeditation" means that the defendant intended to kill another human being, . . . and that after forming that intent . . . , reflected on the decision before killing. It is this reflection, regardless of the length of time in which it occurs, that distinguishes first degree murder from second degree mur-der. An act is not done with premeditation if it is the instant effect of a sud-den quarrel or heat of passion.

Id. at 428.

Many of the courts that decline to follow *Carroll* take the position that the pro-cess of premeditation requires an "appreciable" amount of time. In *Bullock v. United States*, 122 F.2d 213, 213–14 (D.C. Cir. 1941), for example, the court noted:

> To speak of premeditation and deliberation which are instantaneous, or which take no appreciable time, is a contradiction in terms. . . . There is nothing deliberate and premeditated about a killing which is done within a second or two after the accused first thinks of doing it. . . .

See also State v. Hall, 722 N.W.2d 472, 477 (Minn. 2006) ("In order to prove premedi-tation, 'the state must always prove that, after the defendant formed the intent to kill, some appreciable time passed during which the consideration, planning, preparation or determination required . . . prior to the commission of the act took place.'"); *State v. Ros*, 973 A.2d 1148, 1161 (R.I. 2009) (observing that the difference between first-degree murder and "momentary-intent-based second-degree murder is the duration of the defendant's intent to kill" and "[i]n order to prove first-degree murder, the state must show that the accused formed an intent to kill, thought about or deliberated on that intent to kill for some appreciable length of time (premeditation), and then engaged in homicidal conduct"). *But cf. Watson v. United States*, 501 A.2d 791, 793 (D.C. 1985) (noting that the appreciable time requirement does not necessitate a "lapse of days or hours, or even minutes" and, in fact, "the time involved may be as brief as a few seconds").

Do the courts that reject *Carroll* have a point? On the other hand, are these cases subject to criticism because the prosecution is constitutionally barred from requiring the defendant to testify and therefore may be unable to prove precisely what happened at the time of the killing—especially where only the defendant and the deceased were present? In such cases, can the prosecution only speculate as to whether an intentional killing was impulsive or premeditated?

Is there a difference between "premeditation" and "deliberation"? If so, does the "appreciable amount of time" approach risk conflating the two concepts instead of analyzing them as "separate standards with, respectively, a quantitative element (how much time elapsed) and a qualitative one (how maturely the actor . . . reflected)"? Joshua Dressler, *Rethinking Criminal Homicide Statutes: Giving Juries More Discretion*, 47 Tex. Tech L. Rev. 89, 92 (2014).

2. Subsequent Application of the *Anderson* Test. One other court has explicitly endorsed the standards outlined in *Anderson*. *See Mattern v. State*, 151 P.3d 1116, 1129–30 (Wyo. 2007); *see also State v. Ortega*, 813 N.W.2d 86, 100–01 (Minn. 2012) (likewise considering evidence of planning, motive, and method of killing relevant in measuring premeditation). It is open to question, however, how closely California still adheres to that approach.

In *People v. Perez*, 831 P.2d 1159, 1163 (Cal. 1992), the California Supreme Court observed that *Anderson* merely created "a framework to aid in appellate review" of first-degree murder convictions, and "did not propose to define the elements of first degree murder or alter the substantive law of murder in any way":

> In identifying categories of evidence bearing on premeditation and deliberation, *Anderson* did not purport to establish an exhaustive list that would exclude all other types and combinations of evidence that could support a finding of premeditation and deliberation. . . . The *Anderson* factors, while helpful for purposes of review, are not a sine qua non to finding first degree premeditated murder, nor are they exclusive.

The court upheld the first-degree murder conviction in *Perez*, a case that—like *Anderson*—involved a very bloody crime scene, with blood found in almost every room of the victim's house. The victim, who had attended high school 10 years earlier with the defendant, was beaten and stabbed with two different knives. Her body had some 38 knife wounds, including 26 stabbing or slashing wounds (inflicted by a steak knife matching the knives in the victim's kitchen) and about a dozen puncture wounds (inflicted by a second knife). Although the second knife did not match any of the knives in the victim's kitchen and was used after the victim was already dead, the *Perez* court found the manner of killing "indicative of premeditation and deliberation":

> The evidence of blood in the kitchen knife drawer supports an inference that defendant went to the kitchen in search of another knife after the steak knife broke. This action bears similarity to reloading a gun or using another gun when the first one has run out of ammunition. . . .
>
> . . . Defendant dismisses reliance on the use of the second knife by noting that the coroner's testimony indicated that the wounds inflicted by it were post mortem and in nonvital areas. There is no indication, however, that it would have been readily apparent, at the time of the assault, that the victim was already dead. . . . Moreover, the jury could reasonably infer that the post mortem wounds were inflicted to make certain the victim was dead. . . . Given that the post mortem wounds were inflicted after defendant had broken the first knife and used a second knife to inflict these wounds, it is difficult to characterize defendant's conduct as "mere rash and unconsidered impulse." Some period of time necessarily must have elapsed between the first and second set of wounds. While this conduct, in itself, may not necessarily support a finding of premeditation, in conjunction with the manner of killing, it could easily have led the jury to infer premeditation and deliberation.

Id. at 1164–65.

The California Supreme Court continues to cite *Anderson*'s three categories of evidence and three tests for premeditation, *see, e.g., People v. Sandoval*, 363 P.3d 41, 65 (Cal. 2015), and has not replaced *Anderson* with any alternative definition of premeditation. According to one California appellate court, however, *Anderson*, "although not overruled by *People v. Perez*, has been construed to insignificance." *People v. Caldwell*, 11 Cal. Rptr. 2d 752, 756 (Cal. Ct. App. 1992).[6]

3. The Manner of Killing. In *Anderson*, the court concluded that the method of killing there — more than 60 knife wounds — suggested "a 'random,' violent, indiscriminate attack rather than . . . deliberately placed wounds inflicted according to a preconceived design." Likewise, in *State v. Brown*, 836 S.W.2d 530, 542, 543–44 (Tenn. 1992), a case involving "a shocking history of physical [child] abuse," the court found insufficient evidence that a father had premeditated the death of his four-year-old son, noting that "[r]epeated blows can be delivered in the heat of passion, with no design or reflection." *See also Austin v. United States*, 382 F.2d 129, 139 (D.C. Cir.

---

6. In denying review in *Caldwell*, the California Supreme Court ordered that the Court of Appeal's opinion not be published.

1967) (observing that "many murders most brutish and bestial are committed in a consuming frenzy or heat of passion," rather than as the result of the "calmly calculated plan to kill requisite for premeditation and deliberation").

In *Booth v. State*, 507 A.2d 1098, 1108 (Md. 1986), *vacated and remanded on other grounds,* 482 U.S. 496 (1987), by contrast, the court thought that "[t]he intervals between the [12] stab wounds inflicted on [the victim] evidence[d] sufficient time for reflection and decision." *See also State v. Beck*, 487 S.E.2d 751, 754 (N.C. 1997) (finding that a "brutal manner" of killing is evidence of premeditation); David Crump, *"Murder, Pennsylvania Style": Comparing Traditional American Homicide Law to the Statutes of the Model Penal Code*, 109 W. Va. L. Rev. 257, 264, 274 (2007) (referring to *Anderson* as the "poster child for what is wrong with the premeditation-deliberation formula," and criticizing the California court for ignoring "the brutality and violence of the killing").

In comparison, consider killings accomplished by more exacting means. In one such case, *Hunt v. State*, 691 A.2d 1255 (Md. 1997), the defendant fired two shots at a police officer who was trying to handcuff him. Characterizing the evidence of premeditation as "overwhelming," the court pointed to "the methodical process" used in firing the weapon involved in that case:

> In order to fire the gun, Hunt took several deliberate and conscious actions to place it in an operational mode: He pulled the hammer of the weapon toward him. He pointed the weapon at [the officer], and he pulled the trigger. We reject the notion that this weapon, a .357 single-action revolver, may be fired in any other but a deliberate manner. Further, this Court has held that the delay between firing a first and second shot is enough time for reflection and decision to justify a finding of premeditation and deliberation.

Id. at 1272, 1274.

In *State v. Bingham*, 719 P.2d 109 (Wash. 1986), however, the court found insufficient evidence of premeditation where death was caused by strangulation, a process that took approximately three to five minutes. Noting that there was no evidence of premeditation prior to the time the defendant began strangling the victim, the court held that "[h]aving the opportunity to deliberate is not evidence the defendant did deliberate." Otherwise, the court feared, "any form of killing which took more than a moment could result in a finding of premeditation, without some additional evidence showing reflection." *Id.* at 113. *But cf. Hounshell v. State*, 486 A.2d 789, 795 (Md. Ct. Spec. App. 1985) (concluding that the time required to strangle a victim offers "a significant opportunity for reflection and a change of heart" and thus by itself constitutes sufficient evidence of premeditation).

Considering this group of cases as a whole, what relevance should the manner of killing have on the question of premeditation?

4. The Defendant's Actions Subsequent to the Killing. In *Anderson*, the court held that the defendant's efforts to cover up the crime were "irrelevant" to the question whether he acted with premeditation at the time of the killing. In *People v. Perez*, 831 P.2d 1159, 1165 (Cal. 1992), by contrast, which is discussed above in Note 2, the court thought that the defendant's conduct after the killing helped prove premeditation:

> Additionally, the conduct of defendant *after* the stabbing, such as the search of dresser drawers, jewelry boxes, kitchen drawers and the changing of a Band-Aid on his bloody hand, would appear to be inconsistent with a state of mind that would have produced a rash, impulsive killing.

Other courts have likewise considered a defendant's evasive tactics following the killing evidence of premeditation. *See, e.g., State v. Helmer*, 545 N.W.2d 471, 478 (S.D. 1996) (noting that "attempts to conceal or dispose of evidence support an implicit finding of premeditation"). Is such evidence relevant? Consider the views of the *Perez* dissent:

> Despite the contrary language in *Anderson*, *some* conduct after a murder can prove premeditation. A payoff to a hit man after the killing will do that nicely, so might cashing in a large life insurance policy recently purchased without the victim's knowledge. But mere flight or other efforts to avoid capture where one is culpable to some degree in a homicide case do not necessarily suggest the killing was premeditated.
>
> Persons involved in second degree murder are no less likely to adopt evasive tactics than those who planned the crime at the outset.

Perez, 831 P.2d at 1175 (Mosk, J., dissenting) (quoting the Court of Appeal's opinion).

5. The Appropriateness of Using Premeditation to Distinguish First- and Second-Degree Murder. Statutes like those interpreted in *Carroll* and *Anderson*, which use premeditation to separate first-degree and second-degree murder, "reflect a belief that one who meditates an intent to kill and then deliberately executes it is more dangerous, more culpable or less capable of reformation than one who kills on sudden impulse; or that the prospect of the death penalty is more likely to deter men from deliberate than from impulsive murder." *Bullock v. United States*, 122 F.2d 213, 214 (D.C. Cir. 1941). Does this reasoning make sense? Do the purposes of punishment support treating premeditated killers more harshly than impulsive or spontaneous killers?

In considering this issue, two questions arise: first, whether it is possible to separate premeditated killings from intentional killings that are not premeditated; second, if such a line can be drawn, whether it accurately divides murderers according to their relatively culpability.

The materials above discuss the first question. In addition, consider the following excerpt from *Selected Writings of Benjamin Nathan Cardozo* 383–84 (Margaret E. Hall ed. 1947):

> A long series of decisions, beginning many years ago, has given to these words [premeditation and deliberation] a meaning that differs to some extent

from the one revealed upon the surface. To deliberate and premeditate . . . , one does not have to plan the murder days or hours or even minutes in advance, as where one lies in wait for one's enemy or places poison in his food and drink. . . . "If there is hesitation or doubt to be overcome, a choice made as the result of thought, however short the struggle between the intention and the act," there is . . . deliberation and premeditation . . . .

I think the distinction is much too vague to be continued in our law. . . . The presence of a sudden impulse is said to mark the dividing line, but how can an impulse be anything but sudden when the time for its formation is measured by the lapse of seconds? Yet the decisions are to the effect that seconds may be enough. . . . If intent is deliberate and premeditated whenever there is choice, then in truth it is always deliberate and premeditated, since choice is involved in the hypothesis of the intent. What we have is merely a privilege offered to the jury to find the lesser degree when the suddenness of the intent, the vehemence of the passion, seems to call irresistibly for the exercise of mercy. I have no objection to giving them this dispensing power, but it should be given to them directly and not in a mystifying cloud of words. The present distinction is so obscure that no jury hearing it for the first time can fairly be expected to assimilate and understand it. I am not at all sure that I understand it myself after trying to apply it for many years.

In connection with the second question, consider *State v. Forrest*, 362 S.E.2d 252 (N.C. 1987). The defendant in that case was convicted of first-degree murder and sentenced to life in prison after he shot his dying father. In affirming the conviction and finding sufficient evidence of premeditation, the court noted that the defendant brought a gun to the hospital, cocked the gun before firing each of four shots, and later admitted that he had thought about putting his father out of his misery and had promised not to let him suffer. *See id.* at 258. *See also Boyle v. State*, 214 S.W.3d 250, 254 (Ark. 2005) (refusing to create "a 'mercy-killing' exception," explaining that "[a]bsent a legally-recognized defense, where a person intentionally causes the death of another, his act constitutes murder, and it is completely irrelevant that the act was motivated by love rather than malice"). The dissenting justice in *Forrest*, however, thought that "[o]ur law of homicide should not be so roughly hewn as to be incapable of recognizing the difference" between "someone who kills because of a desire to end a loved one's physical suffering caused by an illness which is both terminal and incurable" and "one who kills because of unmitigated spite, hatred or ill will." *Forrest*, 362 S.E.2d at 260 (Exum, C.J., dissenting).

6. The Model Penal Code Approach. The drafters of the Model Penal Code were critical of the view that premeditated killers generally tend to be more culpable than spontaneous or impulsive killers:

Prior reflection may reveal the uncertainties of a tortured conscience rather than exceptional depravity. The very fact of a long internal struggle may be evidence that the homicidal impulse was deeply aberrational and far more the product of extraordinary circumstances than a true reflection of the actor's normal character. . . .

It also seems clear, moreover, that some purely impulsive murders will present no extenuating circumstances. The suddenness of the killing may simply reveal callousness so complete and depravity so extreme that no hesitation is required.

Model Penal Code § 210.6 Comment at 127. Accordingly, the Model Penal Code does not recognize degrees of murder. Instead, it defines murder to encompass all purposeful or knowing killings (as well as those committed recklessly with extreme indifference to life). *See id.* § 210.2(1)(a).

Most states have rejected the MPC's position: they continue to separate murder into degrees, using premeditation as the dividing line. *See* 2 Wayne R. LaFave, Substantive Criminal Law § 14.7, at 476–77 (2d ed. 2003).

7. **Diminished Capacity.** Following the lead of the California Supreme Court, some jurisdictions recognize a diminished capacity defense to first-degree murder. In these states, defendants are allowed to argue that they suffered from some mental disease that, while insufficient to make out an insanity defense, made them incapable of premeditation and thus reduces their crime from first- to second-degree murder. *See, e.g., Commonwealth v. Garcia,* 479 A.2d 473 (Pa. 1984); *State v. Ellis,* 963 P.2d 843 (Wash. 1998). Other jurisdictions, however, have rejected this defense. In *Chestnut v. State,* 538 So. 2d 820, 825 (Fla. 1989), for example, the court explained that "many, if not most, crimes are committed by persons with mental aberrations," and those with "less serious mental deficiencies" that do not rise to the level of insanity "should be held accountable for their crimes just as everyone else." (For further discussion of diminished capacity and its relationship with the insanity defense, see Chapter 15, Section C.2, Note 3.)

In *People v. Wolff,* 394 P.2d 959 (Cal. 1964), the California Supreme Court went even further, reversing a first-degree murder conviction in a case involving a 15-year-old schizophrenic boy who killed his mother. The court held that the defendant was guilty only of second-degree murder because his "diminished capacity" rendered him incapable of satisfying the "true test" of premeditation, which, the court explained, "must include consideration of the somewhat limited extent to which this defendant could *maturely and meaningfully reflect* upon the gravity of his contemplated act." *Id.* at 975. Although "dressed . . . in '*mens rea* clothing,'" the court's decision essentially adopted a "strained definition[]" of premeditation and "creat[ed] a mini-insanity defense." Joshua Dressler, Understanding Criminal Law § 26.03[A][2], at 369–70 (7th ed. 2015) (quoting Peter Arenella, *The Diminished Capacity and Diminished Responsibility Defenses: Two Children of a Doomed Marriage,* 77 Colum. L. Rev. 827, 831 (1977)). In 1981, the California legislature passed a statute rejecting *Wolff* and providing that premeditation does not require evidence that the defendant "maturely and meaningfully reflected upon the gravity of his or her act." Cal. Penal Code § 189 (reprinted above in Section A).

[2] Voluntary Manslaughter: Heat of Passion

Maher v. People

10 Mich. 212 (1862)

CHRISTIANCY, JUSTICE.

. . . .

To give the homicide the legal character of murder, all the authorities agree that it must have been perpetrated with malice prepense or aforethought. . . . It is not necessary here to enumerate all the elements which enter into the legal definition of malice aforethought. It is sufficient to say that, within the principle of all the recognized definitions, the homicide must, in all ordinary cases, have been committed with some degree of coolness and deliberation, or, at least, under circumstances in which ordinary men, or the average of men recognized as peaceable citizens, would not be liable to have their reason clouded or obscured by passion; and the act must be prompted by, or the circumstances indicate that it sprung from, a wicked, depraved or malignant mind—a mind which, even in its habitual condition, and when excited by no provocation which would be liable to give undue control to passion in ordinary men, is cruel, wanton or malignant, reckless of human life, or regardless of social duty.

But if the act of killing, though intentional, be committed under the influence of passion or in heat of blood, produced by an adequate or reasonable provocation, and before a reasonable time has elapsed for the blood to cool and reason to resume its habitual control, and is the result of the temporary excitement, by which the control of reason was disturbed, rather than of any wickedness of heart or cruelty or recklessness of disposition; then the law, out of indulgence to the frailty of human nature, or rather, in recognition of the laws upon which human nature is constituted, very properly regards the offense as of a less heinous character than murder, and gives it the designation of manslaughter.

. . . .

. . . [In order to justify a conviction for manslaughter, the defendant's] reason should, at the time of the act, be disturbed or obscured by passion to an extent which *might render* ordinary men, of fair average disposition, *liable* to act rashly or without due deliberation or reflection, and from passion, rather than judgment.

To the question, what shall be considered in law a reasonable or adequate provocation for such state of mind, so as to give to a homicide, committed under its influence, the character of manslaughter? [O]n principle, the answer, as a general rule, must be, anything the natural tendency of which would be to produce such a state of mind in ordinary men, and which the jury are satisfied did produce it in the case before them—not such provocation as must, by the laws of the human mind, produce such an effect with the *certainty that physical effects follow from physical causes;* for then the individual could hardly be held morally accountable. Nor, on the other hand, must the provocation, in every case, be held sufficient or reasonable, because such a state of excitement has followed from it; for then, by habitual and long continued indulgence of evil passions, a bad man might acquire a claim to mitigation which would not be available to better men, and on account of that very wickedness of heart which, in itself, constitutes an aggravation both in morals and in law.

In determining whether the provocation is sufficient or reasonable, *ordinary human nature*, or the average of men recognized as men of fair average mind and disposition, should be taken as the standard . . . .

State v. Thornton
730 S.W.2d 309 (Tenn. 1987)

Harbison, Justice.

Appellant was convicted of murder in the first degree as a result of shooting his wife's paramour. . . . Appellant found his wife and the victim, Mark McConkey, engaged in sexual relations in the front bedroom of appellant's home. He fired a single shot which struck McConkey in the left hip. The victim died sixteen days later as a result of a massive infection resulting from the bullet wound. Before the night in question appellant had never been acquainted with McConkey or had any previous contact with him.

Appellant and his wife had been married just under four years, and their three-year-old son was in the home in an upstairs bedroom when the shooting occurred in a downstairs bedroom. Appellant and his wife had been separated for about six weeks, but no divorce action had been filed and appellant had been making a serious effort toward reconciliation with his wife.

Under these undisputed facts, in our opinion, the case does not warrant a conviction of homicide greater than that of voluntary manslaughter. . . .

A. *The Factual Background*

. . . Appellant, James Clark Thornton, III, was thirty-one years of age at the time of the trial of this case in June 1984. His wife, Lavinia, was twenty-seven years of age. . . . Appellant was a second-year law student at Memphis State University. . . . His wife had not completed her undergraduate work when the parties married, but at the time of the homicide she was taking some additional class work toward her undergraduate degree. The victim, Mark McConkey, was twenty-five years of age, single, and a third-year student at the University of Tennessee Medical School in Memphis.

As stated, appellant had never met McConkey and did not even know his name. Mrs. Thornton had met him four days before the homicide and had engaged in sexual relations with him in the home belonging to her and appellant every night since that time, including the night of the homicide. She testified that she thought that when she told her husband that she might want to "date" someone else, that this, in modern society, indicated that she intended to have sexual relations. In that manner she sought to mitigate her infidelity and misconduct toward a husband who had never been unfaithful to her insofar as disclosed by the record.

The marriage of the parties was in some difficulty, apparently as a result of dissatisfaction of Mrs. Thornton. She had advised her husband in March 1983 that she wanted to be separated from him for a time, and he had voluntarily taken an apartment about two miles away from their home. He visited the home almost daily, however, and there has been no suggestion that he was ever guilty of violence, physical misconduct or mistreatment toward his wife or son. He was particularly devoted to the child, and frequently kept the child with him at his apartment on weekends or in the evenings.

. . . During [appellant's] junior year [of high school,] it was discovered that he had developed a severe case of scoliosis, or curvature of the spine, and he had undergone surgery to correct that condition. He was disabled to the point that he received a vocational rehabilitation grant which enabled him to attend undergraduate school at the University of Tennessee at Chattanooga. He was slightly built, being only five feet six inches in height and weighing about 125 to 130 pounds. McConkey was an athlete, a former basketball and football player in high school. He was five feet nine inches in height and weighed about 183 pounds.

Mrs. Thornton testified that she told McConkey when she first met him that she was married but separated from her husband. She had consulted an attorney and had signed a divorce petition, but the same apparently had not been filed on the date of the homicide.

Appellant, according to uncontradicted testimony, was deeply disturbed over the separation of the parties. He had sought assistance from a marriage counselor, and had persuaded his wife to go with him to the marriage counselor on several occasions. They had a joint meeting scheduled with the counselor on May 4, the day after the homicide. Appellant testified that the parties had agreed to a separation of six months, and both he and the marriage counselor testified that the parties had agreed that they would not have sexual relations with each other or with anyone else during that period. Mrs. Thornton denied making that agreement, but she did admit meeting with the marriage counselor on several occasions.

. . . .

The record indicates that as early as May 1, two days before the homicide, Mrs. Thornton had stated to her husband that she did not think that the parties would ever be reconciled. On the evening of May 3, appellant picked her and their child up at their home, and the three went to dinner. Again on that occasion Mrs. Thornton reiterated that she thought that the marriage was over, and on this occasion she told appellant that she planned to date someone else whom she had met. Appellant was concerned over the situation, but on a previous occasion his wife had told him that she had had sexual relations with another student, and this had proved to be false.

He returned his wife and child to their home at about 7:30 p.m. and then went to his apartment to study for a final examination in the law school. He called two close friends of the parties, however, and discussed his marital situation with them. Both of them verified that he was very concerned about the situation, but both told him that they believed that his wife was serious about going through with a divorce. One of them advised him that his wife apparently did not believe his feelings about a reconciliation were sincere.

Acting on that suggestion, appellant returned to the home of the parties in his automobile, stating that he wanted to try once more to convince his wife that he was indeed sincere. When he arrived at the home he saw an automobile parked in the driveway. He did not recognize the car as being one belonging to any of his wife's friends. Accordingly he parked around the corner and walked back to the house. Observing from the rear of the house, he saw his wife and McConkey in the kitchen with the child. He observed as Mrs. Thornton washed some laundry for McConkey and as they were eating dinner. Thereafter they sat and read. They drank wine and smoked some marijuana, and appellant saw them kissing.[7]

He decided to go home to get his camera, but before doing so he let the air out of one of the tires on McConkey's car. He went to his apartment, and obtained his camera and an old pistol which had belonged to his father. He visited a convenience store in an attempt to find film for the camera, and finally obtained some at a drugstore. He then returned to the marital residence, arriving at about 9:30 p.m. He testified that he intended to take pictures for the purpose of showing them to the marriage counselor on the next day and possibly also for use in evidence if divorce proceedings did ensue.

Appellant spent more than an hour in the backyard of his home observing his wife and McConkey in the den and kitchen. Thereafter they left the den area, but appellant remained behind the house, thinking that McConkey was about to leave. When he went around the house, however, he found that McConkey's car was still in the driveway and saw the drapes in the front guest bedroom downstairs had been closed. He listened near the window and heard unmistakable sounds of sexual intercourse. He then burst through the front door and into the bedroom where he found the nude couple and attempted to take some pictures.[8] At that point he testified that he thought McConkey was attempting to attack him. In all events he drew his pistol and fired a single shot, striking McConkey in the left hip. Appellant did not harm either his wife or child, although Mrs. Thornton said that he did make some threats against her. . . .

Appellant testified that he simply lost control and "exploded" when he found his wife in bed with the victim. He testified that he had armed himself because McConkey was much larger than he, and he felt that he needed protection if there was trouble when he returned to the residence with the camera.

---

7. Justice Drowota, who concurred in part and dissented in part, noted that the defendant felt "shock and a sickening fear" upon seeing his wife kiss McConkey; he "was upset at seeing his wife being embraced by another man in front of his child."

8. Justice Drowota observed that appellant's efforts were unsuccessful because he could not focus the camera.

Appellant testified that he did not intend to kill McConkey, but simply to shoot him in order to disable him and also because of his outrage at the situation which he had found. The single shot was not aimed at a vital organ, but the victim ultimately died because of the spread of a massive infection from the wound.

. . . .

Appellant attempted to interpose alternative defenses of self-defense and insanity. The jury rejected both of these defenses, and we agree with the Court of Criminal Appeals that this was entirely within their province. . . .

B. *The Legal Issues*

. . . .

. . . [I]t has long been a well-settled legal principle that the commission of unlawful sexual intercourse with a female relative is an act obviously calculated to arouse ungovernable passion, and that the killing of the seducer or adulterer under the influence or in the heat of that passion constitutes voluntary manslaughter, and not murder, in the absence of evidence of actual malice.

One of the leading cases in this jurisdiction is *Toler v. State,* 152 Tenn. 1, 260 S.W. 134 (1924). There the defendant learned during a noon hour that on a previous occasion the victim had seduced his teenage daughter and had attempted to molest his nine-year-old daughter. The defendant immediately armed himself, walked a quarter of a mile to a field in which the unarmed victim was working, and shot him several times, killing him instantly.

There, as here, the jury rejected a theory of self-defense. It returned a verdict of murder in the second degree. Reversing and remanding for a new trial, this Court said:

> . . . It is undisputed that within less than an hour before he killed the deceased defendant had been informed of the outrage by the deceased of his young daughter. He was convinced of its truth, and, in all probability, it was true. This greatly shocked him and greatly aroused his passion, as it was calculated to do. Defendant, no doubt, from the time he was informed of this assault upon his young daughter until the shooting was done, was greatly agitated and was not capable of cool and deliberate thinking and reasoning, and killed the deceased while in this state of mind . . . . At any rate his mental stress must have been great, and in view of the fact that less than an hour had elapsed between the time he received information of the assault by deceased upon his daughter and the shooting, there was hardly time for his passion to subside or cool . . . .

. . . .

The facts of the present case are far stronger. Appellant actually discovered his wife *in flagrante delicto* with a man who was a total stranger to him, and at a time when appellant was trying to save his marriage and was deeply concerned about both his wife and his young child. He did not fire a shot or in any way harm the victim until he actually discovered the victim and his wife engaged in sexual intercourse in appellant's own home. In our opinion the passions of any reasonable person would have been inflamed and intensely aroused by this sort of discovery, given the factual background of this case. . . .

We are of the opinion that . . . the appellant acted under legally sufficient provocation. The conviction of murder in the first degree is set aside, and the cause will be remanded to the trial court for sentencing of the defendant for voluntary manslaughter. . . .

Drowota, Justice, concurring in part and dissenting in part.

While I concur with the result of the majority opinion insofar as the evidence in this case will not sustain the jury's finding that Defendant is guilty of murder in the first degree, I must respectfully dissent from the holding of the majority that the conviction should be reduced to voluntary manslaughter. . . . [T]he killing constitutes murder in the second degree.

   . . . .

None of the evidence in this case is sufficient to sustain a verdict of first degree murder. As this Court observed in *State v. Bullington*, 532 S.W.2d 556, 559–60 (Tenn. 1976):

> The premeditation-deliberation element of first degree murder requires that the act be performed with a cool purpose. . . . In order to constitute murder in the first degree, the cool purpose must be formed and the deliberate intention conceived in the mind of the accused, in the absence of passion, to take the life of the person slain. . . .

I think that Defendant did not act after a cooling off period and thus a conviction of first degree murder cannot be supported on these facts. Although the State argues with force and logic that these facts demonstrate premeditation and sustain the jury's verdict, as this Court observed in *Drye v. State,* 181 Tenn. 637, 646, 184 S.W.2d 10, 13 (1944):

> That [defendant's] actions in procuring the weapon and seeking contact with his wife appeared deliberate and determined, is not persuasive that his passion had cooled. Suppressed anger is a common accompaniment of passion, the deepest and most powerful emotion. . . . Nor is the fact that he was relatively calm after the event inconsistent. Having discharged the weapon, his mind recoiled into calm. . . .

The law is well established that the presence and amount of passion will affect the degree of a homicide; however, "[i]n order to reduce second degree murder to voluntary manslaughter, it must be shown that the defendant acted upon a sudden heat of passion, *without malice.*" Malice is evident on the facts of this case. . . .

... Defendant threatened the victim immediately before the weapon discharged, striking the victim precisely where Defendant threatened to shoot.[9] Defendant intentionally aimed the weapon at the victim to avoid a fatal wound, but this inadequate precaution was insufficient to prevent the foreseeable consequence of death from a serious wound at close range with a large caliber weapon. Other evidence ... exists in this record as well,[10] but these two facts are sufficient to negate the majority's conclusion[] that ... Defendant is guilty of voluntary manslaughter.

Furthermore, assuming that Defendant was provoked to act when he heard the sounds of sexual relations emanating from the guest room and was provoked to such an extent that he was able to break through the locked front doors, he did not fire immediately upon entering the bedroom but instead attempted to take photographs and then threatened the victim before the gun discharged. These actions preceding the shooting do not indicate that Defendant's reason had been so overcome by passion and excitement to make him incapable of malice. ...

Notes and Questions

1. The Rationale for the Heat of Passion Defense. What is the justification for mitigating murder to voluntary manslaughter when a defendant kills in the heat of passion? Provocation has never been considered a defense to any other crime. Do the purposes of punishment support creating an exception for murder cases? Note that the common law's original justification for dividing the crime of homicide into murder and manslaughter—in order to limit the reach of the then-mandatory death penalty for unjustifiable homicides—is no longer applicable given the discretionary nature of capital sentencing today.

Is heat of passion a "partial justification" or a "partial excuse"? Joshua Dressler, Understanding Criminal Law § 31.07[C][1], at 538 (7th ed. 2015). Consider Professor Dressler's observations:

> In partial-justification terms, do we say that a heat-of-passion killing is a less serious offense than an ordinary homicide, because the decedent (partially) deserved to die because of the provocation? Or, instead, do we partially *excuse* the killer because—although the killing is ... unjustified—we believe that the passion she experienced at the moment of the fatal act makes her less responsible—less to blame—for her conduct? Or is it reduced because the homicide is less wrong than the ordinary homicide *and* because the killer is less to blame than the ordinary killer ...?

Id.

---

9. Elsewhere in his opinion, Justice Drowota noted that the defendant screamed at McConkey, "I ought to teach you screwing around with somebody else's wife. I ought to shoot you in the ass."

10. [n.1] For instance, Mr. McConkey asked Defendant not to shoot; he was retreating at the time the Defendant's weapon discharged and was shot from the rear. That Defendant deflated one of Mr. McConkey's tires may also be some evidence of malice.

Do any of these rationales for the provocation defense make sense? Why aren't defendants who intended to kill culpable enough to be convicted of murder? If other "overwhelming emotions" — "despair [and] compassion," for example — "do not reduce perpetrators' culpability for killing . . . , why should rage be treated differently"? Vera Bergelson, *Justification or Excuse? Exploring the Meaning of Provocation*, 42 Tex. Tech L. Rev. 307, 311 (2009). *But cf.* Stephen P. Garvey, *Passion's Puzzle*, 90 Iowa L. Rev. 1677, 1684 (2005) (arguing that the heat of passion doctrine enables the criminal law to differentiate between killings committed in "willful defiance of the law" (murder) and those that involve a different type of culpability, i.e., "failure to control the desire to kill" (manslaughter)).

Is the heat of passion doctrine subject to criticism on feminist grounds because it primarily benefits male defendants and it is "largely from a male-centered perspective that the reduction of an intentional killing from murder to manslaughter is capable of being regarded as a compassion to human infirmity"? Jeremy Horder, Provocation and Responsibility 194 (1992) (advocating abolition of the provocation doctrine). *See also* Emily L. Miller, Comment, *(Wo)manslaughter: Voluntary Manslaughter, Gender, and the Model Penal Code*, 50 Emory L.J. 665, 667–68 (2001) (concluding that voluntary manslaughter "has never been a female-friendly doctrine" and even today "continues to perpetrate a violent form of male subordination of women"). *But cf.* Joshua Dressler, *Why Keep the Provocation Defense?: Some Reflections on a Difficult Subject*, 86 Minn. L. Rev. 959, 976 (2002) (responding that "the victims of male violence are more often than not other men," and heat of passion is no different from other criminal law defenses, which likewise are most useful to men "because men, far more often than women, kill people for *all* reasons"); Aya Gruber, *A Provocative Defense*, 103 Cal. L. Rev. 273, 332 (2015) (arguing that the provocation doctrine "does not necessarily burden women unfairly" because their "status as presumed victims rather than culpable wrongdoers largely protects them from the penal state," and charging that "the feminist critique of provocation . . . may unwittingly . . . contribute to mass incarceration").

Note that defendants in some states have the burden of proving that they killed in the heat of passion. *See* 720 Ill. Comp. Stat. 5/9-2. The Texas legislature went even further, eliminating voluntary manslaughter as a separate offense in 1993. Instead, defendants convicted of murder who are able to prove at sentencing by a preponderance of the evidence that they killed in the heat of passion receive a reduced sentence: they are sentenced for a second-degree felony rather than a first-degree felony. *See Beltran v. State*, 472 S.W.3d 283 (Tex. Crim. App. 2015) (applying Tex. Penal Code § 19.02).

2. Intent to Kill. In the typical voluntary manslaughter case, the defendant probably intended to kill. Nevertheless, most modern statutes consider voluntary manslaughter the appropriate verdict even if intent to kill is absent (as purportedly was the case in *Thornton*). *See, e.g., People v. Lasko*, 999 P.2d 666 (Cal. 2000). Thus, a defendant acting in the heat of passion who intended to inflict only serious bodily harm or who acted with extreme recklessness may be convicted of voluntary manslaughter. *See* 2 Wayne R. LaFave, Substantive Criminal Law § 15.2(a), at 492–93 (2d ed. 2003).

3. Actual Provocation. The "passion" with which the defendant acted in a voluntary manslaughter case is typically rage, although it may also be "fear or any violent and intense emotion sufficient to dethrone reason." Model Penal Code § 210.3 Comment at 60. Was Thornton actually acting in the heat of passion when he shot McConkey?

In determining whether defendants were actually provoked, is it proper to consider their conduct following the killing? *See People v. Mills*, 226 P.3d 276, 307–08 (Cal. 2010) (permitting the prosecution to introduce evidence describing a murder defendant's sightseeing and travel activities in the days following the killing, on the grounds that the fact that he "was behaving normally, engaging in leisure activity," was relevant to prove that he "intended to kill the victim in cold blood": "a person who had acted under the influence of a passionate impulse would not have behaved in so cavalier a fashion so recently after committing such a violent and transgressive act"). For discussion of the use of similar evidence in first-degree murder cases to establish premeditation, see Note 4 in Section B.1.

4. Reasonable Provocation. Under traditional common-law rules, only a limited set of events was deemed sufficient to provoke the reasonable person: a serious assault or battery; witnessing an act of adultery by one's wife; mutual combat;[11] an unlawful arrest; and commission of a crime against a close relative. *See* Joshua Dressler, Understanding Criminal Law § 31.07[B][2][a], at 531 (7th ed. 2015).

The modern approach, reflected in *Maher*, is less restrictive and makes no attempt to come up with an exhaustive list of provoking events sufficient to mitigate murder to voluntary manslaughter. Instead, the existence of reasonable provocation depends on the facts of the particular case, and the jury is simply asked whether the circumstances would have provoked a reasonable person. *See People v. Beltran*, 301 P.3d 1120, 1130 (Cal. 2013) (quoting extensively from *Maher* and rejecting a standard asking whether the reasonable person "would be moved to kill" because "[t]he proper focus is placed on the defendant's state of mind, not on his particular act" — i.e., "the provocation must be one that would cause an emotion so intense that an ordinary person would simply react, without reflection [and] with his reason and judgment obscured").

5. Adultery as Reasonable Provocation. Even Justice Drowota's separate opinion in *Thornton* did not question the common-law principle that a reasonable husband would be provoked by finding his wife in bed with another man. One court explained the traditional rule as follows: "if the husband shall stab the adulterer, or knock out his brains, this is bare manslaughter: for jealousy is the rage of a man, and adultery is the highest invasion of property. . . . [A] man cannot receive a higher provocation."

---

11. For an interesting discussion of the history and modern significance of this concept, see *United States v. Martinez*, 988 F.2d 685, 690–96 (7th Cir. 1993).

The Queen v. Mawgridge, 84 Eng. Rep. 1107, 1115 (Q.B. 1708). Under the traditional view, however, a woman who witnessed an act of adultery by her husband was not considered reasonably provoked. *See* Susan D. Rozelle, *Controlling Passion: Adultery and the Provocation Defense*, 37 Rutgers L.J. 197, 198 & n.3 (2005).

Assuming a gender-neutral standard, does it make sense to say that reasonable people would be provoked by discovering that their spouse is one of the significant number of people who have extramarital affairs? *See* Kristen P. Mark et al., *Infidelity in Heterosexual Couples: Demographic, Interpersonal, and Personality-Related Predictors of Extradyadic Sex*, 40 Archives Sexual Behav. 971 (2011) (citing statistics reporting that 19 percent of married women and 23 percent of married men have extramarital sex). Is a gender-neutral standard "a shallow concession to equality" given that "women rarely react to their husband's infidelity with deadly violence," whereas "men who kill their wives or lovers frequently act after accusing them of infidelity"? Laurie J. Taylor, Comment, *Provoked Reason in Men and Women: Heat-of-Passion Manslaughter and Imperfect Self-Defense*, 33 UCLA L. Rev. 1679, 1697 (1986).

In response to several Maryland cases where a husband successfully avoided a murder conviction by claiming he was provoked to kill his wife because he discovered or suspected she was having an affair, the Maryland legislature passed legislation in 1997 foreclosing this defense. Specifically, the statute provides that "[t]he discovery of one's spouse engaged in sexual intercourse with another does not constitute legally adequate provocation for the purpose of mitigating a killing from the crime of murder to voluntary manslaughter even though the killing was provoked by that discovery." Md. Crim. Law Code Ann. §2-207(b). *See* Joan Jacobson, *Bill Seeks to Repeal Law on Infidelity*, Balt. Sun, Mar. 28, 1997, at B1. *See also* Coroners and Justice Act, 2009, c. 25, §55 (revision to English manslaughter statute providing that "[i]n determining whether [the defendant's] loss of self-control had a qualifying trigger" necessary to mitigate murder to manslaughter, "the fact that a thing done or said constituted sexual infidelity is to be disregarded"). *But cf. R. v. Clinton*, [2013] Q.B. 1 (2012) (allowing the defendant to argue that his wife's infidelity, in combination with other factors, led to a reasonable loss of self-control).

6. Words as Reasonable Provocation. Defendants who kill in response to provocative words—insults, slurs, and taunts, for example—often have difficulty raising a voluntary manslaughter defense. For instance, an African-American man was convicted of first-degree murder when he shot his next-door neighbor after the neighbor admitted killing one of the defendant's dogs and threatened to kill the other one because "it was bad enough living around n*****, much less dogs." *People v. Green*, 519 N.W.2d 853, 856–57 (Mich. 1994) (Levin, J., dissenting from denial of leave to appeal); *see also State v. Perez*, 912 A.2d 944, 948 (Vt. 2006) (likewise rejecting a voluntary manslaughter claim based on the same racial slur).

Many states take the position that words, no matter how hurtful, can never rise to the level of reasonable provocation. *See, e.g., People v. Garcia*, 651 N.E.2d 100, 110 (Ill. 1995); *Girouard v. State*, 583 A.2d 718, 722–23 (Md. 1991); *State v. Kulzer*, 979

A.2d 1031, 1039 (Vt. 2009). But some states treat words like other forms of provocation, allowing the jury to decide whether they would have provoked a reasonable person. *See People v. Lee*, 971 P.2d 1001, 1007 (Cal. 1999); *Smith v. State*, 965 S.W.2d 509, 513 (Tex. Crim. App. 1998). Does the latter approach make sense because "sometimes words may be even more inflammatory than aggressive actions"? *State v. Shane*, 590 N.E.2d 272, 277 (Ohio 1992).

Still other jurisdictions take a middle position, believing that words generally do not constitute adequate provocation unless they "convey inflammatory information," such as a "sudden oral revelation of infidelity." *Commonwealth v. LeClair*, 708 N.E.2d 107, 111 (Mass. 1999); *see also Lynn v. State*, 765 S.E.2d 322, 324 (Ga. 2014). In *State v. Shane*, however, the Ohio Supreme Court refused to give "special treatment" to disclosures of adultery. Noting the "archaic" foundations of the traditional rule that adultery constitutes reasonable provocation, the court explained that killing one's spouse "is not an acceptable response to the confession of infidelity." *Shane*, 590 N.E.2d at 278.

7. Other Forms of Provocation. In considering how the concept of reasonable provocation should be applied, compare the following cases.

(a) *State v. Turgeon*, 676 A.2d 339 (Vt. 1996): The defendant had "a heated verbal exchange" with his wife, during which she "tormented" him about the fact that she had a protective order prohibiting him from visiting their son. Angered by the altercation, he left the scene, and his "erratic driving" attracted the attention of several police officers. The officers gave chase, and the defendant shot and killed one of them. Upholding the trial court's refusal to give a voluntary manslaughter instruction, the court observed that the defendant's "fit of anger . . . was not directed at his wife," but instead at a "third party who was not involved in the initial altercation," and thus was not "a reasonable reaction to a domestic confrontation." *Id.* at 342.

(b) *People v. McInerney*: In 2008, 15-year-old Brandon McInerney killed Larry King, an eighth-grade classmate who was gay and possibly transgender and who had been the victim of substantial bullying from McInerney and other classmates. In response to the bullying, King pretended to flirt with McInerney, although there was disagreement whether King interrupted a basketball game to ask McInerney to be his Valentine, or just said "I love you" as they passed in the halls and possibly blew McInerney a kiss. The following day, McInerney brought a loaded gun to school and shot King twice in the head while King was sitting in a classroom. At McInerney's 2011 trial on first-degree murder charges, an expert psychologist testified for the defense that, "of course, if a boy comes on to another boy, that would be like the ultimate humiliation" and "the tipping point for McInerney was when King returned to class and allegedly said, 'I've changed my name to Leticia.'" A jury of nine women and three men was unable to reach a verdict, though seven jurors thought McInerney had acted in the heat of passion. McInerney eventually agreed to plead guilty to second-degree murder and voluntary manslaughter with a gun and was sentenced to 21 years in prison. *See* J. Kelly Strader, *Gay Panic, Gay Victims, and the Case for Gay Shield Laws*, 36 Cardozo L. Rev. 1473, 1478, 1484–85 (2015).

In 2014, following McInerney's trial, the California legislature passed a statute foreclosing a voluntary manslaughter defense based on the "discovery of . . . the victim's actual or perceived gender, gender identity, gender expression, or sexual orientation, including under circumstances in which the victim made an unwanted nonforcible romantic or sexual advance towards the defendant." Cal. Penal Code § 192(f) (reprinted above in Section A). *See also People v. Page*, 737 N.E.2d 264, 274 (Ill. 2000) (finding that same-sex advances do not constitute adequate provocation); *Commonwealth v. Pierce*, 642 N.E.2d 579, 582 (Mass. 1994) (concluding that a "nonthreatening physical gesture and verbal invitation" to engage in homosexual sex are insufficient provocation to justify a voluntary manslaughter instruction, and noting that while "the grabbing of the defendant's testicles . . . was perhaps offensive, it was not the type of behavior that would provoke a reasonable person"). *But see Schick v. State*, 570 N.E.2d 918 (Ind. Ct. App. 1991) (affirming voluntary manslaughter conviction where a 17-year-old hitchhiker stomped to death the man who had picked him up after the man made a sexual advance). *See generally* Robert B. Mison, Comment, *Homophobia in Manslaughter: The Homosexual Advance as Insufficient Provocation*, 80 Calif. L. Rev. 133, 178 (1992) (arguing that "[t]he courts' continued acceptance of the homosexual-advance defense is an unacceptable judicial affirmation of homophobia" and "perpetuates society's heterocentric view of acceptable behavior"). *But cf.* Joshua Dressler, *When "Heterosexual" Men Kill "Homosexual" Men: Reflections on Provocation Law, Sexual Advances, and the "Reasonable Man" Standard*, 85 J. Crim. L. & Criminology 726, 754 (1995) (replying that "an unwanted sexual advance is a basis for justifiable indignation," and one who kills in response is not necessarily homophobic); Cynthia Lee, *The Gay Panic Defense*, 42 U.C. Davis L. Rev. 471, 481 (2008) (opposing the prohibition of the "gay panic" defense on the grounds that "rid[ding] society of the cultural norms that make gay panic arguments persuasive" requires "openly battl[ing] the assumptions that underlie such claims" and allowing "prosecutors [to] expose the flaws in such arguments"). For discussion of the "trans panic" defense, where a heterosexual man claims that he was reasonably provoked upon discovering his trans female sex partner was biologically male, see Cynthia Lee & Peter Kwan, *The Trans Panic Defense: Masculinity, Heteronormativity, and the Murder of Transgender Women*, 66 Hastings L.J. 77 (2014).

(c) *People v. Oropeza*, 59 Cal. Rptr. 3d 653, 660 (Cal. Ct. App. 2007): Jorge Oropeza appealed his first-degree murder conviction, arguing that another driver cut off the truck in which Oropeza was riding and then "continued to provoke [Oropeza] with his aggressive driving, his yelling and his obscene gestures." The appellate court rejected Oropeza's contention that the jury should have been instructed on voluntary manslaughter and affirmed his conviction. Although the court thought there "certainly" was evidence that Oropeza was acting in the heat of passion and he showed "an abundance of human weakness, it was not of a type such that the law is willing to declare his acts less culpable." "[A]n ordinarily reasonable person might be angered by the act" of being "intentionally cut off," the court explained, but once the other driver left, a reasonable person would not have made "extraordinary efforts to catch up to him and then engage in [the] alcohol-infused, ego-inspired act of mutual road rage" that led to the shooting. *Id.* at 661. *See generally* Andrew Ferguson, *Road Rage*, TIME, Jan. 12, 1998, at 64 (finding a dramatic increase in the number of road rage incidents, and concluding that 80 percent of people are angry most or all of the time they are driving); Ashley Halsey III & Bonnie S. Berkowitz, *Got Road Rage? You're Not Alone*, WASH. POST, Sept. 2, 2013, at B1 (reporting that 12 percent of D.C. drivers surveyed acknowledged feeling "uncontrollable anger toward another driver," double the 2005 figure).

8. Mistaken Provocation. Is voluntary manslaughter an appropriate verdict even when a defendant is mistaken in thinking that the victim engaged in provoking behavior? Would the result in *Thornton* have been different, for example, if Lavinia Thornton had not been guilty of "infidelity and misconduct toward a husband who had never been unfaithful to her"—if instead of finding his wife and McConkey in bed together, the defendant had mistakenly thought the two of them were having an affair when in fact they were just friends?

Do concerns about mistakes explain the traditional common-law rule that the defendant must actually witness an act of adultery in order to mitigate murder to voluntary manslaughter, as well as the reluctance of many courts to consider words adequate provocation? Consider the views of Justice Manning, dissenting in *Maher*, 10 Mich. at 227–28:

> To make that manslaughter which would otherwise be murder, the provocation . . . must be given in the presence of the person committing the homicide. . . . It would, it seems to me, be extremely mischievous to let passion engendered by suspicion, or by something one has heard, enter into and determine the nature of a crime committed while under its influence. The innocent as well as the guilty, or those who had not as well as those who had given provocation, might be the sufferers.

9. A Series of Provoking Events as Reasonable Provocation. In *Commonwealth v. Stonehouse*, 555 A.2d 772 (Pa. 1989), the court reversed a battered woman's murder conviction on the grounds that her attorney had provided ineffective assistance of counsel by failing to seek an instruction advising the jury to consider the combined effect of the three years of abuse she had suffered at the hands of the victim in determining the sufficiency of the provocation she faced. "The cumulative impact of a series of related events" can constitute reasonable provocation, the court observed. *Id.* at 782 (quoting *Commonwealth v. McCusker*, 292 A.2d 286, 290 (Pa. 1972)). *See also People v. Borchers*, 325 P.2d 97, 102 (Cal. 1958) (affirming the trial judge's decision to overturn the jury's second-degree murder conviction and enter a verdict of voluntary manslaughter because "a series of events over a considerable period of time" could have reasonably provoked the defendant to kill his fiancée).

Other courts, however, have rejected similar claims of voluntary manslaughter. In *Girouard v. State*, 583 A.2d 718, 722 (Md. 1991), the court dismissed the idea that "prolonged stress, anger and hostility caused by marital problems" can justify a voluntary manslaughter conviction. "Domestic arguments easily escalate into furious fights," the court explained, and there is "no reason for a holding in favor of those who find the easiest way to end a domestic dispute is by killing the offending spouse." *Id.* at 723.

Which is the better view? Is it reasonable to recognize that "a course of ill treatment . . . can induce a homicidal response in a person of ordinary firmness," given "the undoubted capacity of events to accumulate a detonating force, no different from that of a single blow or injury"? *State v. Guido*, 191 A.2d 45, 56 (N.J. 1963). Alternatively, even though "the long-smoldering grudge . . . may be psychologically just as compelling a force as the sudden impulse," is it, "unlike the impulse, . . . a telltale characteristic of premeditation"? *Girouard*, 583 A.2d at 722–23.

10. Cooled Passion. Both *Maher* and *Thornton* note that voluntary manslaughter is not an appropriate verdict if sufficient time elapsed between the provocation and the killing so that either the defendant's emotions had cooled or the passion of a reasonable person would have cooled. As the court observed in *People v. Harris*, 134 N.E.2d 315, 317 (Ill. 1956), "no yardstick of time can be used by the court to measure a reasonable period of passion but it must vary as do the facts of every case." "Humans react violently to the infliction of a serious injury," the court explained, "and the degree of pain which results therefrom not only governs the passion itself but also influences the duration of the cooling period." *Id.* Does this doctrine make sense, or does the passage of time tend to aggravate rather than cool passion?

In thinking about how the cooling standard should be applied, consider the following cases.

(a) *State v. Gounagias*, 153 P. 9 (Wash. 1915): Just over two weeks before the killing, Dan George (who was the defendant's coworker and at that time also his housemate) sodomized the defendant while he was helpless and almost unconscious and then, despite the defendant's request, told others about the incident. As a result, the defendant was subjected to a series of teasing, insulting comments and vulgar gestures. On the night of the killing, he was once again teased about the assault as he entered a coffeehouse. He returned home, retrieved a gun, went to George's house, and shot him five times. The court found insufficient evidence to make out a case of voluntary manslaughter and therefore affirmed the trial judge's decision to exclude all evidence of provocation. The court indicated that the evidence would have been admissible had the defendant killed George immediately after the assault, or after seeing him the next day—or perhaps even after he first discovered that George was spreading the story to others. Because several weeks intervened, however, and the defendant was not subjected to any new provocation on the night of the killing, but only to "a mere reminder by the words or acts of others of an old provocation long condoned," the court concluded that there was no "sudden anger and resentment," but only "brooding thought, resulting in the design to kill." *Id.* at 15, 14.

(b) *People v. Berry*, 556 P.2d 777 (Cal. 1976): The victim, defendant's wife of two months, told him that she wanted a divorce because she had fallen in love with another man. During the next two weeks, the victim "alternately taunted defendant with her involvement with [the other man] and at the same time sexually excited defendant, indicating her desire to remain with him." *Id.* at 779. Several days prior to the killing, the defendant choked the victim until she was unconscious after she said that she had intended to have sex with him that night but then had decided against it because she was saving herself for the other man. On the day before the killing, the defendant went to the couple's apartment to talk to the victim. She was out, and he waited in the apartment until she returned the next morning. After they exchanged a few words, she began screaming and he strangled her with a telephone cord. The court held that the defendant was entitled to a voluntary manslaughter instruction, finding that the 20-hour interval during which he waited for the victim in the apartment was insufficient cooling time because "the long course of provocatory conduct, which had resulted in intermittent outbreaks of rage under specific provocation in the past, reached its final culmination in the apartment when [the victim] began screaming." *Id.* at 781.

(c) *State v. Furlough*, 1993 Tenn. Crim. App. Lexis 769 (Tenn. Crim. App. Nov. 18, 1993): The defendant, a battered woman, awoke one morning and found her husband "standing over their daughter with her diaper off, his pants down and his penis erect." The husband pushed the defendant on the bed and told her to "forget what she had seen." Later that day, he "threatened 'to do it' with their baby" and said he was going to "'have [the child]' when they got home." *Id.* at *3. The defendant went to the truck, grabbed a gun, and shot him. In rejecting the defendant's voluntary manslaughter defense and affirming her first-degree murder conviction and life sentence, the court reasoned, "assuming that the incident about which the appellant testified occurred, it occurred early that morning and the victim was not at the time of the shooting attempting to engage in any sort of sexual act with their daughter." *Id.* at *8. *But cf. State v. Felton*, 329 N.W.2d 161, 173 (Wis. 1983) (reversing a battered woman's conviction for murdering her abusive husband on the grounds that her attorney's failure to investigate a manslaughter defense rendered his representation ineffective, and finding insufficient cooling time because "at most, the last assault or provocation occurred within two or three hours").

(d) *People v. Nesler*: In the summer of 1988, Daniel Driver molested the defendant's six-year-old son Willie and three other boys. Driver had previously been convicted on molestation charges in 1983, as a result of which he had served three months in jail. The police were unable to find Driver for some time, but his preliminary hearing on the charges involving the defendant's son was eventually scheduled for April 2, 1992. On the morning of the hearing, Willie could not stop vomiting as he prepared to testify. When Driver walked into the courtroom prior to the hearing, he smirked at Nesler and Willie. Later, outside the courtroom, another mother who had testified told Nesler that Driver "was going to walk." At that point, Nesler retrieved a gun—purportedly from her sister's purse, although on one occasion Nesler told the police she had brought the gun to the courthouse in her car. She walked into the courtroom, and fired five shots at Driver, who sat handcuffed at the defense table. Nesler argued that she was "pushed over the edge by a series of fast-moving events" on the morning of the killing, while the prosecution contended that she was "making good on a promise of vengeance that she had uttered many times" during the preceding three years. The jury returned a verdict of voluntary manslaughter, and the judge imposed a 10-year sentence, calling the crime "an execution." *See* Mark Arax, *Ellie Nesler Gets 10 Years in Court Killing*, L.A. Times, Jan. 8, 1994, at A1. The jury's finding that Nesler was sane was ultimately reversed on the grounds of juror misconduct, and she pled guilty in exchange for a seven-year sentence. She was released on parole after serving nearly four years.

(e) *People v. Williams*, 576 N.E.2d 68 (Ill. App. Ct. 1991): When the defendant came home one day, she found her husband naked and two women leaving the bedroom. The couple argued, and the defendant went into the kitchen and began cooking. Her husband came into the kitchen, and they continued to argue. When the husband slapped the defendant's head, she grabbed a knife and stabbed him. In affirming her murder conviction, the court concluded that the jury could have found sufficient cooling time to reject a manslaughter verdict, noting that "no one knows exactly how much time elapsed during the . . . sequence of events." *Id.* at 74.

11. The Reasonable Person. In evaluating voluntary manslaughter claims, the jury must determine whether a reasonable person would have been provoked and whether that person would have cooled off in the interval between the provocation and the killing. Who is this "reasonable person," and which of the defendant's characteristics— if any—does the reasonable person share? In *Keenan v. Commonwealth*, 44 Pa. 55, 58 (1863), the court concluded that the defendant's intoxicated condition was not relevant:

> [M]easured by this rule, the crimes of a proud, or captious, or selfish, or habit- ually ill-natured man, or of one who eats or fasts too much, or of one who is habitually quarrelsome, covetous, dishonest, or thievish, or who, by any sort of indulgence, fault, or vice, renders himself very easily excitable, or very sub- ject to temptation, are much less criminal than those of a moderate, well- tempered, and orderly citizen, because to the former a very small provocation or temptation becomes adequate to excuse or palliate any crime. If such were the rule, a defendant would be much more likely to injure than to benefit his case by showing a good character, and the law would present no inducement to men to try to rise to the standard of even ordinary social morality.
>
> Of course it is impossible that such a principle can be a rule of law. If it were admitted, it could not be administered, for no judicial tribunal can have time or competence for such a thorough investigation of the special charac- ter or state of each individual mind as the rule requires, and therefore it would necessarily jump to a conclusion such as the caprice, or prejudice, or other influence of the moment would dictate.

Thus, in *Bedder v. Director of Public Prosecutions*, [1954] 1 W.L.R. 1119, 1122, the House of Lords rejected the defendant's argument that the hypothetical reasonable person must be one with "the personal physical peculiarities of the accused." The defendant in that case, an 18-year-old man who was impotent, killed a prostitute under circumstances described by the Lords as follows:

> [The defendant] attempted in vain to have intercourse with [the victim], whereupon . . . she jeered at him and attempted to get away. He tried still to hold her, and then she slapped him in the face and punched him in the stomach: he grabbed her shoulders and pushed her back from him where[upon] (I use his words), "She kicked me in the privates. Whether it was her knee or foot, I do not know. After that I do not know what happened till she fell." She fell, because he had taken a knife from his pocket and stabbed her with it twice, the second blow inflicting a mortal injury.

Id. at 1120. In refusing to require that the jury be instructed to consider how a reasonable man suffering from the defendant's disability would have reacted in those circumstances, the Lords explained:

> It would be plainly illogical not to recognise an unusually excitable or pugnacious temperament in the accused as a matter to be taken into account but yet to recognize for that purpose some unusual physical characteristic, be it impotence or another. Moreover, . . . the temper of a man which leads him to react in such and such a way to provocation, is or may be itself conditioned by some physical defect. It is too subtle a refinement for . . . a jury to grasp that the temper may be ignored but the physical defect taken into account.

Id. at 1123.

Subsequently, however, in *Director of Public Prosecutions v. Camplin*, 1978 App. Cas. 705, 718, the House of Lords held that jurors should be told that the reasonable person is "a person having the power of self-control to be expected of an ordinary person of the sex and age of the accused, but in other respects sharing such of the accused's characteristics as they think would affect the gravity of the provocation to him." The defendant in that case, who was 15 years old, killed a middle-aged man by hitting him over the head with a chapati pan after the man forcibly sodomized the boy and then laughed at him. Concluding that the trial judge had erred in instructing the jury that the defendant's acts should be evaluated by a "reasonable man" standard, rather than a "reasonable boy" or a "reasonable lad" standard, the Lords considered the defendant's age a relevant factor. "It is a characteristic which may have its effects on temperament as well as physique," the Lords explained, and "to require old heads upon young shoulders is inconsistent with the . . . compassion to human infirmity" on which the provocation doctrine is based. *Id.* at 717. In addition, the Lords noted that "the gravity of verbal provocation may well depend upon the particular characteristics or circumstances of the person to whom a taunt or insult is addressed":

> To taunt a person because of his race, his physical infirmities or some shameful incident in his past may well be considered by the jury to be more

offensive to the person addressed, however equable his temperament, if the facts on which the taunt is founded are true than it would be if they were not.

Id.

Accepting the House of Lords' rationale for considering the age of a 15-year-old defendant, in what sense is gender also relevant? Which way does gender cut in determining whether a reasonable person would have been provoked? *See* Joshua Dressler, *When "Heterosexual" Men Kill "Homosexual" Men: Reflections on Provocation Law, Sexual Advances, and the "Reasonable Man" Standard*, 85 J. Crim. L. & Criminology 725, 757 n.164 (1995) (observing that the decision in *Camplin* "could inadvertently result in the law holding men, simply because of their gender, to a lesser standard of control than it holds women"). Under *Camplin*'s standard, would *Bedder* have been decided differently?

Almost 20 years after *Camplin*, in *The Queen v. Morhall*, 1996 App. Cas. 90, 99 (1995), the House of Lords made clear that even "transitory" and "discreditable" traits may be relevant in assessing the gravity of the provocation a defendant faced. The defendant in that case stabbed a friend who had been teasing him about his glue-sniffing addiction. The Lords reversed the defendant's murder conviction because the trial judge had failed to instruct the jury "to take into account the fact of the defendant's addiction to glue-sniffing when considering whether a person with the ordinary person's power of self-control would have reacted to the provocation as the defendant did." *Id.* at 100. Rejecting the prosecution's view that the jury should not consider characteristics that are "inconsistent with the concept of a reasonable man," the Lords explained:

> [T]he "reasonable person test" is concerned not with ratiocination, nor with the reasonable man whom we know so well in the law of negligence (where we are concerned with reasonable foresight and reasonable care), nor with reasonable conduct generally. The function of the test is only to introduce, as a matter of policy, a standard of self-control which has to be complied with if provocation is to be established in law.

Id. at 96, 97–98.

Following *Morhall*, the English courts issued conflicting decisions concerning the relevance of a defendant's mental illness in applying manslaughter's reasonable person standard. In *The Queen v. Smith*, [2001] 1 App. Cas. 146 (2000), the House of Lords disapproved of instructions informing the jury that it should consider the defendant's severe depression only in assessing the gravity of the provocation he faced, and not in "deciding whether an ordinary man sharing [his] characteristics would have lost his self-control." Lord Clyde, one of the three Lords in the majority, explained that "justice cannot be done without regard to the particular frailties of particular individuals where their capacity to restrain themselves in the face of provocation is lessened by some affliction which falls short of a mental abnormality." Noting that "[s]ome groups of people may be seen to be by nature more susceptible to provocation than others [and] [s]ome races may be more hot-blooded than others," Lord Clyde concluded that "the standard of reasonableness in this context should refer to a person exercising the ordinary power of self-control over his passions which someone in his position is able to exercise and is expected by society to exercise," with the defendant's "position" including "all the characteristics which the particular individual possesses and which may in the circumstances bear on his power of control other than those influences which have been self-induced."

In *Attorney General v. Holley*, [2005] 3 All E.R. 371, however, the court was critical of the position taken in *Smith* and rejected the defendant's argument that the jury, in evaluating his manslaughter defense, ought to take into account that his serious chronic alcoholism was a disease that made his consumption of alcohol involuntary. The court acknowledged that "[t]he powers of self-control possessed by ordinary people vary according to their age and, more doubtfully, their sex," and that those characteristics therefore ought to be considered. But the court distinguished "abnormalities, that is, features not found in a person having ordinary powers of self-control," which the court concluded were irrelevant in "identifying and applying the objective standard of self-control."

In the wake of *Holley* and opposition to the House of Lords' decision in *Smith*, Parliament's 2009 redefinition of manslaughter — as a killing resulting from the defendant's "loss of self-control," where that "loss of self-control had a qualifying trigger" — included a caveat requiring that someone of the defendant's gender and age "with a normal degree of tolerance and self-restraint and in the circumstances of [the defendant] might have reacted in the same or in a similar way." The statute went on to define "circumstances" as "all of [the defendant's] circumstances other than those whose only relevance to [the defendant's] conduct is that they bear on [the defendant's] general capacity for tolerance or self-restraint." Coroners and Justice Act, 2009, c. 25, § 54. For discussion of this statute, see Simon Parsons, *The Loss of Control Defence — Fit for Purpose?*, 79 J. CRIM. L. 94 (2015). *See also Masciantonio v. The Queen*, (1995) 183 C.L.R. 58, 67 (Austl.) (noting that "[t]he provocation must be put into context and it is only by having regard to the attributes or characteristics of the accused that this can be done"); *The Queen v. Tran*, [2010] 3 S.C.R. 350 (Can.) (concluding that characteristics like age, race, and gender are not "peculiar or idiosyncratic" and "can be ascribed to an ordinary person without subverting the logic of the objective test of provocation"); *The Queen v. Thibert*, [1996] S.C.R. 37 (Can.) (holding that the reasonable person must also "share with the accused such other factors as would give the act or insult in question a special significance" — in that case, for example, "an ordinary person who was a married man, faced with the break-up of his marriage").

Are these decisions sensible? Or are all of these efforts to single out particular characteristics of the reasonable person "doomed to failure because no physical, psychological or emotional trait is [always relevant or] always irrelevant to reasonableness" in voluntary manslaughter cases? Peter Westen, *Individualizing the Reasonable Person in Criminal Law*, 2 Crim. L. & Phil. 137, 148 (2008). Is a generic reasonable person standard preferable in order to "avoid different applications of the law of manslaughter to defendants of different races, creed, color, sex or social status"? *Gonzales v. State*, 689 S.W.2d 900, 903 (Tex. Crim. App. 1985). Is a more individualized standard also subject to criticism because "[i]f the reasonable person were defined to be just like the defendant in every respect, he would arguably do exactly what the defendant did under the circumstances"? George P. Fletcher, Rethinking Criminal Law 513 (1978). *See also People v. Steele*, 47 P.3d 225, 241 (Cal. 2002) (rejecting the defendant's argument that the jury should have asked "how an otherwise ordinary person, having [his] Vietnam War background, his resulting clear symptoms of post-traumatic stress disorder, and his brain function abnormalities which led him to misinterpret and overreact to events, would have acted in the situation in which [he] found himself at the time of the killing," explaining that "because only he fits this particular description, defendant would be setting his own standard of conduct [and] would eliminate the objective standard in favor of a subjective one").

On the other hand, consider the following comments:

> The result of taking into account the social reality of an accused is a more realistic assessment of his or her culpability.
>
> . . . .
>
> The law, by abstracting human beings out of their social reality, confers upon them a formal equality. But this formal equality is illusory and in fact leads to unjust consequences, for the "systematic application of an equal scale to systemically unequal individuals necessarily tends to reinforce systemic inequalities." Thus, the Anglo-American premise of abstract equality serves to perpetuate inequality.

Dolores A. Donovan & Stephanie M. Wildman, *Is the Reasonable Man Obsolete? A Critical Perspective on Self-Defense and Provocation*, 14 Loy. L.A. L. Rev. 435, 449–50, 465 (1981). *See also* Jonathan Herring, *Provocation and Ethnicity*, 1996 Crim. L. Rev. 490, 492 (noting that individuals of some cultural backgrounds tend to be short-tempered, and therefore "[i]n some cases the defendant can clearly be regarded as not fully responsible for her shortness of temper"). For a general discussion of critical jurisprudence and its application to criminal law, see Chapter 16, Section C.

12. Applying the Reasonable Person Standard. In thinking about how the reasonable person should be defined, consider the following cases.

(a) *State v. Felton*, 329 N.W.2d 161 (Wis. 1983): The defendant, a battered woman, killed her sleeping husband after he had subjected her to years of abuse. The court held that the relevant inquiry in evaluating her voluntary manslaughter defense was "how an ordinarily constituted person who was a battered spouse would have reacted to the provocation." Although the court thought that "a defendant's background is not in general relevant to the objective test for heat of passion, the question is how an ordinary person faced with a similar provocation would react" and "[i]t is proper in applying the objective test, therefore, to consider how other persons similarly situated with respect to that type, or history, of provocation would react." *Id.* at 172. For discussion of the similar issues that arise in self-defense cases involving battered women, see *State v. Norman* and the accompanying Notes in Chapter 14, Section B.

(b) *State v. McKinney*: In 1998, Aaron McKinney and Russell Henderson lured University of Wyoming student Matthew Shepard from a bar and drove him outside of town, where they robbed him, beat him on the head repeatedly with a pistol, tied him to a fence, and left him for dead. Shepard died several days later, and McKinney and Henderson were charged with murder. Henderson pleaded guilty, but McKinney went to trial, arguing that Shepard made sexual advances that reminded McKinney of homosexual abuse he had experienced as a child. The trial judge refused to admit evidence of McKinney's history of abuse, and he was convicted and sentenced to two consecutive life terms after Shepard's parents asked that his life be spared. *See* Michael Janofsky, *Judge Rejects "Gay Panic" as Defense in Murder Case,* N.Y. Times, Nov. 2, 1999, at A14. Matthew Shepard's death, which fueled efforts to expand hate-crime statutes to include crimes motivated by sexual orientation, is the subject of Moises Kaufman's play and movie, *The Laramie Project. See also Commonwealth v. Carr,* 580 A.2d 1362, 1363 (Pa. Super. Ct. 1990) (refusing to admit evidence of defendant's "psychosexual history," including child abuse and "a history of constant rejection by women," offered in support of defendant's claim that he was reasonably provoked by a lesbian couple's "nude homosexual lovemaking"); *The Queen v. Tran,* [2010] 3 S.C.R. 350 (Can.) (noting that "it would be appropriate to ascribe to the ordinary person relevant racial characteristics if the accused were the recipient of a racial slur, but it would not be appropriate to ascribe to the ordinary person the characteristic of being homophobic if the accused were the recipient of a homosexual advance"). *But see The Queen v. Green,* (1997) 191 C.L.R. 334 (Austl.) (McHugh, J.) (in reversing murder conviction in homosexual-advance case, one of the justices in the majority concluded that, "[i]n the present case, [the manslaughter statute's reference to 'an ordinary person in the position of the accused'] translates to a person with the minimum powers of self-control of an ordinary person who is subjected to a sexual advance that is aggravated because of the accused's special sensitivity to a history of violence and sexual assault within his family").

(c) *Freddo v. State,* 155 S.W. 170 (Tenn. 1912): Raymond Freddo, a 19-year-old orphan who had been raised by a foster mother, had an unusual respect for women and was very sensitive to language that was obscene or disrespectful toward women. James Higginbotham, one of Freddo's coworkers, repeatedly called Freddo a "son of a bitch" despite numerous warnings from Freddo himself as well as others. On the day of the killing, Higginbotham repeated the comment, and Freddo killed him by striking him on the head with a steel bar. In reviewing the adequacy of the provocation, the court refused to consider Freddo's sensitivity to the epithet and concluded that a reasonable person would not have been provoked by Higginbotham's conduct.

(d) *People v. Wu*, 286 Cal. Rptr. 868 (Cal. Ct. App. 1991):[12] The defendant, a Chinese woman, strangled her nine-year-old son Sidney and then unsuccessfully attempted to kill herself after Sidney told her that his father (with whom the boy had lived for most of his life) did not love him and mistreated him. Defense experts testified that committing suicide and "leav[ing] the children alone" is considered "totally irresponsible behavior" for an Asian mother, and that "in her culture, . . . there [were] no options . . . but to kill herself and take the son along with her so that they could step over to the next world where she could devote herself . . . to the caring of the son." *Id.* at 885, 886. In ruling that the trial court had erred in refusing to instruct the jury that it could take the defendant's cultural background into account, the court reasoned that this background was relevant to explain both "the source of her [emotional] stress" and "how [her son's] statements could have constituted 'sufficient provocation'" to lead her to kill him in the heat of passion. *Id.* at 884. Does the court's ruling "reduce[]" "culture . . . to stereotype" by "rel[ying] on a stereotype of Asian women as the self-sacrificing woman/mother"? Leti Volpp, *(Mis)identifying Culture: Asian Women and the "Cultural Defense"*, 17 Harv. Women's L.J. 57, 90 (1994). Or does it recognize that "provocation doctrine is, in essence, a dominant cultural defense," which "makes allowances for the ways in which reasonable people are influenced and compelled by dominant cultural conceptions of natural honor," such that "denying foreign defendants the right to introduce cultural evidence effectively denies them use of the provocation doctrine"? James J. Sing, Note, *Culture as Sameness: Toward a Synthetic View of Provocation and Culture in the Criminal Law*, 108 Yale L.J. 1845, 1869, 1878 (1999).

More generally, given the difficulty of defining the "reasonable person," would it be preferable to abolish the objective component of voluntary manslaughter? Does "a reasonableness standard, . . . by its nature, preclude[] consideration of the defendant's personal culpability"? Dolores A. Donovan & Stephanie M. Wildman, *Is the Reasonable Man Obsolete? A Critical Perspective on Self-Defense and Provocation*, 14 Loy. L.A. L. Rev. 435, 456 (1981). Should the jury simply be instructed to determine "whether, in light of all the evidence in the case, the accused was honestly and understandably aroused to the heat of passion"? *Id.* at 467. Is this essentially the effect of the Model Penal Code formulation, described in the following Note?

13. The Model Penal Code Approach. The Model Penal Code defines manslaughter to include "homicide which would otherwise be murder . . . committed under the influence of extreme mental or emotional disturbance for which there is reasonable explanation or excuse." Model Penal Code § 210.3(1)(b). The MPC further provides that the reasonableness of the defendant's explanation or excuse "shall be

---

12. In denying review in *Wu*, the California Supreme Court ordered that the Court of Appeal's opinion not be published.

determined from the viewpoint of a person in the actor's situation under the circumstances as he believes them to be." *Id.*

The Comments explain that this provision "reflects the trend of many modern decisions to abandon preconceived notions of what constitutes adequate provocation and to submit that question to the jury's deliberation." *Id.* § 210.3 Comment at 61. The MPC goes beyond even that modern trend, however, by incorporating "a larger element of subjectivity." *Id.* at 49. Although the "reasonable explanation or excuse" requirement "preserves the essentially objective character of the inquiry and erects a barrier against debilitating individualization of the legal standard," "[t]he trier of fact must evaluate the actor's conduct under the circumstances that the actor believed to exist." *Id.* at 62. In so doing, the MPC instructs the trier of fact to consider "the viewpoint of a person in the actor's situation." The Comments explain that the term "situation" is "designedly ambiguous":

> On the one hand, it is clear that personal handicaps and some external circumstances must be taken into account. Thus, blindness, shock from traumatic injury, and extreme grief are all easily read into the term "situation." . . . On the other hand, it is equally plain that idiosyncratic moral values are not part of the actor's situation. An assassin who kills a political leader because he believes it is right to do so cannot ask that he be judged by the standard of a reasonable extremist. Any other result would undermine the normative message of the criminal law. In between these two extremes, however, there are matters neither as clearly distinct from individual blameworthiness as blindness or handicap nor as integral a part of moral depravity as a belief in the rightness of killing. Perhaps the classic illustration is the unusual sensitivity to the epithet "bastard" of a person born illegitimate. An exceptionally punctilious sense of personal honor or an abnormally fearful temperament may also serve to differentiate an individual actor from the hypothetical reasonable man, yet none of these factors is wholly irrelevant to the ultimate issue of culpability. The proper role of such factors cannot be resolved satisfactorily by abstract definition of what may constitute adequate provocation. The Model Code endorses a formulation that affords sufficient flexibility to differentiate in particular cases between those special aspects of the actor's situation that should be deemed material for purpose of grading and those that should be ignored. There thus will be room for interpretation of the word "situation," and that is precisely the flexibility desired. . . . In the end, the question is whether the actor's loss of self-control can be understood in terms that arouse sympathy in the ordinary citizen.

Id. at 62–63. For a description of the impact of the MPC's approach to voluntary manslaughter, see 2 WAYNE R. LAFAVE, SUBSTANTIVE CRIMINAL LAW § 15.2(b)(10), at 506 (2d ed. 2003) (citing about a dozen jurisdictions that have adopted this provision at least in part). For a study suggesting, however, that jury verdicts are not influenced by whether the jury instructions follow the common law or the Model Penal Code's formulation, see Matthew P. Spackman et al., *An Analysis of the Effects of*

Subjective and Objective Instruction Forms on Mock-Juries' Murder/Manslaughter Distinctions, 26 LAW & HUM. BEHAV. 605 (2002).

14. Applying the Model Penal Code. In *People v. Shelton*, 385 N.Y.S.2d 708 (N.Y. Sup. Ct. 1976), *aff'd mem.*, 434 N.Y.S.2d 649 (N.Y. App. Div. 1980), the court recognized that the New York manslaughter statute, modeled after the Model Penal Code, was broader than the common-law formulation because the killing need not necessarily be spontaneous: "[r]ather, it may be that a significant mental trauma has affected a defendant's mind for a substantial period of time, simmering in the unknowing conscious and then inexplicably coming to the fore." *Id.* at 715; *see also State v. White*, 251 P.3d 820, 826 (Utah 2011) (noting that the Utah statute, also patterned on the Model Penal Code, was "enacted . . . in response to the unworkable nature of the heat of passion defense" and was meant to "substantially enlarge[] the class of cases that might be reduced to manslaughter") (emphasis omitted). The *Shelton* court defined "extreme emotional disturbance" as

> the emotional state of an individual, who . . . is exposed to an extremely unusual and overwhelming stress . . . and . . . has an extreme emotional reaction to it, as a result of which there is a loss of self-control and reason is overborne by intense feelings, such as passion, anger, distress, grief, excessive agitation, or other similar emotions. In evaluating this, consideration is given to whether the actor is able to reflect dispassionately, the time interval between the provocation and the act and whether the intensity of these feelings is such that his usual intellectual controls fail and the normal rational thinking for that individual no longer prevail[s] at the time of the act. Perhaps the key factor in this determination is the loss of self-control.

Shelton, 434 N.Y.S.2d at 717–18.

Applying that standard to the facts before it, the court concluded that Willard Shelton, a school drug counselor, was not acting under the influence of extreme emotional disturbance at the time he killed Nilda Cruz, a student who threatened to reveal that Shelton had smoked marijuana with her. Although the court found that Shelton was exposed to "an unusual stress," it felt that the stress was "neither extremely unusual nor overwhelming" because "in the last analysis, he knew that it was his word against hers, a 14 year old student." *Id.* at 718. In addition, the court thought that Shelton had not lost his self-control, but instead had made a calm, calculated decision to kill after failing to convince Cruz not to report him. Given this finding, the court had no need to consider the reasonableness of the defendant's reaction.

The question of reasonableness did come up, however, in *People v. Casassa*, 404 N.E.2d 1310 (N.Y. 1980). The defendant in that case was "devastated" when Victoria Lo Consolo, whom Casassa had dated, told him that she did not love him. He engaged in a "bizarre series of actions," including breaking into the apartment below Lo Consolo's apartment to eavesdrop on her conversations and breaking into her apartment when she was out, undressing, and lying on her bed. *Id.* at 1312. On the day of the killing, Casassa brought Lo Consolo several bottles of liquor. When she rejected his gift, he pulled out a steak knife, stabbed her several times, and then submerged her body in the bathtub to "make sure she was dead." *Id.* He was convicted of murder despite psychiatric testimony suggesting that he was obsessed with Lo Consolo and that their relationship, "combined with several personality attributes peculiar to [him]," caused him to act from extreme emotional disturbance. *Id.* at 1313. The Court of Appeals found the evidence sufficient to support the conviction, concluding that although Casassa was acting as the result of an extreme emotional disturbance, there was no reasonable explanation or excuse for his emotional condition: "each of the mitigating factors put forward by the defendant, including his claimed mental disability, . . . was so peculiar to him" that the court attributed the killing to his "malevolence rather than an understandable human response deserving of mercy." *Id.* at 1317. *But cf. People v. Owens*, 611 N.Y.S.2d 67, 68 (N.Y. App. Div. 1994) (reversing murder conviction as against the weight of the evidence, and instead entering manslaughter conviction (without citing *Casassa*), in a case where a defendant suffering from multiple personality disorder claimed that "one of the 'alter' personalities manifested itself" at the time of the shooting).

For other examples of cases applying the Model Penal Code's approach, see *State v. Person*, 673 A.2d 463, 469–71 (Conn. 1996) (concluding that the trial judge should have instructed the jury on extreme emotional disturbance manslaughter where the victim had broken off her engagement with the defendant and obtained a restraining order against him, and then confronted him with a can of mace and two knives after returning home to find that he had broken into her apartment to retrieve his belongings; he stabbed her in the struggle that ensued after she sprayed him with the mace); *People v. Harris*, 740 N.E.2d 227, 230, 231 (N.Y. 2000) (likewise holding that the jury should have been instructed on extreme emotional disturbance where the defendant killed an old friend with a machete and then dismembered his body, after the victim—who had previously had a sexual relationship with the defendant's girlfriend, Monique Lloyd—"began taunting defendant by expressing in crude terms that he could still have sex with Lloyd at anytime and that Lloyd would leave defendant for him merely at his beck and call"; the court concluded that the jury "could reasonably infer that [the defendant] was provoked to rage over the emotionally charged subject of his lover's past and potentially future infidelity" with the victim); *State v. Shumway*, 63 P.3d 94, 97 (Utah 2002) (reversing murder conviction on the grounds that a 15-year-old boy who stabbed his friend 39 times during a sleepover was entitled to a jury instruction on extreme emotional disturbance where the defendant "had been bullied and pushed around by his peers since he was in the third grade, and . . . all of this 'came out on [the victim]' when the boys fought over [a] knife" the victim had been using to poke the defendant).

For the view that the Model Penal Code's definition of manslaughter offers less protection to women than the common-law formulation because trial judges are more likely to give extreme emotional disturbance instructions based simply on "the desire of the killer's victim to leave a miserable relationship," thus "[tying] women to relationships that they do not want," see Victoria Nourse, *Passion's Progress: Modern Law Reform and the Provocation Defense*, 106 YALE L.J. 1331, 1332, 1335, 1396 (1997) (advocating that manslaughter be restricted to cases where the defendant is provoked by "a wrong that the law would independently punish" and therefore is "in a position of normative equality vis-à-vis [the] victim"). *See also State v. Person*, 673 A.2d at 473 n.1 (Callahan, J., dissenting) (criticizing the majority for "essentially establish[ing] a per se rule that anyone who kills a former girlfriend or boyfriend is entitled to a jury instruction on extreme emotional disturbance"). Note, however, that both Person and Harris were ultimately convicted of murder. *See State v. Person*, 761 A.2d 269 (Conn. App. Ct. 2000); *People v. Harris*, 777 N.Y.S.2d 762 (N.Y. App. Div. 2004).

15. **Diminished Capacity.** Some jurisdictions permit defendants to argue that their diminished capacity negated not only premeditation, thus foreclosing a first-degree murder conviction, but also malice, thus reducing murder to manslaughter. As was true with the diminished capacity defense to first-degree murder, which is discussed in Note 7 following *People v. Anderson* in Part 1 above, the California Supreme Court took this defense the furthest. In *People v. Conley*, 411 P.2d 911, 918 (Cal. 1966), the court reversed a first-degree murder conviction because the trial judge had failed to instruct the jury that the defendant was entitled to a voluntary manslaughter verdict if his diminished capacity rendered him "unable to comprehend his duty to govern his actions in accord with the duty imposed by law" and thus unable to act with malice. *But cf. State v. Congress*, 114 A.3d 1128, 1139 (Vt. 2014) (rejecting this approach, reasoning that "'malice' is not some separate state of mind independent of" the mens rea necessary to commit murder and, because voluntary manslaughter is a provoked killing that would otherwise be murder, "a defendant who defeats the State's burden with respect to the state-of-mind element for second-degree murder cannot be convicted of any degree of homicide more serious than involuntary manslaughter").

In 1978, Dan White, a member of the San Francisco Board of Supervisors, successfully raised a diminished capacity defense when he was charged with murdering George Moscone, the mayor of San Francisco, and Harvey Milk, another member of the Board of Supervisors and a prominent figure in the city's LGBTQ community. Twelve hours after learning from a reporter that Moscone had decided to follow Milk's urging and refuse to reappoint White to the Board, White armed himself and went to City Hall, ostensibly to talk to Moscone about the possibility of reappointment. He entered the building through a basement window to avoid the metal detectors, shot Moscone four times after being told that he would not be reappointed to the Board, reloaded the gun, went to Milk's office, and shot him five times. At trial, the defense argued that White was under severe pressure and suffered from depression, and that he lacked the capacity to harbor malice. The jury acquitted him of first-degree murder and instead returned a verdict of voluntary manslaughter. Harvey Milk's story is the subject of the 2008 award-winning film *Milk*. For additional background on the case, see WILLIAM J. WINSLADE & JUDITH W. ROSS, THE INSANITY PLEA 21–51 (1983).

The outrage engendered by the verdict in White's case led to riots and ultimately to abolition of the diminished capacity defense in California. In 1981, the state legislature passed a statute overruling *Conley* and providing that "[n]either an awareness of the obligation to act within the general body of laws regulating society nor acting despite such awareness is included within the definition of malice." Cal. Penal Code § 188 (reprinted above in Section A). The following year, the California electorate likewise voted in favor of an initiative abolishing the diminished capacity defense. *See id.* § 25(a). For a history of the diminished capacity defense in California, see *People v. Saille*, 820 P.2d 588, 591–96 (Cal. 1991).

[C] Unintentional Homicide

[1] Second-Degree Murder: Depraved Heart/ Extreme Indifference

Commonwealth v. Malone
47 A.2d 445 (Pa. 1946)

MAXEY, CHIEF JUSTICE.

This is an appeal from the judgment and sentence under a conviction of murder in the second degree. William H. Long, age 13 years, was killed by a shot from a 32-caliber revolver held against his right side by the defendant, then aged 17 years. These youths were on friendly terms at the time of the homicide. The defendant and his mother, while his father and brother were in the U.S. Armed Forces, were residing in Lancaster, Pa., with the family of William H. Long, whose son was the victim of the shooting.

On the evening of February 26, 1945, when the defendant went to a moving picture theater, he carried in the pocket of his raincoat a revolver which he had obtained at the home of his uncle on the preceding day. In the afternoon preceding the shooting, the decedent procured a cartridge from his father's room and he and the defendant placed it in the revolver.

After leaving the theater, the defendant went to a dairy store and there met the decedent. Both youths sat in the rear of the store ten minutes, during which period the defendant took the gun out of his pocket and loaded the chamber to the right of the firing pin and then closed the gun. A few minutes later, both youths sat on stools in front of the lunch counter and ate some food. The defendant suggested to the decedent that they play "Russian Poker."[13] Long replied: "I don't care; go ahead." The

---

13. [n.1] It has been explained that "Russian poker" is a game in which the participants, in turn, place a single cartridge in one of the five chambers of a revolver cylinder, give the latter a quick twirl, place the muzzle of the gun against the temple and pull the trigger, leaving it to chance whether or not death results to the trigger puller.

defendant then placed the revolver against the right side of Long and pulled the trigger three times. The third pull resulted in a fatal wound to Long. The latter jumped off the stool and cried: "Oh! Oh! Oh!" and Malone said: "Did I hit you, Billy? Gee, Kid, I'm sorry." Long died from the wounds two days later.

The defendant testified that the gun chamber he loaded was the first one to the right of the firing chamber and that when he pulled the trigger he did not "expect to have the gun go off." He declared he had no intention of harming Long, who was his friend and companion. The defendant was indicted for murder, tried and found guilty of murder in the second degree and sentenced to a term in the penitentiary for a period not less than five years and not exceeding ten years. . . .

Appellant . . . contends that the facts did not justify a conviction for any form of homicide except involuntary manslaughter. This contention we over-rule. A specific intent to take life is, under our law, an essential ingredient of murder in the first degree. At common law, the "grand criterion" which "distinguished murder from other killing" was malice on the part of the killer and this malice was not necessarily "malevolent to the deceased particularly" but "any evil design in general; the dictate of a wicked, depraved and malignant heart"; 4 Blackstone 199. Among the examples that Blackstone cites of murder is "coolly discharging a gun among a multitude of people," causing the death of someone of the multitude.

. . . When an individual commits an act of gross recklessness for which he must reasonably anticipate that death to another is likely to result, he exhibits that "wickedness of disposition; hardness of heart; cruelty; recklessness of consequences and a mind regardless of social duty" which proved that there was at that time in him "that state or frame of mind termed malice." This court has declared that if a driver "wantonly, recklessly, and in disregard of consequences" hurls "his car against another, or into a crowd" and death results from that act "he ought . . . to face the same consequences that would be meted out to him if he had accomplished death by wantonly and wickedly firing a gun."

. . . .

The killing of William H. Long by this defendant resulted from an act intentionally done by the latter, in reckless and wanton disregard of the consequences which were at least sixty per cent certain from his thrice attempted discharge of a gun known to contain one bullet and aimed at a vital part of Long's body. This killing was, therefore, murder, for malice in the sense of a wicked disposition is evidenced by the intentional doing of an uncalled-for act in callous disregard of its likely harmful effects on others. The fact that there was no motive for this homicide does not exculpate the accused. In a trial for murder proof of motive is always relevant but never necessary.

Notes and Questions

1. The Justifications for Punishing Unintentional Homicide as Murder. Given that Malone apparently had no intent to hurt, much less kill, his friend Long, were murder charges appropriate? Are the drafters of the Model Penal Code correct in thinking "there is a kind of reckless homicide that cannot fairly be distinguished in grading terms from homicides committed purposely or knowingly"? Model Penal Code § 210.2 Comment at 21.

2. Other Russian Roulette Cases. In a subsequent Pennsylvania case, *Commonwealth v. Ashburn*, 331 A.2d 167 (Pa. 1975), the victim was the first to suggest playing Russian Roulette. The defendant then loaded a gun and fired two shots, the second of which proved fatal. The court affirmed the second-degree murder conviction, refusing to interpret *Malone* as mandating acquittal of murder charges if the risk of death was less than 60 percent. Rather, the court explained, the result in *Malone* did "not depend on any precise mathematical calculation of the probable consequences of the defendant's acts." *Id.* at 170. Does this ruling make sense because "[i]n terms of moral culpability, there is no reason for punishing the discharge on the third pull any differently from the discharge on the first"? Alan C. Michaels, Note, *Defining Unintended Murder*, 85 Colum. L. Rev. 786, 798 (1985). *See also State v. Boyce*, 718 A.2d 1097 (Me. 1998) (affirming depraved-heart murder conviction and 40-year prison sentence in Russian Roulette case without specifying which shot was fatal); *Commonwealth v. Ward*, 688 N.E.2d 227 (Mass. 1997) (finding second-degree murder conviction appropriate in Russian Roulette case where the first shot was fatal); *People v. Roe*, 542 N.E.2d 610 (N.Y. 1989) (same).

Does it matter who initiated the Russian Roulette game — the defendant, as in *Malone*, or the victim, as in *Ashburn*? Would it have made a difference in *Malone* if Long had shot himself while playing the game? In *People v. Hansen*, 68 Cal. Rptr. 2d 897 (Cal. Ct. App. 1997), the court affirmed a conviction on the lesser charge of involuntary manslaughter where the defendant proposed the Russian Roulette game but the victim shot himself. *Cf. Minor v. State*, 605 A.2d 138, 141, 139 (Md. 1992) (affirming conviction on misdemeanor reckless endangerment charges where the defendant and his 42-year-old brother had been drinking and discussing playing Russian Roulette, the brother asked the defendant to give him the loaded shotgun, the defendant did so "in order to 'call his bluff,'" "daring him to play" the game, and the brother fatally shot himself). For discussion of the causation issues that arise in this type of case, see Chapter 10, Section B.3.

People v. Knoller
158 P.3d 731 (Cal. 2007)

Kennard, Justice.

On January 26, 2001, two dogs owned by defendant Marjorie Knoller and her husband, codefendant Robert Noel, attacked and killed Diane Whipple in the hallway of an apartment building in San Francisco. Defendant Knoller was charged with second degree murder and involuntary manslaughter; codefendant Noel, who was not present at the time of the attack on Whipple, was charged with involuntary manslaughter but not murder. Both were also charged with owning a mischievous animal that caused the death of a human being, in violation of section 399 [of the California Penal Code].

After a change of venue to Los Angeles County, a jury convicted defendants on all counts. Both moved for a new trial. The trial court denied Noel's motion. It granted Knoller's motion in part, giving her a new trial on the second degree murder charge. . . .

. . . .

The trial court sentenced both defendants to four years' imprisonment, the maximum term for involuntary manslaughter, staying the sentences for the section 399 violations. . . .

The Court of Appeal reversed the trial court's order granting Knoller a new trial on the second degree murder charge. . . . In all other respects, the Court of Appeal affirmed the convictions of both defendants.

. . . .

. . . [W]e reaffirm the test of implied malice we set out in *People v. Phillips*, (1966) 414 P.2d 353, and . . . reiterated in many later cases: Malice is implied when the killing is proximately caused by "an act, the natural consequences of which are dangerous to life, which act was deliberately performed by a person who knows that his conduct endangers the life of another and who acts with conscious disregard for life." In short, implied malice requires a defendant's awareness of engaging in conduct that endangers the life of another — no more, and no less.

. . . .

I. Facts and Proceedings

In 1998, Pelican Bay State Prison inmates Paul Schneider and Dale Bretches, both members of the Aryan Brotherhood prison gang, sought to engage in a business of buying, raising, and breeding Presa Canario dogs. This breed of dog tends to be very large, weighing over 100 pounds, and reaching over five feet tall when standing on its hind legs. A document found in defendants' apartment describes the Presa Canario as "a gripping dog . . . always used and bred for combat and guard . . . [and] used extensively for fighting. . . ."

. . . .

Defendants Knoller and Noel, who were attorneys representing a prison guard at Pelican Bay State Prison, met inmate Schneider at the prison sometime in 1999. . . .

Defendant Knoller thereafter contacted Dr. Donald Martin, a veterinarian for 49 years, and on March 26, 2000, he examined and vaccinated the [two Presa Canario dogs, Bane and Hera]. With his bill to Knoller, Dr. Martin included a letter, which said in part: "I would be professionally amiss [*sic*] if I did not mention the following, so that you can be prepared. These dogs . . . have had no training or discipline of any sort. They were a problem to even get to, let alone to vaccinate. . . . To add to this, these animals would be a liability in any household, reminding me of the recent attack in Tehama County to a boy by large dogs. He lost his arm and disfigured his face. . . ." Knoller thanked Dr. Martin for the information and said she would pass it on to her client.

On April 1, 2000, both defendants and a professional dog handler took custody of the dogs . . . . Bane then weighed 150 pounds and Hera 130 pounds. . . .

. . . .

Between the time defendants Noel and Knoller brought the dogs to their sixth-floor apartment in San Francisco and the date of the fatal mauling of Diane Whipple on January 26, 2001, there were about 30 incidents of the two dogs being out of control or threatening humans and other dogs. Neighbors mentioned seeing the two dogs unattended on the sixth floor and running down the hall. Codefendant Noel's letters to prisoner Schneider confirmed this, mentioning one incident when defendant Knoller had to let go of the two dogs as they broke from her grasp and ran to the end of the hall. Noel described how the dogs even pushed past him and "took off side by side down the hall toward the elevator in a celebratory stampede!! 240 lbs. of Presa wall to wall moving at top speed!!!" In a letter to inmate Schneider, defendant Knoller admitted not having the upper body strength to handle Bane and having trouble controlling Hera.

When neighbors complained to defendants Noel and Knoller about the two dogs, defendants responded callously, if at all. . . .

There were also instances when defendants' two dogs attacked or threatened people. David Moser, a fellow resident in the apartment building, slipped by defendants Knoller and Noel in the hallway only to have their dog Hera bite him on the "rear end." When he exclaimed, "Your dog just bit me," Noel replied, "Um, interesting." Neither defendant apologized to Moser or reprimanded the dog. . . .

One time, codefendant Noel himself suffered a severe injury to his finger when Bane bit him during a fight with another dog. The wound required surgery, and Noel had to wear a splint on his arm and have two steel pins placed in his hand for eight to 10 weeks.

Mauling victim Diane Whipple and her partner Sharon Smith lived in a sixth-floor apartment across a lobby from defendants. Smith encountered defendants' two dogs as often as once a week. In early December 2000, . . . Whipple had come upon codefendant Noel in the lobby with one of the dogs, which lunged at her and bit her in the hand. . . . Whipple made every effort to avoid defendants' dogs, checking the hallway before she went out and becoming anxious while waiting for the elevator for fear the dogs would be inside. She and Smith did not complain to apartment management because they wanted nothing to do with defendants Knoller and Noel.

On January 26, 2001, Whipple telephoned Smith to say she was going home early. At 4:00 p.m., Esther Birkmaier, a neighbor who lived across the hall from Whipple, heard dogs barking and a woman's "panic-stricken" voice calling, "Help me, help me." Looking through the peephole in her front door, Birkmaier saw Whipple lying facedown on the floor just over the threshold of her apartment with what appeared to be a dog on top of her. Birkmaier saw no one else in the hallway. Afraid to open the door, Birkmaier called 911, the emergency telephone number, and at the same time heard a voice yelling, "No, no, no" and "Get off." . . .

. . . .

The officers [who responded] called for an ambulance. Shortly thereafter, defendant Knoller emerged from her apartment. She did not ask about Whipple's condition but merely told the officers she was looking for her keys, which she found just inside the door to Whipple's apartment.

. . . .

An autopsy revealed over 77 discrete injuries covering Whipple's body "from head to toe." The most significant were lacerations damaging her jugular vein and her carotid artery and crushing her larynx, injuries typically inflicted by predatory animals to kill their prey. . . .

On February 8, 2001, both defendants appeared on the television show *Good Morning America* and basically blamed mauling victim Whipple for her own death.[14] Defendant Knoller claimed that Whipple had already opened her apartment door when something about her interested Bane. . . . Knoller claimed that Whipple had ample opportunity to just slam the door of her apartment or stay still on the floor.

Codefendant Noel did not testify, but he presented evidence of positive encounters between the two dogs and veterinarians, friends, and neighbors. Defendant Knoller did testify in her own defense. She referred to herself, her husband, and Pelican Bay prisoner Schneider as the "triad," and she spoke of Schneider as her "son." The two dogs had become a focal point in the relationship. She denied reading literature in the apartment referring to the vicious nature of the dogs. She thought the dogs had no personality problems requiring a professional trainer. She denied receiving or otherwise discounted any warnings about the two dogs' behavior and she maintained that virtually all the witnesses testifying to incidents with the dogs were lying. . . . Knoller said she threw herself on Whipple to save her. . . . She acknowledged not calling 911 to get help for Whipple.

Asked whether she denied responsibility for the attack on Whipple, Knoller gave this reply: "I said in an interview that I wasn't responsible but it wasn't . . . in regard to what Bane had done, it was in regard to knowing whether he would do that or not. And I had no idea that he would ever do anything like that to anybody. How can you anticipate something like that? It's a totally bizarre event. I mean how could you anticipate that a dog that you know that is gentle and loving and affectionate would do something so horrible and brutal and disgusting and gruesome to anybody? How could you imagine that happening?"

---

14. Excerpts from the defendants' appearance on *Good Morning America* can be viewed at https://www.youtube.com/watch?v=uOFRsFS2lCE.

In rebuttal, the prosecution presented evidence that the minor character of defendant Knoller's injuries—principally bruising to the hands—indicated that she had not been as involved in trying to protect mauling victim Whipple as she had claimed. Dr. Randall Lockwood, the prosecution's expert on dog behavior, testified that good behavior by a dog on some occasions does not preclude aggressive and violent behavior on other occasions, and he mentioned the importance of training dogs such as Bane and Hera not to fight.

. . . [I]n granting Knoller's motion for a new trial on the second degree murder count[,] [t]he trial court observed: ". . . [W]ith all of the information that had come out dealing with the dogs, the defendants were fully on notice that they had a couple of wild, uncontrollable and dangerous dogs that were likely going to do something bad. Is the 'something bad' death? That is the ultimate question in the case. There is no question but that the something bad was going to be that somebody was going to be badly hurt. I defy either defendant to stand up and tell me they had no idea that those dogs were going to hurt somebody one day. But can they stand up and say that they knew subjectively—not objectively and that's an important distinction—that these dogs were going to stand up and kill somebody?"

The trial court continued: . . . "There was one time on the stand, Ms. Knoller, when I truly believed what you said. You broke down in the middle of a totally scripted answer and you actually, instead of crying, you actually got mad and you said you had no idea that this dog could do what he did and pounded the table. I believed you. That was the only time, but I did believe you." The court then described the definition of second degree murder as requiring that one "*subjectively knows, based on everything, that the conduct that he or she is about to engage in has a high probability of death to another human being.*" (Italics added.)

. . . .

. . . The Court of Appeal reversed the trial court's order granting Knoller's motion for a new trial on the second degree murder count. . . . The Court of Appeal held that a second degree murder conviction can be based simply on a defendant's "subjective appreciation and conscious disregard of a likely risk of . . . serious bodily injury." In all other respects, the Court of Appeal affirmed both defendants' convictions.

II. The Elements of Implied Malice

. . . .

. . . Second degree murder is the unlawful killing of a human being with malice aforethought but without the additional elements, such as willfulness, premeditation, and deliberation, that would support a conviction of first degree murder. Section 188 provides: "[M]alice may be either express or implied. It is express when there is manifested a deliberate intention to take away the life of a fellow creature. It is implied, when no considerable provocation appears, or when the circumstances attending the killing show an abandoned and malignant heart."

The statutory definition of implied malice, a killing by one with an "abandoned and malignant heart," is far from clear in its meaning. Indeed, an instruction in the statutory language could be misleading, for it "could lead the jury to equate the malignant heart with an evil disposition or a despicable character" instead of focusing on a defendant's awareness of the risk created by his or her behavior. . . .

III. The Court of Appeal's Test for Implied Malice

. . . [T]he great majority of this court's decisions establish that a killer acts with implied malice only when acting with an awareness of endangering human life. This principle has been well settled for many years, and it is embodied in the standard jury instruction given in murder cases, including this one. The Court of Appeal here, however, held that a second degree murder conviction, based on a theory of implied malice, can be based simply on a defendant's awareness of the risk of causing serious bodily injury to another. . . . In holding that a defendant's conscious disregard of the risk of serious bodily injury suffices to sustain such a conviction, the Court of Appeal erred.

IV. The Trial Court's Grant of a New Trial on the Second Degree Murder Charge

. . . .

Here, the trial court properly instructed the jury. . . . But when the court evaluated defendant Knoller's new trial motion, it . . . stated that . . . the issue in this case was "whether or not as a *subjective* matter and as a matter of law Ms. Knoller *knew* that there was *a high probability*" that her conduct would result in someone's death. (Italics added.) But . . . the *Phillips* test [for implied malice does not] require a defendant's awareness that his or her conduct has *a high probability* of causing death. Rather, it requires only that a defendant acted with a "conscious disregard for human life."

. . . .

. . . It is uncertain whether the trial court would have reached the same result using correct legal standards.

The Court of Appeal's judgment is reversed and the matter is remanded to that court, with directions to return the case to the trial court for reconsideration of defendant Knoller's new trial motion in accord with the views expressed in this opinion.

Notes and Questions

1. **Subsequent Developments in the *Knoller* Case.** On remand, a different trial judge refused Knoller's request for a new trial and reinstated the second-degree murder conviction. Rejecting the argument that she was bound by the original trial judge's conclusions and applying the standard for implied malice laid out in the California Supreme Court's opinion, Judge Charlotte Woolard found that the prosecution's evidence showed that Knoller "knew her conduct endangered life" and knew that "both dogs 'singularly or together were capable of killing a person and, if not properly restrained, would kill a person.'" *See* Bob Egelko, *Murder Conviction*

Reinstated in '01 Dog Mauling, S.F. Chron., Aug. 23, 2008, at B1. Citing the fact that Knoller made "only 'minimal efforts' at intervention and 'left Ms. Whipple in the hallway to die alone,'" and then "blamed the victim" in her interview on *Good Morning America*, the judge sentenced Knoller to a prison term of 15 years to life. *See* Bob Egelko, *Knoller Gets 15 to Life in Mauling Death*, S.F. Chron., Sept. 23, 2008, at B1.

The California Court of Appeal unanimously rejected Knoller's appeal in an unpublished opinion. The court explained:

> Defendant's deliberate act of leaving her apartment with an unmuzzled Bane knowing that she could not control him, as well as the evidence that she knew he was dangerous to human life provided substantial support for the jury's finding that she acted with conscious disregard for human life. The question was not whether Bane would probably kill someone but whether defendant was aware that her act of taking him into the hallway without a muzzle created a substantial risk that someone would be killed.

People v. Knoller, 2010 Cal. App. Unpub. Lexis 6668, at *124 (Cal. Ct. App. Aug. 20, 2010). The state supreme court denied review, *see People v. Knoller*, 2010 Cal. Lexis 12088 (Cal. Dec. 1, 2010), and the federal courts rejected Knoller's habeas petition. *See Knoller v. Miller*, 633 F. App'x 418 (9th Cir. 2016).

2. Other Dog Bite Cases. In *Berry v. Superior Court*, 256 Cal. Rptr. 344 (Cal. Ct. App. 1989), a case that preceded *Knoller*, the California Court of Appeal refused to dismiss second-degree murder charges filed against a dog owner, finding sufficient evidence of implied malice to justify a trial for murder. The victim in that case, a 2½-year-old who lived next door to the defendant, wandered into the defendant's backyard and was mauled to death by a pit bull the defendant had raised for fighting purposes. In denying review in *Berry*, the California Supreme Court ordered that the appellate court's opinion not be officially published. Berry was ultimately acquitted of second-degree murder, but he was convicted on the lesser charge of involuntary manslaughter, as well as cultivating marijuana, keeping a mischievous animal that killed, and keeping a fighting dog. He was sentenced to a prison term of three years and eight months, and the Court of Appeal affirmed his conviction. *See People v. Berry*, 2 Cal. Rptr. 2d 416 (Cal. Ct. App. 1991).

In *State v. Davidson*, 987 P.2d 335 (Kan. 1999), the Kansas Supreme Court affirmed a second-degree murder conviction and 12-year prison sentence in a case where the defendant's three Rottweiler dogs escaped from her fenced-in yard while she was sleeping and attacked an 11-year-old boy who was waiting for a school bus. The court concluded that the defendant "created an unreasonable risk and then consciously disregarded it in a manner and to the extent that it reasonably could be inferred that she was extremely indifferent to the value of human life." Specifically, the court reasoned that the defendant "selected powerful dogs with a potential for aggressive behavior," "ignored the advice from experts on how to properly train her dogs and their warnings of the dire results which could occur from improper training," "fail[ed] to properly secure the gate," and "ignored the aggressive behavior her dogs displayed toward her neighbors and their children." *Id.* at 344–45.

3. Putting Content into the Definition of Depraved-Heart Murder. What precisely is the definition of depraved-heart murder? The term "abandoned and malignant heart," described by the California Supreme Court in *Knoller* as "far from clear," has also been characterized as "crime definition by literary metaphor." David Crump, *"Murder, Pennsylvania Style": Comparing Traditional American Homicide Law to the Statutes of the Model Penal Code*, 109 W. Va. L. Rev. 257, 305 (2007). *But cf. Leonard v. State*, 17 P.3d 397, 413 (Nev. 2001) (calling the term "archaic but essential"). One commentator has likewise questioned the value of the concept of "extreme indifference":

> To speak of extreme indifference is pointless, because indifference is itself the ultimate extremity. You may want a thing with diminishing degrees of fervour, but once you have become indifferent to it you have reached the end of the road. You are dead to it.

Glanville L. Williams, The Mental Element in Crime 92 (1965).

Are these criticisms well taken? Would it help to confine depraved-heart murder to cases where the defendant "accepted causing a death" — i.e., where the defendant would still have committed the act "had he known a death would result"? Alan C. Michaels, *Acceptance: The Missing Mental State*, 71 S. Cal. L. Rev. 953, 1016 (1998). Alternatively, should the jury be instructed to conduct "an objective examination of the nature of the defendant's risk-creating activity" and to convict of depraved-heart murder only if that activity "objectively had no purpose outside of threatening or causing harm"? Hannah B. Schieber, Comment, *Utter Confusion: Why "Utter Disregard for Human Life" Should Be Replaced with an Objective Analysis of the Defendant's Activity*, 2011 Wis. L. Rev. 691, 694, 724. Or are these approaches too narrow?

Perhaps efforts to define depraved-heart murder more precisely are doomed to fail because these cases essentially involve a value judgment that turns on four factors:

> (1) the social utility of the actor's conduct; (2) the magnitude of the risk his conduct creates including both the nature of foreseeable harm and the likelihood that the conduct will result in that harm; (3) the actor's knowledge of the risk; and (4) any precautions the actor takes to minimize the risk.

Jeffries v. State, 169 P.3d 913, 916 (Alaska 2007) (quoting *Neitzel v. State*, 655 P.2d 325, 336–37 (Alaska Ct. App. 1982)). For a comprehensive examination of how various states conceptualize depraved-heart murder, see John C. Duffy, Note, *Reality Check: How Practical Circumstances Affect the Interpretation of Depraved Indifference Murder*, 57 Duke L.J. 425, 433–44 (2007).

4. Awareness of the Risk. According to the Alaska courts cited in the prior Note, a defendant's knowledge of the risk is one of the factors to be used in determining the appropriateness of depraved-heart murder charges. Similarly, the California Supreme Court's opinion in *Knoller* considered "an awareness of endangering human life" a prerequisite for a depraved-heart murder conviction. Did the court in *Malone* likewise require awareness of the risk of death? Was Malone aware of the risk?

Does it make sense to focus on awareness of risk as one of the critical factors in determining a murder defendant's culpability? Or does "emphasizing cognitive awareness of a risk . . . ignore[] or conceal[] the moral quality that 'culpable indifference' expresses," i.e., the notion of "not-caring" and "callousness" that signals "not a desire to harm, but an insufficiently strong aversion to harm, or a desire or willingness to create a risk of harm"? Kenneth W. Simons, *Rethinking Mental States*, 72 B.U. L. Rev. 463, 466–67 (1992).

5. The Model Penal Code Approach. The Model Penal Code defines murder to include homicide "committed recklessly under circumstances manifesting extreme indifference to the value of human life." Model Penal Code § 210.2(1)(b). The drafters explain their choice of this particular definition as follows:

> The significance of purpose or knowledge as a standard of culpability is that . . . purposeful or knowing homicide demonstrates precisely such indifference to the value of human life. Whether recklessness is so extreme that it demonstrates similar indifference is not a question, it is submitted, that can be further clarified. It must be left directly to the trier of fact under instructions which make it clear that recklessness that can fairly be assimilated to purpose or knowledge should be treated as murder and that less extreme recklessness should be punished as manslaughter.

Id. § 210.2 Comment at 21–22.

6. Intent to Cause Serious Bodily Harm as Second-Degree Murder. Under the common law, proof that a defendant intended to inflict serious or grievous bodily harm was another way to establish the malice necessary for second-degree murder. The common-law rule is based on the theory that intent to cause serious bodily harm is "equivalent in legal character to a criminal purpose aimed against life." *Wellar v. People*, 30 Mich. 16, 19 (1874).

Is it inappropriate to equate an intent to inflict serious bodily harm with an intent to kill? Are murder charges excessive in cases where an assault fortuitously leads to death? Or is "the outcome of intentionally inflicting serious harm . . . so unpredictable that anyone prepared to act so wickedly has little ground for complaint if . . . he is convicted and punished as severely as one who intended to kill"? *The Queen v. Cunningham*, 1982 App. Cas. 566, 584 (H.L. 1981) (Lord Edmund-Davies).

In *Commonwealth v. Dorazio*, 74 A.2d 125, 130 (Pa. 1950), the court adopted a very loose definition of serious bodily harm, observing that "it is not necessary that the injury be intended to be permanent or dangerous to life[;] it is malicious to intend injury such as to seriously interfere with health and comfort." Dorazio, a former professional heavyweight prize fighter, attacked a coworker who was a member of a rival union. Dorazio pursued the victim when he attempted to flee, and then "punch[ed] him repeatedly in and about the head and body" as he lay on the floor. *Id.* at 127. Affirming the second-degree murder conviction, the court acknowledged that the use of fists would typically justify only a conviction for involuntary manslaughter. But it held that malice can be implied in such cases under certain circumstances, depending on "[t]he size of the assailant, the manner in which the fists [were] used, the ferocity of the attack and its duration[,] and the provocation." *Id.* at 130. On these facts, the court found sufficient evidence that Dorazio intended to inflict serious bodily harm, concluding that the "events show a brutal, persistent attack upon a helpless, non-resisting victim; they show a measure of depravity and hardness of heart, a recklessness of consequences and a mind regardless of social duty which imports malice." *Id. See also People v. Cravens*, 267 P.3d 1113, 1119–20 (Cal. 2012) (affirming second-degree murder conviction on the grounds that the defendant committed an act "predictably dangerous to human life" when he threw a "very hard . . . sucker punch" with sufficient force that his victim, who was "smaller and shorter" as well as "intoxicated, exhausted, and vulnerable," was "unconscious . . . even before [his head] . . . hit the pavement with an audible cracking sound that even the neighbors could hear, . . . caus[ing] skull fractures the forensic pathologist likened to the force experienced in a motor vehicle crash or from being struck in the head with a hammer, baseball bat, or tire iron").

Most jurisdictions define serious bodily harm more narrowly than the *Dorazio* court. In *Wellar*, for example, the court interpreted serious bodily harm to mean "such an injury as may be expected to involve serious consequences, either periling life or leading to great bodily harm"; the injury must be "of a very serious character which might naturally and commonly involve loss of life, or grievous mischief." *Wellar*, 30 Mich. at 19. *See also Thornton v. State*, 919 A.2d 678, 728–30 (Md. 2007) (holding that this form of murder requires proof that the defendant intended "to cause such severe harm that death would be *the* likely result, not merely a possible result"). Would *Dorazio* and *Cravens* have been decided differently under the Michigan and Maryland formulations?

The Model Penal Code does not recognize intent to cause serious bodily harm as a separate category of murder, and most of the modern criminal codes have followed that lead. *See* 2 Wayne R. LaFave, Substantive Criminal Law § 14.3, at 435 (2d ed. 2003). The drafters of the MPC thought it preferable to convict those who intended serious bodily harm of either extreme-indifference murder or manslaughter. They explain their reasoning as follows:

> That the actor intended to cause injury of a particular nature or gravity is, of course, a relevant consideration in determining whether he acted with "extreme indifference to the value of human life" under Section 210.2(1)(b) or "recklessly" with respect to death of another under Section 210.3(1). Most traditional illustrations of murder based on intent to injure will fall within the recklessness category as defined in the Model Code. In the rare case of purposeful infliction of serious injury not involving recklessness with respect to death, the actor should be prosecuted for some version of aggravated assault or, perhaps, for negligent homicide.

Model Penal Code § 210.2 Comment at 28–29.

[2] Involuntary Manslaughter: Criminal Negligence/ Recklessness

Commonwealth v. Welansky
55 N.E.2d 902 (Mass. 1944)

LUMMUS, JUSTICE.

[Barnett Welansky was the owner of the Cocoanut Grove, a Boston nightclub where a fire broke out in November of 1942. The fire, the second deadliest in this country's history, claimed the lives of 492 people. Although Welansky typically spent evenings at the club, he was not present at the time of the fire, having been hospitalized about two weeks earlier. The ceilings of the nightclub were lined with flammable satin, and the prosecution's evidence showed, among other things, that the number of customers at the club that evening exceeded the legal capacity and that many of the emergency exits were blocked, hidden, or locked, possibly to prevent customers from leaving without paying. On this evidence, Welansky was found guilty of multiple counts of involuntary manslaughter. He was sentenced to 12 to 15 years in prison, but was pardoned two months before he died, after serving almost four years of his sentence.]

. . . .

The Commonwealth disclaimed any contention that the defendant intentionally killed or injured the persons named in the indictment as victims. It based its case on involuntary manslaughter through wanton or reckless conduct. . . .

To define wanton or reckless conduct so as to distinguish it clearly from negligence and gross negligence is not easy. Sometimes the word "willful" is prefaced to the words "wanton" and "reckless" in expressing the concept. That only blurs it. Wilful means intentional. . . . Wilfully causing harm is a wrong, but a different wrong from wantonly or recklessly causing harm. . . . What must be intended is the conduct, not the resulting harm. The words "wanton" and "reckless" are practically synonymous in this connection, although the word "wanton" may contain a suggestion of arrogance or insolence or heartlessness that is lacking in the word "reckless." But intentional conduct to which either word applies is followed by the same legal consequences as though both words applied.

The standard of wanton or reckless conduct is at once subjective and objective. . . . Knowing facts that would cause a reasonable man to know the danger is equivalent to knowing the danger. The judge charged the jury correctly when he said, "To constitute wanton or reckless conduct, as distinguished from mere negligence, grave danger to others must have been apparent and the defendant must have chosen to run the risk rather than alter his conduct so as to avoid the act or omission which caused the harm. If the grave danger was in fact realized by the defendant, his subsequent voluntary act or omission which caused the harm amounts to wanton or reckless conduct, no matter whether the ordinary man would have realized the gravity of the danger or not. But even if a particular defendant is so stupid [or] so heedless . . . that in fact he did not realize the grave danger, he cannot escape the imputation of wanton or reckless conduct in his dangerous act or omission, if an ordinary normal man under the same circumstances would have realized the gravity of the danger. A man may be reckless within the meaning of the law although he himself thought he was careful."

The essence of wanton or reckless conduct is intentional conduct, by way either of commission or of omission where there is duty to act, which conduct involves a high degree of likelihood that substantial harm will result to another. Wanton or reckless conduct amounts to what has been variously described as indifference to or disregard of probable consequences. . . .

The words "wanton" and "reckless" are thus not merely rhetorical or vituperative expressions used instead of negligent or grossly negligent. They express a difference in the degree of risk and in the voluntary taking of risk so marked, as compared with negligence, as to amount substantially and in the eyes of the law to a difference in kind. . . .

. . . [A]t common law conduct does not become criminal until it passes the borders of negligence and gross negligence and enters into the domain of wanton or reckless conduct. . . .

Judgments affirmed.

Notes and Questions

More Recent Parallels. In 2003, another of the deadliest nightclub fires in American history occurred in the Station nightclub in Rhode Island. One hundred people died and more than 200 others were injured in the overcrowded club when fireworks were set off during a heavy metal band's performance, sparking a fire that quickly spread to the flammable, sound-proofing polyurethane foam installed in the club. The band manager who actually set off the pyrotechnics pleaded guilty to 100 counts of involuntary manslaughter and received a four-year prison sentence.

In a very controversial decision, and over the objection of prosecutors and the victims' families, a judge allowed the two brothers who owned the club to plead no contest to 100 counts of involuntary manslaughter. The brother who bought the foam was sentenced to four years in prison, and the other was ordered to perform 500 hours of community service. Although the Governor of Rhode Island commented after the sentencing hearing that "[n]obody who witnessed today's emotional testimony could believe that the punishment fit the crime," the judge explained that his decision was influenced by the fear that "horrifying and gruesome" photos from the night of the fire "could further traumatize the public," the "uncertain prospects" for conviction, the defendants' "clean criminal records," and "the difficulty of selecting an impartial jury in a state where most people know someone touched by the disaster." *See* Jonathan Saltzman & Megan Tench, *A Day of Tears and Anger in R.I. Court*, Bos. GLOBE, Sept. 30, 2006, at A1.

The two defendants sentenced to prison ultimately served about half of their four-year sentences, but civil suits were also filed in the wake of the fire by more than 300 survivors and family members. They sued dozens of defendants, including the manufacturers of the flammable foam, brewer Anheuser Busch, the town of West Warwick, and the state of Rhode Island. Eventually all of the defendants agreed to settlements totaling $176 million. *See* Eric Tucker, *Funds Set for R.I. Club Fire Victims' Children*, Bos. Globe, Nov. 25, 2009, at 2.

Commonwealth v. Feinberg

253 A.2d 636 (Pa. 1969)

Jones, Justice.

Appellant Max Feinberg owned and operated a cigar store in the skid-row section of Philadelphia. One of the products he sold was Sterno, a jelly-like substance composed primarily of methanol and ethanol and designed for cooking and heating purposes. Sterno was manufactured and sold in two types of containers, one for home use and one for industrial use.[15] Before September, 1963, both types of Sterno contained approximately 3.75% methanol, or wood alcohol, and 71% ethanol, or grain alcohol; of the two types of alcohols, methanol is far more toxic if consumed internally. Beginning in September of 1963, the Sterno company began manufacturing a new type of industrial Sterno which was 54% methanol. The cans containing the new industrial Sterno were identical to the cans containing the old industrial Sterno except in one crucial aspect: on the lids of the new 54% methanol Sterno were imprinted the words "Institutional Sterno. Danger. Poison. For use only as a Fuel. Not for consumer use. For industrial and commercial use. Not for home use." A skull and crossbones were also lithographed on the lid.[16] The carton in which the new Sterno cans were packaged and shipped did not indicate that the contents differed in any respect from the old industrial Sterno.

According to its records, Sterno Corporation sent only one shipment of the new Sterno to the Philadelphia area; that shipment went to the Richter Paper Company and was received on December 17, 1963. Charles Richter, president of the firm, testified that his company, in turn, made only one sale of the new industrial Sterno, and that was to appellant. Richter testified that his records indicated that appellant

15. The Superior Court inferred that Feinberg sold industrial Sterno because it was cheaper than the product designed for home use and thus more profitable for him. *See Commonwealth v. Feinberg*, 234 A.2d 913, 917 (Pa. Super. Ct. 1967).

16. The Superior Court observed:

The containers of the regular Sterno [designed for home use] and the institutional type previously sold contained no such warning and were merely marked "Caution. Flammable. For use only as a fuel." The only difference in the containers previously sold was that the institutional type was so marked but had no wrap around label as was affixed to the container intended for regular use. Both containers were the same size, as were the containers sold after December 21st which did not contain wrap around labels.

Id. at 914.

received the Sterno on December 21 and, since Richter had not opened any of the cartons, he was unaware that he was selling appellant a new type of industrial Sterno. On December 27, Richter received a call from appellant informing him that the cartons contained a new type of Sterno and that appellant wished to return the portion of his order that he had not sold. The unused cartons were picked up by Richter's deliveryman the next day.

Meanwhile, between December 21 and December 28, appellant had sold approximately 400 cans of the new industrial Sterno. Between December 23 and December 30, thirty-one persons died in the skid-row area as a result of methanol poisoning. In many of the cases the source of the methanol was traced to the new industrial Sterno. Since appellant was the only retail outlet of this type of Sterno in Philadelphia, he was arrested and indicted on thirty-one counts charging involuntary manslaughter. . . .[17]

. . . The Penal Code defines involuntary manslaughter as a death "happening in consequence of an unlawful act, or the doing of a lawful act in an unlawful way. . . ."[18] . . . When a death results from the doing of an act lawful in itself but done in an unlawful manner, in order to sustain a conviction for manslaughter the Commonwealth must present evidence to prove that the defendant acted in a rash or reckless manner. The conduct of the defendant resulting in the death must be such a departure from the behavior of an ordinary and prudent man as to evidence a disregard of human life or an indifference to the consequences. Furthermore, there must be a direct causal relationship between the defendant's act and the deceased's death.

. . . .

We conclude . . . that the Commonwealth has made out all the elements necessary to warrant a conviction for involuntary manslaughter. First, the record establishes that appellant sold the Sterno with the knowledge that at least some of his customers would extract the alcohol for drinking purposes. Witnesses for the Commonwealth testified that when they purchased the Sterno from appellant, they would merely say "make one" or hold up fingers to indicate how many cans they wanted; one witness testified that appellant referred to the Sterno as shoe polish and on one occasion shouted to him on the street asking how he and his wife were making out with their shoe polish; finally, the witnesses testified that appellant asked them to conceal the Sterno under their coats when leaving his store. Such conduct does not square with the conclusion that appellant was merely selling the Sterno for cooking and heating

---

17. Feinberg was convicted on 17 counts, apparently because the trial judge found insufficient evidence of causation linking him to the other deaths. The judge imposed consecutive prison sentences of one to three years on five of the counts, and suspended the sentence on the remaining 12 counts. *See United States ex rel. Feinberg v. Rundle*, 316 F. Supp. 1129, 1130 (E.D. Pa. 1970), *aff'd*, 444 F.2d 402 (3d Cir. 1971). Feinberg appealed on those five counts, and the Superior Court affirmed four, finding insufficient proof of causation as to the fifth. *See Commonwealth v. Feinberg*, 234 A.2d 913 (Pa. Super. Ct. 1967). (The causation issues raised by cases like *Feinberg* are considered in Chapter 10, Section B.3.b.)

18. The current version of the statute is reprinted above in Section A.

purposes. Second, appellant was aware, or should have been aware, that the Sterno he was selling was toxic if consumed. The new industrial Sterno was clearly marked as being poisonous. Even the regular Sterno is marked "Caution. Flammable. For Use only as a Fuel" and if consumed internally may have serious consequences. Furthermore, when appellant was informed about the first deaths from methanol poisoning, he told the boy who worked in his shop to tell any police who came around that there was no Sterno in the store. Appellant also told the police that he had never purchased any Sterno from the Richter Paper Company. This evidence indicates to us that appellant was aware that he was selling the Sterno for an illicit purpose.

Appellant presses several contentions for our consideration. First, he claims that the Commonwealth has not established the necessary causal link between the sale of the Sterno and the deaths. We cannot agree. First, appellant sold the Sterno knowing, or having reason to know, that some of his customers would consume it. Second, some of his customers did consume the new industrial Sterno and died as a result. The Commonwealth's expert toxicologist testified that in several of the cases death could only have resulted from consumption of the new as opposed to the regular Sterno. Since appellant was the only retail outlet for the new Sterno in Philadelphia, these persons must have died from drinking Sterno purchased in appellant's store. Third, . . . [t]he court in *Thiede [v. State*, 182 N.W. 570 (Neb. 1921)], in answering an argument similar to the one now made by appellant, stated: "Defendant contends that the drinking of liquor by deceased was his voluntary act and served as an intervening cause, breaking the causal connection between the giving of the liquor by defendant and the resulting death. The drinking of the liquor, in consequence of defendant's act, was, however, what the defendant contemplated. Deceased, it is true, may have been negligent in drinking, but, where the defendant was negligent, then the contributory negligence of the deceased will be no defense in a criminal action."

Appellant next criticizes the following sentence in [the Superior Court's] opinion: "In the light of the *recognized weaknesses* of the purchasers of the product, and appellant's greater concern for profit than with the results of his actions, he was grossly negligent and demonstrated a wanton and reckless disregard for the welfare of those *whom he might reasonably have expected* to use the product for drinking purposes." Appellant argues that the Superior Court is here imposing an inequitable burden on sellers of Sterno by requiring them to recognize the "weaknesses" of their customers. Appellant has exaggerated the import of this sentence. The Superior Court was not imposing a duty on all sellers of Sterno to determine how their customers will use the product. The Court was merely saying that if a seller of Sterno is aware that the purchaser is an alcoholic and will use Sterno as a source of alcohol, then the seller is grossly negligent and wantonly reckless in selling Sterno to him. We do not think this imposes an intolerable burden on sellers of Sterno.

Notes and Questions

1. **Putting Content into the Definition of Involuntary Manslaughter.** As the *Welansky* and *Feinberg* opinions demonstrate, courts have used a number of

different terms to describe the mens rea necessary for involuntary manslaughter: wantonness, willfulness, recklessness, indifference, disregard, culpable negligence, criminal negligence, gross negligence. Often courts use more than one of these terms in the same breath.

Regardless of the particular terminology used, how does one determine the bounds of the involuntary manslaughter charge? Is it possible to answer that question in any meaningful way, or are terms like "criminal negligence" "largely a matter of degree, incapable of precise definition"? *Gian-Cursio v. State*, 180 So. 2d 396, 399 (Fla. Dist. Ct. App. 1965).

Would it help to consider the four factors that the Alaska courts have suggested for depraved-heart murder cases, simply requiring a lower level of culpability for involuntary manslaughter? *See* Note 3 following *People v. Knoller* in Section C.1 above.

2. Comparing Civil Tort Liability. In the great majority of states, involuntary manslaughter requires a higher degree of culpability than necessary to impose civil tort liability. Given that an involuntary manslaughter conviction cannot be premised on simple tort negligence in Pennsylvania, was it appropriate to convict Feinberg of involuntary manslaughter for selling Sterno to customers who should have known better than to drink it? Is *Feinberg* a case that would have better been left to tort litigation?

What exactly is the difference between involuntary manslaughter and civil tort negligence? As one court noted, "[c]riminal negligence and recklessness have always required something more than simple [tort] negligence," but "what that extra something is has always troubled the courts." *People v. Cruciani*, 334 N.Y.S.2d 515, 521 (N.Y. Suffolk Cnty. Ct. 1972).

3. Comparing Depraved-Heart Murder. If criminal sanctions were appropriate in *Feinberg*, why stop at involuntary manslaughter? Should Feinberg have been charged with depraved-heart murder? What is the difference between involuntary manslaughter and depraved-heart murder?

In attempting to answer that question, the Fourth Circuit observed in *United States v. Fleming*, 739 F.2d 945, 949 n.5 (4th Cir. 1984), that confusion has arisen because phrases like "wanton and reckless disregard for human life" are often used in describing both involuntary manslaughter and depraved-heart murder. The Fourth Circuit acknowledged that the difference between malice (murder) and gross negligence (manslaughter) is "one of degree rather than kind," but explained that "[t]he key point is that malice requires that . . . the jury could conclude that defendant's entering into the risk created by his conduct evidenced a depraved mind without regard for human life." *Id.* at 948, 949 n.5.

In distinguishing involuntary manslaughter and depraved-heart murder, other courts have focused instead on the riskiness of the defendant's actions. In *Commonwealth v. Lyons*, 828 N.E.2d 1, 6 (Mass. 2005), for example, the Massachusetts Supreme Judicial Court described the difference between involuntary manslaughter and depraved-heart murder in terms of "the degree of risk of physical harm" associated with the defendant's conduct. Conceding that there is a "fine line" between the two crimes, the court explained that depraved-heart murder requires "a plain and strong likelihood of death," whereas manslaughter involves "a high degree of likelihood [of] substantial harm."

Compare *People v. Roe*, 542 N.E.2d 610, 611 (N.Y. 1989), where the New York Court of Appeals said that both involuntary manslaughter and depraved-heart murder require a mens rea of recklessness, but that the difference between the two turns on the dangerousness of the defendant's conduct:

> Depraved indifference murder . . . differs from manslaughter . . . in that it must be shown that the actor's reckless conduct is imminently dangerous and presents a grave risk of death; in manslaughter, the conduct need only present the lesser "substantial risk" of death. Whether the lesser risk sufficient for manslaughter is elevated into the very substantial risk present in murder depends upon . . . "an objective assessment of the degree of risk presented by defendant's reckless conduct."

This court also acknowledged, however, that this assessment is ultimately "a qualitative judgment to be made by the trier of the facts." *Id.* at 612.

Subsequently, however, the New York court retreated from *Roe* and described the depraved indifference to life necessary for murder as "a culpable mental state":

> "[D]epraved indifference is best understood as an utter disregard for the value of human life—a willingness to act not because one intends harm, but because one simply doesn't care whether grievous harm results or not" . . . . "[A] depraved and utterly indifferent actor is someone who does not care if another is injured or killed" . . . . [T]he words "utter disregard," "willingness," and "does not care" can only describe a state of mind.

People v. Feingold, 852 N.E.2d 1163, 1168 (N.Y. 2006).

Do any of these distinctions help?

4. Awareness of the Risk. Some jurisdictions expressly require proof that the defendant was aware of the risk in order to support an involuntary manslaughter conviction. *See, e.g., Bussard v. State*, 288 N.W. 187, 189 (Wis. 1939) (reversing involuntary manslaughter conviction because, although the defendant was "negligent in a high degree," "[g]ross negligence . . . cannot rest on inadvertence").

Other courts disagree. In *Walker v. Superior Court*, 763 P.2d 852, 868 (Cal. 1988), for example, the court ruled that "criminal negligence must be evaluated objectively": "[t]he question is whether 'a reasonable person in defendant's position would have been aware of the risk involved.'" "If so," the court continued, the "defendant is presumed to have had such an awareness." *Id.* In reaching the same conclusion in *Commonwealth v. Pierce*, 138 Mass. 165, 179 (1884), then-Judge Oliver Wendell Holmes explained, "we cannot recognize a privilege to do acts manifestly endangering human life, on the ground of good intentions alone." Recall the similar views expressed in

Commonwealth v. Welansky, which is excerpted above. *See also Commonwealth v. Walker*, 812 N.E.2d 262, 270 (Mass. 2004) (reaffirming *Welansky*'s holding that subjective awareness of risk is not required for an involuntary manslaughter conviction).

Is it appropriate to impose criminal liability for a serious crime like manslaughter on those who are unaware of the risk created by their actions? For a general discussion of the propriety of punishing negligence, see Note 7 following *United States v. Villegas* in Chapter 4, Section B.2.

5. Defining the Reasonable Person. If an involuntary manslaughter conviction can be premised on the theory that a reasonable person would have recognized the riskiness of the defendant's conduct, what characteristics should be ascribed to that reasonable person?

In *State v. Williams*, 484 P.2d 1167 (Wash. Ct. App. 1971), the parents of a 17-month-old child were convicted of involuntary manslaughter when the child died after an abscessed tooth became infected, causing gangrene and eventually pneumonia. The defendants did not seek medical treatment for the baby because they thought he had a toothache and did not realize how ill he was—despite the fact that his cheek was swelling and turned "a bluish color" and "the odor generally associated with gangrene" was present. *Id.* at 1174, 1173. There was also evidence, however, that the defendants "did not take the baby to a doctor because of fear that the Welfare Department would take the baby away from them." *Id.* at 1170. They testified that "they had heard that the defendant husband's cousin lost a child that way." *Id.* at 1174. (Note that the defendants may have "had good reason to be afraid," given that "[w]elfare authorities were at the time quick to remove Native American children from their families and place them with non-Native American families." Stephen P. Garvey, *What's Wrong with Involuntary Manslaughter?*, 85 Tᴇx. L. Rᴇv. 333, 334–35 (2006). In fact, Congress passed the Indian Child Welfare Act, 25 U.S.C. §§ 1901, 1901(4), in 1978 in response to evidence that "an alarmingly high percentage of Indian families are broken up by the removal, often unwarranted, of their children . . . by nontribal public and private agencies." *See* H.R. Rep. No. 95-1386, at 10 (1978) (reporting that 25 to 35 percent of Native-American children were separated from their families and placed in foster care, adoptive homes, or institutions before the statute was enacted).

In affirming the involuntary manslaughter conviction in *Williams* using a simple tort negligence standard,[19] the court described the father as a "24-year-old full-blooded Sheshont Indian with a sixth-grade education" whose "sole occupation is that of laborer," and the mother as a "20-year-old part Indian with an 11th grade education." *Williams*, 484 P.2d at 1169–70. Are any of those factors relevant in evaluating whether the defendants "fail[ed] to exercise the 'ordinary caution' . . . that a man

---

19. Subsequent to *Williams*, however, the state legislature adopted the majority view, requiring more than simple tort negligence to support an involuntary manslaughter conviction. *See State v. Norman*, 808 P.2d 1159, 1163–64 (Wash. Ct. App. 1991) (citing Wash. Rev. Code § 9A.32.070).

of reasonable prudence would exercise under the same or similar conditions"? *Id.* at 1171. (The concept of the reasonable person is addressed in greater detail in the discussion of voluntary manslaughter and reasonable provocation appearing in Notes 11–12 in Section B.2 above.)

6. The Model Penal Code Approach. The Model Penal Code defines manslaughter to include homicide that is "committed recklessly." Model Penal Code § 210.3(1)(a). It also creates a separate crime, negligent homicide, for homicide that is "committed negligently." *Id.* § 210.4(1).

The Comments offer the following explanation for the decision to create two different offenses: "Statutes derived from the common law classify unintentional homicide as involuntary manslaughter without any attempt to distinguish conscious disregard of homicidal risk from inadvertent risk creation. This failure to differentiate across a broad spectrum of culpability raises serious grading difficulties." *Id.* § 210.3 Comment at 53. *See also* David Crump, *"Murder, Pennsylvania Style": Comparing Traditional American Homicide Law to the Statutes of the Model Penal Code*, 109 W. Va. L. Rev. 257, 323, 324 (2007) (commending the MPC's drafters for narrowing the common law's "murder-skip-to-negligence gap," i.e., the "sharp falloff — all the way from murder to a relatively minor offense defined only by gross negligence" — "with no offense in between these two extremes").

In justifying the decision to punish criminally negligent conduct, the drafters of the Model Penal Code observe:

> It has been urged that inadvertent negligence is not a sufficient basis for criminal conviction, both on the utilitarian ground that threatened sanctions cannot influence the inadvertent actor and on the moral ground that criminal punishment should be reserved for cases involving conscious fault. . . .
>
> . . . [N]either contention was regarded by the Institute as persuasive. Criminal punishment of negligent homicide is not impotent to stimulate care that might otherwise not be taken, nor is a person's failure to use his faculties for the protection of others an improper basis for condemnation. The Model Code's definition of negligence insists on proof of substantial fault and limits penal sanctions to cases where "the significance of the circumstances of fact would be apparent to one who shares the community's general sense of right and wrong." Justice is safeguarded by insisting upon that gross deviation from ordinary standards of conduct which is contemplated by the Model Code definition of negligence. Liability for inadvertent risk creation is thus properly limited to cases where the actor is grossly insensitive to the interests and claims of other persons in society.

Model Penal Code § 210.4 Comment at 86–87.

Does the Model Penal Code's approach help clarify the differences between the various categories of unintentional homicide? In distinguishing manslaughter from murder "committed recklessly under circumstances manifesting extreme indifference to the value of human life," *id.* § 210.2(1)(b), the drafters explain that the definition of murder "describes a kind of culpability that differs in degree but not in kind from the ordinary recklessness required for manslaughter." "[U]ltimately," the Comments admit, "this issue must depend on an assessment of blameworthiness by the trier of fact." *Id.* § 210.3 Comment at 53.

Likewise, in defining "recklessness" (the mens rea required for both manslaughter and extreme-indifference murder) as "consciously disregard[ing] a substantial and unjustifiable risk," *id.* § 2.02(2)(c), the drafters note:

> "[S]ubstantial" and "unjustifiable" . . . are terms of degree, and the acceptability of a risk in a given case depends on a great many variables. Some standard is needed for determining *how* unjustifiable the risk must be in order to warrant a finding of culpability. There is no way to state this value judgment that does not beg the question in the last analysis; the point is that the jury must evaluate the actor's conduct and determine whether it should be condemned. The Code proposes, therefore, that this difficulty be accepted frankly, and that the jury be asked to measure the substantiality and unjustifiability of the risk by asking whether its disregard, given the actor's perceptions, involved a gross deviation from the standard of conduct that a law-abiding person in the actor's situation would observe.

Id. § 2.02 Comment at 237. The Comments make the same point when defining "negligence." *See id.* at 241.

Given that the Model Penal Code requires recklessness—and thus conscious awareness of risk—in order to support a manslaughter conviction, the difficulties associated with defining the reasonable person arise only in negligent homicide cases. The MPC considers defendants "negligent" if they "should be aware of a substantial and unjustifiable risk" and the "failure to perceive [that risk] . . . involves a gross deviation from the standard of care that a reasonable person would observe in the actor's situation." *Id.* § 2.02(2)(d). The Comments concede the "inevitable ambiguity" in the term "situation":

> If the actor were blind or if he had just suffered a blow or experienced a heart attack, these would certainly be facts to be considered in a judgment involving criminal liability, as they would be under traditional law. But the heredity, intelligence or temperament of the actor would not be held material in judging negligence, and could not be without depriving the criterion of all its objectivity.

Id. § 2.02 Comment at 242. For a summary of the drafters' similar comments in discussing the word "situation" in § 210.3's definition of extreme emotional disturbance (the MPC's analogue to voluntary manslaughter), see Note 13 in Section B.2 above.

7. **Other Examples of Unintentional Killing.** Consider the following cases with an eye towards distinguishing those where depraved-heart murder charges are

appropriate (extreme-indifference murder under the MPC's formulation); those where involuntary manslaughter is the proper charge (manslaughter or negligent homicide under the MPC); and those where only civil liability should be imposed.

(a) *State v. Jones*, 538 S.E.2d 917 (N.C. 2000): Thomas Richard Jones, who had a previous drunk driving conviction as well as another similar charge pending, was driving with a blood alcohol level of .046, "well below" the state's .08 limit. He had also been taking prescription painkillers, however, despite being told that he should not drink or drive while medicated. Prosecution witnesses testified that shortly before the fatal accident, Jones was speeding, drove up on a curb, and bumped into another vehicle. When he bent down to put a country music tape into his car stereo, he crossed the median and hit an oncoming vehicle, killing two of the college students riding in that car. Jones was convicted of first-degree felony murder (based on the theory that he committed the felony of assault with a deadly weapon — i.e., his car — on three students who survived the accident). He was sentenced to life in prison without parole, apparently the most severe sentence that had ever been imposed in a drunk-driving case, after the jury declined the prosecution's request for the death penalty. The state supreme court reversed, concluding that first-degree murder requires "a mens rea greater than culpable or criminal negligence" — in the case of first-degree felony murder, "an actual intent to commit the underlying felony." Jones subsequently pled guilty to two counts of depraved-heart murder and received a prison sentence of 15 to 18 years. *See* John Hinton, *Guilty Plea Averts Verdict*, WINSTON-SALEM J., Jan. 23, 2003, at A1.

Although convicting drunk drivers of second-degree murder was controversial at one time, such cases are no longer unusual, especially when the defendants were driving in a very reckless fashion or ignored warning signals suggesting that their driving was impaired. *See, e.g., United States v. Sheffey*, 57 F.3d 1419 (6th Cir. 1995) (affirming second-degree murder conviction where the defendant, whose blood alcohol level was .22 two hours after the accident, crossed over a double yellow line on a narrow mountain road, hitting an oncoming car and killing a passenger in that vehicle); *Jeffries v. State*, 90 P.3d 185 (Alaska Ct. App. 2004) (cataloguing cases from other jurisdictions and summarizing the situations in which drunk drivers have been convicted of murder), *aff'd*, 169 P.3d 913 (Alaska 2007). *But cf. People v. Pomykala*, 784 N.E.2d 784 (Ill. 2003) (striking down as unconstitutional a state statute creating a presumption that driving under the influence constitutes the recklessness necessary for reckless homicide). (For a general discussion of the connection between intoxication and criminal liability, see Chapter 4, Section C.3.)

(b) *People v. Choi*: Sung Soo Choi, a Korean Presbyterian missionary, told Kyung-Ja Chung that she was possessed by demons, which were making her arrogant and disobedient to her husband. With Chung's consent, and her husband's assistance, Choi conducted a five-hour exorcism ritual, during which the two men repeatedly stomped and pushed on Chung's abdomen, chest, and thighs with their hands and feet as well as a large spoon. Chung died after suffering massive internal injuries: 16 ribs were fractured, her heart was crushed against her back, and parts of her intestine had shut down. In the first homicide trial in recent times stemming from an exorcism, the judge found the two men guilty of involuntary manslaughter, but acquitted them of second-degree murder. The judge reasoned that the defendants "may have been misguided and blinded by their religious zeal, but were focused on 'saving [the woman] from the demons they believed possessed her.'" Choi received the maximum four-year prison term, and Chung's husband was sentenced to two years in prison. *See* Ann W. O'Neill, *Judge Rules Exorcism Death Manslaughter*, L.A. TIMES, Apr. 17, 1997, at A1.

(c) *State v. McKnight*, 576 S.E.2d 168 (S.C.), *cert. denied*, 540 U.S. 819 (2003): Regina McKnight, a homeless cocaine addict with an I.Q. of 72, gave birth to a stillborn baby girl who had traces of cocaine in her body. McKnight was convicted of homicide by child abuse, defined as "causing the death of a child under the age of 11 while committing child abuse or neglect, . . . under circumstances manifesting an extreme indifference to human life." The state supreme court upheld McKnight's conviction and 20-year prison sentence, rejecting her argument that the statute was not meant to apply to unborn children and reasoning that "the fact that McKnight took cocaine knowing she was pregnant was sufficient evidence to submit to the jury on whether she acted with extreme indifference to her child's life." *Id.* at 173. *But cf. State v. Aiwohi*, 123 P.3d 1210 (Haw. 2005) (holding that a fetus is not a person under the state's manslaughter statute, and therefore reversing manslaughter conviction of a mother whose baby died two days after birth from the toxic effects of crystal meth she smoked during her pregnancy); *State v. Louk*, 786 S.E.2d 219 (W. Va. 2016) (likewise reversing conviction for child neglect resulting in death).

For the view that "legislative fetal protection efforts are on the rise, . . . dramatically exceed[ing] prior limits," and that these statutes "do very little to promote fetal health" and tend to target poor women and women of color, "signify[ing] an eerie return to the eugenics-era past," see Michele Goodwin, *Fetal Protection Laws: Moral Panic and the New Constitutional Battlefront*, 102 CALIF. L. REV. 781, 786, 794 (2014). For a description of these criminal statutes, see 2 WAYNE R. LAFAVE, SUBSTANTIVE CRIMINAL LAW § 14.1, at 95–97 (2d ed. Supp. 2015). See also Chapter 1, Section A.4.b, for a general discussion of the appropriateness of using the criminal law to punish addicted mothers.

(d) *State v. Neumann*, 832 N.W.2d 560 (Wis. 2013): Dale and Leilani Neumann were the parents of an 11-year-old girl who died from juvenile-onset diabetes mellitus, a condition that was still treatable even on the day of her death. The defendants knew their daughter's medical condition was worsening, to the point that she was "pale, limp, unconscious, and unresponsive," but they "identif[ied] as Pentecostals" and believed that "there are spiritual root causes to sickness," that "their prayer and strong religious beliefs [would] cure any health problems," and that seeking medical treatment "would be 'putting the doctor before God,' amounting to idolatry and sin." *Id.* at 571, 570. The couple was convicted of reckless homicide and sentenced to six months in prison and 10 years' probation, and the state supreme court affirmed their convictions. *See also Commonwealth v. Schaible*, 2015 Pa. Super. Unpub. Lexis 3377 (Pa. Super. Ct. Sept. 15, 2015) (rejecting the prosecution's challenge to a prison sentence of 3½ to 7 years imposed after parents pled nolo contendere to depraved-heart murder in a similar case, where a seven-month-old baby died from untreated pneumonia and the parents had been sentenced to 10 years' probation on involuntary manslaughter charges when another of their nine children had died from untreated pneumonia several years earlier). For a discussion of other comparable cases and a description of the laws in some states that immunize parents from prosecution for withholding medical treatment because of religious beliefs, see Suzanne Sataline, *A Child's Death and a Crisis for Faith*, Wall Street J., June 12, 2008, at D1.

(e) *People v. Murray*, 2014 Cal. App. Unpub. Lexis 281 (Cal. Ct. App. Jan. 15, 2014): In a police interview following Michael Jackson's death in 2009, the 50-year-old singer's personal physician, cardiologist Conrad Murray, admitted giving Jackson propofol, an anesthetic usually used during surgery, as a sleeping aid shortly before he stopped breathing. At Murray's trial on involuntary manslaughter charges, however, the defense argued that Jackson took a sedative and injected himself with propofol. In addition to challenging this version of the facts, the prosecution introduced evidence that Murray delayed calling for help after Jackson went into cardiac arrest, instead texting and talking on his cellphone. The coroner's report concluded that Jackson died of acute propofol intoxication, and the autopsy revealed that he had received an amount of propofol equivalent to that administered during major surgery. *See* Randal C. Archibold, *Doctor Is Charged in Death of Jackson*, N.Y. Times, Feb. 9, 2010, at A12; Harriet Ryan & Victoria Kim, *Jury Convicts Murray in Jackson Death*, L.A. Times, Nov. 8, 2011, at A1. The jury convicted Murray and the trial judge sentenced him to the maximum term of four years in prison, citing the doctor's complete lack of remorse and accusing him of practicing "horrible medicine" and being "more concerned with collecting his $150,000-a-month salary than following the Hippocratic oath." *See* Harriet Ryan, *Murray Gets the Maximum*, L.A. Times, Nov. 30, 2011, at A1. The California Court of Appeal rejected Murray's appeal, concluding, inter alia, that sufficient evidence supported his conviction and that the trial judge did not err in refusing to sequester the jury and exclude cameras from the trial. *See People v. Murray*, 2014 Cal. App. Unpub. Lexis 281 (Cal. Ct. App. Jan. 15, 2014), *review denied*, 2014 Cal. Lexis 3018 (Cal. Apr. 23, 2014).

(f) *State v. Mangano*: In the only homicide prosecution stemming from Hurricane Katrina, Mabel and Salvador Mangano, the owners of a New Orleans nursing home that was the site of the largest loss of life during the 2005 hurricane, were charged with negligent homicide after 35 of their residents, some of whom were bedridden, drowned in the home. The prosecution alleged that the defendants acted negligently by ignoring warnings and by refusing (possibly because of concerns about cost) to follow the lead of three other nursing homes, which had successfully evacuated their residents. The government also challenged the adequacy of the defendants' emergency evacuation procedures: they had only a nine-passenger van for a home that accommodated 100 people, and they turned down an offer of two buses the day before the storm. The defense, on the other hand, portrayed the Manganos as caring individuals who chose to stay in the home for fear that leaving would traumatize the elderly residents, and as "victims of a 'government who let us down so terribly'" by failing to take proper care of the New Orleans levees and then failing to issue an evacuation order. After four hours of deliberation, the jury voted to acquit the defendants. As one juror explained, "There were a lot of mistakes made, and it should have been a lot of people answering for it. . . . So why just these two people?" Adam Nossiter, *Trial Starts for Owners of Nursing Home Hit by Storm*, N.Y. TIMES, Aug. 17, 2007, at A19; Adam Nossiter, *Nursing Home Owners Are Acquitted in Deaths*, N.Y. TIMES, Sept. 8, 2007, at A12.

(g) *United States v. SabreTech, Inc.*, 271 F.3d 1018 (11th Cir. 2001): In the first criminal prosecution in this country arising from an airplane accident, both federal and state charges were brought against SabreTech, an aircraft maintenance company that was responsible for packing oxygen generators without safety caps in the cargo hold of a ValuJet airplane. The oxygen generators allegedly heated up, causing a fire in the cargo hold, and the plane ultimately crashed in the Florida Everglades, killing all 110 people on board. The 1996 crash was described by the Eleventh Circuit as "a tragic accident that could have been avoided" and SabreTech was indicted on numerous federal charges, but the jury convicted the company only of willfully failing to train its employees and eight counts of recklessly transporting hazardous materials. The federal judge's original sentence — $2 million in fines and $9 million in restitution — was reduced to three years' probation and a $500,000 fine after the Eleventh Circuit reversed the convictions on the reckless transportation charges, finding that they were based on hazardous materials regulations that had not been properly authorized by the Federal Aviation Act. A separate indictment charging SabreTech with 110 counts of murder and manslaughter was brought in state court. The homicide charges were all dismissed when SabreTech pled no contest to one count of transporting hazardous waste and its parent company agreed to make a $500,000 donation to airline safety and victim services organizations.

Consider also *State v. Ford Motor Co.*, No. 5234 (Ind. Super. Ct., Mar. 13, 1980): in the first U.S. prosecution of a corporation for a death resulting from a defective product, Ford Motor Company was charged with reckless homicide when a safety defect in the fuel system of the Ford Pinto, which tended to cause massive fuel leakages when the car was involved in a rear-end collision at low or moderate speeds, led to the death of three teenagers. Ford's critics claimed that the company had foreseen the problem but decided not to spend the $10 required to alter the car's design after doing "cost-benefit studies on the Pinto that assigned specific value to human life — that, in a word, Ford had callously traded dollars for lives, and was prepared to sacrifice human life for corporate profit." Richard A. Epstein, *Is Pinto a Criminal?*, 4 REGULATION, Mar.–Apr. 1980, at 15. The jury voted to acquit on all charges, reasoning that Ford had done everything possible to recall the car several months before the accident.

[D] Felony Murder

[1] The Policy Issues Surrounding Felony Murder

Nelson E. Roth & Scott E. Sundby, *The Felony-Murder Rule: A Doctrine at Constitutional Crossroads,* 70 Cornell L. Rev. 446, 446–59 (1985)[20]

Few legal doctrines have been as maligned and yet have shown as great a resiliency as the felony-murder rule. Criticism of the rule constitutes a lexicon of everything that scholars and jurists can find wrong with a legal doctrine: it has been described as "astonishing" and "monstrous," an unsupportable "legal fiction," "an unsightly wart on the skin of the criminal law," and . . . an "anachronistic remnant" that has "no logical or practical basis for existence in modern law." . . .

Despite the widespread criticism, the felony-murder rule persists in the vast majority of states. Most states have attempted to limit the rule's potential harshness either by limiting the scope of its operation or by providing affirmative defenses. Such patchwork attempts to mitigate the rule's harshness, however, have been legitimately criticized because "they do not resolve [the rule's] essential illogic." . . . The United States thus remains virtually the only western country still recognizing a rule which makes it possible "that the most serious sanctions known to law might be imposed for accidental homicide."[21]

. . . .

A. The Rule's Historical Development

The origins of the felony-murder rule are disputed. . . .

The purpose of the felony-murder rule at common law is also vague. It is frequently argued that the rule's purpose was not fully articulated because all felonies at common law were punished by death and, therefore, the rule had little practical impact. Further research has revealed, however, the execution rates varied widely according to the felony. One suggested purpose is that the rule served as a means of more severely punishing incomplete or attempted felonies, which were only misdemeanors at common law, if a killing occurred. The rule thus enabled the courts to impose the same punishment as if the felony had succeeded. This purpose, of course, has little

---

20. Copyright © 1985 by the Cornell Law Review. Reprinted with permission.

21. [n.12] England, where the doctrine originated, abolished the felony-murder rule in 1957. The rule apparently never existed in France or Germany. [In a more recent article, another commentator argued that the whole notion of "the harsh 'common law' felony murder rule" is "a myth" because "early [English and American] felony murder rules almost always conditioned murder liability on causing death with fault, even if they did not explicitly require proof of a culpable mental state," and they "certainly did not punish felons for 'accidental' death." Guyora Binder, *The Origins of American Felony Murder Rules*, 57 Stan. L. Rev. 59, 63, 68 (2004). Binder therefore concluded that "it is deeply misleading to say that early felony murder rules imposed strict liability" and "flat wrong to say that they imposed strict liability for accidental death in the course of all felonies." *Id.*]

relevance in modern criminal justice systems, which recognize attempted felonies as serious punishable crimes.

Whatever the felony-murder rule's justification at common law, courts have attempted to provide the rule with a contemporary rationale. These post hoc rationalizations fall into four general categories: deterrence, transferred intent, retribution, and general culpability.

B. Deterrence

The deterrence rationale consists of two different strains. The first approach views the felony-murder rule as a doctrine intended to deter negligent and accidental killings during commission of felonies. Proponents argue that co-felons will dissuade each other from the use of violence if they may be liable for murder. Justice Holmes attempted to justify the rule on this basis by arguing that the rule would be justified if experience showed that death resulted disproportionately from the commission of felonies. . . .

The second view focuses not on the killing, but on the felony itself, and endorses the felony-murder rule as a deterrent to dangerous felonies. From this perspective, punishing both accidental and deliberate killings that result from the commission of a felony is "the strongest possible deterrent" to "undertaking inherently dangerous felonies."

Both of the deterrence justifications are logically flawed and neither has proven to have a basis in fact. The illogic of the felony-murder rule as a means of deterring killing is apparent when applied to accidental killings occurring during the commission of a felony. Quite simply, how does one deter an unintended act? . . . Moreover, any potential deterrence effect on unintentional killings is further reduced because few felons either will know that the felony-murder rule imposes strict liability for resulting deaths or will believe that harm will result from commission of the felony. Finally, statistical evidence has not borne out Holmes's proposed justification that a disproportionate number of killings occur during felonies.

The purpose of deterring the commission of dangerous felonies through the felony-murder rule also lacks a legitimate basis. First, considerable doubt exists that serious crimes are deterred by varying the weight of the punishment. Second, the rule from this perspective uses the sanctions for murder to deter felonies, and "it is usually accepted as wiser to strike at the harm intended by the criminal rather than at the greater harm possibly flowing from his act which was neither intended nor desired by him." Where the killing is unintended, it would be far more sensible to enhance the sentence for conduct over which the felon had control, such as the carrying of a deadly weapon, rather than automatically to elevate the killing to murder. . . .

    . . . .

C. Transferred Intent and Constructive Malice:
The Felony-Murder Rule's Presumption of Culpability

The felony-murder rule may be conceptualized as a theory of "transferred or constructive intent." This theory posits that the intent to commit the felony is "transferred" to the act of killing in order to find culpability for the homicide. . . .

Judges and commentators have criticized the transferred intent theory of felony murder as "an anachronistic remnant" that operates "fictitiously" to broaden unacceptably the scope of murder. . . .

The inapplicability of transferred intent to felony murder becomes evident when the crime's two different mens rea elements are examined: the intent to commit the felony and the culpability for the killing. The mental patterns are . . . distinct and separate; for example, the intent to burglarize cannot be equated with the malice aforethought required for murder. The non-transferability of culpability is even more evident where the felony-murder rule allows elevation of the killing to first degree murder. In such a situation, the rule equates the intent to commit the felony with premeditation and deliberation. . . .

D. Retribution and General Culpability:
A Strict Liability View of the Felony-Murder Rule

. . . .

The "evil mind" theory of felony murder finds its roots in seventeenth and eighteenth century English notions of criminology. Mens rea was a less developed concept and judges focused on the harm resulting from a defendant's illegal act, rather than the maliciousness of his intent. The felony-murder rule thus partly operated on an unarticulated rationale that one who does bad acts cannot complain about being punished for their consequences, no matter how unexpected. Moreover, the felony-murder rule conceived from an "evil mind" perspective comported with the retribution theory of punishment prevailing at the time of the rule's development, which focused on the resulting harm, not on the actor's mental state, in deciding the appropriate punishment. A convict, therefore, bore responsibility for his felony and for any harmful result arising from the crime regardless of his specific intentions.

Continued reliance on a general culpability theory to justify the felony-murder rule has been described as a rather "primitive rationale" and as "a tribute to the tenacity of legal conceptions rooted in simple moral attitudes." The "evil mind" theory conflicts with the basic premise that "the criminal law is concerned not only with guilt or innocence in the abstract but also with the degree of criminal liability." Although the general culpability rationale was perhaps sufficient as long as a general intent of wrongdoing established malice aforethought, it conflicts with the progressive trend of categorizing homicide according to the degree of culpability. Indeed, the felony-murder rule viewed from a general culpability perspective effectively eliminates a mens rea element in convicting a felon for a killing occurring during the commission of a felony, and results in the rule operating as a strict liability crime: the occurrence of a killing is punished as murder regardless of the defendant's culpability.

David Crump & Susan W. Crump,
In Defense of the Felony Murder Doctrine,
8 Harv. J.L. & Pub. Pol'y 359, 361–71 (1985)

A. *Rational Classification and Proportional Grading of Offenses . . .*

. . . .

. . . Felony murder reflects a societal judgment that an intentionally committed robbery that causes . . . death . . . is qualitatively more serious than an identical robbery that does not. . . .

Scholarly criticisms of felony murder have tended . . . to regard mens rea as the only legitimate determinant of the grade of a homicide resulting from a felony. . . . The fallacy of this approach is its denigration of actus reus and its failure to include the result of defendant's conduct . . . . [I]f one must categorize a robbery causing death as either a robbery or a murder, it is the latter category that is the "better fit"; calling such a crime robbery, and robbery only, would distort its significance in the scheme of crime grading.

B. *Condemnation . . .*

A purpose of sentencing closely related to proportionality is that of condemnation. . . . [C]haracterizing a robbery-homicide solely as robbery . . . communicat[es] to the citizenry that the law does not consider a crime that takes a human life to be different from one that does not—a message that would be indistinguishable, in the minds of many, from a devaluation of human life.

Another aspect of condemnation is the expression of solidarity with the victims of crime. If we as a society label a violent offense in a manner that depreciates its significance, we communicate to the victim by implication that we do not understand his suffering. . . .

. . . .

C. *Deterrence*

. . . .

. . . There is mounting evidence that serious crime is subject to deterrence if consequences are adequately communicated. The felony murder rule is just the sort of simple, commonsense, readily enforceable, and widely known principle that is likely to result in deterrence.

. . . .

The argument against deterrence often proceeds on the . . . assumption that felony murder is addressed only to accidental killings . . . . By facilitating proof and simplifying the concept of liability, however, felony murder may deter intentional killings as well. The robber who kills intentionally, but who might claim under oath to have acted accidentally, is thus told that he will be deprived of the benefit of this claim. . . . Furthermore, the . . . proposition that accidental killings cannot be deterred is inconsistent with the widespread belief that the penalizing of negligence, and even the imposition of strict liability, may have deterrent consequences.[22]

Notes and Questions

1. Accidental Deaths Occurring in the Course of a Felony. In *People v. Stamp*, 82 Cal. Rptr. 598 (Cal. Ct. App. 1969), three defendants were convicted of felony murder and sentenced to life imprisonment when the owner of a business they robbed died of a heart attack approximately 15 minutes after the armed robbery. In affirming the convictions, the court thought it irrelevant that the victim, an overweight 60-year-old man with a history of heart problems, might have died soon anyway.

Likewise, in *State v. McClain*, 623 A.2d 280 (N.J. Super. Ct. App. Div. 1993), the defendant was convicted of felony murder and sentenced to 30 years in prison when his accomplice snatched the purse of a 69-year-old woman, who went into cardiac arrest while pursuing him. Although the woman was resuscitated, she never regained consciousness and died seven months later. The court observed that "[f]elony murder is an absolute-liability crime because the actor need not have contemplated or consciously risked the victim's death." *Id.* at 282.

Is felony murder an appropriate verdict in these cases because "the robber takes his victim as he finds him"? *Stamp*, 82 Cal. Rptr. at 603. Or is it unreasonable to bring murder charges in cases where the victim of a felony fortuitously dies, especially if the defendant treated the victim politely and gently in an effort to minimize any risk of harm? *Cf.* J. Michael Kennedy, *"Gentleman Bandit" Turns Self in After 100 Robberies*, L.A. TIMES, Aug. 28, 1991, at A1 (describing a series of robberies committed by an unemployed computer programmer in Texas, who used a small antique revolver that "wouldn't fire because the hammer was frozen," who "would apologize as he tied people up, make them as comfortable as possible, return pictures of the grand-kids that he found in wallets, [and] call the front desk of hotels to tell them the guest in Room 319 could use some help getting untied," and who called for an ambulance when one of his victims had a heart attack).

2. The Model Penal Code Approach. The drafters of the Model Penal Code would have preferred to abandon the common-law doctrine of felony murder, but they concluded that outright abolition was "impolitic, given the weight of prosecutive opposition." Herbert Wechsler, *Codification of Criminal Law in the United States: The Model Penal Code*, 68 COLUM. L. REV. 1425, 1446 (1968). Instead, the MPC provides that the elements of recklessness and extreme indifference to life necessary to make out a case of murder under §210.2(1)(b)—homicide "committed recklessly under circumstances manifesting extreme indifference to the value of human

---

22. Note that in a subsequent article, Professor Crump advocated limiting felony murder charges to cases where the felons themselves "engage in an act that is 'clearly dangerous to human life.'" David Crump, *Reconsidering the Felony Murder Rule in Light of Modern Criticisms: Doesn't the Conclusion Depend upon the Particular Rule at Issue?*, 32 HARV. J.L. & PUB. POL'Y 1155, 1166 (2009).

life"—are "presumed" to exist if the defendant was committing one of the specific felonies listed in § 210.2(1)(b). For a description of the practical impact of this rebuttable presumption, see MPC § 1.12(5).

The Comments explain:

> This doctrine aside, the criminal law does not predicate liability simply on conduct causing the death of another. Punishment for homicide obtains only when the deed is done with a state of mind that makes it reprehensible as well as unfortunate. . . . [The felony murder rule] bases conviction of murder not on any proven culpability with respect to homicide but on liability for another crime. The underlying felony carries its own penalty and the additional punishment for murder is therefore gratuitous. . . .

Id. § 210.2 Comment at 36.

The Comments do acknowledge that "[f]or the vast majority of cases it is probably true that homicide occurring during the commission or attempted commission of a felony is murder independent of the felony-murder rule." *Id.* at 37. Nevertheless, they continue, "criminal liability attaches to individuals not generalities," and "[i]t is a weak rejoinder to a complaint of unjust conviction to say that for most persons in the defendant's situation the result would have been appropriate." *Id.* In addition, the Comments point out:

> First, there is no basis in experience for thinking that homicides *which the evidence makes accidental* occur with disproportionate frequency in connection with specified felonies.[23] Second, it remains indefensible in principle to

---

23. [n.96] In fact, the number of all homicides which occur in the commission of such crimes as robbery, burglary, or rape is lower than might be expected. For example, comparison of the figures for solved and unsolved homicides from M. Wolfgang, Criminal Homicide (1985), with statistics on basic felonies taken from the FBI Uniform Crime Reports reveals the following for Philadelphia from 1948–1952:

Relation of Total Felonies to Homicides Occurring
During the Felony Philadelphia 1948–1952

Offense	No. of Crimes Reported	No. Accompanied by Homicide	%	No. per 1000
Robbery	6,432	38	0.59	5.9
Rape	1,133	4	0.35	3.5
Burglary	27,669	1	0.0036	.36
Auto Theft	10,315	2	0.019	1.9

. . . More recent statistics derived from N.J. State Police, Crime in New Jersey: Uniform Crime Reports 42–45 (1975) reveal strikingly similar percentages. In 1975, 16,273 robberies were committed in New Jersey, and 66 homicides resulted from these robberies, only .41 per cent, a figure even lower than the earlier statistics from . . . Philadelphia. When other violent felonies are taken into account, this percentage drops even lower. In 1975, there were 1,382 forcible rapes and 111,264 forcible breaking-and-enterings in New Jersey in addition to the 16,273 robberies. These crimes resulted in 136 deaths. Thus only .10 per cent of these serious felonies resulted in homicide.

use the sanctions that the law employs to deal with murder unless there is at least a finding that the actor's conduct manifested an extreme indifference to the value of human life. The fact that the actor was engaged in a crime of the kind that is included in the usual first-degree felony-murder enumeration or was an accomplice in such crime . . . will frequently justify such a finding. Indeed, the probability that such a finding will be justified seems high enough to warrant the presumption of extreme indifference. . . . But liability depends, as plainly it should, upon the crucial finding.

Id. at 38–39.

Professors Crump and Crump offered several responses to these comments:

First, the very data offered by the Code's Reporter give precisely such a "basis in experience" by showing that homicides during robberies are more than thirty times as likely as homicides during auto thefts. "Robbery victims run a high risk of injury . . . [,]" [with the] likelihood of injury rang[ing] from 53% if the weapon is a stick to 17% if it is a gun. . . . Second, felony-homicides are the most serious kind of homicides in terms of public concern, even if they do comprise a small percentage of total homicides. Third, the Model Penal Code begs the question by addressing homicides "which the evidence makes accidental." Usually, the evidence in this regard is ambiguous, and that is a major point of the felony murder rule.

David Crump & Susan W. Crump, *In Defense of the Felony Murder Doctrine*, 8 Harv. J.L. & Pub. Pol'y 359, 370 n.43 (1985). *See also* David Crump, *Reconsidering the Felony Murder Rule in Light of Modern Criticisms: Doesn't the Conclusion Depend upon the Particular Rule at Issue?*, 32 Harv. J.L. & Pub. Pol'y 1155, 1164 (2009) (criticizing the MPC approach as "an odd combination" of "a confusing concept of recklessness coupled with a presumption," which is "likely to produce inconsistency and arbitrariness in verdicts").

Only New Hampshire has adopted a felony murder statute modeled on the Model Penal Code. *See* N.H. Rev. Stat. Ann. §630:1-b (presuming the recklessness and extreme indifference necessary for second-degree murder if the defendant "causes the death by the use of a deadly weapon in the commission of . . . any class A felony"). *Cf.* Guyora Binder, *Felony Murder and Mens Rea Default Rules: A Study in Statutory Interpretation*, 4 Buff. Crim. L. Rev. 399, 433 (2000) (noting that the "practical consequence" of the New Hampshire statute has been "the abolition of felony murder" in that state).

[*See also* Federal Bureau of Investigation, Crime in the United States 2015: Uniform Crime Reports, https://ucr.fbi.gov/crime-in-the-u.s/2015/crime-in-the-u.s.-2015/home (taking into account the murders reported in 2015 for which information was available, .18 percent of robberies, .046 percent of arsons, .013 percent of rapes, .0065 percent of burglaries, and .0058 percent of auto thefts resulted in death).]

The lack of enthusiasm for the MPC's approach prompted one commentator to observe that "[o]f all the reforms proposed by the Model Penal Code, perhaps none has been less influential." George P. Fletcher, *Reflections on Felony-Murder*, 12 Sw. U. L. Rev. 413, 413 (1981). *Cf.* Binder, *supra*, at 485 (arguing that states which have adopted default mens rea rules like those contained in MPC §§ 2.02(3) and 2.02(4) cannot consistently adhere to the traditional strict-liability approach to felony murder).

3. The Deterrent Rationale for the Felony Murder Rule. Even though the felony murder doctrine contravenes modern notions of culpability and mens rea, is it nevertheless justifiable because of its deterrent effect — either because it discourages potential offenders from committing felonies, or because it encourages those who commit felonies to do so carefully in order to avoid accidental deaths?

Consider Oliver W. Holmes, The Common Law 57–58 (1881):

> [I]f a man does an act with intent to commit a felony, and thereby accidentally kills another, . . . [t]he fact that the shooting is felonious does not make it any more likely to kill people. If the object of the rule is to prevent such accidents, it should make accidental killing with firearms murder, not accidental killing in the effort to steal; while, if its object is to prevent stealing, it would be better to hang one thief in every thousand by lot.

4. Constitutional Issues. Some commentators have questioned the constitutionality of the felony murder doctrine. For example, Professors Roth and Sundby have argued that the felony murder rule violates both the Due Process Clause's presumption of innocence (by conclusively presuming malice from the commission of a felony) and the Eighth Amendment's prohibition of cruel and unusual punishment (by imposing strict liability for a serious, nonregulatory crime like murder). *See* Nelson E. Roth & Scott E. Sundby, *The Felony-Murder Rule: A Doctrine at Constitutional Crossroads*, 70 Cornell L. Rev. 446, 469–71, 490–91 (1985).

In a similar vein, the Canadian Supreme Court ruled that the felony murder doctrine violated two portions of Canada's Charter of Rights and Freedoms: the presumption of innocence and the provision prohibiting deprivations of life, liberty, or security without fundamental justice. *See The Queen v. Vaillancourt*, [1987] 2 S.C.R. 636 (Can.).

Nevertheless, constitutional challenges to the felony murder doctrine have not proven particularly successful in this country, and most courts have rejected such constitutional arguments outright. These courts respond to the due process concerns by explaining that felony murder statutes do not unconstitutionally create a conclusive presumption or shift the burden of proof to the defendant, but merely eliminate malice or mens rea as an element of the crime. And they reason that the sentences imposed for felony murder are not so grossly disproportionate to the crime in all cases as to violate the Eighth Amendment. *See, e.g., People v. Dillon*, 668 P.2d 697, 716–18 (Cal. 1983); *State v. Hernandez*, 528 A.2d 794, 798–800 (Conn. 1987); *State v. Burkhart*, 103 P.3d 1037, 1046–48 (Mont. 2004); *State v. Oimen*, 516 N.W.2d 399, 408–09

(Wis. 1994); *Mares v. State*, 939 P.2d 724, 728–30 (Wyo. 1997). *See also People v. Chun*, 203 P.3d 425, 431 (Cal. 2009) (rejecting separation of powers challenge to the state's second-degree felony murder rule and upholding its constitutionality as a judicial interpretation of the murder statute's requirement of "malice aforethought" even though "no statute specifically spells it out").

Several courts, however, have sidestepped such constitutional challenges by interpreting their felony murder statutes to require proof of one of the mental states necessary to constitute murder. *See People v. Aaron*, 299 N.W.2d 304, 326 (Mich. 1980); *State v. Ortega*, 817 P.2d 1196, 1201–08 (N.M. 1991); *State v. Doucette*, 470 A.2d 676, 682 (Vt. 1983). In addition, at least one state legislature has included a mens rea requirement in its felony murder statute. *See* Del. Code Ann. tit. 11, §§ 635–636 (requiring proof that defendants recklessly caused death for first-degree felony murder and that they acted with criminal negligence for second-degree felony murder).

5. The Persistence of Felony Murder. Despite the academic criticisms leveled at felony murder, the rule remains in effect in most American jurisdictions. In addition to New Hampshire and the handful of states described in the prior Note, Hawaii and Kentucky are the only states whose homicide statutes contain no felony murder rule. *See* Haw. Rev. Stat. § 707-701.5 (limiting murder to intentional or knowing killings); Ky. Rev. Stat. Ann. § 507.020 (requiring intent to kill in most murder cases). Moreover, unintentional deaths resulting from felonies are punished only as involuntary manslaughter in Ohio. *See* Ohio Rev. Code Ann. § 2903.04.

As described in the following Section, however, the jurisdictions that retain the felony murder doctrine have imposed various limits on its reach. Given these exceptions, one critic of felony murder believes that it can be "rationally support[ed] as necessary to impose deserved punishment" if it is confined to cases "involv[ing] both the negligent imposition of risk" and an independent and "distinct malicious purpose." Guyora Binder, *Making the Best of Felony Murder*, 91 B.U. L. Rev. 403, 409 (2011). After reading the discussion that follows, ask yourself whether you agree with that assessment.

[2] Limitations on the Felony Murder Doctrine

[a] Inherently Dangerous Felonies

People v. Howard
104 P.3d 107 (Cal. 2005)

Kennard, Justice.

. . . .

I

At 12:40 a.m. on May 23, 2002, California Highway Patrol Officer Gary Stephany saw defendant driving a Chevrolet Tahoe (a sport utility vehicle) without a rear license plate, and signaled him to pull over. Defendant stopped on the side of the road. But when Officer Stephany and his partner, Officer Wayne Bernard, got out of their patrol car, defendant restarted the engine and sped to a nearby freeway. The officers gave chase at speeds of up to 90 miles per hour and radioed for assistance. . . .

Minutes later, Officer Anthony Arcelus and his partner, Officer Bret Boss, who had been monitoring the pursuit on their car radio, saw the Tahoe . . . and took up the chase. Officer Arcelus, who was driving, estimated the Tahoe's speed at more than 80 miles per hour, and he saw it run a stop sign and a traffic light. By then, the car's headlights were . . . turned off. Up to that point, the chase had taken place in rural parts of Fresno County. When the Tahoe started heading toward downtown Fresno, Officer Arcelus gave up the pursuit, fearing that the high-speed chase might cause an accident.

About a minute after Officer Arcelus stopped chasing the Tahoe, he saw it run a red light half a mile ahead of him and collide with a car driven by Jeanette Rodriguez. Rodriguez was killed and her husband [Robert], a passenger in the car, was seriously injured. It turned out that the Tahoe that defendant was driving had been stolen earlier that day. Defendant, who was also injured in the crash, was arrested and charged with murder [of Jeanette], with causing serious bodily injury [to Robert] while evading a police officer ([Vehicle Code] § 2800.3), and with evading a police officer in willful or wanton disregard for the safety of persons or property (§ 2800.2).

At trial, . . . [a]n accident reconstruction expert testified that at the time of the accident the Tahoe was traveling over 80 miles per hour, and Rodriguez's car was traveling close to the posted speed limit of 35 miles per hour. . . .

Forensic toxicologist Roger Peterson, a witness for the defense, testified that defendant had a "high amount" of methamphetamine in his bloodstream at the time of the accident. A person under the influence of methamphetamine, Peterson said, might drive at excessive speeds, might have trouble staying in a single lane, and might not notice traffic lights and signs. Defendant also had marijuana in his bloodstream, but not enough to be under the influence. Victim [Jeanette] Rodriguez's bloodstream contained morphine (a metabolite of heroin) and benzoyleconine (a metabolite of cocaine). Based on this evidence, toxicologist Peterson expressed his opinion that [she] was under the influence of heroin and possibly cocaine when the accident occurred.

Defendant testified on his own behalf. He admitted stealing the Tahoe and fleeing from the Highway Patrol officers. He did so because his probation officer had told him he would go to prison if he was again caught in a stolen car. He could only remember bits and pieces of the chase. He described himself as a skilled driver; his cousin, a race car driver, had taught him to drive "sprint cars" at a racetrack. He saw the victims' car before the accident but could not recall hitting it. . . .

The jury convicted defendant of all counts [and he received a prison sentence of 15 years to life]. The Court of Appeal affirmed. . . .

II

Because the second degree felony-murder rule is a court-made rule, it has no statutory definition. This court has described it thusly: "A homicide that is a direct causal result of the commission of a felony inherently dangerous to human life (other than the . . . felonies enumerated in Pen. Code, § 189[24]) constitutes at least second degree murder." The rule "eliminates the need for proof of malice in connection with a charge of murder." It is not an evidentiary presumption but a substantive rule of law, which is based on the theory that "when society has declared certain inherently dangerous conduct to be felonious, a defendant should not be allowed to excuse himself by saying he was unaware of the danger to life because, by declaring the conduct to be felonious, society has warned him of the risk involved."

Because the second degree felony-murder rule is "a judge-made doctrine without any express basis in the Penal Code," its constitutionality has been questioned. And, as we have noted in the past, legal scholars have criticized the rule for incorporating "an artificial concept of strict criminal liability that 'erodes the relationship between criminal liability and moral culpability.'" Therefore, we have repeatedly stressed that the rule "deserves no extension beyond its required application."

"In determining whether a felony is inherently dangerous [under the second degree felony-murder rule], the court looks to the elements of the felony in the abstract, 'not the "particular" facts of the case,' i.e., not to the defendant's specific conduct." That is, we determine whether the felony "by its very nature . . . cannot be committed without creating a substantial risk that someone will be killed. . . ."

Felonies that have been held inherently dangerous to life [in this state] include shooting at an inhabited dwelling, poisoning with intent to injure, arson of a motor vehicle, grossly negligent discharge of a firearm, manufacturing methamphetamine, kidnapping, and reckless or malicious possession of a destructive device.

Felonies that have been held not inherently dangerous to life [in this state] include practicing medicine without a license under conditions creating a risk of great bodily harm, serious physical or mental illness, or death; false imprisonment by violence, menace, fraud, or deceit; possession of a concealable firearm by a convicted felon; possession of a sawed-off shotgun; escape; grand theft; conspiracy to possess methedrine; extortion; furnishing phencyclidine; and child endangerment or abuse.

III

In determining whether section 2800.2 is an offense inherently dangerous to life, we begin by reviewing the statutory scheme. Three statutes punish those who flee from police officers: sections 2800.1, 2800.2, and 2800.3.

---

24. Section 189, which is reprinted above in Section A, defines first-degree murder to include killings committed in the course of specific enumerated felonies: arson, rape, carjacking, robbery, burglary, mayhem, kidnapping, train wrecking, torture, and various sex offenses.

Section 2800.1 states that any motorist who "with the intent to evade, willfully flees or otherwise attempts to elude" a peace officer pursuing on a motor vehicle or bicycle is, under specified circumstances, guilty of a misdemeanor.

Under section 2800.3, when "willful flight or attempt to elude a pursuing peace officer in violation of Section 2800.1 proximately causes death or serious bodily injury to any person," the offense is a wobbler (an offense that can be a felony or a misdemeanor, at the trial court's discretion), punishable by up to five years in prison.

Section 2800.2, which was the basis for defendant's conviction under the second degree felony-murder rule, provides:

> "(a) If a person flees or attempts to elude a pursuing peace officer in violation of Section 2800.1 and the pursued vehicle is driven in a willful or wanton disregard for the safety of persons or property, the person driving the vehicle, upon conviction, shall be punished by imprisonment in the state prison [for 16 months, two years, or three years], or by confinement in the county jail [for not less than six months nor more than one year]. The court may also impose a fine . . . or may impose both that imprisonment or confinement and fine.

> "(b) For purposes of this section, a willful or wanton disregard for the safety of persons or property includes, but is not limited to, driving while fleeing or attempting to elude a pursuing peace officer during which time either three or more violations that are assigned a traffic violation point count under Section 12810 occur, or damage to property occurs."

> . . . .

Violations that are assigned points under section 12810 and can be committed without endangering human life include driving an unregistered vehicle owned by the driver, driving with a suspended license, driving on a highway at slightly more than 55 miles per hour when a higher speed limit has not been posted, failing to come to a complete stop at a stop sign, and making a right turn without signaling for 100 feet before turning.

. . . [Thus,] subdivision (b) [which was added in 1996] greatly expanded the meaning of the . . . statutory phrase ["willful or wanton disregard for the safety of persons or property"] to include conduct that ordinarily would not be considered particularly dangerous.[25]

. . . [A] violation of section 2800.2 is not, in the abstract, inherently dangerous to human life. Therefore, the second degree felony-murder rule does not apply when a killing occurs during a violation of section 2800.2. . . .

---

25. [n.2] Justice Baxter's dissenting opinion stresses that the trial court's instructions to the jury left the phrase "willful or wanton disregard for the safety of persons or property" undefined, and did not mention the Legislature's broad definition of that phrase. . . . But in determining whether a felony is inherently dangerous, we must consider the law enacted by the Legislature, regardless of the jury instructions in a particular case. . . .

Nothing here should be read as saying that a motorist who kills an innocent person in a hazardous, high-speed flight from a police officer should not be convicted of murder. A jury may well find that the motorist has acted with malice by driving with conscious disregard for the lives of others, and thus is guilty of murder. But, as we have explained, not all violations of section 2800.2 pose a danger to human life. Therefore, the prosecution may not (as it did here) resort to the second degree felony-murder rule to remove from the jury's consideration the question whether a killing that occurred during a violation of section 2800.2 was done with malice.

BROWN, JUSTICE, concurring and dissenting.

. . . .

Here, defendant was convicted solely on a second degree felony-murder theory. The majority appears to acknowledge the rule is constitutionally and analytically suspect. . . . I agree, but I would go farther and abrogate the rule entirely. As the facts of this case conclusively demonstrate, the application of the second degree felony-murder rule remains irredeemably arbitrary.

The majority concludes, based on a technical parsing of the provision's grammar, that a violation of Vehicle Code section 2800.2 is not an inherently dangerous felony for purposes of second degree felony murder. However, a commonsense construction of the statute's language leads to the opposite conclusion—a conclusion that is considerably less counterintuitive. As one lower court stated in addressing the same issue we review here, "It would seem clear as a matter of logic that any felony whose key element is 'wanton disregard' for human life necessarily falls within the scope of 'inherently dangerous' felonies. . . . [A]part from the 'wanton disregard' element, one must also be engaged in the act of fleeing from a pursuing peace officer whose vehicle is displaying lights and sirens. Any high-speed pursuit is inherently dangerous to the lives of the pursuing police officers. In even the most ethereal of abstractions, it is not possible to imagine that the 'wanton disregard' of the person fleeing does not encompass disregard for the safety of the pursuing officers." . . .

Indeed, I agree with Justice Baxter that if any offense should easily qualify as inherently dangerous, Vehicle Code section 2800.2 certainly would. Although it is possible to imagine slow motion pursuits where neither people nor property are harmed, the facts of this case present the more likely scenario . . . .

. . . Two other [California] Court of Appeal decisions have concluded that a violation of Vehicle Code section 2800.2 is an inherently dangerous felony. In this case, two members of this court and a unanimous Court of Appeal reached the same conclusion. The fact that such variations are not just possible, but actually inevitable, suggests a level of arbitrariness we should make every effort to eliminate from the criminal law. For that reason, as well as other concerns discussed more fully in [my dissenting opinion in *People v. Robertson* (2004) 95 P.3d 872], I would abrogate the nonstatutory second degree felony-murder rule and leave it to the Legislature to define precisely what conduct subjects a defendant to strict criminal liability.

[Justice Brown's dissent in *Robertson* had this to say about the inherently dangerous felony limitation:

. . . [The second-degree felony murder rule] requires the court to determine both how the predicate felony is to be defined and what threshold of dangerousness is sufficient. Even when a court agrees to look at the elements of the felony in the abstract, i.e., whether the commission of the crime as defined by the statute poses a danger to human life, reasonable judges can disagree about the legitimacy of contracting or expanding the statutory definition of a felony in order to conclude that a particular violation should be deemed inherently dangerous. . . .

Moreover, which felonies are inherently dangerous to human life is not self-evident. When a homicide results, it is clear that, in the particular circumstances, the predicate felony was dangerous to human life, but that does not tell us whether it should be deemed so in the abstract. (*See, e.g., People v. Lopez* (1971) 489 P.2d 1372 [since Pen. Code, § 4532, relating to escape, draws no relevant distinction between sneaking away and killing a guard to obtain a key, it proscribes an offense, which considered in the abstract, is not inherently dangerous to human life]; *People v. Henderson*, [(1977) 560 P.2d 1180] [predicate felony of false imprisonment, viewed as a whole in the abstract, is not inherently dangerous to human life]; *but see People v. Patterson*, [(1989) 778 P.2d 549] [the fact that Health & Saf. Code, § 11352 includes a variety of offenses does not preclude the court from determining that the "primary element" of furnishing a dangerous drug is inherently dangerous].)

Nor does the phrase "inherently dangerous" tell us exactly how dangerous a felony has to be to justify obviating the malice requirement. Over time, the court has shifted from a standard that only required a showing that the predicate felony posed an inherent danger to human life, to one requiring that the predicate felony involve "a substantial risk that someone will be killed," and then to a more recent position that an act is "inherently dangerous" to human life when there is a high probability that it will result in death. In this case [*Robertson*], the majority cites both standards, reasoning that a high probability does not mean a greater than 50 percent chance.]

BAXTER, JUSTICE, dissenting.

. . . .

The majority invoke the premise that second degree felony murder only occurs in the commission of a felony which is inherently dangerous in the abstract—one which, by its very nature, cannot be committed without creating a substantial risk, or a high probability, that someone will be killed. . . .

The majority focus upon subdivision (b) of section 2800.2, which was added in 1996. . . .

I am not persuaded. Subdivision (a) of section 2800.2 gives clear and specific notice that one who, in order to elude police pursuit, drives with reckless indifference to safety is guilty of a felony. Such reckless driving is, of course, inherently dangerous—by definition, it creates a substantial risk that someone will be killed. Moreover, there is no doubt that defendant committed exactly the reckless endangerment of human life forbidden by the statute. . . .

Conversely, the principal reason for applying the felony-murder rule is present. The purpose of the felony-murder doctrine "is to deter those engaged in felonies from killing negligently or accidentally." Because the doctrine absolves the prosecution from proving malice, it properly applies when "the killer is engaged in a felony whose inherent danger to human life renders logical an imputation of malice on the part of all who commit it."

 . . . .

Under such circumstances, it perverts reason to refuse to apply the felony-murder rule simply because subdivision (b) of section 2800.2 may additionally describe a nondangerous felony. Where society has warned, in plain statutory words, that the particular conduct committed by the defendant is both dangerous and felonious, it should not matter that the statute may forbid nondangerous conduct as well.

 . . . .

Notes and Questions

1. **Competing Ways of Defining Inherently Dangerous Felonies.** Unlike California, the majority of states that have adopted the inherently dangerous rule determine which felonies are sufficiently dangerous by looking at the facts and circumstances of the particular case. In most such jurisdictions, a felony is considered inherently dangerous if it is either inherently dangerous in the abstract or was committed in an inherently dangerous fashion. *See, e.g.*, *Metts v. State*, 511 S.E.2d 508, 510 (Ga. 1999); *State v. Jacques*, 14 P.3d 409, 417 (Kan. 2000); *Fisher v. State*, 786 A.2d 706, 733 (Md. 2001); *Commonwealth v. Ortiz*, 560 N.E.2d 698, 701 (Mass. 1990).

2. **The Rationale Underlying the Inherently Dangerous Felony Limitation.** What is the justification for limiting the felony murder doctrine to inherently dangerous felonies? Justice Baxter's dissent in *Howard* suggested that only an intent to commit an inherently dangerous felony can be deemed sufficiently culpable to impute the malice required for murder. If so, why should it matter whether the defendant's felony was inherently dangerous in the abstract or under the particular circumstances of the case? For the view that felony murder is no longer a strict liability crime in jurisdictions following the inherently dangerous felony rule, see Kenneth W. Simons, *When Is Strict Criminal Liability Just?*, 87 J. Crim. L. & Criminology 1075, 1121–22 (1997).

3. **The Function of the Felony Murder Doctrine.** Does a court's view of the felony murder rule's purpose determine which definition of inherently dangerous felonies it favors? As reflected in Justice Baxter's dissenting opinion in *Howard*, the California Supreme Court has generally taken the position that the felony murder doctrine is intended to deter felons from killing negligently or accidentally, not to deter them from committing the underlying felonies themselves. *See, e.g.*, *People v. Patterson*, 778 P.2d 549, 557 (Cal. 1989); *People v. Burroughs*, 678 P.2d 894, 900 (Cal. 1984).

Does this theory of felony murder support the court's adoption of the abstract approach?

4. The Impact of the Competing Definitions of Inherently Dangerous Felonies. Was the California Supreme Court wise to choose to define inherently dangerous felonies using the abstract approach? Consider that court's critique of the circumstances approach:

> If . . . a court were to examine the particular facts of the case prior to establishing whether the underlying felony is inherently dangerous, the court might well be led to conclude the rule applicable despite any unfairness which might redound to the defendant by so broad an application: the existence of the dead victim might appear to lead inexorably to the conclusion that the underlying felony is exceptionally hazardous.

People v. Patterson, 778 P.2d 549, 554 (Cal. 1989) (quoting *People v. Burroughs*, 678 P.2d 894, 897–98 (Cal. 1984)).

On the other hand, is the abstract approach subject to criticism because so few felonies are inherently dangerous when viewed in the abstract? Reconsider the felonies listed by the *Howard* majority that are not considered inherently dangerous in California. If some of these decisions seem wrong, is the standard adopted by the California courts to blame or the way that standard has been applied?

Recall, as explained by Justice Brown, that the California Supreme Court has changed its view over time as to how "inherently" dangerous a felony needs to be in the abstract in order to support a felony murder conviction. For the view that California's felony murder rule has become unconstitutionally vague as a result of these inconsistencies, particularly on the question whether courts should engage in a "theoretical" analysis of what "minimum conduct (in terms of dangerousness)" is necessary to commit the felony, or alternatively an "empirical" analysis of how the felony is "ordinar[ily]" committed, see Evan Tsen Lee, *Why California's Second-Degree Felony-Murder Rule Is Now Void for Vagueness*, 43 Hastings Const. L.Q. 1, 28 (2015).

Note that some other courts that use the abstract approach to define inherently dangerous felonies have reached conclusions comparable to those reached in California, while others have disagreed. *Compare State v. Lucas*, 759 P.2d 90 (Kan. 1988) (finding that child abuse is an inherently dangerous felony in the abstract), *with State v. Anderson*, 666 N.W.2d 696 (Minn. 2003) (holding that weapons possession offenses—possession of a weapon by an ex-felon and possession of a stolen firearm— are not inherently dangerous in the abstract).

5. Drug Trafficking as an Inherently Dangerous Felony. In *People v. Patterson*, 778 P.2d 549 (Cal. 1989), the victim died of a drug overdose after consuming cocaine supplied by the defendant. The California Supreme Court declined to decide whether the felony of furnishing cocaine is inherently dangerous, although it indicated that the inquiry should not focus on the entire range of conduct prohibited by the statute, which included transporting, importing, selling, furnishing, and administering a variety of controlled substances, but instead on whether the specific drug (cocaine) and criminal act (furnishing) involved in the particular case created "a high probability of death." *Id.* at 558. Does *Howard* deviate from this approach in analyzing the dangerousness of the flight crime at issue there?

Other courts that have wrestled with the drug trafficking question have reached conflicting results. In *People v. Taylor*, 8 Cal. Rptr. 2d 439 (Cal. Ct. App. 1992), the California Court of Appeal applied the standard set out in *Patterson* and concluded that furnishing PCP is not an inherently dangerous felony. The court explained that "[m]erely conveying the drug to another does not require that it be consumed." *Id.* at 449. In addition, the court reasoned, "[e]ven when consumed, PCP does not carry a high probability of death" because "[i]t is almost impossible to overdose on it" and "the vast majority of users, 90 to 95 percent, do not suffer any untoward effects on any given occasion." *Id.*

Likewise, in *State v. Wesson*, 802 P.2d 574, 579 (Kan. 1990), the Kansas Supreme Court applied the abstract approach and determined that "[t]here is nothing inherently violent or forcible in the sale of crack cocaine." The court observed that "[t]he violence accompanying drug sales is coincidental rather than necessarily inherent," and, in fact, "violence is only involved in an extremely small percentage of the sales of illicit drugs." *Id.* at 580, 581. The court therefore held that felony murder charges could not be brought in that case, where the defendant stabbed a customer who tried to run off with the defendant's drugs without paying for them. *See also State v. Aarsvold*, 376 N.W.2d 518, 522 (Minn. Ct. App. 1985) (refusing to characterize the sale of cocaine as inherently dangerous because the "use of cocaine, even when injected, does not generally cause death").

By contrast, other courts have applied the circumstances approach and reached the opposite conclusion. *See Williams v. State*, 779 S.E.2d 304, 309 (Ga. 2015) (finding possession with intent to distribute inherently dangerous where the defendant's one-year-old daughter "ingested [a] deadly dose of cocaine" after discovering it "inside a hole in the living room sofa," a place "accessible" to the child where the defendant "typically hid[]" the drugs he was planning to sell); *State v. Taylor*, 626 A.2d 201, 202 (R.I. 1993) (per curiam) (concluding that it was inherently dangerous for the defendant to administer methadone without a doctor's advice to a five-year-old child who had a respiratory infection); *Heacock v. Commonwealth*, 323 S.E.2d 90, 94 (Va. 1984) (reasoning in dictum that the distribution of cocaine was inherently dangerous because the defendant, who supplied the cocaine and also helped prepare the dose for the victim to inject, had seen another person react violently to the same drugs; because injecting any amount of cocaine can lead to cardiac arrest; and because the state had considered the "risk to the public health" in classifying cocaine as a controlled substance).

Recently, a number of state legislatures have intervened, amending their homicide statutes to make clear that felony drug charges can lead to a felony murder conviction.

See, e.g., Fla. Stat. Ann. §782.04(1)(a)(3); Kan. Stat. Ann. §21-5402(c)(1)(N) (thus superseding *Wesson*); Minn. Stat. Ann. §§609.185(a)(3), 609.195(b) (nullifying *Aarsvold*); N.J. Stat. Ann. §2C:35–9.

[b] The Merger Exception

Rose v. State

255 P.3d 291 (Nev. 2011)

DOUGLAS, CHIEF JUSTICE.

In this appeal, we address whether a charge of assault with a deadly weapon merges with a charged homicide so that it cannot be used as the basis for second-degree felony murder. To maintain the narrow confines of second-degree felony murder, wherein the felonies that can be used to support a conviction are not statutorily enumerated and the use of the felony-murder rule has "the potential for untoward prosecutions," we hold that assaultive-type felonies that involve a threat of immediate violent injury merge with a charged homicide for purposes of second-degree felony murder and therefore cannot be used as the basis for a second-degree felony-murder conviction. Whether the felony is assaultive must be determined by the jury based on the manner in which the felony was committed. Because the crime at issue here, assault with a deadly weapon, could be assaultive based on the manner in which it was committed, we conclude that the district court erred when it failed to instruct the jury to determine whether the felony underlying the second-degree felony-murder theory was assaultive based on the manner in which the felony was committed. . . .

Appellant Brian Rose was convicted of second-degree murder with the use of a deadly weapon for shooting his girlfriend, Jackie Watkins, in the head. On the day of the killing, Rose and his friend, Jake Timms, went target shooting in the desert with Rose's .40 caliber Smith & Wesson semiautomatic handgun. Afterwards, they picked up Watkins and went to a barbeque at the home of another friend, Julius Castano. Rose brought the gun inside the house and placed it in the family room because he claimed he feared someone might break into his car and steal his registered gun.

Throughout the evening, Rose, Timms, and Julius handled the gun. At one point, Rose took the magazine out of the gun and pulled the slide back to make sure the chamber was empty. . . .

Later in the evening, Rose shot Watkins in the head while she spoke on the phone to her friend Erin Fragoso. . . . According to Rose's voluntary statement to police, he aimed the gun at or near Watkins while she was talking to Fragoso and told her to get off the phone. He then shot a single round from his gun and hit the top of Watkins's head. Fragoso could hear Rose's voice in the background and could tell that it was firm and forceful, but she could not hear his exact words. Fragoso ended the call after a long silence from Watkins; she did not hear a gunshot.

Although witnesses in the home heard the gunshot, none of them saw Rose fire the gun. Julius's father, Joseph Castano, was upstairs in his room at the time and heard laughing from downstairs right before the gunshot was fired. Julius heard the gunshot and turned around to see Watkins on the couch, not moving. Rose was standing right next to Watkins with the gun in his hand. Julius testified that "there was no stiff pointing the gun at nobody . . . . It was in [Rose's] hand like he wanted me to take it from his hands." . . .

. . . At the Castano home, officers found an ejected cartridge on the floor against the wall, behind a couch. Officers also found Rose's loaded Smith & Wesson handgun upstairs in a bedroom.

. . . Rose admitted to knowing how to use his gun and knowing that the gun had no hammer. Rose told the detectives that he did not know his gun was loaded and that he accidentally shot Watkins. He also told them that he considered fleeing to Mexico. When the detectives asked Rose if he intended to shoot Watkins, he responded, "God no."

Rose acknowledged that he must have pulled the trigger when he turned, but there was no witness testimony presented that Rose purposefully aimed and fired at Watkins. In his voluntary statement to detectives, Rose claimed that he had pointed the gun at the chair next to Watkins to be "a dick." He said he gave Watkins "a squinted look" and smiled to let her know he was playing around. Rose stated that he "looked back the other way and, and then when [he] looked back, that's when it actually went off." Rose asserted that he did not care whether Watkins got off the phone or not, and, at the time, he believed the gun was empty. At the end of the interrogation, the detectives told Rose that Watkins died, and Rose became very upset and cried.

. . . .

[T]he jury returned a general verdict finding Rose guilty of second-degree murder with the use of a deadly weapon. . . . Rose was sentenced to 10 to 25 years in prison, plus an equal and consecutive term for the use of a deadly weapon. . . .

The record indicates that the State relied on the felony-murder rule as one of its theories for second-degree murder. During closing argument, the State argued that malice could be established in four ways: (1) express malice (intent to kill), (2) implied malice (reckless disregard of consequences and social duty), (3) felony murder based on assault with a deadly weapon, and (4) commission of an unlawful act that naturally tends to destroy the life of a human being. It argued that if the killing occurred during "the prosecution of committing a felony," specifically, assault with a deadly weapon, the crime was second-degree murder. . . .

The felony-murder rule makes a killing committed in the course of certain felonies murder, without requiring the State to present additional evidence as to the defendant's mental state. The rule takes two forms in Nevada: first-degree felony murder and second-degree felony murder. The Legislature has specified the felonies that provide the malicious intent necessary to characterize a killing as first-degree murder. In contrast, there are no statutorily enumerated felonies with respect to second-degree felony murder . . . . [Our] statutes broadly provide that killings occurring in the commission of an unlawful act that naturally tends to destroy human life or committed in the "prosecution of a felonious intent" are . . . murder of the second degree. Despite that broad language, this court has placed restrictions on the use of the felony-murder rule to establish second-degree murder in order to avoid the potential for "untoward" prosecutions that a broad application of the felony-murder rule would allow. In particular, we have required that "two elements [be] satisfied: (1) . . . 'the [predicate] felony [must be] inherently dangerous, where death or injury is a directly foreseeable consequence of the illegal act,' and (2) . . . 'there [must be] an immediate and direct causal relationship — without the intervention of some other source or agency — between the actions of the defendant and the victim's death.'" The question presented by Rose is whether we should further narrow the use of the felony-murder rule to establish second-degree murder by applying the merger doctrine.

The merger doctrine developed in the felony-murder context as a means of restricting the scope of the felony-murder rule, particularly when it is used to support a second-degree murder conviction. *People v. Sarun Chun*, 203 P.3d 425, 434 (Cal. 2009). "The merger doctrine developed due to the understanding that the underlying felony must be an independent crime and not merely the killing itself. Thus, certain underlying felonies 'merge' with the homicide and cannot be used for purposes of felony murder." *Id.* at 434–35.

. . . .

The merger doctrine was first articulated and applied to second-degree felony murder in California in *People v. Ireland*, 450 P.2d 580 (Cal. 1969). The issue arose in *Ireland* in response to a trial court instruction allowing second-degree felony murder based on assault with a deadly weapon as the predicate felony. The California Supreme Court held that such an instruction was improper because "[t]o allow such use of the felony-murder rule would effectively preclude the jury from considering the issue of malice aforethought in all cases wherein homicide has been committed as a result of a felonious assault — a category which includes the great majority of all homicides."

Recently, in *Sarun Chun*, the California Supreme Court further clarified when an underlying felony merges with murder in the context of second-degree felony murder. It plainly stated that an underlying felony that is assaultive in nature necessarily merges with the homicide and cannot be the basis for a second-degree felony-murder instruction. The court went on to define an assaultive felony as any felony that involves a threat of immediate violent injury. "Accordingly, if the elements of the crime have an assaultive aspect, the crime merges with the underlying homicide even if the elements also include conduct that is not assaultive." The *Sarun Chun* court declined to enumerate which felonies are assaultive but held that shooting at an occupied vehicle is assaultive and cannot be used as the underlying felony to support a second-degree felony-murder charge; therefore, it concluded that the trial court erred in instructing the jury on second-degree felony murder.

. . . [Our] Legislature has not specified the felonies that can be used for purposes of second-degree felony murder, and absent such clear direction, we are convinced that the merger doctrine has a worthwhile place in restricting the scope of the second-degree felony-murder rule to avoid the potential for "untoward" prosecutions that has led us to restrict the rule in other ways.

We are persuaded by the California Supreme Court's reasoning that allowing assaultive-type felonies to form the basis for a second-degree murder conviction based on the felony-murder rule would mean that virtually every homicide would occur in the commission of a felony and therefore be murder, unless otherwise justifiable or excusable or committed upon a sudden irresistible impulse. [*Accord People v. Moran*, 158 N.E. 35, 36 (N.Y. 1927)] (addressing felony-murder rule and holding that felonious assault that culminated in homicide could not be used to apply the felony-murder rule because the result would be that almost every homicide would be committed in the course of a felony so that no further evidence of intent would ever be required for a murder conviction; therefore, the felony "must be one that is independent of the homicide and of the assault merged therein"). . . .

Under our decision today, the application of the merger doctrine turns on a determination of whether the underlying felony is assaultive in nature. We therefore also must determine whether that question presents a factual determination for the jury or a legal determination for the trial court. We faced a similar decision as to the question of whether a felony is inherently dangerous for purposes of second-degree felony murder. Recently, . . . we abandoned earlier cases that had suggested that that question is a legal one to be determined in the abstract based on the elements of the underlying felony; we instead held that the jury must determine whether the felony underlying a second-degree felony-murder charge is inherently dangerous based on the manner in which the felony was committed. In applying the merger doctrine, we are similarly persuaded that the jury should determine whether the underlying felony is assaultive—i.e., involves a threat of immediate violent injury—based on the manner in which the felony was committed.

In the present case, the predicate felony for the second-degree felony-murder theory was assault with a deadly weapon. At the time that Rose shot Watkins, NRS 200.471 defined assault as "[u]lawfully attempting to use physical force against another person" or "[i]ntentionally placing another person in reasonable apprehension of immediate bodily harm." The offense was a felony if the assault was made with the use of a deadly weapon. The assault here is based on Rose's act of aiming the gun at or near Watkins and telling her to get off the phone. The conduct could be viewed as using a deadly weapon to intentionally place the victim in reasonable apprehension of immediate bodily harm by threatening her with immediate violent injury. A jury therefore could find that the felony was assaultive and merged with the homicide. Alternatively, a properly instructed jury could have found implied malice based on the circumstances of the killing, and still convicted Rose of second-degree murder. But based on the facts of this case and the conflicting evidence as to Rose's state of mind, we cannot conclude beyond a reasonable doubt that a rational jury would have found Rose guilty of second-degree murder absent the omitted instruction.[26]

. . . .

Notes and Questions

1. **The Deterrent Rationale for the Merger Exception.** In addition to the arguments advanced in *Rose*, do the deterrence rationales underlying the felony murder rule support the merger doctrine? In cases of assault, for example, does the felony murder rule have no deterrent effect because "there is no way . . . to convince" a defendant who wants to "physically attack" a victim "to achieve her felonious purpose . . . in a safer manner," whereas the felony murder rule can "warn[] [a defendant] that if she chooses to go ahead with her felonious plan to take another person's property, she should do so in a comparatively non-dangerous manner"? Joshua Dressler, Understanding Criminal Law § 31.06[C][2], at 524 (7th ed. 2015). Or is that reasoning "demonstrably erroneous" because "a person [who] has formed the intent to engage in a relatively mild assault . . . can, as much as the rapist or robber, be restrained from life-endangering actions"? David Crump & Susan W. Crump, *In Defense of the Felony Murder Doctrine*, 8 Harv. J.L. & Pub. Pol'y 359, 378 (1985). *Cf. People v. Mattison*, 481 P.2d 193, 198–99 (Cal. 1971) ("While the felony-murder rule can hardly be much of a deterrent to a defendant who has decided to assault his victim with a deadly weapon, . . . knowledge that the death of a person to whom heroin is furnished may result in a conviction for murder should have some effect on the defendant's readiness to do the furnishing").

2. **The Merger Exception's Convoluted History in California.** In tracing the development of the merger doctrine in California, the Nevada Supreme Court's opinion in *Rose* omitted a number of California Supreme Court decisions issued in the 40 years intervening between *People v. Ireland*, 450 P.2d 580 (Cal. 1969), and *People v. Chun*, 203 P.3d 425 (Cal. 2009). During that period, the California Supreme Court, which has devoted more attention to the merger doctrine than any other court, adopted a number of different approaches to the exception.

In first applying the merger exception to assault with a deadly weapon in *Ireland*, the court held that the merger doctrine foreclosed the use of felony murder charges

---

26. [n.2] . . . We also have considered Rose's claim that there was insufficient evidence to support his conviction and conclude that it lacks merit. *See* . . . NRS 200.020(2) ("Malice shall be implied when no considerable provocation appears, or when all the circumstances of the killing show an abandoned and malignant heart."); *Keys v. State*, 104 Nev. 736, 738, 766 P.2d 270, 271 (1988) (explaining that malice may be implied from "the intentional use of a deadly weapon in a deadly and dangerous manner"). . . .

for any felony that was "an integral part of the homicide" or "included in fact" within the homicide. *Ireland*, 450 P.2d at 590 (emphasis omitted). Does that standard make sense, or is it inconsistent with the inherently dangerous felony exception because it applies to "those felonies that are most likely to result in death"? *People v. Hansen*, 885 P.2d 1022, 1030 (Cal. 1994).

In *People v. Mattison*, 481 P.2d 193 (Cal. 1971), the court adopted a different merger standard, holding that felony murder charges could be brought so long as the underlying felony had a "collateral and independent felonious design" — that is, the felony "was not done with the intent to commit injury which would cause death." *Id.* at 198 (allowing felony murder conviction where the defendant gave methyl alcohol to an alcoholic and thereby committed the felony of "wilfully mingl[ing] any poison with any food, drink or medicine, with intent that the same shall be taken by any human being to his injury"); *see also People v. Smith*, 678 P.2d 886, 891 (Cal. 1984) (noting, in reversing felony murder conviction based on the felony of child abuse, that the crime involved no independent purpose, i.e., "the purpose here was the very assault that resulted in death"). Does this standard have the "anomalous result" of punishing a felon "who actually intends to injure" the victim less severely than one "who acts with a purpose other than specifically to inflict injury upon someone"? *Hansen*, 885 P.2d at 1030. Or is it the merger doctrine itself that creates any such anomaly?

The California Supreme Court changed course again in *Hansen*. After criticizing the two previous formulations of the merger exception, the *Hansen* court chose to focus on whether use of the felony murder rule for a particular felony would "elevate all felonious assaults to murder or otherwise subvert the legislative intent." *Id.* The court went on to affirm a felony murder conviction based on the underlying felony of willfully shooting at an occupied dwelling on the theory that "[m]ost homicides do not result from violations" of that offense and therefore, unlike the assault charge involved in *Ireland*, use of the felony murder rule would not "have the effect of 'preclud[ing] the jury from considering the issue of malice aforethought . . . [in] the great majority of homicides.'" *Id.* (quoting *Ireland*, 450 P.2d at 590). Is this a preferable approach, or is asking judges to "speculat[e] — futilely and undoubtedly inaccurately — about how many homicides are committed in what way . . . the legal equivalent of the theological debate about how many angels can dance on the head of a pin"? *People v. Robertson*, 95 P.3d 872, 894 (Cal. 2004) (Brown, J., dissenting). Did *Hansen* come close to eviscerating the merger doctrine — or at least limiting it to the crime of assault in its generic form?

The California Supreme Court's qualms about the approach taken in *Hansen* surfaced a decade later when it resolved two cases involving the same predicate felony — discharging a firearm in a grossly negligent manner — by returning to *Mattison*'s independent purpose test. In the first, *People v. Robertson*, 95 P.3d at 881, the court affirmed the felony murder conviction because the defendant's "asserted underlying purpose was to frighten away the young men who were burglarizing his automobile" by firing warning shots in the air, "a purpose collateral to the resulting homicide." But the court reached the opposite conclusion in the second case, *People v. Randle*, 111 P.3d 987, 999 (Cal. 2005), distinguishing *Robertson* because the defendant admitted that he had shot directly at the victim and the fact that he may have fired in order to rescue another person was "simply . . . a *motive* for the shooting" rather than "a purpose independent of the shooting." Do these decisions create an "anomaly" by "putting the person who merely intends to frighten the victim in a worse legal position than the person who actually intended to shoot at the victim"? *Chun*, 203 P.3d at 443. Are the two cases also subject to criticism because "[i]t is not clear how a future court should decide whether a given intent is a purpose or merely a motive"? *Id.* at 442. (For a discussion of the distinction between the concepts of purpose and motive, see Chapter 4, Section B.2, Note 4.)

In a bit of an understatement, the court in *Chun* characterized this line of cases as "problematic" and undertook to revisit the merger exception. *Chun*, 203 P.3d at 440. In deciding to focus the merger analysis on whether the underlying felony was "assaultive in nature," *id.* at 443, the court was critical of the disparate outcomes in *Robertson* and *Randle* and expressly overturned *Hansen*. In addition to finding that Chun's felony — willfully discharging a firearm at an occupied automobile — could not support a felony murder charge, the court also indicated that its new definition of the merger doctrine would have foreclosed felony murder charges in *Smith* (child abuse, whether based on assault or neglect) and *Hansen* (willfully shooting at an occupied dwelling), as well as *Robertson* and *Randle* (discharging a weapon in a grossly negligent manner). Was the Nevada Supreme Court right in *Rose* to conclude that the California Supreme Court has finally settled on the proper standard for evaluating the reach of the merger exception?

3. Who Determines the Scope of the Merger Exception? In *Rose*, the Nevada Supreme Court concluded that jurors should make the "factual determination" whether or not a particular defendant's crime was "assaultive in nature," and thus covered by the merger doctrine, "based on the manner in which the felony was committed." In *People v. Chun*, 203 P.3d 425, 442 (Cal. 2009), by contrast, one of the reasons the California Supreme Court was troubled by the *Robertson-Randle* disparity and chose to adopt the "assaultive in nature" formulation was its view that the merger exception raises "a legal question with little or no factual content": "an underlying felony either never or always merges" regardless of the facts of a particular case. Accordingly, the court held that trial judges in California should conduct the merger analysis and should not instruct the jury on the merger doctrine.

Do the different views taken by the two courts reflect the fact that California uses the abstract approach to define inherently dangerous felonies whereas, as the court pointed out in *Rose*, juries make that determination in Nevada by looking at "the manner in which the felony was committed"? Or should a state's allocation of decisionmaking authority in applying the inherently dangerous felony exception be irrelevant here? (The inherently dangerous felony limitation is discussed above in Part 2.a.)

4. Child Abuse. As discussed above in Note 2, the California Supreme Court relied on the merger doctrine in *People v. Smith*, 678 P.2d 886 (Cal. 1984), in reversing the felony murder conviction of a mother charged with beating her three-year-old daughter to death. The court concluded that the felony child abuse statute at issue there was indistinguishable from assault for purposes of the merger doctrine, noting that "[i]t would be wholly illogical to allow this kind of assaultive child abuse to be bootstrapped into felony murder merely because the victim was a child rather than an adult, as in *Ireland*." *Id.* at 891. *See also People v. Pelt*, 800 N.E.2d 1193 (Ill. 2003) (reaching the same conclusion).

Some state legislatures, however, have worded their homicide statutes to make clear that child abuse can be the basis for felony murder charges. *See, e.g.*, Ariz. Rev. Stat. § 13-1105(A)(2); Fla. Stat. Ann. § 782.04(1)(a)(2)(h); Kan. Stat. Ann. § 21-3436(a)(7).

5. Discharge of a Weapon. In *People v. Morgan*, 758 N.E.2d 813 (Ill. 2001), the Illinois Supreme Court decided that the felony of aggravated discharge of a firearm cannot serve as the basis for a felony murder charge in that state. The court reasoned that the defendant's aggravated discharge of a weapon was an act that was "inherent in, and arose out of, the fatal shootings": "every shooting necessarily encompasses conduct constituting . . . aggravated discharge of a firearm, i.e., discharging a firearm in the direction of another. Potentially, then, all fatal shootings could be charged as felony murder based upon aggravated battery and/or aggravated discharge of a firearm." *Id.* at 838. *Cf. People v. Davison*, 923 N.E.2d 781, 788 (Ill. 2010) (noting that *Morgan* also required that the underlying felony have an "independent felonious purpose" in order to survive the merger doctrine).

In *State v. Millbrook*, 788 N.W.2d 647, 652 (Iowa 2010), the Iowa Supreme Court applied a definition of the merger exception similar to *Morgan*, analyzing "whether the act constituting the predicate felony was independent of the act causing death," i.e., "whether there were separate, independent acts supporting the charges of felony murder" and the underlying felony. The predicate felony in that case, "intimidation with a dangerous weapon," was defined by statute to prohibit discharging a dangerous weapon at an occupied building or vehicle or "within an assembly of people" "with the intent to injure or provoke fear or anger," "thereby plac[ing] the occupants or people in reasonable apprehension of serious injury." Iowa Code § 708.6. In affirming the defendant's felony murder conviction, the court explained that "a separate, independent act constituting intimidation with a dangerous weapon . . . occurred prior to the assault that resulted in the victim's death" because the defendant testified that he fired the fatal shot only after opening the door to the van in which he was riding, thus "enabl[ing] [his accomplice's] initial shot" and "aid[ing] and abet[ting] [the accomplice's] commission of intimidation with a dangerous weapon." *Millbrook*, 788 N.W.2d at 652–53.

Consider also *In re Bowman*, 172 P.3d 681 (Wash. 2007), which held that the merger doctrine did not prevent use of the state's drive-by shooting statute as the predicate for a felony murder conviction. The statute defined drive-by shooting as recklessly firing a weapon "from a motor vehicle or from the immediate area of a motor vehicle" "in a manner which creates a substantial risk of death or serious physical injury to another person." Wash. Rev. Code § 9A.36.045. In refusing to apply the merger exception, the Washington Supreme Court reasoned that the drive-by shooting statute prohibits "specific *reckless conduct* that . . . creates a risk that a person might be injured." *Bowman*, 172 P.3d at 684–85. Unlike assault, therefore, drive-by shooting "does not require a victim" and "does not criminalize conduct that causes bodily injury or fear of such injury." *Id.* In addition, the court explained, "[d]rive-by shooting and homicide are two separate and distinct crimes": although homicide invariably involves an assault, it "can be committed without reckless discharge of a firearm." *Id.* at 685.

Given the holding in *Chun*, described above in Note 2, the California Supreme Court would presumably agree with the result in *Morgan*. But how would that court have ruled in *Millbrook* and *Bowman*?

6. Burglary. In *People v. Wilson*, 462 P.2d 22 (Cal. 1969), the California Supreme Court held that the merger exception forecloses a felony murder conviction in burglary cases where the defendant was breaking and entering with the intent to commit an assault. A majority of other courts, however, have rejected the California court's decision. Does the majority view make sense because the crime of burglary includes an independent element — breaking and entering — and therefore does not merge with the homicide? Or is the fortuity of an entry insufficient to distinguish the crimes of assault and burglary?

Consider the explanation for the majority position offered in *People v. Miller*, 297 N.E.2d 85, 87–88 (N.Y. 1973), the leading case espousing that view:

> [P]ersons within domiciles are in greater peril from those entering the domicile with criminal intent, than persons on the street who are being subjected to the same criminal intent. . . . Where, as here, the criminal act underlying the burglary is an assault with a dangerous weapon, the likelihood that the assault will culminate in a homicide is significantly increased by the situs of the assault. When the assault takes place within the domicile, the victim may be more likely to resist the assault; the victim is also less likely to be able to avoid the consequences of the assault, since his paths of retreat and escape may be barred or severely restricted by furniture, walls and other obstructions incidental to buildings. Further, it is also more likely that when the assault occurs in the victim's domicile, there will be present family or close friends who will come to the victim's aid and be killed. Since the purpose of the felony-murder statute is to reduce the disproportionate number of accidental homicides which occur during the commission of the enumerated predicate felonies by punishing the party responsible for the homicide . . . for murder, the Legislature, in enacting the burglary and felony-murder statutes, did not exclude from the definition of burglary, a burglary based upon the intent to assault. . . .

Is *Miller*'s reasoning persuasive, or is the relative dangerousness of assaults inside and outside the home irrelevant to the applicability of the merger doctrine?

Relying in part on *Miller* and in part on the fact that the California legislature listed burglary as one of the felonies that can lead to a first-degree felony murder conviction, the California Supreme Court overturned its holding in *Wilson. See People v. Farley*, 210 P.3d 361 (Cal. 2009). In so doing, the court was critical of *Wilson*'s conclusion that felony murder charges "serve[] no purpose" in these circumstances: "a person who enters a building with the intent to assault, rather than to kill (in which case the felony-murder rule would be unnecessary), may be deterred by the circumstance that if the victim of the assault dies, the burglar 'will be deemed guilty of first degree murder.'" *Id.* at 410. Does that argument apply equally to felony murder cases where assault is the underlying felony?

7. Rejection of the Merger Exception. Some courts have rejected the merger doctrine altogether, often on the grounds that the legislature intended the felony murder rule to be available in assault cases. *See, e.g., Edge v. State*, 414 S.E.2d 463 (Ga. 1992); *Roary v. State*, 867 A.2d 1095 (Md. 2005); *Barnett v. State*, 263 P.3d 959 (Okla. Crim. App. 2011); *Rodriguez v. State*, 953 S.W.2d 342 (Tex. App. 1997) (limiting the merger exception to prohibit only the use of manslaughter as the underlying felony). *But cf. State v. Heemstra*, 721 N.W.2d 549 (Iowa 2006) (overturning precedent and adopting the merger doctrine despite statutory language including assault among the predicate felonies for felony murder).

[c] *The Agency Doctrine*

Commonwealth v. Tejeda

41 N.E.3d 721 (Mass. 2015)

Gants, Chief Justice.

The primary issue in this appeal is whether a defendant who joins with others to commit an armed robbery may be found guilty of murder on the theory of felony-murder for the killing of his accomplice by someone resisting the armed robbery. We conclude that he may not.

. . . On January 14, 2012, the defendant and two friends, Christopher Pichardo and Stephane Etienne, met with Frederick Reynoso, who was to sell them one-half pound of marijuana for $2,200. Together, they traveled in a vehicle that the defendant had borrowed from his girl friend to a residence in the Dorchester section of Boston, where the transaction was to take place. Pichardo, Etienne, and Reynoso entered the home through a basement door; the defendant remained outside in the parked vehicle. Reynoso's cousin, Jonathan Santiago, was waiting for them in the basement. Once inside, Santiago weighed the marijuana, placed it into eight one-ounce bags, and handed the bags to Pichardo. Pichardo told Santiago that Etienne would pay him for the marijuana. Etienne dropped his cellular telephone to distract Santiago, and Pichardo then pulled out a .40 caliber semiautomatic handgun from his waistband and told Santiago, "You know what time it is." Reynoso responded by pulling out his own .32 caliber revolver, and a gun battle between Pichardo and Reynoso followed in which shots were fired from both weapons. A bullet struck Pichardo on the right side of his chest.

Etienne and Pichardo attempted to leave the basement, but Pichardo collapsed while still inside. Etienne took Pichardo's firearm and cellular telephone, as well as the marijuana, and ran to the defendant's vehicle, which was parked around the corner. Etienne and the defendant then returned to the basement and attempted to carry Pichardo back to the vehicle, but they were unable to lift his body. They ran back to the vehicle and left the scene. The defendant telephoned 911 from Pichardo's cellular telephone shortly thereafter to inform the police that Pichardo had been shot. Pichardo was taken from the scene by ambulance and was pronounced dead shortly after arriving at Boston Medical Center.

. . . The police later . . . executed a search warrant on the defendant's girl friend's vehicle and found approximately thirty bags of marijuana in the trunk.

A Superior Court jury convicted the defendant of murder in the second degree on the theory of felony-murder, with armed robbery as the underlying felony. The jury also convicted the defendant of the armed robbery of Santiago, . . . home invasion, . . . and possession of marijuana with intent to distribute . . . .

The felony-murder [rule] . . . incorporates two implicit premises. The first is constructive malice: the substitution of "the intent to commit the underlying felony for the malice aforethought required for murder." The second is vicarious criminal liability for every act resulting in death committed by a joint venturer in furtherance of the joint venture, that is, the act of one is treated as the act of all. These two legal constructions have defined felony-murder since it was first articulated in English common law in the Eighteenth Century. *See Rex v. Plummer*, 84 Eng. Rep. 1103, 1105 (K.B. 1701) ("if divers persons be engaged in an unlawful act, and one of them kills another, it shall be murder in all the rest" provided that "[t]he killing must be in pursuance of that unlawful act, and not collateral to it").

In *Commonwealth v. Campbell*, 89 Mass. 541, 7 Allen 541, 543 (1863), the Commonwealth sought to expand the scope of felony-murder by claiming that a defendant should be vicariously responsible for the act of someone who was not a joint venturer during the commission of the underlying felony. In *Campbell*, the defendant had participated in a draft riot during the Civil War where a person was shot and killed, but the evidence was unclear whether the fatal shot had been fired by one of the rioters "with whom the prisoner was acting in concert," or by a soldier inside the armory who was resisting the attack by the rioters. The Commonwealth sought a jury instruction that the defendant may be found guilty of homicide regardless of who fired the shot. We rejected the Commonwealth's argument, declaring, "[n]o person can be held guilty of homicide unless the act is either actually or constructively his, and it cannot be his act in either sense unless committed by his own hand or by some one acting in concert with him or in furtherance of a common object or purpose." . . .

A century later, this court reaffirmed the principle that vicarious liability in felony-murder is limited to the acts resulting in death committed by a joint venturer. *Commonwealth v. Balliro*, 349 Mass. 505, 515, 209 N.E.2d 308 (1965). In *Balliro*, the defendants broke and entered a home in the night with the intent to commit an assault with a dangerous weapon, but the police were waiting for them inside, and a gunfight resulted in which a mother and her son were killed. Over the defendants' objection, the judge instructed the jury that, if the defendants "entered and shot first," the death of the two victims was "imputable to these defendants and they are guilty of murder." The judge denied the defendants' request for an instruction that they could not be found guilty unless it were proved that the bullets that caused the deaths of the victims were fired by one of the defendants, and not by the police. . . . After carefully examining the relevant case law, we reaffirmed the rule in *Campbell*, "which has been the law of this Commonwealth for more than one hundred years," and declared that a defendant cannot be found guilty of felony-murder "for the death of any person killed by someone resisting the commission of the felony." We therefore concluded that the judge erred in his instructions to the jury and in declining to give the defendants' requested instructions.

Now, more than fifty years after our *Balliro* opinion, the Commonwealth again asks us to expand the scope of felony-murder by expanding the scope of vicarious liability to make every joint venturer criminally responsible for every act that results in death that is proximately caused by the underlying felony. Under the Commonwealth's "proximate cause theory," a joint venturer would be vicariously liable for an act resulting in death even if it were committed by a person who was resisting the underlying felony or attempting to apprehend the persons committing it, provided that resistance or an attempt to apprehend would be reasonably foreseeable by a person initiating the underlying felony, which it always would be. The Commonwealth concedes, correctly, that the majority of other States follow what has become known as the "agency theory" of felony-murder under which the act causing death must be committed in furtherance of the joint venture by the defendant or someone acting in concert with him or her. The Commonwealth asks that we join the minority of jurisdictions that impose felony-murder according to the "proximate cause theory."

. . . [T]he common law of felony-murder is already an exception to . . . two basic principles of our criminal jurisprudence. First, generally we require proof of a defendant's intent to commit the crime charged, and do not conclusively presume such intent from the intent to commit another crime.

Second, generally "[o]ne is punished for his own blameworthy conduct, not that of others." Only where a dangerous felony results in death do we adopt a principle that we otherwise have "firmly rejected" — that a person who knowingly participates in one crime as part of a joint venture is "ipso facto also guilty" of all other crimes committed by an accomplice in furtherance of the joint venture.

Adoption of the Commonwealth's proximate cause theory would essentially cause our law of felony-murder to depart even further from the second basic principle: it would extend vicarious accomplice liability to acts that were not committed by accomplices, and that were committed not to further the joint venture but to thwart it. We need not decide here whether our common law of felony-murder should continue to be an exception to our basic principles of criminal jurisprudence, or whether we should join those who have abolished or redefined felony-murder. But we would need persuasive reasons to justify an expansion of what is already an unusual doctrine. The reasons offered by the Commonwealth are not persuasive.

First, the Commonwealth contends that the proximate cause theory should be applied to the common law of felony-murder because it comports with the scope of liability in civil cases and reflects the causation standard that would apply in a civil case brought by the decedent against the joint venturers.[27] The purpose of civil liability, however, is to fairly compensate a plaintiff for injuries caused by the wrongful or negligent conduct of another. In light of that purpose, it is reasonable that, where a person is killed during the course of an armed robbery by someone seeking to resist it, the burden of loss should be imposed on those who committed the armed robbery and thereby set in motion the chain of events that proximately caused the death. In contrast, the purpose of criminal liability is to punish persons found culpable for their wrongful conduct, and that punishment is most severe when a person is found guilty of murder. Given the "fundamentally different purposes of criminal law and tort law," and the extreme penalties and infamy associated with a conviction of murder, it is not reasonable to expand the scope of felony-murder to punish a defendant for conduct that neither the defendant nor an accomplice committed or intended. *See State v. Canola*, 73 N.J. 206, 226, 374 A.2d 20 (1977) ("Tort concepts of foreseeability and proximate cause have shallow relevance to culpability for murder in the first degree").

Second, the Commonwealth argues that, "[b]y holding defendants responsible for deaths caused when they engage in activities which are 'inherently dangerous to human life,' we deter individuals from creating scenarios which may result in death." We doubt that persons contemplating a dangerous felony would be significantly deterred by the possibility that, if a person were to be killed by someone seeking to thwart or apprehend them, they might be found guilty of felony-murder. If they thought that they likely faced the risk of death from someone seeking to resist or arrest them, that risk would be the more potent deterrent.

---

27. [n.10] We note that causation may also be an issue under the agency theory of felony-murder. . . . [I]f a police officer suffered a heart attack attributable to the stress of confronting armed robbers and died after receiving negligent medical care, the question whether there was a sufficient causal relationship between the joint venturers' act and the resulting death would arise under both the agency and proximate cause theories.

Third, the Commonwealth contends that someone should be found guilty of murder for a violent death and, without the proximate cause theory of felony-murder, there is the risk that no one will be punished for the death of a bystander mistakenly shot by an armed robbery victim or by a police officer, because the victim and the police officer may have been justified in their use of force against the robbers. It is true that, in these circumstances, it is likely that no one will be found guilty of murder. But that does not mean that the joint venturers will escape punishment. Armed robbery is a life felony under Massachusetts law, and the death is likely to be treated as an aggravating factor by a judge imposing sentence on the armed robbery conviction. Moreover, a tragic death does not always justify a murder conviction; the law recognizes that a person is guilty of manslaughter, not murder, punishable by up to twenty years in prison rather than a life sentence, where the killing is committed intentionally under mitigating circumstances or unintentionally but recklessly. . . .

Notes and Questions

1. **The Proximate Cause and Agency Approaches.** Did the court in *Tejeda* make a persuasive case for rejecting the proximate cause approach and instead endorsing the agency approach, which limits the felony murder doctrine to killings committed by one of the felons? Does the proximate cause approach improperly "discriminate between robbers, not on the basis of any difference in their own conduct, but solely on the basis of the response by others that the robber's conduct happened to induce"? *People v. Washington*, 402 P.2d 130, 133 (Cal. 1965). Or is any such discrimination of little concern because "[e]very robber or burglar knows when he attempts to commit his crime that he is inviting dangerous resistance," and "[h]e therefore should be held responsible for *any death* which by direct and almost inevitable sequence results from the initial criminal act"? *Commonwealth v. Thomas*, 117 A.2d 204, 205 (Pa. 1955), *overruled by Commonwealth v. Redline*, 137 A.2d 472 (Pa. 1958).

Was the *Tejeda* court right to be critical of the proximate cause approach because "the tort liability concept of proximate cause has no proper place in prosecutions for criminal homicide," given that "[t]ort law is primarily concerned with who shall bear the burden of loss, while criminal law is concerned with the imposition of punishment"? *Campbell v. State*, 444 A.2d 1034, 1041 (Md. 1982). Or are "the analogies between civil and criminal cases in which individuals are injured or killed . . . so close that the principle of proximate cause applies to both classes of cases"? *People v. Lowery*, 687 N.E.2d 973, 976 (Ill. 1997).

Does a court's view of the purposes served by the felony murder doctrine help determine its stance on this issue? Was the *Tejeda* court wrong in seeing little deterrent value in the proximate cause approach because "if potential felons realize that they will be culpable as murderers for a death that occurs during the commission of a felony, they will be less likely to commit the felony"? *State v. Martin*, 573 A.2d 1359, 1368 (N.J. 1990). Does the persuasiveness of the deterrence argument turn on whether one views the felony murder rule's function as deterring accidental deaths that might occur during the course of a felony or deterring the felonies themselves?

Although the agency approach is followed in most jurisdictions, some states continue to adhere to the proximate cause approach. *See, e.g., State v. Jackson*, 697 S.E.2d 757 (Ga. 2010) (overturning precedent to the contrary); *People v. Klebanowski*, 852 N.E.2d 813 (Ill. 2006); *Palmer v. State*, 704 N.E.2d 124 (Ind. 1999); *State v. Martin*, 573 A.2d at 1370–71 (noting that amendments to the felony murder statute were meant to abolish the agency rule). *But cf. Layman v. State*, 42 N.E.3d 972, 979–80 (Ind. 2015) (distinguishing *Palmer* and reversing felony murder conviction where a homeowner killed a burglar on the ground that the felons, who were unarmed and thought the house was empty, did not "engage[] in violent and threatening conduct" that was "'clearly the mediate or immediate cause' of their friend's death") (quoting *Palmer*, 704 N.E.2d at 126).[28]

2. The Deaths of Cofelons. Whichever position they take on the issue addressed in the prior Note — i.e., whether they follow the agency or the proximate cause approach — most courts apply the felony murder doctrine even in cases where the victim was one of the cofelons. *See* Martin J. McMahon, Annotation, *Application of Felony-Murder Doctrine Where Person Killed Was Co-felon*, 89 A.L.R.4TH 683. As the Pennsylvania Supreme Court explained in *Commonwealth ex rel. Smith v. Myers*, 261 A.2d 550, 558 (Pa. 1970), "[t]he probability that a felon will be killed seems at least as great as the probability that the victim will be an innocent bystander.... Indeed, to make the result hinge on the character of the victim is, in many instances, to make it hinge on the marksmanship of resisters."

Nevertheless, some courts refuse to apply the felony murder doctrine to deaths of cofelons. Does the minority position make sense because "the obvious ultimate purpose of the felony-murder statute... is... to prevent the deaths of innocent persons," and "it would be incongruous to... plac[e] the perpetrators themselves beneath its mantle"? *State v. Williams*, 254 So. 2d 548, 550, 551 (Fla. Dist. Ct. App. 1971). Or is the better view that applying the felony murder rule irrespective of the victim's identity ultimately does protect innocent people by maximizing felony murder's deterrent value and reducing the number of felonies committed? *See United States v. Tham*, 118 F.3d 1501, 1510 (11th Cir. 1997). *See also People v. Billa*, 79 P.3d 542, 546 (Cal. 2003) ("Making [felons] guilty of murder if anyone, including an accomplice, dies... gives them an incentive to do whatever is necessary to make sure no one dies" and thus serves the purpose of deterring felons from killing negligently or accidentally).

Alternatively, is the minority approach justifiable on the ground that the cofelon assumed the risk of being killed or "forfeited any right to the law's protection" by

---

28. In jurisdictions that follow the agency approach and therefore foreclose a felony murder conviction where a killing was committed by someone other than a cofelon, such killings may nevertheless lead to a conviction of depraved-heart murder if one of the felons initiated a gun battle or committed some other act, beyond merely participating in the felony, "sufficiently provocative of lethal resistance to support a finding of... conscious disregard for human life." *Taylor v. Superior Court*, 477 P.2d 131, 134 (Cal. 1970).

agreeing to participate in the felony? *Commonwealth v. Thomas*, 117 A.2d 204, 221 (Pa. 1955) (Jones, J., dissenting). Or is the assumption of risk argument unpersuasive given that neither consent nor contributory negligence on the part of a victim is generally a valid defense to murder charges? *See Commonwealth ex rel. Smith v. Myers*, 261 A.2d at 558. *See also Billa*, 79 P.3d at 546 ("One may have less sympathy for [a felon] who dies . . . , but an accomplice's participation in a felony does not make his life forfeit or compel society to give up all interest in his survival.").

3. The "in the Commission" Requirement. Homicide statutes are often worded so as to allow felony murder charges if a death occurs either while a felony is being committed (or attempted) or while the felons are fleeing after committing (or attempting to commit) the crime. Many courts interpret such language to require that the felony and the fatal act be "part of one continuous transaction," such that the duration of the felony continues until the felons reach "a place of temporary safety." *People v. Wilkins*, 295 P.3d 903, 907 (Cal. 2013). Thus, in *Auman v. People*, 109 P.3d 647, 651 (Colo. 2005), the court held that "arrest, by itself, does not terminate a co-participant's liability for felony murder." The court therefore left to the jury the question whether Auman's arrest five minutes before her cofelon killed a police officer "terminate[d] . . . her immediate flight from the commission of the predicate felony." *Id.* at 650. *See also People v. Gillis*, 712 N.W.2d 419 (Mich. 2006) (finding sufficient evidence to support a felony murder conviction where a police officer who received a report of home invasion began pursuing the defendant 10 miles from the scene of the crime, and the defendant ran into another car, killing two people, almost 20 minutes after the emergency call was placed and 10 minutes after the officer first spotted him).

What if the defendant first kills the victim and then decides to steal some of the victim's property in order to cover up the real motive for the homicide? Are felony murder charges still appropriate so long as the " 'one-continuous-transaction' rule" is satisfied, even if the defendant had no "intent to rob prior to the killing"? *Batiste v. State*, 121 So. 3d 808, 831–32 (Miss. 2013) (affirming conviction where defendant returned to the scene of the homicide more than an hour later and took the victim's wallet during his "clean-up effort"). Or is that view inconsistent with the basic premise of the felony murder doctrine because if the defendant "lacks the intent to commit the predicate felony at the time of the killing, then no malice is supplied to support murder"? *Nay v. State*, 167 P.3d 430, 435, 431 (Nev. 2007) (discussing conflicting cases and "adopt[ing] the majority position that . . . the intent to commit the predicate enumerated felony must have arisen before or during the conduct resulting in death"). *See also State v. Hacheney*, 158 P.3d 1152, 1161 (Wash. 2007) (observing that "the *death* must have been a probable consequence of the felony, not the other way around").

4. The "in Furtherance" Requirement. A number of jurisdictions follow the traditional English practice cited in *Tejeda*, limiting the felony murder doctrine to cases where the killing occurred in furtherance of the underlying felony. *See* 2 Wayne R. LaFave, Substantive Criminal Law § 14.5(f), at 461 (2d ed. 2003). Questions surrounding the in furtherance requirement obviously arise in cases like *Tejeda*. *See*

Commonwealth v. Bolish, 113 A.2d 464, 479 (Pa. 1955) (Musmanno, J., concurring and dissenting in part) (taking the position that the felony murder rule should not apply when cofelons are killed because those deaths are "in hindrance" rather than "in furtherance of the criminal design").

These issues also arise when a killing by one cofelon goes beyond the scope of the plan agreed to by the others. A felony murder conviction is inappropriate in such cases, some courts have held, because "the slaying must be causally related to the objects of the felony"; "mere coincidence of time and place between the felony and the murder" is not enough. *United States v. Heinlein*, 490 F.2d 725, 733 (D.C. Cir. 1973). Absent the in furtherance limitation, these courts reason, a felon could conceivably be convicted of felony murder if "one of his cofelons during the course of the robbery looked out a window, saw a passerby down the street, and shot and killed him even though the passerby had no connection to the robbery whatsoever." *Commonwealth v. Waters*, 418 A.2d 312, 317 n.10 (Pa. 1980). *See also State v. Montgomery*, 759 A.2d 995, 1020 (Conn. 2000) (observing that the function of the "in furtherance" requirement is to limit felony murder charges to "those circumstances which were within the contemplation of the confederates to the undertaking").

Although the California Supreme Court endorsed each of these concepts in *People v. Cavitt*, 91 P.3d 222 (Cal. 2004), it affirmed felony murder convictions entered against two defendants who contended that a third cofelon, the stepdaughter of the victim, took it upon herself for her own personal reasons to kill her stepmother after the defendants helped tie the victim up and rob her house, and then left with the proceeds of the robbery. The in furtherance limitation requires a "logical connection between the felony and the act resulting in death," the court observed, but "the requisite connection has not depended on proof that the homicidal act furthered or facilitated the underlying felony." *Id.* at 230. Thus, the court held, "[e]vidence that Betty was intentionally murdered by Mianta because of a private grudge, instead of killed accidentally or killed intentionally to facilitate the burglary-robbery," did not weaken "the undisputed logical nexus between the burglary-robbery and the homicide," given that "the crimes involved the same victim, occurred at the same time and place, and were each facilitated by binding and gagging Betty." *Id.* at 236.

5. **Causation.** Closely related to the in furtherance doctrine is the requirement that the underlying felony must have caused the death in order to support a felony murder conviction. *See, e.g., State v. Montgomery*, 759 A.2d 995, 1020 (Conn. 2000) (equating the two, noting that "[t]he phrase 'in furtherance of' was intended to impose the requirement of a relationship between the underlying felony and the homicide beyond that of mere causation in fact, similar to the concept of proximate cause in the law of torts"). Causation questions obviously arise in cases like *Tejeda*, where the fatal act was performed by someone other than a felon, but they arise in other felony murder cases as well.

In *State v. Leech*, 790 P.2d 160 (Wash. 1990), for example, a firefighter died from carbon monoxide poisoning while battling a fire set by the defendant. The defendant challenged the causal link between his act of arson and the death, contending that the firefighter was negligent in failing to obey state safety regulations and obtain a new air bottle when the alarm in his breathing apparatus sounded. Rejecting this argument, the court explained that "the arsonist can anticipate that firemen will be endangered," "human error in fighting a fire is [not] an extraordinary occurrence," and the firefighter's alleged negligence was not the sole cause of his death. *Id.* at 162.

Likewise, in *People v. Taylor*, 169 Cal. Rptr. 290 (Cal. Ct. App. 1980), the victim died from the combined effects of consuming alcohol and injecting himself with heroin (the latter was supplied by the defendant). Even though the heroin itself would not have been fatal, the court concluded there was adequate evidence of causation for felony murder purposes because a felon is "criminally liable for a result directly caused by his act, even though there is another contributing cause." *Id.* at 295. *See also Hulme v. State*, 544 S.E.2d 138, 141 (Ga. 2001) (finding sufficient evidence of causation in drug distribution case where the defendant was "actively involved with controlling the victim's dosages [of methadone], . . . the victim routinely took the dosages that Hulme provided to her, . . . the victim took the potentially lethal dosage from Hulme on the day of her death, and . . . the potentially lethal dose of methadone contributed to the victim's death"). *But cf. State v. Mauldin*, 529 P.2d 124, 126 (Kan. 1974) (observing that a "'direct causal relation' within the meaning of the felony-murder rule" requires "something more . . . beyond the fact the death sequentially followed the sale of the heroin," and therefore dismissing felony murder charges brought against a drug dealer who did not assist in administering the drugs and was not present when the victim injected himself); *Sheriff, Clark County v. Morris*, 659 P.2d 852, 859 (Nev. 1983) (holding that "the causal relationship must extend beyond the unlawful sale of the drugs to an involvement by commission or omission in the ingestion of a lethal dosage by the decedent").

Consider also *King v. Commonwealth*, 368 S.E.2d 704 (Va. Ct. App. 1988), where a plane carrying a load of marijuana encountered foul weather and crashed, killing the copilot, Mark Bailey, who was flying the plane at the time. The pilot, Nelson King, was charged with felony murder. The court noted that felony murder charges are appropriate only where "the killing is so closely related to the felony in time, place, and causal connection as to make it a part of the same criminal enterprise." *Id.* at 706. "Death must be a consequence of the felony and not merely coincidence," the court continued. *Id.* at 707. Applying that standard to the facts before it, the court found insufficient evidence of causation. Although it acknowledged that "but for the felony, King and Bailey probably would not have been in the plane," it pointed out that the felony murder doctrine requires more than but for causation. *Id.* at 708. The court observed that the plane would have crashed even if its cargo had been legal, and concluded that Bailey's death was caused by "fog, low cloud cover, pilot error, and inexperience," not by an act "which was an integral part of the felony or . . . in direct furtherance of the felony." *Id.* The court noted, however, that its decision might have been different "[h]ad the plane been flying low or recklessly to avoid detection." *Id.*

For a more extensive discussion of the causation issues that arise in criminal cases, see Chapter 10.

6. The Affirmative Defense for Unforeseeable Deaths. Cases may arise where a death was caused by a felony, and occurred during and in furtherance of the crime, but nevertheless was not reasonably foreseeable. Approximately 10 states have created an affirmative defense in such circumstances if certain conditions are met: the defendant did not commit or aid the fatal act; the defendant was not armed and had no reason to believe any of the cofelons were armed; and the defendant had no reason to believe any of the cofelons intended to commit an act likely to lead to death or serious bodily injury. For an illustration of such a statute, see N.Y. Penal Law § 125.25(3), reprinted above in Section A. *See generally* 2 Wayne R. LaFave, Substantive Criminal Law § 14.5(c), at 452 (2d ed. 2003). *But cf. Mares v. State*, 939 P.2d 724 (Wyo. 1997) (refusing to judicially create such a defense).

7. Misdemeanor Manslaughter. The misdemeanor manslaughter rule, a cousin of the felony murder doctrine, punishes as involuntary manslaughter any killing that occurs in the commission of an unlawful act. Typically, the unlawful act is a misdemeanor — often a traffic violation, such as speeding or failing to obey a traffic signal. But in some jurisdictions, it can also be a felony that is not deemed dangerous or serious enough to serve as the basis for a felony murder charge, or even the violation of a civil ordinance.

The misdemeanor manslaughter rule raises the same policy issues as the felony murder doctrine, but has fared less well. The Model Penal Code rejects the rule, and a substantial number of state statutes have followed that lead. *See* 2 Wayne R. LaFave, Substantive Criminal Law § 15.5, at 530 (2d ed. 2003). *But compare State v. Weitbrecht*, 715 N.E.2d 167, 171 (Ohio 1999) (refusing to dismiss involuntary manslaughter charges on the grounds that the misdemeanor manslaughter doctrine constitutes cruel and unusual punishment violative of the Eighth Amendment, reasoning that "[w]here human lives are lost, the gravity of the crime is serious and is not lessened by the fact that the underlying crime consists of a minor misdemeanor"), *with id.* at 172 (Pfeifer, J., dissenting) (disagreeing on the facts there, where a fatal collision occurred after the defendant "apparently suffered a cardiac event [and] lost consciousness," and then committed the misdemeanors of failing to maintain control of the car and driving in the wrong lane, and the prosecution "stipulated that there was no evidence of criminal recklessness or criminal negligence on her part").

In those jurisdictions where it survives, the misdemeanor manslaughter rule has been limited in a variety of ways. Some states have, for example: (1) imposed causation requirements, demanding proof that the misdemeanor was the cause of death; (2) required the prosecution to prove that the defendant was culpably negligent or reckless; (3) limited the doctrine to misdemeanors that involve a danger of injury; (4) restricted the doctrine to misdemeanors that are *mala in se* rather than *mala prohibita*, at least absent evidence that the defendant was negligent or that death was the natural and probable result of the defendant's conduct; and (5) refused to apply the doctrine where the underlying misdemeanor was a strict liability crime and the defendant was not criminally negligent. Most states do not recognize a merger exception in this context, however, and misdemeanor assault and battery charges can therefore lead to a misdemeanor manslaughter verdict. *See* LaFave, *supra*, § 15.5.

[E] The Death Penalty

[1] The Policy Considerations Underlying the Death Penalty

Thirty-one states and the federal government currently authorize imposition of the death penalty; 19 states and the District of Columbia do not. Between 1976, when the Supreme Court reinstated the death penalty in *Gregg v. Georgia*, 428 U.S. 153 (1976), and the end of 2016, 8,276 persons were sentenced to die in this country. At the end of September 2016, 2,902 prisoners were on death row awaiting execution. *See* Bureau of Justice Statistics Bulletin, U.S. Dep't of Justice, Capital Punishment, 2013 (2014), http://www.bjs.gov/content/pub/pdf/cp13st.pdf; *Facts About the Death Penalty*, Death Penalty Information Center, http://www.deathpenaltyinfo.org/documents/FactSheet.pdf. In general, fewer than two percent of defendants convicted of murder are sentenced to die. *See* Joshua Marquis, *The Myth of Innocence*, 95 J. Crim. L. & Criminology 501, 518 (2005).

Between 1930 and the end of 2016, 5,301 prisoners were executed in this country, 1,442 of them since 1976. Almost two-thirds of the executions since 1976 have taken place in five states—with Texas in the lead, having executed 538 individuals, more than one-third of the nationwide total.

After the Supreme Court reinstated the death penalty in 1976, the number of annual executions rose steadily, until 1999 when 98 prisoners were put to death (the highest number since 1951). Since then, however, there has been a reduction in both death sentences and executions. In 2014, 73 defendants received a death sentence, the lowest number in 40 years and more than 200 fewer than 20 years earlier. The following two years, the number of death sentences dropped still further, to 49 in 2015 and 30 in 2016. Likewise, the 28 executions in 2015 and the 20 in 2016 were the smallest number since 1991. *See* Bureau of Justice Statistics Bulletin, *supra*; *Facts About the Death Penalty*, *supra*.

The recent decline in the number of executions mirrors political developments in a number of jurisdictions. In 2000, George Ryan, then-Governor of Illinois, declared a moratorium on all executions in that state, and then, shortly before leaving office three years later, granted a blanket commutation of all 164 death sentences then in effect in Illinois. In 2007, the New Jersey legislature passed a bill repealing the death penalty, making that state the first to do so in 40 years. *See* New Jersey Death Penalty Study Commission Report (2007), http://www.njleg.state.nj.us/committees/dpsc_final.pdf. Four other state legislatures have since followed New Jersey's lead and abolished the death penalty: New Mexico (2009), Illinois (2011), Connecticut (2012), and Maryland (2013). The Nebraska legislature passed similar legislation in 2015, overriding Governor Pete Ricketts' veto, but in 2016 the voters passed a referendum funded largely by Ricketts that reinstated the death penalty. *See* Joe Duggan, *Nebraska's Death Penalty Still Has Roadblocks to Clear*, Omaha World-Herald, Nov. 10, 2016, at 1A. In addition to these legislative developments, moratoriums on the death penalty have been imposed by the governors of four additional states: Oregon (2011), Colorado (2013), Washington (2014), and Pennsylvania (2015). *See Commonwealth v. Williams*, 129 A.3d 1199, 1215 (Pa. 2015) (interpreting the term "reprieve" in the state constitution to include "any temporary postponement of sentence," and rejecting the prosecution's argument that the governor's power is "limited to granting reprieves with a specific end date or for a purpose relating only to the prisoner's unique circumstances").

In thinking about whether capital punishment is justifiable from a policy perspective, consider the Supreme Court's opinions in *Glossip v. Gross* and *McCleskey v. Kemp*, which are excerpted below, as well as the materials in Chapter 2, Section C.3.

Glossip v. Gross
135 S. Ct. 2726 (2015)

Justice Alito delivered the opinion of the Court.

Prisoners sentenced to death in the State of Oklahoma filed an action in federal court under 42 U.S.C. § 1983, contending that the method of execution now used by the State violates the Eighth Amendment because it creates an unacceptable risk of severe pain. They argue that midazolam, the first drug employed in the State's current three-drug protocol, fails to render a person insensate to pain. After holding an evidentiary hearing, the District Court denied four prisoners' application for a preliminary injunction, finding that they had failed to prove that midazolam is ineffective. The Court of Appeals for the Tenth Circuit affirmed . . . .

For two independent reasons, we also affirm. First, the prisoners failed to identify a known and available alternative method of execution that entails a lesser risk of pain, a requirement of all Eighth Amendment method-of-execution claims. *See Baze v. Rees*, 553 U.S. 35, 61 (2008) (plurality opinion). Second, the District Court did not commit clear error when it found that the prisoners failed to establish that Oklahoma's use of a massive dose of midazolam in its execution protocol entails a substantial risk of severe pain.

[The Court's reasoning and Justice Sotomayor's dissenting views on this issue are summarized below in Note 4.]

Justice Scalia, with whom Justice Thomas joins, concurring.

I join the opinion of the Court, and write to respond to Justice Breyer's plea for judicial abolition of the death penalty.

Welcome to Groundhog Day. The scene is familiar: Petitioners, sentenced to die for the crimes they committed (including, in the case of one petitioner since put to death, raping and murdering an 11-month-old baby), come before this Court asking us to nullify their sentences as "cruel and unusual" under the Eighth Amendment['s ban on "cruel and unusual punishments"]. . . . They were afforded counsel and tried before a jury of their peers—tried twice, once to determine whether they were guilty and once to determine whether death was the appropriate sentence. . . . And now, acknowledging that their convictions are unassailable, they ask us for clemency, as though clemency were ours to give.

The response is also familiar: A vocal minority of the Court, waving over their heads a ream of the most recent abolitionist studies (a superabundant genre) as though they have discovered the lost folios of Shakespeare, insist that *now*, at long last, the death penalty must be abolished for good. Mind you, not once in the history of the American Republic has this Court ever suggested the death penalty is categorically impermissible. The reason is obvious: It is impossible to hold unconstitutional that which the Constitution explicitly *contemplates*. The Fifth Amendment provides that "[n]o person shall be held to answer for a capital . . . crime, unless on a presentment or indictment of a Grand Jury," and that no person shall be "deprived of life . . . without due process of law." . . .

Historically, the Eighth Amendment was understood to bar only those punishments that added "terror, pain, or disgrace" to an otherwise permissible capital sentence. *Baze v. Rees*, 553 U.S. 35, 96 (2008) (Thomas, J., concurring in judgment). Rather than bother with this troubling detail, Justice Breyer elects to contort the constitutional text. Redefining "cruel" to mean "unreliable," "arbitrary," or causing "excessive delays," and "unusual" to include a "decline in use," he proceeds to offer up a white paper devoid of any meaningful legal argument.

Even accepting Justice Breyer's rewriting of the Eighth Amendment, his argument is full of internal contradictions and (it must be said) gobbledy-gook. He says that the death penalty is cruel because it is unreliable; but it is *convictions*, not *punishments*, that are unreliable. Moreover, the "pressure on police, prosecutors, and jurors to secure a conviction," which he claims increases the risk of wrongful convictions in capital cases, flows from the nature of the crime, not the punishment that follows . . . . That same pressure would exist, and the same risk of wrongful convictions, if horrendous death-penalty cases were converted into equally horrendous life-without-parole cases. The reality is that any innocent defendant is infinitely better off appealing a death sentence than a sentence of life imprisonment. . . . The capital convict will obtain endless legal assistance from the abolition lobby (and legal favoritism from abolitionist judges), while the lifer languishes unnoticed behind bars.

Justice Breyer next says that the death penalty is cruel because it is arbitrary. To prove this point, he points to a study of 205 cases that "measured the 'egregiousness' of the murderer's conduct" with "a system of metrics" . . . . Egregiousness is a moral judgment susceptible of few hard-and-fast rules. More importantly, egregiousness of the crime is only one of several factors that render a punishment condign — culpability, rehabilitative potential, and the need for deterrence also are relevant. That is why this Court has required an individualized consideration of all mitigating circumstances, rather than formulaic application of some egregiousness test.

It is because these questions are contextual and admit of no easy answers that we rely on juries to make judgments about the people and crimes before them. The fact that these judgments may vary across cases is an inevitable consequence of the jury trial . . . . [T]he fact that some defendants receive mercy from their jury no more renders the underlying punishment "cruel" than does the fact that some guilty individuals are never apprehended, are never tried, are acquitted, or are pardoned.

Justice Breyer's third reason that the death penalty is cruel is that it entails delay . . . . Life without parole is an even lengthier period than the wait on death row . . . . As for the argument that delay undermines the penological rationales for the death penalty . . . , Justice Breyer apparently forgets that one of the plaintiffs *in this very case* was already in prison when he committed the murder that landed him on death row. Justice Breyer further asserts that "whatever interest in retribution might be served by the death penalty as currently administered . . . can be served almost as well by a sentence of life in prison without parole." . . . If he thinks the death penalty not much more harsh (and hence not much more retributive), why is he so keen to get rid of it? With all due respect, whether the death penalty and life imprisonment constitute more-or-less equivalent retribution is a question far above the judiciary's pay grade. . . . I would not presume to tell parents whose life has been forever altered by the brutal murder of a child that life imprisonment is punishment enough.

And finally, Justice Breyer speculates that it does not "seem likely" that the death penalty has a "significant" deterrent effect. It seems very likely to me, and there are statistical studies that say so. *See, e.g.,* Zimmerman, *State Executions, Deterrence, and the Incidence of Murder*, 7 J. APPLIED ECON. 163, 166 (2004) ("[I]t is estimated that each state execution deters approximately fourteen murders per year on average"); Dezhbakhsh, Rubin, & Shepherd, *Does Capital Punishment Have a Deterrent Effect? New Evidence from Postmoratorium Panel Data*, 5 AM. L. & ECON. REV. 344 (2003) ("[E]ach execution results, on average, in eighteen fewer murders" per year); Sunstein & Vermeule, *Is Capital Punishment Morally Required? Acts, Omissions, and Life-Life Tradeoffs*, 58 STAN. L. REV. 703, 713 (2005) ("All in all, the recent evidence of a deterrent effect from capital punishment seems impressive, especially in light of its 'apparent power and unanimity'"). . . . [W]e federal judges live in a world apart from the vast majority of Americans. . . . We are not confronted with the threat of violence that is ever present in many Americans' everyday lives. . . . Let the People decide how much incremental deterrence is appropriate.

Of course, th[e] delay [in executions] is a problem of the Court's own making [due to] the proliferation of labyrinthine restrictions on capital punishment, promulgated by this Court under an interpretation of the Eighth Amendment that empowered it to divine "the evolving standards of decency that mark the progress of a maturing society"—a task for which we are eminently ill suited. . . . Amplifying the surrealism of his argument, Justice Breyer uses the fact that many States have abandoned capital punishment—have abandoned it precisely because of the costs those suspect decisions have imposed—to conclude that it is now "unusual." . . .

If we were to travel down the path that Justice Breyer sets out for us and once again consider the constitutionality of the death penalty, I would ask that counsel also brief whether our cases that have abandoned the historical understanding of the Eighth Amendment . . . should be overruled. . . . Justice Breyer's dissent is the living refutation of [the] assumption that this Court has the capacity to recognize "evolving standards of decency." Time and again, the People have voted to exact the death penalty as punishment for the most serious of crimes. . . . And time and again, a vocal minority of this Court . . . has sought to replace the judgments of the People with their own standards of decency. . . .

JUSTICE THOMAS, with whom JUSTICE SCALIA joins, concurring.

I agree with the Court that petitioners' Eighth Amendment claim fails. That claim has no foundation in the Eighth Amendment, which prohibits only those "method[s] of execution" that are "deliberately designed to inflict pain." *Baze v. Rees*, 553 U.S. 35, 94 (2008) (Thomas, J., concurring in judgment). Because petitioners make no allegation that Oklahoma adopted its lethal injection protocol "to add elements of terror, pain, or disgrace to the death penalty," they have no valid claim.

I write separately to respond to Justice Breyer's dissent . . . . Justice Breyer's assertion that the death penalty in this country has fallen short of the aspiration that capital punishment be reserved for the "worst of the worst"—a notion itself based on an implicit proportionality principle that has long been discredited, *see Harmelin v. Michigan*, 501 U.S. 957, 966 (1991) (opinion of Scalia, J.)—merits further comment. His conclusion is based on an analysis that itself provides a powerful case against enforcing an imaginary constitutional rule against "arbitrariness."

The thrust of Justice Breyer's argument is that empirical studies performed by death penalty abolitionists reveal that the assignment of death sentences does not necessarily correspond to the "egregiousness" of the crimes, but instead appears to be correlated to "arbitrary" factors, such as the locality in which the crime was committed. . . . The Donohue study, on which Justice Breyer relies most heavily, measured the "egregiousness" (or "deathworthiness") of murders by asking lawyers to identify the legal grounds for aggravation in each case, and by asking law students to evaluate written summaries of the murders and assign "egregiousness" scores based on a rubric designed to capture and standardize their moral judgments. Donohue, *An Empirical Evaluation of the Connecticut Death Penalty System Since 1973, Are There Unlawful Racial, Gender, and Geographic Disparities?* 11 J. EMPIRICAL LEGAL STUDIES 637, 644–45 (2014). . . . The law students make their moral judgments based on written summaries—they do not . . . have an opportunity to assess the credibility of witnesses, to see the remorse of the defendant, to feel the impact of the crime on the victim's family; they do not bear the burden of deciding the fate of another human being; and they are not drawn from the community whose sense of security and justice may have been torn asunder by an act of callous disregard for human life. . . .

There is a reason the choice between life and death, within legal limits, is left to the jurors and judges who sit through the trial, and not to legal elites (or law students). . . . [The constitutional] provisions [guaranteeing a right to jury trial] ensure that capital defendants are given the option to be sentenced by a jury of their peers who, collectively, are better situated to make the moral judgment between life and death than are the products of contemporary American law schools.

It should come as no surprise, then, that the primary explanation a regression analysis revealed for the gap between the egregiousness scores and the actual sentences was not the race or sex of the offender or victim, but the locality in which the crime was committed. . . . The [Sixth Amendment] . . . , which place[s] such decisions in the hands of jurors and trial courts located where "the crime shall have been committed," seem[s] deliberately designed to introduce that factor.

In any event, the results of these studies are inherently unreliable because they purport to control for egregiousness by quantifying moral depravity in a process that is itself arbitrary, not to mention dehumanizing. One such study's explanation of how the author assigned "depravity points" to identify the "worst of the worst" murderers proves the point well. McCord, *Lightning Still Strikes*, 71 Brooklyn L. Rev. 797, 833–34 (2005). Each aggravating factor received a point value based on the "blameworth[iness]" of the action associated with it. Killing a prison guard, for instance, earned a defendant three "depravity points" because it improved the case for complete incapacitation, while killing a police officer merited only two, because, "considered dispassionately," such acts do "not seem be a *sine qua non* of the worst criminals." . . . Killing a child under the age of 12 was worth two depravity points, because such an act "seems particularly heartless," but killing someone over the age of 70 earned the murderer only one, for although "elderly victims tug at our hearts," they do so "less" than children "because the promise of a long life is less." Killing to make a political statement was worth three depravity points; killing out of racial hatred, only two. . . . [T]his small sample . . . shows just how unsuitable this evidence is to serve as a basis for a judicial decision declaring unconstitutional a punishment duly enacted in more than 30 States, and by the Federal Government.

. . . In my decades on the Court, I have not seen a capital crime that could not be considered sufficiently "blameworthy" to merit a death sentence (even when genuine constitutional errors justified a vacatur of that sentence).[29] [Justice Thomas goes on here to describe the facts of a number of the Court's death penalty cases.]

---

29. [n.3] For his part, Justice Breyer explains that his experience on the Court has shown him "discrepancies for which [he] can find no rational explanations." Why, he asks, did one man receive death for a single-victim murder, while another received life for murdering a young mother and nearly killing her infant? The outcomes in those two cases may not be morally compelled, but there was certainly a rational explanation for them: The first man, who had previously confessed to another murder, killed a disabled man who had offered him a place to stay for the night. The killer

Whatever one's views on the permissibility or wisdom of the death penalty, I doubt anyone would disagree that each of these crimes was egregious enough to merit the severest condemnation that society has to offer. . . . [30] To the extent that we are ill at ease with . . . disparate outcomes, it seems to me that the best solution is for the Court to stop making up Eighth Amendment claims in its ceaseless quest to end the death penalty through undemocratic means.

Justice Breyer, with whom Justice Ginsburg joins, dissenting.

. . . .

Nearly 40 years ago, this Court upheld the death penalty under statutes that, in the Court's view, contained safeguards sufficient to ensure that the penalty would be applied reliably and not arbitrarily. *See Gregg v. Georgia*, 428 U.S. 153, 187 (1976) (joint opinion of Stewart, Powell, and Stevens, JJ.). The circumstances and the evidence of the death penalty's application have changed radically since then. Given those changes, I believe that it is now time to reopen the question. . . .

I. *"Cruel"*—Lack of Reliability

This Court has specified that the finality of death creates a "qualitative difference" between the death penalty and other punishments (including life in prison). That "qualitative difference" creates "a corresponding difference in the need for reliability in the determination that death is the appropriate punishment in a specific case." There is increasing evidence, however, that the death penalty as now applied lacks that requisite reliability.

For one thing, despite the difficulty of investigating the circumstances surrounding an execution for a crime that took place long ago, researchers have found convincing evidence that, in the past three decades, innocent people have been executed. *See, e.g.*, Liebman, *Fatal Injustice; Carlos DeLuna's Execution Shows That a Faster, Cheaper Death Penalty Is a Dangerous Idea*, L.A. Times, June 1, 2012, p. A19 (describing results of a 4-year investigation, later published as *The Wrong Carlos: Anatomy of a Wrongful Execution* (2014), that led its authors to conclude that Carlos DeLuna, sentenced to death and executed in 1989, six years after his arrest in Texas for stabbing a single mother to death in a convenience store, was innocent); Grann, *Trial By Fire: Did Texas Execute An Innocent Man?* The New Yorker, Sept. 7, 2009, p. 42 (describing evidence that Cameron Todd Willingham was convicted, and ultimately executed in 2004, for the apparently motiveless murder of his three children as the result of

---

stabbed his victim's throat and prevented him from seeking medical attention until he bled to death. The second man expressed remorse for his crimes and claimed to suffer from mental disorders. The other "discrepancies" similarly have "rational" explanations, even if reasonable juries could have reached different results.

30. [n.4] Justice Breyer appears to acknowledge that our decision holding mandatory death penalty schemes unconstitutional, *Woodson v. North Carolina*, 428 U.S. 280 (1976) (plurality opinion), may have introduced the problem of arbitrary application. I agree that *Woodson* eliminated one reliable legislative response to concerns about arbitrariness. Because that decision was also questionable on constitutional grounds, I would be willing to revisit it in a future case.

invalid scientific analysis of the scene of the house fire that killed his children). *See also, e.g.,* Press Release: Gov. Ritter Grants Posthumous Pardon in Case Dating Back to 1930s, Jan. 7, 2011, p. 1 (Colorado Governor granted full and unconditional posthumous pardon to Joe Arridy, a man with an IQ of 46 who was executed in 1936, because, according to the Governor, "an overwhelming body of evidence indicates the 23-year-old Arridy was innocent, including false and coerced confessions, the likelihood that Arridy was not in Pueblo at the time of the killing, and an admission of guilt by someone else"); R. Warden, Wilkie Collins's The Dead Alive: The Novel, the Case, and Wrongful Convictions 157–58 (2005) (in 1987, Nebraska Governor Bob Kerrey pardoned William Jackson Marion, who had been executed a century earlier for the murder of John Cameron, a man who later turned up alive; the alleged victim, Cameron, had gone to Mexico to avoid a shotgun wedding).

For another, the evidence that the death penalty has been wrongly *imposed* (whether or not it was carried out), is striking. . . . (I use "exoneration" to refer to relief from all legal consequences of a capital conviction through a decision by a prosecutor, a Governor or a court, after new evidence of the defendant's innocence was discovered.) Since 2002, the number of exonerations in capital cases has risen to 115. Last year, in 2014, six death row inmates were exonerated based on actual innocence. All had been imprisoned for more than 30 years (and one for almost 40 years) at the time of their exonerations.[31] . . .

. . . [R]esearchers estimate that about 4% of those sentenced to death are actually innocent. *See* Gross, O'Brien, Hu, & Kennedy, *Rate of False Conviction of Criminal Defendants Who Are Sentenced to Death*, 111 Proceeding of the National Academy of Sciences 7230 (2014) (full-scale study of all death sentences from 1973 through 2004 estimating that 4.1% of those sentenced to death are actually innocent); Risinger, *Innocents Convicted: An Empirically Justified Factual Wrongful Conviction Rate*, 97 J. Crim. L. & C. 761 (2007) (examination of DNA exonerations in death penalty cases for murder-rapes between 1982 and 1989 suggesting an analogous rate of between 3.3% and 5%).

Finally, if we expand our definition of "exoneration" (which we limited to errors suggesting the defendant was actually innocent) and thereby also categorize as "erroneous" instances in which courts failed to follow legally required procedures, the numbers soar. Between 1973 and 1995, courts identified prejudicial errors in 68% of the capital cases before them. Gelman, Liebman, West, & Kiss, *A Broken System: The Persistent Patterns of Reversals of Death Sentences in the United States*, 1 J. Empirical L. Studies 209, 217 (2004). State courts on direct and postconviction review overturned 47% of the sentences they reviewed. Federal courts, reviewing capital cases in habeas corpus proceedings, found error in 40% of those cases. . . .

---

31. As this book went to press in June 2017, 159 death row prisoners had been exonerated since 1973 "with evidence of their innocence." *See Facts About the Death Penalty*, Death Penalty Information Center, http://www.deathpenaltyinfo.org/documents/FactSheet.pdf.

II. *"Cruel"* — Arbitrariness

. . . .

When the death penalty was reinstated in 1976, this Court acknowledged that the death penalty is (and would be) unconstitutional if "inflicted in an arbitrary and capricious manner."

The Court has consequently sought to make the application of the death penalty less arbitrary by restricting its use to those whom Justice Souter called "the worst of the worst." *Kansas v. Marsh*, 548 U.S. [163, 206 (2006)] (dissenting opinion); *see also Roper v. Simmons*, 543 U.S. 551, 568 (2005) ("Capital punishment must be limited to those offenders who commit a narrow category of the most serious crimes and whose extreme culpability makes them the most deserving of execution").

Despite the *Gregg* Court's hope for fair administration of the death penalty, 40 years of further experience make it increasingly clear that the death penalty is imposed arbitrarily, *i.e.*, without the "reasonable consistency" legally necessary to reconcile its use with the Constitution's commands.

. . . A recent study, for example, examined all death penalty sentences imposed between 1973 and 2007 in Connecticut, a State that abolished the death penalty in 2012. Donohue, *An Empirical Evaluation of the Connecticut Death Penalty System Since 1973: Are There Unlawful Racial, Gender, and Geographic Disparities?* 11 J. EMPIRICAL LEGAL STUDIES 637 (2014). The study reviewed treatment of all homicide defendants. It found 205 instances in which Connecticut law made the defendant eligible for a death sentence. Courts imposed a death sentence in 12 of these 205 cases, of which 9 were sustained on appeal. The study then measured the "egregiousness" of the murderer's conduct in those 9 cases, developing a system of metrics designed to do so. . . . Application of the studies' metrics made clear that only 1 of those 9 defendants was indeed the "worst of the worst" (or was, at least, within the 15% considered most "egregious"). The remaining eight were not. Their behavior was no worse than the behavior of at least 33 and as many as *170* other defendants (out of a total pool of 205) who had not been sentenced to death.

. . . Other studies show that circumstances that ought *not* to affect application of the death penalty, such as race, gender, or geography, often do. Numerous studies, for example, have concluded that individuals accused of murdering white victims, as opposed to black or other minority victims, are more likely to receive the death penalty. Fewer, but still many, studies have found that the gender of the defendant or the gender of the victim makes a not-otherwise-warranted difference.

Geography also plays an important role in determining who is sentenced to death. . . . [W]*ithin* a death penalty State, the imposition of the death penalty heavily depends on the county in which a defendant is tried. [S]*ee* . . . Donohue, *supra*, at 673 ("[T]he single most important influence from 1973–2007 explaining whether a death-eligible defendant [in Connecticut] would be sentenced to death was whether the crime occurred in Waterbury [County]"). . . . Some studies indicate that the disparity reflects the decisionmaking authority, the legal discretion, and ultimately the power of the local prosecutor. Others suggest that the availability of resources for defense counsel (or the lack thereof) helps explain geographical differences. Still others indicate that the racial composition of and distribution within a county plays an important role. Finally, some studies suggest that political pressures, including pressures on judges who must stand for election, can make a difference. . . .

Justice Thomas catalogues the tragic details of various capital cases, but this misses my point. Every murder is tragic, but unless we return to the mandatory death penalty struck down in *Woodson*, the constitutionality of capital punishment rests on its limited application to the worst of the worst. And this extensive body of evidence suggests that it is not so limited. . . .

The studies bear out my own view, reached after considering thousands of death penalty cases and last-minute petitions over the course of more than 20 years. I see discrepancies for which I can find no rational explanations. Why does one defendant who committed a single-victim murder receive the death penalty (due to aggravators of a prior felony conviction and an after-the-fact robbery), while another defendant does not, despite having kidnapped, raped, and murdered a young mother while leaving her infant baby to die at the scene of the crime. Why does one defendant who committed a single-victim murder receive the death penalty (due to aggravators of a prior felony conviction and acting recklessly with a gun), while another defendant does not, despite having committed a "triple murder" by killing a young man and his pregnant wife? For that matter, why does one defendant who participated in a single-victim murder-for-hire scheme (plus an after-the-fact robbery) receive the death penalty, while another defendant does not, despite having stabbed his wife 60 times and killed his 6-year-old daughter and 3-year-old son while they slept? In each instance, the sentences compared were imposed in the same State at about the same time. . . .

III. *"Cruel"* — Excessive Delays

. . . Given the special need for reliability and fairness in death penalty cases, the Eighth Amendment does, and must, apply to the death penalty "with special force." . . . [T]he Constitution insists that "every safeguard" be "observed" when "a defendant's life is at stake." *Gregg*, 428 U.S. at 187 (joint opinion of Stewart, Powell, and Stevens, JJ.).

These procedural necessities take time to implement. . . . In 2014, 35 individuals were executed. Those executions occurred, on average, nearly 18 years after a court initially pronounced its sentence of death. In some death penalty States, the average delay is longer. In an oral argument last year, for example, the State admitted that the last 10 prisoners executed in Florida had spent an average of nearly 25 years on death row before execution.

The length of the average delay has increased dramatically over the years. In 1960, the average delay between sentencing and execution was two years. Ten years ago (in

2004) the average delay was about 11 years. By last year the average had risen to about 18 years. Nearly half of the 3,000 inmates now on death row have been there for more than 15 years. And, at present execution rates, it would take more than 75 years to carry out those 3,000 death sentences; thus, the average person on death row would spend an additional 37.5 years there before being executed. . . .

These lengthy delays create two special constitutional difficulties. First, a lengthy delay in and of itself is especially cruel because it "subjects death row inmates to decades of especially severe, dehumanizing conditions of confinement." . . . [N]early all death penalty States keep death row inmates in isolation for 22 or more hours per day. . . .

The dehumanizing effect of solitary confinement is aggravated by uncertainty as to whether a death sentence will in fact be carried out. . . . Several inmates have come within hours or days of execution before later being exonerated. . . . Indeed, one death row inmate, who was later exonerated, still said he would have preferred to die rather than to spend years on death row pursuing his exoneration. Nor is it surprising that many inmates consider, or commit, suicide. . . .

The second constitutional difficulty resulting from lengthy delays is that those delays undermine the death penalty's penological rationale, perhaps irreparably so. . . . Capital punishment by definition does not rehabilitate. . . . [T]he major alternative to capital punishment — namely, life in prison without possibility of parole — also incapacitates.

Thus, as the Court has recognized, the death penalty's penological rationale in fact rests almost exclusively upon a belief in its tendency to deter and upon its ability to satisfy a community's interest in retribution. Many studies have examined the death penalty's deterrent effect; some have found such an effect, whereas others have found a lack of evidence that it deters crime. *Compare* [the studies cited by Justice Scalia] *with e.g.*, Sorensen, Wrinkle, Brewer, & Marquart, *Capital Punishment and Deterrence: Examining the Effect of Executions on Murder in Texas*, 45 Crime & Delinquency 481 (1999) (no evidence of a deterrent effect); Bonner & Fessenden, *Absence of Executions: A Special Report, States with No Death Penalty Share Lower Homicide Rates*, N.Y. Times, Sept. 22, 2000, p. A1 (from 1980–2000, homicide rate in death-penalty States was 48% to 101% higher than in non-death-penalty States); Radelet & Akers, *Deterrence and the Death Penalty: The Views of the Experts*, 87 J. Crim. L. & C. 1, 8 (1996) (over 80% of criminologists believe existing research fails to support deterrence justification); Donohue & Wolfers, *Uses and Abuses of Empirical Evidence in the Death Penalty Debate*, 58 Stan. L. Rev. 791, 794 (2005) (evaluating existing statistical evidence and concluding that there is "profound uncertainty" about the existence of a deterrent effect).

Recently, the National Research Council . . . reviewed 30 years of empirical evidence and concluded that it was insufficient to establish a deterrent effect and thus should "not be used to inform" discussion about the deterrent value of the death penalty. NATIONAL RESEARCH COUNCIL, DETERRENCE AND THE DEATH PENALTY 2 (D. Nagin & J. Pepper eds. 2012).

I recognize that a "lack of evidence" for a proposition does not prove the contrary. But suppose that we add to these studies the fact that, today, very few of those sentenced to death are actually executed, and that even those executions occur, on average, after nearly two decades on death row. . . . Of the 8,466 inmates under a death sentence at some point between 1973 and 2013, 16% were executed, 42% had their convictions or sentences overturned or commuted, and 6% died by other causes; the remainder (35%) are still on death row.

Thus an offender who is sentenced to death is two or three times more likely to find his sentence overturned or commuted than to be executed; and he has a good chance of dying from natural causes before any execution (or exoneration) can take place. In a word, executions are *rare*. . . . These facts, when recurring, must have some offsetting effect on a potential perpetrator's fear of a death penalty. . . .

But what about retribution? Retribution is a valid penological goal. . . . *But see* A. SARAT, MERCY ON TRIAL: WHAT IT MEANS TO STOP AN EXECUTION 130 (2005) (Illinois Governor George Ryan explained his decision to commute all death sentences on the ground that it was "cruel and unusual" for "family members to go through this . . . legal limbo for [20] years").

The relevant question here, however, is whether a "community's sense of retribution" can often find vindication in "a death that comes," if at all, "only several decades after the crime was committed." By then . . . [t]he offenders and the victims' families have grown far older. Feelings of outrage may have subsided. The offender may have found himself a changed human being. And sometimes repentance and even forgiveness can restore meaning to lives once ruined. . . .

. . . [T]his Court has said that, if the death penalty does not fulfill the goals of deterrence or retribution, "it is nothing more than the purposeless and needless imposition of pain and suffering and hence an unconstitutional punishment." *Atkins* [*v. Virginia*, 536 U.S. 304, 319 (2002)]; *see also Gregg*, 428 U.S. at 183 (joint opinion of Stewart, Powell, and Stevens, JJ.) ("sanction imposed cannot be so totally without penological justification that it results in the gratuitous infliction of suffering").

Indeed, Justice Lewis Powell (who provided a crucial vote in *Gregg*) came to much the same conclusion, albeit after his retirement from this Court. . . . Chief Justice Rehnquist appointed him to chair a committee addressing concerns about delays in capital cases . . . . The Committee presented a report to Congress, and Justice Powell testified that "[d]elay robs the penalty of much of its deterrent value." Justice Powell, according to his official biographer, ultimately concluded that capital punishment . . . "serves no useful purpose." . . . In short, the problem of excessive delays led Justice Powell, at least in part, to conclude that the death penalty was unconstitutional. . . .

One might ask, why can Congress or the States not deal directly with the delay problem? . . . For one thing, delays have helped to make application of the death penalty more reliable. . . . [I]t is difficult for judges, as it would be difficult for anyone, not to apply legal requirements punctiliously when the consequence of failing to do so may well be death, particularly the death of an innocent person. . . . .

In this world, or at least in this Nation, we can have a death penalty that at least arguably serves legitimate penological purposes or we can have a procedural system that at least arguably seeks reliability and fairness in the death penalty's application. We cannot have both. And that simple fact, demonstrated convincingly over the past 40 years, strongly supports the claim that the death penalty violates the Eighth Amendment. . . .

IV. *"Unusual"* — Decline in Use of the Death Penalty

. . . [I]n the last two decades, the imposition and implementation of the death penalty have increasingly become unusual. . . . Between 1986 and 1999, 286 persons on average were sentenced to death each year. But, approximately 15 years ago, the numbers began to decline, and they have declined rapidly ever since. In 1999, 279 persons were sentenced to death. Last year, just 73 persons were sentenced to death.

That trend . . . also holds true with respect to the number of annual executions. In 1999, 98 people were executed. Last year, that number was only 35.

. . . Often when deciding whether a punishment practice is, constitutionally speaking, "unusual," this Court has looked to the number of States engaging in that practice. . . . In 1972, when the Court decided *Furman*, the death penalty was lawful in 41 States. Nine States had abolished it. As of today, 19 States have abolished the death penalty (along with the District of Columbia), although some did so prospectively only. In 11 other States that maintain the death penalty on the books, no execution has taken place for more than eight years . . . .

. . . Of the 20 States that have conducted at least one execution in the past eight years, 9 have conducted fewer than five in that time, making an execution in those States a fairly rare event. That leaves 11 States in which it is fair to say that capital punishment is not "unusual." And just three of those States (Texas, Missouri, and Florida) accounted for 80% of the executions nationwide (28 of the 35) in 2014. Indeed, last year, only seven States conducted an execution. . . .

In terms of population, if we ask how many Americans live in a State that at least occasionally carries out an execution (at least one within the prior three years), the answer two decades ago was 60% or 70%. Today, that number is 33%.

At the same time, use of the death penalty has become increasingly concentrated geographically. . . . [B]etween 2004 and 2009, only 35 counties imposed 5 or more death sentences, *i.e.*, approximately one per year. . . . [B]etween 2010 and 2015 (as of June 22), only 15 counties imposed five or more death sentences. . . . Between 1976 and 2007, there were no executions in 86% of America's counties. Liebman & Clarke[, *Minority Practice, Majority's Burden: The Death Penalty Today*, 9 Ohio S. J. Crim. L.

255, 265–66 & n.47 (2011)]; *cf. ibid.* (counties with less than 5% of the Nation's population carried out over half of its executions from 1976–2007). . . .

Moreover, we have said that it "is not so much the number of these States that is significant, but the consistency of the direction of change." . . . Seven States have abolished the death penalty in the last decade, including (quite recently) Nebraska. And several States have come within a single vote of eliminating the death penalty. . . .

These circumstances perhaps reflect the fact that a majority of Americans, when asked to choose between the death penalty and life in prison without parole, now choose the latter. Wilson, *Support for Death Penalty Still High, But Down*, Washington Post, GovBeat, June 5, 2014, online at www.washingtonpost.com/blogs/govbeat /wp/2014/06/05/support-for-death-penalty-still-high-but-down [(reporting that, while 60% of those polled generally support capital punishment — down from 80% in 1994 — a majority (52%) would prefer life in prison, compared to 42% who would choose the death penalty over life imprisonment)].

I rely primarily upon domestic, not foreign events, in pointing to changes and circumstances that tend to justify the claim that the death penalty, constitutionally speaking, is "unusual." . . . I note, however, that many nations — indeed, 95 of the 193 members of the United Nations — have formally abolished the death penalty and an additional 42 have abolished it in practice. In 2013, only 22 countries in the world carried out an execution. No executions were carried out in Europe or Central Asia, and the United States was the only country in the Americas to execute an inmate in 2013. Only eight countries executed more than 10 individuals (the United States, China, Iran, Iraq, Saudi Arabia, Somalia, Sudan, Yemen). And almost 80% of all known executions took place in three countries: Iran, Iraq, and Saudi Arabia. (This figure does not include China, which has a large population, but where precise data cannot be obtained.)

V

I recognize a strong counterargument that favors constitutionality. . . . The Constitution foresees a country that will make most important decisions democratically. Most nations that have abandoned the death penalty have done so through legislation, not judicial decision. And legislators, unlike judges, are free to take account of matters such as monetary costs, which I do not claim are relevant here. [*See*] California Commission on the Fair Administration of Justice, Report and Recommendations on the Administration of the Death Penalty in California 117 (June 30, 2008) (death penalty costs California $137 million per year; a comparable system of life imprisonment without parole would cost $11.5 million per year); Dáte, *The High Price of Killing Killers*, Palm Beach Post, Jan. 4, 2000, p. 1A (cost of each execution is $23 million above cost of life imprisonment without parole in Florida).

The answer is that the matters I have discussed . . . are quintessentially judicial matters. They concern the infliction — indeed the unfair, cruel, and unusual infliction — of a serious punishment upon an individual. I recognize that in 1972 this Court, in a sense, turned to Congress and the state legislatures in its search for standards that would increase the fairness and reliability of imposing a death penalty. The legislatures responded. But, in the last four decades, considerable evidence has accumulated that those responses have not worked.

Thus we are left with a judicial responsibility. The Eighth Amendment sets forth the relevant law, and we must interpret that law. . . . For the reasons I have set forth in this opinion, I believe it highly likely that the death penalty violates the Eighth Amendment. At the very least, the Court should call for full briefing on the basic question. . . .

Notes and Questions

1. The Policy Debate. Is capital punishment justifiable from a policy perspective? Do you find Justice Breyer or Justices Scalia and Thomas more convincing?

2. Execution Delays. Justice Breyer cited delays in implementing the death penalty as evidence that current capital sentencing procedures are "cruel" within the meaning of the Eighth Amendment. A federal district judge in California likewise relied on the "inordinate and unpredictable period of delay preceding . . . execution" in striking down the state's death penalty statute, *see Jones v. Chappell*, 31 F. Supp. 3d 1050, 1053 (C.D. Cal. 2014), but the decision was reversed by the Ninth Circuit on procedural grounds. *See Jones v. Davis*, 806 F.3d 538 (9th Cir. 2015). In the November 2016 elections, the California voters narrowly approved a referendum designed to shorten the appeals process in capital cases to five years. The California Supreme Court is considering the constitutionality of the measure. *See Briggs v. Brown*, 387 P.3d 1254 (Cal. 2017).

The Florida legislature acted with similar motives when it passed the "Timely Justice Act" in 2013, requiring the governor to sign a death warrant 30 days after the state supreme court certifies that all legal appeals have been exhausted in a capital case. Under the terms of the statute, the prisoner must then be executed within six months. The law gives the governor some discretion in that the death warrant cannot be signed until after clemency review is completed and the governor has the sole authority to order a clemency investigation. But the state's parole commission typically completes clemency investigations in less than a year. *See* Mary Ellen Klas, *Scott Speeds Executions*, Tampa Bay Times, June 15, 2013, at 1A. The Florida Supreme Court upheld the constitutionality of the statute in *Abdool v. Bondi*, 141 So. 3d 529 (Fla. 2014), and the number of executions has recently increased in Florida, though the governor has not signed death warrants for every death row prisoner whose appeals have been exhausted. *See* Steve Bousquet, *Vigils to Protest Death Penalty*, Tampa Bay Times, Jan. 12, 2015, at 1A.

3. Methods of Execution. Almost all executions in this country today are performed by lethal injection, the method used by the federal government and each of the states that permits capital punishment. The last holdout was Nebraska, where the legislature turned to lethal injection following the state supreme court's ruling that use of the electric chair violated the state constitution. *See State v. Mata*, 745 N.W.2d 229 (Neb. 2008).

Until recently, most executions by lethal injection followed a three-drug protocol, originally adopted in 1977 by the Oklahoma legislature "after consulting with the head of the anesthesiology department at the University of Oklahoma College of Medicine," and then embraced by other states "without significant independent review." *Baze v. Rees*, 553 U.S. 35, 42 & n.1 (2008) (plurality opinion). The *Baze* plurality described this protocol as follows:

> The first drug, sodium thiopental (also known as Pentathol), is a fast-acting barbiturate sedative that induces a deep, comalike unconsciousness . . . . The second drug, pancuronium bromide (also known as Pavulon), is a paralytic agent that inhibits all muscular-skeletal movements and, by paralyzing the diaphragm, stops respiration. Potassium chloride, the third drug, interferes with the electrical signals that stimulate the contractions of the heart, inducing cardiac arrest.

Id. at 44.

In addition to lethal injection, 15 states authorize an alternative method of execution to be used if, for example, lethal injection is ruled unconstitutional or the prisoner prefers the other method. *See* Bureau of Justice Statistics Bulletin, U.S. Dep't of Justice, Capital Punishment, 2013, at 7 (2014), http://www.bjs.gov /content/pub/pdf/cp13st.pdf. The controversies surrounding lethal injection and the scarcity of drugs described in the following Notes have led several states in recent years to reinstate an alternative method of execution in the event that the drugs become unavailable, including Tennessee (electric chair), Utah (firing squad), and Oklahoma (nitrogen gas). *See Methods of Execution: Authorized Methods*, Death Penalty Information Center, http://www.deathpenaltyinfo.org/methods -execution.

4. Challenges to Execution Methods. As the majority noted in *Glossip*, the Supreme Court "has never invalidated a State's chosen procedure for carrying out a sentence of death as the infliction of cruel and unusual punishment." *Glossip v. Gross*, 135 S. Ct. 2726, 2732 (2015). Challenges to particular execution methods have generally been unsuccessful in the lower courts as well. *See, e.g., Hunt v. Nuth*, 57 F.3d 1327, 1337–38 (4th Cir. 1995) (upholding the constitutionality of the gas chamber); *Campbell v. Wood*, 18 F.3d 662 (9th Cir. 1994) (en banc) (same re hanging); *Provenzano v. Moore*, 744 So. 2d 413 (Fla. 1999) (same regarding electric chair). *But see Fierro v. Gomez*, 77 F.3d 301, 308–09 (9th Cir.) (concluding that the gas chamber violated the Eighth Amendment because it involves "intense, visceral pain, . . . akin to the experience of a major heart attack, or to being held under water," and "the substantial risk that inmates will suffer this extreme pain for several minutes"), *vacated and remanded*, 519 U.S. 918 (1996); *Dawson v. State*, 554 S.E.2d 137, 144 (Ga. 2001) (finding that the electric chair—"with its specter of excruciating pain and its certainty of cooked brains and blistered bodies"—violated the state constitution's prohibition of cruel and unusual punishment by "inflict[ing] purposeless physical violence and needless mutilation that makes no measurable contribution to accepted goals of punishment"); *State v. Mata*, 745 N.W.2d 229, 278 (Neb. 2008) (likewise holding that the state constitution foreclosed use of the electric chair, explaining that "early assumptions about an instantaneous and painless death were simply incorrect and . . . there are more humane methods of carrying out the death penalty").

In *Baze v. Rees*, 553 U.S. 35 (2008) (plurality opinion), the Supreme Court upheld the constitutionality of the three-drug protocol used until recently in most lethal injections. The Oklahoma procedures subsequently challenged in *Glossip v. Gross* replaced the first drug (sodium thiopental) with midazolam, with the amount of that sedative increased from 100 to 500 milligrams following the state's botched execution of Clayton Lockett in 2014. The *Glossip* majority described the Lockett execution as follows:

> [T]he execution team spent nearly an hour making at least one dozen attempts to establish intravenous (IV) access to Lockett's cardiovascular system, including at his arms and elsewhere on his body. The team eventually believed that it had established intravenous access through Lockett's right femoral vein, and it covered the injection access point with a sheet, in part to preserve Lockett's dignity during the execution. After the team administered the midazolam and a physician determined that Lockett was unconscious, the team next administered the paralytic agent (vecuronium bromide) and most of the potassium chloride. Lockett began to move and speak, at which point the physician lifted the sheet and determined that the IV had "infiltrated," which means that "the IV fluid, rather than entering Lockett's blood stream, had leaked into the tissue surrounding the IV access point." The execution team stopped administering the remaining potassium chloride and terminated the execution about 33 minutes after the midazolam was first injected. About 10 minutes later, Lockett was pronounced dead.

Glossip, 135 S. Ct. at 2734. *See also id.* at 2782 (Sotomayor, J., dissenting) (noting that "[v]arious witnesses reported that Lockett began to writhe against his restraints, saying, '[t]his s*** is f***ing with my mind,' 'something is wrong,' and '[t]he drugs aren't working'"). *But cf. Estate of Lockett v. Fallin*, 841 F.3d 1098 (10th Cir. 2016) (finding that Lockett's execution did not constitute cruel and unusual punishment).

In upholding the Oklahoma lethal injection procedures, the *Glossip* majority reasoned that the prisoners failed to establish "'a substantial risk of serious harm,' an 'objectively intolerable risk of harm,'" "when compared to a known and reliable alternative method of execution." *Glossip*, 135 S. Ct. at 2737–38 (quoting *Baze*, 553 U.S. at 50). The Court relied on a doctor of pharmacy who testified as an expert in the court below that "the proper administration of a 500-milligram dose of midazolam would make it 'a virtual certainty' that any individual would be 'at a sufficient level of unconsciousness to resist the noxious stimuli which could occur from application of the 2nd and 3rd drugs' used in the Oklahoma protocol." *Id.* at 2741. The majority also cited "important safeguards" Oklahoma had adopted in the wake of the Lockett execution "to ensure that midazolam is properly administered": "[t]he execution team must secure both a primary and backup IV access site, it must confirm the viability of the IV sites, and it must continuously monitor the offender's level of consciousness." *Id.* at 2742.

The four dissenters criticized the majority for "credit[ing] the scientifically unsupported and implausible testimony of a single expert witness" and for adopting "the wholly novel requirement" that death row inmates must "prov[e] the availability of an alternative means for their own executions." *Id.* at 2781 (Sotomayor, J., dissenting). The dissent pointed out that all three experts who testified before the district judge agreed that midazolam has a ceiling effect, meaning that "more is not necessarily better," and that the prisoners' experts testified that, while the drug undoubtedly induces unconsciousness, it does not reliably "keep[] a condemned inmate unconscious" when the inmate experiences "the extreme pain and discomfort associated with administration of the second and third drugs" and for that reason is not used as the sole anesthetic during surgery. *Id.* at 2788, 2783. The dissent was also skeptical of the value of the state's procedural safeguards, noting that once the second drug—"a powerful paralytic"—is administered, it becomes "impossible to tell whether the condemned inmate in fact remain[s] unconscious." *Id.* at 2791.

Given the understandable lack of experimental evidence measuring the efficacy of lethal drugs, how confident can any court be in their effectiveness during an execution? Was the *Glossip* majority right in warning that "federal courts should not 'embroil [themselves] in ongoing scientific controversies beyond their expertise'"? *Id.* at 2740 (majority opinion). Or did the dissenters have the stronger argument in urging that the Justices should not "abdicat[e] our duty to examine critically the factual predicates for the District Court's finding"? *Id.* at 2786 (Sotomayor, J., dissenting). *See also* Deborah W. Denno, *The Lethal Injection Quandary: How Medicine Has Dismantled the Death Penalty*, 76 FORDHAM L. REV. 49, 58–59 (2007) (condemning the "constitutionally vulnerable" lethal injection procedures used around the country, and concluding that "states have continued to produce grossly inadequate protocols that severely restrict understanding of how executions are performed and heighten the likelihood of unconstitutionality"); Steven D. Schwinn, *The Wonderland Rules for Method-of-Execution Claims*, SCOTUSBLOG (June 30, 2015, 3:16 PM), http://www.scotusblog.com/2015/06/symposium-the-wonderland-rules-for-method-of-execution-claims/ (criticizing the *Glossip* majority for allowing "non-medical state officials [to] essentially experiment with lethal injection cocktails" and for requiring "a lay *plaintiff*... to show a lack of viable alternatives *to his own execution*," an "extraordinary burden" that "a challenger never bears... in protecting other enumerated fundamental rights"). Glossip's case was the subject of the docu-series *Killing Richard Glossip*, which aired on Investigation Discovery in April 2017.

5. Shortages of Lethal Injection Drugs. A number of states in addition to Oklahoma have revised their lethal injection protocols as the supply of drugs has dwindled. In 2011, the sole American manufacturer of sodium thiopental announced that it would no longer produce the drug, and Britain and other European countries have banned the exportation of drugs to be used for executions in the United States. *See* John Schwartz, *Legal Questions Are Raised as States Seek Death Penalty Drug*, N.Y. Times, Apr. 14, 2011, at A14. In addition, the D.C. Circuit blocked the FDA from allowing prisons to import sodium thiopental on the grounds that the agency had not approved or reviewed the drug for safety and effectiveness. *See Cook v. FDA*, 733 F.3d 1 (D.C. Cir. 2013).

In 2009, Ohio became the first state to abandon the three-drug cocktail and instead use a massive dose of a single anesthetic in its lethal injections. The move came after an unsuccessful attempt to execute Romell Broom, who "sobbed with pain as prison officials repeatedly stuck him with a needle for nearly two hours in a failed effort to find a usable vein." *See* Ian Urbina, *Ohio Is First to Change to One Drug in Executions*, N.Y. Times, Nov. 14, 2009, at A10. The Ohio Supreme Court subsequently ruled that the Eighth Amendment does not bar a second attempt to execute Broom, who is the only prisoner in almost 70 years to survive a failed execution in this country. *See State v. Broom*, 51 N.E.3d 620 (Ohio), *cert. denied*, 137 S. Ct. 590 (2016).

Lethal injections in a number of other death penalty states now consist of a single drug, including pentobarbital and midazolam. *See State by State Lethal Injection*, Death Penalty Information Center, http://www.deathpenaltyinfo.org/state-lethal-injection. But Pfizer's recent announcement that it would no longer allow any of its products to be used in lethal injections "closes off the last remaining open-market source of drugs used in executions," as every FDA-approved drug company now bans the sale of drugs for such purposes. *See* Erik Eckholm, *Pfizer Prohibits Use of Its Drugs for Executions*, N.Y. Times, May 14, 2016, at A1.

As a result, a number of states are turning to compounding pharmacies, which are not regulated by the FDA, to obtain their lethal injection drugs. *See State by State Lethal Injection, supra.* In the wake of numerous challenges to lethal injection protocols, some states have refused to disclose the source of the drugs used in executions. Constitutional challenges to this lack of transparency have largely been rejected. *See, e.g., Ryan v. Wood*, 135 S. Ct. 21 (2014) (mem.) (vacating the Ninth Circuit's decision to stay an execution until the State revealed the names of the lethal injection drugs to be used and the qualifications of the executioners); *Jones v. Commissioner*, 811 F.3d 1288 (11th Cir.) (rejecting challenge to the Georgia Lethal Injection Secrecy Act), *rehearing en banc denied*, 812 F.3d 923 (11th Cir. 2016) (denying rehearing by a vote of six to five). For the view that the Eighth Amendment "should encompass a due process right to know the method by which the state plans to execute" death row prisoners because "due process and basic fairness demand that litigants receive notice of the state's plans for them and an opportunity to challenge those plans," see Eric Berger, *Lethal Injection Secrecy and Eighth Amendment Due Process*, 55 B.C. L. Rev. 1367, 1375, 1373 (2014). *But cf.* Mary D. Fan, *The Supply-Side*

Attack on Lethal Injection and the Rise of Execution Secrecy, 95 B.U. L. Rev. 427, 435 (2015) (responding that protecting the identity of drug suppliers "reduces the need to resort to questionable backroom sources abroad, eleventh-hour substitutions, or reversion to older — and arguably more brutal — methods of execution").

McCleskey v. Kemp

481 U.S. 279 (1987)

Justice Powell delivered the opinion of the Court.

This case presents the question whether a complex statistical study that indicates a risk that racial considerations enter into capital sentencing determinations proves that petitioner McCleskey's capital sentence is unconstitutional under the Eighth or Fourteenth Amendment.

I

McCleskey, a black man, was convicted of two counts of armed robbery and one count of murder in the Superior Court of Fulton County, Georgia, on October 12, 1978. McCleskey's convictions arose out of the robbery of a furniture store and the killing of a white police officer during the course of the robbery. . . .

The jury convicted McCleskey of murder. At the penalty hearing, the jury heard arguments as to the appropriate sentence. . . . The jury in this case found two aggravating circumstances to exist beyond a reasonable doubt: the murder was committed during the course of an armed robbery; and the murder was committed upon a peace officer engaged in the performance of his duties. McCleskey offered no mitigating evidence. The jury recommended that he be sentenced to death. . . . The court followed the jury's recommendation and sentenced McCleskey to death.

. . . .

McCleskey filed a petition for a writ of habeas corpus in the Federal District Court for the Northern District of Georgia. His petition raised 18 claims, one of which was that the Georgia capital sentencing process is administered in a racially discriminatory manner in violation of the Eighth and Fourteenth Amendments to the United States Constitution. In support of his claim, McCleskey proffered a statistical study performed by Professors David C. Baldus, Charles Pulaski, and George Woodworth (the Baldus study) that purports to show a disparity in the imposition of the death sentence in Georgia based on the race of the murder victim and, to a lesser extent, the race of the defendant. The Baldus study is actually two sophisticated statistical studies that examine over 2,000 murder cases that occurred in Georgia during the 1970s. The raw numbers collected by Professor Baldus indicate that defendants charged with killing white persons received the death penalty in 11% of the cases, but defendants charged with killing blacks received the death penalty in only 1% of the cases. The raw numbers also indicate a reverse racial disparity according to the race of the defendant: 4% of the black defendants received the death penalty, as opposed to 7% of the white defendants.

Baldus also divided the cases according to the combination of the race of the defendant and the race of the victim. He found that the death penalty was assessed in 22% of the cases involving black defendants and white victims; 8% of the cases involving white defendants and white victims; 1% of the cases involving black defendants and black victims; and 3% of the cases involving white defendants and black victims. Similarly, Baldus found that prosecutors sought the death penalty in 70% of the cases involving black defendants and white victims; 32% of the cases involving white defendants and white victims; 15% of the cases involving black defendants and black victims; and 19% of the cases involving white defendants and black victims.

Baldus subjected his data to an extensive analysis, taking account of 230 variables that could have explained the disparities on nonracial grounds. One of his models concludes that, even after taking account of 39 nonracial variables, defendants charged with killing white victims were 4.3 times as likely to receive a death sentence as defendants charged with killing blacks. According to this model, black defendants were 1.1 times as likely to receive a death sentence as other defendants. Thus, the Baldus study indicates that black defendants, such as McCleskey, who kill white victims have the greatest likelihood of receiving the death penalty.[32]

. . . .

II

McCleskey's first claim is that the Georgia capital punishment statute violates the Equal Protection Clause of the Fourteenth Amendment.[33] . . . As a black defendant who killed a white victim, McCleskey claims that the Baldus study demonstrates that he was discriminated against because of his race and because of the race of his victim. In its broadest form, McCleskey's claim of discrimination extends to every actor in the Georgia capital sentencing process, from the prosecutor who sought the death penalty and the jury that imposed the sentence, to the State itself that enacted the

---

32. [n.5] Baldus' 230-variable model divided cases into eight different ranges, according to the estimated aggravation level of the offense. Baldus argued in his testimony to the District Court that the effects of racial bias were most striking in the midrange cases. "[W]hen the cases become tremendously aggravated so that everybody would agree that if we're going to have a death sentence, these are the cases that should get it, the race effects go away. It's only in the mid-range of cases where the decision-makers have a real choice as to what to do. If there's room for the exercise of discretion, then the [racial] factors begin to play a role." Under this model, Baldus found that 14.4% of the black-victim midrange cases received the death penalty, and 34.4% of the white-victim cases received the death penalty. According to Baldus, the facts of McCleskey's case placed it within the midrange.

33. [n.7] Although the District Court rejected the findings of the Baldus study as flawed, the Court of Appeals assumed that the study is valid and reached the constitutional issues. Accordingly, those issues are before us. As did the Court of Appeals, we assume the study is valid statistically without reviewing the factual findings of the District Court. . . .

capital punishment statute and allows it to remain in effect despite its allegedly discriminatory application. We agree with the Court of Appeals, and every other court that has considered such a challenge, that this claim must fail.

A

Our analysis begins with the basic principle that a defendant who alleges an equal protection violation has the burden of proving "the existence of purposeful discrimination." Thus, to prevail under the Equal Protection Clause, McCleskey must prove that the decisionmakers in *his* case acted with discriminatory purpose. He offers no evidence specific to his own case that would support an inference that racial considerations played a part in his sentence. Instead, he relies solely on the Baldus study. McCleskey argues that the Baldus study compels an inference that his sentence rests on purposeful discrimination. McCleskey's claim that these statistics are sufficient proof of discrimination, without regard to the facts of a particular case, would extend to all capital cases in Georgia, at least where the victim was white and the defendant is black.

The Court has accepted statistics as proof of intent to discriminate in certain limited contexts. First, this Court has accepted statistical disparities as proof of an equal protection violation in the selection of the jury venire in a particular district. . . . Second, this Court has accepted statistics in the form of multiple-regression analysis to prove statutory [employment discrimination] violations under Title VII of the Civil Rights Act of 1964.

But the nature of the capital sentencing decision, and the relationship of the statistics to that decision, are fundamentally different from the corresponding elements in the venire-selection or Title VII cases. Most importantly, each . . . jury is unique in its composition, and the Constitution requires that its decision rest on consideration of innumerable factors that vary according to the characteristics of the individual defendant and the facts of the particular capital offense. Thus, the application of an inference drawn from the general statistics to a specific decision in a trial and sentencing simply is not comparable to the application of an inference drawn from general statistics to a specific venire-selection or Title VII case. In those cases, the statistics relate to fewer entities, and fewer variables are relevant to the challenged decisions.

. . . .

B

McCleskey also suggests that the Baldus study proves that the State as a whole has acted with a discriminatory purpose. He appears to argue that the State has violated the Equal Protection Clause by adopting the capital punishment statute and allowing it to remain in force despite its allegedly discriminatory application. But "'[d]iscriminatory purpose' . . . implies more than intent as volition or intent as awareness of consequences. It implies that the decisionmaker, in this case a state legislature, selected or reaffirmed a particular course of action at least in part 'because of,' not merely 'in spite of,' its adverse effects upon an identifiable group." For this claim to prevail, McCleskey would have to prove that the Georgia Legislature enacted or maintained the death penalty statute *because* of an anticipated racially discriminatory effect. In *Gregg v. Georgia,* this Court found that the Georgia capital sentencing system could operate in a fair and neutral manner. There was no evidence then, and there is none now, that the Georgia Legislature enacted the capital punishment statute to further a racially discriminatory purpose.[34]

Nor has McCleskey demonstrated that the legislature maintains the capital punishment statute because of the racially disproportionate impact suggested by the Baldus study. As legislatures necessarily have wide discretion in the choice of criminal laws and penalties, and as there were legitimate reasons for the Georgia Legislature to adopt and maintain capital punishment, we will not infer a discriminatory purpose on the part of the State of Georgia.

. . . .

IV

. . . [Turning to the Eighth Amendment,] McCleskey argues that the sentence in his case is disproportionate to the sentences in other murder cases.

. . . .

Although our decision in *Gregg* as to the facial validity of the Georgia capital punishment statute appears to foreclose McCleskey's disproportionality argument, he . . . contends that the Georgia capital punishment system is arbitrary and capricious in *application*, and therefore his sentence is excessive, because racial considerations may influence capital sentencing decisions in Georgia. . . .

To evaluate McCleskey's challenge, we must examine exactly what the Baldus study may show. Even Professor Baldus does not contend that his statistics *prove* that race enters into any capital sentencing decisions or that race was a factor in McCleskey's particular case. Statistics at most may show only a likelihood that a particular factor entered into some decisions. There is, of course, some risk of racial prejudice influencing a jury's decision in a criminal case. There are similar risks that other kinds of prejudice will influence other criminal trials. The question "is at what point that risk becomes constitutionally unacceptable." . . .

McCleskey's argument that the Constitution condemns the discretion allowed decisionmakers in the Georgia capital sentencing system is antithetical to the fundamental role of discretion in our criminal justice system. Discretion in the

---

34. [n.20] McCleskey relies on "historical evidence" to support his claim of purposeful discrimination by the State. This evidence focuses on Georgia laws in force during and just after the Civil War. Of course, the "historical background of the decision is one evidentiary source" for proof of intentional discrimination. But unless historical evidence is reasonably contemporaneous with the challenged decision, it has little probative value. Although the history of racial discrimination in this country is undeniable, we cannot accept official actions taken long ago as evidence of current intent.

criminal justice system offers substantial benefits to the criminal defendant. Not only can a jury decline to impose the death sentence, it can decline to convict or choose to convict of a lesser offense. Whereas decisions against a defendant's interest may be reversed by the trial judge or on appeal, these discretionary exercises of leniency are final and unreviewable. Similarly, the capacity of prosecutorial discretion to provide individualized justice is "firmly entrenched in American law." . . . Of course, "the power to be lenient [also] is the power to discriminate," but a capital punishment system that did not allow for discretionary acts of leniency "would be totally alien to our notions of criminal justice."

At most, the Baldus study indicates a discrepancy that appears to correlate with race. Apparent disparities in sentencing are an inevitable part of our criminal justice system. The discrepancy indicated by the Baldus study is "a far cry from the major systemic defects identified in *Furman*." . . . Where the discretion that is fundamental to our criminal process is involved, we decline to assume that what is unexplained is invidious. In light of the safeguards designed to minimize racial bias in the process, the fundamental value of jury trial in our criminal justice system, and the benefits that discretion provides to criminal defendants, we hold that the Baldus study does not demonstrate a constitutionally significant risk of racial bias affecting the Georgia capital sentencing process.

V

Two additional concerns inform our decision in this case. First, McCleskey's claim, taken to its logical conclusion, throws into serious question the principles that underlie our entire criminal justice system. The Eighth Amendment is not limited in application to capital punishment, but applies to all penalties. Thus, if we accepted McCleskey's claim that racial bias has impermissibly tainted the capital sentencing decision, we could soon be faced with similar claims as to other types of penalty.[35] Moreover, the claim that his sentence rests on the irrelevant factor of race easily could be extended to apply to claims based on unexplained discrepancies that correlate to membership in other minority groups, and even to gender. If arbitrary and capricious punishment is the touchstone under the Eighth Amendment, such a claim could—at least in theory—be based upon any arbitrary variable, such as the defendant's facial characteristics, or the physical attractiveness of the defendant or the victim, that some statistical study indicates may be influential in jury decisionmaking. As these examples illustrate, there is no limiting principle to the type of challenge brought by McCleskey. The Constitution does not require that a State eliminate any demonstrable disparity that correlates with a potentially irrelevant factor in order to operate a criminal justice system that includes capital punishment. . . .

Second, McCleskey's arguments are best presented to the legislative bodies. . . . Legislatures are better qualified to weigh and "evaluate the results of statistical

---

35. [n.38] Studies already exist that allegedly demonstrate a racial disparity in the length of prison sentences.

studies in terms of their own local conditions and with a flexibility of approach that is not available to the courts." . . .

Justice Brennan, with whom Justice Marshall joins, and with whom Justice Blackmun and Justice Stevens join in all but Part I, dissenting.

I

Adhering to my view that the death penalty is in all circumstances cruel and unusual punishment forbidden by the Eighth and Fourteenth Amendments, I would vacate the decision below insofar as it left undisturbed the death sentence imposed in this case. . . .

Even if I did not hold this position, however, I would reverse the Court of Appeals, for petitioner McCleskey has clearly demonstrated that his death sentence was imposed in violation of the Eighth and Fourteenth Amendments. . . .

II

At some point in this case, Warren McCleskey doubtless asked his lawyer whether a jury was likely to sentence him to die. A candid reply to this question would have been disturbing. First, counsel would have to tell McCleskey that few of the details of the crime or of McCleskey's past criminal conduct were more important than the fact that his victim was white. . . . In addition, frankness would compel the disclosure that it was more likely than not that the race of McCleskey's victim would determine whether he received a death sentence: 6 of every 11 defendants convicted of killing a white person would not have received the death penalty if their victims had been black, while, among defendants with aggravating and mitigating factors comparable to McCleskey's, 20 of every 34 would not have been sentenced to die if their victims had been black. . . . The story could be told in a variety of ways, but McCleskey could not fail to grasp its essential narrative line: there was a significant chance that race would play a prominent role in determining if he lived or died.

. . . .

III

It is important to emphasize at the outset that the Court's observation that McCleskey cannot prove the influence of race on any particular sentencing decision is irrelevant in evaluating his Eighth Amendment claim. Since *Furman v. Georgia,* the Court has been concerned with the *risk* of the imposition of an arbitrary sentence, rather than the proven fact of one. . . .

Defendants challenging their death sentences thus never have had to prove that impermissible considerations have actually infected sentencing decisions. We have required instead that they establish that the system under which they were sentenced posed a significant risk of such an occurrence. McCleskey's claim does differ, however, in one respect from these earlier cases: it is the first to base a challenge not on speculation about how a system *might* operate, but on empirical documentation of how it *does* operate.

. . . .

Evaluation of McCleskey's evidence cannot rest solely on the numbers them-selves. . . . Georgia's legacy of a race-conscious criminal justice system, as well as this Court's own recognition of the persistent danger that racial attitudes may affect criminal proceedings, indicates that McCleskey's claim is not a fanciful product of mere statistical artifice.

For many years, Georgia operated openly and formally precisely the type of dual system the evidence shows is still effectively in place. The criminal law expressly differentiated between crimes committed by and against blacks and whites, distinc-tions whose lineage traced back to the time of slavery. During the colonial period, black slaves who killed whites in Georgia, regardless of whether in self-defense or in defense of another, were automatically executed.

By the time of the Civil War, a dual system of crime and punishment was well-established in Georgia. The state criminal code contained separate sections for "Slaves and Free Persons of Color," and for all other persons. The code provided, for instance, for an automatic death sentence for murder committed by blacks, but declared that anyone else convicted of murder might receive life imprisonment if the conviction were founded solely on circumstantial testimony *or* simply if the jury so recommended. . . .

This historical review of Georgia criminal law is not intended as a bill of indict-ment calling the State to account for past transgressions. Citation of past practices does not justify the automatic condemnation of current ones. But it would be unre-alistic to ignore the influence of history in assessing the plausible implications of McCleskey's evidence. "Americans share a historical experience that has resulted in individuals within the culture ubiquitously attaching a significance to race that is irrational and often outside their awareness." . . .

IV

. . . .

The Court maintains that petitioner's claim "is antithetical to the fundamental role of discretion in our criminal justice system." . . .

Reliance on race in imposing capital punishment, however, is antithetical to the very rationale for granting sentencing discretion. Discretion is a means, not an end. It is bestowed in order to permit the sentencer to "trea[t] each defendant in a capital case with that degree of respect due the uniqueness of the individual." . . .

Considering the race of a defendant or victim in deciding if the death penalty should be imposed is completely at odds with this concern that an individual be eval-uated as a unique human being. . . .

The Court next states that its unwillingness to regard petitioner's evidence as suf-ficient is based in part on the fear that recognition of McCleskey's claim would open the door to widespread challenges to all aspects of criminal sentencing. Taken on its face, such a statement seems to suggest a fear of too much justice. . . . The prospect that there may be more widespread abuse than McCleskey documents may be dismaying, but it does not justify complete abdication of our judicial role. . . .

Finally, the Court justifies its rejection of McCleskey's claim by cautioning against usurpation of the legislatures' role in devising and monitoring criminal punishment. . . . The judiciary's role in this society counts for little if the use of governmental power to extinguish life does not elicit close scrutiny, . . . for those granted constitutional protection in this context are those whom society finds most menacing and opprobrious. . . .

For these reasons, "[t]he methods we employ in the enforcement of our criminal law have aptly been called the measures by which the quality of our civilization may be judged." Those whom we would banish from society or from the human community itself often speak in too faint a voice to be heard above society's demand for punishment. It is the particular role of courts to hear these voices, for the Constitution declares that the majoritarian chorus may not alone dictate the conditions of social life.

Justice Blackmun, with whom Justice Marshall and Justice Stevens join, and with whom Justice Brennan joins in all but Part IV-B,[36] dissenting.

. . . .

A criminal defendant alleging an equal protection violation must prove the existence of purposeful discrimination. He may establish a prima facie case of purposeful discrimination "by showing that the totality of the relevant facts gives rise to an inference of discriminatory purpose." Once the defendant establishes a prima facie case, the burden shifts to the prosecution to rebut that case. "The State cannot meet this burden on mere general assertions that its officials did not discriminate or that they properly performed their official duties." The State must demonstrate that the challenged effect was due to "permissible racially neutral selection criteria."

. . . .

There can be no dispute that McCleskey has made the requisite showing. . . . The Baldus study demonstrates that black persons are a distinct group that are singled out for different treatment in the Georgia capital sentencing system. . . .

. . . The most persuasive evidence of the constitutionally significant effect of racial factors in the Georgia capital sentencing system is McCleskey's proof that the race of the victim is more important in explaining the imposition of a death sentence than is the factor whether the defendant was a prime mover in the homicide.[37] Similarly,

---

36. Part IV-B of Justice Blackmun's opinion endorsed the views expressed in Justice Stevens' dissent, which is excerpted below.

37. [n.9] A defendant's chances of receiving a death sentence increase by a factor of 4.3 if the victim is white, but only by 2.3 if the defendant was the prime mover behind the homicide.

the race-of-victim factor is nearly as crucial as the statutory aggravating circumstance whether the defendant had a prior record of a conviction for a capital crime.[38] . . .

The above-described evidence, considered in conjunction with the other record evidence outlined by Justice Brennan, gives rise to an inference of discriminatory purpose. . . . [A]bsent evidence to the contrary, one must conclude that racial factors entered into the decisionmaking process that yielded McCleskey's death sentence.

JUSTICE STEVENS, with whom JUSTICE BLACKMUN joins, dissenting.

. . . .

The Court's decision appears to be based on a fear that the acceptance of McCleskey's claim would sound the death knell for capital punishment in Georgia. If society were indeed forced to choose between a racially discriminatory death penalty (one that provides heightened protection against murder "for whites only") and no death penalty at all, the choice mandated by the Constitution would be plain. But the Court's fear is unfounded. One of the lessons of the Baldus study is that there exist certain categories of extremely serious crimes for which prosecutors consistently seek, and juries consistently impose, the death penalty without regard to the race of the victim or the race of the offender. If Georgia were to narrow the class of death-eligible defendants to those categories, the danger of arbitrary and discriminatory imposition of the death penalty would be significantly decreased, if not eradicated. . . .

Notes and Questions

1. **The Composition of the Death Row Population.** Of the 2,902 prisoners on death row in this country at the end of September 2016, 42 percent were white, 42 percent were African-American, and 13 percent were Latino. Women make up about two percent of the death row population. *See* DEATH PENALTY INFORMATION CENTER, FACTS ABOUT THE DEATH PENALTY, http://www.deathpenaltyinfo .org/documents/FactSheet.pdf; BUREAU OF JUSTICE STATISTICS BULLETIN, DEP'T OF JUSTICE, CAPITAL PUNISHMENT, 2013, at 10 (2014), http://www.bjs.gov/content/pub/ pdf/cp13st.pdf.

Of the 1,452 prisoners executed between the beginning of 1977 and the end of April 2017, 55.6 percent (808) were white, 34.5 percent (501) were African-American, and 8.3 percent (120) were Latino. Sixteen women (1%) were executed during this period. More than three-quarters (75.6%, or 1,612) of the 2,130 victims in these cases were white; 15.3 percent (324) were African-American, and 6.9 percent (149) were Latino. *See* DEATH PENALTY INFORMATION CENTER, RACE OF DEATH ROW INMATES EXECUTED SINCE 1976, http://www.deathpenaltyinfo.org/race-death-row-inmates-executed-1976 #defend; BUREAU OF JUSTICE STATISTICS BULLETIN, *supra*, at 14.

---

38. [n.10] A prior record of a conviction for murder, armed robbery, rape, or kidnaping with bodily injury increases the chances of a defendant's receiving a death sentence by a factor of 4.9.

2. Evaluating the Court's Ruling in *McCleskey*. Commentators have criticized the Court's opinion in *McCleskey* as "logically unsound, morally reprehensible, and legally unsupportable," *The Supreme Court, 1986 Term — Leading Cases*, 101 Harv. L. Rev. 119, 158 (1987), and, like *Plessy v. Ferguson*, 163 U.S. 537 (1896), "wrong the day it was decided." John H. Blume & Sheri Lynn Johnson, *Unholy Parallels Between* McCleskey v. Kemp *and* Plessy v. Ferguson: *Why* McCleskey *(Still) Matters*, 10 Ohio St. J. Crim. L. 37, 63 (2012). Others, however, have argued that the Court's decision was "all too predictable" given the judiciary's "staunch resistance" to sentencing challenges alleging racial discrimination. Randall L. Kennedy, McCleskey v. Kemp: *Race, Capital Punishment, and the Supreme Court*, 101 Harv. L. Rev. 1388, 1408, 1403 (1988).

Was the Court's ruling in *McCleskey* dictated by the long-standing doctrine that only purposeful discrimination violates the Equal Protection Clause? *See id.* at 1405, 1419 (noting that this intent requirement "insulates entirely many of the unconscious ways in which prejudiced social values give rise to differential treatment on the basis of race," and is therefore "hopeless[ly] inadequa[te] as a tool for responding to racial oppression in its subtle modern guises"). *But cf.* John H. Blume et al., *Post-*McCleskey *Racial Discrimination Claims in Capital Cases*, 83 Cornell L. Rev. 1771, 1807–08 (1998) (observing that "in other classes of race cases, courts do find intentional discrimination with less evidence than has been accumulated in some of [the death penalty] cases"). Was the Court's insistence on evidence of intent justifiable only in resolving McCleskey's equal protection claim, and not his argument that the death penalty was administered in an arbitrary fashion in violation of the Eighth Amendment? Consider Samuel R. Gross & Robert Mauro, *Patterns of Death: An Analysis of Racial Disparities in Capital Sentencing and Homicide Victimizing*, 37 Stan. L. Rev. 27, 37 (1984):

> "Arbitrariness" . . . is not the description of an affirmative act; it is a wholly negative legal concept, the absence of a legitimate justification for an action or a pattern of actions. Not surprisingly, none of the Supreme Court opinions that condemn arbitrariness in the imposition of the death penalty suggests that intent is relevant to the issue.

Researchers studying the administration of the death penalty in other areas have reached the same conclusion as the Baldus study. *See, e.g.,* U.S. General Accounting Office, Death Penalty Sentencing: Research Indicates Pattern of Racial Disparities 5–6 (1990) (reviewing 28 empirical studies conducted in the 1970s and 1980s, and reporting that 82 percent of them found that the victim's race influenced the likelihood a defendant would be charged with a capital crime or receive a death sentence, a "finding . . . remarkably consistent across data sets, states, data collection methods, and analytic techniques"); Gross & Mauro, *supra*, at 105, 61–62 (concluding, based on a study of capital sentencing patterns in eight states between 1976 and 1980, that "discrimination . . . based on the race of the victim . . . is a remarkably stable and consistent phenomenon," and cannot be explained by nonracial variables, including the three "most important [nonracial] predictors of capital sentencing" — killing in the course of another felony, killing a stranger, and killing more than one person); Glenn L. Pierce & Michael L. Radelet, *Empirical Analysis: The Impact of Legally Inappropriate Factors on Death Sentencing for California Homicides, 1990–1999,* 46 Santa Clara L. Rev. 1, 37–38 (2005) (studying death sentences imposed in California for homicides committed during the 1990s, and finding, after "controlling for all other predictor variables, [that] those who kill non-Hispanic African Americans are 59.3 percent less likely to be sentenced to death than those who kill non-Hispanic whites," and that the "disparity increases to 67 percent when comparing the death sentencing rates of those who kill whites with those who kill Hispanics"); Steven F. Shatz & Terry Dalton, *Challenging the Death Penalty with Statistics:* Furman, McCleskey, *and a Single County Case Study,* 34 Cardozo L. Rev. 1227, 1244–51 (2013) (citing more than 20 studies conducted between 1990 and 2013 from "different jurisdictions, with differing methodologies, covering a variety of time periods" that "produced results remarkably consistent with the Baldus study" concerning the impact of the victim's race on capital sentencing). *See also* Justin D. Levinson et al., *Devaluing Death: An Empirical Study of Implicit Racial Bias on Jury-Eligible Citizens in Six Death Penalty States,* 89 N.Y.U. L. Rev. 513, 521 (2014) (finding, in mock juror study conducted in six leading death penalty states, that "jury-eligible citizens harbored . . . implicit racial stereotypes about Blacks and Whites generally, as well as implicit associations between race and the value of life"—i.e., that "White people are more valuable than Black people").

Does *McCleskey*'s refusal to attach constitutional significance to these statistics "effectively condone the expression of racism in a profound aspect of our law"? Anthony Lewis, *Bowing to Racism,* N.Y. Times, Apr. 28, 1987, at A31. Or do these studies simply mean that "the death penalty is sought and imposed less often in jurisdictions with high black populations," which reflects not discrimination but the "empowerment of black people," who, as "the only demographic segment of America with a majority opposed to the death penalty," are exercising their "clout in the election of prosecutors and in the verdicts of juries"? Kent Scheidegger, *Rebutting the Myths About Race and the Death Penalty,* 10 Ohio St. J. Crim. L. 147, 164–65 (2012).

Even if Scheidegger is right, do the statistical disparities suggest that the death penalty should be abolished because it cannot be operated in a race-neutral fashion? Late in his tenure on the Court, Justice Blackmun came to believe that the death penalty "as currently administered" is unconstitutional, in part because "we may not be capable of devising procedural or substantive rules to prevent the more subtle and often unconscious forms of racism from creeping into the system." *Callins v. Collins,* 510 U.S. 1141, 1159, 1154 (1994) (Blackmun, J., dissenting from the denial of certiorari). Additionally, Justice Powell, the author of the majority opinion in *McCleskey,* reported five years later (after he had left the Court) that he wished he had voted differently in the case, and in fact had "come to think that capital punishment should be abolished." John C. Jeffries, Jr., *A Change of Mind That Came Too Late,* N.Y. Times, June 23, 1994, at A23.

3. The Congressional Response to *McCleskey.* Congressional efforts to overturn the Court's decision in *McCleskey* proved unavailing. Although the House of

Representatives twice voted in favor of bills that would have given capital defendants the right to challenge their death sentences by presenting statistical evidence of racial discrimination, the Senate refused to go along on each occasion. For a description of the various bills and the legislative debate, see David C. Baldus et al., *Reflections on the "Inevitability" of Racial Discrimination in Capital Sentencing and the "Impossibility" of Its Prevention, Detection, and Correction*, 51 Wash. & Lee L. Rev. 359, 376–405 (1994).

In 1994, Congress did pass a law mandating that juries in federal capital cases be instructed not to consider the race, national origin, religion, or gender of the defendant and victim in choosing whether to impose the death penalty. The statute also required that all jurors sign certificates attesting that such factors did not affect their sentencing decision. *See* 18 U.S.C. § 3593(f). Nevertheless, a 12-year study of the federal death penalty issued by the Justice Department in 2000 revealed racial disparities that "sorely troubled" then-Attorney General Janet Reno. *See* Rory K. Little, *Why a Federal Death Penalty Moratorium?*, 33 Conn. L. Rev. 791, 808 (2001).

4. The States' Response to *McCleskey*. Although several state supreme courts indicated a willingness to entertain statistical claims like that made by McCleskey, ultimately these challenges proved unsuccessful. *See State v. Cobb*, 663 A.2d 948, 951 n.4, 961 n.20 (Conn. 1995) (leaving open whether evidence like that presented in *McCleskey* would suffice to show that the death penalty was disproportionately applied, though noting that this case involved only "preliminary data" that had not been "subjected to a rigorous statistical analysis" to control for nonracial variables); *State v. Wakefield*, 921 A.2d 954, 1041 (N.J. 2007) (although the court had acknowledged that disparities based on the race of the defendant or victim would violate the state constitution, and had called for studies to test whether racial considerations were influencing death penalty decisions, it found no "persuasive evidence" of racial differences in the operation of New Jersey's death penalty); *see also State v. Russell*, 477 N.W.2d 886, 888 n.2 (Minn. 1991) (rejecting, in the context of a racial challenge brought in a noncapital case, *McCleskey*'s requirement of intentional discrimination because it "places a virtually insurmountable burden" on defendants).

In 2009, the North Carolina legislature passed the Racial Justice Act, which barred use of the death penalty if defendants could prove that "race was a significant factor in decisions to seek or impose the sentence of death in the county, the prosecutorial district, the judicial division, or the State at the time the death sentence was sought or imposed" in their case. N.C. Gen. Stat. § 15A-2012(a)(3). Almost all of the more than 150 prisoners on death row in North Carolina sought relief under the statute, citing a study which found that capital defendants in the state were 2.6 times more likely to be sentenced to die in cases where at least one of the victims was white. For additional discussion of racial disparities in North Carolina's use of the death penalty, see Catherine M. Gross et al., *A Stubborn Legacy: The Overwhelming Importance of Race in Jury Selection in 173 Post-Batson North Carolina Capital Trials*, 97 Iowa L. Rev. 1531 (2012); Seth Kotch & Robert P. Mosteller, *The Racial Justice Act and the Long Struggle with Race and the Death Penalty in North Carolina*, 88 N.C. L. Rev. 2031 (2010).

In the first Racial Justice Act challenge decided on the merits, a North Carolina judge reduced a capital sentence to life in prison without parole, after finding that race was a "significant factor" in the prosecution's use of peremptory challenges in the state from 1990 to 2010. *See State v. Robinson*, No. 91-CRS-23143 (N.C. Super. Ct. Apr. 20, 2012), *available at* http://www.deathpenaltyinfo.org/north-carolina-racial -justice-act-ruling-summary. Meanwhile, the North Carolina legislature took steps to limit the reach of the Racial Justice Act so that relief could no longer be granted based on proof of racial disparities tied to the race of the victim, any statistical evidence had to relate to the particular county or prosecutorial district where the defendant was tried, and statistical evidence was insufficient by itself to make the required showing. Three additional death sentences were invalidated under this amended version of the act in 2012, but the legislature voted to repeal it the following year. *See* Campbell Robertson, *Judge in North Carolina Voids 3 Death Sentences*, N.Y. Times, Dec. 14, 2012, at A25. The North Carolina Supreme Court agreed to review the four cases that had led to sentence reductions while the Racial Justice Act was still in effect. Twenty months after oral argument, the court reversed the lower courts' rulings on procedural grounds and remanded the cases for reconsideration without expressing any views on the merits. *See State v. Robinson*, 780 S.E.2d 151 (N.C. 2015), *cert. denied*, 137 S. Ct. 67 (2016); *State v. Augustine*, 780 S.E.2d 552 (N.C. 2015).

5. Subsequent Developments on Race and the Death Penalty in the Supreme Court. In *Foster v. Chatman*, 136 S. Ct. 1737 (2016), the Supreme Court reversed a capital conviction based on the constitutional principle first recognized in *Batson v. Kentucky*, 476 U.S. 79 (1986), which prohibits the use of peremptory challenges to strike prospective jurors (in any type of case) because of their race. The Supreme Court concluded by a vote of seven to one that the prosecution's decision to strike all eligible African-American jurors in Foster's case had been "motivated in substantial part by race." In support of its finding that prosecutors made "a concerted effort to keep black prospective jurors off the jury," Chief Justice Roberts' majority opinion cited evidence that the prosecution's files identified the race of the African-Americans in the jury pool, that "no" was written next to the names of prospective African-American jurors, and that the reasons offered for excusing several African-Americans from the jury applied equally to white members of the pool who were allowed to sit on the jury.

The Supreme Court also ruled that a capital defendant was denied effective assistance of counsel when his attorney chose to introduce the testimony of an expert psychologist who the lawyer knew would testify (and who did testify) that the defendant was more likely to pose a future danger to society because he is African-American. *See Buck v. Davis*, 137 S. Ct. 759 (2017).

[2] The Constitutionality of the Death Penalty and Capital Sentencing Procedures

1. The History of the Death Penalty. At early English common law, all felony convictions resulted in a mandatory death sentence, unless the defendant was entitled to the benefit of clergy (thus transferring jurisdiction of the case to the ecclesiastical courts, which had more lenient penalties). Beginning in about 1353, the benefit of clergy was extended to every man who could read — or memorize, given that the defendant was generally asked to read Psalm 51 from the Bible. The benefit of clergy was not made available to women (except "professed nuns") until 1624, however, because women "were incapable of being ordained." ROLLIN M. PERKINS & RONALD N. BOYCE, CRIMINAL LAW 1020–21 (3d ed. 1982).

As noted earlier in this Chapter, the history of the criminal law's efforts to grade homicides according to culpability reflected a desire to limit the number of defendants eligible for the mandatory death penalty. Beginning in 1794, when Pennsylvania became the first state to divide murder into first- and second-degree, the death penalty was reserved for defendants convicted of first-degree murder. Thereafter, a number of states eliminated the death penalty altogether — starting with Michigan, which abolished the death penalty for all crimes except treason in 1846 — although some states seesawed back and forth between abolishing and reinstating capital punishment.

The states that retained the death penalty gradually moved from mandatory death sentences to a system of discretion, beginning with Tennessee in 1838. By 1963, all capital punishment statutes in this country envisioned that the sentencing judge or jury would have discretion to determine whether or not to sentence a defendant to death. Under these discretionary statutes, the sentencer had complete latitude, unaided by any standards or guidelines. Judges and juries were extremely reluctant to impose death sentences, however, and no executions occurred between 1968 and 1977. *See* WILLIAM J. BOWERS, LEGAL HOMICIDE: DEATH AS PUNISHMENT IN AMERICA, 1864–1982, at 7–11, 15, 25–26 (1984).

2. The Early Constitutional Cases. *McGautha v. California*, 402 U.S. 183 (1971), was the first Supreme Court opinion to explore the constitutionality of a discretionary death penalty model. By a vote of six to three, the Court rejected the defendant's argument that "committing to the untrammeled discretion of the jury the power to pronounce life or death in capital cases" violated the Due Process Clause. *Id.* at 207. The Court explained that any effort to "catalog the appropriate factors in this elusive area" would be unwise because "[t]he infinite variety of cases . . . would make general standards either meaningless 'boiler-plate' or a statement of the obvious that no jury would need." *Id.* at 208.

Just one year later, however, the Court held that the exercise of standardless discretion in capital cases did violate the Eighth Amendment's prohibition of cruel and unusual punishment. *See Furman v. Georgia*, 408 U.S. 238 (1972). The vote in *Furman* was five to four, with Justices Potter Stewart and Byron White switching sides from *McGautha*. There was no majority opinion in *Furman*, and each Justice filed a separate opinion articulating his particular views. Two of the five Justices in the majority, Justices Brennan and Marshall, thought that any use of the death penalty violated the Eighth Amendment. The other three — Justices Douglas, Stewart, and White — were unwilling to completely ban capital punishment, but expressed concern that the death penalty was "wantonly and . . . freakishly imposed" in only a "random handful" of cases, *id.* at 309–10 (Stewart J., concurring), with "no meaningful basis for distinguishing the few cases in which it is imposed from the many cases in which it is not." *Id.* at 313 (White, J., concurring). *Furman* had the effect of striking down every death penalty statute then in existence in this country without providing much guidance as to when, if ever, the Court would deem capital punishment constitutional.

Within five years after *Furman*, however, 35 states and the federal government had enacted new death penalty statutes. These statutes fell into two groups of roughly equal size: those that imposed mandatory death sentences in certain cases, and those that articulated guidelines in an effort to limit the sentencer's discretion.

3. The Constitutionality of Mandatory Death Sentences. In *Woodson v. North Carolina*, 428 U.S. 280 (1976), the Court struck down a statute mandating death for any defendant convicted of first-degree murder. Justice Stewart announced the judgment of the Court and wrote an opinion joined by Justices Powell and Stevens. Given the pre-*Furman* trend away from mandatory death sentences, Justice Stewart concluded that the North Carolina statute was inconsistent with contemporary standards of decency. In addition, he reasoned, a mandatory death penalty "simply paper[s] over the problem of unguided and unchecked jury discretion" because many juries simply refuse to convict in cases where they deem a death sentence inappropriate. *Id.* at 302.

The Court reached the same conclusion in *Sumner v. Shuman*, 483 U.S. 66 (1987), striking down a statute that imposed a mandatory death sentence on any prisoner who committed first-degree murder while already serving a life sentence without possibility of parole. The Court explained that the statute was inconsistent with *Woodson*'s holding that "the fundamental respect for humanity underlying the Eighth Amendment . . . requires consideration of the character and record of the individual offender and the circumstances of the particular offense." *Id.* at 75 (quoting *Woodson*, 428 U.S. at 304 (opinion of Stewart, J.)).

4. The Constitutionality of Guided Discretion. Given the Court's response to the mandatory death sentencing schemes, most death penalty statutes today provide for a system of guided discretion, enumerating aggravating factors and permitting imposition of the death penalty so long as the sentencer finds that one such aggravating circumstance exists and that the aggravating factors are not outweighed by any relevant mitigating factors. For an illustration of a statute of this type, see Model Penal Code § 210.6.[39]

---

39. The American Law Institute voted to withdraw MPC § 210.6 in 2009. Although the Institute decided not to express disapproval of capital punishment, it chose to withdraw the provision "in light of the current intractable institutional and structural obstacles to ensuring a minimally adequate system for administering capital punishment." Carol S. Steiker & Jordan M. Steiker, *No More Tinkering: The American Law Institute and the Death Penalty Provisions of the Model Penal Code*, 89 Tex. L. Rev. 353, 354 (2010) (quoting American Law Institute, Report of the Council to the

In *Gregg v. Georgia*, 428 U.S. 153 (1976), the Court upheld the constitutionality of one such statute. The Georgia procedures at issue in *Gregg* called for a separate sentencing hearing once the jury voted to convict in a capital case. At that hearing, evidence was presented on the appropriateness of the death sentence. The statute listed 10 aggravating circumstances, and the jury was instructed to consider any other relevant aggravating or mitigating factors. The jury did not need to find any mitigating circumstances in order to vote against the death penalty, but it was required to find at least one statutory aggravating circumstance beyond a reasonable doubt before imposing the death penalty. Any defendant sentenced to death under this procedure had the right to an automatic appeal to the state supreme court. (The procedural issues surrounding this type of death penalty statute are addressed below in *Lockett v. Ohio* and the accompanying Notes.)

Although again there was no majority opinion in *Gregg*, seven Justices rejected the argument that the death penalty is under all circumstances cruel and unusual punishment. In the opinion announcing the judgment of the Court, Justice Stewart, joined by Justices Powell and Stevens, applied the standards articulated in the Court's Eighth Amendment precedents, which required, first, "an assessment of contemporary values" to determine whether capital punishment was consistent with "'evolving standards of decency,'" and, second, an evaluation whether the death penalty was "excessive," considering both whether it "involve[d] the unnecessary and wanton infliction of pain" and whether it was "grossly out of proportion to the severity of the crime." *Id.* at 173 (quoting *Trop v. Dulles*, 356 U.S. 86, 101 (1958) (plurality opinion)). In finding no violation of these constitutional standards, Justice Stewart cited this country's long acceptance of the death penalty in murder cases—for example, the Fifth Amendment's guarantee of a right to grand jury indictment in "capital cases" and the "deprived of life" language contained in the Due Process Clauses of the Fifth and Fourteenth Amendments. Justice Stewart also pointed to the post-*Furman* enactment of death penalty statutes in a majority of states. In addition, he reasoned that the death penalty does not result in "the gratuitous infliction of suffering" because it serves the purposes of deterrence and retribution. *Id.* at 183. Finally, he noted that a death sentence is not necessarily disproportionate for the crime of murder given that the defendant took life.

Turning to the specifics of the Georgia statute, Justice Stewart concluded that it reduced the likelihood of arbitrary sentencing by giving the jury "guidance regarding the factors about the crime and the defendant that the State, representing organized society, deems particularly relevant to the sentencing decision." *Id.* at 192. He rejected the defendant's contention that the new statute made only "cosmetic" changes in capital sentencing procedures and continued to allow for capriciousness at various stages: the prosecutor had "unfettered authority" in deciding whether to bring capital charges against a particular defendant and whether to agree to a plea bargain; the jury

Membership of the American Law Institute on the Matter of the Death Penalty 4 (2009), *available at* http://www.deathpenaltyinfo.org/documents/alicoun.pdf).

could vote to convict of a lesser-included offense that was not subject to the death penalty; and the governor and parole board could commute a death sentence. *Id.* at 198, 199. "Nothing in any of our cases suggests that the decision to afford an individual defendant mercy violates the Constitution," Justice Stewart responded. *Id.* at 199.

5. Revisiting the Court's Eighth Amendment Precedents. Are you persuaded by Justice Breyer's call in *Glossip v. Gross* for reconsideration of the constitutionality of the death penalty? Is Justice Scalia right that the references to capital punishment in the Constitution definitively foreclose any such constitutional challenge? If the Court is to rethink its death penalty jurisprudence, should its review also encompass, as Justice Thomas proposed, the decisions striking down mandatory death sentences for certain crimes and, per Justice Scalia's suggestion, the basic premise that "evolving standards of decency" are relevant in adjudicating Eighth Amendment claims?

Since Justices Brennan and Marshall left the Court, no other Supreme Court Justice has dissented in every capital case on the grounds that the Eighth Amendment bars use of the death penalty under all circumstances. In his final Term, however, Justice Blackmun (who had dissented from *Furman*'s holding striking down the death penalty) came to believe that "the death penalty, as currently administered, is unconstitutional." *Callins v. Collins*, 510 U.S. 1141, 1159 (1994) (Blackmun, J., dissenting from the denial of certiorari). Noting that "the death penalty remains fraught with arbitrariness, discrimination, caprice, and mistake," Justice Blackmun announced that "[f]rom this day forward, I no longer shall tinker with the machinery of death." *Id.* at 1144, 1145.

Two years before he left the Court, Justice Stevens (who had joined the plurality opinion in *Gregg* reinstating the death penalty) criticized the continued reliance on capital punishment as "the product of habit and inattention," and concluded that the death penalty "represents 'the pointless and needless extinction of life with only marginal contributions to any discernible social or public purposes'" and therefore is "patently excessive and cruel and unusual punishment." *Baze v. Rees*, 553 U.S. 35, 78, 86 (2008) (Stevens, J., concurring in the judgment). Nevertheless, Justice Stevens joined the judgment of the Court, rejecting the challenge to Kentucky's lethal injection protocol, because he could not "justify a refusal to respect precedents that remain a part of our law." *Id.* at 87. *See also Kansas v. Marsh*, 548 U.S. 163, 207–08, 210 (2006) (Souter, J., dissenting) (citing the "repeated exonerations" of death row prisoners as "a new body of fact [that] must be accounted for in deciding what . . . the Eighth Amendment guarantees should tolerate," though concluding that "it is far too soon for any generalization about the soundness of capital sentencing across the country").

Note that since *Glossip* was decided, Justices Breyer and Ginsburg have written dissents from the denial of certiorari in cases questioning the constitutionality of the death penalty. *See, e.g., Tucker v. Louisiana*, 136 S. Ct. 1801 (2016).

Despite the views expressed by these individual Justices, the Court has never retreated from the ruling in *Gregg v. Georgia* that the Constitution does not bar use of the death penalty under all circumstances. But subsequent decisions, which are discussed in the Notes that follow, make clear that a death sentence may not constitutionally be imposed for certain crimes or on certain types of defendants.

6. Executing Defendants for Crimes Other than Murder. Although *Gregg* upheld the constitutionality of the Georgia death penalty statute as applied to murder, a year later the Supreme Court struck down the portion of the Georgia statute that authorized the death penalty in certain rape cases: where the defendant had a prior conviction for a capital felony; where the rape occurred while the defendant was also committing another capital felony or aggravated battery; or where the rape was "outrageously or wantonly vile, horrible or inhuman in that it involved torture, depravity of mind, or an aggravated battery to the victim." *Coker v. Georgia*, 433 U.S. 584, 598–99 (1977) (plurality opinion).

The four Justices in the *Coker* plurality found the death penalty "grossly disproportionate and excessive punishment for the crime of rape" and thus violative of the Eighth Amendment. *Id.* at 592. Although the plurality opinion characterized rape as the "ultimate violation of self" "[s]hort of homicide," it concluded that rape "does not compare with murder" "in terms of moral depravity and . . . the injury to the person and to the public." *Id.* at 597–98.

Justices Brennan and Marshall adhered to the view they had expressed in *Furman* that capital punishment was, under all circumstances, cruel and unusual punishment. Justice Powell agreed that the death penalty for rape was unconstitutional "in the absence of excessive brutality or severe injury," but preferred not to rule out imposing a death sentence in cases of aggravated rape because "[t]he deliberate viciousness of the rapist may be greater than that of the murderer." *Id.* at 604, 603 (Powell, J., concurring in the judgment in part and dissenting in part). Chief Justice Burger and Justice Rehnquist dissented, reasoning that "[t]he long-range effect [of rape] upon the victim's life and health is likely to be irreparable" and therefore rape "is not a crime 'light years' removed from murder in the degree of its heinousness." *Id.* at 611–12, 620 (Burger, C.J., dissenting). For additional discussion of *Coker* and a description of the racially discriminatory manner in which the death penalty was historically imposed in rape cases, see Note 10 following *Commonwealth v. Berkowitz* in Chapter 7, Section B.3.

Thirty years later, in *Kennedy v. Louisiana*, 554 U.S. 407 (2008), the Supreme Court extended *Coker*'s reasoning in striking down a Louisiana statute that made oral, anal, or vaginal intercourse with a child under the age of 13 a capital offense. Reversing the death sentence imposed on a defendant convicted of raping his eight-year-old stepdaughter, Justice Kennedy's opinion for the five Justices in the majority found a "national consensus" against executing a defendant for the crime of child rape: only five other states had followed the 1995 Louisiana statute in making that crime a capital offense; there was no evidence of "a consistent direction of change in support of the death penalty for child rape"; and "contemporary norms" could not be "based upon state legislation that ha[d] been proposed but not yet enacted" in five states (two of which had rejected the bills). *Id.* at 426, 431. In addition, although nine states had at some point made adult or child rape a capital crime since *Furman* was decided in 1972, the Court pointed out that "no individual ha[d] been executed for the rape of an adult or child since 1964, . . . no execution for any other nonhomicide offense ha[d] been conducted since 1963," and Kennedy and one other Louisiana prisoner were the only two people on death row for a crime other than homicide. *Id.* at 433. Echoing *Coker*, the majority also saw "a distinction between intentional first-degree murder . . . and nonhomicide crimes against individual persons, even including child rape," in terms of their "severity and irrevocability." *Id.* at 438.

Writing for the four dissenters, Justice Alito disputed the majority's national consensus argument, pointing out that dicta in *Coker* "stunted legislative consideration of the question whether the death penalty for . . . raping a young child is consistent with prevailing standards of decency." *Id.* at 448 (Alito, J., dissenting). The dissent also questioned whether it is "really true that every person who is convicted of capital murder and sentenced to death is more morally depraved than every child rapist," and argued that the fact that "the loss of human life represents a unique harm . . . does not explain why other grievous harms are insufficient to permit a death sentence." *Id.* at 466, 467.

Given the Court's reasoning in *Coker* and *Kennedy*, does the Constitution prohibit executing defendants for any crime other than murder? What about espionage or treason? *See* 18 U.S.C. § 794 (authorizing death penalty for espionage); *id.* § 2381 (authorizing death penalty for treason). Note that the majority in *Kennedy* warned that its decision was "limited to crimes against individual persons" and did not reach crimes like "treason, espionage, terrorism, and drug kingpin activity, which are offenses against the State." *Kennedy*, 554 U.S. at 437. For a list of federal and state crimes eligible for the death penalty, see Bureau of Justice Statistics Bulletin, U.S. Dep't of Justice, Capital Punishment, 2013, at 6, 8 (2014), http://www.bjs .gov/content/pub/pdf/cp13st.pdf.

7. **Executing Murder Defendants Who Did Not Intentionally Kill.** If *Coker* and *Kennedy* call into question the constitutionality of imposing the death penalty for crimes other than murder, may the state execute a defendant convicted of murder who did not actually perform the killing? In *Enmund v. Florida*, 458 U.S. 782 (1982), for example, the defendant waited in the getaway car while two accomplices robbed and murdered an elderly couple. He was convicted of first-degree felony murder and sentenced to death. By a five-to-four vote, the Court held that the Eighth Amendment prohibits executing one "who does not himself kill, attempt to kill, or intend that a killing take place or that lethal force will be employed." *Id.* at 797. The Court reasoned that "causing harm intentionally must be punished more severely than causing the same harm unintentionally," and that Enmund was therefore "plainly different" from his accomplices who actually killed. *Id.* at 798.

In *Tison v. Arizona*, 481 U.S. 137 (1987), another five-to-four opinion, however, the Court explained that *Enmund* does not limit the death penalty to cases where the defendant demonstrably intended to kill. Although the Court did not attempt to "precisely delineate the particular types of conduct and states of mind warranting imposition of the death penalty," it held that "major participation in the felony committed, combined with reckless indifference to human life, is sufficient to satisfy the *Enmund* culpability requirement." *Id.* at 158. The Court reasoned that "reckless indifference to the value of human life may be every bit as shocking to the moral sense as an 'intent to kill'":

> [S]ome nonintentional murderers may be among the most dangerous and inhumane of all—the person who tortures another not caring whether the victim lives or dies, or the robber who shoots someone in the course of the robbery, utterly indifferent to the fact that the desire to rob may have the unintended consequence of killing the victim as well as taking the victim's property.

Id. at 157. Distinguishing *Enmund*, the *Tison* Court upheld death sentences imposed on two brothers whose father murdered four people. The brothers provided weapons and a getaway car to aid their father's escape from prison, helped him lock up the prison guards, fled with him and assisted in flagging down a passing car when they got a flat tire, and then stood by while he shot the four people in the car. The Court concluded that the brothers "could have foreseen that lethal force might be used, particularly since [they] knew that [their] father's previous escape attempt had resulted in murder." *Id.* at 152.

Does *Tison*'s reasoning make sense, or is reckless indifference to life an insufficiently culpable mens rea for a capital sentence? For the argument that *Tison* is "no longer constitutionally sound" given that only nine states and the federal government "maintain their adherence to *Tison*'s minimal requirements" and only five of those jurisdictions "are actively pursuing . . . the death penalty for felony-murder non-triggermen who lack intent to kill," see Joseph Trigilio & Tracy Casadio, *Executing Those Who Do Not Kill: A Categorical Approach to Proportional Sentencing*, 48 Am. Crim. L. Rev. 1371, 1399, 1401, 1403–04 (2011) (citing statistics showing that "only three felony-murder non-triggermen" have been put to death since *Tison* was decided and another five are on death row).

Assuming *Tison* is still good law, does the *Tison* Court's narrow reading of *Enmund* mean that a robber who killed accidentally or whose victim died of a heart attack could receive the death penalty? *See People v. Contreras*, 314 P.3d 450, 480–81 (Cal. 2013) (holding that "[p]roof that a defendant who is guilty of felony murder was the actual killer of the victim—by itself—establishes the degree of culpability required to impose the death penalty," and refusing to interpret *Enmund-Tison* as requiring evidence of either intent to kill or reckless indifference to human life in such cases). *But cf.* Steven F. Shatz, *The Eighth Amendment, the Death Penalty and Ordinary Robbery-Burglary Murderers: A California Case Study*, 59 Fla. L. Rev. 719, 723 (2007) (arguing that California and the five other states that authorize the execution of "the 'ordinary' robbery-burglary murderer—one whose murder involved no more aggravating statutorily defined death-eligibility factor than the fact that the murder occurred during a robbery or burglary"—are acting in violation of Eighth Amendment standards).[40]

8. Executing Prisoners Who Are Mentally Incompetent. In *Ford v. Wainwright*, 477 U.S. 399 (1986), the Court determined that imposing the death penalty on someone who is insane at the time of execution is cruel and unusual punishment. In so ruling, the majority "question[ed] the retributive value of executing a person who has no comprehension of why he has been singled out and stripped of his fundamental right to life," and cited the importance of "protect[ing] the dignity of society itself from the barbarity of exacting mindless vengeance." *Id.* at 409, 410. The Court did not attempt, however, to define insanity for these purposes.

Twenty years later, in *Panetti v. Quarterman*, 551 U.S. 930 (2007), the Court considered the scope of its holding in *Ford v. Wainwright*. Panetti alleged that although he understands " 'the state is saying that [it wishes] to execute him for [his] murders,' he believes in earnest that the stated reason is a 'sham' and the State in truth wants to execute him 'to stop him from preaching.' " *Id.* at 954–55. Writing for the five Justices in the majority, Justice Kennedy concluded that Panetti had "made a substantial showing of incompetency," and the state courts had "failed to provide [him] with a constitutionally adequate opportunity to be heard" by finding him eligible for the death penalty without giving him "an opportunity to submit psychiatric evidence as a counterweight to the report filed by the court-appointed experts." *Id.* at 948, 952. In addition, the majority in *Panetti* concluded that the court below had used "an improperly restrictive test" in defining competency under *Ford v. Wainwright*. *Id.* at 935. "A prisoner's awareness of the State's rationale for an execution is not the same as a rational understanding of it," the Court observed, and "*Ford* does not foreclose inquiry into the latter." *Id.* at 959. The Court stopped short of defining competency for purposes of *Ford v. Wainwright* or ruling whether Panetti was in fact competent to be executed, instead remanding the case for the lower courts to reconsider his claim.

On remand, the Fifth Circuit affirmed the district court's conclusion that Panetti "has both a factual and rational understanding of his crime, his impending death, and the causal retributive connection between the two." *Panetti v. Stephens*, 727 F.3d 398, 410 (5th Cir. 2013), *cert. denied*, 135 S. Ct. 47 (2014). But the Fifth Circuit subsequently granted a stay of execution while it considers Panetti's claim that the Due Process Clause constitutionally obligates the State to provide him with a lawyer and an expert to evaluate his mental condition. *See Panetti v. Stephens*, 586 F. App'x 163 (5th Cir. 2014).

In *Singleton v. Norris*, 319 F.3d 1018, 1027 (8th Cir.) (en banc), *cert. denied*, 540 U.S. 832 (2003), the Eighth Circuit held that *Ford v. Wainwright* does not bar the execution of "a prisoner who became incompetent during his long stay on death row

---

40. Note that the death penalty was subsequently abolished in one of those six states (Maryland).

but who subsequently regained competency through appropriate medical care"—
in that case, by the administration of antipsychotic medication. *See also Commonwealth v. Sam*, 952 A.2d 565 (Pa. 2008) (permitting the involuntary administration
of medication for purposes of rendering a prisoner competent to be executed), *cert.
denied*, 558 U.S. 828 (2009). By contrast, some state supreme courts, interpreting their
own state constitutions, have reached the opposite conclusion. *See State v. Perry*, 610
So. 2d 746 (La. 1992); *Singleton v. State*, 437 S.E.2d 53 (S.C. 1993).

A number of lower courts have held that the Eighth Amendment does not prohibit executing a defendant found guilty but mentally ill in one of the states that authorizes that verdict as an alternative to an insanity acquittal. *See Sanders v. State*, 585
A.2d 117 (Del. 1990); *People v. Crews*, 522 N.E.2d 1167 (Ill. 1988); *Harris v. State*,
499 N.E.2d 723 (Ind. 1986); *State v. Wilson*, 413 S.E.2d 19 (S.C. 1992). (For a general
description of the guilty but mentally ill verdict, see Chapter 15, Section C.1, Note 12.)

9. Executing Prisoners Who Are Intellectually Disabled. In *Atkins v. Virginia*,
536 U.S. 304 (2002), the Supreme Court overruled its prior decision in *Penry v.
Lynaugh*, 492 U.S. 302 (1989), and held that the Eighth Amendment forecloses the
execution of intellectually disabled individuals. The Court found a "national consensus" supporting its decision, observing that 18 of the 38 states that had a death
penalty at that time, as well as the federal government, barred the execution of intellectually disabled defendants. *Id*. at 316, 313–15. In addition, the Court explained
that "[t]his national consensus unquestionably reflects widespread judgment about
the relative culpability of mentally retarded offenders, and the relationship between
mental retardation and the penological purposes served by the death penalty":

> Mentally retarded persons frequently know the difference between right and
> wrong and are competent to stand trial. Because of their impairments, however, by definition they have diminished capacities to understand and process information, to communicate, to abstract from mistakes and learn from
> experience, to engage in logical reasoning, to control impulses, and to understand the reactions of others. There is no evidence that they are more likely
> to engage in criminal conduct than others, but there is abundant evidence
> that they often act on impulse rather than pursuant to a premeditated plan,
> and that in group settings they are followers rather than leaders.

Id. at 317, 318. Noting that the parties disagreed whether Atkins suffered from an
intellectual disability, the majority did not resolve that question, "leav[ing] to the
State[s] the task of developing appropriate ways to enforce the constitutional restriction." *Id*. at 317 (quoting *Ford v. Wainwright*, 477 U.S. 399, 416–17 (1986)).

The three *Atkins* dissenters criticized the majority for "miraculously extract[ing]"
a national consensus based on "agreement among 47 percent of the death penalty
jurisdictions." *Id*. at 342, 343 (Scalia, J., dissenting). On the question of relative blameworthiness, the dissent argued that "[s]urely culpability, and deservedness of the
most severe retribution, depends not merely (if at all) upon the mental capacity of
the criminal (above the level where he is able to distinguish right from wrong) but

also upon the depravity of the crime." *Id.* at 350. For an empirical study finding that just under eight percent of capital defendants raised *Atkins* claims between 2002 and 2013, more than half of whom were successful, see John H. Blume et al., *A Tale of Two (And Possibly Three)* Atkins*: Intellectual Disability and Capital Punishment Twelve Years After the Supreme Court's Creation of a Categorical Bar*, 23 WM. & MARY BILL RTS. J. 393, 398 (2014) (concluding that *Atkins* did not "generate[] a substantial amount of litigation, much less frivolous litigation").

One of the issues left open in *Atkins*—the proper definition of intellectual disability—returned to the Court in *Hall v. Florida*, 134 S. Ct. 1986 (2014), where the majority overturned a Florida statute that required a death row prisoner to have an IQ no higher than 70 in order to present evidence of intellectual disability. Writing for the five Justices in the majority, Justice Kennedy observed that "the medical community defines intellectual disability according to three criteria: significantly subaverage intellectual functioning, deficits in adaptive functioning (the inability to learn basic skills and adjust behavior to changing circumstances), and onset of these deficits during the developmental period." *Id.* at 1994. The majority went on to find that the Florida statute "disregards established medical practice in two interrelated ways": by "tak[ing] an IQ score as final and conclusive evidence of a defendant's intellectual capacity, when experts in the field would consider other evidence"; and by failing to recognize that an IQ score is "imprecise" and, because of the "standard error of measurement" (SEM), is "best understood as a range of scores on either side of the recorded score" rather than "a single fixed number." *Id.* at 1995. Accordingly, the Court held that "when a defendant's IQ test score falls within the test's acknowledged and inherent margin of error [typically five points], the defendant must be able to present additional evidence of intellectual disability, including testimony regarding adaptive deficits." *Id.* at 2001.

The four dissenters accused the majority of overturning *Atkins*' holding that the Eighth Amendment "does not mandate the use of a single method for identifying" intellectually disabled death row prisoners. *Id.* at 2002 (Alito, J., dissenting). The dissent also criticized the Court for ignoring that the Eighth Amendment concept of "evolving standards of decency" refers to "the standards of *American society as a whole*," not the "standards of *professional societies*," which "at best represent the views of a small professional elite." *Id.* at 2002, 2005. The dissent defended the Florida statute as "a sensible standard that comports with the longstanding belief that IQ tests are the best measure of intellectual functioning" and "takes into account the inevitable risk of testing error by permitting defendants to introduce multiple scores." *Id.* at 2007.

In another post-*Atkins* case, *Brumfield v. Cain*, 135 S. Ct. 2269 (2015), the Supreme Court determined that the Louisiana courts had erred in denying a death row inmate an evidentiary hearing on his *Atkins* claim. Specifically, Justice Sotomayor's opinion for the five Justices in the majority reasoned that, "[a]ccounting for th[e] margin of error," an IQ test score of 75 was "squarely in the range of potential intellectual disability" and impairment of adaptive functioning was shown by evidence that

Brumfield "was placed in special education classes at an early age, was suspected of having a learning disability, and can barely read at a fourth-grade level." *Id.* at 2278, 2280. *See also Moore v. Texas*, 137 S. Ct. 1039, 1053 (2017) (concluding that a Texas appellate court "failed adequately to inform itself of the 'medical community's diagnostic framework'" in finding that a defendant was not intellectually disabled based on a 1992 definition of intellectual disability that the American Association on Intellectual and Developmental Disabilities has sincce abandoned) (quoting *Hall*, 134 S. Ct. at 2000).

In the wake of *Atkins* and *Hall*, the lower courts have also struggled with the procedures to be used in complying with the Supreme Court's decisions. Many states require defendants to prove intellectual disability by a preponderance of the evidence. *See, e.g., In re Hawthorne*, 105 P.3d 552 (Cal. 2005); *State v. Johnson*, 244 S.W.3d 144 (Mo. 2008). But others have imposed more stringent burdens of proof on the defense. *See, e.g., People v. Vasquez*, 84 P.3d 1019 (Colo. 2004) (clear and convincing evidence); *Hill v. Humphrey*, 662 F.3d 1335 (11th Cir. 2011) (en banc) (upholding Georgia statute requiring proof beyond a reasonable doubt). Likewise, the states are divided on the question whether determinations of intellectual disability are to be made by the trial judge or the jury. *See Commonwealth v. Sanchez*, 36 A.3d 24, 60–61 (Pa. 2011) (citing conflicting state rules).

10. Executing Minors. In *Roper v. Simmons*, 543 U.S. 551 (2005), the Court overruled its decision in *Stanford v. Kentucky*, 492 U.S. 361 (1989), and held that the Eighth Amendment bars the execution of defendants who were under 18 years old at the time of their crime. Writing for the five Justices in the majority, Justice Kennedy found "evidence of [a] national consensus against the death penalty for juveniles." Specifically, the majority noted that "30 States prohibit the juvenile death penalty" (i.e., the 12 states that at that time had no death penalty at all and 18 others that had a death penalty but exempted juveniles), and that, even in the remaining 20 states, the execution of juveniles is "infrequent": "[s]ince *Stanford*, six States have executed prisoners for crimes committed as juveniles. In the past 10 years, only three have done so: Oklahoma, Texas, and Virginia." *Id.* at 564–65.

The majority also relied on "differences between juveniles and adults" which it thought "render suspect any conclusion that a juvenile falls among the worst offenders":

> The susceptibility of juveniles to immature and irresponsible behavior means "their irresponsible conduct is not as morally reprehensible as that of an adult." Their own vulnerability and comparative lack of control over their immediate surroundings mean juveniles have a greater claim than adults to be forgiven for failing to escape negative influences in their whole environment. The reality that juveniles still struggle to define their identity means it is less supportable to conclude that even a heinous crime committed by a juvenile is evidence of irretrievably depraved character.

Id. at 569–70. Given "the diminished capacity of juveniles," the Court continued, "the penological justifications for the death penalty apply to them with lesser force than to adults": "[r]etribution is not proportional if the law's most severe penalty is imposed on one whose culpability or blameworthiness is diminished . . . by reason of youth and immaturity," and "the same characteristics that render juveniles less culpable than adults suggest as well that juveniles will be less susceptible to deterrence." *Id.* at 571. Finally, the majority noted that "[o]ur determination that the death penalty is disproportionate punishment for offenders under 18 finds confirmation in the stark reality that the United States is the only country in the world that continues to give official sanction to the juvenile death penalty." *Id.* at 575.

Justice O'Connor, who had cast the critical fifth vote in *Stanford v. Kentucky*, dissented in *Roper v. Simmons*, concluding that "the evidence . . . fails to demonstrate conclusively that any such [national] consensus has emerged in the brief period since . . . *Stanford*." *Id.* at 588 (O'Connor, J., dissenting). Moreover, Justice O'Connor argued that "the Court has adduced no evidence impeaching the seemingly reasonable conclusion reached by many state legislatures: that at least some 17-year-old murderers are sufficiently mature to deserve the death penalty in an appropriate case." *Id.* Is Justice O'Connor's criticism well-taken? Is any line arbitrary, given that "age is simply a 'proxy,' and an imperfect one at that, for a combination of factors that determines the relative culpability of a juvenile murderer"? Joseph L. Hoffmann, *On the Perils of Line-Drawing: Juveniles and the Death Penalty*, 40 HASTINGS L.J. 229, 233 (1989).

In a separate dissent written for himself, Chief Justice Rehnquist, and Justice Thomas, Justice Scalia accused the *Roper* majority of "presum[ing] to be the authoritative conscience of the Nation" as well as "mak[ing] the type of legislative judgments" that "judges are ill-equipped to make." *Roper*, 543 U.S. at 616 (Scalia, J., dissenting). Justice Scalia's dissent was also particularly critical of the Court's reliance on foreign law, chiding the majority for allowing "the views of other countries and the so-called international community [to] take center stage" while making "the views of our own citizens . . . essentially irrelevant." *Id.* at 622. For a discussion of subsequent Supreme Court opinions that applied *Roper* to cases where juveniles were sentenced to life in prison without parole, see Chapter 2, Section D.3, Note 6.

Lockett v. Ohio

438 U.S. 586 (1978)

MR. CHIEF JUSTICE BURGER delivered . . . an opinion (Part III), in which MR. JUSTICE STEWART, MR. JUSTICE POWELL, and MR. JUSTICE STEVENS joined, . . . and announced the judgment of the Court.

We granted certiorari in this case to consider, among other questions, whether Ohio violated the Eighth and Fourteenth Amendments by sentencing Sandra Lockett to death pursuant to a statute that narrowly limits the sentencer's discretion to consider the circumstances of the crime and the record and character of the offender as mitigating factors.

I

Lockett was charged with aggravated murder with the aggravating specifications (1) that the murder was "committed for the purpose of escaping detection, apprehension, trial, or punishment" for aggravated robbery, and (2) that the murder was "committed while . . . committing, attempting to commit, or fleeing immediately after committing or attempting to commit . . . aggravated robbery." That offense was punishable by death in Ohio. . . .

[The prosecution's evidence showed that Lockett drove the getaway car for three men who were robbing a pawnshop. The pawnbroker grabbed a gun from one of the men and it went off, killing the pawnbroker.] . . . The jury found Lockett guilty as charged.

Once a verdict of aggravated murder with specifications had been returned, the Ohio death penalty statute required the trial judge to impose a death sentence unless, after "considering the nature and circumstances of the offense" and Lockett's "history, character, and condition," he found by a preponderance of the evidence that (1) the victim had induced or facilitated the offense, (2) it was unlikely that Lockett would have committed the offense but for the fact that she "was under duress, coercion, or strong provocation," or (3) the offense was "primarily the product of [Lockett's] psychosis or mental deficiency."

In accord with the Ohio statute, the trial judge requested a presentence report as well as psychiatric and psychological reports. The reports contained detailed information about Lockett's intelligence, character, and background. The psychiatric and psychological reports described her as a 21-year-old with low-average or average intelligence, and not suffering from a mental deficiency. One of the psychologists reported that "her prognosis for rehabilitation" if returned to society was favorable. The presentence report showed that Lockett had committed no major offenses although she had a record of several minor ones as a juvenile and two minor offenses as an adult. It also showed that she had once used heroin but was receiving treatment at a drug abuse clinic and seemed to be "on the road to success" as far as her drug problem was concerned. It concluded that Lockett suffered no psychosis and was not mentally deficient.[41]

After considering the reports and hearing argument on the penalty issue, the trial judge concluded that the offense had not been primarily the product of psychosis or mental deficiency. Without specifically addressing the other two statutory mitigating factors, the judge said that he had "no alternative, whether [he] [liked] the law or not" but to impose the death penalty. He then sentenced Lockett to death.

. . . .

---

41. [n.2] The presentence report also . . . indicated that [one of her accomplices] told the police that Lockett had not followed his order to keep the car running during the robbery and instead had gone to get something to eat.

III

Lockett [argues] that her death sentence is invalid because the statute under which it was imposed did not permit the sentencing judge to consider, as mitigating factors, her character, prior record, age, lack of specific intent to cause death, and her relatively minor part in the crime. . . . [42]

We begin by recognizing that the concept of individualized sentencing in criminal cases generally, although not constitutionally required, has long been accepted in this country. Consistent with that concept, sentencing judges traditionally have taken a wide range of factors into account. . . . And where sentencing discretion is granted, it generally has been agreed that the sentencing judge's "possession of the fullest information possible concerning the defendant's life and characteristics" is "[highly] relevant — *if not essential* — [to the] selection of an appropriate sentence. . . ."

. . . .

Although legislatures remain free to decide how much discretion in sentencing should be reposed in the judge or jury in noncapital cases, the plurality opinion in *Woodson* [*v. North Carolina*], after reviewing the historical repudiation of mandatory sentencing in capital cases, concluded that

> "in capital cases the fundamental respect for humanity underlying the Eighth Amendment . . . requires consideration of the character and record of the individual offender and the circumstances of the particular offense as a constitutionally indispensable part of the process of inflicting the penalty of death."

That declaration rested "on the predicate that the penalty of death is qualitatively different" from any other sentence. We are satisfied that this qualitative difference between death and other penalties calls for a greater degree of reliability when the death sentence is imposed.

We . . . conclude that the Eighth and Fourteenth Amendments require that the sentencer, in all but the rarest kind of capital case, not be precluded from

---

42. [n.7] The limits on the consideration of mitigating factors in Ohio's death penalty statute which Lockett now attacks appear to have been a direct response to *Furman*. Prior to *Furman*, . . . [t]he Ohio House of Representatives had passed a bill abandoning the practice of unbridled sentencing discretion and instructing the sentencer to consider a list of aggravating and mitigating circumstances in determining whether to impose the death penalty. The list of mitigating circumstances permitted consideration of any circumstance "tending to mitigate the offense, though failing to establish a defense."

. . . After *Furman*, the [Senate Judiciary] Committee decided to retain the death penalty but to eliminate much of the sentencing discretion permitted by the House bill. As a result, the Ohio Senate developed the current sentencing procedure which requires the imposition of the death penalty if one of seven specific aggravating circumstances and none of three specific mitigating circumstances is found to exist. Confronted with what reasonably would have appeared to be the questionable constitutionality of permitting discretionary weighing of mitigating factors after *Furman*, . . . the statute under which Lockett was sentenced was enacted.

considering, *as a mitigating factor,* any aspect of a defendant's character or record and any of the circumstances of the offense that the defendant proffers as a basis for a sentence less than death. . . .

. . . .

The Ohio death penalty statute does not permit the type of individualized consideration of mitigating factors we now hold to be required by the Eighth and Fourteenth Amendments in capital cases. . . . [O]nly the three factors specified in the statute can be considered in mitigation of the defendant's sentence. We see, therefore, that once it is determined that the victim did not induce or facilitate the offense, that the defendant did not act under duress or coercion, and that the offense was not primarily the product of the defendant's mental deficiency, the Ohio statute mandates the sentence of death. The absence of direct proof that the defendant intended to cause the death of the victim is relevant for mitigating purposes only if it is determined that it sheds some light on one of the three statutory mitigating factors. Similarly, consideration of a defendant's comparatively minor role in the offense, or age, would generally not be permitted, as such, to affect the sentencing decision.

The limited range of mitigating circumstances which may be considered by the sentencer under the Ohio statute is incompatible with the Eighth and Fourteenth Amendments. To meet constitutional requirements, a death penalty statute must not preclude consideration of relevant mitigating factors. . . .

Mr. Justice Rehnquist, concurring in part and dissenting in part.

. . . .

. . . As a practical matter, I doubt that today's opinion will make a great deal of difference in the manner in which trials in capital cases are conducted, since I would suspect that it has been the practice of most trial judges to permit a defendant to offer virtually any sort of evidence in his own defense as he wished. But . . . the theme of today's opinion, far from supporting those views expressed in *Furman* which did appear to be carried over to the *Woodson* cases, tends to undercut those views. If a defendant as a matter of constitutional law is to be permitted to offer as evidence in the sentencing hearing any fact, however bizarre, which he wishes, even though the most sympathetically disposed trial judge could conceive of no basis upon which the jury might take it into account in imposing a sentence, the new constitutional doctrine will not eliminate arbitrariness or freakishness in the imposition of sentences, but will codify and institutionalize it. By encouraging defendants in capital cases, and presumably sentencing judges and juries, to take into consideration anything under the sun as a "mitigating circumstance," it will not guide sentencing discretion but will totally unleash it. . . .

Notes and Questions

1. Statutory Aggravating Circumstances. Most death penalty statutes, like the one before the Court in *Lockett*, require the sentencer to find the presence of at least one statutory aggravating circumstance beyond a reasonable doubt before sentencing a defendant to die. Typical statutory aggravating circumstances include: killing for financial gain; killing a police officer or prison guard; killing more than one person; killing in order to escape from lawful custody or to avoid arrest; and a history of violence. *See* Model Penal Code § 210.6(3); *id.* § 210.6 Comment at 168. In the wake of the terrorist attacks of September 11, 2001, the New York legislature also made a killing "in furtherance of an act of terrorism" a capital offense. *See* N.Y. Penal § 125.27(1)(a), reprinted above in Section A. *Cf. United States v. Caro*, 597 F.3d 608, 622–24 (4th Cir. 2010) (upholding two of the 16 aggravating circumstances listed in the federal death penalty statute — "'[c]onviction for two felony drug offenses . . . committed on different occasions, involving the distribution of a controlled substance,'" and "'[c]onviction for [a] serious Federal drug offense[]'" carrying a sentence of at least five years — on the grounds that "recidivism justifies harsher sentencing . . . to provide increased retribution and deterrence" and, while the defendant's convictions "might be considered 'nonviolent' by themselves, illegal drugs have long and justifiably been associated with violence") (quoting 18 U.S.C. §§ 3592(c)(10), 3592(c)(12)).

In *Godfrey v. Georgia*, 446 U.S. 420, 428–32 (1980), the Supreme Court held that one common aggravating circumstance — a killing that was "outrageously or wantonly vile, horrible, or inhuman" — was unconstitutionally vague. But the Court indicated that this aggravator would provide sufficient guidance to the jury to meet constitutional standards if narrowed to require torture or aggravated battery. *Cf. Arave v. Creech*, 507 U.S. 463, 471 (1993) (rejecting vagueness challenge to aggravating circumstance for defendants who showed "utter disregard for life," in light of the state supreme court's interpretation narrowing it to "cold-blooded, pitiless" killers).

In *Lowenfield v. Phelps*, 484 U.S. 231 (1988), the Court approved of an aggravating circumstance that completely overlapped with one of the elements of the crime. Lowenfield was convicted of first-degree murder, defined by the Louisiana homicide statute to require an "intent to kill or inflict great bodily harm upon more than one person." He was then sentenced to death based on the sole aggravating circumstance that he "knowingly created a risk of death or great bodily harm to more than one person." Upholding the sentence, the Court noted that "[t]he use of 'aggravating circumstances' is not an end in itself, but a means of genuinely narrowing the class of death-eligible persons and thereby channeling the jury's discretion." The majority saw "no reason why this narrowing function may not be performed by jury findings at either the sentencing phase of the trial or the guilt phase." *Id.* at 244–45. The Court explained:

> [T]he narrowing function required for a regime of capital punishment may be provided in either of . . . two ways: The legislature may itself narrow the definition of capital offenses, as . . . Louisiana [has] done, so that the jury finding of guilt responds to this concern, or the legislature may more broadly define capital offenses and provide for narrowing by jury findings of aggravating circumstances at the penalty phase.

Id. at 246.

Does this reasoning make sense, or was the dissent right in thinking that the Court's opinion unconstitutionally and "inevitably tilt[ed] the sentencing scales toward the imposition of the death penalty"? *Id.* at 255 (Marshall, J., dissenting). Justice Marshall reasoned that the jury will deliberate at trial "unaware that [its] finding will make the defendant eligible for the death penalty at the sentencing phase," with the result that the prosecution "enters the sentencing hearing with the jury already across the threshold of death eligibility, without any awareness on the jury's part that it . . . crossed that line." *Id.* at 258.

Does *Lowenfield* imply that it is permissible to include in the list of statutory aggravating circumstances the fact that a murder occurred during the course of a felony, as some states do? For criticism of this practice, see Richard A. Rosen, *Felony Murder and the Eighth Amendment Jurisprudence of Death*, 31 B.C. L. Rev. 1103 (1990). (For further discussion of the death penalty and felony murder, see Note 7 above.)

More generally, do the aggravating circumstances described above accurately separate out those murderers who are "the worst of the worst" and thus deserving of execution? *Kansas v. Marsh*, 548 U.S. 163, 206 (2006) (Souter, J., dissenting). In evaluating the use of felony murder as an aggravating circumstance, for example, is it relevant that felony murder cases most often involve African-American defendants who killed white victims and that some studies suggest that "the defendant who killed a white victim during a felony is the defendant most likely to receive the death penalty"? Rosen, *supra*, at 1118–19. Is the list of common aggravating circumstances subject to critique on feminist grounds because "the most reprehensible murders as depicted by the capital statutes do not include domestic murder," reflecting "a bias against treating domestic homicide as seriously as some other categories of arguably no more reprehensible homicide, notably predatory crime"? Elizabeth Rapaport, *Capital Murder and the Domestic Discount: A Study of Capital Murder in the Post-Furman Era*, 49 SMU L. Rev. 1507, 1512 (1996). Note that some death penalty statutes have added an aggravating circumstance covering cases where the murder victim had obtained an order of protection against the defendant. *See* 42 Pa. Cons. Stat. § 9711(d)(18). For the argument that "the current use of aggravators to narrow the pool of death-eligible defendants by choosing those most deserving of death is an inherently flawed method" and proposing that sentencers instead "us[e] mitigating factors to weed out those not deserving of the death penalty," see Andy T. Wang, *Deserving of Life: A Mitigating Factor Approach to the Narrowing Mandate in Capital Sentencing*, 52 Harv. J. on Legis. 509, 510 (2015).

2. Nonstatutory Aggravating Circumstances. Although the sentencer must find at least one statutory aggravating circumstance in order to vote in favor of the death penalty, it may also consider nonstatutory aggravating circumstances in deciding whether a death sentence is appropriate.

In *Payne v. Tennessee*, 501 U.S. 808 (1991), for example, the Court ruled that the Eighth Amendment does not prohibit the prosecution from introducing "victim impact" evidence describing the victim's personal characteristics and the emotional impact the crime has had on the victim's family. In so ruling, the Court overruled a four-year-old precedent that had excluded such testimony from capital sentencing hearings on the ground that it was irrelevant to a defendant's blameworthiness. *See Booth v. Maryland*, 482 U.S. 496 (1987). Rather, the Court concluded in *Payne*, victim impact evidence informs the jury of the harm caused by the defendant's crime and also acts to counterbalance the fact that "virtually no limits are placed on the relevant mitigating evidence a capital defendant may introduce concerning his own circumstances." *Payne*, 501 U.S. at 822. Although some commentators have endorsed the use of victim impact statements on the grounds that they "invite empathetic concern in a way that abstractions and general rules do not," Paul Gewirtz, *Victims and Voyeurs: Two Narrative Problems at the Criminal Trial, in* Law's Stories: Narrative and Rhetoric in the Law 135, 142–43 (Peter Brooks & Paul Gewirtz eds., 1996), others have argued that such evidence "evoke[s] emotions inappropriate in the context of criminal sentencing" by "appeal[ing] to hatred, the desire for undifferentiated vengeance, and even bigotry." Susan Bandes, *Empathy, Narrative, and Victim Impact Statements*, 63 U. Chi. L. Rev. 361, 365 (1996). For further discussion of victim impact evidence and victims' rights generally, see Chapter 1, Section B.2.d.

3. Mitigating Circumstances. The plurality opinion in *Lockett v. Ohio* concluded that "a death penalty statute must not preclude consideration of relevant mitigating factors." Obviously, as the *Lockett* plurality noted, a death sentence is "qualitatively different" from other penalties. But is it really so different from life imprisonment without parole to justify the Court's insistence that the state go to such lengths to guide the sentencer's discretion and ensure that it consider all mitigating circumstances, when these safeguards are not required in non-capital cases? *Cf. Abdul-Kabir v. Quarterman*, 550 U.S. 233, 284 (2007) (Scalia, J., dissenting) (endorsing the view that "limiting a jury's discretion to consider all mitigating evidence" is not unconstitutional because "the understanding of the American people who adopted [the Eighth Amendment] did not remotely include any requirement that a capital jury be permitted to consider all mitigating factors").

Is Justice Rehnquist's criticism of the plurality opinion in *Lockett* well-taken? Was Justice Stewart right when he noted in *Gregg v. Georgia*, 428 U.S. 153, 199 (1976) (plurality opinion), that "[n]othing in any of our cases suggests that the decision to afford an individual defendant mercy violates the Constitution"? Or did Justice Thomas have the better argument when he said that "withhold[ing] the death penalty out of sympathy for a defendant who is a member of a favored group is no different from . . . impos[ing] the penalty on the basis of negative bias"? *Graham v. Collins*, 506 U.S. 461, 495 (1993) (Thomas, J., concurring). Has Justice Thomas now revised his views given that he joined Justice Scalia's concurring opinion in *Glossip v. Gross* (excerpted in Part 1 above), which analogized capital defendants who receive mercy from a sentencing jury to those who are "never apprehended, . . . never tried, . . . acquitted, or . . . pardoned"?

Twenty years after *Lockett*, in *Buchanan v. Angelone*, 522 U.S. 269, 270 (1998), Chief Justice Rehnquist wrote an opinion for the Court holding that *Lockett* does not require jury instructions to mention either "the concept of mitigating evidence generally, or . . . particular statutory mitigating factors" urged by the defendant. Accordingly, the Court held that the trial judge in that case had complied with the dictates of *Lockett* by generally instructing the jurors to base their decision on "all the evidence" presented at the sentencing hearing and by not foreclosing their consideration of any mitigating evidence.

Most recently, in *Kansas v. Carr*, 136 S. Ct. 633 (2016), the Supreme Court held that trial judges are not required to explicitly instruct the jury that mitigating circumstances need not be proven beyond a reasonable doubt. The Court reasoned that the jurors were told that aggravating circumstances must be established beyond a reasonable doubt whereas mitigating circumstances "must merely 'be found to exist' " and that the jury was "repeatedly" instructed "to consider any mitigating factor." *Id.* at 643.[43] Do these later cases imply that Justice Rehnquist's views in *Lockett* have now prevailed, and that the Court has "significantly eroded the principle of individualized consideration"? Phyllis L. Crocker, *Feminism and Defending Men on Death Row*, 29 St. Mary's L.J. 981, 997 (1998) (discussing *Buchanan*). Or are such criticisms exaggerated?

More generally, is there an unavoidable tension between the Court's desire to minimize the arbitrary and capricious exercise of discretion in the capital sentencing process (evidenced in *Furman* and *Gregg*) and its requirement of individualization (evidenced in *Woodson*, *McCleskey*, and *Lockett*)? (Recall, as pointed out in footnote 7 of the *Lockett* plurality's opinion, that the Ohio legislature passed the statute invalidated by the Court because of its perception that "permitting discretionary weighing of mitigating factors" was of "questionable constitutionality" in the wake of *Furman*.) If this inherent tension exists, what is the solution? Justice Blackmun suggested that the only answer is to "accept the fact that the death penalty cannot be administered in accord with our Constitution." *Callins v. Collins*, 510 U.S. 1141, 1157 (1994) (Blackmun, J., dissenting from the denial of certiorari). "[T]he consistency promised in *Furman* and the fairness to the individual demanded in *Lockett* are not only inversely related, but irreconcilable in the context of capital punishment," he explained, and "the proper course when faced with irreconcilable constitutional commands is not to ignore one or the other, nor to pretend that the dilemma does not exist, but to admit the futility of the effort to harmonize them." *Id.* at 1155, 1157.

4. Doubts About Guilt as a Mitigating Circumstance. Empirical evidence suggests that residual doubts about a defendant's guilt are "[b]y far, the strongest mitigating factor" in jurors' minds. William J. Bowers et al., *Foreclosed Impartiality in Capital Sentencing: Jurors' Predispositions, Guilt-Trial Experience, and Premature Decision Making*, 83 Cornell L. Rev. 1476, 1534 (1998) (citing a survey of 916 people who had sat on juries in 257 capital trials in 11 states); *see also* Stephen P. Garvey, *Aggravation and Mitigation in Capital Cases: What Do Jurors Think?*, 98 Colum. L. Rev.

---

43. The Court also ruled in *Carr* that the Eighth Amendment did not mandate separate capital sentencing hearings for two brothers who were tried jointly.

1538, 1563–64 (1998) (citing interviews of jurors from 41 capital trials in South Carolina). Nevertheless, a plurality of the Court suggested in *Franklin v. Lynaugh*, 487 U.S. 164 (1988), that capital juries are not required to consider such "residual doubts" at sentencing because they do not involve "any aspect of [a defendant's] 'character,' 'record,' or a 'circumstance of the offense,'" which was all that the Court's opinion in *Lockett* required. *Id.* at 174 (quoting *Lockett*, 438 U.S. at 604); *see also id.* at 187–88 (O'Connor, J., concurring in the judgment) (making the same point).

The *Franklin* plurality did not need to resolve that issue, however, and the Court has continued to leave open the question whether there is "a constitutional right to introduce residual doubt evidence at sentencing." *Oregon v. Guzek*, 546 U.S. 517, 525 (2006) (holding that even if such a right existed, the defendant there was not entitled to present new alibi evidence that he did not claim was unavailable at trial). Writing separately in *Guzek*, Justices Scalia and Thomas complained that the majority missed "the opportunity to put to rest, once and for all, the mistaken notion that the Eighth Amendment requires" admission of residual doubt evidence at capital sentencing hearings. *Id.* at 528 (Scalia, J., concurring in the judgment). Are these Justices correct, or were the original drafters of the Model Penal Code right to bar imposition of the death penalty in cases where the evidence "does not foreclose all doubt respecting the defendant's guilt" as "an accommodation to the irrevocability of the capital sanction"? Model Penal Code § 210.6 Comment at 134.

Several Supreme Court opinions have also considered capital defendants' efforts to present residual doubt evidence that comes to light after they have already been convicted and sentenced to death. In *Herrera v. Collins*, 506 U.S. 390 (1993), for example, the defendant filed a habeas petition challenging the state's refusal to consider newly discovered evidence purportedly demonstrating that someone else had committed the murders for which he had been sentenced to die 10 years earlier. Among other things, the defendant claimed that the Eighth Amendment prohibits executing one who is actually innocent. The Court affirmed his sentence, observing that "federal habeas courts sit to ensure that individuals are not imprisoned in violation of the Constitution — not to correct errors of fact." *Id.* at 400. Although the majority assumed that "a truly persuasive demonstration of 'actual innocence' made after trial would render the execution of a defendant unconstitutional," it found it unnecessary to resolve that question. *Id.* at 417. Noting that "the threshold showing for such an assumed right would necessarily be extraordinarily high" — both because of "the very disruptive effect that entertaining claims of actual innocence would have on the need for finality in capital cases" and because of "the enormous burden that having to retry cases based on stale evidence would place on the States" — the Court concluded that "[t]he showing made by petitioner in this case falls far short of any such threshold." *Id.*

Writing separately, Justices Scalia and Thomas argued that "[t]here is no basis in text, tradition, or even in contemporary practice (if that were enough) for finding in the Constitution a right to demand judicial consideration of newly discovered evidence of innocence brought forward after conviction." *Id.* at 427–28 (Scalia, J., concurring). Nevertheless, they joined the Court's opinion, noting that they under-stood "the reluctance of the present Court to admit publicly that Our Perfect Constitution lets stand any injustice, much less the execution of an innocent man who has received, though to no avail, all the process that our society has tradition-ally deemed adequate." *Id.* at 428. Justice Blackmun, joined by Justice Stevens and in large part by Justice Souter, dissented, concluding that it is "contrary to any standard of decency to execute someone who is actually innocent." *Id.* at 435 (Blackmun, J., dissenting).

Subsequently, in *House v. Bell*, 547 U.S. 518, 554, 541 (2006), the Court unani-mously agreed that the defendant had not met the "extraordinarily high" standard *Herrera* required to show "freestanding innocence"—even though House had presented, among other things, newly discovered DNA evidence rebutting "the only forensic evidence at the scene . . . linking him to the crime." A majority of the Court concluded, however, that House had produced enough evidence of his innocence to satisfy the lesser standard required to pursue a habeas petition raising constitutional claims that would otherwise have been procedurally barred under state law—i.e., that, "in light of new evidence, 'it is more likely than not that no reasonable juror would have found petitioner guilty beyond a reasonable doubt.'" *Id.* at 537 (quoting *Schlup v. Delo*, 513 U.S. 298, 327 (1995)).

5. Other Mitigating Circumstances. Other relevant mitigating circumstances include: "severe emotional disturbance," "a turbulent family history," and "beatings by a harsh father," *Eddings v. Oklahoma*, 455 U.S. 104, 115 (1982); good behavior in prison while awaiting trial, *see Skipper v. South Carolina*, 476 U.S. 1 (1986); "post-crime religious conversion," *Brown v. Payton*, 544 U.S. 133 (2005); a clean prior record, *see* Model Penal Code § 210.6(4)(a); a minor role in the crime, *see id.* § 210.6(4)(e); and commission of a crime under duress or the influence of drugs or alcohol, *see id.* §§ 210.6(4)(f)–(g).

In *McKoy v. North Carolina*, 494 U.S. 433 (1990), the Court invalidated a require-ment that mitigating circumstances be supported by a unanimous jury verdict. Not-ing that *Lockett* required that "each juror be permitted to consider and give effect to mitigating evidence," the Court concluded that "such consideration of mitigating evidence may not be foreclosed by one or more jurors' failure to find a mitigating circumstance." *Id.* at 442–43. The Court also endorsed a broad definition of "rele-vant" mitigating evidence as "evidence which tends logically to prove or disprove some fact or circumstance which a fact-finder could reasonably deem to have mitigating value." *Id.* at 440.

6. Weighing the Aggravating and Mitigating Circumstances. Once the jury iden-tifies the relevant aggravating and mitigating circumstances, it must then weigh them in determining whether or not to impose the death penalty. In *Kansas v. Marsh*, 548 U.S. 163, 174 (2006), the Court observed that, assuming a capital sentencing scheme "rationally narrow[s] the class of death-eligible defendants" and follows *Lock-ett*'s mandate for "a reasoned, individualized sentencing determination," "a State enjoys a range of discretion in imposing the death penalty, including the manner in which aggravating and mitigating circumstances are to be weighed."

Justice Thomas' majority opinion in *Marsh* upheld a Kansas statute that required jurors to impose a death sentence if they found beyond a reasonable doubt that the "aggravating circumstances [were] not outweighed by any mitigating circumstance"—even if they believed the "aggravating evidence and mitigating evidence [were] in equipoise." *Id.* at 166. Noting that the Court had previously held in *Walton v. Arizona*, 497 U.S. 639 (1990), that a capital defendant may constitutionally be required to shoulder the burden of proving that the mitigating circumstances outweighed the aggravating circumstances, the *Marsh* majority reasoned that, "[a] *fortiori*, Kansas' death penalty statute . . . may direct imposition of the death penalty when the State has proved beyond a reasonable doubt that mitigators do not outweigh aggravators." *Marsh*, 548 U.S. at 173. And the Court dismissed the defendant's reliance on its precedents striking down mandatory death penalty schemes, suggesting that those cases govern only statutes that "automatically impose death upon conviction for certain types of murder." *Id.* at 171 (quoting *Walton*, 497 U.S. at 652).

Writing for the four dissenters, Justice Souter criticized the Kansas statute's "tie breaker in favor of death," calling it "morally absurd" to mandate a death sentence "when the case for aggravation has failed to convince the sentencing jury." *Id.* at 207 (Souter, J., dissenting).

7. Judges Versus Juries as Sentencing Authorities. Most death penalty statutes delegate the sentencing function in capital cases to the jury, although in a few states the jury makes a recommendation that the trial judge may overturn. In *Gregg v. Georgia*, 428 U.S. 153, 190 (1976) (plurality opinion), Justice Stewart noted that "[j]ury sentencing has been considered desirable in capital cases in order 'to maintain a link between contemporary community values and the penal system—a link without which the determination of punishment could hardly reflect "the evolving standards of decency that mark the progress of a maturing society."'"

Despite this language, the Court subsequently held in *Spaziano v. Florida*, 468 U.S. 447 (1984), that the Constitution did not mandate that death sentences be imposed by a jury. Although juries made the sentencing determination in 30 of the 37 jurisdictions that allowed the death penalty at that time, and only three states permitted judges to override a jury's recommendation of life, the Court refused to hold that "contemporary standards of decency are offended . . . every time a State reaches a conclusion different from a majority of its sisters over how best to administer its criminal laws." *Id.* at 464.

In *Ring v. Arizona*, 536 U.S. 584, 609 (2002), however, the Court relied on the Sixth Amendment right to jury trial in deciding that "a sentencing judge, sitting without a jury," may not "find an aggravating circumstance necessary for imposition of the death penalty." Thus, the defendant in that case—who had been convicted of felony murder—could not be sentenced to death based on the trial judge's finding that the crime was committed for pecuniary gain, a statutory aggravating factor that was not reflected in the jury's verdict. The Court's decision in *Ring* built on its earlier ruling in *Apprendi v. New Jersey*, 530 U.S. 466 (2000), that the Constitution requires a jury determination of any fact (other than a prior conviction) that enhances a sentence beyond the maximum the defendant could have received under the facts reflected in the jury's verdict. The Court concluded in *Ring* that statutory aggravating factors in capital cases "operate as 'the functional equivalent of an element of a greater offense,'" and thus must be found by a jury beyond a reasonable doubt. *Ring*, 536 U.S. at 609 (quoting *Apprendi*, 530 U.S. at 494). (*Apprendi* and the line of cases following it are described in greater detail above in Chapter 2, Section D.2.b.)

The *Ring* Court was careful to limit its holding, however, noting that the defendant's challenge in that case was limited to findings of aggravating circumstances. Thus, the Court pointed out, Ring made "no Sixth Amendment claim with respect to mitigating circumstances," he did not "argue that the Sixth Amendment required the jury to make the ultimate determination whether to impose the death penalty," and he did not challenge a state supreme court's "authority to reweigh the aggravating and mitigating circumstances" after striking down one of the aggravating factors found by the jury. *Id.* at 597 n.4. *But cf.* William J. Bowers et al., *The Decision Maker Matters: An Empirical Examination of the Way the Role of the Judge and the Jury Influence Death Penalty Decision-Making*, 63 WASH. & LEE L. REV. 931, 940 (2006) (arguing that *Ring* had broader implications because findings of aggravating circumstances are "no more essential" than other findings in making death penalty determinations).

Most recently, in *Hurst v. Florida*, 136 S. Ct. 616 (2016), the Court relied on *Ring* in striking down Florida's death penalty scheme, which first asked the jury to make a nonbinding sentencing recommendation based on a majority vote, and then authorized the trial judge to independently evaluate the aggravating and mitigating circumstances and ultimately determine the sentence. Noting that the Sixth Amendment "requires a jury, not a judge, to find each fact necessary to impose a sentence of death," the Court refused to distinguish *Ring* on the ground that Florida, unlike Arizona, "incorporated an advisory jury verdict." *Id.* at 619, 622. Under the Florida procedures, the Court reasoned, the jury did not "make specific factual findings with regard to the existence of mitigating or aggravating circumstances and its recommendation [was] not binding on the trial judge." *Id.* at 622 (quoting *Walton v. Arizona*, 497 U.S. 639, 648 (1990)). The *Hurst* Court therefore overruled *Spaziano* "to the extent that [it] allow[ed] a sentencing judge to find an aggravating circumstance, independent of a jury's factfinding, that is necessary for imposition of the death penalty." *Id.* at 624.

In the wake of the Court's decision in *Hurst*, the Florida legislature revised its death penalty statute to permit judges to impose a death sentence only if the jury unanimously found at least one statutory aggravating circumstance and 10 jurors favored a death sentence. Does this statute satisfy the dictates of *Ring* and *Hurst*? *See State v. Perry*, 210 So. 3d 630 (Fla. 2016) (striking the statute down on the grounds that *Hurst* requires a unanimous jury recommendation of death). *See also Woodward v.*

Alabama,134 S. Ct. 405 (2013) (Sotomayor, J., dissenting from the denial of certiorari) (arguing that *Ring* calls into question the Alabama statute, which allows the judge to reweigh the aggravating and mitigating circumstances and to reverse even a unanimous jury vote against the death penalty); *Ex parte Bohannon*, 2016 Ala. Lexis 114 (Ala. Sept. 30, 2016) (upholding the Alabama statute on the grounds that *Hurst* requires a unanimous jury finding only on the statutory aggravating circumstance), *cert. denied*, 137 S. Ct. 831 (2017); *Rauf v. State*, 145 A.3d 430 (Del. 2016) (per curiam) (striking down Delaware's death penalty procedures, interpreting *Hurst* to require that a unanimous jury find beyond a reasonable doubt both that an aggravating circumstance exists and that the aggravating circumstances outweigh the mitigating circumstances). For an empirical study finding that Delaware judges were more likely than juries to impose a death sentence, see Valerie P. Han et al., *The Death Penalty: Should the Judge or the Jury Decide Who Dies?*, 12 J. Empir. Stud. 70 (2015). For a description of how the various states allocate the decisionmaking in capital sentencing hearings, see Death Penalty Information Center, *U.S. Supreme Court:* Ring v. Arizona, http://www.deathpenaltyinfo.org/us-supreme-court-ring-v-arizona.

8. Death-Qualified Juries. In *Witherspoon v. Illinois*, 391 U.S. 510, 522 (1968), the Court held that the Sixth Amendment right to an impartial jury barred prosecutors from excluding prospective jurors for cause in capital cases simply because they "voiced general objections to the death penalty or expressed conscientious or religious scruples against its infliction." In *Wainwright v. Witt*, 469 U.S. 412, 424 (1985), the Court clarified the *Witherspoon* standard, concluding that the relevant question in determining whether a capital juror may be excluded for cause is "whether the juror's views would 'prevent or substantially impair the performance of his duties as a juror in accordance with his instructions and his oath.'" *See also Morgan v. Illinois*, 504 U.S. 719, 729 (1992) (holding that a defendant may challenge prospective jurors for cause who would automatically vote to impose the death penalty in all capital cases).

Although the Court overturned the death sentence in *Witherspoon*, it refused to reverse the conviction, finding the evidence "too tentative and fragmentary to establish that jurors not opposed to the death penalty tend to favor the prosecution in the determination of guilt." *Witherspoon*, 391 U.S. at 517. But the Court left open the possibility that a defendant convicted by a death-qualified jury "in some future case might still attempt to establish that the jury was less than neutral with respect to guilt." *Id.* at 520 n.18.

In *Lockhart v. McCree*, 476 U.S. 162 (1986), the Court revisited the question left open in *Witherspoon*. In the 18-year interval between the two cases, "[s]ocial scientists perceived *Witherspoon* . . . as an invitation to produce data relevant to the prosecution proneness issue," and a number of sophisticated studies were conducted, "[a]ll [of which] supported the view that a death-qualified jury differs from a non-death-qualified jury in that its attitudes are more favorable to the prosecution and that it is in fact more likely to convict a criminal defendant." Welsh S. White, The

Death Penalty in the Eighties: An Examination of the Modern System of Capital Punishment 167 (1987). In addition, McCree presented expert testimony consistent with those studies, which showed that "death qualification significantly decreases the proportion of women and blacks eligible to serve as jurors." *Id.* at 168. Nevertheless, the Court rejected the defendant's empirical evidence and then went on to say that, even if the evidence had demonstrated that death-qualified juries are "somewhat more 'conviction-prone,'" the Sixth Amendment did not prohibit the prosecution from excluding prospective jurors who did not satisfy the *Witherspoon/Witt* standard from the guilt phase of capital trials. *Lockhart v. McCree*, 476 U.S. at 173. *But cf. Baze v. Rees*, 553 U.S. 35, 84 (2008) (Stevens, J., concurring in the judgment) (arguing that "the process of obtaining a 'death qualified jury' is really a procedure that has the purpose and effect of obtaining a jury that is biased in favor of conviction" and therefore "deprive[s] the defendant of a trial by jurors representing a fair cross section of the community"); Aliza Plener Cover, *The Eighth Amendment's Lost Jurors: Death Qualification and Evolving Standards of Decency*, 92 Ind. L.J. 113 (2016) (reporting the results of an empirical study of 11 Louisiana death penalty trials held between 2009 and 2013, which found that 22.5 percent of prospective jurors were excluded because they were opposed to the death penalty, almost 60 percent of whom were African-American).

Since *Lockhart v. McCree*, the Supreme Court has on several occasions reviewed the propriety of specific exclusions of jurors under the *Witherspoon/Witt* standard. In *Uttecht v. Brown*, 551 U.S. 1, 15 (2007), for example, the Court upheld the exclusion of a juror who was "confused about the conditions under which death could be imposed." The majority observed that "when there is ambiguity in the prospective juror's statements, 'the trial court, aided as it undoubtedly [is] by its assessment of [the venireman's] demeanor, [is] entitled to resolve it in favor of the State.'" *Id.* at 7 (quoting *Witt*, 469 U.S. at 434). The four dissenters, by contrast, charged that the majority "appear[ed] to be under the impression that trial courts should be encouraging the inclusion of jurors who will impose the death penalty rather than only ensuring the exclusion of those who say that, in all circumstances, they cannot." *Id.* at 44 (Stevens, J. dissenting). *See also White v. Wheeler*, 136 S. Ct. 456, 461 (2015) (per curiam) (finding that a state court did not violate clearly established law in rejecting a capital defendant's challenge to the trial judge's decision to exclude a juror whose "answers . . . were at least ambiguous as to whether he would be able to give appropriate consideration to imposing the death penalty").

9. Educating Capital Sentencing Juries. In noncapital cases, juries typically receive no information about sentencing issues because the trial judge has primary responsibility for sentencing. In capital cases, where juries play a role in sentencing, controversies have arisen concerning the type and amount of information about sentencing that should be given to the jury.

In *California v. Ramos*, 463 U.S. 992 (1983), for example, the Court upheld the constitutionality of an instruction informing a capital jury that the governor had the power to commute a life imprisonment sentence (even though they were not told about the governor's comparable power with respect to a death sentence). On remand, however, the state supreme court struck down the instruction as violative of the state constitution, reasoning that it was "a misleading 'half-truth'" and also "invite[d] the jury to consider speculative and impermissible factors in reaching its decision." *People v. Ramos*, 689 P.2d 430, 440 (Cal. 1984).

In *Shafer v. South Carolina*, 532 U.S. 36 (2001), a majority of the Supreme Court endorsed the plurality's conclusion in *Simmons v. South Carolina*, 512 U.S. 154 (1994), that in capital cases where the defendant's future dangerousness is at issue and the jury must choose between death and life imprisonment without parole, the Due Process Clause requires the trial judge to inform the jury that the defendant is ineligible for parole under state law. In support of its conclusion, the *Simmons* plurality relied on public opinion research suggesting that jurors are likely to be confused about the practical impact of a "life" sentence. *See id.* at 170 & n.9. *See also Lynch v. Arizona*, 136 S. Ct. 1818 (2016) (per curiam) (holding that the possibility of executive clemency did not justify a different conclusion).

These rulings are limited, however, and do not necessarily require that juries be given all relevant information about parole. Thus, in *Brown v. Texas*, 522 U.S. 940 (1997), the Court denied certiorari in a case upholding a Texas law that required capital juries to assess a defendant's future dangerousness but prohibited them from receiving information about when the defendant would be eligible for parole if sentenced to life in prison (even though jurors that had responsibility for sentencing in *noncapital* cases in Texas were given this information). Justice Stevens wrote an opinion joined by three other Justices, noting the "obvious tension" between the Court's precedents and the Texas practice, and observing that it "unquestionably tips the scales in favor of a death sentence that a fully informed jury might not impose." *Id.* at 941, 942 (Stevens, J., opinion respecting the denial of certiorari).

10. Automatic State Supreme Court Review. The overwhelming majority of death penalty statutes provide for automatic review of all capital sentences, usually by the state's highest court. This review typically covers the defendant's challenges to both the conviction and the sentence. For example, the death penalty statute upheld in *Gregg v. Georgia*, 428 U.S. 153 (1976) (plurality opinion), allowed an automatic appeal of all death sentences to the state supreme court. The Georgia statute required that court to make three determinations: that the death sentence was not "imposed under the influence of passion, prejudice, or any other arbitrary factor"; that the evidence supported the jury's finding of a statutory aggravating circumstance; and that the sentence was not "excessive or disproportionate to the penalty imposed in similar cases" (the so-called "proportionality review"). *Id.* at 166–67.

Although Justice Stewart's opinion in *Gregg* characterized this automatic appeal provision as "an important additional safeguard against arbitrariness and caprice," *id.* at 198, the Court later held in *Pulley v. Harris*, 465 U.S. 37 (1984), that state supreme courts are not constitutionally required to conduct a proportionality review and compare the defendant's death sentence to the sentences imposed in other similar cases. A number of states abandoned the requirement of proportionality review in the wake of *Pulley*, although it is still required in 17 states. *See* William Berry, *Ending the Death Lottery: A Case Study of Ohio's Broken Proportionality Review,* 76 Ohio St. L.J. 67, 98 (2015).

Even in those jurisdictions, however, the state supreme courts' record has been subject to criticism. *See, e.g., Walker v. Georgia*, 555 U.S. 979, 982 (2008) (Stevens, J., opinion respecting the denial of certiorari) (accusing the Georgia Supreme Court of conducting "an utterly perfunctory" proportionality review, "consist[ing] of a single paragraph . . . stated . . . in the most conclusory terms," which failed to consider "numerous cases involving offenses very similar" to the defendant's where the jury did not impose a capital sentence or the prosecution did not even seek the death penalty); Berry, *supra*, at 71 (arguing that proportionality review in Ohio is a matter of "form, not substance," and finding that more than 40 percent of capital sentences imposed in that state between 1996 and 2011 were "comparatively excessive"); Brooks Emanuel, *North Carolina's Failure to Perform Comparative Proportionality Review*, 39 N.Y.U. Rev. L. & Soc. Change 419, 431 (2015) (charging that the North Carolina Supreme Court has been comparing too few cases and thus "has not been faithfully performing this review").

11. Congressional Limits on Habeas Corpus. The Antiterrorism and Effective Death Penalty Act of 1996 (AEDPA), passed in the wake of the 1995 bombing of the Oklahoma City federal building masterminded by Timothy McVeigh, imposed new limits on habeas corpus petitions and thereby restricted the ability of death row inmates to challenge the constitutionality of their convictions and sentences in federal court. For the first time, Congress created a statute of limitations for habeas petitions, requiring that they be filed within one year. *See* 28 U.S.C. §§ 2244(d), 2255(f). *But cf. McQuiggin v. Perkins*, 133 S. Ct. 1924, 1928 (2013) (relying on *House v. Bell*, described above in Note 4, in holding that "actual innocence, if proved," creates an exception to the AEDPA statute of limitations).

In addition, AEDPA requires that state prisoners must now do more than prove that their constitutional rights were violated in order to obtain habeas relief. Rather, they cannot prevail on a claim already "adjudicated on the merits" in state court unless the state court's decision was either "contrary to, or involved an unreasonable application of, clearly established" Supreme Court doctrine or was "based on an unreasonable determination of the facts." 28 U.S.C. § 2254(d).

AEDPA also restricts a prisoner's right to file more than one habeas petition, requiring that any successive petition must present a new claim not previously raised on habeas and must be based on either (A) "a new rule of constitutional law, made retroactive to cases on collateral review by the Supreme Court, that was previously unavailable" or (B) new facts that could not reasonably have been discovered before and that "would be sufficient to establish by clear and convincing evidence" that "no reasonable factfinder" would have convicted the defendant but for the constitutional error. *Id.* §§ 2244(b)(2), 2255(h). *See also Felker v. Turpin*, 518 U.S. 651, 664 (1996) (upholding the constitutionality of the statute's limits on successive petitions as "well within the compass of th[e] evolutionary process" surrounding efforts to alleviate "abuse of the writ" of habeas corpus).

Finally, AEDPA creates specific rules for death penalty cases that apply in any state that "opts in" by affording indigent capital defendants a right to counsel in state collateral attack proceedings. *See* 28 U.S.C. § 2261. These provisions, among other things, impose an even shorter statute of limitations (180 days) for habeas petitions filed by death row inmates in those jurisdictions, and also create strict time deadlines by which the federal courts must dispose of those petitions (typically, 60 days after the case is submitted to the district court and 120 days after the last brief is filed in the court of appeals). *See id.* §§ 2263, 2266. A few states have attempted to satisfy the opt-in requirements, but their efforts have been unsuccessful. *See* Carol S. Steiker & Jordan M. Steiker, *A Tale of Two Nations: Implementation of the Death Penalty in "Executing" Versus "Symbolic" States in the United States*, 84 Tex. L. Rev. 1869, 1925 (2006).

Chapter 7

Rape

[A] Statutory Rape

People v. Hernandez

393 P.2d 673 (Cal. 1964)

PEEK, JUSTICE.

. . . .

Section 261 of the Penal Code provides in part as follows: "Rape is an act of sexual intercourse, accomplished with a female not the wife of the perpetrator, under . . . the following circumstances: 1. Where the female is under the age of eighteen years . . . ." [The defendant was convicted under this provision and sentenced to two years' probation and a $150 fine.]

The sole contention raised on appeal is that the trial court erred in refusing to permit defendant to present evidence for the purpose of showing that he had in good faith a reasonable belief that the prosecutrix was 18 years or more of age.

The undisputed facts show that the defendant and the prosecuting witness were not married and had been companions for several months prior to January 3, 1961 — the date of the commission of the alleged offense. Upon that date the prosecutrix was 17 years and 9 months of age and voluntarily engaged in an act of sexual intercourse with defendant.

. . . .

. . . We are dealing here, of course, with statutory rape where, in one sense, the lack of consent of the female is not an element of the offense. In a broader sense, however, the lack of consent is deemed to remain an element but the law makes a conclusive presumption of the lack thereof because she is presumed too innocent and naive to understand the implications and nature of her act. The law's concern with her capacity or lack thereof to so understand is explained in part by a popular conception of the social, moral and personal values which are preserved by the abstinence from sexual indulgence on the part of a young woman. An unwise disposition of her sexual favor is deemed to do harm both to herself and the social mores by which the community's conduct patterns are established. Hence the law of statutory rape intervenes in an effort to avoid such a disposition. This goal, moreover, is not accomplished by penalizing the naive female but by imposing criminal sanctions against the male, who is conclusively presumed to be responsible for the occurrence.

The assumption that age alone will bring an understanding of the sexual act to a young woman is of doubtful validity. Both learning from the cultural group [of] which she is a member and her actual sexual experiences will determine her level of comprehension. The sexually experienced 15-year-old may be far more acutely aware of the implications of sexual intercourse than her sheltered cousin who is beyond the age of consent. A girl who belongs to a group whose members indulge in sexual intercourse at an early age is likely to rapidly acquire an insight into the rewards and penalties of sexual indulgence. Nevertheless, even in circumstances where a girl's actual comprehension contradicts the law's presumption, the male is deemed criminally responsible for the act, although himself young and naive and responding to advances which may have been made to him.[1]

The law as presently constituted does not concern itself with the relative culpability of the male and female participants in the prohibited sexual act. Even where the young woman is knowledgeable it does not impose sanctions upon her. The knowledgeable young man, on the other hand, is penalized and there are none who would claim that under any construction of the law this should be otherwise. However, the issue raised by the rejected offer of proof in the instant case goes to the culpability of the young man who acts without knowledge that an essential factual element exists and has, on the other hand, a positive, reasonable belief that it does not exist.

The primordial concept of mens rea, the guilty mind, expresses the principle that it is not conduct alone but conduct accompanied by certain specific mental states which concerns, or should concern, the law. . . .

Statutory rape has long furnished a fertile battleground upon which to argue that the lack of knowledgeable conduct is a proper defense. The law in this state now rests, as it did in 1896, with this court's decision in *People v. Ratz*, 115 Cal. 132, where it is stated: ". . . The protection of society, of the family, and of the infant, demand that one who has carnal intercourse under such circumstances shall do so in peril of the fact, and he will not be heard against the evidence to urge his belief that the victim of his outrage had passed the period which would make his act a crime." The age of consent at the time of the *Ratz* decision was 14 years, and it is noteworthy that the purpose of the rule, as there announced, was to afford protection to young females therein described as "infants." The decision on which the court in *Ratz* relied was *The Queen v. Prince*, L.R. 2 Crown Cas. 154. However England has now, by statute,

---

1. [n.1] The inequitable consequences to which we may be led are graphically illustrated by the following excerpt from *State v. Snow* (Mo. 1923) 252 S.W. 629, 632: "We have in this case a condition and not a theory. This wretched girl was young in years but old in sin and shame. A number of callow youths, of otherwise blameless lives . . . fell under her seductive influence. They flocked about her, . . . like moths about the flame of a lighted candle and probably with the same result. The girl was a common prostitute. . . . The boys were immature and doubtless more sinned against than sinning. They did not defile the girl. She was a mere 'cistern for foul toads to knot and gender in.' Why should the boys, misled by her, be sacrificed? What sound public policy can be subserved by branding them as felons? Might it not be wise to ingraft an exception in the statute?"

departed from the strict rule, and excludes as a crime an act of sexual intercourse with a female between the ages of 13 and 16 years if the perpetrator is under the age of 24 years, has not previously been charged with a like offense, and believes the female "to be of the age of sixteen or over and has reasonable cause for the belief."

The rationale of the *Ratz* decision, rather than purporting to eliminate intent as an element of the crime, holds that the wrongdoer must assume the risk; that, subjectively, when the act is committed, he consciously intends to proceed regardless of the age of the female and the consequences of his act, and that the circumstances involving the female, whether she be a day or a decade less than the statutory age, are irrelevant.[2] There can be no dispute that a criminal intent exists when the perpetrator proceeds with utter disregard of, or in the lack of grounds for, a belief that the female has reached the age of consent. But if he participates in a mutual act of sexual intercourse, believing his partner to be beyond the age of consent, with reasonable grounds for such belief, where is his criminal intent? In such circumstances he has not consciously taken any risk. . . . If it occurs that he has been misled, we cannot realistically conclude that for such reason alone the intent with which he undertook the act suddenly becomes more heinous. . . .

. . . Our departure from the views expressed in *Ratz* is in no manner indicative of a withdrawal from the sound policy that it is in the public interest to protect the sexually naive female from exploitation. No responsible person would hesitate to condemn as untenable a claimed good faith belief in the age of consent of an "infant" female whose obviously tender years preclude the existence of reasonable grounds for that belief. However, the prosecutrix in the instant case was but three months short of 18 years of age and there is nothing in the record to indicate that the purposes of the law as stated in *Ratz* can be better served by foreclosing the defense of a lack of intent. This is not to say that the granting of consent by even a sexually sophisticated girl known to be less than the statutory age is a defense. We hold only that, in the absence of a legislative direction otherwise, a charge of statutory rape is defensible wherein a criminal intent is lacking.

. . . .

---

2. [n.3] "When the law declares that sexual intercourse with a girl under the age of ten years is rape, it is not illogical to refuse to give any credence to the defense, 'I thought she was older, and I therefore did not believe that I was committing a crime when I had sexual intercourse with her.' . . . But when age limits are raised to sixteen, eighteen, and twenty-one, when the young girl becomes a young woman, when adolescent boys as well as young men are attracted to her, the sexual act begins to lose its quality of abnormality and physical danger to the victim. Bona fide mistakes in the age of girls can be made by men and boys who are no more dangerous than others of their social, economic and educational level. . . . Even if the girl looks to be much older than the age of consent fixed by the statute, even if she lies to the man concerning her age, if she is a day below the statutory age sexual intercourse with her is rape. The man or boy who has intercourse with such girl still acts at his peril. *The statute is interpreted as if it were protecting children under the age of ten.*" (Emphasis added.) (PLOSCOWE, SEX AND LAW (1951) at pp. 184 and 185.)

. . . It is not our purpose here to make a determination that the defendant entertained a reasonable belief. Suffice to state that . . . it was reversible error to reject the [defendant's] offer [of proof].

Garnett v. State

632 A.2d 797 (Md. 1993)

Murphy, Chief Judge.

. . . .

Raymond Lennard Garnett is a young retarded man. At the time of the incident in question he was 20 years old. He has an I.Q. of 52. His guidance counselor from the Montgomery County public school system, Cynthia Parker, described him as a mildly retarded person who read on the third-grade level, did arithmetic on the 5th-grade level, and interacted with others socially at school at the level of someone 11 or 12 years of age. . . . As Raymond was unable to pass any of the State's functional tests required for graduation, he received only a certificate of attendance rather than a high-school diploma.

In November or December 1990, a friend introduced Raymond to Erica Frazier, then aged 13; the two subsequently talked occasionally by telephone. On February 28, 1991, Raymond, apparently wishing to call for a ride home, approached the girl's house at about nine o'clock in the evening. Erica opened her bedroom window, through which Raymond entered; he testified that "she just told me to get a ladder and climb up her window." The two talked, and later engaged in sexual intercourse. Raymond left at about 4:30 a.m. the following morning. On November 19, 1991, Erica gave birth to a baby, of which Raymond is the biological father.

Raymond was tried . . . on one count of second degree rape under § 463(a)(3) proscribing sexual intercourse between a person under 14 and another at least four years older than the complainant. . . . The court found Raymond guilty. It sentenced him to a term of five years in prison, suspended the sentence and imposed five years of probation, and ordered that he pay restitution to Erica and the Frazier family. . . .

Section 463(a)(3) does not expressly set forth a requirement that the accused have acted with a criminal state of mind, or mens rea. The State insists that the statute, by design, defines a strict liability offense, and that its essential elements were met in the instant case when Raymond, age 20, engaged in vaginal intercourse with Erica, a girl under 14 and more than 4 years his junior. Raymond replies that the criminal law exists to assess and punish morally culpable behavior. He says such culpability was absent here. He asks us either to engraft onto subsection (a)(3) an implicit mens rea requirement, or to recognize an affirmative defense of reasonable mistake as to the complainant's age. Raymond argues that it is unjust, under the circumstances of this case which led him to think his conduct lawful, to brand him a felon and rapist. . . .

Raymond asserts that the events of this case were inconsistent with the criminal sexual exploitation of a minor by an adult. . . . With an I.Q. of 52, Raymond functioned at approximately the same level as the 13-year-old Erica; he was mentally an adolescent in an adult's body. Arguably, had Raymond's chronological age, 20, matched his socio-intellectual age, about 12, he and Erica would have fallen well within the four-year age difference obviating a violation of the statute, and Raymond would not have been charged with any crime at all.

The precise legal issue here rests on Raymond's unsuccessful efforts to introduce into evidence testimony that Erica and her friends had told him she was 16 years old, the age of consent to sexual relations, and that he believed them. Thus the trial court did not permit him to raise a defense of reasonable mistake of Erica's age, by which defense Raymond would have asserted that he acted innocently without a criminal design. . . . The requirement that an accused have acted with a culpable mental state is an axiom of criminal jurisprudence. . . .

To be sure, legislative bodies since the mid-19th century have created strict liability criminal offenses requiring no mens rea. Almost all such statutes responded to the demands of public health and welfare arising from the complexities of society after the Industrial Revolution. Typically misdemeanors involving only fines or other light penalties, these strict liability laws regulated food, milk, liquor, medicines and drugs, securities, motor vehicles and traffic, the labeling of goods for sale, and the like. . . . Statutory rape, carrying the stigma of [a] felony as well as a potential sentence of 20 years in prison, contrasts markedly with the other strict liability regulatory offenses and their light penalties.

Modern scholars generally reject the concept of strict criminal liability. . . .

The commentators similarly disapprove of statutory rape as a strict liability crime. . . . [T]hey observe that statutory rape prosecutions often proceed even when the defendant's judgment as to the age of the complainant is warranted by her appearance, her sexual sophistication, her verbal misrepresentations, and the defendant's careful attempts to ascertain her true age. Voluntary intercourse with a sexually mature teen-ager lacks the features of psychic abnormality, exploitation, or physical danger that accompanies such conduct with children.

. . . .

We think it sufficiently clear, however, that Maryland's second degree rape statute defines a strict liability offense that does not require the State to prove mens rea; it makes no allowance for a mistake-of-age defense. The plain language of § 463, viewed in its entirety, and the legislative history of its creation lead to this conclusion. [The court's discussion of the statutory language and legislative history is omitted.]

This interpretation is consistent with the traditional view of statutory rape as a strict liability crime designed to protect young persons from the dangers of sexual exploitation by adults, loss of chastity, physical injury, and, in the case of girls, pregnancy. The majority of states retain statutes which impose strict liability for sexual acts with underage complainants. . . . [E]ven among those states providing for a mistake-of-age defense in some instances, the defense often is not available where the sex partner is 14 years old or less; the complaining witness in the instant case was only 13. . . .

Maryland's second degree rape statute is by nature a creature of legislation. Any new provision introducing an element of mens rea, or permitting a defense of reasonable mistake of age, with respect to the offense of sexual intercourse with a person less than 14, should properly result from an act of the Legislature itself, rather than judicial fiat. Until then, defendants in extraordinary cases, like Raymond, will rely upon the tempering discretion of the trial court at sentencing.

[Dissenting opinions by Justices Eldridge and Bell omitted.]

Notes and Questions

1. **The Historical Explanation for Statutory Rape Laws.** Although today statutory rape laws are defended as a way of "protect[ing] children from predators and from themselves," on the theory that individuals under the agent of consent "are not competent to consent to sexual contact or sexual intercourse," *State v. Jadowski*, 680 N.W.2d 810, 817 (Wis. 2004), the traditional justification for these laws was very different. "[T]he crime originated in thirteenth century England in order to conserve a girl's eligibility for marriage, and thus her value to her father as a means to enhance the family's wealth. What was being protected was not the girl's freedom, but precisely her status as an object . . . ." Kenneth L. Karst, *Woman's Constitution*, 1984 Duke L.J. 447, 458. *See also The Queen v. Prince*, [1874–1880] All E.R. 881, 886, 887–88 (Cr. Cas. Res. 1875) (opinions of Blackburn, J., and Brett, J.) (nine of the 16 judges hearing the case acknowledged that the purpose underlying a similar statute — which prohibited "unlawfully tak[ing] . . . any unmarried girl" under 16 years of age "out of the possession and against the will of her father or mother" — was to recognize the father's "legal right" to "the possession" of his daughter). *Cf.* Kay L. Levine, *The External Evolution of Criminal Law*, 45 Am. Crim. L. Rev. 1039 (2008) (tying the prosecution rates for statutory rape in California to the state's economic interest in reducing the welfare costs associated with teenage pregnancy).

2. **Statutory Rape and Mens Rea.** As the *Garnett* court noted, most states refuse to recognize a mistake-of-age defense in statutory rape cases. Even the California Supreme Court, in a case decided subsequent to *Hernandez*, concluded that a mistake regarding the complainant's age is no defense to the charge of lewd or lascivious conduct with a child under the age of 14. *See People v. Olsen*, 685 P.2d 52, 57 (Cal. 1984). *See also* Catherine L. Carpenter, *On Statutory Rape, Strict Liability, and the Public Welfare Offense Model*, 53 Am. U. L. Rev. 313, 385–91 (2003) (noting that a substantial minority of states follow a similar hybrid model, allowing a mistake-of-age defense only for statutory rape charges involving older victims).

Is there any justification for convicting a defendant who took steps to ascertain the complainant's age—by demanding a driver's license, for example? Is it time to "reclassify[y]" statutory rape "as a true crime," requiring proof of mens rea, because "the public welfare offense model's application to statutory rape is, by current standards, strained and outmoded"? *Id.* at 322, 318. *Cf.* Criminal Code, R.S.C., ch. C-46, § 150.1(4) (Can.) (recognizing a defense if the defendant "took all reasonable steps to ascertain the age of the complainant"); *CC v. Ireland*, [2006] IESC 33 (Ir. S.C.) (finding strict liability statutory rape law unconstitutional).

Do you agree with commentators who have questioned the California Supreme Court's reliance on "sexual, and possibly racial, stereotypes" to support its decision in *Hernandez*? Nancy S. Erickson & Nadine Taub, *Final Report: Sex Bias in the Teaching of Criminal Law*, 42 RUTGERS L. REV. 309, 398 (1990). *See also* Michele Goodwin, *Law's Limits: Regulating Statutory Rape Law*, 2013 WIS. L. REV. 481, 494, 485 n.8 (describing statutory rape laws as "rooted in assumptions about white women's vulnerability, chastity, and agency," and observing that race continues to have an impact on "the probability of being charged and convicted for violating age of consent laws").

Should consent be an affirmative defense to statutory rape charges? *See* Heidi Kitrosser, *Meaningful Consent: Toward a New Generation of Statutory Rape Laws*, 4 VA. J. SOC. POL'Y & L. 287, 331 (1997) (advocating such an approach, with a "progressive definition of consent" depending on the age of the parties). *Cf. State v. Rife*, 789 So. 2d 288 (Fla. 2001) (concluding that consent is a mitigating factor in sentencing).

3. Chastity as an Element of Statutory Rape. Traditionally, proof of the complainant's chastity was required in order to support a charge of statutory rape. One court offered the following explanation for this requirement: "The object of the statute is to protect the virtuous maidens and the undefiled virgins of the State and not the unchaste female. The act which constitutes the crime of statutory rape is depriving a female within the age limits of her virginal chastity." *State v. Vicars*, 183 N.W.2d 241, 243 (Neb. 1971).

Even after chastity was eliminated as an essential element of statutory rape, a number of states continued to allow defendants to raise the complainant's promiscuity either as a complete defense to the crime or to mitigate their sentence. *See* Kristine Cordier Karnezis, *Modern Status of Admissibility, in Statutory Rape Prosecution, of Complainant's Prior Sexual Acts or General Reputation for Unchastity*, 90 A.L.R.3D 1300.

4. Gender-Neutral Statutory Rape Laws. All statutory rape laws in this country are now gender-neutral. Idaho was the last holdout, *see* Catherine L. Carpenter, *The Constitutionality of Strict Liability in Sex Offender Registration Laws*, 86 B.U. L. REV. 295, 313 (2006), but the statute in that state was amended in 2016. *See* Idaho Code § 18-6101.

In *Michael M. v. Superior Court*, 450 U.S. 464 (1981) (plurality opinion), however, the U.S. Supreme Court rejected a claim that the Equal Protection Clause requires gender-neutral statutory rape laws. In explaining its conclusion, the plurality reasoned that "young men and young women are not similarly situated with respect to the problems and the risks of sexual intercourse" because "[o]nly women may become pregnant, and they suffer disproportionately the profound physical, emotional, and psychological consequences of sexual activity." *Id.* at 471. In addition, the plurality noted, "the risk of pregnancy itself constitutes a substantial deterrence to young females"; "[a] criminal sanction imposed solely on males thus serves to roughly 'equalize' the deterrents on the sexes." *Id.* at 473. Finally, the plurality observed that "a gender-neutral statute would frustrate [the state's] interest in effective enforcement" because "a female is surely less likely to report violations of the statute if she herself would be subject to criminal prosecution." *Id.* at 473–74.

Three of the dissenting Justices suggested, however, that the real basis for gender-based statutory rape laws was "to further [the] outmoded sexual stereotypes" that "young women, in contrast to young men, were to be deemed legally incapable of consenting to an act of sexual intercourse" because "their chastity was considered particularly precious." *Id.* at 496, 494–95 (Brennan, J., dissenting). In addition, these Justices rejected the plurality's deterrence argument, noting that "[c]ommon sense . . . suggests that a gender-neutral statutory rape law is potentially a *greater* deterrent of sexual activity than a gender-based law, for the simple reason that a gender-neutral law subjects both men and women to criminal sanctions and thus arguably has a deterrent effect on twice as many potential violators." *Id.* at 493–94. *Cf. State v. Limon*, 122 P.3d 22 (Kan. 2005) (striking down as a violation of equal protection the state's "Romeo and Juliet statute," which imposed shorter prison sentences on teenagers convicted of statutory rape if the victim and defendant were members of the opposite sex, on the grounds that there was no rational basis for distinguishing between same-sex and opposite-sex relationships) (citing *Lawrence v. Texas*, 539 U.S. 558 (2003) (finding same-sex sodomy laws unconstitutional)).

Commenting on the Supreme Court's decision in *Michael M.*, one author observed:

> Gender-based statutory rape laws reinforce the sexual stereotype of men as aggressors and women as passive victims. The laws perpetuate the double standard of sexual morality. For males, sex is an accomplishment; they gain something through intercourse. For women, sex entails giving something up.
>
> . . . .
>
> . . . By refusing to grant women autonomy and by protecting them in ways that men are not protected, the state treats women's bodies — and therefore women themselves — as objects. Men are treated differently. Their bodies are regarded as a part of them, subject to their free control.

Frances Olsen, *Statutory Rape: A Feminist Critique of Rights Analysis*, 63 Tex. L. Rev. 387, 405–06 (1984).

Another commentator, though critical that the Supreme Court's "antiquated and perverse cost-benefit approach to sexuality and statutory rape laws" has "almost nothing to do with protecting the vulnerable from abuse," warned:

> [S]cholars have documented the passivity associated with the onset of adolescence in girls, particularly in terms of their interactions with men.... [D]uring adolescence, girls' self-esteem, body image, academic confidence, and willingness to speak out declines sharply.... In their yearning for femininity, they may become compliant and cooperative when pressured for sex. In this light, [a] recent study ... suggests that a considerable proportion of adolescents experience their first sexual intercourse under coercive conditions.

Michelle Oberman, *Girls in the Master's House: Of Protection, Patriarchy and the Potential for Using the Master's Tools to Reconfigure Statutory Rape Law*, 50 DePaul L. Rev. 799, 806, 820 (2001). *But cf.* Michele Goodwin, *Law's Limits: Regulating Statutory Rape Law*, 2013 Wis. L. Rev. 481, 516 (arguing that "false consciousness and broad-scale female vulnerability arguments deny the agency of young women, creating a strange double-bind that on one end demands that girls and young women be taken seriously across various social, economic, academic settings, and even sexual contexts, and on the other end firmly entraps them in victimology").

The facts of *Michael M.* illustrate Oberman's point: although at first the complainant in that case willingly kissed the defendant, she eventually asked him to "slow down and stop"; when he told her to take her pants off, she refused and tried to get up; and she ultimately "let him do what he wanted to do" only after he "slugged [her] in the face" with his fist two or three times. *Michael M.*, 450 U.S. at 483 n.* (Blackmun, J., concurring in the judgment). Olsen noted that the intercourse in *Michael M.* was "not even voluntary by any reasonable definition." Olsen, *supra*, at 416.

5. Abolishing Statutory Rape Laws. Given the controversies surrounding statutory rape laws, should they be abolished altogether? Do the archaic bases of these laws — the outmoded notion of children as the property of their parents and the concern for preserving the virginity of young women — counsel in favor of decriminalizing statutory rape, especially considering the incidence of teenage sex today? *See* Centers for Disease Control & Prevention, *Youth Risk Behavior Surveillance — United States, 2015*, 65 Morbidity & Mortality Wkly. Rep., June 10, 2016, at 26, *available at* http://www.cdc.gov/healthyyouth/data/yrbs/pdf/2015/ss6506_updated .pdf (reporting that 43 percent of male and 39 percent of female high school students had had sexual intercourse, with the percentages rising between ninth and twelfth grade from 27 percent to 59 percent for males and from 21 percent to 57 percent for females).

Even if statutory rape laws remain on the books, should the age of consent be substantially lowered? Currently, the age of consent varies, with 16 being the most popular choice — although almost every state statute also requires an age difference (most commonly four years) between the defendant and the complainant. *See United States v. Gomez*, 757 F.3d 885, 906–08 (9th Cir. 2014).

Note that several courts have struck down as unconstitutional the use of statutory rape laws when the defendant and complainant were about the same age. *See B.B. v. State*, 659 So. 2d 256 (Fla. 1995) (16-year-old male charged with having intercourse with 16-year-old female); *In re D.B.*, 950 N.E.2d 528 (Ohio 2011) (two 13-year-olds). *But cf. J.A.S. v. State*, 705 So. 2d 1381 (Fla. 1998) (distinguishing *B.B.* and finding no constitutional barrier to filing statutory rape charges against a 15-year-old male who had intercourse with a 12-year-old female); *People ex rel. J.L.*, 800 N.W.2d 720 (S.D. 2011) (allowing statutory rape charges to be brought against a 14-year-old male who had sex with his girlfriend, who was only 15 months younger but under the age of consent of 13). *See generally* Michele Goodwin, *Law's Limits: Regulating Statutory Rape Law*, 2013 Wis. L. Rev. 481, 530 (arguing that "[s]ex between consenting teenagers should not be considered a crime" because "it is morally wrong to subject children to criminal punishment for [conduct for] which adults in similar circumstance are afforded privacy . . . grounded in the Constitution").

6. **Sentencing in Statutory Rape Cases.** Garnett faced a maximum sentence of 20 years' imprisonment. At the time Hernandez was tried, the maximum sentence for statutory rape in California was 50 years in prison. Nevertheless, neither of them went to prison. Even if defendants found guilty of statutory rape receive relatively lenient sentences, the conviction may trigger the state's sex offender registry requirements. *See* Catherine L. Carpenter, *On Statutory Rape, Strict Liability, and the Public Welfare Offense Model*, 53 Am. U. L. Rev. 313, 376–80 (2003). *See also Humphrey v. Wilson*, 652 S.E.2d 501 (Ga. 2007) (finding mandatory 10-year prison term imposed on a 17-year-old defendant who had oral sex with a 15-year-old girl cruel and unusual punishment).

7. **The Model Penal Code Approach.** The Model Penal Code punishes a male for *rape* if he has sexual intercourse with a female who is under 10 years of age. *See* Model Penal Code § 213.1(1)(d). Any person, male or female, can be punished for the crime of *deviate sexual intercourse by force* if they engage in deviate sexual intercourse (e.g., oral or anal sex) with someone under 10. *See id.* § 213.2(1)(d). A male who has sexual intercourse with a female, or anyone who engages in deviate sexual intercourse, is guilty of the lesser felony of *corruption of minors* if the complainant is under 16 and the defendant is at least four years older. *See id.* § 213.3(1)(a). In addition, the misdemeanor of *sexual assault* includes sexual contact with any person who is under 10, or with anyone who is under 16 if the defendant is at least four years older. *See id.* §§ 213.4(4), 213.4(6). Finally, corruption of minors (or sexual assault) charges can be brought against a defendant who has sexual or deviate sexual intercourse (or sexual contact), either with someone under the age of 21 for whom the defendant is acting as guardian or with someone "in custody" or otherwise "detained" over whom the defendant has "supervisory or disciplinary authority." *See id.* §§ 213.3(1)(b)–(c), 213.4(7)–(8).

These MPC provisions were drafted so as to avoid "an extravagant use of penal sanctions to inhibit sexual experimentation among contemporaries." *Id.* § 213.3 Comment at 383. The Comments explain:

> The age of 10 was selected in order to limit these serious offenses to persons who seek sexual gratification with pre-pubescent children. These extremely young children are obviously incapable of meaningful consent to sexual intercourse. Older children may have attained physical manifestations of sexual maturity and an interest in sexual experience, but they are still likely to lack full appreciation of the nature and consequences of such conduct. For these reasons, the early adolescent who willingly engages in sexual activity with an older person may be regarded as a victim of adult depredation deserving state protection. On the other hand, those who engage in intercourse with adolescents are neither as dangerous nor as morally reprehensible as those who engage in such conduct with very young children. In part this is true because the post-pubescent child is a more plausible, though certainly not an acceptable, target of sexual desire. More importantly, the sexually mature though underage adolescent may play such an active role in encouraging sexual relations that the conduct of the older participant in yielding to temptation must be viewed as evidencing a less grievous moral default than exhibited by the exploiter of a very young child.
>
> . . . .
>
> . . . The chief significance of punishing consensual relations with a late adolescent lies not in redressing victimization of an immature person but rather in vindicating community standards of ethically acceptable behavior. The Model Code foregoes any such attempt to legislate private morality.

Id. at 379–80.

The Model Penal Code elects not to make the complainant's chastity an element of statutory rape—both because "[a] rule of chastity embodies an outdated notion of virginity as the essential female virtue" and because, "[i]f the female is too young or too naive to be deemed responsible for her conduct, the fact of one previous experience does not render the male's conduct any less an imposition." *Id.* at 384. Nevertheless, the Code recognizes a defense to the charges that set the age of consent at 16—corruption of a minor (§ 213.3) and sexual assault involving a person younger than 16 (§ 213.4(6))—if "the alleged victim had, prior to the time of the offense charged, engaged promiscuously in sexual relations with others." *Id.* § 213.6(3). The Comments justify this defense on the ground that "[i]n such cases, proof of prior sexual promiscuity rebuts the presumption of naivete and inexperience that supports the imposition of criminal liability." *Id.* § 213.6 Comment at 420.

The Model Penal Code takes a compromise position on the mistake-of-age question. A reasonable mistake is recognized as a defense to crimes that set the age of consent higher than 10; where the age of consent is 10 or younger, however, no such defense is allowed. *See id.* § 213.6(1). The Comments explain that "[a] man who engages in consensual intercourse in the reasonable belief that his partner has reached her eighteenth birthday evidences no abnormality, no willingness to take advantage of immaturity, no propensity to the corruption of minors." On the other hand, "[t]he actor who is mistaken as to the age of a child under 10 can make no such claim, for no credible error of perception would be sufficient to recharacterize a child of such tender years as an appropriate subject of sexual gratification." *Id.* § 213.6 Comment at 415, 414. For a discussion of the Model Penal Code's stance on gender neutrality in defining sex offenses, see Note 4 in Section B.4 below.

8. The Proposed Revisions to the Model Penal Code. As explained in greater detail in Note 13 following *Commonwealth v. Berkowitz* in Section B.3 below, the Model Penal Code provisions governing sexual offenses are currently undergoing revision. Under the most recent proposal, *rape of a child*, a second-degree felony punishable by up to 20 years in prison, is defined as sexual penetration where the defendant knows or recklessly disregards the risk that the victim is under 12 years old and more than two years younger than the defendant. *See* Model Penal Code: Sexual Assault and Related Offenses § 213.5(1) (Tentative Draft No. 2, 2016). *Sexual penetration of a minor*, a third-degree felony punishable by a maximum sentence of 10 years, would include cases of sexual penetration where the defendant knows or recklessly disregards the risk that the victim is under 16 and more than four years younger than the defendant (and not the defendant's spouse). *See id.* § 213.5(3). A defendant who knows or recklessly disregards the risk that the victim is under 18 years of age and the defendant is the victim's parent, foster parent, guardian, grandparent, aunt, or uncle would be guilty of *incest*, a second-degree felony, for an act of sexual penetration and *incestuous sexual contact with a child*, a third-degree felony, for an act of sexual contact. *See id.* §§ 213.5(2), 213.7(2).

The proposed revisions would also create two additional offenses for sexual contact with a child, which, as described below, includes sexual touching. *Aggravated criminal sexual contact with a child*, a third-degree felony, applies when the defendant knows or recklessly disregards the risk that the victim is under 12 years of age and more than four years younger than the defendant. This charge also encompasses cases where a person under the age of 16 is the victim of the crimes of aggravated criminal sexual contact or offensive criminal sexual contact (the elements of which are also described below). *See id.* § 213.7(1) (citing *id.* §§ 213.6(1)–(2)). *Inappropriate sexual contact with a minor*, a misdemeanor punishable by a maximum prison sentence of one year, is defined as sexual contact with someone other than a spouse where the defendant knows or recklessly disregards the risk that the victim is under 16 and more than 10 years younger than the defendant. *See id.* § 213.7(3).

The drafters of the proposed revisions explain the decision to require at least recklessness in statutory rape cases by calling "strict liability of any sort in this context . . . unconscionable." Model Penal Code: Sexual Assault and Related Offenses 77 (Tentative Draft No. 1, 2014). They reject a mens rea of negligence as "unnecessarily expansive" given that "most sexual relationships between pre-adolescent children and older persons are almost certain to be captured by" the provisions prohibiting sexual penetration of a minor because it would be "a nearly insurmountable hurdle" for defendants over 20 to argue that they were not aware of a substantial risk the complainant was under 16. *Id.* at 77–78. Acknowledging the possibility that a younger defendant could escape liability, the drafters of the revisions nevertheless conclude that "the need to deter or punish teenagers for consensual sex with other children believed (even unreasonably) to be peers is insufficient reason to depart from the general principle requiring moral culpability as a prerequisite to criminal punishment, especially in light of the severe penalties and collateral consequences associated with sex offenses and the increasing awareness of the ongoing cognitive development of juvenile offenders." *Id.* at 78.

The proposed statutory rape provisions, like the rest of the Model Penal Code's sex offenses, would be entirely gender-neutral. In addition, the proposed revisions foreclose convicting defendants younger than 12 for any sex offenses other than aggravated forcible rape and aggravated criminal sexual contact (the elements of which are described below). *See* Model Penal Code: Sexual Assault and Related Offenses § 213.0(9) (Tentative Draft No. 2, 2016) (citing *id.* §§ 213.1(1), 213.6(1)(a)).

[B] Forcible Rape

[1] Perspectives

The Violence Against Women Act of 1991, S. Rep. No. 197, 102d Cong., 1st Sess. 36–39 (1991)

Violent attacks by men now top[] the list of dangers to an American woman's health. . . . [E]very 6 minutes, a woman is raped in the United States. . . . 1990 saw a record high number of rapes reported to the police. . . . [3]

Unfortunately, as the figures have skyrocketed, our attention has waned. Problems of lesser scope and danger have received far more public concern and attention. Drunk driving, heart attacks, and cancer — not violent attacks by men — are commonly perceived to be the most serious health threats to women. Yet the figures

---

3. In 2015, 112,966 rapes were reported to the police (one every five minutes). *See* Federal Bureau of Investigation, Crime in the United States 2015: Uniform Crime Reports, *available at* https://ucr.fbi.gov/crime-in-the-u.s/2015/crime-in-the-u.s.-2015/tables/table-16. Some of these reports (7,340) were based on the FBI's traditional definition of rape ("the carnal knowledge of a female forcibly and against her will"), but the overwhelming majority used the FBI's 2011 revised definition ("penetration, no matter how slight, of the vagina or anus with any body part or object, or oral penetration by a sex organ of another person, without the consent of the victim"). The FBI's figures include attempted rape and assault with intent to rape, but not statutory rape or incest. By comparison, the National Crime Victimization Survey (NCVS), which also includes unreported crimes, estimated that 431,840 rapes and sexual assaults occurred in 2015. *See* Jennifer L. Truman & Rachel E. Morgan, Bureau of Justice Statistics, Criminal Victimization, 2015, at 2 (2016), *available at* http://www.bjs.gov/content/pub/pdf/cv15.pdf.

clearly demonstrate that violence puts women at greater risk.[4] Our society has, up until now, chosen not to appreciate the significance of these figures. We have systematically underestimated the problem, in seriousness, in scope, and intensity. We have inadvertently accepted this violence as somehow "normal" and, as a result, we have been too quick to accept a system that places greater burdens on some female crime victims than on male victims.

> . . . .

In part, we have been unable to see the enormity of the problem because we have failed to measure the problem fully or accurately. . . .

Substantial undercounting plagues the estimates we do have for some of the most serious crimes against women. As one witness put it, "it is almost certain that the national estimate of . . . rape . . . understates the total number." "[V]irtually all rape experts agree that the NCS [National Crime Survey] estimates of the number of rape cases are substantially inaccurate and low." . . .[5]

> . . . .

Unfortunately, our unwillingness to see violence against women as criminal behavior of enormous scope and seriousness is encouraged by the unwilling silence of many survivors. Rape [is one] of the most underreported crimes in America. For a host of reasons—including fear of retaliation and the lingering stigma of sex crimes . . . —vast numbers of these crimes are left unreported to police or other authorities. . . .[6]

> . . . .

-----

4. [n.15] For example, a woman is 10 times more likely to be raped than she is to die in a car crash. . . .

5. Some studies estimate that the actual incidence of rape is significantly higher than the Uniform Crime Reports or even the NCVS figures. *See, e.g.,* Patricia Tjaden & Nancy Thoennes, Office of Justice Programs, Extent, Nature, and Consequences of Rape Victimization: Findings from the National Violence Against Women Survey 9 (2006) (reporting figures at least four times higher than the NCVS figures), *available at* http://www.ojp.usdoj.gov/nij/pubs -sum/210346.htm; Corey Rayburn Yung, *How to Lie with Rape Statistics: America's Hidden Rape Crisis,* 99 Iowa L. Rev. 1197, 1204, 1201–02 (2014) (concluding that "America is in a crisis of sexual violence that has gone undetected because police departments across the country systemically underreport rape," by, for example, "aggressively interrogat[ing] and harass[ing] rape victims" so that they will "recant their allegations," "label[ing] a large percentage of cases as 'unfounded' while performing little or no investigation," "regularly classifying rape complaints as lesser offenses" that are not reported to the FBI, and "fail[ing] to create any written record that a victim made a rape complaint to eliminate the incident from the . . . data").

6. The Bureau of Justice Statistics estimates that only about one-third of rape victims report the crime to the police. *See* Jennifer L. Truman & Rachel E. Morgan, Bureau of Justice Statistics, Criminal Victimization, 2015, at 6 (2016), *available at* http://www.bjs.gov/content/pub/pdf /cv15.pdf. Other research suggests that the percentage of rapes actually reported is even lower. *See, e.g.,* Patricia Tjaden & Nancy Thoennes, Office of Justice Programs, Extent, Nature, and Consequences of Rape Victimization: Findings from the National Violence Against Women Survey 33 (2006), *available at* http://www.ojp.usdoj.gov/nij/pubs-sum/210346.htm (finding that 19% of female and 13% of male victims report the crime).

We have also underestimated the effect these crimes have on every woman in society. The cost of violence against women must be measured not only in the lives scarred or lost by violence itself, but the lives left unfulfilled because of the fear of violence. Recent studies estimate, for example, the "fear of rape is central to the day-to-day concerns of about a third of women. . . ."

This fear takes a substantial toll on the lives of all women, in lost work, social, and even leisure opportunities. For example, one recent study showed that three-quarters of women never go to the movies alone after dark because of the fear of rape and nearly 50 percent do not use public transit alone after dark for the same reason. . . . Due in large part to the fear of rape, a woman is eight times more likely than a man to avoid walking in her own neighborhood after dark. . . . [W]hile 52 percent of women surveyed never walked by parks or empty lots alone after dark, only 13 percent of men employed this strategy to avoid crime.

The White House Council on Women and Girls, Rape and Sexual Assault: A Renewed Call to Action 7, 9, 1–2, 5–6 (2014)[7]

The numbers alone are stunning: nearly 1 in 5 women—or almost 22 million—have been raped in their lifetimes. . . . Women and girls are the vast majority of victims . . . . Men and boys, however, are also at risk: 1 in 71 men—or almost 1.6 million—have been raped during their lives.

. . . .

Most victims know their perpetrators: 51% of female victims were raped by a current or former intimate partner, and 41% were raped by an acquaintance. Stranger rape, in contrast, accounts for 14% of the total. Of men and boys, 52% report being raped by an acquaintance and 15% by a stranger.[8] . . .

The majority of perpetrators are male: 98% of female and 93% of male rape survivors report that their assailants were male. . . .

Young people are especially at risk: nearly half of female survivors were raped before they were 18, and over one-quarter of male survivors were raped before they were 10. College students are particularly vulnerable: 1 in 5 women has been sexually assaulted while in college.

. . . .

Rape and sexual assault survivors often suffer from a wide range of physical and mental problems that can follow them for life . . . . Although hard to quantify, several

7. This report, which is available at https://www.whitehouse.gov/sites/default/files/docs/sexual_assault_report_1-21-14.pdf, describes federal efforts to combat sexual violence in connection with the third reauthorization of the Violence Against Women Act, which was signed in 2013.

8. [n.6] Some women are raped by multiple perpetrators in different relationships. Because a woman may be raped both by an intimate partner and a stranger, the overall percentages do not sum to 100.

studies have calculated the economic costs of a rape, accounting for medical and victim services, loss of productivity, decreased quality of life, and law enforcement resources. Each used a slightly different methodology, but all found the costs to be significant: ranging from $87,000 to $240, 776 per rape. . . .

. . . Across all demographics, rapists and sexual offenders are too often not made to pay for their crimes, and remain free to assault again. Arrest rates are low and meritorious cases are still being dropped — many times because law enforcement officials and prosecutors are not fully trained on the nature of these crimes or how best to investigate and prosecute them . . . .

. . . Sexual assault is pervasive because our culture still allows it to persist. . . . [I]n order to put an end to this violence, we as a nation must see it for what it is: a crime. Not a misunderstanding, not a private matter, not anyone's right or any woman's fault.

Nancy S. Erickson & Nadine Taub, *Final Report: "Sex Bias in the Teaching of Criminal Law"*, 42 RUTGERS L. REV. 309, 341–43 (1990)[9]

Many people do not realize that rape usually causes physical pain; they reason that if consensual sexual intercourse is not generally painful, then neither is forced intercourse. Some people even assume that rape must give some sexual pleasure to the victim; hence the jokes such as "rape is assault with a friendly weapon," and "he [the rapist] was just giving her a good time." Not surprisingly, this failure to accurately perceive the female victim's experience seems much more common among men than among women, and perhaps originates in physiological differences:

> Physiologically, male sexuality . . . is dependent upon penile reactions. Thus the male must experience some stimulation, and the result must be physically pleasurable even if the situation is psychologically distasteful. Therefore it may be difficult for a man to comprehend rape as anything but a basically sexual experience for anyone who is engaged in it. . . . The woman's claim that the rape was physically only painful and without any pleasurable sensation . . . may be unintelligible to a man. . . .

The truth about rape can be discovered only by listening to its victims:

> Forcible rape is not in any normal sense intercourse. In most cases, the lubrication . . . required for normal completed intercourse does not exist. . . . As a result of this crucial aspect, as well as the fact that the victim is usually in a traumatized state immediately preceding the rape and, thus, the muscles at the entrance to the vagina are not relaxed, penetration cannot either easily or immediately occur. What does happen is that the rapist repeatedly batters . . . the very delicate and sensitive features lying *outside* the vagina,

---

causing the tissues to tear and to bleed. [After penetration,] . . . the tissues (this time, the lining of the vagina) are repeatedly, with each thrust, ripped and torn.

As can be imagined, forcible rape is traumatically painful. I believe that it is the most physically painful ordeal that an individual can undergo and still live afterward. When I was being raped I felt as though I were being repeatedly stabbed with a knife in one of the most sensitive areas of my body. Near the end, I was in shock. I felt numb and could feel no pain, but I knew that the rapist was tearing me apart inside. Hours after the attack, the pain returned, and I felt as though I had been set on fire. Although I bled for only a few days, the pain lasted for weeks.

    . . . .

This rape victim sums it up by saying: "[T]here is no 'sex' in rape. There is only pain . . . ."

In addition to physical pain, the victim experiences severe psychological trauma. . . . [C]urrent studies show that "men and women share the same basic responses to rape—including depression, nightmares, flashbacks, self-blame, and a sometimes overwhelming sense of vulnerability. . . ." Such responses are understandable when one sees rape for what it really is—a violent crime that deprives a victim of feelings of autonomy, security, and personhood. Many women have also reported additional consequences that may be more common for female than male victims, such as fear of men in general. Whatever the particular effects of rape may be on an individual, it is clear that the psychological trauma is often severe and long-lasting.

Susan Estrich, Real Rape 1–4 (1987)[10]

In May 1974 a man held an ice pick to my throat and said: "Push over, shut up, or I'll kill you." I did what he said, but I couldn't stop crying. When he was finished, I jumped out of my car as he drove away.

I ended up in the back seat of a Boston police car. I told the two officers I had been raped by a man who came up to the car door as I was getting out in my own parking lot (and trying to balance two bags of groceries and kick the car door open). He took the car, too.

They asked me if he was a crow. That was their first question. A crow, I learned that day, meant to them someone who is black. . . .

They asked me if I knew him. That was their second question. They believed me when I said I didn't. Because, as one of them put it, how would a nice (white) girl like me know a crow?

---

10. Reprinted with permission from the publisher of Real Rape: How the Legal System Victimizes Women Who Say No by Susan Estrich, Cambridge, Mass.: Harvard University Press, Copyright © 1987 by the President and Fellows of Harvard College.

Now they were really listening. They asked me if he took any money. He did; but though I remember virtually every detail of that day and night, I can't remember how much. It doesn't matter. I remember their answer. He did take money; that made it an armed robbery. Much better than a rape. They got right on the radio with that.

We went to the police station first, not the hospital, so I could repeat my story (and then what did he do?) to four more policemen. . . .

By the time we went to the hospital, they were really on my team. I could've been one of their kids. . . .

Late that night, I sat in the Police Headquarters looking at mug shots. I was the one who insisted on going back that night. My memory was fresh. I was ready. . . . But it wasn't any one of them. After that, they couldn't help me very much. . . . I didn't have a great description of identifying marks or the like: no one had ever told me that if you're raped, you should not shut your eyes and cry for fear that this really is happening, but should keep your eyes open and focus so you can identify him when you survive. . . .

　　　. . . .

At first, being raped is something you simply don't talk about. Then it occurs to you that people whose houses are broken into or who are mugged in Central Park talk about it *all* the time. Rape is a much more serious crime. If it isn't my fault, why am I supposed to be ashamed? If I'm not ashamed, if it wasn't "personal," why look askance when I mention it?

　　　. . . .

In many respects I am a very lucky rape victim, if there can be such a thing. Not because the police never found him: looking for him myself every time I crossed the street, as I did for a long time, may be even harder than confronting him in a court-room. No, I am lucky because everyone agrees that I was "really" raped. When I tell my story, no one doubts my status as a victim. No one suggests that I was "asking for it." No one wonders, at least out loud, if it was really my fault. No one seems to identify with the rapist. His being black, I fear, probably makes my account more believable to some people, as it certainly did with the police. But the most important thing is that he was a stranger; that he approached me not only armed but uninvited; that he was after my money and car, which I surely don't give away lightly, as well as my body. . . .

　　　. . . .

But most rape cases are not as clear-cut as mine, and many that are, like mine, simply are never solved. It is always easier to find the man when the woman knows who he is. But those are the men who are least likely to be arrested, prosecuted, and convicted. Those are the cases least likely to be considered real rapes.

Many women continue to believe that men can force you to have sex against your will and that it isn't rape so long as they know you and don't beat you nearly to death in the process. Many men continue to act as if they have that right. In a very real sense, they do. That is not what the law says. . . . [But] [w]hat the law seems to say and what it has been in practice are two different things. In fact, the law's abhorrence of the rapist in stranger cases like mine has been matched only by its distrust of the victim who claims to have been raped by a friend or neighbor or acquaintance.

Lorenne M.G. Clark & Debra J. Lewis, Rape: The Price of Coercive Sexuality 112–17 (1977)[11]

From its beginnings in ancient Greece, western political and legal theory has rested on two main assumptions. The first is the assumption that individuals have a right to own private property and that inequality in the distribution of such property can be traced to natural differences among men. . . . The second is the assumptions that men are naturally superior to women and that this inequality can be traced to natural differences between the sexes. . . . The first assumption laid the basis for a class society characterized by inequality between individuals and, ultimately, between classes of individuals. . . . The second assumption . . . made women the objects rather than the subjects of property rights: women were among the forms of private property owned and controlled by individual men.

. . . .

As is well known, a system of private property under individual ownership necessitated ownership of the means and products of production by the propertied classes. But as is much less well known or appreciated, it also required control of the means and products of *re*production, in order to ensure that there would be determinate heirs to function as the designatable future owners of individually-held accumulations of private property.

. . . [S]ince the personality of the family was vested in the husband alone, this meant that certainty of paternity was necessary if biological inheritance was to be an adequate institution for the preservation of family property across generations. Certainty of paternity was . . . possible only if the male property owner had exclusive access to one (or more) women. The husband had to be protected in his right of exclusive sexual access and in his right to control over the products of reproduction, and so he became the owner of his wife and children.

. . . .

. . . Under Anglo-Saxon law, rape, along with most other offences, was punished by orders to pay compensation and reparation. If a woman was raped, a sum was paid to either her husband or father, depending on who still exercised rights of ownership over her, and the exact amount of compensation depended on the woman's economic position and her desirability as an object of an exclusive sexual relationship. The sum was not paid to the woman herself; it was paid to her father or husband because he was the person who was regarded as having been wronged by the act.

Rape is simply theft of sexual property. . . . In having intercourse with a woman who does not belong to him, a man is guilty of trespassing on the property of whoever does own her, and of stealing access to female sexuality to which he has no legal right. From the beginning, rape was perceived as an offence against property, not an offence against the person on whom the act was perpetrated, and it has not lost the shrouds of these historical origins.

. . . .

. . . The punishment of rape has never lost its connections with the economic status of the rape victim. The higher the socio-economic status of the victim, the greater the likelihood that she will be considered "credible," and granted her day in court.

Angela P. Harris, *Race and Essentialism in Feminist Legal Theory*, 42 STAN. L. REV. 581, 598–600 (1990)

[T]he paradigm experience of rape for black women has historically involved the white employer in the kitchen or bedroom as much as the strange black man in the bushes. During slavery, the sexual abuse of black women by white men was commonplace. Even after emancipation, the majority of working black women were domestic servants for white families, a job which made them uniquely vulnerable to sexual harassment and rape.

Moreover, as a legal matter, the experience of rape did not even exist for black women. During slavery, the rape of a black woman by any man, white or black, was simply not a crime. Even after the Civil War, rape laws were seldom used to protect black women against either white or black men, since black women were considered promiscuous by nature. In contrast to the partial or at least formal protection white women had against sexual brutalization, black women frequently had no legal protection whatsoever. "Rape," in this sense, was something that only happened to white women. . . .

Finally, for black people, male and female, "rape" signified the terrorism of black men by white men, aided and abetted, passively (by silence) or actively (by "crying rape"), by white women. . . . [B]oth the law of rape and Southern miscegenation laws were part of a patriarchal system through which white men maintained their control over the bodies of all black people . . . . [T]hough many white women encouraged interracial sexual relationships, white women, protected by the patriarchal idealization of white womanhood, were able to remain silent, unhappily or not, as black men were murdered by mobs.

I. Bennett Capers, *Real Rape Too*, 99 Calif. L. Rev. 1259, 1261–63, 1265 (2011)[12]

. . . In a 2007 study, the Bureau of Justice Statistics found that 4.5 percent of the inmates surveyed reported being sexually abused in the previous twelve months. Extrapolating nationally, the study estimated that more than 60,000 inmates are sexually abused each year.[13] In all likelihood these numbers are conservative. Because of the stigma of appearing weak and the fear of retaliation, male victims of prison rape often choose not to report their victimization to prison authorities or counselors. In addition, the findings fail to reflect the impact of repeated assaults. Prisoners who are raped rarely have access to safe spaces. Instead, they are subjected to repeated, if not daily, sexual assaults.

As a society, we rarely think of male-victim rape. On the few occasions that we do, we assume male rape victimization occurs only in prisons. That assumption is wrong. In fact, even outside of prisons, males are victims of rape. A study conducted by the Bureau of Justice Statistics, based on surveys of households, estimated that more than 36,000 males age twelve and over were victims of completed rape or attempted rape during 2008 alone and that one in thirty-three men in the United States has been the victim of rape or attempted rape. Again, this number probably underestimates the frequency of male-victim rape. Even more than female victims, male rape victims are likely to encounter disbelief or derision when they report their

---

12. Copyright © 2011 by I. Bennett Capers. Reprinted with permission.

13. In 2003, Congress passed the Prison Rape Elimination Act, 42 U.S.C. § 15601, which provides for the collection of data on the incidence of prison rape, training of the government officials "responsible for the prevention, investigation, and punishment" of prison rape, and issuance of "national standards for the detection, prevention, reduction, and punishment of prison rape." *Id.* §§ 15604(a)(2), 15607(a)(1). Although the statute received unanimous approval from Congress, the Justice Department did not issue the final standards required by the statute until 2012 and most state prisons do not comply with those standards. *See Jails, Prisons Still Trying to Meet Federal Anti-rape Rules*, Bos. Globe, Sept. 12, 2016, at A9 (reporting that 12 states are in complete compliance with the federal standards). Moreover, the incidence of prison rape remains high. A 2013 Bureau of Justice Statistics report summarized the results of a survey of more than 90,000 inmates conducted pursuant to the statute:

> In 2011–12, an estimated 4.0% of state and federal prison inmates and 3.2% of jail inmates reported experiencing one or more incidents of sexual victimization by another inmate or facility staff in the past 12 months . . . . Among non-heterosexual inmates, 12.2% of prisoners and 8.5% of jail inmates reported being sexually victimized by another inmate; 5.4% of prisoners and 4.3% of jail inmates reported being victimized by staff.
>
> Rates of inmate-on-inmate sexual victimization among prisoner [and jail] inmates were higher among females (6.9% [and 3.6%]) than males (1.7% [and 1.4%]) . . . . Patterns of staff sexual misconduct were different, with higher rates among males in jails [and prisons] (1.9% [and 2.4%]) than among females in jails [and prisons] (1.4% [and 2.3%]) . . . .

Allen J. Beck et al., Bureau of Justice Statistics, Sexual Victimization in Prisons and Jails Reported by Inmates, 2011–12, at 6–7 (2013), *available at* http://bjs.gov/content/pub/pdf/svpjri1112.pdf. For an "insider's account" of prison rape, see Michael Johnson, *Institutionalized Indifference: Rape with a View*, 23 J. Prisoners on Prisons 11 (2014).

victimization. In addition, male victims, both straight and gay, face the added risk of homophobia. . . .

. . . As a society we have been largely indifferent to the prevalence of male rape victimization. In the prison context, we dismiss it as par for the course, as "just deserts," or, worse yet, as a rarely stated but widely known component of deterrence.[14] . . . We treat prisons as invisible zones, as lawless zones, as zones that need not concern us.

Outside the prison context, our response is no better. We tell ourselves male rape victimization is "exceedingly rare" or perhaps something that happens only to gay men. In short, we render male rape victimization invisible. . . .

. . . .

[R]ape law has been gendered for too long. Originally, it was gendered in a way that tilted the scales to benefit men — men as fathers, men as husbands, and men as rapists. . . . Many rape statutes have been reformed so that they are gender neutral, but the application of those laws is still very much gendered.

Margo Kaplan, *Rape Beyond Crime*,
66 Duke L.J. 1045, 1063–67, 1073–74 (2017)[15]

Rape law is particularly stymied by the common understanding that sex is something to be negotiated or won from partners, specifically from women by men. The idea that sex with a woman is something that an aggressive, sexual male achieves is deeply embedded in our understanding of sex, rape, femininity, and masculinity. It characterizes men as driven by a strong natural sex drive that women have a responsibility to resist. A man's ability to obtain sex from a woman — to "score" — is a measure of his masculinity and self-worth. This understanding pits women against men in a "mating dance," where women are the gatekeepers to sex and men the pursuers. Women who want sex — or who do not object to sex — fulfill their role as gatekeepers by putting up some token resistance or passively acquiescing to sex. This understanding of sex and consent therefore deems it normal and acceptable for men to persist, cajole, or simply continue despite a woman's protests or disengagement. A woman who wants sex will eventually accede; a woman who does not want sex will actively and continuously resist absent serious threat of harm.

Social norms about women's sexual activity also influence perceptions of rape. Women who have engaged in sexual activity, who have flirted with the perpetrator, or who were drinking at the time are often perceived as less likely to have been raped or as responsible for their own rapes. . . .

. . . .

---

14. [n.21] As recently as 1994, half of surveyed Americans agreed with the proposition that prison rape is part of the punishment criminals pay for their wrongdoing.

15. Copyright © 2017 by Margo Kaplan. Reprinted with permission.

The role of these norms in sexual violence is evident from the research on those who commit rape. . . . Perpetrators are often unaware that their actions were anything other than ordinary and acceptable behavior for seducing women.

A recent study . . . reported nearly one-third of men surveyed stated that they intended to use force to achieve sex. Yet the majority of these men expressed that they had no intention to "rape a woman," indicating that most men who force women into sex do not view it as rape. These men did not demonstrate high levels of hostility toward women. Instead, they demonstrated high levels of attitudes objectifying women and embraced the idea that men should exhibit sexual dominance over women. . . . Based on their findings, researchers hypothesized that these men might perceive women's "no" as token resistance consistent with gender norms and consider force as an acceptable means to achieve sex.

An even more recent study examines anonymous online content to demonstrate how these norms contribute to rape. In 2012, Reddit.com asked individuals in its community who had committed rape to discuss their motivations, thoughts, and feelings about the encounters. The responses later became the basis for a qualitative study on rape. One man explained why he persisted with sex despite his partner's verbal protest: "At the time I had this impression that girls didn't want to be seen as sluts or whores so they would pretend that they didn't want to have sex when really they did." Another similarly described misjudging his partner's desire and assuming she was engaging in token resistance: "I was horny and I misjudged the girl completely, thought she was just being reserved." Another anonymous poster described overcoming his girlfriend's verbal and physical resistance through persistent badgering. He did not realize that she felt violated until he discovered her crying in another room. He acknowledged some responsibility, but also insisted that she maintained some degree of responsibility for not resisting him sufficiently.

. . . .

Unfortunately, dominant social norms discourage partners from reading cues of nonconsent. Men are socialized to view sex with women—even reluctant women— as a victory to be achieved. They are taught to dismiss or ignore a woman's signs of nonconsent and to perceive neutral or negative cues as indicators of either consent or an invitation to persuasion. . . . They are also taught to infer future consent from past sexual consent.

Social conventions for women also increase the likelihood of miscommunication. Women are repeatedly taught to be polite, to equivocate, hide their feelings, and even simply "go through with sex" rather than outright reject advances in a way that leads to a confrontation. Women are also encouraged to hesitate even if they want sex, and to feign resistance in order to seem as though they have been persuaded. Male consent is rarely a consideration; women are taught that men are inherently pleasure-seeking beings who always crave sex.

Richard A. Posner, Sex and Reason 384–88, 391 (1992)[16]

Contrary to a view held by many feminists, rape appears to be primarily a substitute for consensual sexual intercourse rather than a manifestation of male hostility toward women or a method of establishing or maintaining male domination. . . . [T]he incidence of rape rises with brideprice; thus, the more expensive it is to obtain marital sex, the more likely men are to resort to force. Granted, the infrequency of resort to force in male homosexual encounters, even encounters between an adult and a minor, lends some credence to the view that misogyny is an element in many rapes, as does the fact that rape is rare among animals and virtually unknown among man's closest relatives, the nonhuman primates. Still, much rape is sexual in motive, as would be clearer were it not a crime, for studies of persons convicted of rape are by definition heavily weighted toward people who have neither been deterred by a threat of heavy punishment nor able to elude punishment.

What is the next best thing from a scientific standpoint, however, is that rape is an underreported crime. When it is studied from the point of view of the victims of rape (whether women who have filed complaints of rape or women who have filled out crime-victimization questionnaires), thereby bringing into the study many rapists who are not caught, including many who, given the circumstances of the rape, are unlikely to be caught, we get a clearer picture of the nature of the conduct as it might exist in the absence of criminal sanctions; and we find confirmed the impression that most rapists want to have sex, not to make a statement about, or contribute to, the subordination of women. This is not to deny that rape attracts the violent (those prone to use force to achieve their goals) and the sadistic (who may derive an extra [fillip] of pleasure from the rape victim's agony), for those are men to whom, respectively, the costs of rape are lower, and the benefits of rape greater . . . . But it does suggest that a rational model of "normal" human behavior can be used to analyze the behavior of rapists, including their response to punishment. . . .

. . . .

Since the degree to which rape is underreported is unknown, a reliable estimate of its magnitude cannot be made, but it appears to be greater in the United States than in any developed country—perhaps any other country, period. . . . It is possible to speculate . . . that a country such as the United States, in which permissive and repressive attitudes mingle, would indeed have more rape than a country that was either consistently permissive or consistently repressive. In a permissive society, sexual gratification is widely available to men and the incentive to seek it by force is therefore reduced. Since, moreover, nonmarital intercourse carries no stigma, women are not reluctant to complain to the police if they are raped, and so the probability of apprehension and punishment is high, which increases deterrence. In a repressive

---

16. Reprinted with permission from the publisher of Sex and Reason by Richard A. Posner, Cambridge, Mass.: Harvard University Press, Copyright © 1992 by the President and Fellows of Harvard College.

society, women are sequestered, or at least do not mingle freely with men. Not only are the opportunities for rape therefore reduced, but so is the number of ambiguous social situations in which rape is difficult to prove and (for that reason, among others) common; this is the problem of "date rape" . . . . In addition, there are strong incentives not to report a rape to the authorities in a society in which virginity and chastity are prized; this may be the principal reason why . . . reported rapes are higher in permissive than in repressive societies.

. . . .

We can expect date rape to be frequent in a society, such as ours, in which sexual mores are not uniform — and apparently it is. The reason is not just differences between the mores of sexually active women on the one hand and of police officers and judges on the other, but differences between the mores of men and of their dates. Suppose, as is in fact the case, that some women in our society believe that the courtship ritual requires them to pretend to resist a man's sexual advances, that others are not coy and when they say no do not intend finally to succumb, and that still others dress and [deport] themselves in a manner that seems provocative but in fact they adhere to traditional values. Insofar as men find it difficult to distinguish among these groups of women (search costs again), they will make mistakes with respect to the existence of consent. The result will be sexual acts perceived as rape by the victim and reported as rape in victim surveys.

Katharine K. Baker, *Once a Rapist?*
Motivational Evidence and Relevancy in Rape Law,
110 HARV. L. REV. 563, 566, 599–612 (1997)[17]

All rapes are not alike. They are not alike in the eyes of the men who commit them, and they are not alike in the eyes of the jurors and the public who judge them. . . . All rapes are, in part, about sex and masculinity and domination. But some rapes are predominantly about sex, some rapes are predominantly about masculinity, and some rapes are predominantly about domination. . . .

. . . .

A. Sex

1. Sex and Lovemaking. Some men rape because they want sex. . . . Consider . . . the numerous date rapists who seem to expect a dating relationship to continue notwithstanding the fact that they have raped the woman that they want to date. On the evenings of the rapes in question, these men might well . . . have been looking for shared sexual pleasure and intimacy. . . .

Immature or inexperienced men, unfamiliar with what lovemaking is but looking for it and cast by culture into the role of pursuer, go experimenting. The

---

experimenting can become coercive because many boys are taught that power, dominance, and violence can be arousing to women. . . .

Even when boys do not presume that power and coercion are pleasurable for women, their use of physical strength to get what they want is comprehensible and common. Consider a typical response to the candy machine that refuses to dispense the candybar for which one has inserted seventy-five cents. . . . Maybe one puts in another seventy-five cents; maybe one just pushes the buttons again, this time with more force. . . . Finally, one slams the palm of one's hand against the machine in an effort to get the candybar to fall. This is a common use of force to get what one wants and feels entitled to. . . .

Many rapes involve comparable uses of force. The kinds of encounters that are marked by brief assertions of power, constant cajoling, or infusion of a great deal of alcohol often involve force, coercion, and domination as an instrumental means of getting sex. . . .

2. Sex and Shoplifting. . . . For some, sex is a commodity, and if sex is a commodity, then taking it is theft. . . . We live in a culture that rarely discusses sex as anything other than a commodity. . . .

This cultural endorsement and marketing of sex as a commodified good leads to an increased desire for, and sense of entitlement to, sex. Most men are taught that sexual desire is like hunger: when it is there, you satisfy it. . . .

Men know that taking sex without consent is wrong, but many men do not perceive it as really bad. . . . In one study of college men who had committed sexual assault, seventy-five percent said that they had used alcohol or drugs prior to the assault. Another study of convicted rapists found a comparable seventy-five percent who admitted to using drugs or alcohol prior to the attack. . . . What may explain the correspondence between alcohol use and rape . . . is . . . alcohol's tendency to decrease inhibitions against taking that to which one has no right. . . .

B. Relationships Among Men

1. Uniting. . . . [M]en use rape to relate to other men. Men often rape women to demonstrate their strength, virulence, and masculinity to other men. . . . The authors of one of the first extensive studies of men who rape conclude that "men do not rape women out of a sexual desire for other men, but they may rape women, in part, as a way to relate to men." . . .

2. Dividing. Men also rape women in order to establish power over, or distinction from, other men. . . . These rapists rape not because they want or need the good — i.e., the sex or the woman — but because the good belongs to a man whom they wish to insult. . . . This view explains why rapes during war time often take place in public or are committed in front of civilian witnesses, and it explains why rape and war have gone hand in hand since there has been war. . . .

C. Power and Anger

1. Power. . . . Power rapists rape because they want to establish control over their victims. They rarely exert more strength than is necessary to force their victims into submission. Rape—the act of controlling—not sex, is critical to their motivation to rape.

. . . For instance, the prison rapist may rape to establish himself above his victim in the prison hierarchy; by dominating his victim, he elevates his own position. . . . There is no evidence that prison rapists become chronic rapists or that they choose to have sex with other men once they leave prison.

. . . .

This kind of motivation also explains much marital rape. A husband rapes in order to assert control over a wife who is somehow defying his command. His wife may not want to have sex, or she may simply have annoyed him. . . .

2. Anger and Sadism. . . . The anger rapist . . . uses much more violence than is necessary to force her into submission. "The aim of this type of rapist is to vent his rage on his victim and to retaliate for perceived wrongs or rejections he has suffered at the hands of women. . . . This offender displays a great deal of anger and contempt toward women." The offender "does not seek out a specific victim but instead discharges his anger onto someone who is immediately available." . . .

. . . Many of these men suffer from psychopathology. . . . Everybody agrees that these men should be punished. . . . Most rape victims are not victims of angry, sadistic rapists. This does not mean that most rape victims are not raped; it does not mean that rape victims fabricate their stories; and it does not mean that what happens to them is okay. It does belie the common belief that rapists are crazy men whose sadistic hunger for sex or hatred of women compels them to rape.

[2] Mens Rea

Director of Public Prosecutions v. Morgan
[1976] App. Cas. 182 (1975)

[The facts of the case were summarized by Lord Hailsham as follows:]

The four appellants were all convicted at the Stafford Crown Court of various offences connected with alleged rapes upon the person of Daphne Ethel Morgan of whom the first appellant is, or, at the material time was, the husband. The second, third and fourth appellants were convicted each of a principal offence against Mrs. Morgan, and each of aiding and abetting the principal offences alleged to have been committed by each of the other two. The appellant Morgan, who also had connection with his wife allegedly without her consent as part of the same series of events, was not charged with rape, the prosecution evidently accepting and applying the ancient common law doctrine that a husband cannot be guilty of raping his own wife. Morgan was therefore charged with and convicted of aiding and abetting the rapes alleged to have been committed by the other three. [Morgan was sentenced to ten years in prison, and the three other appellants were each sentenced to four years.]

. . . .

The appellant Morgan and his three co-defendants, who were all members of the R.A.F., spent the evening of August 15, 1973, in one another's company. The appellant Morgan was significantly older than the other three, and considerably senior to them in rank. He was, as I have said, married to the alleged victim, but not, it seems, at the time habitually sleeping in the same bed. At this time, Mrs. Morgan occupied a single bed in the same room as her younger son aged about 11 years, and by the time the appellants arrived at Morgan's house, Mrs. Morgan was already in bed and asleep, until she was awoken by their presence.

According to the version of the facts which she gave in evidence, and which was evidently accepted by the jury, she was aroused from her sleep, frog-marched into another room where there was a double bed, held by each of her limbs, arms and legs apart, by the four appellants, while each of the three young appellants in turn had intercourse with her in the presence of the others, during which time the other two committed various lewd acts upon various parts of her body. When each had finished and had left the room, the appellant Morgan completed the series of incidents by having intercourse with her himself.

According to Mrs. Morgan she consented to none of this and made her opposition to what was being done very plain indeed. In her evidence to the court, she said that her husband was the first to seize her and pull her out of bed. She then "yelled" to the little boy who was sleeping with her to call the police, and later, when the elder boy came out on the landing, she called to him also to get the police, and "screamed." Her assailants, however, covered her face and pinched her nose, until she begged them to let her breathe. She was held, wrists and feet, "dragged" to the neighbouring room, put on the bed where the various incidents occurred. At this stage she was overcome by fear of "being hit." There was never a time when her body was free from being held. When it was all over she grabbed her coat, ran out of the house, drove straight to the hospital and immediately complained to the staff of having been raped. This last fact was fully borne out by evidence from the hospital.

In their evidence in court, the appellants made various damaging admissions which certainly amounted to some corroboration of all this. They admitted that some degree of struggle took place in the bedroom, that Mrs. Morgan made some noise which was forcibly suppressed, and that she was carried out forcibly into the other bedroom, and that her arms and legs were separately held. . . .

All four defendants explained in the witness box that they had spent the evening together in Wolverhampton, and by the time of the alleged offences had had a good deal to drink. Their original intention had been to find some women in the town, but when this failed, Morgan made the surprising suggestion to the others that they should all return to his home and have sexual intercourse with his wife. According to the three younger appellants (but not according to Morgan who described this part of their story as "lying") Morgan told them that they must not be surprised if his wife struggled a bit, since she was "kinky" and this was the only way in which she could get "turned on." However this may be, it is clear that Morgan did invite his three companions home in order that they might have sexual intercourse with his wife, and, no doubt, he may well have led them in one way or another to believe that she would consent to their doing so. . . .

I need not enter into the details of what the defendants said happened after they had arrived at the house. As I have said they admitted that some degree of struggle took place in the wife's bedroom. But all asserted that after she got into the double bedroom she not merely consented to but actively co-operated with and enjoyed what was being done. . . .

[In summing up,] the learned [trial] judge said:

> [T]he prosecution have to prove that each defendant intended to have sexual intercourse with this woman without her consent, not merely that he intended to have intercourse with her but that he intended to have intercourse without her consent. Therefore if the defendant believed or may have believed that Mrs. Morgan consented to him having sexual intercourse with her, then there would be no such intent in his mind and he would be not guilty of the offence of rape, but such a belief must be honestly held by the defendant in the first place. He must really believe that. And, secondly, his belief must be a reasonable belief; such a belief as a reasonable man would entertain if he applied his mind and thought about the matter. . . .

[The Court of Appeal affirmed the defendants' convictions, but certified the following question to the House of Lords: "Whether in rape the defendant can properly be convicted, notwithstanding that he in fact believed that the woman consented, if such belief was not based on reasonable grounds."]

[Three Lords answered this question in the negative, agreeing with the defendants that a conviction would not be proper if a defendant honestly but unreasonably believed that a woman had consented to sex. The other two Lords responded affirmatively, agreeing with the prosecution that a defendant could be convicted under such circumstances. Excerpts from the five opinions follow.]

LORD CROSS.

The Sexual Offences Act 1956 which provides by section 1(1) that it is an offence "for a man to rape a woman" contains no definition of the word "rape." No one suggests that rape is an "absolute" offence to the commission of which the state of mind of the defendant with regard to the woman's consent is wholly irrelevant. The point in dispute is as to the quality of belief which entitles the defendant to be acquitted. . . .

. . . Rape is not a word in the use of which lawyers have a monopoly and the first question to be answered in this case, as I see it, is whether according to the ordinary use of the English language a man can be said to have committed rape if he believed that the woman was consenting to the intercourse and would not have attempted to have it but for this belief, whatever his grounds for so believing. I do not think that he can. Rape, to my mind, imports at least indifference as to the woman's consent. . . . That being my view as to the meaning of the word "rape" in ordinary parlance, I next ask myself whether the law gives it a different meaning. There is very little English authority on the point but what there is . . . accords with what I take to be the ordinary meaning of the word. . . . For these reasons, I think that the summing-up contained a misdirection.

The question which then arises as to the application of the proviso[18] is far easier of solution. I suppose that cases may occur in which the problem which was discussed at such length on this appeal may be of more than academic interest but on the facts of this case it was of no practical importance whatever. If the appellants when they came to give evidence had said that what Mrs. Morgan had said was perfectly true, that she had never at any stage given any sign that she was consenting to — let alone enjoying — the intercourse, but that they were so much influenced by what her husband had told them that they believed throughout that her manifestations of unwillingness were only play acting, then it is conceivable that a jury, on a proper direction, might have acquitted them. They might, that is to say, have said to themselves that though it was almost incredible that any young men could have been so stupid yet, having seen and heard them, they would give them the benefit of the doubt. But the appellants chose — most unwisely — to challenge the truth of Mrs. Morgan's evidence and to assert that although to start with she manifested some unwillingness when it came to the point she co-operated in the proceedings with evident relish. . . . The jury obviously considered that the appellants' evidence as to the part played by Mrs. Morgan was a pack of lies and one must assume that any other jury would take the same view as to the relative credibility of the parties. That any jury which thought that the grounds for a belief in consent put forward by the defendants, which if truly held would have been eminently reasonable, were in fact never entertained by them at all, should in the same breath hold that they may have had an honest belief in consent based on different and unreasonable grounds is inconceivable. So I would apply the proviso and dismiss the appeal.

LORD HAILSHAM.

    . . . .

    . . . The prohibited act in rape is to have intercourse without the victim's consent. The minimum mens rea or guilty mind in most common law offences, including rape, is the intention to do the prohibited act. . . .

---

18. The proviso to §2(1) of the Criminal Appeal Act 1968 provided that "the Court may, notwithstanding that they are of opinion that the point raised in the appeal might be decided in favour of the appellant, dismiss the appeal if they consider that no miscarriage of justice has actually occurred." In 1995, the statute was amended and now provides that appellate courts should affirm a conviction unless "they think [it] is unsafe."

The only qualification I would make . . . is . . . that if the intention of the accused is to have intercourse nolens volens, that is recklessly and not caring whether the victim be a consenting party or not, that is equivalent on ordinary principles to an intent to do the prohibited act without the consent of the victim.

. . . I believe that "mens rea" means "guilty or criminal mind", and if it be the case, as seems to be accepted here, that [the] mental element in rape is not knowledge but intent, to insist that a belief must be reasonable to excuse it is to insist . . . on an objective element in the definition of intent, and this is a course which I am extremely reluctant to adopt. . . .

. . . .

For the above reasons I would answer the question certified in the negative, but would apply the proviso to §2(1) of the Criminal Appeal Act 1968 on the ground that no miscarriage of justice has or conceivably could have occurred. In my view, therefore these appeals should be dismissed.

LORD SIMON.

. . . .

To say that, to establish a charge of rape, the Crown must show on the part of the accused "an intention to have sexual intercourse with a woman without her consent" is ambiguous. It can denote either, first, an intention to have sexual intercourse with a woman who is not, in fact, consenting to it. This was the contention advanced on behalf of the Director of Public Prosecutions before your Lordships; but, for the reasons given by my noble and learned friends, I do not think that it is acceptable. Or, secondly, it can mean an intention to have sexual intercourse with a woman with knowledge that she is not consenting to it (or reckless as to whether or not she is consenting). I believe that this second meaning indicates what it is that the prosecution must prove.

The problem which faces your Lordships arises when the accused raises a case fit for the jury's consideration that he believed that the woman was consenting to sexual intercourse, though in fact she was not doing so. Does an honest *but unreasonable* belief that the woman is consenting to sexual intercourse suffice to negative the charge of rape?

. . . .

[T]he law requires . . . that the [defendant's] belief . . . must be held on reasonable grounds. One reason was given by Bridge J. in the Court of Appeal:

> The rationale of requiring reasonable grounds for the mistaken belief must lie in the law's consideration that a bald assertion of belief for which the accused can indicate no reasonable ground is evidence of insufficient substance to raise any issue requiring the jury's consideration.

I agree; but I think there is also another reason. The policy of the law in this regard could well derive from its concern to hold a fair balance between victim and accused. . . . A respectable woman who has been ravished would hardly feel that she was vindicated by being told that her assailant must go unpunished because he believed, quite unreasonably, that she was consenting to sexual intercourse with him. . . .

I would therefore answer the question certified for your Lordships' consideration, Yes. But, even did I consider that it should be answered No, I would, for the reasons given by my noble and learned friends, think this a suitable case to apply the proviso.

> . . . .

LORD EDMUND-DAVIES.

> . . . .

[Various authorities] all indicate that knowledge by the accused of the woman's unwillingness to have intercourse is essential to the crime of rape. . . . And it will be recalled that . . . "the prosecution have to prove that each defendant intended to have sexual intercourse with this woman without her consent. Not merely that he intended to have intercourse with her but that he intended to have intercourse without her consent." . . . I would add that the man would have the necessary mens rea if he set about having intercourse either against the woman's will or recklessly, without caring whether or not she was a consenting party. . . .

> . . . .

. . . Honest belief, however foolishly formed, that the woman was willing seems to me incompatible with an intention to rape her. Here, as in any other crime where knowledge is an essential ingredient, this should connote actual knowledge and not merely what the accused ought to have known. . . .

> . . . .

In this country a long line of authorities and numerous dicta indicate that, when an accused challenges that he had the necessary mens rea involved in the offence charged by asserting that he committed the actus reus under a mistake of fact, his belief must have been based on reasonable grounds. . . .

> . . . .

. . . [H]ad I felt free to do so I would have acceded to the invitation . . . that we "should decide that a mistake of a relevant fact is a defence if the mistake was honest and genuine, even if it was also unreasonable." But . . . the conclusion I have come to is that the necessary course is to uphold, as being in accordance with established law, the direction given in this case by the learned trial judge as to the necessity for the mistake of fact urged to be based on reasonable grounds. The approach which I should have preferred must, I think, wait until the legislature reforms this part of the law. . . . But, the law being as it now is and for a long time has been, I find myself obliged to say that the certified point of law should be answered in the affirmative.

Lord Fraser.

My Lords, the answer to the general question raised in this case depends, in my opinion, on the nature of the mens rea or mental element in the definition of the crime of rape. . . .

All the definitions of rape quoted to us which made any reference to the state of mind required of the rapist included a statement to the effect that: "one of the elements of the crime of rape is an intention on the part of an accused person to have intercourse without consent." . . .

. . . If the defendant believed (even on unreasonable grounds) that the woman was consenting to intercourse then he cannot have been carrying out an intention to have intercourse without her consent.

The Court of Appeal . . . appear to have read . . . earlier dicta . . . as meaning that the intention was related only to the intercourse and not to the absence of consent. . . . With all respect, I cannot regard that as the proper reading. . . . For one thing, it would be unnecessary because the act of intercourse by its nature inevitably is intentional. . . . If the effect of the evidence as a whole is that the defendant believed, or may have believed, that the woman was consenting, then the Crown has not discharged the onus of proving commission of the offence. . . . Of course, the reasonableness or otherwise of the belief will be important as evidence tending to show whether it was really held by the defendant, but that is all.

. . . .

. . . I would therefore answer the question in the negative—that is in favour of the accused. But, for the reasons stated by my noble and learned friends, I would apply the proviso [and] refuse the appeal.

Reynolds v. State

664 P.2d 621 (Alaska Ct. App. 1983)

Singleton, Judge.

Randall C. Reynolds was convicted of sexual assault in the first degree, [defined as "sexual penetration with another person without consent." AS 11.41.410(a)(1). "Without consent" means that "a person with or without resisting, is coerced by the use of force against a person or property, or by the express or implied threat of death, imminent physical injury, or kidnapping to be inflicted on anyone." AS 11.41.470(8)(A).] . . .

. . . Reynolds testified that he had intercourse with J.D. with her consent. He contends that he did not notice anything about her behavior or demeanor which would indicate that she did not wish to have intercourse with him. . . .

In order to place Reynolds' arguments in context, it is necessary to briefly consider the history of our first-degree sexual assault statute. At common law, rape, the predecessor to first-degree sexual assault, required that the defendant have intercourse with a woman forcibly and against her will. The phrase "forcibly and against her will" was interpreted to mean without her consent. Rape was a general intent crime. The state was required to prove that the defendant intentionally engaged in the prohibited conduct, i.e., sexual intercourse to which the complaining witness had not consented. However, it was not necessary for the state to prove that the defendant knew or should have known that the victim did not consent. The potential harshness of this rule was mitigated by the common law requirement that in order for the state to prove the absence of consent, it must show that the victim "resisted to the utmost." . . .

More recent cases have substantially diluted the requirement of "resistance to the utmost," increasing the risk that a jury might convict a defendant under circumstances where lack of consent was ambiguous. To counteract this risk, some courts, notably the Supreme Court of California, have held that the defendant is entitled to an instruction on reasonable mistake of fact. *See People v. Mayberry*, 542 P.2d 1337 (Cal. 1975). . . .

Under *People v. Mayberry*, when a defendant argues "consent" as a defense, the state must prove that he intentionally engaged in intercourse and was at least negligent regarding his victim's lack of consent.

. . . .

[The Alaska] legislature has substantially enhanced the risk of conviction in ambiguous circumstances by eliminating the requirement that the state prove "resistance" and by substantially broadening the definitions of "force" and "physical injury." We are satisfied, however, that the legislature counteracted this risk through its treatment of mens rea. It did this by shifting the focus of the jury's attention from the victim's resistance or actions to the defendant's understanding of the totality of the circumstances. Lack of consent is a "surrounding circumstance" which under the Revised Code, requires a complementary mental state. . . . No specific mental state is mentioned in AS 11.41.410(a)(1) governing the surrounding circumstance of "consent." Therefore, the state must prove that the defendant acted "recklessly" regarding his putative victim's lack of consent.[19] This requirement serves to protect the defendant against conviction for first-degree sexual assault where the circumstances regarding consent are ambiguous at the time he has intercourse with the complaining witness. While the legislature has substantially reduced the state's burden of proof regarding the actus reus of the offense, it has at the same time made it easier for the defendant to argue the defense of mistake of fact. . . .

In order to prove a violation of AS 11.41.410(a)(1), the state must prove that the defendant knowingly engaged in sexual intercourse and recklessly disregarded his victim's lack of consent. . . .

---

19. At this point, the court cited *Neitzel v. State*, 655 P.2d 325 (Alaska Ct. App. 1982), which indicated that "if a statute does not specify any culpable mental state, conduct is required to be engaged in 'knowingly' and results and circumstances are required to be engaged in 'recklessly.'" *Id.* at 334 (citing the commentary to the state statute governing mens rea, Alaska Stat. § 11.81.610). *Cf.* Model Penal Code § 2.02(3).

Notes and Questions

1. Later Developments in England. The House of Lords' decision in *Morgan* created tremendous controversy, ultimately leading to adoption of the Sexual Offences (Amendment) Act in 1976. Section 1(1) of that statute provided:

> [A] man commits rape if (a) he has unlawful sexual intercourse with a woman who at the time of the intercourse does not consent to it; and (b) at the time he knows that she does not consent to the intercourse or he is reckless as to whether she consents to it.

If the House of Lords had been applying this statute in *Morgan*, would their views have changed? Note that § 1(1) of the Sexual Offences Act 2003 amended the English rape statute so that it now prohibits intentional penetration where the victim "does not consent" and the defendant "does not reasonably believe" the victim is consenting.

2. The Mistake Defense in Other Jurisdictions. In 1980, the Supreme Court of Canada held that a rape defendant could not be convicted if he honestly thought the victim was consenting, even if his belief was unreasonable. *See Pappajohn v. The Queen*, [1980] 2 S.C.R. 120 (Can.). Reminiscent of the legislative response to *Morgan*, the Canadian Parliament amended the rape statute to provide that a mistake about consent is no defense if it was caused by the defendant's "self-induced intoxication," "recklessness," or "wilful blindness," or if the defendant "did not take reasonable steps, in the circumstances known to the accused at the time, to ascertain that the complainant was consenting." Criminal Code, R.S.C., ch. C-46, § 273.2 (Can.).

In this country, a number of states have followed the California Supreme Court's lead in *People v. Mayberry*, 542 P.2d 1337, 1344–46 (Cal. 1975) (described in *Reynolds*), recognizing a defense only where the defendant's belief in the victim's consent was both honest and reasonable. *See* Joshua Dressler, Understanding Criminal Law § 33.05, at 591 (7th ed. 2015) (describing *Mayberry* as "the general rule"). *See generally* Robin Charlow, *Bad Acts in Search of a Mens Rea: Anatomy of a Rape*, 71 Fordham L. Rev. 263, 272–82 (2002) (surveying "the morass" of mens rea rules applied in various states).

In jurisdictions where a mistaken belief about consent constitutes a defense to rape, the question arises as to when defendants are entitled to a jury instruction on the mistake defense. For example, the California Supreme Court has refused to require a *Mayberry* instruction in every rape case where consent is at issue. Rather, the court held in *People v. Williams*, 841 P.2d 961, 966 (Cal. 1992), that an instruction must be given only if the defendant produced "substantial evidence of equivocal conduct [on the part of the victim] that would have led a defendant to reasonably and in good faith believe consent existed where it did not." In that case, the court decided that the defendant had no right to a mistake instruction: he testified that the victim had consented, she testified that he had punched and threatened her, and the court concluded that these "wholly divergent accounts create[d] no middle ground from which [he] could argue he reasonably misunderstood [her] conduct." *Id.* at 966. *But cf.* I. Bennett Capers, *The Unintentional Rapist*, 87 WASH. U. L. REV. 1345, 1380 (2010) (pointing out that *Williams* involved interracial rape charges and arguing that the court improperly "discount[ed]" Williams' testimony, which, "if credited," would "objectively . . . support[] both a finding of consent and a finding that he reasonably and honestly believed . . . consent was present"; concluding that "[a] white woman's allegation of rape may still be open to question," but "perhaps not as much as a black man's claim" of consent or a mistaken belief in consent). For the view that *Williams* "virtually eliminates the defense of mistake of fact" in rape cases and imposes a requirement of "equivocal evidence [that] has never been necessary" for a mistake defense in other contexts, see Rosanna Cavallaro, *A Big Mistake: Eroding the Defense of Mistake of Fact About Consent in Rape*, 86 J. CRIM. L. & CRIMINOLOGY 815, 838, 840 (1996).

When the Supreme Court of Canada faced this issue in *Pappajohn*, it held that a rape defendant is not entitled to a jury instruction on the mistake defense unless "some evidence beyond [defense counsel's] mere assertion of belief in consent" gives the defense an "air of reality." *Pappajohn*, [1980] 2 S.C.R. at 133. The court subsequently elaborated on this standard in *The Queen v. Ewanchuk*, [1999] 1 S.C.R. 330, 356–57 (Can.):

> [A] belief that silence, passivity or ambiguous conduct constitutes consent is a mistake of law, and provides no defence. Similarly, an accused cannot rely upon his purported belief that the complainant's expressed lack of agreement to sexual touching in fact constituted an invitation to more persistent or aggressive contact. An accused cannot say that he thought "no meant yes".

> . . . .

> Common sense should dictate that, once the complainant has expressed her unwillingness to engage in sexual contact, the accused should make certain that she has truly changed her mind before proceeding with further intimacies. The accused cannot rely on the mere lapse of time or the complainant's silence or equivocal conduct to indicate that there has been a change of heart and that consent now exists, nor can he engage in further sexual touching to "test the waters". Continuing sexual contact after someone has said "No" is, at a minimum, reckless conduct which is not excusable.

3. The Appropriateness of Punishing Negligent Behavior. Is it unfair to punish a defendant who honestly but unreasonably thought that the victim consented? Consider the following excerpt from a letter to the editor written by Professor Glanville Williams following the House of Lords' decision in *Morgan*:

> To convict the stupid man would be to convict him for what lawyers call inadvertent negligence—honest conduct which may be the best that this man can do but that does not come up to the standard of the so-called

reasonable man. People ought not to be punished for negligence except in some minor offences established by statute.

Lords' Decision on the Law of Rape, LONDON TIMES, May 8, 1975, at 15.

Compare SUSAN ESTRICH, REAL RAPE 97–98, 103 (1987):

> It is not unfair . . . to demand that men behave "reasonably" and to impose criminal penalties when they do not. . . .
>
> If inaccuracy or indifference to consent is "the best that this man can do" because he lacks the capacity to act reasonably, then it might well be unjust and ineffective to punish him for it. But such men will be rare, at least so long as voluntary drunkenness is not equated with inherent lack of capacity. More common is the case of the man who could have done better but did not; could have paid attention, but did not; heard her refusal or saw her tears, but decided to ignore them. The man who has the inherent capacity to act reasonably but fails to has, through that failure, made a blameworthy choice for which he can justly be punished. The law has long punished unreasonable action which leads to the loss of human life as manslaughter—a lesser crime than murder, but a crime nonetheless. By holding out the prospect of punishment for negligence, the Model Penal Code commentators point out, the law provides an additional motive to men to "take care before acting . . . ." The injury of sexual violation is sufficiently great, the need to provide that additional incentive pressing enough, to justify negligence liability for rape as for killing.
>
> . . . .
>
> . . . [U]nreasonableness as to consent, understood to mean ignoring a woman's words, should be sufficient for liability. Reasonable men should be held to know that no means no; and unreasonable mistakes, no matter how honestly claimed, should not exculpate.

See also Andrew E. Taslitz, *Willfully Blinded: On Date Rape and Self-Deception*, 28 HARV. J.L. & GENDER 381, 388–89, 446 (2005) (observing that "the mind consists of a spectrum or continuum of varying degrees of consciousness," without a "sharp dichotomy between the 'conscious' and 'unconscious' minds," and then using the 2003 rape charges brought against basketball star Kobe Bryant to illustrate the "widespread" phenomenon of "male self-deception" about women's willingness to have sex, which is "morally worse than the simple ignorance involved in ordinary criminal negligence" and supports "a duty of reasonable inquiry to determine an intended sexual partner's desires").

4. Strict Liability. A few jurisdictions have refused to attach any mens rea requirement to the element of nonconsent, believing that even an honest, reasonable mistake is no defense. In explaining this position in *Commonwealth v. Lopez*, 745 N.E.2d 961, 965–66 (Mass. 2001), the court reasoned that the only elements of the crime are force and absence of consent:

Although the Commonwealth must prove lack of consent, the "elements necessary for rape do not require that the defendant intend the intercourse be without consent." Historically, the relevant inquiry has been limited to consent in fact, and no mens rea or knowledge as to the lack of consent has ever been required.

A mistake of fact as to consent, therefore, has very little application to our rape statute. Because [the statute] does not require proof of a defendant's knowledge of the victim's lack of consent or intent to engage in nonconsensual intercourse as a material element of the offense, a mistake as to that consent cannot, therefore, negate a mental state required for commission of the prohibited conduct. Any perception (reasonable, honest, or otherwise) of the defendant as to the victim's consent is consequently not relevant to a rape prosecution.

See also Commonwealth v. Williams, 439 A.2d 765, 769 (Pa. Super Ct. 1982) ("The crux of the offense of rape is force and lack of victim's consent. . . . If the element of the defendant's belief as to the victim's state of mind is to be established as a defense to the crime of rape then it should be done by our legislature . . . ."); *Commonwealth v. Hairston*, 2015 Pa. Super. Unpub. Lexis 3425, at *46–55 (Pa. Super. Ct. Sept. 17, 2015) (declining to overrule *Williams*); *State v. Walden*, 841 P.2d 81, 84 (Wash. Ct. App. 1992) (finding no reason to read a mens rea requirement into the rape statute "in order to prevent nonculpable conduct from being criminal" because "one cannot accidentally or innocently induce another person to engage in sexual intercourse by means of force or threat").

Is the best solution to create degrees of rape, punishing negligent rape (or imposing strict liability) as a lesser-included offense of reckless or knowing rape?

5. The Impact of the Choice of Mens Rea. Is the controversy concerning the appropriate mens rea for rape strictly an academic one, or is it likely to have an impact on the outcome of actual cases? In his letter to the *London Times*, Glanville Williams wrote:

Many charges of rape fail because of a clash of evidence; if there is a doubt the jury have to give the man the benefit of it. . . . It would make almost no difference even if rape were turned by statute into an offense of strict liability . . . ; there would still be conflicts of evidence on whether the man had intercourse with the woman or whether the woman consented. . . .

. . . No one who uses threats against a woman will be heard to say that he thought she consented. If the man does not use threats, even by implication, the only way that anyone can tell whether the woman consents or not is by her words or behavior. . . . There is nothing in the Lords' decision [in *Morgan*] to prevent a judge directing the jury that if anyone would have realised from what the woman said and did that she was not consenting, then they are entitled to conclude that the defendant realised it, unless there are some other facts to raise a doubt in their minds. What the judge must not tell the jury, on a charge of rape or any other serious crime, is that they can convict the defendant although he did not know that the vital facts existed and was not reckless as to those facts, if he was stupid in not realising that they existed.

Lords' Decision on the Law of Rape, London Times, May 8, 1975, at 15.

Once again, compare Susan Estrich, Real Rape 98 (1987):

> The real significance of saying that negligence is enough — or that unreasonable mistakes will not exculpate — will depend on how we define what is reasonable. If the "reasonable" attitude to which a male defendant is held is defined according to a "no means yes" philosophy that celebrates male aggressiveness and female passivity . . . , little is accomplished for women by expanding liability to negligence and requiring that mistakes be reasonable. . . . On the other hand, if the reasonable man is the one who . . . understands that "no means no" . . . , a great deal may be accomplished.

See also Robin Weiner, Note, *Shifting the Communication Burden: A Meaningful Consent Standard in Rape*, 6 Harv. Women's L.J. 143, 147, 148 (1983) (arguing that "a gender gap in sexual communication exists," creating the possibility that a reasonable woman would think the victim "communicated her unwillingness to have sex" but a reasonable man would "still believe she is willing").

6. Requiring Express Consent. Given the difficulties involved in determining what the man thought the woman thought at the time of sexual activity, and the problems that consequently arise in evaluating a defendant's claim that he mistakenly believed the victim consented, is the better approach to require express consent? The Wisconsin rape statute, for example, defines "consent" as "words or overt actions by a person who is competent to give informed consent indicating a freely given agreement to have sexual intercourse or sexual contact." Wis. Stat. §940.225(4). Similarly, the California legislature has defined "consent" as "positive cooperation in act or attitude pursuant to an exercise of free will." Cal. Penal Code §261.6. *See also* Michelle J. Anderson, *Campus Sexual Assault Adjudication and Resistance to Reform,* 125 Yale L.J. 1940, 1979–81 (2016) (noting that about 1,400 colleges and universities have now adopted so-called "yes means yes" disciplinary codes that require "affirmative consent" to sexual activity, and legislation making such provisions mandatory has been passed in California and New York and is under consideration in a number of other states) (citing, e.g., Cal. Educ. Code §67386, which defines "affirmative consent" as "affirmative, conscious, and voluntary agreement to engage in sexual activity").[20]

---

20. The procedures used in these college disciplinary proceedings have recently been the subject of much discussion. In 2011, the Department of Education's Office for Civil Rights (OCR) issued a "Dear Colleague Letter," requiring schools to "take immediate and effective steps to end . . . sexual violence" in order to protect students' rights under Title IX's prohibition of gender discrimination in education. *See* Office for Civil Rights, Dear Colleague Letter from Assistant Secretary for Civil Rights Russlynn Ali, U.S. Dep't of Education (Apr. 4, 2011), http://perma.cc/DB7V-5UBD. The letter specified, for example, that the accuser and accused should be given equal treatment, that

Is requiring express consent preferable because it shifts the burden of communication from the woman to the man — that is, "it suggests that a man has a duty to ascertain his partner's consent before proceeding with sexual activity," whereas "current law . . . suggests just the opposite, namely, that a woman has a duty to convey her nonconsent if she wishes to retain her right to deny sexual access to her body"? Lani A. Remick, *Read Her Lips: An Argument for a Verbal Consent Standard in Rape*, 141 U. Pa. L. Rev. 1103, 1130 (1993). *See also The Queen v. Esau*, [1997] 2 S.C.R. 777 (Can.) (rejecting the notion that "passivity amounts to consent" because "equat[ing] submission with consent" "presume[s] consent" and "overlook[s] the essential character of consent as a social act whereby one person confers on another person the right to do something," and therefore concluding that "[f]ailure to indicate yes or no is no communication at all and hence cannot amount to communication of consent").

Or does an express consent requirement "patronize" and "overprotect[]" women "instead of empowering" them? Vivian Berger, *Not So Simple Rape*, 7 Crim. Just. Ethics, Winter-Spring 1988, at 69, 75–76. Is this approach also open to criticism because it is unrealistic and improperly intrudes on the privacy of sexual relationships? Consider the objections that have been leveled at the "yes means yes" disciplinary codes recently adopted by many colleges: "interpreting a party's signals in a sexual encounter . . . is . . . hopelessly confusing and ambiguous"; affirmative consent requirements "detract from the spontaneity of sexual encounters" and "greater awkwardness . . . will result from communication around sex"; men should not be punished for "fail[ing] to conform their sexual practices to an idealized vision, given how dramatically this vision . . . depart[s] from reality"; and "all or most sex would count as rape" under an affirmative consent rule. Deborah Tuerkheimer, *Rape on and off Campus*, 65 Emory L.J. 1, 12–13 (2015) (citing critics).

If express consent ought to be necessary, are even the Wisconsin and California definitions flawed because they allow men — and juries — to "misinterpret women's nonverbal behavior" and "impute erotic innuendo and sexual intent where there is none," thereby "construct[ing] consent out of stereotype and hopeful imagination"? Michelle J. Anderson, *Negotiating Sex*, 78 S. Cal. L. Rev. 1401, 1406 (2005). In 1992, for example, a grand jury in Austin, Texas, composed of seven women and five men refused to indict a man who had sex with a woman after breaking into her

---

schools should ensure "adequate, reliable, and impartial investigation of complaints," that a preponderance of the evidence standard of proof should be used in disciplinary hearings, and that the accused should not be permitted to personally question the accuser. For a discussion of the pros and cons of these procedures, see Anderson, *Campus Sexual Assault, supra*, at 1982–98. *See also* Katharine K. Baker, *Campus Sexual Misconduct as Sexual Harassment: A Defense of the DOE*, 64 Kan. L. Rev. 861, 864 (2016) (arguing that OCR was attempting to address not only sexual assault on college campuses but hostile environment sexual harassment more broadly, and, "because the regulation of sexual harassment is not a criminal matter, the substantive definition of unacceptable conduct and the process used to evaluate that conduct need not conform to criminal law safeguards").

apartment, assaulting her with a knife, and breaking down the door to the bathroom where she was hiding. Some of the grand jurors apparently believed that the woman impliedly consented when she encouraged the man to wear a condom so that she would not contract AIDS. *See* Ross E. Milloy, *Furor over a Decision Not to Indict in a Rape Case*, N.Y. Times, Oct. 25, 1992, at A30. A second grand jury issued an indictment, and the man was eventually convicted and sentenced to 40 years in prison. *See Rapist Who Agreed to Use Condom Gets 40 Years*, N.Y. Times, May 15, 1993, at A6.

Likewise, in a 1989 rape trial in Florida, a jury of three men and three women acquitted a man who allegedly abducted the victim at knifepoint from a restaurant parking lot and then repeatedly raped her. At the time of the incident, the woman was wearing a lace miniskirt and no underwear. In explaining the jury's verdict, the foreman said: "We felt . . . she was asking for it the way she was dressed. . . . The way she was dressed with that skirt, you could see everything she had. She was advertising for sex." *Jury: Woman in Rape Case 'Asked for It'*, Chi. Trib., Oct. 6, 1989, at 11. Two months later, the same man pleaded guilty to unrelated rape charges in Georgia and was sentenced to life in prison. *See Rape Guilty Plea, After Acquittal*, N.Y. Times, Dec. 7, 1989, at B21.

Are these cases outdated, or do they still reflect prevailing attitudes toward rape victims? *See* Richard L. Clark & Rebecca Casey, Castleton Polling Institute, Male Attitudes Regarding Domestic and Sexual Violence: Survey Data Report 12 (2012), http://www.vtnetwork.org/wp-content/uploads/Male-Attitudes -Survey-FINAL-REPORT-Color2012.pdf (reporting that 46 percent of adult men participating in a 2012 Vermont survey believed that it was at least "sometimes true" that "[w]omen who wear tight or revealing clothing are inviting sexual comments or advances," including 60 percent of respondents between the ages of 18 and 24); Chen Shen, Comment, *Study: From Attribution and Thought-Process Theory to Rape-Shield Laws: The Meanings of Victim's Appearance in Rape Trials*, 5 J.L. & Fam. Stud. 435, 436 (2003) (citing studies finding that "many people, including some judges, jurors, law enforcement officers, lawyers, and professional psychiatrists, believe that the provocative victim invites attack through her appearance").

Given this evidence, should the law of rape require express *verbal* consent? *See* Remick, *supra*, at 1105, 1128–29 (suggesting that the absence of express verbal consent should create a rebuttable presumption of nonconsent); Cathy Young, *On Campus, An Absurd Overregulation of Sexual Conduct*, Bos. Globe, May 22, 2006, at A11 (describing policy implemented initially at Antioch College in the early 1990s, and subsequently adopted in "less extreme" form by other schools, that required "explicit verbal consent every step of the way in a sexual encounter"). *Cf.* Anderson, *Negotiating Sex*, *supra*, at 1407 (advocating that "the law should eliminate the requirement of nonconsent [and] [i]n its place . . . should recognize the centrality of negotiation, in which individuals would be required to consult with their partners before sexual penetration occurs").

7. Withdrawn Consent. Under the traditional view, a defendant cannot be convicted on rape charges so long as the victim consented to the initial penetration. *See State v. Way*, 254 S.E.2d 760, 761–62 (N.C. 1979); Matthew R. Lyon, Comment, *No Means No?: Withdrawal of Consent During Intercourse and the Continuing Evolution of the Definition of Rape*, 95 J. Crim. L. & Criminology 277, 291–99 (2004).

Recently, however, a number of states have adopted the contrary position. *See* 2 Wayne R. LaFave, Substantive Criminal Law § 17.4, at 140–41 (2d ed. Supp. 2015). In *State v. Flynn*, 329 P.3d 429, 438, 431 (Kan. 2014), for example, the court reasoned that the rape statute "proscribes *all* nonconsensual intercourse that is accomplished by force or fear, not just the initial penetration," and therefore encompasses "nonconsensual sexual intercourse occurring when a person communicates his or her withdrawal of consent after penetration and the other person continues the intercourse through compulsion." *See also State v. Baby*, 946 A.2d 463, 486 (Md. 2008) (rejecting the notion that "initial penetration completes the act of intercourse," and concluding that "the continuation of vaginal intercourse by force or the threat of force" after the victim withdrew consent "may constitute rape").

8. Incapacity to Consent. Absence of consent can be demonstrated not only by proof that the victim refused consent, but also by evidence showing an inability to consent. For example, statutory rape laws, discussed above in Section A, deem individuals under a certain age incapable of consent. Likewise, victims are commonly considered incapable of consent when they are "asleep, unconscious, or otherwise incapacitated and therefore could not resist or give consent." *State v. Moorman*, 358 S.E.2d 502, 505–06 (N.C. 1987).

Incapacity issues can therefore arise in situations where the victim has "a mental disease or defect which renders her incapable of appraising the nature of her conduct." Model Penal Code § 213.1(2)(b). One such case was the highly publicized sexual assault trial in Glen Ridge, N.J., where the victim, a 17-year-old girl with an IQ of 64 and the intellectual capacity of an eight-year-old, was persuaded to accompany some high school boys to a nearby house, remove her clothes, perform oral sex on five of the boys, and allow three of them to insert a broomstick and baseball bat into her vagina, while a larger group watched from chairs they had set up, crowding around "like a tank of piranhas" and yelling for her to go "further, further, further." *State v. Scherzer*, 694 A.2d 196, 209–11, 214 (N.J. Super. Ct. App. Div. 1997). Despite the defendants' argument that this was simply a case of "boys will be boys," Anna Quindlen, *Public and Private*, N.Y. Times, Dec. 13, 1992, at D17 (quoting defense attorney's opening statement), the court concluded that the defendants "were aware of [the victim's] acquiescent nature in sexual and other matters and . . . had taken advantage of that aspect of her personality in the past," and thus knew or should have known that she was "incapable of understanding or exercising the right to refuse to engage in such conduct." *Scherzer*, 694 A.2d at 216. Three of the four defendants received prison sentences in connection with the incident, and they ultimately served between two and five years in jail. *See generally* Bernard Lefkowitz, Our Guys: The Glen Ridge Rape and the Secret Life of the Perfect Suburb (1997).

Some statutes, like the New Jersey provision at issue in *Scherzer* and the North Carolina statute applied in *Moorman*, expressly require proof that the defendant knew or should have known of the victim's incapacity. *See Scherzer*, 694 A.2d at 214; *Moorman*, 358 S.E.2d at 505. Other statutes do not specify whether any mens rea attaches to the victim's incapacity, although at times the courts have read in such a requirement. *See Commonwealth v. Carter*, 418 A.2d 537, 539 (Pa. Super. Ct. 1980) (interpreting 18 Pa. Cons. Stat. § 302(c), a provision similar to Model Penal Code § 2.02(3), to require that "the defendant acted at least recklessly with regard to every material element of the section, including that the victim was so mentally deranged or deficient that she was incapable of consent").

9. Mens Rea, Incapacity, and Intoxication. Mens rea and capacity questions can also arise in the substantial number of rape cases where intoxication plays a role. *See* Valerie M. Ryan, *Intoxicating Encounters: Allocating Responsibility in the Law of Rape*, 40 CAL. W. L. REV. 407, 411 nn.33–34 (2004) (citing studies finding that alcohol was consumed by 34 to 74 percent of rape defendants and 30 to 79 percent of victims; the rates in acquaintance rape cases were approximately 75 percent for defendants and 55 percent for victims). Where the victim was intoxicated, rape charges can be based on statutes prohibiting intercourse with someone who is unconscious or, in some states, on statutes specifically barring intercourse with one who is unable to consent because of intoxication. *See generally* Allison C. Nichols, Note, *Out of the Haze: A Clearer Path for Prosecution of Alcohol-Facilitated Sexual Assault*, 71 N.Y.U. ANN. SURV. AM. L. 213 (2015).

One question that has arisen in some of these cases is the meaning of the concept "unconscious." In *Commonwealth v. Blache*, 880 N.E.2d 736, 742–43 (Mass. 2008), for example, the court ruled that the victim need not have been "rendered 'unconscious or nearly so' before she may be deemed past the point of consent." The court therefore concluded that a jury finding that a victim was "so impaired as to be incapable of consenting to intercourse," due to "the consumption of drugs or alcohol or for some other reason (for example, sleep, unconsciousness, mental retardation, or helplessness), . . . satisfies the element of lack of consent" and thus requires that the prosecution "need only prove the amount of force necessary to accomplish intercourse" in order to convict a defendant of rape. *Id.* at 743. *See also Commonwealth v. Erney*, 698 A.2d 56, 58–59 (Pa. 1997) (refusing to restrict the term "unconscious" in the state's rape statute to cases where the victim was "completely unaware of the event throughout the duration of the sexual assault," and therefore affirming rape conviction where the victim was so intoxicated that she was unable to respond to questions and thought she was telling the defendant to stop even though all that could be heard was "unintelligible mumbling," on the grounds that she was "intermittently unconscious throughout the assault and was at all relevant times in such impaired physical and mental condition so as to be unable to knowingly consent").

The courts have also recently confronted the controversial mens rea issues that arise in cases involving intoxicated rape victims. In *State v. Jones*, 804 N.W.2d 409, 414 (S.D. 2011), for example, the court held that the prosecution must prove that a defendant charged with "rape by intoxication" (sex with someone incapable of giving consent because of drugs or alcohol) "knew or reasonably should have known that the complainant's intoxicated condition rendered her incapable of consenting." The court distinguished other types of incapacity on the grounds that "youth, unconsciousness, or mental deficiency [are] conditions [that] are readily apparent or reasonably discoverable, justifying strict liability for those who take advantage of such incapacities," whereas "the line . . . between conscious intoxication and incapacitating intoxication" is more difficult to draw. *Id. See also United States v. Bruguier*, 735 F.3d 754, 760–61 (8th Cir. 2013) (en banc) (concluding that the mens rea term "knowingly" in 18 U.S.C. § 2242(2) applies to the part of that statute criminalizing sexual conduct with one who is "physically incapable of declining participation in, or communicating unwillingness to engage in, th[e] sexual act"); *Commonwealth v. Blache*, 880 N.E.2d at 744–45 (requiring the prosecution to prove that a defendant "knew or reasonably should have known that the complainant's [intoxicated] condition rendered her incapable of consenting to the sexual act" even though mistakes about consent are generally not a defense in Massachusetts, because proof of force " 'should negate any possible mistake as to consent' " in cases where the complainant is "capable of giving or refusing consent," but "the possibility of a defendant's reasonable mistake about the complainant's consent could increase," thus "creating the potential for injustice," when "the prosecution is not required to prove the use of force beyond that necessary for penetration") (quoting *Commonwealth v. Lopez*, 745 N.E.2d 961, 966 (Mass. 2001)). *But cf.* Nichols, *supra*, at 254–55 (advocating a mens rea of recklessness).

Similarly controversial is the question whether defendants in these cases can argue that they lacked the requisite mens rea as to the victim's incapacity to consent because they too were drunk. In *Commonwealth v. Mountry*, 972 N.E.2d 438, 446–47 (Mass. 2012), the court held that even though a defendant's intoxication usually "has no mitigating effect on general intent crimes such as rape," "when proof of knowledge is an element of the crime charged, as here, a defendant's mental impairment by intoxication or otherwise 'bears on [his] ability to possess the requisite knowledge of the circumstances in which he acted.' " Elaborating on its prior ruling in *Blache*, the Massachusetts court explained:

> The instruction in *Blache* has two alternative elements of knowledge. The first, actual knowledge [of the victim's incapacity], is a subjective element for which a defendant's state of intoxication has relevance. The second alternative, that the *defendant* reasonably should have known of the victim's incapacity, contains a mix of subjective and objective components . . . . The subjective component focuses on the defendant's capacity to possess the requisite knowledge, for which his state of intoxication has relevance. The objective component focuses on what the average prudent person possessing the defendant's knowledge would have understood regarding the victim's incapacity.

Id. at 447. The court then went on to disapprove of jury instructions requiring the jurors to evaluate "what 'the average, reasonable person, *not intoxicated*, and observing the situation as it existed, would have known' concerning the victim's capacity to consent." *Id.* The court reasoned as follows:

> [This instruction] effectively foreclosed consideration of evidence of the defendant's intoxication as to the [second] alternative element of knowledge. Contrary to the judge's instruction, this element of knowledge is not purely objective. The Commonwealth had to prove what '*the defendant* reasonably should have known,' not what the average reasonable unintoxicated person would have known. A defendant's impaired state of mind is relevant to the jury's determination of this element. . . . [T]he judge should have instructed the jury that the Commonwealth must prove that in the circumstances known to the defendant, a reasonable person would have known that the victim was incapable of consent, and that when deciding whether the Commonwealth has met its burden of proof, they could consider any credible evidence that the defendant was affected by the voluntary consumption of alcohol.

Id. at 447–48. *See also State v. Smith*, 178 P.3d 672, 678–79 (Kan. Ct. App. 2008) (concluding that, although rape is usually a general intent crime that does not recognize an intoxication defense, the provision in the rape statute criminalizing intercourse with a victim incapable of giving consent expressly requires proof of "a further state of mind . . . beyond the general criminal intent required for rape"—i.e., "knowledge of [the victim's intoxicated] condition" unless it was "reasonably apparent"—and therefore permits a defendant to argue that he was "incapable of forming the requisite state of mind for the knowledge element of the crime" because he was drunk). *But cf.* Nichols, *supra*, at 248 (noting that "[s]tudies suggest that men use alcohol 'as an alibi'" and therefore "an intoxication defense to rape raises the concern that would-be perpetrators will use alcohol as an excuse for aggressive behaviors in which they intend to engage all along"); Steve Bellshaw, *Sexual Assault Investigations: An Offender-Focused, Victim-Centered Approach*, in INSIDE THE MINDS: INVESTIGATING SEX CRIMES 9 (Jo Alice Darden ed., 2011) (finding that rape defendants tend to target victims who are vulnerable and can be "made to lack credibility").

Under the court's opinion in *Mountry*, how exactly is a rape defendant's intoxication relevant to the inquiry into what a defendant reasonably should have known? Is the court's opinion consistent with other definitions of the reasonable person in criminal law? Compare the discussions of voluntary manslaughter in Chapter 6, Section B.2, and self-defense in Chapter 14, Section B. For further discussion of intoxication as a defense to criminal charges generally, see Chapter 4, Section C.3.

Do the problems generated by the combination of alcohol and sex call for an express consent requirement, at least in certain cases? *See* Christine Chambers Goodman, *Protecting the Party Girl: A New Approach for Evaluating Intoxicated Consent*, 2009 B.Y.U. L. REV. 57, 58, 126 (2009) (endorsing a "sliding-scale approach" that would require "more explicit consent" "the more the female has had to drink," but that would deem "silence . . . inadequate to constitute consent when either party has consumed more than a de minimis amount of alcohol").

All of these issues arose in a very public setting during the 2016 trial of Brock Turner, a 19-year-old Stanford University freshman and varsity swimmer charged with assault with the intent to commit rape, sexual penetration with a foreign object of an intoxicated person, and sexual penetration with a foreign object of an unconscious person. Shortly after Turner met the 22-year-old victim at a fraternity party, two graduate students found him outside behind a dumpster "thrusting" on top of her. The graduate students, who said the victim "appeared motionless" with "her eyes closed and her head tilted to the side," stopped and yelled, and then pursued and tackled Turner when he attempted to run away. Police reports indicated that both Turner and the victim were heavily intoxicated, and the victim did not regain consciousness until three hours later.

At trial, Turner claimed that the victim, who could not remember the incident, had consented, but the jury convicted him of all three felonies. At Turner's sentencing hearing, the victim read a 12-page letter in which she responded to the defendant's claim that alcohol and peer pressure explained his conduct. "[Y]ou were not wrong for drinking," she told Turner. "You were wrong for doing what nobody else was doing": "[e]veryone around you was not sexually assaulting me." In addition, the victim's letter detailed her experience and its lasting impact:

> [Turner] admitted to kissing other girls at th[e] party, one of whom was my own sister who pushed him away. He admitted to wanting to hook up with someone. I was the wounded antelope of the herd, completely alone and vulnerable, physically unable to fend for myself, and he chose me. Sometimes I think, if I hadn't gone, then this never would've happened. But then I realized, it would have happened, just to somebody else. . . .
>
> [At the trial,] I was pummeled with narrowed, pointed questions that dissected my personal life, love life, past life, family life, . . . accumulating trivial details to try and find an excuse for this guy who didn't even take the time to ask me for my name, who had me naked a handful of minutes after seeing me. . . .
>
> According to him, the only reason we were on the ground was because I fell down. [I]f a girl falls help her get back up. If she is too drunk to even walk and falls, do not mount her, hump her, take off her underwear, and insert your hand inside her vagina. . . .
>
> . . . I have nightmares of being touched where I cannot wake up . . . . I am afraid to go on walks in the evening, to attend social events with drinking among friends where I should be comfortable . . . . It took me eight months to even talk about what happened. I could no longer connect with friends, with everyone around me. . . .

[In recommending a sentence of no more than a year in jail,] [t]he probation officer weighed the fact that [Turner] surrendered a hard earned swimming scholarship. If I had been sexually assaulted by an un-athletic guy from a community college, what would his sentence be? If a first time offender from an underprivileged background was accused of three felonies and displayed no accountability for his actions other than drinking, what would his sentence be?

See Lindsey Bever, *'You Took Away My Worth': A Sexual Assault Victim's Powerful Message to Her Stanford Attacker*, WASH. POST (June 4, 2016), https://www.washingtonpost.com/news/early-lead/wp/2016/06/04/you-took-away-my-worth-a-rape-victim-delivers-powerful-message-to-a-former-stanford-swimmer/ (reprinting the victim's letter).

Turner faced a maximum 14-year prison term, but the trial judge, reasoning that the case involved "less moral culpability" because Turner had been intoxicated, sentenced him to six months in jail and three years' probation. Turner lost his athletic scholarship and withdrew from Stanford, and he must register as a sex offender. He was released after serving three months of his prison sentence. According to Turner's father, his son's life has been ruined for "20 minutes of action." *See* Thomas Fuller, *Court Records Fill in Details of Stanford Sexual Assault*, N.Y. TIMES, June 13, 2016, at A8; Liam Stack, *In Stanford Rape Case, Brock Turner Blamed Drinking and Promiscuity*, N.Y. TIMES (June 8, 2016), http://www.nytimes.com/2016/06/09/us/brock-turner-blamed-drinking-and-promiscuity-in-sexual-assault-at-stanford.html.

In the wake of the critical reaction to the sentence imposed on Turner, a campaign to recall the trial judge was initiated and he asked to be assigned to the civil docket. The California legislature also acted in response to the case, passing bills providing that "all forms of nonconsensual sexual assault may be considered rape for purposes of the gravity of the offense," and adding cases where the victim was "either unconscious or incapable of giving consent due to intoxication" to the list of sex offenses ineligible for probation and suspended prison sentences. Cal. Penal Code §§ 263.1, 1203.065. In addition, the California legislature recently eliminated any statute of limitations for rape and certain other sex offenses. *See* Cal. Penal Code § 8.01.1.

10. The Proposed Revisions to the Model Penal Code. As discussed in greater detail in Note 13 following *Commonwealth v. Berkowitz* in Part 3 below, the MPC's provisions on sex offenses are currently undergoing revision. In the only part of the proposed revisions that has been approved thus far, "consent" is defined for the first time, as an individual's "willingness to engage in a specific act of sexual penetration or sexual contact." Model Penal Code: Sexual Assault and Related Offenses § 213.0(3)(a) (approved Oct. 2016), http://www.thealiadviser.org/sexual-assault/updated-consent-definition/. This provision specifies that consent can be "express" or "inferred from behavior — both action and inaction — in the context of all the circumstances." *Id.* § 213.03(b). This section also provides that consent can be "revoked or withdrawn any time before or during the [sexual] act," and that the absence or withdrawal of consent can be "overridden by subsequent consent." *Id.* § 213.0(3)(e). Finally, the provision indicates that a "clear verbal refusal" (such as saying "no" or "stop") "establishes the lack of consent" as well as "the revocation or withdrawal of previous consent." *Id.*

The proposed revisions that are still under consideration would recognize a defense of consent to the use of force if a defendant charged with forcible rape, aggravated forcible rape, sexual penetration without consent, or aggravated criminal sexual contact (the elements of which are described below) reasonably believed that the victim "gave explicit prior verbal consent to the use of physical force, threats, or restraint, and/or permission to ignore general expressions of unwillingness." Model Penal Code: Sexual Assault and Related Offenses § 213.9(1) (Tentative Draft No. 2, 2016) (citing *id.* §§ 213.1, 213.2, 213.6(1)). The defendant has the burden of proving this defense by a preponderance of the evidence, and it is not available either if the defendant knew or recklessly disregarded the risk that the victim withdrew consent or if the defendant "knowingly or recklessly caused serious bodily injury." *Id.*

The proposed revisions would explicitly require a mens rea of at least recklessness for every material element of the new sex offenses. *See* Model Penal Code: Sexual Assault and Related Offenses 71 (Tentative Draft No. 1, 2014). The drafters of the revisions reject strict liability as "unconscionable" in these circumstances, given that it could lead to the imposition of severe sentences and collateral consequences on defendants who reasonably believed they were engaged in "constitutionally protected" behavior — "sexual relations between *consenting* adults." *Id.* at 73. The drafters further believe that negligence is an inappropriate standard of liability in a context where "social norms" are not "widely shared, stable, and subjectively just," and therefore they would require "proof of subjective awareness of the relevant risks." *Id.* at 74, 73.

Although MPC § 2.08(2) does not allow a criminal defendant to use "self-induced intoxication" to argue lack of awareness of a risk "of which he would have been aware had he been sober," the proposed revisions would create an exception to § 2.08(2) for sex offenses. *See* Model Penal Code: Sexual Assault and Related Offenses § 213.0(4) (Tentative Draft No. 2, 2016). The drafters of the revisions explain that "sexual intercourse often occurs when both the accused and the complainant are intoxicated" and intoxication "clouds . . . the capacity" of both parties, and therefore they made "a deliberate choice not to impose liability for negligent acts, even when such negligence is the product of voluntary intoxication." Model Penal Code: Sexual Assault and Related Offenses 76 (Tentative Draft No. 1, 2014). For further discussion of the MPC's general position on intoxication as a defense, see Chapter 4, Section C.3, Note 3.

11. Mens Rea and Force. Mens rea questions in rape cases typically surround the consent element of the crime; almost no attention has been paid to the question of mens rea as it applies to the force element (the subject of the following Section). For an analysis of cases that have discussed what mens rea attaches to the element of force, and the widely varying conclusions they have reached, see Kit Kinports, *Rape and Force: The Forgotten Mens Rea*, 4 Buff. Crim. L. Rev. 755 (2001). One such case, *People v. Evans*, is described in Note 5 following *State v. Rusk* in Part 3 below.

[3] Actus Reus

State v. Rusk
424 A.2d 720 (Md. 1981)

Murphy, Chief Judge.

Edward Rusk was found guilty by a jury of second degree rape in violation of Maryland Code, Art. 27, §463(a)(1), [and was sentenced to ten years in prison. Section 463(a)(1)] provides in pertinent part:

"A person is guilty of rape in the second degree if the person engages in vaginal intercourse with another person:

(1) By force or threat of force against the will and without the consent of the other person. . . ."[21]

On appeal, the Court of Special Appeals, sitting en banc, reversed the conviction; it concluded by an 8-5 majority that in view of the prevailing law as set forth in *Hazel v. State*, 221 Md. 464, 157 A.2d 922 (1960), insufficient evidence of Rusk's guilt had been adduced at the trial to permit the case to go to the jury. *Rusk v. State*, 43 Md. App. 476, 406 A.2d 624 (1979) . . . .

At the trial, the 21-year-old prosecuting witness, Pat, testified that on the evening of September 21, 1977, she attended a high school alumnae meeting where she met a girl friend, Terry. After the meeting, Terry and Pat agreed to drive in their respective cars to Fells Point to have a few drinks. . . .

The women arrived in Fells Point about 9:45 p.m. They went to a bar where each had one drink. After staying approximately one hour, Pat and Terry walked several blocks to a second bar, where each of them had another drink. After about thirty minutes, they walked two blocks to a third bar known as E.J. Buggs. The bar was crowded and a band was playing in the back. Pat ordered another drink and as she and Terry were leaning against the wall, Rusk [who was 31 years old] approached and said "hello" to Terry. Terry, who was then conversing with another individual, momentarily interrupted her conversation and said "Hi, Eddie." Rusk then began talking with Pat and during their conversation both of them acknowledged being separated from their respective spouses and having a child. Pat told Rusk that she had

---

21. The current version of the statute omits the clause "against the will" and prohibits vaginal intercourse "by force, or the threat of force, without the consent of the other" person. Md. Code Ann., Criminal §3-304(a)(1).

to go home because it was a weeknight and she had to wake up with her baby early in the morning.

Rusk asked Pat the direction in which she was driving and after she responded, Rusk requested a ride to his apartment. Although Pat did not know Rusk, she thought that Terry knew him. She thereafter agreed to give him a ride. Pat cautioned Rusk on the way to the car that "I'm just giving a ride home, you know, as a friend, not anything to be, you know, thought of other than a ride;" and he said, "Oh, okay." They left the bar between 12:00 and 12:20 a.m.

. . . After a twenty-minute drive, they arrived at Rusk's apartment. Pat testified that she was totally unfamiliar with the neighborhood. She parked the car at the curb on the opposite side of the street from Rusk's apartment but left the engine running. Rusk asked Pat to come in, but she refused. He invited her again, and she again declined. She told Rusk that she could not go into his apartment even if she wanted to because she was separated from her husband and a detective could be observing her movements. Pat said that Rusk was fully aware that she did not want to accompany him to his room. Notwithstanding her repeated refusals, Pat testified that Rusk reached over and turned off the ignition to her car and took her car keys. He got out of the car, walked over to her side, opened the door and said, "Now, will you come up?" Pat explained her subsequent actions:

> "At that point, because I was scared, because he had my car keys. I didn't know what to do. I was someplace I didn't even know where I was. It was in the city. I didn't know whether to run. I really didn't think at that point, what to do.
>
> "Now, I know that I should have blown the horn. I should have run. There were a million things I could have done. I was scared, at that point, and I didn't do any of them."

Pat testified that at this moment she feared that Rusk would rape her. She said: "[I]t was the way he looked at me, and said 'Come on up, come on up;' and when he took the keys, I knew that was wrong."

It was then about 1 a.m. Pat accompanied Rusk across the street into a totally dark house. She followed him up two flights of stairs. She neither saw nor heard anyone in the building. Once they ascended the stairs, Rusk unlocked the door to his one-room apartment, and turned on the light. According to Pat, he told her to sit down. She sat in a chair beside the bed. Rusk sat on the bed. After Rusk talked for a few minutes, he left the room for about one to five minutes. Pat remained seated in the chair. She made no noise and did not attempt to leave. She said that she did not notice a telephone in the room. When Rusk returned, he turned off the light and sat down on the bed. Pat asked if she could leave; she told him that she wanted to go home and "didn't want to come up." She said, "Now, [that] I came up, can I go?" Rusk, who was still in possession of her car keys, said he wanted her to stay.

Rusk then asked Pat to get on the bed with him. He pulled her by the arms to the bed and began to undress her, removing her blouse and bra. He unzipped her slacks and she took them off after he told her to do so. Pat removed the rest of her clothing, and then removed Rusk's pants because "he asked me to do it." After they were both undressed Rusk started kissing Pat as she was lying on her back. Pat explained what happened next:

> "I was still begging him to please let, you know, let me leave. I said, 'you can get a lot of other girls down there, for what you want,' and he just kept saying, 'no'; and then I was really scared, because I can't describe, you know, what was said. It was more the look in his eyes; and I said, at that point—I didn't know what to say; and I said, 'If I do what you want, will you let me go without killing me?' Because I didn't know, at that point, what he was going to do; and I started to cry; and when I did, he put his hands on my throat, and started lightly to choke me; and I said, 'If I do what you want, will you let me go?' And he said, yes, and at that time, I proceeded to do what he wanted me to."

Pat testified that Rusk made her perform oral sex and then vaginal intercourse.

Immediately after the intercourse, Pat asked if she could leave. She testified that Rusk said, "Yes," after which she got up and got dressed and Rusk returned her car keys. She said that Rusk then "walked me to my car, and asked if he could see me again; and I said, 'Yes'; and he asked me for my telephone number; and I said, 'No, I'll see you down Fells Point sometime,' just so I could leave." Pat testified that she "had no intention of meeting him again." She asked him for directions out of the neighborhood and left.

. . . .

Rusk and two of his friends, Michael Trimp and David Carroll, testified on his behalf. According to Trimp, they went in Carroll's car to Buggs' bar to dance, drink and "tr[y] to pick up some ladies." Rusk stayed at the bar, while the others went to get something to eat.

Trimp and Carroll next saw Rusk walking down the street arm-in-arm with a lady whom Trimp was unable to identify. Trimp asked Rusk if he needed a ride home. Rusk responded that the woman he was with was going to drive him home. . . .

Carroll's testimony corroborated Trimp's. He saw Rusk walking down the street arm-in-arm with a woman. He said "[s]he was kind of like, you know, snuggling up to him like. . . . She was hanging all over him then." Carroll was fairly certain that Pat was the woman who was with Rusk.

. . . .

According to Rusk, when they arrived in front of his apartment Pat parked the car and turned the engine off. They sat for several minutes "petting each other." Rusk denied switching off the ignition and removing the keys. He said that they walked to the apartment house and proceeded up the stairs to his room. Rusk testified that

Pat came willingly to his room and that at no time did he make threatening facial expressions. . . . Rusk explained that after the intercourse, Pat "got uptight."

> "Well, she started to cry. She said that — she said, 'You guys are all alike,' she says, 'just out for,' you know, 'one thing.'
>
> "She started talking about — I don't know, she was crying and all. I tried to calm her down and all; and I said, 'What's the matter?' And she said, that she just wanted to leave; and I said, 'Well, okay;' and she walked out to the car. I walked out to the car. She got in the car and left."

Rusk denied placing his hands on Pat's throat or attempting to strangle her. He also denied using force or threats of force to get Pat to have intercourse with him.

In reversing Rusk's second degree rape conviction, the Court of Special Appeals . . . said:

> "In all of the victim's testimony we have been unable to see any resistance on her part to the sex acts and certainly can we see no fear as would overcome her attempt to resist or escape as required by *Hazel*. Possession of the keys by the accused may have deterred her vehicular escape but hardly a departure seeking help in the rooming house or in the street. We must say that 'the way he looked' fails utterly to support the fear required by *Hazel*."

. . . .

. . . [D]ue process requirements mandate that a criminal conviction not be obtained if the evidence does not reasonably support a finding of guilt beyond a reasonable doubt. However, as the Supreme Court made clear in *Jackson v. Virginia*, 443 U.S. 307 (1979), the reviewing court does not ask itself whether *it* believes that the evidence established guilt beyond a reasonable doubt; rather, the applicable standard is "whether, after viewing the evidence in the light most favorable to the prosecution, *any* rational trier of fact could have found the essential elements of the crime beyond a reasonable doubt." . . .

Hazel, which was decided in 1960, . . . recognized that force and lack of consent are distinct elements of the crime of rape. It said:

> "Force is an essential element of the crime and to justify a conviction, the evidence must warrant a conclusion either that the victim resisted and her resistance was overcome by force or that she was prevented from resisting by threats to her safety. But no particular amount of force, either actual or constructive, is required to constitute rape. Necessarily that fact must depend upon the prevailing circumstances. As in this case force may exist without violence. If the acts and threats of the defendant were reasonably calculated to create in the mind of the victim — having regard to the circumstances in which she was placed — a real apprehension, due to fear, of imminent bodily harm, serious enough to impair or overcome her will to resist, then such acts and threats are the equivalent of force."

As to the element of lack of consent, the Court said in *Hazel*:

"[I]t is true, of course, that however reluctantly given, consent to the act at any time prior to penetration deprives the subsequent intercourse of its criminal character. There is, however, a wide difference between consent and a submission to the act. Consent may involve submission, but submission does not necessarily imply consent. Furthermore, submission to a compelling force, or as a result of being put in fear, is not consent."

The Court noted that lack of consent is generally established through proof of resistance or by proof that the victim failed to resist because of fear. . . . *Hazel* thus made it clear that lack of consent could be established through proof that the victim submitted as a result of fear of imminent death or serious bodily harm. In addition, if the actions and conduct of the defendant were reasonably calculated to induce this fear in the victim's mind, then the element of force is present. *Hazel* recognized, therefore, that the same kind of evidence may be used in establishing both force and nonconsent, particularly when a threat rather than actual force is involved.

. . . .

Hazel did not expressly determine whether the victim's fear must be "reasonable." . . . The vast majority of jurisdictions have required that the victim's fear be reasonably grounded in order to obviate the need for either proof of actual force on the part of the assailant or physical resistance on the part of the victim. We think that, generally, this is the correct standard.

. . . [T]he Court of Special Appeals . . . did not believe that the evidence was legally sufficient to demonstrate the existence of "a reasonable fear" which overcame Pat's ability to resist. In support of the Court's conclusion, Rusk maintains that the evidence showed that Pat voluntarily entered his apartment without being subjected to a "single threat nor a scintilla of force"; that she made no effort to run away nor did she scream for help; that she never exhibited a will to resist; and that her subjective reaction of fear to the situation in which she had voluntarily placed herself was unreasonable and exaggerated. Rusk claims that his acts were not reasonably calculated to overcome a will to resist; that Pat's verbal resistance was not resistance within the contemplation of *Hazel*; that his alleged menacing look did not constitute a threat of force; and that even had he pulled Pat to the bed, and lightly choked her, as she claimed, these actions, viewed in the context of the entire incident—no prior threats having been made—would be insufficient to constitute force or a threat of force or render the intercourse nonconsensual.

We think the reversal of Rusk's conviction by the Court of Special Appeals was in error. . . . In view of the evidence adduced at the trial, the reasonableness of Pat's apprehension of fear was plainly a question of fact for the jury to determine. . . . Of course, it was for the jury to observe the witnesses and their demeanor, and to judge their credibility and weigh their testimony. Quite obviously, the jury disbelieved Rusk and believed Pat's testimony. From her testimony, the jury could have reasonably concluded that the taking of her car keys was intended by Rusk to immobilize her alone, late at night, in a neighborhood with which she was not familiar; that after Pat had repeatedly refused to enter his apartment, Rusk commanded in firm tones that she do so; that Pat was badly frightened and feared that Rusk intended to rape her; that unable to think clearly and believing that she had no other choice in the circumstances, Pat entered Rusk's apartment; that once inside Pat asked permission to leave but Rusk told her to stay; that he then pulled Pat by the arms to the bed and undressed her; that Pat was afraid that Rusk would kill her unless she submitted; that she began to cry and Rusk then put his hands on her throat and began "lightly to choke" her; that Pat asked him if he would let her go without killing her if she complied with his demands; that Rusk gave an affirmative response, after which she finally submitted.

. . . That a victim did not scream out for help or attempt to escape, while bearing on the question of consent, is unnecessary where she is restrained by fear of violence.

Considering all of the evidence in the case, with particular focus upon the actual force applied by Rusk to Pat's neck, we conclude that the jury could rationally find that the essential elements of second degree rape had been established and that Rusk was guilty of that offense beyond a reasonable doubt.

COLE, JUDGE, [joined by Judges Smith and Digges,] dissenting.

I agree with the Court of Special Appeals that the evidence . . . was insufficient to convict [Rusk] of rape. . . .

. . . It seems to me that . . . the defendant's conduct under the circumstances [must be] reasonably calculated to give rise to a fear on [the prosecutrix's] part to the extent that she was unable to resist. In other words, the fear must stem from his articulable conduct, and equally, if not more importantly, cannot be inconsistent with her own contemporaneous reaction to that conduct. . . . In my view, there is no evidence to support the majority's conclusion that the prosecutrix was forced to submit to sexual intercourse, certainly not fellatio.

. . . .

While courts no longer require a female to resist to the utmost or to resist where resistance would be foolhardy, they do require her acquiescence in the act of intercourse to stem from fear generated by something of substance. She may not simply say, "I was really scared," and thereby transform consent or mere unwillingness into submission by force. These words do not transform a seducer into a rapist. She must follow the natural instinct of every proud female to resist, by more than mere words, the violation of her person by a stranger or an unwelcomed friend. She must make it plain that she regards such sexual acts as abhorrent and repugnant to her natural sense of pride. She must resist unless the defendant has objectively manifested his intent to use physical force to accomplish his purpose. . . .

Here we have a full grown married woman who meets the defendant in a bar under friendly circumstances. They drink and talk together. She agrees to give him a ride home in her car. When they arrive at his house, located in an area with which she was unfamiliar but which was certainly not isolated, he invites her to come up to his apartment and she refuses. According to her testimony he takes her keys, walks around to her side of the car, and says "Now will you come up?" She answers, "yes." . . . There is no evidence descriptive of the tone of his voice; her testimony indicates only the bare statement quoted above. How can the majority extract from this conduct a threat reasonably calculated to create a fear of imminent bodily harm? There was no weapon, no threat to inflict physical injury.

She also testified that she was afraid of "the way he looked," and afraid of his statement, "come on up, come on up." But what can the majority conclude from this statement coupled with a "look" that remained undescribed? There is no evidence whatsoever to suggest that this was anything other than a pattern of conduct consistent with the ordinary seduction of a female acquaintance who at first suggests her disinclination.

. . . .

The majority relies on the trial court's statement that the defendant responded affirmatively to her question "If I do what you want, will you let me go without killing me?" . . . The facts belie such inference since by the prosecutrix's own testimony the defendant made *no* response. *He said nothing!*

She then testified that she started to cry and he "started lightly to choke" her, whatever that means. Obviously, the choking was not of any persuasive significance. During this "choking" she was able to talk.[22] She said "If I do what you want will you let me go?" It was at this point that the defendant said yes.

I find it incredible for the majority to conclude that on these facts, without more, a woman was *forced* to commit oral sex upon the defendant and then to engage in vaginal intercourse. In the absence of any verbal threat to do her grievous bodily harm or the display of any weapon and threat to use it, I find it difficult to understand how a victim could participate in these sexual activities and not be willing.

. . . .

As the defendant well knew, this was not a child. This was a married woman with children, a woman familiar with the social setting in which these two actors met.[23] It was an ordinary city street, not an isolated spot. He had not forced his way into her car; he had not taken advantage of a difference in years or any state of intoxication

---

22. The Court of Special Appeals noted that "[a]t oral argument it was brought out that the 'lightly choking' could have been a heavy caress." 406 A.2d at 628.

23. According to the dissenting judge in the Court of Special Appeals, Pat had gone to Fells Point with Terry on a few occasions prior to the time she encountered Rusk, but she testified that "I've never met anybody [there] I've gone out with." *Id.* at 631 (Wilner, J., dissenting). On the night in question, "Pat conversed only with Terry, and did not strike up any other acquaintanceships" before she spoke to Rusk. *Id.*

or mental or physical incapacity on her part. He did not grapple with her. She got out of the car, *walked with him* across the street and *followed* him up the stairs to his room. She certainly had to realize that they were not going upstairs to play *Scrabble*.

Once in the room she waited while he went to the bathroom where he stayed for five minutes. In his absence, the room was lighted but she did not seek a means of escape. She did not even "try the door" to determine if it was locked. She waited.

Upon his return, he turned off the lights and pulled her on the bed. There is no suggestion or inference to be drawn from her testimony that he yanked her on the bed or in any manner physically abused her by this conduct. As a matter of fact there is no suggestion by her that he bruised or hurt her in any manner, or that the "choking" was intended to be disabling.

He then proceeded to unbutton her blouse and her bra. He did not rip her clothes off or use any greater force than was necessary to unfasten her garments. He did not even complete this procedure but requested that she do it, which she did "because he asked me to." However, she not only removed her clothing but took his clothes off, too.

Then for a while they lay together on the bed kissing, though she says she did not return his kisses. However, without protest she then proceeded to perform oral sex and later submitted to vaginal intercourse. . . .

In my judgment the State failed to prove the essential element of force beyond a reasonable doubt and, therefore, the judgment of conviction should be reversed.

Notes and Questions

1. **Acquaintance Rape.** *Rusk* is not at all unusual in involving acquaintance, or nonstranger, rape. Despite the mythical view of the rapist as a stranger who jumps out of the bushes or accosts his victim in a dark alley, most rapes are committed by nonstrangers. *See* Michelle C. Black et al., Centers for Disease Control and Prevention, The National Intimate Partner and Sexual Violence Survey: 2010 Summary Report 22-23 (2011), *available at* http://www.cdc.gov/Violence Prevention/pdf/NISVS_Report2010-a.pdf (reporting that only about 15 percent of female and male victims were raped by strangers).

2. **Fear.** In *Rusk*, the court held that a victim's fear of the defendant suffices to establish the existence of force and excuses her failure to resist only if that fear is reasonable as well as honest. In *People v. Iniguez*, 872 P.2d 1183, 1188 (Cal. 1994), by contrast, the court observed that an unreasonable fear may be sufficient to demonstrate that intercourse was "accomplished by means of force, violence, or fear of immediate and unlawful bodily injury" within the terms of the California rape statute, so long as the defendant "knowingly takes advantage of that fear." *See also Salsman v. Commonwealth*, 565 S.W.2d 638, 641 (Ky. Ct. App. 1978) (reasoning that a rape defendant "who takes advantage of a victim's unreasonable fears of violence should not escape punishment any more than the swindler who cheats gullible people by false statements which they should have found incredible").

Is the approach taken in *Iniguez* and *Salsman* analogous to the doctrine that a defendant charged with felony murder "takes his victim as he finds him"? *People v. Stamp*, 82 Cal. Rptr. 598, 603 (Cal. Ct. App. 1969) (discussed in Chapter 6, Section D.1, Note 1).

3. Resistance. Traditionally, the law of rape required that a rape victim resist "to the utmost." One court offered the following justification for this rule:

> Can the mind conceive of a woman, in the possession of her faculties and powers, revoltingly unwilling that this deed should be done upon her, who would not resist so hard and so long as she was able? And if a woman, aware that it will be done unless she does resist, does not resist to the extent of her ability on the occasion, must it not be that she is not entirely reluctant?

People v. Dohring, 59 N.Y. 374, 384 (1874).

Almost every state has abolished the requirement of utmost resistance. *But cf.* La. Rev. Stat. Ann. § 14:42(A)(1) (including that language in the definition of aggravated rape). But a number of jurisdictions follow the approach taken in *Rusk* and require some reasonable resistance by the victim unless the defendant's threats prevented her from resisting. One court explained the rationale for the reasonable resistance requirement as follows:

> [O]nce complainant became aware that defendant intended to engage in sexual relations it was incumbent upon her to resist. This resistance would have the effect of giving defendant notice that his acts were being performed without her consent. . . . Complainant's failure to resist when it was within her power to do so conveys the impression of consent regardless of her mental state, amounts to consent and removes from the act performed an essential element of the crime. We do not mean to suggest, however, that the complainant did in fact consent; however, she must communicate in some objective manner her lack of consent.

People v. Warren, 446 N.E.2d 591, 594 (Ill. App. Ct. 1983).

Was there sufficient evidence of reasonable resistance on the facts of *Rusk*? Compare *State v. Jones*, 299 P.3d 219, 225 (Idaho 2013), where the court was interpreting a rape statute requiring that a victim "resists but her resistance is overcome by force or violence." Reasoning that the statute did not "differentiate between physical or verbal resistance," the court held that verbal resistance—for example, "repeated pleas for [the defendant] to stop"—was sufficient. *Id.* at 227–28. But the court found inadequate evidence of resistance where the victim "'didn't respond' physically, or even verbally," but "just froze." In so holding, the court rejected the prosecution's argument that "feigning sleep" amounted to "passive resistance" on the grounds that "[s]atisfying [the resistance] element with inactivity . . . essentially nullif[ies] the resistance requirement." *Id.* at 229. For discussion of the move in some states to eliminate resistance as a requirement in rape cases, see Note 2 below following *Commonwealth v. Berkowitz*.

4. Force. According to a study conducted by the Law Enforcement Assistance Administration in the late 1970s, approximately one-half of reported rapes involved no use of physical force by the defendant, and about one-third did not involve a weapon. *See* BATTELLE MEMORIAL INSTITUTE LAW AND JUSTICE STUDY CENTER, FORCIBLE RAPE, POLICE VOLUME 1, at 21 (1977–1978). More recent figures confirm that most rapists do not use a weapon. *See* SHANNON M. CATALANO, BUREAU OF JUSTICE STATISTICS, CRIMINAL VICTIMIZATION, 2005, at 10 (2006), *available at* http://www.bjs.gov/content/pub/pdf/cv05.pdf (reporting that no weapon was involved in 85 percent of rapes and sexual assaults).

Even though Rusk did not wield a weapon, his rape conviction was ultimately upheld. In finding sufficient evidence of force in that case, the majority placed "particular focus" on the evidence of choking. Would the case have come out differently without this evidence? Note that 13 Court of Appeals judges and seven judges on the intermediate Court of Special Appeals, as well as the trial judge, considered the adequacy of the evidence in *Rusk*; of those 21 judges, 10 thought the evidence was sufficient to convict, 11 did not. Consider SUSAN ESTRICH, REAL RAPE 65–66 (1987):

> The emphasis on the light choking/heavy caresses is perhaps understandable: it is the only "objective" (as the dissent put it) force in the victim's testimony; it is certainly the only "force" that a schoolboy might recognize. As it happens, however, that force was not applied until the two were already undressed and in bed. Whatever it was — choking or caressing — was a response to the woman's crying as the moment for intercourse approached. It was not the only force that produced that moment.

Cf. State v. Magel, 268 P.3d 666, 668, 671 (Or. Ct. App. 2011) (reversing rape conviction under statute requiring "forcible compulsion," defined to include force or an express or implied threat of force, where the defendant had sex with a girl aged 12 or 13, who told him she "didn't want to do it," but "did not 'put up a fight' because she believed that if she tried to do so, 'he would just fight right back,'" and rejecting the prosecution's argument that a threat was implied because the defendant had concededly "used physical force to compel [the victim] to engage in sexual contact" when she was nine or 10 years old because the "forcible compulsion by threat occurred several years before" and "[t]he record does not reflect that defendant referred in any way to the prior sexual contact").

5. *People v. Evans.* In exploring the contours of the force requirement and evaluating whether there was sufficient evidence of force in *Rusk*, consider also *People v. Evans*, 379 N.Y.S.2d 912 (N.Y. Sup. Ct. 1975), *aff'd*, 390 N.Y.S.2d 768 (N.Y. App. Div. 1976). Lucy Peterson was a 20-year-old college student who was described by the court as "petite, attractive," "unworldly," "gullible, trusting and naive." Upon her arrival in New York City, she met the defendant, Martin Evans, a 37-year-old man whom the court described as "glib," "crafty, scheming, [and] manipulative." *Id.* at 915, 918. Evans pretended to be a psychologist interested in interviewing Peterson for a magazine article. After stopping at a singles bar for the ostensible purpose of conducting a sociological experiment where Evans was to observe Peterson's "reactions and the reactions of males towards her," they went to an apartment that Evans claimed served as one of his offices. *Id.* at 915. When Peterson resisted his attempts to undress her, Evans expressed "disappointment that she had failed the test, that this was all part of his psychological experiment." *Id.* at 916. He then "took steps to cause doubt and fear to arise in [her] mind" by saying: "Look where you are. You are in the apartment of a strange man. How do you know that I am really who I say I am? How do you know that I am really a psychologist? . . . I could kill you. I could rape you. I could hurt you physically." *Id.* at 917. He then made an "abrupt switch" and "attempted to play on [her] sympathy" by telling her a story about a former girlfriend who had died in a car accident. When Peterson "instinctively" stepped forward and put a sympathetic hand on Evans' shoulders, he "grabbed" her. *Id.* An act of intercourse followed, as well as two more before Peterson left the apartment.

On these facts, the court found insufficient evidence of the "forcible compulsion" required by New York's rape statute — i.e., "physical force that overcomes earnest resistance; or a threat, express or implied, that places a person in fear of immediate death or serious physical injury to himself." *Id.* at 915 (quoting N.Y. Penal Law §130.00(8)).[24] In examining the relevance of the defendant's comment that he "could kill [or] rape" the victim, the court concluded that his words were "susceptible to two possible and diverse interpretations":

> The first would be in essence that — you had better do what I say, for you are helpless and I have the power to use ultimate force should you resist. That clearly would be a threat which would induce fear and overcome resistance. The second possible meaning of those words is, in effect, that — you are a foolish girl. You are in the apartment of a strange man. You put yourself in the hands of a stranger, and you are vulnerable and defenseless. The possibility would exist of physical harm to you were you being confronted by someone other than the person who uttered this statement.

Id. at 920. Although the court admitted that it was "entirely possible" the victim interpreted the defendant's words as a threat, and that that interpretation was reasonable, the court concluded that "the controlling state of mind must be that of the speaker":

> [T]his being a criminal trial, it is basic that the criminal intent of the defendant must be shown beyond a reasonable doubt. It is his intent when he acts, his intent when he speaks, which must therefore be controlling. And so, if he utters words which are taken as a threat by the person who hears them, but are not intended as a threat by the person who utters them, there would be no basis for finding the necessary criminal intent to establish culpability under the law.

Id. at 921.

---

24. The New York statute now defines "forcible compulsion" as compulsion by either the "use of physical force" or by "a threat, express or implied," that puts the victim "in fear of immediate" death, physical injury, or kidnapping. N.Y. Penal Law §130.00(8).

The court in *Evans* suggested that force may be in the eye of the beholder — that women might find some behavior threatening that men would not. Was the court right to conclude that it is the defendant's perspective that ought to control? *See* Meredith J. Duncan, *Sex Crimes and Sexual Miscues: The Need for a Clearer Line Between Forcible Rape and Nonconsensual Sex*, 42 Wake Forest L. Rev. 1087, 1112 (2007) (agreeing that "whether the victim actually was raped should turn on what was going on in the perpetrator's mind, not on how the victim felt"). (Evans' use of deceit and trickery is discussed below in Note 7 following *Commonwealth v. Berkowitz*.)

Commonwealth v. Berkowitz

641 A.2d 1161 (Pa. 1994)

[The following summary of the facts of the case is taken from the Superior Court's fuller recitation, *Commonwealth v. Berkowitz*, 609 A.2d 1338, 1339–42 (Pa. Super. Ct. 1992):

In the spring of 1988, appellant and the victim were both college sophomores at East Stroudsburg State University, ages twenty and nineteen years old, respectively. They had mutual friends and acquaintances. . . .

During a one-day jury trial held on September 14, 1988, the victim gave the following account during direct examination by the Commonwealth. At roughly 2:00 on the afternoon of April 19, 1988, after attending two morning classes, the victim returned to her dormitory room. There, she drank a martini to "loosen up a little bit" before going to meet her boyfriend, with whom she had argued the night before. Roughly ten minutes later she walked to her boyfriend's dormitory lounge to meet him. He had not yet arrived.

Having nothing else to do while she waited for her boyfriend, the victim walked up to appellant's room to look for Earl Hassel, appellant's roommate. She knocked on the door several times but received no answer. She therefore wrote a note to Mr. Hassel, which read, "Hi Earl, I'm drunk. That's not why I came to see you. I haven't seen you in a while. I'll talk to you later, [victim's name]." She did so, although she had not felt any intoxicating effects from the martini, "for a laugh."

After the victim had knocked again, she tried the knob on the appellant's door. Finding it open, she walked in. She saw someone lying on the bed with a pillow over his head, whom she thought to be Earl Hassel. After lifting the pillow from his head, she realized it was appellant. She asked appellant which dresser was his roommate's. He told her, and the victim left the note.

Before the victim could leave appellant's room, however, appellant asked her to stay and "hang out for a while." She complied because she "had time to kill" and because she didn't really know appellant and wanted to give him "a fair chance." Appellant asked her to give him a back rub but she declined, explaining that she did not "trust" him. Appellant then asked her to have a seat on his bed. Instead, she found a seat on the floor, and conversed for a while about a mutual friend.[25] No physical contact between the two had, to this point, taken place.

Thereafter, however, appellant moved off the bed and down on the floor, and "kind of pushed [the victim] back with his body. It wasn't a shove, it was just kind of a leaning-type of thing." Next appellant "straddled" and started kissing the victim. The victim responded by saying, "Look, I gotta go. I'm going to meet [my boyfriend]." Then appellant lifted up her shirt and bra and began fondling her. The victim then said "no."

After roughly thirty seconds of kissing and fondling, appellant "undid his pants and he kind of moved his body up a little bit." The victim was still saying "no" but "really couldn't move because [appellant] was shifting at [her] body so he was over [her]." Appellant then tried to put his penis in her mouth. The victim did not physically resist, but rather continued to verbally protest, saying "No, I gotta go, let me go," in a "scolding" manner.

Ten or fifteen more seconds passed before the two rose to their feet. Appellant disregarded the victim's continual complaints that she "had to go," and instead walked two feet away to the door and locked it so that no one from the outside could enter.

Then, in the victim's words, "[appellant] put me down on the bed. It was kind of like—he didn't throw me on the bed. It's hard to explain. It was kind of like a push but no. . . ." She did not bounce off the bed. "It wasn't slow like a romantic kind of thing, but it wasn't a fast shove either. It was kind of in the middle."

Once the victim was on the bed, appellant began "straddling" her again while he undid the knot in her sweatpants. He then removed her sweatpants and underwear from one of her legs. The victim did not physically resist in any way while on the bed because appellant was on top of her, and she "couldn't like go anywhere." She did not scream out at anytime because, "[i]t was like a dream was happening or something."

Appellant then used one of his hands to "guide" his penis into her vagina. At that point, after appellant was inside her, the victim began saying "no, no to him softly in a moaning kind of way . . . because it was just so scary." After about thirty seconds, appellant pulled out his penis and ejaculated onto the victim's stomach.

Immediately thereafter, appellant got off the victim and said, "Wow, I guess we just got carried away." To this the victim retorted, "No, we didn't get carried away, you got carried away." The victim then quickly dressed, grabbed her school books and raced downstairs to her boyfriend who was by then waiting for her in the lounge.

Once there, the victim began crying. Her boyfriend and she went up to his dorm room where, after watching the victim clean off appellant's semen from her stomach, he called the police.

---

25. [n.1] On cross-examination, the victim testified that during this conversation she had explained she was having problems with her boyfriend.

Defense counsel's cross-examination elicited more details regarding the contact between appellant and the victim before the incident in question. The victim testified that roughly two weeks prior to the incident, she had attended a school seminar entitled, "Does 'no' sometimes mean 'yes'?" Among other things, the lecturer at this seminar had discussed the average length and circumference of human penises. After the seminar, the victim and several of her friends had discussed the subject matter of the seminar over a speaker-telephone with appellant and his roommate Earl Hassel. The victim testified that during that telephone conversation, she had asked appellant the size of his penis. According to the victim, appellant responded by suggesting that the victim "come over and find out." She declined.

When questioned further regarding her communications with appellant prior to the April 19, 1988 incident, the victim testified that on two other occasions, she had stopped by appellant's room while intoxicated. During one of those times, she had laid down on his bed. When asked whether she had asked appellant again at that time what his penis size was, the victim testified that she did not remember.

Appellant took the stand in his own defense and offered an account of the incident and the events leading up to it which differed only as to the consent involved. According to appellant, the victim had begun communication with him after the school seminar by asking him of the size of his penis and of whether he would show it to her. Appellant had suspected that the victim wanted to pursue a sexual relationship with him because she had stopped by his room twice after the phone call while intoxicated, laying down on his bed with her legs spread and again asking to see his penis. He believed that his suspicions were confirmed when she initiated the April 19, 1988 encounter by stopping by his room (again after drinking), and waking him up.

Appellant testified that, on the day in question, he did initiate the first physical contact, but added that the victim warmly responded to his advances by passionately returning his kisses. He conceded that she was continually "whispering . . . no's," but claimed that she did so while "amorously . . . passionately" moaning. In effect, he took such protests to be thinly veiled acts of encouragement. When asked why he locked the door, he explained that "that's not something you want somebody to just walk in on you [doing.]"

According to appellant, the two then laid down on the bed, the victim helped him take her clothing off, and he entered her. He agreed that the victim continued to say "no" while on the bed, but carefully qualified his agreement, explaining that the statements were "moaned passionately." According to appellant, when he saw a "blank look on her face," he immediately withdrew and asked "is anything wrong, is something the matter, is anything wrong." He ejaculated on her stomach thereafter because he could no longer "control" himself. Appellant testified that after this, the victim "saw that it was over and then she made her move. She gets right off the bed . . . she just swings her legs over and then she puts her clothes back on." Then, in wholly corroborating an aspect of the victim's account, he testified that he remarked, "Well, I guess we got carried away," to which she rebuked, "No, we didn't get carried, you got carried away."

After hearing both accounts, the jury convicted appellant of rape and indecent assault. . . . Appellant was then sentenced to serve a term of imprisonment of one to four years for rape and a concurrent term of six to twelve months for indecent assault.]

CAPPY, JUSTICE.

. . . .

. . . For the reasons that follow, we affirm the Superior Court's reversal of the conviction for rape . . . and reinstate the verdict of the jury as to indecent assault.

. . . .

In reviewing the sufficiency of the evidence, this Court must view the evidence in the light most favorable to the Commonwealth as verdict winner, and accept as true all evidence and reasonable inferences that may be reasonably drawn therefrom, upon which, if believed, the jury could have relied in reaching its verdict. . . .

The crime of rape is defined as follows:

§ 3121. Rape

A person commits a felony of the first degree when he engages in sexual intercourse with another person not one's spouse:

(1) by forcible compulsion;

(2) by threat of forcible compulsion that would prevent resistance by a person of reasonable resolution. . . .

The victim of a rape need not resist. 18 Pa. C.S.A. § 3107.[26] "The force necessary to support a conviction of rape . . . need only be such as to establish lack of consent and to induce the [victim] to submit without additional resistance. . . . The degree of force required to constitute rape is relative and depends on the facts and particular circumstance of the case." *Commonwealth v. Rhodes*, 510 Pa. 537, 510 A.2d 1217 (1986).

In regard to the critical issue of forcible compulsion, the complainant's testimony is devoid of any statement which clearly or adequately describes the use of force or the threat of force against her. In response to defense counsel's question, "Is it possible that [when Appellee lifted your bra and shirt] you took no physical action to discourage him," the complainant replied, "It's possible." When asked, "Is it possible that [Appellee] was not making any physical contact with you . . . aside from attempting to untie the knot [in the drawstrings of complainant's sweatpants]," she answered, "It's possible." She testified that "He put me down on the bed. It was kind of like — He didn't throw me on the bed. It's hard to explain. It was kind of like a push but not — I can't explain what I'm trying to say." She concluded that "it wasn't

---

26. Although the court did not quote the language of this statute anywhere in its opinion, it provides that "[t]he alleged victim need not resist the actor in prosecutions under this chapter: [p]rovided, however, [t]hat nothing in this section shall be construed to prohibit a defendant from introducing evidence that the alleged victim consented to the conduct in question." 18 Pa. Cons. Stat. § 3107.

much" in reference to whether she bounced on the bed, and further detailed that their movement to the bed "wasn't slow like a romantic kind of thing, but it wasn't a fast shove either. It was kind of in the middle." She agreed that Appellee's hands were not restraining her in any manner during the actual penetration, and that the weight of his body on top of her was the only force applied. She testified that at no time did Appellee verbally threaten her. The complainant did testify that she sought to leave the room, and said "no" throughout the encounter. As to the complainant's desire to leave the room, the record clearly demonstrates that the door could be unlocked easily from the inside, that she was aware of this fact, but that she never attempted to go to the door or unlock it.

As to the complainant's testimony that she stated "no" throughout the encounter with Appellee, we point out that, while such an allegation of fact would be relevant to the issue of consent, it is not relevant to the issue of force. . . . [W]here there is a lack of consent, but no showing of either physical force, a threat of physical force, or psychological coercion, the "forcible compulsion" requirement under 18 Pa. C.S. § 3121 is not met.

Moreover, we find it instructive that in defining the related but distinct crime of "indecent assault" under 18 Pa. C.S. § 3126, the Legislature did not employ the phrase "forcible compulsion" but rather chose to define indecent assault as "indecent contact with another . . . without the consent of the other person." . . . The choice by the Legislature to define the crime of indecent assault utilizing the phrase "without the consent of the other" and to not so define the crime of rape indicates a legislative intent that the term "forcible compulsion" under 18 Pa. C.S. § 3121, be interpreted as something more than a lack of consent. . . .

Reviewed in light of the above described standard, the complainant's testimony simply fails to establish that the Appellee forcibly compelled her to engage in sexual intercourse as required under 18 Pa. C.S. § 3121. Thus, even if all of the complainant's testimony was believed, the jury, as a matter of law, could not have found Appellee guilty of rape. Accordingly, we hold that the Superior Court did not err in reversing Appellee's conviction of rape.

. . . .

. . . The evidence described above is clearly sufficient to support the jury's conviction of indecent assault. . . . The victim testified that she repeatedly said "no" throughout the encounter. Viewing that testimony in the light most favorable to the Commonwealth as verdict winner, the jury reasonably could have inferred that the victim did not consent to the indecent contact. Thus, the evidence was sufficient to support the jury's verdict finding Appellee guilty of indecent assault. . . .

Notes and Questions

1. **Consent and Force.** Does the *Berkowitz* court "create[] a paradox" by finding sufficient evidence that the sexual intercourse was nonconsensual but inadequate evidence of force? Is it a "clear contradiction" to say that a woman "was not forced to

engage in sex (as proven by her failure to resist), but the sex she engaged in was against her will"? Susan Estrich, Real Rape 62 (1987). Even if the Pennsylvania court's conclusion makes sense in the abstract, was it wrong to find insufficient evidence of force on the facts of *Berkowitz*? Did Estrich have a valid point when she commented that "[t]he body of a man who's 50 pounds heavier than you, stronger than you, a more experienced fighter than you, ignoring your words, determined to have sex, can certainly feel like force from the bottom"? Susan Estrich, *Rape: A Question of Force*, USA Today, Aug. 11, 1994, at 13A. Consider also Michelle J. Anderson, *Negotiating Sex*, 78 S. Cal. L. Rev. 1401, 1428–29 (2005):

> Berkowitz did not need to employ force. By pinning and straddling his victim, Berkowitz made it clear that he intended to penetrate her despite her clear and repeated expressions of nonconsent. He thereby intimidated her into a state of "depersonalization," in which she felt as if she were in a dream.

2. Resistance After Rape Reform. The *Berkowitz* court observed that rape victims "need not resist." Likewise, other states have repealed statutory requirements of resistance as part of rape reform legislation. *See* John F. Decker & Peter G. Baroni, *"No" Still Means "Yes": The Failure of the "Non-Consent" Reform Movement in American Rape and Sexual Assault Law*, 101 J. Crim. L. & Criminology 1081, 1106, 1103, 1109 (2011) (citing 14 statutes that have expressly abolished a resistance requirement, eight that still include it, and 16 others that "do not formally require resistance" but "continue to define the elements of force and consent in terms of a victim's resistance by requiring the victim to be 'incapable of resisting,' 'unable to resist,' 'prevented from resisting,' or some variant thereof").

In *People v. Iniguez*, 872 P.2d 1183, 1186–87 (Cal. 1994), the court described the California legislature's 1980 amendment to that state's rape statute, which eliminated the requirement that rape victims "either resist or be prevented from resisting because of threats":

> Prior to 1980, [California law] "defined rape as an act of sexual intercourse under circumstances where the person resists, but where 'resistance is overcome by force or violence' or where 'a person is prevented from resisting by threats of great and immediate bodily harm . . . .'"
>
> . . . .
>
> In discussing the significance of the 1980 amendments in [*People v. Barnes*, 721 P.2d 110 (Cal. 1986)], we noted that "studies have demonstrated that while some women respond to sexual assault with active resistance, others 'freeze,'" and "become helpless from panic and numbing fear." In response to this information, "For the first time, the Legislature has assigned the decision as to whether a sexual assault should be resisted to the realm of personal choice." "By removing resistance as a prerequisite to a rape conviction, the Legislature has brought the law of rape into conformity with other crimes such as robbery, kidnapping and assault, which require force, fear, and nonconsent to convict. In these crimes, the law does not expect falsity

from the complainant who alleges their commission and thus demand resistance as a corroboration and predicate to conviction."

See also Michelle J. Anderson, *Negotiating Sex*, 78 S. Cal. L. Rev. 1401, 1415–17 (2005) (citing studies finding that rape victims commonly "experience[] moderate or high levels of paralysis during the assault" or "dissociate from [their] bod[ies] as an adaptive means to escape").

Other researchers have found that most women do not physically resist sexual assaults, although they typically offer some other form of resistance. *See* Lawrence A. Greenfeld, Bureau of Justice Statistics, Sex Offenses and Offenders: An Analysis of Data on Rape and Sexual Assault (1997) (finding that 71.7 percent of rape and sexual assault victims take some self-protective measure, although only 25.4 percent attack the offender, resist by struggling, or try to chase and capture the offender). A report issued in the late 1970s by the Law Assistance Administration explained:

> Perhaps because most women's experience and expertise with violence tends to be minimal, they are unlikely to engage in physical combat or succeed when they do. Many women employ what is referred to as "passive resistance." This can include crying, being slow to respond, feigning an inability to understand instructions or telling the rapist they are pregnant, diseased or injured.

Battelle Memorial Institute Law and Justice Study Center, Forcible Rape, Prosecutor Volume 2, at 4 (1977–1978).

The Battelle Report also concluded that physical resistance was dangerous: approximately 70 percent of the victims who resisted physically were injured in some way, and about 40 percent of them required medical treatment or hospitalization. *Id.*, Police Volume 1, at 22. Although these statistics are not without their critics, *see* Michelle J. Anderson, *Reviving Resistance in Rape Law*, 1998 U. Ill. L. Rev. 953, 977–79, 981–85 (1998) (citing other studies which found that physical resistance can deter rape and is not more likely to lead to serious injury), it is clear that women have been advised by rape counselors, the media, and government agencies not to physically resist rapists. *See id.* at 957–58 (citing various publications offering such advice, as well as cases where rape victims testified that such warnings prompted their failure to offer physical resistance).

Given this evidence, is it best to repeal any requirement of resistance? Even if resistance is not expressly required by the rape statute, does the resistance requirement effectively sneak in the back door—both because nonconsent is an element of the crime and because a defense is often afforded to those who mistakenly believe the victim consented? In *People v. Barnes*, for example, the court observed that the statutory amendments to the California rape statute "do not mean that when resistance does exist, it is irrelevant to nonconsent. Absence of resistance may also continue to be probative of whether the accused honestly and reasonably believed he was engaging in consensual sex." *Barnes*, 721 P.2d at 121 n.19 (citing *People v. Mayberry*, which is described above in Part 2, Note 2). *See also Iniguez*, 872 P.2d at 1188 ("[T]he trier of fact 'should be permitted to measure consent by weighing both the acts of the alleged attacker and the response of the alleged victim, rather than being required to focus on one or the other.'") (quoting *Barnes*, 721 P.2d at 122). Did the Pennsylvania Supreme Court require resistance on the part of the victim in *Berkowitz*? If so, was it wrong to do so given the language in § 3107 of the state statutes (quoted above in n.26)? *See generally* Decker & Baroni, *supra*, at 1111–12 (concluding that whether or not "a state codifies a resistance requirement . . . , for many courts a victim's resistance still determines whether she consented or whether the defendant used force").

3. *People v. Iniguez.* In *People v. Iniguez*, 872 P.2d 1183 (Cal. 1994), as in *Berkowitz*, the case arrived at the state supreme court after the intermediate court of appeals had reversed the defendant's rape conviction on sufficiency of the evidence grounds. In *Iniguez*, however, the California Supreme Court disagreed with the appellate court and reinstated the defendant's conviction and six-year prison sentence. The court described the facts of the case as follows:

> Around 11:30 p.m. [on the night before her wedding], Mercy went to bed in the living room [of Sandra S., a close family friend]. She slept on top of her sleeping bag. She was wearing pants with an attached skirt, and a shirt. She fell asleep at approximately midnight.
>
> Mercy was awakened between 1:00 and 2:00 a.m. when she heard some movements behind her. She was lying on her stomach, and saw defendant [Sandra's fiancé], who was naked, approach her from behind. Without saying anything, defendant pulled down her pants, fondled her buttocks, and inserted his penis inside her. Mercy weighed 105 pounds. Defendant weighed approximately 205 pounds. Mercy "was afraid, so I just laid there." "You didn't try to resist or escape or anything of that nature because of your fear?" "Right." Mercy further explained that she "didn't know how it was at first, and just want[ed] to get on with my wedding plans the next day." Less than a minute later, defendant ejaculated, got off her, and walked back to the bedroom. Mercy had not consented to any sexual contact.
>
> Officer Fragoso, who interviewed Mercy several days after the attack, testified that she told him she had not resisted defendant's sexual assault because, "She said she knew that the man had been drinking. She hadn't met him before [that day]; he was a complete stranger to her. When she realized what was going on, she said she panicked, she froze. She was afraid that if she said or did anything, his reaction could be of a violent nature. So she decided just to lay still, wait until it was over with and then get out of the house as quickly as she could. . . ."
>
> Mercy immediately telephoned her fiancé Gary and left a message for him. She then telephoned her best friend Pam, who testified that Mercy was so distraught she was barely comprehensible. Mercy asked Pam to pick her up, grabbed her purse and shoes, and ran out of the apartment. Mercy hid in

the bushes outside the house for approximately half an hour while waiting for Pam because she was terrified defendant would look for her.

Id. at 1184–85.

Iniguez acknowledged at trial that the victim did not consent, but contended there was inadequate evidence that sex was "accomplished against a person's will by means of force, violence, or fear of immediate and unlawful bodily injury" as required by the California rape statute.[27] In rejecting that argument, the court explained:

> In *Barnes*, we . . . addressed the question of the role of force or fear of immediate and unlawful bodily injury in the absence of a resistance requirement. We stated that "[a]lthough resistance is no longer the touchstone of the element of force, the reviewing court still looks to the circumstances of the case, including the presence of verbal or nonverbal threats, or the kind of force that might reasonably induce fear in the mind of the victim, to ascertain sufficiency of the evidence . . . ."
>
> . . . [T]he element of fear of immediate and unlawful bodily injury has two components, one subjective and one objective. . . . Applying these principles, . . . [f]irst, there was substantial evidence that Mercy genuinely feared immediate and unlawful bodily injury. Mercy testified that she froze because she was afraid, and the investigating police officer testified that she told him she did not move because she feared defendant would do something violent.
>
> . . . Moreover, even absent the officer's testimony, the prosecution was not required to elicit from Mercy testimony regarding what precisely she feared. "Fear" may be inferred from the circumstances despite even superficially *contrary* testimony of the victim. (*See People v. Renteria* (1964) 61 Cal. 2d 497, 499, 39 Cal. Rptr. 213, 393 P.2d 413 [in robbery prosecution, People not bound by clerk's testimony that he was not in fear, since there was other evidence to support conclusion "that he acted in fear and would not have disgorged the contents of his employer's till except in fear of the harm which might come to him or his employer if he failed to comply with defendant's demands"]; . . . *see also People v. Brew* (1991) 2 Cal. App. 4th 99, 104, 2 Cal. Rptr. 2d 851 [cashier in retail store robbed when defendant, considerably larger than she, with alcohol on his breath, stood close to her, without barrier or counter between them, causing cashier to step back from cash register drawer in fear] . . . .)
>
> In addition, immediately after the attack, Mercy was so distraught her friend Pam could barely understand her. . . .
>
> Second, there was substantial evidence that Mercy's fear of immediate and unlawful bodily injury was reasonable. The Court of Appeal's statement[]

---

27. The current version of the statute also criminalizes sex accomplished by "duress" or "menace." Cal. Penal Code § 261(a)(2).

that defendant "did nothing to suggest that he intended to injure" Mercy . . . ignores the import of the undisputed facts. Defendant, who weighed twice as much as Mercy, accosted her while she slept in the home of a close friend, thus violating the victim's enhanced level of security and privacy.

. . . Any man or woman awakening to find himself or herself in [Mercy's] situation could reasonably react with fear of immediate and unlawful bodily injury. Sudden, unconsented-to groping, disrobing, and ensuing sexual intercourse while one appears to lie sleeping is an appalling and intolerable invasion of one's personal autonomy that, in and of itself, would reasonably cause one to react with fear.

The Court of Appeal's suggestion that Mercy could have stopped the sexual assault by screaming and thus eliciting Sandra S.'s help, disregards both the Legislature's 1980 elimination of the resistance requirement and our express language in *Barnes* upholding that amendment. It effectively guarantees an attacker freedom to intimidate his victim and exploit any resulting reasonable fear so long as she neither struggles nor cries out. There is no requirement that the victim say, "I am afraid, please stop," when it is the defendant who has created the circumstances that have so paralyzed the victim in fear and thereby submission. Moreover, it is sheer speculation that Mercy's assailant would have responded to screams by desisting the attack, and not by causing her further injury or death.

Id. at 1187–90. "In light of [its] disposition on the issue of the sufficiency of the evidence of fear of immediate and unlawful bodily injury," the court felt it was "unnecessary . . . to address the issue" whether the rape conviction could also be sustained under the portion of the California rape statute prohibiting intercourse "accomplished against a person's will by means of force." *Id.* at 1190 n.7.

Are the facts of *Berkowitz* sufficiently distinguishable from this case to justify the difference in outcome?

4. The Force Incidental to Intercourse. Do the ambiguities surrounding questions of force suggest that the force requirement should be satisfied by "the 'force' incidental to the act of intercourse"? SUSAN ESTRICH, REAL RAPE 60 (1987). In *State ex rel. M.T.S.*, 609 A.2d 1266, 1267 (N.J. 1992), the court concluded that "the element of 'physical force' is met simply by an act of non-consensual penetration involving no more force than necessary to accomplish that result." The court reasoned that the New Jersey statute, which defines sexual assault as "'sexual penetration [where] [t]he actor uses physical force or coercion,'" was intended to "focus exclusively on the forceful or assaultive conduct of the defendant" and to "eliminate any consideration of whether the victim resisted or expressed non-consent." *Id.* at 1269 n.1, 1276 (quoting N.J. Stat. Ann. § 2C:14-2c(1)). *See also People v. Griffin*, 94 P.3d 1089, 1094 (Cal. 2004) (rejecting the view that force "means force 'substantially different from or substantially greater than' the physical force normally inherent in an act of consensual sexual intercourse," and noting that, in light of the legislature's elimination of the resistance requirement and omission of a definition of the term "force," "the prosecution need only show the defendant used physical force of a degree sufficient to support a finding that the act of sexual intercourse was against the will of the [victim]") (emphasis omitted).

Other courts, however, have sided with *Berkowitz*, where the court's comparison of the definitions of rape and the lesser offense of indecent assault led it to infer "a legislative intent that the term 'forcible compulsion' [in the rape statute] . . . be interpreted as something more than a lack of consent." *See, e.g., Gibbins v. State*, 495 S.E.2d 46, 48 (Ga. Ct. App. 1997) (observing that "[i]n the ordinary case the force to which reference is made [in the rape statute] is not the force inherent in the act of penetration but is the force used to overcome the resistance of the female"), *overruled on other grounds by Hulett v. State*, 766 S.E.2d 1 (Ga. 2014); *State v. Elias*, 337 P.3d 670, 674, 676 (Idaho 2014) (requiring proof of "extrinsic force" on the grounds that otherwise "the use of force would become mere surplusage," and therefore finding insufficient evidence that digital penetration of a sleeping victim was "accomplished . . . against [her] will by use of force" given that "there was no evidence that [she] was aware of the impending penetration or that her will was rendered ineffective by [the defendant's] use of force"). *Cf. State v. Jones*, 299 P.3d 219, 229 (Idaho 2013) (finding the "extrinsic force" standard met where the defendant "leaned forward" such that the victim "was pushed down . . . to where [she] couldn't get up," with her hands "pinn[ed] underneath her so she could not turn around," and then "removed her underwear to the side," reasoning that the defendant's "use of his body weight to trap [the victim's] hands under her, and effectively forestall any struggle, seems in particular less 'incidental' to sex and far more like force employed to overcome her resistance").

5. Punishing Nonconsensual Sex. If decisions like *Berkowitz* can be justified based on statutory language requiring proof of force, should legislatures amend their criminal statutes to punish nonforcible, nonconsensual sex? In response to the controversy generated by the court's ruling in *Berkowitz*, the Pennsylvania legislature created a new crime in 1995 called "sexual assault," which it defined as "sexual intercourse or deviate sexual intercourse with a complainant without the complainant's consent." 18 Pa. Cons. Stat. § 3124.1. Sexual assault is a second-degree felony in Pennsylvania, punishable by a maximum prison term of 10 years, compared to rape, which is a first-degree felony generally punishable by 20 years. (Indecent assault, the crime for which Berkowitz was convicted, is a second-degree misdemeanor punishable by two years in prison.) For an illustration of a case prosecuted under the sexual assault provision, see *Commonwealth v. Smith*, 863 A.2d 1172, 1176–77 (Pa. Super. Ct. 2004) (affirming conviction where defendant threatened to reveal 16-year-old victim's lesbian relationship to her mother unless the girl had sex with him).

Like Pennsylvania, almost all state legislatures have now made sexual intercourse or contact without consent a separate crime. *See* Corey Rayburn Yung, *Rape Law Gatekeeping*, 58 B.C. L. Rev. 206, 211 n.32 (2017) (citing statutes from every state except Iowa and Maryland). In some jurisdictions, however, the impact of this legislation is limited, either because the provisions are included only in the less serious sex offenses that criminalize sexual contact and not penetration, or because the statute's definition of "nonconsent" requires proof of either forcible compulsion or the victim's incapacity to consent. *See* John F. Decker & Peter G. Baroni, *"No" Still Means "Yes": The Failure of the "Non-Consent" Reform Movement in American Rape and Sexual Assault Law*, 101 J. Crim. L. & Criminology 1081, 1084–85 (2011); *see also* Deborah Tuerkheimer, *Rape on and off Campus*, 65 Emory L.J. 1, 15 & nn.73–74 (2015) (noting that 37 states plus the District of Columbia still include a force requirement in their definition of either rape or nonconsent).

New Hampshire is one of the minority of jurisdictions that does not require proof of force for its most serious sex offense. In that state, aggravated felonious sexual assault includes cases where "the victim indicates by speech or conduct that there is not freely given consent to performance of the sexual act." N.H. Rev. Stat. Ann. §632-A:2(m). New Hampshire was the site of the highly publicized 2015 sexual assault trial of Owen Labrie, an 18-year-old senior at St. Paul's, an exclusive prep school. Prosecutors contended that Labrie sexually assaulted a 15-year-old freshman as part of a school ritual called the Senior Salute, a competition to see which student could "slay" the most girls before graduation (meaning sexual behavior ranging from kissing to intercourse). The victim agreed to meet Labrie after hours in a school building and allowed him to remove her shirt and shorts, but she testified that he ignored her when she told him several times that she wanted to go no further and instead penetrated her with his penis, fingers, and tongue. The victim admitted exchanging friendly notes with Labrie after the incident, but said that they did not reflect her consent, but instead her fear of Labrie and efforts to appease him. At trial, Labrie denied that they had had sex. The jury acquitted him of aggravated felonious sexual assault, but convicted him of misdemeanor statutory rape and the felony charge of using the Internet to solicit sex from a minor. He was sentenced to a year in jail and five years' probation, and is required to register as a sex offender. Labrie is out on bail pending appeal. *See* Matthew Cooper, *How a '90s Internet Law Determined a 2014 Rape Case*, Newsweek, Jan. 8, 2016, *available at* http://www.newsweek.com/2016/01/08/owen-labrie-breaks -his-silence-internet-sex-solicitation-case-st-pauls-406683.html.

Are states like New Hampshire wise to move away from the traditional focus on force because "the fundamental wrong at which the law of rape is aimed is not the application of physical force that causes physical harm" but rather the violation of "the integrity of a woman's will and the privacy of her sexuality"? *People v. Griffin*, 94 P.3d 1089, 1094 (Cal. 2004). Or is "[t]he turn to consent . . . essentially lawless, because there is no determinate and widely-shared understanding of what constitutes consent"? Donald Dripps, *After Rape Law: Will the Turn to Consent Normalize the Prosecution of Sexual Assault?*, 41 Akron L. Rev. 957, 958 (2008). Does the Labrie verdict illustrate Dripps' point or the jury's unwillingness to follow the letter of the law?

6. Threats of Nonphysical Force. Traditionally, rape's "force" requirement has been satisfied only by evidence that the defendant used or threatened *physical* force.

In *Commonwealth v. Mlinarich*, 542 A.2d 1335 (Pa. 1988), for example, the 63-year-old defendant had custody of the victim, a 14-year-old girl who had previously been living in a detention home. The defendant engaged in "sustained, systematic sexual abuse" of the victim, threatening to send her back to the detention home if she refused to have intercourse with him. *Id.* at 1342 (Larsen, J., dissenting). The Pennsylvania Supreme Court affirmed the Superior Court's reversal of the defendant's rape conviction by an equally divided vote. Although the three justices who voted to reverse the conviction thought that the "forcible compulsion" required by the Pennsylvania statute encompassed both "physical force" and "psychological duress," they concluded:

> The critical distinction is where the compulsion overwhelms the will of the victim in contrast to a situation where the victim can make a deliberate choice to avoid the encounter even though the alternative may be an undesirable one. Indeed, the victim in this instance apparently found the prospect of being returned to the detention home a repugnant one. Notwithstanding, she was left with a choice and therefore the submission was a result of a deliberate choice and was not an involuntary act.

Id. at 1338, 1341 (Nix, C.J., concurring).

Likewise, in *State v. Thompson*, 792 P.2d 1103 (Mont. 1990), *overruled on other grounds by State v. Spreadbury*, 257 P.3d 392 (Mont. 2011), the Montana Supreme Court affirmed the dismissal of two counts of rape filed against a principal who threatened to prevent a high school senior from graduating unless she had sex with him. Although the court acknowledged that the defendant had "intimidated" the victim, it was reluctant to "stretch the definition of force to include intimidation, fear, or apprehension." *Id.* at 1106.

The Superior Court's opinion in *Mlinarich* defended this traditional approach as follows:

> If a man takes a destitute widow into his home and provides support for her and her family, [a broader] definition of forcible compulsion will convict him of attempted rape if he threatens to withdraw his support and compel her to leave unless she engages in sexual intercourse. Similarly, a person may be guilty of rape if he or she extorts sexual favors from another person upon threat of discharging the other or his or her spouse from a position of employment, or upon threat of foreclosing the mortgage on the home of the other's parents, or upon threat of denying a loan application, or upon threat of disclosing the other's adultery or submission to an abortion. . . .
>
> . . . To allow a conviction for rape where the alleged victim has deliberately chosen intercourse in preference to some other unpleasant sensation not amounting to physical injury or violence would be to trivialize the plight of the helpless victim of a violent rape. . . . The two scenarios, although reprehensible, are not the same.

People v. Mlinarich, 498 A.2d 395, 402 (Pa. Super. Ct. 1985), *aff'd by an equally divided court*, 542 A.2d 1335 (Pa. 1988).

Recently, some state legislatures have abandoned this limited view of force and have criminalized sex obtained by certain nonphysical forms of coercion. *See* John F. Decker & Peter G. Baroni, *"No" Still Means "Yes": The Failure of the "Non-Consent" Reform Movement in American Rape and Sexual Assault Law*, 101 J. Crim. L. & Criminology 1081, 1120 (2011) (listing 18 states that include threats of non-physical force in their sex offense statutes). Following the Montana Supreme Court's decision in *Thompson*, for example, the legislature in that state amended the definition of "force" to include "the threat of substantial retaliatory action that causes the victim to reasonably believe that the offender has the ability to execute the threat." Mont. Code Ann. § 45-5-501(2)(b). Likewise, the Pennsylvania legislature defined "forcible compulsion" in the wake of the *Berkowitz* decision as "[c]ompulsion by use of physical, intellectual, moral, emotional or psychological force, either express or implied." 18 Pa. Cons. Stat. § 3101. *But cf.* Decker & Baroni, *supra*, at 1125 (charging that many of these statutes "lack teeth" because, for example, they do not define the terms "coercion" and "extortion" or classify the crime as a misdemeanor, and inferring from the fact that "[t]he case law is very scarce in this area" that most defendants are not charged or are acquitted).

For illustrations of cases applying a broader conception of force, see *Halton v. Hesson*, 803 F. Supp. 1272, 1278–79 (M.D. Tenn. 1992) (applying the Tennessee rape statute, which criminalizes intercourse accomplished by means of "force or coercion" and defines "coercion" to include a "threat of kidnapping, extortion, force or violence," and finding sufficient evidence of "coercion" to support conviction of juvenile detention center guard who threatened to keep 15-year-old inmate at the detention center); *Gibbins v. State*, 495 S.E.2d 46, 49 (Ga. Ct. App. 1997) (holding that "evidence of force through intimidation" satisfies the rape statute, and thus affirming conviction of defendant who told his stepdaughter that "she and her mother would be out on the streets" if she told anyone about his sexual abuse); *State v. Meyers*, 799 N.W.2d 132, 146–47 (Iowa 2011) (concluding that "psychological force . . . may give rise to a conviction under the 'against the will' element" of a statute prohibiting sex "by force or against the will" of the victim, and finding sufficient evidence there, where the defendant "engaged in a sexual and romantic relationship with his high-school-age stepdaughter while she was in a very vulnerable psychological state . . . due to her crack cocaine addiction, her estrangement from her mother, . . . her need for support and shelter, [and] the history of sexual and physical abuse [he had] inflicted [on her] in the past"); *State v. Brooks*, 317 P.3d 54, 65 (Kan. 2014) (affirming conviction where defendant threatened to divulge the victim's affair with a married coworker under the portion of the rape statute criminalizing "nonconsensual intercourse . . . under circumstances when [the victim] was overcome by fear"); *State v. Lovely*, 480 A.2d 847, 849, 850 (N.H. 1984) (applying sexual assault statute that prohibits "coerc[ing] the victim to submit by threatening to retaliate"—where "retaliation" is defined to include threats of "extortion" or "[p]ublic humiliation or disgrace"—and affirming conviction of defendant who threatened his male employee with loss of employment and housing if he did not submit to sex).

Is the broader concept of force applied in these opinions preferable because limiting rape to cases involving physical violence means that "the only men who are labeled 'rapists' are those men with a limited repertoire, who lack the power, money or training to employ more sophisticated strategies of persuasion/coercion"? Lorenne M.G. Clark & Debra J. Lewis, Rape: The Price of Coercive Sexuality 143 (1977). Or is the traditional approach more appropriate because "[i]f the ability 'to constrain [by] moral or intellectual means or by the exigencies of the circumstances' is sufficient, then rape (by one party or another) lurks in the background of most intimate relationships"? Stephen J. Schulhofer, *Taking Sexual Autonomy Seriously: Rape Law and Beyond*, 11 Law & Phil. 35, 51–52 (1992).

7. Fraud. Consistent with the traditional view that rape must be accomplished by physical force is the notion that fraud or deception on the part of the defendant is insufficient to support a rape charge. For example, in *People v. Evans*, 379 N.Y.S.2d 912, 914 (N.Y. Sup. Ct. 1975) (described above in Note 5 following *State v. Rusk*), the court commented that "there are some patterns of aggression or aggressive male sexual behavior towards females which do not deserve [the] extreme penalties" that flow from a rape conviction—for example, the court said, cases in which "the male objective [is] achieved through charm or guile or protestations of love, promises or deceit." The court explained:

> Where force is not employed to overcome reluctance, and where consent, however reluctant initially, can be spelled out, this we label "seduction," which society may condone, even as it disapproves.
>
> . . . .
>
> . . . The prevailing view in this country is that there can be no rape which is achieved by fraud, or trick, or stratagem. Provided there is actual consent, the nature of the act being understood, it is not rape, absent a statute, no matter how despicable the fraud. . . . "Fraud cannot be allowed to supply the place of the force which the statute makes mandatory."

Id. at 914, 918–19.

Compare Jane E. Larson, *"Women Understand So Little, They Call My Good Nature 'Deceit'": A Feminist Rethinking of Seduction*, 93 Colum. L. Rev. 374, 418–19 (1993):

> A victim's will may be bent to the coercer's ends by means other than physical force. Force, fear, and fraud work in much the same way: The wrongdoer arranges the victim's world so that the act he wants her to perform appears as her best choice. The victim then makes the desired choice and does what the coercer wants. Yet the victim's perceptions have been manipulated so as to bend her will to another's purposes. . . . Only a shallow and formalistic understanding of moral agency and rational action would allow us to believe that the victim has "chosen" anything under these circumstances.

As the *Evans* court implied, deception as to the nature of the act itself—fraud in the factum—was deemed to vitiate consent even under the traditional approach. Thus, for example, rape convictions have been upheld in cases where women undergoing gynecological examinations were unexpectedly penetrated. Such cases involve fraud in the factum because the women consented to a medical examination, not to sexual intercourse. *See, e.g., People v. Minkowski*, 23 Cal. Rptr. 92, 94 (Cal. Ct. App. 1962); *McNair v. State*, 825 P.2d 571, 574–75 (Nev. 1992). In some states, impersonating the victim's husband is also considered fraud in the factum. *See* John F. Decker & Peter G. Baroni, *"No" Still Means "Yes": The Failure of the "Non-Consent" Reform Movement in American Rape and Sexual Assault Law*, 101 J. Crim. L. & Criminology 1081, 1136–37 (2011) (citing seven state statutes). *But cf. Suliveres v. Commonwealth*, 865 N.E.2d 1086 (Mass. 2007) (dismissing rape charges on the grounds that impersonating the victim's boyfriend was not fraud in the factum).

On the other hand, fraud in the inducement—where the victim understood the sexual nature of the act, but consented to it because of some fraudulent misrepresentation—has traditionally been insufficient to support a rape conviction. *But cf.* Jed Rubenfeld, *The Riddle of Rape-by-Deception and the Myth of Sexual Autonomy*, 122 Yale L.J. 1372, 1398 (2013) (arguing that this distinction "makes no sense" because "countless cases involving larceny, trespass, and contract" demonstrate that "it's simply false that 'fraud in the inducement' fails to vitiate consent elsewhere in the law").

An illustration of a case applying the traditional approach is *Boro v. Superior Court*, 210 Cal. Rptr. 122 (Cal. Ct. App. 1985), where the court dismissed a rape charge brought against a man who made random phone calls to numerous women, posing as a doctor and claiming to have results of blood tests and pap smears showing that the women had a fatal blood disease. Boro told the women that the disease could be cured only by a costly and painful surgical procedure or by the less expensive alternative of having sex with a man who had been injected with a special serum. While most of the women Boro called refused to talk to him, he used this ruse to persuade at least seven women to have sex with him over a three-year period (and some of them paid him sums ranging up to $1,500). *See* Lauren Blau, *Police Seek More Victims in 'Cure' Fraud*, L.A. Times, Mar. 31, 1987, at B12. In dismissing the rape charge, the court explained that the victim "precisely understood the 'nature of the act,' but, motivated by a fear of disease, and death, succumbed to petitioner's fraudulent blandishments." *Boro*, 210 Cal. Rptr. at 126. *See also State v. Bolsinger*, 709 N.W.2d 560, 562, 564 (Iowa 2006) (concluding that defendant's sexual abuse of boys at the camp where he worked was accomplished by means of fraud in the inducement, rather than fraud in the factum, given that the boys were told the defendant was going to "touch their genitals," purportedly to "check for bruises, scratches, hernias, and testicular cancer," and "the victims were touched in exactly the manner represented to them").

The court's decision in *Boro* prompted the California legislature to make it a crime, punishable by a maximum prison term of four years, to "induce[] any other person to engage in sexual intercourse . . . by false or fraudulent representation or pretense that is made with the intent to create fear [of physical injury or death to the victim or a relative], and which does induce fear, and that would cause a reasonable person in like circumstances to act contrary to the person's free will, and does cause the victim to so act." Cal. Penal Code § 266c. Boro was subsequently arrested and charged under that statute; he pled guilty to lesser misdemeanor charges. *See also* Decker & Baroni, *supra*, at 1137–40 (describing other state statutes that likewise punish "medical" or "therapeutic deception").

The Tennessee legislature has gone even further, including within its definition of rape "sexual penetration . . . accomplished by fraud," with "fraud" broadly defined to include "deceit, trickery, misrepresentation and subterfuge." Tenn. Code Ann. §§ 39-13-503(a)(4), 39-11-106(a)(13). A 45-year-old businessman was convicted under this provision and sentenced to 15 years in prison after calling hundreds of women in the middle of the night, pretending to be their boyfriends, and asking them in whispered tones to indulge his sexual fantasy based on the movie *9½ Weeks*. Although most of the women hung up on him, eight followed his instructions, unlocked their doors, blindfolded themselves, removed their clothes, and then had intercourse with him. The appellate court affirmed the conviction, rejecting the defendant's argument that the Tennessee statute is unconstitutionally vague and overbroad. *See State v. Mitchell*, 1999 Tenn. Crim. App. Lexis 772 (Tenn. Crim. App. July 30, 1999); *Jury Sees Fantasy as Rape*, Newsday, Jan. 20, 1996, at A13. *See also The Queen v. Cuerrier*, [1998] 2 S.C.R. 371 (Can.) (holding that failure to disclose HIV status is a type of fraud that vitiates consent); Decker & Baroni, *supra*, at 1133–35, 1146 (listing eight states in addition to Tennessee that criminalize sex obtained by fraud, but noting that these cases are "rarely prosecuted").

Does the Tennessee statute create intractable line-drawing problems? Is "deceptive sex, however bad it may be," not "that bad" because even if it is "a gross exaggeration to say that everyone lies on the way to sex, in the sense of verbally stating untruths," "almost all of us surely conceal" and "many of us . . . tacitly mislead"? Rubenfeld, *supra*, at 1416. *See also* David P. Bryden, *Redefining Rape*, 3 Buff. Crim. L. Rev. 317, 463 (2000) (arguing that the fact that "sex is typically pleasurable in itself" makes it "less clear whether the sexual encounter would have occurred without the deception and also whether the deception destroyed the value of the encounter to the victim"). On the other hand, is it possible to distinguish "material" misrepresentations that would be "important to an ordinary man or woman's decision to consent to sex" from "trivial lies . . . or forms of politeness that mislead few"? Larson, *supra*, at 462. *See also* Deborah Tuerkheimer, *Sex Without Consent*, 123 Yale L.J. Online 335, 343 (2013) (observing that "lines can surely be drawn . . . [j]ust as in other contexts in which consent must be evaluated, [where] what constitutes being 'informed' is a matter of degree"). (Compare the standards of materiality used in defining the crime of theft by false pretenses, discussed in Chapter 8, Section D.)

8. Comparing Other Crimes. In distinguishing between force and deception in *People v. Evans*, 379 N.Y.S.2d 912, 919 (N.Y. Sup. Ct. 1975) (described in the prior Note), the court observed:

> The law recognizes that there are some crimes where trickery and deceit do constitute the basis for a criminal charge. Since the common law, we have recognized the existence of larceny by trick. But of course, for a larceny there has to be a taking of property of value. I do not mean to imply that a woman's right to her body is not a thing of value, but it is not property in the sense which is defined by law.

In *Commonwealth v. Caracciola*, 569 N.E.2d 774, 777 (Mass. 1991), by contrast, the court concluded that force encompasses forms of coercion that do not rise to the level of physical violence, relying in part on the fact that the element of force required in robbery cases includes both actual and constructive force:

> In robbery cases, we said that "[w]hether actual or constructive force is employed, the degree of force is immaterial so long as it is sufficient to obtain the victim's property 'against his will.'" Thus, a purse snatching that is accomplished with force "sufficient to produce awareness, although the action may be so swift as to leave the victim momentarily in a dazed condition," is considered a robbery rather than a larceny which is theft without force. Moreover, a victim's statement that "I was scared to death" is sufficient to show the use of force if the jury decides that "her fear aided the defendant in effecting the taking." The defendant's argument that physical force is a required element in rape cases asks us to assume that the Legislature intended to give greater protection to property than to bodily integrity. We decline to make such an unwarranted assumption.

Consider also Susan Estrich, Real Rape 40–41, 70 (1987):

> The requirement that the victim of a simple rape do more than say no was virtually without precedent in the criminal law. Many other crimes encompass a consent defense; none other has defined it so as to mandate actual physical resistance. In trespass, the posting of a sign or the offering of verbal warnings generally suffices to meet the victim's burden of nonconsent. . . .

> In robbery, claims that the victim cooperated with the taking of the money or eased the way, and thus consented, have been generally unsuccessful. Only where the owner of the property actively participates in planning and committing the theft will consent be found; mere "passive submission" or "passive assent" does not amount to consent—except in the law of rape. . . .

> . . . .

> [Moreover, the] breadth of "seduction" in the context of sexual relations is without parallel in criminal law. Had the men in these cases been seeking money instead of sex, their actions would be in plain violation of traditional

state criminal prohibitions. . . . [H]ad [Mr. Evans] sought money as part of his "sociological test" rather than sex, he . . . could have been guilty of theft. Neither could [he] have escaped liability on the grounds that a "reasonable person" would not have been deceived, any more than a victim's leaving his front door unlocked or his keys in the automobile ignition serves as a defense to burglary or larceny. Had Mr. Rusk . . . simply taken the woman's car, he would have been guilty of larceny or theft. And had Mr. Mlinarich threatened to send the victim to reform school were he not paid off with money instead of sex, he might well have been guilty of state law extortion.

Are these analogies persuasive, or is the crime of rape different in some respect? Recall that the California Supreme Court in *People v. Iniguez* (described above in Note 3) looked to robbery cases in defining the California rape statute's reference to "fear." (For a discussion of robbery, see Chapter 9, Section A. For a discussion of extortion, see Chapter 9, Section B.)

9. Grading Nonforcible, Nonconsensual Intercourse. If it is appropriate to criminalize nonconsensual intercourse that does not involve the use or threat of physical force, what is the appropriate penalty? Recall that, as discussed above in Note 5, the jurisdictions that punish sexual activity without consent often grade that offense as a misdemeanor. One commentator offered the following justification for that model:

> Physical violence in general does far more harm to the victim's welfare than an unwanted sex act. Physical violence in general expresses a more complete indifference, or a more intense hostility, to the victim's humanity. . . .
>
> . . . [P]eople generally, male and female, would rather be subjected to unwanted sex than be shot, slashed, or beaten with a tire iron. . . . [W]hether measured by the welfare or by the dignity of the victim, as a general matter unwanted sex is not as bad as violence. I think it follows that those who press sexual advances in the face of refusal act less wickedly than those who shoot, or slash, or batter.

Donald A. Dripps, *Beyond Rape: An Essay on the Difference Between the Presence of Force and the Absence of Consent*, 92 Colum. L. Rev. 1780, 1792, 1800–01 (1992).

Compare Susan Estrich, Real Rape 103–04 (1987):

> What makes both the "violent rapist" and the stepfather whose feelings "get out of hand" different and more serious offenders than those who commit assault or robbery is the injury to personal integrity involved in forced sex. That injury is the reason that forced sex should be considered a serious crime even where there is no weapon or beating. Whether one adheres to the "rape as sex" school or the "rape as violence" school, the fact remains that what makes rape, whether "simple" or "aggravated," different from other crimes is that rape is a sexual violation—a violation of the most personal, most intimate, and most offensive kind.

Consider also Robin L. West, *Legitimating the Illegitimate: A Comment on* Beyond Rape, 93 Colum. L. Rev. 1442, 1448 (1993):

> Dripps's [argument] wildly misdescribes the experience of rape. . . . What it rather strikingly omits is the violence, and hence the injury, of the penetration itself. *From the victim's perspective*, unwanted sexual penetration involves unwanted force, and unwanted force *is* violent. . . . Th[at] offense . . . is *itself* a forceful, physical, and . . . assaultive penetration of one person's body by another.

10. Rape and the Death Penalty. In *Coker v. Georgia*, 433 U.S. 584 (1977) (plurality opinion), the Supreme Court struck down a Georgia statute that authorized the death penalty in some rape cases. The four Justices in the plurality thought that "[s]hort of homicide, [rape] is the 'ultimate violation of self,' " but they ultimately concluded that the death penalty is "grossly disproportionate and excessive punishment for the crime of rape" and thus violative of the Eighth Amendment's ban on cruel and unusual punishment. *Id.* at 597, 592.

In a separate opinion, Justice Powell agreed that the death penalty was "unacceptable . . . in the absence of excessive brutality or severe injury," but he believed that it might be constitutional if limited to cases of "aggravated rape":

> "[T]here is extreme variation in the degree of culpability of rapists." The deliberate viciousness of the rapist may be greater than that of the murderer. Rape is never an act committed accidentally. Rarely can it be said to be unpremeditated. There is also wide variation in the effect on the victim. . . . Some victims are so grievously injured physically or psychologically that life *is* beyond repair.

Id. at 604, 603 (Powell, J., concurring in the judgment in part and dissenting in part).

Although they agreed that rape is a very serious crime, women's organizations sided with the defendant in *Coker* given the racially discriminatory fashion in which the death penalty had historically been imposed in rape cases. Noting that rape was traditionally a crime of property, the amicus brief filed by the American Civil Liberties Union in *Coker* observed:

> Rape of white women by black men threatened the white man's status by decreasing the value of his sexual possession . . . and by jeopardizing the "purity" of his race, and it was therefore necessary to take extreme measures to prevent this result. Lynching was one such measure; a double standard of justice for weighing rape by white men and by black men was another; and the death penalty for rape—particularly when perpetrated by blacks—was yet a third.

Brief Amici Curiae of the American Civil Liberties Union at 14–16, *quoted in* Nancy S. Erickson & Nadine Taub, *Final Report: "Sex Bias in the Teaching of Criminal Law"*, 42 Rutgers L. Rev. 309, 373–74 (1990). *See also* Jennifer Wriggins, Note, *Rape, Racism, and the Law*, 6 Harv. Women's L.J. 103, 105–06, 112–13 (1983) (noting that rape laws in effect prior to the Civil War imposed the death penalty on African-American men who raped white women, but did not even criminalize the rape of African-American women; that 36 percent of African-American men convicted of raping white women between 1930 and 1967 were executed, compared to only two percent of all other rape defendants; and that judges tend to impose harsher sentences on African-American men who rape white women and more lenient sentences when the victim is African-American). (Recall as well the excerpt from Angela Harris' article reprinted above in Part 1.)

Almost 20 years after *Coker*, six state legislatures—beginning with Louisiana in 1995—amended their death penalty statutes to make the rape of a child a capital offense. The Supreme Court struck down the Louisiana statute in *Kennedy v. Louisiana*, 554 U.S. 407 (2008), refusing to limit *Coker* to adult victims and concluding that imposing a death sentence for the crime of child rape is likewise cruel and unusual punishment. For a discussion of *Coker* and *Kennedy* in the context of the Supreme Court's death penalty jurisprudence, see Chapter 6, Section E.2, Note 6 preceding *Lockett v. Ohio*.

11. The Model Penal Code Approach. The Model Penal Code separates sexual offenses into various categories in an attempt to distinguish among defendants of differing culpability. The most serious crime under the MPC is *rape*, which is defined to encompass cases where the defendant "compels [the victim] to submit [to intercourse] by force or by threat of imminent death, serious bodily injury, extreme pain or kidnapping, to be inflicted on anyone." Model Penal Code § 213.1(1)(a). The MPC thus fails to include absence of consent as an element of rape. Although the Comments recognize that the victim's consent is not irrelevant—"[c]ompulsion plainly implies non-consent"—the drafters chose to focus on the actions of the defendant rather than the victim. *Id.* § 213.1 Comment at 306. The MPC also rejects any statutory requirement of resistance on the part of the victim, both because resistance may be dangerous and because "it is wrong to excuse the male assailant on the ground that his victim failed to protect herself with the dedication and intensity that a court might expect of a reasonable person in her situation." *Id.* at 305. Likewise, the MPC refuses to require that the victim's fear was reasonable: "Neither the blameworthiness of the actor nor the gravity of the insult to the victim is ameliorated by a finding that the threat was implausible or that the actor lacked capacity to carry it out." *Id.* at 310.

Rape is normally a second-degree felony under the Model Penal Code, but it is elevated to a first-degree felony when the defendant "inflicts serious injury upon anyone," or when "the victim was not a voluntary social companion of the actor upon the occasion of the crime and had not previously permitted him sexual liberties." *Id.* § 213.1(1). Although the MPC does not define the terms "voluntary social companion" and "sexual liberties," the Comments explain the "voluntary social companion" limitation on two grounds: "the gravity of the wrong is arguably less severe" when the defendant and the victim had a prior sexual relationship; and "the fact that the actor is a stranger to the victim, or the fact that sexual liberties have not been permitted in the past, is strong objective corroboration of the fact that the sexual act was accomplished by imposition." *Id.* § 213.1 Comment at 307.

The Model Penal Code also punishes sexual intercourse with certain incapacitated victims. Rape charges can be brought where the victim is unconscious or where her "power to appraise or control her conduct" is "substantially impaired" due to drugs or alcohol the defendant "administer[ed] . . . without her knowledge . . . for the purpose of preventing resistance." *Id.* § 213.1(1)(b)-(c). *Gross sexual imposition*, a third-degree felony, includes cases where the defendant knows the victim is "incapable of appraising the nature of her conduct" because of a "mental disease or defect." *Id.* § 213.1(2)(b).

The definition of gross sexual imposition also encompasses some cases of non-physical force: where the defendant "compels [the victim] to submit [to sexual intercourse] by any threat that would prevent resistance by a woman of ordinary resolution." *Id.* § 213.1(2)(a). Although the drafters recognized that "the distinction between coercion and bargain . . . is a task of surpassing subtlety . . . in borderline situations," they concluded that threats like the loss of a job or a "valued possession" "may be sufficient to deny the freedom of choice that the law of rape and related offenses seeks to protect and to subject a woman to unwanted and degrading sexual intimacy." *Id.* § 213.1 Comment at 314, 312.

Gross sexual imposition also includes those cases of deception where the defendant "knows that [the victim] is unaware that a sexual act is being committed on her or that she submits because she mistakenly supposes that he is her husband." *Id.* § 213.1(2)(c). In addition, the MPC includes within the misdemeanor crime of *seduction* cases where a woman "is induced to participate [in intercourse] by a promise of marriage which the actor does not mean to perform." *Id.* § 213.3(1)(d). The MPC refuses to punish other forms of deceptive conduct on the ground that they are not easily distinguishable from "many instances of ordinary seduction." *Id.* § 213.1 Comment at 331.

Each of these offenses is written in gendered terms, envisioning a male defendant and female victim. The gender-neutral counterpart to rape, which applies to anyone who has deviate sexual intercourse (e.g., oral or anal sex) under circumstances that would otherwise qualify as rape, is called *deviate sexual intercourse by force* and is a second-degree felony. *See id.* § 213.2(1). *Deviate sexual intercourse by imposition* is the comparable gender-neutral equivalent for gross sexual imposition and is graded as a third-degree felony. *See id.* § 213.2(2). The misdemeanor *sexual assault*, also a gender-neutral crime, punishes "sexual contact"—sexual touching of "intimate parts of the [victim] for the purpose of arousing or gratifying sexual desire"—where, for example, the defendant knows the sexual contact is "offensive" to the victim. *Id.* § 213.4.

12. Special Procedural Rules for Rape Cases. The Model Penal Code endorses three procedural requirements that were traditionally applied in rape cases but have now been eliminated or relaxed in most jurisdictions. Although these three rules are likewise being reconsidered during the MPC's revision process, the Model Penal Code prohibits prosecution of any sexual offense unless the victim filed a complaint within three months. *See* Model Penal Code § 213.6(4). The Comments offer two rationales for this prompt-complaint requirement: that it protects against the danger that "unwanted pregnancy or bitterness at a relationship gone sour might convert a willing participant in sexual relations into a vindictive complainant"; and that it "limits the opportunity for blackmailing another by threatening to bring a criminal charge of sexual aggression." *Id.* § 213.6 Comment at 421. Although no state adheres to this strict rule today, the timeliness of a victim's complaint is still admissible in most jurisdictions to shed light on her credibility. *See, e.g., People v. Brown,* 883 P.2d 949 (Cal. 1994); *Commonwealth v. Dillon,* 925 A.2d 131 (Pa. 2007). *See generally* Michelle J. Anderson, *The Legacy of the Prompt Complaint Requirement, Corroboration Requirement, and Cautionary Instructions on Campus Sexual Assault,* 84 B.U. L. Rev. 945, 964–68 (2004).

Second, the Model Penal Code endorses a form of the so-called Hale instruction, which warns juries to view a rape victim's testimony with caution. *See* Model Penal Code § 213.6(5). Until the 1970s, a majority of states required trial judges to give such an instruction, even though it was not used in other criminal trials where victims testified for the prosecution. Although most states have now abandoned the instruction, it is still given in some jurisdictions where a rape victim's testimony is not corroborated. *See* Anderson, *supra*, at 976–77 (citing eight states).

Third, the Model Penal Code retains for felony sex offenses the traditional rule that the victim's uncorroborated testimony is insufficient to support a rape conviction (even though her unsubstantiated testimony could support an assault or theft conviction). *See* Model Penal Code § 213.6(5). The Comments explain this rule as "an attempt to skew resolution of . . . disputes in favor of the defendant," given "the difficulty of defending against false accusation of a sexual offense." *Id.* § 213.6 Comment at 428. Every state except Mississippi has now abolished the corroboration requirement, *see* Miss. Code Ann. § 97-3-69, although a few jurisdictions still adhere to it in certain cases. *See* John F. Decker & Peter G. Baroni, *"No" Still Means "Yes": The Failure of the "Non-Consent" Reform Movement in American Rape and Sexual Assault Law,* 101 J. Crim. L. & Criminology 1081, 1148–49, 1151 (2011) (citing three state statutes that retain a corroboration rule in limited circumstances and case law in another 10 states that requires corroboration if "the victim's story is physically impossible or so inherently improbable that no reasonable person could believe it").

For the view that, "contrary to the assumptions of legal scholars formulating these [three] doctrines, most victims of rape do not promptly complain to the police or other authorities, most rapes do not produce corroborating evidence, and most jurors are already cautioned by an underlying societal bias against those who claim rape," see Anderson, *supra*, at 952–53.

In addition to abandoning these special procedural rules, most legislatures enacted rape-shield laws as part of rape reform legislation passed during the 1970s. Although the specific contours of these statutes vary greatly among the states, their primary purpose is to limit the admissibility of evidence describing the victim's sexual history. Such evidence had traditionally been considered relevant both to support the defendant's claim of consent and to cast doubt on the credibility of the victim's testimony. *See generally* Harriet R. Galvin, *Shielding Rape Victims in the State and Federal Courts: A Proposal for the Second Decade*, 70 Minn. L. Rev. 763 (1986); J. Alexander Tanford & Anthony J. Bocchino, *Rape Victim Shield Laws and the Sixth Amendment*, 128 U. Pa. L. Rev. 544 (1980). For a discussion of the rape-shield issues that arose when rape charges were brought against basketball star Kobe Bryant, see Richard I. Haddad, *Shield or Sieve?* People v. Bryant *and the Rape Shield Law in High-Profile Cases*, 39 Colum. J.L. & Soc. Probs. 185 (2005).

13. The Proposed Revisions to the Model Penal Code. Apparently agreeing with the view that the 50-year-old Model Penal Code provisions on sex offenses are "outdated," Deborah W. Denno, *Why the Model Penal Code's Sexual Assault Provisions Should Be Pulled and Replaced*, 1 Ohio St. J. Crim. L. 207, 207 (2003), the American Law Institute decided in 2012 to reconsider the MPC's approach to these crimes. Like the current version of the Model Penal Code, the revisions would create a number of distinct crimes, but the names and elements of those offenses differ greatly from the existing MPC provisions.

The process is still ongoing, but the most recent proposal, released in 2016, has seven offenses linked to sexual penetration (in addition to the three described above in Note 8 in Section A's materials on statutory rape). "Sexual penetration" is defined to include "any act involving penetration, however slight, of the anus or vulva by any object or body part, unless done for bona fide medical, hygienic, or law-enforcement purposes," as well as "direct contact between the mouth or tongue of one person and the anus, penis, or vulva of another." Model Penal Code: Sexual Assault and Related Offenses § 213.0(7) (Tentative Draft No. 2, 2016).

The proposed revisions would define *forcible rape*, a second-degree felony punishable by up to 20 years in prison, to include cases where the defendant knowingly or recklessly (1) "uses physical force, physical restraint, or an implied or express threat of physical force, bodily injury, or physical restraint to cause another person to engage in an act of sexual penetration," or (2) "threatens to inflict bodily injury" on someone other than the victim or "to commit any other crime of violence." *Id.* § 213.1(2). The crime would be elevated to *aggravated forcible rape*, a first-degree felony punishable by up to life in prison, if it is committed under certain aggravating circumstances: where the defendant knowingly or recklessly "uses a deadly weapon," "causes serious bodily injury," or is assisted by another person who is "present at the time." *Id.* § 213.1(1).

The proposed revisions would define *sexual penetration without consent*, a fourth-degree felony punishable by up to five years in prison, as nonconsensual penetration where the defendant acts knowingly or recklessly with respect to the absence of consent. *See* Model Penal Code: Sexual Assault and Related Offenses § 213.2 (Tentative

Draft No. 2 — Errata, 2016). The definition of consent, which is set out in Note 10 in Part 2 above and is the only part of the revisions that has been approved thus far, makes clear that no verbal or physical resistance is necessary to prove nonconsent, but that lack of resistance "may be considered, in the context of all the circumstances," in evaluating whether consent was given. Model Penal Code: Sexual Assault and Related Offenses §213.0(3)(c) (approved Oct. 2016), http://www.theali adviser.org/sexual-assault/updated-consent-definition/.

The revisions include two charges related to penetration of a "vulnerable person." *Rape of a vulnerable person*, a second-degree felony, occurs when the defendant knowingly or recklessly disregards a risk that the victim: (1) is "sleeping, unconscious, or physically unable to communicate . . . refusal" "by words or actions"; (2) is "unable to express refusal, by words or actions, . . . because of mental disorder or disability, whether temporary or permanent"; or (3) "lacks substantial capacity to appraise or control his or her conduct" because of drugs or alcohol that the defendant "administered" without the victim's knowledge "for the purpose of impairing [that] person's capacity to communicate . . . refusal." Model Penal Code: Sexual Assault and Related Offenses §213.3(1) (Tentative Draft No. 2, 2016).

The second such charge, *sexual penetration of a vulnerable person*, is a third-degree felony punishable by a maximum 10-year sentence and encompasses cases of penetration where the defendant knowingly or recklessly disregards a risk that the victim: (1) is "mentally [or] developmentally disabled, or mentally incapacitated, whether temporarily or permanently," such that the victim is "incapable of understanding the physiological nature of sexual penetration, its potential for causing pregnancy, or its potential for transmitting disease"; (2) is "mentally or developmentally disabled" such that the victim's "social and intellectual capacity" is no greater than that of someone under 12 years of age and the defendant's "social and intellectual capacity" is greater than that of a 16-year-old; or (3) is "passing in and out of consciousness" or is in "a state of mental torpor" because of voluntary or involuntary intoxication, irrespective of who administered the substance. *Id.* §213.3(2).

The proposed revisions would also criminalize penetration involving certain threats of nonphysical force. The crime of *sexual penetration by coercion*, a third-degree felony, includes cases where the defendant knowingly or recklessly "obtains . . . consent by threatening," for example, to accuse someone of a crime or noncompliance with immigration regulations or to "inflict any substantial economic or financial harm that would not benefit" the defendant. *Id.* §213.4(1)(a). This crime is also committed if the defendant knows or recklessly disregards the risk that someone other than a spouse or intimate partner is either "detained in a . . . custodial institution" where the defendant has "a position of authority" or is under arrest or on probation, parole, or some "other status involving state-imposed restrictions on liberty" and the defendant "holds any position of authority or supervision" over the victim. *Id.* §213.4(1)(b).

The revisions would define *sexual penetration by exploitation*, a fourth-degree felony, to include knowingly penetrating a patient who is not the defendant's spouse or intimate partner and whom the defendant is contemporaneously treating for "a mental or emotional illness, symptom, or condition" (unless "the therapy is held out as sex-based at its inception"). *Id.* §213.4(2)(a). This section would also criminalize two cases of fraud: where the defendant knowingly (1) "misrepresents that the ... penetration has curative or preventative medical properties," or (2) "leads" the victim to "believe falsely" that the defendant is "personally known" to the victim. *Id.* §213.4(2)(b)-(c).

The proposed revisions would also punish "sexual contact" in two circumstances (in addition to the three described above in Note 8 in Section A's materials on statutory rape). The term "sexual contact" includes certain acts "done for the purpose of sexual gratification, sexual arousal, or sexual degradation": for example, "touching the clothed or unclothed intimate parts" of the victim "with any body part or object"; "touching the clothed or unclothed intimate parts" of the defendant to the victim; "touching" the victim with "ejaculate, urine, or feces"; and "lifting or removing the [victim's] clothing ... to reveal intimate parts." *Id.* §213.0(6).

Aggravated criminal sexual contact, a fourth-degree felony, occurs in three circumstances: (1) where the defendant knowingly or recklessly "causes" the victim "to submit" by using a deadly weapon or by causing or threatening to cause serious bodily injury; (2) where the defendant knowingly or recklessly uses "physical force," "physical restraint," "an express or implied threat of physical force, bodily injury, or physical restraint," or "a threat to commit a crime of violence ... for the purpose of causing [another] person to submit"; or (3) where the defendant knows or recklessly disregards a risk that the victim "lacks substantial capacity to appraise or control his or her conduct" because of drugs or alcohol that the defendant "administered" without the victim's knowledge "for the purpose of impairing [that] person's capacity to communicate ... refusal." *Id.* §213.6(1).

Offensive criminal sexual contact, a petty misdemeanor punishable by up to six months in prison, criminalizes sexual contact when the defendant (1) knows the contact is "offensive" to the victim or (2) knows or recklessly disregards the risk that the victim (A) "has communicated refusal to consent," (B) is "incapable of giving consent" because he or she is "sleeping, unconscious, or physically unable to communicate ... refusal" "by words or actions," or (C) is "unable to communicate refusal ... because of mental disorder or disability, whether temporary or permanent." *Id.* §213.6(2)(a)-(b). This charge may also be brought when the defendant knowingly or recklessly "obtained ... consent" by threatening to accuse someone of a crime or noncompliance with immigration regulations, or by misrepresenting either that the sexual contact was "medical treatment" or that the victim was "in danger of physical injury or illness" that the contact might "serve to mitigate or prevent." *Id.* §213.6(2)(d). Finally, this crime is committed if the defendant knows or recklessly disregards the risk that the victim is within the defendant's "custodial care" as defined in the provision described above that criminalizes sexual penetration by coercion. *Id.* § 213.6(2)(c) (citing *id.* § 213.4(1)(b)). Spouses and intimate partners cannot be charged with offensive criminal sexual contact.

As described in greater detail in Note 10 in Part 2 above, the proposed revisions would recognize a consent defense to charges of forcible rape, aggravated forcible rape, sexual penetration without consent, or aggravated criminal sexual contact in cases where defendants establish by a preponderance of the evidence that they reasonably believed their sex partners "gave explicit prior verbal consent to the use of physical force, threats, or restraint, and/or permission to ignore general expressions of unwillingness." *Id.* § 213.9(1) (citing *id.* §§ 213.1, 213.2, 213.6(1)).

The proposed revisions would eliminate the Hale instruction and the traditional rule about uncorroborated victim testimony. But the revisions would allow the prosecutor to introduce evidence describing where and when the victim made an "[o]fficial [c]omplaint" to "a person in authority, along with evidence tending to establish the reasons for any delay," so long as that evidence was not "substantially more prejudicial than probative" and "avoid[ed] reference to the details alleged in the complaint." *Id.* § 213.10(4)(a). Evidence concerning complaints to anyone who was not "in authority" could not be introduced, however, unless they were "deemed admissible by generally applicable rules of evidence" or were used to "rebut an express or implied argument" that the victim failed to report the crime. *Id.* § 213.10(4)(b). In addition, the revisions would add a rape-shield provision to the Model Penal Code. *See id.* § 213.10(1).

14. The Impact of Rape Reform. Studies measuring the effect of rape reform legislation have reached conflicting results. Some researchers have concluded that reform efforts have had little impact on the percentage of rapes reported to the police, the percentage of complaints leading to arrest, or the percentage of arrests resulting in conviction. *See, e.g.,* Cassia C. Spohn & Julie Horney, *The Impact of Rape Law Reform on the Processing of Simple and Aggravated Rape Cases*, 86 J. Crim. L. & Criminology 861, 862–63, 882–83 (1996) (summarizing a number of studies). By contrast, others have found that certain reforms have substantially increased the number of rapes considered meritorious by the police. *See* Stacy Futter & Walter R. Mebane, Jr., *The Effects of Rape Law Reform on Rape Case Processing*, 16 Berk. Women's L.J. 72, 105–07 (2001) (concluding that rape-shield laws, elimination of the marital exemption, and rejection of defenses based on mistakes about the victim's capacity to consent had a positive impact).

More recent statistics, however, have been more pessimistic. *See, e.g.,* Jody Raphael, Rape Is Rape: How Denial, Distortion, and Victim Blaming Are Fueling a Hidden Acquaintance Rape Crisis 138 (2013) (citing studies reporting that, in contrast to other violent crimes, "the gap" between reported rapes and arrests widened between 1971 and 2006); Kathleen Daly & Brigitte Bouhours, *Rape and Attrition in the Legal Process: A Comparative Analysis of Five Countries*, 39 Crime & Just. 565, 580–81 (2010) (noting that the number of reported rapes increased in the 1970s but then declined by 15 percent between 1996 and 2006); *id.* at 602–07 (finding no change between 1970 and 2005 in the percentage of rapes that led to a conviction (about 14 percent) or the percentage of cases that were dismissed by police and prosecutors before going to court (80 percent), but an increase in the conviction rate from 69 percent to 82 percent for those cases that did go to trial); Corey Rayburn Yung, *Rape Law Gatekeeping*, 58 B.C. L. Rev. 206, 207–09 (2017) (observing that "police gatekeeping is the rule, not the exception," in rape cases — that law enforcement officials refuse to investigate rape complaints, "systematic[ally] fail[] to test rape kits," subject complainants to "a level of scrutiny and disbelief unique among crime victims," and tend to subscribe to rape myths — and concluding that the police are "the largest obstacle to the prosecution and conviction of rapists").

One commentator offered the following explanation for these findings:

> In part, the difficulty lies embedded in contemporary culture. Widespread attitudes about acceptable male behavior fall short of legal definitions of rape and in some respects seem impervious to change in statutory wording. Particularly striking is the finding that many men and women assume that in some dating situations male pressure (including force) to compel intercourse either is not "rape" or is "justified" in some measure by the behavior of the woman.

Stephen J. Schulhofer, *Taking Sexual Autonomy Seriously: Rape Law and Beyond*, 11 Law & Phil. 35, 40 (1992). *See also* Dan M. Kahan, *Culture, Cognition, and Consent: Who Perceives What, and Why, in Acquaintance-Rape Cases*, 158 U. Pa. L. Rev. 729, 794–95 (2010) (finding, in mock juror study based on the facts of *Commonwealth v. Berkowitz*, that cultural differences, not gender, affected participants' view of the case and that "variations in the legal definition of rape ha[d] a minimal influence"); Eric R. Carpenter, *Patriarchy, Not Hierarchy: Rethinking the Effect of Cultural Attitudes in Acquaintance Rape Cases*, 68 Hastings L.J. 225, 258 (2016) (challenging Kahan's methodology and concluding that "traditional gender role or patriarchal beliefs" "rather than worldviews related to hierarchy" determine one's view of acquaintance rape cases). *But cf.* Stephen J. Schulhofer, Unwanted Sex: The Culture of Intimidation and the Failure of Law 39 (1998) (observing that, although "[s]ocial attitudes sometimes control legal outcomes, . . . those attitudes are shaped in turn by legal rules," and blaming "the language of the reform statutes" for "remain[ing] tied to the traditional conception of rape as a crime of physical violence").

Disappointed with the results of 40 years of rape reform, some commentators have recently advocated less reliance on the criminal justice system. *See* Katharine K. Baker, *Why Rape Should Not (Always) Be a Crime*, 100 Minn. L. Rev. 221, 222 (2015) (suggesting that "recast[ing] rape as a civil wrong — a discriminatory act" — might "meet with more success in reducing the amount of nonconsensual sex," and thereby "destabilize[]" "the norm of male entitlement . . . enough to enable the criminal law as reformed to be enforced"); Margo Kaplan, *Rape Beyond Crime*, 66 Duke L.J. 1045, 1048–49 (2017) (arguing that "public health law's focus [on] evidence-based prevention" can "explore positive models of sex," "address[] the full spectrum of sexual attitudes and behaviors, including those that should not be criminal but nonetheless contribute to sexual aggression," and thus help "change the social norms that promote sexual violence and thwart its successful prosecution").

[4] Marital Rape

People v. M.D.

595 N.E.2d 702 (Ill. App. Ct.), *appeal denied*, 602 N.E.2d 467 (Ill. 1992)

DUNN, JUSTICE.

. . . .

Defendant and L.D. were married in August 1978 and had two children. At trial, L.D. testified as follows. Defendant arrived home at 5:30 p.m. on January 10, 1990. He had to leave shortly thereafter to call on a client. Defendant asked if L.D. would be awake later on so they could have sex. They argued for awhile, and defendant then left to meet the client.

Defendant returned home after midnight. L.D. was in bed at the time. Defendant went into the bedroom and asked if L.D. had something for him. After L.D. failed to respond defendant went downstairs. About 20 minutes later, defendant went back to the bedroom, removed his clothes, and laid down next to L.D. He accused L.D. of having an affair with a man who belonged to her church group. Defendant then jumped out of the bed and said that he was not going to wait any longer. He punched L.D. in the back four times, jumped back onto the bed, and began choking her.

L.D. tried to get away, but was unable to do so. Defendant took her pants off, held her down with his forearm, and started to pry her legs apart. He inserted his penis into L.D.'s vagina and asked her to talk dirty. After about 10 minutes, L.D. was able to push defendant away. She went into the bathroom and then went downstairs to the living room. Defendant followed her.

At about 3 a.m., . . . Defendant . . . asked how often L.D. felt they should have sex. When she responded by saying once a week, he became enraged because he felt they should have sex four times a week. Defendant pulled L.D. off the chair by her legs, dragged her across the living room floor, and forced her to go upstairs. He told L.D. that she had better do it right this time.

After L.D. got into bed, defendant grabbed a bedpost, banged it against the end of the bed a few times, and threatened to kill her. He got into bed and told L.D. to perform oral sex on him. Defendant then pried her legs apart and inserted his penis into her vagina. After about 15 minutes, defendant withdrew his penis. He went downstairs while L.D. remained in bed. . . .

Defendant returned to the bedroom shortly thereafter and sat on the end of the bed. He grabbed L.D.'s legs, and she felt something cold. Defendant then placed his weight on top of her and jammed his fist into her vagina. According to L.D., all of defendant's hand entered her vagina up to his wrist. L.D. screamed and tried to get away. Defendant removed his fist, continued to hold L.D. down, and then jammed the fist into her vagina again.

Defendant then pulled L.D. off the bed, took her into the bathroom, and forced her to go into the shower with him. Defendant began masturbating and told her to perform oral sex on him. He left the shower after L.D. told him to get away from her. L.D. then put a sanitary napkin inside her panties because she was bleeding heavily. After L.D. left the bathroom, defendant went inside it. L.D. took this opportunity to run downstairs to call the police. . . .

. . . .

. . . L.D. went to the emergency room of a Rockford hospital. A doctor performed surgery on her and placed sutures inside her vagina. . . . Because of defendant's actions on January 11, L.D. will suffer from urinary incontinence for the rest of her life and will need to take medication daily to prevent her from urinating uncontrollably.

. . . .

[At trial Defendant testified that he and L.D.] had sexual intercourse once, and he later performed oral sex on her. Defendant felt that L.D. was cold and "standoffish" while they had sex. After he performed oral sex on her, defendant decided to stimulate her by using an egg. He had seen this done in pornographic films.

. . . .

Defendant got an egg from the refrigerator and brought it up to the bedroom. He tried to stimulate L.D. by placing fingers from one hand into her vagina. He was holding the egg in the same hand. While he was doing this, L.D. grabbed his testicles. As a result, his entire hand accidentally went into her vagina, and the egg broke outside her vagina. . . .

. . . .

Defendant had been charged with one count of battery, two counts of criminal sexual assault, and three counts of aggravated criminal sexual assault. The jury acquitted him of both counts of criminal sexual assault. These counts involved the two alleged incidents of forcible intercourse. It also acquitted defendant of the aggravated criminal sexual assault count which alleged that defendant had placed his fist and an egg into his wife's vagina and the count which alleged that he had endangered L.D.'s life. The jury found defendant guilty of the aggravated sexual assault count which alleged that he had placed his fist in L.D.'s vagina, and it found him guilty of battery. The trial court sentenced defendant to a 12-year term of imprisonment. Defendant now appeals.

Under section 12-18(c) of the Criminal Code of 1961, [now 720 Ill. Comp. Stat. 5/11-1.10], a person may not be charged by his or her spouse with the offenses of criminal sexual abuse [forcible sexual touching or fondling] or aggravated criminal sexual abuse [forcible sexual touching or fondling accompanied by aggravating circumstances, for example, causing the victim bodily harm]. This exemption does not apply to aggravated criminal sexual assault [forcible penetration accompanied by aggravating circumstances, for example, causing the victim bodily harm], the offense of which defendant was convicted, or criminal sexual assault [forcible penetration]. Defendant argues that applying the marital exemption only to the former two offenses violates the equal protection and due process clauses of the United States and Illinois Constitutions.

. . . .

. . . [T]he applicable standard [of review in evaluating defendant's equal protection challenge] is the rational basis test. When this standard is employed a statutory classification will be upheld if it [is] rationally related to a legitimate governmental interest. . . .

. . . .

The purpose of the statutory scheme we are considering is to protect the personal dignity of potential victims of sex offenses. Sexual assaults are generally violent, degrading acts which cause severe physical and emotional damage to the victims. . . . The four statutes in question are designed to protect individuals from the physical and emotional harm resulting from sexual assaults and to preserve their personal bodily integrity.

Equal projection challenges have been brought in several States to statutes banning forcible sexual assaults and containing marital exemptions similar to the one we are considering. The Colorado Supreme Court held that a marital exemption to the State's first degree sexual assault statute did not violate the equal protection or due process clauses. (*People v. Brown* (Colo. 1981), 632 P.2d 1025, 1027.)[28] Other States have held, however, that marital exemptions in similar statutes violated the equal protection clause. (*See, e.g., Merton v. State* (Ala. Crim. App. 1986), 500 So. 2d 1301, 1302–05 (marital exemption to forcible rape statute unconstitutional); *Williams v. State* (Ala. Crim. App. 1986), 494 So. 2d 819, 830 (marital exemption to forcible sodomy statute unconstitutional); *People v. Liberta* (1984), 64 N.Y.2d 152, 474 N.E.2d 567, 575, 485 N.Y.S.2d 207, 215 (marital exemption to rape and sodomy statutes unconstitutional.) . . .

We recognize that the above out-of-State cases are arguably distinguishable from the one at bar because . . . Illinois does not recognize a marital exemption for its most serious sex offenses.

Nevertheless, we believe the above cases are of significant value because they discuss the source of marital exemptions in sexual offense statutes and analyze possible justifications for the continued existence of such exemptions. . . . A marital exemption for the offense of rape existed at common law. The idea of recognizing

---

28. In 1988, however, the Colorado legislature repealed the marital exemption upheld in *Brown*. *See* Colo. Rev. Stat. § 18-3-409.

this exemption originated with Lord Hale, the 17th century jurist, who, without citing any authority, wrote as follows:

> The husband cannot be guilty of a rape committed by himself upon his lawful wife, for by their mutual matrimonial consent and contract the wife hath given up herself in this kind unto her husband, which she cannot retract.

Other traditional justifications for the marital exemption were the common-law doctrines that a woman was her husband's property and that her legal existence was consolidated into her husband's existence.

The above archaic doctrines simply have no place in modern society. . . . Lord Hale's implied consent theory appears to be based largely upon the other two doctrines and is equally objectionable as it leads to the same result, depriving women of their dignity by refusing to recognize them as whole human beings who are entitled to decide whether or when they will engage in sexual relations.

. . . Furthermore, as other courts have pointed out with respect to Lord Hale's theory, it is irrational to imply consent to a sexual assault, which is generally a violent, degrading act that results in severe physical and psychological harm. A marriage license should not be viewed as a license to forcibly sexually assault one's spouse with impunity. A married individual has the same right to control his or her body as does an unmarried person. For these reasons, we conclude that the above traditional justifications do not provide a rational basis for marital exemptions in sexual assault statutes.

As the court pointed out in *Liberta*, other justifications have been raised in recent times for marital exemptions in sexual assault statutes, including the arguments that such exemptions protect against governmental intrusion into marital privacy and promote reconciliation between spouses. . . . There is no suggestion . . . that the right to marital privacy was meant to apply outside the context of consensual marital relations. . . .

. . . As the court stated in *Liberta*, while protection of marital privacy is a legitimate State interest, there is no rational relationship between this interest and allowing an individual to commit a forcible sexual assault upon his or her spouse . . . .

The Colorado Supreme Court held in *People v. Brown* that the interest in promoting marital reconciliation and preserving family relationships provided a rational basis for the marital exception in that State's first-degree sexual assault statute. The courts in *Williams* and *Liberta* concluded that this rationale was untenable, however, and we agree. It is the violent act of committing a forcible sexual assault which disrupts a marriage and not the injured spouse's attempt to seek redress in the criminal justice system. Additionally, if a marriage has deteriorated to the point where one spouse commits a forcible sexual assault upon the other and the victim desires to see the perpetrator imprisoned, reconciliation is hardly a likely prospect.

Equally untenable is the contention that forcible sexual assault is not as serious an offense if the victim and perpetrator are married and can therefore be addressed adequately by other statutes, such as the battery and aggravated battery statutes. It would seem that a forcible sexual assault committed by a person's spouse would be even more traumatic than one committed by another individual as the perpetrator would be someone with whom the victim had once shared a loving, intimate relationship. As we have previously stated, a married person should have the same right to control his or her body as does an unmarried person. Moreover, the existence of the [sexual abuse and assault] statutes . . . results from a recognition that the nature of the harm resulting from a forcible sexual assault is different than that resulting from an ordinary assault. . . .

The final rationales that have been asserted in support of the marital exemption are that a marital sexual assault would be difficult to prove and that a possibility of fabricated complaints from vindictive spouses exists. The former argument is based upon the problem of proving lack of consent. What this argument fails to take into account is that the problem of proving lack of consent is likely to be present in most cases in which the alleged victim and perpetrator have had a prior consensual sexual relationship regardless of whether they were married or unmarried. With regard to the other contention, we find no basis for believing that a vindictive spouse is more likely to fabricate a sexual assault charge than a vindictive unmarried former lover. . . .

. . . [T]here is no rational basis for a statutory scheme which protects an individual from acts of forcible sexual penetration committed by a spouse but does not protect the individual from other acts of forcible sexual exploitation by his or her spouse. The marital exemption is completely contrary to the statutory objectives of protecting people from the physical and emotional harm resulting from forcible sexual assaults and preserving their personal bodily integrity.

. . . .

Defendant argues that his conviction must be reversed because the statutory scheme under which he was convicted is unconstitutional. We disagree. The fact that a statute contains an unconstitutional provision does not render the entire enactment unconstitutional unless it is determined that the legislature would not have enacted the statute without the invalid portion. The question of whether the remaining portions of an enactment are severable from the unconstitutional portion is thus a question of legislative intent.

. . . In light of the importance of [the] interests [underlying these statutes], we have no doubt that the legislature would have enacted [them] without a marital exemption. . . . Accordingly, we conclude that the invalidity of the marital exemption . . . does not affect the validity of the [sexual abuse and assault] statutes. . . .

Although our decision has the effect of expanding the scope of a criminal statute, this does not deprive defendant of due process of law. Defendant did not come within the marital exemption which we have held to be invalid in part, and he therefore had fair warning at the time of his alleged conduct that it was prohibited under the aggravated criminal sexual assault statute. . . .

Defendant next contends that the trial court erred by ruling that certain evidence he wished to introduce regarding past consensual sexual practices with L.D. was inadmissible. More specifically, defendant wished to introduce evidence that he had engaged in consensual sexual acts with L.D. during which he placed cucumbers, whipped cream, and peaches into her vagina in order to stimulate her. . . .

. . . .

Defendant contends that the trial court's refusal to admit the proffered evidence denied him an opportunity to develop a defense of consent. The evidence was relevant, according to defendant, because it related to sexual conduct involving food, thus tending to show that L.D. may have consented to having the egg placed in her vagina.

The problem with defendant's argument is that the explanation he gave at trial for his conduct was that it was an accident, not that L.D. consented. Defendant stated during his testimony that L.D. did not consent to his use of the egg. He also testified that his hand accidentally slipped into her vagina after she squeezed his testicles. Therefore, consent was not an issue at trial; instead, the determinative issue was whether defendant's conduct was deliberate or accidental. The trial court did not err by ruling that the proffered evidence was inadmissible as it shed no light on the above issue.

. . . .

Notes and Questions

1. The Incidence of Marital Rape. One Justice Department study found that approximately one-fifth of rape victims are assaulted by a spouse or former spouse. *See* Patricia Tjaden & Nancy Thoennes, Office of Justice Programs, Extent, Nature, and Consequences of Rape Victimization: Findings from the National Violence Against Women Survey 21 (2006), *available at* http://www.ojp.usdoj.gov /nij/pubs-sum/210346.htm. Other researchers report that nine percent to 14 percent of married women have been raped by their husbands, *see* Diana E.H. Russell, Rape in Marriage 57 (1990), and that the figures are much higher for battered women, *see id.* at 61 (34% to 37%); Angela Browne, When Battered Women Kill 95–96 (1987) (59%), and for women who are separated or divorced, *see* David Finkelhor & Kersti Yllo, License to Rape: Sexual Abuse of Wives 8, 205 (1985) (25%). *Cf.* Michelle C. Black et al., Centers for Disease Control and Prevention, The National Intimate Partner and Sexual Violence Survey: 2010 Summary Report 42, 21 (2011), *available at* http://www.cdc.gov/ViolencePrevention/pdf /NISVS_Report2010-a.pdf (reporting that almost one in 10 women are raped by an intimate partner during their lifetimes, and that more than half of all rapes are perpetrated by a current or former intimate partner).

2. The Marital Exemption. As the court in *M.D.* pointed out, husbands were traditionally immune from prosecution for raping their wives. Challenges to the marital exemption began in this country in the 1970s, and by 1993 marital rape was punishable to some extent in all 50 states.

Although most states have completely abolished the marital exemption, some continue to treat spouses differently from other rape defendants in certain respects. The South Carolina laws draw the most significant distinction, criminalizing marital rape for married couples living together only if the defendant used "aggravated force" and the victim reported the crime within 30 days. *See* S.C. Code Ann. § 16-3-615. Other states limit marital rape charges to cases involving some use of force or the threat of force. *See, e.g.,* Conn. Gen. Stat. § 53a-706 ("actual physical force"); Miss. Code Ann. § 97-3-99 ("forcible sexual penetration"); Okla. Stat. tit. 21, § 1111(c) ("force or violence"). In addition to the jurisdictions that exempt spouses from the laws governing sex with persons under a certain age, those suffering from mentally incapacity, and those for whom the defendant is in a position of supervisory authority, some states continue to follow the approach struck down in *M.D.* and refuse to prosecute husbands for certain less serious sex offenses. *See, e.g.,* Minn. Stat. § 609.349 ("physically helpless" victim); Ohio Rev. Code Ann. § 2907.03 (sexual battery); W. Va. Code § 61-813-7 (sexual abuse). *See also* Va. Code Ann. § 18.2-61(c) (allowing judges to defer a marital rape prosecution without entering a guilty verdict and to put the defendant on "probation pending the completion of counseling" if the victim and prosecutor agree). *See generally* John F. Decker & Peter G. Baroni, *"No" Still Means "Yes": The Failure of the "Non-Consent" Reform Movement in American Rape and Sexual Assault Law,* 101 J. Crim. L. & Criminology 1081, 1156–62 (2011).

Do any of the arguments addressed in *M.D.* justify retaining some distinction between marital and other forms of rape? Does "a long-standing sexual relationship" carry an "implied authorization" for sex? Donald A. Dripps, *Beyond Rape: An Essay on the Difference Between the Presence of Force and the Absence of Consent,* 92 Colum. L. Rev. 1780, 1801 (1992). Or is "consent to sexual intercourse . . . temporally constrained permission that is specific as to act and non-transferable to others," so that "consent[] to sex with [a] lover in the past does not mean . . . consent[] in the future" and "consent[] to vaginal intercourse does not mean . . . consent[] to anal sex"? Michelle J. Anderson, *Marital Immunity, Intimate Relationships, and Improper Inferences: A New Law on Sexual Offenses by Intimates,* 54 Hastings L.J. 1465, 1546 (2003).

Even if you agree with *M.D.,* is even the "formal neutrality on marital status" reflected in the majority of state statutes that treat husbands no differently from other rape defendants insufficient because wives raped by their husbands continue to "face police, prosecutors, judges, and juries who infer that, absent extraordinary violence, the wives' prior consent to sexual intercourse implied ongoing consent to the alleged rape"? *Id.* at 1514. Is *M.D.* one such case? *See also* Matt Pearce, *No Prison Time for Indiana Man Convicted of Drugging, Raping Wife,* L.A. Times, May 19, 2014 (reporting that a trial judge, in imposing a sentence of eight years' home confinement despite the prosecutor's request for a 40-year prison term, told the victim she "needed to forgive" her husband, who was convicted of six felony charges after drugging her over a period of three years and videotaping himself having sex with her in her sleep).

3. Gender-Neutral Rape Laws. The New York Court of Appeals' opinion in *People v. Liberta,* 474 N.E.2d 567 (N.Y. 1984), cited in *M.D.,* also addressed a challenge to the constitutionality of the gender line drawn in traditional rape statutes, which punished only cases involving male defendants and female victims. Using the higher standard of scrutiny the Equal Protection Clause applies to gender classifications — that the classification must be "substantially related to the achievement of an important governmental objective" — the *Liberta* court rejected the state's contention that "the discrimination is justified because a female rape victim 'faces the probability of medical, sociological, and psychological problems unique to her gender.'" Specifically, the court noted that an "'"archaic and overbroad" generalization' . . . which is evidently grounded in long-standing stereotypical notions of the differences between the sexes, simply cannot serve as a legitimate rationale for a penal provision that is addressed only to adult males." Likewise dismissing the state's argument that women rarely commit the crime of rape, the court responded that "[w]omen may well be responsible for a far lower number of all serious crimes than are men" and "[a] gender-neutral law would indisputably better serve, even if only marginally, the objective of deterring and punishing forcible sexual assaults." Finally, the court concluded that cases involving similar challenges to gender-specific statutory rape laws were "not decisive" given that statutory rape and forcible rape statutes are designed to address different interests, and there was "no evidence . . . that preventing pregnancies is a primary purpose of the statute prohibiting forcible rape." *Id.* at 576–77 (citing *Michael M. v. Superior Court*, 450 U.S. 464 (1981) (plurality opinion)). (For a description of *Michael M.* and a discussion of these issues in the context of statutory rape, see Note 4 in Section A above.).

The New York Court of Appeals' conclusion that gender neutrality is mandated by the Equal Protection Clause was rejected by the Second Circuit on habeas. *See Liberta v. Kelly*, 839 F.2d 77, 83 (2d Cir. 1988) (reasoning that the rape of men by women is "a hypothetical problem" and "only male rape of a female can impose on the victim an unwanted pregnancy"). Nevertheless, all but two states now have completely gender-neutral rape statutes. *See* Ga. Code Ann. § 16-6-1; Miss. Code Ann. § 97-3-71. In the overwhelming majority of jurisdictions, therefore, rape is subject to the same punishment irrespective of the gender of the defendant and the victim.

4. The Model Penal Code Approach. The Model Penal Code retains the marital exemption for all sexual offenses, even if a couple is "living apart under an informal separation arrangement." Model Penal Code § 213.6(2) Comment at 418. So long as the couple remains legally married, the exemption applies unless they are "living apart under a decree of judicial separation." *Id.* § 213.6(2). The marital exemption extends to all "persons living together as man and wife, regardless of the legal status of their relationship." *Id.* It therefore applies to common-law marriages as well as cases where a couple has "purported to contract a marriage that is for some reason invalid." *Id.* § 213.6(2) Comment at 418.

In explaining the decision to retain the marital exemption, the Comments note that marriage, "while not amounting to a legal waiver of the woman's right to say 'no,' does imply a kind of generalized consent": "[t]he relationship itself creates a presumption of consent, valid until revoked." As a result, the Comments conclude that "husbands must be exempt from those categories of liability based not on force or coercion but on a presumed incapacity of the woman to consent"—for example, cases where the woman is unconscious or otherwise unaware that a sexual act is being performed on her. With respect to rape accomplished by force or threat, the Comments reason that the marital exemption "avoids [an] unwarranted intrusion of the penal law into the life of the family." In addition, the Comments take the position that assault charges can adequately deal with cases of marital rape because "the voluntary association of husband and wife . . . affect[s] the nature of the harm involved in unwanted intercourse": "[t]he gravity of the crime of forcible rape derives not merely from its violent character but also from its achievement of a particularly degrading kind of unwanted intimacy," and "that evil, as distinct from the force used to compel submission, may well be thought to be qualitatively different" "[w]here the attacker stands in an ongoing relationship of sexual intimacy." *Id.* § 213.1 Comment at 344–46. (See also Note 11 following *Commonwealth v. Berkowitz* in Part 3 above, which describes the MPC provision elevating rape to a first-degree felony when the victim was not "a voluntary social companion" of the defendant and "had not previously permitted him sexual liberties." *Id.* § 213.1(1).)

The Model Penal Code takes a compromise position on the question of gender neutrality. While it limits the crimes of rape and gross sexual imposition to male defendants and female victims, the crimes of deviate sexual intercourse by force or imposition and sexual assault are drafted in gender-neutral terms. *Compare id.* § 213.1 *with id.* §§ 213.2, 213.4. The drafters recognized the "symbolic" value of gender neutrality in "help[ing] to abrogate certain sex stereotypes," but they concluded that "[p]hysical strength, role conception, and the mechanics of intercourse make sexual aggression an overwhelmingly male phenomenon." *Id.* § 213.1 Comment at 337–38. In addition, the Comments observe that although "the male who is forced to engage in intercourse is denied freedom of choice in much the same way as the female victim of rape," "the potential consequences of coercive intimacy do not seem so grave"—both because male victims do not face a danger of unwanted pregnancy and because, "however devalued virginity has become for the modern woman, it is difficult to believe that its loss constitutes a comparable injury to the male." *Id.* at 338.

The Comments offer the following explanation for the decision to exclude forcible same-sex intercourse from the definitions of rape and gross sexual imposition, thereby foreclosing the possibility of a first-degree felony conviction in those cases:

> Economy in the use of the most severe sanctions of the criminal law suggests that perhaps the punishment of rape as a first-degree felony should be limited to those cases where public outcry is likely to be the greatest, where the harm to the victim is likely to be perceived as the most severe, both by the victim and by society, and where the frequency of the offense has caused the greatest public apprehension.

Id.

5. The Proposed Revisions to the Model Penal Code. The proposed revisions to the Model Penal Code's sexual offenses would be completely gender neutral. *See* Model Penal Code: Sexual Assault and Related Offenses (Tentative Draft No. 2, 2016).

Although earlier drafts of the revisions would also have eliminated any form of marital exception, *see* Model Penal Code: Sexual Assault and Related Offenses (Tentative Draft No. 1, 2014), the most recent draft, described in Note 13 following *Commonwealth v. Berkowitz* in Part 3 above, does exempt spouses and intimate partners from prosecution for certain sex offenses. But the revisions provide that any such defense must be "specifically provided" and does not apply to any crime involving "the use or threat of physical force, physical restraint, bodily injury, or any other crime of violence . . . or coercion." Model Penal Code: Sexual Assault and Related Offenses § 213.9(2)(a) (Tentative Draft No. 2, 2016) (citing *id.* §§ 213.1, 213.4(1)(a)).

Thus, under the most recent draft of the revisions, spouses could not be charged with sexual penetration of a minor, *see id.* § 213.5(3), or inappropriate sexual contact with a minor, *see id.* § 213.7(3). In addition, both spouses and intimate partners would be exempt from prosecution for offensive criminal sexual contact, *see id.* § 213.6(2), as well as for the charges of sexual penetration by exploitation and sexual penetration by coercion that involve, respectively, a defendant who is providing mental health services to the victim and a defendant who holds a position of authority over the victim in connection with, for example, prison, probation, or parole. *See id.* §§ 213.4(2)(a), 213.4(1)(b).

The proposed revisions also give spouses and intimate partners an affirmative defense in prosecutions for the charges of rape or sexual penetration of a vulnerable person that involve no "use or threat of physical force," but instead are based on a lack of consent on the part of a victim who is, for example, asleep or unconscious. *Id.* § 213.9(2)(b) (citing *id.* §§ 213.3(1)(a), 213.3(2)(c)). The defense is available if the defendant reasonably believes, "in light of the specific facts and circumstances of th[e] relationship and the context surrounding the disputed act," that the victim "would welcome the act." *Id.*

Under the most recent proposal, the term "spouse" includes common-law marriages and domestic partnerships, *see id.* § 213.0(8)(a), and an "intimate partner[ship]" requires "a sexually intimate relationship involving cohabitation." *Id.* § 213.0(8)(b). But neither term applies if a temporary or permanent order of protection or separation has been issued or if the two people "no longer liv[e] together because of estrangement in the relationship." *Id.* § 213.0(8)(c).

Chapter 8

Theft

[A] Introduction

When should the "wrongful" acquisition of property be subject to criminal sanction? The borderline between clever commercial skills worthy of praise in a capitalist society and "criminal" acquisition is one that any society must carefully consider and define. The traditional common-law theft crimes suggest one possible line, although, as the materials below indicate, they have been modified by both courts and legislatures in some states. The question of what conduct ought to be criminalized has been at the center of the debate throughout the history of larceny and other property crimes:

> One problem that dogs the law of theft . . . is that in a commercial society no clear line can be drawn between greedy antisocial acquisitive behavior on the one hand and, on the other hand, aggressive selling, advertising, and other entrepreneurial activity that is highly regarded or at least commonly tolerated. Here two important principles of constitutional and criminal law come into play to restrict the scope of the law of theft. A criminal law must not be so comprehensive as to jeopardize the ordinary behavior of decent citizens. Nor may a criminal law be so vague that it fails to warn the citizen what is forbidden and leaves to the discretion of enforcement officers or judges whether certain behavior should be punishable. The tension between these principles, and the impulse to penalize all egregious greed, account for the fact that theft law inevitably falls short of penalizing all rascality.

Louis B. Schwartz, *Theft, in* 4 Encyclopedia of Crime and Justice 1537, 1537 (Sanford H. Kadish ed., 1983).

Even a decision to disapprove of certain kinds of acquisitive conduct does not necessarily mean criminal punishment is appropriate. Civil penalties, including tort liability or simply private institutional sanctions (such as expulsion from a university or stock exchange), can deter and punish conduct without resorting to criminal condemnation. Arguably, more ambiguous or less serious wrongs should be addressed in a noncriminal manner in order to avoid the hazards of excessive prosecutorial discretion and the other risks Professor Schwartz outlines above. Unlike a crime like murder, where punishment depends almost entirely on the defendant's mens rea, the borderline between the criminal and noncriminal acquisition of property depends on a variety of physical as well as mental elements. Commentators have long questioned the rationality of these lines:

The common law crime of larceny differs from such a crime as homicide in that it shades off on every side into the region of mere tort. When one human being is killed by another, the question of crime depends solely upon the intent with which the act was committed. But when a man's property is wrongfully interfered with, the act is criminal only under certain conditions; and the line between such interference as is criminal and such as is a mere tort is purely arbitrary, being founded on no distinction in the nature of things. As a result, there is on all sides a debatable ground, where the act may conceivably be held a crime, or with equal inherent reason may not. The difficulty is not diminished by the fact that the borders of criminality have been extended by statutes whereby such crimes have been created as embezzlement, cheating, cheating by false pretenses, malicious mischief, forcible trespass, etc. The question still remains, whether the act is a crime by the common law or by statute.

Joseph H. Beale, Jr., *The Borderland of Larceny*, 6 Harv. L. Rev. 244, 244 (1892). *See also* John L. Diamond, *Reviving Lenity and Honest Belief at the Boundaries of Criminal Law*, 44 U. Mich. J. L. Ref. 1 (2010) (discussing the subtle and fluid distinctions between criminal and non-criminal conduct in theft and other crimes and the dangers of overcriminalization and excessive prosecutorial discretion).

As you study larceny and the other property offenses, consider whether the various elements of these crimes reflect rational or "purely arbitrary" distinctions.

[B] Larceny

[1] The History and Elements of Larceny and the Type of Property That Can Be Stolen

Lund v. Commonwealth

232 S.E.2d 745 (Va. 1977)

I'Anson, Chief Justice.

Defendant, Charles Walter Lund, was charged in an indictment with the theft of keys, computer cards, computer print-outs and using "without authority computer operation time and services of Computer Center Personnel at Virginia Polytechnic Institute and State University [V.P.I. or University] . . . with intent to defraud, such property and services having a value of one hundred dollars or more." . . . Defendant pleaded not guilty and waived trial by jury. He was found guilty of grand larceny and sentenced to two years in the State penitentiary. The sentence was suspended, and defendant was placed on probation for five years.

Defendant was a graduate student in statistics and a candidate for a Ph.D. degree at V.P.I. The preparation of his dissertation on the subject assigned to him by his faculty advisor required the use of computer operation time and services of the computer center personnel at the University. His faculty advisor neglected to arrange for defendant's use of the computer, but defendant used it without obtaining the proper authorization.

The computer used by the defendant was leased on an annual basis by V.P.I. from the IBM Corporation. The rental was paid by V.P.I. which allocates the cost of the computer center to various departments within the University by charging it to the budget of that department. This is a bookkeeping entry, and no money actually changes hands. The departments are allocated "computer credits [in dollars] back for their use [on] a proportional basis of their [budgetary] allotments." Each department manager receives a monthly statement showing the allotments used and the running balance in each account of his department.

An account is established when a duly authorized administrator or "department head" fills out a form allocating funds to a department of the University and an individual. When such form is received, the computer center assigns an account number to this allocation and provides a key to a locked post office box which is also numbered to the authorized individual and department. The account number and the post office box number are the access code which must be provided with each request before the computer will process a "deck of cards" prepared by the user and delivered to computer center personnel. The computer print-outs are usually returned to the locked post office box. When the product is too large for the box, a "check" is placed in the box, and it is used to receive the print-outs at the "computer center main window."

Defendant came under surveillance on October 12, 1974, because of complaints from various departments that unauthorized charges were being made to one or more of their accounts. When confronted by the University's investigator, defendant initially denied that he had used the computer service, but later admitted that he had. He gave to the investigator seven keys for boxes assigned to other persons. One of these keys was secreted in his sock. He told the investigating officer he had been given the keys by another student. A large number of computer cards and print-outs were taken from defendant's apartment.

The director of the computer center testified that the unauthorized sum spent out of the accounts associated with the seven post office box keys, amounted to $5,065. He estimated that on the basis of the computer cards and print-outs obtained from the defendant, as much as $26,384.16 in unauthorized computer time had been used by the defendant. He said, however, that the value of the cards and print-outs obtained from the defendant was "whatever scrap paper is worth."

Defendant testified that he used the computer without specific authority. He stated that he knew he was a large computer user, but, because he was doing work on his doctoral dissertation, he did not consider this use excessive or that "he was doing anything wrong."

Four faculty members testified in defendant's behalf. They all agreed that computer time "probably would have been" or "would have been" assigned to defendant

if properly requested. Dr. Hinkleman, who replaced defendant's first advisor, testified that the computer time was essential for the defendant to carry out his assignment. He assumed that a sufficient number of computer hours had been arranged
by Lund's prior faculty advisor.

The head of the statistics department, at the time of the trial, agreed with the testimony of the faculty members that Lund would have been assigned computer time
if properly requested. He also testified that the committee which recommended
the awarding of degrees was aware of the charges pending against defendant when
he was awarded his doctorate by the University.

The defendant contends that his conviction of grand larceny of the keys, computer
cards, and computer print-outs cannot be upheld under the provisions of Code § 18.1-
100 because (1) there was no evidence that the articles were stolen, or that they had
a value of $100 or more, and (2) computer time and services are not the subject of
larceny under the provisions of Code § 18.1-100. . . .

Code § 18.1-100 (now § 18.2-95) provides as follows:

> "Any person who: (1) Commits larceny from the person of another of money
> or other thing of value of five dollars or more, or

> (2) Commits simple larceny not from the person of another of goods and
> chattels of the value of one hundred dollars or more, shall be deemed guilty
> of grand larceny. . . ."

. . . The Commonwealth concedes that the defendant could not be convicted of
grand larceny of the keys and computer cards because there was no evidence that
those articles were stolen and that they had a market value of $100 or more. The Com-
monwealth argues, however, that the evidence shows the defendant [committed
grand larceny] when he obtained . . . the computer print-outs which had a value of
over $5,000.

. . . .

At common law, larceny is the taking and carrying away of the goods and chattels
of another with intent to deprive the owner of the possession thereof permanently. . . .
The phrase "goods and chattels" cannot be interpreted to include computer time and
services in light of the often repeated mandate that criminal statutes must be strictly
construed.

At common law, labor or services could not be the subject of the crime of [lar-
ceny] because neither time nor services may be taken and carried away. . . .

Furthermore, the unauthorized use of the computer is not the subject of larceny.
Nowhere in Code § 18.1-100 . . . do we find the word "use." The language of the statute[] connotes more than just the unauthorized use of the property of another. It
refers to a taking and carrying away of a certain concrete article of personal property. *See People v. Ashworth*, 220 A.D. 498, 222 N.Y.S. 24, 27 (1927). There it was held
that the unauthorized use of machinery and spinning facilities of another to process
wool did not constitute larceny under New York's false pretense statute.

We hold that labor and services and the unauthorized use of the University's computer cannot be construed to be subjects of larceny under the provisions of Code § 18.1-100. . . .

The Commonwealth argues that even though the computer print-outs had no market value, their value can be determined by the cost of the labor and services that produced them. We do not agree.

The cost of producing the print-outs is not the proper criterion of value for the purpose here. Where there is no market value of an article that has been stolen, the better rule is that its actual value should be proved.

Here the evidence shows that the print-outs had no ascertainable monetary value to the University or the computer center. Indeed, the director of the computer center stated that the print-outs had no more value than scrap paper. Nor is there any evidence of their value to the defendant, and value to him could only be based on pure speculation and surmise. Hence, the evidence was insufficient to convict the defendant of grand larceny. . . .

For the reasons stated, the judgment of the trial court is reversed, and the indictment is quashed.

Notes and Questions

1. Larceny's Common-Law Origins. The common-law crime of larceny is the root of all modern property crimes. Larceny and the crimes of embezzlement and false pretenses, which were later created by statute (see Sections C and D below for a discussion of these crimes), constitute the traditional "theft" crimes.

Generally, larceny requires proof of each of the following elements: (1) a trespassory (wrongful) (2) taking (3) and carrying away (4) of the personal property (5) of another person (6) with the intent to permanently deprive the other person of that property. *See* Wayne R. LaFave, Criminal Law § 19.3, at 979–95 (5th ed. 2010). As the materials in this section will explore, these seemingly simple elements, which originally defined the "criminal" acquisition of property, actually weave a complex web of rules and exceptions.

2. The Historical Development of Larceny. The Comments accompanying the Model Penal Code's theft provision briefly retrace the history of larceny:

> That history begins with the concern for crimes of violence—in the present context, the taking of property by force from the possession of another, i.e., robbery. The criminal law then expanded, by means of the ancient quasi-criminal writ of trespass, to cover all taking of another's property from his possession without his consent, even though no force was used. This misconduct was punished as larceny. The law then expanded once more, through some famous judicial manipulation of the concept of possession, to embrace misappropriation by a person who with the consent of the owner already had physical control over the property. . . .

Model Penal Code § 223.1 Comment at 128.

What forces fueled the persistent expansion of the common law by judges and legislatures? Commentators and scholars have advanced several theories to explain the development of property crimes. Professor Jerome Hall believes that the forces of history and economics shaped both the emergence and the development of larceny and related property crimes. As commerce and banking played increasingly important roles in society, he argues, the law of theft came to include more types of dishonest takings of property:

> [T]he last twenty years of the eighteenth century produced the most rapid and extensive growth in the entire law of theft. What conditions influenced this accelerated development? To the continuing and cumulative effects of . . . social and economic conditions . . . , it is necessary to add that trade was increasing at enormous strides as the Commercial Revolution advanced to its peak. But most important were the effects of the Industrial Revolution. Both of these factors were aspects of the same movement.

> . . . Whether regarded as the peak of the Commercial Revolution or regarded partly as the era which also ran well into the Industrial Revolution or as a transition, there is unanimity that with reference to the volume of business done, the nature of commerce, and the prevailing types of social and economic organization, the [eighteenth] century, as a whole, stands out clearly against all preceding periods in English history. It would be extraordinary if this had left no mark on the growth of the law on crimes against property without violence.

> In each development of the law, the particular step taken was a resultant of forces determined largely by social and economic conditions, the existing legal sanctions, the whole body of precedent, and the established judicial techniques. The interplay of law, case, and conditions can be understood only when the meaning of each factor is known.

JEROME HALL, THEFT, LAW AND SOCIETY 77–79 (2d ed. 1952). An alternative view, explored in the Notes that follow, is that the development of the law of larceny reflects mere historical happenstance rather than history or principle.

3. The Interests Protected by Larceny. What is the nature of the interest protected by the criminalization of larceny? Most commentators view the laws against larceny as protecting property interests. *See* Louis B. Schwartz, *Theft, in* 4 ENCYCLOPEDIA OF CRIME AND JUSTICE 1537, 1537 (Sanford H. Kadish ed., 1983). Section 223.1(2) of the Model Penal Code and most states, for example, grade the crime of larceny according to the value of the property taken. The Comments accompanying the Model Penal Code's theft provision frame the law of larceny "in terms of a long history of expansion of the role of the criminal law in protecting property." Model Penal Code § 223.1 Comment at 128. Professor George Fletcher believes otherwise:

It is important to realize that an act of thieving might endanger a range of interests other than wealth. In the traditional view, the thief upset the social order not only by threatening property, but by violating the general sense of security and well-being of the community; in this broader sense, theft was feared as a socially unnerving event. . . . Thus, the harm in . . . larceny . . . was primarily relational: The thief endangered the established order of community. . . . The transition to the modern concept of theft witnessed the dissolution of these relational aspects of larceny . . . [and larceny] came to be seen primarily as [an] offense[] against property interests. The modern vision of the criminal law seems to be that the proper allocation of each item of property enjoys the full concern of the community; the dishonest displacement of wealth from one person to another therefore becomes a public harm.

George P. Fletcher, *The Metamorphosis of Larceny*, 89 Harv. L. Rev. 469, 474 (1976).

Which view makes more sense? Note that under ancient common law, a person who caught a thief in the act of stealing was justified in killing the thief. However, one who was caught in possession of stolen goods rather than actually stealing was required only to pay multiple damages. *See id.* at 477; Michael E. Tigar, *The Right of Property and the Law of Theft*, 62 Tex. L. Rev. 1443, 1446–47 (1984). Does the authority to kill a thief who was caught stealing support Fletcher's view that the act of theft endangers the established order of the community?

4. The Type of Property Protected by Larceny. What kinds of property can be the subject of larceny? As Professor Patrick Fitzgerald writes, the common law answered this question in a rather narrow way:

By no means all the property which a person may own is legally capable of being stolen. A man's wealth may consist, not only of land, goods, and money, but also shares in companies, patent rights, and other intangibles, but the law of larceny is restricted to tangible objects. It is not possible at common law to steal an idea for a book, an invention, a ride on a horse, or a peep at a football match. . . . Within the category of tangible things, larceny was yet further restricted to movable objects. Unlike land, which remains where it is, movable property could be easily disposed of and would in many cases be of too little value to make it worth the loser's while to sue, even if he could catch the thief. For these reasons, it was obviously desirable to afford movables the extra protection of the criminal law.

P.J. Fitzgerald, Criminal Law and Punishment 38–39 (1962).

Consider a few of the major areas in which statutory and judicial extensions during this century have substantially broadened common-law larceny:

(a) *Use of Personal Property, Including Computer Time.* As *Lund* illustrates, any use of personal property (including, in the contemporary context, computer time) is not traditionally considered property within the reach of larceny laws. Should it be? In

State v. McGraw, 480 N.E.2d 552 (Ind. 1985), the court vacated the defendant's conviction on two counts of larceny for using city computer facilities in his own private sales venture. Even assuming that "property," as defined in the relevant statute, was meant to include computer use, the court held that the defendant did not deprive the city of any value or use of its computer because the computer's capacity was not reached or likely to be reached. The dissenting justice made the case for the other side:

> Time and use are at the very core of the value of a computer system. To say that only the information stored in the computer plus the tapes and discs and perhaps the machinery involved in the computer system, are the only elements that can be measured as the value or property feature of that system, is incorrect. . . . Thus, when the defendant used the computer system, putting on data from his own private business and taking it out on printouts, he was taking that which was property of the City and converting it to his own use, thereby depriving the City of its use and value.

Id. at 555 (Pivarnik, J., dissenting).

Does the dissent's position have merit? The majority likened the defendant's use of the city's computer to a mechanic's use of an employer's hammer. Is that analogy valid? Are there any other arguments for extending the scope of larceny to include the use of personal property? Should it matter whether the value lost by the owner is less than the value gained by the taker? In response to *Lund*, some states, including Virginia, have now enacted statutes specifically defining computer services as property within the scope of larceny, embezzlement, or false pretenses statutes. (*See, e.g.,* Cal. Penal Code § 502, which is excerpted below following *Oxford v. Moss.*)

Should it be a crime for an employee to violate an employer's computer policy? Should an employee's unauthorized use of a company computer to access personal email or check college basketball scores be criminal if it violates company policy? Should it matter what the motive for the unauthorized use is? In *United States v. Rodriguez*, 628 F.3d 1258 (11th Cir. 2010), the defendant utilized his computer access at the Social Security Administration to obtain information about former girlfriends and other women with whom he sought a romantic relationship. He was convicted under the federal Computer Fraud and Abuse Act (CFAA) on 17 misdemeanor counts of "intentionally access[ing] a computer without authorization or exceed[ing] authorized access, and thereby obtain[ing] . . . information from any department or agency of the United States." 18 U.S.C. § 1030(a)(2)(B). The Eleventh Circuit held that under that provision of the statute, "use of information is irrelevant if [the defendant] obtained the information without authorization or as a result of exceeding authorized access." Accordingly, the court rejected the defendant's argument that he did not obtain the information to defraud anyone or realize financial gain, observing that the statute's misdemeanor penalty provision (unlike the felony provision) "does not contain any language regarding purposes for committing the offense."

In *United States v. John*, 597 F.3d 263 (5th Cir. 2010), the Fifth Circuit likewise held that an employee of Citigroup could be convicted under subsection (a)(2) of the statute for "exceeding authorized access" if the defendant exceeded "limits placed on *the use* of information obtained by permitted access to a computer system and data available on that system," "at least when the user knows or reasonably should know that he or she is not authorized to access a computer and information obtainable from that access in furtherance of or to perpetrate a crime."

By contrast, the en banc Ninth Circuit read the CFAA more narrowly in *United States v. Nosal*, 676 F.3d 854 (9th Cir. 2012) (en banc), concluding that the statutory term "exceeds authorized access" "is limited to violations of restrictions on *access* to information, and not restrictions on its *use*." The statute's purpose, the court reasoned, was "to punish hacking—the circumvention of technological access barriers—not misappropriation of trade secrets," and the court therefore was not persuaded that Congress intended to criminalize "minor dalliances" like "g-chatting with friends, playing games, shopping or watching sports highlights" on work computers. "If Congress meant to expand the scope of criminal liability to everyone who uses a computer in violation of computer use restrictions—which may well include everyone who uses a computer—we would expect it to use language better suited to that purpose," the court noted. The Ninth Circuit was critical of decisions in *Rodriguez* and *John*, observing that the courts in those cases "looked only at the culpable behavior of the defendants before them, and failed to consider the effect on millions of ordinary citizens caused by the statute's unitary definition of 'exceeds authorized access.'"

(b) *Real Property.* At common law it was not larceny to take and carry away in one continuous act anything adhering to the soil. According to one court, the curious rationale for this principle was that "upon severance the property was converted into personality within the possession of the wrongdoer." *Commonwealth v. Meinhart*, 98 A.2d 392, 394 (Pa. Super Ct. 1953). Because larceny is a wrong against possession, meaning that defendants cannot steal from their own possession, "thieves who severed and carried away things attached to real property by one continuous act escaped criminal liability on a technicality." *Id.* Thus, in *State v. Jackson*, 11 S.E.2d 149 (N.C. 1940), the court held that the defendant could not be convicted of larceny for taking a tombstone from a cemetery. Where the acts of severance and asportation were distinct, however, such as where trees were cut down one day and removed at a later time, the common-law crime of larceny did apply. Many states, by statute or court decision, now consider it larceny to take items adhering to real property without requiring separate acts of severance and asportation. *See* Wayne R. LaFave, Criminal Law § 19.4, at 982–83 (5th ed. 2010).

(c) *Services.* At common law, larceny did not cover the use of the labor or services of another, as such "property" was not capable of asportation. Thus, in *Chappell v. United States*, 270 F.2d 274 (9th Cir. 1959), the court reversed the larceny conviction of an Air Force master sergeant who used soldiers under his command to paint his house. Some modern statutes, however, specifically make it a crime to steal labor or services. *See, e.g.,* Model Penal Code § 223.7. In *People v. Topino,* 573 N.Y.S.2d 848 (N.Y. Sup. Ct. 1991), the court held that while the defendant's refusal to pay his taxi fare could conceivably have violated New York's traditional larceny statute, the more appropriate charge would have been the separate crime of "theft of services."

Should the theft of services be criminalized? What about summer associates who make unauthorized use of their law firm's resources by making photocopies of their resumes on their own time? What if a summer associate deceptively engages the help of the firm's librarians, secretaries, and paralegals, who spend dozens of hours researching, typing, and proofreading the student's law journal note?

What about a professor's unauthorized use of a research assistant? In *United States v. Croft,* 750 F.2d 1354 (7th Cir. 1984), the court held that a University of Wisconsin professor knowingly converted to his own use a "thing of value" belonging to the United States (thereby violating 18 U.S.C. § 641) when he misappropriated a student's services for his own personal research project, using federal grant money to remunerate the student.

(d) *Electricity, Gas, Water, and Power.* Metered electricity, natural gas, water in pipes, heat, power, and similar forms of intangible energy are generally considered "tangible property" for purposes of larceny, and unauthorized diversion of such resources is deemed sufficient to support a larceny conviction. According to *People v. Menagas,* 11 N.E.2d 403, 406 (Ill. 1937), the modern seminal case in this area, "the true test of what is a proper subject of larceny seems to be not whether the subject is corporeal or incorporeal, but whether it is capable of appropriation by another than the owner." In finding that larceny charges could be brought against a defendant who wrongfully took electrical energy by attaching wires to a conductor belonging to another, the court explained that "[e]lectricity, the same as gas, is a valuable article of merchandise, bought and sold like other personal property and is capable of appropriation by another." *Id.* at 407. *See also People v. McLaughlin,* 402 N.Y.S.2d 137 (N.Y. Sup. Ct. 1978) (holding that electric current may be the subject of larceny, and thus one who tampers with a meter and diverts electricity has committed larceny).

Some states, such as New York, use both larceny statutes and theft-of-service statutes to protect this type of property. In tracing the development of the definition of "property" under New York penal law, the court in *People v. Neiss,* 423 N.Y.S.2d 942, 944 (N.Y. App. Div. 1980), observed a "plain dichotomy between the concept of gas as an identifiable substance of intrinsic value, and the concept of affording the service of supplying that commodity by utilization of other property such as metering equipment and supply lines." That dichotomy, the court concluded, allows defendants to be prosecuted for both larceny (for the actual taking of property, i.e., the gas) and theft-of-services (for the wrongful receipt of the service of having gas supplied).

(e) *Animals.* At common law, domestic animals were covered by larceny while animals of a base nature were not. Thus, the theft of a cow, horse, hog, or chicken was deemed larceny, while the theft of a dog, cat, monkey, or fox was not. Under more recent court decisions and legislation, all animals reduced to possession are now considered personal property in most states. California, for example, previously considered the taking of an animal to be larceny only if the animal was a "horse, mare, gelding, any bovine animal, any caprine animal, mule, jack, jenny, sheep, lamb, hog, sow, boar, gilt, burro or pig." Cal. Penal Code § 487. In 1982, the California legislature amended the statute to include dogs, *see* Cal. Penal Code §§ 487e, 487f, 487g, and now cats are also considered "personal property" in California.

In *People v. Sadowski*, 202 Cal. Rptr. 201 (Cal. Ct. App. 1984), for example, the defendant was carrying Veronica Meleson's Balinese Lynx Point cat "Truffle" to his car when Meleson saw him. She ran out her front door, yelling "kitty, kitty," and the defendant dropped the cat, which ran back to Meleson. The court, in affirming the defendant's grand theft conviction, found "no reason to distinguish between the theft of a $200 cat and a $200 dog or [to subject] the theft of one . . . to greater punishment than the theft of the other." *Id.* at 203.

Why might the law have protected "domestic" animals but not "base" animals? Does the common-law distinction among animals suggest that the law of larceny is really designed to protect victims' livelihood rather than their property? How does such an interpretation comport with Fletcher's views (described in the prior Note) about the interests protected by larceny? Should the criminal law protect some kinds of property more than others?

(f) *Intangibles.* The theft of personal property that has only symbolic value, such as stocks, bonds, checks, and promissory notes, was not considered larceny at common law. Many states have now adopted statutes broadening the scope of larceny to include such property. For example, the definition of property in New York's larceny statute includes any "computer data, computer program, thing in action, [or] evidence of debt or contract." N.Y. Penal Law § 155.00(1).

Should "contractual rights" also be considered personal property? In *People v. Podolsky*, 496 N.Y.S.2d 619 (N.Y. Sup. Ct. 1985), the court held that tenants' leasehold interests in their apartments could be stolen if they were wrongfully evicted by their landlords. The court concluded that the landlords could be charged with grand larceny, but cautioned that "nonpossessory or indefinite interests are not property susceptible of larceny." *Id.* at 624. Should the "theft" of a customer who is under a nonterminable contract with a competitor constitute larceny? *See People v. Spatarella*, 313 N.E.2d 38 (N.Y. 1974) (holding that a customer is "property" for purposes of the state's extortion statute).

5. The Model Penal Code's Definition of Property. The Model Penal Code takes an expansive view of the type of property that ought to be protected by the theft laws. Section 223.0(6) of the Code provides:

> "[P]roperty" means anything of value, including real estate, tangible and intangible personal property, contract rights, choses-in-action and other interests in or claims to wealth, admission or transportation tickets, captured or domestic animals, food and drink, electric and other power.

6. The Value of the Property. So long as the property that is taken is one of the types protected by the larceny laws, only minimal value is required. Thus, a California appellate court held that an empty cigarette carton has intrinsic value and therefore could be stolen under the state's theft statute. *See People v. Franco*, 84 Cal. Rptr. 513 (Cal. Ct. App. 1970).

What about a free newspaper? Suppose *A* notices his picture on the cover of a free newspaper and, wanting to impress friends and relatives with his new-found fame, scoops up every copy he can find across the city. Is that larceny? Consider the curious case of San Francisco Police Chief Richard Hongisto, who was fired in 1992 for allegedly ordering the removal from sidewalk newsstands of a controversial Bay Area newspaper that had lampooned him on its cover. Despite the fact that police officers confiscated more than 2,000 copies of the paper, no charges were filed against Hongisto. "Since the newspapers were given away free, the fair-market value was zero, and thus the newspaper doesn't constitute property which would be chargeable under the [California] theft statute," the District Attorney explained. David Dietz, *Hongisto Blasts Panel on Firing*, S.F. Chron., May 16, 1992, at A1. Indeed, the state statute's definition of theft provides that "[i]n determining the value of the property obtained . . . , the reasonable and fair market value shall be the test." Cal. Penal Code § 484. Does it make sense to say that an empty cigarette carton has value but not a free newspaper? Was the District Attorney right in refusing to charge Hongisto? Would it make a difference if the left-over newspapers were typically removed from the newsstands and redeemed for compensation at a recycling plant?

It is important to note that the absence of criminal charges does not necessarily mean wrongful conduct has no remedy. Police Chief Hongisto and the City of San Francisco were sued civilly by the Bay Times' publishers, and damages were awarded after a jury trial. In addition, almost $700,000 in legal fees were awarded against the City. *See City Socked for $700,000 in Paper's Suit Against Hongisto*, The Recorder (Mar. 9, 1995); *Coming Up, Inc. v. City of San Francisco*, 857 F. Supp. 711 (N.D. Cal. 1994) (denying qualified immunity).

In some jurisdictions, even property that has no intrinsic or market value can still be the subject of larceny if it has any value to its owner. Thus, if homeowners spread garbage across their lawn for aesthetic reasons, someone who removed the garbage could be guilty of larceny in those jurisdictions. *See* Rollin M. Perkins & Ronald N. Boyce, Criminal Law 296 (3d ed. 1982). Does this rule make sense? Does the fact that the homeowners "invested" time and thought about where to put the pieces of garbage indicate that the placement of the items does in fact have value? What about the fact that the owners would have to replace the garbage in order to restore their aesthetic plan?

7. Grand Versus Petty Larceny. Practically all jurisdictions in the United States distinguish thefts according to the monetary value of the property stolen, although the particular dividing line between grand and petty larceny varies. California, for example, uses $950 as the benchmark in most cases. *See* Cal. Penal Code § 487. A common justification for such distinctions is that they help ensure the appropriate amount of deterrence. Thieves who realize greater gains should receive longer sentences to deter their criminal activity, whereas shorter sentences should be sufficient to deter petty thieves. *See* Wayne R. LaFave, Criminal Law § 18.4(b), at 983–86 (5th ed. 2010); Model Penal Code § 223.1(2).

In *Lund*, the court found the evidence insufficient to establish that the computer print-outs had a value of $100, the statutory minimum in Virginia for grand larceny. Although Lund could possibly have been prosecuted for petty larceny, the constitutional protections against double jeopardy precluded the prosecution from bringing that charge after he had already been tried for grand larceny.

English law, by contrast, does not distinguish larceny offenses according to the amount stolen. Professor C.M.V. Clarkson explains:

> [I]t is as much theft to steal a can of beans as to steal, 10 million. . . . The argument in support of the English approach is that the value of the property is only one way of assessing the extent of the harm and it cannot be made decisive. For instance, the following could be cited as possible indicators of the gravity of an offence: the characteristics of the offender (e.g., theft by a person in a position of trust); the characteristics of the victim (e.g., theft from the old or disabled; theft from individuals as opposed to theft from companies); the circumstances of the offence (e.g., pickpocketing—an "offensive and frightening type of theft"; thefts committed jointly with others); and the non-monetary value of the goods (e.g., a key to be used subsequently for a more serious offence; property of purely sentimental value to the victim).

C.M.V. Clarkson, Understanding Criminal Law 159 (1987).

In the federal system, the Federal Sentencing Guidelines governing economic crimes (most of which are fraud convictions of one type or another) have treated "loss" as a key component determining the length of a defendant's sentence. Many of these cases involve conspiracies in which each participant is treated as being responsible for all losses generated by the conspiracy. As a result, federal sentences in many large-scale fraud conspiracy cases can be incredibly high, even for relatively low-level participants. An American Bar Association Task Force recently endorsed an alternative sentencing model that makes loss less important and focuses more on the culpability of each defendant's acts. *See* A Report on Behalf of the American Bar Association Criminal Justice Section Task Force on the Reform of Federal Sentencing for Economic Crimes (Nov. 10, 2014), http://www.americanbar.org/content/dam/aba/uncategorized/criminal_justice/economic_crimes.authcheckdam.pdf. Some federal judges have relied on the ABA Report in departing from the guidelines. *See, e.g., United States v. Faibish*, 2015 U.S. Dist. Lexis 101200 (E.D.N.Y. Aug. 3, 2015). For further discussion of the Federal Sentencing Guidelines, see Chapter 2, Section D.2.b.

8. The Debate Among Economic Theorists. As you study the theft crimes, evaluate whether the criminal law protects all property interests equitably or whether instead it reflects an inappropriate bias by securing the status quo without regard to how society's wealth is distributed. Consider the following critique of the current laws:

> In its delineation of offenses against property and the application of general "principles" of liability and excuse, criminal law helps to construct a particular conception of legitimate interests in property and a particular image of illegitimate threats to those interests. Hence criminal laws focus on a relatively "conventional" conception of property, which, although it has slightly different scope in different areas, generally excludes many forms of "intangible property" and certainly fails to accommodate the interests in welfare and social security provision which have been dubbed the "new property."
>
> . . . True to its general form, criminal law constructs property offending as an issue of individual responsibility which abstracts the defendant from her social context and thus from potentially embarrassing contextual conditions such as poverty, discrimination and radical inequalities of wealth. In this way, the legal institution is enabled not only to protect property rights but to express and reinforce the legitimacy of the property system in doing so.
>
> . . . Our reflections on the protection of property again lead us away from a simple view of criminal law as even-handedly protecting a conception of valued interests underpinned by social consensus. Rather, our study suggests a broader and subtler set of functions for criminal law, encompassing the expression and underpinning of the perceived social legitimacy of a particular conception of the interests which it serves. Criminal law defends not property at large, but certain kinds of highly unevenly distributed property.
>
> It thereby defends not only property, but the power of certain interests and the authority of the social order which maintains that narrow conception and that inegalitarian distribution.

Nicola Lacey, Celia Wells & Dirk Meure, Reconstructing Criminal Law: Critical Perspectives on Crime and the Criminal Process 501–02 (1990).

On the other hand, consider the economic perspective offered by Judge Richard Posner:

> The major function of criminal law in a capitalist society is to prevent people from bypassing the system of voluntary, compensated exchange — the "market," explicit or implicit — in situations where, because transaction costs are low, the market is a more efficient method of allocating resources than forced exchange. Market bypassing in such situations is inefficient — in the sense in which economists equate efficiency with wealth maximization — no matter how much utility it may confer on the offender.
>
> Much of this market bypassing cannot be deterred by tort law — that is, by privately enforced damage suits. The optimal damages that would be required for deterrence would so frequently exceed the offender's ability to

pay that public enforcement and nonmonetary sanctions such as imprisonment are required.

 . . . This means that the criminal law is designed primarily for the nonaffluent; the affluent are kept in line, for the most part, by tort law. This may seem to be a left-wing kind of suggestion ("criminal law keeps the lid on the lower classes"), but it is not. It is efficient to use different sanctions depending on an offender's wealth. The suggestion is not refuted by the fact that fines are a common criminal penalty. They are much lower than the corresponding tort damage judgments, and hence usable even against relatively nonaffluent offenders, for two reasons. The government invests resources in raising the probability of criminal punishment above that of a tort suit, which makes the optimal fine lower than the punitive damages that would be optimal in the absence of such an investment. Second, a fine is a more severe punishment than its dollar cost. Almost every criminal punishment imposes some nonpecuniary disutility in the form of a stigma, enhanced by such rules as forbidding a convicted criminal to vote. There is no corresponding stigma to a tort judgment.

Richard A. Posner, *An Economic Theory of Criminal Law*, 85 Colum. L. Rev. 1193, 1195, 1204–05 (1985). For another economic perspective, see Guido Calabresi & A. Douglas Melamed, *Property Rules, Liability Rules and Inalienability: One View of the Cathedral*, 85 Harv. L. Rev. 1089, 1124–27 (1972) (arguing that criminal sanctions deter would-be thieves — including, presumably, wealthy ones — from simply bypassing market negotiations and accepting civil damages liability for what they wrongfully take).

Is economic theory helpful in explaining what kinds of property acquisitions are criminalized? Consider Professor Jules Coleman's critique of economic theory:

[I]n crimes the question is whether the state has the right to deprive a particular person of his liberty by incarcerating him. . . . [T]he State must be satisfied that the individual deserves to be punished. . . . So, in order for the state to take the extraordinary step of imposing this burden on someone, it must show that in some sense he deserves it. That argument requires an inquiry not only into what a person does but also into his responsibility and guilt for having done it. These are essential features of the criminal law, and it is not surprising that an economic analysis of crimes that focuses on the inducement aspect of the criminal law in terms of securing compliance with transfer mechanisms should miss it entirely. Such a theory has no place for the moral sentiments and virtues appropriate to matters of crime and punishment: guilt, shame, remorse, forgiveness and mercy, to name a few. A purely economic theory of crime can only impoverish, not enrich, our understanding of the nature of crime.

Jules L. Coleman, Markets, Morals and the Law 164–65 (1988).

Oxford v. Moss

68 Crim. App. R. 183 (Div'l Ct. 1978)

SMITH, JUSTICE.

This is a prosecutor's Appeal by way of Case Stated.

On May 5, 1976, an information was preferred by the prosecutor against the defendant alleging that the defendant stole certain intangible property, namely, confidential information being examination questions for a Civil Engineering Examination to be held in the month of June 1976 at Liverpool University, the information being the property of the Senate of the University, and the allegation being that the respondent intended permanently to deprive the said Senate of the said property.

The facts can be stated very shortly indeed. They were agreed facts. . . . In May 1976 the defendant was a student at Liverpool University. He was studying engineering. Somehow (and this Court is not concerned precisely how) he was able to acquire the proof of an examination paper for an examination in Civil Engineering to be held in the University during the following month, that is to say June 1976. Without doubt the proof, that is to say the piece of paper, was the property of the University. It was an agreed fact, as set out in the case, that the respondent at no time intended to steal what is described as "any tangible element" belonging to the paper; that is to say it is conceded that he never intended to steal the paper itself.

In truth and in fact, and in all common sense, what he was about was this. He was borrowing a piece of paper hoping to be able to return it and not be detected in order that he should acquire advance knowledge of the questions to be set in the examination and thereby, I suppose, he would be enabled to have an unfair advantage as against other students who did not possess the knowledge that he did.

By any standards, it was conduct which is to be condemned, and to the layman it would readily be described as cheating. The question raised is whether it is conduct which falls within the scope of the criminal law.

. . . The question for this Court, shortly put, is whether confidential information can amount to property within the meaning of the Theft Act 1968. By section 1(1) of the statute: "A person is guilty of theft if he dishonestly appropriates property belonging to another with the intention of permanently depriving the other of it . . . ."

By section 4(1): "'property' includes money and all other property, real or personal, including things in action and other intangible property."

The question for this Court is whether confidential information of this sort falls within that definition contained in section 4(1). We have been referred to a number of authorities emanating from the area of trade secrets and matrimonial secrets. In particular, we were referred to *Peter Pan Manufacturing Corporation v. Corsets Silhouette Ltd.* [1963] 3 All E.R. 402, to *Seager v. Copydex Ltd.* [1967] 2 All E.R. 415, to the case of *Argyll v. Argyll* [1965] 2 W.L.R. 790, and *Fraser v. Evans* [1968] 3 W.L.R. 1172.

Those are cases concerned with what is described as the duty to be of good faith. They are clear illustrations of the proposition that, if a person obtains information which is given to him in confidence and then sets out to take an unfair advantage of it, the courts will restrain him by way of an order of injunction or will condemn him in damages if an injunction is found to be inappropriate. . . . [T]hey are of little assistance in the present situation in which we have to consider whether there is property in the information which is capable of being the subject of a charge of theft. . . . [I]t is clear that the answer to that question must be no. . . .

. . . Appeal dismissed.

California Penal Code §§ 499c, 502

§ 499c. Trade secrets; theft; solicitation or bribery to acquire; punishment; defenses

(a) As used in this section:

(1) "Access" means to approach, a way or means of approaching, nearing, admittance to, including to instruct, communicate with, store information in, or retrieve information from a computer system or computer network.

(2) "Article" means any object, material, device, or substance or copy thereof, including any writing, record, recording, drawing, sample, specimen, prototype, model, photograph, micro-organism, blueprint, map, or tangible representation of a computer program or information, including both human and computer readable information and information while in transit.

(3) "Benefit" means gain or advantage, or anything regarded by the beneficiary as gain or advantage, including benefit to any other person or entity in whose welfare he or she is interested.

. . . .

(7) "Copy" means any facsimile, replica, photograph or other reproduction of an article, and any note, drawing or sketch made of or from an article.

(8) "Representing" means describing, depicting, containing, constituting, reflecting or recording.

(9) "Trade secret" means information, including a formula, pattern, compilation, device, method, technique, or process, that:

(A) Derives independent economic value, actual or potential, from not being generally known to the public or to other persons who can obtain economic value from its disclosure or use; and

(B) Is the subject of efforts that are reasonable under the circumstances to maintain its secrecy.

(b) Every person is guilty of theft who, with intent to deprive or withhold the control of a trade secret from its owner, or with an intent to appropriate a trade secret to his or her own use or to the use of another, does any of the following:

(1) Steals, takes, carries away, or uses without authorization a trade secret.

(2) Fraudulently appropriates any article representing a trade secret entrusted to him or her.

(3) Having unlawfully obtained access to the article, without authority makes or causes to be made a copy of any article representing a trade secret.

(4) Having obtained access to the article through a relationship of trust and confidence, without authority and in breach of the obligations created by that relationship, makes or causes to be made, directly from and in the presence of the article, a copy of any article representing a trade secret.

(c) Every person who promises, offers or gives, or conspires to promise or offer to give, to any present or former agent, employee or servant of another, a benefit as an inducement, bribe or reward for conveying, delivering or otherwise making available an article representing a trade secret owned by his or her present or former principal, employer or master, to any person not authorized by the owner to receive or acquire the trade secret and every present or former agent, employee, or servant, who solicits, accepts, receives or takes a benefit as an inducement, bribe or reward for conveying, delivering or otherwise making available an article representing a trade secret owned by his or her present or former principal, employer or master, to any person not authorized by the owner to receive or acquire the trade secret, shall be punished by imprisonment in the state prison, or in a county jail not exceeding one year, or by a fine not exceeding five thousand dollars ($5,000), or by both that fine and imprisonment.

(d) In a prosecution for a violation of this section, it shall be no defense that the person returned or intended to return the article.

§ 502. Unauthorized access to computers, computer systems and computer data

(a) It is the intent of the Legislature in enacting this section to expand the degree of protection afforded to individuals, businesses, and governmental agencies from tampering, interference, damage, and unauthorized access to lawfully created computer data and computer systems. The Legislature finds and declares that the proliferation of computer technology has resulted in a concomitant proliferation of computer crime and other forms of unauthorized access to computers, computer systems, and computer data.

The Legislature further finds and declares that protection of the integrity of all types and forms of lawfully created computers, computer systems, and computer data is vital to the protection of the privacy of individuals as well as to the well-being of financial institutions, business concerns, governmental agencies, and others within this state that lawfully utilize those computers, computer systems, and data.

. . . .

(c) Except as provided in subdivision (h), any person who commits any of the following acts is guilty of a public offense:

(1) Knowingly accesses and without permission alters, damages, deletes, destroys, or otherwise uses any data, computer, computer system, or computer network in order to either (A) devise or execute any scheme or artifice to defraud, deceive, or extort, or (B) wrongfully control or obtain money, property, or data.

(2) Knowingly accesses and without permission takes, copies, or makes use of any data from a computer, computer system, or computer network, or takes or copies any supporting documentation, whether existing or residing internal or external to a computer, computer system, or computer network.

(3) Knowingly and without permission uses or causes to be used computer services.

(4) Knowingly accesses and without permission adds, alters, damages, deletes, or destroys any data, computer software, or computer programs which reside or exist internal or external to a computer, computer system, or computer network.

(5) Knowingly and without permission disrupts or causes the disruption of computer services or denies or causes the denial of computer services to an authorized user of a computer, computer system, or computer network.

(6) Knowingly and without permission provides or assists in providing a means of accessing a computer, computer system, or computer network in violation of this section.

(7) Knowingly and without permission accesses or causes to be accessed any computer, computer system, or computer network.

(8) Knowingly introduces any computer contaminant into any computer, computer system, or computer network.

. . . .

(h)(1) Subdivision (c) does not apply to any person who accesses his or her employer's computer system, computer network, computer program, or data when acting within the scope of his or her lawful employment.

(2) Paragraph (3) of subdivision (c) does not apply to any employee who accesses or uses his or her employer's computer system, computer network, computer program, or data when acting outside the scope of his or her lawful employment, so long as the employee's activities do not cause an injury . . . to the employer or another, or so long as the value of supplies and computer services . . . which are used do not exceed an accumulated total of one hundred dollars ($100).

(i) No activity exempted from prosecution under paragraph (2) of subdivision (h) which incidentally violates paragraph (2), (4), or (7) of subdivision (c) shall be prosecuted under those paragraphs.

[The punishment varies for the different offenses described in subdivision (c). The maximum punishment is three years' imprisonment and a $10,000 fine, although subdivision (k) of the statute instructs sentencing courts to "consider prohibitions on access to and use of computers" as well as "alternate sentencing, including community service, if the defendant shows remorse and recognition of the wrongdoing, and an inclination not to repeat the offense." In addition, subdivision (g) provides that any computer owned by the defendant and used in committing a crime under this statute is subject to forfeiture.]

Notes and Questions

1. **Should Information Be Subject to Theft?** Traditionally, information, including trade secrets, was not protected by larceny statutes. A number of state and federal statutes have been amended or interpreted, however, to cover some kinds of information. In *United States v. Girard*, 601 F.2d 69 (2d Cir. 1979), Girard, a former agent of the Drug Enforcement Administration, sought to sell to one James Bond secret information from DEA files that identified certain government informants. Girard obtained this information from Lambert, a DEA agent who had access to the agency's computer. Unfortunately for Girard and Lambert, James Bond (true to his fictional namesake) became an informant for the DEA, and the two men were convicted of violating 18 U.S.C. § 641, the federal statute prohibiting the theft of public money, property, or records. In affirming their conviction, the court of appeals upheld the district court's decision that the information qualified as a "thing of value," and thus fell within the property covered by § 641.

One newspaper columnist was not impressed by the case:

> It does not matter if the original government document remains in the files. Anyone who copies it or makes notes from it without official approval has still stolen "property."
>
> For advocates of secrecy, the beauty of that legal theory is that it applies no matter what kind of government information is involved. National security need not have a thing to do with it. The price of food in the White House mess, the Amtrak deficit — any fact that leaked could be the subject of a criminal prosecution.
>
> In short, the government property theory of information would give this country an Official Secrets Act.

Anthony Lewis, Int'l Herald Trib., June 20, 1978.

Criticizing the expansive definition of property in § 641, Professor Michael Tigar writes:

> [T]he government's view . . . defines a concept of property that strikes directly at the citizenry's customary use [of information] rights. . . . One had simply assumed that, in a democratic society, government would not stand itself in opposition to its citizens and claim an exclusive proprietary right in its information without some further showing that the character of a particular item of information entitled it to special protection.

Michael E. Tigar, *The Right of Property and the Law of Theft*, 62 Tex. L. Rev. 1443, 1468 (1984). Do Lewis and Tigar have legitimate concerns about criminalizing the exchange of information in a free society? Should we be even more concerned today given the adoption of the federal Computer Fraud and Abuse Act, discussed above in Note 4(a) following *Lund v. Commonwealth*? Does Cal. Penal Code § 502(c)(2), which is quoted above, mean that anyone who has access to, but not specific permission to use, information stored in a computer of a government agency or a private entity might be committing a crime by disclosing that information, because disclosure is use?

Consider the controversy generated by Procter and Gamble's use of an Ohio law to protect information about the company from being disclosed by the media:

> From its twin towers marking the start of downtown to the corporate-subsidized flowerpots that brighten the sidewalks, the imprint of the Procter & Gamble Company on this city is as strong as a Pete Rose slide into second base.
>
> Until this summer, few people here questioned the company's influence in the city where it was founded, in 1837. But the news that the Cincinnati police had conducted an electronic search of all telephone records in the metropolitan area at the behest of Procter & Gamble to help stop news disclosures brought to the surface an old but seldom-discussed complaint.
>
> . . . Procter & Gamble officials have said the investigation was prompted by two articles in The Wall Street Journal in June. The articles, about a pending resignation of a top executive and the possible sale of one division, were written by Alecia Swasy, who is based in Pittsburgh. She quoted unidentified current and former company employees as her sources.
>
> Under a 1974 Ohio law, it is a misdemeanor for an employee of a company to "furnish or disclose confidential matter or information" to "any person not privileged to acquire it."
>
> Many legal experts, inside and outside of Ohio, were surprised that such a law was on the books. They said it appears to violate First Amendment protection of free speech. Edward Fletcher, a law professor at the University of Cincinnati who specializes in trade law, said he had never heard of anyone in Ohio being prosecuted under the law. It was intended to stop business secrets from getting into the hands of competitors, not to prevent sources from talking to newspapers, he said.
>
> "This application is certainly a novel use of the law," Mr. Fletcher said . . . .

Timothy Egan, *Vast Influence of Procter & Gamble Revives Old Questions in Cincinnati*, N.Y. Times, Sept. 1, 1991, at A18. Although several P & G employees were questioned in connection with the leaks, the source of the leaks was never identified and Artzt ultimately wrote a letter to P & G employees admitting that the company had committed "'an error of judgment' that turned into an 'embarrassing experience.'" *The Pampers Police*, St. Petersburg Times, Sept. 9, 1991, at A10.

2. Theft of Trade Secrets. In an information-oriented economy, is it appropriate to protect trade secrets from "theft"? Is it possible to define those secrets in a way that preserves the rights of free speech and press and also protects economic investments? Does the California trade secrets act strike an appropriate balance? Could it be applied as broadly as the Ohio statute was in the Procter & Gamble case described in the prior Note?

Is criminalizing the theft of trade secrets likely to intimidate employees from moving to another company in the same industry? *See, e.g.,* Al Goodman, *A Lopez in Every Garage*, N.Y. TIMES, Oct. 26, 1999, at C1 (reporting the story of Jose Ignatio Lopez, who left an executive position at General Motors in 1993 to join Volkswagen because G.M. was not interested in building the cost-efficient manufacturing plant he envisioned, and was then accused of passing G.M.'s trade secrets to Volkswagen; criminal charges filed against Lopez in Germany were dropped when he paid a $230,000 fine, and the civil dispute between the two car manufacturers was settled in 1997 after Volkswagen paid G.M. $100 million and agreed to buy $1 billion in G.M. parts).

3. Theft of One's Own Trade Secret. Peter Taborsky, a former student lab assistant at the University of South Florida, was convicted of grand theft of trade secrets for stealing a process for extracting ammonia from clay that he himself had invented. The University took the position that the process, arguably worth millions of dollars, belonged to a company that had funded the research. Taborsky, on the other hand, maintained that he worked on the project on his own time after it was terminated. He was originally sentenced to probation and a year under house arrest and was ordered not to make any use of his invention. When he defied the court's order and applied for (and received) two patents for his invention, the court gave him the choice of assigning his patents to the University or going to prison. Taborsky refused to turn over the patents, and he was sentenced to 3½ years in prison. He subsequently declined, on principle, a pardon offered by the Governor and ultimately served 18 months in jail. *See* Leon Jaroff, *Intellectual Chain Gang: Convicted of Stealing His Own Ideas and Notebooks, an Idealistic Young Scientist Sits in Jail*, TIME, Feb. 10, 1997, at 64; Sue Carlton, *Probation Waived for Once-Jailed Researcher*, ST. PETERSBURG TIMES, Oct. 29, 1997, at B3.

4. Cheating on Exams. Should cheating on an exam be a criminal offense? In 1984, a New Jersey appeals court upheld a lower court ruling that the Educational Testing Service (ETS) had the right to invalidate the Scholastic Aptitude Test (SAT) scores of four high school students suspected of cheating on the test. *See Appeals Court Backs Invalidating S.A.T.'s of 4 in Cheating Inquiry*, N.Y. TIMES, July 15, 1984, at A41. ETS challenged the students' scores after a guidance counselor at the high school reported that he had heard rumors the four students had stolen a copy of the test. The students were members of the tennis team and had received permission to take the test earlier in the day because they were supposed to play a tennis match at the regularly scheduled time for the test. Assuming there was sufficient reason to doubt the validity of the students' scores—there was some talk that one of the students had even bragged about the misdeed—and given the considerable interest in preserving the integrity of an exam that plays such a crucial role in the college admissions process, could the state have brought criminal charges against the students? Would the test questions qualify as "trade secrets" under the California "trade secrets" statute reprinted above? For a recent example of students attempting to steal an exam, see Christopher Mele, *Student Arrested After Crawling into a Duct to Steal an Exam*, N.Y. Times, May 5, 2017.

Apparently the first criminal prosecution arising from cheating on the SAT occurred in 1992, when 19-year-old Laurence Adler pleaded guilty to perjury charges after testifying falsely at a hearing in a civil suit he had brought against ETS challenging the cancellation of his test score. Adler testified that he had taken the test, but later admitted that he had paid a college freshman $200 to take the exam for him. Although Adler was initially sentenced to six months in prison, the judge later reduced the jail sentence to 10 days, allowing Adler to serve the remainder of the term in a work-release program. *See* Veronica T. Jennings, *Teen Gets Six Months in SAT Scandal*, Wash. Post, Oct. 24, 1992, at A1; Veronica T. Jennings, *SAT Cheater's Jail Time Cut to 10 Days After New Plea*, Wash. Post, Dec. 24, 1992, at B1. For another extensive report on cheating practices, see Gary Putka, *Blackboard Jungle: A Cheating Epidemic at a Top High School Teaches Sad Lesson*, Wall St. J., June 29, 1992, at A1.

Is the case for criminalization stronger when cheating occurs on an admission examination for professional school or on a professional licensing examination? Given the potential for significant economic gain and even public safety concerns, why is this "wrong" behavior so infrequently addressed by criminal law?

5. Altering Law School Transcripts. A provision of the California Education Code, § 44360, makes it a misdemeanor to alter or use an altered transcript "with fraudulent intent." In 1999 a law school graduate pled guilty to this crime, after having obtained a job offer from a law firm based in part on his submission of another student's transcript, which showed a "more impressive . . . GPA" than his own. The student was sentenced to three years' probation and 200 hours of community service, was ordered to pay restitution to the law firm, and "face[d] possible disciplinary action by the State Bar." *See Grad Pleads No Contest to Doctoring Transcript*, The Daily Journal, Nov. 1999.

[2] Property "of Another"

Henry v. State
36 S.E. 55 (Ga. 1900)

Lewis, Justice.

Sherman Henry was placed upon trial in the city court of Albany, upon an accusation charging him with entering the dwelling-house of one Tempie Mack with intent to steal, and with wrongfully, fraudulently, and privately taking and carrying away therefrom, with intent to steal the same, one suit of clothes and one bicycle of the value of fifteen dollars, the personal property of said Mack. To this accusation he

plcadcd not guilty. Bricfly stated, the following is the substance of the testimony introduced on the trial: Tempie Mack, the prosecutrix, testified that the accused came to
her to engage board. She replied to him that he would have to pay her in advance, as
she had lost so much by boarders. Accused replied that he had a trunk full of clothes
and a bicycle, and that he would deliver them to her as security for the board. This
conversation took place during the day, and that night the accused came back to the
home of prosecutrix, bringing with him his trunk and bicycle, and said, "Here is a
suit of clothes that cost me $8.00, and a bicycle, that I turn over to you as security
for my board." She accordingly received these chattels, and had them placed in a room
in her house occupied by her son. The accused also was assigned to this room, where
he lodged as a boarder. He kept the key to his trunk, wore the clothes, and rode the
bicycle occasionally. In the trunk was a new suit of clothes. He agreed to pay $2.00
per week for board, and he remained in the house as a boarder a little over three
weeks, for which [Mack] was due $7.00. A demand was made on him for the money.
He left the house, leaving the bicycle and trunk therein. Two or three days afterward
the landlady missed the bicycle. She then examined his trunk, and found the new
suit of clothes had also been taken away. It further appeared from the testimony that
the accused had sold the bicycle, and was wearing the new suit of clothes in another
place where he was engaged in work. The accused introduced no evidence, but made
a statement, in which he admitted that he told the landlady his trunk and clothes
would be responsible for his board, but denied delivering them to her, stating that
he kept the key to his trunk, wore his clothes, and rode his bicycle whenever he wished;
said he did not intend to steal anything, but he put on the new suit of clothes to attend
to a job in Arlington, where he was working when arrested, and simply desired to
make some money so that he could pay his board. The judge of the city court, before
whom the case was tried without a jury, after hearing the evidence, found the accused
guilty; whereupon he made a motion for a new trial, on the general grounds that the
verdict was contrary to law and evidence. To the judgment of the court overruling
this motion the accused excepts.

There can be no question about the soundness of the proposition that property
stolen from a bailee may be charged in an indictment to be his property, and authorities have even gone to the extent of holding that property stolen from one who had
himself stolen it could be alleged as his. It is equally true that property in the hands
of a bailee may be stolen by the general owner.

. . . From these principles it necessarily follows that when property has been delivered by the owner to one as a pledge to secure a debt, the pledgee has sufficient interest in the same to maintain a prosecution against any one, even the general owner, by
charging that the property belonged to him, the pledgee. We do not understand, however, that this principle is denied. Counsel for plaintiff in error seeks a reversal in this
case upon the idea that the testimony does not show such a delivery of the property in
question as would constitute a valid pledge in law. We think there is sufficient testimony for the judge to infer an actual delivery by the accused of this property as security for the payment of his board. The fact that he was permitted to use it does not

deprive the pledgee in this case of the right to its custody and control. Nothing can be gathered from the evidence in the record to indicate that she ever consented to such a use or disposition of the same as to absolutely deprive her of such possession. A portion of the property pledged was actually sold to another party by the pledgor without her knowledge and consent; and the circumstances developed by the evidence touching the manner of its disposition by the pledgor were amply sufficient for the judge to infer that he had a fraudulent purpose of depriving his creditor of this security.

. . . Applying these principles to the facts in this case, we think the court did right in overruling the motion for a new trial.

Notes and Questions

1. Distinguishing Possession and Ownership. As *Henry* suggests, even the owner of a piece of property commits larceny by taking that property from someone who has a superior right of possession (e.g., property used as security for a debt). The element of larceny requiring that the property be "of another" is met under such circumstances.

Do cases like *Henry* suggest that the crime of larceny is intended to protect the right of possession and not simply ownership? Is the nonviolent wrongful taking of property a public wrong more deserving of criminal condemnation than other ways of wrongfully taking another person's wealth?

Was the landlady really in possession of Henry's bicycle and suit? How much evidence did the court have? Under the common law, the failure to pay a lodging bill despite a promise to do so would not constitute theft. Is there a reason to distinguish Henry's behavior from a breach of a promise to pay?

2. Stolen Property. The taking of stolen property or contraband falls within the scope of larceny. Thus, in *City of Bremerton v. Smith*, 199 P.2d 95 (Wash. 1948), the court affirmed the larceny conviction of four defendants who "mutilated and injured" certain illegal slot machines belonging to the Moose Lodge and then pilfered money from them. Rejecting the defendants' argument that slot machines are lotteries and not property, the court explained: "Though a possessor of a thing of value be unable to make good in court a legal right to possess it, still, one with no claim of right may not . . . by stealth, trick, force or threats take it from him." *Id.* at 96. Likewise, in *Levin v. United States*, 338 F.2d 265 (D.C. Cir. 1964), the president of a union gave the defendant $35,000, which was to be used to bribe the jurors sitting on the union president's perjury trial. Instead, the defendant appropriated the money for his own use. The court held that the fact that the union president had embezzled the funds from the union was irrelevant for purposes of the charges filed against the defendant because "it is well settled that one who steals money or property which itself [has] been stolen by another may be prosecuted notwithstanding the illegality of his victim's possession." *Id.* at 268.

Are these cases consistent with *Henry*? Should a defendant with no claim to the property who wrongfully takes possession be able to argue as a defense that the victim was not the rightful owner? If a third person subsequently steals stolen property, could the original thief bring a successful suit for damages against the third party? If not, why should the third party be subject to criminal prosecution? Is there any reason to give a thief an opportunity to profit from theft? Is there a deterrence rationale for prosecuting any thief, even one who steals from another thief?

3. Joint and Community Property. The traditional common-law view holds that a partner who steals from the partnership has not taken the "property of another" and therefore cannot be convicted of larceny. As one court explained:

> We conclude that, without specific statutory authority, the unauthorized taking by a partner of partnership assets is not a crime.

> Other factors indicate a need for caution in extending criminal liability to partnership disputes. The misuse of partnership money, in this case to pay a debt to a former partner, is the type of partnership dispute commonly seen in civil courts. The defendant argues that [the] partnership agreement implies that the partners anticipated that separate debts of individual partners might be paid out of partnership funds. . . . Interpretation of the partnership agreement is best left to a civil court or to arbitration, as required by the partnership agreement. If a civil court finds that the $1500 payment constituted a misuse of partnership funds, the aggrieved partners have adequate remedies. . . .

People v. Clayton, 728 P.2d 723, 726 (Colo. 1986).

The dissenter in *Clayton* argued that a "partner should not be immune from prosecution for theft because the property he steals belongs to the partnership." *Id.* at 726 (Vollack, J., dissenting). Likewise, other courts have recognized the partnership as a legal entity that satisfies the "of another" requirement and have therefore allowed partners to be charged with criminal theft. *See, e.g., People v. Sobiek*, 106 Cal. Rptr. 519 (Cal. Ct. App. 1973). Should the criminal law become involved in disputes among partners, or is the controversy better left to civil law?

Theft from a spouse, like theft from a partnership, was also not recognized as larceny under traditional common law. Because the common law considered the wife a mere chattel of the husband, it is not surprising that spouses could not steal from each other. Under the law of torts, spouses could not sue each other either, although most states have now abrogated this rule. Likewise, there are now court opinions and statutes rejecting the common-law rule in criminal theft cases as well. In *People v. Wallace*, 434 N.W.2d 422 (Mich. Ct. App. 1988), for example, Mr. Wallace snatched from Mrs. Wallace's neck a gold chain she had received as a gift from a male friend. Mr. Wallace was charged with larceny from the person. (For a detailed discussion of the distinction between larceny and robbery in "snatching" cases, see Chapter 9, Section A, Note 3.) The court held that the Married Women's Property Acts changed the common-law rule and "gave married women the power to protect, control and dispose of property in their own name, free from their husbands' interference." *Id.* at 428. *See also People v. Morton*, 123 N.E.2d 790 (N.Y. 1954) (holding that the

Married Women's Acts destroyed the fiction of legal unity between husband and wife, thus qualifying the wife as "another" person for purposes of property).

To what extent is the common-law exception for stealing from a spouse simply the natural outgrowth of the unwillingness to criminalize stealing among partners? To what extent does it reflect society's hesitancy to take seriously crimes committed by one family member against another? To what extent does it reflect sexism?

The Model Penal Code and an increasing number of modern courts reject the common-law rule protecting partners and spouses from criminal theft prosecutions. Section 223.0(7) of the Code provides that " 'property of another' includes property in which any person other than the actor has an interest which the actor is not privileged to infringe, regardless of the fact that the actor also has an interest in the property." *See also id.* § 223.1(4).

[3] The Asportation and Caption Requirements

State v. Carswell

249 S.E.2d 427 (N.C. 1978)

COPELAND, JUSTICE.

The Court of Appeals held that the movement of the air conditioner in this case was an insufficient taking and asportation to constitute a case of larceny against the defendant. Because we believe that there was enough evidence to send the larceny charge to the jury, we reverse the Court of Appeals on this point and reinstate the judgment of Judge Thornburg [convicting defendant of felonious larceny and felonious breaking and entering, and imposing consecutive sentences of five years and ten years respectively].

This case comes to the Court only on the contention that the judge erroneously denied defendant's motion for nonsuit on the larceny charge. It is well settled that in ruling on such a motion, the evidence is considered in the light most favorable to the State, and the State is given the benefit of all reasonable inferences.

Larceny has been defined as "a wrongful taking and carrying away of the personal property of another without his consent, . . . with intent to deprive the owner of his property and to appropriate it to the taker's use fraudulently." *State v. Griffin*, 239 N.C. 41, 45, 79 S.E.2d 230, 232 (1953). "A bare removal from the place in which he found the goods, though the thief does not quite make off with them, is a sufficient asportation, or carrying away." 4 W. BLACKSTONE, COMMENTARIES 231.

In *State v. Green*, 81 N.C. 560 (1879), the defendant unlocked his employer's safe and completely removed a drawer containing money. He was stopped before any of the money was taken from the drawer. This Court found these actions sufficient to constitute asportation of the money, and we upheld the larceny conviction.

The movement of the air conditioner in this case off its window base and four to six inches toward the door clearly is "a bare removal from the place in which the thief found [it]." The Court of Appeals apparently agreed; however, it correctly recognized that there is a taking element in larceny in addition to the asportation requirement. The Court of Appeals stated that "here the problem with the State's case is that the evidence of asportation does not also constitute sufficient evidence of taking."

This Court has defined "taking" in this context as the "severance of the goods from the possession of the owner." *State v. Roper*, 14 N.C. 473, 474 (1832). Thus, the accused must not only move the goods, but he must also have them in his possession, or under his control, even if only for an instant. This defendant picked the air conditioner up from its stand and laid it on the floor. This act was sufficient to put the object briefly under the control of the defendant, severed from the owner's possession.

In rare and somewhat comical situations, it is possible to have an asportation of an object without taking it, or gaining possession of it.

> "In a very famous case a rascal walking by a store lifted an overcoat from a dummy and endeavored to walk away with it. He soon discovered that the overcoat was secured by a chain and he did not succeed in breaking the chain. This was held not to be larceny because the rascal did not at any time have possession of the garment. He thought he did until he reached the end of the chain, but he was mistaken." R. PERKINS, CRIMINAL LAW 222 (1957) (discussing *People v. Meyer*, 75 Cal. 383, 17 P. 431 (1888)).

The air conditioner in question was not permanently connected to the premises of Day's Inn Motel at the time of the crime. It had previously been pried up from its base; therefore, when defendant and his companion moved it, they had possession of it for that moment. Thus, there was sufficient evidence to take the larceny charge to the jury.

The defendant's and the Court of Appeals' reliance on *State v. Jones*, 65 N.C. 395 (1871), is misplaced. In that case, the defendant merely turned a large barrel of turpentine, that was standing on its head, over on its side. This Court held that shifting the position of an object without moving it from where it was found is insufficient asportation to support a larceny conviction. The facts of this case show that there was an actual removal of the air conditioner from its base in the window to a point on the floor four to six inches toward the door. Thus, *Jones* is not controlling.

For the reasons stated above, the decision of the Court of Appeals is reversed, and the larceny judgment reinstated.

Notes and Questions

1. **Carrying Away (Asportation).** In *Rogers v. State*, 458 S.W.2d 369 (Ark. 1970), the defendant allegedly cut a chain connecting a boat and trailer to a light pole and then lifted the trailer's tongue off the concrete block upon which it rested. As *Carswell* indicates, the "carrying away" element of larceny was satisfied in this case, even though the defendant never actually removed the property from the owner's lot, because asportation requires only some movement of the property, regardless of degree. Affirming the defendant's conviction for larceny of both the boat and the

trailer, the Arkansas Supreme Court cited precedent from other jurisdictions indicating that any of the following may be sufficient to constitute an asportation: "the slightest removal of goods from the place where they were left by the owner" (Arkansas); "removal of only a hair's breadth" (Nebraska); "the least removal of a thing from the place it was located" (Georgia); "when the property taken is moved from its original position regardless of however slight may be the change of position" (Alabama). *Id.* at 370–71. Do such formulations represent viable standards that courts can use in evaluating the question of asportation?

The asportation requirement generally demands that every part of the property be moved. Thus, in *State v. Jones*, 65 N.C. 395 (1871), which is described in *Carswell*, there was no asportation, and hence no larceny, when a barrel standing on its head was placed on its side. The "fine distinction" between cases like *Jones* and cases like *Carswell*, "which makes not a bit of sense today, has been described as the distinction between rotating a doughnut (every part moves, as is required for larceny) and rotating a pie (the exact center portion, infinitely small, does not move)." Wayne R. LaFave, Criminal Law § 19.3, at 981 n.11 (5th ed. 2010). Can this distinction be defended? To what extent does requiring proof of total movement help ensure that a jury will not erroneously conclude that merely touching another person's property constitutes a taking with the intent to deprive permanently?

Asportation is very often an element of the crime of kidnapping. The amount of movement required to sustain a kidnapping conviction, however, is sometimes held to be more substantial than that required for simple larceny. *See, e.g., People v. Dominguez*, 13 Cal. Rptr. 3d 212 (Cal. Ct. App. 2004) (concluding that movement of victim 10 to 12 feet down an embankment, which appeared to be "incidental" to the offenses of rape and murder, was "not substantial" enough to support kidnapping conviction). Nevertheless, in some jurisdictions, even an insubstantial movement may suffice to sustain a kidnapping charge if it "increased the risk of harm to a victim." *People v. Owens*, 97 P.3d 227 (Colo. Ct. App. 2004). *See also* John L. Diamond, *Kidnapping: A Modern Definition*, 13 Am. J. Crim. L. 1 (1985) (criticizing the use of "asportation" in defining kidnapping).

2. Taking (Caption). In *People v. Meyer*, 17 P. 431 (Cal. 1888), which is cited in *Carswell*, there was sufficient evidence of asportation, but the "taking" element was not satisfied because the defendant never had actual possession or control of the overcoat. In *People v. Rivera*, 566 N.E.2d 220 (Ill. 1990), by contrast, the Illinois Supreme Court held that the defendant was "in possession" of a stolen car even though a chain across the owner's lot prevented the defendant from driving the car off the owner's property. Are these two cases distinguishable?

Does a shoplifter "take" an item for purposes of larceny by picking it up and carrying it around the store with no intent to pay for it? In *Lee v. State*, 474 A.2d 537 (Md. Ct. Spec. App. 1984), the court upheld the larceny conviction of a defendant who took two bottles of cognac from the shelves of a self-service liquor store, concealed one of the bottles in his pants and held the other in his hand, and, when approached by an employee, returned both bottles to the shelf and left the store. According to the court, a person who knowingly obtains or exerts control over another person's property with the purpose of depriving the owner of that property can be convicted of theft even if no attempt is made to remove the property from the premises.

Most cases in this area, like *Lee,* involve some sort of concealment on the part of the defendant. *See also Commonwealth v. Balboni,* 532 N.E.2d 706 (Mass. App. Ct. 1989) (defendant concealed several cigarette cartons in a previously unopened bag); *People v. Britto,* 402 N.Y.S.2d 546 (N.Y. Crim. Ct. 1978) (defendant concealed six or seven ham steaks under his belt).

Suppose instead that the defendant in *Lee* simply placed the bottles of cognac in a shopping cart, though still with every intention of stealing them (i.e., suppose he did nothing manifestly inconsistent with the rights of the storeowner). Could Lee still be convicted of larceny if he was arrested before the bottles were removed from the store? Could the prosecution establish his guilt beyond a reasonable doubt if he acted just like other customers who planned to pay for their liquor purchases? In *The Queen v. Morris*, [1983] 3 All E.R. 288 (H.L.), the House of Lords ruled that an appropriation must involve an act objectively inconsistent with the rights of the owner. Is the concept of an objectively inconsistent act a valid standard? Is it workable in practice? Is it necessary to avoid punishing individuals who are thinking about stealing but have not yet made up their minds?

Consider also *People v. Davis*, 965 P.2d 1165 (Cal. 1998), where the defendant went into a Mervyn's department store and took a shirt displayed for sale from its hanger. He then carried the shirt into the women's department, where he falsely claimed he was returning the shirt (without the receipt) and received a store voucher for the purchase price. The California Supreme Court rejected his argument that there was no trespassory taking and affirmed his larceny conviction. Specifically, the court reasoned that a "self-service store like Mervyn's impliedly consents to a customer picking up and handling an item displayed for sale and carrying it from the display area to a sales counter with the intent of purchasing it," but "manifestly does not consent . . . to a customer's removing an item from a shelf or hanger if the customer's intent in taking possession of the item is to steal it." *Id*. at 1168. The court also held that the defendant had the requisite intent to deprive permanently since he asserted ownership of the shirt and sought a reward in the form of a refund for its return. (For further discussion of the mens rea requirements for larceny, see Part 5 below.)

3. Abolishing the Asportation Requirement. Section 223.2(1) of the Model Penal Code abandons the common-law requirement of asportation and instead defines theft to include "unlawfully tak[ing] or exercis[ing] unlawful control" over another person's movable property. The drafters explained that this change means that the distinction between a completed theft and an attempt no longer depends on "the criminologically insignificant fact of slight movement of the object." Model Penal Code § 223.2 Comment at 164.

Although many states have adopted the Model Penal Code's position, Professor Hall has criticized it, arguing that asportation is a more precise way to differentiate an attempt from the completed crime:

> [I]t seems odd to say that one who, in the absence of the owner, stood *animo furandi* [with the intent to steal] near an automobile whose door was not locked was guilty of theft. On the other hand, one who *animo furandi* took hold of the handle of the door of an automobile, opened it and sat inside the car would certainly be acting in "negation" of the owner's dominion. Turning on the ignition seems unnecessary; indeed, taking hold of the handle would seem to suffice. Thus, at many points doubts would arise as to where noncriminal action ends or where "control" begins, and there would be no established way to resolve them objectively.

Jerome Hall, Law, Social Science and Criminal Theory 269–70 (1982).

Is asportation a "criminologically insignificant" element, as the drafters of the Model Penal Code thought? Is it merely evidence that may be needed in some cases to prove the element of caption, or should it be required even in cases where that element can be proved by other evidence? To what extent should the law of larceny demand proof of physical manifestations like asportation in addition to a culpable mens rea? How persuasive is Professor Hall's criticism of the Model Penal Code's position?

4. Liability Without Asportation. If all the other elements of larceny are present, the absence of asportation and caption does not foreclose the possibility of criminal liability. An attempted larceny charge can still be brought as long as the defendant went beyond mere preparation toward committing the larceny. For example, although the defendant in *Meyer* (which is described both in *Carswell* and Note 2) could not be convicted of larceny because he did not "take" the overcoat, he could be found guilty of attempted larceny. Does the availability of an attempt charge, which typically carries a penalty at least half as long as the completed crime, support the Model Penal Code's approach or Professor Hall's defense of the common-law requirement? (For a discussion of the crime of attempt, see Chapter 11.)

[4] Extensions of Larceny

[a] Lost or Mislaid Property

Brooks v. State

35 Ohio St. 46 (1878)

WHITE, JUSTICE.

The plaintiff in error, George Brooks, at the February term, 1879, of the Court of Common Pleas of Trumbull county, was convicted of larceny in stealing $200 in bank bills, the property of Charles B. Newton. It appears from the evidence, that Newton resided at Newton Falls, in the county of Trumbull, and that, on the 24th of

October, 1878, he came to the city of Warren in a buggy to attend to some business. He fastened his horse to a hitching post on Market street. On his way home, in the forenoon of the same day, he discovered that he had lost the package of bank bills in question. He made search for it in various places where he had been, but failed to find it. He looked where he hitched his horse on Market street, but he states that he did not look there very carefully, as there was a team of horses hitched there at the time. Notice of the loss was published in the two newspapers printed in Warren, and in one printed in Leavittsburgh, which also had a circulation in Warren.

On Wednesday, the 20th of November following, the defendant, who resided in Warren, while working on Market street, near the post at which Newton hitched his horse, found the roll or package of bank bills. The package was found "five or six feet from the hitching post." He was, at the time, working in company with several other laborers. At the time he found the money one of these laborers was within ten feet and another within twenty feet of him, but he did not let any of them know that he had found the money. He states, in his testimony, that he put it in his pocket as soon as he found it. Just after finding the package, he picked up a one dollar bill, which he did show to them. This bill was wet and muddy, and he sold it to one of them for twenty-five cents, saying if none of them bought it he would keep it himself. He testifies the reason he sold it was that he did not want them to know at the time that he had found the other money. This bill was shown to several persons at the time, and was put on the hitching post to dry. Within a half hour after finding the money, at the time of stopping for dinner, he quit work, and, at his request, was paid off. He spent part of the money, the same day, for a pair of boots, and for other purposes, and let a Mrs. Lease have fifty dollars of it the same day, with which to purchase furniture for his wife, and for other purposes. Mrs. Lease saw him have the money at his house the afternoon of the same day. At the time of receiving the money she told him that she did not want to take the money if it was stolen or was counterfeit. He told her he received it from an uncle, and, another time, on being asked by her about it, said, "what if I found it?"

Evidence was also given that the defendant, with his wife, shortly afterward left Warren, and that he attempted to secrete himself before he left. The evidence did not show that the defendant saw any of the notices of the loss of the money published in the newspapers, or that he had any notice of the loss by Newton at the time it was found. Much other evidence was given, but the foregoing is sufficient to show the character of the legal questions raised.

. . . The question is, under what circumstances does such property become the subject of larceny by the finder?

In *Baker v. The State*, 29 Ohio St. 184, the rule stated by Baron Park, in *Thurborn's case,* was adopted. It was there laid down, that "when a person finds goods that have actually been lost, and takes possession with intent to appropriate them to his own use, really believing, at the time, or having good ground to believe, that the owner can be found, it is larceny."

It must not be understood from the rule, as thus stated, that the finder is bound to use diligence or to take pains in making search for the owner. His belief, or grounds of belief, in regard to finding the owner, is not to be determined by the degree of diligence that he might be able to use to accomplish that purpose, but by the circumstances apparent to him at the time of finding the property. If the property has not been abandoned by the owner, it is the subject of larceny by the finder, when, at the time he finds it, he has reasonable ground to believe, from the nature of the property, or the circumstances under which it is found, that if he does not conceal but deals honestly with it, the owner will appear or be ascertained. But before the finder can be guilty of larceny, the intent to steal the property must have existed at the time he took it into his possession.

There are cases in conflict with the foregoing view; but we believe it correct in principle, and well supported by authority.

The case was fairly submitted to the jury; and from an examination of the evidence, we find no ground for interfering with the action of the court below in refusing a new trial.

Judgment affirmed.

OKEY, JUSTICE (dissenting).

I do not think the plaintiff was properly convicted. A scavenger, while in the performance of his duties in cleaning the streets, picked up from the mud and water in the gutter, a roll of money, consisting of bank bills of the denominations of five, ten, and twenty dollars, and amounting, in the aggregate, to two hundred dollars. It had lain there several weeks, and the owner had ceased to make search for it. The evidence fails to show that the plaintiff had any information of a loss previous to the finding, and in his testimony he denied such notice. There was no mark on the money to indicate the owner, nor was there any thing in the attending circumstances pointing to one owner more than another. He put the money in his pocket, without calling the attention of his fellow-workmen to the discovery, and afterward, on the same day, commenced applying it to his own use.

No doubt the plaintiff was morally bound to take steps to find the owner. An honest man would not thus appropriate money, before he had made the finding public, and endeavored to find the owner. But in violating the moral obligation, I do not think the plaintiff incurred criminal liability.

Baker's Case, 29 Ohio St. 184, was correctly decided. It is stated in the opinion, not only that when he took the goods he intended to appropriate them to his own use, but that he had reasonable ground for believing that Alden was the owner. A passage from *Regina v. Thurborn*, 1 Den. C.C. 387, is cited in that case as containing a correct statement of the law. But a careful examination of *Regina v. Thurborn* will show that the court which rendered the decision would not have sustained this conviction; and that case has been repeatedly followed in England and this country.

The obligation, stated in the syllabus, that the finder must deal "honestly" with the money, is too indefinite; and the opinion contains no satisfactory explanation of it. This leaves both law and fact to the jury, without any rule to guide them. What one jury might think was honest dealing, another jury might think was the reverse. The adverb *properly* or *rightfully* would have been as certain.

Model Penal Code § 223.5

Section 223.5. Theft of Property Lost, Mislaid, or Delivered by Mistake

A person who comes into control of property of another that he knows to have been lost, mislaid, or delivered under a mistake as to the nature or amount of the property or the identity of the recipient is guilty of theft if, with purpose to deprive the owner thereof, he fails to take reasonable measures to restore the property to a person entitled to have it.

Model Penal Code § 223.5 Comment at 228–29

The common-law view of larceny as an infringement of the possession of another required a determination of the actor's state of mind at the moment of finding. An honest state of mind at that point would preclude the felony conviction. Moreover, the subsequent formation of a purpose to deprive would not be criminal since the actor would already be in possession. The search for an initial fraudulent intent appears to be largely fictional, and in any event poses the wrong question. The realistic objective in this area is not to prevent initial appropriation but to compel subsequent acts to restore to the owner. The section therefore permits conviction even where the original taking was honest in the sense that the actor then intended to restore; if he subsequently changes his mind and determines to keep the property, he will then be guilty of theft. Similarly, the section bars conviction where the finder acts with reasonable promptness to restore the property, even though he may have entertained a purpose to deprive at the time he acquired the property or at some other time during his possession. Section 223.5 thus focuses on the operative event of a purpose to deprive accompanied by the failure to take reasonable measures to restore. A few recent codes follow this view by including a provision that the actor must have "the purpose to deprive the owner of such property when he obtains the property or at any time prior to taking reasonable measures" to return the same to the owner.

Notes and Questions

1. **Larceny of Lost Property.** At common law, one who took property that had been lost could be convicted of larceny if the prosecution proved the following, in addition to the six traditional elements of larceny (set out in Note 1 following *Lund v. Commonwealth* in Section B.1 above): (1) that, at the time the defendant took the property, the defendant had a clue suggesting that the owner could reasonably be found; and (2) that the defendant had the intent to permanently deprive the owner of the property at the time it was taken. Without these two elements, a defendant who took lost property had not committed the "trespassory" (or wrongful) taking required for larceny.

Do these rules make sense if the larceny laws are designed to protect property? What if they are designed to protect possession?

2. Cultural Differences. Consider the cultural differences between the United States and Japan in attitudes about the discovery of lost property. Ever since a statute addressing lost property was adopted in Japan in 718, Japanese law has required that finders of lost property turn it over to governmental authorities within five days. Since at least the eighteenth century, finders had the right to claim some value of the property they returned — typically 10 percent — even if the true owner reclaimed it. On the other hand, those who failed to turn in lost property were "severely punished." In 2002, $23 million in found cash was turned in in Tokyo, almost three-fourths of which was returned to its owners. The same year, 330,000 lost umbrellas were turned in (although only 0.3 percent were reclaimed). Japanese children are "taught from early on to hand in anything they find to the police." One waitress who turned in $250 cash explained, "I always hand in something I find. . . . I imagine that a person might be in trouble, losing money or a purse." Another man who turned in $120 cash said, "I feel uncomfortable holding another person's money." Norimitsu Onishi, *Never Lost, but Found Daily: Japanese Honesty*, N.Y. Times, Jan. 8, 2004, at A1.

3. Constructive Possession. The concept of "constructive" possession was developed to expand the reach of larceny to include finders of mislaid and lost property:

> It had long been recognized that an owner possessed goods, in the sense that he asserted continued dominion over them even if he were far from them and thus in no position to exert immediate physical control. Ingenious judges availed themselves of this idea by drawing a distinction between lost and "mislaid" property. Thus, a cab driver who appropriates a wallet that a passenger has inadvertently left on the seat or dropped to the floor takes "mislaid" rather than "lost" property, trespassing against the owners' continued "possession." Nevertheless, there was reluctance to extend the harsh penalties of larceny to finders, who do not aggressively act against the property security of others.

Louis B. Schwartz, *Theft, in* 4 Encyclopedia of Crime and Justice 1537, 1540 (Sanford H. Kadish ed., 1983).

Thus, the law of larceny was first extended to reach finders of mislaid property (property that the owner intentionally put in a certain place and then inadvertently forgot) on the theory that the property remained under the "constructive" possession of the true owner. Any taking of such goods with the intent to appropriate them permanently was characterized as a trespassory taking from the owner's possession, provided there was a reasonable basis at the time of the taking for believing the owner could be found. Only later was this notion extended to lost property.

4. Clues to Ownership. The argument between the majority and the dissent in *Brooks* turned on the question whether there were any clues that would have reasonably led Brooks to believe the owner of the bank roll could be identified. In *Baker v. State*, 29 Ohio St. 184 (1876), which is cited by both the dissent and the majority, the defendant found a pocketbook containing a $10 bill on a public road near his work site. Several hours before, "at the time [the owner] lost the pocket-book, [he] had been detained for a short time and within full sight of the defendant. . . . It was also shown by an admission of defendant, that the appearance of the pocket-book at the time he found it, indicated that it had been very recently lost." *Id.* at 185. The court held that these facts were sufficient to establish that the defendant had a clue as to ownership at the time of finding. Does *Baker* lend more support to the majority or the dissent in *Brooks*?

As the conflicting opinions in *Brooks* suggest, determining what constitutes a reasonable clue to ownership can be a difficult issue and may depend on the uniqueness of the item and the location where it was found. Consider *Rich v. State*, 22 So. 2d 617, 617 (Ala. Ct. App. 1945), where a dry-cleaner left some clothes that had been cleaned (and that "bore marks identifying them as the property of [W.H.] Battles") in a box on the side of the road near Battles' mailbox, where they were picked up by the defendant. In affirming her larceny conviction, the court analyzed the case as one involving lost property. Does this opinion suggest that the line between traditional snatching cases (which are clearly larceny) and cases involving the failure to return a lost item is a very fine one?

5. Continuous Taking. In the context of "lost" and "mistakenly delivered" personal property (see Section B.4.b below for a discussion of mistakenly delivered property), the common law is rigorous in enforcing the requirement that "intent to deprive permanently" exist at the actual time of taking. In other, more traditional forms of larceny, however, the fiction of "continuous taking" defines the act of taking to continue so long as the defendant continues to possess the property. Although the intent must still exist at the time of "taking," this fiction substantially extends the period of the "taking." Thus, for example, if *A* wrongfully takes *B*'s watch while *B* is looking the other way, intending only to "borrow" the watch without permission, but subsequently decides to keep it, *A* would be guilty of larceny due to the doctrine of "continuous taking."

Under the common-law principles noted above, the rule is different for those who find lost goods. In those cases, the fiction does not apply and the intent to deprive permanently must therefore exist at the actual time of the taking.

6. The Model Penal Code. As the excerpt from the Comments to Model Penal Code § 223.5 indicates, the Code considers the common-law distinctions pertaining to lost property irrational. To a large extent, the Code eliminates these distinctions by expanding criminality for those who fail to return lost property. Is this the best solution? Should those who keep lost property be grouped and punished with more traditional thieves? Consider the following examples:

(a) Suppose *A* finds a valuable pendant with *B*'s name inscribed on the back. *A* decides to keep the pendant for himself, but changes his mind a minute later and decides to find *B* and return the pendant. Under the common law, *A* is guilty of larceny despite his change of heart because he had both a reasonable clue to ownership and the intent to deprive at the time of the taking. Under § 223.5 of the Model Penal Code, however, *A* could avoid a larceny charge if he took reasonable measures to restore the pendant to its true owner.

(b) Suppose the same facts as above except that when *A* finds the pendant, his first inclination is to try and find *B*, the true owner. A moment later, he changes his mind and decides to keep the pendant. At common law, *A* would not be guilty of larceny because he did not have the requisite intent to steal at the time he found the pendant. *See State v. Belt*, 119 S.E. 576 (S.C. 1923) (holding that one who found a lost suitcase and other lost property was not guilty of larceny if he did not have the intent to steal at the time the property was taken). *See generally* WAYNE R. LaFave, CRIMINAL LAW § 19.2(f), at 976–78 (5th ed. 2010). Under the Model Penal Code, however, *A* would probably be guilty of theft because § 223.5 rejects the common-law requirements that both a reasonable clue to ownership and the requisite intent must exist at the time of the finding and instead provides that one who finds property is guilty of theft if he "fails to take reasonable measures to restore the property to a person entitled to have it."

(c) Suppose *A* finds the pendant and decides to keep it. But the pendant is so dirty and rusty that *A* does not see *B*'s name inscribed on the back. Two days later, after he cleans the pendant, *A* notices the inscription. Under the common law, *A* would not be guilty of larceny (assuming no other circumstances making it likely that the owner's identity could be determined) because the intent to appropriate the pendant and the clues to ownership did not coincide at the time he found the pendant. Under § 223.5 of the Model Penal Code, *A* would probably be guilty for failing to take reasonable measures to return the pendant to *B* once he discovered the inscription.

7. The Metamorphosis of Larceny. Professor Fletcher regrets the "metamorphosis" by which the common-law crime of larceny was expanded and legislation creating new theft crimes was enacted, thereby tending to criminalize every wrongful deprivation of property without considering the specific method by which the defendant acquired the property. Although larceny punishes "wrongful takings" short of violent robbery, the concept of "constructive possession" allows the failure to return lost goods to be included within the crime. Yet, does the failure to return lost property constitute the kind of misconduct larceny was originally designed to address?

Professor Fletcher criticizes the increasing criminalization of wrongful property acquisition:

> The traditional approach to larceny was built on two structural principles which expressed the distinction between a public sphere of criminal conduct and a private sphere subject at most to regulation by the rules of private

law. One of these structural principles, possessorial immunity, was the explicit rule of the courts that transferring possession of an object conferred immunity from the criminal law on the party receiving possession, for subsequent misuse or misappropriation of the entrusted object. This rule was fundamental in defining the contours of larceny as well as the boundary between larceny and the newer offenses that developed in the eighteenth and nineteenth centuries.

The second structural principle of the common law was the implicit rule that criminal liability should attach to all conduct conforming to a collective image of acting like a thief and only to such conduct. In its expansive aspect, this principle meant that acting like a thief created a prima facie case of liability. In its limiting aspect, the rule meant that objectively unincriminating conduct was not subject to criminal sanctions. Thus, if the actor's intent to steal did not manifest itself in an externally identifiable act of stealing, no larceny could be committed, and, therefore, alternative proof of the actor's criminal intent would be irrelevant.

The premise of the traditional approach to larceny was that it was possible to perceive thievery directly as an event in the world and that the courts should rely on this unanalyzed perception in framing the law of theft. Modern legal theory rejects unanalyzed perceptions as a proper source of law. Today we are inclined to analyze the phenomenon of theft into the twin elements of harm and intent. The harm is the unlicensed acquisition of another's property; the intent is defined derivatively as the intent to effect this harm. The implication of so analyzing the crime of theft is that no particular conduct is necessary in order to prove the required intent. Intent may be established by a variety of means, including confessions, admissions, past criminal conduct, and other circumstantial evidence, all of which presuppose an intrusive and open-ended investigation into the life of the accused.

These two approaches to the law of larceny merit our detailed attention, for they signal two clashing conceptions of the proper scope of the criminal law. The traditional approach reflected a deep commitment to working out the realm of public harms, subject only to redress by means of private actions. The view that some harms do not meet the threshold of potentially criminal events remains one of the background assumptions of the legal system. The private nature of at least some harms is a consequence of the relationship in which they occur. This is reflected in our taking for granted that cheating in the university should not be a crime. The principle of possessorial immunity analogously expressed the privacy of harms that occurred in the context of relationships in which one party entrusted an object to another. Further, the limitation of liability to conduct that appeared manifestly to be thievery exempted another set of deprivations from the scope of the criminal law. These deprivations were private in the sense that the process of acquisition was not a public or socially disturbing event. Rejecting both possessorial immunity and the principle of objective criminality, the modern law of theft offenses verges on treating every deprivation of property as a public harm.

George P. Fletcher, *The Metamorphosis of Larceny*, 89 Harv. L. Rev. 469, 472–74 (1976).

[b] Mistaken Delivery

United States v. Rogers

289 F.2d 433 (4th Cir. 1961)

Haynsworth, Circuit Judge.

The defendant has appealed from his conviction under the "bank robbery statute," complaining that the proof did not show the commission of larceny and that the verdict of the jury was coerced by the Court's instructions. We think the proof did support the conviction, but that a new trial should be granted because of the possibly coercive effect of the Court's instructions designed to produce agreement of the jurors upon a verdict.

There was testimony showing that, at the request of his brother, the defendant took a payroll check, payable to the brother in the face amount of $97.92, to a bank where the brother maintained an account. In accordance with the brother's request, he asked the teller to deposit $80 to the credit of the brother's account and to deliver to him the balance of the check in cash. The teller was inexperienced. She first inquired of another teller whether the check could be credited to an account in part and cashed in part. Having been told that this was permissible, she required the defendant's endorsement on the check, and, misreading its date (12/06/59) as the amount payable, she deducted the $80 deposit and placed $1,126.59 on the counter. There were two strapped packages, each containing $500, and $126.59 in miscellaneous bills and change. The defendant took the $1,126.59 in cash thus placed upon the counter and departed.

There was also testimony that when the day's business was done, the teller who handled the transaction was found to be short in her accounts by $1,108.67, the exact amount of the difference between the $1,206.59, for which she had supposed the check to have been drawn, and $97.92, its actual face amount, and that her adding machine tape showed that she had accepted the check as having been drawn for $1,206.59.

There was corroboration from other witnesses of some phases of this story as told by the tellers and the bookkeeper.

The defendant agreed that he took the check to the bank for his brother, asked that $80 be credited to his brother's account, and that the excess be paid to him in cash. He stated, however, that he received in cash only the $17.92, to which he was entitled, denying that he had received the larger sum.

The case was submitted to the jury under instructions that they should find the defendant guilty if they found the much larger sum was placed upon the counter and was taken by the defendant with the intention to appropriate the overpayment, or if he thereafter formed the intention to, and did, appropriate the overpayment to his own use.

. . . We accept the defendant's premise that paragraph (b) of the bank robbery act reaches only the offense of larceny as that crime has been defined by the common law. It does not encompass the crimes of embezzlement from a bank, reached by another statute, or obtaining goods by false pretense. That this is so is indicated by the use of the words, "(whoever) takes and carries away, with intent to steal and purloin . . . ," borrowed from the Act of April 30, 1790, which had been construed as a larceny statute. It is further indicated by the title of the act and its legislative history.

. . . The defendant's premise that the prosecution was required to show the commission of larceny does not lead, however, to the conclusion that he should have been acquitted. The indictment charged larceny and the evidence offered by the prosecution, if accepted by the jury, proved the commission of that crime, not false pretense, embezzlement or some other lesser offense.

An essential element of the crime of larceny, the " 'felonious taking and carrying' away the personal goods of another," is that the taking must be trespassory. It is an invasion of the other's right to possession, and therein is found the principal distinction between larceny and other related offenses.

. . . It has long been recognized, however, that when the transferor acts under a unilateral mistake of fact, his delivery of a chattel may be ineffective to transfer title or his right to possession. If the transferee, knowing of the transferor's mistake, receives the goods with the intention of appropriating them, his receipt and removal of them is a trespass and his offense is larceny.

Such a situation was presented in *Regina v. Middleton*, 28 Law Times (N.S.) 777, 12 Cox C.C. 417 (1873). There it appeared that the defendant had a credit balance of 11 s. in a postal savings account. He obtained a warrant for the withdrawal of 10 s. which he presented to the postal clerk. The clerk mistakenly referred to the wrong letter of advice, one which had been received in connection with the prospective withdrawal of a much larger sum by another depositor. The clerk then placed upon the counter a 5 L note, 3 sovereigns, a half crown and silver and copper amounting altogether to 8 L 16 s. 10 d. The defendant gathered up the money and departed. The jury found that the defendant was aware of the clerk's mistake and took the money with intent to steal it. His conviction of larceny was affirmed by the Court of Criminal Appeals, the fifteen judges dividing eleven to four.

. . . The District Court went too far, however, when it told the jury it might convict if, though his initial receipt of the overpayment was innocent, the defendant thereafter formed the intention to, and did, convert the overpayment.

The charge as given finds support in earlier cases. There was a dictum to that effect in *Wolfstein v. People*, 1875, 6 Hun, N.Y., 121, upon which the Oregon Court relied in deciding *State v. Ducker*, 8 Or. 394, 34 Am. Rep. 590. In England, a similar result was reached in *Regina v. Ashwell*, 16 Q.B. 190 (1883), Lord Coleridge declaring there could be in law no delivery and no receipt if giver and receiver labored under a mutual mistake as to the thing being given and received. Subsequent cases in the United States and in England, however, have consistently held that, if there is a mutual mistake and the recipient is innocent of wrongful purpose at the time of his initial receipt of the overpayment, its subsequent conversion by him cannot be larceny.

Upon the retrial, therefore, the jury should be instructed that among the essential elements of the offense are (1) that the defendant knew when he received the money from the teller or picked it up from the counter that it was more than his due and (2) that he took it from the bank with the intention of converting it.

The judgment is reversed and the case remanded for further proceedings not inconsistent with this opinion.

Notes and Questions

1. Mistaken Delivery. At common law, one who took property that had been delivered by mistake could be convicted of larceny if the prosecution proved the following, in addition to the six traditional elements of larceny (set out in Note 1 following *Lund v. Commonwealth* in Section B.1 above): (1) that a mistake as to the nature or the amount of the property was made at the time of taking; and (2) that the defendant had the intent to permanently deprive the owner of the property at the time it was taken. Without these additional requirements, the taking was not "trespassory" (or wrongful) and thus was not larceny. *See* WAYNE R. LaFAVE, CRIMINAL LAW § 19.3(g), at 978–79 (5th ed. 2010).

As is true in the case of lost property, bringing larceny charges in mistaken delivery cases represents a significant extension of traditional notions of larceny. Is this extension warranted? Have defendants like Rogers violated society's norms by failing to return mistakenly delivered property? How would most people behave in this situation? Is this conduct properly equated with the crime of larceny? In cases involving lost property, the defendant affirmatively acts by taking the property rather than passing it by. Does it matter that the defendant's guilt in mistaken delivery cases can be based on inaction or the failure to correct another's mistake?

2. The Point of Delivery. The cases are divided as to when a person actually receives—i.e., takes—delivered property. In *Robinson v. State*, 11 Tex. Ct. App. 403 (1882), the defendant purchased a trunk. Upon arriving home and opening the trunk, the defendant discovered for the first time that it was not empty, but contained some clothing. At that point, the defendant decided to steal the clothing. Affirming the defendant's larceny conviction, the court concluded that the defendant intended to steal the clothing at the time of the taking—that is, when the clothing was first discovered.

Other courts, by contrast, have held that the receipt of property occurs at the time of delivery, regardless of the time of discovery. Thus, in *Cooper v. Commonwealth*, 60 S.W. 938 (Ky. 1901), a larceny conviction was reversed where the defendant was given a wrapped roll of 20 $5 gold pieces (which both parties thought was a roll of 20 nickels) in exchange for $1. Even though the defendant discovered the mistake when he unwrapped the roll of coins and decided to keep the gold, he was not guilty of larceny because his intent to steal did not coincide with the earlier taking.

Some courts have distinguished among mistaken delivery cases by asking whether the delivered item was a "container." The delivery of a "container" constitutes delivery of its contents as well, thereby precluding a larceny conviction if the recipient later finds some mistakenly delivered contents in the container. Delivery of an item that is not meant as a container, however, is not delivery of the contents, and thus a larceny conviction is possible because the recipient takes possession of the contents only upon discovering them. *See* Rollin M. Perkins & Ronald N. Boyce, Criminal Law 317 (3d ed. 1982).

3. The Model Penal Code. Under the Model Penal Code, a crime can be committed even if the defendant formed the intent to deprive at some point after the time of the mistaken delivery. Specifically, § 223.5 of the Code provides that "a person who comes into control of property of another . . . delivered under a mistake as to the nature or amount of the property or identity of the recipient is guilty of theft if, with the purpose to deprive the owner thereof, he fails to take reasonable measures to restore the property to a person entitled to have it."

4. Comparing the Common Law and the Model Penal Code. As indicated in *Rogers*, *A* is not subject to criminal liability under the common law if she learned about the mistaken delivery after the fact. Alternatively, even if *A* was aware of the mistake at the time of delivery, she cannot be convicted if she initially planned to notify the victim of the mistake—whether or not she ever actually did so. On the other hand, *A* is guilty if she intended to keep the property and was aware of the mistake at the time of delivery, but had a guilty conscience and returned it minutes later. Can these distinctions be justified, or are they purely arbitrary?

Is the Model Penal Code's approach an improvement? Under the Code, the precise timing of both the discovery of the mistake and the formation of the intent to deprive is no longer critical. On the other hand, if *A* learns of the mistaken delivery weeks or months later, is she criminally liable under the Code if she fails to notify the "victim"? Which approach conforms more closely to our perceptions of criminal wrongdoing? Are there more attractive alternatives? (Note that the criminal laws have no impact on how the civil law of property determines ownership and liability.)

5. Distinguishing Mistakes About Value. The crime of larceny does not occur when both parties understand what items are the subject of their transaction but one of them makes a mistake about the value of those items. There is a difference between a thief and a smart purchaser. But what if the valuation error results from a mistaken impression as to exactly what sort of property is involved? For example, suppose *B* offers to sell a priceless Picasso painting for $5. *A* realizes *B*'s mistake and purchases the painting. Should *A* be liable for larceny? Is this mistaken delivery or just good business sense?

Consider the interesting case of Brian Wrzesinski, a 12-year-old boy who paid $12 for a Nolan Ryan rookie baseball card that was actually marked $1,200. The boy, who admittedly knew that the valuable collector's item was worth at least $600, obtained it from an inexperienced salesclerk at a Ball-Mart store who was not familiar with the trading card business. Wrzesinski said he thought he had simply gotten a "great deal" for the card. *See* John Leptich, *Boy Sued Over Baseball Card*, Chi. Trib., Nov. 10, 1990, at C1. Should criminal sanctions or civil remedies apply in this case? Is it wrong or admirable to make good deals in the free market? Would your views change if the store had paid the boy $12 for a card worth $1,200? (The owner of the store filed a civil suit against Wrzesinski, and the suit was eventually settled when the parties agreed that the card would be auctioned off, with the proceeds going to charity. The card fetched a price of $5,000 at the auction. *See* Steve Woodward, *Disputed Ryan Card Gets $5,000*, USA Today, June 24, 1991, at C2.)

Does criminalizing the failure to return mistakenly delivered property blur the distinction between praiseworthy business skills and larceny? Consider the Model Penal Code's analysis:

> Taking advantage of a known mistake that is influencing the other party to a bargain is not criminal under existing law in the absence of special circumstances imposing a duty to correct the mistake. The miner who discovers that his mine is nearly exhausted of ore may sell it to a stranger although he is fully aware that the stranger is buying under the mistaken belief that the property is still valuable as a mine. The prospector who discovers oil under the land of a stranger may buy the land without informing the stranger of his discovery although he knows that the stranger was satisfied by previous tests indicating there was no oil on the property.

> Section 223.3 does not attempt to make this behavior criminal, primarily because the borderline between desirable and disapproved behavior in this area is so ill-defined that criminal sanctions are likely to impinge on conduct well within the bounds of approved commercial activity. For example, suppose a "book scout" finds what appears to be a rare edition in a dusty attic, and pays the unwitting owner 25 cents, hoping to resell to a rich bibliophile for $100. There is no community consensus on whether he should be obliged to disclose his opinion to the original owner that the volume was worth $10 or to the bibliophile that it was worth no more than $25. The book scout's argument, that when he is not retained as appraiser or counselor he should not be required to volunteer valuable professional opinion, would be received favorably in many quarters. Before resolving this as a matter of the criminal

law, inquiry would have to be made into the extent to which book-scouting as a trade can survive only if this kind of transaction is tolerated, how important it is to preserve the trade, and so forth. This kind of elaborate balancing is beyond the appropriate purview of the penal statute.

Model Penal Code § 223.3 Comment at 197–98.

If *A* purchases a pair of glasses from *B* at a price that reflects both parties' belief that the frame is not made of gold, has *A* committed larceny if she does not return the glasses when she later discovers that the frame is gold? How clear or correct is the distinction between mistakes about value versus identity?

[c] Larceny by Trick

State v. Robington

75 A.2d 394 (Conn. 1950)

O'SULLIVAN, JUSTICE.

. . . The third count, upon which the defendant was . . . found guilty, charged that "on the 20th day of September, 1948 . . . the said Margaret Robington did commit larceny of a 1948 Chrysler Sedan, of the value of $3,000.00, the property of the Bonded Auto Sales Inc. and the Par Motor Sales Inc., Connecticut corporations."

The court could reasonably have found, as it did, that during August, 1948, the defendant approached Benjamin Banet, the president of the Bonded Auto Sales, Inc., a corporation dealing in new and used cars; that she told Banet she wanted a new black Chrysler sedan; that, not having one in stock, he took her to the Par Motor Sales, Inc., where an official of that company named Kramer showed her the model she had in mind; that Kramer turned the Chrysler over to her upon her assurance as well as upon Banet's oral guarantee that she would return the car on the following Monday morning or pay the sum of $3015; that she did neither but, on the contrary, used it for her own purposes for over two months and then removed it from Connecticut and concealed it in New Jersey; and that at no time did she intend to pay for the Chrysler. The court further found that when Par Motor Sales, Inc., delivered possession of the car it did not intend to transfer title. The last finding is vigorously challenged by the defendant.

The state was attempting to establish the crime of larceny by trick. This crime is committed when one obtains "the possession of personal property of another by deception, artifice, fraud or force, with the intent on the part of the person obtaining it to convert it to his own use and permanently to deprive the owner of his property." It should be added, however, that "if the owner intends to part with the title to the property as well as possession, whatever other crime may have been committed, it will not be theft." The importance of the finding that the owner did not part with title is obvious. If support for this was lacking, the defendant was improperly convicted of larceny even though the evidence established, as it did, the other essential elements of the crime.

Whether title passed to the defendant depended on the intention of Par Motor Sales, Inc., as disclosed by the statements and acts of its authorized agent. The court found with reason that the Chrysler was placed in the defendant's possession conditionally. She was to return it or pay for it on the following Monday. This condition, attached to the delivery, destroys the theory of a completed sale. The transaction was not dissimilar to one where an automobile is entrusted to a would-be purchaser who is to try it out by driving it around the block but who then makes off with it. The allegation in the information of title in both Bonded Auto Sales, Inc., and Par Motor Sales, Inc., did not prejudice the defendant. The court's conclusion of guilt was justified. . . .

Notes and Questions

1. Larceny by Trick. As the court's opinion in *Robington* illustrates, the crime of larceny by trick occurs when a defendant uses deceptive means to obtain *possession*, but not title or ownership, of another's personal property. Trickery is simply another method (albeit more verbal) used to commit larceny, and thus all the basic elements of larceny apply. *See State v. Freitag*, 802 P.2d 502 (Kan. 1990) (upholding the larceny conviction of a defendant who asked to test-ride a $700 bicycle in the parking lot adjacent to a bicycle store and then absconded with the bike).

The notion that a wrongful taking of possession could be effectuated other than by some form of snatching—in fact, where the owner freely handed over possession to the defendant—represented a major expansion of the law of larceny. The expansion can be traced to *The King v. Pear*, 168 Eng. Rep. 208 (Cr. Cas. Res. 1780), where the defendant stole a horse by misrepresenting to the owner that he wanted to lease it. As a result of the decision in this case, deception and trickery were added as ways of taking property that were criminalized by the law of larceny. Professor Fletcher's discussion of the metamorphosis of larceny, which is excerpted in Note 7 in Section B.4.a above, is critical of this expansion.

Are Professor Fletcher's concerns well-taken? Should the crime of larceny include takings accomplished by trickery? Are such takings comparable to those accomplished by stealth?

2. Comparing the Crime of False Pretenses. The first element of common-law larceny is that the taking must be "trespassory" (wrongful). A trespassory taking is one that occurs without the owner's consent and *without any transfer of title by the owner*. A defendant who receives title (ownership) from the owner has not committed larceny, although she may have committed the crime of false pretenses, a crime which has been added by statute to supplement the judicially created crime of larceny. Transfer of title is what distinguishes the crime of false pretenses from the other theft crimes, including larceny. *See* Wayne R. LaFave, Criminal Law § 19.7, at 1006–07 (5th ed. 2010). (The crime of false pretenses is discussed in Section D below.)

Although larceny by trick was originally punishable as a felony, whereas false pretenses was only a misdemeanor, many states now impose the same punishment for both crimes. *See, e.g.,* Cal. Penal Code §§ 484, 532. Why would the common law initially refuse to criminalize deceptive acts that led to the transfer of title and then, even after they were prohibited, punish them less severely?

3. Questioning the Distinction. Suppose *A* says to *B*, "Your luggage is beautiful. If you give it to me, I will pay you for it next week." *B* turns over the luggage, but *A* fails to pay. *A* has not committed larceny because *B* gave *A* title to the luggage. *See People v. Phebus*, 323 N.W.2d 423 (Mich. Ct. App. 1982) (finding that a shopper who switched the price tag on merchandise and was therefore able to purchase it for a lower price had not committed larceny because the cashier effectively transferred title to the merchandise to the shopper). Indeed, *A* would be guilty of the crime of false pretenses only in jurisdictions that criminalize a misrepresentation of present intentions. In other states, no crime would have been committed at all. (See the discussion in Note 3 following *Chaplin v. United States* in Section D below.)

Suppose instead that *A* says to *B*, "Your luggage is beautiful. May I hold it for a minute?" *B* allows *A* to hold the luggage, and *A* runs off with it. In this case, *A* is definitely guilty of larceny. In both hypotheticals, *A* used a trick to gain possession of *B*'s property. Why should the two situations be treated differently even though *B* was deprived of his property in both cases? Is the concept of "caveat emptor" ("let the buyer beware") relevant in one instance but not the other?

[5] The Specific Intent to Deprive Another of Property Permanently

People v. Kunkin
507 P.2d 1392 (Cal. 1973)

Wright, Chief Justice.

The Los Angeles Free Press (Free Press), its editor and owner, Arthur Glick Kunkin, and its reporter, Gerald Robert Applebaum, were each indicted on two counts of receiving stolen property (Pen. Code § 496) for allegedly taking possession of two documents which had been removed from the Los Angeles office of the Attorney General by Jerry M. Reznick. At trial, after the close of the prosecution's case, the court on defense motion acquitted Free Press and Kunkin on the count pertaining to one of the documents. The related charge against Applebaum for receipt of the same document was dismissed with the prosecutor's consent after the jury was unable to agree on a verdict as to that count. The jury found each defendant guilty of one count of receiving stolen property, and defendants appeal from the judgment entered as to the Free Press and the orders granting probation to Kunkin and Applebaum. For reasons hereinafter set forth, we conclude that there was no substantial evidence to support one of the essential elements of the crime of receiving stolen property and, accordingly, we reverse the judgment.

While Jerry Reznick was employed as a mail clerk at the Los Angeles office of the Attorney General he removed a copy of a personnel roster of the Bureau of Narcotic Enforcement which listed the names, home addresses and home telephone numbers of undercover narcotics agents throughout the state. It was not marked "secret" or "confidential." The copy of such document constitutes the "property" found by the jury to have been received by defendants.

Reznick took the roster to the office of the Free Press where he met Applebaum. Reznick asked Applebaum whether the Free Press would publish the roster and Applebaum replied that he did not know. Although Applebaum feared "there might be trouble" if such a document were published, he said that he would nevertheless consult his editor. When Reznick asked if he would be paid for providing the roster, Applebaum explained that, subject to approval by his superiors, the standard fee paid for information actually used in an article was $20. Reznick then departed.

Reznick returned a week later with the roster. Although Applebaum still could not promise that the Free Press would publish the roster, Reznick left the document on the reporter's desk and insisted that the newspaper not reveal its source of information. No agent of the newspaper promised to pay for the roster and Reznick was never paid for it.

On August 8, 1969, the Free Press published the roster verbatim in its feature article. The following headlines, inter alia, accompanied the article: "Narcotics Agents Listed," "There should be no secret police," and "Know your local Narc." The text editorialized that police personnel should live openly in the community which they serve. On an ensuing television interview, Kunkin acknowledged his role in publishing the list and stated that he was satisfied as to its authenticity. He explained that the roster was appended to the editorial "for dramatic effect."

After the list was published, Reznick went to Applebaum and asked for the return of the copy of the roster he had provided. Applebaum refused but assured Reznick that the document was locked in a safe place. Following requests made by a deputy attorney general to the Free Press, an attorney of undetermined authorization delivered the copy of the roster to the Attorney General's office. Fingerprints of Reznick, Applebaum and Kunkin were found on the document.

Section 496 provides in subdivision 1: "Every person who buys or receives any property which has been stolen or which has been obtained in any manner constituting theft or extortion, knowing the property to be so stolen or obtained, or who conceals, withholds or aids in concealing or withholding any such property from the owner, knowing the property to be so stolen or obtained, is punishable by imprisonment. . . ."

A conviction for receiving stolen property cannot withstand appellate scrutiny unless substantial evidence was presented to the trier of fact that (1) the property was received, concealed, or withheld by the accused; (2) such property had been obtained by theft or extortion; and (3) the accused knew that the property had been so obtained.

We will assume, without deciding, that one of the several copies of the roster of personnel of the bureau distributed to the Los Angeles office of the Attorney

General was "property" within the meaning and intended scope of section 496. We will also assume, without deciding, that the receipt of the roster by defendants was a "receiving" of property within the meaning and intended scope of section 496. Our discussion will focus on the evidence adduced at trial to prove the latter two elements of the crime of receiving: the received property's stolen status and the receiver's knowledge of this status.

. . . Section 496 applies to the receipt of "any property which has been stolen or which has been obtained in any manner constituting theft or extortion." This broad language is intended to include property which has been obtained not only by theft by larceny (i.e., stealing) but also by such other forms of theft as embezzlement. We note at the outset, however, that the jury in this case was instructed on the elements of theft by larceny only. Thus even though section 496 applies by its terms to the receipt of property obtained by embezzlement, the convictions below could only have been predicated on the jury's finding that the roster was stolen, not embezzled. We, of course, cannot look to legal theories not before the jury in seeking to reconcile a jury verdict with the substantial evidence rule. The immediate question, accordingly, is whether there is substantial evidence that Reznick committed a theft by larceny. . . .

It has been settled for at least 78 years that theft by larceny requires a specific intent permanently to deprive the rightful owner of his property. "While the felonious intent of the party taking need not necessarily be an intention to convert the property to his own use, still it must in all cases be an intent to wholly and permanently deprive the owner thereof." (*People v. Brown* (1894) 105 Cal. 66, 69 [38 P. 518].)

There is scant evidence in the instant case that Reznick intended a permanent deprivation. In the typical case the thief's sale of the property is persuasive proof of such an intention, but one of the many distinctive features of this case is that the alleged receiving involved no sale, at least of the stolen item itself. Reznick did leave the roster with defendants in the expectation that he would receive $20 should the roster result in a published story, but Reznick insisted in all his dealings with defendants that the roster be returned to him after they had made whatever use they cared to of the information it contained. By Reznick's uncontradicted testimony, defendants never offered to pay money for the roster or for the information it contained, nor did they actually pay Reznick any money. Thus nothing inherent in the transaction itself bears a necessary or even likely inference that Reznick intended to keep the roster away from the office of the Attorney General permanently.

It appears, however, that after Reznick testified that he had only caused the roster "to be removed," he answered in the affirmative, over objection, a prosecution question whether he had stolen it. We have heretofore recognized that words of common usage do not necessarily reflect the subtle distinctions they bear before bench and bar. Thus an affirmative answer to a leading question whether the witness stole something, when that witness himself has characterized the taking as a removal, is not dispositive of the issue whether the removal was accompanied by a specific intent to steal, that is, to remove permanently.

Were there no more evidence in the record than Reznick's acquiescence in the use of the word "steal," and his account of his tender of the roster to defendants with simultaneous insistence that it be returned to him, we would deem excruciatingly close the question whether there was substantial evidence in support of the jury's finding that the roster was stolen property. A final item of evidence convinces us, however, that there was sufficient circumstantial evidence for the finder of fact to reasonably draw the inference that Reznick took the roster with intent to steal. This dispositive circumstance is that Reznick had in fact ceased working for the office of the Attorney General at the time of his tender of the roster to defendants. Thus he was no longer in a position conveniently to return the roster to the office following its perusal by defendants. We thus conclude that there is substantial evidence in support of the finding that the property was stolen.

We turn now to the question whether there is also substantial evidence from which the jury could reasonably have drawn an inference that defendants knew the roster was stolen when Reznick tendered it to them.

Crucial to consideration of this question is the fact that defendants were not made aware by Reznick that he was no longer employed by the office of the Attorney General.

Besides misleading defendants about his employment status, Reznick maintained throughout his conversations with defendants that he was giving them a roster to look at only.

. . . Since Reznick's testimony regarding his failure to inform defendants that he had ceased to work for the Attorney General and his insistence that the roster be returned was uncontradicted, and since the suspicious circumstances relied upon by the People will not in the peculiar circumstances of this case support an inference of guilty knowledge that the roster had been stolen, we conclude that there was no substantial evidence to support the jury's finding that defendants knew the roster was stolen.

The judgment and orders granting probation are reversed.

Notes and Questions

1. Receipt of Stolen Property. The statutory crime of receipt of stolen property generally includes the following elements: (a) the property was received, concealed, or withheld by the accused; (b) such property had been stolen; and (c) the accused knew the property had been stolen. *See* Wayne R. LaFave, Criminal Law § 20.2, at 1035–45 (5th ed. 2010). For the Model Penal Code's version of this offense, see Model Penal Code § 223.6.

2. Comparing Theft by Embezzlement. Reznick was charged only with theft by larceny and not with theft by embezzlement. Thus, Kunkin and Applebaum could not be convicted of receiving stolen property unless the prosecution proved that they knew Reznick had committed larceny in removing the documents. The prosecution was unable to satisfy this burden once the court found insufficient evidence that Kunkin and Applebaum knew that Reznick had the requisite intent to deprive permanently when he took the documents.

Intent to deprive permanently is not an element of embezzlement in many states, including California. *See* Cal. Penal Code § 503. Therefore, if Reznick had instead been charged with theft by embezzlement, the court might well have upheld the conviction (assuming the other elements of embezzlement had been established). Kunkin and Applebaum would only have had to know that the property was embezzled, and knowledge of an intent to deprive permanently would not have been required. (For further discussion of embezzlement, see Section C below.)

3. Defining "Permanently." The specific intent required for larceny is the intent to deprive an owner of property permanently. "Permanently" has been interpreted to mean the following:

> (a) *For the property's useful life.* In *State v. Lanier*, 477 So. 2d 889, 891 (La. Ct. App. 1985), the court noted that "[t]he man who borrows a tool that he plans to return as soon as it wears out intends to deprive the owner of the tool." Suppose, for example, that *A* walks into *B*'s office while *B* is at lunch and sees two tickets to Sunday's football game lying on *B*'s desk. Seizing the opportunity to take revenge for *B*'s unreasonable demands that *A* work overtime on the weekends, *A* grabs the tickets. Monday morning, before *B* arrives at work, *A* surreptitiously "returns" the tickets to *B*'s office. *See also* Model Penal Code § 223.0(1)(a).

> (b) *Exposing the property to risk such that its return could be impossible.* In *State v. Davis*, 38 N.J.L. 176 (1875), some Princeton students took their professor's horse and buggy, drove it recklessly, and then abandoned it, leaving it to chance whether or not the horse and buggy would be returned to the professor. The students' larceny convictions were upheld. In *State v. Ward*, 10 P. 133 (Nev. 1886), the defendant took another person's horses and abandoned them 12 miles away. Although the defendant hoped that the horses would return to their owner, which in fact they did, the court upheld a larceny conviction because that hope was not well-founded. *See* Wayne R. LaFave, Criminal Law § 19.5(b), at 990 n.15 (5th ed. 2010).

> (c) *Placing an unacceptable condition upon the property's return.* In *Commonwealth v. Mason*, 105 Mass. 163 (1870), the defendant took another's horse with the intention of hiding it until the owner offered a reward for it. The defendant then planned to return the horse and claim the reward. The defendant's conviction of larceny was affirmed. In *State v. Hauptmann*, 180 A. 809 (N.J. 1935), the defendant carried the Lindbergh baby off in his nightdress.

The court found that the defendant committed larceny by taking the night-dress and making its return conditional on the parents' payment of ransom for the baby. (This finding enabled the court to uphold a conviction of felony murder — murder in the commission of burglary (breaking and entering with intent to commit the felony of larceny) — and then impose the death penalty for felony murder. Note that the court did not rely on kidnapping to trigger the felony murder doctrine because it was not a felony at common law.) *See also* Model Penal Code § 223.0(1)(a). *See generally* WAYNE R. LAFAVE, CRIMINAL LAW § 19.5, at 988 (5th ed. 2010).

On the other hand, a defendant who places reasonable conditions on the return of property is not guilty of larceny. In *City of Cincinnati v. Herron*, 274 N.E.2d 461, 462 (Ohio Ct. App. 1971), for example, a storeowner removed four hubcaps from an automobile that was parked on his private property "at a time of night when all businesses in the vicinity [were] closed." Reversing his larceny conviction, the court held that he did not have the necessary mens rea for larceny because he did not intend to deprive the car owner of the hubcaps permanently, but was holding on to them only until the owner "show[ed] me that he was [a] customer of that property." *Id.* at 463.

4. A Claim of Right. Those who take property to collect on a debt, or who for some other reason believe they have a right to the property, have no intent to permanently deprive another person of the property and therefore have not committed larceny. *See, e.g.*, Model Penal Code § 223.1(3). In *Roark v. State*, 130 N.E.2d 326 (Ind. 1955), the defendants loaned $5 to a Mrs. Weisenhan, who offered to repay the debt in the following manner: the defendants were to drive to Weisenhan's farm the next day, sack three bags of wheat, and sell them at a nearby mill. Unfortunately for the defendants, Weisenhan failed to appear at the farm at the appointed time and they entered the barn and went about sacking the wheat on their own. Mr. Dall, who leased the farm from Weisenhan, was not privy to the arrangement, and, suspecting the defendants of burglary, fired a 12-gauge shotgun into the barn, critically injuring both of them. The defendants were tried and convicted of "automobile banditry" (use of an automobile in the commission of larceny) and sentenced to 10 years' imprisonment. The Indiana Supreme Court reversed, concluding that the defendants lacked larcenous intent because they were taking the wheat under a bona fide claim of right.

Suppose that one of *A*'s paintings is stolen from his home. Later, *A* sees a painting hanging in a museum that he believes is the one that was stolen from him. *A* takes the painting and goes to Brazil to safeguard it. In fact, the painting was not stolen from *A*'s home but actually belongs to the museum. *A* does not have the mens rea to commit larceny because he honestly believed the painting was his — even if his belief was unreasonable. *See The King v. Nundah*, (1916) 16 NSW St. R. 482 (Austl.); WAYNE R. LAFAVE, CRIMINAL LAW § 19.5, at 987–95 (5th ed. 2010).

Highly publicized prosecutions of corporate CEOs and other executives often focus on whether a claim of right negates the larceny, embezzlement, and other conduct characterized as corporate looting. Under this theory, extraordinary bonuses and expense reimbursements cannot constitute theft if the defendant believed, even incorrectly, that the corporation had legitimately (even if unwisely) authorized such payments. Such arguments may be particularly strong when the corporate board of directors is fully apprised of the disbursements, although prosecutors may then argue that board members also betrayed the company's trust. Furthermore, executives below the CEO level can argue that they relied on the apparent authority of the CEO to authorize generous payments on behalf of the corporation.

Claim-of-right arguments were made, for example, in the criminal case against two Tyco officials, CEO Dennis Kozlowski and Chief Financial Officer Mark Swartz, who allegedly misspent more than $600 million in corporate funds, including $6,000 for a gold inlaid shower curtain for Kozlowski's apartment and a $2 million birthday party for his wife. After an initial mistrial due to juror intimidation, the defendants were convicted of grand larceny as well as fraud and conspiracy. They received prison sentences of 8 to 25 years and were ordered to pay fines and restitution totaling more than $235 million. *See People v. Kozlowski*, 846 N.Y.S.2d 44 (N.Y. App. Div. 2007) (affirming convictions). Is the line between excessive generosity to corporate executives and criminal theft of corporate funds clear to you? Do you think the distinction between criminality and bad corporate judgments regarding compensation has been inappropriately blurred? Or is the distinction unimportant in the murky world of high corporate finance?

5. The English Requirement of "Dishonesty." In the United States, the intent to deprive permanently represents larceny's only special mens rea element, but notions of "honest belief" play a far greater role in English criminal law because prosecutors must also show that the defendant acted "dishonestly" as a separate and additional element of any theft crime. Professor Ashworth describes this "dishonesty" requirement:

> Dishonesty may be easily recognized in some situations, but it is far more difficult in situations with which a jury or magistrate are unfamiliar — such as alleged business fraud or financial misdealing. Moreover, much depends on who is responsible for characterizing conduct as dishonest. . . . [T]he most fruitful line of development is likely to be a general legislative definition, interpreted by the courts. One proposal for a general definition is that a person is dishonest when acting "knowing that the appropriation will or may be detrimental to the interests of the owner in a significant practical way."

ANDREW ASHWORTH, PRINCIPLES OF CRIMINAL LAW 338–39 (1991). What are the advantages and disadvantages of the "dishonesty" requirement? Would courts in this country benefit from drawing on the English model? Would adding such a requirement have affected the result of any of the larceny cases we have considered in this Chapter?

Although "the finding of dishonesty may often make the difference between conviction and acquittal" in England, oddly enough the Theft Act of 1968 does not define the concept of "dishonesty." *Id.* at 336. Rather, apart from a few legislative clues covering only the most basic situations, "the definition of dishonesty is at large, and the courts have been left to develop an approach." The result has been a complex and controversial three-part test:

> First, the court must ascertain [the defendant's] beliefs in relation to the appropriation — the reasons, motivations, explanations. Second, the jury or magistrate must decide whether a person acting with those beliefs would be regarded as dishonest according to the current standards of ordinary decent people. Third, if there is evidence that [the defendant] thought that the conduct was not dishonest according to those general standards, [the defendant] should be acquitted if the court is left in reasonable doubt on the matter.

Id. at 337. Are there inherent vagueness problems in such a "dishonesty" requirement?

6. Borrowing. One who takes property intending to borrow it and then return it within a reasonable amount of time does not have the specific intent required for larceny. In *People v. Brown*, 38 P. 518 (Cal. 1894), for example, the defendant took a bike to get "even" with another boy. The defendant planned to return the bike the next night, but was caught before he was able to do so. The defendant's conviction of burglary with the intent to commit larceny was reversed because he lacked the mens rea to commit larceny.

On the other hand, where the defendant's actions are blatantly larcenous, the requisite intent may be inferred by the court. In *State v. Langford*, 483 So. 2d 979 (La. 1986), the defendant was able to withdraw nearly $850,000 from his bank account due to a bank computer error that assigned him a code allowing unlimited overdrafts at no charge. (This occurred after the bank had denied defendant's $225,000 loan application.) When the bank realized its mistake, the defendant claimed that he had intended only to borrow the money but was unable to repay it at the present time. The court affirmed his theft conviction.

If the defendant in the *Brown* case had taken the bike with the intent to return it, but then had changed his mind and decided to keep it, he would still be guilty of larceny. *See* Wayne R. LaFave, Criminal Law § 19.5(b), at 989–91 n.8 (5th ed. 2010). In *Commonwealth v. White*, 65 Mass. (11 Cush.) 483 (1853), the court held that a defendant who took another's property with the intent to return it had committed the crime of trespass, though not larceny, and that the trespass continued as long as the wrongful possession. When the defendant later formed the intent to steal, the trespass became larceny. (Compare the stricter common-law rules for larceny of lost and mistakenly delivered property, which are described above in Sections B.4.a and B.4.b.)

Suppose *A* takes a painting from a museum, intending only to borrow it for the weekend. On the way home, however, *A* accidentally drops the painting in the street, and it is run over and destroyed by a passing bus. *A* did not commit larceny because an intent to borrow does not suffice even if some unforeseen event prevents the return of the property. *See, e.g., Saferite v. State*, 93 P.2d 762 (Okla. Crim. App. 1939) (finding that larceny had not been committed where an automobile accident prevented the defendant from returning another's car); LaFave, *supra*, § 19.5(b), at 989–91.

Suppose instead that *A* takes the painting, intending to keep it permanently, but changes her mind at the end of the weekend and returns the painting to the museum in perfect condition. Under these circumstances, *A* is guilty of larceny. Her later intent to return the painting does not erase the crime of larceny, which was complete when the intent to deprive coincided with the trespassory taking. *See, e.g., Brennan v. Commonwealth*, 185 S.W. 489 (Ky. 1916) (affirming larceny conviction where the defendant took a car with the intent to steal it, but later changed his mind).

7. **Statutes that Criminalize Borrowing.** Suppose that *A* takes *B*'s criminal law book with the intent to return it and then taunts *B* by denying her possession of the book. This situation raises the issue whether the law should criminalize borrowing without the owner's consent under some circumstances.

Many state legislatures have enacted statutes that make temporary takings of specific property a crime, though not one punished as severely as larceny. For example, almost every state has a "joyriding" statute that punishes temporary takings of motor vehicles. *See, e.g.,* Cal. Penal Code § 499b; Va. Code § 18.2-102; Model Penal Code § 223.9.

In California, it is a misdemeanor to remove or be in possession of any shopping or laundry cart that has a permanently affixed sign indicating that removal from the premises or the parking area without the consent of the owner is unauthorized. Furthermore, these statutes only require an "intent to temporarily or permanently deprive the owner or retailer of possession of the cart." Cal. Bus. & Prof. Code §§ 22435–22435.4. Why do cars, and in some states shopping carts, receive special protection under the criminal law?

8. **The Propriety of Punishing Wrongful Borrowing.** Intent to deprive permanently is a well-established element of the crime of larceny. The Model Penal Code, while acknowledging certain generally accepted refinements (*see* Model Penal Code § 223.0(1)), has not advocated its elimination. Professor Glanville Williams, however, is critical of the strict mens rea requirement:

> Only two arguments against making the proposed extension of the Theft Act [which would eliminate the requirement of intent to "permanently" deprive] are worth consideration. The first, that it would be contrary to tradition, or that people would not recognize temporary appropriation as theft, can perhaps be answered by pointing to the legal systems that have this concept already. Many of the illustrations . . . would, I think, readily be regarded as theft by many people. For example, it would, I am sure, generally be regarded as theft for a person to take a bicycle, use it for several weeks, and then abandon it on the street even if the owner eventually recovers it. In

the debate on the Theft Bill in the House of Lords, Viscount Dilhorne made the interesting point that none of the definitions of the word "steal" in the Oxford English Dictionary required an intent to deprive the owner permanently; they spoke only of the dishonest taking or appropriating of the property of another. In one respect the definition of theft has always gone far beyond popular usage, the slightest moving of the article with the necessary intent is traditionally theft, though the ordinary man would not regard the theft as complete at that stage. . . . It is strange to swallow this camel while straining at the gnat of saying that it is theft to decamp with someone's valuable article and to conceal it from him dishonestly for what may be a considerable period of time.

It may be that the reader, while accepting some of the arguments of this article, has throughout been afflicted by one other doubt. Is it seriously suggested that trivial cases of dishonestly using the property of another should be subject to prosecution as theft? The absurdity of this . . . was elaborated by Lord Stonham, speaking for the government, in the debate on the Theft Bill in the House of Lords. He gave, as examples of trivial cases, using one's neighbor's lawn mower against his expressed wishes, taking a book from a public library beyond one's borrowing limit, and using a friend's dinner jacket without his consent.

The argument about trivial cases is frequently used to oppose extension of the law, but it is never conclusive in itself, because practically every offence covers some trivial matters. If an offence is needed to deal with serious misconduct, that is sufficient to justify it. Even the present law could be abused by prosecuting for trivial thefts, but in practice a sensible discretion is generally exercised. . . .

Glanville Williams, *Temporary Appropriation Should Be Theft*, 1981 Crim. L. Rev. 129, 138.

Are there other reasons to continue requiring proof of "intent to deprive permanently" to support a conviction for larceny? Should wrongful borrowing generally be criminalized?

Mason v. State

32 Ark. 238 (1877)

Harrison, Justice.

Brier Mason the appellant, and Mid Jones and Riley Beavers, were indicted for larceny in breaking and entering the house of Nathan Dixon, and also for grand larceny in stealing therefrom a keg of beer, the property of said Dixon.

The appellant was separately tried, and acquitted of the charge of burglary, but convicted on the second count, of petit larceny.

He filed a motion for a new trial upon the ground that the evidence did not sustain the verdict, which was refused.

Nathan Dixon, . . . the only witness for the State, testified, that on the second Saturday in April, 1876, the defendant, and the said Jones and Beavers, came to his house in Cincinnati, in Washington County, after eleven o'clock at night, and called for some beer. He had then gone to bed, and refused to get up and let them have it. They insisted, and told him if he did not let them have it they would steal all he had. He did not get up and they left. The witness was sleeping in the house in which he kept his beer for sale. The next morning he discovered that a window of the room in which he kept the beer had been prized up, and a keg of beer which set on the opposite side of the room, had been taken out, and was setting by the window on the porch, and about a gallon of the beer, worth about 30 cents, had been taken. He suspected the defendant and Jones and Beavers of the act but said nothing about it that day to any one except Mr. Scoy, a justice of the peace, who lived about two miles from town; Mr. Scoy told him it was a grand jury case. On the following Monday morning and before he had mentioned the matter to any other person, the defendant and Jones and Beavers came to him, and told him that they had taken the beer, and offered to pay him for it. They offered $3, which he refused to receive, but offered to take $30, and give them a full receipt against the grand jury. They refused to pay $30.

The witness had been selling cakes, and beer and cider as a business in Cincinnati ten years, and had been long intimately acquainted with all the said parties, and had known the defendant, who was raised there since he was ten years old, and from the time the witness came there and engaged in said business. That all had been, for years, customers of his, and the defendant ever since he commenced selling cakes, and beer and cider, and that he lived about a hundred yards from him, and Jones near by.

A felonious or criminal intent, is an essential constituent of larceny. It must always be averred in the charge, and is as necessary to be proven as the taking and carrying away. Proof of one without the other will not suffice.

The mere fact of the taking and carrying away, does not raise a presumption of guilt, or that the taking was to steal, or *lucri causa,* for the sake of profit or gain; but such felonious or criminal intent must be shown by circumstances connected with the taking.

. . . The beer was taken on Saturday night; on Monday morning, before any complaint was made, the parties went to the owner and told him they had taken the beer, and offered to pay him for it. No one had seen them take it; it was not found in their possession, and the fact that they took it was known only to themselves. Dixon kept beer for sale; they applied to him as they had often before done for some; they had been his customers for years; the defendant for ten years ever since he was ten years old; and he was intimately acquainted with all of them; there is no proof that they did not intend to pay for it, and the only reason for not letting them have it, so far as the evidence discloses any, was that he had retired to bed, and did not wish to get up.

Where is the evidence of a design to fraudulently deprive Dixon of his property, or of an intention to take it without giving him a *quid pro quo* of equal value? If they intended to pay for the beer, how did they intend to defraud him, or what gain to themselves did they contemplate?

. . . The judgment of the court below is reversed and the cause remanded to it, that the appellant may have a new trial.

Notes and Questions

1. **The Intention to Pay for Taken Goods.** As *Mason* illustrates, a person who gives or intends to give an equal or more valuable substitute for a fungible good does not have the intent to permanently deprive another of property.

Why should the intent to pay or substitute negate the intent to deprive permanently and constitute a defense to larceny? Is the person who is too impatient to wait in line at a store and instead leaves money on the counter a thief? What about a shopper who breaks into a store after hours but leaves payment for the items that were taken? (For a discussion why the crime of burglary would be committed only if the defendant was guilty of larceny, see Chapter 9, Section D.) Do cases like *Mason* suggest that the law of larceny is protecting more than "possession"?

2. **Defining Fungible Goods.** The doctrine set out in *Mason* is widely applied to takings of goods that merchants have offered for sale. There is less consensus on when to apply the rule in other contexts because difficulties arise in determining precisely what constitutes a fungible good other than one offered for sale.

In *Pylee v. State*, 136 S.W. 464 (Tex. Crim. App. 1911), the defendant took oats from another's field to feed his horses. The defendant claimed that he would have paid for the oats but for the fact that he was driving a young and foolish team of horses that could not be left alone. Therefore, the defendant asserted (as did his wife, who was accompanying him at the time) that he planned to give the money for the oats to his father-in-law, who was following in another buggy led by a gentler horse. The defendant was intercepted, however, as he was heading in the direction of the owner's house. The court held that if the defendant did in fact intend to pay for the oats, he could not be guilty of larceny. *See* WAYNE R. LaFAVE, CRIMINAL LAW § 19.5(c), at 991 n.24 (5th ed. 2010).

Suppose that *A* is attending a "bring your own beer" party at *B*'s house and runs out of beer. *A* opens *B*'s refrigerator and takes the one beer he finds there, leaving a dollar in its place. *B*, who has been busy hosting the party and is by now really thirsty, goes to her refrigerator to get the one beer she had bought for herself to drink that night. She is furious when she finds that her beer is missing. Is *A* guilty of larceny? Some courts, following the approach taken in *Pylee*, would find that *A*'s intent to pay for the beer negated the mens rea for larceny. But other courts would not recognize intent to pay as a defense because the beer was not for sale. Consider, in this context, the following passage from *State v. Kelley*, 563 P.2d 749, 753 (Or. Ct. App. 1977):

> A defendant's actual return of the property after it is obtained may shed some light on his intent at the time of the taking . . . , but a defendant's restitution, repayment or promise to repay is totally irrelevant. . . . There is a distinction between taking property with the intent to return it and taking property with the intent to make restitution or repayment. In the former situation the individual intends to restore the specific property taken to its owner and therefore there can be no intent to permanently deprive. In the latter case the individual intends to pay to the owner the value of the property taken but not the property itself. Theft involves the taking of a specific thing and not the taking of an abstraction such as value. . . . Thus the intent to restore value to the owner while keeping the specific property taken does not preclude a theft conviction.

Which view is more persuasive?

3. The Model Penal Code's Approach. Section 223.1(3)(c) of the Model Penal Code considers intent to pay a defense only where the defendant "took property exposed for sale, intending to purchase and pay for it promptly, or reasonably believing that the owner, if present, would have consented."

[C] Embezzlement

People v. Talbot
28 P.2d 1057 (Cal. 1934)

PER CURIAM.

A hearing was granted in this case after decision by the District Court of Appeal, Second Appellate District, Division Two, to consider the question whether the appropriation of corporate funds by the defendants was made with fraudulent intent, an element necessary to constitute embezzlement. We have painstakingly re-examined the record on this issue. Certain evidence tended to show that defendants were not conscious that their acts amounted to embezzlement even if they did constitute bad business practice. The record shows that each of the defendants and numerous employees had drawing accounts with the corporation; that the withdrawals by defendants were made openly, with no attempt at concealment; that the canceled checks were returned to the corporation; that defendants were charged on the books with all of the expenditures; and that no manipulation of accounts took place. It is further contended, and we may assume that it is true, that the practice of making advances of this sort to corporate officers and employees during this period was common, not only in the Richfield company but in other corporations as well. The prevalence of this unlawful practice cannot, of course, justify it.

These and other facts were before the trial court, and that court was permitted to draw the inference of fraudulent intent from the admitted fact that the funds were appropriated and used for the personal purposes of the defendants. In this state of the record, the appellate court may not disturb the findings and judgment.

We therefore adopt the opinion prepared by Mr. Justice pro tem. Archbald, of the District Court of Appeal, as the opinion of this court. It reads as follows:

> . . . At the time the nine alleged acts of grand theft were committed, Talbot was chairman of the board of directors of the Richfield Oil Company of California. . . .
>
> "For the purpose of proving 'felonious intent' evidence was introduced of fourteen Richfield company checks ordered by Talbot aggregating the sum of $186,886.10, which apparently went entirely for the personal use of said appellant and not for any company expense. One of the checks was for $80,000, the balance of the purchase price of his private yacht, and others aggregating approximately $15,000 were for insurance thereon. The evidence also shows that such withdrawals were not authorized by the board of directors and were without the personal knowledge of the directors, with the possible exception of one of the $50,000 checks which was brought to the attention of director Newberger after it reached the hands of the brokerage firm. . . . It likewise appears that the withdrawals made were charged in the personal accounts of the respective officers, which were kept under the heading, 'Due from officers and employees. Account 418 A.' Up to 1927 it was apparently the practice of Peat, [Marwick], Mitchell & Company, who audited the books of the Richfield company semi-annually, to submit a detailed report of such account to the board of directors, but after that year the practice was changed and two types of balance sheets were made, one 'a detailed report supporting the certified statements and giving in greater detail all of the assets and liabilities and discussing them,' and the other a 'condensed balance sheet,' which did not contain the details of the officers' accounts. This 'condensed balance sheet usually goes to the stockholders and is printed, published.' The detailed report 'is a sort of confidential balance sheet for the executive of the company' or 'for reference.'
>
> "As bearing on the question of fraudulent intent and showing his good faith and lack of motive for wrongdoing as charged, appellant Talbot introduced evidence of his financial condition. Such evidence tended to show that his net worth on August 31, 1929, was approximately $5,439,000. . . .
>
> "Appellant contends that it had been his custom, not only in the Richfield company but in other companies of which he had been an executive, to have drawing accounts against which were charged advances made to officers and employees; that both sums of money he is charged with taking openly and without concealment or any of the other usual indicia of fraudulent acts.

"The taking charged as grand theft was on the theory of embezzlement. Section 484 of the Penal Code, so far as material to such theory, provides: 'Every person . . . who shall fraudulently appropriate property which has been entrusted to him . . . is guilty of theft.' Section 503 of the same code defines embezzlement as 'the fraudulent appropriation of property by a person to whom it has been entrusted.' Section 504 provides that 'every officer, director, trustee, clerk, servant or agent of any . . . corporation (public or private) who fraudulently appropriates to any use or purpose not in the due and lawful execution of his trust, any property which he has in his possession or under his control by virtue of his trust . . . is guilty of embezzlement.' From these sections it clearly appears that fraudulent intent is an essential element of the offense of embezzlement, and such is the ruling of our courts. Appellant says that the element of concealment is lacking, and points to the case of *People v. O'Brien*, 106 Cal. 104, 39 P. 325, as one emphasizing the necessity of concealment as a fact from which fraudulent intent may be inferred. We do not read the case that way. The court decided in effect that the evidence showed simply a case of disputed mutual accounts, which might have been embezzlement if the defendant had not acted openly and without any attempt at concealment.

"While secrecy or concealment is evidence of a criminal or felonious intent, nevertheless there may be embezzlement where the appropriation is openly made and consequently without concealment.

"It is urged that such fraudulent intent must be shown by facts or circumstances independent of and in addition to the act of conversion, and among other cases cited in support of the contention is *People v. Royce*, 106 Cal. 173, 37 P. 630, 39 P. 524. In that case the treasurer of a corporation received a draft for $10,350 and deposited it in his personal account at a bank, notifying the bookkeeper of that fact. No depository bank had ever been named by the directors of the corporation. Three days after the deposit was made the company received from him the sum of $8,310.35. He was charged with embezzlement. The evidence apparently did not show what became of the balance or that defendant did not have it ready to be produced when called for, and there was no evidence that a demand to produce was made upon him. Under such circumstances no felonious intent was shown.

"The element of felonious intent in every contested criminal case must necessarily be determined from the facts and circumstances of the case. In our opinion the law is well expressed in the case of *Mangham v. State*, 11 Ga. App. 427, 75 S.E. 512, 516, where the court says: 'An officer or agent of a corporation cannot take money of the corporation which is entrusted to him, or which comes into his possession by virtue of his office or agency, and use it even temporarily for his personal benefit and avoid criminal responsibility by calling it a loan. The law calls such a transaction a wrongful conversion, from which a fraudulent intent can be inferred.'

"The crime of embezzlement is purely statutory, and legislation with reference thereto resulted from the failure of prosecutions under the common law crime of larceny to reach a case where the possession of property was obtained by consent, and the resulting breach of trust by the agent, officer or bailee, although it as effectually deprived the owner of his property as though it had been taken out of his possession by stealth, was not punishable at common law. In the case of *People v. Gordon*, 133 Cal. 328, 65 P. 746, 747, speaking of our Code definition of embezzlement, the court says: 'The essential elements of embezzlement are the fiduciary relation arising where one intrusts property to another, and the fraudulent appropriation of the property by the latter.' There would seem to be no hidden meaning in the use of the word fraudulent in such definition. It is true that where, as in the cases of *People v. Royce*, 106 Cal. 173, 37 P. 630, 39 P. 524, and *People v. Page*, 116 Cal. 386, 48 P. 326, the money is deposited in the personal account of the defendant but no evidence is introduced showing that it was ever converted to his own use, no 'fraudulent appropriation' is shown. But we are sure that if the evidence in such cases showed, without question, an appropriation of the money to the personal use of the defendants, and contrary to the purposes of the trusts, the fraudulent intent would have been imputed to them.

"One of the definitions of 'fraud' given by the Standard Dictionary is: 'Any act . . . that involves a breach of duty, trust, or confidence, and which is injurious to another, or by which an undue advantage is taken of another,' and an act is declared to be fraudulent that is characterized by fraud. We think the Legislature used the word 'fraudulent,' in its definition of embezzlement, to distinguish an 'appropriation' by an agent of money or property under circumstances that might be merely tinged with suspicion as to the agent's intent, from an appropriation for purely personal uses of the agent, as contrasted with the purpose for which the money or property was entrusted to him. In other words, in every case where the officers of a corporation who are necessarily entrusted with the money and property of the concern use it, knowingly and intentionally, for their own purposes, there is a 'fraudulent appropriation' thereof which is termed embezzlement by the statute, and the fact that such officers intended to restore the money or property is of no avail to them if it has not been restored before information laid or indictment found charging them with embezzlement (Pen. Code sec. 512), and even if prior to the bringing of such charges the officers *voluntarily and actually* restore the property, such fact does not constitute a defense but merely authorizes the court in its discretion to mitigate the offense (sec. 513). It would seem that the legislature here has shown in very clear terms that it is the immediate breach of trust that makes the offense, rather than the permanent deprivation of the owner of his property.

"In the recent case of *People v. Gordon*, 206 Cal. 29, 273 P. 568, 571, the defendant, an attorney, was entrusted with the collection of amounts due on certain bonds. The money was collected but only about half of it was paid over to his client by the defendant. When the balance was demanded the attorney claimed that he was to receive one-half as his fee for collection. The court there said: 'Defendant claims there is no showing of fraudulent intent on his part, as his actions were unconcealed and were based on his understanding that he was to receive half of the sum collected. In our opinion, however, the evidence was amply sufficient to establish the fraud. Defendant's testimony at most raised a conflict which was resolved by the verdict of the jury in favor of the people. The jury was properly instructed on the subject of the element of specific intent, and its determination of the matter is final.' We think the reasoning of that case applies with great force to the one before us. Under the evidence produced by the prosecution serious misappropriations of funds of the corporation are shown, contrary to all authority given and in violation of the trust imposed. The fact that this appellant intended to repay the money taken, or was amply able to do so, is of no avail in the face of the fact that the money was not replaced prior to indictment found. The claim that he used the money in an honest effort to stabilize the price of stock on the market, for the benefit of the corporation and its stockholders and not for the selfish purpose of making his own holdings more valuable, created but a conflict in the evidence which the court, trier of the facts, decided against him, and that determination is final so far as an appellate court is concerned. Neither does the claim that appellant had been accustomed to drawing and using the funds of the corporation for his personal needs, having such withdrawals charged to his personal account and eventually paying the money back by credits due him or payments made by him, relieve the acts from the stain of criminality. Nor can we subscribe to the doctrine that long-continued wrongdoing sanctifies or purifies such conduct. Even if all of the directors of the corporation knew of such custom, the wrong was not made right. They were each charged with the trust to use the funds of the company for company needs, and it might be seriously questioned whether an authorization or ratification by the board of such acts would not have resulted in involving the directors rather than in excusing the officers. That the trial judge understood the law as to intent clearly appears from the record, and in our opinion the evidence amply sustains the conclusion he must have reached thereon. . . .

Notes and Questions

1. **The Elements of the Crime.** Under the rules of common-law larceny, a person who was entrusted with another person's property and misappropriated that property could not be convicted of larceny because of the absence of a trespassory taking. The modern statutory crime of embezzlement was created to fill that gap. Today, most states define embezzlement as (1) the fraudulent (2) appropriation (3) of property (4) of another (5) by one who has been entrusted with possession.

For the purposes of this crime, "fraudulent" usually means "with the intent to deprive" and thus encompasses cases like *Talbot* where the defendant intended only to borrow the property. Some jurisdictions, however, define "fraudulent" as "the intent to deprive permanently." The term "fraudulent" also requires proof that the defendant knew the property belonged to another person: a claim of right is a defense to embezzlement. "Appropriation" means the use of property in a manner inconsistent with what the owner has authorized. *See* Wayne R. LaFave, Criminal Law § 19.6, at 995–1006 (5th ed. 2010). (See Note 4 below for further discussion of the fraudulent intent requirement.)

Note that three of the elements of larceny are not required for embezzlement: trespass, taking, and carrying away.

2. **The History and Development of the Crime.** The statutory crime of embezzlement appears to have emerged from difficulties that arose in applying the rules of larceny to cases where servants misappropriated their masters' property. As Professor Hall describes, the tension finds its roots in the earliest English larceny cases:

> [W]hile the idea of embezzlement is ancient, and instances of its incidence are continuous in the criminal law, legal control of the type of criminal behavior which has become a commonplace in modern times—the violation of private financial trust—dates definitely from the eighteenth century.
>
> The eighteenth century law of embezzlement grew out of the need to overcome the limited utility of the custody concept. The rule that a servant who converted goods or money received from a third person for his master committed merely a civil breach of trust, provided a constantly recurring problem until 1799. Only then was the required legislation enacted. Prior to that time, indeed, the courts were narrowing this area of trust considerably. The technique was to expand the "possession of the master" at every conceivable opportunity. Thus, if the servant placed the money or goods received from a third person into any receptacle owned by the master, that was held enough to constitute possession in the latter, and subsequent conversion larceny. There were limits, however, beyond which even the constructive possession of the master could not be extended, while for over two centuries business increased very rapidly and "servants" became clerks and cashiers who dealt constantly with third persons.

The climax of this situation was reached in the case of *The King v. Joseph Bazeley* in 1799. Bazeley was the principal teller for a firm of bankers. In that capacity he received for deposit a note for one hundred pounds which, after crediting it to the customer's account along with additional sums deposited, he put into his pocket and used to meet a personal obligation. In deciding this case the court said:

> It is clear that the prosecutors had not, upon the present occasion, the actual possession of the Bank-note, and therefore the inquiry must be, whether they had the constructive possession of it? or, in other words, whether the possession of the servant was, under the circumstances of this case, the possession of the master? ... The prosecutors in the present case had only a right or title to possess the note, and not the absolute or even qualified possession of it. It was never in their custody or under their control. . . . At the time, therefore, of the supposed conversion of this note, it was in the legal possession of the prisoner. To divest the prisoner of this possession, it certainly was not necessary that he should have delivered this note into the hands of the prosecutors, or of any other of their servants personally; for if he had deposited it in the drawer, kept for the reception of this species of property, it would have been a delivery of it into the possession of his masters; but he made no such deposit. . . . After these determinations it cannot be contended that the possession of the servant is the possession of the master; for, independently of these authorities, the rule that the possession of the servant is the possession of the master, cannot be extended to a case in which the property never was in the master's possession. . . .

The case was argued on April 24, 1799 and the defendant was discharged shortly thereafter. That same year, 39 Geo. III, c. 85, the first general embezzlement statute, was passed.

JEROME HALL, THEFT, LAW AND SOCIETY 37–38 (2d ed. 1952).

3. The Limits of the Criminal Sanction. The question whether to extend the criminal law to cover embezzlement has been a fertile issue for debate among commentators. Professor Hall (quoted in the prior Note and in Note 2 following *Lund v. Commonwealth* in Section B.1 above) has argued that the entire law of theft, including embezzlement, developed in response to social, political, and economic changes. Consider whether the emergence of the industrial economy and the modern corporate structure necessitated the expansion of the criminal sanction into private business relationships:

> The embezzlement legislation and the extension of the concept of taking from constructive possession were designed to protect class interests. England

was moving from mercantile to industrial capitalism. Units of trade and commerce were growing larger; the image of the solitary merchant or artisan gave way to corporate and partnership forms employing wage labor. A misappropriation between partners or joint venturers might be the stuff of which civil law suits could be made, but the hired clerk's defalcation was a matter for criminal prosecution, a hanging matter.

Michael E. Tigar, *The Right of Property and the Law of Theft*, 62 Tex. L. Rev. 1443, 1454–55 (1984).

Professor Schwartz has commented on the difficulties that arise in determining what constitutes "criminal" misappropriation under the embezzlement laws:

> One of the objections to expanding theft law—the harshness of larceny penalties—was met by providing milder although still heavy sanctions for embezzlement, thus introducing the somewhat surprising phenomenon that different forms of theft would be treated with varying degrees of severity depending on the historic moment when a particular expansion of theft law was effectuated. A major peculation by a trustee or bank official might carry a lesser penalty than a minor trespassory larceny, although many would consider that the former was the more heinous and harmful behavior. Over a period of time the severity of larceny penalties gradually moderated; and ultimately, when various forms of theft were consolidated into a single offense, the same statutory maximum would become applicable to both larceny and embezzlement.
>
> . . . "Misappropriation" is the criminal act that characterizes embezzlement, just as "taking" characterizes larceny. It is generally more difficult to decide whether misappropriation occurred than to decide whether property was unlawfully taken. A real estate broker or a lawyer, for example, may receive the proceeds of a sale of property or money recovered in a lawsuit. It is easy to say that such monies are misappropriated if the broker or lawyer pockets the whole fund and spends it for his personal needs. But what if the broker deposits the buyer's check in the broker's personal bank account, meaning to write a check later payable to the client for the amount of the proceeds less commission? That way of handling the transaction may violate standards of professional behavior which explicitly require clients' funds to be deposited and held in separate accounts; but it would be a harsh rule that transformed every violation of prophylactic professional regulations into a severely punishable theft. Ethical codes of the professions generally provide lesser sanctions, such as reprimand or suspension from practice, and no ethics committee of a professional association should have the power to redefine crime by changing its rules of ethics. On the other hand, the mere fact that an act violates professional standards should not immunize professional misbehavior from criminal sanctions that apply to identical conduct engaged in by nonprofessionals . . . .

Louis B. Schwartz, *Theft, in* 4 Encyclopedia of Crime and Justice 1537, 1543–44 (Sanford H. Kadish ed., 1983).

4. Fraudulent Intent. The term "fraudulent intent" as applied to embezzlement is the specific intent required for the crime—the intent to deprive another of property. Some states require that the mens rea for embezzlement be the intent to deprive "permanently," as is required for larceny.

Other jurisdictions disagree and instead consider an intent to deprive for any period of time, no matter how short, sufficient for embezzlement as long as all the other elements of the crime are present. In these jurisdictions, even borrowing would constitute embezzlement. In *United States v. Powell*, 294 F. Supp. 1353 (E.D. Va. 1968), for example, a postal clerk was charged under a federal statute with having embezzled $1,393.56 entrusted to his care. According to the court, the fact that the clerk intended to return the property or to make restitution was irrelevant because the crime of embezzlement was complete the moment he appropriated property belonging to the Post Office for his own use. As *Talbot* illustrates, some of the courts that refuse to require proof of an intent to deprive "permanently" in embezzlement cases fear that otherwise corporate officers and agents will be able to take property entrusted to them, use it for their personal benefit, and escape criminal liability by claiming that they intended to return the property. Which definition of "fraudulent intent" is preferable? What are the underlying policies at issue?

Unlike the law of larceny (*see Mason v. State* and the accompanying Notes in Section B.5 above), the common law of embezzlement—even in jurisdictions requiring an intent to deprive permanently—does not afford a defense to defendants who substituted equivalent property for the embezzled property. *See State v. Pratt,* 220 P. 505 (Kan. 1923) (affirming embezzlement conviction of loan association treasurer who sold bonds belonging to his employer, even though he intended to replace them or their value). *See generally* Wayne R. LaFave, Criminal Law § 19.6(f), at 1005 n.69 (5th ed. 2010).

In the highly publicized prosecution of Adelphia Cable Company founder John Rigas and his sons, the defendants were accused of wrongfully borrowing $2.3 billion based on the corporation's credit in order to personally purchase Adelphia stock (which later lost substantial value). The defendants argued that they were only borrowing the company's access to credit, and that they intended and had the ability to repay. *See* Peter Grant, *Adelphia Ex-Officials' Defense Has Rocky Start,* Wall St. J., June 2, 2004, at C1. Rigas and one of his sons were convicted of conspiracy, securities fraud, and bank fraud, and they received prison sentences of 15 to 20 years. *See United States v. Rigas*, 490 F.3d 208 (2d Cir. 2007) (affirming convictions).

5. Entrustment. The crime of embezzlement requires that property be appropriated by one who was entrusted with its possession. The entrustment requirement refers to the special legal relationship that must exist between the defendant and the goods that were appropriated. The relationship must be "one of special trust and confidence; a relationship in which there inheres, either for the particular transaction or for all purposes, a special right of access to, or control or possession of, the money, article, or thing of value which is appropriated." *Warren v. State,* 62 N.E.2d 624, 625 (Ind. 1945) (quoting *Vinnedge v. State,* 79 N.E. 355 (Ind. 1906)).

The facts of *Warren* illustrate the important distinction between one who merely has access to property and one who is actually entrusted with that property. The defendant in that case, a maintenance employee, illegally engineered the removal of dozens of drums of Prestone from the General Motors plant where he worked and then shared in the profits generated by their resale. Because the defendant merely had access to the building where the Prestone was stored, and there was no "relation of special trust in regard to the article appropriated," the court upheld his conviction for larceny, not embezzlement. Analogizing the defendant's position to that of a security guard, the court wrote that "[w]here there is at most but a naked possession or control . . . or where the access consists of a mere physical propinquity as an incident of the employment, the felonious appropriation should be regarded as larceny." *Id.*

6. Practical Considerations. In addition to the theoretical problems associated with extending the criminal sanction to include embezzlement, there are a number of practical enforcement problems. First, embezzlement is seriously underreported; employers often choose to handle embezzlement internally rather than to prosecute. Professor Hall suggests several reasons for this phenomenon. Among them are the following:

> (1) "The embezzler does not fall within the popular conception of 'criminal.' That is obviously true of the white collar embezzlers, including bankers and public officials who, far from suggesting criminal types, are regarded as models of success to be imitated. And the embezzler in shirt sleeves, the truck driver and warehouse employee . . . are respected members of their group. All are distinguished from the prototype of the 'criminal' to whom otherness and malevolence are attributed."

> (2) Employers and managers, even in large corporations, often have developed personal relationships with embezzlers. Such relationships make them reluctant to file criminal charges, especially when they are aware that the employee has personal problems that explain the embezzlement.

> (3) Embezzlement prosecutions often attract unwanted publicity for employers, whose business success depends upon a positive public image. Additionally, employers with management problems do not want to attract additional investigations into other possible improprieties within or by the company.

JEROME HALL, THEFT, LAW AND SOCIETY 306–07, 309–10 (2d ed. 1952). Is the meaningfulness of the criminal sanction diminished if it cannot be effectively administered? Or should the principles governing criminal law be established independent of practical enforcement considerations?

7. Is Embezzlement Ambiguous? A second potential practical problem, especially in light of the infrequency of embezzlement prosecutions, is the possibility that audits to detect embezzlement and subsequent prosecutions may be politically motivated. When FBI Director William Sessions was dismissed by President Clinton, one of the primary allegations was that Sessions had used FBI airplanes and cars to transport himself and his family on trips having limited connection to official FBI business. Sessions claimed that the criminal and ethical investigation into his activities was politically motivated. *See* David Johnston, *Defiant F.B.I. Chief Removed from Job by the President*, N.Y. Times, July 20, 1993, at A1.

Is it always clear where courts should draw the line between business practices that are on the borderline of acceptability, on the one hand, and improper business practices that should give rise to embezzlement liability, on the other? In *People v. Sperl*, 126 Cal. Rptr. 907 (Cal. Ct. App. 1976), the Los Angeles County Marshal, among other improprieties, gave a state assemblyman and his family unrestricted access to a county automobile. According to the Court of Appeal, which affirmed the defendant's conviction on a number of embezzlement-type charges, such activity resulted in substantial monetary losses to the county and was "clearly outside the scope" of proper county business. *Id.* at 919. In his defense, the Marshal contended that "there was no definable standard for the court's finding that the free transportation of [the assemblyman] was 'significantly beyond the scope of courtesy commonly extended mutually by public officials.'" *Id.* at 921. Did the defendant have a legitimate vagueness challenge, or was the court right in concluding that a reasonableness standard should control and that the use of a publicly owned vehicle for unauthorized private use clearly constitutes a misappropriation of public funds?

Should the law of embezzlement require proof of a dishonest intent or intent to deceive? Would such a requirement help alleviate some of the ambiguity surrounding the courts' interpretation of this crime? Reconsider the English requirement of dishonesty described in Note 5 following *People v. Kunkin* in Section B.5 above.

8. Property of Another. Defendants are liable for embezzlement only when they convert to their own use the property of another. In *People v. Yannett*, 401 N.E.2d 410 (N.Y. 1980), the defendant owned and operated a nursing home. Each new resident of the nursing home was required to pay all the home's fees until Medicare determined whether it would pay the resident's costs. If Medicare subsequently decided that it would cover the resident, the home was obligated to refund the money it had received from the resident. On several occasions, however, the home failed to return the money or refunded only part of it, even after it had been repaid by Medicare. The jury found the defendant guilty of embezzlement, but the appellate court reversed. Because the money had been paid to the nursing home, not merely entrusted to it, the funds became the property of the nursing home. The nursing home may have acted in bad faith and may have breached a contract, but it could not embezzle its own property.

9. The Model Penal Code. Section 223.8 of the Model Penal Code expands the concept of "property of another" beyond that typically applied in embezzlement cases:

A person who purposely obtains property upon agreement, or subject to a known legal obligation, to make specified payment or other disposition, whether from such property or its proceeds or from his own property to be reserved in equivalent amount, is guilty of theft if he deals with the property obtained as his own and fails to make the required payment or disposition. . . .

The Comments to § 223.8, while acknowledging that most states have not adopted similar provisions, offer the following explanation for the Code's approach:

Section 223.8 is designed to bring within the law of theft certain situations that traditionally have occasioned difficulty. The problem arises whenever the actor's behavior arguably constitutes merely a breach of contract rather than a misappropriation of another's property. Section 223.8 recognizes that in some situations one who promises to make certain payments or otherwise dispose of property should be punished for using the property as his own. At the same time, the provision does not purport generally to substitute criminal prosecutions for civil contract remedies. The challenge, therefore, is to distinguish defaults that should be assimilated to theft from non-performance that should be left to the traditional remedies for breach of contract.

Model Penal Code § 223.8 Comment at 255–56. Does this provision represent an appropriate extension of the criminal law? Would the defendant in *Yannett* (described in the prior Note) have been guilty under the Model Penal Code?

[D] False Pretenses

Chaplin v. United States
157 F.2d 697 (D.C. Cir. 1946)

CLARK, ASSOCIATE JUSTICE.

This is an appeal from a conviction under the first count of an indictment charging appellant and his wife with obtaining money by false pretenses.

. . . [T]he indictment . . . charged that appellant and his wife, ". . . with intent to defraud, feloniously did pretend and represent to one Violette McMullen . . . that they, the said Sydney A. Chaplin and the said Dorothy Chaplin, were engaged in the wine and liquor business in Alexandria, Virginia, and that if she, the said Violette McMullen, would advance certain money, they . . . *would* purchase certain liquor stamps with said money and . . . *would* return . . . any money so advanced. . . ." In the traversing clause, it is charged that the defendants ". . . would not purchase such liquor stamps and would not return . . . the money advanced . . . as they . . . well knew."

It appears from the indictment that the prosecution's case was necessarily founded on the defendants' *intention,* at the time of acquiring the money, not to do two things promised: (1) buy stamps, and (2) repay the money. Both of these promises relate to things the defendants were to do in the future. The prosecution did not prove that the defendants misrepresented their business connection. On the contrary, it appears from the record that the appellant and his wife were in the liquor business, that they did own a large quantity of wine for which state stamps were required and that they did buy some small amount of tax stamps. The question for our decision comes down to whether the "present intention" of the defendants not to return the money and not to buy the stamps as they said they would relates to a "present or past existing fact" such as will support a conviction for the crime of false pretenses. The rule stated in *Wharton's Criminal Law,* 12th Ed., § 1439, is that: "A false pretense, under the statute, must relate to a past event or existing fact. Any representation with regard to a future transaction is excluded. Thus, for instance, a false statement, that a draft which the defendant exhibits to the prosecutor has been received from a house of good credit abroad, and is for a valuable consideration, on the faith of which he obtains the prosecutor's goods, is within the law; a promise to deposit with him such a draft at some future time, though wilfully and intentionally false, and the means of prosecutor's parting possession with his property, is not. So a pretense that the party would do an act that he did not mean to do (as a pretense that he would pay for goods on delivery) was ruled by all the judges not to be a false pretense under the Statute of Geo. II., and the same rule is distinctly recognized in this country, it being held that the statement of an intention is not a statement of an existing fact." We think the great weight of authority sustains this statement of the rule and compels us to answer the question in the negative.

In its brief, the government was most candid on this point, stating that *Commonwealth v. Althause*, 207 Mass. 32, 93 N.E. 202, from which a quotation of dictum was taken did not represent the weight of authority. The same may be said for the other two cases cited to support the prosecution's position on the point. It appears from a study of these cases that the courts concerned found no difficulty in applying the rule on "intention" which has long been used in actions at law for fraud and deceit. We think it unnecessary to discuss the advisability of transplanting this concept to criminal actions. There is a vast difference between subjecting a defendant to criminal penalties and providing for the redress of wrongs through civil actions.

A majority of the courts having this problem placed before them have not subscribed to the theory that "intention," as manifest by false and misleading promises, standing alone, is a *fact* in the sense required for a conviction on the charge of false pretenses.

Not only is the rule deeply rooted in our law, but moreover, we think the reasons upon which it is founded are no less cogent today than they were when the early cases were decided under the English statute cited by Wharton, *supra*. It is of course true that then, as now, the intention to commit certain crimes was ascertained by looking backward from the act and finding that the accused intended to do what he did do. However, where, as here, the act complained of—namely, failure to repay money or use it as specified at the time of borrowing—is as consonant with ordinary commercial default as with criminal conduct, the danger of applying this technique to prove the crime is quite apparent. Business affairs would be materially incumbered by the ever present threat that a debtor might be subjected to criminal penalties if the prosecutor and jury were of the view that at the time of borrowing he was mentally a cheat. The risk of prosecuting one who is guilty of nothing more than a failure or inability to pay his debts is a very real consideration. It is not enough to say that if innocent the accused would be found not guilty. The social stigma attaching to one accused of a crime as well as the burdens incident to the defense would, irrespective of the outcome, place a devastating weapon in the hands of a disgruntled or disappointed creditor.

The business policy, as well as the difficulties and dangers inherent in a contrary rule are illustrated by the earlier English cases. In *The King v. Goodhall*, 1821, Russ. & R.C.C. 461, the accused was found to have obtained a quantity of meat, promising to pay for it but not so intending. In reversing the jury's verdict of guilty the court said: "It was merely a promise for future conduct, and common prudence and caution would have prevented any injury arising from the breach of it." Again, in *Reg. v. Oates*, 1855, Dears C.C. 459, 6 Cox C.C. 540, where the accused was charged with making a fraudulent overcharge for work performed the court discharged the prisoner saying: "Is a shopkeeper who knowingly charges for an article more than it is worth, liable to an indictment under this statute? . . . [T]o hold the statute applicable to such a case would shake many transactions which, though certainly not fair in themselves are still not indictable."

In *Reg. v. Woodman*, 1879, 14 Cox C.C. 179, the prosecution advanced precisely the same argument that is urged here, contending that the defendant's intention was the existing fact about which the misrepresentation had been made. To this the court responded: "How can you define a man's mind? It is a mere promissory false pretense."

If we were to accept the government's position the way would be open for every victim of a bad bargain to resort to criminal proceedings to even the score with a judgment proof adversary. No doubt in the development of our criminal law the zeal with which the innocent are protected has provided a measure of shelter for the guilty. However, we do not think it wise to increase the possibility of conviction by broadening the accepted theory of the weight to be attached to the mental attitude of the accused. . . .

Reversed.

EDGERTON, ASSOCIATE JUSTICE (dissenting).

The court holds that "the great weight of authority . . . compels us." This is a new rule and an important one. I think it is erroneous.

Usually there are good reasons for a doctrine which is widely accepted, and uniformity itself has some value even in criminal law. Accordingly we should consider the weight of authority elsewhere for what it may be worth. But we should not determine our action by a count of foreign cases regardless of logic, consistency, and social need. "The social value of a rule has become a test of growing power and importance." We should decide the question before us "in accordance with present-day standards of wisdom and justice rather than in accordance with some outworn and antiquated rule of the past" which was never adopted here. To let judges who lived and died in other times and places make our decisions would be to abdicate as judges and serve as tellers.

. . . Considered without regard to the foreign cases on which the court relies, the indictment is plainly valid. No doubt a promise is commonly an undertaking, but it is always an assertion of a present intention to perform. "I will" means among other things "I intend to." It is so understood and it is meant to be so understood. Intention is a fact and present intention is a present fact. A promise made without an intention to perform is therefore a false statement about a present fact. This factual and declarative aspect of a promise is not a new discovery. It has come to be widely recognized in civil actions for deceit.

In criminal cases most courts and text writers have clung to an old illusion that the same words cannot embody both a promise and a statement of fact. But this tradition that in a criminal case "the statement of an intention is not a statement of an existing fact" has begun to break down. It is an obvious fiction. The meaning of words is the same whether their author is prosecuted civilly or criminally or not at all. The fiction that a promise made without intent to perform does not embody a misrepresentation conflicts with the facts, with the deceit cases, and with the interest of society in protecting itself against fraud. An Act of Congress makes it a crime in the District of Columbia to obtain money "by any false pretense, with intent to defraud." Congress did not exempt, and the court should not exempt, a pretense conveyed by words which also convey a promise. As a matter of plain English there could be no clearer case of false and fraudulent pretense than a borrower's pretense that he intends to repay money which he actually does not intend to repay.

The old illusion that a promise states no facts is not the only source of the old tolerance of falsehoods regarding intention. That a fool and his money are soon parted was once accepted as a sort of natural law. In 1821 the fact that "common prudence and caution would have prevented any injury" seemed to an English court a good reason for refusing to penalize an injury which had been intentionally inflicted by a false promise. The fact that common agility in dodging an intentional blow would have prevented any injury would not have seemed a reason for refusing to penalize a battery. Fools were fair game though cripples were not. But in modern times, no one not talking law would be likely to deny that society should protect mental as well as physical helplessness against intentional injuries.

Though the court decides the case on the basis of authority, the opinion concludes with a defense of the prevailing rule. But to justify this rule it would be necessary to show that false pretenses regarding intention are a harmless way of obtaining money, or else that intention cannot be proved in prosecutions for false pretenses as it is constantly proved in other criminal prosecutions and in civil actions for deceit.

Difficulties of proof are seldom greater in criminal cases than in civil, except that the prosecution must prove its case beyond a reasonable doubt. No peculiar difficulty of proof distinguishes this crime from others. Intentions of one sort or another must be proved in most criminal cases. They are usually proved by conduct. It is inherently no more difficult to prove an intent not to perform a promise than, for example, an intent to monopolize, to commit a felony, or to receive goods knowing them to be stolen. Appellant's conduct showed his intent. After getting $375 from a nurse by promising to buy liquor stamps and repay the money, he made the same promise a few days later and got $700 more. He said he needed the money to get the stamps. Yet he bought less than $40 worth of stamps, if any, during the next six weeks, and there is no evidence that he bought any stamps at any later time. Meanwhile he continued to borrow money from the woman. He made no repayments at any time. The jury might well conclude, as it did, that the difference between his promises and his performance was not accidental but was part of his original plan. The court does not suggest that the proof of his original intention was insufficient. If it were thought to be insufficient, the conviction should be reversed on that ground. The rule which the court adopts will make prosecutions impossible even when admissions or other evidence make guilt obvious.

No peculiar danger to innocent men distinguishes this crime from others. No honest borrower who fails to repay a loan, or changes his mind about the use which he intended to make of the money, is likely to be charged with obtaining it by false pretenses. Prosecutions are not undertaken without evidence and convictions do not withstand attack unless they are supported by sufficient evidence. The danger of a counter suit for malicious prosecution is always present to discourage unfounded charges. The court's picture of a flood of indictments against honest business men is unconvincing. No such flood has been observed in the few jurisdictions which have adopted the modern rule. It is true that innocent men are sometimes accused of crime. Innocent men have been convicted of murder. . . . Since it is impossible to prevent occasional miscarriage of justice, every criminal statute jeopardizes innocent people in some degree. The court suggests that the law should not jeopardize legitimate business. But this is the unavoidable price of public protection against illegitimate business. If the suggestion is sound the anti-trust law, the pure food law, the child labor law, the law against receiving stolen goods, and many others should be repealed, for malicious and damaging charges and erroneous convictions are possible under all of them. If the suggestion is sound the entire law of false pretenses and not merely a part of it should be repealed, for legal machinery is fallible with respect to the making, the falsity, and the maker's knowledge of the falsity, of representations of every kind.

There is, as the court says, a vast difference between criminal penalties and civil redress. It is the more unfortunate to hold, as the court does, that a common sort of fraud is not a crime. Since civil redress is not punitive but compensatory, the decision means that the law of the District of Columbia offers no deterrent to this sort of fraud. If a swindler has property which can be taken in execution on a civil judgment, he may not always win by practicing this fraud. But he cannot lose. If he perseveres he will win in the long run, for he will not always be sued to judgment. And one who has no property on which execution can be levied is bound to win as often as he can find a victim.

Notes and Questions

1. The Elements of the Crime. The crime of false pretenses consists of obtaining title to property by lies (i.e., false pretenses). In most jurisdictions, the crime has the following five elements: (1) a misrepresentation by the defendant (2) of a present or past material fact (3) with the intent to defraud the victim, (4) where the victim relies on the misrepresentation in (5) transferring title to some property. *See* Wayne R. LaFave, Criminal Law § 19.7, at 1006 (5th ed. 2010).

2. The History and Development of the Crime. The "trespassory taking" requirement of the common-law of larceny greatly limited its scope and left other types of wrongful appropriations uncovered by the criminal laws—including not only embezzlement (which is discussed in the prior Section), but also false pretenses. *See* Wayne R. LaFave, Criminal Law § 19.7, at 1006–21 (5th ed. 2010).

Professors Perkins and Boyce explain why obtaining property through false pretenses was not punished criminally for such a long time:

> Until the rise of modern commerce, commercial transactions were ordinarily fairly simple and infrequent. Individuals had the time and the responsibility to investigate their own deals. If a buyer was able to fool a seller, the buyer was not considered a thief but, rather, a clever man. "In those days a person who deprived another of his property by force or stealth was regarded by all as a very evil person, but he who got the better of another in a bargain by means of a falsehood was more likely to be regarded by his neighbors as clever than criminal."

Rollin M. Perkins & Ronald N. Boyce, Criminal Law 289 (3d ed. 1982).

The harshness of the penalties for larceny also discouraged courts from considering false pretenses a form of larceny. For larceny involving more than twelve pence, the punishment was death. At early common law, twelve pence was a considerable sum of money, the cost of a sheep, but over time its value was considerably reduced by inflation. Judges were reluctant to sentence a person to death for stealing an insignificant sum, and therefore they applied the elements of larceny very strictly, using loopholes to avoid convictions. One such loophole applied to theft by false pretenses: because title was transferred at the time the property was taken, the property belonged to the defendant, and thus the "property of another" element of larceny was missing. *See id.*

As commerce became more important and more complex, merchants no longer had the time or the ability to investigate each transaction closely. It became necessary to rely on a person's word, and perceptions shifted about the use of false pretenses to obtain property. "Once regarded as only mildly wrong, [it was] now branded as definitely and gravely antisocial." *Id.* at 290. Thus, in 1757, Parliament created the crime of false pretenses to plug the loophole created by the law governing larceny. The statute was invented to punish one who "[k]nowingly and designedly, by false pretence or pretences, shall obtain from any person or persons, money, goods, wares, or merchandise, with intent to cheat or defraud any person or persons of the same." 30 Geo. II, c. 24 (1757). Similar statutes have now been enacted in most American jurisdictions. *See* LaFave, *supra*, § 19.7(a), at 1006–07.

Does it make sense to create the crime of false pretenses? Does the notion of false pretenses contradict the principle of *caveat emptor* (let the buyer beware)? Should the crime be punished as severely as larceny?

3. Misrepresentations of Future Fact. As *Chaplin* illustrates, misrepresentations of future facts were traditionally excluded from the prohibition of false pretenses because the courts were unwilling to punish criminally every person who failed to follow through on a promise. In *Commonwealth v. Bomersbach*, 302 A.2d 472 (Pa. Super. Ct. 1973), for example, the defendant obtained $10,000 from a pair of investors, purportedly to form a company that would make use of a secret chemical process for refining hydraulic fluid. The investors knew that the secret process was known only to one Nappi and that Nappi was under no obligation to allow the proposed company to use the process. Nevertheless, when Nappi refused to join the venture and the company failed, the defendant was convicted of false pretenses. The court reversed, holding that a defendant does not commit the crime of false pretenses by representing that certain actions will occur in the future—in this case, the defendant's intent to form the company—even if the defendant has no present intention of performing that promise. *See also James v. State*, 236 S.W.2d 429, 430 (Ark. 1951) (noting that "[a] postdated check taken by the payee with full knowledge that it is postdated, and where it is not represented by the maker as being good at the time given, . . . is a promise to do something in the future, and is not a representation upon which a charge of false pretense can be successfully based").

Do you agree with the majority in *Chaplin*, or does Justice Edgerton have the better argument when he writes in his dissenting opinion that "[i]ntention is a fact and present intention is a present fact"?

The Model Penal Code rejects the traditional approach, including false promises in § 223.3, the provision governing theft by deception. In the Comments accompanying § 223.3, the drafters of the Code explained that "the alternative of excluding [false promises] by rule of law presents the unattractive possibility of allowing the clever to evade liability for theft." Model Penal Code § 223.3 Comment at 189. The Code's formulation is also designed to ease the business-related fears expressed by the majority in *Chaplin:*

> The concern is that businessmen may be unjustly subjected to criminal liability when they make contracts intending in the alternative to perform or to pay liquidated damages or such other damages as the law allows. Not every promise implies an unequivocal intention to perform. Businessmen know when they make contracts that it is sometimes more profitable to breach and to pay the required damages than it is to perform the contract as originally drawn. Promisees know this as well as promisors, and indeed the private law of contract is designed in a manner that frequently makes nonperformance the more attractive alternative. Plainly, it would be an unwarranted interference with the careful balance achieved by this law if a theft prosecution for false pretenses could be substituted for ordinary contract remedies. Among businessmen, especially in certain trades, there will be a general understanding that words of promise mean only that the promisor will perform or submit to civil remedies. In such a context, the promisor could be convicted of theft only if he clearly intended to do neither, as in the case where he accepts the benefits of the promise and then flees the country in order to avoid performance or damages on his part. In short, there as elsewhere, the actor is to be understood in the sense in which he expected and desired his hearer to understand him and in the context of general understandings that surround the particular dealings involved. It is only where the actor did not believe what he purposely caused his victim to believe, and where this can be proved beyond a reasonable doubt, that the actor can be convicted of theft.

Id. at 190.

Would these Comments have swayed the *Chaplin* court? Do they adequately address, or merely underscore, the potential hazards associated with criminalizing commercial breaches of contract? Is there also a danger that consumers who fail to pay their bills will be threatened with criminal prosecution under the Model Penal Code's approach?

The overwhelming modern trend—including the federal courts in mail fraud prosecutions, *see Durland v. United States,* 161 U.S. 306 (1896)—now considers a false statement about one's present intentions to be a misrepresentation of present, not future, fact. Consider *People v. Ashley,* 267 P.2d 271 (Cal. 1954), where the defendant persuaded two elderly women to give him their life savings. He promised to use the money to build a theater, but instead used it for his own regular expenses. In affirming his conviction, the court held that "a promise made without intention to perform is a misrepresentation of a state of mind, and thus a misrepresentation of an existing fact, and is a false pretense." *Id.* at 281. *See also State v. Kaufman,* 112 A.2d

721, 723 (N.J. 1955) ("A promise is not only an undertaking as to the future, but it is necessarily also an assertion of an existing state of mind, a present intention to perform. And the statutory crime based upon a false promise must of necessity refer to this existing state of mind, since the only thing which can be false about a promise is the present intention, or existing state of mind, of the declarant not to perform.").

In *State v. Love*, 271 S.E.2d 110 (S.C. 1980), a former county magistrate obtained $5,500 after promising to perform certain "services" for a client who had been charged with drunk driving. The promised "services" included providing the client a "valid" driver's license, removing evidence from the court clerk's office, and preventing the prosecution of the drunk driving offense. Although the promises all involved acts to be performed in the future, the court affirmed a conviction for false pretenses:

> There is contained in these promises the implied representation or pretense that [the defendant] could do the things promised. This pretense of authority or ability constituted a representation or pretense of fact . . . and supports the charge of obtaining goods under false pretenses. . . . By falsely pretending that he was in a position to aid [the client] in evading prosecution and the penalties for driving under the influence, and by obtaining money for that purpose, the defendant was guilty of obtaining money by false pretenses.

Id. at 114. Do the facts of cases like *Ashley* and *Love* persuade you that the Model Penal Code's approach is correct, or is it too difficult to distinguish between legitimate businesspeople and criminals?

4. Intent to Defraud. Intent to defraud is an element of the crime of false pretenses. Although the nature of the defendants' intent may differ depending on the context, the concept of intent to defraud generally means that: (A) the defendants knew the misrepresentation was false, or knew they did not know whether it was true or false, and nevertheless represented it as true; or (B) the defendants intended to take something they knew belonged to someone else, or to which they had no right. *See State v. Houchins*, 46 S.W.2d 891 (Mo. 1932) (reversing false pretenses conviction because the defendant did not know that his partner was misrepresenting the age and weight of the sheep they were selling). *See generally* Wayne R. LaFave, Criminal Law § 19.6(f), at 1003–05 (5th ed. 2010).

In addition, intent to defraud requires proof that the defendants intended to use the falsehood to deprive the victim of property for which the defendants had no claim of right. The requisite intent is therefore missing if, for example, the defendants believe they are collecting on a debt owed by the victim. In addition, intent to defraud is not satisfied if the defendants intend unconditionally to return the property within a reasonable period. *See id.*

Consider the situation of Bert Look, a Maine lobsterman. John Kostandin, a seafood wholesaler, allegedly owed Look $30,000 and appeared to have no intention of paying him. A friend of Look's, "Deep Homard," posed as a representative of the novelist Stephen King, approached Kostandin, and told him that King wanted to buy three and a half tons of lobsters for his annual lobster bake. Three and a half tons of lobster just happened to have a market value of $30,000. Kostandin delivered the lobster and was then driven by limousine to a Chinese restaurant, supposedly to meet Stephen King. By the time he discovered the hoax, the lobsters had been sold. *See* David Margolick, *A Maine Lobsterman's Justice*, N.Y. Times, Sept. 17, 1993, at B8. Did Look commit the crime of false pretenses? Did he have an intent to defraud? In fact, Look was convicted of theft, fined $15,000, and ordered to pay Kostandin the money he had received from the sale of the lobsters. Should claim of right appropriately constitute a defense here? *See* Jules Crittenden, *Lobsterman Pays for King-Sized Scam*, Bos. Herald, Dec. 4, 1994, at 4.

United States v. Skilling

554 F.3d 529 (5th Cir. 2009), *aff'd in part and vacated in part*, 561 U.S. 358 (2010)

Prado, Circuit Judge.

A jury convicted former Enron Corporation CEO Jeffrey K. Skilling ("Skilling") for conspiracy [and] making false representations to auditors, . . . [and he was sentenced to 292 months in prison, three years' supervised release, and $45 million in restitution]. Skilling argues that the government prosecuted him using an invalid legal theory, [and] that the district court used erroneous jury instructions . . . . We affirm the convictions, vacate the sentence, and remand for resentencing.

I. Factual Background

Skilling's rise at Enron began when he founded Enron's Wholesale business in 1990. In 1997, he became Enron's President and Chief Operating Officer and joined the Board of Directors. In February 2001, he became Enron's CEO, and on August 14, 2001, Skilling resigned from Enron.

About four months after Skilling's departure, Enron crashed into sudden bankruptcy. An initial investigation uncovered an elaborate conspiracy to deceive investors about the state of Enron's fiscal health. That conspiracy allegedly included overstating the company's financial situation for more than two years in an attempt to ensure that Enron's short-run stock price remained artificially high. With Congress looking on, the President appointed a team of investigators, the Enron Task Force. The investigation led to criminal charges against Skilling and many others.

According to the government, the conspiracy, led by Skilling and Ken Lay ("Lay"), Enron's CEO until Skilling took over (and again after his abrupt exit), worked to manipulate Enron's earnings to satisfy Wall Street's expectations. Other top Enron officials were key players in the unlawful scheme, including Richard Causey ("Causey"), the Chief Accounting Officer ("CAO"); Andrew Fastow ("Fastow"), the Chief Financial Officer ("CFO"); and Ben Glisan ("Glisan"), the Treasurer.

. . . The government presented evidence that Skilling engaged in fraud in several of Enron's business endeavors. As an international, multi-billion dollar enterprise, Enron had elaborate financial dealings. At the time of its bankruptcy, the company was comprised of four major businesses: Wholesale, which bought and sold energy; Transportation and Distribution, which owned energy networks; Retail, or Enron Energy Services ("EES"), which sold energy to end-users; and Broadband, or Enron Broadband Services ("EBS"), which bought and sold bandwidth capacity. The government alleged that Skilling took specific fraudulent actions with respect to Wholesale, EES, and EBS.

. . . .

B. False Representations About Enron's Finances

Many of the allegations of fraud . . . stem from Skilling's representations to investors about the financial standing of Wholesale, EES, and EBS. Skilling, as a high ranking corporate officer, held conference calls with investors to update them on the company's progress. The government claims that Skilling misled investors during these calls. For example, on January 22, 2001, Enron released its earnings report for the previous quarter, and Skilling told investors that "the situation in California [regarding the utilities] had little impact on fourth quarter results. Let me repeat that. For Enron, the situation in California had little impact on fourth quarter results." Skilling also stated that "nothing can happen in California that would jeopardize" earnings targets.

However, when he made these statements, Skilling allegedly knew that the California utilities likely could not pay the fees that Enron was expecting and that Enron might have to write off a loss of hundreds of millions of dollars. He also listened silently as Mark Koenig ("Koenig"), Enron's Director of Investor Relations, assured investors that non-core business revenues were a "fairly small" amount of EBS's earnings, which the government alleges was not actually the case.

. . . .

Three days later, Skilling spoke at Enron's annual analysts conference, claiming that EES and EBS, like Enron's other major businesses, had "sustainable high earnings power." Skilling argues that this statement was merely harmless puffery. . . .

On March 23, 2001, Enron held a special conference call with analysts. Enron's stock price had been declining, and investors began surmising that EBS was having financial difficulties. Skilling comforted investors, saying that EBS was "having a great quarter" and that Enron was "highly confident" that EES would meet its earning target. According to the government, however, Skilling knew both divisions were in extreme financial turmoil.

. . . .

On July 17, 2001, Skilling told investors that EES "had an outstanding second quarter" and was "firmly on track to achieve" its earnings targets. That quarter alone, EES lost hundreds of millions of dollars. Skilling reiterated that [an] EES reorganization was based on a concern for management efficiency, while the government contends that the only purpose of the EES reorganization was to hide EES's losses.

C. Manipulating Enron's Reserves

Skilling also allegedly committed fraud when he manipulated Enron's reserves to hit specific earnings targets in the fourth quarter of 1999, the second quarter of 2000, and the fourth quarter of 2000. Stock analysts made various projections regarding the earnings that Enron would announce each quarter, and the average of these estimates was known as the "consensus estimate." The government claims that Skilling was particularly committed to hitting or beating the consensus estimate. In January 2000, the consensus estimate for the fourth quarter of 1999 was earnings of 30¢ per share, which Enron could meet based on its earnings for that quarter. The day before the company was to announce its earnings, however, Koenig brought Skilling unwelcome news: the consensus estimate had jumped a penny per share. Skilling purportedly decided to announce earnings high enough to reach the estimate, even though the increase was not merited by any change in Enron's underlying financial portrait.

Skilling allegedly took a similar unwarranted action at the end of the second quarter of 2000. At that time, the consensus estimate was 32¢ per share. A draft earnings report showed that Enron was going to announce earnings that met the estimate. Skilling, however, wanted to beat the consensus estimate by reporting 34¢ per share. To do that, he allegedly told Wholesale to increase its earnings by $7 million, and then by an additional $7 million. Wholesale acquiesced both times, reopening its books and adding $14 million from a reserve account that it had set aside to cover potential liabilities. The government claims that Enron did not have a business reason for using its reserves to increase Wholesale's earnings, instead doing so solely to exceed analysts' expectations.

. . . .

IV. Jury Instructions

. . . .

B. Materiality

Skilling . . . asserts that the district court erred in failing to provide the jury with adequate guidance on the legal meaning of "materiality" with regard to the charges against him. After explaining to the jury that false statements or omissions can support a fraud conviction only if they are material, the court instructed the jury on the definition of materiality. Skilling argues that the instruction was insufficient to convey to a "lay juror who has never invested in stock in his or her life" what a reasonable investor would consider important. In particular, Skilling contends that the court erred by . . . refusing to instruct the jury about statements that constitute "puffery" and are immaterial as a matter of law . . . . He argues that [such] instructions were necessary because "reasonable investors disregard all sorts of information that a lay juror might mistakenly consider material, especially when viewed in hindsight," and that the district court's refusal to give [the puffery instruction] constitutes reversible error . . . .

. . . .

Skilling . . . sought to have the court tell the jury that even if a statement is false or misleading, it is mere "puffery" and therefore immaterial if it is "so lacking in specificity, or so clearly constituting the opinions of the speaker, that no reasonable investor could find the statement important to the total mix of information he or she would consider when making an investment decision." Such statements, he notes, include "generalized, positive statements about [a] company's competitive strengths . . . and future prospects." *Rosenzweig v. Azurix Corp.*, 332 F.3d 854, 869 (5th Cir. 2003).

Although Skilling is correct that "an expression of opinion not made as a representation of fact," can constitute puffery, *Mfg. Research Corp. v. Greenlee Tool Co.*, 693 F.2d 1037, 1040 (11th Cir. 1982) (citing *Gulf Oil Corp. v. FTC*, 150 F.2d 106, 109 (5th Cir. 1945)), not all such statements of opinion are properly classified as puffery. Similarly, although Skilling correctly points out that "generalized, positive statements about [a] company's competitive strengths . . . and future prospects" can in some cases constitute immaterial puffery, such statements of opinion by corporate insiders are not *per se* immaterial. In *Virginia Bankshares, Inc. v. Sandberg*, 501 U.S. 1083, 1090, 1098 (1991), the Supreme Court considered statements that a merger proposal would give shareholders "a high value for their shares," and held that such statements could be deemed material.

. . . .

Skilling's statements about the financial health of Enron were similar to those deemed potentially material in *Virginia Bankshares*. For example, at the 2001 analyst conference . . . , Skilling claimed that all of Enron's businesses, including EES and EBS, were "uniquely strong franchises with sustainable high earnings power." He also characterized Wholesale as a "stable, high-growth business" and "not a trading business." Similarly, on the March 23, 2001 analyst call . . . , he claimed EBS was having "a great quarter on the intermediation side of the bandwidth business." Summarizing EBS, he said that there was "essentially strong growth on the intermediation side, strong growth on the content services side, in terms of people, budgets, the whole thing."

The jury was entitled to find those and similar statements material. The government presented evidence of contrary, verifiable historical facts regarding the actual condition of EES, EBS, and Wholesale at the time Skilling made these statements: EES was facing a potentially enormous loss; EBS had an unsupportable cost structure, was losing money, was reducing the number of its employees, and had few customers or profitable deals; and Wholesale was heavily dependent on unstable, speculative trading.

. . . .

Skilling unsurprisingly challenges the government on the meaning of his statements and on the actual condition of the businesses to which the statements referred.
But those are fact questions for the jury to resolve. A reasonable jury could find that
Skilling's statements were strongly contrary to verifiable historical facts about the
conditions of the businesses, that he misstated his true opinion, and that his statements were misleading to a reasonable investor who would have considered them
important. Accordingly, the statements were not immaterial [puffery] as a matter of
law, and the evidence is sufficient to support the verdict.

. . . .

Skilling failed to demonstrate that the government's case rested on an incorrect
theory of law or that any reversible errors infected his trial. Accordingly, we affirm
Skilling's convictions in all respects. We vacate Skilling's [sentencing enhancement
for endangering financial institutions] and remand for resentencing.

Notes and Questions

1. Subsequent Developments in Skilling's Case. The Supreme Court reversed other
portions of the Fifth Circuit's decision (rejecting the theory that the federal honest-
services fraud statute extended beyond "bribery and kickback schemes"). *Skilling v.
United States*, 561 U.S. 358, 368 (2010). On remand, however, the Fifth Circuit
concluded that the error was harmless. *See United States v. Skilling*, 638 F.3d 480 (5th
Cir. 2011), *cert. denied*, 132 S. Ct. 1905 (2012). Skilling and prosecutors agreed that
he would forego any further appeals and pay $42 million to the victims of the Enron
collapse in exchange for a 10-year reduction in his sentence. *See* Peter Lattman, *Ex-
Enron Chief's Sentence Is Cut by 10 Years, to 14*, N.Y. Times, June 22, 2013, at B2.

2. Statements of Opinion. Generally expressions of opinion or "puffing" in the
sale of goods are not considered misrepresentations of fact. In *State v. Binette*, 190
A.2d 744, 745 (Me. 1963), for example, the defendant received a political contribution after telling the donor that he "had, through color of his office [of City Clerk],
been one of the persons who had worked very hard to get the new Biddeford High
School project started." The prosecutor indicted him for false pretenses, alleging that
he did no actual work on the project. Noting that "the ordinary affairs of business
involve so many instances of difference of opinion, or the understandable over-
appraisal of one's own efforts or the desirability of one's own product," the court
dismissed the indictment. *Id.* Besides, the court continued, "we are dealing with the
solicitation of political contributions, an activity not infrequently accompanied by
some form of political puffing. We are not convinced that the vague and indefinite
inducements to make such a contribution in the instant case were capable of deceiv-
ing or defrauding anyone." *Id.* at 746. *See also* Model Penal Code § 223.3.

In certain instances, however, courts will treat opinions given by "experts" or those
with greater knowledge of the circumstances as misrepresentations of facts. Thus,

in *State v. Nash*, 204 P. 736 (Kan. 1922), the court affirmed a stockbroker's conviction for false pretenses. The stockbroker misrepresented the value of certain assets in order to obtain a windfall in a stock transaction. In affirming his conviction, the court rejected the argument that the defendant's statements about the value of the assets were merely an expression of opinion:

> Whether or not an assertion of value is to be regarded as an expression of opinion or a statement of fact depends on the circumstances. If a farmer were to ask a grain dealer what wheat is worth today, the answer would not express an opinion. If the grain dealer were to ask the farmer what his farm is worth today, the answer would express an opinion. In one instance value would be understood to be a known market price; in the other, the elements of value would be so numerous and varied that farmers and real estate men would differ in their estimates, and necessarily no more than an opinion could be expressed. . . . Whether a statement is one of fact or one of opinion, in the sense indicated, is a question for the jury.

Id. at 739.

3. The Materiality of the Misrepresented Fact. The fact misrepresented by the defendant must be material in order to support a conviction for false pretenses. In *Sweeton v. Commonwealth*, 275 S.W. 827 (Ky. 1925), the defendant, P.B. Sweeton, was convicted of false pretenses when he obtained a surety's signature on a note that he was tendering as payment for two mules. The two sureties on the note were Baker and Gilbert. When Sweeton approached Gilbert about acting as a surety, he falsely claimed that Baker (Gilbert's former business partner) had asked Gilbert to sign the note. The court reversed the conviction on the grounds that the misrepresentation was not material. Given that Sweeton did not suggest that Baker had any personal interest in Sweeton's receipt of the loan, the court explained, Gilbert would have assumed that Baker wanted to protect himself and therefore wanted Gilbert to sign the note so that he would bear some of the risk. Consequently, the court concluded, the misrepresentation was not likely to have had an impact on Gilbert's decision to sign the note and therefore was not material.

4. Reliance by the Victim. The crime of false pretenses requires a belief, however slight, on the part of the victim that the misrepresented fact is as the defendant represents it. If the victim knows the defendant is lying, there can be no reliance. In *Eason v. State*, 320 S.W.2d 11, 12 (Tex. Crim. App. 1959), the defendant told a café owner that the café's business was hurting because "someone [had] planted some 'hoodoo stuff' on his premises which [the defendant] would locate and remove for a fee of $25." The defendant collected $25 after digging up a jar of crawfish legs and hair. The café owner testified that he did not believe the defendant, but that he paid the money because his wife urged that "if there was anything around the house she wanted to pay him to get it up." *Id.* The court reversed the defendant's conviction, holding that there was no reliance because the café owner did not believe the defendant.

Furthermore, one does not commit the crime of false pretenses by lying about something that could not have induced the victim's reliance. *See, e.g., Beyl v. State*, 85 N.W.2d 653 (Neb. 1957) (reversing a conviction for false pretenses where a purchaser bought some grain, knowing that it had been weighed on falsely calibrated scales, because the purchaser could not have been tricked by the misrepresented weights).

Due in part to the belief that it is the fool who needs the greatest protection, the prevailing view in most jurisdictions is that the victim's reliance need not be reasonable, regardless of the outrageousness of the misrepresentation. *See Palotta v. State*, 199 N.W. 72, 74 (Wis. 1924) (affirming the conviction of a defendant who represented himself as a spiritual healer with magical powers and obtained money from a mentally impaired woman suffering from "nervousness," because the law was "designed to protect the unwise and the credulous as well as the able and the vigilant").

The prosecution, however, has the burden of proving that the victim did, in fact, rely on the defendant's misrepresentation. The jury may consider the absurdity of the misrepresentation in determining whether the victim was actually deceived. *See State v. Nash,* 204 P. 736 (Kan. 1922). A jury may find a misrepresentation so absurd that the victim could not possibly have relied on it—if, for example, the defendant claims that a painting is an original Picasso and then sells it to the victim for a nickel. In *State v. Donohue*, 201 A.2d 413 (N.J. Super. Ct. 1964), the defendant allegedly represented to Young, an alleged co-conspirator, that he could get Young admitted to the Louisiana state bar even though Young had not taken the bar exam. Dismissing the indictment, the court held as a matter of law that the assertion could not have induced reliance by Young. The court thought it "'absurd' and 'incredible' that a person who desires to become a member of the bar of any state would believe that he could become such a member without taking a legal and proper examination and test as required by law." *Id.* at 415.

5. Acts Versus Omissions. The courts have traditionally held that the defendant must commit an affirmative act in order to be guilty of the crime of false pretenses. Silence does not suffice because the law imposes no obligation to divulge material facts. *See McCorkle v. State*, 278 S.W. 965 (Ark. 1926) (reversing false pretenses conviction where the defendant sold six bales of cotton without disclosing that they had a mortgage on them). Yet, under some circumstances, a court may find that the defendant had a positive duty to correct an obvious misapprehension held by the other party. The modern trend is to expand the situations where an affirmative duty to disclose exists. Under the Model Penal Code, for example, such a duty arises when the defendant stands in a fiduciary or confidential relationship to the other person, fails to correct a false impression that the defendant previously created or reinforced, or fails to disclose an adverse claim to the property. *See* Model Penal Code § 223.3.

When should a defendant have a duty to disclose? "Is there a duty to disclose to one's customers that one's competitors are offering a better bargain? If not, is it still possible to be criminally convicted of fraud for 'concealing' such a price disparity from customers, even if comparative price levels were easily discoverable in the market?" John C. Coffee, Jr., *If Silence Equals Fraud, the Rules Shift*, Nat'l L.J., Oct. 5, 1992, at 18. The majority of jurisdictions clearly would find no duty to disclose such information. In *United States v. Brown*, 79 F.3d 1550 (11th Cir. 1996), for example, several real estate developers were convicted of mail fraud after they sold thousands of Florida homes to out-of-state residents, concealing from their buyers that the homes were substantially more expensive than other comparable homes. The court of appeals reversed the conviction, taking the traditional view that sellers have no duty to disclose price disparities to their customers and finding insufficient evidence that a reasonable buyer would have relied on the defendants' representations about the value of the homes. *See id*. at 1557–59.

6. The Monetary Impact on the Victim. Suppose *A* tells *B* that he has a valuable time machine for sale. Actually, *A* believes he has a worthless pile of metal and intends to defraud *B*. *B* relies on *A*'s misrepresentation and buys the "time machine" for $5,000. Though not a time machine, the pile of metal turns out to be a modern art sculpture worth $10,000. *A* is guilty of false pretenses. All the elements of the crime are met, and it is irrelevant whether the result of his misrepresentation was a pecuniary loss or gain for *B*. In *State v. Mills*, 396 P.2d 5 (Ariz. 1964), the Arizona Supreme Court responded as follows to the defendants' claim that they were not guilty of false pretenses because the victim had suffered no pecuniary loss:

> The defendants focus on the wrong part of the transaction. They direct attention to what the victim obtains. The gist of the offense, however, is concerned with what the defrauder obtains. . . . Judge Learned Hand put it as follows: "A man is none the less cheated out of his property, when he is induced to part with it by fraud, because he gets a quid pro quo of equal value. It may be impossible to measure his loss by the gross scales available to a court, but he has suffered a wrong; he has lost his chance to bargain with the facts before him. That is the evil against which the statute is directed."

Id. at 8 (quoting *United States v. Rowe*, 56 F.2d 747, 749 (2d Cir. 1932)). *See also* Wayne R. LaFave, Criminal Law § 19.7(i)(3), at 1020–21 (5th ed. 2010).

7. Bad Checks. A check without sufficient funds in the account to cover the check amount is colloquially called a "bad" check. Though obtaining property by bad check is often deemed a sub-species of false pretenses, most if not all jurisdictions have enacted statutes creating a separate crime specifically covering such cases, which generally carries less severe penalties than the crime of false pretenses. *See* Wayne R. LaFave, Criminal Law § 19.7(j)(1), at 1021 (5th ed. 2010). Most of these statutes require only knowledge of insufficient funds, though some require an actual intent to defraud, and most do not require that anything actually be obtained from the victim. Consequently, bad-check statutes cover some cases that would not constitute false pretenses.

In *Bray v. Commonwealth*, 388 S.E.2d 837 (Va. Ct. App. 1990), the court affirmed a bad-check conviction where the defendant gave her landlady a check drawn on a closed account as a security deposit for an apartment. The court explained: "To prove a bad check offense [under Va. Code § 18.2-181], it is not necessary that anything be received in return for the check. The offense is complete when, with intent to defraud, a person makes or draws or utters a check he knows to be worthless." *Id.* at 840. On the other hand, the court concluded that it was wrong to convict the defendant for using false pretenses in obtaining the key to the premises. The court reasoned that the crime of false pretenses requires a change of ownership (title) as well as possession, and actual ownership of the key always remained with the landlady.

8. Misrepresentations to Obtain Educational Services. Individuals who misrepresent material facts in order to obtain access to schooling for themselves or their children have been prosecuted under false pretenses statutes. In one such case, Yale University brought theft charges against a transfer student who fabricated his transcript and other supporting documents in order to obtain admission. The University accused him of effectively stealing $61,475 in educational loans and scholarships under false pretenses. *See* Raymond Hernandez, *Yale Says It Sees an Impostor in the Ivy*, N.Y. Times, Apr. 12, 1995, at B1.

Similar charges have been brought against parents who falsified their children's addresses to obtain access to better public schools. In one such case, a woman from Cleveland, Ohio, who illegally sent her son to kindergarten in the neighboring town of Euclid, was convicted of fraud and served five days in jail. *See* Rochelle Riley, *More Equity in Education Would Deter District Hopping*, The Courier-Journal, Feb. 11, 1997, at C1.

U.S. Department of Justice   FOR IMMEDIATE RELEASE
Office of Public Affairs   Thursday, February 11, 2016

Morgan Stanley Agrees to Pay $2.6 Billion Penalty in Connection with Its Sale of Residential Mortgage Backed Securities

The Justice Department today announced that Morgan Stanley will pay a $2.6 billion penalty to resolve claims related to Morgan Stanley's marketing, sale and issuance of residential mortgage-backed securities (RMBS). This settlement constitutes the largest component of the set of resolutions with Morgan Stanley entered by members of the RMBS Working Group, which have totaled approximately $5 billion. As part of the agreement, Morgan Stanley acknowledged in writing that it failed to disclose critical information to prospective investors about the quality of the mortgage loans underlying its RMBS and about its due diligence practices.

Investors, including federally insured financial institutions, suffered billions of dollars in losses from investing in RMBS issued by Morgan Stanley in 2006 and 2007.

"Today's settlement holds Morgan Stanley appropriately accountable for misleading investors about the subprime mortgage loans underlying the securities it sold," said Acting Associate Attorney General Stuart F. Delery. "The Department of Justice will not tolerate those who seek financial gain through deceptive or unfair means, and we will take appropriately aggressive action against financial institutions that knowingly engage in improper investment practices."

. . . .

An RMBS is a type of security comprised of a pool of mortgage loans created by banks and other financial institutions. The expected performance and price of an RMBS is determined by a number of factors, including the characteristics of the borrowers and the value of the properties underlying the RMBS. Morgan Stanley was one of the institutions that issued RMBS during the period leading up to the economic crisis in 2007 and 2008.

As acknowledged by Morgan Stanley in a detailed statement of facts that is a part of this agreement (and is quoted below), the company made representations to prospective investors about the characteristics of the subprime mortgage loans underlying its RMBS—representations with which it did not comply:

- In particular, Morgan Stanley told investors that it did not securitize underwater loans (loans that exceeded the value of the property). However, Morgan Stanley did not disclose to investors that in April 2006 it had expanded its "risk tolerance" in evaluating loans in order to purchase and securitize "everything possible." As Morgan Stanley's manager of valuation due diligence told an employee in 2006, "please do not mention the 'slightly higher risk tolerance' in these communications. We are running under the radar and do not want to document these types of things." As a result, Morgan Stanley ignored information—including broker's price opinions (BPOs), which are estimates of a property's value from an independent real estate broker—indicating that thousands of securitized loans were underwater, with combined-loan-to-value ratios over 100 percent. . . .

- Morgan Stanley also told investors that it did not securitize loans that failed to meet originators' guidelines unless those loans had compensating factors. . . . Morgan Stanley has now acknowledged, however, that "Morgan Stanley did not disclose to securitization investors that employees of Morgan Stanley received information that, in certain instances, loans that did not comply with underwriting guidelines and lacked adequate compensating factors . . . were included in the RMBS sold and marketed to investors." So, in fact, "Morgan Stanley . . . securitized certain loans that neither comported with the originators' underwriting guidelines nor had adequate compensating factors."

- Likewise, "Morgan Stanley also prepared presentation materials . . . that it used in discussions with potential investors that described the due diligence process for reviewing pools of loans prior to securitization," but "certain of Morgan Stanley's actual due diligence practices did not conform to the description of the process set forth" in those materials.

. . . .

"In today's agreement, Morgan Stanley acknowledges it sold billions of dollars in subprime RMBS certificates in 2006 and 2007 while making false promises about the mortgage loans backing those certificates," said Acting U.S. Attorney Brian J. Stretch of the Northern District of California. "Morgan Stanley touted the quality of the lenders with which it did business and the due diligence process it used to screen out bad loans. All the while, Morgan Stanley knew that in reality, many of the loans backing its securities were toxic. Abuses in the mortgage-backed securities industry such as these helped bring about the most devastating financial crisis in our lifetime. Our office is committed to dedicating the resources necessary to hold those who engage in such reckless actions responsible for their conduct."

The $2.6 billion civil monetary penalty resolves claims under the Financial Institutions Reform, Recovery and Enforcement Act (FIRREA). FIRREA authorizes the federal government to impose civil penalties against financial institutions that violate various predicate offenses, including wire and mail fraud. The settlement expressly preserves the government's ability to bring criminal charges against Morgan Stanley, and likewise does not release any individuals from potential criminal or civil liability. In addition, as part of the settlement, Morgan Stanley promised to cooperate fully with any ongoing investigations related to the conduct covered by the agreement.

. . . .

Notes and Questions

1. **Criminal versus Civil Sanctions.** When should criminal penalties, in addition to civil sanctions, be imposed? Consider the following analysis:

> Federal prosecutors have their own explanation for how [only] one Wall Street executive landed in jail in the wake of the financial crisis. The cases were complex to investigate and would have been infernally difficult to explain to juries, some told me. Much of the crisis and banker transgressions stemmed from recklessness, not criminality. They also suggest that deferred prosecutions—with their billions in settlements and additional oversights—can be stricter punishments than indictments. Still, while the Department of Justice has not been without its successes—it won a guilty plea from BP in the Deepwater Horizon spill, and it's currently going after traders in the wake of the JPMorgan Chase London Whale trading loss—these remain

exceptions even beyond the financial sector. Federal prosecutors almost never bring criminal charges against top executives of large corporations, from banking to pharmaceuticals to technology. In March, the Justice Department entered into a deferred prosecution against Toyota but did not indict the company or any top executives. As the economy limps back from the Great Recession, compensation has recovered, corporate profits are at record levels and executives see that few, if any, of their peers ever go to prison anymore. Perhaps one reason Americans have come to begrudge the wealthy is a resentment of their culture of impunity.

. . . [B]ack in the Clinton administration, the deputy attorney general Eric Holder laid out his own memo for strengthening corporate prosecutions. But he undermined his own words by also explaining that prosecutors needed to take into account the collateral economic consequences. In testimony in front of the Senate in March, Holder, who is now the U.S. attorney general, seemed to lament the position government enforcers had found themselves in. "I am concerned that the size of some of these institutions becomes so large that it does become difficult for us to prosecute them when we are hit with indications that if we do prosecute—if we do bring a criminal charge— it will have a negative impact on the national economy, perhaps even the world economy."

Jesse Eisinger, *The Fall Guy*, N.Y. Times, May 4, 2014, at MM34. Do you agree or disagree with the New York Times editorial excerpted below?

When the Justice Department recently closed its criminal investigation of Goldman Sachs, it became all but certain that no major American banks or their top executives would ever face criminal charges for their role in the financial crisis.

Justice [Department] officials and even President Obama have defended the lack of prosecutions, saying that even though greed and other moral lapses were evident in the run-up to the crisis, the conduct was not necessarily illegal.

But that characterization of the financial industry's actions has always defied common sense—and all the more so now that a fuller picture is emerging of the range of banks' reckless and lawless activities, including interest-rate rigging, money laundering, securities fraud and excessive speculation.

Which is not to say that prosecuting wrongdoing in the financial crisis is easy. Proving federal fraud requires evidence of intent, no small lift. But proving intent does not require a smoking gun. The financial crisis, fomented over years by big banks and presided over by executives, involved reckless lending, heedless securitizations, exorbitant paydays and illusory profits, all of which led to the government bailouts and economic calamity. Is it plausible that none of that broke the law and that none of the people in positions of power and authority knew what was going on?

No Crime, No Punishment, N.Y. TIMES, Aug. 26, 2012, at SR10.

[E] Theft: Consolidation of the Property Acquisition Offenses

Model Penal Code § 223.1

Section 223.1. Consolidation of Theft Offenses; Grading;
Provisions Applicable to Theft Generally

(1) *Consolidation of Theft Offenses.* Conduct denominated theft in this Article constitutes a single offense. An accusation of theft may be supported by evidence that it was committed in any manner that would be theft under this Article, notwithstanding the specification of a different manner in the indictment or information, subject only to the power of the Court to ensure fair trial by granting a continuance or other appropriate relief where the conduct of the defense would be prejudiced by lack of fair notice or by surprise.

California Penal Code § 484

§ 484. What constitutes theft; Determination of value of property; Presumptions

(a) Every person who shall feloniously steal, take, carry, lead, or drive away the personal property of another, or who shall fraudulently appropriate property which has been entrusted to him or her, or who shall knowingly and designedly, by any false or fraudulent representation or pretense, defraud any other person of money, labor or real or personal property, or who causes or procures others to report falsely of his or her wealth or mercantile character and by thus imposing upon any person, obtains credit and thereby fraudulently gets or obtains possession of money, or property or obtains the labor or service of another, is guilty of theft. In determining the value of the property obtained, for the purposes of this section, the reasonable and fair market value shall be the test, and in determining the value of services received the contract price shall be the test. If there be no contract price, the reasonable and going wage for the service rendered shall govern. For the purposes of this section, any false or fraudulent representation or pretense made shall be treated as continuing, so as to cover any money, property or service received as a result thereof, and the complaint, information or indictment may charge that the crime was committed on any date during the particular period in question. The hiring of any additional employee or employees without advising each of them of every labor claim due and unpaid and every judgment that the employer has been unable to meet shall be prima facie evidence of intent to defraud.

. . . .

Notes and Questions

1. The Problem. Courts are often faced with situations in which the defendant is clearly guilty of appropriating the victim's property in a criminal manner, but it is unclear whether the crime committed was false pretenses, embezzlement, or just plain larceny. In such cases, the defendant may avoid conviction by "claim[ing] that he did not misappropriate property by the means alleged but in fact misappropriated the property by some other means." Model Penal Code § 223.1 Comment at 133. Alternatively, the jury may convict the defendant of one offense only to have the conviction overturned because the appellate court believes that the defendant is guilty of a different offense.

In *People v. Phebus*, 323 N.W.2d 423 (Mich. Ct. App. 1982), for example, the defendant switched the price-tags on several items in a store and then bought one of the items at the incorrect, lower price. The prosecution charged the defendant with larceny, but the court dismissed the charges on the ground that he had committed the crime of false pretenses, not larceny, because title to the property had changed when he bought the item.

In a similar case, *Agnew v. State*, 526 P.2d 1158 (Okla. Crim. App. 1974), the defendant had 29 cases of beer loaded onto his pick-up truck. He then told the cashier that he was buying 29 six-packs and paid the correct price for that amount of beer. He was convicted of false pretenses, but the court of appeals reversed. The court explained that the defendant had committed larceny by trick, not false pretenses, because, unlike Phebus, the defendant had been given title to only 29 six-packs of beer, not 29 cases.

Finally, in *Commonwealth v. O'Malley*, 97 Mass. 584 (1867), the defendant's embezzlement conviction was reversed on appeal. The appellate court thought that the evidence proved larceny rather than embezzlement because the victim had not entrusted her money to the defendant, but had merely given it to him temporarily so that he could count it for her.

2. The Solution. In order to alleviate such problems, the Model Penal Code and some state statutes consolidate the crimes of larceny, embezzlement, and false pretenses into one offense generally referred to as "theft." *See* Model Penal Code § 223.1(1); Cal. Penal Code §§ 484, 490a, 952. Other examples in addition to the Model Penal Code and California provisions set out above are Kan. Stat. Ann. § 21-3701 and Wash. Rev. Code § 9.54.010. (The Model Penal Code also punishes extortion, which is discussed in Chapter 9, Section B, and receipt of stolen property, which is discussed above in Note 1 following *People v. Kunkin* in Section B.5.)

In jurisdictions that have adopted this approach, the prosecution must prove that the defendant committed one of the crimes listed in the theft statute, but anyone who does so is convicted of "theft." The California Supreme Court explained the practical impact of the state's consolidated theft statute as follows:

[I]t was not necessary for the information to allege the particular type of theft involved, such as false pretenses, embezzlement, or larceny by trick. . . .

Similarly, there was no error in failing to instruct the jury that they must agree upon the method by which the theft was committed. If [the victim] intended that only possession of the property should pass at the time of the sale, defendant was guilty of larceny by trick . . . , but if [the victim] intended that title should pass, defendant was guilty of obtaining property by false pretenses. Irrespective of [the victim's] intent, however, defendant could be found guilty of theft by one means or another, and since by the verdict the jury determined that he did fraudulently appropriate the property, it is immaterial whether or not they agreed as to the technical pigeonhole into which the theft fell.

People v. Nor Woods, 233 P.2d 897, 898 (Cal. 1951).

Thus, consolidation helps reduce the number of hung juries because members of the jury can disagree as to the exact type of common-law property offense the defendant committed and nevertheless agree to find the defendant guilty of theft. Likewise, the conviction can be upheld on appeal even if the court of appeals disagrees with the jury as to the particular type of theft the defendant committed.

In defending consolidation, the Comments to §223.1 of the Model Penal Code point out:

Prevailing moral standards do not differentiate sharply between the swindler and other "thieves." To that extent, at least, consolidation conforms to the common understanding of what is substantially the same kind of undesirable conduct. Consolidation also has advantages in the administration of the criminal law if it eliminates procedural problems arising from nice distinctions between closely related types of misbehavior. Differences in the treatment of thieves can be determined on an individual basis by taking into account many factors which are at least as significant as whether fraud or stealth was the means employed to deprive another of his property.

Model Penal Code § 223.1 Comment at 132.

Those who oppose consolidation argue that it covers up the question whether a defendant was properly convicted of the correct offense. Consider Professor Fletcher's views:

The contemporary trend in Anglo-American jurisdictions is to merge larceny and embezzlement in one overarching offense committed by anyone "[w]ho dishonestly appropriates the property of another." . . . This is the language of the 1968 English Theft Act, which has been incorporated as well in the 1973 Crimes Act in Australia. . . . The economy of the merger represented by the 1968 English innovation is that it dispenses with the distinction between taking from possession and taking while in possession. Lost in the process of merger is the crisp, directive language of "taking" and "trespass." It is true that both German and Soviet law treat the concept of "appropriation" as the element common to the distinct crimes of larceny and embezzlement. What makes the 1968 English Statute different is the attempt to abolish the two offenses and to rely exclusively upon the murky concept of appropriation as the criterion of criminality.

GEORGE P. FLETCHER, RETHINKING CRIMINAL LAW 9–10 (1978).

Obviously, the issue of consolidation raises some difficult questions. Those who oppose consolidation argue that there must be a reasonable doubt about guilt in any case where the members of the jury, or the jury and appellate court, are unable to agree precisely what type of theft the defendant committed. Those who favor consolidation respond that such cases reflect disagreement only about the details of the crime and are of little consequence because the distinctions between larceny, embezzlement, and false pretenses are so trivial.

While defendants have tried to raise a lack of fair notice defense when they are charged with one theft offense but convicted of another, the Nebraska Supreme Court rejected such a claim in *State v. Jonusas*, 694 N.W.2d 651 (Neb. 2005), holding that the state's consolidation of theft statute gives defendants sufficient notice of the charges they are facing.

Chapter 9

Aggravated Property Crimes

[A] Robbery

State v. Mejia
662 A.2d 308 (N.J. 1995)

POLLOCK, JUSTICE.

Defendant, Rigoberto Mejia, also known as Martin Gamez, and the victim, Balbino Garcia, were undocumented workers employed at the Breakers Hotel in Spring Lake. Mejia had entrusted Garcia with $750 from Mejia's earnings. When Mejia learned that Garcia was about to leave the United States, Mejia demanded the return of the money. Although Garcia had placed $1,201 in his eyeglass case, he denied possession of Mejia's money. After a dispute, Garcia fled down a basement hallway. Mejia fired a single shot, which struck Garcia in the back. A short time later, Garcia died. The State claimed the shot was purposeful; Mejia claimed it was accidental. [Mejia was convicted of murder, armed robbery, and several other charges. In a portion of the opinion omitted here, the court reversed the death sentence imposed on the murder charge. Mejia was sentenced to 20 years in prison without parole on the armed robbery charge.] . . .

III

Mejia contends that the trial court should have charged the jury that if it found that he had sought to recover his money under a claim of right, it could find him not guilty of robbery. We disagree.

On the State's case, a police officer read into evidence Mejia's statement to the police. The statement indicated that Garcia owed Mejia $750 that Mejia had entrusted to him for safekeeping. Mejia stated further that he went to the Breakers Hotel to "collect the money [Garcia] owed me," and that he threatened Garcia with a gun "so he would give me the money." According to Mejia, neither he nor Garcia had bank accounts because they feared that account records might lead to disclosure of their status as undocumented workers. . . .

A

The common law defined robbery generally as theft of property from the victim by force or by putting the victim in fear of immediate bodily injury. Common law robbery consisted of the combination of the common law crimes of assault and larceny. *State v. McDonald*, 91 N.J.L. 233, 236, 103 A. 165 (E. & A. 1918) (holding that robbery consists of combination of theft and actual or threatened injury). . . .

When adopting the New Jersey Code of Criminal Justice (the Code), the Legislature intended to "revise and codify the [criminal] law in a logical, clear and concise manner." Patterned after the Model Penal Code (MPC), the Code abolished all common law crimes, including robbery. In determining whether the defense of claim-of-right applies to robbery, we must ascertain the intent of the Legislature. . . .

B

N.J.S.A. 2C:15-1a defines robbery:

A person is guilty of robbery if, in the course of committing a theft, he:

(1) Inflicts bodily injury or uses force upon another; or

(2) Threatens another with or purposely puts him in fear of immediate bodily injury; or

(3) Commits or threatens immediately to commit any crime of the first or second degree.

The statute defines "in the course of committing a theft" to include attempts to commit theft and immediate flight after an attempted or completed theft. By so defining "theft," the Legislature broadened the common law of "robbery." The Legislature further broadened the common law definition by providing that the requisite force, although less than that needed for an assault, could satisfy the requirement of "injury" and "force." One authority explains: "The phrase 'or uses force' broadens the definition of robbery to include situations without threat or injury, such as 'the blindside muggings typical of many purse-snatchings.'"

The MPC expressly links robbery and theft, differentiating the two offenses only by requiring the use of threat or force as an element of robbery. Thus, the MPC implies that robbery and theft share the same requirement of criminal intent. Most state statutes, like the MPC, define robbery as a specific-intent crime.

The [New Jersey] Code, like the MPC, incorporates theft as an element of robbery. In this sense, all robberies are thefts, but not all thefts are robberies. *See State v. Sein*, 124 N.J. 209, 229, 590 A.2d 665 (1991) (Wilentz, C.J., dissenting) (stating that "[a]ll robberies are thefts; robbery is simply a greater offense that always includes theft"). . . . Consequently, the intent required for theft also is required for robbery. . . .

The Code makes clear that for an act to constitute theft the stolen property must belong to another. . . . More specifically, a defendant charged with theft or robbery may present evidence proving that the property taken was the defendant's and not the "property of another."

C

Mejia contends that the trial court's anticlaim-of-right charge may have led the jury to believe that it could convict him of robbery even if it found that he had attempted to recover his own property. If the jury charge had that effect, however, the error was harmless. The jury could not have concluded rationally either that Mejia was attempting to recover his own specific property or that Garcia did not possess a protectible interest in it.

Here, moreover, Mejia was not attempting to recover specific currency, such as antique coins. Nothing suggests that Mejia would have been dissatisfied with anything but the specific $750 that he had delivered to Garcia. As Mejia stated, he went to "collect the money [Garcia] owed me." In sum, Mejia attacked Garcia to collect a $750 debt.

D

Apart from arguing that he sought to recover his own specific property, defendant also relies on the affirmative defense of claim of right. To establish the claim-of-right defense, defendant need prove only that he honestly believed that he was recovering his own property, not that the alleged victim actually possessed his property. . . .

New Jersey has long recognized a claim-of-right defense. *See, e.g., State v. Mayberry*, 52 N.J. 413, 431, 245 A.2d 481 (1968), *cert. denied*, 393 U.S. 1043 (1969). Before the enactment of the Code, however, in *State v. Ortiz*, 124 N.J. Super. 189, 305 A.2d 800 (1973), the Appellate Division refused to accept a claim-of-right defense to the charge of robbery, stating:

> In our view, the proposition [that a bona fide but mistakenly held belief that one has a right or claim to property negates the mens rea element of robbery] not only is lacking in sound reason and logic, but it is utterly incompatible with and has no place in an ordered and orderly society such as ours, which eschews self-help through violence. Adoption of the proposition would be but one step short of accepting lawless reprisal as an appropriate means of redressing grievances, real or fancied. . . .

. . . At issue is whether the Legislature implicitly intended the claim-of-right defense to apply to robbery.

In one pre-Code case, the Appellate Division held that the claim-of-right defense so applies. *See State v. D'Agostino*, 176 N.J. Super. 49, 53, 422 A.2d 97 (1980), *certif. denied*, 85 N.J. 494, 427 A.2d 583 (1981). The court reasoned that "[r]obbery . . . is an aggravated form of larceny and when a person cannot be convicted of theft, then he cannot be convicted of robbery."

We disagree with *D'Agostino* and *Bull* [a case similar to *D'Agostino*]. Consequently, we overrule them to the extent that they hold that claim-of-right is a defense to robbery. Those decisions hinge on the following syllogism. Robbery equals theft plus assault. Claim of right is a defense to theft. Therefore, it is a defense to robbery.

Robbery, however, is a more complex crime than theft plus assault. As we recently noted, "the shorthand understanding that robbery equals theft plus assault is inconsistent with the clear, albeit complicated, language of the Code." *State v. Sewell*, 127

N.J. 133, 147, 603 A.2d 21 (1992). Our reading of the Code leads us to conclude that the Legislature did not intend to treat robbery simply as the combination of theft plus the use of unprivileged force.

. . . Furthermore, the emerging trend in other jurisdictions rejects the claim-of-right defense to robbery. *People v. Reid*, 69 N.Y.2d 469, 515 N.Y.S.2d 750, 752, 508 N.E.2d 661, 664 (1987); *see also, e.g., State v. Schaefer*, 163 Ariz. 626, 790 P.2d 281, 284 (1990) (rejecting claim-of-right defense because "[i]t encourages disputants to resolve disputes on the street through violence instead of through the judicial system"); *Commonwealth v. Sleighter*, 495 Pa. 262, 433 A.2d 469, 471 (1981) (asserting that persons with adequate remedy at law should not try to recover property by force or violence); *Austin v. State*, 86 Wis. 2d 213, 271 N.W.2d 668, 670 (1978) (holding that the defendant's belief he was recovering his own money did not bar conviction for armed robbery), *overruled on other grounds, State v. Poellinger*, 153 Wis. 2d 493, 451 N.W.2d 752, 757 (1990).

From the words and structure of the Code, and for sound reasons of public policy, we conclude that the Legislature did not intend to extend the claim-of-right defense to robbery. We hold that Mejia was not entitled to a claim-of-right charge on the guilt phase. Accordingly we affirm his robbery and felony-murder convictions.

. . . .

Notes and Questions

1. The Elements of Robbery. Common-law robbery contains all of the elements of larceny (a trespassory taking and carrying away of another's property with the intent to deprive the owner of the property permanently). In addition, common-law robbery requires proof of two additional elements: (a) the taking must be accomplished by force or by causing the victim to fear the possibility of immediate force; and (b) the taking must be from the person or from the immediate presence and control of the victim. *See* Wayne R. LaFave, Criminal Law, § 20.3, at 1046–64 (5th ed. 2010).

Contrast the common-law definition with the approach taken in § 222.1 of the Model Penal Code:

(1) *Robbery Defined*. A person is guilty of robbery if, in the course of committing a theft, he:

(a) inflicts serious bodily injury upon another; or

(b) threatens another with or purposely puts him in fear of immediate serious bodily injury; or

(c) commits or threatens immediately to commit any felony of the first or second degree.

An act shall be deemed "in the course of committing a theft" if it occurs in an attempt to commit theft or in flight after the attempt or commission.

2. Force. Suppose *A*, while jogging in the park early one morning, finds *B* lying face down in a pool of blood. Finding no pulse, *A* removes $150 from *B*'s wallet and continues on his way. *A* has not committed robbery because the requisite use of force or fear is missing when one steals from the body of a dead person. One line of cases does suggest, however, that if *A* killed *B*, and the time interval between the fatal blow and the taking of property was short, *A* could be convicted of robbery even if the intent to steal was formed after the victim's death. *See Carey v. United States*, 296 F.2d 422 (D.C. Cir. 1961); WAYNE R. LaFAVE, CRIMINAL LAW § 20.3(c), at 1052 & n.33 (5th ed. 2010).

Most jurisdictions agree that the administration of drugs or intoxicating liquors so as to render one's victim helpless constitutes "constructive force" sufficient for robbery. In *State v. Snyder*, 172 P. 364 (Nev. 1918), the defendant administered a drug to a bartender and then, while the bartender was unconscious, took money from the cash register. The court concluded that administration of the drug satisfied the force requirement because it overcame the victim's resistance:

> "Force" is the power or energy by which resistance is overcome. . . . When, to take the personal effects of another, a blow is struck with a bludgeon, thereby paralyzing the victim's power of resistance, the taking will constitute robbery. The same effect might be produced on the victim by the physical act of administering a deadly potion. . . . The agency through which the force operates is immaterial. The result in either case is the overcoming of resistance without the voluntary cooperation of the subject whose resistance is repressed: this is the test.

Id. at 364, 366–67.

On the other hand, if the victim takes the drug knowingly and voluntarily, there is no force. Thus, in *People v. Kelley*, 269 Cal. Rptr. 900 (Cal. Ct. App. 1990), the defendants conspired to get the victim intoxicated so that they could steal his money. They did so by engaging the victim in a drinking game. Because he participated in the game voluntarily, and knew that he was imbibing alcohol, the court concluded that there was no force.

3. The Distinction Between Robbery and Larceny. Some dispute exists as to whether "snatching" cases constitute larceny or robbery. Most courts hold that the force required for robbery does not exist in cases where the defendant snatches property from the owner's grasp or control so suddenly that the owner does not have time to offer any resistance. *See, e.g., People v. Patton*, 389 N.E.2d 1174 (Ill. 1979) (no robbery where defendant grabbed victim's purse very quickly, throwing her arm back "a little bit"). Relying on the specific language of the New Jersey robbery statute, *Mejia* departs from the majority view and expands the crime of robbery to include the minimal contact involved in snatching cases.

Section 222.1(1) of the Model Penal Code favors the majority approach, requiring the infliction or threat of immediate "serious bodily injury" to make out a case of robbery (unless, under § 222.1(1)(c), the defendant commits or threatens a first- or second-degree felony). According to the Comments accompanying this provision, the word "serious" was specifically added "to avoid the result of making a robber out of a man who snatches a bag and thus inflicts some pain or wrench in running off with the bag." Model Penal Code § 222.1 Comment at 108.

Does the majority approach make sense, or should purse-snatching be considered robbery? Do the larceny statutes adequately punish such behavior?

4. Putting in Immediate Fear. Note that using force, on the one hand, and putting in fear, on the other, are alternative requirements: they are not both needed to support a robbery charge. In most jurisdictions, the fact that the victim was actually frightened by the defendant is sufficient evidence of the fear required for robbery— even if an ordinary person would not have been frightened under the same circumstances. In *State v. Parsons*, 87 P. 349, 350 (Wash. 1906), the court observed: "no matter how slight . . . the cause creating the fear may be, nor by what other circumstances the taking may be accompanied," "[i]t is enough that . . . the putting in fear . . . is sufficient to overcome resistance on the part of the person from whom the property is taken, and is the moving cause inducing him to part unwillingly with his property."

Some states, however, use an objective standard to measure fear, allowing a robbery conviction to stand without any showing that the victim was actually placed in fear, so long as the circumstances surrounding the robbery would ordinarily have induced fear in the mind of a reasonable person. For example, in *Brown v. State*, 397 So. 2d 1153 (Fla. Dist. Ct. App. 1981), the court upheld the robbery conviction of a defendant who handed a bank teller a note indicating that a holdup was in progress, made a statement suggesting harm to the teller's family, and kept his hands out of the teller's sight. Given that a reasonable person under those circumstances would have felt sufficiently threatened to accede to the defendant's demands, the court affirmed the conviction. The court explained: "actual fear need not be strictly and precisely shown. . . . This is so even where the victim specifically states that he was never in fear during the course of the robbery." *But see Breedlove v. State*, 482 So. 2d 1277, 1281 (Ala. Crim. App. 1985) (holding that "the test to be applied is a 'subjective' one which focuses on the 'reaction of the victim to the threats of the robber'") (quoting *State v. Hopson*, 362 N.W.2d 166, 169 (Wis. 1984)). *Cf.* WAYNE R. LaFAVE, CRIMINAL LAW § 20.3(d), at 1058 (5th ed. 2010) (suggesting that the term "fear" "does not so much mean 'fright' as it means 'apprehension,'" so that "one too brave to be frightened may yet be apprehensive of bodily harm").

What are the advantages and disadvantages of focusing on the subjective reaction of the robbery victim? Note that § 222.1(1)(b) of the Model Penal Code focuses instead on the defendant's "purposeful behavior" in an effort to "assure that the robbery offense properly identifies those offenders who pose the risks of serious harm to which the crime is addressed." Model Penal Code § 222.1 Comment at 114. "It is not the victim's reaction to the actor's conduct that controls, but the purposeful behavior by the actor in communicating the threat of injury," the drafters explained. *Id.* (Compare the treatment in rape cases of similar issues that arise concerning the reasonableness of victims' fears, which is discussed in Note 2 following *State v. Rusk* in Chapter 7, Section B.3.)

5. Threats to Other Persons or Property. The threat need not necessarily be directed at the defendant in order to support a robbery charge; rather, a threat of immediate force directed at a third person can also suffice for robbery. *See* Wayne R. LaFave, Criminal Law § 20.3(d), at 1056–57 (5th ed. 2010). There are older cases suggesting that a threat to destroy the victim's dwelling or to accuse the victim of sodomy (though not other crimes) can be intimidating enough to support a robbery charge, but this view is generally not accepted today. *See id.* at 1057.

The Model Penal Code partially resurrects these cases, however, by expanding the definition of robbery to include takings accomplished by the commission or threat of a first- or second-degree felony. *See* Model Penal Code § 222.1(1)(c).

6. From the Person or the Immediate Presence and Control of the Victim. Suppose *A* knows that *B* hides money in her house but does not know where. *A* accosts *B* on the street and, holding a gun to her side, forces her to telephone her house and tell *C*, *A*'s partner, where the money is hidden. Arguably this is not a case of common-law robbery because *B*'s property is not being taken from her immediate presence and control. The defendants would, however, be guilty of robbery under the Model Penal Code. Section 222.1 does not incorporate the common-law requirement that the taking must be from the person or immediate presence and control of the victim. *See* Model Penal Code § 222.1 Comment at 112. Were the drafters of the Code right to think that the presence and control requirement is unnecessary?

7. Armed Robbery. Defendants are guilty of armed robbery when they commit a robbery while possessing a dangerous weapon. Armed robbery carries a heavier sentence than simple robbery, and a number of jurisdictions refer to armed robbery as "first-degree robbery" and simple robbery as "second-degree robbery." *See* Wayne R. LaFave, Criminal Law § 20.3(f), at 1061–64 (5th ed. 2010).

8. The Definition of a Dangerous Weapon. A major issue in armed robbery cases is what constitutes a "dangerous" weapon. As one court explained, the dangerousness of a weapon "is determined not only by its design, construction, or purpose, but also by its capability to be used in such a way as to cause injury or death." *Wright v. State*, 528 A.2d 498, 500 (Md. Ct. Spec. App. 1987). For example, the following have been held to constitute dangerous weapons for purposes of a first-degree/armed robbery statute: a German shepherd dog (*Commonwealth v. Tarrant*, 326 N.E.2d 710 (Mass. 1975)); a hammer (*Goolsby v. State*, 492 So. 2d 635 (Ala. Crim. App. 1986)); and a shoe (*People v. Graham*, 455 P.2d 153 (Cal. 1969)).

Definitions like that articulated in *Wright*—that a dangerous weapon is anything that could potentially cause harm—can be applied quite broadly. In *Commonwealth v. Johnson*, 543 N.E.2d 22 (Mass. 1989), the court concluded that the defendant used a "dangerous weapon" when he pointed a concealed hairbrush at a restaurant cashier who had seen him with a real gun during at least four prior robberies. The defendant reasonably represented "an objective threat of danger," the court explained. *Id.* at 23. The court refused to require that a "dangerous weapon" be inherently dangerous, "so long as that object, from the perspective of the victim, reasonably appears capable of inflicting bodily harm, and the accused intends the victim to be intimidated." *Id.* at 23. Similarly, in *State v. Felix*, 737 P.2d 393, 395 (Ariz. 1986), a nasal inhaler pressed against the victim's body to simulate the barrel of a gun was considered a "simulated deadly weapon" and thus was sufficient to support a conviction for first-degree robbery.

If a hairbrush and a nasal inhaler can qualify as dangerous weapons, why not a contact lens or a head of cauliflower? In part to avoid such absurdities, some jurisdictions have sought to narrow the definition of "dangerous or deadly weapon." For example, in *Brooks v. State*, 552 A.2d 872, 880 (Md. 1989), the court held that an instrument would qualify as a dangerous or deadly weapon only if it was "(1) . . . 'anything used or designed to be used in destroying, defeating, or injuring an enemy, or [designed] as an instrument of offensive or defensive combat'; (2) under the circumstances of the case, immediately useable to inflict serious or deadly harm (e.g., unloaded gun or starter's pistol useable as a bludgeon); or (3) actually used in a way likely to inflict that sort of harm (e.g., microphone cord used as a garrote)." While such a limiting construction enabled the court to find that the lightweight plastic toy pistol used by the defendant in *Brooks* was not a dangerous weapon, does its definition cover all cases in which the aggravated offense should apply?

Courts are split as to whether a toy or "simulated" gun qualifies as a dangerous weapon for purposes of armed robbery. In *State v. Davis*, 605 P.2d 572 (Kan. 1980), the Kansas Supreme Court held that a .22 caliber starter pistol, though incapable of firing a projectile, was nevertheless a dangerous weapon when used to accomplish a robbery. Again, some states look to the objective use of the device while others consider the subjective view of the victim. For example, in *State v. Rines*, 413 A.2d 643 (N.J. Super. Ct. 1980), the court held that a defendant who merely showed part of a toy pistol to a robbery victim in order to convince her to turn over her property, but who did not use the toy pistol or threaten to use it as a bludgeon, could not be convicted of armed robbery.

9. Concealed Weapons. A defendant may be guilty of armed robbery even when a weapon was concealed during the robbery and was not brought to the attention of the victim. In *Commonwealth v. Goldman*, 367 N.E.2d 1181, 1182 (Mass. App. Ct. 1977), for example, the court responded to the claim that the victim was unaware that one of the defendants had a revolver by noting that "possession of a dangerous weapon, rather than its use, is the essential element" of armed robbery. The court reasoned as follows: "The fact that the dangerous weapon is concealed rather than exposed does not significantly decrease the potential for victim resistance and the resulting use of the weapon. The mere possession of a dangerous weapon indicates the robber's willingness to use that weapon if necessary to accomplish his criminal undertaking." *Id. See also State v. Buggs*, 547 P.2d 720 (Kan. 1976) (upholding aggravated robbery conviction on the grounds that the defendant was carrying a knife, even though the victims were unaware of it).

Some jurisdictions have gone one step further, holding that defendants can be convicted of first-degree robbery even in the absence of any evidence that they were armed at all. In *People v. Lopez*, 535 N.E.2d 1328 (N.Y. 1989), the defendant confronted his victim on the street, announced "this is a stick-up," and put his hand in his vest as he demanded the victim's radio. Although the victim only saw the defendant move his hand inside his vest and did not see a gun, any other object, or even a bulge, the court affirmed the defendant's conviction for robbery in the first degree, finding that he "[displayed] what appear[ed] to be a . . . firearm," as required by the state's first-degree robbery statute. *Id.* at 1330. "By his gesture the defendant conspicuously and consciously conveyed the impression that he was reaching for something which, under the circumstances, the victim could reasonably conclude was a firearm," the court explained. *Id.* at 1332.

10. Armed Robbery Under the Model Penal Code. The Model Penal Code rejects distinctions based on whether the robber was "armed with a deadly weapon," but instead elevates robbery to a first-degree felony "if in the course of committing the theft the actor attempts to kill anyone, or purposefully inflicts or attempts to inflict serious bodily injury." Model Penal Code § 222.1(2).

11. Use of Force to Escape. As a general rule, the criminal law requires that the defendant's criminal act be contemporaneous with the mens rea needed to commit the crime. Following this principle, the traditional view is that a thief who used force after taking the property in order to effect an escape did not thereby escalate the crime from larceny to robbery, or from simple robbery to armed robbery (if a dangerous weapon was used). *See* Wayne R. LaFave, Criminal Law § 20.3(d), at 1053–56 (5th ed. 2010). The Model Penal Code departs from that view, however, providing in § 222.1(1) that "[a]n act shall be deemed 'in the course of committing a theft' if it occurs in an attempt to commit theft or in flight after the attempt or commission." The drafters of the Code thought that "[t]he thief's willingness to use force against those who would restrain him in flight suggests that he would have employed force to effect the theft had the need arisen." Model Penal Code § 222.1 Comment at 104.

The New Jersey statute applied in *Mejia* adopted the Model Penal Code's approach to this issue, as have a number of other jurisdictions. In *People v. Heller*, 267 N.E.2d 685 (Ill. App. Ct. 1971), for example, the defendant took some money and a gun from a bar and then threatened the bartender with the gun as he left the premises. The court held that these facts could support an armed robbery conviction: "We feel that the use of a dangerous weapon at any point of a robbery, so long as it can reasonably be said to be a part of a single occurrence or incident . . . , will constitute armed robbery." *Id.* at 689.

Many courts, however, still adhere to the traditional rule that the escape is separate from the taking, and therefore require that the use or threat of immediate force coincide with the taking in order to support a robbery charge. In *State v. Richardson*, 302 S.E.2d 799 (N.C. 1983), the defendant threatened the victim and hit him with a stick. Acting in self-defense, the victim threw his duffel bag at the defendant. When the victim tried to retrieve the bag, the defendant chased him away with the stick. When the victim returned to the site two days later, he found that the defendant had taken some items from the duffel bag. On these facts, the court held that the evidence was insufficient to sustain a robbery conviction because the defendant did not use force prior to or at the time of the taking "such as to induce the victim to part with his or her property." *Id.* at 803.

12. **Claim of Right.** Traditionally, the courts held that the specific intent necessary for robbery could not exist if defendants took property which they believed was their own or to which they in good faith (even if incorrectly) believed they had a claim of right. The crime of larceny requires a specific intent to permanently deprive another of property, and a claim of right therefore negates that intent. (*See* Note 4 following *People v. Kunkin* in Chapter 8, Section B.5.) Given that common-law robbery is an aggravated form of larceny and includes all the elements of larceny, a claim of right likewise negated the mens rea required for robbery. The Model Penal Code reflects the traditional view and considers a claim of right a defense to robbery. *See* Model Penal Code § 223.1 Comment at 155–57 & n.99 (discussing Model Penal Code § 223.1(3)(b)). Under this rule, defendants who use force to collect payment for what they honestly believe is a debt owed to them are not guilty of robbery.

Is there a strong policy argument in favor of the traditional rule recognizing a claim of right as a defense to robbery? Are the countervailing policies served by punishing any violence that accompanies a robbery under the laws governing assault, battery and, where relevant, homicide?

Increasingly, the courts, like the New Jersey Supreme Court in *Mejia*, are interpreting robbery statutes to exclude a claim-of-right defense. Consequently, defendants can be convicted of robbery in these jurisdictions even though they could not be convicted of larceny. Often the court decisions rejecting the traditional view are strongly motivated by policy concerns. Consider Justice Mosk's colorful comments in *People v. Butler*, 421 P.2d 703 (Cal. 1967), where he dissented from the majority's decision recognizing a claim of right as a defense to robbery:

> In a bucolic western scene or in the woolly atmosphere of the frontier in the nineteenth century, the six-shooter may have been an acceptable device for do-it-yourself debt collection. If the law permitted a might-make-right doctrine in that milieu, it is of dubious adaptability to urban society in this final third of the twentieth century.

Id. at 709 (Mosk, J., dissenting).

The California Supreme Court ultimately did overrule *Butler* in 1999, holding that the common-law claim-of-right defense does not extend to "forcible takings perpetrated to satisfy, settle or otherwise collect on a debt." *People v. Tufunga*, 987 P.2d 168, 170 (Cal. 1999). The court reaffirmed, however, that when the California legislature enacted the robbery statute in 1872, it apparently intended to incorporate the common-law claim-of-right defense to takings of specific property believed in good faith to be one's own. Therefore, claim of right remains a defense in those robbery cases, whether or not this "continues to reflect sound public policy as we enter the 21st Century." *Id. See also People v. Cabrera*, 61 Cal. Rptr. 3d 373 (Cal. Ct. App. 2007) (refusing to recognize a claim-of-right defense to the crime of carjacking).

The California Court of Appeal added another wrinkle to the *Tufunga* claim-of-right defense in *People v. Smith*, 100 Cal. Rptr. 3d 24 (Cal. Ct. App. 2009), a case in which the owner of a jewelry store allegedly consented to its armed robbery in order to claim insurance proceeds. Two men robbed the store, forcing employees to open the store's safes at gunpoint and leaving them bound and gagged. The robbers argued that the owner of the store (who was not present during the robbery) had actually consented to the taking of the property, having arranged the apparent robbery in order to commit insurance fraud. The defendants therefore maintained that their actions could not be larceny because they took the property with the property owner's consent. The appellate court, however, rejected this argument, holding that when an owner is not present, a forcible taking from unknowing persons who are lawfully in possession of the property can be robbery, even if the robbers believe they have a "right" to the property because of the owner's consent.

Exactly 13 years after he was acquitted of murdering his ex-wife, O.J. Simpson was convicted on 12 felony counts, including armed robbery and kidnapping, in connection with a 2007 raid where Simpson and five others took sports memorabilia worth thousands of dollars from two dealers in a Las Vegas hotel room. Simpson claimed that the items had been stolen from him and denied knowing that his accomplices were armed. He was sentenced to nine to 33 years in prison, and a panel of the Nevada Supreme Court affirmed his conviction in 2010. *See Simpson v. State*, 2010 Nev. Unpub. Lexis 297 (Nev. Oct. 22, 2010). Five years later, the same court rejected Simpson's habeas claim that both his trial and appeal were infected by ineffective assistance of counsel. *See Simpson v. State*, 2015 Nev. Unpub. Lexis 1047 (Nev. Sept. 10, 2015).

13. Unit of Prosecution for Robbery. In *State v. Tvedt*, 107 P.3d 728 (Wash. 2005), Tvedt challenged his conviction on four counts of first-degree robbery, alleging a violation of the double jeopardy provisions in the state and federal constitutions. Tvedt contended that he engaged in only two acts when he robbed two different gas stations. In the first robbery, Tvedt forced two employees to the floor and demanded money while brandishing a knife. The gas station owner told Tvedt the only money was in a deposit box, which Tvedt took. Tvedt then ordered the owner to give him the keys to the owner's truck, and left in the truck. In the second robbery, Tvedt again brandished a knife and forced two employees to lie on the floor. One of the employees told Tvedt where the money was located. In addition to the money, Tvedt took the cellphone of the other employee. In defending the four counts filed against Tvedt, the prosecution contended that the unit of prosecution is defined by the number of persons placed in fear. Disagreeing with both parties, the Washington Supreme Court held that the legislature had intended to make robbery both a property crime and a crime against the person, and that "the unit of prosecution for robbery is each separate forcible taking of property from or from the presence of a person having an ownership, representative, or possessory interest in the property, against that person's will." Because Tvedt forcibly took property from two people in each of the two incidents, the court upheld his conviction on all four counts.

[B] Extortion

State v. Harrington

260 A.2d 692 (Vt. 1969)

HOLDEN, CHIEF JUSTICE.

The respondent John B. Harrington has been tried and found guilty of the offense of threatening to accuse Armand Morin of Littleton, New Hampshire, of the crime of adultery. The indictment charges that the threat was maliciously made with the intent to extort $175,000 and to compel Morin to do an act against his will in violation of 13 V.S.A. § 1701.

At the outset the respondent acknowledges that there is no serious conflict in the material evidence presented to the jury. The main effort of his appeal challenges the jurisdiction and the sufficiency of the evidence to sustain the conviction.

At the time of the alleged offense the respondent was engaged in the general practice of law in a firm with offices in Burlington, Vermont. Early in March, 1968, he was consulted by Mrs. Norma Morin, the wife of the alleged victim, Armand E. Morin. Mrs. Morin had separated from her husband because of his recent and severe physical abuse. Prior to their separation they owned and operated the Continental 93 Motel in Littleton, New Hampshire, where the Morins maintained a residential apartment. The respondent learned the marital estate of the parties had a net value of approximately $500,000. Mrs. Morin reported to the respondent that her husband had also been guilty of numerous marital infidelities with different women at the motel. Mrs. Morin also disclosed that she had been guilty of marital misconduct which apparently had been condoned.

During the first conference the respondent advised Mrs. Morin that, because of her residence in New Hampshire, she could not undertake divorce proceedings in Vermont for at least six months and for her to obtain a divorce in New Hampshire it would be necessary that she obtain counsel from that state. Mrs. Morin indicated she wished to retain Mr. Harrington to represent her.

On one of the subsequent conferences a friend of Mrs. Morin's, who accompanied her to the respondent's office, suggested that an effort should be made to procure corroborative evidence of Mr. Morin's marital misconduct. To this end, the floor plan of the motel was discussed and a diagram prepared. At this time a scheme was designed to procure the services of a girl who would visit the motel in an effort to obtain corroborative evidence of Morin's infidelity.

After some screening, a Mrs. Mazza, who had been suggested by the respondent, was selected to carry out the assignment. The respondent explained to Mrs. Mazza the purpose of her employment and the results she was expected to accomplish and provided her with a "cover story" to explain her registration and presence as a guest at the Continental 93 Motel. Warning Mrs. Mazza against enticement and entrapment, the respondent instructed the employee to be "receptive and available," but not aggressive. The agreement with Mrs. Mazza was that she would be paid one hundred dollars at the time she undertook the assignment and one hundred dollars when her mission was completed.

Mrs. Morin was without funds at the time. A contingent fee agreement was signed by Mrs. Morin and the firm of Harrington and Jackson, by the respondent. The agreement was dated March 5, 1968 and provided that in the event a satisfactory property settlement was obtained, the respondent's firm was to receive twelve and a half percent of the settlement, in addition to reimbursement for expenses advanced by counsel. Electronic listening and recording equipment was ordered and delivered by air.

On the afternoon of March 6 the respondent and two office associates traveled to St. Johnsbury in two vehicles. Mrs. Mazza continued on to Littleton unaccompanied. She registered on arrival at the Continental 93 Motel under the name of Jeanne Raeder. She called the respondent at St. Johnsbury from a public telephone and informed him of her room number and location. Mrs. Mazza later delivered the key to her room to the respondent to enable him to procure a duplicate. The respondent, representing that he was a book salesman, registered at the motel and procured a room directly above that occupied by Mrs. Mazza. He was accompanied by a junior associate and an investigator—both employed by the respondent's law firm.

During the next day Mrs. Mazza attracted Mr. Morin's attention. The sequence of events which followed led to an invitation by Morin for her to join him at his apartment for a cocktail. Mrs. Mazza accepted. Later she suggested that they go to her room because Mr. Morin's young son was asleep in his quarters. Morin went to Mrs. Mazza's room about midnight. Soon after the appointed hour the respondent and his associates entered the room. With one or more cameras, several photographs were taken of Morin and Mrs. Mazza in bed and unclothed. Morin grabbed for one camera and broke it.

During the time of her stay at the motel Mrs. Mazza carried an electronic transmitter in her handbag. By means of this device, her conversations with Morin were monitored by the respondent and his associates.

The respondent and his companions checked out of the motel at about one in the morning. Before doing so, there was a brief confrontation with Morin. According to Morin's testimony, the respondent demanded $125,000. Morin testified—"at that time I made him an offer of $25,000 to return everything he had, and in a second breath I retracted the offer."

The following day the respondent conferred with Mrs. Morin and reported the events of the trip to New Hampshire. He asked Mrs. Morin to consider reconciliation over the weekend. On March 11, 1968, Mrs. Morin informed the respondent she decided it was too late for reconciliation. With this decision, the respondent dictated, in the presence of Mrs. Morin, a letter which was received in evidence as State's Exhibit 1. The letter was addressed to Armand Morin at Littleton, New Hampshire, and was placed in the United States mail at Burlington the same day.

The communication is designated personal and confidential. The following excerpts are taken from the full text:

> "Basically, your wife desires a divorce, and if it can be equitably arranged, she would prefer that the divorce be as quiet and as undamaging as possible.
>
> This letter is being written in your wife's presence and has been completely authorized by your wife. The offer of settlement contained herein is made in the process of negotiation and is, of course, made without prejudice to your wife's rights.
>
> It is the writer's thinking that for the children's sake, for your sake, and for Mrs. Morin's sake, that neither the courts in New Hampshire nor in Vermont should become involved in this potentially explosive divorce. If a suitable "stipulation or separation agreement" can be worked out, the writer would recommend a Mexican, Stipulation-Divorce. This divorce would be based upon the catch-all grounds "Incompatability [*sic*]." A Mexican divorce of this type can be obtained when both parties have agreed as to terms of separation and have executed certain powers of attorney, etc., which this office can provide. With incompatability [*sic*] as the grounds, it is actually immaterial who goes down for the 48 hour period necessary to obtain the divorce in the State of Chihuahua. Mrs. Morin is willing to go; however, if a settlement can be reached, she has no objection to your going.
>
> Mrs. Morin is willing to give up the following:
>
> 1. All of her marital rights, including her rights to share in your estate.
>
> 2. All of her right, title and interest, jointly or by reason of marital status, that she has in and to, any or all property of the marriage, including the Continental 93 Motel, the three (3) farms in Vermont, the capital stock that you own, the house in Lindenville, the joint venture in land in East Burke, all personal property except as is specifically hereinafter mentioned and in short, all rights that she may now have or might acquire in the future, as your wife. Furthermore, any such settlement would include the return to you of all tape recordings, all negatives, all photographs and copies of photographs that might in any way, bring discredit upon yourself. Finally, there would be an absolute undertaking on the part of your wife not to divulge any information of any kind or nature which might be embarrassing to you in your business life, your personal life, your

financial life, [or] your life as it might be affected by the Internal Revenue Service, the United States Customs Service, or any other governmental agency."

The letter goes on to specify the terms of settlement required by Mrs. Morin, concerning custody of the minor child, her retention of an automobile and the disposition of certain designated personal effects. It further provides:

"5. Mrs. Morin would waive all alimony upon receipt of One Hundred Seventy Five Thousand Dollars ($175,000)."

The sum of $25,000 is specified to be paid at the signing of the separation agreement, with the balance due according to a schedule of payments over the period of eighteen months.

The letter continues:

"At the present time Mrs. Morin is almost without funds. She did have the $200 that you gave her when she left and she does have the $1500 in Canadian bills from the 'found' money. Because of her shortage of money, and, because she is badly missing David, and finally, because she cannot continue for any substantial period of time to live in the present vacuum, the writer must require prompt communication from you with respect to the proposed settlement contained herein. This letter is being dictated on March 11 and you should have it in your possession by March 13, at the latest. Unless the writer has heard from you on or before March 22, we will have no alternative but to withdraw the offer and bring immediate divorce proceedings in Grafton County. This will, of course, require the participation by the writer's correspondent attorneys in New Hampshire. If we were to proceed under New Hampshire laws, without any stipulation, it would be necessary to allege, in detail, all of the grounds that Mrs. Morin has in seeking the divorce. The writer is, at present, undecided as to advising Mrs. Morin whether or not to file for "informer fees" with respect to the Internal Revenue Service and the United States Customs Service. In any event, we would file, alleging adultery, including affidavits, alleging extreme cruelty and beatings, and asking for a court order enjoining you from disposing of any property, including your stock interests, during the pendency of the proceeding.

The thought has been expressed that you might, under certain circumstances, decide to liquidate what you could and abscond to Canada or elsewhere. The writer would advise you that this would in no way impede Mrs. Morin's action. You would be served by publication and under those circumstances, I am very certain that all property in New Hampshire and in Vermont, would be awarded, beyond any question, to Mrs. Morin.

With absolutely no other purpose than to prove to you that we have all of the proof necessary to prove adultery beyond a reasonable doubt, we are enclosing a photograph taken by one of my investigators on the early morning of March 8. The purpose of enclosing the photograph as previously stated, is simply to show you that cameras and equipment were in full operating order."

It was stipulated that the letter was received by Morin in Littleton, New Hampshire "in the due course of the mail."

Such is the evidence upon which the respondent was found guilty. . . .

. . . 13 V.S.A. § 1701 provides:

> A person who maliciously threatens to accuse another of a crime or offense, or with an injury to his person or property, with intent to extort money or other pecuniary advantage, or with intent to compel the person so threatened to do an act against his will, shall be imprisoned in the state prison not more than two years or fined not more than $500.00.

The gist of the offense is the attempt to extort money or other gain. It was not essential to the crime, described in the statute, nor to the court's power to deal with it, that the threat be communicated in Vermont. The instruction, sought by the respondent to the contrary when the case was submitted, was correctly denied.

. . . Turning to the other grounds advanced in the motion for acquittal, the respondent maintains his letter (State's Exhibit 1) does not constitute a threat to accuse Morin of the crime of adultery. He argues the implicit threats contained in the communication were "not to accuse of the CRIME of adultery but to bring an embarrassing, reputation-ruining divorce proceeding in Mr. Morin's county of residence unless a stipulation could be negotiated."

In dealing with a parallel contention in *State v. Louanis*, 79 Vt. 463, 467, 65 A. 532 (1907), the Court answered the argument in an opinion by Chief Judge Rowell. "The statute is aimed at blackmailing, and a threat of any public accusation is as much within the reason of the statute as a threat of a formal complaint, and is much easier made, and may be quite as likely to accomplish its purpose. There is nothing in the statute that requires such a restricted meaning of the word 'accuse'; and to restrict it thus, would well nigh destroy the efficacy of the act."

The letter, marked "personal and confidential," makes a private accusation of adultery in support of a demand for a cash settlement. An incriminating photograph was enclosed for the avowed purpose of demonstrating "we have all of the proof necessary to prove adultery beyond a reasonable doubt." According to the writing itself, cost of refusal will be public exposure of incriminating conduct in the courts of New Hampshire where the event took place.

In further support of motion for acquittal, the respondent urges that the totality of the evidence does not exclude the inference that he acted merely as an attorney, attempting to secure a divorce for his client on the most favorable terms possible. This, of course, was the theory of the defense.

The case presented by the State did not require the court to accept the hypothesis of innocence claimed by the respondent. The acts which he performed and the words that he wrote are established by direct and documentary evidence that is not contradicted. The doctrine of *State v. Levy*, 113 Vt. 459, 461, 35 A.2d 853 (1944), and *State v. Goodhart*, 112 Vt. 154, 158, 22 A.2d 151 (1941), advanced by the defense to the effect that the evidence must exclude every reasonable hypothesis except that the respondent is guilty, does not avail him. The rule applies only where the evidence is entirely circumstantial.

The law affords him a presumption of innocence which attends him until the jury returns its verdict. As in all criminal causes, consistent with the right to trial by jury, it was within the province of the triers of the fact to accept the defendant's claim of innocence. After weighing all the evidence in the area of reasonable doubt, the jury might have been persuaded to infer that the accused acted without malicious intent. But the evidence contains the requisite proof to convince the jury to a contrary conclusion.

At the time of the writing, the respondent was undecided whether to advise his client to seek "informer fees." One of the advantages tendered to Morin for a "quiet" and "undamaging" divorce is an "absolute undertaking" on the part of the respondent's client not to inform against him in any way. The Internal Revenue Service, the United States Customs Service and other governmental agencies are suggested as being interested in such information. Quite clearly, these veiled threats exceeded the limits of the respondent's representation of his client in the divorce action. Although these matters were not specified in the indictment, they have a competent bearing on the question of intent.

Apart from this, the advancement of his client's claim to the marital property, however well founded, does not afford legal cause for the trial court to direct a verdict of acquittal in the background and context of his letter to Morin. A demand for settlement of a civil action, accompanied by a malicious threat to expose the wrongdoer's criminal conduct, if made with intent to extort payment, against his will, constitutes the crime alleged in the indictment.

The evidence at hand establishes beyond dispute the respondent's participation was done with preconceived design. The incriminating evidence which his letter threatens to expose was wilfully contrived and procured by a temptress hired for that purpose. These factors in the proof are sufficient to sustain a finding that the respondent acted maliciously and without just cause, within the meaning of our criminal statutes. The sum of the evidence supports the further inference that the act was done with intent to extort a substantial contingent fee to the respondent's personal advantage.

The pronouncement of the jury, in resolving guilt against innocence, does not result from pyramiding inference on inference. Whether the letter threatened to accuse Morin of a crime must be determined from its text. The question of malicious intent similarly depends on the language of the letter. It can also be referred to extraneous facts and circumstances which occurred prior to the writing.

A given state of facts, proven to the satisfaction of the jury, may support several separate conclusions without constructing one inference upon another. It was legally permissible for the jury to find the separate elements of the crime by independently reasoning these factors from the complete evidence.

. . . Judgment affirmed.[1]

Notes and Questions

1. The Elements of the Crime. Definitions of extortion vary widely among different jurisdictions, and they are uniformly general and vague. Consider, for example, the Vermont statute at issue in *Harrington*. What does "maliciously threatens" mean? Compare the Vermont statute with California's definition of extortion:

> Extortion is the obtaining of property from another, with his consent, or the obtaining of an official act of a public officer, induced by a wrongful use of force or fear, or under color of official right.

Cal. Penal Code § 518. Also compare Model Penal Code § 223.4, which defines the crime of "theft by extortion" as "purposely obtain[ing] the property of another by threatening" to inflict one of a specific list of harms.

Most extortion statutes require the following elements: (1) the use of a threat (2) in an attempt to obtain (or, in some states, actually obtaining) (3) property from another person, or some action by another person. *See* WAYNE R. LAFAVE, CRIMINAL LAW § 20.4(a), at 1065 (5th ed. 2010); ROLLIN M. PERKINS & RONALD N. BOYCE, CRIMINAL LAW 448 (3d ed. 1982).

2. The Common-Law Approach. At common law, extortion was a misdemeanor and solely concerned official misconduct. Basically, the extortion charge applied to public officials who corruptly collected an unlawful fee under the color of their office. In *Commonwealth v. Bagley*, 24 Mass. (7 Pick.) 279, 279 (1828), for example, a jailer was convicted of extortion when he demanded and received a fee "for turning the key of the gaol" at the time prisoners entered the jail instead of waiting to collect the fee until they were discharged. "[I]t is extortion at the common law to receive, by color of office, a fee before it is due," the court concluded, even though "no more is taken than will in all probability soon become due." *Id.* at 281.

Most commentators attribute the promulgation of broader extortion statutes to dissatisfaction with the limited scope of common-law robbery. Because robbery was a capital felony at common law, the courts were reluctant to expand the offense to include those who acquired property by threatening something other than immediate violence to the person. *See* WAYNE R. LAFAVE, CRIMINAL LAW § 20.4, at 1064–68 (5th ed. 2010).

---

1. Harrington was sentenced to serve ten to fifteen months in prison, but was paroled after six months. He subsequently received a pardon from the Governor, and eventually his license to practice law was reinstated. *See In re Harrington*, 367 A.2d 161 (Vt. 1976). (Note that the man who prosecuted Harrington, Patrick Leahy, was subsequently elected to the United States Senate.)

3. The Type of Threats That Constitute Extortion. The crux of the crime of extortion is the use of a threat to obtain some sort of financial or other advantage. Although some type of threat is required, the California Court of Appeal has noted that "[n]o precise or particular form of words is necessary in order to constitute a threat" for these purposes. *People v. Massengale*, 68 Cal. Rptr. 415, 419 (Cal. Ct. App. 1968). Rather, the court continued, "[t]hreats can be made by innuendo and the circumstances under which the threat is uttered and the relations between [the defendant and victim] may be taken into consideration" in determining whether a threat was made. *Id.* at 419–20.

The following is a list of the threats commonly included in modern extortion statutes:

(1) threats to injure the victim;

(2) threats to accuse the victim of a crime;

(3) threats to reveal something that would disgrace the victim;

(4) threats to publish defamatory matter about the victim, or to injure his or her business reputation, or to slight his or her personal character;

(5) threats to injure the victim's family or relatives; and

(6) threats to injure anyone.

See Wayne R. LaFave, Criminal Law § 20.4(a), at 1064–67 (5th ed. 2010).

Not all jurisdictions include the same list of threats in their extortion statutes. It is therefore essential to determine whether the defendant's alleged "threat" is included in the relevant statute. For example, California's general extortion statute encompasses five threats:

1. To do an unlawful injury to the person or property of the individual threatened or of a third person.

2. To accuse the individual threatened, or any relative of his or her, or member of his or her family, of any crime.

3. To expose, or to impute to him, her, or them a deformity, disgrace, or crime.

4. To expose a secret affecting him, her, or them.

5. [Or] [t]o report his, her, or their immigration status or suspected immigration status.

Cal. Penal Code § 519. Compare the list of threats included in Model Penal Code § 223.4.

Under the California statute, therefore, *A* would not be guilty of extortion if she threatened to build a stable on her own land unless *B*, her neighbor, paid her $1,000. *A*'s threatened injury to *B*'s property (the only arguably applicable threat) is not "an unlawful injury" as required by the California statute. On the other hand, if *A* and *B* had previously entered into a contract whereby *A* agreed not to build a stable on her land, her threat to do so might constitute a threat to do "an unlawful injury" to *B*'s property. *See People v. Schmitz*, 94 P. 419 (Cal. Ct. App. 1908) (reversing the conviction of defendants who threatened to object to a restaurant's application for a liquor license on the ground that there was insufficient evidence that the defendants were threatening to cause "unlawful injury" within the terms of the extortion statute because any citizen has the right to go to the liquor board and oppose a liquor license).

The Comments accompanying § 223.4 of the Model Penal Code criticize broadly worded extortion provisions because they "appear to embrace breach of contract and similar conduct for which a civil remedy is available." Model Penal Code § 223.4 Comment at 210. The drafters of the Code thought it "clearly unwarranted to permit an extortion charge in such a context, where breach and renegotiation to avoid breach are a normal part of ordinary business dealings." *Id.* To what extent should threats made in the course of a commercial dispute be subject to criminal prosecution? Should athletes who demand renegotiation of multi-year contracts be prosecuted for extortion if they threaten to breach those contracts?

4. **The Definition of "Property."** There is some dispute as to whether the actual right to contract should be considered a form of "property" that can be obtained by extortionate means. In resolving this issue, the language used in the particular state's extortion statute is likely to be determinative. For example, in *People v. Squillante*, 185 N.Y.S.2d 357 (N.Y. Sup. Ct. 1959), a union official threatened to picket a number of stores unless they started using garbage collectors that hired union workers. The union official was convicted of extortion, along with the owners of one of the nine garbage-collection businesses on the union's approved list. In granting bail to the defendants pending appeal, the court questioned the validity of the extortion convictions, commenting that "[o]btaining property from another imports not only that he give up something but that the obtainer receive something" as well. *Id.* at 361. The court was skeptical that "the freedom to contract with the cartmen of their choices" was a type of "property" within the meaning of the extortion statute, noting that the victims in this case did not pay any more for garbage-collection services than they had previously paid the non-union shops. *Id.* The convictions were eventually reversed on appeal. *See People v. Squillante*, 169 N.E.2d 425 (N.Y. 1960).

An Alabama court reached a different conclusion in *Chisler v. State*, 553 So. 2d 654 (Ala. Crim. App. 1989), where the Alabama extortion statute, unlike the New York provision applied in *Squillante*, was broadly worded to include the use of threats to obtain control over intangible property or any "thing of value of any kind" belonging to another person. The court affirmed the defendant's extortion conviction, holding that a liquor manufacturer's contractual right to name its own agents and brokers without fear of official retaliation from the state liquor control board qualified as "property" under the state's extortion statute.

In *Sekhar v. United States*, 133 S. Ct. 2720 (2013), the Supreme Court unanimously agreed that threats intended to induce a General Counsel to recommend that a state employee pension fund invest in certain funds could not be prosecuted as an extortion attempt under the Hobbs Act, 18 U.S.C. § 1951. Six Justices joined the majority opinion written by Justice Scalia, which held that "attempting to compel a person to recommend that his employer approve an investment" does not qualify as "obtaining of property from another." The Court presumed that Congress intended to incorporate the traditional common-law definition of extortion, noting that property must be *transferrable*—that is, capable of passing from one person to another." The remaining three Justices joined an opinion written by Justice Alito, which concurred only in the judgment and concluded that "internal recommendations regarding government decisions are not property." The concurrence therefore declined to reach the majority's argument that "the alleged property . . . was not transferable" and thus "not capable of being 'obtained.'"

Should extortion cover threats attempting to alter contract terms? Does an entertainment lawyer commit extortion by threatening to instruct a client to breach a contract unless the actor receives a raise?

5. Negotiations and Extortion. Was the Vermont Supreme Court right to conclude that Harrington committed the crime of extortion? What should he have done differently?

Harrington is not the only case involving lawyers who have faced extortion charges arising from their behavior during settlement negotiations. In *People v. Beggs*, 172 P. 152 (Cal. 1918), which is discussed more fully below in Note 1 following *United States v. Jackson*, the court upheld an extortion conviction entered against an attorney representing an employer who sought reimbursement for goods allegedly stolen by an employee.

Even prominent attorneys have not been immune from accusations that they committed extortion in the negotiation process. The trial judge in the child-custody dispute between Woody Allen and Mia Farrow required Harvard Law professor and criminal defense attorney Alan Dershowitz to respond on the witness stand to allegations made by Allen's attorney that Dershowitz had attempted to extort a payment of between five and seven million dollars in exchange for Farrow's promise to make criminal child-abuse charges against Allen "go away." Dershowitz claimed that the payment was meant as compensation for child support, tuition, and medical and psychiatric expenses, and possibly for the damages suffered by the child who had allegedly been molested:

> The combatants were celeb lawyer Alan Dershowitz, testifying for Farrow with soapbox expansiveness, and Allen's attorney Elken Abramowitz, cross-examining Dershowitz with the relish of a starving man happening across a Big Mac.

> At issue was the nagging matter of what had happened at a settlement conference held in New York last August, during the tense days after 7-year-old

Dylan Farrow reported being molested by her father but before Allen made that and his affair with her half-sister, Soon-Yi, public. Both parties' lawyers were present, with Dershowitz acting on Farrow's behalf as a sort-of-but-not-exactly mediator.

Abramowitz tried again today to portray the several-million-dollar sums that were tossed around as extortion, a payoff in exchange for keeping the abuse allegations quiet and out of court. Dershowitz resisted that interpretation. He protested at length that discussion of child support and other payments had never been linked with his proposal that both parties approach the Connecticut authorities to argue that prosecution was not in the children's best interest. As for the numbers, "everyone there was in a negotiating posture," he said.

Paula Span, *The Brawling Barristers*, WASH. POST, Apr. 17, 1993, at C1. Although a team of investigators hired by the state police concluded that Dylan Farrow had not been molested, Farrow ultimately won custody of the children. *See* Peter Marks, *Allen Loses to Farrow in Bitter Custody Battle*, N.Y. TIMES, June 8, 1993, at A1.

In another well-publicized case, attorneys representing celebrity singer Michael Jackson held a press conference in which they accused the attorney representing a boy who had sued Jackson for allegedly tortious conduct of "intentionally [making] false accusations against Jackson in order to extort money from him." *Rothman v. Jackson*, 57 Cal. Rptr. 2d 284, 287 (Cal. Ct. App. 1996). Is the truth or falsity of the accusations relevant to the validity of the extortion charge? The boy's tort suit against Jackson was eventually settled for a sum "reputed to be over $25 million," *id.*, and his attorney filed a defamation claim against Jackson and his attorneys in connection with the extortion accusation.

Civil extortion charges were also filed against Martin Singer, a high-profile Hollywood attorney, in a suit filed by reality television star Mike "Boogie" Malin of *Big Brother* fame. The extortion claim was based on a demand letter Singer sent to Malin on behalf of a client, threatening to sue Malin for embezzlement and conversion and to disclose that Malin had spent the allegedly stolen funds on various sexual encounters. The California Court of Appeal dismissed the extortion claim on the grounds that the letter did not make an "overt threat to report Malin to prosecuting agencies or the Internal Revenue Service" and therefore did not "fall under the narrow exception . . . for a letter so extreme in its demands that it constituted criminal extortion as a matter of law." *Malin v. Singer*, 159 Cal. Rptr. 3d 292, 304 (Cal. Ct. App. 2013). The court also concluded that the letter was protected by the litigation privilege, which protects communications related to litigation from civil liability.

Finally, consider a case involving a former collegiate football player, Ryan Loftin. The 22-year-old graduate student and former starting linebacker for the University of Iowa was charged with extortion after he threatened, among other things, to engage in "mudslinging" about the University's football program and coach, to disclose the school's athletic rules violations, and to provide inside information to its football opponents unless he was allowed to keep his athletic scholarship after he quit the team. *See* Tom Witosky, *Extortion Alleged in Loftin Case*, Des Moines Register, Oct. 12, 1999, at 1. Loftin ultimately pled guilty to a "serious misdemeanor" of "trespass causing damage," and was sentenced to two years' probation in addition to 120 hours of community service, restitution, and court costs. He apparently had stolen team playbooks, in addition to making the threats described above. *See* Brian Sharp, *Loftin Apologizes, Gets Community Service*, Iowa City Press-Citizen, Feb. 5, 2000.

6. Distinguishing Extortion from Robbery. In extortion cases that involve a threat of physical injury, the threat is typically a threat to use force at some point in the future. Robbery, on the other hand, is limited to the threat of immediate force. Nevertheless, extortion includes immediate as well as non-immediate threats and, furthermore, unlike common-law robbery, never recognizes a claim-of-right defense for threats of physical injury. Certain types of extortion involving physical threats consequently may either overlap with robbery or serve as a backup crime when all the requirements of robbery are not met. For further discussion of the claim-of-right defense in extortion prosecutions, see Note 1 following *United States v. Jackson* below.

7. Distinguishing Extortion from Compounding. The crime of "compounding," under both the common law and modern statutes, consists of receiving property or some other valuable consideration in exchange for agreeing to conceal or not to prosecute a crime. *See, e.g.,* Model Penal Code § 242.5; Cal. Penal Code § 153; N.J. Stat. Ann. § 2C:29-4. *See generally* Wayne R. LaFave, Criminal Law § 13.6(c), at 759 (5th ed. 2010). Unlike extortion, where the defendant uses a threat in an effort to obtain the other person's property, compounding occurs when the defendant receives some benefit from an agreement not to prosecute, regardless of who initiated the agreement. Hence, in *People v. Pic'l*, 646 P.2d 847 (Cal. 1982), the court held that the grand jury had probable cause to believe an attorney was guilty of compounding a felony when he offered to return property that had been stolen from a professional drag racer if the drag racer agreed to seek the dismissal of charges filed against the defendant's client in connection with the theft.

Traditionally, only the person who received the property was charged with compounding, although some statutes now punish both parties. A wrongdoer's payment to the victim of a crime does not constitute compounding unless it involves an agreement (whether written or not) that the victim will not report or prosecute the crime. Applying this principle to the case involving Michael Jackson (discussed above in Note 5), it was not compounding for the boy to receive the "reputed" $25 million settlement unless he agreed not to testify about Jackson's alleged criminal acts in return for the money. *See Rothman v. Jackson*, 57 Cal. Rptr. 2d 284, 287 (Cal. Ct. App. 1996).

Section 242.5 of the Model Penal Code creates an affirmative defense to the crime of compounding if "the pecuniary benefit did not exceed an amount which the actor believed to be due as restitution or indemnification for harm caused by the offense."

Many states do not recognize such a defense, and some limit it to cases where a court approved the payment. Do these limitations on the reach of compounding statutes properly encourage private restitution and dispute settlement, or do they allow the wealthy to buy off their victims and thereby avoid criminal sanctions? Note that the Model Penal Code tries to discourage excessive payoffs to crime victims by allowing a defense only for payments that do not exceed the victim's perceived loss.

United States v. Jackson

180 F.3d 55 (2d Cir. 1999)

KEARSE, CIRCUIT JUDGE.

Defendant[] Autumn Jackson . . . appeal[s] from [a] conviction entered in the United States District Court for the Southern District of New York following a jury trial before Barbara S. Jones, Judge. Jackson . . . [was] convicted of threatening to injure another person's reputation with the intent to extort money, in violation of 18 U.S.C. § 875(d) . . . [and sentenced to 26 months in prison].

I. Background

The present prosecution arises out of defendant['s] attempts to obtain up to $40 million from William H. ("Bill") Cosby, Jr., a well-known actor and entertainer, by threatening to cause tabloid newspapers to publish Jackson's claim to be Cosby's daughter out-of-wedlock. . . .

In the early 1970s, Cosby had a brief extramarital affair with Jackson's mother, Shawn Thompson. After Jackson was born in 1974, Thompson told Cosby that he was the father. Cosby disputed that assertion, and according to Jackson's birth certificate, her father was one Gerald Jackson. Jackson's grandmother testified, however, that she and Thompson told Jackson, as Jackson was growing up, that Cosby was her biological father. The grandmother told Jackson that Cosby had said that, so long as they "didn't tell anyone about it, that he would take care of her mother and her, and take care of his responsibility."

For more than 20 years after Jackson's birth, Cosby provided Thompson with substantial sums of money, provided her with a car, and paid for her admission to substance-abuse treatment programs. Thompson repeatedly telephoned him saying that she needed money, and in the course of the conversations she would usually reiterate her claim that Cosby was Jackson's father and state that she did not want to embarrass Cosby's wife. Between 1974 and mid-1994, Cosby gave Thompson a total of more than $100,000, typically having traveler's checks or cashier's checks issued in the name of an employee rather than his own name. In 1994, Cosby established a trust fund for Thompson, which was administered by John P. Schmitt, a partner in the New York City law firm that represented Cosby. The trust fund provided Thompson with $750 a week for as long as Cosby chose to fund the trust. Thompson received approximately $100,000 in payments from this fund from mid-1994 until the fund was exhausted, and not replenished, in early 1997.

In addition, Cosby, who had funded college educations for some 300 persons outside of his own immediate family, and had spoken with Jackson by telephone at least once during her childhood, had offered to pay for the education of Jackson and Thompson's other two children. . . . Cosby thereafter also created a trust to pay for Jackson's college tuition and for certain personal expenses such as food, rent, utilities, and medical costs while Jackson was attending college. This trust was administered by Schmitt's law partner Susan F. Bloom. Jackson subsequently enrolled in a community college in Florida. While Jackson was in school, Cosby spoke with her by telephone approximately 15 times to encourage her to pursue her education, telling her that although he was not her father, he "loved her very, very much" and would be a "father figure" for her. . . .

In April 1995, Bloom learned that Jackson had dropped out of college, and Bloom therefore ceased making payments to Jackson from the college education trust. . . .

. . . On January 2 and 3, 1997, Jackson spoke with . . . Schmitt by telephone and asked that she be sent money for food, lodging, and tuition. . . . Schmitt reiterated that Cosby would not pay for Jackson's support until she enrolled in school and secured employment for eight hours a week. . . .

Following this rejection of her request for money, Jackson made a series of calls to business associates of Cosby, threatening to publicize her claim to be his daughter and thereby harm his reputation. . . .

. . . On January 15, 1997, after the telephone calls and letters of the week before had failed to produce the desired results, . . . Jackson contacted Christopher Doherty, a reporter for The Globe tabloid newspaper. . . . After some negotiation of terms, Doherty agreed that The Globe would purchase the rights to Jackson's story of her relationship to Cosby for $25,000.

. . . The agreement with The Globe was never signed. Instead, on the following morning, January 16, Jackson faxed a copy of the agreement, after obliterating the $25,000 price, to Schmitt. In addition, Jackson faxed Schmitt a letter stating, "I need monies and I need monies now." Jackson's letter stated that it was "urgent" that Schmitt contact her and "make certain arrangements" and asked Schmitt to have Cosby call her that day. . . .

. . . Schmitt called Jackson later that morning. . . . Jackson and Schmitt had the following conversation, in which Jackson asked for $40 million:

SCHMITT: I, I received your letter, Autumn.

JACKSON: Okay.

SCHMITT: [Clears throat] How, how much money are you asking for, Autumn?

JACKSON: I'm wanting to settle, once and finally.

SCHMITT: What, what are you asking for?

JACKSON: I'm asking for 40 million, to settle it completely [pause].

SCHMITT: And if our answer to that is no?

JACKSON: Well, like I said, I have offers, and I will go through with those offers.

SCHMITT: And those offers are to sell your story to the Globe? [Pause]. Autumn, are you there?

JACKSON: Yes I am.

SCHMITT: Is that what you're referring to, the contract that you sent me, that, for sale to the Globe of your story?

JACKSON: Them, as well as any others. [Pause].

SCHMITT: Well, I'm, I'm sure you know the answer to that is no, Autumn. Thank you very much.

. . . That afternoon, Cosby instructed Schmitt to report Jackson's threats to the Federal Bureau of Investigation. . . .

II. Discussion

On appeal, Jackson . . . contend[s] principally that the district court gave an erroneous jury charge on the elements of extortion as prohibited by § 875(d) because it omitted any instruction that, in order to convict, the jury must find that the threat to injure Cosby's reputation was "wrongful." Alternatively, [she argues] that if that section does not include an element of wrongfulness, it is unconstitutionally overbroad and vague. . . .

Section 875.(d), the extortion statute under which Jackson [was] convicted, provides as follows:

> (d) Whoever, with intent to extort from any person . . . any money or other thing of value, transmits in interstate or foreign commerce any communication containing any threat to injure the property or reputation of the addressee or of another . . . shall be fined under this title or imprisoned not more than two years, or both.

18 U.S.C. § 875(d). This statute does not define the terms "extort" or "intent to extort."

. . . [I]n sections of the Criminal Code other than § 875(d), the words "extort," "extortionate," and "extortion" either are defined to have a wrongfulness component or implicitly contain such a component. If Congress had meant the word "extort" in § 875(d) to have a different connotation, we doubt that it would have chosen to convey that intention by means of silence. Given its silence and given the plain connotation of extortion in other sections, we decline to infer that "extort" as used in § 875(d) lacks a component of wrongfulness.

. . . The congressional discussions make clear that Congress meant to adopt the traditional concept of extortion, which includes an element of wrongfulness. . . . Like threats of economic harm, not every threat to make a disclosure that would harm another person's reputation is wrongful. . . . We conclude that not all threats to reputation are within the scope of § 875(d), that the objective of the party employing fear of economic loss or damage to reputation will have a bearing on the lawfulness of its use, and that it is material whether the defendant had a claim of right to the money demanded.

We do, however, view as inherently wrongful the type of threat to reputation that has no nexus to a claim of right. There are significant differences between, on the one hand, threatened disclosures of such matters as consumer complaints and non-payment of dues, as to which the threatener has a plausible claim of right, and, on the other hand, threatened disclosures of such matters as sexual indiscretions that have no nexus with any plausible claim of right. In the former category of threats, the disclosures themselves — not only the threats — have the potential for causing payment of the money demanded; in the latter category, it is only the threat that has that potential, and actual disclosure would frustrate the prospect of payment. Thus, if the club posts a list of members with unpaid dues and its list is accurate, the dues generally will be paid; if the consumer lodges her complaint and is right, she is likely to receive her refund; and both matters are thereby concluded. In contrast, if a threatener having no claim of right discloses the victim's secret, regardless of whether her information is correct she normally gets nothing from the target of her threats. And if the victim makes the demanded payment, thereby avoiding disclosure, there is nothing to prevent the threatener from repeatedly demanding money even after prior demands have been fully met.

Where there is no plausible claim of right and the only leverage to force the payment of money resides in the threat, where actual disclosure would be counterproductive, and where compliance with the threatener's demands provides no assurance against additional demands based on renewed threats of disclosure, we regard a threat to reputation as inherently wrongful. We conclude that where a threat of harm to a person's reputation seeks money or property to which the threatener does not have, and cannot reasonably believe she has, a claim of right, or where the threat has no nexus to a plausible claim of right, the threat is inherently wrongful and its transmission in interstate commerce is prohibited by § 875(d).

Within this framework, we conclude that the district court's instruction to the jury on the meaning of "extort" as that term is used in § 875(d) was erroneous. The court instructed simply that "to extort means to obtain money or a thing of value from another by use of threats to reputation." The court gave no other explanation of the term "extort" and did not limit the scope of that term to the obtaining of property to which the defendant had no actual, or reasonable belief of, entitlement. Rather, the court added that "it makes no difference whether the defendant was actually owed any money by" the victim of the threats. While it would have been correct to instruct that it makes no difference whether the defendant was actually owed money by the threat victim if the threat has no nexus to the defendant's claim, the instruction as given lacked this essential component. Issues of whether a defendant has a plausible claim of right and whether there is a nexus between the threat and the defendant's claim are questions of fact for the factfinder, and we conclude that the jury was not properly instructed as to the elements of a § 875(d) offense.

The evidence at trial was plainly sufficient to support verdicts of guilty had the jury been properly instructed. Even if Jackson were Cosby's child, a rational jury could find that her demand, given her age (22) and the amount ($40 million), did not reflect a plausible claim for support. The evidence supported an inference that Jackson had no right to demand money from Cosby pursuant to a contract or promise and no right to insist that she be included in his will. The jury thus could have found that her threat to disclose was the only leverage she had to extract money from him; that if she sold her story to The Globe, she would lose that leverage; and that if Cosby had capitulated and paid her in order to prevent disclosure, there was no logical guarantee that there would not be a similar threat and demand in the future. Thus, had the jury been instructed that the "with intent to extort" element meant that defendant[] could be found guilty of violating § 875(d) only if Jackson's threat to disclose was issued in connection with a claim for money to which she was not entitled or which had no nexus to a plausible claim of right, the jury could permissibly have returned verdicts of guilty on that count.

We conclude, however, that the court's failure to inform the jury of the proper scope of the intent-to-extort element of § 875(d) erroneously allowed the jury to find defendant[] guilty of violating that section on the premise that any and every threat to reputation in order to obtain money is inherently wrongful. Accordingly, Jackson [is] entitled to a new trial on the § 875(d) count. . . . [On rehearing, however, the court decided that the error in the jury instructions was harmless, and thus affirmed Jackson's conviction. *See United States v. Jackson*, 196 F.3d 383 (2d Cir. 1999).]

Notes and Questions

1. **Claim of Right.** Even though the traditional view is that a claim of right negates the intent to permanently deprive another person of property, and thus constitutes a defense to robbery (*see* Note 12 in Section A above), traditionally most states did not recognize a claim of right as a defense to extortion. In *People v. Beggs*, 172 P. 152 (Cal. 1918), for example, a store employee was caught stealing, and the store owner's lawyer threatened him with prosecution unless he paid $2,000. In upholding the lawyer's conviction for extortion, the court rejected his claim-of-right defense. The court explained:

> [W]e cannot escape the conclusion that, assuming [the employee] had in fact stolen goods of the value of two thousand dollars . . . , the threats made by defendant to prosecute [him] unless he paid the value of said goods . . . constitutes the crime of extortion. It is the means employed which the law denounces, and though the purpose may be to collect a just indebtedness arising from and created by the criminal act for which the threat is to prosecute the wrongdoer, it is nevertheless within the statutory inhibition. The law does not contemplate the use of criminal process as a means of collecting a debt.

Id. at 154.

Nevertheless, an increasing number of state and federal statutes recognize a claim of right as a defense to extortion under certain circumstances — for example, if the property or action that is the subject of the extortionate threat is owed to the defendant as a right "in fact" (*e.g.*, Miss. Code Ann. §97-3-81) or if the defendant's conduct was reasonable (*e.g.*, Ohio Rev. Code Ann. §2905.12 (recognizing such a defense for the lesser crime of coercion)).

Section 223.4 of the Model Penal Code recognizes a limited claim-of-right defense to extortion. The defense is restricted to cases where the defendant threatened (i) to accuse another person of a crime, (ii) to divulge a secret, or (iii) "to take or withhold action as an official, or cause an official to take or withhold action." No claim-of-right defense is available if, for example, the defendant threatened to inflict physical harm.

Does it make sense to allow at least a limited claim-of-right defense to extortion, or does that approach allow debt collectors to circumvent the legal avenues available to adjudicate their claims? Does the position taken in *Jackson* and the Model Penal Code inappropriately encourage the use of threats to settle private disputes? Is it possible to conduct negotiations without committing extortion if a claim of right is no defense? How would a claim-of-right defense have affected the outcome in *Harrington*?

2. Why Criminalize Blackmail? Blackmail is the colloquial term for extortionate threats to reveal the commission of a crime or some other social disgrace. Theorists have had a difficult time trying to explain why this form of extortion (even in the absence of a claim of right) should be criminalized, although intuitively most observers agree that it should be. Consider Professor Lindgren's observation:

> For the past fifty years law professors and philosophers have been trying to explain why blackmail is a crime. The problem with blackmail is this: Why can't you threaten to do what you have a legal right to do? For example, it is blackmail if you seek a job from a prospective employer by threatening to expose his extramarital affair or criminal fraud. Yet you have a legal right to seek a job and a legal right to threaten to expose a prospective employer's affair or fraud. Why then is it blackmail to combine these otherwise legal ends and means? This puzzle — perhaps the most difficult in all of the substantive criminal law — has been termed the paradox of blackmail.

James Lindgren, *More Blackmail Ink: A Critique of* Blackmail, Inc., *Epstein's Theory of Blackmail*, 16 Conn. L. Rev. 909, 909 (1984).

Indeed, two economists have argued that blackmail should not be punished criminally:

> As defined, blackmail should not be accorded the legal sanctions usually meted out in response to criminal behavior since it does not entail the violation of rights. Rather, it consists of the offer of a commercial trade. The blackmailer will remain silent about the humiliating, embarrassing or even

criminal secret of the blackmailee, accepting payment in return. If the offer to trade money for silence is rejected, the blackmailer will publicize the secret, which is part of his rights of free speech. In these terms the distinction between extortion and blackmail may be made as follows: extortion utilizes a threat to do something illicit, such as commit murder, arson or kidnapping. The threat of blackmail is limited to what would otherwise be licit—[to] commit an act of free speech. If a person has the right to do X, he necessarily has the right to give warning of the fact that he will do or may do X—that is, to threaten to do X. Blackmail is thus a noncriminal act.

Blackmail, then, is a "capitalist act between consenting adults," to use the felicitous phrase introduced by Robert Nozick. As such, according to the laws of economics, it must benefit both parties. It is easy to see how the blackmailer gains from the trade. He is paid merely for holding his tongue. But the "victim" also gains. Both parties gain from a voluntary trade, and this is as true of the exchange of money for silence as it is for any other case. The payment extracted must be worth less to the victim than the costs of having his secret uncovered. Otherwise he or she would reject the deal, stating in effect, "Publish and be damned!" In contrast to the gossip, who tells the secret without even affording the victim the opportunity of purchasing silence, the blackmailer can be seen as a benefactor.

Also, blackmail has social, or spillover, benefits. Were it legalized, the presumption is that more people would engage in this activity. If this occurred, real criminal activity would be retarded. The miscreants would now have to share their ill-gotten gains with the blackmailer. This would reduce the expected gain from criminal activity, since the apprehended perpetrator would not only have to give up his booty, but would also be penalized up to the value he places on not going to jail, which may well be higher than the proceeds of any specific crime.

Walter Block & David Gordon, *Blackmail, Extortion and Free Speech: A Reply to Posner, Epstein, Nozick and Lindgren*, 19 LOY. L.A. L. REV. 37, 38–39 (1985). Reprinted with permission.

Professor Epstein responds that "blackmail is criminal because of its tendency to induce deception and other wrongs," and he speculates about the complications that would arise if blackmail were legalized and corporations hypothetically named "Blackmail, Inc." were formed to solicit negative information about people and then contract to keep the information secret for a fee. Richard A. Epstein, *Blackmail, Inc.*, 50 U. CHI. L. REV. 553, 565 (1983).

Professor Landes and Judge Posner give an economic defense for punishing blackmail:

A more persuasive explanation of why blackmail is a crime is that the decision to discourage blackmail follows directly from the decision to rely on a public monopoly of law enforcement in some areas of enforcement, notably criminal law. Were blackmail, a form of private enforcement, lawful, the public monopoly of enforcement would be undermined. Over-enforcement of the law would result if the blackmailer were able to extract the full fine from the offenders. . . . Alternatively, the blackmailer might sell his incriminating information to the offender for a price lower than the statutory cost of punishment to the criminal, which would reduce the effective cost of punishment to the criminal below the level set by the legislature.

Consistently with this analysis, we observe that practices indistinguishable from blackmail, though not called by that name, are permitted in areas where the law is enforced privately rather than publicly because the over-enforcement problem is not serious. No one seems to object to a person's collecting information about his or her spouse's adulterous activities, and threatening to disclose that information in a divorce proceeding or other forum, in order to extract maximum compensation for the offending spouse's breach of the marital obligations. A third party is not permitted to "blackmail" the offending spouse (unless the third party is the victimized spouse's agent) because permitting him to enforce the marital contract would undermine the assignment of the exclusive right to enforce such contracts to the victim of the breach. It is also consistent with our analysis that blackmail is forbidden in areas where there are no legal prohibitions at all—where the information would humiliate, but not incriminate, the blackmailer's victim. The social decision not to regulate a particular activity is a judgment that the expenditure of resources on trying to discover and punish it would be socially wasted. That judgment is undermined if blackmailers are encouraged to expend substantial resources on attempting to apprehend and punish people engaged in the activity.

William M. Landes & Richard A. Posner, *The Private Enforcement of Law*, 4 J. LEGAL STUD. 1, 42 (1975). Reprinted with permission of William Landes.

Can Landes and Posner's analysis be reconciled with the result in *Harrington*? Professor Lindgren offers another explanation for why blackmail is a crime:

Under my theory, blackmail is the seeking of an advantage by threatening to press an actual or potential dispute that is primarily between the blackmail victim and someone else. The blackmailer threatens to bring others into the dispute but typically asks for something for himself; he turns someone else's power, usually group power, to personal benefit. The bargaining is unfair in that the threatener uses leverage that is less his than someone else's.

James Lindgren, *Unraveling the Paradox of Blackmail*, 84 COLUM. L. REV. 670, 703 (1984). Questions about the rationale for criminalizing blackmail continue to fascinate scholars. *See, e.g.,* Symposium, *Blackmail*, 141 U. PA. L. REV. 1565 (1993).

McCormick v. United States

500 U.S. 257 (1991)

JUSTICE WHITE delivered the opinion of the Court.

This case requires us to consider whether the Court of Appeals properly affirmed the conviction of petitioner, an elected public official, for extorting property under color of official right in violation of the Hobbs Act, 18 U.S.C. § 1951. . . .

I

Petitioner Robert L. McCormick was a member of the West Virginia House of Delegates in 1984. He represented a district that had long suffered from a shortage of medical doctors. For several years, West Virginia had allowed foreign medical school graduates to practice under temporary permits while studying for the state licensing exams. Under this program, some doctors were allowed to practice under temporary permits for years even though they repeatedly failed the state exams. McCormick was a leading advocate and supporter of this program.

In the early 1980s, following a move in the House of Delegates to end the temporary permit program, several of the temporarily licensed doctors formed an organization to press their interests in Charleston. The organization hired a lobbyist, John Vandergrift, who in 1984 worked for legislation that would extend the expiration date of the temporary permit program. McCormick sponsored the House version of the proposed legislation and a bill was passed extending the program for another year. Shortly thereafter, Vandergrift and McCormick discussed the possibility of introducing legislation during the 1985 session that would grant the doctors a permanent medical license by virtue of their years of experience. McCormick agreed to sponsor such legislation.

During his 1984 reelection campaign, McCormick informed Vandergrift that his campaign was expensive, that he had paid considerable sums out of his own pocket, and that he had not heard anything from the foreign doctors. Vandergrift told McCormick that he would contact the doctors and see what he could do. Vandergrift contacted one of the foreign doctors and later received from the doctors $1,200 in cash. Vandergrift delivered an envelope containing nine $100 bills to McCormick. Later the same day, a second delivery of $2,000 in cash was made to McCormick. During the fall of 1984, McCormick received two more cash payments from the doctors. McCormick did not list any of these payments as campaign contributions nor did he report the money as income on his 1984 federal income tax return. And although the doctors' organization kept detailed books of its expenditures, the cash payments were not listed as campaign contributions. Rather, the entries for the payments were accompanied only by initials or other codes signifying that the money was for McCormick.

In the spring of 1985, McCormick sponsored legislation permitting experienced doctors to be permanently licensed without passing the state licensing exams. McCormick spoke at length in favor of the bill during floor debate and the bill ultimately was enacted into law. Two weeks after the legislation was enacted, McCormick received another cash payment from the foreign doctors.

Following an investigation, a federal grand jury returned an indictment charging McCormick with five counts of violating the Hobbs Act, by extorting payments under color of official right, and with one count of filing a false income tax return in violation of 26 U.S.C. § 7206(1), by failing to report as income the cash payments he received from the foreign doctors. At the close of a 6-day trial, the jury was instructed that to establish a Hobbs Act violation the Government had to prove that Mc-Cormick induced a cash payment and that he did so knowingly and willfully by extortion. . . .

The next day the jury informed the court that it "would like to hear the instructions again with particular emphasis on the definition of extortion under the color of official right and on the law as regards the portion of moneys received that does not have to be reported as income." The court then reread most of the extortion instructions to the jury, but reordered some of the paragraphs and made the following significant addition:

> Extortion under color of official right means the obtaining of money by a public official when the money obtained was not lawfully due and owing to him or to his office. Of course, extortion does not occur where one who is a public official receives a legitimate gift or a voluntary political contribution even though the political contribution may have been made in cash in violation of local law. Voluntary is that which is freely given without expectation of benefit.

It is also worth noting that with respect to political contributions, the last two paragraphs of the supplemental instructions on the extortion counts were as follows:

> It would not be illegal, in and of itself, for Mr. McCormick to solicit or accept political contributions from foreign doctors who would benefit from this legislation.

> In order to find Mr. McCormick guilty of extortion, you must be convinced beyond a reasonable doubt that the payment alleged in a given count of the indictment was made by or on behalf of the doctors with the expectation that such payment would influence Mr. McCormick's official conduct, and with knowledge on the part of Mr. McCormick that they were paid to him with that expectation by virtue of the office he held.

The jury convicted McCormick of the first Hobbs Act count (charging him with receiving the initial $900 cash payment) and the income tax violation but could not reach verdicts on the remaining four Hobbs Act counts. The District Court declared a mistrial on those four counts.

The Court of Appeals affirmed, observing that nonelected officials may be convicted under the Hobbs Act without proof that they have granted or agreed to grant some benefit or advantage in exchange for money paid to them and that elected officials should be held to the same standard when they receive money other than "legitimate" campaign contributions. After stating that McCormick could not be prosecuted under the Hobbs Act for receiving voluntary campaign contributions, the court rejected McCormick's contention that conviction of an elected official under the Act requires, under all circumstances, proof of a *quid pro quo*, i.e., a promise of official action or inaction in exchange for any payment or property received. Rather, the court interpreted the statute as not requiring such a showing where the parties never intended the payments to be "legitimate" campaign contributions. After listing seven factors to be considered in making this determination[2] and canvassing the record evidence, the court concluded:

> Under these facts, a reasonable jury could find that McCormick was extorting money from the doctors for his continued support of the 1985 legislation. Further, the evidence supports the conclusion that the money was never intended by any of the parties to be a campaign contribution. Therefore, we refuse to reverse the jury's verdict against McCormick for violating the Hobbs Act.

. . . We agree with the Court of Appeals that in a case like this it is proper to inquire whether payments made to an elected official are in fact campaign contributions, and we agree that the intention of the parties is a relevant consideration in pursuing this inquiry. But we cannot accept the Court of Appeals' approach to distinguishing between legal and illegal campaign contributions. The Court of Appeals stated that payments to elected officials could violate the Hobbs Act without proof of an explicit *quid pro quo* by proving that the payments "were never intended to be legitimate campaign contributions." This issue, as we read the Court of Appeals' opinion, actually involved two inquiries; for after applying the factors the Court of Appeals considered relevant, it arrived at two conclusions: first, that McCormick was extorting money for his continued support of the 1985 legislation and "further" that the money was never intended by the parties to be a campaign contribution at all. The first conclusion, especially when considered in light of the second, asserts that the campaign contributions were illegitimate, extortionate payments.

This conclusion was necessarily based on the factors that the court considered, the first four of which could not possibly by themselves amount to extortion.

---

2. Later in the opinion, the Supreme Court quoted the portion of the Court of Appeals' opinion listing those factors:

"Some of the circumstances that should be considered in making this determination include, but are not limited to, (1) whether the money was recorded by the payer as a campaign contribution, (2) whether the money was recorded and reported by the official as a campaign contribution, (3) whether the payment was in cash, (4) whether it was delivered to the official personally or to his campaign, (5) whether the official acted in his official capacity at or near the time of the payment for the benefit of the payer or supported legislation that would benefit the payer, (6) whether the official had supported similar legislation before the time of the payment, and (7) whether the official had directly or indirectly solicited the payer individually for the payment."

500 U.S. at 269 n.7 (quoting 896 F.2d 61, 66 (4th Cir. 1990)).

Neither could they when considered with the last three more telling factors, namely, whether the official acted in his official capacity at or near the time of the payment for the benefit of the payer; whether the official had supported legislation before the time of the payment; and whether the official had directly or indirectly solicited the payer individually for the payment. Even assuming that the result of each of these seven inquiries was unfavorable to McCormick, as they very likely were in the Court of Appeals' view, we cannot agree that a violation of the Hobbs Act would be made out, as the Court of Appeals' first conclusion asserted.

Serving constituents and supporting legislation that will benefit the district and individuals and groups therein is the everyday business of a legislator. It is also true that campaigns must be run and financed. Money is constantly being solicited on behalf of candidates, who run on platforms and who claim support on the basis of their views and what they intend to do or have done. Whatever ethical considerations and appearances may indicate, to hold that legislators commit the federal crime of extortion when they act for the benefit of constituents or support legislation furthering the interests of some of their constituents, shortly before or after campaign contributions are solicited and received from those beneficiaries, is an unrealistic assessment of what Congress could have meant by making it a crime to obtain property from another, with his consent, "under color of official right." To hold otherwise would open to prosecution not only conduct that has long been thought to be well within the law but also conduct that in a very real sense is unavoidable so long as election campaigns are financed by private contributions or expenditures, as they have been from the beginning of the Nation. It would require statutory language more explicit than the Hobbs Act contains to justify a contrary conclusion.

This is not to say that it is impossible for an elected official to commit extortion in the course of financing an election campaign. Political contributions are of course vulnerable if induced by the use of force, violence, or fear. The receipt of such contributions is also vulnerable under the Act as having been taken under color of official right, but only if the payments are made in return for an explicit promise or undertaking by the official to perform or not to perform an official act. In such situations the official asserts that his official conduct will be controlled by the terms of the promise or undertaking. This is the receipt of money by an elected official under color of official right within the meaning of the Hobbs Act.

This formulation defines the forbidden zone of conduct with sufficient clarity. As the Court of Appeals for the Fifth Circuit observed in *United States v. Dozier*, 672 F.2d 531, 537 (5th Cir. 1982):

> A moment's reflection should enable one to distinguish, at least in the abstract, a legitimate solicitation from the exaction of a fee for a benefit conferred or an injury withheld. Whether described familiarly as a payoff or with the Latinate precision of *quid pro quo*, the prohibited exchange is the same: a public official may not demand payment as inducement for the promise to perform (or not to perform) an official act.

The United States agrees that if the payments to McCormick were campaign contributions, proof of a *quid pro quo* would be essential for an extortion conviction, and quotes the instruction given on this subject in 9 Department of Justice Manual §9-85A.306, p. 9-1938.134 (Supp. 1988-2): "campaign contributions will not be authorized as the subject of a Hobbs Act prosecution unless they can be proven to have been given in return for the performance of or abstaining from an official act; otherwise any campaign contribution might constitute a violation."

We thus disagree with the Court of Appeals' holding in this case that a *quid pro quo* is not necessary for conviction under the Hobbs Act when an official receives a campaign contribution. By the same token, we hold, as McCormick urges, that the District Court's instruction to the same effect was error.

. . . Accordingly, we reverse the judgment of the Court of Appeals and remand for further proceedings consistent with this opinion.

JUSTICE SCALIA, concurring.

I agree with the Court's conclusion and, given the assumption on which this case was briefed and argued, with the reasons the Court assigns. If the prohibition of the Hobbs Act against receipt of money "under color of official right" includes receipt of money from a private source for the performance of official duties, that ambiguously described crime assuredly need not, and for the reasons the Court discusses should not, be interpreted to cover campaign contributions with anticipation of favorable future action, as opposed to campaign contributions in exchange for an explicit promise of favorable future action.

I find it unusual and unsettling, however, to make such a distinction without any hint of a justification in the statutory text: §1951 contains not even a colorable allusion to campaign contributions or *quid pro quos*. I find it doubly unsettling because there is another interpretation of §1951, contrary to the one that has been the assumption of argument here, that would render the distinction unnecessary. While I do not feel justified in adopting that interpretation without briefing and argument, neither do I feel comfortable giving tacit approval to the assumption that contradicts it. I write, therefore, a few words concerning the text of this statute, and the history that has produced the unexamined assumption underlying our opinion.

Section 1951(a) provides: "Whoever in any way or degree obstructs, delays, or affects commerce or the movement of any article or commodity in commerce, by robbery or extortion . . . shall be fined not more than $10,000 or imprisoned not more than twenty years, or both." Section 1951(b)(2) defines "extortion" as "the obtaining of property from another, with his consent, induced by wrongful use of actual or threatened force, violence, or fear, or under color of official right." The relevant provisions were enacted as part of the Anti-Racketeering Act of 1934, and were carried forward without change in the Hobbs Act of 1948. For more than 30 years after enactment, there is no indication that they were applied to the sort of conduct alleged here.

When, in the 1960s, it first occurred to federal prosecutors to use the Hobbs Act to reach what was essentially the soliciting of bribes by state officials, courts were unimpressed with the notion. They thought that public officials were not guilty of extortion when they accepted, or even when they requested, *voluntary* payments designed to influence or procure their official action. *United States v. Hyde*, 448 F.2d 815, 833 (CA5 1971) ("The distinction from bribery is therefore . . . the fear and lack of voluntariness on the part of the victim"); *United States v. Addonizio*, 451 F.2d 49, 72 (CA3 1971) ("While the essence of bribery is voluntariness, the essence of extortion is duress"); *United States v. Kubacki*, 237 F. Supp. 638, 641 (E.D. Pa. 1965) (same). Not until 1972 did any court apply the Hobbs Act to bribery. *See United States v. Kenny*, 462 F.2d 1205, 1229 (CA3 1972) ("kickbacks" by construction contractors to public officials established extortion "under color of official right," despite absence of "threat, fear, or duress"). That holding was soon followed by the Seventh Circuit in *United States v. Braasch*, 505 F.2d 139, 151 (1974), which said that "so long as the motivation for the payment focuses on the recipient's office, the conduct falls within the ambit of 18 U.S.C. § 1951." While *Kenny, Braasch*, and subsequent cases were debated in academic writing, compare Ruff, *Federal Prosecution of Local Corruption: A Case Study in the Making of Law Enforcement Policy*, 65 Georgetown L.J. 1171 (1977) (criticizing *Kenny*), with Lindgren, *The Elusive Distinction Between Bribery and Extortion: From the Common Law to the Hobbs Act*, 35 UCLA L. Rev. 815 (1988) (defending *Kenny*), the Courts of Appeals accepted the expansion with little disagreement, and this Court has never had occasion to consider the matter.

It is acceptance of the assumption that "under color of official right" means "on account of one's office" that brings bribery cases within the statute's reach, and that creates the necessity for the reasonable but textually inexplicable distinction the Court makes today. That assumption is questionable. "The obtaining of property . . . under color of official *right*" more naturally connotes some false assertion of official *entitlement* to the property. This interpretation might have the effect of making the § 1951 definition of extortion comport with the definition of "extortion" at common law. One treatise writer, describing "extortion by a public officer," states: "At common law it was essential that the money or property be obtained under color of office, that is, under the pretense that the officer was entitled thereto by virtue of his office. The money or thing received must have been claimed or accepted in right of office, and the person paying must have yielded to official authority." 3 R. Anderson, Wharton's Criminal Law and Procedure 790–91 (1957).

It also appears to be the case that under New York law, which has long contained identical "under color of official right" language and upon which the Hobbs Act is said to have been based, bribery and extortion were separate offenses. An official charged with extortion could defend on the ground that the payment was voluntary and thus he was guilty only of bribery. I am aware of only one pre-Hobbs Act New York prosecution involving extortion "under color of official right," and there the defendant, a justice of the peace, had extracted a payment from a litigant on the false ground that it was due him as a court fee. *People v. Whaley*, 6 Cow. (N.Y.) 661, 661–63 (Sup. Ct. 1827).

Finally, where the United States Code explicitly criminalizes conduct such as that alleged in the present case, it calls the crime bribery, not extortion—and like all bribery laws I am aware of (but unlike § 1951 and all other extortion laws I am aware of) it punishes not only the person receiving the payment but the person making it. *See* 18 U.S.C. § 201(b) (criminalizing bribery of and by federal officials). *Compare* 18 U.S.C. § 872 (criminalizing extortion by federal officials, making no provision for punishment of person extorted). McCormick, though not a federal official, is subject to federal prosecution for bribery under the Travel Act, 18 U.S.C. § 1952, which criminalizes the use of interstate commerce for purposes of bribery—and reaches, of course, both the person giving and the person receiving the bribe.

I mean only to raise this argument, not to decide it, for it has not been advanced and there may be persuasive responses. *See, e.g.,* Lindgren, *supra*, at 837–89 (arguing that under early common law bribery and extortion were not separate offenses and that extortion did not require proof of a coerced payment). But unexamined assumptions have a way of becoming, by force of usage, unsound law. Before we are asked to go further down the road of making reasonable but textually unapparent distinctions in a federal "payment for official action" statute—as we unquestionably will be asked—I think it well to bear in mind that the statute may not exist.

JUSTICE STEVENS, with whom JUSTICE BLACKMUN and JUSTICE O'CONNOR join, dissenting.

. . . The extortion was completed on June 1, 1984, when Vandergrift personally delivered an envelope containing nine $100 bills to petitioner. The fact that the payment was not reported as a campaign contribution, as required by West Virginia law, or as taxable income, as required by federal law, together with other circumstantial evidence, adequately supports the conclusion that the money was intended as a payment to petitioner personally to induce him to act favorably on the licensing legislation. His covert acceptance of the cash—indeed, his denial at trial that he received any such payment—supports the conclusion that petitioner understood the payers' intention and that he had implicitly (at least) promised to provide them with the benefit that they sought.

As I understand its opinion, the Court would agree that these facts would constitute a violation of the Hobbs Act if the understanding that the money was a personal payment rather than a campaign contribution had been explicit rather than implicit and if the understanding that, in response to the payment, petitioner would endeavor to provide the payers with the specific benefit they sought had also been explicit rather than implicit. In my opinion there is no statutory requirement that illegal agreements, threats, or promises be in writing, or in any particular form. Subtle extortion is just as wrongful—and probably much more common—than the kind of express understanding that the Court's opinion seems to require.

Nevertheless, to prove a violation of the Hobbs Act, I agree with the Court that it is essential that the payment in question be contingent on a mutual understanding that the motivation for the payment is the payer's desire to avoid a specific threatened harm or to obtain a promised benefit that the defendant has the apparent power to deliver, either through the use of force or the use of public office. In this sense, the crime does require a "*quid pro quo*." Because the use of the Latin term "*quid pro quo*" tends to confuse the analysis, however, it is important to clarify the sense in which the term was used in the District Court's instructions.

As I have explained, the crime of extortion was complete when petitioner accepted the cash pursuant to an understanding that he would not carry out his earlier threat to withhold official action and instead would go forward with his contingent promise to take favorable action on behalf of the unlicensed physicians. What he did thereafter might have evidentiary significance, but could neither undo a completed crime or complete an uncommitted offense. When petitioner took the money, he was either guilty or not guilty. For that reason, proof of a subsequent *quid pro quo*—his actual support of the legislation—was not necessary for the Government's case. And conversely, evidence that petitioner would have supported the legislation anyway is not a defense to the already completed crime. The thug who extorts protection money cannot defend on the ground that his threat was only a bluff because he would not have smashed the shopkeeper's windows even if the extortion had been unsuccessful. It was in this sense that the District Court correctly advised the jury that the Government did not have to prove the delivery of a postpayment *quid pro quo*. . . .

Notes and Questions

1. Extortion or Bribery? As indicated in Justice Scalia's concurrence, the common-law crime of public official extortion was committed when "money or property [was] obtained under color of office, that is, under pretense that the officer was entitled thereto by virtue of his office." The classic example is a public official who is ostensibly collecting a government fee but instead unlawfully pockets the money.

The prosecution of McCormick illustrates how dramatically the common-law crime has been expanded so that it now can cover behavior that overlaps with the crime of bribery discussed in the next Section. As a result of this expansion, public official extortion can encompass cases where: (1) a public official (2) obtains money or property (3) improperly (4) by using the official's government office (expanding the common law's "under color of office") (5) to perform or not to perform an official act. As the Court concludes in *McCormick*, a *quid pro quo* is required and, in the case of campaign contributions, the *quid pro quo* must be explicit. In the tradition of general extortion statutes and unlike bribery, only the public official seeking the property is guilty of the crime. *See* James Lindgren, *The Elusive Distinction Between Bribery and Extortion: From the Common Law to the Hobbs Act*, 35 UCLA L. Rev. 815 (1988).

Public official ("color of office") extortion should be distinguished from the general statutory crime of extortion defined and discussed above in *Harrington* and

Jackson. (For further discussion of the early common-law view, see Note 2 following *Harrington.*)

2. Campaign Contributions. Can a principled distinction be made between legitimate and criminal solicitations of campaign contributions by public officials? Is the current line sufficiently clear?

[C] Bribery

McDonnell v. United States
136 S. Ct. 2355 (2016)

CHIEF JUSTICE ROBERTS delivered the opinion of the Court.

In 2014, the Federal Government indicted former Virginia Governor Robert McDonnell and his wife, Maureen McDonnell, on bribery charges. The charges related to the acceptance by the McDonnells of $175,000 in loans, gifts, and other benefits from Virginia businessman Jonnie Williams, while Governor McDonnell was in office. . . .

To convict the McDonnells of bribery, the Government was required to show that Governor McDonnell committed (or agreed to commit) an "official act" in exchange for the loans and gifts. The parties did not agree, however, on what counts as an "official act." The Government alleged in the indictment, and maintains on appeal, that Governor McDonnell committed at least five "official acts." Those acts included "arranging meetings" for Williams with other Virginia officials to discuss [a] product [developed by Williams's company], "hosting" events for [the company] at the Governor's Mansion, and "contacting other government officials" concerning studies of [the product]. The Government also argued more broadly that these activities constituted "official action" because they related to Virginia business development, a priority of Governor McDonnell's administration. Governor McDonnell contends that merely setting up a meeting, hosting an event, or contacting an official — without more — does not count as an "official act."

At trial, the District Court instructed the jury according to the Government's broad understanding of what constitutes an "official act," and the jury convicted both Governor and Mrs. McDonnell on the bribery charges. The Fourth Circuit affirmed Governor McDonnell's conviction, and we granted review to clarify the meaning of "official act."

I

A

On November 3, 2009, petitioner Robert McDonnell was elected the 71st Governor of Virginia. His campaign slogan was "Bob's for Jobs," and his focus in office was on promoting business in Virginia. As Governor, McDonnell spoke about economic development in Virginia "on a daily basis" and attended numerous "events, ribbon cuttings," and "plant facility openings." He also referred thousands of constituents to meetings with members of his staff and other government officials. According to longtime staffers, Governor McDonnell likely had more events at the Virginia Governor's Mansion to promote Virginia business than had occurred in "any other administration."

This case concerns Governor McDonnell's interactions with one of his constituents, Virginia businessman Jonnie Williams. Williams was the CEO of Star Scientific, a Virginia-based company that developed and marketed Anatabloc, a nutritional supplement made from anatabine, a compound found in tobacco. Star Scientific hoped to obtain Food and Drug Administration approval of Anatabloc as an anti-inflammatory drug. An important step in securing that approval was initiating independent research studies on the health benefits of anatabine. Star Scientific hoped Virginia's public universities would undertake such studies, pursuant to a grant from Virginia's Tobacco Commission.

Governor McDonnell first met Williams in 2009, when Williams offered McDonnell transportation on his private airplane to assist with McDonnell's election campaign. Shortly after the election, Williams had dinner with Governor and Mrs. McDonnell at a restaurant in New York. The conversation turned to Mrs. McDonnell's search for a dress for the inauguration, which led Williams to offer to purchase a gown for her. Governor McDonnell's counsel later instructed Williams not to buy the dress, and Mrs. McDonnell told Williams that she would take a rain check.

In October 2010, Governor McDonnell and Williams met again on Williams's plane. During the flight, Williams told Governor McDonnell that he "needed his help" moving forward on the research studies at Virginia's public universities, and he asked to be introduced to the person that he "needed to talk to." Governor McDonnell agreed to introduce Williams to Dr. William Hazel, Virginia's Secretary of Health and Human Resources. Williams met with Dr. Hazel the following month, but the meeting was unfruitful; Dr. Hazel was skeptical of the science behind Anatabloc and did not assist Williams in obtaining the studies.

Six months later, Governor McDonnell's wife . . . offered to seat Williams next to the Governor at a political rally. Shortly before the event, Williams took Mrs. McDonnell on a shopping trip and bought her $20,000 worth of designer clothing. The McDonnells later had Williams over for dinner at the Governor's Mansion, where they discussed research studies on Anatabloc.

Two days after that dinner, Williams had an article about Star Scientific's research e-mailed to Mrs. McDonnell, which she forwarded to her husband. Less than an hour later, Governor McDonnell texted his sister to discuss the financial situation of certain rental properties they owned in Virginia Beach. Governor McDonnell also e-mailed his daughter to ask about expenses for her upcoming wedding.

The next day, Williams returned to the Governor's Mansion for a meeting with Mrs. McDonnell. At the meeting, Mrs. McDonnell described the family's financial problems, including their struggling rental properties in Virginia Beach and their daughter's wedding expenses. Mrs. McDonnell, who had experience selling nutritional supplements, told Williams that she had a background in the area and could help him with Anatabloc. According to Williams, she explained that the "Governor says it's okay for me to help you and — but I need you to help me. I need you to help me with this financial situation." Mrs. McDonnell then asked Williams for a $50,000 loan, in addition to a $15,000 gift to help pay for her daughter's wedding, and Williams agreed.

Williams testified that he called Governor McDonnell after the meeting and said, "I understand the financial problems and I'm willing to help. I just wanted to make sure that you knew about this." According to Williams, Governor McDonnell thanked him for his help. Governor McDonnell testified, in contrast, that he did not know about the loan at the time, and that when he learned of it he was upset that Mrs. McDonnell had requested the loan from Williams. Three days after the meeting between Williams and Mrs. McDonnell, Governor McDonnell directed his assistant to forward the article on Star Scientific to Dr. Hazel.

In June 2011, Williams sent Mrs. McDonnell's chief of staff a letter containing a proposed research protocol for the Anatabloc studies. The letter was addressed to Governor McDonnell, and it suggested that the Governor "use the attached protocol to initiate the 'Virginia Study' of Anatabloc at the Medical College of Virginia and the University of Virginia School of Medicine." Governor McDonnell gave the letter to Dr. Hazel. Williams testified at trial that he did not "recall any response" to the letter.

In July 2011, the McDonnell family visited Williams's vacation home for the weekend, and Governor McDonnell borrowed Williams's Ferrari while there. Shortly thereafter, Governor McDonnell asked Dr. Hazel to send an aide to a meeting with Williams and Mrs. McDonnell to discuss research studies on Anatabloc. The aide later testified that she did not feel pressured by Governor or Mrs. McDonnell to do "anything other than have the meeting," and that Williams did not ask anything of her at the meeting. After the meeting, the aide sent Williams a "polite blow-off" e-mail.

At a subsequent meeting at the Governor's Mansion, Mrs. McDonnell admired Williams's Rolex and mentioned that she wanted to get one for Governor McDonnell. Williams asked if Mrs. McDonnell wanted him to purchase a Rolex for the Governor, and Mrs. McDonnell responded, "Yes, that would be nice." Williams did so, and Mrs. McDonnell later gave the Rolex to Governor McDonnell as a Christmas present.

In August 2011, the McDonnells hosted a lunch event for Star Scientific at the Governor's Mansion. According to Williams, the purpose of the event was to launch

Anatabloc. According to Governor McDonnell's gubernatorial counsel, however, it was just lunch.

The guest list for the event included researchers at the University of Virginia and Virginia Commonwealth University. During the event, Star Scientific distributed free samples of Anatabloc, in addition to eight $25,000 checks that researchers could use in preparing grant proposals for studying Anatabloc. Governor McDonnell asked researchers at the event whether they thought "there was some scientific validity" to Anatabloc and "whether or not there was any reason to explore this further." He also asked whether this could "be something good for the Commonwealth, particularly as it relates to economy or job creation." When Williams asked Governor McDonnell whether he would support funding for the research studies, Governor McDonnell "very politely" replied, "I have limited decision-making power in this area."

In January 2012, Mrs. McDonnell asked Williams for an additional loan for the Virginia Beach rental properties, and Williams agreed. On February 3, Governor McDonnell followed up on that conversation by calling Williams to discuss a $50,000 loan.

Several days later, Williams complained to Mrs. McDonnell that the Virginia universities were not returning Star Scientific's calls. She passed Williams's complaint on to the Governor. While Mrs. McDonnell was driving with Governor McDonnell, she also e-mailed Governor McDonnell's counsel, stating that the Governor "wants to know why nothing has developed" with the research studies after Williams had provided the eight $25,000 checks for preparing grant proposals, and that the Governor "wants to get this going" at the universities. According to Governor McDonnell, however, Mrs. McDonnell acted without his knowledge or permission, and he never made the statements she attributed to him.

On February 16, Governor McDonnell e-mailed Williams to check on the status of documents related to the $50,000 loan. A few minutes later, Governor McDonnell e-mailed his counsel stating, "Please see me about Anatabloc issues at VCU and UVA. Thanks." Governor McDonnell's counsel replied, "Will do. We need to be careful with this issue." The next day, Governor McDonnell's counsel called Star Scientific's lobbyist in order to "change the expectations" of Star Scientific regarding the involvement of the Governor's Office in the studies.

At the end of February, Governor McDonnell hosted a healthcare industry reception at the Governor's Mansion, which Williams attended. Mrs. McDonnell also invited a number of guests recommended by Williams, including researchers at the Virginia universities. Governor McDonnell was present, but did not mention Star Scientific, Williams, or Anatabloc during the event. That same day, Governor McDonnell and Williams spoke about the $50,000 loan, and Williams loaned the money to the McDonnells shortly thereafter.

In March 2012, Governor McDonnell met with Lisa Hicks-Thomas, the Virginia Secretary of Administration, and Sara Wilson, the Director of the Virginia Department of Human Resource Management. The purpose of the meeting was to discuss

Virginia's health plan for state employees. At that time, Governor McDonnell was taking Anatabloc several times a day. He took a pill during the meeting, and told Hicks-Thomas and Wilson that the pills "were working well for him" and "would be good for" state employees. Hicks-Thomas recalled Governor McDonnell asking them to meet with a representative from Star Scientific; Wilson had no such recollection. After the discussion with Governor McDonnell, Hicks-Thomas and Wilson looked up Anatabloc on the Internet, but they did not set up a meeting with Star Scientific or conduct any other follow-up. It is undisputed that Virginia's health plan for state employees does not cover nutritional supplements such as Anatabloc.

In May 2012, Governor McDonnell requested an additional $20,000 loan, which Williams provided. Throughout this period, Williams also paid for several rounds of golf for Governor McDonnell and his children, took the McDonnells on a weekend trip, and gave $10,000 as a wedding gift to one of the McDonnells' daughters. In total, Williams gave the McDonnells over $175,000 in gifts and loans.

B

In January 2014, Governor McDonnell was indicted for accepting payments, loans, gifts, and other things of value from Williams and Star Scientific in exchange for "performing official actions on an as-needed basis, as opportunities arose, to legitimize, promote, and obtain research studies for Star Scientific's products." The charges against him comprised one count of conspiracy to commit honest services fraud, three counts of honest services fraud, one count of conspiracy to commit Hobbs Act extortion, six counts of Hobbs Act extortion, and two counts of making a false statement. *See* 18 U.S C. §§ 1343, 1349 (honest services fraud); § 1951(a) (Hobbs Act extortion); § 1014 (false statement). Mrs. McDonnell was indicted on similar charges, plus obstructing official proceedings, based on her alleged involvement in the scheme. *See* § 1512(c)(2) (obstruction).

The theory underlying both the honest services fraud and Hobbs Act extortion charges was that Governor McDonnell had accepted bribes from Williams.

The parties agreed that they would define honest services fraud with reference to the federal bribery statute, 18 U. S. C. § 201. That statute makes it a crime for "a public official or person selected to be a public official, directly or indirectly, corruptly" to demand, seek, receive, accept, or agree "to receive or accept anything of value" in return for being "influenced in the performance of any official act." § 201(b)(2). An "official act" is defined as "any decision or action on any question, matter, cause, suit, proceeding or controversy, which may at any time be pending, or which may by law be brought before any public official, in such official's official capacity, or in such official's place of trust or profit." § 201(a)(3).

The parties also agreed that obtaining a "thing of value . . . knowing that the thing of value was given in return for official action" was an element of Hobbs Act extortion, and that they would use the definition of "official act" found in the federal bribery statute to define "official action" under the Hobbs Act.

As a result of all this, the Government was required to prove that Governor McDonnell committed or agreed to commit an "official act" in exchange for the loans and gifts from Williams.

The Government alleged that Governor McDonnell had committed at least five "official acts":

(1) "arranging meetings for [Williams] with Virginia government officials, who were subordinates of the Governor, to discuss and promote Anatabloc";

(2) "hosting, and . . . attending, events at the Governor's Mansion designed to encourage Virginia university researchers to initiate studies of anatabine and to promote Star Scientific's products to doctors for referral to their patients";

(3) "contacting other government officials in the [Governor's Office] as part of an effort to encourage Virginia state research universities to initiate studies of anatabine";

(4) "promoting Star Scientific's products and facilitating its relationships with Virginia government officials by allowing [Williams] to invite individuals important to Star Scientific's business to exclusive events at the Governor's Mansion"; and

(5) "recommending that senior government officials in the [Governor's Office] meet with Star Scientific executives to discuss ways that the company's products could lower healthcare costs."

The case proceeded to a jury trial, which lasted five weeks. Pursuant to an immunity agreement, Williams testified that he had given the gifts and loans to the McDonnells to obtain the Governor's "help with the testing" of Anatabloc at Virginia's medical schools. Governor McDonnell acknowledged that he had requested loans and accepted gifts from Williams. He testified, however, that setting up meetings with government officials was something he did "literally thousands of times" as Governor, and that he did not expect his staff "to do anything other than to meet" with Williams.

. . . .

The jury convicted Governor McDonnell on the honest services fraud and Hobbs Act extortion charges, but acquitted him on the false statement charges. Mrs. McDonnell was also convicted on most of the charges against her. Although the Government requested a sentence of at least ten years for Governor McDonnell, the District Court sentenced him to two years in prison. Mrs. McDonnell received a one-year sentence.

. . . .

II

The issue in this case is the proper interpretation of the term "official act." . . .

According to the Government, "Congress used intentionally broad language" in § 201(a)(3) to embrace "*any* decision or action, on *any* question or matter, that may at *any time* be pending, or which may by law be brought before *any* public official, in such official's official capacity." The Government concludes that the term "official act" therefore encompasses nearly any activity by a public official. In the Government's view, "official act" specifically includes arranging a meeting, contacting another public official, or hosting an event — without more — concerning any subject, including a broad policy issue such as Virginia economic development.

Governor McDonnell, in contrast, contends that statutory context compels a more circumscribed reading, limiting "official acts" to those acts that "direct[ ] a particular resolution of a specific governmental decision," or that pressure another official to do so. He also claims that "vague corruption laws" such as § 201 implicate serious constitutional concerns, militating "in favor of a narrow, cautious reading of these criminal statutes."

Taking into account the text of the statute, the precedent of this Court, and the constitutional concerns raised by Governor McDonnell, we reject the Government's reading of § 201(a)(3) and adopt a more bounded interpretation of "official act." Under that interpretation, setting up a meeting, calling another public official, or hosting an event does not, standing alone, qualify as an "official act."

A

The text of § 201(a)(3) sets forth two requirements for an "official act": First, the Government must identify a "question, matter, cause, suit, proceeding or controversy" that "may at any time be pending" or "may by law be brought" before a public official. Second, the Government must prove that the public official made a decision or took an action "on" that question, matter, cause, suit, proceeding, or controversy, or agreed to do so. The issue here is whether arranging a meeting, contacting another official, or hosting an event — without more — can be a "question, matter, cause, suit, proceeding or controversy," and if not, whether it can be a decision or action on a "question, matter, cause, suit, proceeding or controversy."

The first inquiry is whether a typical meeting, call, or event is itself a "question, matter, cause, suit, proceeding or controversy." The Government argues that nearly any activity by a public official qualifies as a question or matter—from workaday functions, such as the typical call, meeting, or event, to the broadest issues the government confronts, such as fostering economic development. We conclude, however, that the terms "question, matter cause, suit, proceeding or controversy" do not sweep so broadly.

The last four words in that list — "cause," "suit," "proceeding," and "controversy" — connote a formal exercise of governmental power, such as a lawsuit, hearing, or administrative determination.

. . . .

But what about a "question" or "matter"? A "question" could mean any "subject or aspect that is in dispute, open for discussion, or to be inquired into," and a "matter" any "subject" of "interest or relevance." Webster's Third New International Dictionary 1394, 1863 (1961). If those meanings were adopted, a typical meeting, call, or event would qualify as a "question" or "matter." A "question" may also be interpreted more narrowly, however, as "a subject or point of debate or a proposition being or to be voted on in a meeting," such as a question "before the senate." *Id.* at 1863. Similarly, a "matter" may be limited to "a topic under active and usually serious or practical consideration," such as a matter that "will come before the committee." *Id.* at 1394.

To choose between those competing definitions, we look to the context in which the words appear. Under the familiar interpretive canon *noscitur a sociis*, "a word is known by the company it keeps." While "not an inescapable rule," this canon "is often wisely applied where a word is capable of many meanings in order to avoid the giving of unintended breadth to the Acts of Congress."

. . . .

Applying that . . . approach here, we conclude that a "question" or "matter" must be similar in nature to a "cause, suit, proceeding or controversy." Because a typical meeting, call, or event arranged by a public official is not of the same stripe as a lawsuit before a court, a determination before an agency, or a hearing before a committee, it does not qualify as a "question" or "matter" under § 201(a)(3).

. . . .

For its part, the Fourth Circuit found at least three questions or matters at issue in this case:

(1) "whether researchers at any of Virginia's state universities would initiate a study of Anatabloc"; (2) "whether the state-created Tobacco Indemnification and Community Revitalization Commission" would "allocate grant money for the study of anatabine"; and (3) "whether the health insurance plan for state employees in Virginia would include Anatabloc as a covered drug." We agree that those qualify as questions or matters under § 201(a)(3). Each is focused and concrete, and each involves a formal exercise of governmental power that is similar in nature to a lawsuit, administrative determination, or hearing.

The question remains whether — as the Government argues — merely setting up a meeting, hosting an event, or calling another official qualifies as a decision or action on any of those three questions or matters. Although the word "decision," and especially the word "action," could be read expansively to support the Government's view, our opinion in *United States v. Sun-Diamond Growers of Cal.*, 526 U. S. 398 (1999), rejects that interpretation.

In *Sun-Diamond*, the Court stated that it was not an "official act" under § 201 for the President to host a championship sports team at the White House, the Secretary of Education to visit a high school, or the Secretary of Agriculture to deliver a speech to "farmers concerning various matters of USDA policy." We recognized that "the Secretary of Agriculture *always* has before him or in prospect matters that affect farmers, just as the President always has before him or in prospect matters that affect college and professional sports, and the Secretary of Education matters that affect high schools." But we concluded that the existence of such pending matters was not enough to find that any action related to them constituted an "official act." It was possible to avoid the "absurdities" of convicting individuals on corruption charges for engaging in such conduct, we explained, "*through the definition of that term,*" i.e., by adopting a more limited definition of "official acts."

It is apparent from *Sun-Diamond* that hosting an event, meeting with other officials, or speaking with interested parties is not, standing alone, a "decision or action" within the meaning of § 201(a)(3), even if the event, meeting, or speech is related to a pending question or matter. Instead, something more is required: § 201(a)(3) specifies that the public official must make a decision or take an action *on* that question or matter, or agree to do so.

. . . .

Under this Court's precedents, a public official is not required to actually make a decision or take an action on a "question, matter, cause, suit, proceeding or controversy"; it is enough that the official agree to do so. The agreement need not be explicit, and the public official need not specify the means that he will use to perform his end of the bargain. Nor must the public official in fact intend to perform the "official act," so long as he agrees to do so. A jury could, for example, conclude that an agreement was reached if the evidence shows that the public official received a thing of value knowing that it was given with the expectation that the official would perform an "official act" in return. It is up to the jury, under the facts of the case, to determine whether the public official agreed to perform an "official act" at the time of the alleged *quid pro quo.* . . .

Setting up a meeting, hosting an event, or calling an official (or agreeing to do so) merely to talk about a research study or to gather additional information, however, does not qualify as a decision or action on the pending question of whether to initiate the study. Simply expressing support for the research study at a meeting, event, or call—or sending a subordinate to such a meeting, event, or call—similarly does not qualify as a decision or action on the study, as long as the public official does not intend to exert pressure on another official or provide advice, knowing or intending such advice to form the basis for an "official act." Otherwise, if every action somehow related to the research study were an "official act," the requirement that the public official make a decision or take an action on that study, or agree to do so, would be meaningless.

Of course, this is not to say that setting up a meeting, hosting an event, or making a phone call is always an innocent act, or is irrelevant, in cases like this one. If an official sets up a meeting, hosts an event, or makes a phone call on a question or matter that is or could be pending before another official, that could serve as evidence of an agreement to take an official act. A jury could conclude, for example, that the official was attempting to pressure or advise another official on a pending matter. And if the official agreed to exert that pressure or give that advice in exchange for a thing of value, that would be illegal.

The Government relies on this Court's decision in [*United States v. Birdsall*, 223 U.S. 223 (1914),] to support a more expansive interpretation of "official act," but *Birdsall* is fully consistent with our reading of § 201(a)(3). We held in *Birdsall* that "official action" could be established by custom rather than "by statute" or "a written rule or regulation," and need not be a formal part of an official's decisionmaking process. That does not mean, however, that every decision or action customarily performed by a public official—such as the myriad decisions to refer a constituent to another official—counts as an "official act." The "official action" at issue in *Birdsall* was "advis[ing] the Commissioner of Indian Affairs, contrary to the truth," that the facts of the case warranted granting leniency to certain defendants convicted of "unlawfully selling liquor to Indians." That "decision or action" fits neatly within our understanding of § 201(a)(3): It reflected a decision or action to advise another official on the pending question whether to grant leniency.

In sum, an "official act" is a decision or action on a "question, matter, cause, suit, proceeding or controversy." The "question, matter, cause, suit, proceeding or controversy" must involve a formal exercise of governmental power that is similar in nature to a lawsuit before a court, a determination before an agency, or a hearing before a committee. It must also be something specific and focused that is "pending" or "may by law be brought" before a public official. To qualify as an "official act," the public official must make a decision or take an action on that "question, matter, cause, suit, proceeding or controversy," or agree to do so. That decision or action may include using his official position to exert pressure on another official to perform an "official act," or to advise another official, knowing or intending that such advice will form the basis for an "official act" by another official. Setting up a meeting, talking to another official, or organizing an event (or agreeing to do so)—without more—does not fit that definition of "official act."

B

In addition to being inconsistent with both text and precedent, the Government's expansive interpretation of "official act" would raise significant constitutional concerns. Section 201 prohibits *quid pro quo* corruption—the exchange of a thing of value for an "official act." In the Government's view, nearly anything a public official accepts—from a campaign contribution to lunch—counts as a *quid*; and nearly anything a public official does—from arranging a meeting to inviting a guest to an event—counts as a *quo*.

But conscientious public officials arrange meetings for constituents, contact other officials on their behalf, and include them in events all the time. The basic compact underlying representative government *assumes* that public officials will hear from their constituents and act appropriately on their concerns—whether it is the union official worried about a plant closing or the homeowners who wonder why it took five days to restore power to their neighborhood after a storm. The Government's position could cast a pall of potential prosecution over these relationships if the union had given a campaign contribution in the past or the homeowners invited the official to join them on their annual outing to the ballgame. Officials might wonder whether they could respond to even the most commonplace requests for assistance, and citizens with legitimate concerns might shrink from participating in democratic discourse.

. . . .

None of this, of course, is to suggest that the facts of this case typify normal political interaction between public officials and their constituents. Far from it. But the Government's legal interpretation is not confined to cases involving extravagant gifts or large sums of money, and we cannot construe a criminal statute on the assumption that the Government will "use it responsibly." The Court in *Sun-Diamond* declined to rely on "the Government's discretion" to protect against overzealous prosecutions under § 201, concluding instead that "a statute in this field that can linguistically be interpreted to be either a meat axe or a scalpel should reasonably be taken to be the latter."

A related concern is that, under the Government's interpretation, the term "official act" is not defined "with sufficient definiteness that ordinary people can understand what conduct is prohibited," or "in a manner that does not encourage arbitrary and discriminatory enforcement." Under the "standardless sweep" of the Government's reading, public officials could be subject to prosecution, without fair notice, for the most prosaic interactions. "Invoking so shapeless a provision to condemn someone to prison" for up to 15 years raises the serious concern that the provision "does not comport with the Constitution's guarantee of due process." Our more constrained interpretation of § 201(a)(3) avoids this "vagueness shoal."

. . . .

III

Governor McDonnell argues that his convictions must be vacated because the jury was improperly instructed on the meaning of "official act" under § 201(a)(3) of the federal bribery statute. According to Governor McDonnell, the District Court "refused to convey any meaningful limits on 'official act,' giving an instruction that allowed the jury to convict [him] for lawful conduct." We agree.

The jury instructions included the statutory definition of "official action," and further defined the term to include "actions that have been clearly established by settled practice as part of a public official's position, even if the action was not taken pursuant to responsibilities explicitly assigned by law." The instructions also stated that "official actions may include acts that a public official customarily performs," including acts "in furtherance of longer-term goals" or "in a series of steps to exercise influence or achieve an end." In light of our interpretation of the term "official acts," those instructions lacked important qualifications, rendering them significantly overinclusive.

First, the instructions did not adequately explain to the jury how to identify the "question, matter, cause, suit, proceeding or controversy." . . .

Second, the instructions did not inform the jury that the "question, matter, cause, suit, proceeding or controversy" must be more specific and focused than a broad policy objective. The Government told the jury in its closing argument that "[w]hatever it was" Governor McDonnell had done, "it's all official action." Based on that remark, and the repeated references to "Bob's for Jobs" at trial, the jury could have thought that the relevant "question, matter, cause, suit, proceeding or controversy" was something as nebulous as "Virginia business and economic development," as the District Court itself concluded. To avoid that misconception, the District Court should have instructed the jury that the pertinent "question, matter, cause, suit, proceeding or controversy" must be something specific and focused that is "pending" or "may by law be brought before any public official," such as the question whether to initiate the research studies.

Third, the District Court did not instruct the jury that to convict Governor McDonnell, it had to find that he made a decision or took an action — or agreed to do so — on the identified "question, matter, cause, suit, proceeding or controversy," as we have construed that requirement. At trial, several of Governor McDonnell's subordinates testified that he asked them to attend a meeting, not that he expected them to do anything other than that. If that testimony reflects what Governor McDonnell agreed to do at the time he accepted the loans and gifts from Williams, then he did not agree to make a decision or take an action on any of the three questions or matters described by the Fourth Circuit.

The jury may have disbelieved that testimony or found other evidence that Governor McDonnell agreed to exert pressure on those officials to initiate the research studies or add Anatabloc to the state health plan, but it is also possible that the jury convicted Governor McDonnell without finding that he agreed to make a decision or take an action on a properly defined "question, matter, cause, suit, proceeding or controversy." To forestall that possibility, the District Court should have instructed the jury that merely arranging a meeting or hosting an event to discuss a matter does not count as a decision or action on that matter.

Because the jury was not correctly instructed on the meaning of "official act," it may have convicted Governor McDonnell for conduct that is not unlawful. . . .

There is no doubt that this case is distasteful; it may be worse than that. But our concern is not with tawdry tales of Ferraris, Rolexes, and ball gowns. It is instead with the broader legal implications of the Government's boundless interpretation of the federal bribery statute. A more limited interpretation of the term "official act" leaves ample room for prosecuting corruption, while comporting with the text of the statute and the precedent of this Court.

Notes and Questions

1. Introduction. Bribery is a crime committed by both the giver and the recipient of a payment, and its definition therefore depends on which party's point of view is being described. As the Supreme Court explained in *United States v. Sun-Diamond Growers*, 526 U.S. 398, 404 (1999), bribery exists when "something of value is corruptly given, offered or promised to a public official (as to the giver) or corruptly demanded, sought, received, accepted or agreed to be received or accepted by the public official (as to the recipient) with intent . . . to influence any official act (giver) or in return for being influenced in the performance of any official act (recipient)."

Given this language and the prior decision in *McCormick* (excerpted above in Section B), should anyone have been surprised by the Court's unanimous ruling in *McDonnell*? Justice Scalia wrote the Court's unanimous opinion in *Sun-Diamond Growers*, and Chief Justice Roberts relied upon that decision in *McDonnell*. Note, however, that *McDonnell* does not cite *McCormick*. Is that because *McCormick* had three dissenters, or because Justice Scalia's concurring opinion in *McCormick* suggested the Court might have interpreted the Hobbs Act differently if the case had been briefed and argued differently? Is it surprising that the trial judge and the Fourth Circuit in *McDonnell* reasoned as they did in light of the prior two cases?

Before the 14-count indictment was filed against the McDonnells, the Governor reportedly refused to accept the prosecution's offer to let him plead guilty to one felony fraud count and to forgo prosecution of his wife. *See* Rosalind S. Helderman & Carol D. Leonnig, *Ex-Va. Governor Rejected Plea Deal*, WASH. POST, Jan. 24, 2014, at A1. Following the Supreme Court's decision, prosecutors dropped all charges against the McDonnells. *See* Alan Blinder, *U.S. Ends Corruption Case Against Former Governor of Virginia*, N.Y. TIMES, Sept. 9, 2016, at A11.

2. The Mens Rea Requirement. As one commentator noted, a bribery charge requires proof of "a corrupt intent, i.e., from the standpoint of the briber, an intent to influence official action, or, from the standpoint of the bribee, an intent to use his public office as a means of acquiring an unlawful benefit." CHARLES E. TORCIA, 4 WHARTON'S CRIMINAL LAW § 646, at 469–70 (15th ed. 1996). Those who pay money to a public employee therefore do not commit the crime of bribery unless they intended to influence the public employee's performance of official duties. Consequently, in *People v. Powell*, 362 N.E.2d 1329 (Ill. App. Ct. 1977), a lawyer who gave a police officer $250 was acquitted because it could not be proven that the payment was intended to influence an investigation. In *United States v. Kim*, 738 F. Supp. 1002 (E.D. Va. 1990), on the other hand, a defendant was convicted of bribery when he wrote the Immigration and Naturalization Service (INS) to report a man illegally residing in this country, later called INS agents to check on the status of the investigation, and then sent them $500 in cash to do him a "favor . . . quicker."

3. The Model Penal Code. The Model Penal Code's approach to bribery abandons the common-law focus on "corrupt" agreements and "corrupt" motives. Instead, §§ 240.1–240.7 of the Code specify with particularity the types of arrangements that are prohibited. For example, § 240.1, which governs bribery in official and political matters, provides as follows:

> A person is guilty of bribery, a felony of the third degree, if he offers, confers or agrees to confer upon another, or solicits, accepts or agrees to accept from another:
>
> (1) any pecuniary benefit as consideration for the recipient's decision, opinion, recommendation, vote or other exercise of discretion as a public servant, party official or voter; or
>
> (2) any benefit as consideration for the recipient's decision, vote, recommendation or exercise of official discretion in a judicial or administrative proceeding; or
>
> (3) any benefit as consideration for a violation of a known legal duty as public servant or party official.
>
> It is no defense to prosecution under this section that a person whom the actor sought to influence was not qualified to act in the desired way whether because he had not yet assumed office, or lacked jurisdiction, or for any other reason.

4. The Crime Is Complete with the Offer or Solicitation. A defendant is guilty of committing bribery once a bribe is offered or solicited. Thus, the prosecution need not prove that the purpose for which the bribe was offered was actually accomplished. In *State v. Walker*, 657 S.W.2d 704 (Mo. Ct. App. 1983), for example, the defendant offered the mayor of Pagedale, Missouri, money and other benefits if the city would withdraw from a lawsuit challenging the legality of a tax increase measure that the defendant wanted placed on the ballot. The defendant was found guilty of bribery even though the mayor did not act on his request.

In *United States v. Mazzio*, 501 F. Supp. 340 (E.D. Pa. 1980), the defendants were convicted of bribing police officers in order to further their gambling activities. The defendants contended that they could not be found guilty of bribery because they had given money to an undercover police officer who had no intention to perform any "service" in return for the money. The court held that the unwillingness of the recipient of a bribe to perform the actions desired by the payer is not a defense because "the gravamen of the offense of bribery is the solicitation or acceptance of a bribe, not the delivery of its quid pro quo." *Id.* at 343. *See* ROLLIN M. PERKINS & RONALD N. BOYCE, CRIMINAL LAW 536 (3d ed. 1982).

Likewise, it is irrelevant whether or not the bribe was ever paid. In *United States v. Rasco*, 853 F.2d 501 (7th Cir. 1988), the defendant challenged his bribery conviction on the ground that the government failed to establish the exact value of the bribe. The court rejected this argument, noting that the prosecution was only required to "prove that a thing of value was offered." *Id.* at 504.

Finally, the crime is committed even if the public official was legally bound to perform the act or would have done so even without the inducement of a bribe. In

United States v. Jannotti, 673 F.2d 578 (3d Cir. 1982) (en banc), two members of the Philadelphia City Council accepted money from undercover FBI agents in exchange for their support and influence in voting on a proposed hotel project. In rejecting the defendants' argument that their concerns about the legitimacy of the hotel project helped establish that the payments were benign, the court observed that "it is neither material nor a defense to bribery that 'had there been no bribe, the [public official] might, on the available data, lawfully and properly have made the very recommendation that [the briber] wanted him to make.'" *Id.* at 601.

5. Using Official Influence. The Supreme Court's decision in *McConnell* defined "official acts" to exclude the procurement of government access by itself. Do you agree with the Court that a more expansive definition of official acts would blur the line between criminality and constituent services? When is it bribery to make a contribution to a state attorney general who is investigating allegations against one's business? When is it bribery to give a donor to a private foundation access to government officials who have ties to the foundation?

Consider also *State v. Bowling*, 427 P.2d 928 (Ariz. Ct. App. 1967), where the court held that a state legislator who accepted $5,000 to advocate on behalf of a client seeking a new liquor license before the state superintendent of liquor licenses was not guilty of bribery because procurement of liquor licenses was not part of state legislators' official acts — even though the liquor board's budget was allocated by the state legislature. The *Bowling* court took a narrow view of what functions fall within a legislator's official duties. Indeed, the Arizona legislature subsequently passed a statute criminalizing "influence peddling" by state employees. *See* Ariz. Rev. Stat. § 13-2606 (provision added in 1980 making it a felony to "intentionally or knowingly obtain or seek to obtain any benefit from another person upon a claim or representation that he can or will improperly influence the action of a public servant").

Consider, in contrast, *Commonwealth v. Bellis*, 399 A.2d 397 (Pa. 1979), where a member of Philadelphia's City Council was convicted of bribery for accepting a total of $62,000 in exchange for representing several corporations that were seeking licenses and contracts from the city. Unlike the bribery statute at issue in *Bowling*, *Bellis* was decided under Pennsylvania's broad bribery statute, which was intended to secure employees' "undivided loyalty" to their employer. *Id.* at 400. Bellis represented these companies before various city departments and agencies, although it was undisputed that he did not actually do anything in the city council for them. Nevertheless, the court concluded that the bribery statute did "not require that the bribe influence or intend to influence a matter that is within the [public official's] official duties," but instead required only that the official accept money "as an inducement, bribe or reward . . . for showing any favor or disfavor in relation to the affairs or business of his principal, employer, or master." *Id.* at 399. Given that the defendant helped negotiate contracts between the city and private parties, and these contracts certainly related to the city's affairs, the court affirmed his bribery conviction.

It is common for state legislators, as well as county and local officials, to maintain private law practices. Should public officials be allowed to practice law? Under what circumstances would their representation of clients run afoul of the bribery laws?

6. Hiring Children of Foreign Government Officials. JPMorgan Chase bank and its Hong Kong subsidiary agreed in a civil settlement with the Securities and Exchange Commission and the Federal Reserve to pay $264 million and avoid criminal punishment for the *quid pro quo* hiring of Chinese government officials' children in exchange for contracts from Chinese government-run companies. Federal officials are also reportedly investigating the hiring practices of other major banks as well. *See* Ben Protess & Alexandra Stevenson, *For Using Jobs to Entice China's Elite, Chase Agrees to Pay a $264 Million Penalty*, N.Y. Times, Nov. 18, 2016, at B1. When should a firm's hiring of the child of a client or potential client constitute bribery? Should *quid pro quo* be required to impose criminal liability? Should such hiring decisions be viewed as acceptable client development or favors among business associates?

7. Illegal Gratuities. The federal illegal gratuity statute makes it a crime to "directly or indirectly give, offer, or promise anything of value to any public official, former public official, or person selected to be a public official, for or because of any official act performed or to be performed by such public official." 18 U.S.C. § 201(c)(1)(A). In *United States v. Sun-Diamond Growers*, 526 U.S. 398 (1999), a trade association was convicted of violating that statute because it gave then-Secretary of Agriculture Michael Espy gratuities worth $5,900, including tickets to the U.S. Open Tennis Tournament, luggage, meals, a framed print, and a crystal bowl. The Supreme Court contrasted the illegal gratuity statute with the federal bribery statute, which requires that something of value be offered or sought "to influence any official act":

> The distinguishing feature of each crime is its intent element. Bribery requires intent "to influence" an official act or "to be influenced" in an official act, while illegal gratuity requires only that the gratuity be given or accepted "for or because of" an official act. In other words, for bribery there must be a *quid pro quo* — a specific intent to give or receive something of value *in exchange* for an official act. An illegal gratuity, on the other hand, may constitute merely a reward for some future act that the public official will take (and may already have determined to take), or for a past act that he has already taken. The punishments prescribed for the two offenses reflect their relative seriousness: Bribery may be punished by up to 15 years' imprisonment, a fine of $250,000 ($500,000 for organizations) or triple the value of the bribe, whichever is greater, and disqualification from holding government office. Violation of the illegal gratuity statute, on the other hand, may be punished by up to two years' imprisonment and a fine of $250,000 ($500,000 for organizations).

Id. at 404–05.

The prosecution maintained that any gratuity given to Espy because of his "official position" (for example, to build a reservoir of good will) violated the illegal gratuity law. The Supreme Court rejected this argument, interpreting the statute to require proof of "a link" between the gratuity and "a specific 'official act' for or because of which it was given." *Id.* at 414. Otherwise, the Court noted, the statute would criminalize "token gifts to the President based on his official position and not linked to any identifiable act." *Id.* at 406. Because the jury instructions had not accurately defined the crime, the Court reversed the trade association's conviction.

8. Extortion as a Defense to Bribery. The Model Penal Code does not recognize "extortion" or economic duress as a defense to bribery. The Comments accompanying § 240.1 explain:

> [D]enial of the extortion defense for the bribe giver seems clearly correct as a matter of policy. The private citizen who responds to an official's threat of adverse action by paying money to secure more favorable treatment evidences thereby a willingness to subvert the legitimate processes of government. It is not acceptable to pay kick-backs or under-the-table compensation to a public servant, even if such payment is required in order to obtain official action that is rightfully due. Such conduct constitutes a degree of cooperation in the undermining of governmental integrity that is inconsistent with complete exoneration from criminal liability. The correct decision, of course, is to refuse the illicit overture and to report it to the appropriate authorities. Only by refusing to immunize the payer from criminal liability can the penal law encourage resort to this option.

Model Penal Code § 240.1 Comment at 41.

Many, but not all, court decisions follow the Model Penal Code's approach. In *United States v. Colacurcio*, 659 F.2d 684, 690 (5th Cir. 1981), for example, the court rejected the defendants' argument that "they were coerced by the police into offering bribes [to shield their gambling and prostitution operation from prosecution] and that such economic coercion . . . is a complete defense to the bribery charge." The court noted that the defendants could have reported the alleged coercion to the police department's internal affairs office and concluded, in any event, that extortion is not a defense to bribery.

Is it fair to view the victims of police extortion as criminals rather than victims? Does the Model Penal Code's position demand too much?

9. Determining Who Can Be Bribed. Modern bribery statutes have expanded the general common-law definition of bribery by criminalizing the bribery of witnesses and jurors as well as commercial bribery and bribery in sports. *See, e.g.,* Model Penal Code § 224.8 (prohibiting commercial bribery).

10. Does Prosecutorial Leniency in Return for Testimony Constitute Bribery? In 1998, a panel of the U.S. Court of Appeals for the Tenth Circuit sent shock waves through the federal criminal bar when it held that federal prosecutors commit bribery when they enter into cooperation "deals" with criminal informants, promising them leniency in return for (truthful) testimony. A number of other federal courts quickly rejected the panel's holding, and the Tenth Circuit agreed to reconsider the ruling en banc. The full 12-judge court then reversed the panel's ruling. *See United States v. Singleton*, 165 F.3d 1297 (10th Cir. 1999) (en banc). The majority held that the federal bribery statute simply "does not apply to the United States or an Assistant United States Attorney functioning within the official scope of the office." Two judges concurred more narrowly, reasoning that although prosecutors' longstanding practice of agreeing to deals in exchange for truthful testimony fit the language of the federal bribery statute, Congress never intended to implicate that practice when it enacted the statute (finding this confirmed by subsequent federal statutes that recognize the practice). Interestingly, three judges still dissented, concluding that the government's conduct falls within the plain language of the federal statute and is therefore bribery.

The federal bribery statute provides in relevant part that "whoever . . . directly or indirectly, gives, offers, or promises anything of value to any person, for or because of the testimony . . . given or to be given by such person as a witness upon a trial," may be imprisoned for up to two years. 18 U.S.C. § 201(c)(2). Should this language apply to federal prosecutors offering leniency for truthful testimony? Which of the three opinions (if any) in *Singleton* do you agree with?

———————

[D] Burglary

People v. Gauze

542 P.2d 1365 (Cal. 1975)

MOSK, JUSTICE.

Can a person burglarize his own home? That is the quandary which emerges in the case of James Matthew Gauze, who appeals from a judgment of conviction of assault with a deadly weapon and burglary.

Defendant shared an apartment with Richard Miller and a third person and thus had the right to enter the premises at all times. While visiting a friend one afternoon, defendant and Miller engaged in a furious quarrel. Defendant directed Miller to "Get your gun because I am going to get mine." While Miller went to their mutual home, defendant borrowed a shotgun from a neighbor. He returned to his apartment, walked into the living room, pointed the gun at Miller and fired, hitting him in the side and arm. Defendant was convicted of assault with a deadly weapon and burglary; the latter charge was predicated on his entry into his own apartment with the intent to commit the assault.

Common law burglary was generally defined as "the breaking and entering of the dwelling of *another* in the nighttime with intent to commit a felony." The present burglary statute, Penal Code section 459, provides in relevant part that "Every person who enters *any* house, room, apartment . . . with intent to commit grand or petit larceny or any felony is guilty of burglary."

Facially the statute is susceptible of two rational interpretations. On the one hand, it could be argued that the Legislature deliberately revoked the common law rule that burglary requires entry into the building of another.[3] On the other hand, the Legislature may have impliedly incorporated the common law requirement by failing to enumerate one's own home as a possible object of burglary. No cases directly on point have been found. Therefore, in determining which statutory interpretation should be adopted it is necessary to examine the purposes underlying common law burglary and how they may have been affected by the enactment of the Penal Code.

Common law burglary was essentially an offense "against habitation and occupancy." By proscribing felonious nighttime entry into a dwelling house, the common law clearly sought to protect the right to peacefully enjoy one's own home free of invasion. In the law of burglary, in short, a person's home was truly his castle. It was clear under common law that one could not be convicted of burglary for entering his own home with felonious intent. This rule applied not only to sole owners of homes, but also to joint occupants. The important factor was occupancy, rather than ownership.

California codified the law of burglary in 1850. That statute and subsequent revisions and amendments preserved the spirit of the common law, while making two major changes. First, the statute greatly expanded the type of buildings protected by burglary sanctions. Not only is a person's home his castle under the statute, but so, inter alia, are his shop, tent, airplane, and outhouse. This evolution, combined with elimination of the requirement that the crime be committed at night, signifies that the law is no longer limited to safeguarding occupancy rights. However, by carefully delineating the type of structures encompassed under section 459, the Legislature has preserved the concept that burglary law is designed to protect a possessory right in property, rather than broadly to preserve any place from all crime.

The second major change effected by codification of the burglary law was the elimination of the requirement of a "breaking": under the statute, every person who *enters* with felonious intent is a burglar. This means, at a minimum, that it no longer matters whether a person entering a house with larcenous or felonious intent does so through a closed door, an open door or a window.[4] The entry with the requisite intent constitutes the burglary.

---

3. [n.1] The term "building" is used throughout this opinion for literary convenience; section 459 actually encompasses entry into a variety of structures, not all of them buildings.

4. [n.3] At common law, entry through a closed door or window, whether locked or unlocked, was a breaking, but further opening a partially opened window was not.

The elimination of the breaking requirement was further interpreted in *People v. Barry* (1892) 94 Cal. 481, 29 P. 1026, to mean that trespassory entry was no longer a necessary element of burglary. In *Barry*, this court held a person could be convicted of burglary of a store even though he entered during regular business hours. A long line of cases has followed the *Barry* holding.

Barry and its progeny should not be read, however, to hold that a defendant's right to enter the premises is irrelevant. Indeed, the court in *Barry*, by negative implication, substantiated the importance of determining the right of an accused to enter premises. When the defendant thief in *Barry* argued he had a right to be in the store, the court could have replied that his right to enter the store was immaterial. Instead the court declared, "To this line of reasoning we can only say, a party who enters with the intention to commit a felony enters without an invitation. He is not one of the public invited, nor is he entitled to enter. Such a party could be refused admission at the threshold, or ejected from the premises after the entry was accomplished." Thus, the underlying principle of the *Barry* case is that a person has an implied invitation to enter a store during business hours for legal purposes only. The cases have preserved the common law principle that in order for burglary to occur, "The entry must be *without consent*. If the possessor actually invites the defendant, or actively assists in the entrance, e.g., by opening a door, there is no burglary."

Thus, section 459, while substantially changing common law burglary, has retained two important aspects of that crime. A burglary remains an entry which invades a possessory right in a building. And it still must be committed by a person who has no right to be in the building.

Applying the foregoing reasoning, we conclude that defendant cannot be guilty of burglarizing his own home. His entry into the apartment, even for a felonious purpose, invaded no possessory right of habitation; only the entry of an intruder could have done so. More importantly, defendant had an absolute right to enter the apartment. This right, unlike that of the store thief in *Barry*, did not derive from an implied invitation to the public to enter for legal purposes. It was a personal right that could not be conditioned on the consent of defendant's roommates. Defendant could not be "refused admission at the threshold" of his apartment, or be "ejected from the premises after the entry was accomplished." He could not, accordingly, commit a burglary in his own home.

The People argue, however, that a contrary conclusion is compelled by a dictum in *People v. Sears* (1965) 62 Cal. 2d 737, 44 Cal. Rptr. 330, 401 P.2d 938. In *Sears*, defendant was convicted of felony murder. For three years prior to the murder, defendant had slept in a garage nearby the cottage occupied by his wife. Then the spouses separated and defendant moved to a hotel. Three weeks later, he returned to the cottage, looking for his wife and hiding a reinforced steel pipe under his shirt. In an ensuing struggle, he killed his wife's daughter. This court reversed his conviction because a confession was improperly admitted, but for guidance upon retrial we declared valid a felony-murder instruction based on burglary—entering the cottage with intent to assault his wife—as the felony. In answer to defendant's argument that he could not be guilty of burglary because he had a right to enter the house, the court replied, "One who enters a room or building with the intent to commit a felony is guilty of burglary even though permission to enter has been extended to him personally or as a member of the public. The entry need not constitute a trespass. Moreover, since defendant had moved out of the family home three weeks prior to the crime, he could claim no right to enter the residence of another without permission. Even if we assume that defendant could properly enter the house for a lawful purpose (*cf.* Civ. Code, § 157), such an entry still constitutes burglary if accomplished with the intent to commit a felonious assault within it."

As the above quotation indicates, our opinion that Sears could be convicted of burglary was based on two separate considerations. First, Sears had no right to enter his wife's house; that fact alone supported the conviction. Second, even if he had a right to enter, the right was based on former section 157 of the Civil Code (now § 5102), which gave a person the right to enter the *separate* property of his or her spouse, subject to certain conditions. Thus Sears' "right" to enter his wife's house, like the "right" of the felon to enter the store in *Barry*, was at best conditional. An entry for anything but a legal purpose was a breach of his wife's possessory rights, in marked contrast to the entry in the present case.

Only if the *Sears* dictum is read in an expansive manner can it be used to support the prosecution theory that a person can burglarize his own home. Such a reading would be entirely inconsistent with the purposes of section 459. As aptly articulated by the Court of Appeal in *People v. Lewis* (1969) 274 Cal. App. 2d 912, 920, 79 Cal. Rptr. 650, 655, "Burglary laws are based primarily upon a recognition of the dangers to personal safety created by the usual burglary situation—the danger that the intruder will harm the occupants in attempting to perpetrate the intended crime or to escape and the danger that the occupants will in anger or panic react violently to the invasion, thereby inviting more violence. The laws are primarily designed, then, not to deter the trespass and the intended crime, which are prohibited by other laws, so much as to forestall the germination of a situation dangerous to personal safety." Section 459, in short, is aimed at the danger caused by the unauthorized entry itself.

In contrast to the usual burglary situation, no danger arises from the mere entry of a person into his own home, no matter what his intent is. He may cause a great deal of mischief once inside. But no emotional distress is suffered, no panic is engendered, and no violence necessarily erupts merely because he walks into his house. To impose sanctions for burglary would in effect punish him twice for the crime he committed while in the house. In such circumstances it serves no purpose to apply section 459.

It has been urged that the purpose of burglary laws is to protect persons inside buildings because indoor crime is more dangerous than outdoor crime. It is true that in *People v. Wilson* (1969) 1 Cal. 3d 431, 440, 82 Cal. Rptr. 494, 500, 462 P.2d 22, 28, we said, "We have often recognized that persons within dwellings are in greater peril from *intruders* bent on stealing or engaging in other felonious conduct." However, we have never categorized all indoor crimes to be more dangerous than all outdoor crimes. Nor would such a conclusion be relevant to the purposes of section 459. The statute protects against *intruders* into indoor areas, not persons committing crimes in their own homes.

To hold otherwise could lead to potentially absurd results. If a person can be convicted for burglarizing his own home, he could violate section 459 by calmly entering his house with intent to forge a check. A narcotics addict could be convicted of burglary for walking into his home with intent to administer a dose of heroin to himself. Since a burglary is committed upon entry, both could be convicted even if they changed their minds and did not commit the intended crimes.

In positing such hypotheticals, we indulge in no idle academic exercise. The differing consequences are significant, for the punishment for burglary is severe. First degree burglary is punishable by imprisonment for five years to life,[5] while a second degree burglar is subject to imprisonment in the county jail for a one-year maximum or in state prison for one to fifteen years. (Pen. Code, §461.) In contrast, the punishment for assault with a deadly weapon, the underlying crime committed in this case, is less severe: imprisonment in state prison for six months to life or in county jail for a maximum of one year, or a fine.[6] (Pen. Code, §245, subd. (a).) [The California burglary statutes have been amended, and the maximum sentences reduced, since this opinion was issued. The current versions are described in Note 9 below.]

For the foregoing reasons, we conclude defendant cannot be guilty of burglarizing his own home, and the judgment of conviction for burglary must therefore be reversed. . . .

Notes and Questions

1. Common-Law Burglary. The common-law crime of burglary consists of the following elements: (a) breaking and (b) entering (c) the dwelling house (d) of another person (e) in the nighttime (f) with the intent to commit a felony. *See* WAYNE R. LAFAVE, CRIMINAL LAW §21.1, at 1069–81 (5th ed. 2010).

2. Modern Burglary Statutes. Most modern burglary statutes require only the following elements: (a) the unauthorized entering (b) of a building or structure (c) of another person (d) with the intent to commit any crime. *See, e.g.*, Model Penal Code §221.1(1). *See generally* WAYNE R. LAFAVE, CRIMINAL LAW §21.1, at 1069–81 (5th ed. 2010).

Does the crime of burglary serve a purpose? Should an indoor crime be punished more severely than an outdoor crime? What special interests does the law of

---

5. [n.6] First degree burglary, the crime charged in the present case, includes nighttime burglaries of dwellings and armed burglaries. (Pen. Code, §460.)

6. [n.7] The penalties for both burglary and assault with a deadly weapon are substantially increased when a firearm is used in commission of the crime. (Pen. Code, §12022.5.)

burglary protect? Is the modern extension of burglary to include entries into all buildings appropriate, or was the common law right to limit the crime to entries into dwellings? Should a shoplifter be considered a burglar?

3. Breaking. Most jurisdictions have now eliminated the "breaking" requirement. When still required as an element of burglary, the breaking may be either actual or constructive. An actual breaking requires the creation of a breach or opening into the structure. A defendant who merely trespasses through a preexisting opening has not committed an actual breaking. But any minimal force used to gain an unauthorized entry—such as opening a closed door or raising an unlocked window—can satisfy the "breaking" requirement.

A constructive breaking occurs when the defendant uses some trick or artifice to gain entry. *See, e.g., State v. Maxwell*, 672 P.2d 590 (Kan. 1983) (after gaining entry into an antique dealer's home on the pretext of wanting to discuss a watch, the defendant robbed the occupants); *State v. Van Meveren*, 290 N.W.2d 631 (Minn. 1980) (defendant gained entry by claiming that he needed to use the bathroom and, immediately after entering, commenced an assault); *Commonwealth v. Hayes*, 460 A.2d 791 (Pa. Super. Ct. 1983) (defendant gained entry by pretending that he had come to read the meter in the basement, and then stole a bucket of pennies). A constructive breaking also occurs when entrance is gained by threat of violence or by conspiracy. In *State v. Bray*, 365 S.E.2d 571, 577 (N.C. 1988), for example, the court observed that "[a] defendant has made a constructive breaking when another person who is under the defendant's direction or who is acting in concert with the defendant actually makes the opening."

Ironically, the courts' countless refinements of the "breaking" requirement—resulting in such meaningless distinctions as whether or not a window was left open half an inch—contributed to its eventual demise, and most jurisdictions today have dispensed with the breaking requirement entirely. *See* Michael M. Pacheco, Comment, *The Armed Career Criminal Act: When Burglary Is Not Burglary*, 26 WILLA-METTE L. REV. 171 (1989).

4. Entering. An entry occurs as soon as any part of the defendant's body is within the structure. Thus, in *Franco v. State*, 42 Tex. 276, 279 (1875), the court found sufficient evidence of entry where the defendant "raised the window in the dwelling of an aged lady, and was holding it up with his hand in such a way that his fingers were within the house, his elbow resting on the sill of the window, and his body outside of the house."

In *Magness v. Superior Court*, 278 P. 3d 259 (Cal. 2012), the California Supreme Court unanimously found insufficient evidence of entry when a defendant stood in a driveway and used a remote control to open the garage door. "[S]omething that is *outside* must go *inside* for an entry to occur," the court explained, and therefore the defendant could only be charged with attempted burglary.

As the court's opinion in *Gauze* illustrates, the entry must be wrongful. The person must not have a possessory right to be in the building. A person's right to enter a store or place of business is usually conditional upon entering with a purpose consistent with the reason the building is open. Entering with an intent to commit a crime violates this condition and is therefore wrongful. *See, e.g., People ex rel. McLain v. Housewright*, 293 N.E.2d 911 (Ill. App. Ct. 1973) (affirming burglary conviction where the defendant entered a supermarket during business hours with the intent to steal).

The Model Penal Code, however, advocates narrowing the modern notion of burglary by excluding any entries to premises that "are at the time open to the public or [that] the actor is licensed or privileged to enter." Model Penal Code § 221.1(1). Is the Model Penal Code's position persuasive?

5. Dwelling House. Modern statutes have departed from the notion that the target of a burglary must be a "dwelling house." The crime now encompasses entries into other buildings and structures, including offices, shops, garages, warehouses, and telephone booths. Thus, in *De Albuquerque v. State*, 712 S.W.2d 809 (Tex. App. 1986), the court affirmed the burglary conviction of a defendant who climbed six feet over the counter and protective shield of a currency exchange booth that was a permanent structure in the Houston airport. In *State v. Bybee*, 781 P.2d 316 (N.M. 1989), however, a soft drink vending machine located outside a building was not considered a structure under New Mexico's burglary statute.

Although the court in *Crews v. Commonwealth*, 352 S.E.2d 1 (Va. Ct. App. 1987), reversed a burglary conviction on the grounds that a school bus not permanently affixed to the ground was not a storehouse, warehouse, or other house as required by the Virginia burglary statute, today motor vehicles, trucks, trailers, watercraft, aircraft, and tents are often considered "structures" for purposes of burglary statutes. Moreover, in *State v. Cloud*, 324 N.W.2d 287 (S.D. 1982), the court held that even an entry into the open, uncovered box of a pickup truck constituted burglary.

Even though most modern statutes no longer limit the crime of burglary to dwellings, some statutes distinguish between first- and second-degree burglary depending on whether the structure the defendant entered was an inhabited dwelling. A dwelling is generally defined as someone's residence. *People v. Ramos*, 60 Cal. Rptr. 2d 523, 524–25 (Cal. Ct. App. 1997), elaborated on that concept:

> On November 23, 1994, Virgil Wagner died at home from natural causes. His daughter-in-law, Marilyn Ball, was notified of his death, and when she went to Wagner's house two days later, she found that a microwave and a VCR were missing. Although Ball locked the house when she left, there were at least two more unauthorized entries into the house and other items were taken. When the police investigated, they found Ramos' fingerprints inside Wagner's house. When he was arrested, Ramos told the police that he went to Wagner's house on November 23, knocked on the front door and, when no one answered, walked around to the back of the house. Since it appeared that no one was home, Ramos decided to go in and take something he could sell to obtain money to buy drugs. Ramos broke a window,

entered the house, walked by Wagner's bedroom, looked in and saw a body on the bed. The body did not move, so [Ramos] entered the bedroom to get a closer look. When he saw Wagner's stiff body and his face "turned to the left with the eyes open," Ramos ran out the door, grabbing the VCR on his way.

Ramos was charged with five counts of first degree burglary. At trial, the People presented evidence of the November 23 entry plus others occurring before and after Wagner's death. During argument, the prosecutor conceded the later entries were second degree burglaries but argued that the November 23 entry was a first degree burglary because the house was "occupied" until Wagner's remains were removed. The jury convicted Ramos of three counts, finding the November 23 entry was a first degree burglary and two other entries (after Wagner's death) were second degree burglaries.

. . . .

To prove first degree burglary of an inhabited dwelling, the People must present evidence that the house is "currently being used for dwelling purposes, whether occupied or not." (Pen. Code, § 459.) What this means is that a dwelling is inhabited if the occupant is absent but intends to return to use the house as a dwelling. To put it plainly, a dead body is not using a house for a "dwelling" and there is no way to say that a dead man is going to return or that he has an "intent" of any kind. It follows that, at the time of Ramos' entry on November 23, the house was not occupied within the meaning of section 459.

We reject as metaphysical sophistry the Attorney General's suggestion that the house was inhabited because Wagner "went to sleep, fully intending to remain in his house." By the time Ramos got there, Wagner was dead and, to the best of our knowledge, unable to entertain any intent of any kind. The house was no longer occupied.

It follows that Ramos' first degree burglary conviction must be reduced to second degree burglary.

6. **Of Another.** As the court's opinion in *Gauze* illustrates, a defendant cannot burglarize his own residence. *See also State v. Altamirano*, 803 P.2d 425, 428 (Ariz. 1990) (concluding that the defendant could not burglarize his own residence since he had "an absolute right to remain [there] at all times"). Do these decisions make sense? Is burglary primarily an offense against the right of habitation or the ownership of property?

The Ohio Supreme Court has ruled that "[b]ecause the purpose of burglary law is to protect the dweller, . . . custody and control, rather than legal title, is dispositive." Thus a husband was convicted of burglarizing the apartment that his estranged wife occupied, despite an unusual Ohio statute providing that "neither [husband nor wife] can be excluded from the other's dwelling, except by [court] decree." *State v. Lilly*, 717 N.E.2d 322 (Ohio 1999).

7. In the Nighttime. The common-law doctrine limiting burglary to nighttime entries rested upon two rationales. First, night was the time when individuals could more easily fall prey to criminals. *See* 4 BLACKSTONE, COMMENTARIES ON THE LAWS OF ENGLAND 224 (1769). Second, a distinction was drawn between day and night because the intruder's countenance could be discerned by daylight but not during the night. As the court explained in *State v. Billings*, 242 N.W.2d 726, 729 (Iowa 1976):

> [N]ighttime in a charge of burglary under [the Iowa Code] is, as it was at common law, a period between sunset and sunrise during which there is not daylight enough by which to discern a man's face. . . . At common law, the circumstance of aggravation signified by the "nighttime" factor was not sunset but the concealment afforded by darkness. . . .

Today most jurisdictions have dispensed with the "nighttime" requirement, thus envisioning that the crime of burglary can occur at any time of the day or night. *See, e.g., Griffin v. Commonwealth*, 412 S.E.2d 709, 711 (Va. Ct. App. 1991) ("[T]he timing of the offense is not an essential element of the offense. . . . [T]he indictment's allegation that the offense occurred in the daytime is nothing more than surplusage."). Nevertheless, several states consider nighttime entry one of the factors that elevates a burglary to a higher grade of the offense. *See, e.g.*, Model Penal Code § 221.1(2).

8. Intent to Commit a Felony. The common-law crime of burglary required proof that the defendant entered with the intent commit a felony. Section 221.1(1) of the Model Penal Code and many modern codes have expanded burglary to include an entry with the intent to commit any crime.

Whatever mens rea is required, that criminal intent must exist at the time of the entry (and also at the time of the breaking, where that element is still included in the definition of burglary). Suppose *A* enters a department store intending to do some shopping but later changes her mind and steals an expensive watch. *A* would be guilty of theft but not burglary because she did not have the intent to steal when she entered the store. If, instead, *A* entered the store with the intent to steal the watch, she would be guilty of burglary even if she changed her mind after she entered the store.

Consider *Auman v. People*, 109 P.3d 647 (Colo. 2005), where the Colorado Supreme Court reversed burglary and felony murder convictions entered against Lisa Auman, who along with several other people, broke into her ex-boyfriend's room and removed some of her belongings as well as his, ultimately leading to a high-speed chase and the death of a police officer. The burglary charge was based on the theory that Auman broke into the room with the intent to commit the felony of theft, a crime that can be negated by a claim of right. Auman claimed that she intended to take only her own possessions when she broke into the room. Because the jury instructions failed to require the jury to find that Auman intended to take the property of another without authorization when she entered the room, the court concluded that she did not receive fair consideration of her defense that she lacked the requisite intent to commit a felony.

Under the common law, a mere trespass (an unprivileged entry onto land) was only a tort and not a crime. Many states have now criminalized trespass, although the crime is often limited to certain circumstances — for example, entries into a structure or other specified types of property. Consider the problems the restrictions on the crime of trespass created when an unauthorized visitor entered the Queen of England's bedroom at night without any demonstrable intent to commit a crime in the palace:

> When Michael Fagan dropped in on Queen Elizabeth in her bedroom last July, it is unlikely that he had in mind making British jurisprudential history. But that is what he has done by getting acquitted of any wrongdoing in the incident — a case, said one outraged British newspaper today, that is the craziest since the "Knave of Hearts in Alice in Wonderland."

Peter Osnos, *'Bonkers,' Says Britain, as Fagan Is Acquitted*, WASH. POST, Sept. 25, 1982, at C9. British prosecutors had difficulty determining what charges to bring against the successful palace intruder, who bragged that he had "sat on the throne." Because trespass into the palace was not a crime in England, the prosecutors settled on a charge of burglary. The prosecutorial effort was unsuccessful, and the jury found the defendant not guilty after only 14 minutes of deliberation. British newspapers reacted with disdain:

> . . . "Bonkers" said the *Sun*. Fumed the *Mirror*: "There are times when to call the law an ass is to insult asses." "What can we say of British justice?" the *Daily Mail* exhorted. "That truly it is the eighth wonder of the world."
>
> . . . .
>
> The *Sun*, Britain's biggest-selling tabloid, which invoked "Alice in Wonderland" in its denunciation, said today that the verdict "solemnly declared open house at the Queen's residence."

Id. British authorities promised the public that both palace security and British criminal law would be reappraised.

9. The Penalties for Burglary. Due to the breadth of modern burglary statutes, there has been a gradual trend in some states to reduce the penalties for the crime. For instance, the California legislature has created degrees of burglary. First-degree burglary applies to entries into inhabited dwellings and is now punishable by a maximum of six years in prison (instead of life imprisonment, the maximum sentence at the time *Gauze* was decided). Second-degree burglary encompasses all other forms of burglary and is punishable by a maximum of one year in prison (compared to 15 years at the time of the *Gauze* decision). *See* Cal. Penal Code §§ 460, 461. In 2014, California voters enacted Proposition 47, which forecloses burglary charges against those who enter a commercial establishment during regular business hours with intent to steal property valued at less than $950. As a result, this conduct instead constitutes the crime of shoplifting, which, unlike burglary, is only a misdemeanor. *See* Cal. Penal Code § 459.5. On the other hand, first-degree burglary is one of the dangerous felonies included in the "three strikes" legislation enacted in California in 1994. Three convictions of any such felony lead to a minimum prison sentence of 25 years to life. *See* Cal. Penal Code § 667. (For further discussion of "three strikes" laws, see Chapter 2, Section D.3, Note 4.)

Consider what happened to a teenage boy who, along with his younger brother and a friend, broke into his school's cafeteria and stole a box of ice cream bars. Since the entry amounted to burglary in addition to the less serious crime of larceny, the boy was sentenced to three years in prison. The ensuing public outcry led the Georgia Board of Pardons to reduce the sentence to probation, although the burglary conviction remained on his record. *See Georgia Teen Granted Probation in Theft of Ice Cream*, L.A. Times, Sept. 26, 1993, at A7.

Chapter 10

Causation

[A] When Is Causation an Issue?

[1] Culpability and "But-For" Causation

Compare the following situations:

(a) Assailant *A* holds up victim at gunpoint, demanding victim's wallet and gold watch. Victim, terrorized, collapses and dies of a heart attack prompted by acute fear for his life.

(b) Assailant *B* holds up victim at gunpoint, demanding victim's wallet and gold watch. Victim collapses and dies of a brain aneurism, a cerebral accident that would have happened at precisely the same moment whether or not the victim had been mugged.

How are these situations different? Is the difference legally significant in determining the assailants' responsibility for the victims' deaths?

In (a), but not in (b), the acts of the assailant cause the victim's death. As a result, in (a), but not in (b), the assailant may *possibly* be held culpable for the victim's death. A final determination of *A*'s culpability depends on the answer to additional questions, ones about the assailant's state of mind, about the presence or absence of possible defenses, and so on. But *B* cannot possibly be held liable for the victim's death because *B* had nothing to do with bringing it about. In (b), inquiry into homicide liability ends as soon as it begins.

The term used to describe this somewhat obvious requirement is "but for" causation. As one crucial element of establishing culpability, we must always be able to show that *but for* the accused's relevant act or omission the harmful result would not have occurred. In situation (b) this condition is not met. The victim's death would have occurred at the same time in the same way whether or not the assailant had acted.

The requirement of "but for" causation is so obvious that, up to this point, it has been subsumed in our presentation of criminal law: one can only be held culpable for those results that one has contributed to bringing about. Think back on the presence of "but for" causation in the cases in previous Chapters.

Obvious as it is, the requirement is not mandated by *logic*. That is, one can imagine a legal system that punishes persons who did not cause harm, a system that, for example, punishes scapegoats. Thus, one can imagine a highly effective system of deterrence based on imprisoning or executing the relatives or friends of offenders. Those who know that their relatives or friends might be harmed as a result of their criminal acts are quite likely to refrain. Our reasons for shunning the practice of scapegoating come from morality and from legal requirements rather than logic. It seems unfair to subject anyone to institutionalized sanctions for results that that person did not have a role in producing.

Obviously, the requirement of "but for" causation is a very weak requirement in the sense that any event has countlessly many antecedent causes, earlier events that made possible the later event that is in question. To say that one event caused another is to say very little about legal responsibility; it merely leaves open the *possibility* of such responsibility.

In the following selection from his *Textbook of Criminal Law*, Professor Glanville Williams considers the implications of "but for" causation.

GLANVILLE WILLIAMS, TEXTBOOK OF CRIMINAL LAW
379, 380–81 (2d ed. 1983)[1]

Surely the notion of but-for causation is ridiculously wide, because it takes us back to Adam and Eve. The criminal's mother is a but-for cause of his crimes, and so is his grandmother, and all his ancestors to infinity.

That is perfectly true, but two factors limit the judicial enquiry. First, one starts with the defendant who is charged; his mother does not come into it, much less Adam and Eve. Secondly, but-for causation is only half the story; the defendant who was the but-for cause of the harm is not responsible unless his conduct was also the *imputable* cause. We still have to deal with imputable causation.

Is the notion of but-for cause a useful one? Where the cause is a positive act, isn't it too obvious to be worth stating? If D shoots V and V drops dead, surely you don't have to prove that the bullet entering V's heart caused him to die?

When but-for causation is obvious (as it usually is), it is not discussed. Certainly the answer to your last question is in the negative. But occasionally an issue of this kind may require expert assistance.

D may administer poison to V, who may die shortly afterwards, yet an autopsy may reveal that V died not of the poison but of heart disease. There will then be medical evidence at D's trial to the effect that the poison did not cause the death, meaning that V would in any case have died at the time and in the way he did, and that the poison did not play any contributory part. If the jury believe this evidence, or, rather, if they are not sure that it is untrue, they must acquit of murder—though D may, of course, be convicted of the attempt.

---

1. Reprinted with permission of Sweet & Maxwell, Ltd.

We may summarise, then, by saying that but-for causation is of legal interest only in the comparatively rare cases where, notwithstanding appearances, it is absent; that when it is alleged to be absent, this raises a question of fact for the jury, who may decide by ordinary experience but may have to be assisted by expert evidence; and that the burden is on the Crown to prove beyond reasonable doubt that the defendant's act (or omission) was a but-for cause.

[Professor Williams addresses further implications of the "but for" requirement in special situations. One kind of special situation is that in which two actors simultaneously deliver fatal blows.]

What about two but-for causes contributed by different defendants? Doesn't your definition imply the paradox that if two persons independently cause an event, neither causes it?

To provide for this, an exception for causes of multiple causation has to be inserted into the definition. It is possible for two sufficient causes, C1 and C2, to be present together, so that E follows both, when usually it follows only one or the other. Both C1 and C2 are causes, even though in the particular situation one or other (as the case may be) was not necessary to be present. An example is where two fatal wounds are given independently at the same time.

[A different kind of special situation is that in which a second actor accelerates the death of the first actor's victim.]

What of accelerating the victim's death?

This is a "killing" in law. Since we are all fated to die at some time, every instance of killing is an instance of accelerating death; and even if death is hastened by as little as five minutes it is still a criminal homicide. So it is no defence to a person who stabs another to death to show that the victim was already dangerously ill.

Suppose that D1's shot entered the lung and would have caused the victim's death in an hour, but D2's entered the heart and killed him instantaneously?

Then, of course, only D2 has killed him. D1 is guilty of an attempt.

The but-for cause is sometimes referred to as the factual cause, or the de facto cause, or the scientific cause. The important thing is to distinguish it from cause in another sense, the "imputable" (or "legal" or "effective" or "direct" or "proximate") cause.

———————

In *State v. Muro*, 695 N.W.2d 425 (Neb. 2005), an eight-month-old child died, apparently from a skull fracture resulting from a beating by defendant's husband. Defendant was convicted of felony child abuse on the theory that she intentionally or knowingly deprived the child of medical care after the injury and that neglect of the injury resulted in death. The conviction was reversed on the ground that no proof was offered that the child would have survived if treated in a timely way. Thus, defendant's inaction was not shown to be a "but-for" cause of death.

[2] Intervening Actors and Events

"But for" causation is a necessary condition but not a sufficient condition for liability for a criminal result. It merely sets the stage for a second inquiry into the sufficiency of the connection between the act and the result. There are many ways to express this criterion for liability. Section 2.03 of the Model Penal Code, for example, says that the act must not be too "remote" or "accidental" in its relationship to the result. The following sections explore the parameters of this requirement.

People v. Kibbe

321 N.E.2d 773 (N.Y. 1974)

Gabrielli, Judge.

The factual setting of the bizarre events of a cold winter night of December 30, 1970, as developed by the testimony, including the voluntary statements of the defendants, reveals the following: During the early evening the defendants were drinking in a Rochester tavern along with the victim, George Stafford. The bartender testified that Stafford was displaying and "flashing" one hundred dollar bills, was thoroughly intoxicated and was finally "shut off" because of his inebriated condition. At some time between 8:15 and 8:30 p.m., Stafford inquired if someone would give him a ride to Canandaigua, New York, and the defendants, who, according to their statements, had already decided to steal Stafford's money, agreed to drive him there in Kibbe's automobile. The three men left the bar and proceeded to another bar where Stafford was denied service due to his condition. The defendants and Stafford then walked across the street to a third bar where they were served, and each had another drink or two.

After they left the third bar, the three men entered Kibbe's automobile and began the trip toward Canandaigua. Krall drove the car while Kibbe demanded that Stafford turn over any money he had. In the course of an exchange, Kibbe slapped Stafford several times, took his money, then compelled him to lower his trousers and to take off his shoes to be certain that Stafford had given up all his money; and when they were satisfied that Stafford had no more money on his person, the defendants forced Stafford to exit the Kibbe vehicle.

As he was thrust from the car, Stafford fell onto the shoulder of the rural two-lane highway on which they had been traveling. His trousers were still down around his ankles, his shirt was rolled up towards his chest, he was shoeless and he had also been stripped of any outer clothing. Before the defendants pulled away, Kibbe placed Stafford's shoes and jacket on the shoulder of the highway. Although Stafford's eyeglasses were in the Kibbe vehicle, the defendants, either through inadvertence or perhaps by specific design, did not give them to Stafford before they drove away. It was sometime between 9:30 and 9:40 p.m. when Kibbe and Krall abandoned Stafford on the side of the road. The temperature was near zero, and, although it was not snowing at the time, visibility was occasionally obscured by heavy winds which intermittently blew previously fallen snow into the air and across the highway; and there was snow on both sides of the road as a result of previous plowing operations. The structure nearest the point where Stafford was forced from the defendants' car was a gasoline service station situated nearly one-half of a mile away on the other side of the highway. There was no artificial illumination on this segment of the rural highway.

At approximately 10:00 p.m. Michael W. Blake, a college student, was operating his pickup truck in the northbound lane of the highway in question. Two cars, which were approaching from the opposite direction, flashed their headlights at Blake's vehicle. Immediately after he had passed the second car, Blake saw Stafford sitting in the road in the middle of the northbound lane with his hands up in the air. Blake stated that he was operating his truck at a speed of approximately 50 miles per hour, and that he "didn't have time to react" before his vehicle struck Stafford. After he brought his truck to a stop and returned to try to be of assistance to Stafford, Blake observed that the man's trousers were down around his ankles and his shirt was pulled up around his chest. A Deputy Sheriff called to the accident scene also confirmed the fact that the victim's trousers were around his ankles, and that Stafford was wearing no shoes or jacket.

At the trial, the Medical Examiner of Monroe County testified that death had occurred fairly rapidly from massive head injuries. In addition, he found proof of a high degree of intoxication with a .25%, by weight, of alcohol concentration in the blood.

For their acts, the defendants were convicted of murder, robbery in the second degree and grand larceny in the third degree. However, the defendants basically challenge only their convictions of murder, claiming that the People failed to establish beyond a reasonable doubt that their acts "caused the death of another," as required by the statute. As framed by the Appellate Division the only serious question raised by these appeals "is whether the death was caused by [the defendants'] acts." In answering this question, we are required to determine whether the defendants may be convicted of murder for the occurrences which have been described. They contend that the actions of Blake, the driver of the pickup truck, constituted both an intervening and superseding cause which relieves them of criminal responsibility for Stafford's death.

. . . [T]o be a sufficiently direct cause of death so as to warrant the imposition of a criminal penalty therefor, it is not necessary that the ultimate harm be intended by the actor. It will suffice if it can be said beyond a reasonable doubt, as indeed it can be here said, that the ultimate harm is something which should have been foreseen as being reasonably related to the acts of the accused.

. . . We subscribe to the requirement that the defendants' actions must be *a sufficiently direct cause* of the ensuing death before there can be any imposition of criminal liability, and recognize, of course, that this standard is greater than that required to serve as a basis for tort liability. Applying these criteria to the defendants' actions, we conclude that their activities on the evening of December 30, 1970 were a sufficiently direct cause of the death of George Stafford so as to warrant the imposition of criminal sanctions. In engaging in what may properly be described as a despicable course of action, Kibbe and Krall left a helplessly intoxicated man without his eyeglasses in a position from which, because of these attending circumstances, he could not extricate himself and whose condition was such that he could not even protect himself from the elements. The defendants do not dispute the fact that their conduct evinced a depraved indifference to human life which created a grave risk of death, but rather they argue that it was just as likely that Stafford would be miraculously rescued by a good Samaritan. We cannot accept such an argument. There can be little doubt but that Stafford would have frozen to death in his state of undress had he remained on the shoulder of the road. The only alternative left to him was the highway, which in his condition, for one reason or another, clearly foreboded the probability of his resulting death.

Under the conditions surrounding Blake's operation of his truck (i.e., the fact that he had his low beams on as the two cars approached; that there was no artificial lighting on the highway; and that there was insufficient time in which to react to Stafford's presence in his lane), we do not think it may be said that any supervening wrongful act occurred to relieve the defendants from the directly foreseeable consequences of their actions. In short, we will not disturb the jury's determination that the prosecution proved beyond a reasonable doubt that their actions came clearly within the statute and "[caused] the death of another person."

Notes and Questions

1. Causation and Foreseeability. The court in *Kibbe* rejects the argument that the acts of the driver constitute an intervening and superseding cause. It concludes instead that the acts of Kibbe and Krall were a "sufficiently direct" cause of death for them to be convicted of murder.

What makes their acts sufficiently direct? Is it simply the fact that their criminal acts placed Stafford in a situation that turned out to be fatal, indeed that their acts were *very important* in placing him in such a situation? What is the significance of Stafford not having his eyeglasses? Does it matter whether Kibbe and Krall realized that Stafford's glasses remained in the car, or is that irrelevant to the question of causation?

Suppose that rather than being run over by a driver, Stafford had been attacked and killed by a rabid dog. Would Kibbe and Krall still be responsible for his death? Note that in this new situation their acts turn out to have the same role as before in placing him in a dangerous situation.

The court appears to draw a distinction between the situation in *Kibbe* and our hypothetical one when it refers to the "ultimate harm [in *Kibbe* as] something which should have been foreseen." Surely the acts of the dog, unlike those of the driver, could not have been foreseen. Thus, Kibbe and Krall's treatment of Stafford seems to be a sufficiently direct cause of death when the driver is involved but not when the immediate cause of death is the dog.

2. Foreseeability and Recklessness. The court's reliance on foreseeability implies that Kibbe and Krall's homicide liability rests on a high degree of recklessness. Arguably, they were reckless with regard to the kind of risk represented by the driver but not the kind of risk represented by the dog.

3. Relevance of Agency. Note that the difference between the actual facts of *Kibbe* and the dog hypothetical does not depend on the fact that one situation involves human agency (the driver) and the other does not (the dog). Had Kibbe and Krall left Stafford in a field known to be the hunting grounds of carnivorous animals, an attack by such an animal might be foreseeable and therefore not a superseding cause.

4. Residual Charges. Assume that Kibbe and Krall intended that Stafford freeze to death. Assume also that the unexpected happens, that he is killed by the dog or by an enemy who comes across his inert form. In these circumstances, in which the immediate actor is a superseding cause, are Kibbe and Krall nonetheless responsible for homicide under a multiple cause analysis?

5. Should Causation Matter? Note that, in one sense, the difference between these two hypothetical situations is anomalous. Why should Kibbe and Krall be treated differently in the two cases if their acts and states of mind are the same? In both situations they intended that Stafford should die by freezing to death and placed him in a situation in which that was likely to happen, and in both cases death came about in a different way than they were in a position to anticipate.

Part of the problem is derived from the fact that the *actual result* is an element of some offenses, including homicide. If liability were based *solely* on conduct and state of mind, there would be no occasion to distinguish between attempts and successes, no occasion to take the actual result into account in determining liability. But here the legal analysis is even more complicated because it depends not only on the actual result (the victim's death) but on how the result came about — on the foreseeability of the way in which the result came about.

Commentators disagree about whether the legal rules about causation are anomalous. The argument in favor of them is usually said to be intuitive. It is said that our intuition is that one who intentionally causes harm is more blameworthy than one who acts with the intention of causing the same harm but fails. And it is said that one who intends to cause harm is more blameworthy if the harm occurs in a foreseeable way than in an unforeseeable way.

[3] Causation in the Model Penal Code

Model Penal Code § 2.03

Section 2.03. Causal Relationship Between Conduct and Result; Divergence Between Result Designed or Contemplated and Actual Result or Between Probable and Actual Result.

(1) Conduct is the cause of a result when:

> (a) it is an antecedent but for which the result in question would not have occurred; and
>
> (b) the relationship between the conduct and result satisfies any additional causal requirements imposed by the Code or by the law defining the offense.

(2) When purposely or knowingly causing a particular result is an element of an offense, the element is not established if the actual result is not within the purpose or the contemplation of the actor unless:

> (a) the actual result differs from that designed or contemplated, as the case may be, only in the respect that a different person or different property is injured or affected or that the injury or harm designed or contemplated would have been more serious or more extensive than that caused; or
>
> (b) the actual result involves the same kind of injury or harm as that designed or contemplated and is not too remote or accidental in its occurrence to have a [just] bearing on the actor's liability or on the gravity of his offense.

(3) When recklessly or negligently causing a particular result is an element of an offense, the element is not established if the actual result is not within the risk of which the actor is aware or, in the case of negligence, of which he should be aware unless:

> (a) the actual result differs from the probable result only in the respect that a different person or different property is injured or affected or that the probable injury or harm would have been more serious or more extensive than that caused; or
>
> (b) the actual result involves the same kind of injury or harm as the probable result and is not too remote or accidental in its occurrence to have a [just] bearing on the actor's liability or on the gravity of his offense.

(4) When causing a particular result is a material element of an offense for which absolute liability is imposed by law, the element is not established unless the actual result is a probable consequence of the actor's conduct.

Explanatory Note

Subsection (1) states the minimum requirement for a finding of causation when a crime is defined in terms of conduct causing a particular result; the actor's conduct must be an antecedent but for which the result would not have occurred. It also provides that additional causal requirements may be imposed by the Code or by the law defining the offense. This is not to say, however, that but-for causation is sufficient by itself; the later subsections impose additional requirements or limitations that may preclude a finding of liability with respect to consequences of which the actor's conduct is a but-for cause.

Subsection (2) is concerned with offenses in which causing a result purposely or knowingly is an element. If the actual result is within the purpose or contemplation of the actor (i.e., events transpire as the actor intended or knew that they would), the case presents no difficulty. Problems arise only if there is a divergence between the actual and contemplated result. If the divergence is only that a different person or property is affected, or that the contemplated harm would have been more serious, the difference is declared to be legally immaterial. If, however, there are other differences, the causality element is established only if the actual result involves the same kind of injury as the contemplated result and the actual result is not too remote or accidental in its occurrence to have a [just] bearing on the actor's liability or the gravity of his offense. The traditional language of proximate causation is replaced by language that focuses on the relationship between the purpose or contemplation of the actor and the actual result of his conduct. This is a fresh approach, justifying legislative treatment of an issue traditionally left to the courts.

Subsection (3) performs the same function for offenses in which recklessness or negligence is an element. Liability is predicated on but-for causation, subject to limitations based on the relationship between the risks created by the actor's conduct that support a finding of recklessness or negligence and the consequences that in fact ensued.

Subsection (4) is addressed to strict liability offenses. It provides that the causal element is not established unless the actual result is a probable consequence of the actor's conduct, a minimal protection against the limitless extrapolation of liability without fault.

Comment

. . . What will usually turn on determinations under this section is not the criminality of the defendant's conduct, but the gravity of his offense. For example, when the actor's purpose is to cause the death of another, the lack of an adequate relation between his conduct and the death of his intended victim results in conviction for attempted murder rather than murder. Similarly, when the actor recklessly creates a risk of death, escape from responsibility for criminal homicide under the present section does not bar criminal liability for lesser offenses.

How far the penal law ought to attribute importance in the grading of offenses to the actual result of conduct, as opposed to results attempted or threatened, presents a significant and difficult issue. Distinctions of this sort are essential, at least when severe sanctions are involved, for it cannot be expected that jurors will lightly return verdicts leading to severe sentences in the absence of the resentment aroused by the infliction of serious injuries. Whatever abstract logic may suggest, a prudent legislator cannot disregard these facts in the enactment of a penal code.

Attributing importance to the actual result does not, moreover, usually detract from the deterrent efficacy of the law, at least in cases of purposeful misconduct. One who attempts to kill, risking the gravest penalty, is unlikely to be influenced in his behavior by the treatment that the law provides for those who fail in such attempts; his expectation is that he will succeed. . . .

Subsection (2)(b) deals with situations in which the actual result involves the same kind of injury or harm as that designed or contemplated, but in which the precise injury inflicted was different or occurred in a different way. Here the Code makes no attempt to catalogue the possibilities — intervening or concurrent causes, natural or human; unexpected physical conditions; distinctions between mortal and non-mortal wounds; and so on. It deals only with the ultimate criterion by which the significance of such factors ought to be judged — whether the actual result is too remote or accidental in its occurrence to have a [just] bearing on the actor's liability or the gravity of his offense.

The purpose of this qualification is to exclude situations in which the manner in which the actual result occurs, or the nature of the actual result, is so remote from the actor's purpose or contemplation that it should have no bearing on the gravity of the offense for which he is convicted.

It has been argued that this formulation gives insufficient attention to the problem of intervention by a responsible human agent. Consider, for example, the case of a gunshot wound, followed by an operation that brings about the victim's death. Death may have resulted from intentional killing by the surgeon, or from the surgeon's recklessness or negligence, or from the victim's contracting an infection (through no one's fault) in the course of the operation. Even if it is assumed that each of these occurrences is equally probable under the circumstances, Hart and Honore contend that it is not sufficient in cases of human intervention to put the issues of liability to the jury in terms of whether the result was "too accidental" in its occurrence to have a just bearing on the actor's liability or the gravity of his offense. Rather, relying on what they perceive to be deeply ingrained common sense ideas about causality and responsibility, they see the issue as properly turning on the voluntariness of the intervening actor's conduct — to the extent that his intervention is independent and voluntary, the defendant's liability should be diminished.

In response to criticisms that the word "accidental" alone might lead to too narrow an inquiry, the words "remote or" were added to the section. But given that two results are equally remote or accidental in their occurrence, the question remains whether it should be significant that they are brought about by human or nonhuman intervention, or by human acts that are volitional or nonvolitional. The language of Subsection (2)(b) does not accept the view that volitional human intervention should be treated differently from other intervening causes, but neither does it mandate a contrary position. It is up to the trier of fact to give weight to such variables if it is persuaded that these considerations are significant in determining whether the occurrence of the actual result had a [just] bearing on the actor's liability or the gravity of this offense.

Notes and Questions

1. **"Remote and Accidental" Consequences as Unforeseeable.** In subsection (2)(b) of § 2.03, the drafters of the Model Penal Code chose to provide that the actual result not be "too remote or accidental in its occurrence." In the *Kibbe* case, the court achieves the same result by requiring that the actual result be foreseeable. What, if any, are the advantages of the MPC approach?

Note that the wording of subsection (2)(b) makes it clear that the judgment is an objective one. A court applying the MPC standard is not concerned with what is or is not foreseeable from the standpoint and situation of the actors. Rather it is concerned with commonly shared standards of remoteness. But is the standard really objective? Can one expect general agreement on what is too remote or accidental?

2. **Applications of Causation Theory.** Consider two illustrations of the straightforward workings of the causation doctrine. In *Tyus v. State*, 845 So. 2d 318 (Fla. Dist. Ct. App. 2003), the defendant burglarized the residence of an elderly woman, who died of cardiac dysrhythmia when confronted by the burglar. The court affirmed his manslaughter conviction and held that the victim's death was not too remote and accidental, i.e., was not caused by the acts of an independent, supervening cause other than the defendant.

Suppose, by contrast, that after the defendants store a gun in their bedroom, a minor intrudes on the bedroom twice (to find ammunition and the gun) and then goes to the victim's house with the gun and shoots the victim in a culpably negligent way. The defendants had no knowledge or control over the shooter's actions, and the minor is therefore an independent, supervening cause of the victim's death. *Cf. Finocchio v. Mahler*, 37 S.W.3d 300 (Mo. Ct. App. 2000) (finding a lack of causation on these facts in a civil wrongful death action).

3. **Moral Aspects of Causation.** Note that the MPC provision contains the word "just" in brackets. This signals that some of the drafters wished to include the word in the final formulation, but that there was no consensus. How does the inclusion of this term change the meaning and implications of § 2.03?

Among other factors, saying that the actual result must not be too remote or accidental to have a *just* bearing on liability implies that the determination is *moral* rather than descriptive or conceptual. Do you agree that the question is essentially a moral one?

4. Causation and Voluntary Intermediaries. In their Comment to subsection (2)(b), the drafters remind us of Professors H.L.A. Hart and A.M. Honore's criticism (based on their book, Causation in the Law (1959)) of the MPC position. Echoing many other writers, Hart and Honore argue for two separate criteria for intervening cause: they contend that a cause should be superseding if either (a) it produces the result in a way that is too remote or accidental or (b) it is the voluntary act of a responsible actor.

The following legislative proposal, which was not adopted, incorporates this suggestion:

Tentative Draft, California Joint Legislative Committee

for Revision of the Penal Code (1968)

Section 408. Causation: Responsibility for Causing a Result

(1) An element of an offense which requires that the defendant have caused a particular result is established when his conduct is an antecedent but for which the result would not have occurred, and,

(a) if the offense requires that the defendant intentionally or knowingly cause the result, that the actual result, as it occurred,

(i) is within the purpose or contemplation of the defendant, whether the purpose or contemplation extends to natural events or to the conduct of another, or, if not,

(ii) involves the same kind of injury or harm as that designed or contemplated and is not too remote, accidental in its occurrence or dependent on another's volitional act to have a just bearing on the defendant's liability or on the gravity of his offense;

(b) if the offense requires that the defendant recklessly or negligently cause the result, that the actual result, as it occurred,

(i) is within the risk of which the defendant was or should have been aware, whether that risk extends to natural events or to the conduct of another, or, if not,

(ii) involves the same kind of injury or harm as that recklessly or negligently risked and is not too remote, accidental in its occurrence or dependent on another's volitional act to have a just bearing on the defendant's liability or on the gravity of his offense;

(c) if the offense imposes strict liability, that the actual result, as it occurred, is a probable consequence of the actor's conduct.

———

Why do Hart and Honore insist that "deeply ingrained common sense ideas about causality and responsibility" support their analysis? The underlying philosophical claim seems to be that voluntary acts of responsible persons initiate causal chains but are not themselves parts of causal chains. On this view it is a contradiction to talk about a voluntary act as caused. It follows therefore that a voluntary act severs a causal chain; in doing so it becomes a supervening cause.

This philosophical claim, however, is nonsense in both theory and practice. When we describe acts as "voluntary," we do not imply that they are uncaused. Consider acts both large (the choice of a career as, say, a lawyer or lion tamer) and small (the choice of an anchovy sandwich, say, over a dish of pistachio ice cream). Every such choice has causes. One does not have to be a psychologist to be certain that the choice to be a lawyer or lion tamer, to eat anchovies or ice cream, is not random and can be explained causally in terms of the actor's history and nature. None of this makes the choice involuntary, nor does it imply that the actor is not responsible. (Consider the selection from Professor Feinberg, *Causing Voluntary Acts*, excerpted below in Section C.)

In practice, the argument that a voluntary act severs the causal chain is similarly unsatisfactory. Suppose actor *A* knowingly sends the victim to a barber who, in the manner of the protagonist of the story *Sweeney Todd*, turns his clients into meat pies. The barbarous barber is surely liable, and his act is the voluntary act of a responsible agent. Nonetheless, his liability hardly absolves actor *A*, hardly severs the causal chain. The reason, as our MPC-honed intuitions tell us, is that the relationship between *A*'s acts and the victim's death is not at all remote or accidental.

The California draft, but not the Hart-Honore formula, gives us the same result as the MPC in this situation. The draft does not treat the voluntary acts of the homicidal barber as a superseding cause as long as they are "within the purpose or contemplation of the defendant."

The suggestion that the voluntary act of a responsible agent, however foreseeable, severs a causal chain, has special application in the cases in which the would-be superseding cause is a suicidal act. We will look more closely at such cases in the next Section.

[B] Determining the Limits of Causation

[1] Introduction

Questions about superseding causes arise in three distinguishable kinds of situations. First, they may be prompted by the acts of third parties. *Kibbe* and the hypothetical about a Sweeney Todd-like barber are both examples of this. Third parties may include nonhuman agents, such as the rabid dog in our variation on *Kibbe*.

Second, such questions may come up as a result of acts committed by victims. Suicidal acts by victims often raise these kinds of concerns. But other circumstances do so as well. Suppose, for example, that *A* attacks *V* in a homicidal rage and, after battering him with his fists, thinks that he has killed him—but is mistaken. *A* leaves *V* in a cave where *V*, lacking the strength to find help, decides to wait until his capacities improve. Instead he dies of neglect and starvation. In the words of Model Penal Code § 2.03, although the actual result occurs in a way not contemplated by *A*, "the actual result involves the same kind of . . . harm as that designed" and thus the only question is whether it is "too remote or accidental to have a [just] bearing on the actor's liability or the gravity of his offense."

In a third kind of situation, we may be uncertain whether the actor's mens rea does or does not embrace the kind of harm that results.

We will consider each of these categories in turn.

[2] Acts of Third Parties

[a] Expected or Planned Acts of Third Parties

Imagine a gang war among rival gangs involved in organized crime. One gang has hired a professional killer (*K*) to assassinate the operational head (*A*) of the rival gang. *A*, the would-be victim, knowing of the plan, hires a look-alike (*V*) to impersonate him in public. *K* kills *V*, the substitute.

K is clearly liable for intentionally killing *V*. Is *A* also liable or is *K* a superseding cause?

Under both the Model Penal Code and the California draft, the answer is clear. In the words of the MPC, the actual result *is* "within the purpose or the contemplation of the actor [*A*]" and therefore there is no need to consider whether *K*'s acts are "too remote or accidental," etc. The California draft gives the same result, under virtually the same rule.

Notes and Questions

1. **Characterizing the Foreseeable Intervenor.** This example raises terminological and conceptual problems. In Chapter 12, we will explore the distinction between the principal actor in a crime and accomplices. Even without a formal analysis, we can anticipate that the players in the hypothetical just given will be hard to characterize. For example, who is the principal in the homicidal act resulting in *V*'s demise?

K seems clearly to be the principal since his act brings about *V*'s death. But *A*'s role is hard to label. (1) He is not an accomplice. In the words of Model Penal Code § 2.06, he does not "aid," "attempt to aid," "agree to aid," or "solicit" *V*'s killing. (2) Moreover, he is not a co-principal, working cooperatively with *K* to kill *V*. (3) Thirdly, he is not a principal working through an innocent agent since *K* is hardly that. Thus, his role is hard to label.

2. **Can There Be Multiple Independent and Responsible Causal Agents?** The example demonstrates that there is nothing inconsistent about saying both (1) that *K* is a responsible, self-determining actor and is responsible for killing *V* and (2) that *K*'s actions are the result of a causal chain that includes *A*'s actions. (We have already looked at the relationship between these claims in discussing Hart and Honore on voluntary acts. See further discussion in Section C of this chapter.)

3. Causing and Hoping. It is important not to confuse the impersonation/assassination example with the following kind of situation. Suppose S sends T to California hoping that T will be killed in an earthquake. Against all odds, T, while in California, is at the epicenter of a quake and is killed. Is S liable for T's death?

Note that "but for" causation is present. But is that enough to establish S's liability? What is missing from this example that is present in the prior one?

[b] *Coincidental Acts of Third Parties*

This category of situations is anticipated by *Kibbe*, above, and our discussion of it. The following case typifies the way in which the issue of causation arises and reviews the applicable principles.

Commonwealth v. Rementer

598 A.2d 1300 (Pa. Super. Ct. 1991)

BECK, JUDGE.

[The appellant, a social acquaintance of the victim (Ms. Berry), accompanied her to a bar, where they began arguing. After they left the bar, he assaulted her and, ultimately, chased her through the streets of Philadelphia.]

. . . Vito Michielli and his wife and two small children were on Water Street that evening driving home from a shopping trip. Berry and appellant approached his car forcing him to stop. Berry was screaming "help me" and "let me in" and attempted to open the back door of the station wagon. Michielli and his wife were frightened and the children began to cry. The Michiellis' reaction was to lock all the doors and attempt to close the windows of the car. Mr. Michielli reached out of his window, pushed Berry away and sped off. Not until several days later, when a local newspaper reported the incident and Berry's tragic death, did Michielli realize that in leaving the scene his car had run over Berry.

. . . At trial, appellant testified on his own behalf. He stated that both he and Berry had injected cocaine earlier on the day of her death. He testified that they were arguing and that they had also been drinking. . . . According to appellant, Berry's pleas for help were entirely unprovoked by him. . . . Appellant admitted striking Berry but claimed that he did so out of anger because his attempts to calm her down by talking rationally had failed. He also claimed that he hit her only once, did not mean to hurt her and did not intend to kill her.

The trial court found appellant guilty of murder in the third degree. . . . [See Chapter 6, Section A, for Pennsylvania's statutory definition of third-degree murder.]

The issue regarding causation plainly arises in the instant case because the immediate cause of Berry's death was the crushing blow received under the wheels of Michielli's station wagon. Appellant argues that by the time Berry ran over to Michielli's car the "unfortunate domestic dispute" had ended and that therefore Berry's death had an accidental and intervening cause. Thus, according to appellant, the chain of causation between his assault on Berry and her resulting death had been broken. . . .

Many cases have grappled with the concept of what constitutes a legally sufficient causal connection where, as here, the immediate cause of death was not the blow dealt by the defendant's hand. We have concluded, from a careful reading of these cases and from analysis provided by criminal law commentators, that the resolution of the causation issue here and in analogous cases involves a two part inquiry. The first part of the inquiry requires us to decide whether the defendant's conduct was an operative cause of the victim's death. With respect to establishing a causal relationship between conduct and result, our crimes code poses a threshold factual requirement and that is, the conduct must be "an antecedent but for which the result in question would not have occurred." Thus, if the victim's death is attributable *entirely* to other factors and not at all brought about by the defendant's conduct, no causal connection exists and no criminal liability for the result can attach. The second part of the test raises the question of whether the result of defendant's actions were so extraordinarily remote or attenuated that it would be unfair to hold the defendant criminally responsible.

In discussing the first part of the test we point out that the defendant's conduct need not be the sole cause of the victim's death in order to establish causal connection. . . .

However, causation-in-fact, the "but for" element of assessing the causal connection, alone will not necessarily determine criminal culpability. If it did, little would distinguish tort liability from criminal liability. . . . Thus not only do we demand that the defendant's conduct actually cause the victim's death in that "it is an antecedent but for which the result in question would not have occurred," we also question, in cases such as the instant one, whether the fatal result was so extraordinary, remote or attenuated that it would be unfair to hold the defendant criminally responsible for it.

In our view, it is this second prong of the causation inquiry which is in fact at issue when our cases impose a "stricter" or "more direct" test for criminal causation than is needed for tort liability. . . .

In light of the foregoing principles, we examine appellant's claim that the evidence at trial was insufficient to establish the necessary causal connection between his conduct and Berry's resulting death. Appellant first contends that the argument he was having with Berry was over by the time she approached Michielli's car for aid and that, therefore, her actions in seeking refuge in the station wagon cannot be attributed to him. Berry's actions were not provoked by his assault but were spontaneous and unrelated to the "earlier dispute," appellant argues, and therefore, his conduct cannot be said to have caused her death.

This argument that there was no dispute occurring at the time Berry ran to Michielli's car is belied by considerable evidence which, when viewed in the light most favorable to the Commonwealth, establishes quite the contrary. As described above, several witnesses testified to the ferocity and tenacity of appellant's assault on Berry and all the observations attested to occurred within minutes of Berry's death. Campbell testified that he saw Berry shouting and running for help. He said appellant punched Berry in the head no more than two minutes before she fell to her death beneath the wheels of the car. Smith, Campbell and the Michiellis all testified that Berry's actions right up until the instant of her death were accompanied by cries for help, a fact which completely refutes appellant's claim that her actions were not taken in response to his conduct. Finally, Mrs. Michielli stated that when Berry approached their car, appellant was chasing her and was right behind her. Appellant's contention that the "dispute" had ended is wholly without support in the record.

Appellant further argues that Berry's death occurred through such an unforeseeable chain of events that his conduct cannot be said to have caused the fatal result. We disagree. The evidence at trial plainly established that appellant subjected Berry to a brutal and persistent assault from which she continually attempted to escape. In the first place, it is completely natural and foreseeable that any victim of an assault would respond to the danger by trying to escape it. In fact, it is difficult to imagine behavior which is more responsive or more predictable than fleeing from a deadly assault. Moreover, Berry's actions were particularly likely in the context of the instant case. Berry was clearly intent upon escaping her assailant at any cost and attempted to do so repeatedly. . . . The risk that Berry might suffer serious injury or death either during the assault or in her attempt to avoid it, was inherent in the situation appellant's attack created. In our view, the fatal result of appellant's assault is not rendered unforeseeable merely because the precise agency of death, i.e., the Michielli[s'] station wagon, could not have been foretold. Appellant perpetrated a deadly assault on the decedent in and around an automobile on a public street with other moving vehicles in close proximity. It is absurd to argue that the fatal result was so extraordinary or accidental that appellant should not be held criminally liable for the consequences of his conduct. We find that more than sufficient evidence was adduced at trial from which the factfinder could conclude that appellant's conduct was the legal cause of Berry's death.

Notes and Questions

1. The Foreseeability of Responsive Acts. Somewhat distinguishable from *coincidental* acts of third parties are what may be called *unexpected but responsive* acts. For example, *A*, intending to kill *B*, batters him severely and causes him to be hospitalized. Events—expected or unexpected—that affect *B* in the hospital are responsive, i.e., responses to the injuries caused by *A*.

When does maltreatment in a hospital constitute a superseding cause? Is maltreatment always a superseding cause?

On one hand, many cases stress that "a person who inflicts a serious wound upon another, calculated to destroy or endanger his life, will not be relieved of responsibility, even though unskilled or improper medical treatment aggravates the wound and contributes to the death." *Hall v. State*, 159 N.E. 420 (Ind. 1928). Thus, some of the risks encountered as maltreatment in hospitals are so-called normal risks and do not count as superseding. Among these are common infections contracted through normal contact with hospital personnel and illnesses frequently transmitted through blood transfusions.

On the other hand, if the patient is subjected to a wholly unconventional and dangerous procedure and dies as a result, or if the hospital in other ways creates unusual risks, then such conduct may well sever the causal connection.

In *Pittman v. State*, 528 N.E.2d 67 (Ind. 1988), the victim, who weighed between 400 and 500 pounds, was stabbed by the defendant/appellant, who had broken into his home to steal coins. The stab wound appeared to have done minimal damage, but the doctor decided to perform an exploratory laparotomy to determine whether vital organs had been damaged. In light of the victim's obesity and circulatory problems, this was a high risk procedure. About two weeks later, the victim died of a pulmonary embolism, a blood clot attributable to his obesity and post-operative immobility. Testimony indicated that the original stab wound was not serious and that the victim would probably have survived if the laparotomy had not been performed. The Supreme Court of Indiana affirmed a lower court conviction for voluntary manslaughter, finding that the performance of the laparotomy was not a superseding cause.

2. Human and Natural Interventions. Note that the principles discussed in *Rementer* apply to cases in which the coincidental acts are of nonhuman agency or result from forces of nature. If a battered victim is left in a violent hailstorm to die of the wounds inflicted by the assailant, and the victim instead is killed by large ice pellets, this intervention is hardly remote and accidental. On the other hand, if the victim is struck and killed by an asteroid, a court may well find that this is a superseding cause.

3. Odd Case, Odder Result. The *Rementer* case is discussed and distinguished in a bizarre Montana case, *State v. Sherer*, 60 P.3d 1010 (Mont. 2002). The defendant, practicing medicine under a false name and impersonating a doctor, advised several "patients" to cut and mutilate themselves. Having pled guilty to other charges, he appealed his conviction for aggravated assault on the grounds that the victims chose to injure themselves, that they acted on his advice by their own will. The Montana Supreme Court rejected the causal argument that the harmful results were too remote and unforeseeable to bear on the offender's liability.

Note that this case, which alludes to *Rementer*, refers to self-harming by victims, a topic that is discussed in detail in the next Section.

[3] Acts of Victims

[a] Suicidal Acts of Victims

Rex v. Beech

23 Cox Crim. Cas. 181 (1912)

The appellant was indicted before Lord Coleridge, J. at Cheshire Assizes for unlawfully and maliciously inflicting bodily harm upon the prosecutrix. He was found guilty and sentenced to twelve months' imprisonment in the second devision.

It appeared that the prosecutrix was the village nurse and lived alone. At 11:45 p.m. on an evening in November the appellant came to her house when she was in bed. He entered the house by breaking a window, and went upstairs to the bedroom occupied by the prosecutrix.

The door was locked and the appellant threatened to break it open if the prosecutrix would not let him in. She refused, and the appellant then tried to burst open the door. The prosecutrix called out that if he got in he would not find her in the room, and as the appellant continued his attack upon the door, the prosecutrix jumped out of the window, sustaining injuries. In giving evidence the prosecutrix stated that the appellant had attempted to interfere with her on a previous occasion when she had threatened to take poison if he touched her.

[Argument for appellant:] There was no evidence to show that the appellant had any reason to think the prosecutrix would jump out of the window, and therefore there was no evidence that he intended to do her any harm. It is essential that an intention to make her jump should have been shown. . . .

DARLING, JUSTICE. (after stating the evidence for the prosecution). It is complained that the learned judge did not put certain points to the jury, but we are unable to say that any material point was omitted or that anything was put incorrectly. Undoubtedly the tendency of the summing up was unfavourable to the appellant, but when that occurs it is not necessarily the fault of the judge; the facts may be too strong for him. What the learned judge told the jury was this: "Will you consider whether the conduct of the prisoner amounted to a threat of causing injury to this young woman; was the act of jumping the natural consequence of the conduct of the prisoner; and was the grievous bodily harm the result of the conduct of the prisoner? If you answer these three questions in the affirmative, your verdict will be one of guilty. If you answer them, or any one of them, in the negative, your verdict will be one of not guilty." We think that was a proper direction. The appeal must be dismissed.

Notes and Questions

1. Acts of Victims as Superseding Causes. Is it obvious why the acts of the victim in *Beech* are not a superseding cause? A similar result was reached in the Canadian case of *Rex v. Valade*, 26 Can. Cr. Cas. 233 (1915), in which a girl under the age of consent was compelled by the defendant to have sexual intercourse, jumped through a window to escape her assailant, and was killed.

These cases stand in contrast to *State v. Preslar*, 48 N.C. 421 (1956), in which the victim, the wife of the defendant, left home after a fight, with her father's house as her destination. Mysteriously, she chose to spend the night sleeping by the road outside her father's house and eventually died of the effects of exposure. Her acts were held to be a superseding cause of her death.

2. Factors in *Stephenson*. The cases just discussed play a role in the deliberations of the Supreme Court of Indiana in *Stephenson v. State*, excerpted below. In considering whether the defendant should be held liable for the victim's death, consider the foreseeability of the victim's acts, the responsibility of the victim, and the immediacy of the victim's acts.

Stephenson v. State

179 N.E. 633 (Ind. 1932)

Per Curiam. [Madge Oberholtzer, a young woman of 28, had seen the defendant socially several times between January and March 1925. On March 15, defendant and a few of his friends forced her against her will to accompany them on a train trip from Indianapolis to Chicago. During the trip, defendant forced Ms. Oberholtzer to suffer violent sexual assaults; her wounds included severe bites. During a stopover at a hotel in Hammond, Indiana, Ms. Oberholtzer, though guarded by one of Stephenson's friends, managed to obtain bichloride of mercury and swallowed the poison in a suicide attempt. She became violently ill. Stephenson, having discovered her suicide attempt and rejecting her calls for a doctor, drove her home to Indianapolis on March 17. She had many wounds and serious infections affecting internal organs. Notwithstanding regular medical treatment, she was warned on March 28 by her physician that "she had no chance of recovery . . . and that she was going to die." She died on April 14, almost exactly a month after her abduction.]

[Stephenson was convicted of second-degree murder.]

Appellant very earnestly argues that the evidence does not show appellant guilty of murder. He points out in his brief that, after they reached the hotel, Madge Oberholtzer left the hotel and purchased a hat and the poison, and voluntarily returned to his room, and at the time she took the poison she was in an adjoining room to him, and that she swallowed the poison without his knowledge, and at a time when he was not present. From these facts he contends that she took her life by committing suicide; that her own act in taking the poison was an intervening responsible agent which broke the causal connection between his acts and the death; that his acts were not the proximate cause of her death, but the taking of the poison was the proximate cause of death. . . .

Bishop in his work on Criminal Law, vol. 2, (9th Ed.) page 484, says: "When suicide follows a wound inflicted by the defendant his act is homicidal, if deceased was rendered irresponsible by the wound and as a natural result of it." We do not understand that by the rule laid down by Bishop, *supra*, that the wound which renders the deceased mentally irresponsible is necessarily limited to a physical wound. We should think the same rule would apply if a defendant engaged in the commission of a felony such as rape or attempted rape, and inflicts upon his victim both physical and mental injuries, the natural and probable result of which would render the deceased mentally irresponsible and suicide followed, we think he would be guilty of murder. In the case at bar, appellant is charged with having caused the death of Madge Oberholtzer while engaged in the crime of attempted rape. The evidence shows that appellant, together with Earl Gentry and the deceased, left their compartment on the train and went to a hotel about a block from the depot, and there appellant registered as husband and wife, and immediately went to the room assigned to them. This change from their room on the train to a room in the hotel is of no consequence, for appellant's control and dominion over the deceased was absolute and complete in both cases. The evidence further shows that the deceased asked for money with which to purchase a hat, and it was supplied her by "Shorty," at the direction of appellant, and that she did leave the room and was taken by Shorty to a shop and purchased a hat and then, at her request, to a drug store where she purchased the bichloride of mercury tablets, and then she was taken back to the room in the hotel, where about 10 o'clock a.m. she swallowed the poison. Appellant argues that the deceased was a free agent on this trip to purchase a hat, etc., and that she voluntarily returned to the room in the hotel. This was a question for the jury, and the evidence would justify them in reaching a contrary conclusion. Appellant's chauffeur accompanied her on this trip, and the deceased had, before she left appellant's home in Indianapolis, attempted to get away, and also made two unsuccessful attempts to use the telephone to call help. She was justified in concluding that any attempt she might make, while purchasing a hat or while in the drug store, to escape or secure assistance would be no more successful in Hammond than it was in Indianapolis. We think the evidence shows that the deceased was at all times from the time she was entrapped by the appellant at his home on the evening of March 15th till she returned to her home two days later, in the custody and absolute control of appellant. Neither do we think the fact that the deceased took the poison some four hours after they left the drawing-room on the train or after the crime of attempted rape had been committed necessarily prevents it from being a part of the attempted rape. Suppose they had not left the drawing-room on the train, and, instead of the deceased taking poison, she had secured possession of appellant's revolver and shot herself or thrown herself out of the window of the car and died from the fall. We can see no vital difference. At the very moment Madge Oberholtzer swallowed the poison she was subject to the passion, desire, and will of appellant. She knew not what moment she would be subject to the same demands that she was while in the drawing-room on the train. What would have prevented appellant from compelling her to submit to him at any moment? The same forces, the same impulses, that would impel her to shoot herself during the actual attack or throw herself out of the car window after the attack had ceased, [were] pressing and overwhelming her at the time she swallowed the poison. The evidence shows that she was so weak that she staggered as she left the elevator to go to the room in the hotel, and was assisted by appellant and Gentry. That she was very ill, so much so that she would not eat, all of which was the direct and proximate result of the treatment accorded her by appellant. We think the situation no different here than we find in the *Beech* Case or the *Valade* Case, *supra*. To say that there is no causal connection between the acts of appellant and the death of Madge Oberholtzer, and that the treatment accorded her by appellant had no causal connection with the death of Madge Oberholtzer would be a travesty on justice. The whole criminal program was so closely connected that we think it should be treated as one transaction, and should be governed by the same principles of law as was applied in the case of *Rex v. Beech* and *Rex v. Valade, supra*. We therefore conclude that the evidence was sufficient and justified the jury in finding that appellant by his acts and conduct rendered the deceased distracted and mentally irresponsible, and that such was the natural and probable consequence of such unlawful and criminal treatment, and that the appellant was guilty of murder in the second degree as charged in the first count of the indictment. . . .

Instruction No. 43, given by the court of his own motion, told the jury that "one who inflicts an injury on another is deemed by the law to be guilty of homicide, if the injury contributes mediately or immediately to the death of such other. The fact that other causes contribute to the death does not relieve the actor from responsibility. While it is true that a person cannot be killed twice, yet it is equally true that two persons can contribute to cause the death of another, in which case each will be responsible for such death."

We think the evidence justified the court in submitting the question to the jury, as there was evidence that the deceased died from the joint effect of the injuries inflicted on her, which, through natural cause and effect, contributed mediately to the death. We think the proposition of law stated in this instruction is well supported by authority. "The general rule, both of law and reason, is, that whenever a man contributed to a particular result, brought about, either by sole volition of another, or by such volition added to his own, he is to be held responsible for the result, the same as if his own unaided hand had produced it. The contribution, however, must be of such magnitude and so near the result that sustaining to it the relation of cause and effect, the law takes it within its cognizance. Now, these propositions conduct us to the doctrine, that whenever a blow is inflicted under circumstances to render the party inflicting it criminally responsible, if death follows, he will be holden for murder or manslaughter, though the person beaten would have died from other causes, or would not have died from this one, had not others operated with it; provided, that the blow really contributed mediately or immediately to the death as it actually took place in a degree sufficient for the law's notice." . . .

MARTIN, JUSTICE (dissenting in part, concurring in part, dissenting in the conclusion).

Unlawful act must be the proximate cause of death. "To render a person responsible for the death of another . . . his unlawful act or omission must be the proximate cause of the death of the person killed." . . . In the case at bar the evidence is not sufficient to show that the bite or the infection resulting therefrom was the proximate cause responsible for decedent's death, but it appears that bichloride of mercury poisoning was the supervening, proximate, and responsible cause thereof.

Responsibility for deceased's having taken poison. While the state maintains that the wound inflicted during the attempted rape and the infection resulting therefrom was the cause of death and that appellant was guilty of murder by reason thereof, "even though the poison as a concurrent cause of death were taken by her without legal responsibility therefor by appellant"; yet it also contends that appellant is guilty of murder for the reason that he is legally responsible for deceased's having taken the poison.

It is unnecessary to consider here the much-mooted question as to whether suicide is a crime, or to consider the criminal liability of one who advises or aids another to commit suicide. . . . There was no evidence that appellant "administered" the poison or "caused the same to be administered" to deceased, or that at the time the deceased took the poison she was under any restraint or compulsion by appellant, which would cause her act to be considered in law the act of the appellant.

Where, upon deliberation, one commits suicide because of shame, humiliation, or remorse, the one who caused such mental state, although he may be morally responsible for the death in the sight of God, is not guilty of murder under the law, unless he in some way procured, advised, compelled, assisted, or exercised control over the person performing the act. . . .

Taking of poison as a natural consequence of the rape, attempted rape or bite. Only one argument by which the state sought to sustain the verdict of guilty under the first count of the indictment remains for consideration, viz., that one who inflicts a wound is held to contemplate and be responsible for the natural consequence of his act, and that at the time appellant committed the rape, or the attempted rape, he was bound to anticipate deceased's act of taking bichloride of mercury. I do not find any evidence to justify a finding that the taking of poison by deceased was such an act as a reasonable person under similar circumstances would have committed. . . .

After a consideration of all the foregoing propositions by the court, the per curiam opinion was adopted, which holds that the allegation in the indictment that Miss Oberholtzer was "distracted with pain and shame" when she took bichloride of mercury was sufficient to charge that she was mentally irresponsible when she took the poison; and that the evidence was sufficient to show the infliction of physical and mental injuries which rendered the deceased mentally irresponsible at the time of her "suicide." I do not believe the adjective clause of the indictment "distracted with pain and shame" is equivalent to a charge that the deceased was of unsound mind or was mentally unbalanced. Charges in an indictment must be clear and plain, and if the grand jury had intended to make a charge that the appellant had by his acts caused Madge Oberholtzer to become mentally unbalanced and of unsound mind they would have done so by a definite and certain charge to that effect.

The trial was not had on any such theory, and there is no evidence to indicate that at any time the mind of the deceased was not clear and sound. We cannot assume otherwise without proof. An assumption that every person who commits suicide is insane as well as an unqualified holding that one who mistreats another so as to cause insanity is responsible for the criminal acts thereafter committed by such person, would lead to most dangerous legal consequences. . . .

I do not believe that the evidence is sufficient to sustain a finding of guilty under the first count of the indictment, and for that reason . . . believe that the judgment should be reversed . . . .

Notes and Questions

1. **The Context of *Stephenson*.** The publicity and notoriety that accompanied *Stephenson* can be explained not merely by the horrific facts of the case but also by Stephenson's status as Grand Dragon of the Ku Klux Klan. Some historians attribute the beginning of the decline of the KKK's power to this case. *Cross of Fire*, a 1989 made-for-television docudrama, was based on the circumstances that gave rise to *Stephenson*.

2. **Pushing the Limits of Doctrine.** Note that this case required the court to reach beyond such cases as *Beech* and *Valade* in finding that Stephenson had "control" over Oberholtzer's actions. In the earlier cases, the immediacy, spontaneity, and unthinking character of the victim's self-destructive acts are crucial to this kind of finding. The dissent in *Stephenson* assumes that control is the relevant criterion and questions whether the facts of the case support such a finding.

3. **The Reasoning in *Stephenson*.** How does the court determine that Stephenson was legally responsible for Oberholtzer's death? Is it essential to their reasoning that she was not "mentally responsible" and that therefore her suicidal act was not voluntary?

4. ***Stephenson* and the MPC.** What is the relationship between the criteria used in *Stephenson* and Model Penal Code § 2.03's requirement that the actual result "involve . . . the same kind of injury or harm as the probable result" of Stephenson's assault and that the actual result not be "too remote or accidental in its occurrence"? Does Stephenson's conduct meet these tests?

———————

The following case involves liability for the consequences of another person's suicide.

State v. Bauer
471 N.W.2d 363 (Minn. Ct. App. 1991)

SHORT, JUDGE.

Eighteen-year-old Rachelle Cazin died of a single gunshot wound to the head. Justin Bauer, then 17, was with Cazin when she died. At the time of her death, Cazin was pregnant with a six to six-and-one-half month old fetus. Bauer did not deny paternity, but testified he did not believe Cazin was pregnant. There was testimony at trial that Bauer made threats against Cazin because she was spreading rumors she was pregnant with his child. Bauer admitted he was angry with Cazin.

On April 9, Cazin asked Bauer to meet her in the woods near their home and to bring his gun. The couple met as planned and agreed to commit suicide together. Bauer testified Cazin put the gun in her mouth and he counted to three, but nothing happened. Bauer claims he then tried to talk Cazin out of shooting herself. As he walked away from her, he heard a gunshot. Bauer hid Cazin's body under a layer of brush, ran home, changed his clothes, unloaded the gun, threw the remaining shells outside and cleaned the gun.

That evening, a priest in Mountain Iron received an anonymous call. The caller said his girlfriend had committed suicide after he backed out of the suicide pact. He admitted to the priest that he had hidden the girl's body and was afraid no one would believe him. When police associated this call with Cazin's disappearance, they obtained a search warrant for Bauer's home. At first, Bauer told them Cazin had not shown up for the arranged meeting. When confronted with the call to the priest, Bauer admitted his involvement. He showed them the rifle in his bedroom, and led them to the scene where Cazin's body was located.

The jury found Bauer not guilty of second degree (intentional) murder and fetal homicide. He was found guilty of aiding a suicide and of felony fetal homicide. . . .

Bauer challenges the state's proof of causation on the fetal homicide offense. Bauer was convicted of "causing the death of an unborn child, without intent to effect the death of any unborn child or person, while committing or attempting to commit a felony offense." Expert testimony established that the fetus died from asphyxiation caused by cessation of blood flow from its mother. This death was certainly a foreseeable consequence of her suicide. Although Bauer testified he did not know Cazin was pregnant, there was much evidence from which the jury could have inferred otherwise. Nor are we persuaded Cazin's decision to commit suicide was an intervening independent force. . . . Cazin's suicide was not an "intervening cause," as Bauer argues, because he participated in it and could reasonably have foreseen it. An accomplice can be guilty of felony murder even though his accomplice commits an intentional act which more proximately causes the death. . . .

We find no causation problem with applying the felony murder rule to these facts.

Notes and Questions

1. **Felony Murder and the Problem of Causation.** Note that one function of felony murder statutes is to evade the limits of causation provisions like those in the Model Penal Code. Consequences that might otherwise be "too remote and accidental" thus become legitimate bases for liability. Minnesota's "felony fetal homicide" provision seems to have this role in *Bauer*. (For further discussion of the causation issues that arise in felony murder cases, see Chapter 6, Section D.2.c.)

2. Alternative View of *Bauer*. In the absence of the felony fetal homicide provision, would Bauer's claim that Cazin's acts were a superseding cause be a successful argument, absolving him of liability for the death of the fetus?

3. Facilitating Suicide. In *State v. Marti*, 290 N.W.2d 570 (Iowa 1980), the defendant provided the victim with the means to shoot herself by loading a gun and putting it beside her. The victim did indeed commit suicide immediately thereafter, and the Supreme Court of Iowa held that the jury was properly instructed to determine whether the victim's act was a superseding and intervening cause. The jury found that it was not, and the defendant was convicted of involuntary manslaughter.

A different situation also involving a victim's decision to end his life was presented in *State v. Fox*, 810 N.W.2d 888 (Iowa Ct. App. 2011). The defendant, Troy Fox, was driving a car with his friend, Ruben Mayo, as his passenger and crashed into a utility pole on the highway. The two men had both been drinking. Mayo sustained spinal cord injuries and traumatic brain damage and could only communicate by blinking. After Mayo decided to discontinue his life support, Fox was convicted of homicide by vehicle. Following the view taken by many courts, the appellate court held that Mayo's conscious decision to remove life-sustaining medical assistance was not an intervening and superseding cause of death that relieved Fox's criminal culpability for homicide, and it affirmed the conviction. *See also State v. Pelham*, 824 A.2d 1082 (N.J. 2003).

[b] Other Self-Destructive Acts of Victims

Shirah v. State

555 So. 2d 807 (Ala. Crim. App. 1989)

Tyson, Judge.

On the night of April 13, 1987, Michael Shane Nelson (the victim), Marlene Nelson (the victim's sister), Karland Thompson, and the appellant gathered at Angela Davis's apartment. At some point, the group went to a liquor store where Davis purchased some beer and the appellant bought some whiskey. On the way back to Davis's apartment, the group smoked a joint of marijuana. Once back at Davis's apartment, everyone began drinking. Several other people came by during the course of the night. When the liquor ran out, the appellant stated that he knew where he could get some morphine. Shortly thereafter, the appellant and the victim left the apartment. When they returned, the appellant had a glass with a clear liquid in it. Thompson asked what was in the glass and the appellant said that it was morphine. The appellant went to the kitchen and mixed the morphine with some Sprite in a glass. He then brought the glass containing the mixture into the living room. Marlene took a sip from the glass, and the victim drank about half the glass. The appellant also drank the mixture.

The group then spent the night at Davis's apartment. When Davis tried to wake the victim the next morning, she could not arouse him. The victim was not breathing and was turning blue. When the victim would not wake up after he was placed in the shower, the police and paramedics were called. . . .

The appellant contends that the State failed to prove that his conduct was the cause-in-fact of the appellant's death. Citing *Lewis v. State*, 474 So. 2d 766 (Ala. Crim. App. 1985), he argues that since the victim voluntarily and knowingly drank the morphine, the victim's conduct was a superseding and intervening cause sufficient to break the chain of causation.

The facts of *Lewis* are clearly distinguishable from the case at bar. In *Lewis*, the victim and the defendant had "played" Russian roulette at the defendant's house on the day in question. After the "game" was over, the defendant put the gun away and went into another room and made a telephone call. During this time, the victim found the gun and shot himself.

This court in *Lewis* held that the victim "exercised his own free will when he got the gun, loaded it and shot himself," and thus, "the victim's conduct was a supervening, intervening cause sufficient to break the chain of causation." *Lewis*, 474 So. 2d at 771. We also stated that:

> If the victim had shot himself while he and the appellant were playing Russian Roulette, or if the appellant was present when the victim was playing the game by himself, the appellant's conduct of influencing the victim to play would have been the cause-in-fact and the proximate cause of the victim's death. . . .

> It also seems clear that the appellant would be responsible for the victim's death if he had left the room while the victim was still playing the game because he should have perceived the result. But, the evidence reveals that the appellant had put the gun away after they finished playing the "game."

Lewis, 474 So. 2d at 771.

In the case at bar, the State's evidence showed that it was the appellant who supplied the morphine to the victim. When the whiskey ran out that night, it was the appellant who told the group that he knew where he could obtain some morphine. The appellant and the victim then went to the appellant's house and got the morphine, which had been prescribed for the appellant's father who was dying of cancer. The two returned to Davis's apartment. The appellant then mixed the morphine and some Sprite in a glass and brought the glass into the living room. The appellant then allowed the victim to drink from the glass.

Section 13A-2-5(a), Code of Alabama 1975, provides that "[a] person is criminally liable if the result would not have occurred but for his conduct, operating either alone or concurrently with another cause, unless the concurrent cause was sufficient to produce the result and the conduct of the actor clearly insufficient."

"If the actual result is not within the contemplation of the actor, or within the area of risk which he should have been aware, he is not deemed to have 'caused' the result. But if the difference is only one concerning which person or what property would be affected by defendant's act, or one of the degree of harm which would result, he is still held to have 'caused' the result." Commentary, Ala. Code, § 13A-2-5 (1975).

In *Lewis*, we found that the victim's conduct was a superseding, intervening cause because we did not believe that the appellant should have perceived that the victim would go get the gun and shoot himself with it after the gun had been put away. Here, the appellant made the morphine available to the victim and was present when the victim drank the morphine mixture. The victim's conduct in voluntarily drinking the morphine was a concurrent cause rather than a superseding, intervening cause. The fact that the appellant only believed the victim would get "high" by drinking the morphine does not change the result. . . .

Thus, we find that the State sufficiently proved the causal relationship between the appellant's conduct and the victim's death [and affirm the defendant's conviction of criminally negligent homicide].

Notes

1. **Causation and Drug Use.** *State v. Wassil*, 658 A.2d 548 (Conn. 1995), likewise affirming a manslaughter conviction, is typical of many cases in which a defendant sold or gave drugs to a friend, who, in turn, consumed or injected the drugs and died of an overdose. In many of these cases, the defense that there was a supervening act by the deceased is rejected and the delivery of the drugs by the defendant is determined to be a reckless act.

Analytically, it is arguable that the death of an individual as a result of the intake of drugs supplied by another person is statistically a highly unusual occurrence and is therefore indeed a "remote and accidental" result, barring special circumstances. Nonetheless, quite a few cases are in accord with *State v. Wassil*. In *Aumuller v. State*, 944 So. 2d 1137 (Fla. 2007), for example, a drug dealer sold heroin to the victim, Jairon Nevius, who overdosed and died after consuming the heroin as well as alcohol and Valium. On appeal, the Florida Supreme Court upheld Aumuller's conviction of first-degree murder by drug distribution.

In *People v. Kidd*, 997 N.E.2d 634 (Ill. App. Ct. 2013), the defendant was convicted of drug-induced homicide when his girlfriend died after inhaling cocaine with him. The charges were based on an Illinois statute that states (ungrammatically) the following: "A person who . . . deliver[s] a controlled substance to another, and any person's death is caused by injection, inhalation, or ingestion of any amount of that controlled substance, commits the offense of drug-induced homicide." 720 ILCS 5/9-3.3(a). The appeals court agreed with the trial court that the defendant's act of providing the victim with cocaine was the "proximate cause" of her death.

2. **Causation in *Feinberg*.** Compare these cases with *Commonwealth v. Feinberg*, 253 A.2d 636 (Pa. 1969). (For other aspects of this case, see Chapter 6, Section C.2.) Feinberg, who operated a tobacco store in a run-down section of Philadelphia, regularly sold Sterno, a product designed to be burned for heat but used commonly as an intoxicant. In the latter part of 1963 Feinberg received and sold a large shipment of

so-called "industrial" Sterno, which had a much higher (and therefore much more dangerous) percentage of methanol. The cans of industrial Sterno bore the warning, "Poison. For use only as fuel. Not for consumer use." Thirty-one persons died from the effects of methanol poisoning, allegedly after drinking from cans sold by Feinberg. Evidence showed both that Feinberg knew his customers drank Sterno as an intoxicant and that he should have been aware that industrial Sterno was poisonous. The Pennsylvania Supreme Court upheld his conviction for manslaughter, holding that the victims' voluntary consumption of the poison was not an intervening/superseding cause because "the drinking of the liquor, in consequence of the defendant's act, was . . . what the defendant contemplated."

[4] Complementary and Concurrent Acts

The case of *Lewis v. State*, discussed in *Shirah*, is one of a family of cases involving such activities as drag racing and Russian Roulette—joint or cooperative activities that involve risk. When one of the participants is killed, what is the criminal liability of the survivor? In the case of Russian Roulette, in which typically the participants each take a turn firing at themselves a gun with *some* chambers filled, two points are ordinarily clear. The acts of each participant are the voluntary acts of a responsible agent, but any act that culminates in death is hardly "remote and accidental." Rather it is in the contemplation of those who play. Thus, liability under the Model Penal Code for reckless homicide (amounting to murder or manslaughter) is appropriate. (Joint participation in the shared activity supplies the actus reus.) The acts of the victim are not a superseding cause.

In the case of drag racing, the analysis is more complicated. On the one hand, one may analogize the activity to Russian Roulette and emphasize the known risk of the activity. On this account, each participant is responsible for the acts of all others, and harm either to a participant or an onlooker is unlikely to act as a superseding cause.

On the other hand, the activity is usually not as risky as Russian Roulette and the danger of drag racing often results from unexpected mistakes made by participants. If this dimension is emphasized, the mistakes of participants are more likely to be superseding causes, acts that, being unexpected, are indeed remote and accidental from the standpoint of surviving co-participants.

(Note that *Commonwealth v. Malone*, discussed in Chapter 6, Section C.1, raises questions about assessing mens rea in Russian Roulette cases. In Chapter 12, Section C, we will look at the relevance of the concept of accomplice liability to drag racing cases.)

Commonwealth v. Root
170 A.2d 310 (Pa. 1961)

Charles Alvin Jones, Chief Justice.

The appellant was found guilty of involuntary manslaughter for the death of his competitor in the course of an automobile race between them on a highway. The trial court overruled the defendant's demurrer to the Commonwealth's evidence and, after verdict, denied his motion in arrest of judgment. On appeal from the judgment of sentence entered on the jury's verdict, the Superior Court affirmed. We granted allocatur because of the important question present as to whether the defendant's unlawful and reckless conduct was a sufficiently direct cause of the death to warrant his being charged with criminal homicide.

The testimony, which is uncontradicted in material part, discloses that, on the night of the fatal accident, the defendant accepted the deceased's challenge to engage in an automobile race; that the racing took place on a rural 3-lane highway; that the night was clear and dry, and traffic light; that the speed limit on the highway was 50 miles per hour; that, immediately prior to the accident, the two automobiles were being operated at varying speeds of from 70 to 90 miles per hour; that the accident occurred in a no-passing zone on the approach to a bridge where the highway narrowed to two directionally-opposite lanes; that, at the time of the accident, the defendant was in the lead and was proceeding in his right-hand lane of travel; that the deceased, in an attempt to pass the defendant's automobile, when a truck was closely approaching from the opposite direction, swerved his car to the left, crossed the highway's white dividing line and drove his automobile on the wrong side of the highway head-on into the oncoming truck with resultant fatal effect to himself.

This evidence would of course amply support a conviction of the defendant for speeding, reckless driving and, perhaps, other violations of The Vehicle Code. . . . In any event, unlawful or reckless conduct is only one ingredient of the crime of involuntary manslaughter. Another essential and distinctly separate element of the crime is that the unlawful or reckless conduct charged to the defendant was the *direct* cause of the death in issue. The first ingredient is obviously present in this case but, just as plainly, the second is not.

While precedent is to be found for application of the tort law concept of "proximate cause" in fixing responsibility for criminal homicide, the want of any rational basis for its use in determining criminal liability can no longer be properly disregarded. When proximate cause was first borrowed from the field of tort law and applied to homicide prosecutions in Pennsylvania, the concept connoted a much more direct casual relation in producing the alleged culpable result than it does today. Proximate cause, as an essential element of a tort founded in negligence, has undergone in recent times, and is still undergoing, a marked extension. More specifically, this area of civil law has been progressively liberalized in favor of claims for damages for personal injuries to which careless conduct of others can in some way be associated. To persist in applying the tort liability concept of proximate cause to prosecutions for criminal homicide after the marked expansion of *civil* liability of defendants in tort actions for negligence would be to extend possible *criminal* liability to persons chargeable with unlawful or reckless conduct in circumstances not generally considered to present the likelihood of a resultant death.

Even if the tort liability concept of proximate cause were to be deemed applicable, the defendant's conviction of involuntary manslaughter in the instant case could not be sustained under the evidence. The operative effect of a supervening cause would have to be taken into consideration. But, the trial judge refused the defendant's point for charge to such effect and erroneously instructed the jury that "negligence or want of care on the part of . . . [the deceased] is no defense to the criminal responsibility of the defendant. . . ."

Under the uncontradicted evidence in this case, the conduct of the defendant was not the proximate cause of the decedent's death as a matter of law. . . .

In the case now before us, the deceased was aware of the dangerous condition created by the defendant's reckless conduct in driving his automobile at an excessive rate of speed along the highway but, despite such knowledge, he recklessly chose to swerve his car to the left and into the path of an oncoming truck, thereby bringing about the head-on collision which caused his own death.

To summarize, the tort liability concept of proximate cause has no proper place in prosecutions for criminal homicide and more direct casual connection is required for conviction. In the instant case, the defendant's reckless conduct was not a sufficiently direct cause of the competing driver's death to make him criminally liable therefor.

The judgment of sentence is reversed and the defendant's motion in arrest of judgment granted. . . .

EAGEN, JUSTICE (dissenting).

The opinion of the learned Chief Justice admits, under the uncontradicted facts, that the defendant, at the time of the fatal accident involved, was engaged in an unlawful and reckless course of conduct. Racing an automobile at 90 miles per hour, trying to prevent another automobile going in the same direction from passing him, in a no-passing zone on a two-lane public highway, is certainly all of that. Admittedly also, there can be more than one direct cause of an unlawful death. To me, this is self-evident. But, says the majority opinion, the defendant's recklessness was not a direct cause of the death. With this, I cannot agree.

If the defendant did not engage in the unlawful race and so operate his automobile in such a reckless manner, this accident would never have occurred. He helped create the dangerous event. He was a vital part of it. The victim's acts were a natural reaction to the stimulus of the situation. The race, the attempt to pass the other car and forge ahead, the reckless speed, all of these factors the defendant himself helped create. He was part and parcel of them. That the victim's response was normal under the circumstances, that his reaction should have been expected and was clearly foreseeable, is to me beyond argument. That the defendant's recklessness was a substantial factor is obvious. All of this, in my opinion, makes his unlawful conduct a direct cause of the resulting collision. . . .

The majority opinion states, "Legal theory which makes guilt or innocence of criminal homicide depend upon such *accidental* and *fortuitous circumstances* as are now embraced by modern tort law's encompassing concept is . . . too harsh to be just." If the resulting death had been dependent upon "accidental and fortuitous circumstances" or, as the majority also say, "in circumstances not generally considered to present the likelihood of a resultant death," we would agree that the defendant is not criminally responsible. However, acts should be judged by their tendency under the known circumstances, *not* by the actual intent which accompanies their performance. Every day of the year, we read that some teen-agers, or young adults, somewhere in this country, have been killed or have killed others, while racing their automobiles. Hair-raising, death-defying, lawbreaking rides, which encompass "racing" are the rule rather than the exception, and endanger not only the participants, but also every motorist and passenger on the road. To call such resulting accidents "accidental and fortuitous," or unlikely to result in death, is to ignore the cold and harsh reality of everyday occurrences. Root's actions were as direct a cause of Hall's death as those in the "shield" cases. Root's shield was his high speed and any approaching traffic in his quest to prevent Hall from passing, which he knew Hall would undertake to do, the first time he thought he had the least opportunity. . . .

While the victim's foolhardiness in this case contributed to his own death, he was not the only one responsible and it is not he alone with whom we are concerned. It is the people of the Commonwealth who are harmed by the kind of conduct the defendant pursued. Their interests must be kept in mind.

Notes and Questions

1. **The Dilemma in *Root*.** How would you resolve the causation issue in *Root*? What bearing should statistical evidence of deaths in cases of drag racing have on the court's decision about causation?

2. **Note on Suicide Pacts.** In a number of reported situations in which one participant to a suicide pact survived and the other did not, the survivors have been charged with first-degree murder or lesser homicide offenses (e.g., manslaughter on a mitigation by extreme emotional distress theory). Because the death of one participant follows directly from the mutual agreement to end life and from joint acts carrying out that agreement, lack of causation defenses are rarely effective. (Compare the facts and resolution of *Bauer* above.)

3. *Parolene v. United States.* In general, causation in criminal law is not partial or proportional. The criteria for causation are either satisfied or they are not. The case of *Parolene v. United States*, 134 S. Ct. 1710 (2014), can be seen as an exception. The victim was abused as a child, and images of her abuse were widely circulated. Parolene pled guilty to possessing child pornography, including two images of the victim. As an adult, the victim sought restitution in the amount of $3 million under 18 U.S.C. § 2259 for continuing hurt and humiliation; the Fifth Circuit held that restitution was not limited to losses proximately caused by Parolene and that each defendant/possessor of the images was liable for the victim's entire loss.

The Supreme Court disagreed and ruled that restitution was mandated in "an amount that comports with the defendant's relative role in the causal process that underlies the victim's general losses." It conceded that this "amount would not be severe in a case like this" because the victim's losses were "the product of the acts of thousands of offenders." But the Court added that the restitution, "a reasonable and circumscribed award," would not be "a token or nominal amount." The Court held as well that the victim's losses were proximately caused by Parolene and endorsed and applied the notion of aggregate causation, a concept not widely developed in prior law.

[C] Changing Conceptions of Responsibility

We have examined the legal scope and implications of causal responsibility. Those of you who are inclined to ask philosophical questions may see these legal distinctions as incomplete and therefore unsatisfactory. What does it mean to say that persons are causally responsible? Does it mean that their acts have no *antecedent* causes? Does responsibility involve free will and, if so, is an act done with free will an *uncaused* act? If any act is caused, does that mean that it occurred *necessarily* or that it was *determined*?

The branch of philosophy that deals with free will and the relationships among responsibility, blame, and causal determination of behavior is often called the philosophy of action.

We have argued that it is essential for criminal law that we be able to say that criminal defendants are responsible for their conduct and that they are therefore deserving of blame. This is often expressed by saying that they acted out of (or with) free will. It seems easy to move from this conclusion to the inference that, if the actor had free will, the conduct was not *determined* by *causes*. The underlying assumption is that either the actor freely chose to act (and is responsible, and held accountable) or the actor was determined to act by causes (and is therefore not responsible, and not to be held accountable).

These assumptions, logical as they may seem, involve significant confusion. Posing freedom and causation (determination) as mutually exclusive alternatives creates a dilemma for common sense. Thus, Professor Sanford Kadish has expressed the exclusivity view as follows:

> While man is total subject under the laws of the natural world, he is total sovereign over his own actions. . . . In the same sense and for the same reasons that a person's genes, upbringing, and social circumstances are not seen as the cause of his actions, neither are the actions of another seen as the cause of his actions. . . . [W]hen we seek to determine the responsibility of one person for the volitional acts of another, the concept of cause is not available to determine the answer.

Sanford H. Kadish, Blame and Punishment: Essays in the Criminal Law 140–45 (1987)

Professor Kadish notwithstanding, we *do not* see the concepts of responsibility and cause as exclusive but rather as complementary. We generally regard the behavior of responsible agents as subject to psychological explanation, sociological explanation, and so on. Offering someone a bargain on a used car may cause the individual to buy it; personal buying habits may help us offer a full causal explanation of that behavior. But the explanation in no way shows that the individual is not responsible for the conduct. If we assume that every choice that can be explained causally in this way is not a free act, then freedom disappears altogether (because every act is amenable to some kind of causal account, or even many kinds: psychological, economic, biological, and so on).

Philosophers of mind try to sort out this dilemma by looking more closely at the idea of causation. They point out that only *some* causal explanations are incompatible with holding actors responsible. In cases of insanity, duress, and sleepwalking, we (for various reasons) conclude that persons are not responsible and therefore not to be held criminally responsible. Other kinds of causal accounts (involving perhaps the sociological background or the emotional characteristics of the actor) are irrelevant to any claim of non-responsibility. The claim that someone was abused in childhood usually does not excuse a rape that the individual committed as an adult, even if it does move us toward a (partial) causal explanation. Why are some causes relevant to a finding of nonresponsibility and others not?

Philosophers offer examples to help explain how causation and freedom/responsibility are related in our general ways of thinking and in criminal law. For the most part, they offer a variety of ways of understanding the compatibility of causation and freedom — and understanding as well that some special kinds of causes are inconsistent with freedom and responsibility. These arguments are related to basic assumptions of criminal law.

Professor Joel Feinberg, in an essay titled *Causing Voluntary Actions,* which appeared in his 1970 book, DOING AND DESERVING, asks us to consider examples of cases in which it is obvious that voluntary, responsible acts are not only caused acts, but *deliberately* caused acts.

> It is my thesis that there is no conceptual barrier, at least none imposed by common sense, to our speaking of the causes of voluntary actions. This is a view in opposition to that of Professors Hart and Honore in their remarkable book *Causation in the Law.* These authors conclude, after a very careful scrutinizing of common sense and ordinary language, that "whatever the metaphysics of the matter may be, a [free and deliberate] human action is never regarded as itself caused." I shall call this thesis of theirs the *first cause principle,* for it asserts that every voluntary human action is a new causal start, a kind of prime mover or uncaused cause.
>
> . . . *Counterexample 1: the foolhardy bank teller.* Jones, a depositor in the defendant's bank, was standing in line before the depositor's window when a bank robber entered, drew his gun, and warned "If anyone moves I'll

shoot." The teller immediately grabbed something and dived to the floor. The bandit shot at him, and the ricocheting bullet struck Jones, still waiting in line, causing him severe injury. Jones than sued the bank (a more likely defendant than the impecunious bandit), charging that the teller's violation of the bandit's order created an unreasonable risk of harm to the customers and that the teller's thoughtless act was thus the cause of Jones's injury. Let us suppose, for the sake of this example, that the teller's act was "negligent" (that is, unreasonably risky) to the customers and that it was a necessary condition of Jones's injury. Let us suppose also that the bandit entered the bank fully informed of the various kinds of things that might happen and fully prepared to shoot if anyone should call his bluff and that, when he did shoot, he was calm, collected, and fully aware of what he was doing. Now, on these facts, he did not intend to injure Jones since he aimed at the teller; but let us assume that, when he shot at the teller, he was aware of the danger he was creating for others but quite indifferent with regard to the possibility that someone else might be hurt. One might well find, it seems to me, that the teller's negligent act was *the cause* of Jones's injury even though that injury would not have occurred but for the reckless and fully voluntary intervention of the bandit.

Counterexample 2: the ingenious suicide. Mr. Blue, tired of life but too squeamish to kill himself, decides to use a more robust kind of person as an unwitting means. He hears about Manley Firmview, who has often announced to his friends that, if he ever encountered a person who would say so-and-so to him, he would kill the rascal. Mr. Blue seeks out Mr. Firmview and says so-and-so to him. Firmview pauses for a moment, calmly considers the consequences, and then shoots the grateful Mr. Blue dead. Would common sense balk at the claim that Mr. Blue caused his own death *by means of* Firmview's free and deliberate "intervention?" That he killed himself or literally committed suicide may be going too far, but that his remarks to Firmview were the cause of his demise could scarcely be denied. . . .

One moral of these . . . stories is that there are many more ways of causing someone to do something than by compelling or forcing him, or persuading and inducing him to do it. One can unintentionally cause him to act by unwisely calling his bluff; or one can "get him to act" by accepting a standing offer, drawing his attention to an inciting situation, or capitalizing on his firmly fixed habits of mind.

Notes and Questions

1. Toward a General Reconciliation of Voluntariness and Causation. Feinberg obviously wants us to generalize from his counterexamples. He cites Hart and Honore as claiming that it never makes sense to talk about "causing voluntary action." Feinberg's reply has two parts. His counterexamples show that, *at least in these cases*, it makes sense to talk about causing voluntary action. In these cases, one person *deliberately* causes another's voluntary action. But by far the more important impli-cation is that in *every* case of voluntary action, it makes sense to look for some kind of causal explanation. In every case of voluntary action, in other words, we can look not only at "our own network of predispositions, expectations, purposes, and values" but also at how these personal characteristics filter "the determining influences."

2. Pragmatic Redescriptions of Voluntariness and Causation. It is one thing to show, as Feinberg does, that free will/voluntariness and causation are compatible aspects of all situations in which persons are held responsible. It is something else to show the practical consequences of using the concepts in this way. So-called prag-matic philosophers try to show how our modes of thought help us achieve useful ways of regarding ourselves and others. In the following selection, Daniel Dennett empha-sizes "the varieties of free will worth wanting" and shows the implications of our ways of thinking about responsibility and causation for the goals of criminal law.

DANIEL DENNETT, ELBOW ROOM: THE VARIETIES OF FREE WILL WORTH WANTING 153, 155, 158–63 (1984)[2]

The distinction between responsible moral agents and beings with diminished or no responsibility is coherent, real, and important. It is coherent, even if in many instances it is hard to apply; it draws an empirically real line, in that we don't all fall on one side; and, most important, the distinction matters: the use we make of it plays a crucial role in the quality and meaning of our lives.

The argument I will give for this view is, of necessity, an argument to the effect that it is rational for us to esteem free will and covet responsibility. No other sort of argument could be a defense of those concepts. . . .

When are people responsible for the bad things they do? To answer this question, we must pause to consider the point of *holding* people responsible. The judgment of responsibility, whether in a court of law, or by a private individual with regard to another, sets the stage for a decision about sanctions: What shall we do? What response should be made to this responsible agent?

Moral assessment of persons is important because of the bearing it has on how to behave *vis-á-vis* the persons assessed. It is offenders, not conduct, we must incarcer-ate or treat or blame, and our behavior is rational only insofar as it fits with what we can discover about offenders from their conduct.

We may decide to forgive, or we may decide to reproach, or denounce, or scold, or even punish the culprit. Each of these alternatives has a distinct place and ratio-nale in our interpersonal economy, and contributes to the depth of our institution of holding people responsible. But for simplicity I will concentrate on the most explicit (public, codified, instituted) response: punishment. . . .

Why do we want to punish people who "commit crimes"? . . .

In an ideal world, it seems, everyone would see the right thing to do and do it, just for that reason, so we would have no need of laws and a system of threatened punishments. Everyone would behave like angels. Heaven on Earth, in short. It might seem that in a somewhat less ideal world ("one step down") we would need the system of laws, since people (if they were like us) would be selfish and aggressive. But this system of laws would deter perfectly, because (unlike us) everyone would be so rational. People—all people—would see as plain as the noses on their faces that crime didn't pay, and hence would all abstain from it. Judges and policemen and jailers would be appointed and trained, and would sit around, like the Swiss Army, waiting to be called into action, but rather doubting that it would ever happen in their lifetimes.

Why isn't that the situation we find ourselves in? If we're really *homo sapiens*, the "rational animal," why are our prisons overcrowded and our judges overworked? One reason seems to be that we skimp on our institutions of enforcement, and hence people, being rational indeed, see that under certain conditions crime *does* pay, or at any rate is likely enough to pay to be worth the risk. The deterrent power of laws is (ideally) a function of people's perception of the likelihood of their being apprehended and the severity of the penalty that might be inflicted. Increasing either factor increases deterrence. The incidence of running red lights could be dramatically reduced by either installing a squad car at every intersection 24 hours a day (making apprehension very likely) or by making the penalty life imprisonment. But again, being rational, the citizenry determines that either option—or indeed any combination of these options watered down—would probably not be worth the cost to society. Better a few red lights should be run than we should have to devote so much of our wealth to enforcement, or to inflict such brutal (and brutalizing) punishments on miscreants. So our skimping is itself rational it seems.

Since rapidly diminishing returns would be the result of any further investment in strengthening our enforcement, the optimal institution will be one in which a certain amount of lawbreaking, apprehension, and conviction is "tolerated." That is not to say our present system needs no serious reform, but—runs this argument—it would be irrational to hold out any hope of devising a system of *perfect* deterrence. So lawbreakers will always be among us; the jailer will never have—should never have—an entirely ceremonial position.

But recognizing the value in minimizing the amount of lawbreaking (while also trying to minimize the costs of enforcement and punishment), we see that there are improvements (fine tuning) of the laws that are called for. Deterrence depends on several factors, and one is "publicity": deterrence has a chance to succeed only with people who *know* the law and *understand* the conditions and sanctions. There may be individuals, we recognize, who fail to meet these conditions, and hence may commit the prohibited deed because the deterrence effect of the law never reaches to them. That is why a part of the cost of the institution of laws is public education; secret laws are useless as deterrents. The cost-effective way of achieving a suitably high level of knowledge is to combine a sufficiently energetic public information program with a somewhat peremptory (and hence bracing) legal wrinkle: ignorance of the law is no excuse.

This latter condition provides a motivation to all to maintain a state of mild inquisitiveness about the law and any new changes in it, and would be outrageous, rationally unacceptable, in the absence of a "sufficiently" energetic public information program. That is why the two elements must operate together; provided that the state does its part in making the information available, it is not asking too much to hold the citizenry responsible for knowing it. It is important to note that the principle that ignorance of the law is no excuse has a measure of arbitrariness about it. It does not suppose that there *couldn't be* intuitively valid grounds for pleading ignorance as an excuse; it simply declares that such pleas *will not (normally) even be entertained*. Life is too short; the law must be efficient, and we have to draw the line somewhere. (This is the strategic idea, illustrated simply in this instance, that we will find as the basis of our sense of personal moral responsibility.) . . .

Our refusal, beyond some arbitrary point, to delve further into causes and circumstances may strike a chord of suspicion in some. Can this policy be fair? Indeed it can. Remember that the breaks average out; we could not improve basketball by disallowing the fluke shots and unlucky breaks. (My claim here is in effect that *holding people responsible* is the best game in town.) Recall that a certain tolerance for risk-taking lawbreakers was built into the rationale for skimping on law enforcement. It is not even a *prima facie* sign of irrationality if our miscreant has simply calculated the odds, decided that on this occasion law breaking is worth a shot, and lost. We cannot conclude from the fact that a wager was lost that it was irrationally made. So long as the risk was taken in full knowledge of the consequences of the loss, the agent can hardly complain that the sanctions now imposed are unfairly applied to him.

The effect of such an institution, with such a rationale, is to create—to *constitute*— a class of legally culpable agents whose subsequent liability to punishment maintains the credibility of the sanctions of the laws. The institution, if it is to maintain itself, must provide for the fine tuning of its arbitrary thresholds as new information (or misinformation) emerges that might undercut its credibility. One can speculate that there is an optimal setting of the competence threshold (for any particular combination of social circumstances, degree of public sophistication, and so on) that maximizes the bracing effect of the law. A higher than optimal threshold would encourage a sort of malingering on the part of defendants, which, if recognized by the populace, would diminish their respect for the law and hence diminish its deterrent effect. And a lower than optimal threshold would yield a diminishing return of deterrence and lead to the punishment of individuals who, in the eyes of society, "really couldn't help it." The public perception of the fairness of the law is a critical factor in its effectiveness.

I take the foregoing sketch to be a version of the standard, presumptive defense of our institution of law, trial, and punishment as an institution of deterrence. (There are other defenses I choose to pass over here.) It exhibits, in the daylight of familiar surroundings, the sort of rationale I suppose to exist for our more fundamental (but probably historically later) "institution": the "moral conceptual world" of personal responsibility.

Notes and Questions

1. Dennett's Premises. Dennett's style of argumentation may seem hard to grasp. As a pragmatist, he assumes and tries to spell out the ways in which the distinction between responsibility and non-responsibility (free will and coercion) has an ongoing function both in our ways of thinking and in maintaining our moral and legal institutions. The explanation of the distinction is no more and no less than an account of how it is used, what work it performs. Dennett admits that some applications of the distinction are controversial and that such controversies will never be wholly resolved. But he wants us to focus attention on the indispensability of the distinction and the usefulness of it.

2. Free Will and Compatibility. Note that Dennett takes for granted the compatibility of causation and free will. He shows how this compatibility is embedded in the ways we think about law. For example, whenever we consider the deterrent effects of law, we see it influencing (causing) the incidence of crimes, the quantity of criminal acts. To say that this causal influence occurs is, of course, perfectly compatible with saying that the persons who are or are not influenced by these deterrent effects may be held responsible for their actions (i.e., are acting with free will).

3. Causation in Jewish Law. An interesting article, *Murder by Gruma: Causation in Homicide Cases Under Jewish Law*, by Irene Merker Rosenberg, Yale L. Rosenberg, and Bentzion S. Turin, 80 B.U. L. Rᴇᴠ. 1017 (2000), explores the significant differences between the Jewish law of homicide under the Torah and the secular common law. The authors point out that, in the interest of avoiding all mistakes, all possibility of convicting and punishing the innocent, "a rabbinic court cannot convict a person of murder unless that person caused the victim's death directly and not by a gruma or indirect cause. One consequence then of Jewish law's focus on direct causation is that solicitation of an offense cannot be criminally punished. Moreover, no matter how much assistance a co-conspirator gives to a principal, accomplice liability is virtually nonexistent in Jewish law." The authors conclude that because "[p]unishment of the innocent is antithetical to the Jewish criminal justice system," the rules of (direct) causation in Jewish law "effectively eliminate . . . the possibility of erroneous conviction, leaving nothing to inference in the determination of guilt."

4. Scholarship on Causation. A complex and provocative discussion of the "metaphysics" of causation can be found in a symposium on the morality of criminal law published in 2000 in the California Law Review. Among the attempts to reconstruct and criticize the doctrine of causation in criminal law are Michael Moore's *The Metaphysics of Causal Intervention*, 88 Calif. L. Rev. 827 (2000), and Stephen Morse's *The Moral Metaphysics of Causation and Results*, 88 Calif. L. Rev. 879 (2000).

Chapter 11

Attempt and Solicitation

Introduction: The Challenge of Inchoate Offenses

The criminal law does not always require a completed offense or actual harm in order to impose criminal liability. Instead, some crimes are "inchoate"—meaning "incipient," "incomplete or imperfectly developed," from the Latin "to begin." Rather than a monolithic whole, a "crime" can often be viewed along a timeline: beginning with the conception of a criminal idea; running through the process of developing a criminal plan, enlisting co-actors, and taking steps to put the plan into effect; and ending with completion of the crime. (Of course, these steps can occur in a very short time, and not all crimes involve all of these steps.) The criminal law has long determined that criminal liability may be imposed backwards along this timeline almost—but not quite—back to the moment the criminal idea was first conceived.

It is also often said that Anglo-American law does not punish the mere formation of a criminal idea absent some overt act—there are no "thought crimes" in American law. *See United States v. Balsys*, 524 U.S. 666, 714 (1998) ("the First Amendment protects against the prosecution of thought crime"); Joshua Dressler, Understanding Criminal Law § 27.01, at 375 (7th ed. 2015). However, when an actor takes steps in furtherance of a criminal idea, in a way that seems dangerous or substantial, we criminalize the "attempt" to commit the crime. Moreover, for crimes that involve more than one actor, the crime of solicitation occurs when the architect of the plan asks another person to help. And if the person solicited agrees, we may call it the crime of "conspiracy." These three crimes—attempt, solicitation, and conspiracy—can all take place before any actual harm occurs. In effect, they extend the reach of the criminal law beyond the scope of the single actor who commits a completed crime. The Model Penal Code addresses these three "Inchoate Crimes" in close succession: § 5.01 (Attempt), § 5.02 (Solicitation), and § 5.03 (Conspiracy).

A number of challenges arise when the criminal law endeavors to criminalize inchoate conduct before the substantive crime is completed or any criminal harm results. At what point is criminal liability appropriate? May actors be punished even though they have given up the effort? And what about crimes that could not possibly have succeeded? In this Chapter, we address such questions regarding the inchoate crimes of attempt and solicitation. Conspiracy, which raises similar issues as well as other interesting questions, is addressed in Chapter 13. (For example, we will consider whether the crime of conspiracy comes too close to punishing mere ideas.) Another theory by which criminal liability is extended, to reach persons who "help" others commit crimes, is addressed in Chapter 12, "Accomplice Liability."

[A] Attempt

[1] Issues in Attempt

The crime of attempt has a distinctive peculiarity. Despite the basic premise that criminal law exists to punish persons who cause harm, the crime of attempt punishes persons who have caused no harm. Rather, their criminal liability consists of *trying* to cause harmful results.

1. Why Punish Attempts at All? It is, of course, logically possible to limit the use of criminal sanctions to actors who succeed in causing harm. What do we achieve by extending the reach of criminal law to those who try but fail? The answer depends on both theoretical and practical considerations. Theoretically, the answer rests on the aims of criminal law. If recognition of blameworthiness and delivering "just deserts" are the goals, then those who try to cause harm can be viewed as equally blameworthy and deserving of punishment as those who succeed. If deterrence is our focus, then those who try to commit crimes generally need restraint, and would-be criminals will be deterred by the sight of attempters going to jail.

The theory of general deterrence here is complicated by the arguments of some theorists that there is no deterrent value in punishing attempts, because all actors intend to succeed. If we punish all those who actually succeed, we will still achieve the maximum amount of deterrence. Other theorists disagree, arguing that more potential offenders will be deterred from committing their completed crimes if they believe they will be punished *whether or not they succeed*.

Perhaps the most common justification for criminalizing attempts is a pragmatic one: it allows law enforcement to intervene earlier, and thereby prevent crime. Note, however, that this represents a tradeoff with the value of certainty. Arresting actors before a crime has occurred runs the risk of criminalizing innocent, or at least nondangerous, behavior.

2. The Appropriate Punishment for Attempt. The question of how severely to punish attempts is as vexing as the question whether to punish attempts at all. In general, three different approaches are used. One position, adopted by § 5.05(1) of the Model Penal Code, is to punish attempts as severely as the completed crime — on the theory that the actors present the same danger, whether or not they succeed, and therefore merit the same degree of blame and deterrence. (The Model Penal Code creates an exception, however, for attempts to commit the most serious crimes — capital offenses and first-degree felonies — which are punished as second-degree felonies.) A second, widely adopted approach is to impose a prison term for attempts only half as severe as that authorized for the completed crime. *E.g.*, Cal.

Penal Code § 664. A more nuanced position is to punish attempts less severely than the completed offense, unless the conduct seems just as threatening. For example, the Federal Sentencing Guidelines recommend reducing the prison sentence for attempt unless the defendant committed all the acts necessary to complete the substantive offense, or was "about to do so" before the plan was interrupted. U.S. Sentencing Commission Guidelines Manual § 2X1.1(b) (2016) (decreasing the substantive "offense level" by three points for attempts).

These alternative approaches appear to place different weight on the various purposes for criminal punishment described in Chapter 2. How severely do you think attempts should be punished? Do attempts that cause no harm call for less retribution than completed offenses? In light of the Kantian saying, "an eye for an eye, a tooth for a tooth," perhaps the full force of criminal sanctions should not be imposed when neither an eye nor a tooth has been lost. Or is individualized case-by-case consideration inevitable? If so, does that suggest keeping the full range of punishment open, up to the maximum for the completed offense?

3. **Merger.** Note that every completed crime is preceded by an "attempt" to complete it. When an attempt actually leads to commission of the target crime, the criminal law "merges" the attempt with the completed offense so that a defendant is not convicted of both. Since every crime involves a (successful) attempt, the attempt is "merged" with (or absorbed into) the completed offense. This merger rule is also applied to the crime of "solicitation" described below in Section B. However, the merger rule is not applied to the crime of conspiracy in most jurisdictions. Rather, a group agreement to commit a crime, that is, a "conspiracy," is said to involve a separate and "distinct evil" from the target offense. *See United States v. Jimenez Recio*, 537 U.S. 270 (2003). (For further consideration of conspiracy, see Chapter 13, Section A.)

4. **Kinds of Attempts.** Some commentators divide attempts into two types: "complete but imperfect" attempts, where all the necessary acts are completed but the attempt fails for some external reason; and "incomplete" attempts, where a significant step is taken but not all acts necessary to complete the crime are performed. *See* Joshua Dressler, Understanding Criminal Law § 27.01, at 376 (7th ed. 2015); Andrew Ashworth, *Criminal Attempts and the Role of Resulting Harm Under the Code, and in the Common Law*, 19 Rutgers L.J. 725, 734 (1988).

Section 5.01(1) of the Model Penal Code divides the situations that give rise to possible attempt liability into three categories, using language that is somewhat more complex. (Ask yourself: is the MPC needlessly convoluted, or does the need for precision mandate somewhat clunky language?)

(a) **Complete Attempts.** The simplest kind, which needs little discussion, is described as follows: "[W]hen causing a particular result is an element of the crime, [the actor] does or omits to do anything with the purpose of causing or with the belief that it will cause such result without further conduct on his part." Model Penal Code § 5.01(1)(b). Note the use of the term "belief" rather than "knowledge" here. An easy example is the terrorist who sets a bomb to go off at noon—but the bomb malfunctions and fails to explode.

(b) **Interrupted Attempts.** Distinguishable from the first category of attempts are those situations in which the actor is interrupted in a course of conduct intended to culminate in criminal harm. Courts and legislators have struggled with the question of how much conduct is enough to constitute an attempt in such cases—that is, when does "mere preparation" turn into a criminal attempt? Here the MPC requires a "substantial step in a course of conduct planned to culminate in . . . commission of the crime." Model Penal Code § 5.01(1)(c).

At one time, some courts tried to incorporate such attempts into category (a), by refusing to impose liability unless the actor had carried out the so-called "last step." But this approach was obviously unsatisfactory in some cases. Consider the poisoner who plans to administer 13 doses of poison, one per day, until the victim is dead. Why shouldn't the poisoner be charged with attempt after administering the twelfth dose, the eighth, or even earlier? Shouldn't the law be permitted to intervene before the actor gets dangerously close to completing the crime?

(c) **Impossible Attempts.** A third kind of attempt involves a mistaken belief on the part of the actor. The actor mistakenly believes that the crime can be completed or the intended harm will occur, when in fact it cannot possibly happen. For example, when the actor tries to kill a "sleeping" victim, but the intended victim is already dead. Alternatively, an absentminded professor is leaving a restaurant in the middle of a sudden rainstorm. Seeing an umbrella that he had left in the restaurant the previous week, and mistakenly thinking it belongs to another customer, the professor takes it to ward off the rain. The professor has not committed the crime of theft, but should he be convicted of attempted theft?

Attempt convictions in such "impossibility" cases are controversial, and many common-law courts were unwilling to find actors criminally liable in (some) such circumstances. The Model Penal Code, however, imposes liability for even "impossible" attempts, providing that "a person is guilty of an attempt to commit a crime if . . . he purposely engages in conduct which would constitute the crime *if the attendant circumstances were as he believes them to be.*" Model Penal Code § 5.01(1)(a) (emphasis added). Many modern codes have adopted the MPC's approach.

Significantly, however, the MPC provides an "escape hatch" in sympathetic "impossibility" cases: when "the particular conduct . . . is *so inherently unlikely* to result or culminate in . . . a crime that neither such conduct nor the actor presents a public danger . . . , the Court shall . . . impose a sentence for a crime of a lower grade . . . or in extreme cases, may dismiss the prosecution." Model Penal Code § 5.05(2) (emphasis added). Part 4 of this Section explores the topic of impossibility.

5. Other Substantive Preparatory Crimes. As suggested in Note 1 above, criminalizing inchoate activity allows society to use criminal law to prevent harm as well as to punish harmful behavior after it has occurred. Attempt is one type of inchoate crime; it criminalizes significant preparatory steps taken toward crime. But because it can be difficult to distinguish non-dangerous preparation from a true criminal attempt, most criminal codes include other more specific crimes to punish inchoate conduct that might be described as "merely preparatory." For example, most jurisdictions make it a crime to possess dangerous weapons or burglary tools. Such statutes normally require a jury to find some criminal mens rea, in order to separate criminal conduct from innocent behavior. *See, e.g.*, Cal. Penal Code §§ 466–469 (criminalizing the possession with criminal intent of specifically listed tools, including motor vehicle or apartment building "master keys").

Some traditional common-law crimes are also preparatory crimes. For example, common-law burglary consists of breaking and entering into another's dwelling with the purpose of committing a felony. Similarly, the common law generally defines assault as an attempt to commit a battery, including a threat that creates a reasonable fear of bodily harm prior to any actual physical touching. And solicitation (discussed below in Section B), while usually held to be insufficient grounds for criminal attempt liability, is a substantive crime in many jurisdictions.

Finally, in order to address the threat of terrorism after September 11, 2001, Congress made it a crime to provide "material support" to terrorists or terrorist organizations. *See* 18 U.S.C. §§ 2339A & B (as amended since it was enacted on Oct. 26, 2001). The conduct prohibited in those statutes may be viewed as preparatory to terrorism itself. *See* Norman Abrams, *The Material Support Terrorism Offenses: Perspectives Derived from the (Early) Model Penal Code*, 1 J. Nat'l Sec. L. & Pol'y 5 (2005). The U.S. Supreme Court has upheld the "material support" criminal statutes in the face of First Amendment challenges. *See Holder v. Humanitarian Law Project*, 561 U.S. 1 (2010).

Note that once a legislature makes preparatory conduct a crime, then an "attempt" to commit that crime may also be subject to prosecution. Thus, for example, a 23-year-old Texas man pled guilty in 2014 to the charge of attempting to provide material support to a foreign terrorist organization after he was caught boarding a plane ultimately bound for Syria. *See* Ben Brumfield, *Texas Man Pleads Guilty to Attempting to Join Isis' Jihad in Syria*, CNN (June 28, 2014), http://www.cnn.com/2014 /06/28/justice/texas-terror-arrests/. (A second man was charged in connection with the case with conspiring to recruit others to support terrorism. For discussion of the use of conspiracy charges to combat terrorism since 9/11, see Chapter 13, Section C.1.)

[2] The Elements of Attempt

The following case presents perhaps the most common criminal attempt scenario: the defendants take some, but not all, steps necessary to complete the substantive offense.

United States v. Jackson

560 F.2d 112 (2d Cir. 1977)

BRYAN, SENIOR DISTRICT JUDGE.

Robert Jackson, William Scott, and Martin Allen appeal from judgments of conviction entered on November 23, 1976 in the United States District Court for the Eastern District of New York after a trial before Chief Judge Jacob Mishler without a jury.[1]

... [Two counts of the indictment] charged appellants with an attempted robbery of [a] branch [of Manufacturers Hanover Trust] on June 14 and on June 21, 1976, respectively, in violation of 18 U.S.C. § 2113(a). ... [The defendants were also charged with, and convicted of, conspiracy and possession of a sawed off shotgun. Jackson was ultimately sentenced to two years in prison, Scott to seven years, and Allen to ten years.]

... Appellants' principal contention is that the court below erred in finding them guilty. ... [T]hey assert that, as a matter of law, their conduct never crossed the elusive line which separates "mere preparation" from "attempt." This troublesome question was recently examined by this court in *United States v. Stallworth*, 543 F.2d 1038 (2d Cir. 1976), which set forth the applicable legal principles. For the reasons which follow, we affirm the convictions of all three. ...

I

The Government's evidence at trial consisted largely of the testimony of Vanessa Hodges, an unindicted co-conspirator, and of various FBI agents who surveilled the Manufacturers Hanover branch on June 21, 1976. Since the facts are of critical importance in any attempt case, we shall review the Government's proof in considerable detail.

On June 11, 1976, Vanessa Hodges was introduced to appellant Martin Allen by Pia Longhorne, another unindicted co-conspirator. Hodges wanted to meet someone who would help her carry out a plan to rob the Manufacturers Hanover branch located at 210 Flushing Avenue in Brooklyn, and she invited Allen to join her. Hodges proposed that the bank be robbed the next Monday, June 14th, at about 7:30 A.M. She hoped that they could enter with the bank manager at that time, grab the weekend deposits, and leave. Allen agreed to rob the bank with Hodges, and told her he had access to a car, two sawed-off shotguns, and a .38 caliber revolver.

The following Monday, June 14, Allen arrived at Longhorne's house about 7:30 A.M. in a car driven by appellant Robert Jackson. A suitcase in the back seat of the car contained a sawed-off shotgun, shells, materials intended as masks, and handcuffs to bind the bank manager. While Allen picked up Hodges at Longhorne's, Jackson filled the car with gas. The trio then left for the bank.

---

1. Why do you think the defendants waived their constitutional right to a jury trial here?

When they arrived, it was almost 8:00 A.M. It was thus too late to effect the first step of the plan, *viz.*, entering the bank as the manager opened the door. They rode around for a while longer, and then went to a restaurant to get something to eat and discuss their next move. After eating, the trio drove back to the bank. Allen and Hodges left the car and walked over to the bank. They peered in and saw the bulky weekend deposits, but decided it was too risky to rob the bank without an extra man.

Consequently, Jackson, Hodges, and Allen drove to Coney Island in search of another accomplice. . . . [O]n 33rd Street they found appellant William Scott, who promptly joined the team. Allen added to the arsenal another sawed-off shotgun . . . and the group drove back to the bank.

When they arrived again, Allen entered the bank to check the location of any surveillance cameras, while Jackson placed a piece of cardboard with a false license number over the authentic license plate of the car. Allen reported back that a single surveillance camera was over the entrance door. After further discussion, Scott left the car and entered the bank. He came back and informed the group that the tellers were separating the weekend deposits and that a number of patrons were now in the bank. Hodges then suggested that they drop the plans for the robbery that day, and reschedule it for the following Monday, June 21. Accordingly, they left the vicinity of the bank and returned to Coney Island where, before splitting up, they purchased a pair of stockings for Hodges to wear over her head as a disguise and pairs of gloves for Hodges, Scott, and Allen to don before entering the bank.

Hodges was arrested on Friday, June 18, 1976 on an unrelated bank robbery charge, and immediately began cooperating with the Government. After relating the events of June 14, she told FBI agents that a robbery of the Manufacturers branch at 210 Flushing Avenue was now scheduled for the following Monday, June 21. . . .

At the request of the agents, Hodges called Allen on Saturday, June 19, and asked if he were still planning to do the job. He said that he was ready. On Sunday she called him again. This time Allen said that he was not going to rob the bank that Monday because he had learned that Hodges had been arrested and he feared that federal agents might be watching. Hodges nevertheless advised the agents that she thought the robbery might still take place as planned with the three men proceeding without her.

At about 7:00 A.M. on Monday, June 21, 1976, some ten FBI agents took various surveilling positions in the area of the bank. At about 7:39 A.M. the agents observed a brown four-door Lincoln, with a New York license plate on the front and a cardboard facsimile of a license plate on the rear, moving in an easterly direction on Flushing Avenue past the bank, which was located on the southeast corner of Flushing and Washington Avenues. . . . The Lincoln circled the block and came to a stop at a fire hydrant situated at the side of the bank facing Washington Avenue, a short distance south of the corner of Flushing and Washington.

. . . The Lincoln pulled out, made a left turn onto Flushing, and proceeded in a westerly direction for one block to Waverly Avenue. It stopped, made a U-turn, and parked on the south side of Flushing between Waverly and Washington—a spot on the same side of the street as the bank entrance but separated from it by Washington Avenue. After remaining parked in this position for approximately five minutes, it pulled out and cruised east on Flushing past the bank again. The Lincoln then made a right onto Grand Avenue, the third street east of the bank, and headed south. It stopped halfway down the block, midway between Flushing and Park Avenues, and remained there for several minutes. During this time Jackson was seen working in the front of the car, which had its hood up.

The Lincoln was next sighted several minutes later in the same position it had previously occupied on the south side of Flushing Avenue between Waverly and Washington. The front license plate was now missing. The vehicle remained parked there for close to thirty minutes. Finally, it began moving east on Flushing Avenue once more, in the direction of the bank.

At some point near the bank as they passed down Flushing Avenue, the appellants detected the presence of the surveillance agents. The Lincoln accelerated down Flushing Avenue and turned south on Grand Avenue again. It was overtaken by FBI agents who ordered the appellants out of the car and arrested them. The agents then observed a black and red plaid suitcase in the rear of the car. The zipper of the suitcase was partially open and exposed two loaded sawed-off shotguns, a toy nickel-plated revolver, a pair of handcuffs, and masks. A New York license plate was seen lying on the front floor of the car. All of these items were seized.

In his memorandum of decision, Chief Judge Mishler . . . characterized the question of whether the defendants had attempted a bank robbery as charged in counts two and three or were merely engaged in preparations as "a close one." After canvassing the authorities on what this court one month later called a "perplexing problem," Chief Judge Mishler applied the following two-tiered inquiry formulated in *United States v. Mandujano*, 499 F.2d 370, 376 (5th Cir. 1974), *cert. denied*, 419 U.S. 1114 (1975):

> First, the defendant must have been acting with the kind of culpability otherwise required for the commission of the crime which he is charged with attempting. . . .

> Second, the defendant must have engaged in conduct which constitutes a substantial step toward commission of the crime. A substantial step must be conduct strongly corroborative of the firmness of the defendant's criminal intent.

He concluded that on June 14 and again on June 21, the defendants took substantial steps, strongly corroborative of the firmness of their criminal intent, toward commission of the crime of bank robbery and found the defendants guilty on each of the two attempt counts. These appeals followed.

II

"[There] is no comprehensive statutory definition of attempt in federal law." *United States v. Heng Awkak Roman*, 356 F. Supp. 434, 437 (S.D.N.Y.), *aff'd*, 484 F.2d 1271 (2d Cir. 1973), *cert. denied*, 415 U.S. 978 (1974). Fed. R. Crim. P. 31(c), however, provides in pertinent part that a defendant may be found guilty of "an attempt to commit either the offense charged or an offense necessarily included therein if the attempt is an offense." 18 U.S.C. § 2113(a) [which prohibits taking or attempting to take any bank property by force and violence or by intimidation] specifically makes attempted bank robbery an offense.

. . . .

Chief Judge Kaufman, writing for th[is] court [in *Stallworth*], selected the two-tiered inquiry of *United States v. Mandujano, supra,* "properly derived from the writings of many distinguished jurists," as stating the proper test for determining whether the foregoing conduct constituted an attempt. He observed that this analysis "conforms closely to the sensible definition of an attempt proffered by the American Law Institute's Model Penal Code." . . .

The draftsmen of . . . Model Penal Code [§ 5.01(1)] recognized the difficulty of arriving at a general standard for distinguishing acts of preparation from acts constituting an attempt. They found general agreement that when an actor committed the "last proximate act," i.e., when he had done all that he believed necessary to effect a particular result which is an element of the offense, he committed an attempt. They also concluded, however, that while the last proximate act is *sufficient* to constitute an attempt, it is not *necessary* to such a finding. The problem then was to devise a standard more inclusive than one requiring the last proximate act before attempt liability would attach, but less inclusive than one which would make every act done with the intent to commit a crime criminal.

The draftsmen considered and rejected the following approaches to distinguishing preparation from attempt, later summarized in *Mandujano*:

> (a) The physical proximity doctrine—the overt act required for an attempt must be proximate to the completed crime, or directly tending toward the completion of the crime, or must amount to the commencement of the consummation.

> (b) The dangerous proximity doctrine—a test given impetus by Mr. Justice Holmes whereby the greater the gravity and probability of the offense, and the nearer the act to the crime, the stronger is the case for calling the act an attempt.

> (c) The indispensable element test—a variation of the proximity tests which emphasizes any indispensable aspect of the criminal endeavor over which the actor has not yet acquired control.

(d) The probable desistance test—the conduct constitutes an attempt if, in the ordinary and natural course of events, without interruption from an outside source, it will result in the crime intended.

(e) The abnormal step approach—an attempt is a step toward crime which goes beyond the point where the normal citizen would think better of his conduct and desist.

(f) The res ipsa loquitur or unequivocality test—an attempt is committed when the actor's conduct manifests an intent to commit a crime.

The formulation upon which the [Model Penal Code] draftsmen ultimately agreed required, in addition to criminal purpose, that an act be a substantial step in a course of conduct designed to accomplish a criminal result, and that it be strongly corroborative of criminal purpose in order for it to constitute such a substantial step. The following differences between this test and previous approaches to the preparation-attempt problem were noted [in the Comments accompanying MPC § 5.01(1)(c)]:

First, this formulation shifts the emphasis from what remains to be done—the chief concern of the proximity tests—to what the actor has already done. The fact that further major steps must be taken before the crime can be completed does not preclude a finding that the steps already undertaken are substantial. It is expected, in the normal case, that this approach will broaden the scope of attempt liability.

Second, although it is intended that the requirement of a substantial step will result in the imposition of attempt liability only in those instances in which some firmness of criminal purpose is shown, no finding is required as to whether the actor would probably have desisted prior to completing the crime. Potentially the probable desistance test could reach very early steps toward crime—depending upon how one assesses the probabilities of desistance—but since in practice this test follows closely the proximity approaches, rejection of probable desistance will not narrow the scope of attempt liability.

Finally, the requirement of proving a substantial step generally will prove less of a hurdle for the prosecution than the *res ipsa loquitur* approach, which requires that the actor's conduct must itself manifest the criminal purpose. The difference will be illustrated in connection with the present section's requirement of corroboration. Here it should be noted that, in the present formulation, the two purposes to be served by the *res ipsa loquitur* test are, to a large extent, treated separately. Firmness of criminal purpose is intended to be shown by requiring a substantial step, while problems of proof are dealt with by the requirement of corroboration (although . . . the latter will also tend to establish firmness of purpose).

The draftsmen concluded that, in addition to assuring firmness of criminal design, the requirement of a substantial step would preclude attempt liability, with its accompanying harsh penalties, for relatively remote preparatory acts. At the same time, however, by not requiring a "last proximate act" or one of its various analogues it would permit the apprehension of dangerous persons at an earlier stage than the other approaches without immunizing them from attempt liability.

. . . .

. . . [In this case,] [o]n two separate occasions, appellants reconnoitered the place contemplated for the commission of the crime and possessed the paraphernalia to be employed in the commission of the crime—loaded sawed-off shotguns, extra shells, a toy revolver, handcuffs, and masks—which was specially designed for such unlawful use and which could serve no lawful purpose under the circumstances. Under the Model Penal Code formulation, approved by the *Stallworth* court, either type of conduct, standing alone, was sufficient as a matter of law to constitute a "substantial step" if it strongly corroborated their criminal purpose. Here both types of conduct coincided on both June 14 and June 21, along with numerous other elements strongly corroborative of the firmness of appellants' criminal intent. The steps taken toward a successful bank robbery thus were not "insubstantial" as a matter of law, and Chief Judge Mishler found them "substantial" as a matter of fact. We are unwilling to substitute our assessment of the evidence for his, and thus affirm the convictions for attempted bank robbery. . . .

. . . .

Notes and Questions

1. The Elements of Attempt. A criminal attempt requires both (a) an intent to do an act or cause a result that constitutes a crime; and (b) an act in furtherance of that intent that goes beyond mere preparation. *See* Wayne R. LaFave, Criminal Law § 11.3(a) (5th ed. 2010); Rollin M. Perkins & Ronald N. Boyce, Criminal Law 611 (3d ed. 1982). For the second element, most jurisdictions have adopted the "substantial step" test suggested in Model Penal Code § 5.01(1) and applied in *Jackson*. *See, e.g., United States v. Resendiz-Ponce*, 549 U.S. 102 (2007) (relying on MPC § 5.01(1)(c)'s "substantial step" language to define the federal offense of attempting to re-enter the United States illegally after removal).

For a recent, thorough exploration of the crime of attempt and the legal issues that have long been raised regarding the crime, see Gideon Yaffe, *Criminal Attempts*, 124 Yale L.J. 92 (2014).

2. Mens Rea. It is generally said that criminal attempt requires a mens rea of purpose; that is, the actor intends or desires to cause the completed criminal offense. But should recklessness or negligence sometimes suffice to satisfy the mens rea for attempt? In *Thacker v. Commonwealth*, 114 S.E. 504 (Va. 1922), the defendant was drunk and became upset when a woman refused to admit him into her tent. After walking a little way down the road, the defendant turned and shot at a lighted lamp shining through the tent. His bullet just missed the heads of the woman and her baby. If the woman or baby had been killed by the bullet, the defendant would have been guilty of some form of unintentional homicide (murder, manslaughter, or negligent homicide). Thacker was not aiming at the woman or the baby, however, and the bullet did not strike anyone. The Virginia Supreme Court ruled that the defendant could not be convicted of attempted murder.

The explanation offered for this holding is that the mens rea required for an attempt conviction is "purpose." Even though Thacker's recklessness could suffice for manslaughter and, in the case of "extreme recklessness," even for murder (see Chapter 6, Section C), attempted murder required that he have purpose regarding both the act *and* the result of death. Model Penal Code § 5.01(1)(b) likewise refuses to punish those who were merely reckless or negligent as to the result required to commit a particular crime. But, in addition to purpose, the MPC also considers "belief that [one's conduct] will cause such result" to be sufficient. *Id.* Is "belief" the same as "knowledge"? The murky distinction between knowledge and purpose when used to differentiate between criminal liability and innocence is examined below in Chapter 12, Section C.

Some commentators have criticized the prevailing rule, arguing that recklessness should suffice for an attempt conviction if it would also suffice for the completed offense. Professor Eugene Meehan explains:

> It is anomalous that a more strict, more culpable state of mind is required for attempt than for the complete offense; whether the accused failed or succeeded, his actual mental state, or criminal purpose, is identical; if there are good and acceptable reasons for recklessness being an acceptable *mens rea* for the complete offense, there are similar good and acceptable reasons for recklessness being an acceptable *mens rea* for the attempt; it is not logical that a *physical* difference between attempt and the complete offense attempted (being non-completion) be reflected in a different *mental* element; and finally, the dividing line between recklessness and intention is barely distinguishable in practice, such that the reality of the situation in the courts is that the necessary intention is often being construed out of what is clearly recklessness.

EUGENE R. MEEHAN, THE LAW OF CRIMINAL ATTEMPT 280 (1984).

Another commentator has argued similarly:

> If a pharmacist is grossly negligent in making up a prescription and the patient dies as a result of taking the dosage on the bottle, the pharmacist is clearly guilty of manslaughter. Surely the policy considerations which dictate such a conviction apply equally if, through chance, the negligent error is discovered before any damage is done. There seems to be every reason for a verdict of attempted manslaughter.

Donald Stuart, *Mens Rea, Negligence, and Attempts*, 1968 CRIM. L. REV. 647, 662.

Do you find these arguments persuasive, or do you support the general rule that recklessness is not a sufficiently culpable mental state for the crime of attempt? Does the logic of "recklessly trying" to commit a crime make sense to you? Or does the concept of "trying" to do something necessarily connote a purpose to achieve the result?

3. Mens Rea and Specific Intent. When an attempt to commit a specific intent crime is charged, the actor's purpose must extend not only to the acts or results constituting that crime, but also to whatever "specific intent" is required. For example, suppose *A* purposefully takes *B*'s lawn mower but plans to return it in a few hours. The police see *A* walking away with the lawn mower and intervene. *A* would not be liable for attempted larceny because *A* lacked the requisite specific intent to deprive *B* of the property permanently. For a general discussion of specific intent, see Chapter 4, Section B.1.

4. Mens Rea and "Attendant Circumstances." In cases where a defendant is charged with attempting to commit a crime that has an attendant circumstance as one of its elements — for example, the age of the victim in a statutory rape prosecution, or the time of day in the common-law definition of burglary as breaking and entering at night — § 5.01(1) of the Model Penal Code provides that the defendant must be proved to have been "acting with the kind of culpability otherwise required for commission of the crime." That is, the same mens rea analysis that applies to that particular circumstance element in cases where the crime was completed applies to attempt prosecutions as well. Thus, for example, if the age of the victim in a statutory rape case is a matter of strict liability in that jurisdiction, it would be a matter of strict liability in an attempted statutory rape prosecution as well. *See* Model Penal Code § 5.01 Comment at 301.

5. Actus Reus: The Model Penal Code's "Substantial Step" Approach. As the court's opinion in *Jackson* illustrates, determining when an attempt is complete — i.e., drawing the line between noncriminal preparation and criminal attempt — poses difficult problems. Why aren't mere thoughts enough to support an attempt conviction? If purpose to commit the crime is established, why shouldn't an individual be arrested long before serious harm results? Although that approach might resolve the inconsistencies that arise in distinguishing preparation from attempt, the courts have refused to punish on the basis of thoughts alone. Rather, they have used various standards to define how far along a criminal plan must proceed before an attempt is said to be criminal. Thus, § 5.01(1)(c) of the Model Penal Code requires "an act or omission constituting a substantial step in a course of conduct planned to culminate in [the actor's] commission of the crime." MPC § 5.01(2) then specifies that the substantial step must be "strongly corroborative of the actor's criminal purpose" and sets out several examples of conduct that can satisfy the "substantial step" test.

Nevertheless, differences in application of the "substantial step" test inevitably occur. Compare the following case to *Jackson*. In *United States v. Buffington*, 815 F.2d 1292 (9th Cir. 1987), three men were charged with attempting to rob a federal bank located in a shopping center. The evidence showed that the defendants had assembled two handguns, female clothing and makeup to disguise one defendant, and a multi-layered clothing disguise for another. After making two advance visits to the bank, they returned with their weapons on the day of the alleged attempt and drove slowly around the parking lot with their attention directed toward the bank. They parked about 150 feet from both the bank and a Payless store, and one of the men went into the Payless store. The other two got out and stood by the car facing the bank. Coincidentally, a power outage occurred in the shopping center at that point, and a bank teller glancing out the window noticed one of the men near the car wrapping a scarf around his face. The three men then returned to the car. They were arrested as they drove out of the parking lot.

In light of the examples enumerated in §5.01(2) of the Model Penal Code—including reconnoitering the site of the crime and possessing materials to be used in committing the crime that can serve no lawful purpose under the circumstances—did the defendants' conduct in *Buffington* constitute a substantial step strongly corroborative of their criminal intent? No, according to the Ninth Circuit, which reversed their convictions for attempted robbery. Calling the conduct here "entirely tentative and unfocused," as distinguished from the "unequivocal" conduct found in other similar cases, the court held that the defendants "did not cross the boundary between preparation and attempt. . . . Not only did [they] not take a single step toward the bank, they displayed no weapons and no indication that they were about to make an entry. Standing alone, their conduct did not constitute . . . a step toward commission of the crime of such substantiality that, unless frustrated, the crime would have occurred." *Id.* at 1303. Although the court purported to be applying the "substantial step" test, does its rationale contain elements of some of the other approaches courts have used to distinguish preparation from attempt (which are described in *Jackson*)?

Many courts do not agree with *Buffington*'s suggestion that defendants need to be moving towards their target in order to be guilty of attempted robbery under the Model Penal Code. In *Adams v. State*, 342 S.E.2d 747 (Ga. 1986), for example, the court upheld an attempt conviction using the "substantial step" test where the defendants discussed robbing someone at a hotel, drove for about an hour in a car containing guns and ski masks until they reached the hotel, and agreed as they drove into the hotel parking lot that they would find someone who was leaving the hotel to rob. They were stopped by the police as they were driving around the parking lot. Although one of them got out of the car, he did so to escape from the police, not to rob anyone.

Consider also *United States v. Howard*, 766 F.3d 414 (5th Cir. 2014), where the defendant was caught in a government sting operation that was investigating Internet crimes against children. Howard arranged to have sex with two underage girls in phone conversations with a government agent posing as the girls' mother. Howard sent explicit photos of himself to these "girls," and offered their "mother" advice on how to prepare them for sex. But he made no travel arrangements and would not commit to a meeting date. When the undercover agent told Howard to book a flight, saying "take it or leave it," Howard responded, "okay, I'll leave it" and never communicated with the agent again. He was arrested three months later. The court affirmed his conviction for attempting to "knowingly persuade, induce, [or] entice" a minor to engage in unlawful sexual activity in violation of 18 U.S.C. § 2422(b). The court acknowledged that the conviction could not rest only on "explicit sex talk" or the transmission of sexually explicit photos and that the government's decision to wait three months and then arrest Howard with no additional evidence was "curious." But it concluded that "grooming behavior plus other acts strongly corroborative of intent to entice illegal sex — such as detailed discussions to arrange a meeting with the minor victim — can suffice to establish [the] substantial step" necessary for attempt liability. 766 F.3d at 422–28 (surveying many prior cases). For discussion of the question whether defendants like Howard would have an "impossibility" defense, see Part 4 below.

6. Actus Reus: The Physical Proximity Approach. By contrast to the Model Penal Code's "substantial step" test, an older, yet prominent, approach for separating mere preparation from criminal attempt is the physical proximity doctrine. Under this test, the defendant must come physically close to completing the crime. The focus here is on what remains to be done to accomplish the crime, and not just on what steps (substantial or otherwise) the defendant has already taken.

For example, the New York Court of Appeals applied the physical proximity approach in the venerable case of *People v. Rizzo*, 158 N.E. 888 (N.Y. 1927). The four defendants in that case planned to rob one Rao, a payroll clerk for a construction company who was to be carrying a large sum of payroll money. Two of the defendants armed themselves, and the four men drove around looking for Rao, first at the bank and then at various construction sites. They were still searching for him when they were eventually spotted and followed by two police officers. When the defendants stopped the car and Rizzo got out to look for Rao in another building, the officers arrested them. The Court of Appeals reversed their attempted robbery conviction, concluding that they had not come "dangerously near" to successfully completing the crime:

> Rao was not found; the defendants were still looking for him; no attempt to rob him could be made, at least until he came in sight; he was not in the building [where they were arrested]. There was no man there with the payroll for the United Lathing Company whom these defendants could rob. Apparently no money had been drawn from the bank for the payroll by anybody at the time of the arrest. In a word, these defendants had planned to commit a crime and were looking around the city for an opportunity to commit it, but the opportunity fortunately never came. Men would not be guilty of an attempt at burglary if they had planned to break into a building and were arrested while they were hunting about the streets for the building not knowing where it was. Neither would a man be guilty of an attempt

to commit murder if he armed himself and started out to find the person whom he had planned to kill but could not find him. So here these defendants were not guilty of an attempt to commit robbery in the first degree when they had not found or reached the presence of the person they intended to rob.

Id. at 889–90.

Decades later, Professor Glanville Williams described the critique of the physical proximity test:

[One] way of supporting the proximity rule is to say that it results from the notion of crime as a punishable wrong. Society has not thought it desirable to extend the scope of punishment too widely. So long as the law was purely deterrent or retributive in its aim, the circumspection of the offense of attempt was perhaps justified. At the present day when the courts have wide powers of probation, there is much to be said for a broader measure of responsibility. Any act done with the fixed intention of committing a crime, and by way of preparation for it, however remote it may be from the crime, might well be treated as criminal. The rational course would be to catch intending offenders as soon as possible, and set about curing them of their evil tendencies: not leave them alone on the ground that their acts are mere preparation.

GLANVILLE L. WILLIAMS, CRIMINAL LAW: THE GENERAL PART 632 (2d ed. 1961).

7. **Comparing Solicitation and Attempt.** Although soliciting another person to commit a crime can be a crime in itself (as discussed below in Section B), "mere solicitation" is often said to be insufficient for attempt liability. Thus, a solicitation was held insufficient to satisfy the substantial step test in *State v. Molasky*, 765 S.W.2d 597 (Mo. 1989). Molasky was serving a 32-year prison sentence for sexual abuse, child abuse, rape, and sodomy, when he became acquainted with another inmate, Ricky Holt. Holt informed the authorities that Molasky had asked Holt to kill Ellen and Ellis Denos, Molasky's ex-wife and her new husband. Holt agreed to wear a hidden microphone to record his conversations with Molasky. In one such conversation, Molasky offered to pay Holt $5,000 if he would kill the couple after his release from prison. A time was set for the killing, and Molasky specified that he wanted the bodies disposed of and did not want the crime committed in front of his son. Molasky did not have a street address for the Denoses or a picture of them. Missouri's criminal statutes did not include an independent crime of solicitation; rather, solicitation was punishable only if it constituted the "substantial step" necessary for attempt. The court indicated that Molasky might have been guilty of attempted murder if he had paid Holt, or perhaps if he had given Holt a picture of the Denoses. But without more, the solicitation was not considered a "substantial step" and his attempted murder conviction was reversed.

When combined with other conduct, however, solicitation can lead to attempt liability. Thus, in *People v. Superior Court (Decker)*, 157 P.3d 1017 (Cal. 2007), the California Supreme Court reversed the dismissal of attempted murder charges brought against a man who had solicited an undercover police detective to kill his sister and her friend. The court concluded that Decker had satisfied the actus reus for attempt—"commission of a direct but ineffectual act toward accomplishing the intended killing"—because his actions extended beyond merely soliciting the murder. In addition, Decker had "tested the level of surveillance" near his sister's home, made a $5,000 down payment with money he "spent months accumulating . . . in small denominations," and provided descriptions to the intended assassin of the sister and her home, car, workplace, and habits.

8. Attempted Murder, HIV-Positive Defendants, and Causation. Although some of the following cases are products of the initial hysteria regarding HIV infection and its "incurable" fatal effect, attempted murder charges have sometimes been successfully prosecuted against defendants infected with the HIV (AIDS) virus. For example, in *Weeks v. Scott*, 55 F.3d 1059 (5th Cir. 1995), an HIV-positive prisoner who threatened to "take somebody with him when he went" and then spit on a prison guard was convicted of attempted murder and sentenced to life imprisonment (based on two prior felony convictions). Applying the Texas state law defining attempt, the Fifth Circuit observed that the crime requires "an act amounting to more than mere preparation [that] tends but fails to effect the commission" of the crime. *Id.* at 1062. Although the district court had acknowledged that "there are no known cases of a person contracting the virus by being deliberately spat on by an HIV-infected person," *Weeks v. Collins*, 867 F. Supp. 544, 547 (S.D. Tex. 1994), and Weeks submitted "a mountain of scientific evidence to support the contention that HIV cannot be transmitted through saliva," the court of appeals affirmed the conviction because "some evidence existed" to support the jury's conclusion and thus, "viewing the evidence in the light most favorable to the prosecution, [a] rational trier of fact could have found, beyond a reasonable doubt, that spitting could transmit HIV." 55 F.3d at 1063–64. *See also State v. Smith*, 621 A.2d 493 (N.J. App. Div. 1993) (affirming attempted murder conviction using the Model Penal Code approach where HIV-positive defendant bit corrections officer).

As these opinions demonstrate, attempt cases can pose interesting questions regarding causation (a topic addressed above in Chapter 10). According to the Centers for Disease Control, there are "rare bite-related instances of HIV transmission from exposure to saliva contaminated with HIV-infected blood," but "exposure to saliva uncontaminated with blood is considered to be a rare mode of HIV transmission." *Transmission of HIV Possibly Associated with Exposure of Mucous Membrane to Contaminated Blood*, 46 Morbidity & Mortality Weekly Report 620 (July 11, 1997), *available at* http://www.cdc.gov/mmwr/preview/mmwrhtml/00048364.htm. It is also true today that HIV is not invariably fatal and can be controlled with various medication regimens. *See HIV/AIDS for Veterans and the Public*, U.S. Dep't of Veterans Affairs, http://www.hiv.va.gov/patient/faqs/index.asp. For discussion of the controversy surrounding prosecution of HIV-positive defendants for assault when they have unprotected sex, see Chapter 1, Section A.4.a.

[3] Abandonment as a Defense to Attempt

For all inchoate offenses involving uncompleted crimes, the law must determine how to handle a claim that the defendant started on the path toward crime, but then "changed his mind" and decided not to go through with the offense. For attempts, such a claim is called "abandonment" or "renunciation" or, sometimes, "withdrawal."

People v. Staples

85 Cal. Rptr. 589 (Cal. Ct. App. 1970)

Reppy, Associate Justice.

Defendant was charged in an information with attempted burglary (Pen. Code, §§ 664, 459). Trial by jury was waived, and the matter submitted on the testimony contained in the transcript of the preliminary hearing together with exhibits. Defendant was found guilty [and sentenced to probation]. . . .

I. *The Facts*

In October 1967, while his wife was away on a trip, defendant, a mathematician, under an assumed name, rented an office on the second floor of a building in Hollywood which was over the mezzanine of a bank. Directly below the mezzanine was the vault of the bank. Defendant was aware of the layout of the building, specifically of the relation of the office he rented to the bank vault. Defendant paid rent for the period from October 23 to November 23. The landlord had 10 days before commencement of the rental period within which to finish some interior repairs and painting. During this prerental period defendant brought into the office certain equipment. This included drilling tools, two acetylene gas tanks, a blow torch, a blanket, and a linoleum rug. The landlord observed these items when he came in from time to time to see how the repair work was progressing. Defendant learned from a custodian that no one was in the building on Saturdays. On Saturday, October 14, defendant drilled two groups of holes into the floor of the office above the mezzanine room. He stopped drilling before the holes went through the floor. He came back to the office several times thinking he might slowly drill down, covering the holes with the linoleum rug. At some point in time he installed a hasp lock on a closet, and planned to, or did, place his tools in it. However, he left the closet keys on the premises. Around the end of November, apparently after November 23, the landlord notified the police and turned the tools and equipment over to them. Defendant did not pay any more rent. It is not clear when he last entered the office, but it could have been after November 23, and even after the landlord had removed the equipment. On February 22, 1968, the police arrested defendant. After receiving advice as to his constitutional rights, defendant voluntarily made an oral statement which he reduced to writing.

Among other things which defendant wrote down were these:

Saturday, the 14th . . . I drilled some small holes in the floor of the room. Because of tiredness, fear, and the implications of what I was doing, I stopped and went to sleep.

At this point I think my motives began to change. The [actual] commencement of my plan made me begin to realize that even if I were to succeed a fugitive life of living off of stolen money would not give the enjoyment of the life of a mathematician however humble a job I might have.

I still had not given up my plan however. I felt I had made a certain investment of time, money, effort and a certain [psychological] commitment to the concept.

I came back several times thinking I might store the tools in the closet and slowly drill down (covering the hole with a rug [or] linoleum square). As time went on (after two weeks or so), [m]y wife came back and my life as bank robber seemed more and more absurd.

II. *Discussion of Defendant's Contentions*

Defendant's position in this appeal is that, as a matter of law, there was insufficient evidence upon which to convict him of a criminal attempt under Penal Code section 664 . . . .

In order for the prosecution to prove that defendant committed an attempt to burglarize as proscribed by Penal Code section 664, it was required to establish that he had the specific intent to commit a burglary of the bank and that his acts toward that goal went beyond mere preparation.

The required specific intent was clearly established in the instant case. Defendant admitted in his written confession that he rented the office fully intending to burglarize the bank, that he brought in tools and equipment to accomplish this purpose, and that he began drilling into the floor with the intent of making an entry into the bank.

. . . .

None of [our cases] provide a litmus-like test [for distinguishing acts of preparation from completed attempts], and perhaps no such test is achievable. Such precision is not required in this case, however. There was definitely substantial evidence entitling the trial judge to find that defendant's acts had gone beyond the preparation stage. Without specifically deciding where defendant's preparations left off and where his activities became a completed criminal attempt, we can say that his "drilling" activity clearly was an unequivocal and direct step toward the completion of the burglary. It was a fragment of the substantive crime contemplated, i.e., the beginning of the "breaking" element. Further, defendant himself characterized his activity as the *actual commencement of his plan*. The drilling by defendant was obviously one of a series of acts which logic and ordinary experience indicate would result in the proscribed act of burglary.

The instant case provides an out-of-the-ordinary factual situation. . . . Usually the actors in cases [involving] attempts are intercepted or caught in the act. Here, there was no direct proof of any actual interception. But it was clearly inferable by the trial judge that defendant became aware that the landlord had resumed control over the office and had turned defendant's equipment and tools over to the police. This was the equivalent of interception.

The inference of this nonvoluntary character of defendant's abandonment was a proper one for the trial judge to draw. However, it would seem that the character of the abandonment in situations of this type, whether it be voluntary (prompted by pangs of conscience or a change of heart) or nonvoluntary (established by inference in the instant case), is not controlling. The relevant factor is the determination of whether the acts of the perpetrator have reached such a stage of advancement that they can be classified as an attempt. Once that attempt is found there can be no exculpatory abandonment. "One of the purposes of the criminal law is to protect society from those who intend to injure it. When it is established that the defendant intended to commit a specific crime and that in carrying out this intention he committed an act that caused harm or sufficient danger of harm, it is immaterial that for some collateral reason he could not complete the intended crime." (*People v. Camodeca*, 52 Cal. 2d 142, 147.)

The order is affirmed.

Notes and Questions

1. The Common Law: No Abandonment Once Attempt Is Complete. The *Staples* decision reflects the traditional — some would say harsh — common-law rule that once a defendant has crossed the line from preparation to attempt, the crime of attempt has been completed and later abandonment is no defense. As Professor Perkins explained long ago, "[a] criminal attempt is a 'complete offense' in the sense that one who has carried a criminal effort to such a point that it is punishable, can no more wipe out his criminal guilt by an abandonment of his plan than a thief can obliterate a larceny by a restoration of the stolen chattel." Rollin M. Perkins, *Criminal Attempt and Related Problems*, 2 UCLA L. REV. 319, 354 (1955).

Thus, in *State v. Workman*, 584 P.2d 382 (Wash. 1978), Lawrence Workman and Steve Hughes were found guilty of attempted robbery when they decided to commit a robbery on their way home after an evening of dancing and drinking. The defendants parked their car in an alley near a gas station and took a .22 caliber rifle, a gunny sack with eye holes, and a stocking cap to a hiding place near the gas station's pay phone. While the defendants were trying to muster the courage to follow through with their plan, the clerk stepped out for a breath of air, saw the defendants, and called the police. A police officer in an unmarked car arrived at the scene. Still unaware that they had been detected, Workman and Hughes decided to abandon their efforts. While walking back to the car, they were arrested. The Washington Supreme Court affirmed their convictions, holding that once a substantial step had been taken, the crime of attempt could not be abandoned.

Would it make sense to allow defendants who were guilty of a crime on Tuesday to "take it back" and nullify their criminality on Wednesday? On the other hand, if the harm never happens, should a voluntary cessation of dangerous conduct constitute a defense? What purpose is served in punishing those who genuinely have decided not to cause criminal harm? Or do criminal actors always have the potential to commit their crimes later?

2. The Modern Trend: Allowing Voluntary Abandonment as a Defense. Since the advent of the Model Penal Code, the common law's "no abandonment" rule has been discarded in many jurisdictions. The clear trend among modern authorities is to recognize a sincere and voluntary abandonment, or "renunciation," as a defense to attempt, as endorsed in § 5.01(4) of the Model Penal Code (creating an "affirmative defense" to attempt where "circumstances manifest a complete and voluntary renunciation of . . . criminal purpose").

The Comments to § 5.01(4) offer two reasons for recognizing this defense. "First, renunciation of criminal purpose tends to negative dangerousness." An actor who voluntarily abandons a crime "has plainly demonstrated his lack of firm purpose." On the other hand, if the abandonment is not voluntary, the criminal intent remains and the actor is still dangerous. "The second reason . . . is to provide actors with a motive for desisting from their criminal designs, thereby diminishing the risk that the substantive crime will be committed." The abandonment defense is therefore used as a carrot to induce criminals to give up their criminal plans. Model Penal Code § 5.01 Comment at 359.

Is the Model Penal Code's reasoning persuasive? What do you think of its psychological "incentive to desist" argument?

Some federal courts continue to question whether an abandonment defense even exists, given that it would have to be implied into federal criminal statutes that contain no express statutory language to that effect. In rejecting such a defense in *United States v. Shelton*, 30 F.3d 702, 706 (6th Cir. 1994), for example, the Sixth Circuit was "not persuaded that the availability of a withdrawal defense would provide an incentive or motive to desist." Noting the vagaries of apprehension, prosecution, and jury verdicts, the court concluded that "a remote chance of acquittal would appear to have an even more remote chance of deterring conduct." *Id.* (holding that a defendant who has "committed the crime of attempt . . . can withdraw only from the commission of the substantive offense"). *See also United States v. Buttrick*, 432 F.3d 373, 377 (1st Cir. 2005) (observing that the availability of an abandonment defense remains an open question in federal cases).

Finally, assuming that abandonment (renunciation) should be a defense to attempt, should it also afford a defense to substantive crimes like theft and burglary? If not, should some sentencing mitigation be mandatory when a sincere renunciation is proved? For a thoughtful analysis of this issue, see Evan Tsen Lee, *Canceling Crime*, 30 CONN. L. REV. 117 (1997).

3. Abandonment: A Difficult Defense to Win. Even when allowed in theory, the defense of abandonment is not an easy one to win. As the court observed in *People v. Kimball*, 311 N.W.2d 343, 349 (Mich. 1981), "[a]bandonment is not 'voluntary' when the defendant fails to complete the attempted crime because of unanticipated difficulties, unexpected resistance, or circumstances which increase the probability of detection or apprehension. Nor is the abandonment 'voluntary' when the defendant fails to consummate the attempted offense after deciding to postpone the criminal conduct until another time or to substitute another victim or another but similar objective." *See also* Model Penal Code § 5.01 Comment at 356–57 (noting that a "voluntary" abandonment is one that is "not influenced by outside circumstances," but admonishing that a defendant's "[r]eappraisal of the [relevant] criminal sanctions" is "presumably" still voluntary "so long as the actor's fear of the law is not related to a particular threat of apprehension or detection").

Even if a defense of "voluntary abandonment" makes sense in the abstract, does MPC § 5.01(4) blur the line between criminal and noncriminal attempts? How should a jury determine whether defendants voluntarily and permanently abandoned their criminal scheme, or merely changed or delayed their plans because they perceived an increased likelihood of apprehension? Consider the following cases:

In *State v. Mahoney*, 870 P.2d 65 (Mont. 1994), the defendant forcibly restrained the victim, stabbed her 12 times, and then attempted to rape her. But the victim was able to resist, and finally the defendant stopped and called the police. Noting that "at this point, substantial harm had been done and acts of actual danger had, indeed, been committed," the court denied an abandonment defense because the defendant "only called the police after observing that the victim was bleeding profusely . . . and because she struggled and successfully prevented" the rape. *Id.* at 72.

In *People v. Johnson*, 585 P.2d 306 (Colo. App. 1978), Johnson rode up to a vacant house on a bicycle and broke a window. A witness saw Johnson riding away from the house and called the police. The police caught Johnson two blocks away, bicycling back toward the house. He was arrested and convicted on charges of attempted burglary. The appellate court reversed the conviction because the trial court failed to instruct the jury on the defense of voluntary abandonment. The court cautioned, however, that the jury should evaluate the completeness of Johnson's abandonment in light of the fact that he was heading back toward the house, and also consider whether the presence of a potential witness indicated that the abandonment was not voluntary but rather based on a fear of apprehension.

4. The Timing of Abandonment. Suppose *A* is in a jurisdiction that recognizes the defense of voluntary abandonment. *A*, while attempting to commit crime *X*, commits the lesser crime *Y*. *A* then voluntarily and completely abandons all criminal purpose. It is important to recognize that even if *A* would not be convicted for an attempt to commit crime *X*, he would still be liable for committing crime *Y*. Even modern authorities recognize the rule that one cannot "abandon" a substantive crime that has already been completed. For example, in *Moore v. State*, 397 S.E.2d 477 (Ga. 1990), the court held that abandonment of an attempted burglary did not preclude convicting the defendant of crimes that were already complete: criminal trespass and possession of burglary tools.

Are there other situations in which voluntary cessation comes too late to allow an abandonment defense? In *State v. Smith*, 409 N.E.2d 1199 (Ind. Ct. App. 1980), Smith stabbed his uncle, Melvin Howell, twice in the chest during a quarrel. Howell fled, and Smith chased after him, still holding the knife and screaming epithets. When Howell collapsed about two blocks away, Smith felt remorse, put his uncle into a car, and raced to the hospital. Howell miraculously survived and lived to testify against Smith, who was convicted of attempted murder. The appellate court ruled that abandonment constitutes a defense to the crime of attempt, but only if it occurs "before the crime is completed or the harm is done," that is, before the crime is "in the process of consummation or has become so inevitable that it cannot reasonably be stayed." *Id.* at 1202, 1201. Here, the court noted, Smith's change of heart came too late because the attempted murder was complete with the first stabbing. "Remorse . . . is not abandonment," the court concluded. *Id.* at 1202.

Section § 5.01(4) of the Model Penal Code allows an abandonment defense after "the last proximate act has occurred" so long as "the criminal result can still be avoided, as for example when the fuse has been lit but can still be stamped out." Model Penal Code § 5.01 Comment at 360. But the defense is unavailable once the defendant "has put in motion forces that he is powerless to stop." *Id.* Thus, a defendant "can gain no immunity for his completed effort, as for example when he fires at the intended victim but misses; all he can do is desist from making a second attempt." *Id.*

[4] Legal and Factual Impossibility

In some cases, it is impossible for an attempt to be completed, even though the defendant purposely (if mistakenly) intends that the crime be committed and takes steps that go beyond "mere preparation." Common-law courts developed the categories of "factual" and "legal" impossibility to attempt to separate "impossible" attempts that should result in conviction from those that should not. According to these common-law decisions, "legal impossibility" is a defense to attempt whereas "factual impossibility" is not. The distinction, however, has proven elusive and inconsistent in application. It is not difficult for articulate lawyers and jurists to recharacterize cases of impossibility as either "legal" or "factual," and the analysis in many cases may seem to be result-oriented rather than clear.

The Model Penal Code disavows any categorical distinction between legal and factual impossibility, providing that even if the completed crime is impossible, the crime of attempt is committed so long as the defendant purposefully engages in conduct that would lead to a crime "if the attendant circumstances were as he believes them to be." Model Penal Code § 5.01(1)(a). This approach embodies logical consistency, but can lead to results that may seem harsh. But don't forget the mitigating "inherently unlikely" escape hatch provided in MPC § 5.05(2).

The following two cases illustrate the struggle and confusion surrounding the common-law notion that impossibility can sometimes constitute a defense to attempt. *Dlugash* reflects the Model Penal Code approach while also describing the common-law distinction; *Thousand* presents an even more refined, modern analysis. But the debate is an unending one. Do not be too distressed if it does not appear perfectly clear to you even after reading both opinions.

People v. Dlugash

363 N.E.2d 1155 (N.Y. 1977)

Jasen, Judge.

The criminal law is of ancient origin, but criminal liability for attempt to commit a crime is comparatively recent. At the root of the concept of attempt liability are the very aims and purposes of penal law. The ultimate issue is whether an individual's intentions and actions, though failing to achieve a manifest and malevolent criminal purpose, constitute a danger to organized society of sufficient magnitude to warrant the imposition of criminal sanctions. Difficulties in theoretical analysis and concomitant debate over very pragmatic questions of blameworthiness appear dramatically in reference to situations where the criminal attempt failed to achieve its purpose solely because the factual or legal context in which the individual acted was not as the actor supposed them to be. Phrased somewhat differently, the concern centers on whether an individual should be liable for an attempt to commit a crime when, unknown to him, it was impossible to successfully complete the crime attempted. For years, serious studies have been made on the subject in an effort to resolve the continuing controversy when, if at all, the impossibility of successfully completing the criminal act should preclude liability for even making the futile attempt. The 1967 revision of the Penal Law approached the impossibility defense to the inchoate crime of attempt in a novel fashion. The statute provides that, if a person engages in conduct which would otherwise constitute an attempt to commit a crime, "it is no defense to a prosecution for such attempt that the crime charged to have been attempted was, under the attendant circumstances, factually or legally impossible of commission, if such crime could have been committed had the attendant circumstances been as such person believed them to be." (Penal Law, § 110.10.) This appeal presents to us, for the first time, a case involving the application of the modern statute. We hold that, under the proof presented by the People at trial, defendant Melvin Dlugash may be held for attempted murder, though the target of the attempt may have already been slain, by the hand of another, when Dlugash made his felonious attempt.

. . . Defendant stated that, on the night of December 21, 1973, he, Bush and Geller had been out drinking. Bush had been staying at Geller's apartment and, during the course of the evening, Geller several times demanded that Bush pay $100 towards the rent on the apartment. According to defendant, Bush rejected these demands, telling Geller that "you better shut up or you're going to get a bullet." All three returned to Geller's apartment at approximately midnight, took seats in the bedroom, and continued to drink until sometime between 3:00 and 3:30 in the morning. When Geller again pressed his demand for rent money, Bush drew his .38 caliber pistol, aimed it at Geller and fired three times. Geller fell to the floor. After the passage of a few minutes, perhaps two, perhaps as much as five, defendant walked over to the fallen Geller, drew his .25 caliber pistol, and fired approximately five shots in the victim's head and face. Defendant contended that, by the time he fired the shots, "it looked like Mike Geller was already dead." . . .

The jury found the defendant guilty of murder. The defendant then moved to set the verdict aside. He submitted an affidavit [which the jury, having already convicted, did not consider], in which he contended that he "was absolutely, unequivocally and positively certain that Michael Geller was dead before [he] shot him." Further, the defendant averred that he was in fear for his life when he shot Geller. "This fear stemmed from the fact that Joseph Bush, the admitted killer of Geller, was holding a gun on me and telling me, in no uncertain terms, that if I didn't shoot the dead body I, too, would be killed." This motion was denied.

On appeal, the Appellate Division reversed the judgment of conviction on the law and dismissed the indictment. The court ruled that "the People failed to prove beyond a reasonable doubt that Geller had been alive at the time he was shot by defendant; defendant's conviction of murder thus cannot stand." Further, the court held that the judgment could not be modified to reflect a conviction for attempted murder because "the uncontradicted evidence is that the defendant, at the time he fired the five shots into the body of the decedent, believed him to be dead, and . . . there is not a scintilla of evidence to contradict his assertion in that regard."

Preliminarily, we state our agreement with the Appellate Division that the evidence did not establish, beyond a reasonable doubt, that Geller was alive at the time defendant fired into his body. . . . While the defendant admitted firing five shots at the victim approximately two to five minutes after Bush had fired three times, all three medical expert witnesses testified that they could not, with any degree of medical certainty, state whether the victim had been alive at the time the latter shots were fired by the defendant. Thus, the People failed to prove beyond a reasonable doubt that the victim had been alive at the time he was shot by the defendant. Whatever else it may be, it is not murder to shoot a dead body. Man dies but once.

. . . .

The most intriguing attempt cases are those where the attempt to commit a crime was unsuccessful due to mistakes . . . on the part of the would-be criminal. A general rule developed in most American jurisdictions that legal impossibility is a good defense but factual impossibility is not. Thus, for example, it was held that defendants who shot at a stuffed deer did not attempt to take a deer out of season, even though they believed the dummy to be a live animal. The court stated that there was no criminal attempt because it was no crime to "take" a stuffed deer, and it is no crime to attempt to do that which is legal. (*State v. Guffey*, 262 S.W.2d 152 [Mo. App.]; *see also State v. Taylor*, 345 Mo. 325, 133 S.W.2d 336 [no liability for attempt to bribe a juror where person bribed was not, in fact, a juror].) These cases are illustrative of legal impossibility. A further example is Francis Wharton's classic hypothetical involving Lady Eldon and her French lace. Lady Eldon, traveling in Europe, purchased a quantity of French lace at a high price, intending to smuggle it into England without payment of the duty. When discovered in a customs search, the lace turned out to be of English origin, of little value and not subject to duty. The traditional view is that Lady Eldon is not liable for an attempt to smuggle.

On the other hand, factual impossibility was no defense. For example, a man was held liable for attempted murder when he shot into the room in which his target usually slept and, fortuitously, the target was sleeping elsewhere in the house that night. Although one bullet struck the target's customary pillow, attainment of the criminal objective was factually impossible. *State v. Moretti*, 52 N.J. 182, 244 A.2d 499, *cert. den.* 393 U.S. 952, presents a similar instance of factual impossibility. The defendant agreed to perform an abortion, then a criminal act, upon a female undercover police investigator who was not, in fact, pregnant. The court sustained the conviction, ruling that "when the consequences sought by a defendant are forbidden by the law as criminal, it is no defense that the defendant could not succeed in reaching his goal because of circumstance unknown to him."

The New York cases can be parsed out along similar lines. One of the leading cases on legal impossibility is *People v. Jaffe*, 185 N.Y. 497, 78 N.E. 169, in which we held that there was no liability for the attempted receipt of stolen property when the property received by the defendant in the belief that it was stolen was, in fact, under the control of the true owner. Similarly, in *People v. Teal*, 196 N.Y. 372, 89 N.E. 1086, a conviction for attempted subornation of perjury was overturned on the theory that the testimony attempted to be suborned was irrelevant to the merits of the case. Since it was not subornation of perjury to solicit false, but irrelevant, testimony, "the person through whose procuration the testimony is given cannot be guilty of subornation of perjury and, by the same rule, an unsuccessful attempt to [do] that which is not a crime when effectuated, cannot be held to be an attempt to commit the crime specified." Factual impossibility, however, was no defense. Thus, a man could be held for attempted grand larceny when he picked an empty pocket.

As can be seen from even this abbreviated discussion, the distinction between "factual" and "legal" impossibility was a nice one indeed and the courts tended to place a greater value on legal form than on any substantive danger the defendant's actions posed for society. The approach of the draftsmen of the Model Penal Code was to eliminate the defense of impossibility in virtually all situations. Under the code provision, to constitute an attempt, it is still necessary that the result intended or desired by the actor constitute a crime. However, the code suggested a fundamental change to shift the locus of analysis to the actor's mental frame of reference and away from undue dependence upon external considerations. The basic premise of the code provision is that what was in the actor's own mind should be the standard for determining his dangerousness to society and, hence, his liability for attempted criminal conduct.

In the belief that neither of the two branches of the traditional impossibility arguments detracts from the offender's moral culpability, the [New York] Legislature substantially carried the [Model Penal Code's] treatment of impossibility into the 1967 revision of the Penal Law. Thus, a person is guilty of an attempt when, with intent to commit a crime, he engages in conduct which tends to effect the commission of such crime. (Penal Law, § 110.00.) It is no defense that, under the attendant circumstances, the crime was factually or legally impossible of commission, "if such crime could have been committed had the attendant circumstances been as such person believed them to be." (Penal Law, § 110.10.) Thus, if defendant believed the victim to be alive at the time of the shooting, it is no defense to the charge of attempted murder that the victim may have been dead.

Turning to the facts of the case before us, we believe that there is sufficient evidence in the record from which the jury could conclude that the defendant believed Geller to be alive at the time defendant fired shots into Geller's head. Defendant admitted firing five shots at a most vital part of the victim's anatomy from virtually point blank range. Although defendant contended that the victim had already been grievously wounded by another, from the defendant's admitted actions, the jury could conclude that the defendant's purpose and intention was to administer the coup de grace. . . .

The jury convicted the defendant of murder. Necessarily, they found that defendant intended to kill a live human being. Subsumed within this finding is the conclusion that defendant acted in the belief that Geller was alive. Thus, there is no need for additional fact findings by a jury. Although it was not established beyond a reasonable doubt that Geller was, in fact, alive, such is no defense to attempted murder since a murder would have been committed "had the attendant circumstances been as [defendant] believed them to be." The jury necessarily found that defendant believed Geller to be alive when defendant shot at him.

The Appellate Division erred in not modifying the judgment to reflect a conviction for the lesser included offense of attempted murder. . . .

People v. Thousand

631 N.W.2d 694 (Mich. 2001)

YOUNG, JUSTICE.

We granted leave in this case to consider whether the doctrine of "impossibility" provides a defense to a charge of attempt . . . or to . . . solicitation. . . .

Deputy William Liczbinski was assigned by the Wayne County Sheriff's Department to conduct an undercover investigation for the department's Internet Crimes

Bureau. Liczbinski was instructed to pose as a minor and log onto "chat rooms" on the Internet for the purpose of identifying persons using the Internet as a means for engaging in criminal activity.

. . . On December 8, 1998, while using the screen name "Bekka," Liczbinski was approached by defendant, who was using the screen name "Mr. Auto-Mag," in an Internet chat room. Defendant described himself as a twenty-three-year-old male from Warren, and Bekka described herself as a fourteen-year-old female from Detroit. Bekka indicated that her name was Becky Fellins, and defendant revealed that his name was Chris Thousand. During this initial conversation, defendant sent Bekka, via the Internet, a photograph of his face. . . . From December 9 through 16, 1998, Liczbinski, still using the screen name "Bekka," engaged in chat room conversation with defendant. During these exchanges, the conversation became sexually explicit. Defendant made repeated lewd invitations to Bekka to engage in various sexual acts, despite various indications of her young age.

During one of his online conversations with Bekka, after asking her whether anyone was "round there," watching her, defendant indicated that he was sending her a picture of himself. Within seconds, Liczbinski received over the Internet a photograph of male genitalia. Defendant asked Bekka whether she liked and wanted it and whether she was getting "hot" yet, and described in a graphic manner the type of sexual acts he wished to perform with her. Defendant invited Bekka to come see him at his house for the purpose of engaging in sexual activity. Bekka replied that she wanted to do so, and defendant cautioned her that they had to be careful, because he could "go to jail." Defendant asked whether Bekka looked "over sixteen," so that if his roommates were home he could lie.

The two then planned to meet at an area McDonald's restaurant. . . . Defendant indicated that they could go to his house, and that he would tell his brother that Bekka was seventeen. Defendant instructed Bekka to wear a "nice sexy skirt," something that he could "get [his] head into." . . . Bekka asked defendant to bring her a present, and indicated that she liked white teddy bears.

. . . On Thursday, December 17, 1998, Liczbinski and other deputy sheriffs were present at the specified McDonald's restaurant when they saw defendant inside a vehicle matching the description given to Bekka by defendant. Defendant . . . got out of the vehicle and entered the restaurant. . . . Defendant looked around for approximately thirty seconds before leaving the restaurant. Defendant was then taken into custody. Two white teddy bears were recovered from defendant's vehicle. . . .

Following a preliminary examination, defendant was bound over for trial on charges of solicitation to commit third-degree criminal sexual conduct, attempted distribution of obscene material to a minor, and child sexually abusive activity. Defendant brought a motion to quash the information, arguing that, because the existence of a child victim was an element of each of the charged offenses, the evidence was legally insufficient to support the charges. The circuit court agreed and dismissed the case, holding that it was legally impossible for defendant to have committed the

charged offenses. The Court of Appeals affirmed the dismissal of the charges of solicitation and attempted distribution of obscene material to a minor, but reversed the
dismissal of the charge of child sexually abusive activity. . . .[2]

A. THE "IMPOSSIBILITY" DOCTRINE

The doctrine of "impossibility" as it has been discussed in the context of inchoate crimes represents the conceptual dilemma that arises when, because of the defendant's mistake of fact or law, his actions could not possibly have resulted in the
commission of the substantive crime underlying an attempt charge. . . . The question, then, becomes whether the defendant can be prosecuted for the attempted
offense, and the answer is dependent upon whether he may raise the defense of
"impossibility."

Courts and legal scholars have drawn a distinction between two categories of
impossibility: "factual impossibility" and "legal impossibility." It has been said that,
at common law, legal impossibility is a defense to a charge of attempt, but factual
impossibility is not. *See* American Law Institute, Model Penal Code and Commentaries (1985), comment to § 5.01, pp 307–17; Perkins & Boyce, Criminal Law
(3d ed), p 632; Dressler, Understanding Criminal Law (1st ed), § 27.07[B],
p 349. However, courts and scholars alike have struggled unsuccessfully over the
years to articulate an accurate rule for distinguishing between the categories of
"impossibility."

"Factual impossibility," which has apparently never been recognized in any American jurisdiction as a defense to a charge of attempt, "exists when [the defendant's]
intended end constitutes a crime but she fails to consummate it because of a factual
circumstance unknown to her or beyond her control." Dressler, *supra*, § 27.07[C][1],
p 350. An example of a "factual impossibility" scenario is where the defendant is
prosecuted for attempted murder after pointing an unloaded gun at someone and
pulling the trigger, where the defendant believed the gun was loaded.

The category of "legal impossibility" is further divided into two subcategories:
"pure" legal impossibility and "hybrid" legal impossibility. Although it is generally
undisputed that "pure" legal impossibility will bar an attempt conviction, the concept of "hybrid legal impossibility" has proven problematic. As Professor Dressler
points out, the failure of courts to distinguish between "pure" and "hybrid" legal
impossibility has created confusion in this area of the law.

"Pure legal impossibility exists if the criminal law does not prohibit D's conduct
or the result that she has sought to achieve." *Id.*, § 27.07[D][2], p 352. In other words,
the concept of pure legal impossibility applies when an actor engages in conduct that

---

2. [n.1] The Court of Appeals concluded that, because the child sexually abusive activity statute
proscribes mere preparation to engage in such activity, the circuit court erred in dismissing that
charge on the basis of the doctrine of legal impossibility. We denied defendant's application for
leave to appeal from this portion of the Court of Appeals opinion, and this charge is not presently
before us.

he believes is criminal, but is not actually prohibited by law: "There can be no conviction of criminal attempt based upon D's erroneous notion that he was committing a crime." PERKINS & BOYCE, *supra*, p 634. As an example, consider the case of a man who believes that the legal age of consent is sixteen years old, and who . . . had consensual sexual intercourse [with a girl who was] fifteen years old. If the law actually fixed the age of consent at fifteen, this man would not be guilty of attempted statutory rape, despite his mistaken belief that the law prohibited his conduct.

When courts speak of "legal impossibility," they are generally referring to what is more accurately described as "hybrid" legal impossibility.

> Most claims of legal impossibility are of the hybrid variety. Hybrid legal impossibility exists if D's goal was illegal, but commission of the offense was impossible due to a factual mistake by her regarding the legal status of some factor relevant to her conduct. This version of impossibility is a "hybrid" because, as the definition implies and as is clarified immediately below, D's impossibility claim includes both a legal and a factual aspect to it.

> Courts have recognized a defense of legal impossibility or have stated that it would exist if D receives unstolen property believing it was stolen; tries to pick the pocket of a stone image of a human; offers a bribe to a "juror" who is not a juror; tries to hunt deer out of season by shooting a stuffed animal; shoots a corpse believing that it is alive; or shoots at a tree stump believing that it is a human.

> Notice that each of the mistakes in these cases affected the legal status of some aspect of the defendant's conduct. The status of property as "stolen" is necessary to commit the crime of "receiving stolen property with knowledge it is stolen"—i.e., a person legally is incapable of committing this offense if the property is not stolen. The status of a person as a "juror" is legally necessary to commit the offense of bribing a juror. The status of a victim as a "human being" (rather than as a corpse, tree stump, or statue) legally is necessary to commit the crime of murder or to "take and carry away the personal property of another." Finally, putting a bullet into a stuffed deer can never constitute the crime of hunting out of season.

> On the other hand, in each example of hybrid legal impossibility D was mistaken about a fact: whether property was stolen, whether a person was a juror, whether the victims were human or whether the victim was an animal subject to being hunted out of season.

[DRESSLER, *supra*, § 27.07[D][3][a], pp 353–54.]

As the Court of Appeals panel in this case accurately noted, it is possible to view virtually any example of "hybrid legal impossibility" as an example of "factual impossibility":

> "Ultimately any case of hybrid legal impossibility may reasonably be characterized as factual impossibility. . . . By skillful characterization, one can

describe virtually any case of hybrid legal impossibility, which is a common law defense, as an example of factual impossibility, which is not a defense."

See also Weiss, *Scope, Mistake, and Impossibility: The Philosophy of Language and Problems of Mens Rea*, 83 COLUM. L. REV. 1029, 1029–30 (1983) ("because ordinary English cannot adequately distinguish among the various kinds of impossible attempts, courts and commentators have frequently misclassified certain types of cases"); *State v. Moretti*, 52 N.J. 182, 189, 244 A.2d 499 (1968) ("our examination of [authorities discussing the doctrine of impossibility] convinces us that the application of the defense of impossibility is so fraught with intricacies and artificial distinctions that the defense has little value as an analytical method for reaching substantial justice").

It is notable that "the great majority of jurisdictions have now recognized that legal and factual impossibility are 'logically indistinguishable' ... and have abolished impossibility as a defense." *United States v. Hsu*, 155 F.3d 189, 199 (CA3 1998). For example, several states [e.g., Colorado, Kansas, and New York] have adopted statutory provisions similar to Model Penal Code, §5.01(1).

In other jurisdictions, courts have considered the "impossibility" defense under attempt statutes that did not include language explicitly abolishing the defense. Several of these courts have simply declined to participate in the sterile academic exercise of categorizing a particular set of facts as representing "factual" or "legal" impossibility, and have instead examined solely the words of the applicable attempt statute [e.g., Nevada, New Jersey, and California].

B. ATTEMPTED DISTRIBUTION OF OBSCENE MATERIAL TO A MINOR

The Court of Appeals panel in this case ... concluded that it was legally impossible for defendant to have committed the charged offense of attempted distribution of obscene material to a minor. The panel held that, because "Bekka" was, in fact, an adult, an essential requirement of the underlying substantive offense was not met (dissemination to a minor), and therefore it was legally impossible for defendant to have committed the crime.

We begin by noting that the concept of "impossibility," in either its "factual" or "legal" variant, has never been recognized by this Court as a valid defense to a charge of attempt. ...

Finding no recognition of impossibility in our common law, we turn now to the terms of the statute:

Any person who shall attempt to commit an offense prohibited by law, and in such attempt shall do any act towards the commission of such offense, but shall fail in the perpetration, or shall be intercepted or prevented in the execution of the same, when no express provision is made by law for the punishment of such attempt, shall be punished. ...

... We have ... explained the elements of attempt under our statute as including "an intent to do an act or to bring about certain consequences which would in law amount to a crime; and . . . an act in furtherance of that intent which, as it is most commonly put, goes beyond mere preparation."

We are unable to discern from the words of the attempt statute any legislative intent that the concept of "impossibility" provide any impediment to charging a defendant with, or convicting him of, an attempted crime, notwithstanding any factual mistake—regarding either the attendant circumstances or the legal status of some factor relevant thereto—that he may harbor. The attempt statute carves out no exception for those who, possessing the requisite criminal intent to commit an offense prohibited by law and taking action toward the commission of that offense, have acted under an extrinsic misconception.

Defendant in this case is not charged with the substantive crime of distributing obscene material to a minor . . . . It is unquestioned that defendant could not be convicted of that crime, because defendant allegedly distributed obscene material not to "a minor," but to an adult man. Instead, defendant is charged with the distinct offense of attempt, which requires only that the prosecution prove intention to commit an offense prohibited by law, coupled with conduct toward the commission of that offense. The notion that it would be "impossible" for the defendant to have committed the completed offense is simply irrelevant to the analysis. . . .

Because the nonexistence of a minor victim does not give rise to a viable defense to the attempt charge in this case, the circuit court erred in dismissing this charge on the basis of "legal impossibility."

C. SOLICITATION TO COMMIT THIRD-DEGREE CRIMINAL SEXUAL CONDUCT

Defendant was additionally charged, on the basis of his Internet conversations with "Bekka," with solicitation to commit third-degree criminal sexual conduct. . . .

The Court of Appeals erred to the extent that it relied on the doctrine of "impossibility" as a ground for affirming the circuit court's dismissal of the solicitation charge. As we have explained, Michigan has never adopted the doctrine of impossibility as a defense in its traditional attempt context, much less in the context of solicitation crimes. Moreover, we are unable to locate any authority, and defendant has provided none, for the proposition that "impossibility" is a recognized defense to a charge of solicitation in other jurisdictions.[3]

. . . .

---

3. [n.18] On the other hand, some courts have had occasion to specifically reject the notion that impossibility is a defense to solicitation. *See, e.g., Benson v. Superior Court of Los Angeles Co.,* 368 P.2d 116 (Cal. 1962) ("if the solicitor believes that the act can be committed 'it is immaterial that the crime urged is not possible of fulfillment at the time when the words are spoken' or becomes impossible at a later time"). *See also* Model Penal Code, § 5.04(1) ("It is immaterial to the liability of a person who solicits or conspires with another to commit a crime that: (b) the person whom he solicits or with whom he conspires is irresponsible or has an immunity to prosecution or conviction for the commission of the crime").

KELLY, JUSTICE [joined by CAVANAUGH, JUSTICE] (concurring in part and dissenting in part).

I respectfully disagree with the majority's conclusion that the doctrine of "legal impossibility" has never been adopted in Michigan. There is ample evidence to the contrary in the case law of the state. Because "legal impossibility" is a viable defense, I would affirm the Court of Appeals decision affirming the circuit court's dismissal of attempted distribution of obscene material to a minor.

. . . .

Examination of the language of the attempt statute leads to a reasonable inference that the Legislature did not intend to punish conduct that a mistake of legal fact renders unprohibited. The attempt statute makes illegal an ". . . attempt to commit an offense prohibited by law . . . ." It does not make illegal an action not prohibited by law. Hence, one may conclude, the impossibility of completing the underlying crime can provide a defense to attempt.

This reasoning is supported by the fact that the attempt statute codified the common-law rule regarding the elements of attempt. . . .

This state's attempt statute, unlike the Model Penal Code and various state statutes that follow it, does not contain language allowing for consideration of a defendant's beliefs regarding "attendant circumstances." Rather, it takes an "objective" view of criminality, focusing on whether the defendant actually came close to completing the prohibited act. 1 ROBINSON, CRIMINAL LAW DEFENSES, §85(a), pp 423–24; §85(b), p 426, n.22. The impossibility of completing the offense is relevant to this objective approach because impossibility obviates the state's "concern that the actor may cause or come close to causing the harm or evil that the offense seeks to prevent."

. . . The underlying offense in this case, disseminating or exhibiting sexual material to a minor, requires a minor recipient. Because the dissemination was not to a minor, it is legally impossible for defendant to have committed the prohibited act.

I further disagree with the majority's conclusion that "legal impossibility" is not a recognized defense to a solicitation charge. . . . The majority states that no authority supports the proposition that "legal impossibility" is a defense to solicitation in other jurisdictions. However, this fact is unremarkable in light of the rarity with which the defense is invoked. Moreover, "the impossibility issue can arise in all inchoate offenses," including solicitation. ROBINSON, supra, at §85(f)(2), p 436. . . .

As judges, we often decide cases involving disturbing facts. However repugnant we personally find the criminal conduct charged, we must decide the issues on the basis of the law. I certainly do not wish to have child predators loose in society. However, I believe that neither the law nor society is served by allowing the end of removing them from society to excuse unjust means to accomplish it. . . .

. . . Of course, if [my] view prevailed, defendant could still be prosecuted for his alleged misconduct. He is to be tried on the most serious of the charges, child sexually abusive activity.

Notes and Questions

1. **Legal Impossibility.** As outlined in *Dlugash* and *Thousand*, those jurisdictions that adhere to the "traditional" common-law approach distinguish between legal impossibility, which is a defense, and factual impossibility, which is not. This approach, as explained in *Dlugash*, is based on the premise that "it is no crime to attempt to do that which is legal."

The following have been called examples of legal impossibility (although consider whether you could articulately describe them as cases of "factual" impossibility):

(a) In the Sherlock Holmes story *The Empty House*, Holmes is being stalked by Colonel Moran, "the best shot in India." Holmes sets a trap for Moran by placing a wax bust of himself in the window of his apartment. Every so often, Holmes' housekeeper moves the bust to make it seem alive. Moran is fooled. From a vacant apartment across the street, he shoots the bust "plumb in the middle of the back of the head and smack through the brain." Holmes and Watson leap from their hiding places and seize him. As Moran is being led away, Holmes asks Inspector Lestrade, "What charge do you intend to prefer?" "What charge, sir? Why, of course, the attempted murder of Mr. Sherlock Holmes," the Inspector replies. "Not so, Lestrade," Holmes answers. Holmes' reasoning was that Moran could not be prosecuted for attempted murder because he was only attempting to shoot a dummy.

(b) Assume an absentminded professor takes an umbrella she covets from the faculty lounge. She brings the umbrella home, and her husband tells her the umbrella is really her own mislaid umbrella. When the professor is charged with attempted larceny, she raises legal impossibility as a defense, arguing that it is no crime to steal one's own umbrella. *See* Ira P. Robbins, *Attempting the Impossible: The Emerging Consensus*, 23 Harv. J. on Legis. 377, 378–79 (1986).

(c) Wielding an axe, *A* strikes his neighbor, who appears to be sleeping in the forest. In the morning, *A* discovers that all that he struck was a log. *A* argues that legal impossibility is a defense to attempted murder because it is no crime to cut a log.

(d) A college student smokes what she thinks is marijuana. Later she discovers it was ordinary tobacco. She raises legal impossibility as a defense to the charge of attempted possession of a controlled substance. *But see Grill v. State*, 651 A.2d 856, 859 (Md. 1995) (concluding on similar facts that "[c]onsistent with the 'factual impossibility' cases, a rational factfinder could have concluded" that the defendant intended to purchase a controlled substance, "failing only to effectuate her intention by a fact unknown to her, i.e., that what she purchased was not heroin but rather a noncontrolled 'look-alike' substance").

(e) A soldier wants to murder his sergeant and shoots at someone who resembles the sergeant but turns out to be an enemy soldier attacking the troops. *See* Robbins, *supra*, at 378–79.

(f) *A* attempts to buy stolen jewelry at an appropriately discounted price. The jewelry is not really stolen. *See People v. Jaffe*, 78 N.E. 169 (N.Y. 1906) (holding that legal impossibility was a defense there because "the immediate act which the defendant had in contemplation (to wit, the purchase of the goods which were brought to his place for sale) could not have been criminal under the statute even if the purchase had been completed because the goods had not in fact been stolen"). *But cf. People v. Rojas*, 358 P.2d 921, 924 (Cal. 1961) (finding sufficient evidence of "specific intent to commit the substantive offense" in a similar case; "'[t]he fact that defendant was mistaken regarding the external realities did not alter his intention, but simply made it impossible to effectuate it'") (quoting Jerome Hall, General Principles of Criminal Law 127 (1947)).

(g) *A* offers a bribe to a person he thinks is a juror. In fact, the person is not a juror at all. *A* argues that it is no crime to offer money to a non-juror, and thus legal impossibility is a defense. *See State v. Taylor*, 133 S.W.2d 336 (Mo. 1939) (accepting this argument).

(h) Agents set up decoy deer to catch those who are hunting before the legal season begins. Defendants shoot at the decoy and are charged with attempting to hunt deer out of season. *See State v. Guffey*, 262 S.W.2d 152 (Mo. Ct. App. 1953) (holding that legal impossibility is a defense). *But see State v. Curtis*, 603 A.2d 356 (Vt. 1991) (using the Model Penal Code's approach to convict).

2. Factual Impossibility. Jurisdictions that accept the traditional doctrine of impossibility do not consider factual impossibility a defense to a charge of attempt because, as the court notes in *Dlugash*, "when the consequences sought by a defendant are forbidden by the law as criminal, it is no defense that the defendant could not succeed in reaching his goal because of circumstances unknown to him." The following have been called examples of factual impossibility:

(a) *A* shoots at *B*, but unbeknownst to *A*, the gun is unloaded. *A* is guilty of attempted murder because she was attempting to fire a bullet at *B*. *See, e.g., State v. Pamms*, 100 N.W.2d 592 (Wis. 1960).

(b) A pickpocket attempts to pick an empty pocket. He has no defense to an attempted theft charge because this is a case of factual impossibility. *See, e.g., People v. Twiggs*, 35 Cal. Rptr. 859 (Cal. Ct. App. 1963).

3. Distinguishing Factual Versus Legal and "Hybrid" Legal Impossibility. Trying to make sense of the distinction between factual and legal impossibility has created headaches for generations of law students. Is there any justification for treating legal impossibility and factual impossibility differently? Can you distinguish the first group of cases from the second?

Under the common-law formulation, the difference between legal and factual impossibility in theory turned on the defendant's intent: if the act the defendant intended to commit was not a crime, the common law defined the case as one of legal impossibility and afforded a defense because the defendant could do "everything he intended to do but yet . . . not commit the completed crime." On the other hand, if what the defendant wanted to do was prohibited by the criminal law but the defendant was "unable to accomplish what he intend[ed] because of some facts unknown to him," the common law defined the case as one of factual impossibility. 2 Wayne R. LaFave, Substantive Criminal Law § 11.5, at 229 (2d ed. 2003).

Despite the purported theoretical distinction drawn by the common law, the examples of factual impossibility set out above in Note 2 seem strikingly similar to the mistaken identity cases in Note 1, which have been called examples of legal impossibility. Can all of the illustrations listed in Note 1 be transformed into cases of factual impossibility simply by recharacterizing the defendant's "intent"? Is the problem that these illustrations can be considered examples of legal impossibility only by "asserting, in effect, that a person's intent is to do what he was actually doing rather than what he thought he was doing"? LaFave, *supra*, § 11.5(a)(1), at 232.

Does it help to subdivide the concept of legal impossibility, as Professor Dressler does, into "pure" legal impossibility and "hybrid" legal impossibility? The *Thousand* court endorses this distinction, and holds that defendants can be convicted of attempt whether completion of the crime they intended to commit was rendered impossible due to their mistake regarding "the legal status" of some person or object ("hybrid legal impossibility") or due to a mistake regarding some other "factual circumstance" ("factual impossibility"). That is, although both types of mistakes might render the completed offense "impossible," both also support criminal conviction for attempt. The Michigan Supreme Court ultimately concludes that the distinction between factual and hybrid legal impossibility is verbal sophistry because "it is possible to view virtually any example of 'hybrid legal impossibility' as an example of 'factual impossibility.'" *See also United States v. Tykarsky*, 446 F.3d 458, 465–66 (3d Cir. 2006) (observing in a similar case that "the distinction between factual and legal impossibility is essentially a matter of semantics, for every case of legal impossibility can reasonably be characterized as a factual impossibility").

Nevertheless, a minority of states still remain loyal to the traditional common-law distinction. Are there public policy reasons to retain the traditional approach?

4. True or "Pure" Legal Impossibility. Suppose *A*, wanting to commit a crime in order to aggravate his parents, does the following:

 (a) Having been told that his singing is a crime, sings outside his house.

(b) Drives 75 miles per hour on the highways in Colorado, mistakenly thinking that the speed limit is 65.

(c) Thinking it is a crime, pulls a tag reading "Warning: do not remove this tag under penalty of law" from the bottom of his living room sofa.

It is never a criminal attempt, under either the Model Penal Code or traditional common law, to try to do something that is *not* a crime—even if the defendant erroneously believes that the law prohibits the conduct in question. Because singing is not a crime, *A* cannot be convicted of attempt, no matter how bad his mistaken intent (or his singing) may be. This is "pure" legal impossibility, in Dressler's terms. Unlike factual impossibility and hybrid legal impossibility, pure legal impossibility involves a mistake of law, rather than a mistake of fact. (See Chapter 4, Sections C.1 and C.2, for further discussion of mistakes of law and fact.)

5. The Model Penal Code Approach: Liability Based on the Facts as the Defendant "Believes Them to Be." The inconsistencies characterizing the common law's approach to impossibility prompted the Model Penal Code and a majority of states to reject any distinction between factual and legal impossibility in attempt prosecutions. Instead, MPC § 5.01(1)(a) punishes attempts so long as the defendant's "conduct . . . would constitute the crime if the attendant circumstances were as he believes them to be." The Comments to the MPC note that "the purpose of [§ 5.01(1)(a)] is to eliminate legal impossibility as a defense." Model Penal Code § 5.01 Comment at 578. The Comments defend this decision as follows:

> The primary rationale of [the legal impossibility defense] is that, judging the actor's conduct in the light of the actual facts, what he intended to do did not amount to a crime. This approach, however, is unsound in that it seeks to evaluate a mental attitude—"intent" or "purpose"—not by looking to the actor's mental frame of reference, but to a situation wholly at variance with the actor's beliefs. In so doing, the courts exonerate defendants in situations where attempt liability most certainly should be imposed. In all of these cases the actor's criminal purpose has been clearly demonstrated; he went as far as he could in implementing that purpose; and, as a result, his "dangerousness" is plainly manifested.
>
>   . . . .
>
> Insofar as it has not rested on conceptual tangles that have been largely independent of policy considerations, the defense of impossibility seems to have been employed to serve a number of functions. First, it has been used to verify criminal purpose; if the means selected were absurd, there is good ground for doubting that the actor really planned to commit a crime. Similarly, if the defendant's conduct, objectively viewed, is ambiguous, there may be ground for doubting the firmness of his purpose to commit a criminal offense. A general defense of impossibility is, however, an inappropriate way of assuring that the actor has a true criminal purpose.

A second function that the defense of impossibility seems to have served in some cases is to supplement the defense of entrapment. In situations in which the technical entrapment rules do not exonerate the defendant, there is a temptation to find that the presence of traps and decoys makes the actor's endeavor impossible. The Model Code has a separate formulation on entrapment which is believed to state the appropriate considerations for a defense on this ground.

A third consideration that has been advanced in support of an impossibility defense is the view that the criminal law need not take notice of conduct that is innocuous, the element of impossibility preventing any dangerous proximity to the completed crime. The law of attempts, however, should be concerned with manifestations of dangerous character as well as with preventive arrests; the fact that particular conduct may not create an actual risk of harmful consequences, though it would if the circumstances were as the defendant believed them to be, should not therefore be conclusive. The innocuous character of the particular conduct becomes relevant only if the futile endeavor itself indicates a harmless personality, so that immunizing the conduct from liability would not result in exposing society to a dangerous person.

Id. at 308–09, 315–16.

Thus, if *A* takes *B*'s briefcase, believing (even unreasonably) that the briefcase is his own, *A* is not guilty of theft, or even attempted theft, because both crimes require an intent to take property that belongs to another. But under MPC § 5.01(1)(a), if *A* takes his own briefcase, believing it belongs to *B*, *A* may be convicted of attempted theft. Is the distinction between these two cases sensible?

6. The MPC's Exception for "Inherent Impossibility." Suppose *A* makes a voodoo image of *B* and then sticks a pin into the voodoo doll, fully intending to kill *B*. Assuming that *B* continues to live, *A* would nevertheless seem to be guilty of attempted murder under § 5.01(1) of the Model Penal Code (as well as possibly under the common law). However, our "justice" intuitions may be offended by the prospect of imposing criminal liability for conduct we believe to be harmless because it cannot (or, we believe, almost certainly cannot) cause criminal harm. (Consider whether this sense of injustice might explain the common law's recognition of a defense for "legal impossibility.")

The Model Penal Code creates a potential escape hatch for such situations, permitting judges to either dismiss attempt charges or impose a reduced sentence following a conviction:

> If the particular conduct charged to constitute a criminal attempt, solicitation or conspiracy is *so inherently unlikely* to result or culminate in the commission of a crime that neither such conduct nor the actor presents a public danger . . . , the Court shall exercise its power . . . to enter judgment and

impose sentence for a crime of lower grade or degree or, in extreme cases, may dismiss the prosecution.

Model Penal Code § 5.05(2) (emphasis added).

7. **"Sting" Operations by Law Enforcement.** The scenario in *Thousand*, where law enforcement sets up an undercover operation to attract would-be offenders, is not unusual. In *United States v. Tykarsky*, 446 F.3d 458 (3d Cir. 2006), for example, the defendant arranged via an Internet chatroom titled "Iloveoldermen2" to meet a woman he believed to be 14 years old (screen name "HeatherJet14") but who was in fact an adult undercover FBI agent. Tykarsky was arrested upon entering the hotel where the meeting had been scheduled and was charged under the federal statute prohibiting attempts to "knowingly persuade, induce, [or] entice" a minor to engage in unlawful sexual activity. 18 U.S.C. § 2422(b). Agreeing with four other federal courts of appeals, the Third Circuit concluded that the federal statute did not embody an impossibility defense: "Congress did not intend to allow the use of an adult decoy . . . to be asserted as a defense." 446 F.3d at 466. "[I]t is common knowledge that law enforcement officials rely heavily on decoys and sting operations," the court reasoned, and the statute is "most naturally read to focus on the subjective intent of the defendant, not the actual age of the victim." *Id*. at 468.

Were the courts in *Thousand* and *Tykarsky* right to reject an impossibility defense in these cases? What do you think of the ethics of these undercover sting operations generally? See Chapter 15, Section B, for discussion of the "entrapment" defense.

8. *Dlugash* **Reprised: Whatever Happened to Bush?** Professor Alan Dershowitz, who represented Dlugash, has provided some interesting background on the case. Joe Bush, the man who initially shot Mike Geller, was nowhere to be found when Dlugash was arrested. Evidently, Bush traveled around the country as a fugitive before eventually returning to New York City. Upon his return, Bush once again got into trouble and was arrested. The police, however, failed to realize that Bush was the man wanted in connection with Geller's death. By a remarkable coincidence, Bush ended up in the same police van as Dlugash. Dlugash immediately informed his lawyers, and Bush was formally charged with Geller's murder. Bush's lawyer worked out a plea bargain, under which the murder charge was dropped in exchange for Bush's plea of guilty to manslaughter. He was sentenced to prison for five to 10 years in connection with his role in Geller's death. *See* Alan M. Dershowitz, The Best Defense 91 (1982). Dlugash, meanwhile, eventually pled guilty to attempted manslaughter in the second degree, a crime that ironically did not exist under New York law, and could not, given the mens rea requirement of "purpose" for attempt. (*See* Note 2 in Section 2 above.) Dlugash was sentenced to five years' probation. *See* Dershowitz, *supra*, at 116.

[B] Solicitation

The crime of solicitation involves purposefully asking or encouraging another person to commit a crime. As the *Thousand* case excerpted above demonstrates, in jurisdictions that criminalize solicitation, the inchoate offenses of attempt and solicitation are often found together. Like attempt, solicitation is viewed as preparatory toward crime. And like conspiracy (discussed in Chapter 13), the crime of solicitation can be misused, due to its very inchoateness, to target groups that are at odds with the authorities. Compare the following two cases. How are they alike? How are they different? What role, if any, do you think the cultural context of the times played in each?

State v. Schleifer

121 A. 805 (Conn. 1923)

WHEELER, CHIEF JUSTICE.

The information before us charges that the accused, intending to endanger the public peace and to incite and procure the commission and perpetration of divers felonies and aggravated crimes akin to felonies, did unlawfully solicit, urge, command, counsel, and endeavor to incite, cause, and procure some or all of a large number of persons assembled, to the state's attorney unknown, to perpetrate or attempt to perpetrate the crimes of murder, robbery, aggravated assault with deadly or dangerous weapons, assault with intent to murder, and assault with intent to rob, the same being felonies or aggravated crimes akin to felonies, by oral address, in language in substance as follows:

> You will never win the strike with soft methods. You young men ought to go out on the bridge. Don't use eggs; use coal or indelible ink. Break foremen's windows at their homes. Watch the scabs when they come from work, lay for them, especially on pay day. Take them in a dark alley and hit them with a lead pipe. That is the softest thing you can use. Reimburse yourselves for what we have sacrificed for five months. Don't forget to bump off a few now and then, so Mr. Pearson will know that you are not getting cold feet. You car men know how to take a brake shoe off. Take the brake shoe and put it under something that will put the cars off the irons. A little sand or emery in the journal boxes will help greatly. Don't be satisfied with trimming the engines. Put some of the cars on the bum. Also, if convenient, put something in between the frames and rods of engines on sidings. Get busy, young fellows, and trim these scabs. Things are running too smooth on the New Haven Road, but let me hear from you while I am here. Go ahead and rip things, and don't let the injunction stop you from trimming these scabs. Don't forget to tie them up with derailments. You boys ought to cut them all up.

To this information the accused filed a motion to quash, which the trial court sustained upon the grounds stated in part therein, viz.:

(1) That said information is insufficient in law. (2) That said information fails to set forth any offense or crime. . . . (8) That said information merely charges the defendant with having uttered certain words set forth in said information, and such utterances do not constitute a crime by virtue of any statute of this state, or at common law. (9) That said information merely states that the defendant entertained certain intentions, as evidenced by certain expressions made by him, and such intentions do not either at common law or by virtue of any statute constitute crime.

In its memorandum on the motion to quash, the court held that in the common-law crime of solicitation "the inducement or invitation" must have been "directed to one individual soliciting the accomplishment of some particular act which, if complied with, would result in the commission of some specific offense." The trial court further held:

> While it cannot be seriously denied that the public utterance in a promiscuous assembly of such entreaties and exhortations as are charged in this information is highly prejudicial to the public peace, and ought to be seriously penalized, it is a situation that should be met by appropriate legislation. I do not feel warranted in view of all the authorities in undertaking to extend the present limitations of the common law crime of solicitation so as to include the acts of the accused now under consideration.

In *Commonwealth v. Flagg*, 135 Mass. 545, 549, the information charged a solicitation to burn a barn, and the judgment of conviction was sustained. The court, by Morton, C.J., held:

> It is an indictable offense at common law for one to counsel and solicit another to commit a felony or other aggravated offense, although the solicitation is of no effect, and the crime counseled is not in fact committed.

In *Commonwealth v. Randolph*, 146 Pa. 83, 23 Atl. 388, it is held that the solicitation to commit murder, accompanied by a money bribe for so doing, is a crime at common law. The case of *Smith v. Commonwealth*, 54 Penn. 209, 93 Am. Dec. 686, upon which the accused in the case at bar especially relies, is distinguished as deciding merely that solicitation to commit a misdemeanor is not a crime at common law, a question which *Commonwealth v. Randolph* does not determine.

. . . The trial court criticizes the information because it does not charge that any particular person was solicited to the commission of any particular crime in any specified place, and the state assigns this among its other alleged errors. It was not necessary to make such an allegation. The solicitation was directed to each one present in the assemblage. It would not have been more direct or more compulsive if each one in the assemblage had been called by name by the accused. . . .

. . . The ground of demurrer that the information merely states that the defendant entertained certain intentions may be answered briefly. The mere intention, unexpressed, of the accused does not, and is not claimed to, subject the accused to criminal punishment. But when the intention be expressed in the form of a solicitation, or incitement, or a command to another to commit a crime, and that crime a felony or a high crime and misdemeanor akin to felony, it is a crime under our common law.

. . . There is error; the judgment is set aside, and the cause remanded, to be proceeded with according to law.

People v. Quentin
296 N.Y.S.2d 443 (N.Y. Dist. Ct. 1968)

Tomson, Judge.

The defendants, Robert Quentin and John Garcia, have been charged . . . with possession and promotion of an obscene brochure . . . and criminal solicitation in the third degree. The defendants move for leave to withdraw their not guilty pleas and interpose a demurrer to the information on the ground that it does not state facts sufficient to constitute a crime.

The brochure in question, although objectionable to the majority of its readers, would appear to be obscene primarily because of the cover. . . . The cover picture is unrelated to the balance of the pamphlet. It is obviously used only to attract attention and in so doing appeals to the prurient interest.

The rest of the brochure is worthy of note. The inside front cover concisely describes the philosophy of the defendants. In part it reads:

> America is carnivorous. She eats the world for dessert. . . . The rich are rich because they are thieves and the poor because they are victims, and the future will condemn those who accept the present as reality. Break down the family, church, nation, city, economy. . . . Subversiveness saves us. . . . [O]ur professors are spies; let us close the schools and flow into the streets. . . . Grow hair long and become too freaky to fit into the machine culture. What's needed is a generation of people who are freaky, crazy, irrational, sexy, angry, irreligious, childish and mad: people who burn draft cards, burn high school and college degrees: people who say: "To hell with your goals"; people who lure the youth with music, pot and acid: people who re-define reality, who re-define the normal. . . . The white youth of America have more in common with Indians plundered, than they do with their own parents. Burn their house down, and you will be free.

This is followed by a paragraph entitled "How to make a fire bomb," and a recipe for Tryptamine, a psychedelic agent. The recipe ends with the statements:

> This last (Tetrahydrofurane) is a very powerful reducing agent; wear safety glasses, add very cautiously, and perform this step with ventilation, away from flames (H2 is evolved). The yield is about 40 grams of DMT, in

tetrahydrofurane solution. This cannot be drunk or injected, but may be smoked by sprinkling on mint or cannabis leaves and letting the solution evaporate. It's evaporated when it starts smelling like DMT instead of tetrahydrofurane.

. . . [The prosecution] alleges a violation of Section 100.00 of the Penal Law which is criminal solicitation in the third degree. It charges that the defendants violated the section in that they attempted to cause persons to whom [the] brochure was distributed to possess a chemical compound known as DET and DMT which violates §229 (429) of the Mental Hygiene Law. The brochure on one of its pages gives a formula for making a fire bomb. Below that is also a formula for making both DET and DMT [both of which are members of the Tryptamine family]. On the page with the formula is no other solicitation, request or advocacy concerning the drugs. The formula taken alone appears to be such as would be found in a chemistry book or encyclopedia. It is clear that Section 100.00 was intended to cover a situation where a particular person importunes another specified individual to do a specific act which constitutes a crime. The purpose was to hold the solicitor criminally responsible even if the one solicited fails to commit the act. It does not appear that Section 100.00 was designed to cover a situation where the defendant makes a general solicitation (however reprehensible) to a large indefinable group to commit a crime.

The defendants' motion is granted and all counts of the information are dismissed with leave to the District Attorney to file a new information.

Model Penal Code § 5.02: Criminal Solicitation

(1) *Definition of Solicitation*. A person is guilty of solicitation to commit a crime if with the purpose of promoting or facilitating its commission he commands, encourages or requests another person to engage in specific conduct which would constitute such crime or an attempt to commit such crime or which would establish his complicity in its commission or attempted commission.

(2) *Uncommunicated Solicitation*. It is immaterial under Subsection (1) of this Section that the actor fails to communicate with the person he solicits to commit a crime if his conduct was designed to effect such communication.

(3) *Renunciation of Criminal Purpose*. It is an affirmative defense that the actor, after soliciting another person to commit a crime, persuaded him not to do so or otherwise prevented the commission of the crime, under circumstances manifesting a complete and voluntary renunciation of his criminal purpose.

Notes and Questions

1. The Elements of Solicitation. The crime of solicitation has two elements: (1) encouraging, requesting, or advising another person to commit a crime, (2) with the intent (purpose) that the other person commit the acts constituting that crime. *See* Wayne R. LaFave, Criminal Law § 11.1, at 602 (5th ed. 2010); Rollin M. Perkins & Ronald N. Boyce, Criminal Law 582–88 (3d ed. 1982).

2. Comparing the Common Law and Modern Statutes. Modern solicitation statutes tend to limit liability to situations where the defendant encourages the commission of particularly serious crimes listed in the statute. For instance, the California statute punishes only the solicitation of bribery, murder, robbery, grand theft, carjacking, burglary, receiving stolen property, extortion, arson, rape by force and violence, perjury, subornation of perjury, forgery, and kidnapping. *See* Cal. Penal Code § 653f. By contrast, § 5.02 of the Model Penal Code and the common law would punish the solicitation of any crime.

3. Punishing Solicitation. Like all inchoate offenses, solicitation does not require that the solicited person actually commit the solicited crime. In fact, because solicitation is typically considered a lesser offense, solicitation charges are usually brought only when the solicited crime was not actually committed. At common law, if the solicited crime was actually committed, solicitation would be "merged" with the completed offense so that a defendant could only be sentenced for the completed offense. The Model Penal Code follows the same approach. *See* Model Penal Code § 1.07(1)(b).

The common law generally treated solicitation as a misdemeanor, even if the target offense was a felony. But § 5.05(1) of the Model Penal Code "grades" solicitation, attempt, and conspiracy equally, and in fact, would punish them as severely (that is, as "crimes of the same grade") as the target offense (unless the target crime is a capital offense or first-degree felony).

4. The Justifications for Punishing Solicitation. The drafters of the Model Penal Code described the debate surrounding the question whether solicitation should be criminalized:

> There has been difference of opinion as to whether a genuine social danger is presented by solicitation to commit a crime. It has been argued, on the one hand, that the conduct of the solicitor is not dangerous since between it and the commission of the crime that is his object is the resisting will of an independent moral agent. By the same token it is urged that the solicitor, manifesting his reluctance to commit the crime himself, is not a menace of significance. Against this is the view that a solicitation is, if anything, more dangerous than a direct attempt, since it may give rise to the cooperation among criminals that is a special hazard. Solicitation may, indeed, be thought of as an attempt to conspire. Moreover, the solicitor, working his will through one or more agents, manifests an approach to crime more intelligent and masterful than the efforts of his hireling. Indeed, examples drawn from the controversial fields of political agitation and labor unrest suggest as a non-controversial lesson that the imposition of liability for criminal solicitation may be an important means by which the leadership of a movement deemed criminal may be suppressed.

Model Penal Code § 5.02 Comment at 365–66.

5. The Requirement That the Solicitation Be Communicated. The traditional common-law rule required that the solicitation actually be communicated to the person solicited. For example, in *State v. Cotton*, 790 P.2d 1050 (N.M. 1990), James Cotton was charged with soliciting his wife to bribe or intimidate a witness. Cotton had been arrested for sexually abusing his 14-year-old stepdaughter. While in prison awaiting trial on those charges, he wrote his wife a letter asking her to talk his stepdaughter out of testifying against him. He asked another inmate to put a stamp on the sealed, addressed envelope. But unbeknownst to Cotton, that inmate removed the letter from the envelope and gave it to the authorities, who put a blank piece of paper in the envelope, resealed and stamped it, and returned it to Cotton. Cotton mailed the envelope. Later, he wrote a second letter asking his wife to convince or even bribe his stepdaughter not to testify against him, but he was arrested before he could mail that letter. The court held that Cotton could not be convicted because his wife never receive either solicitation.

The Model Penal Code disagrees with this approach. Under § 5.02(2), the crime of solicitation is complete even if "the actor fails to communicate with the person he solicits."

6. Comparing Solicitation and Attempt, Conspiracy, and Accomplice Liability. If a solicited person acts on the solicitor's advice or encouragement and actually commits the crime, then the solicitor is also guilty of the completed offense as an accomplice. If the solicited person attempts to commit the crime, then the solicitor may be convicted of the attempt as an accomplice. Furthermore, if the solicited person agrees to the solicitor's criminal plan, both may be convicted of conspiracy (assuming that, if required, a subsequent overt act was performed). The crime of conspiracy is discussed in greater detail in Chapter 13, and accomplice ability is described in Chapter 12.

The question whether the act of solicitation can also constitute a criminal attempt has been controversial, and can be an issue of some importance in jurisdictions that lack a separate solicitation statute. *See* Wayne R. LaFave, Criminal Law § 11.1(f) (5th ed. 2010). Many courts hold that the bare act of solicitation, without more, is mere preparation and therefore insufficient to constitute an attempt. In *Gervin v. State*, 371 S.W.2d 449 (Tenn. 1963), for example, Robert Gervin was charged with attempted murder on the theory that he hired, persuaded, and procured another person to kill the intended victim. But the court held that, as a matter of law, Gervin had engaged only in solicitation and that a charge of attempt could not be sustained.

By contrast, as discussed above in Note 7 in Section A.2, the California Supreme Court ruled in *People v. Superior Court (Decker)*, 157 P.3d 1017 (Cal. 2007), that attempted murder charges could be brought against a defendant who had solicited an undercover detective to kill two people because the defendant had also taken other steps to assist the solicited "assassin." Thus, the evidentiary line between solicitations that are, and are not, criminal attempts can be a thin one that is difficult to draw.

7. Abandonment/Renunciation of Solicitation. Like attempt, the common law held that a completed solicitation could not be renounced. But also like attempt, an increasing number of jurisdictions now follow the approach taken in Model Penal Code § 5.02(3), which recognizes a defense in cases of complete and voluntary renunciation. Here, however, the MPC limits the renunciation defense to cases where the solicitor either successfully persuaded the solicited person not to commit the crime or otherwise prevented its commission. Can you see why this requirement is included in § 5.02(3), but not in § 5.01(4)'s definition of the abandonment defense for attempt? For a discussion of what constitutes a "complete" and "voluntary" renunciation, see the discussion in Section A.3 above.

8. No Defense for Impossibility. As indicated in footnote 18 of the *Thousand* opinion excerpted above in Section A.4, many courts and the Model Penal Code do not recognize impossibility as a defense to solicitation—other than, of course, "pure" legal impossibility.

9. Soliciting a Large Group. Are *Schleifer* and *Quentin* consistent? Do you agree with the *Quentin* court that the criminal law should not punish a solicitation made to a large, indefinable group? Can the two cases be distinguished other than by the size of the group? Suppose *A* appears on television and offers a substantial reward for the murder of *B*. Should *A*'s offer constitute solicitation?

10. Crimes Committed by Talking, and the First Amendment. Are constitutional rights protected by the First Amendment threatened by solicitation prosecutions? Of course, solicitation, as well as some other crimes, for example, conspiracy, perjury, and extortion, are often accomplished by speech. The First Amendment does not bar prosecution for such crimes. Rather, as the U.S. Supreme Court summarized in *United States v. Alvarez*, 132 S. Ct. 2537 (2012), a legislature can properly criminalize speech that is "integral to criminal conduct" or that "presents some grave and imminent threat" (citing for the first proposition, *Giboney v. Empire Storage & Ice Co.*, 336 U.S. 490 (1949), and for the second, *Brandenburg v. Ohio*, 395 U.S. 444 (1969) (per curiam)). Nevertheless, the Court applies "strict scrutiny" to criminal statutes and prosecutions founded on speech.

In *Brandenburg*, for example, the Court reversed the conviction of a Ku Klux Klan leader who spoke at a rally of hooded figures (including Mr. Brandenburg), using hateful speech and burning a cross. Even such reprehensible "advocacy," said the Court, cannot be criminalized "except where [it] is directed to inciting or producing imminent lawless action and is likely to incite or produce such action"—a "clear and present danger" test in the words of Justice Oliver Wendell Holmes. (*Brandenburg* is further discussed in the *Buttorff* decision, excerpted below in Chapter 12, Section B.) By contrast, in *Giboney* the Court affirmed an injunction against labor union picketing because it was inseparable from unlawful conduct (an illegal restraint of trade). *See also Virginia v. Black*, 538 U.S. 343 (2003) (holding that, even though cross burning is a form of "symbolic expression," a Virginia statute did not "run afoul of the First Amendment insofar as it bans cross burning with intent to intimidate," given that "burning a cross is a particularly virulent form of intimidation").

More recently, in *Alvarez*, the Court struck down the so-called "Stolen Valor Act," which made it a crime to "falsely represent" that one had been "awarded any [Congressionally authorized military] decoration or medal." The Court ruled that a statute that prohibited pure falsity, without any harm to others or benefit to the speaker, was too broad to pass muster under the First Amendment. Congress immediately responded, however, by re-enacting the statute with an added element, "intent to obtain . . . [any] tangible benefit." Whether the additional mens rea requirement means the statute would now survive a First Amendment challenge remains to be seen. But the operator of a California gym pled guilty to violating the new statute in 2016, after he falsely claimed to have received multiple military decorations and used those claims to attract business to his gym. *See* Janis Mara, *Purple Heart Impostor Is Guilty*, Marin Indep. J., July 29, 2016, at A1.

Other examples abound. For example, federal criminal law prohibits "advocating the overthrow of the government," 18 U.S.C. §2385, and the related offense of "seditious conspiracy," 18 U.S.C. §2384, which consists of a group advocating to "overthrow, put down, or to destroy by force the Government of the United States, or to levy war against them." In 1999, the Second Circuit affirmed the conviction of a blind Muslim scholar and cleric, Sheik Omar Abdel Rahman, and others for their seditious roles in advocating and conspiring to "wage a war of urban terrorism" that resulted in (among other things) the first World Trade Center bombing in 1993. *See United States v. Rahman*, 189 F.3d 88 (2d Cir. 1999). Relying on *Brandenburg*, the court noted that "to be convicted under Section 2384, one must conspire to use force, not just advocate the use of force."

Similarly, in a closely divided civil en banc decision, *Planned Parenthood of the Columbia/Willamette, Inc. v. American Coalition of Life Activists*, 290 F.3d 1058 (9th Cir. 2002), the court upheld a jury's verdict against anti-abortion activists who had published "Wanted" and "Guilty" posters featuring the photos, names, and addresses of abortion providers, as well as a website "scorecard" with lines drawn through the names of doctors who had been killed or injured. Citing *Brandenburg*, the Ninth Circuit agreed that the posters could reasonably be interpreted as a threat to incite violence against the doctors. (In fact, three doctors had been murdered after their information appeared on the posters. Do you think this "proves" the case?) The defendants were enjoined from further publication and damages were awarded. Five of the 11 Ninth Circuit judges dissented, arguing that "none of the statements on which liability was premised were overtly threatening" and that none of the defendants had personally resorted to, advocated, or appeared to have the capacity or propensity to cause criminal violence. Thus, said the dissenters, there was not a "true threat" unprotected by the First Amendment: "a statement does not become a true threat because it instills fear in the listener; . . . many statements generate fear in the listener (such as 'Stop smoking or you'll die of lung cancer' or 'If you walk in that neighborhood late at night, you're going to get mugged'), yet . . . may not be punished or enjoined consistent with the First Amendment." *Id.* at 1089–91 (Kozinski, J., dissenting).

Do you think soliciting (or inciting) criminal conduct should be protected First Amendment activity that is not subject to prosecution? Where, and perhaps even more critically, how would you draw the line? Do you find the constitutional lines discussed above to be helpful? Clear? Appropriate? For a more extensive discussion of this complicated and controversial area of First Amendment law, see Eugene Volokh, *The 'Speech Integral to Conduct' Exception*, 101 Cornell L. Rev. 981 (2016).

11. Solicitation of Solicitation. In *State v. Grant-Chase*, 837 A.2d 322 (N.H. 2003), the court affirmed a conviction for soliciting the crime of solicitation of murder. The defendant had had an affair with her parole officer (Bruce Ciccone), which Ciccone ended by returning to his wife of almost 30 years. The defendant soon violated her parole and was returned to prison, where she met Carol Carriola, an inmate reputed to have Mafia connections. The two discussed how Carriola might hire a "mob hit-man" to kill Ciccone's wife. Although Carriola testified she never truly intended to attempt to hire a killer, the Supreme Court of New Hampshire ruled that Grant-Chase had clearly violated the state's criminal solicitation statute. She had encouraged Carriola to engage in the crime of solicitation (i.e., to solicit someone to murder Ciccone's wife), and her solicitation of that criminal act of solicitation was itself a crime. Do you agree, or is the crime of solicitation of solicitation "too inchoate" to merit criminal punishment?

Chapter 12

Accomplice Liability

[A] Introduction

Accomplice liability is a theory by which "helpers" to crime may be convicted of the offense they facilitate. "Being an accomplice" is *not* a separate offense; rather, it is a theory of liability. Thus, it is addressed by the Model Penal Code in § 2.06, in an Article separate from the inchoate offenses (attempt, solicitation, and conspiracy).

The common law divided accomplices into different categories—principals in the first and second degree, accessories before and after the fact—and these labels are still used in some jurisdictions today. But the modern trend, as reflected in MPC § 2.06, is to group all accomplices together, while attempting to define the limits of criminal liability for those who help others commit crimes.

This Chapter focuses on: (a) how much participation in the underlying crime is necessary in order to convict an accomplice; (b) what mens rea is required; and (c) when (if ever) accomplices can "cancel" their criminal liability by withdrawing from the crime. The Chapter closes with a brief examination of the offense of obstruction of justice, which can closely resemble the common-law offense of "accessory after the fact," a separate crime that essentially involves "helping" a criminal only after the crime is completed.

WAYNE R. LaFAVE, CRIMINAL LAW §§ 13.1 & 13.6, at 701–04, 753 (5th ed. 2010)[1]

§ 13.1 — *Parties to Crime.*

In the commission of each criminal offense there may be several persons or groups which play distinct roles before, during and after the offense. Collectively these persons or groups are termed the parties to the crime. The common law classification of parties to a felony consisted of four categories: (1) principal in the first degree; (2) principal in the second degree; (3) accessory before the fact; and (4) accessory after the fact.

This classification scheme gave rise to many procedural difficulties, but if they were overcome a person in any one of the four categories could be convicted and subjected to the penalties authorized for commission of the felony. It was later recognized that the accessory after the fact, by virtue of his involvement only after the

[handwritten margin note: 4 categories]

---

felony was completed, was not truly an accomplice in the felony. This category has thus remained distinct from the others, and today the accessory after the fact is not deemed a participant in the felony but rather one who has obstructed justice, subjecting him to different and lesser penalties. The distinctions between the other three categories, however, have now been largely abrogated, although some statutes resort to the common law terminology in defining the scope of complicity. It thus remains important to understand what is collectively encompassed within these three categories.

The common law classification scheme . . . existed only as to felonies. . . . As to misdemeanors, all parties [to the crime were] held to be principals, although conduct which would constitute one an accessory after the fact to a felony was not criminal when the post-crime aid was to a misdemeanant.

. . . .

(a) *Principal in the First Degree.* A principal in the first degree may simply be defined as the criminal actor. He is the one who, with the requisite mental state, engages in the act or omission concurring with the mental state which causes the criminal result. . . .

There can be more than one principal in the first degree. This occurs when more than one actor participates in the actual commission of the offense. Thus, when one man beats a victim and another shoots him, both may be principals in first degree to murder. And when two persons forge separate parts of the same instrument, they are both principals in the first degree to the forgery. While there may be more than one principal in the first degree, there must always be at least one for a crime to have taken place.

Although it has been said that a principal in the first degree must be present at the commission of the offense, this is not literally so. He may be "constructively" present when some instrument which he left or guided caused the criminal result. Thus, when an actor leaves poison for another who later drinks it, he is a first degree principal. . . .

(b) *Principal in the Second Degree.* To be a principal in the second degree, one must be present at the commission of a criminal offense and aid, counsel, command, or encourage the principal in the first degree in the commission of that offense. This requirement of presence may be fulfilled by constructive presence. A person is constructively present when he is physically absent from the situs of the crime but aids and abets the principal in the first degree at the time of the offense from some distance. This may happen when one stands watch for the primary actor, signals to the principal from a distance that the victim is coming, or stands ready (though out of sight) to render aid to the principal if needed. However, one must be close enough to render aid if needed.

The assistance rendered by the principal in the second degree has traditionally been referred to as "aiding and abetting." . . .

(c) *Accessory Before the Fact.* An accessory before the fact is one who orders, counsels, encourages, or otherwise aids and abets another to commit a felony and who is not present at the commission of the offense. The primary distinction between the accessory before the fact and the principal in the second degree is presence. If a person was actually or constructively present at the offense, due to his participation he is a principal in the second degree; if he was not present, he is an accessory before the fact. Through prior counseling followed by appearance at the scene of the crime to aid the primary actor, one may become both an accessory before the fact and also a principal in the second degree.

The aid or counsel may be far removed in time from the commission of the offense, although it must be shown to have retained some relationship to it by causing, encouraging, or assisting the offense. If one contributes specific material aid, he will still be an accessory though it is not used in the offense. The exact time of the commission of the offense is also immaterial. One may intend to aid a crime which is to occur on a certain date but which in fact occurs later, and he will still be an accessory before the fact to the crime. The quantity of the aid is immaterial, and it may come through some intermediary. . . .

Although the accessory before the fact is often the originator of the offense, this need not be the case. Indeed, if one is enlisted by another to lend aid toward the commission of the offense and the aid is given, the person giving the assistance may thereby become an accessory before the fact.

. . . .

§ 13.6 — *Post-Crime Aid: Accessory After the Fact, Misprision and Compounding.*

At common law, one not himself a principal in the commission of a felony was an accessory after the fact if a completed felony had theretofore been committed by another; he knew of the commission of the felony by the other person; and he gave aid to the felon personally for the purpose of hindering the felon's apprehension, conviction, or punishment. Unlike the principal in the second degree and accessory before the fact, the accessory after the fact is generally not treated as a party to the felony nor subject to the same punishment prescribed for the felony.

Misprision of felony, consisting of concealment of a known felony by one who was not a principal or accessory before the fact to the felony, is no longer an offense in most jurisdictions. The offense of compounding crime consists of the receipt of some consideration in return for an agreement not to prosecute or inform on another who is known to have committed an offense.

Notes and Questions

1. **Accomplice Liability: A Multiplicity of Labels and a Theory of Liability, Not a Separate Crime.** Courts and legislatures employ a number of different labels to describe accomplice liability and the defendants who are convicted of crime on an accomplice liability theory. Thus, an accomplice is sometimes referred to as an

"accessory" to the crime, or an "aider and abettor"; and "aiding and abetting" and "complicity" are terms sometimes used to describe accomplice liability.

It is important to recognize that, unlike conspiracy (which is a separate crime that targets people who agree to commit a criminal offense), accomplice liability is not a crime in itself, but rather a way of convicting "helpers." Accomplices are convicted of the underlying offense committed by the principal, and are subject to the full range of penalties authorized for that offense. For example, an accomplice to bank robbery will be convicted of bank robbery, not "being an accomplice." This is true even if the accomplice never went anywhere near the bank: for example, the person who purchased guns and masks for a robbery but was on vacation in the Bahamas when the bank was actually robbed is still guilty of bank robbery via accomplice liability. *E.g., State v. Daniels*, 129 A.3d 1056 (N.J. 2016) (defendant who helped write demand notes was charged with bank robbery although he did not accompany the robber to the bank).

For another example, consider the case of Warren Jeffs, the leader of a polygamous Mormon sect in Utah. Jeffs was convicted of rape on an accomplice liability theory, on the prosecution's proof that he had commanded 14-year-old Elissa Wall to marry another member of the sect (her 19-year-old cousin, Allen Steed) and "give herself" to him "mind, body and soul." *State v. Jeffs*, 243 P.3d 1250 (Utah 2010). Jeffs did not engage in sexual conduct with Wall himself, yet he was convicted of rape and sentenced as severely (10 years to life in prison) as the actual rapist might have been. The Utah Supreme Court overturned Jeffs' conviction due to faulty jury instructions, ruling in part that the jury should have been told that Jeffs could be convicted as an accomplice to rape only if he specifically intended for Steed to rape Wall. (Section C below addresses the mens rea required for accomplice liability.) Utah did not retry Jeffs because he had been convicted in Texas for his own illegal marriages to two young girls and was serving a life sentence for sexual assault. *See Polygamist Leader Gets Life Sentence*, N.Y. TIMES, Aug. 10, 2011, at A15.

Note that because accomplice liability is not a separate crime, an accomplice cannot be convicted absent proof that some principal actor actually committed a crime (as discussed below in Note 5 in Section B). This, too, distinguishes accomplice liability from the inchoate offenses of attempt, solicitation, and conspiracy, all of which may be used to convict an offender even though the object offense was never committed.

2. Persons Who Are Legally Incapable of Committing the Crime. Under both the common law and Model Penal Code § 2.06(5), a person who is legally incapable of committing an offense can still be convicted as an accomplice. For example, rape statutes traditionally exempted husbands from prosecution for raping their wives. *See* Chapter 7, Section B.4. But if the husband hired another man to assault and rape his estranged wife, the husband could be prosecuted as an accomplice to the other man's rape. Likewise, residents of an apartment can be convicted of burglary if they assist an illegal entry into their own dwelling. *See Spriggs v. United States*, 52 A.3d 878 (D.C. 2012).

3. Persons Whose Conduct Is Inevitably Incident to Commission of the Crime. Model Penal Code § 2.06(6)(b) endorses the traditional common-law rule that "a person is not an accomplice . . . if the offense is so defined that his conduct is inevitably incident to its commission." Consider, for example, the crimes of prostitution and extortion. It is impossible to carry out an act of prostitution without a partner, or an act of extortion without the individual who is extorted. The conduct of the prostitute's partner and the extortionist's victim is "inevitably incident" to the commission of the offense," and § 2.06(6)(b) would therefore prohibit charging them as accomplices to those crimes. What policies explain this rule?

[B] Actus Reus: The Extent of Participation Necessary

United States v. Buttorff

572 F.2d 619 (8th Cir. 1978)

Ross, Circuit Judge.

Gordon S. Buttorff and Charles A. Dodge appeal from their convictions, after a joint jury trial, on various counts of aiding and abetting several persons (the principals) in the filing of false or fraudulent income tax related forms, in violation of 26 U.S.C. § 7205 and 18 U.S.C. § 2. Buttorff was indicted on 11 counts and convicted on 9. Dodge was separately indicted on 8 counts and was convicted on all 8. [They were sentenced to serve concurrent one-year prison terms on each count.]

The charges against these defendants arise from their participation in a series of public and private meetings which were held in February and March of 1975, and which were attended by numerous employees of the John Deere Tractor plant in Dubuque, Iowa. Fifteen of those employees subsequently filed income tax withholding forms W-4 or W-4E with John Deere, claiming allowances in excess of those to which they were entitled, or falsely certifying that they received no taxable income during the prior year and expected to receive none during the current year. Those men all either pleaded guilty to, or were convicted by juries of, violations of 26 U.S.C. § 7205.

Dodge was charged with aiding or abetting six of those men and Buttorff was charged with aiding or abetting eight of them.

Both defendants challenge the sufficiency of the evidence on the aiding and abetting charges and raise the issue of their first amendment rights of freedom of assembly and freedom of speech. We agree that the facts here present a close question.

The government's evidence showed that Buttorff and Dodge addressed at least four large public gatherings in northeastern Iowa and western Wisconsin early in 1975. Each of the principals testified that he attended one or more of those meetings. Most of the testimony recalled speeches given by the defendants, the major portion of which dealt with the Constitution, the Bible, and the unconstitutionality of the graduated income tax. The evidence indicates that the discussions of the W-4 and W-4E forms occurred primarily during question and answer sessions following the speeches.

The principals all testified that they submitted false or fraudulent forms because of the defendants' recommendations, advice or suggestions. Some indicated that the defendants told them to divide their yearly salary by 750 to determine the number of claimed allowances necessary to stop withholding. Others testified that they heard the defendants say that 30 or 40 claimed allowances would be sufficient to stop withholding. All the principals claimed between 28 and 40 allowances on their subsequently filed W-4 forms.

Only one principal testified to an affirmative action, other than speaking, by either defendant. Vernon Van Natta testified that Buttorff came to his father's home and provided him with a W-4 form. He stated that the form already had the number 20 written in and either he or Buttorff changed it to 28.

No other principal testified that either defendant actually assisted him in preparing a W-4 or W-4E, or was with him when he filed such a form. Most testified to having other sources of information on tax evasion and other influences on his activity in the tax protest movement. However, all principals indicated that they filed withholding forms as a result of attending these tax protest meetings and many paid various amounts of money to the defendants for a wide range of tax related services.

The Supreme Court has held that to establish aiding or abetting the government need only show "that a defendant 'in some sort associate himself with the venture, that he participate in it as something that he wishes to bring about, that he seek by his action to make it succeed.'" *Nye & Nissen v. United States*, 336 U.S. 613, 619 (1949), quoting *United States v. Peoni*, 100 F.2d 401, 402 (2d Cir. 1938). This court has interpreted that language to mean that "there must exist some affirmative participation which at least encourages the perpetrator."

Under this language we find that the evidence was sufficient to allow the jury to decide whether the defendants' activities constituted aiding and abetting the filing of fraudulent withholding statements. Each was associated with the tax evasion movement; each opposed the graduated income tax and wanted to bring about its demise; and each, by speaking to large groups of persons, sought to advance his ideas and encourage others to evade income taxes.

The problem here, of course, is that each defendant's only participation in the allegedly illegal activity of the principals, except with regard to Van Natta, was to talk about his ideas before gatherings of disgruntled Americans. What this court must decide is whether the first amendment protections of free speech and assembly prohibit the convictions of these defendants for their activities here.

There is no doubt that the right of free speech is fundamental and may not be denied or abridged. That right, however, is not in its nature absolute.

Judge Learned Hand dealt with free speech in the context of counseling or advising others to violate the law in *Masses Publishing Co. v. Patten*, 244 F. 535 (S.D.N.Y. 1917). His language is relevant here:

> One may not counsel or advise others to violate the law as it stands. Words are not only the keys of persuasion, but the triggers of action, and those which have no purport but to counsel the violation of law cannot by any latitude of interpretation be a part of that public opinion which is the final source of government in a democratic state. . . . To counsel or advise a man to an act is to urge upon him either that it is his interest or his duty to do it. . . . Political agitation, by the passions it arouses or the convictions it engenders, may in fact stimulate men to the violation of law. Detestation of existing policies is easily transformed into forcible resistance of the authority which puts them in execution, and it would be folly to disregard the causal relation between the two. Yet to assimilate agitation, legitimate as such, with direct incitement to violent resistance, is to disregard the tolerance of all methods of political agitation which in normal times is a safeguard of free government. The distinction is not a scholastic subterfuge, but a hard-bought acquisition in the fight for freedom . . . . If one stops short of urging upon others that it is their duty or their interest to resist the law, it seems to me one should not be held to have attempted to cause its violation.

More recently, the Supreme Court has distinguished between speech which merely advocates law violation and speech which incites imminent lawless activity. *See Brandenburg v. Ohio*, 395 U.S. 444 (1969). The former is protected; the latter is not.

Although the speeches here do not incite the type of imminent lawless activity referred to in criminal syndicalism cases, the defendants did go beyond mere advocacy of tax reform. They explained how to avoid withholding and their speeches and explanations incited several individuals to activity that violated federal law and had the potential of substantially hindering the administration of the revenue. This speech is not entitled to first amendment protection and, as discussed above, was sufficient action to constitute aiding and abetting the filing of false or fraudulent withholding forms. . . . [2]

Wilcox v. Jeffery

1 All E.R. 464 (King's Bench 1951)

GODDARD, LORD CHIEF JUSTICE.

This is a Case stated by the metropolitan magistrate at Bow Street Magistrate's Court before whom the appellant, Herbert William Wilcox, the proprietor of a periodical called "Jazz Illustrated," was charged on an information that "on Dec. 11, 1949, he did unlawfully aid and abet one Coleman Hawkins in contravening art. 1(4) of

---

2. For further discussion of the First Amendment issues raised by prosecuting crimes accomplished by speech, see Chapter 11, Section B, Note 10.

the Aliens Order, 1920, by failing to comply with a condition attached to a grant of leave to land, to wit, that the said Coleman Hawkins should take no employment paid or unpaid while in the United Kingdom, contrary to art. 18(2) of the Aliens Order, 1920." Under the Aliens Order, art. 1(1), it is provided that

> ... an alien coming ... by sea to a place in the United Kingdom — (a) shall not land in the United Kingdom without the leave of an immigration officer. . . .

It is provided by art. 1(4) that:

> An immigration officer, in accordance with general or special directions of the Secretary of State, may, by general order or notice or otherwise, attach such conditions as he may think fit to the grant of leave to land, and the Secretary of State may at any time vary such conditions in such manner as he thinks fit, and the alien shall comply with the conditions so attached or varied. . . .

If the alien fails to comply, he is to be in the same position as if he has landed without permission, i.e., he commits an offence.

The case is concerned with the visit of a celebrated professor of the saxophone, a gentleman by the name of Hawkins who was a citizen of the United States. He came here at the invitation of two gentlemen of the name of Curtis and Hughes, connected with a jazz club which enlivens the neighbourhood of Willesden. They, apparently, had applied for permission for Mr. Hawkins to land and it was refused, but, nevertheless, this professor of the saxophone arrived with four French musicians. When they came to the airport, among the people who were there to greet them was the appellant. He had not arranged their visit, but he knew they were coming and he was there to report the arrival of these important musicians for his magazine. So, evidently, he was regarding the visit of Mr. Hawkins as a matter which would be of interest to himself and the magazine which he was editing and selling for profit. Messrs. Curtis and Hughes arranged a concert at the Princes Theatre, London. The appellant attended that concert as a spectator. He paid for his ticket. Mr. Hawkins went on the stage and delighted the audience by playing the saxophone. The appellant did not get up and protest in the name of the musicians of England that Mr. Hawkins ought not to be here competing with them and taking the bread out of their mouths or the wind out of their instruments. It is not found that he actually applauded, but he was there having paid to go in, and, no doubt, enjoying the performance, and then, lo and behold, out comes his magazine with a most laudatory description, fully illustrated, of this concert. On those facts the magistrate has found that he aided and abetted. [He was sentenced to pay a fine of £25 and costs of £21.]

Reliance is placed by the prosecution on *R. v. Coney* [[1882] 8 Q.B.D. 534] which dealt with a prize fight. This case relates to a jazz band concert, but the particular nature of the entertainment provided, whether by fighting with bare fists or playing on saxophones, does not seem to me to make any difference to the question which we have to decide. The fact is that a man is charged with aiding and abetting an illegal act, and I can find no authority for saying that it matters what that illegal act is, provided that the aider and abettor knows the facts sufficiently well to know that they would constitute an offence in the principal.

. . . .

There was not accidental presence in this case. The appellant paid to go to the concert and he went there because he wanted to report it. He must, therefore, be held to have been present, taking part, concurring, or encouraging, whichever word you like to use for expressing this conception. It was an illegal act on the part of Hawkins to play the saxophone or any other instrument at this concert. The appellant clearly knew that it was an unlawful act for him to play. He had gone there to hear him, and his presence and his payment to go there was an encouragement. He went there to make use of the performance, because he went there, as the magistrate finds and was justified in finding, to get "copy" for his newspaper. It might have been entirely different, as I say, if he had gone there and protested, saying: "The musicians' union do not like you foreigners coming here and playing and you ought to get off the stage." If he had booed, it might have been some evidence that he was not aiding and abetting. If he had gone as a member of a *claque* to try to drown the noise of the saxophone, he might very likely be found not guilty of aiding and abetting. In this case it seems clear that he was there, not only to approve and encourage what was done, but to take advantage of it by getting "copy" for his paper. In those circumstances there was evidence on which the magistrate could find that the appellant aided and abetted, and for these reasons I am of opinion that the appeal fails.

. . . .

Devlin, Justice.

I agree, and I wish to add only a word on the application of *R. v. Coney*. Counsel for the appellant sought to distinguish that case on the facts inasmuch as in *R. v. Coney* the performance, which was a prize fight, was illegal from beginning to end, whereas in the case we are considering the bulk of the concert was quite legal, the only part of the performance which was illegal being that which involved Mr. Hawkins. That, however, is not, in my judgment, a distinction which affects the application to this case of the principle in *R. v. Coney*. It may well be that if a spectator goes to a concert he may explain his presence during an illegal item by saying that he hardly felt it necessary to get up and go out and then return when the performance resumed its legality, if I may so call it. It is conceivable that in such circumstances (and I should wish to consider it further if it ever arose) the presence of a person during one item might fall within the accidental or casual class. . . . Here there was abundant evidence, apart from the mere fact of the appellant's presence, that he was making use of this item in the performance and that his attendance at that item was, therefore, deliberate. In those circumstances I think the principle in *R. v. Coney* applies, and that the magistrate was justified in drawing the inference which he did draw.

Appeal dismissed with costs.

Notes and Questions

1. The Amount of Aid or Encouragement Necessary for Accomplice Liability. The aid or encouragement provided by an accomplice need not be substantial. There is no requirement, for example, that "but for" the aid or encouragement, the crime would not have occurred. *See* WAYNE R. LAFAVE, CRIMINAL LAW § 13.2(a) (5th ed. 2010). While perhaps somewhat imprecise, Judge Learned Hand's description in *United States v. Peoni*, 100 F.2d 401 (2d Cir. 1938) (quoted in *Buttorff*), has repeatedly been endorsed by many courts, including the U.S. Supreme Court. Accomplice liability, Judge Hand wrote, requires that the defendant "in some sort associate himself with the venture, that he participate in it as something that he wishes to bring about, that he seek by his action to make it succeed." *Id.* at 402. (Note that this definition encompasses not only the actus reus requirement, but also the mens rea component of accomplice liability.)

In the notorious case of *State ex rel. Attorney General v. Tally*, 15 So. 722 (Ala. 1893), for example, Judge Tally's sister-in-law (Annie Skelton) was purportedly seduced by a man named R.C. Ross, who then left town for another city. Determined to exact retribution, the woman's four brothers followed Ross with the intent of killing him. One of Ross' relatives, aware of the Skelton brothers' plan, sent a telegram to warn Ross of the impending danger. Unbeknownst to the Skelton brothers, Judge Tally was keeping watch at the telegraph office and sent a telegram of his own, instructing the telegraph operator (Huddleston) not to deliver the warning. Huddleston complied with the judge's request, and the brothers ultimately caught up with Ross and killed him. The court determined that Judge Tally had sufficiently aided the Skelton brothers to make himself an accomplice to the murder. Specifically, the court noted:

> The assistance given . . . need not contribute to the criminal result in the sense that but for it the result would not have ensued. It is quite sufficient if it facilitated a result that would have transpired without it. It is quite enough if the aid merely renders it easier for the principal actor to accomplish the end intended by him and the aider and abettor, though in all human probability the end would have been attained without it.

Id. at 738–39.

Professor Joshua Dressler has asserted that "American accomplice law is a disgrace" on this point, and that accomplices whose assistance has no causal relationship to a crime should be convicted only of some lesser offense. Joshua Dressler, *Reforming Complicity Law: Trivial Assistance as a Lesser Offense?*, 5 OHIO ST. J. CRIM. L. 427, 428 (2008). He notes, however, that his idea has attracted "no legislative interest." *Id.* at 430.

Still, at least one court has declined to punish an accomplice when there was no proof that her encouragement had any impact on the principal. In *State v. Ulvinen*, 313 N.W.2d 425 (Minn. 1981), the court reversed the conviction of a mother who responded "it would be best for the kids" after her son told her that he was planning on killing his wife. "[A]t best," the court reasoned, the mother "passively acquiesced" in the killing; she engaged in no "active encouragement or instigation," but only "passive approval." She "responded in a way which, while not discouraging him, did not aid, advise, or counsel him to act as he did," and there was no evidence that her statement had "any influence on her son's decision to kill." *Id.* at 428–29. *But cf. State v. Johnson*, 450 N.W.2d 103, 106 (Minn. 1990) (distinguishing *Ulvinen* from the accomplice there because Ulvinen's son had "repeatedly told many people, not just his mother, that he was going to kill his wife").

Would it be preferable to limit accomplice liability to instances where the aid or encouragement actually made a difference? Was *Wilcox v. Jeffrey* wrongly decided (for this or any other reason)? Why do you think the British authorities chose to prosecute this seemingly inconsequential case?

2. Purpose to Aid the Principal. Judge Hand's opinion in *Peoni*, quoted in the previous Note, makes clear that accomplice liability requires proof that the aid or encouragement provided by the defendant was given purposefully. In *Hicks v. United States*, 150 U.S. 442 (1893), for example, the defendant argued that he was trying to dissuade the principal (Rowe) from shooting a man named Colvard, when he laughed and said "take off your hat and die like a man" as Rowe aimed his gun at Colvard. Even though Rowe fired the fatal shot immediately after Hicks' comment, the Court held that Hicks could not be convicted as an accomplice to murder simply because his words had the effect of encouraging Rowe to shoot. Rather, guilt depended on a finding that Hicks intended to encourage Rowe. (Other mens rea issues surrounding accomplice liability are addressed below in Section C.)

3. Agreeing to Aid and Attempting to Aid. Note the variety of ways one can be convicted as an accomplice under § 2.06(3) of the Model Penal Code: by soliciting, aiding, agreeing to aid, attempting to aid, or failing to act when there is a legal duty to prevent the crime. In some respects, this part of § 2.06 goes beyond the traditional common-law formulation. Consider the following two examples:

> (a) Suppose *A* agrees to help *B* commit a bank robbery by driving the getaway car. On the day of the robbery, *A* forgets to set her alarm clock and sleeps through the robbery, and *C* acts as the getaway driver instead. *A* is probably liable as *B*'s accomplice under the common law because her agreement to aid provided some encouragement to *B*. Under the Model Penal Code, her agreement to aid clearly makes her liable, even without proof that it encouraged *B* to commit the crime. Given the result in *Wilcox*, should it make any difference if *A*'s encouragement consisted of applauding when *B* announced his intention to rob the bank?

> (b) Suppose *A* hears that *B* is going to rob a bank. Wanting to help, she mails *B* a self-help guide titled *Seven Easy Ways to Commit Bank Robbery for Fun and Profit*, but the guide is lost by the post office and never delivered. *B* robs the bank, unaware of *A*'s attempt to help. Nonetheless, under the Model Penal

Code, *A* is liable as an accomplice. By contrast, under the common law, attempted aid that is not communicated, and therefore could not provide encouragement to the principal, is insufficient for accomplice liability.

4. Omissions as the Basis for Accomplice Liability. As MPC § 2.06(3)(a)(iii) provides, those who have a duty to prevent a crime can be convicted as accomplices if they fail to perform that duty (assuming the omission is accompanied by the requisite mens rea). In *Powell v. United States*, 2 F.2d 47 (4th Cir. 1924), for example, 55 gallons of liquor were found on a passenger train. Many of the containers were badly hidden; some were even leaking onto the floor. The court found the train conductor guilty of aiding and abetting the illegal transportation of liquor because he so obviously failed in his duty to prevent it.

Although this rule is followed in most states, not every jurisdiction agrees with the MPC's position. In *State v. Jackson*, 976 P.2d 1229 (Wash. 1999), for example, the Washington Supreme Court construed its accomplice statute to foreclose criminal liability based on omissions. The defendants in that case were a couple whose two-year-old foster child died as the result of a head injury allegedly inflicted by at least one of them. They were both prosecuted on an accomplice liability theory, that each of them had failed to aid the child when the other one was assaulting her. In ruling that the Washington statute did not permit accomplice liability for a failure to act, the court found it relevant that the legislature had intentionally chosen not to include a provision like MPC § 2.06(3)(a)(iii) in a statute otherwise modeled on the Model Penal Code.

5. The Relationship Between the Accomplice's Liability and the Principal's Guilt. At common law, an accessory before the fact could not be prosecuted unless the principal had already been convicted. If the principal was acquitted, escaped, or died before trial, the accessory before the fact was free of criminal liability. (There was no such restriction, however, governing the prosecution of principals in the second degree.) *See* Wayne R. LaFave, Criminal Law § 13.1(d)(3) (5th ed. 2010).

This rule created a loophole whereby sophisticated defendants could escape criminal liability by convincing someone who was immune from conviction to commit a crime on their behalf. The doctrine of "innocent agency" was created in order to close that loophole. That doctrine provides that one who uses an innocent agent to commit a crime — i.e., someone who has a defense of insanity, immaturity, duress, or mistake — is deemed to be the principal for the crime and is convicted on that basis. Thus, for example, drug dealers who use young children to sell their wares can still be convicted of distributing narcotics even if the actual sellers cannot be charged because of their age. The doctrine of innocent agency is reflected in § 2.06(2)(a) of the Model Penal Code.

In addition, the common-law rule requiring the government to convict the principal before convicting an accessory before the fact has now been discarded in almost every jurisdiction, and accomplices may be convicted even if the principal is acquitted or absent. This rule is incorporated in Model Penal Code § 2.06(7).

In *Standefer v. United States*, 447 U.S. 10 (1980), for example, the defendant, who was the head of Gulf Oil's tax department, illegally authorized payment for five vacation trips taken by Cyril Niederberger, the IRS agent in charge of auditing Gulf's tax returns. Although Niederberger was acquitted of accepting unauthorized compensation, Standefer was convicted in a separate trial as an accomplice to Niederberger's acceptance of unauthorized compensation. The Supreme Court affirmed, noting that an accomplice may be convicted despite the principal's prior acquittal. The Court explained that "'different juries may reach different results . . . under our jury system'. . . . While symmetry of results may be intellectually satisfying, it is not required." *Id.* at 25.

In fact, an accomplice can sometimes be convicted of a more serious crime than the principal. Consider the Shakespearean illustration suggested by Glanville Williams: the accomplice (Iago) cold-bloodedly deludes the principal (Othello) into suspecting his wife (Desdemona) of infidelity, causing a jealous rage during which the principal kills his wife. Othello's liability for murder may be mitigated to manslaughter because he acted in the heat of passion or from an extreme emotional disturbance. But no such mitigation is available to Iago when he is prosecuted as an accomplice because he was not acting in the heat of passion, and he can therefore be convicted of murder. *See* Glanville L. Williams, Criminal Law: The General Part 391 (2d ed. 1961). Again, this principle is reflected in Model Penal Code § 2.06(7).

Despite these modifications of the common-law rule, an accomplice's liability is still derived from the principal's actions, and an accomplice cannot be convicted unless the principal committed the object crime. Thus, even at the *accomplice's* trial, the prosecution must prove that the conduct the accomplice aided was in fact criminal. In *Shuttlesworth v. City of Birmingham*, 373 U.S. 262 (1963), for example, two African-American ministers incited a group of African-American students to engage in a "sit-down demonstration" at a "whites only" lunch counter. The ministers were convicted of aiding and abetting the students' violation of a municipal criminal trespass ordinance. The ordinance was declared unconstitutional, however, and the Court reversed the ministers' conviction, holding that one cannot be convicted for aiding and abetting a noncriminal act.

6. Accomplice Liability and the "Phantom Principal." Although § 2.06(7) of the Model Penal Code adheres to the rule described in the prior Note and requires "proof of the commission of the offense" in order to establish accomplice liability, other provisions of the Model Penal Code can be used to convict an individual who provided assistance to a principal who never committed a crime. Consider again four ways in which one may become an accomplice under § 2.06(3) of the Model Penal Code — by soliciting the crime, aiding the crime, agreeing to aid the crime, and attempting to aid the crime. Consider, with regard to each of these four alternatives, how the criminal law treats a would-be accomplice if the principal's actions are *not* fundamentally criminal—for example, if the principal is an undercover police officer merely pretending to go along with the crime. (Let's call such persons "apparent principals.") Because no crime is actually committed, there cannot be accomplice liability even though the defendant purposefully sought to help commit an offense.

(a) If one *attempts to aid* an apparent principal, one can be charged with the crime of attempt under § 5.01(3) of the Model Penal Code. Note that the common law has no provision comparable to § 5.01(3) and therefore would not convict the would-be accomplice in this scenario.

(b) If one *solicits* an apparent principal, one can be charged with solicitation under § 5.02 of the Model Penal Code.

(c) If one *agrees to aid* an apparent principal, one can be charged with conspiracy under § 5.03 of the Model Penal Code (and presumably also with attempt under § 5.01(3)). Note that the Model Penal Code takes a "unilateral view" of the agreement that constitutes the actus reus of conspiracy, so that one is said to have reached an agreement to commit a crime even when the other party was merely pretending to go along. The common law rejects this position, however, and requires two willing parties for a conspiracy. For further discussion of this issue, see Chapter 13, Section A.2, Note 4.

(d) And what about the remaining possibility, *aiding* an apparent principal? Arguably, this situation is conceptually impossible: one cannot aid an undercover police officer in committing a crime that the officer, in fact, does not commit. However, it might still be possible to impose criminal liability by describing the would-be accomplice's actions here as an "attempt to aid" the apparent principal, thereby returning to the first category described above.

[C] Mens Rea: The State of Mind Necessary

Should accomplice liability require proof of "purpose"—i.e., proof that the accomplice wanted the principal to succeed in committing the underlying offense? Or is "knowledge" that the offense will be committed with one's aid enough? Most authorities, including § 2.06(3)(a) of the Model Penal Code, impose a mens rea requirement of "purpose." But that rule is not always observed, especially in cases with "hard facts." Compare also § 2.06(4) of the Model Penal Code, described below in Note 5, which allows accomplice liability on proof of a less culpable mental state with respect to the result elements of crimes.

State v. Gladstone

474 P.2d 274 (Wash. 1970)

Hale, Justice.

A jury found defendant Bruce Gladstone guilty of aiding and abetting one Robert Kent in the unlawful sale of marijuana. Deferring imposition of sentence, the court placed defendant on probation. He appeals the order deferring sentencing contending that the evidence as a matter of law was insufficient to sustain a verdict of guilty. His point, we think, is well taken.

. . . .

Gladstone's guilt as an aider and abettor in this case rests solely on evidence of a conversation between him and one Douglas MacArthur Thompson concerning the possible purchase of marijuana from one Robert Kent. There is no other evidence to connect the accused with Kent who ultimately sold some marijuana to Thompson.

When asked by Thompson — an agent of the police — where marijuana could be bought, the defendant did no more than name Kent as an individual who might be willing to sell some and draw a sketch of his location. There was no evidence whatever that the defendant had any association, understanding, agreement or arrangement, direct or indirect, tacit or express with Kent to aid or persuade him in any way in the sale of marijuana.

The conversation between defendant and Thompson occurred at defendant's residence. Douglas MacArthur Thompson, a 25-year-old student at the University of Puget Sound in Tacoma and an employee of the Internal Revenue Service of the United States, had done some investigative work for the government. From time to time, the Tacoma Police Department engaged him to investigate the use, possession and sale of narcotics, principally marijuana, among college students. When working for the Tacoma Police Department, he operated under the control and direction of the department's narcotics detail.

Thompson testified that Lieutenant Seymour and Detective Gallwas of the narcotics detail asked him to attempt a purchase of marijuana from Gladstone. During the evening of April 10, 1967 — between 10 and 11 o'clock — the two officers and Thompson drove in a police car to the vicinity of defendant's apartment. Thompson went to Gladstone's door alone, beyond the hearing and out of the sight of the two officers. He knocked at the door and Gladstone responded. Thompson asked Gladstone if he would sell him some marijuana. Describing this incident, Thompson testified as follows:

> Well, I asked — at the time Gladstone told me that he was — he did not have enough marijuana on hand to sell me any, but he did know an individual who had quite a sufficient quantity and that was very willing to sell and he named the individual as Robert Kent, or Bob Kent as he put it, and he gave me directions to the residence and he — due to the directions I asked him if, you know, if he could draw me a map and he did.

When Thompson said he asked Gladstone to draw the map for him, he added, "I'm not sure whether he did give me the exact address or not, he told me where the residence was." He said that Gladstone then with pencil and paper sketched the location of Kent's place of residence. Thompson had no prior knowledge of where Kent lived, and did not know if he might have marijuana or that he had ever possessed it.

The two officers then took Thompson to Kent's residence where marijuana was purchased. The actual purchase was made by Thompson directly from Kent while Officer Gallwas and Lieutenant Seymour stayed in the police car. Kent was subsequently arrested and convicted of selling Thompson approximately 8 ounces of marijuana — the very sale which defendant here was convicted of aiding and abetting.

That ended the prosecution's case. Even if it were accorded all favorable inferences, there appears at this point a gap in the evidence which we feel as a matter of law is fatal to the prosecution's cause. Neither on direct examination nor under cross-examination did Thompson testify that he knew of any prior conduct, arrangements or communications between Gladstone and Kent from which it could be even remotely inferred that the defendant had any understanding, agreement, purpose, intention or design to participate or engage in or aid or abet any sale of marijuana by Kent. Other than to obtain a simple map from Gladstone and to say that Gladstone told him Kent might have some marijuana available, Thompson did not even establish that Kent and the defendant were acquainted with each other. Testimony of the brief conversation and Gladstone's very crude drawing consisting of 8 penciled lines indicating where Kent lived constitute the whole proof of the aiding and abetting presented.

. . . .

. . . [E]ven without prior agreement, arrangement or understanding, a bystander to a robbery could be guilty of aiding and abetting its commission if he came to the aid of a robber and knowingly assisted him in perpetrating the crime. But regardless of the modus operandi and with or without a conspiracy or agreement to commit the crime and whether present or away from the scene of it, there is no aiding and abetting unless one "in some sort associate himself with the venture, that he participate in it as in something that he wishes to bring about, that he seek by his action to make it succeed."

. . . Whatever information the defendant is shown by the record to have given the police informant, to the effect that Kent might sell him some marijuana, amounted at most to no more than a statement of opinion and possibly no more than campus gossip, rumor or innuendo. That the police ultimately bought marijuana from Kent would not, without more, operate to convert defendant's statement to the police, that Kent would or might sell marijuana, into an aiding, abetting, counseling or encouraging of Kent to make the sale.

... Learned Hand, J., we think, hit the nail squarely when, in *United States v. Peoni*, 100 F.2d 401, 402 (2d Cir. 1938), he wrote that, in order to aid and abet another to commit a crime, it is necessary that a defendant

> in some sort associate himself with the venture, that he participate in it as in something that he wishes to bring about, that he seek by his action to make it succeed. All the words used—even the most colorless, "abet"—carry an implication of purposive attitude towards it.

. . . .

It would be a dangerous precedent indeed to hold that mere communications to the effect that another might or probably would commit a criminal offense amount to an aiding and abetting of the offense should it ultimately be committed.

There being no evidence whatever that the defendant ever communicated to Kent the idea that he would in any way aid him in the sale of any marijuana, or said anything to Kent to encourage or induce him or direct him to do so, or counseled Kent in the sale of marijuana, or did anything more than describe Kent to another person as an individual who might sell some marijuana, or would derive any benefit, consideration or reward from such a sale, there was no proof of an aiding and abetting, and the conviction should, therefore, be reversed as a matter of law. Remanded with directions to dismiss.

HAMILTON, JUSTICE (dissenting).

... I am satisfied that the jury was fully warranted in concluding that appellant, when he affirmatively recommended Kent as a source and purveyor of marijuana, entertained the requisite conscious design and intent that his action would instigate, induce, procure or encourage perpetration of Kent's subsequent crime of selling marijuana to Thompson. ...

... [T]he jury, with the witnesses before it, was in a far better position to evaluate the witnesses' candor, voice inflections, appearance, demeanor, attitude and credibility than this court viewing naught but the cold record. I would sustain the jury's verdict and affirm the judgment.

Notes and Questions

1. Purposeful Versus Knowing Assistance. Accomplice liability requires "intent" to aid or encourage the principal's crime. The majority of authorities describe this as "purpose" regarding the target offense, and this requirement is "sometimes broken down into 'dual intents': (1) the intent to render the conduct that . . . assisted the primary party . . . ; and (2) the intent, by such assistance, that the primary party commit the offense charged"—although proof of one usually follows from proof of the other. JOSHUA DRESSLER, UNDERSTANDING CRIMINAL LAW § 30.05[A], at 474 (7th ed. 2015). The first of these two intent requirements is discussed above in Note 2 in Section B.

Although the term "intent" is often defined to encompass both purpose and knowledge (*see* Chapter 6, Section A), a majority of courts require proof of "purpose" in the context of accomplice liability. Under this view, which the court follows in *Gladstone*, one who sells a gun, knowing that it is to be used for a crime, is not considered an accomplice unless the seller's purpose was to aid that crime.

The original draft of the Model Penal Code would have allowed accomplice liability based on a finding that the defendant "substantially" and "knowingly facilitated" the crime, but in the end § 2.06(3)(a) endorsed the majority approach and required purpose. *See* Model Penal Code § 2.06 Comment at 314–20 (preferring "a narrow formulation in order not to include situations where liability was inappropriate"). Should one who knowingly aids a crime be considered an accomplice? What if *A* gives *B* directions to the chemistry classroom, knowing (but not caring) that *B* intends to bomb it?

2. The Minority View. Cases that deem knowledge sufficient for accomplice liability tend to do so where the defendant assisted a serious crime and/or provided very critical aid. *See* Wayne R. LaFave, Criminal Law § 13.2(d) (5th ed. 2010).

Consider, for example, *People v. Beard*, 431 N.W.2d 232 (Mich. 1988). As the principal (Gregory Allen) and accomplice (Andre Beard) were driving by a restaurant, Beard swerved the car toward a group of pedestrians. One of the pedestrians responded by shooting at the car. Beard and Allen then drove to Beard's house, where Allen obtained a shotgun, and they returned to the restaurant. Beard confronted the person he believed had fired the shot, and a fight broke out. Allen went back to the car, retrieved the shotgun, and fired several times, injuring some bystanders. The court held that Beard could be convicted as an accomplice to Allen's assault with intent to kill so long as he "intended the commission of the crime or had knowledge that [Allen] intended its commission at the time of the giving of aid or encouragement." *Id.* at 234.

Similarly, in *United States v. Ortega*, 44 F.3d 505 (7th Cir. 1995), the court upheld Ortega's conviction for aiding and abetting the possession of heroin with intent to distribute. Writing for the court, Chief Judge Posner observed that the defendant would have been guilty of purposefully assisting the crime if he had, as the prosecution alleged, praised the quality of the heroin to the prospective customer. But the evidence that the defendant had actually made any such comment was "so weak" that the court "hesitated" to affirm the conviction on that basis. *Id.* at 507. Nevertheless, the court concluded that there was sufficient evidence to convict the defendant as an accomplice, even though all he did was provide "one-time assistance by watching over the heroin" while the principal was in a restaurant negotiating the terms of the sale, and even if "he merely rendered assistance without being compensated or otherwise identifying with the goals of the principal." *Id.* at 508. The court reasoned that "[o]ne who, knowing the criminal nature of another's act, deliberately renders what he knows to be active aid in the carrying out of the act is, we think, an aider and abettor even if there is no evidence that he wants the act to succeed — even if he is acting in a spirit of mischief." *Id.*

How do these cases compare with *Gladstone*? For discussion of the similar issues that arise in conspiracy cases, see *People v. Lauria* in Chapter 13, Section A.3.

3. Should Knowing Facilitation be Punished as a Separate Crime? In addition to imposing accomplice liability in cases of purposeful assistance, the New York legislature has created a separate misdemeanor offense that punishes those who knowingly assist a crime:

> A person is guilty of criminal facilitation in the fourth degree when, believing it probable that he is rendering aid . . . to a person who intends to commit a crime, he engages in conduct which provides such person with means or opportunity for the commission thereof and which in fact aids such person to commit a felony. . . .

New York Penal Law § 115.00. In *People v. Llanos*, 570 N.E.2d 1072 (N.Y. 1991), the court reversed a conviction under this provision even though the defendant yelled "police, police" and knocked on the door to the principals' apartment when the police came to search the apartment for drugs. The court reasoned that the defendant's actions did not permit the principals to possess the drugs any longer than they otherwise would have, and therefore she neither provided them with the "means or opportunity" to commit the crime nor in fact aided their commission of the crime.

4. The *Gladstone* Opinion and the "Art" of Appellate Judging. Note that the majority opinion in *Gladstone* stated descriptively, no fewer than six times, that Gladstone had portrayed Kent as someone who only "might" sell marijuana. But the witness' actual testimony was that Gladstone *knew* that Kent "had quite a sufficient quantity [of marijuana] and . . . was very willing to sell." Do you think the majority's characterization of this testimony was accurate? Fair? Intentionally different? Did it make a difference to the outcome of the case? Are there other facts in the case that might have led the majority to reverse the jury's guilty verdict?

Now imagine a slightly different hypothetical: suppose Gladstone drew a "very crude drawing consisting of 8 penciled lines" in order to give Timothy McVeigh directions to the Oklahoma City Federal Building, knowing that he intended to blow up the building when he arrived. Is the result the same as in *Gladstone*—that is, the hypothetical accomplice is not guilty "as a matter of law"? Or can the prosecution make a stronger case in the hypothetical than on the actual facts of *Gladstone* that the jury can infer purpose from one's knowledge that directions will be used to facilitate a bombing? McVeigh was executed in 2001 for the bombing of the federal building, which left 168 people dead. *See United States v. McVeigh*, 153 F.3d 1166 (10th Cir. 1998), *cert. denied*, 526 U.S. 1007 (1999).

Ask yourself—as you read other appellate decisions and not just *Gladstone*—how do appellate judges decide what facts to include and emphasize in their opinions, how to characterize them, and when to omit them? Is there some "art" to that exercise? Consider also whether appellate judges are influenced by factors outside the "four corners" of the applicable legal rules and the specific facts of the case, as adherents of "Legal Realism" and some other contemporary schools of critical jurisprudence believe (discussed in greater detail in Chapter 16, Section C).

5. The Mens Rea Required for Result Elements. Given that accomplice liability generally requires proof of purpose, can one who assists in a reckless act that leads to death be convicted as an accomplice to involuntary manslaughter? In *People v. Abbott*, 445 N.Y.S.2d 344 (N.Y. App. Div. 1981), for example, Abbott and Moon drove separate cars in a "drag race," driving at speeds in excess of 80–90 mph on a four-lane road in a residential neighborhood. Abbott struck another car broadside, killing the driver of that car and her two passengers. Abbott and Moon were both charged with criminally negligent homicide, and Moon was convicted as Abbott's accomplice even though there was no evidence that he had the purpose of causing death. Rather, the prosecution's theory was that Moon "intentionally aided Abbott to engage in the criminally negligent conduct which resulted in the deaths of the three victims." *Id.* at 346. The court affirmed the conviction, finding that "Moon while acting with the culpable mental state of criminal negligence gave assistance or encouragement to Abbott to engage in conduct dangerous to life." *Id.* at 347. *See also Commonwealth v. Roebuck*, 32 A.3d 613 (Pa. 2011) (using the same reasoning to convict an accomplice of depraved-heart murder).

In *People v. Marshall*, 106 N.W.2d 842 (Mich. 1961), by contrast, the court reversed Marshall's involuntary manslaughter conviction. Marshall had loaned his car to one Neal McClary, knowing McClary was drunk, and McClary then drove in the wrong direction on an expressway and crashed head-on into another vehicle, killing the driver of the other car as well as himself. The court concluded that the killing "was not counselled by [the defendant, or] accomplished by another acting jointly with him, nor did it occur in the attempted achievement of some common enterprise." *Id.* at 844. The court observed, however, that the case would have been "entirely different" if Marshall had been in the car with McClary at the time of the accident instead of being at home in bed. *Id.* at 843.

Section 2.06(4) of the Model Penal Code clearly envisions that one can be convicted as an accomplice to involuntary manslaughter without proof of purpose to kill, and the "overwhelming majority" of jurisdictions agree. Joshua Dressler, Understanding Criminal Law § 30.05[B][3], at 478 (7th ed. 2015). MPC § 2.06(4) provides:

> When causing a particular result is an element of an offense, an accomplice in the conduct causing such result is an accomplice in the commission of that offense if he acts with the kind of culpability, if any, with respect to that result that is sufficient for the commission of the offense.

How would Moon and Marshall be treated under this provision? Compare the criminal law's analysis of this issue in attempt cases like *Thacker*, discussed in Chapter 11, Section A.2, Note 2.

6. The Mens Rea Required for Attendant Circumstances. If the crime committed by the principal requires proof of some attendant circumstance — for example, the age of the victim in a statutory rape prosecution — what mens rea must the accomplice have with respect to that circumstance in order to be held criminally liable? That question has rarely been addressed by the courts, *see* Joshua Dressler, Understanding Criminal Law § 30.05[B][4], at 479 (7th ed. 2015), and the drafters of the Model Penal Code observed that "[t]here is deliberate ambiguity as to whether the purpose requirement extends to circumstance elements . . . or whether, as in the case of attempts, the policy of the substantive offense on this point should control." Model Penal Code § 2.06 Comment at 311 n.37. (The Comments are referring here to the language in the MPC that requires proof in an attempt prosecution that the defendant was "acting with the kind of culpability *otherwise required for commission of the crime.*" Model Penal Code § 5.01(1) (emphasis added). Section 5.01(1) is discussed above in Chapter 11, Section A.2, Note 4.)

Note that the MPC's definition of "purpose" when referring to "attendant circumstances" requires proof that the defendant "is aware of the existence of such circumstances or he believes or hopes that they exist." Model Penal Code § 2.02(2)(a)(ii). Does this definition of "purpose" actually require only "knowledge" (awareness of the existence) of attendant circumstances? If so, does it suggest a logical inconsistency in the MPC?

7. The Natural and Probable Consequences Doctrine. Under the traditional common-law view, an accessory before the fact and a principal in the second degree can be held liable for all crimes that were the "natural and probable consequences" of the initial crime they assisted. *See* Wayne R. LaFave, Criminal Law § 13.3(b) (5th ed. 2010). This "natural and probable consequences" doctrine is controversial and is not followed in every jurisdiction. (Compare the felony murder rule, discussed above in Chapter 6, Section D, and the "foreseeability" limitation on the *Pinkerton* doctrine in conspiracy cases, discussed in Chapter 13, Section B.1.)

Where it is applied, the natural and probable consequences doctrine can lead to far-reaching results. For example, in *United States v. Vaden*, 912 F.2d 780 (5th Cir. 1990), two prison guards (Vaden and Slater) were escorting a prisoner named Rivera from the showers when Vaden intentionally walked away in order to permit three other inmates to attack Rivera. During the assault on Rivera, the attackers held off Officer Slater with a knife. Officer Vaden was found guilty of aiding and abetting the assault on Officer Slater on the theory that that crime was the "natural and probable consequence" of the assault on Rivera.

By contrast, in *United States v. Greer*, 467 F.2d 1064 (7th Cir. 1972), the court declined to apply the "natural and probable consequences" doctrine. The principals in *Greer* stole 40,000 pounds of copper from a freight depot in Indiana and then drove it to Chicago. Because Greer had told the thieves where to find the copper, he was convicted as an accomplice to the transportation of stolen copper across state lines. On appeal, the court reversed the conviction, concluding that accomplice liability does not extend to include all "likely consequences":

> To allow a jury to infer intent to aid in the commission of one offense from the demonstrated intent to aid in another earlier offense because the later crime is a foreseeable consequence of the earlier one, is to base criminal liability only on a showing of negligence rather than criminal intent.

Id. at 1069. *Cf. People v. Chiu*, 325 P.3d 972, 980 (Cal. 2014) (limiting the natural and probable consequences doctrine to offenses other than first-degree premeditated murder because "the connection between the [accomplice's] culpability and the perpetrator's premeditative state is too attenuated, . . . especially in light of the severe penalty involved and the . . . public policy concern of deterrence").

The Model Penal Code rejects the natural and probable consequences doctrine outright. The Comments observe: "Whatever may have been the law on th[is] point, in any event, it is submitted that the liability of an accomplice ought not be extended beyond the purposes he shares." Model Penal Code § 2.06 Comment at 312. Is the MPC's position here consistent with § 2.06(4), discussed above in Note 5?

In 2014, the United States Supreme Court issued the following opinion, its first major pronouncement on the reach of accomplice liability in almost 35 years. In addition to providing a "primer" on the law governing accomplice liability, the opinion reflects the complexity of modern criminal statutes.

Rosemond v. United States

134 S. Ct. 1240 (2014)

Justice Kagan delivered the opinion of the Court.

A federal criminal statute, § 924(c) of Title 18, prohibits "us[ing] or carr[ying]" a firearm "during and in relation to any crime of violence or drug trafficking crime." In this case, we consider what the Government must show when it accuses a defendant of aiding or abetting that offense. We hold that the Government makes its case by proving that the defendant actively participated in the underlying drug trafficking or violent crime with advance knowledge that a confederate would use or carry a gun during the crime's commission. . . .

I

This case arises from a drug deal gone bad. Vashti Perez arranged to sell a pound of marijuana to Ricardo Gonzales and Coby Painter. She drove to a local park to make the exchange, accompanied by two confederates, Ronald Joseph and petitioner Justus Rosemond. One of those men apparently took the front passenger seat and the other sat in the back, but witnesses dispute who was where. At the designated meeting place, Gonzales climbed into the car's backseat while Painter waited outside. The backseat passenger allowed Gonzales to inspect the marijuana. But rather than handing over money, Gonzales punched that man in the face and fled with the drugs. As Gonzales and Painter ran away, one of the male passengers—but again, which one is contested—exited the car and fired several shots from a semiauto-matic handgun. . . .

. . . [T]he Government prosecuted the §924(c) charge on two alternative theories. The Government's primary contention was that Rosemond himself used the firearm during the aborted drug transaction. But recognizing that the identity of the shooter was disputed, the Government also offered a back-up argument: Even if it was Joseph who fired the gun as the drug deal fell apart, Rosemond aided and abetted the §924(c) violation. . . . The jury convicted Rosemond of violating §924(c) (as well as all other offenses charged). The verdict form was general: It did not reveal whether the jury found that Rosemond himself had used the gun or instead had aided and abetted a confederate's use during the marijuana deal.

II

The federal aiding and abetting statute, 18 U.S.C. §2, states that a person who furthers—more specifically, who "aids, abets, counsels, commands, induces or procures"—the commission of a federal offense "is punishable as a principal." . . .

We have previously held that under §2 "those who provide knowing aid to persons committing federal crimes, with the intent to facilitate the crime, are themselves committing a crime." . . . As at common law, a person is liable under §2 for aiding and abetting a crime if (and only if) he (1) takes an affirmative act in furtherance of that offense, (2) with the intent of facilitating the offense's commission. *See* . . . *Hicks* v. *United States*, 150 U.S. 442, 449 (1893) (an accomplice is liable when his acts of assistance are done "with the intention of encouraging and abetting" the crime).

The questions that the parties dispute, and we here address, concern how those two requirements—affirmative act and intent—apply in a prosecution for aiding and abetting a §924(c) offense. Those questions arise from the compound nature of that provision. Recall that §924(c) forbids "us[ing] or carr[ying] a firearm" when engaged in a "crime of violence or drug trafficking crime." The prosecutor must show the use or carriage of a gun; so too he must prove the commission of a predicate (violent or drug trafficking) offense. For purposes of ascertaining aiding and abetting liability, we therefore must consider: When does a person act to further this double-barreled crime? And when does he intend to facilitate its commission? We address each issue in turn.

A

Consider first Rosemond's account of his conduct (divorced from any issues of intent). Rosemond actively participated in a drug transaction . . . . But as he tells it, he took no action with respect to any firearm. . . . [M]ust Rosemond, as he claims, have taken some act to assist the commission of the other (firearm) component of §924(c)?

The common law imposed aiding and abetting liability on a person (possessing the requisite intent) who facilitated any part—even though not every part—of a criminal venture. . . . [I]n the words of a[] standard reference: If a person was "present abetting while *any* act necessary to constitute the offense [was] being performed through another," he could be charged as a principal — even "though [that act was] *not the whole thing necessary.*" And so "[w]here several acts constitute[d] together one crime, if each [was] separately performed by a different individual[,] . . . all [were] principals as to the whole." Indeed, . . . a person's involvement in the crime could be not merely partial but minimal too: "The quantity [of assistance was] immaterial," so long as the accomplice did "*something*" to aid the crime. After all, the common law maintained, every little bit helps — and a contribution to some part of a crime aids the whole.

[Thus,] under § 2: As almost every court of appeals has held, "[a] defendant can be convicted as an aider and abettor without proof that he participated in each and every element of the offense." In proscribing aiding and abetting, Congress used language that "comprehends all assistance rendered by words, acts, encouragement, support, or presence" — even if that aid relates to only one (or some) of a crime's phases or elements. . . . The division of labor between two (or more) confederates thus has no significance: A strategy of "you take that element, I'll take this one" would free neither party from liability.

Under that established approach, Rosemond's participation in the drug deal here satisfies the affirmative-act requirement for aiding and abetting a § 924(c) violation. . . . [T]he commission of a drug trafficking (or violent) crime is — no less than the use of a firearm — an "essential conduct element of the § 924(c) offense." . . . Rosemond therefore could assist in § 924(c)'s violation by facilitating either the drug transaction or the firearm use (or of course both). In helping to bring about one part of the offense (whether trafficking drugs or using a gun), he necessarily helped to complete the whole. . . .

. . . .

B

. . . As previously explained, a person aids and abets a crime when (in addition to taking the requisite act) he intends to facilitate that offense's commission. An intent to advance some different or lesser offense is not, or at least not usually, sufficient: Instead, the intent must go to the specific and entire crime charged — so here, to the full scope (predicate crime plus gun use) of § 924(c).[3] And the canonical formulation of that needed state of mind — later appropriated by this Court and oft-quoted in both parties' briefs — is Judge Learned Hand's: To aid and abet a crime, a defendant must not just "in some sort associate himself with the venture," but also "participate in it as in something that he wishes to bring about" and "seek by his action to make it succeed." *Nye & Nissen* v. *United States*, 336 U.S. 613, 619 (1949) (quoting *Peoni*, 100 F.2d at 402).

---

3. [n.7] Some authorities suggest an exception to the general rule when another crime is the "natural and probable consequence" of the crime the defendant intended to abet. . . . We . . . express no view on th[at] issue.

We have previously found that intent requirement satisfied when a person actively participates in a criminal venture with full knowledge of the circumstances constituting the charged offense. . . . In *Pereira* [*v. United States*, 347 U.S. 1 (1954)], we found the requisite intent for aiding and abetting [in a mail fraud case] because the defendant took part in a fraud "know[ing]" that his confederate would take care of the mailing. Likewise, in *Bozza* v. *United States*, 330 U.S. 160, 165 (1947), we upheld a conviction for aiding and abetting the evasion of liquor taxes because the defendant helped operate a clandestine distillery "know[ing]" the business was set up "to violate Government revenue laws." . . . So for purposes of aiding and abetting law, a person who actively participates in a criminal scheme knowing its extent and character intends that scheme's commission.[4]

The same principle holds here: An active participant in a drug transaction has the intent needed to aid and abet a §924(c) violation when he knows that one of his confederates will carry a gun. In such a case, the accomplice has decided to join in the criminal venture, and share in its benefits, with full awareness of its scope—that the plan calls not just for a drug sale, but for an armed one. In so doing, he has chosen (like the abettors in *Pereira* and *Bozza* or the driver in an armed robbery) to align himself with the illegal scheme in its entirety—including its use of a firearm. And he has determined (again like those other abettors) to do what he can to "make [that scheme] succeed." He thus becomes responsible, in the typical way of aiders and abettors, for the conduct of others. He may not have brought the gun to the drug deal himself, but because he took part in that deal knowing a confederate would do so, he intended the commission of a §924(c) offense—i.e., an armed drug sale.

For all that to be true, though, the §924(c) defendant's knowledge of a firearm must be advance knowledge—or otherwise said, knowledge that enables him to make the relevant legal (and indeed, moral) choice. When an accomplice knows beforehand of a confederate's design to carry a gun, he can attempt to alter that plan or, if unsuccessful, withdraw from the enterprise; it is deciding instead to go ahead with his role in the venture that shows his intent to aid an *armed* offense. But when an accomplice knows nothing of a gun until it appears at the scene, he may already have completed his acts of assistance; or even if not, he may at that late point have no realistic opportunity to quit the crime. And when that is so, the defendant has not shown the requisite intent to assist a crime involving a gun. . . .

The Government . . . views [our] standard as met whenever the accomplice, having learned of the firearm, continues any act of assisting the drug transaction. . . .

But that approach, we think, would diminish too far the requirement that a defendant in a §924(c) prosecution must intend to further an *armed* drug deal. Assume,

---

4. [n.8] We did not deal in these cases, nor do we here, with defendants who incidentally facilitate a criminal venture rather than actively participate in it. A hypothetical case is the owner of a gun store who sells a firearm to a criminal, knowing but not caring how the gun will be used. We express no view about what sort of facts, if any, would suffice to show that such a third party has the intent necessary to be convicted of aiding and abetting.

for example, that an accomplice agrees to participate in a drug sale on the express condition that no one brings a gun to the place of exchange. But just as the parties are making the trade, the accomplice notices that one of his confederates has a (poorly) concealed firearm in his jacket. The Government would convict the accomplice of aiding and abetting a §924(c) offense if he assists in completing the deal without incident, rather than running away or otherwise aborting the sale. But behaving as the Government suggests might increase the risk of gun violence—to the accomplice himself, other participants, or bystanders; and conversely, finishing the sale might be the best or only way to avoid that danger. In such a circumstance, a jury is entitled to find that the defendant intended only a drug sale—that he never intended to facilitate, and so does not bear responsibility for, a drug deal carried out with a gun. A defendant manifests that greater intent, and incurs the greater liability of §924(c), when he chooses to participate in a drug transaction knowing it will involve a firearm; but he makes no such choice when that knowledge comes too late for him to be reasonably able to act upon it.[5]

[The Court reversed Rosemond's conviction and remanded because the jury instructions given at his trial "did not explain that Rosemond needed advance knowledge of a firearm's presence."[6]]

Justice Alito, with whom Justice Thomas joins, concurring in part and dissenting in part.

I largely agree . . . [but] I reject the Court's conclusion that a conviction for aiding and abetting a violation of 18 U.S.C. §924(c) demands proof that the alleged aider and abettor had what the Court terms "a realistic opportunity" to refrain from engaging in the conduct at issue. This rule represents an important and, as far as I am aware, unprecedented alteration of the law of aiding and abetting and of the law of intentionality generally.

. . . I begin with our case law on the *mens rea* required to establish aiding and abetting. There is some tension in our cases on this point. Specifically, some of our cases suggest that an aider and abettor must act purposefully or with intent. . . . On the

---

5. [n.10] Contrary to the dissent's view, . . . our decision [does not] remotely deny that the "intent to undertake some act is . . . perfectly consistent with the motive of avoiding adverse consequences which would otherwise occur." Our holding is grounded in the distinctive intent standard for aiding and abetting someone else's act—in the words of Judge Hand, that a defendant must not just "in some sort associate himself with the venture" (as seems to be good enough for the dissent), but also "participate in it as in something that he wishes to bring about" and "seek by his action to make it succeed." . . . [W]e think that intent standard cannot be satisfied if a defendant charged with aiding and abetting a §924(c) offense learns of a gun only after he can realistically walk away—i.e., when he has no opportunity to decide whether "he wishes to bring about" (or make succeed) an *armed* drug transaction, rather than a simple drug crime. . . .

6. On remand, the Tenth Circuit affirmed Rosemond's conviction on the grounds that the erroneous jury instruction did not affect the outcome of the trial. The court reasoned that, by convicting Rosemond as the principal for a different offense—possessing the ammunition fired from the gun—the jury "necessarily found that he was the actual shooter." *United States v. Rosemond*, 615 F. App'x 480, 483 (10th Cir. 2015), *cert. denied*, 136 S. Ct. 1450 (2016).

other hand, there are cases to which the Court also refers, that appear to hold that the requisite *mens rea* is simply knowledge. The Court refers interchangeably to both of these tests and thus leaves our case law in the same, somewhat conflicted state .... But because the difference between acting purposefully (when that concept is properly understood) and acting knowingly is slight, this is not a matter of great concern.

[Then], however, the Court veers off in a new and, to my mind, most unfortunate direction. ... [T]he seriously misguided step occurs [when] the Court says that if the risk of walking away exceeds (by some unspecified degree) the risk created by completing the sale and if the alleged aider and abettor chooses to continue for that reason, the alleged aider and abettor lacks the *mens rea* required for conviction.

. . . .

... The Court justifies its holding [by citing] *Nye & Nissen* .... But the Court, having refrained from deciding whether aiding and abetting requires purposeful, as opposed to knowing, conduct, quickly and without explanation jettisons the "knowing" standard and concludes that purposeful conduct is needed. This is a critical move because if it is enough for an alleged aider and abettor simply to know that his confederate is carrying a gun, then the alleged aider and abettor in the Court's hypothetical case (who spots the gun on the confederate's person) unquestionably had the *mens rea* needed for conviction.

But even accepting the *Nye & Nissen* standard as the exclusive means of proving the required *mens rea*, the Court's analysis is still quite wrong. Under the *Nye & Nissen* standard, the Government must simply prove that a defendant had as his conscious object that the hypothetical drug sale (which, as the defendant knew, included the carrying of a gun by one of the participants) go forward to completion. ...

The Court confuses two fundamentally distinct concepts: intent and motive. ... [T]he intent to undertake some act is of course perfectly consistent with the motive of avoiding adverse consequences which would otherwise occur. ...

Common-law commentators recognized this elementary distinction between intent and motive. ... [I]f "A puts a loaded pistol to B's temple and shoots B through the head deliberately, ... [i]t is obvious that in every such case the intention of A must be to kill B." This fact "throws no light whatever on A's motives for killing B. ... The motive may have been a desire for revenge, or a desire for plunder, or a wish on A's part to defend himself against an attack by B, ... or to put a man already mortally wounded out of his agony." "In all these cases the intention is the same, but the motives are different, and in all the intention may remain unchanged from first to last whilst the motives may vary from moment to moment."

. . . .

Notes and Questions

1. *Rosemond*'s **Actus Reus Analysis.** Is the Court right to hold that the government's actus reus burden was satisfied because Rosemond undeniably aided a drug trafficking crime and thus assisted one part of § 924(c)? Is that result dictated by the traditional rule that any minimal assistance is enough for accomplice liability, even if the crime would have occurred without the accomplice's participation? Or does the "compound nature" of § 924(c) distinguish *Rosemond* from cases like *Wilcox* and *Tally*, which are described above in Section B?

2. *Rosemond*'s Mens Rea Analysis. Is the Court's holding faithful to the "canonical" *Peoni* standard it purports to be applying? Or is Justice Alito correct in asserting that the majority "refers interchangeably" to both purpose and knowledge in articulating the mens rea necessary to convict Rosemond? If so, is the Court simply making the uncontroversial point that a jury may infer the requisite purpose from a defendant's knowledge? Or is the Court saying that knowledge is a sufficiently culpable mens rea in and of itself here?

More generally, does *Rosemond* settle the question whether a mens rea of purpose or knowledge should be required for accomplice liability? Or is the Court's holding limited to § 924(c) cases? Or to the subset of § 924(c) cases where the alleged accomplice provided more than "incidental" assistance?

3. The Controversy Regarding "Advance Knowledge." If you think the Court's mens rea analysis in *Rosemond* is inconsistent with the *Peoni* formulation, are your concerns assuaged by the majority's requirement that an accomplice have "advance knowledge" that a confederate will be armed? Or do you think that Rosemond should be acquitted even if he knew well in advance that his compatriot would be carrying a gun, unless he had "purpose" that the gun be brought to the site of the drug deal? On the other hand, does Justice Alito have the better view when he says that Rosemond is guilty of violating § 924(c) so long as he gained knowledge of the gun at any point during the drug transaction? Under the majority's formulation, when does an accessory's awareness of a firearm "come[] too late" to qualify as "advance knowledge"?

Justice Alito accuses the majority of conflating purpose and motive. Is the majority's response in footnote 10 of its opinion persuasive? What does Justice Kagan mean when she refers to "the distinctive intent standard" applied in accomplice cases?

4. Parsing the Elements of § 924(c). Is the Court right to conclude that Congress intended the language "during and in relation to any crime of . . . drug trafficking" to be "an essential conduct element" of § 924(c)? Or is this phrase better viewed as an "attendant circumstance" element of the crime? How does this distinction affect your evaluation of the mens rea necessary to convict Rosemond?

This is actually a difficult issue, as "separating crimes that simply bar certain conduct from those that also require proof of an attendant circumstance has proven to be notoriously difficult." Kit Kinports, Rosemond, *Mens Rea, and the Elements of Complicity*, 52 San Diego L. Rev. 133, 158 (2015). The Model Penal Code does not expressly define the term "attendant circumstances," although the Comments accompanying the attempt provision mention that circumstances "refer to the objective situation that the law requires to exist, in addition to the defendant's act or any results that the act may cause." Model Penal Code § 5.01 Comment at 301 n.9.

Adding to the complexity, as discussed above in Note 6, the courts have rarely ana-lyzed the question of what mens rea the prosecution must prove an accomplice had with respect to the circumstance elements of a crime, and the drafters of the MPC decided to leave that issue "deliberate[ly] ambigu[ous]." Model Penal Code § 2.06 Comment at 311 n.37.

5. The Cumulative Impact of the Court's Decision. When both the actus reus and mens rea portions of the Court's opinion are combined, does *Rosemond* "expand[] § 924(c) liability to defendants who displayed a striking absence of culpability with respect to the [statute's] firearm" element? Kit Kinports, Rosemond, *Mens Rea, and the Elements of Complicity*, 52 San Diego L. Rev. 133, 170 (2015).

[D] Withdrawal of Aid as a Defense

Commonwealth v. Huber

15 Pa. D. & C.2d 726 (Montgomery Cnty. Ct. 1958)

Groshens, Judge.

Defendant was indicted . . . on the charge of accessory before the fact to rob-bery, and . . . on the charge of accessory after the fact to robbery.

At the trial before the Hon. Harold G. Knight, sitting without a jury, defendant was found guilty of accessory before the fact.

Defendant's motions for a new trial and in arrest of judgment are now before the court for disposition. In support of his motions, defendant contends in his brief: (a) That the Commonwealth failed to prove his guilt beyond a reasonable doubt, and (b) that defendant withdrew from any plan or scheme of robbery so as to make him not guilty as an accessory before the fact.

We have carefully examined the notes of testimony in their entirety and the tran-script of oral arguments at the trial. We are convinced there was ample evidence to support President Judge Knight's verdict of guilty on the charge of accessory before the fact.

The happening of the robbery was not in dispute at the trial, as counsel for defen-dant admitted in open court that a robbery had taken place. The issue was narrowed down to defendant's connection with the robbery.

To prove defendant's implications the Commonwealth called the two police offi-cers who investigated the case and one of the principals to the robbery. Both police officers testified defendant freely admitted to them three days after the robbery that he had furnished the rifle used in the robbery and the naphtha type fluid used on the victim, that he knew a "hold-up" was planned, that he had been asked to accom-pany the principals which he refused to do, that defendant had gone to the police station on the night of the robbery where he learned that the robbery had taken place and that he went forthwith to the home of one of the principals to get his rifle back.

One of the three principals, Ernest Farr, testified that defendant knew of the plan and that defendant furnished the rifle and naphtha (ether).

Defendant took the stand in his own defense and corroborated much of the Commonwealth's evidence. For example defendant testified concerning his rifle and his knowledge of its proposed use in a conversation with John Goodwin, one of the principals:

> "'Sure, you can borrow it,' and I asked him what he was going to do with it, and he said:

"I am going to rob somebody."

By the Court:

> "Q. Going to what?

> "A. He said he was going to rob somebody.

> "Q. Rob somebody?

> "A. That's it."

By Mr. Pearlstine [defense counsel]:

> "Q. And then what did you say to him about that?

> "A. I just laughed right then, and then Landis, Dave Landis came in and I hadn't had a chance to talk to him again till we got down to my place.

> "Q. Did Goodwin at that time say anything about you going with him or where they were going or anything like that or what they planned to [do]?

> "A. Yes, at that time he asked me to go along.

> "Q. What did you say?

> "A. I said no I had a date at first; and then he was persistent and it seemed like he wanted me to go and I says: *'No, I ain't going to get involved in anything like that'* (Italics supplied).

> "Q. Did you or not think he was serious at the time?

> "A. No, I did not."

An accessory before the fact is defined in *Commonwealth v. Habecker*, 113 Pa. Super. Ct. 335, at page 340, as:

> "... one who plans, cooperates, assists, aids, counsels or abets in the perpetration of a felony."

Certainly, the Commonwealth's evidence of aid given by this defendant, supported as it is by defendant's own testimony, amply supports the finding of guilt. The defense of withdrawal remains but to be considered.

> . . . .

The fact that this defendant was asked to participate in the robbery as a principal, and that he refused, does not constitute such a withdrawal as would relieve him of criminal liability as an accessory before the fact. Had this defendant demanded and received back his rifle, or had he reported the principals to the police in time to thwart the robbery, then he could be said to have withdrawn successfully. Having placed the rifle in the hands of John Goodwin who, according to defendant's own testimony, told defendant "he was going to rob somebody," defendant committed himself to a sequence of events from which he could only extricate himself by getting his rifle out of the hands of John Goodwin before the robbery, or by thwarting the robbery in some other way. The "aid" in this case was the rifle. Therefore, to effectively withdraw made it incumbent upon defendant to get the rifle out of the hands of John Goodwin, or the equivalent thereof. He did neither of these things. He did, however, go to the police station where he learned of the perpetration of the robbery. He then rushed posthaste to get his rifle, not to withdraw from the crime, but to get incriminating evidence out of the possession of a principal who was then the object of a police investigation.

The credibility of defendant was for the trial judge, who saw him on the stand and heard him testify; when defendant told Judge Knight that he did not take seriously John Goodwin's declared intention to rob someone with the rifle, Judge Knight obviously did not believe him. . . .

Was it a mere coincidence that defendant happened to be in the police station when he overheard an officer report a robbery? Why was defendant so certain his rifle had been used in the robbery that he rushed to the home of John Goodwin to get his rifle? The actions of defendant, as well as his verbal admissions, indicated a consciousness of his own marginal involvement in the robbery. Defendant's conduct before and after the robbery was inconsistent with innocence. His long and friendly association with John Goodwin, who is conceded to be one of the principal felons, is a circumstance which, together with the other proof submitted, was sufficient to sustain the verdict of guilty.

Notes and Questions

1. Withdrawal of Aid. As *Huber* illustrates, a defense of withdrawal is available, at least in theory, to an accomplice who removes all aid and encouragement in a timely manner or gives the police notice of the impending crime in time for them to intervene. *See* Wayne R. LaFave, Criminal Law § 13.3(d) (5th ed. 2010). *Accord*, Model Penal Code § 2.06(6)(c) (also allowing the option of withdrawing by "otherwise mak[ing] proper effort to prevent the commission of the offense"). But some jurisdictions impose a stricter requirement that the defendant must "thwart the crime." *E.g.*, *State v. Daniels*, 129 A.3d 1056 (N.J. 2016) (requiring that an accomplice "take affirmative steps to successfully prevent" the offense, and therefore "renunciation is not complete when mere abandonment does not prevent the commission of the crime"). In every state, the defense remains largely a jury question, and there are very few reported decisions where accomplices' convictions were reversed on the grounds that they presented a persuasive claim of withdrawal that no reasonable trier of fact would have rejected.

For example, in *State v. Miller*, 513 S.E.2d 147 (W. Va. 1998), the defendant, a long-time victim of domestic violence, was convicted of first-degree murder when she drove her 16-year-old son Christopher to the home where his father was staying and gave the boy the rifle that he used to kill his father. The court rejected the defendant's contention that she had "abandoned any . . . intent [to kill the victim] in a timely fashion" when she "laid the rifle down beside Christopher, told him to move the car, announced that she wanted to talk to [the victim] at her mother's house, and walked in that direction." Arguing that it was "not realistic to expect her to have said specific 'withdrawal' words to Christopher, such as, 'I don't approve of shooting your father,' or 'Let's quit this criminal venture and do something else,'" the defendant maintained that her actions "adequately expressed [the] intention that she wanted Christopher to bring the car to his grandmother's house, where she would be waiting, unarmed, to talk to [the victim]" and "did not want Christopher to wait . . . for his father to come out." But the court explained that "the jury could have concluded that given the appellant's expressed intent, an effective withdrawal or abandonment would have required her either to deprive Christopher of the rifle or to drive him away from [the victim]." *Id.* at 156–57.

Consider also *People v. Cooper*, 332 N.E.2d 453 (Ill. 1975). Cooper and two other men broke into a woman's house in order to rob her. Cooper helped gag the woman and tie her hands, but then "got scared" and left the house without taking anything. *Id.* at 455. Subsequently, one of the other men killed her. Cooper was convicted of burglary, robbery, and murder, and his withdrawal defense was rejected because he had not withdrawn his aid—he had done nothing to untie the woman or remove the gag—and therefore he had not effectively "neutralize[d] the effect of his conduct." *Id.* at 459.

In cases where the accomplice's only aid is to encourage or request that the principal commit the crime, courts have recognized a defense if the defendant withdrew the encouragement or request, and communicated that withdrawal to the principal before the principal went on to commit the crime. In *State v. Peterson*, 4 N.W.2d 826 (Minn. 1942), for example, Peterson initially asked Anderson to burn down her house, but then changed her mind before he started the fire and urged him to leave the house. The court reversed Peterson's conviction, finding that she had taken "the most effective measures within her power to arrest the execution of the plan" and had "made that fact known to Anderson in an unmistakable manner." *Id.* at 828.

2. The Motivation for Withdrawing. States are split on the question whether the availability of this defense depends on the motivation underlying the accomplice's withdrawal. In some jurisdictions, withdrawal of aid is no defense if it is motivated by the fear of apprehension rather than the moral realization that committing the crime would be wrong. But other states consider the motivation for withdrawal irrelevant, in order to induce those who have aided a criminal scheme to try to prevent its success. *See* WAYNE R. LAFAVE, CRIMINAL LAW § 13.3(d) (5th ed. 2010). Model

Penal Code § 2.06(6)(c) takes the latter position and does not inquire into the motivation for withdrawal. Which view makes more sense? Compare the requirements for raising a successful abandonment defense to an attempt charge, which are discussed above in Chapter 11, Section A.3.

[E] Accessory After the Fact and Obstruction of Justice

1. Accessory After the Fact and Its Modern-Day Expansion into Obstruction of Justice. Unlike the theory of liability for accomplices, "accessory after the fact" was traditionally recognized as a separate, substantive crime at common law (usually carrying a less serious penalty than the underlying felony itself). The common-law crime of accessory after the fact has four elements: (1) a felony has been committed; (2) the defendant knows the felon committed the crime; (3) the defendant does something to aid the felon; (4) with the purpose of hindering the felon's apprehension by the authorities. The common-law crime was limited to felonies, and did not extend to assisting misdemeanants. *See* Wayne R. LaFave, Criminal Law § 13.6(a), at 753–54 (5th ed. 2010).

Although many jurisdictions have abandoned "accessory after the fact" as a separate crime, the federal criminal code still includes it, largely as originally enacted by the First Congress in 1790. *See* 18 U.S.C. § 3 (providing that the penalty shall be "not more than one-half the maximum term of imprisonment . . . prescribed for the punishment of the principal," up to a maximum of 15 years). In 2003, a husband and wife were sentenced under this provision to more than two years in prison when they pled guilty to charges that they wired money, and offered their home as a hiding place, to James Kopp, an anti-abortionist who had murdered a doctor. *See* Susan Saulny, *Two Who Helped Doctor's Killer Are Released After 29 Months*, N.Y. Times, Aug. 22, 2003, at B4. *See also* 18 U.S.C. § 2339 (authorizing up to 10 years' imprisonment for one who "harbors or conceals" a terrorist).

Other jurisdictions have merged the crime of being an accessory after the fact into, or combined the concept with, obstruction of justice statutes. These statutes encompass not only conduct that would make one an accessory after the fact, but also many other actions perceived as criminal interference with a proper criminal justice system. Consider, for example, the crime of "hindering apprehension or prosecution" as defined in § 242.3 of the Model Penal Code:

A person commits an offense if, with purpose to hinder the apprehension, prosecution, conviction or punishment of another for crime, he:

(1) harbors or conceals the other; or

(2) provides or aids in providing a weapon, transportation, disguise or other means of avoiding apprehension or effecting escape; or

(3) conceals or destroys evidence of the crime, or tampers with a witness, informant, document or other source of information, regardless of its admissibility in evidence; or

(4) warns the other of impending discovery or apprehension, except that this paragraph does not apply to a warning given in connection with an effort to bring another into compliance with the law; or

(5) volunteers false information to a law enforcement officer.

The offense is a felony in the third degree if the conduct which the actor knows has been charged or is liable to be charged against the person aided would constitute a felony of the first or second degree. Otherwise it is a misdemeanor.

Note that defendants can be convicted under this provision if they purposefully try to hinder the operation of the law. It is not necessary that they aid someone who actually committed a crime; it is sufficient if they help someone who is merely wanted by the authorities.

Of the five ways to obstruct justice listed in MPC § 242.3, the first four can be found in many modern statutes. *See* LaFave, *supra*, § 13.6(a), at 757–58. The fifth — volunteering false information to a law enforcement officer — has been criminalized in only a few states. *See* Model Penal Code § 242.3 Comment at 235–36. The federal criminal code, however, includes a frequently employed statute that prohibits making a "false statement," 18 U.S.C. § 1001, which provides up to five years' imprisonment for any "materially false, fictitious, or fraudulent statement or representation" made by someone, whether or not under oath, "in any matter within the jurisdiction of the executive, legislative, or judicial branch of the Government of the United States." *See, e.g., United States v. Rodgers*, 466 U.S. 475 (1984) (affirming conviction for lying to FBI agents).

Prosecutors' use of statutes that criminalize false statements and obstruction of justice can be far-ranging. In 2004, for example, Martha Stewart, the entrepreneur of home design and tasteful lifestyle (and also a former stockbroker), and her stockbroker Peter Bacanovic were convicted under § 1001 for lying to federal officials who were conducting an insider trading investigation. The government alleged that Stewart had falsely denied that her decision to sell her stock in a biotech company called ImClone, just before it dropped substantially in value, was based on a tip from Bacanovic that ImClone's CEO (also a client of Bacanovic) had decided to dump his stock. Proving the old adage that "the cover-up is worse than the crime," Stewart and Bacanovic were convicted not just of false statements but also of conspiracy and obstructing an agency investigation. *See United States v. Stewart*, 433 F.3d 273 (2d Cir. 2006).

Nevertheless, the courts are sometimes wary of overly extending the reach of these criminal statutes. In *Yates v. United States*, 135 S. Ct. 1074 (2015), for example, the Supreme Court was asked to interpret 18 U.S.C. § 1519, a 2002 federal obstruction statute enacted in response to various financial frauds, which prohibits the knowing destruction of documents or any other "tangible object" with the intent to impede a federal investigation. The Court ruled that the phrase "tangible object" could not be

construed to reach the undersized fish that a commercial fisherman tossed overboard in an effort to destroy evidence that he was fishing in violation of federal fish
and game regulations.

2. Other Federal Obstruction Statutes. In addition to the false statement offense
and the crime of perjury (lying under oath), the federal criminal code contains a
number of obstruction of justice statutes. The oldest, dating back to 1790, includes
the broadly phrased "catchall" offense of "corruptly . . . endeavor[ing] . . . to influence, obstruct, or impede the due administration of justice." 18 U.S.C. § 1503(a).
There are also other, more specific federal statutes — like 18 U.S.C. § 1512, for
example, which addresses the offense of witness tampering:

> (b) Whoever knowingly uses intimidation, threatens or corruptly persuades
> another person, or engages in misleading conduct toward another person, with
> intent to —
>
>> (1) influence, delay or prevent the testimony of any person in an official
>> proceeding;
>>
>> (2) cause or induce any person to —
>>
>>> (A) withhold testimony, or withhold a record, document, or other object,
>>> from an official proceeding;
>>>
>>> (B) alter, destroy, mutilate, or conceal an object with intent to impair the
>>> object's integrity or availability for use in an official proceeding;
>>>
>>> (C) evade legal process summoning that person to appear as a witness, or
>>> to produce a record, document, or other object, in an official proceeding;
>>> or
>>>
>>> (D) be absent from an official proceeding to which such person has been
>>> summoned by legal process; or
>>
>> (3) hinder, delay, or prevent the communication to a law enforcement offi-
>> cer or judge of the United States of information relating to the commis-
>> sion or possible commission of a Federal offense . . .
>
> shall be fined under this title or imprisoned not more than 20 years, or
> both.
>
> . . . .
>
> (e) In a prosecution for an offense under this section, it is an affirmative defense,
> as to which the defendant has the burden of proof by a preponderance of the evi-
> dence, that the conduct consists solely of lawful conduct and that the defendant's
> sole intention was to encourage, induce, or cause the other person to testify
> truthfully.

3. Obstruction of Justice and the Impeachment of President Clinton. In 1998, this
broad array of federal statutes was notoriously used in the investigation of President
Bill Clinton by Independent Counsel Kenneth Starr, formerly a federal judge on the

D.C. Circuit and Solicitor General of the United States under President George H.W. Bush. The "Starr Report" ultimately led to the President's impeachment by the House of Representatives, although Clinton was not convicted by a two-thirds vote on the charges after a trial in the Senate. In reading the excerpts from the Independent Counsel's report that follow, consider whether the conduct alleged in the report would have supported an "accessory after the fact" charge at common law.

The Starr Report: The Official Report of the Independent Counsel's Investigation of the President

(Submitted to Congress, Sept. 9, 1998)

[The Independent Counsel concludes that there exists] substantial and credible information that President [Bill] Clinton obstructed justice during the *Jones v. Clinton* sexual harassment lawsuit by lying under oath and concealing evidence of his relationship with a young White House intern and federal employee, Monica Lewinsky. After a federal criminal investigation of the President's actions began in January 1998, the President lied under oath to the grand jury and obstructed justice during the grand jury investigation. . . .

[The *Jones* case was a civil sexual harassment lawsuit brought by an Arkansas state employee concerning President Clinton's behavior while Governor of Arkansas. It did not involve allegations regarding President Clinton's later conduct while in the White House with Ms. Lewinsky. However, the judge presiding over the *Jones* litigation allowed the plaintiff to ask questions about other extramarital sexual conduct Clinton had allegedly been involved in.]

. . . .

Once the discovery process in the *Jones* case became an issue (particularly after the Supreme Court's unanimous decision . . . that ordered the case to go forward [*Clinton v. Jones*, 520 U.S. 681 (1997) (holding that the Constitution did not require deferring the case until the President left office)]), [President Clinton's and Ms. Lewinsky's] continuing efforts to conceal the relationship took on added legal significance. The risks to the President of disclosure of the relationship dramatically increased.

An effort to obstruct justice by withholding the truth from the legal process — whether by lying under oath, concealing documents, or improperly influencing a witness's testimony — is a federal crime. There is substantial and credible information that President Clinton engaged in such efforts to prevent the truth of his relationship with Monica Lewinsky from being revealed in the *Jones* case.

. . . .

There is substantial and credible information that the President and Ms. Lewinsky reached an understanding that both of them would lie under oath when asked whether they had a sexual relationship (a conspiracy to obstruct justice or to commit perjury, in criminal law terms). . . .

There also is substantial and credible information that President Clinton endeavored to obstruct justice by suggesting that Ms. Lewinsky file an affidavit to avoid her deposition, which would "lock in" her testimony under oath, and to attempt to avoid questions at his own deposition—all to impede the gathering of discoverable evidence in the *Jones v. Clinton* litigation.

During the course of their relationship, the President and Ms. Lewinsky also discussed and used cover stories to justify her presence in the Oval Office area. The evidence indicates—given Ms. Lewinsky's unambiguous testimony and the President's lack of memory, as well as the fact that both planned to lie under oath—that the President suggested the continued use of . . . cover stories even after Ms. Lewinsky was named as a potential witness in the *Jones* litigation. At no time did the President tell Ms. Lewinsky to abandon these stories and to tell the truth about her visits, nor did he ever indicate to her that she should tell the truth about the relationship. . . .

. . . .

At various times during the *Jones* discovery process, the President and those working on his behalf devoted substantial time and attention to help Ms. Lewinsky obtain a job in the private sector.

. . . .

When a party in a lawsuit (or investigation) provides job or financial assistance to a witness, a question arises as to possible witness tampering. The critical question centers on the intent of the party providing the assistance. . . .

One can draw inference about the party's intent from circumstantial evidence. In this case, the President assisted Ms. Lewinsky in her job search in late 1997, at a time when she would have become a witness harmful to him in the *Jones* case *were she to testify truthfully.* The President did not act half-heartedly. His assistance led to the involvement of the Ambassador to the United Nations, one of the country's leading business figures (Mr. Perelman), and one of the country's leading attorneys (Vernon Jordan).

The question, therefore, is whether the President's efforts in obtaining a job for Ms. Lewinsky were to influence her testimony or simply to help an ex-intimate without concern for her testimony. . . .

There is substantial and credible information that the President assisted Ms. Lewinsky in her job search motivated at least in part by his desire to keep her "on the team" in the *Jones* litigation.

. . . .

In a meeting with Betty Currie [the President's personal secretary in the White House] on the day after his deposition and in a separate conversation a few days later, President Clinton made statements to her that he knew were false. The contents of the statements and the context in which they were made indicate that President Clinton was attempting to influence the testimony that Ms. Currie might have been required to give in the *Jones* case or in a grand jury investigation.

. . . .

The President called [Ms. Currie] shortly after the deposition [in the *Jones* case] and met with Ms. Currie the next day. The President appeared "concerned," according to Ms. Currie. He then informed Ms. Currie that questions about Ms. Lewinsky had been asked at the deposition.

The statements the President made to [Ms. Currie] on January 18 and then again on January 20 or 21 — that he was never alone with Ms. Lewinsky, that Ms. Currie could always hear or see them, and that he never touched Ms. Lewinsky — were false, but consistent with the testimony that the President provided under oath at his deposition. The President knew that the statements were false at the time he made them to Ms. Currie. The President's suggestion that he was simply trying to refresh his memory when talking to Ms. Currie conflicts with common sense: Ms. Currie's confirmation of false statements could not in any way remind the President of the facts.

. . . .

The context of the President's statements and the context in which those statements were made provide substantial and credible information that President Clinton sought improperly to influence Ms. Currie's testimony. Such actions constitute an obstruction of justice and improper influence on a witness.

. . . There is substantial and credible information that President Clinton endeavored to obstruct justice during the federal grand jury investigation. While refusing to testify for seven months, he simultaneously lied to potential grand jury witnesses knowing that they would relay the falsehoods to the grand jury.

. . . .

Rather than lie to the grand jury himself, the President lied about his relationship with Ms. Lewinsky to senior aides, and those aides then conveyed the President's false story to the grand jury.

. . . [T]he President lied to, among others, three current senior aides — John Podesta, Erskine Bowles, and Sidney Blumenthal — and one former senior aide, Harold Ickes. The President denied any kind of sexual relationship with Monica Lewinsky; said that Ms. Lewinsky made a sexual demand on him; and denied multiple telephone conversations with Monica Lewinsky. The President, by his own later admission, was aware that his aides were likely to convey the President's version of events to the grand jury.

The President's aides took the President at his word when he made these statements. Each aide then testified to the nature of the relationship between Monica Lewinsky and the President based on those statements — without knowing that they were calculated falsehoods by the President designed to perpetuate the false statements that the President made during his deposition in the *Jones* case.

The aides' testimony provided the grand jury a false account of the relationship between the President and Ms. Lewinsky. Their testimony thus had the potential to affect the investigation . . . .

. . . .

. . . [In summary,] the President made and caused to be made false statements to the American people about his relationship with Ms. Lewinsky. He also made false statements about whether he had lied under oath or otherwise obstructed justice in his civil case. By publicly and emphatically stating in January 1998 that "I did not have sexual relations with that woman" and these "allegations are false," the President also effectively delayed a possible congressional inquiry, and then he further delayed it by asserting Executive Privilege and refusing to testify for six months [before the grand jury]. This represents substantial and credible information that may constitute grounds for an impeachment. . . .

Notes and Questions

1. Obstruction of Justice Crimes. As the Starr Report acknowledges, criminal obstruction of justice charges depend heavily on evidence that the defendant had the mens rea to interfere with a judicial proceeding. The Starr Report claims, for example, that President Clinton misled aides about his affair with Monica Lewinsky in an effort to obstruct the federal grand jury investigation, not merely to avoid personal and political embarrassment or to conceal his sexual misconduct from his family. How would you rank the relative strength of the various allegations of obstruction of justice described in the Starr Report?

Compare the Starr Report's allegations to the Supreme Court's discussion of federal obstruction of justice three years earlier in *United States v. Aguilar*, 515 U.S. 593 (1995). In *Aguilar*, the government prosecuted a sitting federal district court judge under 18 U.S.C. § 1503, for allegedly "corruptly endeavor[ing] to influence, obstruct, and impede [a] grand jury investigation." 515 U.S. at 599. The prosecution's evidence showed that a grand jury had been convened to investigate an alleged conspiracy and the judge had lied about his involvement to FBI agents who were investigating that conspiracy. The Supreme Court interpreted the word "endeavor" in the obstruction statute to require that the defendant's conduct have "the 'natural and probable effect' of interfering with the due administration of justice." *Id.* In affirming the reversal of the judge's conviction, the Court ruled that "uttering false statements to an investigating agent . . . who might or might not testify before a grand jury" is insufficient to prove obstruction of justice. *Id.* at 600. The Court explained:

> We think the [evidence] relied upon by the Government would not enable a rational trier of fact to conclude that respondent knew that his false statement would be provided to the grand jury, and that the evidence goes no further than showing that respondent testified falsely to an investigating agent. Such conduct, we believe, falls on the other side of the statutory line from that of one who delivers false documents or testimony to the grand jury

itself. Conduct of the latter sort all but assures that the grand jury will consider the material in its deliberations. But what use will be made of false testimony given to an investigating agent who has not been subpoenaed or otherwise directed to appear before the grand jury is far more speculative. We think it cannot be said to have the "natural and probable effect" of interfering with the due administration of justice.

Id. at 601. Does the Starr Report's factual account effectively distinguish President Clinton's conduct from *Aguilar*? For a discussion of these issues in the context of the FBI's investigation of possible Russian interference in the 2016 presidential election and President Trump's decision to fire FBI Director James Comey, see Charlie Savage, *Parsing Obstruction of Justice, an Often-Murky Crime*, N.Y. Times, May 17, 2017, at A17.

2. **Vagueness and Adequate Notice.** Recall our earlier discussion in Chapter 1, Section B.2.e, of the constitutional requirement that defendants receive fair notice of what conduct is criminalized. Are some obstruction of justice provisions too vague to provide constitutionally adequate notice? For example, what does "corruptly endeavor" mean in 18 U.S.C. § 1503, as opposed to merely "endeavor"? Compare the Supreme Court's analysis in *Arthur Andersen v. United States*, 544 U.S. 696 (2005), of the phrase "knowingly . . . corruptly persuade" that appears in 18 U.S.C. § 1512, which is quoted above in Note 2 preceding the Starr Report. *Andersen* is discussed in Chapter 4, Section B.1, Note 7.

A different federal obstruction statute was ruled unconstitutionally vague in connection with an earlier White House scandal. In the "Iran Contra Affair" in the 1980s, a number of federal officials, including National Security Advisor John Poindexter, were accused of making false and misleading statements to Congress about military support the United States was providing to rebel "Contras" in Nicaragua in violation of legislation prohibiting such aid. In *United States v. Poindexter*, 951 F.2d 369 (D.C. Cir. 1991), the court reversed Poindexter's conviction for obstruction of justice under 18 U.S.C. § 1505, a statute that criminalizes obstruction of proceedings or investigations of federal agencies and "either House or committee" of Congress. The court ruled that the statute's convoluted language "does not at all clearly encompass lying to the Congress, which is, by way of contrast, clearly a violation of § 1001, the False Statements statute." 951 F.2d at 378. (The statute of limitations, however, precluded prosecuting Poindexter under § 1001.) The court added that "the term 'corruptly' is too vague to provide constitutionally adequate notice that it prohibits lying to Congress." *Id.* at 379.

3. **Compounding Crime.** As noted in the Introduction to this Chapter, the crime of "compounding" is committed when a person receives money, property, or some other consideration in return for agreeing not to prosecute a criminal or not to inform the authorities about a crime. *See* Wayne R. LaFave, Criminal Law § 13.6(c) (5th ed. 2010). Victims of crime, however, do not commit compounding simply by accepting reimbursement for their injuries or agreeing to settle a civil suit they filed against

their assailant. Likewise, the crime is not committed if the assailant settles the civil case hoping that the victim will not report the crime or otherwise pursue criminal prosecution. Rather, some agreement (though not necessarily a written one) is required.

For example, the negotiated civil settlement agreed to by the late pop star Michael Jackson (which was "never disclosed to the public, but . . . reputed to be over $25 million"), arising from Jackson's alleged tortious and criminal behavior toward a young boy, could not give rise to compounding charges in the absence of an "agreement" by the boy's family not to cooperate in a criminal investigation of Jackson. *See Rothman v. Jackson*, 57 Cal. Rptr. 2d 284 (Cal. Ct. App. 1996). For further discussion of the Michael Jackson case and a description of the distinction between compounding and extortion, see Note 5 following *State v. Harrington* in Chapter 9, Section B. Compare also the common-law crime of misprision of felony, which is discussed in Chapter 3, Section B, Note 8.

4. Perjury. Related to obstruction of justice is the crime of perjury. Under the common law, perjury is defined as a "false oath" (i.e., "a willful and corrupt sworn statement made without sincere belief in its truthfulness") that is made "in a judicial proceeding in regard to a material matter." Rollin M. Perkins & Ronald N. Boyce, Criminal Law 511 (3d ed. 1982). Thus, inaccurate sworn testimony is not perjury if the witness honestly believed it was true. Moreover, in *Bronston v. United States*, 409 U.S. 352 (1973), the Supreme Court ruled that even testimony that is intentionally misleading, or completely unresponsive to the question asked, is not perjury (at least not under the federal perjury statute, 18 U.S.C. § 1621), if the words spoken were "literally true." 409 U.S. at 362. This strict requirement for perjury prosecutions, as compared to fraud crimes that prohibit even misleading omissions, is based on the long-standing view that the perjury "offense must not be so severe as to discourage witnesses from appearing." *Id.* at 359.

In addition, the perjury statutes passed by Congress and most state legislatures provide that a sworn answer is not perjurious unless it is "material" to the proceeding. The "materiality" requirement can apply to other obstruction offenses as well. In 2015, for example, an en banc panel of the Ninth Circuit reversed the obstruction of justice conviction of Barry Bonds, baseball's all-time home run hitter, on the ground that his "rambling, non-responsive answer to a simple question" was not "material." *United States v. Bonds,* 784 F.3d 582, 582 (9th Cir. 2015) (en banc) (per curiam). Several of the judges feared that a broader interpretation would mean that "few witnesses or lawyers would be safe from prosecution." *Id.* at 586 (Kozinski, C.J., concurring).

Chapter 13

Conspiracy

The crime of conspiracy is an ancient one, dating back to a British statute enacted in 1285. *See* Francis B. Sayre, *Criminal Conspiracy*, 35 HARV. L. REV. 393 (1922). A separate inchoate offense consisting merely of an agreement between two or more people to commit a crime, conspiracy has long been called the "darling of the modern prosecutor's nursery" because of the procedural advantages and expanded scope of criminal liability that accompany a conspiracy charge. *Harrison v. United States*, 7 F.2d 259, 263 (2d Cir. 1925) (L. Hand, J.); *see* Barry Tarlow, *RICO: The New Darling of the Prosecutor's Nursery*, 49 FORDHAM L. REV. 165 (1980). In addition, the "*Pinkerton* doctrine" permits the government to expand the net of prosecution well beyond the acts actually committed by the defendant, to include foreseeable crimes committed by the defendant's co-conspirators. Conspiracy charges therefore give prosecutors a valuable tool to pursue large corrupt groups such as the Mafia, drug cartels, and even terrorist organizations. Its inchoate nature, however, can also give rise to controversial prosecutions. Still, "more than one-quarter of all federal criminal prosecutions and a large number of state cases involve . . . conspiracy" charges, and the crime is likely to remain a prominent feature of American criminal justice for the foreseeable future. Neal Kumar Katyal, *Conspiracy Theory*, 112 YALE L.J. 1307, 1310 (2003).

[A] The Breadth and Elements of Conspiracy

[1] Elements, Justifications, Advantages, and Sentencing

1. **The Elements of Conspiracy.** A conspiracy is generally defined as an agreement between two or more people to commit a crime. Although there is some variation from state to state, the following elements commonly appear in conspiracy statutes: (1) an agreement between at least two people; (2) purpose to enter into that agreement; (3) an overt act in furtherance of the agreement (not required at common law, but required in a majority of states); and (4) purpose to promote the crime that is the object of the conspiracy. A minority of American jurisdictions also require (5) knowledge that the target of the conspiracy is indeed unlawful. *See generally* WAYNE R. LAFAVE, CRIMINAL LAW 648–99 (5th ed. 2010). Section 5.03 of the Model Penal Code addresses conspiracy as the third "inchoate" crime, after attempt and solicitation.

Conspiracy is, in essence, merely an agreement to commit a substantive crime, without more. Like the crimes of attempt and solicitation, conspiracy can be used to punish inchoate criminal activity; but unlike attempt and solicitation, the crime of conspiracy typically does not "merge" with the completed offense, so it may be charged as an additional, separate crime even after the target offense is complete. Moreover, in most jurisdictions defendants can be convicted of conspiracy even though their conduct has not yet reached the point necessary to support a criminal attempt conviction. Thus, in *United States v. Feola*, 420 U.S. 671, 693–94 (1975), the Supreme Court identified the early "intervention of the criminal law" as an "independent value served by the law of conspiracy": "agreement to engage in a criminal venture," the Court explained, is "an event of sufficient threat to social order to permit the imposition of criminal sanctions for the agreement alone."

2. **The Justification for Criminal Conspiracy Laws.** What is the purpose of the conspiracy laws? What evil does this crime seek to punish that would escape the reach of other criminal laws? The California Supreme Court articulated the conventional rationale in *People v. Zamora*, 557 P.2d 75, 86–87 (Cal. 1976):

> Criminal liability for conspiracy, separate from and in addition to that imposed for the substantive offense which the conspirators agree to commit, has been justified by a "group danger" rationale. The division of labor inherent in group association is seen to encourage the selection of more elaborate and ambitious goals and to increase the likelihood that the scheme will be successful. Moreover, the moral support of the group is seen as strengthening the perseverance of each member of the conspiracy, thereby acting to discourage any reevaluation of the decision to commit the offense which a single offender might undertake. And even if a single conspirator reconsiders and contemplates stopping the wheels which have been set in motion to attain the object of the conspiracy, a return to the status quo will be much more difficult since it will entail persuasion of the other conspirators.

Accord, Callanan v. United States, 364 U.S. 587 (1961) ("Collective criminal agreement—partnership in crime—presents a greater potential threat to the public than individual delicts."); *Krulewitch v. United States*, 336 U.S. 440, 448–49 (1949) (Jackson, J., concurring) ("[T]o unite, back of a criminal purpose, the strength, opportunities and resources of many is obviously more dangerous and more difficult to police than the efforts of a lone wrongdoer.").

Are concerns about the supposed evils of "group danger" well-taken? Consider the views of one critic of conspiracy laws:

> Though these assumed dangers from conspiracy have a romantically individualistic ring, they have never been verified empirically. It is hardly likely that a search for such verification would end in support of . . . [the] suggestion that combination alone is *inherently* dangerous. This view is immediately refuted by reference to our own society, which is grounded in organization and agreement. More likely, empirical investigation would disclose that there is as much reason to believe that a large number of

participants will increase the prospect that the plan will be leaked as that it will be kept secret; or that persons involved will share their uncertainties and dissuade each other as that each will stiffen the others' determination. Most probably, however, the factors ordinarily mentioned as warranting the crime of conspiracy would be found to add to the danger to be expected from a group in certain situations and not others; the goals of the group and the personalities of its members would make any generalization unsafe and hence require some other explanation for treating conspiracy as a separate crime in all cases.

What does seem to lie at the root of conspiracy's continued independent status is the degree of deliberateness of antisocial tendency it seems to evidence.

Abraham S. Goldstein, *Conspiracy to Defraud the United States*, 68 YALE L.J. 405, 414 (1959). *See also* Philip E. Johnson, *The Unnecessary Crime of Conspiracy*, 61 CALIF. L. REV. 1137, 1139 (1973) ("The law of conspiracy is not basically sound. It should be abolished, not reformed.").

In response, Professor (and former Acting U.S. Solicitor General) Neal Katyal has charged that critics "have ignored many of the unique harms that conspiracies pose." Neal Kumar Katyal, *Conspiracy Theory*, 112 YALE L.J. 1307, 1314 (2003). "Conspiracy creates obvious efficiencies" for criminals, he argues, and recent "psychological data demonstrates that criminal groups pose special dangers to society," *Id.* at 1312, 1397. Who has the better argument here?

3. The Prosecutorial Advantages of Conspiracy. Prosecutors often charge conspiracy, in addition to the completed substantive offense, thus earning Judge Learned Hand's colorful description of conspiracy as the "darling of the modern prosecutor's nursery." Indeed, 40 years ago, Professor Paul Marcus reported that a significant percentage of prosecutors surveyed said they filed conspiracy charges not because the defendants had committed no substantive crime, but in order to obtain evidentiary, plea bargaining, or other strategic advantages. *See* Paul Marcus, *Conspiracy: The Criminal Agreement, in Theory and in Practice*, 65 GEO. L.J. 925 (1977). Because criminal liability attaches at an earlier point in time for conspiracy than for criminal attempts, conspiracy charges enable law enforcement to intervene at the earliest signs of criminal combination and well before actual harm occurs. In addition, conspiracy charges offer prosecutors a host of procedural advantages, which are described below.

A. The Exception to the Hearsay Rule for Co-Conspirator Statements. Normally, an out-of-court statement that is offered to prove the truth of its content is inadmissible hearsay. But the law of evidence has created an exception for any statements made by a defendant's co-conspirators during the course of and in furtherance of the conspiracy.

For example, suppose the defendant is facing first-degree murder charges. If one of the defendant's coworkers told a third person that the defendant was planning to kill the victim, the coworker's hearsay statement would not be admissible at the defendant's trial to prove intent to kill. But if the defendant and the coworker were involved in a conspiracy to commit murder, the coworker's statement would be admissible under the co-conspirator exception to the hearsay rule, provided that the statement was made to further the conspiracy in some way (for example, as part of a request that the third person obtain the murder weapon). *See Bourjaily v. United States*, 483 U.S. 171 (1987); Fed. R. Evid. 801(d)(2)(E) (codifying this exception). Moreover, courts have consistently rejected the argument that the co-conspirator hearsay exception violates defendants' right "to be confronted with the witnesses against" them guaranteed by the Sixth Amendment's Confrontation Clause. *See, e.g., United States v. Hargrove*, 508 F.3d 946, 960 (7th Cir. 2007).

B. Wide Choice of Venue. It is a traditional rule of conspiracy law that all co-conspirators may be tried in any jurisdiction where any overt act in furtherance of the conspiracy occurred, in addition to the place where the criminal agreement was formed. *See Hyde & Schneider v. United States*, 225 U.S. 347 (1915). Thus, in large-scale conspiracies, prosecutors often have great latitude in selecting their forum, and can choose the jurisdiction they believe is most likely to convict. *Cf.* Model Penal Code § 5.03(4)(b)(i) (limiting venue in conspiracy cases to jurisdictions where the defendant entered into the agreement, or where the defendant or a co-conspirator committed an overt act).

C. Joint Trial of Multiple Defendants. The normal presumption is that all members of an alleged conspiracy may be tried together; judges rarely grant a conspiracy defendant's motion to sever the trial. *See United States v. Zafiro*, 506 U.S. 534 (1993). The option of a joint multi-defendant trial can expand the potential venue choices. It can also produce a prejudicial "spillover" effect in the eyes of a jury, by associating defendants who were minor members of the conspiracy with the negative evidence and images introduced against co-defendants who were more deeply involved. Professor Marcus has criticized the complexity and potential prejudice of such "mega-trials":

> Perhaps the most striking change in the conspiracy area during the past two decades has been the enormous number of cases involving many defendants, complex evidentiary issues, and dozens and dozens of complicated charges. . . . It is difficult to imagine how a jury goes about sorting the testimony of hundreds of witnesses, or considering evidence it heard more than a year earlier. Indeed, how does a jury begin to apply the reasonable doubt standard when there are more than fifty counts charging more than a dozen different individuals?

Paul Marcus, *Criminal Conspiracy Law: Time to Turn Back from an Ever Expanding, Ever More Troubling Area*, 1 Wm. & Mary Bill Rts. J. 1, 10–11 (1992). *See also* Edward J. Imwinkelried, *Prejudice to the Nth Degree: The Introduction of Uncharged Misconduct Admissible Only Against a Co-Defendant at a Megatrial*, 53 Okla. L. Rev. 35 (2000). Marcus provides as examples cases like *United States v. Casamento*, 887

F.2d 1141 (2d Cir. 1989) (21 defendants, 275 witnesses, thousands of exhibits, 40,000 pages of transcripts, 17-month trial), and *United States v. Accetturo*, 842 F.2d 1408 (3d Cir. 1988) (26 defendants, 15-month trial).

Can justice be served in large, complex conspiracy "mega-trials"? Note that the Supreme Court has approved multi-defendant conspiracy trials, observing that the use of "measures, such as limiting [jury] instructions, often will suffice to cure any risk of prejudice." *Zafiro*, 506 U.S. at 539.

D. *Pinkerton* Liability. As discussed in greater depth in Section B.1 below, the *Pinkerton* doctrine provides that defendants who join a conspiracy may be convicted not only for the crime of conspiracy, but also for any foreseeable crimes committed by any of their co-conspirators in furtherance of the conspiracy—even if a particular defendant did not commit that crime and lacked the personal involvement required to support conviction as an accomplice. *See Pinkerton v. United States*, 328 U.S. 640 (1946). Thus, the larger the group of conspirators charged, the broader the potential criminal liability for every member. Although the MPC affirmatively rejects *Pinkerton* liability, the doctrine is followed in federal and some state courts.

E. Extended Statute of Limitations and "Reaching Back" to Cover Many Years of Activity. A conspiracy can be alleged to cover many years of a group's activity, and the prosecution can "reach back" to introduce evidence of the very earliest actions that led to the criminal conspiracy. Yet as discussed in Note 2 following *Sisselman* in Section B.3, the statute of limitations for the crime of conspiracy does not begin to run when the conspiratorial agreement is formed, but only after the conspiracy has ended. If one of the conspiracy's goals is keeping the conspiracy secret from discovery, the statute of limitations may not begin until many years after the last conspiratorial crime was committed. Thus, the evidence in a conspiracy trial, rather than focusing on a discrete criminal act, can sometimes encompass many years of conduct.

4. Sentencing and Merger. Under the common law, conspiracy was a misdemeanor. Today, the penalty varies widely among different jurisdictions, but in many states conspiracy is a felony. Many jurisdictions treat conspiracy as a less serious offense than the substantive crimes the conspirators were planning to commit, but at least one state takes the opposite view. *See* Cal. Penal Code § 182a (classifying conspiracies to commit certain misdemeanors as a felony). *See also Clune v. United States*, 159 U.S. 590 (1895) (upholding an 18-month prison sentence for conspiring to obstruct the federal mails even though the crime of obstructing the mails was punishable only by a $100 fine). Section 5.05(1) of the Model Penal Code provides that conspiracy is a crime "of the same grade and degree as the most serious offense which is . . . an object of the conspiracy," with the caveat that conspiracies to commit first-degree felonies are treated as second-degree felonies.

At common law, defendants could not be convicted of both a substantive crime and conspiring to commit that crime, just as they could not be convicted of both an attempt and the completed crime. Because the purpose of conspiracy laws was to punish inchoate criminal behavior, conspiracy liability was said to "merge" into liability for the completed crime once the unlawful object of the conspiracy was actually achieved. Today, however, most jurisdictions consider conspiracy a separate and distinct crime, whether or not the target offense has been committed. *See* Wayne R. LaFave, Criminal Law § 12.4(d) (5th ed. 2010). As the Supreme Court observed in *United States v. Jimenez Recio*, 537 U.S. 270, 274 (2003), the "agreement is a distinct evil, which may exist and be punished whether or not the substantive crime ensues."

Thus, in *Callanan v. United States*, 364 U.S. 587 (1961), the Supreme Court held that separate, and even cumulative, sentences may be imposed for conspiracy and the substantive completed crime. Justice Frankfurter's majority opinion justified this view:

> Group association for criminal purposes often, if not normally, makes possible the attainment of ends more complex than those which one criminal could accomplish. Nor is the danger of a conspiratorial group limited to the particular end toward which it has embarked. Combination in crime makes more likely the commission of crimes unrelated to the original purpose for which the group was formed. In sum, the danger which a conspiracy generates is not confined to the substantive offense which is the immediate aim of the enterprise.

Id. at 593–94.

By contrast, § 1.07(1)(b) of the Model Penal Code prohibits conviction for both a conspiracy and its target offense, and prohibits cumulative sentencing unless the conspiracy has "criminal objectives that transcend any particular offenses that have been committed in pursuance of its goals." Model Penal Code § 5.03 Comment at 390. The Federal Sentencing Guidelines are to similar effect, advising against sentencing enhancements for conspiracy convictions "unless they represent additional conduct that is not otherwise accounted for." U.S. Sentencing Commission Guidelines Manual, Ch. 3, Pt. D, Introductory Comment (2016).

[2] Actus Reus: Agreement

The following case focuses on the element of "agreement," which is essential to the crime of conspiracy. It also introduces the topic of mens rea, which is discussed in more detail in Part 3.

State v. Allan

83 A.3d 326 (Conn. 2014)

McDonald, Justice.

[W]e consider what evidence is necessary to support a conviction for conspiracy to sell narcotics in the context of a buyer-seller relationship between the alleged coconspirators. . . . In reaching its verdict, the jury reasonably could have found the following facts.

On the evening of April 15, 2009, officers of the Meriden Police Department conducted surveillance at the corner of West Main Street and Randolph Avenue in Meriden after receiving complaints of drug activity. From their unmarked vehicles, the surveillance team observed the defendant engaging in the following conduct that, in their experience, was consistent with drug dealing. The defendant walked back and forth near the corner of West Main Street and Randolph Avenue while talking on his cell phone. Police officers observed several vehicles periodically stop at this corner, at which point the defendant approached these vehicles, reached inside, and conducted "some sort of transaction" with the vehicles' occupants. Then, while the vehicles idled at this corner, the defendant walked a short distance away to a house located at 20 Maple Branch. That house was the subject of a separate police investigation due to neighbors' complaints about drug dealing occurring on its second floor. From the complaints and subsequent surveillance, the police suspected that this residence served as a "stash house," as drug dealers commonly keep their drugs and money at a location near to where they conduct their drug transactions so as to avoid having any evidence of drug activity on their person in the event of a police stop. Shortly after entering the second floor of the house, the defendant exited the house and returned to the particular vehicle waiting at the street corner. Moments later, the driver of the vehicle would drive away, while the defendant remained at the corner.

During one of these interactions, the officers observed the defendant walk away from a van with money in his hand, which they did not see him possess when he initially approached it. In light of this additional information, once the van departed, the surveillance officers radioed officers in a police cruiser. Upon stopping the van, the driver, Humberto Zarabozo, cooperated with the police and told them that he had just purchased crack cocaine from the defendant and that he had purchased narcotics from the defendant in the past. The officers recovered crack cocaine from the floor of Zarabozo's van. Subsequently, the officers returned to the surveillance area, where they continued to observe the defendant engaging in similar conduct with approaching vehicles . . . .

Soon thereafter, the officers observed the following incident. A tan Acura drove along West Main Street past the corner where the defendant had been meeting vehicles, [and] turned onto Maple Branch. As the Acura drove toward this location, the defendant crossed West Main Street and walked up Maple Street while talking on his cell phone. The Acura turned around and parked in close proximity to 20 Maple Branch, facing Maple Street. As the defendant approached Maple Branch, the driver of the Acura flashed the car's front lights and then turned off the driving lights while leaving the parking lights on. In response to these signals, the defendant approached the passenger side of the vehicle. He then opened the passenger door and leaned into the vehicle. Moments later, the defendant emerged from the Acura and returned to his corner as the Acura drove away. Following their unsuccessful pursuit of the Acura, the officers returned one to two hours after this incident to arrest the defendant.

The officers took the defendant into custody . . . and conducted a search of his person, which yielded no drug related materials. When the officers asked the defendant about the driver of the Acura, he informed them that the driver's name was "Fleet" and that Fleet was a drug supplier from Waterbury. The officers knew the name Fleet as a street level drug supplier, but did not know his real name. The defendant further told them that Fleet had driven to Maple Branch to "resupply" him with crack cocaine. . . . [Later,] the police learned that Fleet's actual name is Kareem Thomas. . . .

Thereafter, while the defendant was being processed at the police station, he asked the booking officer what had happened to "the big fat white guy," . . . "the one that I sold drugs to," presumably referring to Zarabozo . . . . One or two weeks after the defendant's arrest, the police executed a search warrant for the second floor apartment at 20 Maple Branch, where they seized crack cocaine packaged for street sale . . . .

The state charged the defendant with sale of narcotics by a person who is not drug-dependent . . . , possession of narcotics . . . , [and] conspiracy to sell narcotics . . . . The jury returned a verdict finding the defendant guilty of conspiracy to sell narcotics . . . and finding him not guilty of the other charges. The court . . . sentenced the defendant to . . . twelve years [of] imprisonment followed by five years [of] special parole.

. . . On appeal, the defendant urges us to adopt the buyer-seller exception that has been uniformly recognized by the federal courts, as well as several state courts, as part of our conspiracy jurisprudence. In doing so, the defendant asserts that, without this exception, every drug sale or attempted drug sale in Connecticut could be prosecuted as a conspiracy. He further argues that such a result would frustrate the legislative intent of our narcotics laws, in which there are more severe sanctions for the sale or distribution of narcotics than for mere possession or attempted possession. . . . Moreover, the defendant claims that application of this exception to the present case would reveal that there is insufficient evidence to find a conspiracy to sell narcotics because the evidence establishes no more than his attempt to purchase narcotics from Thomas on a single occasion.

. . . .

Conspiracy is the unlawful act of agreeing to commit a crime. . . . [T]he state must prove that there was an agreement between two or more persons to engage in conduct constituting a crime and that the agreement was followed by an overt act in furtherance of the conspiracy. "Conspiracy is a specific intent crime, with the intent divided into two elements: (a) the intent to agree or conspire and (b) the intent to commit the offense which is the object of the conspiracy. Thus, proof of a conspiracy to commit a specific offense requires proof that the conspirators intended to bring about the elements of the conspired offense." Accordingly, when the charged object of the conspiracy is to sell or distribute narcotics, the state is required to prove two distinct elements of intent: (a) that the conspirators intended to agree and (b) that they intended for narcotics to be sold to another person. "The existence of a formal agreement between the parties need not be proved; it is sufficient to show that they are knowingly engaged in a mutual plan to do a forbidden act. . . . Consequently, it is not necessary to establish that the defendant and his coconspirators signed papers, shook hands, or uttered the words we have an agreement. . . . [T]he requisite agreement or confederation may be inferred from proof of the separate acts of the individuals accused as coconspirators and from the circumstances surrounding the commission of these acts."

. . . [F]ederal conspiracy law generally reflects the same fundamental requirements . . . . Like Connecticut law, under federal law, "[a] drug-distribution conspiracy . . . requires proof that the defendant knowingly agreed—either implicitly or explicitly—with someone else to distribute drugs." . . . The Circuit Courts of Appeals uniformly acknowledge that evidence of a mere buyer-seller relationship, without more, does not constitute a conspiracy to distribute drugs.

Two lines of reasoning have emerged for this conclusion. One group of federal Circuit Courts of Appeals have reasoned that, in a buyer-seller relationship, there is no singularity of purpose and thus no meeting of the minds. "Mere proof of a buyer-seller agreement without any prior or contemporaneous understanding does not support a conspiracy conviction because there is no common illegal purpose: In such circumstances, the buyer's purpose is to buy; the seller's purpose is to sell." *United States v. Donnell*, 596 F.3d 913, 924–25 (8th Cir. 2010); *see United States v. Brown*, 726 F.3d 993, 1001 (7th Cir. 2013) ("People in a buyer-seller relationship have not agreed to advance further distribution of drugs; people in conspiracies have. That agreement is the key."). Accordingly, a mere buyer-seller relationship lacks an essential element necessary to form a conspiracy. Another group of federal Circuit Courts of Appeals have reasoned that, under the common-law definition of conspiracy, "when a buyer purchases illegal drugs from a seller, two persons have agreed to a concerted effort to achieve the unlawful transfer of the drugs from the seller to the buyer. [This] would constitute a conspiracy with the alleged objective of a transfer of drugs." Nonetheless, these courts further reason that Congress did not intend to subject buyers, particularly addicts, who purchase drugs for personal use, to the severe liabilities intended for distributors. Accordingly, this latter group has deemed a mere buyer-seller relationship to fall within a "narrow exception to the general conspiracy rule for such transactions."

. . . [W]e view the first group's characterization to be the correct view of the law. . . . [It] stems from two tenets of common-law conspiracy. First, mere association with a member of a conspiracy or acquiescence in the object or purpose of a conspiracy is not sufficient to satisfy the intent elements of conspiracy. Second, conspiracy is a separate and distinct offense from the underlying crime that is the object of the agreement. Accordingly, in the context of a drug sale between two alleged coconspirators, . . . there must be evidence of an agreement to distribute drugs and . . . such an agreement must be in addition to the purchase and sale between the two parties. Liability will arise as a coconspirator, therefore, when "[the buyer and seller] shared a conspiratorial purpose to advance other transfers, whether by the seller or by the buyer."

By contrast, when the government's proof shows no more than a simple sales transaction between alleged coconspirators, its case for conspiracy will fail.

. . . .

. . . In light of this conclusion, we now turn to the question of whether there was sufficient evidence in the present case to support the defendant's conviction of conspiracy to sell narcotics. The defendant argues that the evidence, specifically his statements made to the police, was sufficient to sustain only a conviction of attempted possession of narcotics. We disagree.

. . . [W]e recognize that, due to the clandestine nature of conspiracies, a conviction is usually based on circumstantial evidence. . . . In deliberating [on] the conspiracy charge, the jury was allowed to infer the existence of the requisite agreement between the defendant and Thomas not just from the defendant's statements to the police, but also from proof of the separate acts of each of them and from the circumstances surrounding the commission of these acts. We conclude that the totality of this evidence was sufficient to allow the jury to conclude that the defendant and Thomas conspired to sell narcotics.

There was ample evidence to support the conclusion that the defendant was in the business of selling drugs. . . .

The evidence also supports the conclusion that Thomas, known to the Meriden police as a street level dealer operating under the name Fleet, intended to agree with the defendant to assist him in this enterprise. *See Salinas v. United States*, 522 U.S. 52, 65 (1997) ("[o]ne can be a conspirator by agreeing to facilitate only some of the acts leading to the substantive offense"). The defendant's characterizations of Thomas as a drug dealer from Waterbury and his statement that Thomas' purpose in meeting with him was to "resupply" him with crack cocaine reasonably connotes not only a past relationship but also the procurement of drugs for a purpose and in a quantity consistent with resale versus personal use. Other evidence reflects an established relationship of mutual trust. . . . This evidence in its totality takes the relationship between the defendant and Thomas out of a mere buyer-seller relationship and into a conspiratorial relationship, where both parties agreed and intended to sell narcotics. . . .

Finally, to the extent that the defendant emphasizes that the jury acquitted him of the charges of sale and possession of narcotics, that fact has no bearing on our examination of the sufficiency of the evidence regarding the conspiracy charge. *See State v. Stevens*, 425 A.2d 104 (1979) ("Consistency in the verdict is not necessary. Each count in an indictment is regarded as if it was a separate indictment."); [*accord, United States v. Powell*, 469 U.S. 57 (1984)]. Construing the evidence in the light most favorable to sustaining the verdict, we hold that the evidence was sufficient to support a finding beyond a reasonable doubt that the defendant had conspired with Thomas to sell narcotics . . . .

Notes and Questions

1. **The Jury's Verdict in *Allan*.** Before turning to the definition of *agreement*, which is at the core of the *Allan* opinion, note that the jury acquitted Allan of selling and possessing narcotics. How could the jury find him guilty of conspiracy but not the substantive offenses? Is this an example of what are called inconsistent jury verdicts or compromise verdicts? Perhaps the jurors were in some disagreement and were able to agree to convict Allan on only one charge. The state supreme court speculates that the jury might have been influenced by the discrepancies between Zarabozo's trial testimony and his statements to the police concerning the location where he bought drugs from Allan, but ultimately concludes that "[i]t is unclear whether these inconsistencies, or some other factors, influenced the jury in finding the defendant not guilty of the sale of narcotics." *Allan*, 83 A.3d at 330 n.2.

2. **Proving the Existence of an Agreement.** The "act" that each defendant needs to commit in order to be guilty of the crime of conspiracy is the act of agreement. Although most jurisdictions also require proof that one conspirator committed an overt act in furtherance of the conspiracy (not a particularly onerous requirement, as explained in Part 4 below), agreement among the conspirators remains the essence of the crime.

The evidence of agreement necessary to support a criminal conspiracy conviction is less rigid than the formal "meeting of the minds" necessary to enter into a contract. *See* Wayne R. LaFave, Criminal Law § 12.2(a) (5th ed. 2010). No formal agreement, oral or written, is necessary for conspiracy. As the *Allan* court put it, prosecutors do not need evidence that the conspirators "signed papers, shook hands, or uttered the words we have an agreement." As that same court explained 74 years earlier:

> It is enough that there is a "mutual purpose" to do the forbidden act; . . . that there is a "concurrence of sentiment and cooperative conduct in an unlawful and criminal enterprise." . . . "It is sufficient if there be concert of action, all the parties working together understandingly, with a single design for the accomplishment of a common purpose."

State v. Kemp, 9 A.2d 63, 72 (Conn. 1939). Thus, a conspiracy can be formed by a tacit agreement, with the conspirators never formalizing or even expressly communicating its terms.

In addition, the conspiratorial agreement may be proved by circumstantial, rather than direct, evidence. For example, in *Duffy v. State*, 416 S.E.2d 734, 735 (Ga. 1992), Duffy and two others "each pursued the victim over a fence and, acting together, beat the victim to death." The court found the evidence sufficient to establish the existence of a conspiracy, noting that the defendants' "concerted actions" gave "rise to an inference of a tacit agreement to act in harmony to complete an aggravated assault."

In cases involving such circumstantial evidence, the jury might determine that the defendants were acting independently and that their parallel conduct was simply a matter of coincidence. But the jurors are also entitled to infer that the defendants' parallel conduct was the result of a conspiracy. As one federal court explained in affirming a conspiracy conviction based on evidence of "numerous unrelated and separate violations" of the law committed by police officers in "a police department honeycombed with graft":

> Th[e] evidence [of the officers' parallel conduct] . . . may be likened to the web of the spider. No single strand, or even several strands, would be sufficient. Yet when all these strands are considered together, and their interrelations and connections are considered, they form, we think, a complete web, which was more than sufficient to take to the jury the question of a general conspiracy among the [officers]. . . . [T]he jury might well have found (as we think they did find) that all those acts just could not have happened save on the theory of a consistent pattern of agreement between [the defendants].

Williams v. United States, 218 F.2d 276, 278–79 (4th Cir. 1954).

As the *Allan* court also notes, however, "mere association with a member of a conspiracy . . . is not sufficient." A fact-specific analysis of the evidence, and the reasonable inferences that can be drawn from the evidence, will always be necessary. *See, e.g., Mattingly v. State*, 145 N.E.2d 650, 655–56 (Ind. 1957) (finding insufficient evidence that the defendant joined a conspiracy to rob a barber shop, even though there was "a relationship and association" between him and the two conspirators; as the three of them were driving around, the defendant listened to the other two "talk[] about places," including the barber shop, that "they might 'break into'"; and he dropped them off about a block away from the shop).

3. The Unlawful Object of the Conspiracy. The predominant view today is that the object of a conspiracy must itself be a crime. The common law, however, did not adhere to that approach: an agreement to commit an "unlawful act," including a tort or even an immoral act, could lead to common-law conspiracy liability.

Similarly, the general federal conspiracy statute makes it a crime "either to commit any offense against . . . *or to defraud* the United States." 18 U.S.C. § 371 (emphasis added). Thus, in *United States v. Conover*, 772 F.2d 765 (11th Cir. 1985), Conover allegedly violated his company's conflict of interest policy when he arranged to buy materials for a construction project, which was financed with federal loans, from his codefendant, a friend and business associate. The prosecution did not allege that the government suffered any financial loss or that the defendants violated any federal rules or laws. Nevertheless, the court sustained the defendants' conviction on the ground that there had been fraud: violation of the private corporation's conflict of interest policy constituted "collusive and dishonest business practices" and thus contravened the federal government's interest in "seeing that the entire project [was] administered honestly and efficiently and without corruption and waste." *Id.* at 771.

Consider also *Commonwealth v. Bessette*, 217 N.E.2d 893 (Mass. 1966), involving a state public works official who was charged with conspiring to violate the standards governing the award of state contracts. The court noted that the crime of conspiracy includes "situations where the purpose of a group plan or the proposed means of accomplishing that plan, even if not criminal, involve 'an evil intent to oppress or injure the public' (or, perhaps, third persons) by activity, which is 'illegal, void and against public policy.'" *Id.* at 897. The court emphasized, however, that this type of noncriminal conspiracy charge should be "limited to . . . a narrow range of situations" and dismissed the indictment in that case because it did not allege that the improper contracts were "particularly dangerous to the public interest." *Id.* at 897, 899.

Are conspiracy statutes too broad if they are written or interpreted to criminalize agreements to violate noncriminal statutes or even private corporate policies? Indeed, some conspiracy statutes contain even broader language, such as Cal. Penal Code § 182(a)(5), which criminalizes conspiracies to commit "any act injurious to the public health, to public morals, or to pervert or obstruct justice, or the due administration of the laws." Interpreting a similar provision, however, the U.S. Supreme Court called into question the constitutionality of conspiracy statutes that seem to cover "an agreement to do almost any act which a judge and jury might find at the moment contrary to his or its notion of what was good for health, morals, trade, commerce, justice or order." *Musser v. Utah*, 333 U.S. 95 (1948). On remand, the Utah Supreme Court found the provision unconstitutionally vague. *See State v. Musser*, 223 P.2d 193 (Utah 1950). Justice Tobriner later relied on *Musser* to limit the reach of the California statute, holding (in a notorious conspiracy case charging an attorney who helped publish a book written by a death row inmate that was smuggled out of San Quentin) that the objective of the conspiratorial agreement must at least violate some statute. *See Davis v. Superior Court*, 345 P.2d 513, 517–19 (Cal.1959).

4. The Parties to the Agreement: Unilateral or Bilateral Conspiracies? Just as it "takes two to tango," at least two people are necessary for a conspiracy. And because an actual "agreement" is required, some jurisdictions hold that a defendant who purports to enter into an agreement to commit a criminal act cannot be convicted if the other person turns out to be an undercover police officer who was merely pretending to go along with the scheme. This is known as the "bilateral conspiracy" requirement.

In *Delaney v. State*, 51 S.W.2d 485, 486 (Tenn. 1932), for example, Delaney approached Donovan and offered to pay him to kill someone "against whom Delaney [had] a grudge or grievance on account of several matters." Donovan agreed, but then revealed the plan to the police. At Delaney's trial for conspiracy to commit murder, Donovan testified that although he had told Delaney he would go along with the plot, "such a crime was foreign to his nature and disposition, and . . . he at no time intended to commit the murder." *Id.* The court reversed Delaney's conviction, concluding that there was no conspiracy: "The essence of the offense . . . is a combination of two or more persons, and it would be a contradiction of the very terms of the statutory definition to hold that one person alone may commit the offense. The guilty participation of more than one is obviously necessary." *Id.* (This common-law rule also explains the doctrine, which has now been abandoned, that a husband and wife could not form a conspiracy because marriage united the couple into one person in the eyes of the law. *See* Wayne R. LaFave, Criminal Law § 12.4(c)(2) (5th ed. 2010).)

By contrast, the Model Penal Code and many modern criminal codes reject the traditional "bilateral" rule, in favor of a "unilateral" approach to the conspiratorial relationship that would have convicted Delaney even though the person he believed he was "conspiring" with turned out to be misrepresenting his interest in the scheme. MPC § 5.03(1)(a), for example, provides that "[a] person" can be charged with conspiracy if he or she "agrees" with another person to effectuate a crime. The Comments explain:

> Attention is directed . . . to each individual's culpability by framing the definition in terms of the conduct that suffices to establish the liability of any given actor. . . . [Thus,] the culpable party's guilt would not be affected by the fact that the other party's agreement was feigned. He has conspired, within the meaning of the definition, in the belief that the other party was with him; . . . his culpability is not decreased by the other's secret intention.

Model Penal Code § 5.03 Comment at 398, 400.

The Model Penal Code's unilateral approach views conspiracy as an inchoate crime, treating it primarily as a form of attempt and punishing even a single person's attempt to commit a crime by forming an illegal combination. By contrast, the common law's bilateral approach treats conspiracy as dangerous primarily because it represents the effort of a group to commit crime, and punishes only the formation of an actual illegal combination.

5. Wharton's Rule. Some crimes cannot be committed by one person acting alone — for example, dueling, adultery, incest, gambling, or giving or receiving bribes. If the usual conspiracy rules applied to such crimes, their commission would always, and inevitably, give rise to conspiracy liability as well, thus creating two crimes from a single event. To avoid this presumed anomaly, the common law developed "Wharton's rule," named for the commentator who first explained it. In *Gebardi v. United States*, 287 U.S. 112, 122 (1932), the U.S. Supreme Court described the rule as follows:

> [W]here it is impossible under any circumstances to commit the substantive offense without co-operative action, the preliminary agreement between the same parties to commit the offense is not an indictable conspiracy.

Note an odd exception, however: if a third person enters the picture and agrees to assist in the commission of a two-person crime, then all three may be convicted of conspiracy because *three* persons are not required to commit the object crime. *See* Wayne R. LaFave, Criminal Law 695 (5th ed. 2010). Other narrowing interpretations have also been applied to Wharton's rule in order to limit its reach. *See id.* Four decades after *Gebardi*, the U.S. Supreme Court described the Wharton prohibition not as a "Rule" but as merely a "judicial presumption"—one that can be overridden by a clear legislative intention to criminalize agreements to commit two-person crimes. *Iannelli v. United States*, 420 U.S. 770, 782 (1975). *See also People v. Johnson*, 303 P.3d 379, 390 (Cal. 2013) (relying on *Iannelli* in finding "no justification for applying the presumption of Wharton's Rule" to a conspiracy to participate in a criminal street gang). Nevertheless, some jurisdictions continue to apply the rule as a way of avoiding harsh criminal consequences in some cases.

The drafters of the Model Penal Code believed that the Wharton rule misses the point:

> [T]he rationale [for the rule] that conspiracy "assumes . . . a crime of such a nature that it is aggravated by a plurality of agents" completely overlooks the functions of conspiracy as an inchoate crime. That an offense inevitably requires concert is no reason to immunize criminal preparation to commit it. Further, the rule operates to immunize from a conspiracy prosecution *both* parties to *any* offense that inevitably requires concert, thus disregarding the legislative judgment that at least one should be punishable and taking no account of the varying policies that ought to determine whether the other should be. The rule is supportable only insofar as it avoids cumulative punishment for conspiracy and the completed substantive crime, for it is clear that the legislature would have taken the factor of concert into account in grading a crime which inevitably requires concert.

Model Penal Code § 5.04 Comment at 482–83. The Comments go on to note that because the MPC prohibits cumulative sentencing for conspiracy and the substantive crime (*see* Note 4 in Part 1 above), the only sensible rationale for the rule disappears. *See id.* at 483.

Although the MPC therefore rejects the Wharton rule, it provides in § 5.04(2) that conspiracy charges may not be brought against those who could not be convicted as accomplices to the target offense under § 2.06(6) because their conduct was "inevitably incident" to commission of the crime. (Section 2.06(6) is discussed in Chapter 12, Section A, Note 3.) How does § 5.04(2) differ from the Wharton rule? How would § 5.04(2) have affected the outcome in *Allan*?

6. *Ocasio*: An Interesting Twist. The U.S. Supreme Court recently confronted an interesting twist on the foregoing rules in a case that charged conspiracy to violate the Hobbs Act, a federal statute that prohibits obtaining "property from another" under color of official right. Ocasio, a police officer, was charged with conspiring with the owners of an auto body repair shop to "steer" unsuspecting persons involved in car crashes to the body shop, in return for a kickback. Ocasio argued that because it was the body shop owners' own money that he was receiving, they could not have conspired with him to obtain the property "of another." The Court, however, affirmed Ocasio's conviction. The Court cited the "age-old" principle that "a conspirator need not agree to commit every part of the substantive offense" so long as all the conspirators share "the intent that the underlying crime be committed," and explained that Ocasio and the body shop owners had shared the same "objective" of violating the Hobbs Act—that is, that Ocasio would obtain money from the body shop owners under color of his official right. Additionally, the Court quoted *Gebardi*'s point that a defendant "may be convicted of conspiring to commit a substantive offense that he or she cannot personally commit" in reasoning that the body shop owners were properly included as Ocasio's co-conspirators.

[3] The Requisite Mens Rea — "Purpose" or "Knowledge"?

The following case illustrates the persistent difficulties that arise in trying to pin down the mental state needed to convict defendants of inchoate crimes. These issues have already been discussed in the context of attempt in Chapter 11, Section A.2, and accomplice liability in Chapter 12, Section C.

People v. Lauria
59 Cal. Rptr. 628 (Cal. Ct. App. 1967)

FLEMING, JUSTICE.

In an investigation of call-girl activity the police focused their attention on three prostitutes actively plying their trade on call, each of whom was using Lauria's telephone answering service, presumably for business purposes.

On January 8, 1965, Stella Weeks, a policewoman, signed up for telephone service with Lauria's answering service. Mrs. Weeks, in the course of her conversation with Lauria's office manager, hinted broadly that she was a prostitute concerned with the secrecy of her activities and their concealment from the police. She was assured that the operation of the service was discreet and "about as safe as you can get." It was arranged that Mrs. Weeks need not leave her address with the answering service, but could pick up her calls and pay her bills in person.

On February 11, Mrs. Weeks talked to Lauria on the telephone and told him her business was modelling and she had been referred to the answering service by Terry, one of the three prostitutes under investigation. She complained that because of the operation of the service she had lost two valuable customers, referred to as tricks. Lauria defended his service and said that her friends had probably lied to her about having left calls for her. But he did not respond to Mrs. Weeks' hints that she needed customers in order to make money, other than to invite her to his house for a personal visit in order to get better acquainted. In the course of his talk he said "his business was taking messages."

On February 15, Mrs. Weeks talked on the telephone to Lauria's office manager and again complained of two lost calls, which she described as a $50 and a $100 trick. On investigation the office manager could find nothing wrong, but she said she would alert the switchboard operators about slip-ups on calls.

On April 1, Lauria and the three prostitutes were arrested. Lauria complained to the police that this attention was undeserved, stating that Hollywood Call Board had 60 to 70 prostitutes on its board while his own service had only 9 or 10, that he kept separate records for known or suspected prostitutes for the convenience of himself and the police. When asked if his records were available to police who might come to the office to investigate call girls, Lauria replied that they were whenever the police had a specific name. However, his service didn't "arbitrarily tell the police about prostitutes on our board. As long as they pay their bills we tolerate them." In a subsequent voluntary appearance before the Grand Jury Lauria testified he had always cooperated with the police. But he admitted he knew some of his customers were prostitutes, and he knew Terry was a prostitute because he had personally used her services, and he knew she was paying for 500 calls a month.

Lauria and the three prostitutes were indicted for conspiracy to commit prostitution, and nine overt acts were specified. Subsequently the trial court set aside the indictment as having been brought without reasonable or probable cause. The People have appealed, claiming that a sufficient showing of an unlawful agreement to further prostitution was made.

To establish agreement, the People need show no more than a tacit, mutual understanding between co-conspirators to accomplish an unlawful act. Here the People attempted to establish a conspiracy by showing that Lauria, well aware that his codefendants were prostitutes who received business calls from customers through his telephone answering service, continued to furnish them with such service. This approach attempts to equate knowledge of another's criminal activity with conspiracy to further such criminal activity, and poses the question of the criminal responsibility of a furnisher of goods or services who knows his product is being used to assist the operation of an illegal business. Under what circumstances does a supplier become a part of a conspiracy to further an illegal enterprise by furnishing goods or services which he knows are to be used by the buyer for criminal purposes?

The two leading cases on this point face in opposite directions. In *United States v. Falcone*, 311 U.S. 205 [(1940)], the sellers of large quantities of sugar, yeast, and cans were absolved from participation in a moonshining conspiracy among distillers who bought from them, while in *Direct Sales Co. v. United States*, 319 U.S. 703 [(1943)], a wholesaler of drugs was convicted of conspiracy to violate the federal narcotic laws by selling drugs in quantity to a codefendant physician who was supplying them to addicts. The distinction between these two cases appears primarily based on the proposition that distributors of such dangerous products as drugs are required to exercise greater discrimination in the conduct of their business than are distributors of innocuous substances like sugar and yeast.

In the earlier case, *Falcone*, the sellers' knowledge of the illegal use of the goods was insufficient by itself to make the sellers participants in a conspiracy with the distillers who bought from them. Such knowledge fell short of proof of a conspiracy, and evidence on the volume of sales was too vague to support a jury finding that respondents knew of the conspiracy from the size of the sales alone.

In the later case of *Direct Sales*, the conviction of a drug wholesaler for conspiracy to violate federal narcotic laws was affirmed on a showing that it had actively promoted the sale of morphine sulphate in quantity and had sold codefendant physician, who practiced in a small town in South Carolina, more than 300 times his normal requirements of the drug, even though it had been repeatedly warned of the dangers of unrestricted sales of the drug. The court contrasted the restricted goods involved in *Direct Sales* with the articles of free commerce involved in *Falcone*: "All articles of commerce may be put to illegal ends," said the court. "But all do not have inherently the same susceptibility to harmful and illegal use. . . . This difference is important for two purposes. One is for making certain that the seller knows the buyer's intended illegal use. The other is to show that by the sale he intends to further, promote, and cooperate in it. This intent, when given effect by overt act, is the gist of conspiracy. While it is not identical with mere knowledge that another purposes unlawful action it is not unrelated to such knowledge. . . . The step from knowledge to intent and agreement may be taken. There is more than suspicion, more than knowledge, acquiescence, carelessness, indifference, lack of concern. There is informed and interested cooperation, stimulation, instigation. And there is also a 'stake in the venture' which, even if it may not be essential, is not irrelevant to the question of conspiracy."

While *Falcone* and *Direct Sales* may not be entirely consistent with each other in their full implications, they do provide us with a framework for the criminal liability of a supplier of lawful goods or services put to unlawful use. Both the element of *knowledge* of the illegal use of the goods or services and the element of *intent* to further that use must be present in order to make the supplier a participant in a criminal conspiracy.

Proof of *knowledge* is ordinarily a question of fact and requires no extended discussion in the present case. The knowledge of the supplier was sufficiently established when Lauria admitted he knew some of his customers were prostitutes and admitted he knew that Terry, an active subscriber to his service, was a prostitute. In the face of these admissions he could scarcely claim to have relied on the normal assumption an operator of a business or service is entitled to make, that his customers are behaving themselves in the eyes of the law. Because Lauria knew in fact that some of his customers were prostitutes, it is a legitimate inference he knew they were subscribing to his answering service for illegal business purposes . . . .

The more perplexing issue in the case is the sufficiency of proof of *intent* to further the criminal enterprise. The element of intent may be proved either by direct evidence, or by evidence of circumstances from which an intent to further a criminal enterprise by supplying lawful goods or services may be inferred. Direct evidence of participation, such as advice from the supplier of legal goods or services to the user of those goods or services on their use for illegal purposes . . . , provides the simplest case. . . .

. . . .

In examining precedents in this field we find that sometimes, but not always, the criminal intent of the supplier may be inferred from his knowledge of the unlawful use made of the product he supplies. . . .

Inflated charges, the sale of goods with no legitimate use, sales in inflated amounts, each may provide a fact of sufficient moment from which the intent of the seller to participate in the criminal enterprise may be inferred. In such instances participation by the supplier of legal goods to the illegal enterprise may be inferred because in one way or another the supplier has acquired a special interest in the operation of the illegal enterprise. His intent to participate in the crime of which he has knowledge may be inferred from the existence of his special interest. . . .

It [also] seems apparent that a supplier who furnishes equipment which he *knows* will be used to commit a serious crime may be deemed from that knowledge alone to have intended to produce the result. Such proof may justify an inference that the furnisher intended to aid the execution of the crime and that he thereby became a participant. For instance, we think the operator of a telephone answering service with positive knowledge that his service was being used to facilitate the extortion of ransom, the distribution of heroin, or the passing of counterfeit money who continued to furnish the service with knowledge of its use, might be chargeable on knowledge alone with participation in a scheme to extort money, to distribute narcotics, or to pass counterfeit money. The same result would follow the seller of gasoline who knew the buyer was using his product to make Molotov cocktails for terroristic use.

Logically, the same reasoning could be extended to crimes of every description. Yet we do not believe an inference of intent drawn from knowledge of criminal use properly applies to the less serious crimes classified as misdemeanors. . . .

With respect to misdemeanors, we conclude that positive knowledge of the supplier that his products or services are being used for criminal purposes does not, without more, establish an intent of the supplier to participate in the misdemeanors. With respect to felonies, we do not decide the converse, viz., that in all cases of felony knowledge of criminal use alone may justify an inference of the supplier's intent to participate in the crime. The implications of *Falcone* make the matter uncertain with respect to those felonies which are merely prohibited wrongs. But decision on this point is not compelled, and we leave the matter open.

. . . .

When we review Lauria's activities in the light of this analysis, we find no proof that Lauria took any direct action to further, encourage, or direct the call-girl activities of his codefendants and we find an absence of circumstances from which his special interest in their activities could be inferred. Neither excessive charges for standardized services, nor the furnishing of services without a legitimate use, nor an unusual quantity of business with call girls, are present. The offense which he is charged with furthering is a misdemeanor, a category of crime which has never been made a required subject of positive disclosure to public authority. Under these circumstances, although proof of Lauria's knowledge of the criminal activities of his patrons was sufficient to charge him with that fact, there was insufficient evidence that he intended to further their criminal activities, and hence insufficient proof of his participation in a criminal conspiracy with his codefendants to further prostitution. Since the conspiracy centered around the activities of Lauria's telephone answering service, the charges against his codefendants likewise fail for want of proof.

In absolving Lauria of complicity in a criminal conspiracy we do not wish to imply that the public authorities are without remedies to combat modern manifestations of the world's oldest profession. Licensing of telephone answering services under the police power, together with the revocation of licenses for the toleration of prostitution, is a possible civil remedy. The furnishing of telephone answering service in aid of prostitution could be made a crime. Other solutions will doubtless occur to vigilant public authorities if the problem of call-girl activity needs further suppression.

Notes and Questions

1. Purposefully Versus Knowingly Furthering the Target Offense. It is generally said that conspiracy requires a twofold mens rea: an intent to enter into an agreement, and an intent to further the agreement's unlawful objective. *See* WAYNE R. LaFAVE, CRIMINAL LAW § 12.2(c) (5th ed. 2010). Proof of the defendant's purpose to enter into the agreement is generally satisfied by the same evidence that establishes the act of agreement, as discussed in the previous Section.

In proving intent to further the target offense, however, courts and commentators have long struggled with the issue addressed in *Lauria* (the same issue discussed above in *Gladstone* in the context of accomplice liability): whether the prosecution must establish "purpose" to promote the underlying crime or whether mere knowledge that the other person will commit the crime is sufficient. The Model Penal Code and a majority of states require proof of "purpose to promote or facilitate" the commission of the target crime. Model Penal Code § 5.03(1). As the dictum in *Lauria* indicates, however, others have suggested that knowledge may be sufficient where the object of the conspiracy is a serious felony. *See* LaFAVE, *supra*, § 12.2(c)(3), at 668.

Does the majority view make sense, or should one who knowingly aids criminal activity be guilty of conspiracy as well? Consider the following examples:

(a) A vendor legally sells a weapon to an individual who the vendor knows intends to use it to assassinate a particular politician.

(b) A supplier sells a pen to someone who announces that he intends to use it to commit tax fraud.

(c) An individual gives a known robber an armored truck's delivery schedule.

Note that even if the prosecution must prove that it was the defendant's actual purpose to promote the unlawful objective of the conspiracy, *Lauria* observes that purpose may be inferred if the defendant had "a stake in the venture." Likewise, in another part of the *Allan* opinion excerpted above, the Connecticut Supreme Court listed several factors that courts "have identified . . . as relevant to th[e] inquiry" whether "the step from knowledge to intent" can be made in cases alleging drug distribution conspiracies: "sales on credit or consignment; large quantities of drugs; multiple transactions; standardized dealings; a level of mutual trust; and the continuity of the relationship between the parties." *State v. Allan*, 83 A.3d 326, 338 (Conn. 2014).

Were these two cases correctly decided? Did the Connecticut court properly find adequate evidence that Thomas "intended to agree . . . to assist [Allan] in [his drug dealing] enterprise"? Was the California court right to find insufficient evidence that Lauria had a "special interest" in the prostitutes' activities? The same question regarding purpose versus mere knowledge arises in the context of accomplice liability, which is addressed above in Chapter 12, Section C.

2. The Mens Rea Required for Result Elements of the Target Offense. When the object crime of a conspiracy requires proof of a certain result (for example, death in a conspiracy to commit murder), the purpose requirement described in the prior Note applies to the result element as well. That is, the defendants cannot be convicted of conspiracy unless it was their purpose to cause that result. Here the Model Penal Code's definition of conspiracy differs from its treatment of accomplice liability. MPC §5.03 does not contain a provision comparable to MPC §2.06(4), which governs accomplice liability and is discussed in Note 5 following *Gladstone* in Chapter 12, Section C. Similarly, the MPC's drafters were unwilling to adopt the approach taken in §5.01(1)(b) with respect to attempt, where proof of knowledge suffices as to result elements (discussed above in Chapter 11, Section A.2, Note 2). Rather, the drafters chose to require a consistently high mens rea for result elements in conspiracy cases, citing "the extremely preparatory behavior that may be involved in conspiracy." Model Penal Code §5.03 Comment at 408.

3. Traffic Lights and *Feola*: The Mens Rea Required for Attendant Circumstances. Still more difficult mens rea questions arise in conspiracy prosecutions when the crime that is the object of the conspiracy requires proof of some attendant circumstance. First, even if "purpose" is the required mens rea, the MPC defines "purpose" when applied to attendant circumstances to include "aware[ness] of the existence of such circumstances," which may be difficult to distinguish from mere "knowledge." Model Penal Code §2.02(2)(a)(ii).

Second, is even "knowledge" of attendant circumstances always required for a conspiracy conviction? For example, the federal crime of mail fraud requires proof that the mails were actually used in the commission of a fraud, but does not require that the defendant knew the mails would be used. (Showing how carefully mens rea requirements may be parsed, however, the federal courts uniformly hold that the use of the mails must have been "reasonably foreseeable," thereby imposing a negligence-type standard. *See Pereira v. United States*, 347 U.S. 1, 9 (1954).) Should the crime of conspiring to commit mail fraud require knowledge that the mails will be used, even though the result would be to insist on a higher level of mens rea for conspiracy than for the target offense?

In *United States v. Crimmins*, 123 F.2d 271 (2d Cir. 1941), Judge Learned Hand answered this question affirmatively, at least for the federal offense of conspiring to transport stolen securities *interstate*. In ruling that the government was required to prove that Crimmins knew that the securities he transported not only were stolen but also came from out of state, Judge Hand offered a now-famous analogy:

> While one may, for instance, be guilty of running past a traffic light of whose existence one is ignorant, one cannot be guilty of conspiring to run past such light, for one cannot agree to run past a light unless one supposes that there is a light to run past.

Id. at 273. But can Judge Hand's analogy be criticized as flawed, or too facile? Is the stoplight a circumstance element or part of the actus reus here? If the former, is the relevant circumstance not the existence of the light, but the fact that it is red? Additionally, traffic offenses are typically strict liability crimes. If the driver's failure to realize the light had changed is not a defense to running a red light, should a passenger who was similarly oblivious to the color of the light and was encouraging the driver to keep going and drive faster have a defense to conspiring to run a red light?

In *United States v. Feola*, 420 U.S. 671 (1975), the Supreme Court confronted a similar question: whether conspiring to assault a federal officer required proof that the defendants knew their victim was a federal officer, when the substantive crime of assaulting a federal officer did not require such knowledge. The Court described the facts of the case as follows:

> The facts reveal a classic narcotics "rip-off." . . . [T]he evidence shows that Feola and his confederates arranged for a sale of heroin to buyers who turned out to be [federal] undercover agents. . . . The group planned to palm off on the purchasers, for a substantial sum, a form of sugar in place of heroin and, should that ruse fail, simply to surprise their unwitting buyers and relieve them of the cash they had brought along for payment. The plan failed when one agent, his suspicions being aroused, drew his revolver in time to counter an assault upon another agent from the rear. Instead of enjoying the rich benefits of a successful swindle, Feola and his associates found themselves charged, to their undoubted surprise, with conspiring to assault, and with assaulting, federal officers.

Id. at 674–75. The federal statute defining the target offense the defendants had allegedly conspired to violate punishes anyone who "forcibly assaults, resists, opposes, impedes, intimidates, or interferes with [a federal officer] while engaged in or on account of the performance of his official duties." 18 U.S.C. § 111. Reasoning that the statute's purpose of protecting federal law enforcement personnel "could well be frustrated by the imposition of a strict scienter requirement," the Court concluded that the defendants could be convicted on the assault charge without proof that they knew their victims were even officers, let alone federal ones. 420 U.S. at 678.

The Court then went on to rule, contrary to *Crimmins*, that the conspiracy charge likewise did not require proof that the defendants knew the victims' official status, apparently heeding "[t]he Government's plea . . . for symmetry" between the conspiracy charge and the target offense. *Id.* at 676. The Court reasoned:

> The statute makes it unlawful simply to "conspire . . . to commit any offense against the United States." A natural reading of these words would be that since one can violate a criminal statute simply by engaging in the forbidden conduct, a conspiracy to commit the offense is nothing more than an agreement to engage in the prohibited conduct. Then where, as here, the substantive statute does not require that an assailant know the official status of his victim, there is nothing on the face of the conspiracy statute that would seem to require that those agreeing to the result have a greater degree of knowledge.

Id. at 687. The Justices then rejected Learned Hand's "seductive" traffic light analogy, calling it "effective prose . . . [but], as applied to the facts before us, bad law." *Id.* at 689–90. The Court explained:

> The *Crimmins* rule [is based on the notion] that it is improper to find conspiratorial liability where the parties to the illicit agreement were not aware of the fact giving rise to federal jurisdiction, because the essence of conspiracy is agreement and persons cannot be punished for acts beyond the scope of their agreement. This "reason" states little more than a conclusion, for it is clear that one may be guilty as a conspirator for acts the precise details of which one does not know at the time of the agreement. The question is not merely whether the official status of an assaulted victim was known to the parties at the time of their agreement, but whether the acts contemplated by the conspirators are to be deemed legally different from those actually performed solely because of the official identity of the victim. Put another way, does the identity of the proposed victim alter the legal character of the acts agreed to, or is it no more germane to the nature of those acts than the color of the victim's hair?

> Our analysis of the substantive offense . . . is sufficient to convince us that for the purpose of individual guilt or innocence, awareness of the official identity of the assault victim is irrelevant. We would expect the same to obtain with respect to the conspiracy offense unless one of the policies behind the imposition of conspiratorial liability is not served where the parties to the agreement are unaware that the intended target is a federal law enforcement official. . . .

> That individuals know that their planned joint venture violates federal as well as state law seems totally irrelevant to th[e] purpose of conspiracy law. . . . Indeed, . . . imposition of an "anti-federal" knowledge requirement . . . here would serve only to make it more difficult to obtain convictions on charges of conspiracy, a policy with no apparent purpose.

> . . . Given the level of intent needed to carry out the substantive offense, we fail to see how the agreement is any less blameworthy or constitutes less

of a danger to society solely because the participants are unaware which body of law they intend to violate. . . .

To summarize, . . . we hold that where knowledge of the facts giving rise to federal jurisdiction is not necessary for conviction of a substantive offense embodying a mens rea requirement, such knowledge is equally irrelevant to questions of responsibility for conspiracy to commit that offense.

Id. at 692–94, 696.

In effect, the *Feola* Court viewed the substantive offense as a species of "assault," with the terms "federal" and "officer" merely "jurisdictional element[s]" ("facts that serve only to establish federal jurisdiction"), for which mens rea is typically not required. *Id.* at 690 n.24, 692, 694. But while that may be true of the victims' federal status, is it also true of the fact that they were "officers"?

Is *Feola* consistent with the general rule requiring "agreement" among conspirators regarding the unlawful object? Ultimately, the Court claimed that "[t]he question posed by the traffic light analogy is not before us." *Id.* at 690. But does its preference for "symmetry" suggest that it would convict the defendants of conspiracy in Judge Hand's traffic light hypothetical without requiring evidence that they knew the light they were running was red? What if they did not know there was a stoplight at all? In considering these questions, note that the *Feola* Court relied on its then-recent decision in *United States v. Freed*, 401 U.S. 601 (1971), observing that *Freed* had likewise "declined to require a greater degree of intent for conspiratorial responsibility than for responsibility for the underlying substantive offense" of possessing unregistered hand grenades. *Feola*, 420 U.S. at 688. (Recall that *Freed*, discussed in Chapter 5, Section A, held that knowledge of a hand grenade's unregistered status is not required.)

The Model Penal Code expressly declines to make a recommendation as to what mens rea ought to be required for attendant circumstances in conspiracy cases, saying that the issue is "best left to judicial resolution as cases that present the question may arise." Model Penal Code § 5.03 Comment at 413. For discussion of the mens rea required for attendant circumstances in accomplice liability cases, see Note 6 following *Gladstone* in Chapter 12, Section C.

4. **The "Corrupt Motive" Requirement.** In some jurisdictions, the crime of conspiracy requires proof that the conspirators knew that the agreed-upon conduct was unlawful. (Recall the discussion of the "unlawful object" requirement above in Part 2, Note 3.) This doctrine was first enunciated in *People v. Powell*, 63 N.Y. 88 (1875), a case in which county welfare officials were charged with conspiring to award contracts for the purchase of goods without first advertising for contract bids. The evidence showed that the defendants were unaware of a statute that prohibited them from buying goods without first soliciting bids. In upholding the reversal of their convictions, the court wrote:

> [T]o make an agreement between two or more persons, to do an act inno-
> cent in itself, a criminal conspiracy, it is not enough that it appears that the
> act which was the object of the agreement was prohibited. The confedera-
> tion must be corrupt. The agreement must have been entered into with an
> evil purpose, as distinguished from a purpose simply to do the act prohib-
> ited in ignorance of the prohibition. This is implied in the meaning of the
> word conspiracy. Mere concert is not conspiracy. Persons who agree to do
> an act innocent in itself, in good faith and without the use of criminal means,
> are not converted into conspirators, because it turns out that the contem-
> plated act was prohibited by statute.

Id. at 91–92.

The *Powell* doctrine thus distinguishes conspiracy from most other crimes, in
essence carving out an exception to the general rule that ignorance of the law is no
excuse. Is this additional mens rea requirement appropriate for conspiracy prosecutions? Is an "evil purpose" inherent in the meaning of the term "conspiracy"? If so,
what exactly is the state of mind required by *Powell*? Must the conspirators actually
know that the objective of their agreement is illegal, or does a general understanding that it is "bad" or "corrupt" suffice?

Because of the difficulties raised by these questions, the Model Penal Code abandons any "corrupt motive" requirement:

> The *Powell* rule, and many of the decisions that rely on it, may be viewed as
> a judicial endeavor to import fair mens rea requirements into statutes cre-
> ating regulatory offenses that do not rest on traditional concepts of personal
> fault and culpability. . . . There is no good reason why the fortuity of con-
> cert should be used as a device for limiting criminality in this area. . . . The
> melodramatic and sinister view of conspiracy on which the *Powell* decision
> seems to rest is largely discredited today. [The] uncertain "corrupt motive"
> requirement . . . has little resolving power in particular cases and serves
> mainly to divert attention from clear analysis of the mens rea requirements
> of conspiracy.

Model Penal Code § 5.03 Comment at 417–18.

Most state statutes have followed the Model Penal Code in rejecting the *Powell*
approach. *See* Peter Buscemi, Note, *Conspiracy: Statutory Reform Since the Model
Penal Code*, 75 Colum. L. Rev. 1122, 1131 n.48 (1975). Nonetheless, some state court
opinions proclaim adherence to the "corrupt motive" doctrine, at least in part. In
People v. Marsh, 376 P.2d 300 (Cal. 1962), for example, the California Supreme
Court held that conspiracy requires proof of "a specific intent to violate the law,"
and therefore concluded that the defendants could not be convicted of conspiring
to practice medicine without a license unless they knew a license was necessary.
See also Commonwealth v. Kelley, 268 N.E.2d 132, 139–40 (Mass. 1971) (requiring
proof of a corrupt motive for conspiracies to commit unlawful acts that are not a
crime).

[4] Overt Acts

1. Requiring an Overt Act. At common law, conspiracy did not require proof of an overt act; the crime was therefore complete once the defendants entered into the agreement. *See* Wayne R. LaFave, Criminal Law § 12.2(b) (5th ed. 2010); *Bannon v. United States,* 156 U.S. 464, 468 (1895) ("At common law it was neither necessary to aver nor prove an overt act in furtherance of the conspiracy."). A number of states still follow the common-law approach. *E.g.,* Miss. Code Ann. § 97-1-1. Although § 5.03(5) of the Model Penal Code imposes an overt act requirement, it expressly exempts the most serious conspiracies (conspiracies to commit first- and second-degree felonies) from the requirement.

Many modern conspiracy statutes have likewise departed from the common-law view and require an overt act. For example, the general federal conspiracy statute, 18 U.S.C. § 371, expressly includes an overt act requirement. Nevertheless, a number of other federal conspiracy statutes contain no such language, and the Supreme Court has declined to read an overt act requirement into such statutes. Thus, for example, in *United States v. Shabani,* 513 U.S. 10 (1994), the Supreme Court held that proof of an overt act is not required for convictions under the federal drug distribution conspiracy statute, 21 U.S.C. § 846. Noting that Congress should be presumed to be aware of the common law, the Court ruled that, absent some contrary indication, it would assume that the omission of an overt act requirement from the statute was deliberate and reflected Congress' intent to adopt the common-law approach. *Accord, Whitfield v. United States,* 543 U.S. 209 (2005) (holding that proof of an overt act is not required under 18 U.S.C. § 1956(h) for conspiracies to commit money laundering).

Does requiring an overt act in conspiracy cases serve a useful function? The question is particularly apt given that the requirement is generally quite easy to fulfill (as explained in the following Note). If the gravamen of the crime of conspiracy is the agreement to achieve an unlawful objective, what purpose is served by demanding an additional overt act? Courts have identified at least two functions performed by the requirement. One is "to provide a *locus poenitentiae*—an opportunity for the conspirators to reconsider, terminate the agreement, and thereby avoid punishment for the conspiracy." *People v. Zamora,* 557 P.2d 75, 82 (Cal. 1976). The other is to verify that a true conspiracy actually exists, that is, to corroborate "the operation of the conspiracy." *United States v. Medina,* 761 F.2d 12, 15 (1st Cir. 1985).

2. The Nature of the Overt Act Requirement. In jurisdictions that have departed from the common-law approach, at least one—but only one—of the conspirators must have committed an overt act in furtherance of the agreement before anyone in the group may be convicted of conspiracy. *See* Wayne R. LaFave, Criminal Law § 12.2(b), at 663–64 (5th ed. 2010). That is, only a single overt act need be performed by a single conspirator for criminal liability to be extended to all co-conspirators. *See, e.g., United States v. Robinson,* 503 F.2d 208, 213 (7th Cir. 1974).

Moreover, in most jurisdictions, the overt act need not be an "act beyond mere preparation" (as opposed to the more "substantial step" necessary to support an attempt charge). Indeed, the overt act need not be a criminal, or even a "bad" act, but rather can be *any* act committed by any *one* of the conspirators, so long as it furthers the conspiracy even slightly. As Justice Holmes once observed, "if an overt act is required, it does not matter how remote the act may be from accomplishing the purpose, if done to effect it; that is, I suppose, in furtherance of it in any degree." *Hyde & Schneider v. United States*, 225 U.S. 347, 388 (1912) (dissenting opinion). As a result, the overt act requirement is seldom, if ever, a bar to a meaningful criminal conspiracy prosecution.

Thus, for example, in *Yates v. United States*, 354 U.S. 298 (1957), 14 defendants were convicted under 18 U.S.C. § 371 for allegedly "conspiring (1) to advocate and teach the duty and necessity of overthrowing the Government of the United States by force and violence, and (2) to organize, as the Communist Party of the United States, a society of persons who so advocate and teach, all with the intent of causing the overthrow of the Government by force and violence as speedily as circumstances would permit." The Court found reasons to overturn the convictions of each defendant — a result that perhaps exposes the controversial character of the time, when McCarthyism and the prosecution of individuals for proclaiming belief in a Communist ideology were coming under special scrutiny. *See generally* ELLEN SCHRECKER, MANY ARE THE CRIMES: MCCARTHYISM IN AMERICA (1998). Nevertheless, the *Yates* Court affirmed that the government's allegations were sufficient to meet the overt act requirement:

> . . . [Two] of the 11 overt acts alleged in the indictment . . . were proved. Each was a public meeting held under [Communist] Party auspices at which speeches were made by one or more of the petitioners extolling leaders of the Soviet Union and criticizing various aspects of the foreign policy of the United States. At one of the meetings an appeal for funds was made. Petitioners contend that these meetings do not satisfy the requirement of the statute that there be shown an act done by one of the conspirators "to effect the object of the conspiracy." The Government concedes that nothing unlawful was shown to have been said or done at these meetings, but contends that these occurrences nonetheless sufficed as overt acts under the jury's findings.

> We think the Government's position is correct. It is not necessary that an overt act be the substantive crime charged in the indictment as the object of the conspiracy. Nor, indeed, need such an act, taken by itself, even be criminal in character. The function of the overt act in a conspiracy prosecution is simply to manifest "that the conspiracy is at work," and is neither a project still resting solely in the minds of the conspirators nor a fully completed operation no longer in existence.

354 U.S. at 333–34.

The following cases further illustrate how insubstantial the overt act requirement can be. In *Singer v. United States*, 208 F.2d 477, 480 (6th Cir. 1953), telephoning a prospective buyer of sheet metal was considered a sufficient overt act for the crime of conspiring to possess sheet metal stolen in interstate commerce. Similarly, in *State v. Knight*, 479 N.W.2d 792, 794 (Neb. 1992), the defendant discussed "offing" his former lover's husband in three telephone conversations with an informant, and each conversation was deemed to satisfy the overt act requirement for a murder conspiracy. *See also United States v. Donner*, 497 F.2d 184, 192 (7th Cir. 1974) (a press conference held by the defendants during which they spoke of trashing a draft office was a sufficient overt act to support a conspiracy to damage government property).

In fact, even an omission can qualify as an overt act. Thus, in *Gerson v. United States*, 25 F.2d 49 (10th Cir. 1928), the defendants were charged with conspiring to commit the crime of fraudulently concealing property from a bankruptcy trustee. The court affirmed their convictions, and rejected their argument that the "passive act" of omitting property from a schedule of assets did not constitute an overt act. The court explained that "a continuous and intended concealment from the trustee of property belonging to the estate in bankruptcy, even though the actual concealment of the property took place before the appointment of the trustee, is sufficient as an overt act." *Id.* at 55.

3. Exceptions to the Minimalist Overt Act Approach. A few states require that the overt act be a more "substantial one," although it usually need not be as substantial as necessary to support a conviction for attempt. WAYNE R. LAFAVE, CRIMINAL LAW § 12.2(b), at 663 (5th ed. 2010). Some jurisdictions, for example, use an approach similar to Ohio's, requiring "[an act] of a character that manifests a purpose on the part of the actor that the object of the conspiracy should be completed." Ohio Rev. Code Ann. § 2923.01(B).

The Maine statute goes even further, imposing an overt act requirement that resembles the actus reus needed for the crime of attempt:

> A person may not be convicted of criminal conspiracy unless it is alleged and proved that the actor, or one with whom the actor conspired, took a substantial step toward commission of the crime. A substantial step is any conduct which, under the circumstances in which it occurs, is strongly corroborative of the firmness of the actor's intent to complete commission of the crime; provided that speech alone may not constitute a substantial step.

Me. Rev. Stat. Ann. tit. 17-A, § 151(4); *cf. id.* § 152(1) (using similar language to define attempt). (For discussion of attempt's actus reus requirement, see Chapter 11, Section A.2.)

[B] The Scope of Conspiracy Liability

[1] The *Pinkerton* Doctrine

The doctrine endorsed by the Supreme Court in the following case is a powerful engine of criminal prosecution, particularly in organized crime settings. It is also an extension of traditional criminal law principles that can lead to liability for crimes a defendant did not personally commit and may not have consciously anticipated. While critics of the Supreme Court's opinion abound, Professor (and former Acting U.S. Solicitor General) Neal Katyal has cautioned that "the benefits of *Pinkerton*" should not be ignored. Neal Kumar Katyal, *Conspiracy Theory*, 112 YALE L.J. 1307, 1372 (2003). As you read what follows, ask yourself whether the doctrine makes sense, or whether it unfairly extends criminal liability too far.

Pinkerton v. United States

328 U.S. 640 (1946)

MR. JUSTICE DOUGLAS delivered the opinion of the Court.

Walter and Daniel Pinkerton are brothers who live a short distance from each other on Daniel's farm. They were indicted for violations of the Internal Revenue Code [in connection with the unlawful possession, transportation, and sale of whiskey]. The indictment contained [various] substantive counts and one conspiracy count. . . . [The evidence showed that Walter committed the substantive crimes and that Daniel was in jail, serving a sentence for other crimes, when at least some of those substantive offenses were committed. Following their conviction, Walter was fined $500 and sentenced to 30 months in prison on the substantive counts; he received a two-year concurrent prison sentence for conspiracy. Daniel was fined $1,000 and sentenced to 30 months on the substantive counts; on the conspiracy count, he was sentenced to a two-year concurrent prison term and a $500 fine.] . . .

It is contended that there was insufficient evidence to implicate Daniel in the conspiracy. But we think there was enough evidence for submission of the issue to the jury.

There is, however, no evidence to show that Daniel participated directly in the commission of the substantive offenses on which his conviction has been sustained, although there was evidence to show that these substantive offenses were in fact committed by Walter in furtherance of the unlawful agreement or conspiracy existing between the brothers. The question was submitted to the jury on the theory that each petitioner could be found guilty of the substantive offenses, if it was found at the time those offenses were committed petitioners were parties to an unlawful conspiracy and the substantive offenses charged were in fact committed in furtherance of it.

Daniel relies on *United States v. Sall*, [116 F.2d 745 (3d Cir. 1940)]. That case held that participation in the conspiracy was not itself enough to sustain a conviction for the substantive offense even though it was committed in furtherance of the conspiracy. The court held that, in addition to evidence that the offense was in fact committed in furtherance of the conspiracy, evidence of direct participation in the commission of the substantive offense or other evidence from which participation might fairly be inferred was necessary.

We take a different view. We have here a continuous conspiracy. There is here no evidence of the affirmative action on the part of Daniel which is necessary to establish his withdrawal from it. *Hyde v. United States*, 225 U.S. 347, 369 [(1912)]. As stated in that case, "Having joined in an unlawful scheme, having constituted agents for its performance, scheme and agency to be continuous until full fruition be secured, until he does some act to disavow or defeat the purpose he is in no situation to claim the delay of the law. As the offense has not been terminated or accomplished he is still offending. . . ." And so long as the partnership in crime continues, the partners act for each other in carrying it forward. It is settled that "an overt act of one partner may be the act of all without any new agreement specifically directed to that act." Motive or intent may be proved by the acts or declarations of some of the conspirators in furtherance of the common objective. A scheme to use the mails to defraud, which is joined in by more than one person, is a conspiracy. Yet all members are responsible, though only one did the mailing. The governing principle is the same when the substantive offense is committed by one of the conspirators in furtherance of the unlawful project. The criminal intent to do the act is established by the formation of the conspiracy. Each conspirator instigated the commission of the crime. The unlawful agreement contemplated precisely what was done. It was formed for the purpose. The act done was in execution of the enterprise. The rule which holds responsible one who counsels, procures, or commands another to commit a crime is founded on the same principle. That principle is recognized in the law of conspiracy when the overt act of one partner in crime is attributable to all. An overt act is an essential ingredient of the crime of conspiracy. . . . If that can be supplied by the act of one conspirator, we fail to see why the same or other acts in furtherance of the conspiracy are likewise not attributable to the others for the purpose of holding them responsible for the substantive offense.

A different case would arise if the substantive offense committed by one of the conspirators was not in fact done in furtherance of the conspiracy, did not fall within the scope of the unlawful project, or was merely a part of the ramifications of the plan which could not be reasonably foreseen as a necessary or natural consequence of the unlawful agreement. But as we read this record, that is not this case. Affirmed.

Mr. Justice Rutledge, dissenting in part.

The judgment concerning Daniel Pinkerton should be reversed. In my opinion it is without precedent here and is a dangerous precedent to establish. . . .

. . . The proof showed that Walter alone committed the substantive crimes. There was none to establish that Daniel participated in them, aided and abetted Walter in committing them, or knew that he had done so. . . . There was evidence, however, to show that over several years Daniel and Walter had confederated to commit similar crimes . . . .

. . . Daniel has been held guilty of the substantive crimes committed only by Walter on proof that he did no more than conspire with him to commit offenses of the same general character. There was no evidence that he counseled, advised or had knowledge of those particular acts or offenses. There was, therefore, none that he aided, abetted or took part in them. There was only evidence sufficient to show that he had agreed with Walter at some past time to engage in such transactions generally. As to Daniel this was only evidence of conspiracy, not of substantive crime.

The Court's theory seems to be that Daniel and Walter became general partners in crime by virtue of their agreement and because of that agreement without more on his part Daniel became criminally responsible as a principal for everything Walter did thereafter in the nature of a criminal offense of the general sort the agreement contemplated, so long as there was not clear evidence that Daniel had withdrawn from or revoked the agreement. . . . [T]he result is a vicarious criminal responsibility as broad as, or broader than, the vicarious civil liability of a partner for acts done by a copartner in the course of the firm's business.

Such analogies from private commercial law and the law of torts are dangerous, in my judgment, for transfer to the criminal field. Guilt there with us remains personal, not vicarious, for the more serious offenses. It should be kept so. The effect of Daniel's conviction in this case . . . is either to attribute to him Walter's guilt or to punish him twice for the same offense, namely, agreeing with Walter to engage in crime. Without the agreement Daniel was guilty of no crime on this record. With it and no more, so far as his own conduct is concerned, he was guilty of two.

Notes and Questions

1. *Pinkerton* **Liability.** Under the *Pinkerton* doctrine, a conspirator can be held liable for crimes committed by co-conspirators, even though the conspirator's only involvement in the substantive criminal conduct was the original agreement to the overall conspiratorial objective. Thus, for example, a co-conspirator who agrees to be the getaway car driver for a bank robbery can be convicted of theft if one of the other conspirators steals a gun to be used in the robbery. Although the *Pinkerton* doctrine has been criticized, it is still followed in the federal courts and in a number of state courts as well.

2. **The Limits of *Pinkerton* Liability.** Justice Douglas somewhat mysteriously suggested, in *Pinkerton*'s final paragraph, that "a different case would arise" if the substantive crime committed by another conspirator was not done "in furtherance" of the conspiracy, fell outside "the scope" of the conspiracy, or could not reasonably have been "foreseen as a necessary or natural consequence of the unlawful agreement." The Court presumably intended these three conditions to be limitations on

the reach of *Pinkerton* liability, but is it clear the Court meant for them to be applied in the alternative?

The three limitations mentioned in *Pinkerton* are not obviously coextensive, and they can be linguistically manipulated to reach various results. For example, an act that can be viewed as a "natural consequence" may not always be "in furtherance of" a conspiratorial agreement. Nor will a "natural consequence" always fall within an agreement's scope. And acts within the "scope" of an agreement will not always "further" it. Indeed, Justice Douglas' third category sounds quite similar to the common law's "natural and probable consequences" doctrine for accomplice liability, described above in Note 7 following *Gladstone* in Chapter 12, Section C. In fact, *Pinkerton* and accomplice liability are often discussed together, and the doctrines are frequently linked. *See* Joshua Dressler, Understanding Criminal Law § 30.08, at 489 (7th ed. 2015); Wayne R. LaFave, Criminal Law § 13.3(a) (5th ed. 2010); Wesley M. Oliver, *Limiting Criminal Law's 'In for a Penny, In for a Pound' Doctrine*, 103 Geo. L.J. Online 8 (2013).

Lower courts sometimes apply different formulations in limiting *Pinkerton* liability, depending on the result that seems most fair. A number of them read the Supreme Court's opinion as imposing *two* limits on the reach of *Pinkerton*: the substantive crime must have been in furtherance of the conspiracy *and* it must have been reasonably foreseeable. *E.g.*, *United States v. Irvin*, 2 F.3d 72, 75–78 (4th Cir. 1993).

Moreover, some courts have noted possible "due process limitations on the *Pinkerton* doctrine in cases involving attenuated relationships between the conspirator and the substantive crime." *United States v. Alvarez*, 755 F.2d 830, 850 (11th Cir. 1985); *accord*, *United States v. Castaneda*, 9 F.3d 761, 768 (9th Cir. 1993) (vacating a defendant's firearms conviction, reasoning that "given [her] lack of participation in the drug conspiracy and her lack of involvement with the predicate [drug] offenses, . . . we cannot conclude, without violating the fundamental precepts of due process, that [she] could have foreseen the other conspirators' use of firearms in relation to the predicate offenses").

Because *Pinkerton* liability is already a judicially developed gloss on statutory language that does not obviously include it, perhaps linguistic limitation, and even judicial manipulation, is entirely understandable. Do you think *Pinkerton* liability is fair? If so, what limitations, if any, do you think make sense?

Pinkerton liability is also limited chronologically—a defendant cannot be convicted for a co-conspirator's substantive crime if the defendant had not yet joined the conspiracy or had already withdrawn from it. *See Levine v. United States*, 383 U.S. 265, 266 (1966) (per curiam). (The withdrawal defense is discussed below in Section B.3.) Thus, in determining the extent of a defendant's liability under *Pinkerton* for the crimes committed by other conspirators, it is critical to determine when each defendant joined and left the conspiracy. *See United States v. O'Campo*, 973

F.2d 1015, 1021 (1st Cir. 1992) (concluding that a defendant who joined a drug conspiracy after two sales of marijuana had already occurred could not be held liable for those transactions under *Pinkerton*).

3. The Model Penal Code's Position. The Model Penal Code does not accept the *Pinkerton* doctrine, believing that it is unfair to hold all members of a conspiracy equally liable irrespective of their actual role in particular substantive crimes. *See* Model Penal Code § 2.06 Comment at 307–10. Although no explicit statement rejecting the doctrine can be found in the Code itself, the Comments make clear that a conspirator is liable only for the crime of conspiracy. The MPC then permits punishing a defendant for a substantive crime committed by co-conspirators only if the prosecution can prove the defendant met the requirements for accomplice liability for that specific crime.

The Code's approach arguably offers the advantages of proportioning punishment and focusing on the conspiracy's masterminds or main actors, punishing them more severely than less involved members of the conspiracy. Consider the Arizona Supreme Court's arguments for rejecting the *Pinkerton* doctrine:

> The state argues that whenever one has conspired to commit a crime which is then actually committed by one's co-conspirators, one will inevitably come within the definition of an accomplice and can therefore be held liable for the completed crime. To put the state's case another way, if one "agrees with one or more persons that at least one of them will engage in conduct constituting" a crime, as required by the conspiracy statute, one by definition "aids, counsels, agrees to aid or attempts to aid" in the planning or commission of that crime, as required by the accomplice statute.

> Although this argument has enormous appeal, we think there is a logical distinction between *agreeing to the commission of a crime by another and agreeing to aid another in committing a crime*, the latter being more participatory than the former. The distinction between being an accomplice and being a conspirator to a completed crime is certainly subtle when the crime conspired to is the one actually committed, but there is a difference. *Pinkerton*, in any event, goes well beyond this. Under *Pinkerton*, a conspirator may be held liable for a crime to which the conspirator never agreed, and which is committed by a co-conspirator with whom the conspirator never personally dealt, as long as the crime is reasonably foreseeable and is committed in furtherance of the conspiracy. Clearly, one who has not agreed to the commission of a crime and has not aided in its planning or commission could not be convicted of the crime as an accomplice. *Pinkerton* liability is not, therefore, the equivalent of accomplice liability. A conspirator to a completed offense is not always an accomplice to that offense.

State ex rel. Woods v. Cohen, 844 P.2d 1147, 1150–51 (Ariz. 1992). On the other hand, Rhode Island's Supreme Court has defended the *Pinkerton* doctrine, noting that its perceived "harshness may be considered as an occupational hazard confronting those who might be tempted to engage in a criminal conspiracy." *State v. Barton*, 424 A.2d 1033, 1038 (R.I. 1981).

Do you find the critics of the *Pinkerton* doctrine, or Justice Douglas' "partnership in crime" analogy, more persuasive?

[2] The Structure of Conspiracies: Single versus Multiple Conspiracies, and "Chains" versus "Wheels"

When a number of different people are involved in an ongoing criminal enterprise, it is often difficult to determine the relationship between them, precisely what agreements each of them shares, and whether there are several small conspiracies or one single overarching criminal enterprise. For example, is an international narcotics organization that may commit many crimes along the way a single conspiracy, or a set of separate conspiracies (to import, to transport, to distribute, and to possess narcotics)? What is the relationship between growers or manufacturers in one country and street sellers in another country (or even multiple countries)? These questions can be important for purposes of determining where the trial may be held, how many charges can be brought, which defendants may be tried together, what evidence is admissible against them, when the statute of limitations has run, and ultimately how severely the defendants can be punished. See Section A.1 above (discussing the prosecutorial advantages of conspiracy) and Section B.1 (discussing *Pinkerton* liability). Thus a "diagram" of conspiratorial relationships is often essential, and can be quite complicated as well as disputed. *See, e.g., United States v. Evans*, 970 F.2d 663, 680–81 (10th Cir. 1992) (reproducing two complex diagrams of "an elaborate drug distribution network"). The criminal law must develop general principles to govern the innumerable variations of human, and criminal, associations.

1. **A Single Agreement to Commit Multiple Crimes.** Generally, even though many of the co-conspirators have never met or even communicated with each other, they are considered part of a single conspiracy if the prosecution can show a "community of interest" among them. Wayne R. LaFave, Criminal Law § 12.3(b)(2) (5th ed. 2010). Moreover, MPC § 5.03(2) provides:

> If a person guilty of conspiracy . . . knows that a person with whom he conspires to commit a crime has conspired with another person or persons to commit the same crime, he is guilty of conspiring with such other person or persons, whether or not he knows their identity, to commit such crime.

In *Braverman v. United States*, 317 U.S. 49 (1942), the Supreme Court addressed the question whether an agreement to commit several crimes constitutes one or several conspiracies. The defendants were all involved in various aspects of an illegal bootlegging operation, which violated at least seven separate revenue laws. The prosecution argued that their seven criminal objectives meant they had formed seven different conspiracies (thus permitting at least seven separate conspiracy counts and, possibly, seven consecutive sentences). The Court disagreed, finding only a single conspiracy:

Whether the object of a single agreement is to commit one or many crimes, it is in either case that agreement which constitutes the conspiracy which the statute punishes. The one agreement cannot be taken to be several agreements and hence several conspiracies because it envisages the violation of several statutes rather than one.

... The single agreement is the prohibited conspiracy, and however diverse its objects it violates but a single statute. For such a violation, only the single penalty prescribed by the statute can be imposed.

Id. at 53–54.

Section 5.03(3) of the Model Penal Code embraces the *Braverman* holding, although it extends the doctrine a bit further to encompass any "continuous conspiratorial relationship":

If a person conspires to commit a number of crimes, he is guilty of only one conspiracy so long as such multiple crimes are the object of the same agreement or continuous conspiratorial relationship.

Despite *Braverman*, if the legislature has enacted separate conspiracy statutes that can be read to embrace the same conduct, a single agreement can violate each statute and the conspirators can be punished separately for each conspiracy statute they violated. In *Albernaz v. United States*, 450 U.S. 333 (1981), for example, the defendants' agreement to import and distribute marijuana violated the federal statute criminalizing conspiracies to import marijuana as well as a different statute prohibiting conspiracies to distribute marijuana. The defendants were convicted and separately sentenced under each statute, and the Supreme Court affirmed. *See* Wayne R. LaFave, Criminal Law § 12.3(b)(1) (5th ed. 2010).

2. "Chain" Versus "Wheel" Conspiracies. In order to both determine and limit the liability of members of large criminal organizations, the courts have developed the somewhat oversimplified concepts of "chain" and "wheel" conspiracies. The structure of some multi-party conspiracies resembles a chain, and others more closely resemble a wheel. Still others may resemble a combination of the two.

In a chain conspiracy, the parties are linked together in linear fashion. Chain conspiracies often involve the smuggling and distribution of illicit drugs or other contraband. Typically, each party or link has a specialized function. For a particular person to be criminally associated with the others—and thereby included within the same conspiracy—it must be established that that person knew the others in the "chain" existed, even if their specific identities were unknown, and that all the conspirators shared a community of interest. Because of the inherent interdependence between the "links" in a chain conspiracy, proving that co-conspirators knew that others were necessarily working together in a common enterprise, and knew that their success or failure depended upon the other links, is often relatively straightforward.

Suppose, for example, that: (1) opium growers in Afghanistan supply the drug to (2) distributors in Pakistan, who ship the opium to (3) other distributors in South America, who smuggle the drug into the United States in order to provide it to (4) distributors who provide the drug to (5) street dealers. That is a chain and is similar to the *Bruno* case discussed below. It need not be proven that conspirators in one part of this chain actually knew the other conspirators personally. Thus, the narcotics suppliers in one country can be convicted of conspiring with the off-loaders and distributors in another country—each group knows (or "must have known") that other people were performing the requisite tasks somewhere else. *E.g., United States v. Price*, 258 F.3d 539 (6th Cir. 2001). (Note that the required mens rea may be a controversial part of this analysis and the doctrine of "willful blindness" discussed in Chapter 4, Section B.2, Notes 2–3, may be useful in inferring a conspirator's knowledge.)

By contrast to a chain, in a "wheel" conspiracy, several subsidiary parties are connected to a main central party. The main party serves as the "hub" of the wheel, around which the conspiracy turns, while subsidiary parties connected to the hub— but not necessarily to each other—are the spokes. But like any wheel, it will not work unless the spokes are connected by a rim—that is, by the same single, general agreement. A "wheel" organization will be considered a single conspiracy so long as the spokes are connected by this rim. Suppose, for example, that a methamphetamine manufacturer in Iowa distributes the drug to individuals in five different states. This is a "wheel," with the manufacturer acting as the "hub" and the five individuals as the "spokes." If each "spoke" has only a separate individual agreement with the hub, then there is no overall conspiracy; rather, each "hub and spoke" agreement may be considered a separate chain-like conspiracy. This would be the case if the manufacturer in Iowa agreed to distribute methamphetamine to one seller, later decided to be a co-marketer with another seller, and entered into a separate arrangement with a third seller.

Note that the existence of a "rim" is generally determined from the spokes' point of view. If it can be shown that the spokes shared a community of interest, the existence of a general agreement may be inferred and the spokes can be deemed part of one single conspiracy. Courts are frequently willing to find the requisite community of interest if the success or failure of the spokes is clearly interdependent, or if it appears that the spokes share a common goal. *See* Joshua Dressler, Understanding Criminal Law § 29.07[D][2] (7th ed. 2015); Wayne R. LaFave, Criminal Law § 12.3(b) (5th ed. 2010).

Not surprisingly, the defendants in any conspiracy case will each seek to minimize their own liability. Somewhat perversely, therefore, the "hub" defendant in a wheel conspiracy will often try to demonstrate as broad a conspiracy as possible, with a clear general "rim" agreement among the "spokes," in order to limit the hub's own liability to a single conspiracy count. Conversely, the spokes in such an organization will usually claim a number of single, individualized agreements, in order to limit the charges and evidence admissible against them. Thus, when the prosecutor has charged a large criminal group with conspiracy, defendants who might be described as the "hub" and "spokes" may find themselves at odds with each other.

3. An Exemplary Chain Conspiracy. In the famous case of *United States v. Bruno*, 105 F.2d 921 (2d Cir.) (per curiam), *rev'd on other grounds*, 308 U.S. 287 (1939), the court confronted an indictment that charged 90 defendants with a massive conspiracy "to import, sell and possess narcotics":

> [The conspiracy's] object was to smuggle narcotics into the Port of New York and distribute them to addicts both in this city and in Texas and Louisiana. This required the cooperation of four groups of persons; the smugglers who imported the drugs; the middlemen who paid the smugglers and distributed to retailers; and two groups of retailers—one in New York and one in Texas and Louisiana—who supplied the addicts. . . . The evidence did not disclose any cooperation or communication between the smugglers and either group of retailers, or between the two groups of retailers themselves; however, the smugglers knew that the middlemen must sell to retailers, and the retailers knew that the middlemen must buy of importers of one sort or another. Thus the conspirators at one end of the chain knew that the unlawful business would not, and could not, stop with their buyers; and those at the other end knew that it had not begun with their sellers.

The court ruled that this evidence proved a single joint "venture, in all parts of which each [defendant] was a participant, and an abettor in the sense that the success of that part with which he was immediately concerned, was dependent upon the success of the whole." It made no difference, said the court, that one group of buyers were "retailing" their drugs in New York while the other sold in Texas and Louisiana. For the smugglers, "there was but one conspiracy, for it was of no moment to them whether the middlemen sold to one or more groups of retailers, provided they had a market somewhere." And the court said this was true for each retailer as well: "he knew that he was a necessary link in a scheme of distribution, and the others, whom he knew to be convenient to its execution, were as much parts of a single undertaking or enterprise as two salesmen in the same shop."

Was the *Bruno* court right to characterize the drug organization as a single chain conspiracy? Would two separate "chains" or even a "wheel" have better described the structure of the agreement there? Consider the same court's comment about *Bruno* in a subsequent opinion:

> [I]t is not so clear why the New York and Texas groups of retailers were not in a "spoke" relation with the smugglers and the middleman, so that there would be two conspiracies unless the evidence permitted the inference that each group of retailers must have known the operation to be so large as to require the other as an outlet.

United States v. Borelli, 336 F.2d 376, 383 n.2 (2d Cir. 1964).

4. Inferring the Existence of a Chain. Even if a chain structure exists, it is still necessary to prove that each link was part of a single general agreement. When the purpose of a chain is to obtain and distribute a substantial amount of contraband—either through one large sale or a number of smaller ones—courts are often willing to infer that the buyer and seller were aware they must be part of a larger chain conspiracy. *See, e.g., United States v. Sin Nagh Fong*, 490 F.2d 527 (9th Cir. 1974) (finding the defendant linked to a larger conspiracy because he sold large amounts of heroin and cocaine to a buyer, and must have known from the quantities involved that the buyer would resell it). But when only a few, small-scale sales are made, the existence of a chain conspiracy cannot so easily be inferred. For example, in *United States v. Peoni*, 100 F.2d 401 (2d Cir. 1938), Peoni made a one-time sale of counterfeit bills to Regno, who then resold them to Dorsey. The prosecution tried to implicate Peoni and Dorsey in the same chain conspiracy. But the defense argued that Peoni had no idea Regno would resell the bills, and that from Peoni's point of view it was not necessary for Regno to do so. Thus, the *Peoni* court concluded that Peoni and Dorsey were not co-conspirators. In distinguishing this case from the facts of *Bruno*, which is discussed in the prior Note, the Second Circuit observed that Peoni "had no interest in whether" Regno sold the counterfeit bills to Dorsey or instead "passed them to innocent persons himself." *United States v. Bruno*, 105 F.2d 921 (2d Cir.), *rev'd on other grounds*, 308 U.S. 287 (1939). (*Peoni*'s mens rea analysis is described above in Chapter 12, Section C.)

5. The Final Purchaser in a Chain. Can the final purchaser of contraband be considered part of the conspiratorial chain? If so, would this make street buyers of small quantities of cocaine co-conspirators with the members of a Colombian drug cartel? And liable under *Pinkerton* for all their crimes? In thinking about this question, recall the *Allan* case excerpted above in Section A.2.

6. An Exemplary Wheel Conspiracy. The following case nicely illustrates the difficulties that arise in establishing a wheel conspiracy.

Kotteakos v. United States
328 U.S. 750 (1946)

Mr. Justice Rutledge delivered the opinion of the Court.

The only question is whether petitioners have suffered substantial prejudice from being convicted of a single general conspiracy by evidence which the Government admits proved not one conspiracy but some eight or more different ones of the same sort executed through a common key figure, Simon Brown. Petitioners were convicted under the general conspiracy section of the Criminal Code of conspiring to violate the provisions of the National Housing Act. The judgments were affirmed by the Circuit Court of Appeals. We granted certiorari because of the importance of the question for the administration of criminal justice in the federal courts.

The indictment named thirty-two defendants, including the petitioners. The gist of the conspiracy, as alleged, was that the defendants had sought to induce various financial institutions to grant credit, with the intent that the loans or advances would then be offered to the Federal Housing Administration for insurance upon applications containing false and fraudulent information.

Of the thirty-two persons named in the indictment nineteen were brought to trial and the names of thirteen were submitted to the jury. Two were acquitted; the jury disagreed as to four; and the remaining seven, including petitioners, were found guilty. . . .

Simon Brown, who pleaded guilty, was the common and key figure in all of the transactions proven. He was president of the Brownie Lumber Company. Having had experience in obtaining loans under the National Housing Act, he undertook to act as broker in placing for others loans for modernization and renovation, charging a five per cent commission for his services. Brown knew, when he obtained the loans, that the proceeds were not to be used for the purposes stated in the applications.

In May, 1939, petitioner Lekacos told Brown that he wished to secure a loan in order to finance opening a law office, to say the least a hardly auspicious professional launching. Brown made out the application, as directed by Lekacos, to state that the purpose of the loan was to modernize a house belonging to the estate of Lekacos' father. Lekacos obtained the money. Later in the same year Lekacos secured another loan through Brown, the application being in the names of his brother and sister-in-law. Lekacos also received part of the proceeds of a loan for which one Gerakeris, a defendant who pleaded guilty, had applied.

In June, 1939, Lekacos sent Brown an application for a loan signed by petitioner Kotteakos. It contained false statements. Brown placed the loan, and Kotteakos thereafter sent Brown applications on behalf of other persons. Two were made out in the names of fictitious persons. The proceeds were received by Kotteakos and petitioner Regenbogen, his partner in the cigarette and pinball machine business. Regenbogen, together with Kotteakos, had indorsed one of the applications. Kotteakos also sent to Brown an application for a loan in Regenbogen's name. This was for modernization of property not owned by Regenbogen. The latter, however, repaid the money in about three months after he received it.

The evidence against the other defendants whose cases were submitted to the jury was similar in character. They too had transacted business with Brown relating to National Housing Act loans. But no connection was shown between them and petitioners, other than that Brown had been the instrument in each instance for obtaining the loans. In many cases the other defendants did not have any relationship with one another, other than Brown's connection with each transaction. As the Circuit Court of Appeals said, there were "at least eight, and perhaps more, separate and independent groups, none of which had any connection with any other, though all dealt independently with Brown as their agent." As the Government puts it, the pattern was "that of separate spokes meeting in a common center," though, we may add, without the rim of the wheel to enclose the spokes.

The proof therefore admittedly made out a case, not of a single conspiracy, but of several, notwithstanding only one was charged in the indictment. The Court of Appeals aptly drew analogy in the comment, "Thieves who dispose of their loot to a single receiver — a single 'fence' — do not by that fact alone become confederates: they may, but it takes more than knowledge that he is a 'fence' to make them such." It stated that the trial judge "was plainly wrong in supposing that upon the evidence there could be a single conspiracy; and in the view which he took of the law, he should have dismissed the indictment." Nevertheless the appellate court held the error not prejudicial, saying among other things that "especially since guilt was so manifest, it was 'proper' to join the conspiracies," and "to reverse the conviction would be a miscarriage of justice." . . .

With all deference we disagree with that conclusion and with the ruling that the permeating error did not affect "the substantial rights of the parties." That right, in each instance, was the right not to be tried *en masse* for the conglomeration of distinct and separate offenses committed by others as shown by this record. . . .

We have not rested our decision particularly on the fact that the offense charged, and those proved, were conspiracies. That offense is perhaps not greatly different from others when the scheme charged is tight and the number involved small. But as it is broadened to include more and more, in varying degrees of attachment to the confederation, the possibilities for miscarriage of justice to particular individuals become greater and greater. At the outskirts they are perhaps higher than in any other form of criminal trial our system affords. The greater looseness generally allowed for specifying the offense and its details, for receiving proof, and generally in the conduct of the trial, becomes magnified as the numbers involved increase. Here, if anywhere, extraordinary precaution is required, not only that instructions shall not mislead, but that they shall scrupulously safeguard each defendant individually, as far as possible, from loss of identity in the mass. Indeed, the instructions often become, in such cases, his principal protection against unwarranted imputation of guilt from others' conduct. Here also it is of special importance that plain error be not too readily taken to be harmless.

———————

7. **Difficulties in Proving Wheel Conspiracies.** Proving the existence of a complete wheel conspiracy is more challenging than proving the existence of a complete chain conspiracy. The success or failure of one spoke often appears to be independent of the success or failure of the others. Thus, it is more difficult to demonstrate a community of interest among all the spokes because it is harder to show that the spokes were necessarily aware of each other and shared a common goal. In *Kotteakos*, for example, although each conspirator shared a *similar* goal (falsely obtaining a government loan), they did not have the same *single* goal because they were each interested only in their own particular loan. The Court therefore concluded that the participants were not part of one single conspiracy. Similarly, in *Canella v. United States*, 157 F.2d 470 (9th

Cir. 1946), an army officer was caught accepting bribes. Even though the various people who bribed him (the spokes) were aware of each other, they were considered unconnected because they had separate goals—each separately paid the officer a bribe in order to obtain a different government contract.

Still, when one common goal exists, courts may find sufficient evidence of a single wheel conspiracy even if other connections are weak. In *People v. Quintana*, 540 P.2d 1097 (Colo. 1975), for example, the spokes gave false testimony on behalf of the hub at an extradition hearing. Although the hub had not even met all of the spokes and was unfamiliar with much of their testimony, they were all found to be involved in a single conspiracy to commit perjury because they shared a common goal: to prevent extradition of the hub. Likewise, in *State v. McLaughlin*, 44 A.2d 116 (Conn. 1945), the defendant subscribed to an illegal network that brought horse racing information to New Haven. Because the defendant was aware that four subscribers were necessary to finance the extension of the network to New Haven, he was deemed to be part of a single conspiracy with the other subscribers. *See* Wayne R. LaFave, Criminal Law § 12.3(b) (5th ed. 2010).

8. The Model Penal Code's Approach. Recall that Model Penal Code § 5.03(2) provides:

> If a person guilty of conspiracy . . . knows that a person with whom he conspires to commit a crime has conspired with another person or persons to commit the same crime, he is guilty of conspiring with such other person or persons, whether or not he knows their identity, to commit such crime.

Is this different from the approach described in *Kotteakos* and Note 2 above? The "wheel" and "chain" approach assumes that the boundaries of a conspiracy need to be carefully delineated because, once included in a conspiracy, each party can be held equally liable. The Model Penal Code appears to make no such assumption. In theory, § 5.03(2) envisions that each party may have participated in a unique set of agreements, and liability will be assessed solely on the basis of each defendant's individual situation. Do you think this makes much difference in the real world?

[3] Withdrawal, Renunciation, and the Duration of the Conspiracy

1. Withdrawing from a Conspiracy. As the Supreme Court recently explained, "[u]pon joining a criminal conspiracy, a defendant's membership in the ongoing unlawful scheme continues until he withdraws." *Smith v. United States*, 133 S. Ct. 714, 717 (2013). The Court unanimously concluded in *Smith* that a conspirator's "withdrawal . . . must be active" in order to be effective and that it is the defendant's "burden to show that." *Id.* at 721. This opinion states the rule for federal cases, drawn from common law according to the Court, although another jurisdiction might choose to allocate the burden of proof differently. For discussion of the constitutional implications of requiring criminal defendants to prove defenses, see Note 4 following *Tomlins* in Chapter 14, Section B.

As noted in *Smith*, withdrawal is not a complete defense to the crime of conspiracy. It "terminates the defendant's liability for postwithdrawal acts of his co-conspirators" under *Pinkerton*, but the defendant "remains guilty of conspiracy." 133 S. Ct. at 719. Even in jurisdictions that do not follow *Pinkerton*, a conspirator's withdrawal from the conspiracy can be significant. It starts the statute of limitations running for the crime of conspiracy as to that conspirator. *See id.* In addition, statements made by co-conspirators after the date of a conspirator's withdrawal cannot be admitted against the conspirator under the co-conspirator hearsay exception. *See* Wayne R. LaFave, Criminal Law § 12.4(b) (5th ed. 2010).

In order to demonstrate the "active" withdrawal required by *Smith*, a conspirator is generally required to commit an "affirmative act bringing home the fact of his withdrawal to his confederates" in time for them to abandon the conspiracy. *Loser v. Superior Court*, 177 P.2d 320, 321 (Cal. 1947). "Mere cessation of activity"—even on the part of a conspirator who has been incarcerated—is not sufficient. *United States v. Borelli*, 336 F.2d 376, 388 (2d Cir. 1964). Many courts have interpreted this requirement to mean that the conspirator must inform all of the other co-conspirators of the decision to withdraw (and, obviously, do nothing else to further the conspiracy). *See id.* (holding the defendant's attempt to withdraw from an illegal abortion conspiracy ineffective because he informed only one member of the conspiracy); *United States v. Bostick,* 791 F.3d 127, 143 (D.C. Cir. 2014) ("To withdraw from a conspiracy, an individual must come clean to the authorities or communicate his or her abandonment in a manner reasonably calculated to reach co-conspirators.").

The Model Penal Code uses the term "abandonment" rather than withdrawal, but similarly provides that a conspirator effectively withdraws from a conspiracy "only if and when he advises those with whom he conspired of his abandonment." Model Penal Code § 5.03(7)(c). The MPC does not address how this is to be accomplished in a large chain conspiracy like *Bruno* (described above in Section B.2), where conspirators at one end of the chain do not know the conspirators at the other end. Perhaps because of that difficulty, the MPC provides alternatively that a conspirator can effectively withdraw by "informing the law enforcement authorities of the existence of the conspiracy and of his participation therein." *Id.*

In *United States v. United States Gypsum Co.*, 438 U.S. 422 (1978), the Supreme Court ruled that a conspirator can also withdraw from a conspiracy by nonverbal communication. The defendants were indicted for conspiring to fix the market price of gypsum board in violation of federal antitrust laws. At trial, they argued that they had withdrawn from the conspiracy early enough so that the five-year statute of limitations had already expired by the time they were indicted. In support, the defendants introduced evidence that they had engaged in a price war with their competitors, and thus had obviously withdrawn from the conspiracy to fix prices. The trial judge, however, instructed the jury that a conspirator can withdraw from a conspiracy only by "affirmative notice" to each co-conspirator or "disclosure" to law enforcement. *Id.* at 431. The Supreme Court reversed the convictions, ruling that conspirators can also withdraw by committing "[a]ffirmative acts inconsistent with the object of the conspiracy and communicated in a manner reasonably calculated to reach co-conspirators." *Id.* at 464.

Note that although withdrawal is only a partial defense to conspiracy—cutting off the defendant's liability for co-conspirators' future acts but not relieving the defendant of liability for the conspiracy itself—there is one situation in which withdrawal might afford a complete defense. In jurisdictions where an overt act in furtherance of the conspiracy is necessary to complete the crime (*see* Section A.4 above), courts have ruled that a defendant who withdraws from a conspiratorial agreement before any co-conspirator commits an overt act cannot be convicted of conspiracy, because no conspiracy existed before the defendant withdrew. *See* Model Penal Code § 5.03(7)(b).

2. **Withdrawal versus Renunciation.** As described in the prior Note, withdrawal establishes only a partial defense to conspiracy liability. Withdrawal must therefore be distinguished from "renunciation," which some jurisdictions and the MPC recognize as a complete defense to the crime. A conspirator who takes action amounting to a complete renunciation of the conspiracy has a defense not only to the crimes committed by co-conspirators in furtherance of the conspiracy, but also to the original conspiracy charge itself. The Model Penal Code is quite strict on what is necessary to establish a renunciation defense:

> It is an affirmative defense [to conspiracy] that the actor, after conspiring to commit a crime, *thwarted the success* of the conspiracy, under circumstances manifesting a complete and voluntary renunciation of his criminal purpose.

Model Penal Code § 5.03(6) (emphasis added). The next case explores some ramifications of the concept of renunciation.

People v. Sisselman

542 N.Y.S.2d 801 (N.Y. App. Div. 1989)

YESAWICH, JUSTICE.

Defendant was convicted of conspiracy in the fourth degree and solicitation in the fourth degree for paying Dennis Patterson $250 to break the limbs of Louis Marrero, who defendant suspected was dating his extramarital girlfriend, giving her drugs or both. Patterson, acting as a police agent, recorded two telephone conversations during which defendant solicited Patterson to perform the assault, which in fact was never accomplished. Thereafter, fitted with a concealed body tape recorder, a "wire," Patterson met with defendant who told Patterson that he wanted Marrero beaten with a baseball bat, paid Patterson $250, planned an alibi and made other incriminating statements. Several days later Patterson informed defendant that he had been wearing a wire.

At trial, defendant, through his own testimony and that of his longtime friend, Marty Biederman, asserted that he had renounced the assault scheme prior to finding out that Patterson was a police informant by directing him not to carry out the assault. . . .

County Court gave the jury a renunciation charge suggested by the Committee on Criminal Jury Instructions of the State of New York, which defined the two elements of the affirmative defense as (1) voluntary and complete renunciation of the criminal enterprise, and (2) a substantial and successful effort to prevent the object crime. The jury was further instructed that for the effort to be deemed successful, the "effort must have been the sole and motivating inducement for Dennis Patterson to have abandoned any further effort and intention to commit such a crime." Convicted, defendant now appeals.

Defendant argues that the quoted charge language deprived him of the renunciation defense because he simply could not be the "sole and motivating" factor in preventing the object crime since Patterson, as a police agent, never intended to commit the assault. . . .

"Renunciation does not negate the commission of the inchoate crime," but rather offers those guilty of such crimes an incentive to take steps to prevent the object or substantive crime, in exchange for which the defendant is excused from liability. Unlike charges based upon accessorial conduct or criminal facilitation where only substantial efforts to prevent the object crime are required to invoke the renunciation defense, charges of conspiracy and solicitation give way to the renunciation defense only where "the defendant prevented the commission of such crime." The statute does not go so far as to say that defendant's efforts must be the "sole" reason that the object crime was not committed; indeed, such a reading would thwart the purpose of the provision where, for instance, two coconspirators acted in concert to prevent the consummation of the object crime, and to that extent the pattern instruction is an overstatement of the law.

The real problem here is that defendant was in no position to prevent the object crime since Patterson never intended to carry out the solicited assault. Despite this inability on defendant's part to literally comply with the statute, it would be unfair to deny him the renunciation defense merely because his coconspirator lacked criminal intent, for, in addition to encouraging prevention of the substantive crime, the renunciation defense is predicated upon the premise that complete and voluntary "renunciation manifests a lack of the firmness of purpose that evidences individual dangerousness." Consequently, although defendant was incapable of preventing the object crime, he should be given the opportunity to rebut the prima facie indication of firmness of purpose which follows from the People's proof of solicitation and the overt act in furtherance of the conspiracy. County Court should have charged that defendant's efforts to prevent the object crime would be deemed successful if they would have prevented the crime in the event that Patterson had intended to carry out the object crime. Having been denied this defense by County Court's instruction, a new trial is required.

Notes and Questions

1. Renunciation. Renunciation was not recognized as a defense to conspiracy at common law and is still not accepted in every jurisdiction today. The common-law view was that, as with other inchoate offenses (*see* Chapter 11, Section A.3), once the conduct constituting the crime was committed, the offense could not be renounced. While conspirators could withdraw from the conspiracy, thereby cutting off further *Pinkerton* liability and starting the statute of limitations, they would still be liable for the crime of conspiracy they had already committed.

Like the MPC, however, many states have now adopted a renunciation defense for conspiracy. A number are even less restrictive than MPC § 5.03(6), providing that timely notification of the police, or a substantial attempt to thwart the conspiracy, will suffice. *See* Wayne R. LaFave, Criminal Law § 12.4(b) (5th ed. 2010). But other jurisdictions stick to the MPC's more onerous "thwart the crime" standard. *See, e.g., State v. Daniels,* 129 A.3d 1056 (N.J. 2016) ("A renunciating co-conspirator must prove, by a preponderance of the evidence, that after conspiring to commit the crime, he subsequently informed the authorities about the conspiracy and therein thwarted the crime or caused the crime to be thwarted.") (citing N.J. Stat. Ann. § 2C:5–2(e)). As *Sisselman* indicates, however, the defendant need not be the sole cause of the conspiracy's failure.

2. The Duration of the Conspiracy. It is also a complete defense to the crime of conspiracy that the statute of limitations expired before conspiracy charges were filed against the defendant. The statute of limitations begins running either when the conspiracy ends, *see Grunewald v. United States*, 353 U.S. 391, 396–97 (1957), or for individual conspirators, when they withdraw from the conspiracy. *See United States v. Read*, 658 F.2d 1225, 1233 (7th Cir. 1981).

Determining when a conspiracy ends can be tricky. Do efforts to conceal the scheme serve to keep the conspiracy alive and prevent the statute of limitations from beginning to run? In *Grunewald v. United States*, the defendants were charged with conspiring to commit tax fraud. They argued that the three-year statute of limitations had expired because the fraud was completed six years before they were indicted. The government responded that the conspirators' attempts to conceal the fraud had prolonged the conspiracy. The Supreme Court held that acts of concealment do not function to keep a conspiracy alive unless they were part of the original conspiratorial agreement. *See* 353 U.S. at 402. The Court rejected the government's position because it would mean that the statute of limitations would never begin to run for many conspiracies:

> Every conspiracy is by its very nature secret; a case can hardly be supposed where men concert together for crime and advertise their purpose to the world. And again, every conspiracy will inevitably be followed by actions taken to cover the conspirators' traces. Sanctioning the Government's theory would for all practical purposes wipe out the statute of limitations in conspiracy cases.

Id. See also State v. Yslas, 676 P.2d 1118, 1122 (Ariz. 1984) (holding that a robbery conspiracy ended when the robbers divided the loot, and did not continue during their subsequent attempts to sell the loot and conceal the crime, because it did not appear they had planned that far ahead when they formed the conspiracy).

Note, however, that a prosecutor can avoid the impact of *Grunewald* by alleging that one of the conspirators' goals was to continue to conceal their crimes after the crimes were committed. *See, e.g., United States v. Menendez*, 137 F. Supp. 3d 688, 699 (D.N.J. 2015) ("prosecution . . . is not time-barred if the defendant commits affirmative acts of concealment in furtherance of the scheme within the limitations period"). The prosecution has to prove the allegation that concealment was a goal, of course, but juries often find it to be self-evident.

[C] Modern Applications of Conspiracy Law

[1] Conspiracy Charges in Post 9/11 Terrorism Cases

Since the World Trade Center and the Pentagon were attacked on September 11, 2001, the federal government has made significant efforts to try to detect and prevent further terrorist attacks before they occur. The inchoate offense of conspiracy can be particularly useful in this context, allowing early law enforcement intervention and the filing of criminal charges before harm has actually occurred. *See generally* Alec Walen, *Criminalizing Statements of Terrorist Intent*, 101 J. Crim. L. & Criminology 803 (2011); Robert M. Chesney, *Beyond Conspiracy? Anticipatory Prosecution and the Challenge of Unaffiliated Terrorism*, 80 S. Cal. L. Rev. 425 (2007). But it can also raise significant controversy. *See generally* Aziz Z. Huq, *The Signaling Function of Religious Speech in Domestic Counterterrorism*, 89 Tex. L. Rev. 833 (2011).

In a number of recent cases, the federal courts have struggled in determining how to apply old common-law principles of conspiracy (as well as international law) to modern terrorism threats, and the U.S. Supreme Court will presumably have to weigh in sooner or later. In one recent case, the D.C. Circuit, sitting en banc, affirmed a military commission's conviction of Osama Bin Laden's personal secretary on charges of "conspiracy to commit war crimes." *Al Bahlul v. United States*, 840 F.3d 757 (D.C. Cir. 2016) (en banc) (per curiam) ("*Al Bahlul III*"), *cert. pending*, No. 16-1307; *see also Al Bahlul v. United States*, 767 F.3d 1 (D.C. Cir. 2014) (en banc) ("*Al Bahlul I*").

Ali Hamza Ahmad Suliman al Bahlul was captured in Pakistan in December 2001 and allegedly "worked closely with Osama Bin Laden in plotting al Queda's September 11th attacks." *Al Bahlul III*, 840 F.3d at 759 (Kavanaugh, J., concurring). A U.S. military commission at Guantanamo Bay convicted al Bahlul of conspiring to commit war crimes as well as other offenses and sentenced him to life in prison. In its third en banc decision in the case, the D.C. Circuit, by a vote of six to three, affirmed the conviction; in addition to a brief per curiam opinion, the nine judges participating in the case wrote five separate opinions totaling 160 pages. The *Al Bahlul III* opinions address not only First Amendment and equal protection concerns and the principles and history underlying the law of conspiracy, but also the question whether jurisdiction to prosecute such charges can constitutionally rest with military commissions, as opposed to the federal district courts, given that conspiracy is not an international war crime. A four-judge plurality in *Al Bahlul III* said yes, with two other judges concurring on more limited grounds. An opinion signed by three of the judges in the plurality refused to "incorporate international law into the U.S. Constitution as a judicially enforceable constraint on Congress and the President." *Id.* These judges also observed that "conspiracy has historically been tried by U.S. military commissions," citing the use of military commissions to try conspiracy charges brought against those involved in the assassination of President Abraham Lincoln in 1865 and against alleged Nazi saboteurs arrested on American soil in 1942. *Id.* at 760, 766–67. Meanwhile, the three dissenting judges concluded that "[h]istory and precedent have established a narrow, atextual exception to Article III under which the military may try enemy belligerents for offenses against the international 'laws of war,' but inchoate conspiracy is not such an offense." *Id.* at 804–05 (Rogers, J., dissenting).

Other federal courts of appeals have also issued important opinions affirming terrorism conspiracy convictions. Unlike *Al Bahlul*, these cases have been prosecuted in Article III criminal courts rather than military commissions. *See, e.g., United States v. Ghailani*, 733 F.3d 29 (2d Cir. 2013) (affirming life sentence for conspiring to commit the bombings of U.S. embassies in Kenya and Tanzania in which more than 200 people were killed). *See also United States v. Hassan*, 742 F.3d 104 (4th Cir. 2014) (affirming 45-year prison sentence); *United States v. Amawi*, 695 F.3d 457 (6th Cir. 2012) (affirming three sentences ranging from 8 to 20 years).

Finally, note that unlike the *Al Bahlul* and *Ghailani* cases, the *Hassan* and *Amawi* prosecutions involved undercover investigations in which arrests were made before any violent acts of terrorism were carried out. Such undercover investigations of inchoate conspiracies, which have often involved secret government observation of groups or activities related to the Muslim faith, raise not only questions of entrapment (*see* Chapter 15, Section B, Note 5(c) following *Jacobson*), but also controversial questions beyond the scope of the first-year criminal law curriculum (such as the appropriate balance between permitting broad discussion of political and religious ideas and the desire to prevent criminal violence). *See, e.g.,* David Cole & James X. Dempsey, Terrorism and the Constitution: Sacrificing Civil Liberties in the Name of National Security (2006); Amna Akbar, *Policing "Radicalization,"* 3 U.C. Irvine L. Rev. 809 (2013); Steven R. Morrison, *Conspiracy Law's Threat to Free Speech*, 15 U. Pa. J. Const. L. 865 (2013). But law students can be confident that the old common-law principles remain relevant in the "real world" today.

[2] The RICO Statute: A Complicated Conspiracy Approach to Prosecuting Organized Crime

In 1970, Congress enacted a major new criminal statute to attack criminal organizations, the Racketeer Influenced and Corrupt Organizations ("RICO") Act, 18 U.S.C. § 1961 et seq. Like the conspiracy laws, RICO was designed to combat criminal combinations. As discussed below, the RICO statute has its own conspiracy section, 18 U.S.C. § 1962(d).

United States v. Horak

833 F.2d 1235 (7th Cir. 1987)

CUDAHY, CIRCUIT JUDGE.

Defendant-appellant John Horak was convicted of mail fraud and of conducting the affairs of an enterprise through a pattern of racketeering activity [in violation of RICO, 18 U.S.C. § 1961(c)]. The district court ordered forfeiture of Horak's job, salary, bonuses and corporate pension and profit-sharing plans from the date of the violation, pursuant to 18 U.S.C. § 1963(a)(1), but held that the conviction did not support forfeiture of Horak's stock in Waste Management, Inc. ("Waste").

Horak appeals his conviction on the ground that the evidence was insufficient to establish a violation of section 1962(c) [of RICO]. Horak appeals the order of forfeiture on the grounds that the forfeited interests were not maintained in violation of [RICO] and that the order violates the Eighth Amendment's proscription against cruel and unusual punishment. . . .

I.

HOD Disposal Service ("H.O.D."), a garbage removal company, services portions of Lake County, Illinois and Wisconsin. Prior to 1972, Horak was the sole owner of H.O.D. In 1972 Waste, a Fortune 500 company with foreign and domestic subsidiaries, purchased H.O.D. from Horak. The payment terms included voting shares in Waste (worth approximately $8 million at the time of trial) and an employment contract for Horak as H.O.D.'s manager. H.O.D. is a division of Waste Management of Illinois ("WM-Ill."), a wholly-owned subsidiary of Waste.

H.O.D. has provided garbage collection services to the Village of Fox Lake, Illinois since 1954. In 1981 Fox Lake solicited bids for a new garbage collection contract. Although not the lowest of the four bids received, H.O.D.'s bid nonetheless was approved in June, 1981. The contract, worth approximately $700,000, was awarded to H.O.D. in July, 1981 by the six-member board of trustees, which, together with the mayor, governed Fox Lake.

Richard Hamm, the mayor of Fox Lake, and Richard Gerretsen, the mayor's whip on the board of trustees, were the government's chief witnesses in this case. Their cooperation was obtained during an FBI investigation on a separate indictment under which both men were found guilty of extortion and bribery. According to their testimonies, shortly before the Fox Lake contract was to be awarded, Gerretsen and Horak met and reached an agreement that Hamm and Gerretsen each were to be paid $5,000 in periodic payments in exchange for the 1981 contract. Gerretsen testified that he received $5,000 in small increments. Hamm testified that he received $7,000 in small monthly amounts. The extra $2,000 resulted from a meeting between Hamm and Horak in which a condominium dumpster problem was resolved in H.O.D.'s favor. Horak denied making any payments in response to the dumpster problem.

FBI agents who visited Horak in April, 1985 testified that initially Horak denied any wrongdoing. However, once Horak was informed of Hamm's cooperation with the FBI, he changed his story and admitted to paying Fox Lake officials in the hopes of enhancing H.O.D.'s chances of winning the 1981 contract. He admitted that he knew Hamm and Gerretsen were not authorized to receive the money and agreed to the FBI's characterization of the payoffs as a "bribe."

The WM-Ill. controller, Robert Brach, testified that Horak was considered an H.O.D. employee, with influence over its day-to-day affairs, although "technically" he was a WM-Ill. employee. Brach stated that Horak had nothing to do with Waste or its other subsidiaries, with the exception of WM-Ill. Brach also testified that the revenues WM-Ill. earned from its divisions flowed through to Waste, but that H.O.D.'s revenue generally constituted less than 5% of WM-Ill.'s total revenue. He denied that the amount of Horak's bonus depended solely upon the amount of business H.O.D. generated but rather testified that the bonus was based on H.O.D.'s profits. . . .

The jury returned a verdict of guilty on all counts on February 14, 1986. . . . On March 13, the court sentenced Horak to six months in prison and five years' probation and fined him $25,000 for the RICO violation, with a special condition that he make restitution in an undetermined amount on the basis of the mail fraud convictions. (On December 12, 1986, the district court set an $80,000 maximum on this restitution award.) On April 18, 1986, the district court [entered the forfeiture order]. . . .

II. *Violation of Section 1962(c)*

Horak challenges his section 1962(c) conviction on three grounds.[1] Horak contends that: (1) as an employee of a subsidiary of the charged enterprise, he was not "employed by or associated with" the enterprise; (2) the evidence failed to support a finding that he "conducted the affairs" of the enterprise; and (3) the evidence failed to support a finding that he engaged in a "pattern of racketeering activity." We reject all three contentions and affirm the conviction.

---

1. [n.1] The provision pertinent to this case provides: "It shall be unlawful for any person employed by or associated with any enterprise engaged in, or the activities of which affect, interstate or foreign commerce, to conduct or participate, directly or indirectly, in the conduct of such enterprise's affairs through a pattern of racketeering activity or collection of unlawful debt."

First, the evidence manifestly permitted a jury to conclude beyond a reasonable doubt that Horak was employed by or associated with Waste, the charged RICO enterprise. Horak was employed by H.O.D., a division of WM-Ill., which, in turn, is a wholly-owned subsidiary of Waste. H.O.D.'s revenues flowed through to Waste. Horak's day-to-day control of H.O.D. was monitored by WM-Ill. and Waste, particularly Horak's right to contract on H.O.D.'s behalf. Contracts between $300,000 and $1 million required WM-Ill.'s approval; contracts over $1 million required Waste's approval. This evidence is clearly sufficient.

Second, the evidence permitted the jury to conclude beyond a reasonable doubt that Horak conducted or participated in the conduct of the affairs of Waste. Essentially Horak argues that even assuming a pattern of racketeering activity were shown, he did not "conduct" the affairs of Waste — the evidence showed only that he conducted the affairs of H.O.D. Horak's argument is misplaced: "conduct" in section 1962(c) does not mean "control" or "manage," and, in any event, section 1962(c) also proscribes "participat[ion], directly or indirectly, in the conduct" of the affairs of the enterprise. To establish the relationship required by 1962(c) between racketeering activity and the affairs of the enterprise, this circuit has held that the government must show, first, that the defendant committed racketeering acts, second, that the defendant's position in or relation with the enterprise facilitated commission of the acts and, third, that the acts had some effect on the enterprise. *United States v. Blackwood*, 768 F.2d 131, 138 (7th Cir.), *cert. denied*, 474 U.S. 1020 (1985).

Horak's contention that his position as H.O.D. manager does not adequately establish a relationship with the affairs of Waste fails the *Blackwood* test. Horak's position at H.O.D. facilitated his commission of the racketeering acts used to procure the 1981 contract from the Village of Fox Lake. Because H.O.D.'s regular business was garbage collection and a portion of Waste's regular business was garbage collection through its subsidiaries and divisions, Horak, as manager of H.O.D., was acting on Waste's behalf, thus conducting or participating in its affairs. Also, Horak's procurement of the 1981 contract through his racketeering activity undoubtedly "had some effect" on H.O.D.'s parent corporation, Waste, because the revenues derived from the contract were channeled up to Waste through WM-Ill. *Blackwood*, 768 F.2d at 138; *see also United States v. Ambrose*, 740 F.2d 505, 512 (7th Cir. 1984) (such effect does not have to be monetary), *cert. denied*, 472 U.S. 1017 (1985).

Finally, the evidence permitted a conclusion beyond a reasonable doubt that Horak engaged in a "pattern" of racketeering activity. The statutory definition of the pattern element requires at least two acts of racketeering activity within ten years,[2] but two acts do not necessarily fulfill the pattern requirement. *Sedima, S.P.R.L. v. Imrex Co.*, 473 U.S. 479, 496 n.14 (1985). The *Sedima* Court concluded that the legislative

---

2. [n.2] The pertinent provision states: "'pattern of racketeering activity' requires at least two acts of racketeering activity, one of which occurred after the effective date of this chapter and the last of which occurred within ten years (excluding any period of imprisonment) after the commission of a prior act of racketeering activity."

history of RICO indicates that a confluence of "continuity plus relationship" between or among the predicate acts establishes the requisite pattern. This court recognizes the need to evaluate the facts of each case individually in order to balance properly the two prongs of continuity and relationship. We have held that to require that predicate acts always occur as parts of separate schemes in order to satisfy the continuity prong would effectively negate the relationship prong and allow defendants who participated in one massive ongoing scheme to escape RICO liability.

Evidence of three separate bribes was presented to the jury in this case: (1) a $5,000 payment to Hamm regarding the 1981 contract; (2) a $5,000 payment to Gerretsen regarding the 1981 contract; and (3) a $2,000 payment to Hamm involving a dumpster problem at a condominium complex. We conclude that these acts satisfy the "continuity plus relationship" test and permit a conclusion that Horak engaged in a "pattern" of racketeering activity.

Horak does not dispute that he made the payments, but he claims that the two $5,000 payments were a part of a single scheme to win the 1981 contract and that insufficient evidence was introduced to permit the jury to conclude that the $2,000 payment was a bribe. Without the $2,000 payment, according to Horak, the evidence does not permit a finding of "pattern," but rather only an isolated act of bribery to obtain one contract. Horak appropriately directs attention to *Lipin Enterprises, Inc. v. Lee*, 803 F.2d 322, 324 (7th Cir. 1986), a civil RICO case where this court found no "pattern" established by twelve mail frauds perpetrated over a brief period of several months, relating to a single scheme to defraud a single victim in the sale of a business. However, as was noted in *Lipin*, acts of mail fraud are "perhaps unique" in that a multiplicity of mailings may be no evidence of "the requisite continuity of the underlying fraudulent activity." 803 F.2d at 325 (Cudahy, J., concurring). In the present case, evidence indicated an ongoing relationship built on periodic monthly payments of bribes to officials of Fox Lake. Horak made payments to Gerretsen for several months and then subsequently to Hamm for another period of approximately a year. . . . [W]e believe that the ongoing bribes of two public officials, even if pertinent only to a single ongoing service contract, may well establish a "pattern" for purposes of section 1962(c).

We believe further that a pattern was established by the additional evidence indicating a second bribe related to discussions of a problem that arose in connection with the garbage service contract. Hamm testified that he met with Horak to discuss potential solutions to the problem and that their meeting resulted in an additional $2,000 payment. Horak contends that insufficient proof existed that the $2,000 was a separate bribe concerning a separate problem. However, it is clear that some two years after establishing the initial scheme to pay $10,000, Horak and Hamm met to negotiate about the garbage services, and Hamm received an additional $2,000. This is sufficient to show continuity and relationship—an ongoing scheme to bribe public officials to obtain and perform a service contract over a several year period.

III. *Forfeiture Under Section 1963(a)(1)*

The district court ordered that Horak forfeit, pursuant to section 1963(a)(1), his job with H.O.D., the gross income and bonuses he received from H.O.D. from January, 1981 until his conviction, and all corporate contributions to his pension and profit-sharing plans for the same time period. The version of section 1963(a)(1) in effect at the time of Horak's violation provided:

> (a) Whoever violates any provision of section 1962 of this chapter shall be fined not more than $25,000 or imprisoned not more than twenty years, or both, and shall forfeit to the United States (1) any interest he has acquired or maintained in violation of section 1962. . . .

Horak contends that the (a)(1) forfeiture order was improper because the evidence failed to show that he actually maintained all the interests in violation of section 1962 and because the order violated the Eighth Amendment. We agree that the interests (other than the job) ordered forfeited were not adequately proven to be "acquired or maintained in violation of section 1962" and we therefore remand for further forfeiture proceedings. We do not reach the Eighth Amendment claim as it relates to section (a)(1).

The forfeiture provisions of section 1963(a) are the first revival in modern times of forfeiture as a criminal sanction against a defendant, i.e. forfeiture as applied *in personam*. Congress emphasized that new remedies were needed to attack organized crime and racketeering, and, to accompany the statutory scheme, Congress enacted a provision very rare in criminal law: "The provisions of this title shall be liberally construed to effectuate its remedial purpose." In light of these facts, section (a)(1) has been read broadly to mandate forfeiture of every interest, including proceeds, that a defendant acquired or maintained in violation of section 1962. Thus, presumably, section (a)(1) requires that a convicted defendant forfeit all "ill-gotten gains" or their proceeds. . . .

The forfeiture of Horak's job is consistent with numerous cases that have interpreted section 1963(a). The rationale behind these job forfeiture orders seems to be that section (a)(1) demands that the defendant be separated from any employment position that afforded him the opportunity to engage in the racketeering activity for which he was convicted. Significantly, none of these decisions analyzed the potential forfeiture of defendant's position of employment as Horak suggests: namely, was it shown that the defendant would have lost his position if he had not engaged in the racketeering activity? Rather, in light of the Congressional intent, these courts have construed section (a)(1) to authorize the forfeiture of any employment position that allowed defendant the opportunity to perform the racketeering acts. We agree that such a forfeiture order is consistent with section (a)(1). We do not decide here the scope and duration of job forfeiture permissible in such an order. In the present circumstances, the order is proper under (a)(1).

However, it is not clear to us that Horak should be required to forfeit the *entirety* of his salary, bonuses and corporate profit-sharing and pension plans from 1981 to the present. The district court concluded that these forfeited interests all "depended (in part or whole)" on Horak's performance as H.O.D. manager, which performance was "enhanced" by his criminal activity that violated section 1962. Thus, according to this analysis, any interest that partially depends on, or is in some measure caused by, the criminal activity must be wholly forfeited. We believe that this construction of section (a)(1) is overly expansive. . . .

[A] remand is necessary for the district court to consider whether Horak's salary, bonuses and profit-sharing and pension plans were in fact "acquired or maintained" in violation of section 1962. We do not believe that it is sufficient under section (a) 1) for the court to determine that Horak's racketeering activities "enhanced" his performance as H.O.D. manager, thus affecting the enumerated interests. Instead, on remand, the court must determine what portion of Horak's interests would not have been acquired or maintained "but for" his racketeering activities. That is, in order to win a forfeiture order, the government must show on remand that Horak's racketeering activities were a cause in fact of the acquisition or maintenance of these interests or some portion of them. For example, if the government can prove that Horak would have been fired in 1981 but for his landing the Fox Lake contract (which he accomplished by violating section 1962), the court should order forfeiture of his entire salary thereafter and such other emoluments of his employment as would have been lost by the firing. But, if the government can prove only that Horak received a bonus for his landing of the Fox Lake contract, then only that bonus is forfeitable under (a)(1). Presumably, the pension and profit-sharing issues are also subject to a "but-for" test. When and under what circumstances were these benefits earned?

Notes and Questions

1. The History of RICO. Congress enacted the RICO statute in 1970 in response to growing concerns about organized crime's infiltration of legitimate business and the perceived difficulty of obtaining convictions under traditional conspiracy law. The statute authorized a penalty that was unusually severe at the time: imprisonment up to 20 years. *See* 18 U.S.C. § 1963(a). Yet as is often the case with new statutes, federal prosecutors were slow to learn about RICO and RICO charges were initially rare. *See* G. Robert Blakey & Brian Gettings, *Racketeer Influenced and Corrupt Organizations (RICO): Basic Concepts—Criminal and Civil Remedies*, 53 Temple L.Q. 1009, 1014–15 (1980); Gerard E. Lynch, *A Conceptual, Practical, and Political Guide to RICO Reform*, 43 Vand. L. Rev. 769, 775 n.13 (1990).[3] By 1980, however, the statute had begun to be widely used and appellate decisions addressing RICO began to populate the federal reporters.

---

3. Professor Blakey, a U.S. Senate staffer in 1969 who is credited with authoring much of the RICO statute, has published frequently on the topic in subsequent years. Judge Lynch is a former federal prosecutor from the Southern District of New York, who became a law professor at Columbia and is currently a Senior Judge on the Second Circuit.

RICO is intentionally written broadly and can be used to attack all types of organized criminal behavior, such as political corruption, white-collar crime, health care fraud, and even motorcycle gangs. *See* Nathan Koppel, *Law Targets 'Criminal Enterprise'*, WALL STREET J., Jan. 21, 2011, at A2. Although enacted as part of the Organized Crime Control Act of 1970 and initially aimed at organizations like the Mafia, the Supreme Court ruled in 1981 that no "organized crime" connection is required for a RICO prosecution. *See United States v. Turkette*, 452 U.S. 576 (1981).

2. RICO's Severe Criminal Penalties. As the Seventh Circuit discusses in *Horak*, RICO violators face not only a potential lengthy prison sentence and a fine, but also forfeiture of any gain they acquired through the pattern of racketeering and any interest they hold in the enterprise. *See* 18 U.S.C. § 1963(a). This broad forfeiture remedy was, again, unusual when the statute was enacted in 1970. *See* G. Robert Blakey & Brian Gettings, *Racketeer Influenced and Corrupt Organizations (RICO): Basic Concepts—Criminal and Civil Remedies*, 53 TEMPLE L.Q. 1009, 1035 (1980). One result of RICO's forfeiture penalties is that if RICO is applied against corporate executives who commit fraud in order to further their company's interests, these corporate heads can be forced to give up any profits realized from the fraud, their stock in the corporation, and their jobs. *See Rusello v. United States*, 464 U.S. 16 (1983); Gerard E. Lynch, *A Conceptual, Practical, and Political Guide to RICO Reform*, 43 VAND. L. REV. 769, 782 (1990). In *Alexander v. United States*, 509 U.S. 544 (1993), for example, the Supreme Court ruled that RICO's forfeiture provisions could be applied to $8 million of assets the defendant owned in sexually explicit bookstores and theaters (based on predicate criminal obscenity violations).

Because RICO also authorizes a 20-year prison term, defendants convicted under RICO can receive much heavier sentences than they would have if convicted only of the specific offenses that made up their criminal predicates. In addition, those individual criminal predicates can also be punished separately (assuming the statute of limitations has not expired). Does the "pattern" and organized group context of RICO violations justify such enhanced penalties?

3. The Substantive Elements of RICO. Subsections (a) through (d) of 18 U.S.C. § 1962 describe four different ways that RICO can be violated. These provisions prohibit the following:

(a) using income derived from a pattern of racketeering activity to acquire an interest in an enterprise;

(b) acquiring or maintaining an interest in an enterprise through a pattern of racketeering activity;

(c) conducting the affairs of an enterprise through a pattern of racketeering activity; and

(d) conspiring to commit any of these offenses.

See G. Robert Blakey & Brian Gettings, *Racketeer Influenced and Corrupt Organizations (RICO): Basic Concepts—Criminal and Civil Remedies*, 53 TEMPLE L.Q. 1009, 1021–22 (1980).

Parts (a) and (b) are aimed at preventing criminal organizations from gaining control of legitimate enterprises, while part (c) is aimed at the criminal organizations themselves. Part (d) permits charging conspiracies to violate any of the other three subsections. Most RICO prosecutions are based on parts (c) and (d). Part (c) is heavily relied upon to attack, for example, white-collar crime and government corruption because both the investment banker who commits a series of securities frauds and the politician who accepts a series of bribes may act in violation of that subsection. *See* Gerard E. Lynch, *A Conceptual, Practical, and Political Guide to RICO Reform*, 43 VAND. L. REV. 769, 771–74 (1990).

The complexities of the RICO statute, combined with increased severity of sentences for other federal crimes since 1970, has resulted in fewer uses of RICO in recent years.

4. Defining an "Enterprise." Aimed at group crime, RICO is essentially just a complicated conspiracy statute. The term "enterprise" is broadly defined in 18 U.S.C. § 1961(4) to "include[] any individual, partnership, corporation, association, or other legal entity, and any union or group of individuals associated in fact although not a legal entity." The U.S. Supreme Court ruled early on that RICO can be applied to any "enterprise," whether formed for illegal or entirely legal purposes. *See United States v. Turkette*, 452 U.S. 576 (1981).

In *Boyle v. United States*, 556 U.S. 938 (2009), the Supreme Court again read RICO broadly, affirming that the statute could be applied to a "loosely and informally organized" group of people who had committed bank robberies. The Court concluded that the group could qualify as a RICO enterprise even though "[i]t does not appear to have had a leader or hierarchy; nor does it appear that the participants ever formulated any long-term master plan or agreement." *Id.* at 941. Quoting *Turkette*, the Court noted that "RICO reaches 'a[ny] group of persons associated together for a common purpose of engaging in a course of conduct.'" *Id.* at 944. The Court did agree with Boyle that "an association-in-fact enterprise must have a structure," comprised of "at least three structural features: a purpose, relationships among those associated with the enterprise, and longevity sufficient to permit these associates to pursue the enterprise's purpose." *Id.* at 945–46. But beyond that, the Court found "no basis in the language of RICO" for requiring proof of "a hierarchical structure," "a chain of command," or "a name, regular meetings, dues, established rules and regulations, disciplinary procedures, or induction or initiation ceremonies." *Id.* at 948. A RICO "association-in-fact enterprise is simply a continuing unit that functions with a common purpose," the Court observed. *Id.*

Moreover, in *National Organization for Women v. Scheidler*, 510 U.S. 249 (1994), the Supreme Court held that RICO is not limited to enterprises motivated by an economic purpose. Thus, the Court allowed private plaintiffs to use RICO to sue a group of anti-abortion activists who had allegedly resorted to violence, extortion, and other racketeering acts with the non-monetary goal of effectively shutting down abortion clinics. The *NOW* plaintiffs alleged that the defendants, who had been blockading abortion clinics and harassing patients, conspired to violate RICO through criminally extortionate acts. (Although the plaintiffs prevailed at a jury trial and were awarded a nationwide injunction and damages in excess of $85,000, they ultimately lost when the Supreme Court ruled in two separate opinions that the defendants' underlying conduct had not violated the federal extortion statute and that the criminal violation "predicates" required for RICO liability (*see* Note 5 below) were not established. *See Scheidler v. NOW, Inc.*, 537 U.S. 393 (2003), and 547 U.S. 9 (2006).)

5. **Defining a "Pattern of Racketeering Activity."** As is apparent from the *NOW* cases described in the prior Note, RICO requires that "predicate" criminal acts have been committed. And as the *Horak* court explained, a "pattern of racketeering" predicates is required, defined in the statute as "requir[ing] at least two acts of racketeering" within a 10-year period. 18 U.S.C. § 1961(5). The statute lists numerous crimes that can constitute "racketeering activity," including federal charges of arson, bribery, drug distribution, extortion, obscenity, and mail, wire, or securities fraud. 18 U.S.C. § 1961(1). Significantly, the statute also includes most major crimes that are "chargeable under State law," such as murder, kidnapping, and gambling, thus sweeping in many offenses that otherwise would not trigger federal charges. *See* G. Robert Blakey & Brian Gettings, *Racketeer Influenced and Corrupt Organizations (RICO): Basic Concepts — Criminal and Civil Remedies*, 53 Temple L.Q. 1009, 1021–22 (1980).

In *H.J. Inc. v. Northwestern Bell Telephone Co.*, 492 U.S. 229 (1989), the Supreme Court relied on RICO's use of the term "pattern" and its legislative history in ruling that the predicate RICO crimes must be "related" to one another and must "amount to or pose a threat of continued criminal activity." *Id*. at 239. Writing for the four Justices in the minority, Justice Scalia called this "continuity plus relationship" test — a test not found in the statutory text — "about as helpful . . . as 'life is a fountain,' " and suggested that a "constitutional challenge" might be in order. *Id*. at 252, 254 (Scalia, J., concurring in the judgment).

With this background sketch of the law, do you think it was reasonable for the Seventh Circuit to conclude that Horak had engaged in a pattern of racketeering? Would the court's conclusion have been different without the evidence of the additional $2,000 paid to Hamm?

6. **Who "Conducts" or "Participates in" the Affairs of an Enterprise?** In *Reves v. Ernst & Young*, 507 U.S. 170, 185–86 (1993), the Court held that § 1962(c)'s reference to those who "conduct or participate, directly or indirectly, in the conduct of [an] enterprise's affairs" requires proof that the defendant actually "participate[d] in the operation or management of the enterprise." Thus, an accounting firm was not subject to a RICO claim even though it prepared the audit report for a farming cooperative that went bankrupt, because the firm did not participate in the "operation or management" of the cooperative itself. *Id*. at 186. The Court acknowledged,

however, that a RICO defendant need not hold "a formal position in the enterprise" and need not be part of "upper management," but could be a "lower rung participant . . . in the enterprise who [is] under the direction of upper management." *Id.* at 179, 184. Again, do you think Horak's role in Waste Management satisfied this definition?

7. RICO's Civil Penalties. Unique among federal criminal statutes, RICO allows not only the government, but also private plaintiffs, to sue RICO violators for injunctive relief and damages caused by a RICO violation. *See* 18 U.S.C. § 1964(c). As an added incentive, the statute allows successful plaintiffs to recover treble damages and also attorney's fees. As a result, many of the reported cases interpreting RICO are private civil suits, rather than criminal prosecutions. Examples are the *NOW* and *Ernst & Young* decisions described in the previous Notes. And because use of the statute is not restrained by prosecutorial discretion, some of the applications and interpretations urged by private plaintiffs may seem extreme. Moreover, there is a tremendous incentive for private parties to include a "RICO count" in lawsuits that otherwise merely allege civil corporate fraud. In *Sedima v. Imrex Co.*, 473 U.S. 479 (1985), the Court declined to restrict such civil suits to defendants who had already been convicted on criminal charges because (in what has become a familiar theme in the Supreme Court's RICO opinions) the broad text of the statute contained no such limitation.

In 2016, the Supreme Court distinguished for the first time between government and private RICO lawsuits. In *RJR Nabisco, Inc. v. European Community*, 136 S. Ct. 2090 (2016), the Court agreed unanimously that a RICO pattern of racketeering can be based on "offenses committed abroad," but the seven participating Justices then ruled by a vote of four to three that a private plaintiff must allege "a *domestic* injury" because of the "potential for international friction" that private lawsuits unconstrained by diplomatic concerns might represent.

8. Has RICO Been Extended Too Far? While initially intended to attack traditional forms of organized crime, RICO's expanded application, as illustrated by *Horak*, has generated intense controversy. Do you think the reach of RICO, and its availability to private plaintiffs, goes too far? Or does Congress' continued acceptance of the way the statute has been used by prosecutors and interpreted by courts support the current state of affairs? *See* Michael C. Dorf, *Spandrel or Frankenstein's Monster? The Vices and Virtues of Retrofitting in American Law,* 54 Wm. & Mary L. Rev. 339, 358 (2012) (noting that "[j]udges and scholars have criticized the scope of RICO, but it remains extraordinarily broad," suggesting that Congress perhaps "has, through inaction, ratified the courts' broad construction"). Might the criticisms directed at RICO reflect some implicit distaste for harshly treating certain classes of criminals as opposed to others?

Chapter 14

Justification

[A] Introduction

The criminal law groups defenses into two categories — justifications and excuses. The distinction between the two has been described as follows:

> [A]s H.L.A. Hart writes, the difference between justified and excused acts is the difference between an act which "the law does not condemn, or even welcomes [justification]," and an act "which is deplored, but the psychological state of the agent . . . rule[s] out the public condemnation and punishment [excuse]." That is, a justified act indicates . . . that the conduct is not wrongful; an excuse concedes the wrongfulness of the act, but asserts that the actor should not be punished for her wrongful behavior, primarily because of psychological or situational involuntariness.
>
> Although perhaps too simplistic, it generally is said that while "justification" speaks to the act, "excuse" focuses upon the actor. Justified conduct is external to the actor; excuses are internal.

Joshua Dressler, *New Thoughts About the Concept of Justification in the Criminal Law: A Critique of Fletcher's Thinking and* Rethinking, 32 UCLA L. Rev. 61, 66–67 (1984).

> The nature of a justification is that the claim is grounded in an implicit exception to the prohibitory norm. The "right" of self-defense carves out a set of cases in which violation of the norm is permissible. When the principles of justification are rendered concrete in particular cases, the result is a precedent that other people may properly rely upon in similar cases. . . .
>
> Excuses bear a totally different relationship to prohibitory norms. They do not constitute exceptions or modifications of the norm, but rather a judgment in the particular case that an individual cannot fairly be held accountable for violating the norm.

George P. Fletcher, Rethinking Criminal Law 810–11 (1978).

This Chapter focuses on the defenses that are typically characterized as justifications: self-defense; the use of defensive force to protect one's home or property or to serve law enforcement interests; and necessity. The following Chapter then describes the excuses of duress, entrapment, and insanity. A number of other defenses have already been discussed above: mistake (Chapter 4, Sections C.1 and C.2); intoxication (Chapter 4, Section C.3); and heat of passion (Chapter 6, Section B.2).

[B] Self-Defense

People v. Goetz

497 N.E.2d 41 (N.Y. 1986)

CHIEF JUDGE WACHTLER.

A Grand Jury has indicted defendant on attempted murder, assault, and other charges for having shot and wounded four youths on a New York City subway train after one or two of the youths approached him and asked for $5. The lower courts, concluding that the prosecutor's charge to the Grand Jury on the defense of justification was erroneous, have dismissed the attempted murder, assault and weapons possession charges. We now reverse and reinstate all counts of the indictment.

I

. . . .

On Saturday afternoon, December 22, 1984, Troy Canty, Darryl Cabey, James Ramseur, and Barry Allen boarded an IRT express subway train in The Bronx and headed south toward lower Manhattan. The four youths rode together in the rear portion of the seventh car of the train. Two of the four, Ramseur and Cabey, had screwdrivers inside their coats, which they said were to be used to break into the coin boxes of video machines.

Defendant Bernhard Goetz boarded this subway train at 14th Street in Manhattan and sat down on a bench towards the rear section of the same car occupied by the four youths. Goetz was carrying an unlicensed .38 caliber pistol loaded with five rounds of ammunition in a waistband holster. . . .

It appears from the evidence before the Grand Jury that Canty approached Goetz, possibly with Allen beside him, and stated "give me five dollars." Neither Canty nor any of the other youths displayed a weapon.[1] Goetz responded by standing up, pulling out his handgun and firing four shots in rapid succession. The first shot hit Canty in the chest; the second struck Allen in the back; the third went through Ramseur's arm and into his left side; the fourth was fired at Cabey, who apparently was then standing in the corner of the car, but missed, deflecting instead off of a wall of the conductor's cab. After Goetz briefly surveyed the scene around him, he fired another shot at Cabey, who then was sitting on the end bench of the car. The bullet entered the rear of Cabey's side and severed his spinal cord.

. . . Ramseur and Canty, initially listed in critical condition, have fully recovered[, as has Allen]. Cabey remains paralyzed, and has suffered some degree of brain damage.

On December 31, 1984, Goetz surrendered to police in Concord, New Hampshire, identifying himself as the gunman being sought for the subway shootings in New

---

1. There was no evidence that Goetz knew about the screwdrivers. *See* GEORGE P. FLETCHER, A CRIME OF SELF-DEFENSE 95 (1988).

York nine days earlier. Later that day, after receiving *Miranda* warnings, he made two lengthy statements. . . . In the statements, . . . Goetz admitted that he had been illegally carrying a handgun in New York City for three years. He stated that he had first purchased a gun in 1981 after he had been injured in a mugging. Goetz also revealed that twice between 1981 and 1984 he had successfully warded off assailants simply by displaying the pistol.

According to Goetz's statement, the first contact he had with the four youths came when Canty, sitting or lying on the bench across from him, asked "how are you," to which he replied "fine." Shortly thereafter, Canty, followed by one of the other youths, walked over to the defendant and stood to his left, while the other two youths remained to his right, in the corner of the subway car. Canty then said "give me five dollars." Goetz stated that he knew from the smile on Canty's face that they wanted to "play with me." Although he was certain that none of the youths had a gun, he had a fear, based on prior experiences, of being "maimed."

Goetz then established "a pattern of fire," deciding specifically to fire from left to right. His stated intention at that point was to "murder [the four youths], to hurt them, to make them suffer as much as possible." When Canty again requested money, Goetz stood up, drew his weapon, and began firing, aiming for the center of the body of each of the four. Goetz recalled that the first two he shot "tried to run through the crowd [but] they had nowhere to run." Goetz then turned to his right to "go after the other two." One of these two "tried to run through the wall of the train, but . . . he had nowhere to go." The other youth (Cabey) "tried pretending that he wasn't with [the others]" by standing still, holding on to one of the subway hand straps, and not looking at Goetz. Goetz nonetheless fired his fourth shot at him. He then ran back to the first two youths to make sure they had been "taken care of." Seeing that they had both been shot, he spun back to check on the latter two. Goetz noticed that the youth who had been standing still was now sitting on a bench and seemed unhurt. As Goetz told the police, "I said '[you] seem to be all right, here's another,'" and he then fired the shot which severed Cabey's spinal cord. Goetz added that "if I was a little more under self-control . . . I would have put the barrel against his forehead and fired." He also admitted that "if I had had more [bullets], I would have shot them again, and again, and again."[2]

II

. . . The matter was presented to a Grand Jury in January 1985. . . . Neither the defendant nor any of the wounded youths testified before this Grand Jury. On

---

2. In a television interview conducted 20 years later, Goetz said that he knew the four young men were not "panhandling," explaining, "I was very familiar with the streets of New York. I know a mugging when it's going down." When asked if he thought it was possible that he shot "four innocent people," Goetz responded, "There are many things in my life that I regret and I wish I had taken a different path on. But that is not one of them." *Interview with "Subway Vigilante" Bernhard Goetz*, CNN Larry King Live (Dec. 17, 2004), *available at* http://www.cnn.com/TRANSCRIPTS /0412/17/lkl.01.html.

January 25, 1985, the Grand Jury indicted defendant on one count of criminal possession of a weapon in the third degree, for possessing the gun used in the subway shootings, and two counts of criminal possession of a weapon in the fourth degree, for possessing two other guns in his apartment building. It dismissed, however, the attempted murder and other charges stemming from the shootings themselves.

Several weeks after the Grand Jury's action, the People, asserting that they had newly available evidence, moved for an order authorizing them to resubmit the dismissed charges to a second Grand Jury. . . . Presentation of the case to the second Grand Jury began on March 14, 1985. Two of the four youths, Canty and Ramseur, testified. Among the other witnesses were four passengers from the seventh car of the subway who had seen some portions of the incident. Goetz again chose not to testify, though the tapes of his two statements were played for the grand jurors, as had been done with the first Grand Jury.

On March 27, 1985, the second Grand Jury filed a 10-count indictment, containing four charges of attempted murder, four charges of assault in the first degree, one charge of reckless endangerment in the first degree, and one charge of criminal possession of a weapon in the second degree [possession of a loaded firearm with intent to use it unlawfully against another]. Goetz was arraigned on this indictment on March 28, 1985, and it was consolidated with the earlier three-count indictment.

On October 14, 1985, Goetz moved to dismiss the charges contained in the second indictment alleging, among other things, . . . that the prosecutor's instructions to that Grand Jury on the defense of justification were erroneous and prejudicial to the defendant so as to render its proceedings defective.

 . . . .

III

Penal Law article 35 recognizes the defense of justification, which "permits the use of force under certain circumstances." One such set of circumstances pertains to the use of force in defense of a person, encompassing both self-defense and defense of a third person. Penal Law § 35.15(1) sets forth the general principles governing all such uses of force: "[a] person may . . . use physical force upon another person when and to the extent he *reasonably believes* such to be necessary to defend himself or a third person from what he *reasonably believes* to be the use or imminent use of unlawful physical force by such other person" (emphasis added).

Section 35.15(2) sets forth further limitations on these general principles with respect to the use of "deadly physical force": "A person may not use deadly physical force upon another person . . . unless (a) He *reasonably believes* that such other person is using or about to use deadly physical force . . . or (b) He *reasonably believes* that such other person is committing or attempting to commit a kidnapping, forcible rape, forcible sodomy or robbery" (emphasis added).

 . . . .

Because the evidence before the second Grand Jury included statements by Goetz that he acted to protect himself from being maimed or to avert a robbery, the prosecutor correctly chose to charge the justification defense in section 35.15 to the Grand Jury. The prosecutor properly instructed the grand jurors to consider whether the use of deadly physical force was justified to prevent either serious physical injury or a robbery, and, in doing so, to separately analyze the defense with respect to each of the charges. . . .

When the prosecutor had completed his charge, one of the grand jurors asked for clarification of the term "reasonably believes." The prosecutor responded by instructing the grand jurors that they were to consider the circumstances of the incident and determine "whether the defendant's conduct was that of a reasonable man in the defendant's situation." It is this response by the prosecutor—and specifically his use of "a reasonable man"—which is the basis for the dismissal of the charges by the lower courts. As expressed repeatedly in the Appellate Division's plurality opinion, because section 35.15 uses the term "*he* reasonably believes," the appropriate test, according to that court, is whether a defendant's beliefs and reactions were "reasonable to *him*." Under that reading of the statute, a jury which believed a defendant's testimony that he felt that his own actions were warranted and were reasonable would have to acquit him, regardless of what anyone else in defendant's situation might have concluded. Such an interpretation defies the ordinary meaning and significance of the term "reasonably" in a statute, and misconstrues the clear intent of the Legislature, in enacting section 35.15, to retain an objective element as part of any provision authorizing the use of deadly physical force.

Penal statutes in New York have long codified the right recognized at common law to use deadly physical force, under appropriate circumstances, in self-defense. These provisions have never required that an actor's belief as to the intention of another person to inflict serious injury be correct in order for the use of deadly force to be justified, but they have uniformly required that the belief comport with an objective notion of reasonableness. The 1829 statute, using language which was followed almost in its entirety until the 1965 recodification of the Penal Law, provided that the use of deadly force was justified in self-defense or in the defense of specified third persons "when there shall be a reasonable ground to apprehend a design to commit a felony, or to do some great personal injury, and there shall be imminent danger of such design being accomplished."

. . . .

[T]he Law Revision Commission, in a 1937 Report to the Legislature on the Law of Homicide in New York, summarized the self-defense statute as requiring a "reasonable belief in the imminence of danger," and stated that the standard to be followed by a jury in determining whether a belief was reasonable "is that of a man of ordinary courage in the circumstances surrounding the defendant at the time of the killing." The Report added that New York did not follow the view, adopted in a few States, that "the jury is required to adopt the subjective view and judge from the standpoint of the very defendant concerned."

. . . .

The provisions of the Model Penal Code with respect to the use of deadly force in self-defense reflect the position of its drafters that any culpability which arises from a mistaken belief in the need to use such force should be no greater than the culpability such a mistake would give rise to if it were made with respect to an element of a crime. Accordingly, under Model Penal Code § 3.04(2)(b), a defendant charged with murder (or attempted murder) need only show that he "*believe[d]* that [the use of deadly force] was necessary to protect himself against death, serious bodily injury, kidnapping or [forcible] sexual intercourse" to prevail on a self-defense claim (emphasis added). If the defendant's belief was wrong, and was recklessly, or negligently formed, however, he may be convicted of the type of homicide charge requiring only a reckless or negligent, as the case may be, criminal intent.

. . . .

New York did not follow the Model Penal Code's equation of a mistake as to the need to use deadly force with a mistake negating an element of a crime, choosing instead to use a single statutory section which would provide either a complete defense or no defense at all to a defendant charged with any crime involving the use of deadly force. The drafters of the new Penal Law [which was approved by the legislature in 1965] adopted in large part the structure and content of Model Penal Code § 3.04, but, crucially, inserted the word "reasonably" before "believes."

The plurality below agreed with defendant's argument that the change in the statutory language from "reasonable ground," used prior to 1965, to "he reasonably believes" in Penal Law § 35.15 evinced a legislative intent to conform to the subjective standard contained in Model Penal Code § 3.04. This argument, however, ignores the plain significance of the insertion of "reasonably." Had the drafters of section 35.15 wanted to adopt a subjective standard, they could have simply used the language of section 3.04. "Believes" by itself requires an honest or genuine belief by a defendant as to the need to use deadly force. Interpreting the statute to require only that the defendant's belief was "reasonable to *him*," as done by the plurality below, would hardly be different from requiring only a genuine belief; in either case, the defendant's own perceptions could completely exonerate him from any criminal liability.

We cannot lightly impute to the Legislature an intent to fundamentally alter the principles of justification to allow the perpetrator of a serious crime to go free simply because that person believed his actions were reasonable and necessary to prevent some perceived harm. To completely exonerate such an individual, no matter how aberrational or bizarre his thought patterns, would allow citizens to set their own standards for the permissible use of force. It would also allow a legally competent defendant suffering from delusions to kill or perform acts of violence with impunity, contrary to fundamental principles of justice and criminal law.

. . . .

Goetz also argues that the introduction of an objective element will preclude a jury from considering factors such as the prior experiences of a given actor and thus, require it to make a determination of "reasonableness" without regard to the actual circumstances of a particular incident. This argument, however, falsely presupposes that an objective standard means that the background and other relevant characteristics of a particular actor must be ignored. To the contrary, we have frequently noted that a determination of reasonableness must be based on the "circumstances" facing a defendant or his "situation." Such terms encompass more than the physical movements of the potential assailant. . . . [T]hese terms include any relevant knowledge the defendant had about that person.[3] They also necessarily bring in the physical attributes of all persons involved, including the defendant. Furthermore, the defendant's circumstances encompass any prior experiences he had which could provide a reasonable basis for a belief that another person's intentions were to injure or rob him or that the use of deadly force was necessary under the circumstances.

. . . .

Notes and Questions

1. The Criminal Trial Against Goetz. After the New York Court of Appeals reinstated the indictment, Goetz went to trial in 1987. A jury of eight men and four women returned a verdict of not guilty on all counts except criminal possession of a weapon in the third degree.

Goetz was sentenced to a prison term of one year. Although he was eligible for parole after 60 days, his request for early parole was denied because the parole board thought that his release "would deprecate the seriousness of the crime and undermine respect for the law." He ultimately spent eight months in jail. *See* Ronald Sullivan, *Goetz Parole Denied*, N.Y. TIMES, Mar. 4, 1989, at A31; Ronald Sullivan, *Self-Defense Claim in Subway Death*, N.Y. TIMES, Jan. 24, 1990, at B2.

Goetz now spends his days helping injured squirrels and selling electronic equipment on the Internet. He also ran unsuccessfully for public office in New York City, winning 1,300 votes for mayor in 2001 and 17,000 votes for public advocate in 2005. *See* Jennifer Steinhauer, *Undaunted by Their Slim Prospects, Outsiders Crowd Mayoral Race*, N.Y. TIMES, Aug. 28, 2001, at B1.

2. The Civil Trial Against Goetz. Darrell Cabey, the most seriously injured of Goetz's four victims, filed a civil damages suit against Goetz. Nine years after the criminal trial ended in an acquittal on most charges, the civil jury rejected Goetz's self-defense claim and ruled in favor of Cabey, awarding him $18 million in compensatory damages and $25 million in punitive damages. The award was largely

---

3. Earlier in the opinion, the court explained that this "relevant knowledge" included any information a defendant had about the assailant's prior acts of violence and reputation for violence.

a symbolic one, however, given Goetz's financial status. In fact, Goetz filed for bankruptcy a week after the civil verdict. The bankruptcy court refused to discharge the $43 million debt to Cabey, but to date Goetz has not paid the judgment entered against him and it is unlikely he will ever be able to do so. *See* Lynette Holloway, *Bankrupt, Goetz Still Owes Victim*, N.Y. Times, Aug. 2, 1996, at B3; Adam Nossiter, *Bronx Jury Orders Goetz to Pay Man He Paralyzed $43 Million*, N.Y. Times, Apr. 24, 1996, at A1.

There are various possible explanations for the difference in outcome between the criminal and civil trials. One is the lower standard of proof applied in civil cases. Another is the difference in the evidence presented at the two trials: the civil jury did not hear about the mugging Goetz experienced in 1981, but did hear evidence of racial slurs Goetz had made (including the comment that Cabey's mother should have had an abortion). In addition, the racial composition of the two juries differed: the six-person jury in the civil trial consisted of four African-Americans and two Latinos, whereas the 12-person jury in the criminal trial was composed of nine whites, two African-Americans, and one Latino. Moreover, the New York subways became cleaner and safer in the nine years that intervened between the two trials, perhaps making Goetz's "seemingly obsessive fears about crime . . . seem like a historical curiosity" in a different political atmosphere. *Id.*

3. **The Racial Context of the Goetz Case.** Although the New York subway shootings received a great deal of media attention and the public was well aware that Goetz was white and his four victims were African-American, the New York Court of Appeals failed to mention that fact. Likewise, there was little explicit discussion of race at Goetz's criminal trial, although "indirectly and covertly, the defense played on the racial factor." George P. Fletcher, A Crime of Self-Defense 206 (1988). Fletcher explained:

> [Defense counsel's] strategy of relentlessly attacking the "gang of four," "the predators" on society, calling them "vultures" and "savages," carried undeniable racial undertones. . . .
>
> The covert appeal to racial bias came out most dramatically in the re-creation of the shooting. . . . The defendant called in four props to stand in for the four victims. . . . The nominal purpose of the demonstration was to show the way in which each bullet entered the body of each victim. The defense's real purpose, however, was to re-create for the jury, as dramatically as possible, the scene that Goetz encountered when four young black passengers began to surround him. For that reason [defense counsel] asked the Guardian Angels to send him four young black men to act as the props in the demonstration. In came the four young black Guardian Angels, fit and muscular, dressed in T-shirts, to play the parts of the four victims in a courtroom minidrama.

Is the "implicit message" of defense counsel's tactic—that "[i]n a subway encounter with these four black toughs, any normal, reasonable person would have feared the worst"—impermissible racial stereotyping and an inappropriate appeal to racism? *Id.* at 134. Or is it simply a realistic reflection of the fact that "it is difficult to expect the ordinary person in our time not to perceive race as one—just one—of the factors defining the 'kind' of person who poses a danger"? *Id.* at 206. *Cf.* Cynthia Lee, *Making Race Salient: Trayvon Martin and Implicit Bias in a Not Yet Post-Racial Society*, 91 N.C. L. Rev. 1555, 1562 (2013) (discussing social science research "showing that individuals are more likely to perceive an action as aggressive, violent, and dangerous when committed by a Black person than when the same action is committed by a White person [and] that individuals are more likely to 'see' a weapon in the hands of a Black person than in the hands of a White person, even when the Black person is actually unarmed"). Does our acknowledgment that "racial discrimination violates contemporary social morality" mean that "an actor's failure to overcome his racism . . . is blameworthy and thus unreasonable, independent of whether or not it is 'typical'"? Jody D. Armour, *Race Ipsa Loquitur: Of Reasonable Racists, Intelligent Bayesians, and Involuntary Negrophobes*, 46 Stan. L. Rev. 781, 790 (1994). *See also* Cynthia Kwei Yung Lee, *Race and Self-Defense: Toward a Normative Conception of Reasonableness*, 81 Minn. L. Rev. 367, 495 (1996) (distinguishing a "normative" from a "positivist" (or "descriptive") model of reasonableness, noting that "[a] typical or common belief . . . is not necessarily a reasonable belief").

Was the race of the four victims especially relevant in assessing the reasonableness of Goetz's fear, given that he had received a beating three years earlier from three young African-American men that had permanently damaged his knee? Would it be equally reasonable for an African-American man to fear a group of four young white Skinheads who approached him and said "give me five dollars"? Are the two situations the same? If so, is it better to reject defenses in both cases because "granting legal recognition to [any such] self-defense claim communicates the state's approval of racial bias [and] reinforces derogatory cultural stereotypes"? Armour, *supra*, at 815. Or is that view "inconsistent with the principle that an actor should [not] be punished . . . for possessing or choosing to possess racist or otherwise illiberal beliefs or desires"? Stephen P. Garvey, *Self-Defense and the Mistaken Racist*, 11 New Crim. L. Rev. 119, 129 (2008).

Although the jurors in Goetz's criminal trial denied that race played a factor in their decision, some observers found their claims implausible. "If Goetz were a black man who shot four white youths on a subway train, there would be no doubt of the verdict. The media and the public would be screaming for the most stringent penalty possible." Joseph R. Tybor, *Message of Fear, Goetz's Acquittal Reflects American Beliefs*, Chi. Trib., June 21, 1987, at C1 (quoting N.Y. Assembly member Al Vann). (Compare the description in Chapter 6, Section E.1, of statistical evidence indicating that the race of a murder victim has a substantial impact on the likelihood the killer will be sentenced to die.)

4. Trayvon Martin. Issues of race and self-defense returned to the national spotlight in 2012 when George Zimmerman, a 28-year-old neighborhood watch volunteer, shot and killed Trayvon Martin, an unarmed 17-year-old African-American who was returning to his father's girlfriend's home from a convenience store around 7:00 p.m. Martin was wearing a hoodie, carrying a drink and a box of Skittles, and talking to his girlfriend on his cell phone. Zimmerman called 911 and told the dispatcher, "Hey, we've had some break-ins in my neighborhood . . . [a]nd there's a real suspicious guy" who "looks like he's up to no good, or he's on drugs or something. It's raining and he's just walking around, looking about." Zimmerman asked the 911 dispatcher when the police would arrive because "these assholes, they always get away." He then ignored the dispatcher's instructions to wait for the officers and not to follow Martin, and got out of his car when Martin, apparently having noticed that Zimmerman was following him, began running away from him. Accounts vary as to exactly what occurred at that point, but Zimmerman and Martin exchanged words, leading to a physical confrontation, and Zimmerman shot Martin in the chest. *See* Cynthia Lee, *Making Race Salient: Trayvon Martin and Implicit Bias in a Not Yet Post-Racial Society*, 91 N.C. L. Rev. 1555, 1557–58 (2013); John D. Moore, Note, *Reasonable Provocation: Distinguishing the Vigilant from the Vigilante in Self-Defense Law*, 78 Brook. L. Rev. 1659, 1672–73 (2013).

Zimmerman was charged with second-degree murder, but claimed that he acted in self-defense after Martin knocked him down, banged his head against the sidewalk, and appeared to be reaching for Zimmerman's gun. There were no eyewitnesses to the shooting itself, and those witnesses who did testify offered conflicting accounts of the incident. An all-female jury, one of whom was Latina and the rest white, acquitted Zimmerman of both second-degree murder (a killing "perpetrated by any act imminently dangerous to another and evincing a depraved mind regardless of human life") and manslaughter (a "culpabl[y] negligen[t]" killing). Fla. Stat. §§ 782.04(2), 782.07(1). *See* Lizette Alvarez, *Zimmerman Is Acquitted in Trayvon Martin Killing*, N.Y. Times, July 14, 2013, at A1. For information on the "stand your ground" issues arising in this case, see Note 1 following *People v. Tomlins* below.

5. Subjective Versus Objective Standards of Self-Defense. Although most courts agree with the New York Court of Appeals and require that a defendant's fear be both honest and reasonable in order to make out a claim of self-defense, a minority of states define self-defense to require only an honest fear. *See* 2 Wayne R. LaFave, Substantive Criminal Law § 10.4(c), at 147–49 (2d ed. 2003). Under the minority view, Goetz would have had a valid self-defense claim if he subjectively feared the four young men, even if his fear was unreasonable.

Is the minority approach preferable because it focuses on the "subjective mental culpability of the defendant" rather than the "long-standing fictional [reasonable person] standard," and thus better serves the criminal law's function of "punish[ing] morally culpable actors on the basis of their culpability and . . . their act"? Richard Singer, *The Goetz Case Revives Issue of Self-Defense Standards*, N.Y.L.J., Feb. 18, 1986, at 1.

Or does this argument "misconstrue[] the foundation of criminal responsibility" and undermine the criminal law's role in "enforc[ing] conventional expectations of reasonable behavior"? GEORGE P. FLETCHER, A CRIME OF SELF-DEFENSE 61 (1988). Fletcher was critical of subjective self-defense standards, noting that "[t]he basis for all blaming is not the offender's thoughts, but our judgment about whether he could and should have acted otherwise under the circumstances." *Id.* (For a general discussion of the wisdom of criminalizing negligent acts, see Chapter 4, Section B.2, Note 7 following *Villegas*.)

Even if punishing negligent behavior is justifiable in some circumstances, is it inappropriate in the self-defense context? Consider the views expressed by Glanville Williams in arguing that the Model Penal Code should incorporate a completely subjective approach to self-defense:

> The criminal law of negligence works best when it gives effect to the large number of rules of prudence which are commonly observed though not directly incorporated into the law. Such rules include the rule against pulling out on a blind corner, the rule against carrying a gun in such a way that it is pointing at another person, the rule against deliberately pointing a gun at another person, even in play, and so on. These rules are not part either of enacted or of common law, but as customary standards of behavior they become binding via the law of negligence. Are there any similar rules of behavior applicable when a person acts in self-defense . . . ? It must be recollected that the injury he inflicts on the other is in itself intentional, so that the usual rules of prudence in respect to the handling of weapons are not in question. The only question is whether the defendant was negligent in arriving at the conclusion that the use of force in question was called for. It is hard to imagine what rules of prudence could normally serve in this situation.

Model Penal Code § 3.09 Comment at 152 n.10 (quoting Glanville Williams).

6. The Model Penal Code Approach. As the court indicated in *Goetz,* the Model Penal Code authorizes the use of defensive force when the defendant "believes that such force is immediately necessary for the purpose of protecting himself against the use of unlawful force . . . on the present occasion." Model Penal Code § 3.04(1). The Code thus adopts a subjective definition of self-defense—subject, however, to the important limitations contained in § 3.09(2).

Section 3.09(2) provides that a defendant who "is reckless or negligent in having such belief [that defensive force is necessary] or in acquiring or failing to acquire any knowledge . . . that is material to the justifiability of his use of force" has no defense "in a prosecution for an offense for which recklessness or negligence, as the case may be, suffices to establish culpability." Thus, for example, a defendant who honestly but unreasonably believed that it was necessary to use defensive force—that is, one whose mistake about the need for self-defense was negligent—would be convicted of negligent homicide rather than murder.

The Comments explain the rationale underlying this approach:

> [A] person should not be convicted of a crime of intention where he has labored under a mistake that, had the facts been as he supposed, would have left him free from guilt. . . . To convict for a belief arrived at on an unreasonable ground is to convict for negligence. Where the crime otherwise requires greater culpability for conviction, it is neither fair nor logical to convict when there is only negligence as to the circumstances that would establish a justification.
>
> . . . [I]t makes more sense to assimilate the defendant who is reckless as to the existence of justifying circumstances to one who recklessly takes life than to assimilate him to one who purposefully does so.
>
> . . . Recklessness and negligence as to the factors that establish justification, in short, are treated on a parity with recklessness or negligence as to the other material elements of the offense involved.

Id. § 3.09 Comment at 151–52.

Is it sensible to group those who are negligent in appraising the need for self-defense with those who kill negligently, or does the validity of that comparison depend on how one characterizes cases involving an unreasonable use of defensive force? Consider Mark Kelman, *Interpretive Construction in the Substantive Criminal Law*, 33 Stan. L. Rev. 591, 616 (1981):

> On the one hand, we might view the killing incident as temporally disjoined; a negligent perception of the need to kill is *followed* by an intentional killing. Under this view, the defendant is more blameworthy than the traditional negligent killer (e.g., the bad driver, the person who plays with guns), because he has focused on the issue of whether to take human life and has gone ahead and done it. On the other hand, if the perception of the need to kill and the conduct are unified as a single incident, we will not see the killing as worse than the traditional negligent killing.

7. Imperfect Self-Defense. Some of the states that follow the traditional, objective approach to self-defense have adopted the doctrine of imperfect self-defense. In these jurisdictions, defendants who honestly but unreasonably believed that defensive force was necessary are convicted of manslaughter rather than murder.

In many of these states, cases of imperfect self-defense result in voluntary manslaughter convictions. Even though the killing was not committed in the heat of passion and therefore does not fit the traditional definition of voluntary manslaughter, that charge is considered an appropriate compromise on the grounds that the defendant's honest fear negates malice and, though culpable, the defendant is not as blameworthy as a cold-blooded killer. *See, e.g., Swann v. United States*, 648 A.2d 928, 930–31 (D.C. 1994); *Wilson v. State*, 30 A.3d 955, 960 (Md. 2011); *Commonwealth v. Colandro*, 80 A. 571, 573–75 (Pa. 1911). In other jurisdictions, however, these defendants are convicted of involuntary manslaughter, on the theory that their unreasonable fear makes the killing equivalent to reckless or negligent homicide. *See, e.g., State v. Beeler*, 12 S.W.3d 294, 297–300 (Mo. 2000); *State v. Clark*, 570 N.W.2d 195, 199 (N.D. 1997).

In the states that follow the traditional view of self-defense but do not recognize imperfect self-defense, a defendant who honestly but unreasonably believed defensive force was necessary is guilty of murder. *See, e.g., State v. Abdalaziz*, 729 A.2d 725 (Conn. 1999); *People v. Reese*, 815 N.W.2d 85 (Mich. 2012). *Cf. State v. Head*, 648 N.W.2d 413 (Wis. 2002) (applying state statute making imperfect self-defense second-degree murder).

Questions of imperfect self-defense dominated the South African trial of Olympic runner Oscar Pistorius, who fired four shots through a locked bathroom door in his home, killing his girlfriend, Reeva Steenkamp, on Valentine's Day in 2013. The prosecution argued that Pistorius, also known as "Blade Runner" because both his legs were amputated below the knee when he was an infant, deliberately killed Steenkamp following an argument. But the trial judge acquitted Pistorius of murder and convicted him of culpable (negligent) homicide, apparently believing that Pistorius thought he was acting in self-defense and mistook Steenkamp for an intruder. Pistorius was sentenced to five years in prison. The prosecution appealed the verdict, and South Africa's Supreme Court of Appeal reversed, concluding that the trial judge had misinterpreted the law in acquitting Pistorius of murder because the runner should have realized that his actions would kill whoever was in the bathroom. Although prosecutors sought the 15-year minimum sentence for murder called for by the country's sentencing guidelines, the trial judge imposed a six-year sentence, citing "mitigating factors" that included Pistorius' expressions of remorse and the fact that he "has lost his career and is ruined financially." The judge denied prosecutors' request to appeal what they called a "shockingly too lenient" sentence, and they have asked the Supreme Court of Appeal to impose a harsher sentence. *See* Norimitsu Onishi, *South African Appeals Court Convicts Pistorius of Murder*, N.Y. Times, Dec. 4, 2015, at A17; Norimitsu Onishi, *Pistorius Sentenced to Six Years in Girlfriend's 2013 Murder*, N.Y. Times, July 7, 2016, at A7; Sewell Chan, *Pistorius Prosecutor's Appeal Thwarted*, N.Y. Times, Aug. 27, 2016, at D6.

8. The Use of Excessive Force. As noted by the New York Court of Appeals, the amount of force used to defend oneself must be reasonable. Thus, the law of self-defense generally distinguishes between deadly and nondeadly force:

> In determining how much force one may use in self-defense, the law recognizes that the amount of force which he may justifiably use must be reasonably related to the threatened harm which he seeks to avoid. One may justifiably use *nondeadly* force against another in self-defense if he reasonably believes that the other is about to inflict unlawful bodily harm (it need not be death or serious bodily harm) upon him (and also believes that it is necessary to use such force to prevent it). . . . He may justifiably use *deadly* force against the other in self-defense, however, only if he reasonably believes that the other is about to inflict unlawful death or serious bodily harm upon him (and also that it is necessary to use deadly force to prevent it).

2 Wayne R. LaFave, Substantive Criminal Law § 10.4(a)–(b), at 144 (2d ed. 2003).

Three different approaches are used in drawing the line between deadly and non-deadly force. Some states follow the Model Penal Code, which focuses on the defendant's state of mind, defining deadly force as "force which the actor uses with the purpose of causing or which he knows to create a substantial risk of causing death or serious bodily harm." Model Penal Code § 3.11(2). Under this view, a defendant "uses deadly force if he fires at another with intent to kill him or do him serious bodily harm, though actually he misses him completely or causes him only minor bodily injury. But merely to threaten death or serious bodily harm, without any intention to carry out the threat, is not to use deadly force, so that one may be justified in pointing a gun at his attacker when he would not be justified in pulling the trigger." LaFave, *supra*, at 144. In other jurisdictions, the difference turns on the likely result of the defendant's conduct, so that the use of force is deadly, for example, only if it was "likely to cause" or "readily capable of causing" death or serious bodily injury. Still other states use a combination of the first two approaches, deeming the use of force to be deadly if it was either intended or likely to cause death or serious bodily injury. *See People v. Vasquez*, 148 P.3d 326, 328–29 (Colo. App. 2006) (citing conflicting authorities).

Serious bodily harm has been defined in this context as "bodily injury which creates a substantial risk of death or which causes serious, permanent disfigurement or loss or substantial impairment of the function of any bodily member or organ, or extended convalescence necessary for recovery of physical health." *State v. Sullivan*, 695 A.2d 115, 118 n.6 (Me. 2007) (quoting state statute). *Cf. Manuel v. State*, 667 So. 2d 590, 591–93 (Miss. 1995) (noting that an assailant's fists can create a reasonable fear of serious bodily injury). (For discussion of how the term is defined in cases where a second-degree murder charge is based on the theory that the defendant intended to inflict serious bodily injury, see Note 6 following *People v. Knoller* in Chapter 6, Section C.1.) For the view that a defendant may use deadly force when threatened with rape, see *State v. Havican*, 569 A.2d 1089 (Conn. 1990); Judith Fabricant, *Homicide in Response to a Threat of Rape: A Theoretical Examination of the Rule of Justification*, 11 Golden Gate U. L. Rev. 945 (1981).

Was Goetz confronted with a threat of only nondeadly force, so that he used excessive force by shooting the four victims? Could he have responded with nondeadly force, for example, by displaying his gun or drawing it without firing?

Even if it was reasonable for Goetz to use deadly force, did the fifth shot constitute excessive force? According to Goetz's confession, quoted in the New York Court of Appeals' opinion, he fired the fifth shot at Cabey after checking on the victims and finding that Cabey "seem[ed] to be all right." In acquitting Goetz, the jury apparently decided that he was confused when he made this statement to the police. Instead, the jury seemed to credit testimony introduced at the trial which suggested that the five shots were fired in rapid succession, without much of a break before the last one, and that Goetz was operating on "automatic pilot" when he emptied his gun in a rush of adrenaline. *See* GEORGE P. FLETCHER, A CRIME OF SELF-DEFENSE 105–06, 191–97 (1988).

9. Self-Defense as an Excuse. Although historically self-defense was considered an excuse, most jurisdictions now classify it as a justification. Nonetheless, in some respects, self-defense continues to resemble an excuse. For example, the defense is available even if the defendant's fear of the victim turned out to be mistaken, so long as it was reasonable. In the oft-quoted words of Justice Holmes, "[d]etached reflection cannot be demanded in the presence of an uplifted knife." *Brown v. United States*, 256 U.S. 335, 343 (1921). Likewise, defendants who are threatened with serious bodily harm are entitled to kill in self-defense even if they are in no danger of dying, and they may also kill to protect their homes in some circumstances (*see* Section C.1 below). Thus, as one commentator has noted, "[t]he theory of self-defense . . . oscillates between a rationale of excuse and of justification." GEORGE P. FLETCHER, RETHINKING CRIMINAL LAW 767 (1978). *Cf.* Marcia Baron, *Justifications and Excuses*, 2 OHIO ST. J. CRIM. L. 387 (2005) (arguing that self-defense operates as a justification even in cases where defendants make reasonable mistakes).

10. Defending Third Persons. The New York statute at issue in *Goetz* authorizes a defendant to use defensive force to protect a third person, so long as the defendant reasonably believed that the use of force was necessary to protect the other person from an imminent threat of unlawful physical force. In enacting this statute, the legislature overturned a controversial New York opinion adopting the so-called "alter ego" approach for cases involving the defense of third persons.

In that decision, *People v. Young*, 183 N.E.2d 319 (N.Y. 1962) (per curiam), the defendant was charged with assault when he came to the aid of a young African-American man who was being beaten by two middle-aged white men. Unbeknownst to Young, the two older men were in fact undercover police officers who were lawfully attempting to arrest the young man. The New York Court of Appeals concluded that "the right of a person to defend another ordinarily should not be greater than such person's right to defend himself." *Id.* at 320. Because Young was deemed to step into the shoes of the young man, who had no right to resist a lawful arrest, Young could not justify his use of force on the ground that he was defending a third person.

Was the approach taken in *Young* sensible given that "the potential incidence of mistake in estimating fault or the need for action . . . is increased where the actor is protecting a stranger, because in such circumstances he is less likely to know which party to the quarrel is in the right"? Model Penal Code § 3.05 Comment at 65. Or is it preferable to focus, as the New York statute does, on the reasonableness of the defendant's perceptions in the hopes of "discouraging indifference to the plight of strangers"? *Commonwealth v. Young*, 959 N.E.2d 943, 952 (Mass. 2012). The Model Penal Code takes the latter view, *see id.* § 3.05, as do a majority of states. *See* JOSHUA DRESSLER, UNDERSTANDING CRIMINAL LAW § 19.01, at 258 (7th ed. 2015). The Comments to the Model Penal Code offer the following criticism of the alter ego approach:

The cautious potential actor who knows the law will, in the vast majority of cases, refrain from acting at all, with the result that an innocent person is injured without receiving any assistance from bystanders. If the actor goes to the aid of a seeming victim, however, he will be liable if wrong even without fault on his part in estimating the circumstances.

Model Penal Code § 3.05 Comment at 66.

One controversy surrounding the defense of third persons that has arisen in recent years is whether the defense can be used to protect an unborn child. Courts in different states disagree whether the defense is available to protect a fetus. *See* 2 Wayne R. LaFave, Substantive Criminal Law § 10.5, at 40–41 (2d ed. Supp. 2015).

State v. Norman

378 S.E.2d 8 (N.C. 1989)

Mitchell, Justice.

The defendant [Judy Norman] was tried . . . upon a proper indictment charging her with the first degree murder of her husband [John (J.T.)]. The jury found the defendant guilty of voluntary manslaughter. The defendant appealed from the trial court's judgment sentencing her to six years' imprisonment.

. . . Notwithstanding the uncontroverted evidence that the defendant shot her husband three times in the back of the head as he lay sleeping in his bed, the Court of Appeals held that the defendant's evidence that she exhibited what has come to be called "the battered wife syndrome" entitled her to have the jury consider whether the homicide was an act of perfect self-defense and, thus, not a legal wrong. [Accordingly, the Court of Appeals concluded that the trial judge had erred in refusing to instruct the jury on self-defense and reversed the conviction.]

. . . .

The defendant presented evidence tending to show a long history of physical and mental abuse by her husband due to his alcoholism. At the time of the killing, the thirty-nine-year-old defendant and her husband had been married almost twenty-five years and had several children. The defendant testified that her husband had started drinking and abusing her about five years after they were married. His physical abuse of her consisted of frequent assaults that included slapping, punching and kicking her, striking her with various objects, and throwing glasses, beer bottles and other objects at her. The defendant described other specific incidents of abuse, such as her husband putting her cigarettes out on her, throwing hot coffee on her, breaking glass against her face and crushing food on her face. Although the defendant did not present evidence of ever having received medical treatment for any physical injuries inflicted by her husband, she displayed several scars about her face which she attributed to her husband's assaults.

The defendant's evidence also tended to show other indignities inflicted upon her by her husband. Her evidence tended to show that her husband did not work and forced her to make money by prostitution, and that he made humor of that fact to family and friends. He would beat her if she resisted going out to prostitute herself or if he was unsatisfied with the amounts of money she made. He routinely called the defendant "dog," "bitch" and "whore," and on a few occasions made her eat pet food out of the pets' bowls and bark like a dog. He often made her sleep on the floor. At times, he deprived her of food and refused to let her get food for the family. During those years of abuse, the defendant's husband threatened numerous times to kill her and to maim her in various ways.

. . . .

In the early morning hours on the day before his death, the defendant's husband, who was intoxicated, went to a rest area off I-85 near Kings Mountain where the defendant was engaging in prostitution and assaulted her. While driving home, he was stopped by a patrolman and jailed on a charge of driving while impaired. After the defendant's mother got him out of jail at the defendant's request later that morning, he resumed his drinking and abuse of the defendant.

The defendant's evidence also tended to show that her husband seemed angrier than ever after he was released from jail and that his abuse of the defendant was more frequent. That evening, sheriff's deputies were called to the Norman residence, and the defendant complained that her husband had been beating her all day and she could not take it anymore. The defendant was advised to file a complaint, but she said she was afraid her husband would kill her if she had him arrested. The deputies told her they needed a warrant before they could arrest her husband, and they left the scene.[4]

The deputies were called back less than an hour later after the defendant had taken a bottle of pills. The defendant's husband cursed her and called her names as she was attended by paramedics, and he told them to let her die. A sheriff's deputy finally chased him back into his house as the defendant was put into an ambulance. The defendant's stomach was pumped at the local hospital, and she was sent home with her mother.

While in the hospital, the defendant was visited by a therapist with whom she discussed filing charges against her husband and having him committed for treatment. Before the therapist left, the defendant agreed to go to the mental health center the next day to discuss those possibilities. The therapist testified at trial that the defendant seemed depressed in the hospital, and that she expressed considerable anger toward her husband. He testified that the defendant threatened a number of times

---

4. In fact, however, the police were authorized to make a warrantless arrest for misdemeanor assault, even though the crime was not committed in their presence, so long as they had probable cause to believe that an assault occurred and that J.T. might cause property damage or "physical injury to himself or others" unless "immediately arrested." N.C. Gen. Stat. § 15A-401(b)(2).

that night to kill her husband and that she said she should kill him "because of the things he had done to her."

The next day, the day she shot her husband, the defendant went to the mental health center to talk about charges and possible commitment, and she confronted her husband with that possibility. She testified that she told her husband later that day: "J.T., straighten up. Quit drinking. I'm going to have you committed to help you." She said her husband then told her he would "see them coming" and would cut her throat before they got to him.

The defendant also went to the social services office that day to seek welfare benefits, but her husband followed her there, interrupted her interview and made her go home with him. He continued his abuse of her, threatening to kill and to maim her, slapping her, kicking her, and throwing objects at her. At one point, he took her cigarette and put it out on her, causing a small burn on her upper torso. He would not let her eat or bring food into the house for their children.

That evening, the defendant and her husband went into their bedroom to lie down, and he called her a "dog" and made her lie on the floor when he lay down on the bed. Their daughter brought in her baby to leave with the defendant, and the defendant's husband agreed to let her baby-sit. After the defendant's husband fell asleep, the baby started crying and the defendant took it to her mother's house so it would not wake up her husband. She returned shortly with the pistol and killed her husband.

The defendant testified at trial that she was too afraid of her husband to press charges against him or to leave him. She said that she had temporarily left their home on several previous occasions, but he had always found her, brought her home and beaten her. . . .

The defendant and other witnesses testified that for years her husband had frequently threatened to kill her and to maim her. . . .

Two expert witnesses in forensic psychology and psychiatry who examined the defendant after the shooting, Dr. William Tyson and Dr. Robert Rollins, testified that the defendant fit the profile of battered wife syndrome. This condition, they testified, is characterized by such abuse and degradation that the battered wife comes to believe she is unable to help herself and cannot expect help from anyone else. She believes that she cannot escape the complete control of her husband and that he is invulnerable to law enforcement and other sources of help.

Dr. Tyson, a psychologist, was asked his opinion as to whether, on 12 June 1985, "it appeared reasonably necessary for Judy Norman to shoot J.T. Norman"? He replied: . . . "I think Judy Norman felt that she had no choice, both in the protection of herself and her family, but to engage, exhibit deadly force against Mr. Norman, and that in so doing, she was sacrificing herself, both for herself and for her family."

Dr. Rollins . . . testified that in his opinion the defendant was a typical abused spouse and that "[s]he saw herself as powerless to deal with the situation, that there was no alternative, no way she could escape it." . . .

The killing of another human being is the most extreme recourse to our inherent right of self-preservation and can be justified in law only by the utmost real or apparent necessity. . . . Only if defendants are required to show that they killed due to a reasonable belief that death or great bodily harm was imminent can the justification for homicide remain clearly and firmly rooted in necessity. The imminence requirement ensures that deadly force will be used only where it is necessary as a last resort in the exercise of the inherent right of self-preservation. . . .

The term "imminent" . . . has been defined as "immediate danger, such as must be instantly met, such as cannot be guarded against by calling for the assistance of others or the protection of the law." Black's Law Dictionary 676 (5th ed. 1979). Our cases have sometimes used the phrase "about to suffer" interchangeably with "imminent" to describe the immediacy of threat that is required to justify killing in self-defense.

. . . The evidence tended to show that no harm was "imminent" or about to happen to the defendant when she shot her husband. The uncontroverted evidence was that her husband had been asleep for some time when she walked to her mother's house, returned with the pistol, fixed the pistol after it jammed and then shot her husband three times in the back of the head. The defendant was not faced with an instantaneous choice between killing her husband or being killed or seriously injured. Instead, *all* of the evidence tended to show that the defendant had ample time and opportunity to resort to other means of preventing further abuse by her husband. . . . Additionally, no [violent] action by the decedent had been underway immediately prior to his falling asleep.

. . . .

Dr. Tyson . . . testified that the defendant "believed herself to be doomed . . . to a life of the worst kind of torture and abuse, degradation that she had experienced over the years in a progressive way; that it would only get worse, and that death was inevitable." Such evidence of the defendant's speculative beliefs concerning her remote and indefinite future, while indicating she had felt generally threatened, did not tend to show that she killed in the belief—reasonable or otherwise—that her husband presented a threat of *imminent death or great bodily harm.* Under our law of self-defense, a defendant's subjective belief of what might be "inevitable" at some indefinite point in the future does not equate to what she believes to be "imminent." . . .

The defendant testified that, "I knowed when he woke up, it was going to be the same thing, and I was scared when he took me to the truck stop that night it was going to be worse than he had ever been." . . . Testimony about such indefinite fears concerning what her sleeping husband might do at some time in the future did not tend to establish a fear—reasonable or otherwise—of *imminent death or great bodily harm* at the time of the killing.

We are not persuaded by the reasoning of our Court of Appeals in this case that when there is evidence of battered wife syndrome, neither an actual attack nor threat of attack by the husband at the moment the wife uses deadly force is required to justify the wife's killing of him in perfect self-defense. The Court of Appeals concluded that to impose such requirements would ignore the "learned helplessness," meekness and other realities of battered wife syndrome and would effectively preclude such women from exercising their right of self-defense. . . .

The Court of Appeals suggests that . . . the jury, based on the evidence of the decedent's intensified abuse during the thirty-six hours preceding his death, could have found that the decedent's passive state at the time of his death was "but a momentary hiatus in a continuous reign of terror by the decedent [and] the defendant merely took advantage of her first opportunity to protect herself." . . . Such predictions of future assaults to justify the defendant's use of deadly force in this case would be entirely speculative, because there was no evidence that her husband had ever inflicted any harm upon her that approached life-threatening injury, even during the "reign of terror." It is far from clear in the defendant's poignant evidence that any abuse by the decedent had ever involved the degree of physical threat required to justify the defendant in using deadly force, even when those threats were imminent. The use of deadly force in self-defense to prevent harm other than death or great bodily harm is excessive as a matter of law.

MARTIN, JUSTICE, dissenting.

          . . . .

At the heart of the majority's reasoning is its unsubstantiated concern that to find that the evidence presented by defendant would support an instruction on self-defense would "expand our law of self-defense beyond the limits of immediacy and necessity." Defendant does not seek to expand or relax the requirements of self-defense and thereby "legalize the opportune killing of allegedly abusive husbands by their wives," as the majority overstates. Rather, defendant contends that the evidence as gauged by the existing laws of self-defense is sufficient to require the submission of a self-defense instruction to the jury. . . .

Evidence presented by defendant described a twenty-year history of beatings and other dehumanizing and degrading treatment by her husband. In his expert testimony a clinical psychologist concluded that defendant fit "and exceed[ed]" the profile of an abused or battered spouse, analogizing this treatment to the dehumanization process suffered by prisoners of war under the Nazis during the Second World War and the brainwashing techniques of the Korean War. The psychologist described the defendant as a woman incarcerated by abuse, by fear, and by her conviction that her husband was invincible and inescapable:

> Mrs. Norman didn't leave because she believed, fully believed that escape was totally impossible. There was no place to go. [S]he had left before; he had come and gotten her. She had gone to the Department of Social Services.

He had come and gotten her. [S]he believed the law could not protect her; no one could protect her, and I must admit, looking over the records, that there was nothing done that would contradict that belief. She fully believed that he was invulnerable to the law and to all social agencies that were available; that nobody could withstand his power. As a result, there was no such thing as escape. . . .

In addition to the testimony of the clinical psychologist, defendant presented the testimony of witnesses who had actually seen defendant's husband abuse her. These witnesses described circumstances that caused not only defendant to believe escape was impossible, but that also convinced *them* of its impossibility. Defendant's isolation and helplessness were evident in testimony that her family was intimidated by her husband into acquiescing in his torture of her. Witnesses also described defendant's experience with social service agencies and the law, which had contributed to her sense of futility and abandonment through the inefficacy of their protection and the strength of her husband's wrath when they failed. Where torture appears interminable and escape impossible, the belief that only the death of the oppressor can provide relief is reasonable in the mind of a person of ordinary firmness, let alone in the mind of the defendant, who, like a prisoner of war of some years, has been deprived of her humanity and is held hostage by fear.

. . . .

Evidence presented in the case *sub judice* revealed no letup of tension or fear, no moment in which the defendant felt released from impending serious harm, even while the decedent slept. This, in fact, is a state of mind common to the battered spouse. . . . Psychologists have observed and commentators have described a "constant state of fear" brought on by the cyclical nature of battering as well as the battered spouse's perception that her abuser is both "omnipotent and unstoppable." Constant fear means a perpetual anticipation of the next blow, a perpetual expectation that the next blow will kill. "[T]he battered wife is constantly in a heightened state of terror because she is certain that one day her husband will kill her during the course of a beating. . . . Thus from the perspective of the battered wife, the danger is constantly 'immediate.'" . . . In the context of the doctrine of self-defense, "imminent" is a term the meaning of which must be grasped from the defendant's point of view. Properly stated, . . . the question is not whether the threat was in fact imminent, but whether defendant's belief in the impending nature of the threat, given the circumstances as she saw them, was reasonable in the mind of a person of ordinary firmness.

Defendant's intense fear, based on her belief that her husband intended not only to maim or deface her, as he had in the past, but to kill her, was evident in the testimony of witnesses who recounted events of the last three days of the decedent's life. This testimony could have led a juror to conclude that defendant reasonably perceived a threat to her life as "imminent," even while her husband slept. Over these three days, her husband's anger was exhibited in an unprecedented crescendo of violence. The evidence showed defendant's fear and sense of hopelessness similarly intensifying, leading to an unsuccessful attempt to escape through suicide and culminating in her belief that escape would be possible only through her husband's death.

[At this point, the dissent recited in detail some of the testimony elicited at Norman's trial. In addition to facts already set out above, the dissent described the following evidence:

. . . Mark Navarra [the boyfriend of defendant's daughter Phyllis] testified that at one point [on the day before the killing] defendant's husband threw a sandwich that defendant had made for him on the floor. She made another; he threw it on the floor, as well, then insisted she prepare one without touching it. Defendant's husband had then taken the third sandwich, which defendant had wrapped in paper towels, and smeared it on her face. Both Navarra and Phyllis testified that they had later watched defendant's husband seize defendant's cigarette and put it out on her neck, the scars from which defendant displayed to the jury.

Navarra also testified that "in the year and a half he had lived with the Normans, he had never seen defendant's husband madder than he was on [the day he died], opining that it was the DUI arrest two days before that had ignited [his] fury."

Defendant's mother testified that "her son-in-law had reacted to the discovery that her daughter had taken [an overdose of] pills with cursing and obscenities and threats such as, 'Now, you're going to pay for taking those pills,' and 'I'll kill you, your mother and your grandmother.' His rage was such that defendant's mother feared he might kill the whole family, and knowing defendant's sister had a gun in her purse, she took the gun and placed it in her own."

A friend of defendant's husband who was driving with the couple on the day of the shooting testified that "defendant's husband 'started slapping on her' when she was following a truck too closely, . . . periodically poured his beer . . . on defendant's head . . . and kicked defendant, who was still driving, in the side of the head."

Phyllis testified that "her father had beaten her mother 'all day long'" on the day he died. She also testified that was "the third day defendant's husband had forbidden her to eat any food."

The defendant testified that, after taking Phyllis' baby to her mother's house, she "asked her mother to watch the baby, then asked if her mother had anything for [a] headache, as her head was 'busting.' Her mother responded that she had some pain pills in her purse. Defendant went in to get the pills, 'and the gun was in there, and I don't know, I just seen the gun, and I took it out, and I went back there and shot him.'"]

From this evidence of the exacerbated nature of the last three days of twenty years of provocation, a juror could conclude that defendant believed that her husband's threats to her life were viable, that serious bodily harm was imminent, and that it was necessary to kill her husband to escape that harm. And from this evidence a juror could find defendant's belief in the necessity to kill her husband not merely reasonable but compelling.

The [law of] self-defense [also] requires that there be evidence that the defendant was not the aggressor in bringing on the affray. If the defendant was the aggressor and killed with murderous intent, that is, the intent to kill or inflict serious bodily harm, then she is not entitled to an instruction on self-defense. A hiatus between provocation by the decedent and the killing can mark the initiation of a new confrontation between the defendant and the decedent, such that the defendant's earlier perception of imminent danger no longer appears reasonable and the defendant becomes the aggressor. . . .

Where the defendant is a battered wife, there is no analogue to the victim-turned-aggressor, who . . . turns the tables on the decedent in a fresh confrontation. Where the defendant is a battered wife, the affray out of which the killing arises can be a continuing assault. There was evidence before the jury that it had not been defendant but her husband who had initiated "the affray," which the jury could have regarded as lasting twenty years, three days, or any number of hours preceding his death. . . .

Finally, . . . self-defense poses the question of whether there was any evidence tending to show that the force used by defendant to repel her husband was not excessive, that is, more than reasonably appeared to be necessary under the circumstances. This question is answered in part by abundant testimony describing defendant's immobilization by fear caused by abuse by her husband. Three witnesses, including the decedent's best friend, all recounted incidents in which defendant passively accepted beating, kicks, commands, or humiliating affronts without striking back. From such evidence that she was paralyzed by her husband's presence, a jury could infer that it reasonably appeared to defendant to be necessary to kill her husband in order ultimately to protect herself from the death he had threatened and from severe bodily injury, a foretaste of which she had already experienced.[5]

Notes and Questions

1. **The Incidence and Impact of Domestic Violence.** The Surgeon General has described domestic violence as the "single largest cause of injury to women in the United States," S. Rep. No. 101-545, at 37 (1990), and more than one-fifth of women report having been physically assaulted by their intimate partners at some point in their lives. *See* PATRICIA TJADEN & NANCY THOENNES, U.S. DEP'T OF JUSTICE, EXTENT, NATURE, AND CONSEQUENCES OF INTIMATE PARTNER VIOLENCE 10 (2000), *available at* http://www.ncjrs.gov/pdffiles1/nij/181867.pdf.

---

5. Three months after the court's decision in this case, the Governor commuted Norman's sentence and ordered her release; she had served two months in prison. *See* Kerry A. Shad, State v. Norman: *Self-Defense Unavailable to Battered Women Who Kill Passive Abusers*, 68 N.C. L. REV. 1159, 1162 n.24 (1989).

The Senate Report issued in connection with Congress' consideration of the 1994 Violence Against Women Act elaborated on these points:

> In nineteenth century America, courts drew a curtain around the home, refusing to intervene in cases of spouse abuse. Some courts even sanctioned the "salutary restraint of domestic discipline" but applied the "rule of thumb" limiting "chastisement" to a stick no bigger than a man's thumb. Up until as late as 15 years ago, many jurisdictions refused to arrest and prosecute spouse abusers, even though a comparable assault on the street by a stranger would have led to a lengthy jail term.
>
> ... Statistics present a chilling picture of just how serious—indeed even lethal—spouse abuse may be. Between 2,000 and 4,000 women die every year from abuse. Every day, four women are killed by their male partners and, in many of those cases, the homicides are the culmination of repeated, but lesser, abuse. One-third of all domestic violence cases, if reported, would be classified by police as felony rape, robbery, or aggravated assault; the remaining two-thirds involve bodily injury at least as serious as the injury inflicted in 90 percent of all robberies and aggravated assaults.
>
> Unlike other crimes, spouse abuse is "chronic" violence. It is persistent intimidation and repeated physical injury. Absent intervention "one can almost guarantee that the same woman will be assaulted again and again by the same man." One study showed that, over a 6-month period following a domestic violence incident, one-third of the victims will be subject to another rape, robbery, aggravated or simple assault. And this chronic abuse often escalates. One study showed that in over half of all murders of wives by their husbands, police had been called to the residence five times in the previous year to investigate a domestic violence complaint.
>
> ... The 3 to 4 million women abused each year are not located in any one area, among any one socio-economic group, or from any particular race, ethnic or religious group. The common perception that battering affects only poor, uneducated, and minority populations, is simply incorrect. ...
>
> ... Over 1 million women in the United States seek medical assistance each year for injuries sustained by their husbands or other partners. As many as 20 percent of hospital emergency room cases are related to wife battering.

S. Rep. No. 101-545, at 36–37 (1990).

Although the number of reported incidents of domestic assault has decreased in recent years along with the overall crime rate, current or former intimate partners are responsible for more than a quarter of the serious violent crimes committed against women and almost one-third of the homicides. *See* Jennifer L. Truman & Rachel E. Morgan, U.S. Dep't of Justice, Nonfatal Domestic Violence, 2003–2012, at 5 (2014), *available at* http://www.bjs.gov/content/pub/pdf/ndv0312.pdf; Callie Marie Rennison & Sarah Welchans, Bureau of Justice Statistics,

INTIMATE PARTNER VIOLENCE 1 (2000), http://www.bjs.gov/content/pub/pdf/ipv .pdf. Moreover, domestic violence remains underreported, with some surveys finding that women fail to report almost three-fourths of physical assaults. *See* TJADEN & THOENNES, *supra*, at 49.

2. The Battered Woman Syndrome. The term "battered woman syndrome" referred to in *Norman* describes "a collection of common behavioral and psychological characteristics exhibited in women who repeatedly are physically and emotionally abused over a prolonged length of time by the dominant male figure in their lives." *State v. Hess*, 23 A.3d 373, 378 (N.J. 2011). In an opinion issued almost 30 years earlier, the New Jersey Supreme Court explained the concept as follows, building on theories about learned helplessness and the cycle of violence developed by psychologist Lenore Walker in her path-breaking books, The BATTERED WOMAN (1979) and THE BATTERED WOMAN SYNDROME (1984):

> [R]elationships characterized by physical abuse tend to develop battering cycles. Violent behavior directed at the woman occurs in three distinct and repetitive stages that vary both in duration and intensity depending on the individuals involved.
>
> Phase one of the battering cycle is referred to as the "tension-building stage," during which the battering male engages in minor battering incidents and verbal abuse while the woman, beset by fear and tension, attempts to be as placating and passive as possible in order to stave off more serious violence.
>
> Phase two of the battering cycle is the "acute battering incident." At some point during phase one, the tension between the battered woman and the batterer becomes intolerable and more serious violence inevitable. The triggering event that initiates phase two is most often an internal or external event in the life of the battering male, but provocation for more severe violence is sometimes provided by the woman who can no longer tolerate or control her phase-one anger and anxiety.
>
> Phase three of the battering cycle is characterized by extreme contrition and loving behavior on the part of the battering male. During this period the man will often mix his pleas for forgiveness and protestations of devotion with promises to seek professional help, to stop drinking, and to refrain from further violence. For some couples, this period of relative calm may last as long as several months, but in a battering relationship the affection and contrition of the man will eventually fade and phase one of the cycle will start anew.
>
> The cyclical nature of the battering behavior helps explain why more women simply do not leave their abusers. The loving behavior demonstrated by the batterer during phase three reinforces whatever hopes these women might have for their mate's reform and keeps them bound to the relationship.

. . . .

[Moreover, some] women . . . become so demoralized and degraded by the fact that they cannot predict or control the violence that they sink into a state of psychological paralysis and become unable to take any action at all to improve or alter the situation. There is a tendency in battered women to believe in the omnipotence or strength of their battering husbands and thus to feel that any attempt to resist them is hopeless.

In addition to these psychological impacts, external social and economic factors often make it difficult for some women to extricate themselves from battering relationships. A woman without independent financial resources who wishes to leave her husband often finds it difficult to do so because of a lack of material and social resources.

. . . .

In addition, battered women, when they want to leave the relationship, are typically unwilling to reach out and confide in their friends, family, or the police, either out of shame and humiliation, fear of reprisal by their husband, or the feeling they will not be believed. . . .

Finally, battered women are often hesitant to leave a battering relationship because, in addition to their hope of reform on the part of their spouse, they harbor a deep concern about the possible response leaving might provoke in their mates. They literally become trapped by their own fear. Case histories are replete with instances in which a battered wife left her husband only to have him pursue her and subject her to an even more brutal attack.

State v. Kelly, 478 A.2d 364, 371–72 (N.J. 1984).

The "case histories" referred to by the court in *Kelly* are part of a general trend described by one commentator as follows:

At least half of women who leave their abusers are followed and harassed or further attacked by them. In one study of interspousal homicide, more than half of the men who killed their spouses did so when the partners were separated; in contrast, less than ten percent of women who killed were separated at the time. . . . Men who kill their wives describe their feeling of loss of control over the woman as a primary factor; most frequently, the man expresses the fear that the woman was about to abandon him, though in fact this fear may have been unfounded.

Martha R. Mahoney, *Legal Images of Battered Women: Redefining the Issue of Separation*, 90 MICH. L. REV. 1, 64–65 (1991). *See also* JENNIFER L. TRUMAN & RACHEL E. MORGAN, U.S. DEP'T OF JUSTICE, NONFATAL DOMESTIC VIOLENCE, 2003–2012, at 11 (2014), *available at* http://www.bjs.gov/content/pub/pdf/ndv0312.pdf (reporting that women who are separated from their husbands are 40 times more likely to experience intimate partner abuse than married women, 10 times more likely than women who have never married, and four times more likely than divorced women).

3. Criticism of the Theory. Some commentators have criticized the characterization of battered women as passive and helpless:

[M]any of these "helpless" women attempted

> "to control other people and events in the environment to keep the batterer from losing his temper. . . . One woman interviewed spent an enormous amount of time talking about her efforts to control her mother, his mother, and their children so that none of them would upset her husband. She found that if she kept all these people in check through some interesting manipulations, life was pleasant in their home. The moment someone got out of line, her man began his beatings."

> . . . .

> If these women are so passive, dependent and helpless, where do they get the strength and courage to live, day after day, with the abuse, humiliation and violence? Where do they get the intestinal fortitude to protect their children, pay their bills, maintain their facade of wedded bliss? And, in those rare instances, where do they get the desperation to kill?

Christine A. Littleton, *Women's Experience and the Problem of Transition: Perspectives on Male Battering of Women*, 1989 U. CHI. LEGAL F. 23, 41, 30 (quoting LENORE E. WALKER, THE BATTERED WOMAN 34 (1979)). Pointing out that many victims of domestic violence seek help or try to leave their abusive relationships, another author concluded that it is "the helping professions, rather than battered women, that [are] afflicted with 'helplessness.'" Martha R. Mahoney, *Legal Images of Battered Women: Redefining the Issue of Separation*, 90 MICH. L. REV. 1, 61–62 (1991). *See also* CHRISTOPHER PETERSON ET AL., LEARNED HELPLESSNESS: A THEORY FOR THE AGE OF PERSONAL CONTROL 238–39 (1993) (reporting that passivity, rather than a sign of helplessness, is in fact "instrumental"—a deliberate strategy on the part of the woman to try to placate the abuser).

In response to criticisms of the battered woman syndrome and learned helplessness theories, the term "battered woman syndrome" has now been replaced by the "social agency" theory or simply "battering and its effects." *See, e.g.*, Cal. Evid. Code § 1107(a) (providing for the admissibility of expert testimony regarding "intimate partner battering and its effects"). Experts testifying in support of battered women's self-defense claims today tend to emphasize the social realities facing victims of domestic violence, including the control exercised by the batterer, the lack of alternatives available to the woman, and the dangers of leaving the abusive relationship. They describe the steps victims take to protect themselves and the hurdles they encounter in obtaining help, and their testimony focuses on the non-psychological effects of abusive relationships. *See* MARY ANN DUTTON, UPDATE OF THE "BATTERED WOMAN SYNDROME" CRITIQUE 4, 7–8 (Aug. 2009), http://www.vawnet.org/material/update-battered-woman-syndrome-critique; Sue Osthoff & Holly Maguigan, *Explaining Without Pathologizing: Testimony on Battering and Its Effects, in* CURRENT

Controversies on Family Violence 225, 230–32 (Donileen R. Loseke et al. eds., 2d ed. 2005).

Testimony along these lines is intended to minimize confusion generated by the term "battered woman syndrome," by avoiding the implication that the woman suffers from a "syndrome" or mental impairment or that some sort of profile or model exists that all battered women must match. Jury simulation studies find that this type of expert testimony is more helpful than "battered woman syndrome" testimony in educating juries, especially in cases of non-confrontational killings, and is less likely to lead jurors to view the woman as "psychologically unstable." Regina A. Schuller et al., *Rethinking Battered Woman Syndrome Evidence: The Impact of Alternative Forms of Expert Testimony on Mock Jurors' Decisions*, 36 Can. J. Behav. Sci. 127, 134 (Apr. 2004).

At one time, domestic violence victims encountered evidentiary hurdles when they tried to introduce expert psychological testimony in support of self-defense claims. Such testimony is now routinely admitted in every state, as a result of either legislation or judicial decision. *See* Janet Parrish, *Trend Analysis: Expert Testimony on Battering and Its Effects in Criminal Cases, in* U.S. Dep't of Justice, The Validity and Use of Evidence Concerning Battering and Its Effects in Criminal Trials 3 (1996). *See also, e.g., People v. Brown*, 94 P.3d 574, 581–84 (Cal. 2004) (holding that expert testimony concerning battering and its effects is admissible even when there is evidence of only a single incident of abuse); *State v. Townsend*, 897 A.2d 316, 326–31 (N.J. 2006) (admitting such testimony even in the absence of a diagnosis of battered woman's syndrome). There is some variation from state to state, however, with respect to the issues about which these expert witnesses may testify. *See* Joshua Dressler, Understanding Criminal Law § 18.05[B][3][b], at 245–46 (7th ed. 2015).

4. Battered Women Who Kill. Only a small percentage of battered women kill. In fact, women are much less likely than men to kill their intimate partners. *See Crime in the United States 2015, Expanded Homicide Data Tables, Murder Circumstances by Relationship*, Federal Bureau of Investigation: Uniform Crime Reports, https://ucr.fbi.gov/crime-in-the-u.s/2015/crime-in-the-u.s.-2015/home (Tables 2 & 10) (reporting that fewer than three percent of male murder victims (265 total) were killed by their intimate partners in 2015, compared to more than 35 percent of female victims (1005 total)). *See also* Callie Marie Rennison & Sarah Welchans, Bureau of Justice Statistics, Intimate Partner Violence 1 (2000), http://www.bjs.gov/content/pub/pdf/ipv.pdf (citing comparable figures for 1976–1998); World Health Organization, Global and Regional Estimates of Violence against Women: Prevalence and Health Effects of Intimate Partner Violence and Non-Partner Sexual Violence 2 (2013), *available at* http://www.who.int/reproductivehealth/publications/violence/9789241564625/en/(finding that as many as 38 percent of female murder victims worldwide are killed by their intimate partners).

Moreover, many of the women who kill their intimate partners were in abusive relationships. *See, e.g.*, Elizabeth M. Schneider, *Resistance to Equality*, 57 U. Pitt. L. Rev. 477, 520 (1996) (citing studies reporting that "at least 45 percent and perhaps as many as 97 percent [of women imprisoned for killing a partner] were abused by the person they killed").

It is not entirely clear what percentage of the battered women who kill act, like Norman did, under non-confrontational circumstances. *Compare* Charles P. Ewing, Battered Women Who Kill: Psychological Self-Defense as Legal Justification 31–34 (1987) (finding that only one-third of the 87 killings he studied occurred during a battering incident, and approximately one-fifth of the men were asleep or nearly asleep), *with* Holly Maguigan, *Battered Women and Self-Defense: Myths and Misconceptions in Current Reform Proposals*, 140 U. Pa. L. Rev. 379, 397 (1991) (examining 223 appellate court cases decided between 1902 and 1991 involving women who were convicted of killing an intimate partner despite a history of abuse and a claim of self-defense, and noting that her findings—that three-fourths of these killings occurred under confrontational circumstances and only eight percent involved a sleeping victim—confirmed similar results of other studies), *and* V.F. Nourse, *Self-Defense and Subjectivity*, 68 U. Chi. L. Rev. 1234, 1253 (2001) (reporting similar findings in a survey of 70 cases where battered women charged with homicide raised self-defense claims and imminence was at issue). Whatever their frequency, the cases like *Norman* are the ones that raise the most difficult self-defense questions.

5. Defining the Reasonable Person. As the New York Court of Appeals suggested in *Goetz*, traditional self-defense law provides that the physical attributes of the defendant and victim—their size, age, strength, and physical condition—as well as the victim's prior violent acts and reputation are relevant considerations when evaluating whether a reasonable person in the defendant's situation would have thought the victim posed a threat. *See, e.g., Smith v. United States*, 161 U.S. 85, 88–89 (1896).

Should the defendant's gender likewise be a relevant factor because women and men tend to react very differently in situations calling for the use of defensive force? The court in *State v. Wanrow*, 559 P.2d 548 (Wash. 1977), thought so. In adopting a reasonable woman standard for self-defense cases involving female defendants, the court reasoned that jury instructions phrased in masculine terms "leave[] the jury with the impression the objective standard to be applied is that applicable to an altercation between two men." *Id.* at 558.

Consider also Elizabeth M. Schneider & Susan B. Jordan, *Representation of Women Who Defend Themselves in Response to Physical or Sexual Assault*, 4 Women's Rts. L. Rep. 149, 153, 156 (1978):

> Standards of justifiable homicide have been based on male models and expectations. Familiar images of self-defense are a soldier, a man protecting his home, family, or the chastity of his wife, or a man fighting off an assailant. . . .

> . . . [W]omen are less likely to have had training or experience in hand-to-hand fighting. Socially imposed proscriptions inhibit their ability to fend off an attacker. The fact that women generally are of slighter build also gives a male assailant an advantage. All of these conditions will have an impact on the reasonableness of a woman's perception of an imminent and lethal threat to her life such as would justify the use of deadly force.

Using similar reasoning, some courts have held that the appropriate inquiry in cases involving battered women who kill is whether a reasonable battered woman, or a reasonable person with the defendant's history of abuse, would have thought it necessary to resort to defensive force. *See Smith v. State*, 486 S.E.2d 819, 822–23 (Ga. 1997); *State v. Stewart*, 763 P.2d 572, 579 (Kan. 1988); *Boykins v. State*, 995 P.2d 474, 476 (Nev. 2000); *State v. Gartland*, 694 A.2d 564, 575 (N.J. 1997); *State v. Thomas*, 673 N.E.2d 1339, 1345 (Ohio 1997). *See also The Queen v. Malott*, [1998] 1 S.C.R. 123 (Can.) (taking a similar position).

In *Bechtel v. State*, 840 P.2d 1, 11 (Okla. Crim. App. 1992), the Oklahoma Court of Criminal Appeal went even further, adopting a special jury instruction for battered women's self-defense cases that omitted the standard jury instruction's reference to "a reasonable person" and instead advised the jury to consider whether "a person, in the circumstances and from the viewpoint of the defendant, would reasonably have believed that she was in imminent danger of death or great bodily harm."[6]

Is the approach taken by these courts necessary in order to fairly evaluate self-defense claims in these cases because the reasonable battered woman differs from the reasonable woman in several respects: she is familiar with her partner's attacks and understands the seriousness of his threats; she tends to become hypersensitive to her partner's actions and thus has the ability to predict the onset of a beating; and she understands the futility of relying on other means of protecting herself? *See The Queen v. Lavallee*, [1990] 1 S.C.R. 852, 874 (Can.) (noting that in cases involving battered women, "[t]he definition of what is reasonable must be adapted to circumstances which are, by and large, foreign to the world inhabited by the hypothetical 'reasonable man'"); Lauren Bennett Cattaneo et al., *Intimate Partner Violence Victims'*

---

6. The complete text of the jury instruction the court adopted for cases involving battered women is as follows (with the language omitted from the pattern jury instruction in brackets):

> A person is justified in using deadly force in self-defense if that person [reasonably] believed that use of deadly force was necessary to protect herself from imminent danger of death or great bodily harm. Self-defense is a defense although the danger to life or personal security may not have been real, if a [reasonable] person, in the circumstances and from the viewpoint of the defendant, would reasonably have believed that she was in imminent danger of death or great bodily harm.

The concurring opinion in *Bechtel* called the majority's decision somewhat "puzzling," noting that the modified instruction "includes the reasonableness requirement" in the last clause despite the court's purported intent to "strik[e] the words 'reasonably' and 'reasonable' from [the] instruction." *Bechtel*, 840 P.2d at 15–16 (Parks, J., concurring in the result) (quoting the majority opinion).

Accuracy in Assessing Their Risk of Re-abuse, 22 J. FAM. VIOLENCE 429, 437 (Aug. 2007) (finding that two-thirds to three-quarters of battered women are able to accurately predict the level of danger they face from their abusive partners, and those who are wrong are no more likely to overestimate than to underestimate the risk).

On the other hand, is the "reasonable battered woman" inquiry inadvisable because it "makes a mockery of objective standards and of the entire notion of justification"? Stephen J. Morse, *The "New Syndrome Excuse Syndrome"*, 14 CRIM. JUST. ETHICS, Winter/Spring 1995, at 3, 13. Is the concept of a reasonable battered woman an oxymoron because "we are judging reasonableness from the perspective of someone who, by definition, is experiencing a set of symptoms that renders her state of mind abnormal"? Joshua Dressler, *Battered Women and Sleeping Abusers: Some Reflections*, 3 OHIO ST. J. CRIM. L. 457, 464 (2006). Or is this criticism unfair because the "battered woman syndrome" construct is not necessarily meant to connote some sort of mental disease or defect, but is simply "a convenient way of describing a set of characteristics that are common to many (but not all) battered women"? Janet Parrish, *Trend Analysis: Expert Testimony on Battering and Its Effects in Criminal Cases, in* U.S. DEP'T OF JUSTICE, THE VALIDITY AND USE OF EVIDENCE CONCERNING BATTERING AND ITS EFFECTS IN CRIMINAL TRIALS 2 (1996).

The reasonable battered woman standard has also been criticized for "creat[ing] a new and equally rigid classification." Elizabeth M. Schneider, *Describing and Changing: Women's Self-Defense Work and the Problem of Expert Testimony on Battering*, 9 WOMEN'S RTS. L. REP. 195, 216 (1986). Schneider explained:

> The notion of battered woman syndrome contains the seeds of old stereotypes of women in new form — the victimized and the passive battered woman, too paralyzed to act because of her own incapacity. . . . The effect is that women who depart from this stereotype, because of their own life situations or because the facts of their cases do not fit this perspective, are not likely to be able to take advantage of judicial solicitude.

Id. See also Linda L. Ammons, *Mules, Madonnas, Babies, Bathwater, Racial Imagery and Stereotypes: The African-American Woman and the Battered Woman Syndrome*, 1995 WIS. L. REV. 1003, 1071, 1078 n.279 (observing that the reasonable battered woman standard disproportionately disadvantages certain groups of women — including women of color and women who are financially independent — whom juries are less likely to regard as "helpless"); Anne M. Coughlin, *Excusing Women*, 82 CAL. L. REV. 1, 70, 59 (1994) (calling the defense "misogynist" because it "continues to portray the independent wife as evil, deserving condemnation and blame, and . . . continues to recognize the submissive wife as good and to reward her with familiar patronizing sympathy").

In *People v. Humphrey*, 921 P.2d 1 (Cal. 1996), the California Supreme Court refused to endorse a "reasonable battered woman" standard. The court acknowledged that "the jury, in determining objective reasonableness, must view the situation from the *defendant's perspective*" and "must consider all of the relevant circumstances in which defendant found herself," including her "situation and knowledge." But the court concluded that "the ultimate question is whether a reasonable *person*, not a reasonable battered woman, would believe in the need to kill." *Id.* at 7–9. Does the court's distinction make sense?

The prosecution in *Humphrey* was critical of any move to "chang[e] the [self-defense] standard from objective to subjective," raising the specter of a "reasonable gang member" standard. *Id.* at 9. Is this a legitimate fear? Beginning with *State v. Janes*, 850 P.2d 495 (Wash. 1993), a number of courts have concluded that the psychological impact of prolonged child abuse is analogous to the effects of intimate partner violence and have therefore allowed evidence describing the battered child syndrome to support self-defense claims raised by abused children who kill their parents. *See, e.g., State v. Smullen*, 844 A.2d 429, 445–50 (Md. 2004); *State v. MacLennan*, 702 N.W.2d 219, 233–35 (Minn. 2005). Where should the line be drawn in determining which of a particular defendant's characteristics ought to be incorporated in the reasonable person standard? *Compare State v. Brown*, 573 P.2d 675, 678 (N.M. Ct. App. 1977) (reversing the assault conviction of a defendant who shot at police on the grounds that the trial court erred in excluding expert testimony describing law enforcement's treatment of racial minorities and African-Americans' tendency to perceive the police as a threat), *with People v. Romero*, 81 Cal. Rptr. 2d 823, 826–28 (Cal. Ct. App. 1999) (concluding that testimony from an expert in street violence, Latino culture, and the sociology of poverty offered to describe the Latino culture's notion of "honor" was irrelevant to self-defense claim), *and State v. Hampton*, 558 N.W.2d 884, 890–91 (Wis. Ct. App. 1996) (upholding exclusion of expert testimony describing 15-year-old defendant's "psycho-social history," reasoning that evidence detailing the defendant's repeated exposure to violence as both a witness and victim "'would eviscerate the objective, reasonable person requirement'" and give "[a] person exposed to a lifetime of violence . . . greater latitude to exercise the privilege of self-defense than a person raised in a life free from strife," and distinguishing cases involving battered women because the evidence excluded here described "remote instances of alleged violence committed by third persons not involved in the events surrounding [the] homicide") (quoting the State's brief), *and Osby v. State*, 939 S.W.2d 787, 789–90 (Tex. App. 1997) (affirming murder conviction and finding no error in the trial court's refusal to admit expert testimony concerning the mental state of a 17-year-old who advanced a claim of urban survival syndrome to support his contention that he shot two men who had previously threatened him in self-defense, concluding that a state statute allowed expert testimony only in self-defense cases involving "family violence"). (For discussion of the similar issues that arise in defining reasonable provocation in voluntary manslaughter cases, see Chapter 6, Section B.2, Notes 11–12.)

6. The Imminence Requirement. As the court noted in *Norman*, defensive force is generally considered justifiable only if the defendant reasonably feared an imminent threat. Thus, "[a] preemptive strike against a feared aggressor is illegal force used too soon; and retaliation against a successful aggressor is illegal force used too late." GEORGE P. FLETCHER, A CRIME OF SELF-DEFENSE 20 (1988). *But cf. The Queen v. Pétel*, [1994] 1 S.C.R. 3, 13–14 (Can.) (noting that Canadian self-defense law creates "no formal requirement that the danger be imminent," but instead considers imminence "only one of the factors which the jury should weigh in determining whether the accused had a reasonable apprehension of danger and a reasonable belief that she could not extricate herself otherwise than by killing the attacker").

The Model Penal Code, by contrast, requires that a defendant believe defensive force is "immediately necessary for the purpose of protecting himself against the use of unlawful force . . . on the present occasion." Model Penal Code § 3.04(1). The drafters of the Code thought that this standard afforded greater "latitude for the attainment of a just result" than traditional requirements that the defendant face an "imminent" or "immediate" threat. Under § 3.04, "[t]here would, for example, be a privilege to use defensive force to prevent an assailant from going to summon reinforcements, given a belief that it is necessary to disable him to prevent an attack by overwhelming numbers — so long as the attack is apprehended on the 'present occasion.'" *Id.* § 3.04 Comment at 39–40.

7. Applying the Imminence Requirement in Cases Involving Battered Women. What are the purposes of the imminence requirement? Are those purposes satisfied in a case like *Norman*? Should the trial judge have left that decision to the jury rather than deciding as a matter of law that Norman did not have a viable self-defense claim? Could the jury have fairly viewed Judy Norman as someone "who, quite literally, ha[d] been remitted to a state of nature where the government ha[d] abandoned her to the government of her murderous husband, with no legal recourse"? Victoria Nourse, *Getting over the Subjectivity/Objectivity Question*, 11 NEW CRIM. L. REV. 33, 46 (2008). Even though J.T. Norman was asleep, is it "not quite accurate to say that [he] pose[d] no threat" because "[u]nless actually comatose, a sleeping abuser is merely seconds away from being an awakened abuser"? Joan H. Krause, *Distorted Reflections of Battered Women Who Kill: A Response to Professor Dressler*, 4 OHIO ST. J. CRIM. L. 555, 563 (2007).

On the other hand, does that reasoning allow victims of domestic violence to exact "vigilante justice" and give them a "license to kill" at any time? Donald A. Downs & James Fisher, *Battered Woman Syndrome: Tool of Justice or False Hope in Self-Defense Cases?*, *in* CURRENT CONTROVERSIES ON FAMILY VIOLENCE 241, 249, 252 (Donileen R. Loseke et al. eds., 2d ed. 2005). Is there always a "slight possibility," however "remote in J.T. Norman's case," that a "batterer will change his behavior if permitted to live"? Joshua Dressler, *Battered Women and Sleeping Abusers: Some Reflections*, 3 OHIO ST. J. CRIM. L. 457, 467 (2006). Even if this hope is overly optimistic, was the North Carolina Supreme Court right to think that inevitable harm is not necessarily imminent, or does that view tend to "prevent [a battered woman] from exercising the right of self-defense at the only time it would be effective"? *State v. Kelly*, 478 A.2d 364, 385 n.23 (N.J. 1984); *see also The Queen v. Lavallee*, [1990] 1 S.C.R. 852, 883 (Can.) (requiring a domestic violence victim to "wait until the physical assault is

'underway' before her apprehensions can be validated in law would . . . be tantamount to sentencing her to 'murder by installment' ").

Consider 2 Paul H. Robinson, Criminal Law Defenses § 131(c)(1), at 78 (1984):

> Suppose *A* kidnaps and confines *D* with the announced intention of killing
> him one week later. *D* has an opportunity to kill *A* and escape each morn-
> ing as *A* brings him his daily ration. Taken literally, the *imminent* require-
> ment would prevent *D* from using deadly force in self-defense until *A* is
> standing over him with a knife, but that outcome seems inappropriate. . . .
> The proper inquiry is not the immediacy of the threat but the immediacy of
> the response necessary in defense. If a threatened harm is such that it can-
> not be avoided if the intended victim waits until the last moment, the princi-
> ple of self-defense must permit him to act earlier — as early as is required to
> defend himself effectively.

See also Bechtel v. State, 840 P.2d 1, 12 (Okla. Crim. App. 1992) (analogizing the
battered woman's situation to "the classic hostage situation"); Jane Campbell Mori-
arty, *"While Dangers Gather": The Bush Preemption Doctrine, Battered Women, Imminence, and Anticipatory Self-Defense*, 30 N.Y.U. Rev. L. & Soc. Change 1, 24 (2005)
(comparing domestic violence to terrorism, and noting that "in evaluating the danger of someone carrying out a threat to kill, an intended victim cannot reasonably
assume the danger has permanently ceased simply because the terrorist is momentarily incapacitated"); Lawrence P. Tiffany & Carl A. Anderson, *Legislating the
Necessity Defense in Criminal Law*, 52 Denv. L.J. 839, 846–47 (1975) (pointing out
that the "temporal 'imminence' of the threat may be . . . evidence of a lack of alternatives, but the absence of temporal 'imminence' is not proof of the existence of
alternatives"). *But cf.* Kimberly Kessler Ferzan, *Defending Imminence: From Battered
Women to Iraq*, 46 Ariz. L. Rev. 213, 262, 255 (2004) (arguing that "the imminence
requirement is more than a proxy for necessity," but also "stak[es] out the type of
threats that constitute aggression," and thus is critical in determining "at what point
[it is] fair to construe the putative aggressor as posing a threat").

8. The Initial Aggressor Rule. As the dissenting opinion in *Norman* noted, the
defendant was not entitled to use self-defense if she was the initial aggressor. If she
created the dangerous situation that required her to act in self-defense, it could not
be said that her use of defensive force was "necessary." Is the dissent's characterization of the Normans' relationship as a "continuing assault" initiated by J.T. a persuasive
response to the suggestion that Judy was the initial aggressor?

Various definitions of the term "initial aggressor" are used in different jurisdictions. Some courts interpret the initial aggressor doctrine to require that a defendant
be "entirely free from fault in provoking the altercation." *Perricllia v. Commonwealth*, 326 S.E.2d 679, 685 (Va. 1985). Under this standard, a defendant can forfeit
the right to use defensive force by, for example, using provoking language. *See id.*;
People v. Dunlap, 734 N.E.2d 973, 981 (Ill. App. Ct. 2000). *But see State v. Riley*, 976

P.2d 624, 629 (Wash. 1999) (holding that provocative language does not make one the initial aggressor).

Most jurisdictions take a narrower view, limiting the initial aggressor rule, for example, to cases where the defendant committed "an affirmative unlawful act reasonably calculated to produce an affray foreboding injurious or fatal consequences." *United States v. Peterson*, 483 F.2d 1222, 1233 (D.C. Cir. 1973). *See also State v. Jackson*, 382 P.2d 229, 232 (Ariz. 1963) (requiring that the initial aggressor have committed an act "deliberately calculated to lead to further conflict"). *Cf. Edwards v. United States*, 721 A.2d 938, 943 (D.C. 1998) (applying *Peterson* and concluding that the evidence allowed the jury to find that Edwards "invited and provoked the encounter" by engaging in the "ruse" of trying to pass off soap as cocaine). For a discussion of these various approaches, with an eye towards differentiating between "the vigilant and the vigilante," see John D. Moore, Note, *Reasonable Provocation: Distinguishing the Vigilant from the Vigilante in Self-Defense Law*, 78 Brook. L. Rev. 1659, 1661 (2013).

However the phrase "initial aggressor" is defined, most courts seem to agree that an initial aggressor's right to use defensive force is restored if the aggressor "communicates to his adversary his intent to withdraw and in good faith attempts to do so." *Peterson*, 483 F.2d at 1231. *Cf. Murphy-Bey v. United States*, 982 A.2d 682, 691 (D.C. 2009) (holding that testimony that the defendant "stepped back from [the victim] is 'evidence, however weak' that he withdrew" and "whether those steps constituted both a proper withdrawal and a proper communication of that withdrawal was an issue for the jury"). In some jurisdictions, an initial aggressor also regains the right to use self-defense if the other person overreacts, by responding to the aggressor's use of nondeadly force with deadly force (which constitutes excessive force and is therefore unlawful).

Under the Model Penal Code's version of the initial aggressor rule, an initial aggressor is likewise allowed to use nondeadly force in self-defense in cases where the other person unnecessarily uses deadly force in response to the aggressor's threat of only nondeadly force. Thus, the Model Penal Code's analogue to the initial aggressor doctrine is triggered only if the defendant resorted to deadly force. *See* Model Penal Code § 3.04(2)(b)(i). Moreover, the use of even deadly force is permissible in these circumstances unless the defendant, "with the purpose of causing death or serious bodily injury, provoked the use of force against himself in the same encounter." *Id.* Characterizing this provision as "narrower" than the common law's initial aggressor rule, the Comments explain that "the only case" that implicates the MPC's initial aggressor doctrine is where the defendant "provokes a struggle (whether by assault, battery, insult or other means) with the positive purpose that the outcome shall be the death of his victim or his serious bodily harm":

> The typical case to be imagined is this: *A* attacks *B* with his fists; *B* defends himself, and manages to subdue *A* to the extent of pinning him to the floor. *B* then starts to batter *A*'s head savagely against the floor. *A* manages to rise,

and since *B* is still attacking him and *A* now fears that if he is thrown again to the floor he will be killed, *A* uses a knife. *B* is killed or seriously wounded.

The solution to this situation under the provisions of this section is as follows: *B* is entitled to defend himself against *A*'s attack, but only to the extent of using moderate, nondeadly force. . . . *B* exceeds the bounds of "necessary" force . . . , however, when, after reducing *A* to helplessness, he batters *A*'s head on the floor. Since this excessive force is, in its turn, unlawful, . . . *A* is entitled to defend himself against it and, if he believes that he is then in danger of death or serious bodily harm without apparent opportunity for safe retreat, *A* is also entitled to use his knife in self-protection. *A* of course is criminally liable for his initial battery on *B*, but would have a justifying defense that he could raise against prosecution for the ultimate homicide or wounding. Subsection (2)(b)(i), depriving *A* of his justification on the ground of initial aggression, would not become operative unless *A* entered the encounter with the purpose of causing death or serious bodily harm.

Id. § 3.04 Comment at 49–51. Under the Model Penal Code, an initial aggressor regains the right to use self-defense "by so far breaking off the struggle that any renewal by the other party can be viewed as" a different "encounter." *Id.* at 52.

What is the proper scope of the initial aggressor rule? Should it be restricted to cases where the defendant engaged in a show of physical force, or is that approach too narrow? Should words ever be considered sufficiently provoking to make a defendant the initial aggressor? Should Goetz have been deemed the initial aggressor because there was "[a] strong suggestion of deliberately courting danger run[ning] through [his] personal history," and on the day of the shootings he carried a gun onto the subway and then "'deliberately seated himself in an area of the car that [was] not only in the middle of this group of rambunctious young teens, but . . . [was] in a location where he [was] at least psychologically isolated from all the other passengers on the train'"? GEORGE P. FLETCHER, A CRIME OF SELF-DEFENSE 14, 179 (1988) (quoting the prosecutor's closing argument). Was the jury in George Zimmerman's trial right to reject the prosecution's theory that Zimmerman initiated the confrontation that led to Trayvon Martin's death by wrongly assuming he was a criminal and then following him contrary to the police dispatcher's instructions? What about a battered woman who can no longer tolerate the growing tension in the house and therefore deliberately overcooks her husband's dinner in order to provoke a beating and get it over with?

In addition to the initial aggressor rule, the retreat doctrine can foreclose the right to use defensive force in some jurisdictions. That exception is addressed in the following case.

People v. Tomlins

107 N.E. 496 (N.Y. 1914)

CARDOZO, JUDGE.

The defendant shot and killed his son, a young man of twenty-two. The shooting took place on August 26, 1913, in the little cottage in Stony Point where the son had been born and reared. [At] trial, the father maintained that . . . he had acted justifiably, in lawful self-defense. It will not be helpful to state the details of the tragedy. It is enough to say that the verdict of murder in the first degree is sustained by ample proof. We have, therefore, only to inquire whether there was material error in the court's statement of the law. The jury were properly instructed that homicide in self-defense is not justifiable unless there is reasonable ground to apprehend a design on the part of the person slain to commit a felony, or to do some great personal injury to the slayer, and unless also there is reasonable ground to apprehend that the danger is imminent.

These instructions were coupled, however, with a statement that it was the defendant's duty, if possible, to retreat and escape. "A man," said the court, "has no right to resort to force and violence against another, even where the danger is imminent, even where he has reasonable cause to believe that he is in danger, unless he has no reasonably safe means of escape and retreat. . . . That is the law, gentlemen. We may not feel always like retreating in the face of an attack; it may not seem manly to us, but it is the law that if a man can safely retreat, and thereby escape a conflict with another, he must do so, even though it may not seem dignified and manly. . . . [I]f he could have gotten away from danger by retreating, if he could have gotten off the porch, and gone across the lot, and down the road, or around the house, or anywhere, to a place of safety, then the law says that he should have done so, and that he had no right to use the weapon against his son, unless all reasonable means of retreating were cut off. . . ."

We think that these instructions are erroneous as applied to the case at bar. The homicide occurred in the defendant's dwelling. It is not now and never has been the law that a man assailed in his own dwelling is bound to retreat. If assailed there, he may stand his ground and resist the attack. He is under no duty to take to the fields and the highways, a fugitive from his own home. More than two hundred years ago it was said by Lord Chief Justice Hale: In case a man "is assailed in his own house, he need not fly as far as he can, as in other cases of *se defendendo*, for he hath the protection of his house to excuse him from flying, as that would be to give up the protection of his house to his adversary by his flight." Flight is for sanctuary and shelter, and shelter, if not sanctuary, is in the home. . . . The rule is the same whether the attack proceeds from some other occupant or from an intruder. . . . "Why . . . should one retreat from his own house, when assailed by a partner or co-tenant, any more than when assailed by a stranger who is lawfully upon the premises? Whither shall he flee, and how far, and when may he be permitted to return?" . . .

We think that if the situation justified the defendant, as a reasonable man, in believing that he was about to be murderously attacked, he had the right to stand his ground.

Notes and Questions

1. The Policy Issues Surrounding the Retreat Rule and Stand-Your-Ground Laws. Despite the broader retreat requirement suggested by the trial court's jury instructions in *Tomlins*, the retreat rule in effect in some jurisdictions today requires defendants to retreat before resorting to self-defense only if (1) they are using deadly force and (2) they know they can retreat with complete safety—that is, without incurring even nonserious bodily injury. *See, e.g., State v. Anderson*, 631 A.2d 1149, 1155 (Conn. 1993); *State v. Abbott*, 174 A.2d 881, 885–86 (N.J. 1961).

Leaving aside for one moment cases like *Tomlins* where the defendant is attacked at home, is the retreat rule justifiable because "it is not necessary to kill in self-defense when the assailed can defend himself by the peaceful though often distasteful method of withdrawing to a place of safety"? Joseph H. Beale, Jr., *Retreat from a Murderous Assault*, 16 Harv. L. Rev. 567, 580 (1903). Is it therefore "better that the assailed shall retreat than that the life of another be needlessly spent"? *Abbott*, 174 A.2d at 884. Or is the retreat requirement "unrealistic" and inconsistent "with the behavior of reasonable men"? *Id.* Does requiring retreat "demand what smacks of cowardice" when "the manly thing to do is to hold one's ground"? *Id.* Moreover, if there are compelling reasons to require retreat, why aren't they equally persuasive in cases where a defendant used nondeadly defensive force?

The Model Penal Code imposes a retreat requirement, *see* Model Penal Code § 3.04(2)(b)(ii), as do a minority of states. But the majority rule allows one to stand one's ground and kill an assailant without taking advantage of a ready escape route.

In recent years, the retreat doctrine has lost even more support, as a number of state legislatures—beginning with Florida in 2005—have repealed retreat requirements. Many of these statutes, referred to as "stand your ground" laws by their supporters and "shoot first" laws by their critics, are modeled on the Florida law, which provides that a defendant who is otherwise entitled to use deadly force "does not have a duty to retreat and has the right to stand his or her ground" so long as the defendant "is not engaged in a criminal activity and is in a place where he or she has a right to be." Fla. Stat. § 776.012(2). *Cf. Dawkins v. State*, 252 P.3d 214, 218 (Okla. Crim. App. 2011) (concluding that a defendant who was in possession of a sawed-off shotgun could not take advantage of the state's stand-your-ground law, although "minor infractions" such as parking violations and "outstanding warrants for minor offenses" would not constitute "unlawful activity" that forfeits the right to stand one's ground).

Thirty-three states now have stand-your-ground rules as a result of either legislation or judicial opinion. *See* ABA National Task Force on Stand Your Ground Laws, Preliminary Report and Recommendations (Aug. 8, 2014), *available at*

http://www.americanbar.org/content/dam/aba/administrative/racial_ethnic
_justice/aba_natl_task_force_on_syg_laws_preliminary_report_program_book
.authcheckdam.pdf. For a discussion of the flurry of legislative activity in this area
and the role played by the National Rifle Association, see P. Luevonda Ross, *The
Transmogrification of Self-Defense by National Rifle Association-Inspired Statutes:
From the Doctrine of Retreat to the Right to Stand Your Ground*, 35 S.U. L. REV. 1
(2007).

A subset of these stand-your-ground laws not only eliminate self-defense's retreat
requirement but also grant a defendant immunity from both criminal prosecution
and civil suit. The Florida statute, for example, allows a defendant to file a pretrial
motion to dismiss criminal charges on the ground that the use of force was justified
as self-defense, unless the victim was someone the defendant knew or should have
known was "a law enforcement officer . . . acting in the performance of his or her
official duties." Fla. Stat. § 776.032.

Controversy has surrounded the Florida law since the 2012 death of 17-year-old
Trayvon Martin. Although George Zimmerman declined to file a pretrial motion
asserting his immunity from prosecution, the jury in his murder trial was instructed
on the stand-your-ground statute. On the facts of that case, described above in Note
4 following *People v. Goetz*, did both Martin and Zimmerman have a right to stand
their ground?

In 2015, the American Bar Association's House of Delegates passed a resolution
advocating the repeal of stand-your-ground laws. The move came after an ABA task
force report released the results of empirical studies of the 33 states with such rules.
The ABA task force reported that the laws have increased the number of homicides,
have not deterred crime, and have been most likely to benefit whites who used force
against African-Americans. *See* ABA NATIONAL TASK FORCE ON STAND YOUR GROUND
LAWS, *supra*, at 17–22.

2. The Castle Doctrine. Assuming the validity of a retreat requirement, should it
apply even when one is attacked at home? Judge Cardozo thought not, invoking in
his opinion in *Tomlins* what is referred to as the castle doctrine. Was Cardozo right
to conclude that people should not be forced to be "fugitives" from the "sanctuary
and shelter" of their homes because they have a right to be there and it is the safest
place of retreat? Or are the policies underlying the retreat rule equally applicable when
one is attacked at home?

If Cardozo has the better argument, should the castle doctrine be extended to one's
yard or driveway, or the hallway of an apartment building? What about one's place
of work?

The Model Penal Code recognizes the castle doctrine, *see* Model Penal Code
§ 3.04(2)(b)(ii)(A), as do the overwhelming majority of jurisdictions that impose a
retreat requirement. Although the drafters of the MPC acknowledged that "sentimen-
tal factors relevant to dwellings may not apply to one's place of work," they extended
the castle doctrine to the workplace on the theory that "practical considerations

concerning the two locations were far too similar to sustain a distinction." *Id.* § 3.04 Comment at 56.

3. The Co-Occupant Exception to the Castle Doctrine. Assuming the validity of the castle doctrine, should it apply even in cases like *Tomlins*, where the defendant was attacked at home by a co-occupant? Does Judge Cardozo make a persuasive argument that the policies underlying the castle doctrine are equally relevant in such cases—and perhaps even stronger given the awkwardness of determining when one should return home after fleeing from a co-occupant's assault? On the other hand, do the co-occupant's "equal rights to be in the 'castle'" suggest that one should have to retreat from a co-occupant's attack? *Cooper v. United States*, 512 A.2d 1002, 1006 (D.C. 1986). Or is that argument suspect because it "[p]lac[es] property rights over personal safety," leading to "absurd and deadly consequences"? Judith E. Koons, *Gunsmoke and Legal Mirrors: Women Surviving Intimate Battery and Deadly Legal Doctrines*, 14 J.L. & Pol'y 617, 688 (2006). Regardless of how one weighs the competing policies, does it make sense to opt for a "bright-line rule" that never requires retreat at home so as to "eliminate the need to define and differentiate between residents, nonresidents, invited guests, unwanted guests, etc."? *State v. Glowacki*, 630 N.W.2d 392, 400 (Minn. 2001).

In choosing between these two positions, is the high rate of homicide among family members relevant? *See Crime in the United States 2015, Expanded Homicide Data Tables, Murder Circumstances by Relationship*, Federal Bureau of Investigation: Uniform Crime Reports, https://ucr.fbi.gov/crime-in-the-u.s/2015/crime-in-the-u .s.-2015/home (Table 10) (reporting that at least 1,721 people—12.8 percent of the murder victims for whom information was available—were killed by relatives in 2015). Is it fair to say that the co-occupant exception to the castle doctrine "disadvantage[s] women," especially battered women, because "most men are assaulted and killed outside their homes by strangers, while most women are assaulted and killed within their homes by male intimates"? Marina Angel, *Criminal Law and Women: Giving the Abused Woman Who Kills* A Jury of Her Peers *Who Appreciate* Trifles, 33 Am. Crim. L. Rev. 229, 320 (1996). *See also Glowacki*, 630 N.W.2d at 1053–54 (making this point in rejecting the co-occupant exception); *State v. Gartland*, 694 A.2d 564, 571 (N.J. 1997) (urging the state legislature to rethink the co-occupant exception for this reason); *People v. Jones*, 821 N.E.2d 955, 958 (N.Y. 2004) (reaffirming *Tomlins* and "the castle doctrine['s] application to occupants of the same household," in part because of its "particular importance in cases of domestic violence, most often against women").

Some of the jurisdictions that recognize the castle doctrine have created an exception for co-occupants, but the majority do not distinguish based on the status of the parties—that is, they do not require one to retreat from home under any circumstances, even before using deadly force against a co-occupant. *See, e.g., State v. Harden*, 679 S.E.2d 628, 637–38 (W. Va. 2009) (overruling precedent dating back 100 years and adopting the majority view). The Model Penal Code's version of the castle doctrine takes an intermediate position on this issue, requiring one to retreat before using deadly defensive force against a coworker but not against a co-occupant of the home. *See* Model Penal Code § 3.04(2)(b)(ii)(A).

4. Burden of Proof. Almost every state requires the prosecution to prove beyond a reasonable doubt that the defendant did not act in self-defense — at least once the defendant has satisfied the burden of production on that issue. *See* 2 PAUL H. ROBINSON, CRIMINAL LAW DEFENSES § 132, at 99–100 (1984). Likewise, the Model Penal Code places the burden of disproving self-defense, as well as most other affirmative defenses, on the state once the defendant has shouldered the initial burden of producing some evidence supporting the defense. *See* Model Penal Code §§ 1.12(1)–(2). Nevertheless, an Ohio self-defense statute that imposed the burden of persuasion on the defendant was upheld by the U.S. Supreme Court in *Martin v. Ohio*, 480 U.S. 228 (1987).

The defendant in *Martin* was charged with aggravated murder, defined by state law as "purposely, and with prior calculation and design, caus[ing] the death of another." Although the Due Process Clause demands "proof beyond a reasonable doubt of every fact necessary to constitute the crime," *In re Winship*, 397 U.S. 358, 364 (1970), the Supreme Court concluded in *Martin* that requiring the defendant to prove her self-defense claim by a preponderance of the evidence did not unconstitutionally shift the burden of proof because the defense did not negate any of the elements of aggravated murder. The Ohio self-defense statute was therefore permissible under the Court's ruling in *Patterson v. New York*, 432 U.S. 197, 207 (1977), which held that a criminal defendant may be forced to prove an affirmative defense that "constitutes a separate issue" in the sense that it "does not serve to negative any facts of the crime which the State is to prove in order to convict." (For further discussion of the burden of proof issues that arise in criminal cases, see Chapter 1, Section B.2.c.)

[C] Other Uses of Defensive Force

[1] Defense of Home and Property

State v. Anderson

972 P.2d 32 (Okla. Crim. App. 1998)

LUMPKIN, JUDGE.

Appellee, Aubrey Ivan Anderson, was charged with Murder in the First Degree and Shooting with Intent to Kill. . . . At the close of evidence, the jury was given Oklahoma Uniform Jury Instruction — Criminal 8-15 setting forth the affirmative defense provided in [21 O.S. § 1289.25]. . . . The jury subsequently returned not guilty verdicts on all charges. . . . [T]he State has reserved, as a question of law, the issue of whether the term "occupant" as used in Section 1289.25 can include people other than the home owner or continuous resident of the premises.

. . . .

. . . [T]he only facts from Appellee's trial that now concern us are that he was an invited guest in the home of Joe Alvey and Chris Wilson; that the victims, Joe Younger and Chris Harris, forcibly broke into Alvey and Wilson's home, and that Appellee shot the victims.

Whether the term "occupant" as used in § 1289.25 includes people other than the home owner or continuous resident of the premises presents an issue of first impression for this Court. As we answer this question, we must keep in mind the fundamental rule of statutory construction — to ascertain and give effect to the intention of the Legislature as expressed in the statute. . . . Title 21 O.S. 1991, § 1289.25, also known as the "Make My Day" Law, provides:

> A. The Legislature hereby recognizes that the citizens of the State of Oklahoma have a right to expect absolute safety within their own homes.
>
> B. *Any occupant* of a dwelling is justified in using any degree of physical force, including but not limited to deadly force, against another person who has made an unlawful entry into that dwelling, and when *the occupant* has a reasonable belief that such other person might use any physical force, no matter how slight, against *any occupant* of the dwelling.
>
> C. *Any occupant* of a dwelling using physical force, including but not limited to deadly force, pursuant to the provisions of subsection B of this section, shall have an affirmative defense in any criminal prosecution for an offense arising from the reasonable use of such force and shall be immune from any civil liability for injuries or death resulting from the reasonable use of such force.
>
> D. The provisions of this section . . . shall not be construed to require any person using a pistol pursuant to the provisions of this section to be licensed in any manner (emphasis added).[7]

This statute does not contain a list of definitions. Lacking a specific statutory definition, we must look to the common ordinary meaning of the term "occupant." 25 O.S. 1991, § 1. Webster's II defines "occupant" as "1. One that occupies a place or position, esp. a resident. 2. One who is the first to take possession of previously unowned land or premises." The State argues that under these definitions, and those of "occupancy" and "occupy," section 1289.25 refers only to a person who has a possessory or privacy interest in the premises. While we find these definitions instructive, we do not find they answer the questions before us.

Looking to other statutory uses of the term "occupant," we do not find a requirement for a possessory or privacy interest. *See* 21 O.S. 1991, § 1171 (peeping tom is

---

7. The statute was amended in 2006 with passage of a "stand your ground" law in Oklahoma. The current version, among other things, requires an "unlawful and forcible entry," creates an exception if the defendant was "engaged in an unlawful activity," and allows an "invited guest" to use force to protect a home. *See* Okla. Stat. § 1289.25.

any person who loiters in the vicinity of a private dwelling with the intent to gaze upon occupants therein in a clandestine manner); 21 O.S. 1991, § 1438(B) (malicious mischief is the breaking and entering of a dwelling without permission of the owner or occupant thereof); 47 O.S. 1991, §§ 10–111; 11–507; 11–705; 11–1110 (references to occupants of vehicles). The use of the term "occupied" similarly implies no possessory interest. *See* 21 O.S. 1991, § 1401 (first degree arson committed by willful burning of any building or structure, inhabited or occupied by one or more persons).

Appellant directs us to the Colorado "Make My Day" law, after which Section 1289.25 was patterned. . . . Appellant cites to several cases in which the Colorado courts had held the term "occupant" is synonymous with "homeowner." However, a review of those cases reveals the Colorado courts have not been presented with the question we now have before us and therefore have not addressed whether "occupant" includes a visitor to the home. Likewise, other jurisdictions cited to us by Appellant have not addressed the question before us. . . .

While dictionary definitions, statutory references and case law from Oklahoma and other jurisdictions are helpful in our analysis, the interpretation of the Legislature's intent in Section 1289.25 is ultimately based upon the words in the statute itself. Reading the statute in its entirety, we find it a study in contradiction or compromise. The preamble seems to clearly set forth the intent of the law—"that the citizens of the State of Oklahoma have a right to expect absolute safety within their own homes." However, the terms "resident," "homeowner" or other such restrictive terms were not used in the remainder of the statute. Likewise, the all encompassing term "any person" was not used. Therefore, we are left with the term "occupant," a term with no specific statutory definition. That term is used three times in subsection B. It is the third use of the term "occupant" which leads us to the conclusion that the law was intended to protect anyone legally inside the dwelling, and not just the legal residents of the dwelling. . . . To read it in any other manner would permit only residents or homeowners to protect only other residents or homeowners. Invited guests or employees would be left to fend for themselves. This type of application would lead to many absurd results and is not supported by any statements of legislative intent. There are many fact situations which illustrate this point, but we will look at just two.

The baby-sitter comes to the homeowner's residence to watch the children while the parents (the homeowners) are away. If someone breaks into the house making an unlawful entry, is the [baby-sitter] allowed to protect herself and the children in her care? Under the State's interpretation of the statute, the baby-sitter would not be able to use any physical force, including deadly force, against the intruder because she was not the homeowner or resident. We do not believe the Legislature intended to exclude someone in that position from using physical or deadly force to protect him or herself and those in his or her charge. Another scenario involves that of the invited guest. An unlawful entry is made into the home, the homeowners or residents are either away from the house or unable to defend themselves and only the invited guest is able to muster a defense. . . . Under the State's interpretation of the statute, the invited guest would not be able to . . . defend him or herself. . . . These situations also point out how our interpretation of the statute is consistent with the other laws on self-defense and defense of another.

The Oklahoma statutes addressing self-defense, defense of others, defense of habitation, and defense of property are numerous and often confusing and inconsistent. However, one common aspect is shared. Exoneration is dependent on facts which an innocent defender may not know or be able to know until it is too late, and legal conclusions about those facts which the lay person cannot be expected to make, particularly when one is facing an attacker or unknown intruder. . . . Under Section 1289.25, the person inside the dwelling does not have to determine the intruder's intentions. An unlawful entry and the reasonable belief that the intruder might use any physical force is sufficient to permit the person inside the dwelling to use any physical force, including deadly force, against the person making the unlawful entry. Under Section 1289.25, persons legally inside a dwelling have the right to expect safety and freedom from unlawful intrusion. With the enactment of Section 1289.25 it appears the Legislature was trying to create a place of absolute safety and freedom—the home, whether it be your own home or one in which you are legally present.

The State's argument that including visitors in the term "occupant" will result in some sort of carnage is groundless. The statute has been on the books for approximately a decade without incident. It contains sufficient safeguards to prevent abuse. Under the statute, if the occupant does not "reasonably believe" that the intruder intends to use force, then he or she is not justified in using deadly force. The statute merely tells those who would break into other people's homes that they do so at their own risk. When one is going about his or her business, in the safety of a dwelling, and is suddenly surprised by an intruder breaking into the dwelling, we find the Legislature intended to give the benefit of the doubt to the law-abiding occupant rather than the law breaking intruder. When one intrudes into a dwelling that is not his, the extent of his wrongdoing should not depend on the legal relationship between the dwelling and those lawfully inside it. When one intrudes into the dwelling of another, the harm is the violation of the sanctity of the dwelling itself, not merely to a particular person's property interest. An invited guest in a dwelling has just [as] much right to expect safety therein as the owner.

. . . .

Therefore, we find the Legislature intended for the term "occupant" as used in 21 O.S. 1991, § 1289.25 to include visitors, i.e. persons legally inside the dwelling.

In its second proposition of error, the State contends that [uniform jury instruction] 8–15 omits the element of requiring the force used against the intruder to be reasonable. . . .

. . . .

We reject the State's argument. . . . The uniform instruction is taken directly from subsection B of the statute. When the statute is read as a whole and in its entirety, the only "reasonableness" test set forth is that the occupant "reasonably believes" the intruder might use any force. . . . The Legislature specifically did not limit the amount of force the occupant could use against the intruder. The reference in subsection C to reasonable force . . . merely describes when an accused may claim the defense set out in subsection B. The use of the word "reasonable" in subsection C corresponds to the use of the term "reasonably" in subsection B. The only "reasonableness" pre- requisite to claiming the affirmative defense set forth in section 1289.25 is set out in subsection B, i.e., that the occupant reasonably believes the intruder might use some force, however slight, against the occupant. . . .

CHAPEL, PRESIDING JUDGE, dissenting.

I dissent. Title 21 O.S. 1991, § 1289.25, often referred to as the "Make My Day" Law, provides in Subsection A that it is intended to protect citizens "within their own home." I would therefore limit the application of the Act. In view of Subsection A, I am of the opinion that the word "occupant" which appears in Subsections B and C refers only to residents of a dwelling and no others.

Notes and Questions

1. **Using Force to Protect Property.** As the court's opinion in *Anderson* makes clear, the right to use defensive force is not limited to cases of self-defense. Although defensive force may be used to protect property, the majority view is that defendants may use only nondeadly force to protect property. As the drafters of the Model Penal Code explained, "the preservation of life has such moral and ethical standing in our culture and society, that the deliberate sacrifice of life merely for the protection of property ought not to be sanctioned by law." Model Penal Code § 3.06 Comment at 72.

In 1997, however, the Louisiana legislature became the first to pass the so-called "Shoot the Carjacker" statute, which authorized the use of deadly force to prevent an unlawful entry into one's car (as well as one's home or place of work). *See* La. Rev. Stat. Ann. § 14:20(A)(4). For a discussion of the costs and benefits of this provision, see Jason D. Fisher, Comment, *The "Shoot the Carjacker" Law Under Fire*, 47 EMORY L.J. 1401 (1998).

2. **Using Force to Protect Homes.** Greater leeway is allowed when deadly force is used, as in *Anderson*, to prevent an unlawful entry into the home—although the extent of the defense varies. Some states follow the traditional common-law rule, which broadly allows the use of deadly force to prevent any imminent, unlawful entry into the home. *See, e.g., Fair v. State*, 702 S.E.2d 420, 431–32 (Ga. 2010); *State v. Rye*, 651 S.E.2d 321, 323 (S.C. 2007).

Over time, however, the common-law rule has been narrowed in other jurisdic- tions. For example, some statutes authorize deadly force if the defendant reasonably believed the intruder posed a threat of injury to the occupants, *see, e.g., State v. Jason H.*, 599 S.E.2d 862, 865–66 (W. Va. 2004), and/or was making an unlawful entry in order to commit a felony. *Cf. Mondie v. Commonwealth*, 158 S.W.3d 203, 207–09 (Ky. 2005) (allowing deadly force to prevent a burglary, defined by state statute as an entry to commit any crime, even petty theft or simple assault).

Other states take an even narrower view, allowing the use of deadly force to prevent an unlawful entry into the home only where the defendant reasonably believed the intruder intended to commit a violent or forcible felony or otherwise posed a risk of death or serious bodily harm. *See, e.g., People v. Ceballos*, 526 P.2d 241, 245 (Cal. 1974); *State v. Boyett*, 185 P.3d 355, 358–60 (N.M. 2008).

In recent years, some state legislatures have passed "make my day" statutes like the one at issue in *Anderson* that authorize a relatively broad use of deadly force to protect the home. *See also People v. McNeese*, 892 P.2d 304, 306, 310 (Colo. 1995) (interpreting Colorado's similar statute—which allows the use of deadly force in cases of unlawful entry into a home if the defendant reasonably fears that the intruder "intends to commit a crime against a person or property" and "might use any physical force, no matter how slight"—to require in addition that the intruder actually made an unlawful entry, that is, "a knowing, criminal entry into a dwelling").

Other states have followed Florida's lead, passing "stand your ground"/"shoot first" statutes that not only abolish the retreat requirement for self-defense but also create a presumption that defendants "held a reasonable fear of imminent peril of death or great bodily harm" when they used deadly force against someone who they "knew or had reason to believe" had "unlawfully and forcefully enter[ed] . . . a dwelling, residence, or occupied vehicle." Fla. Stat. §776.013(1). *See also id.* §776.013(4) ("A person who unlawfully and by force enters or attempts to enter a person's dwelling, residence, or occupied vehicle is presumed to be doing so with the intent to commit an unlawful act involving force or violence.") (For a description of the impact "stand your ground" laws have had on the retreat doctrine, see Note 1 following *People v. Tomlins* in Section B above.)

Under most of these approaches—including even the most restrictive, if burglary is considered a forcible felony even when the burglar is breaking and entering in order to commit a nonviolent felony—deadly force may be used to protect a home from an intruder who does not pose any threat of death or serious bodily harm to the occupants. Is it appropriate to ignore the usual limits on deadly force in this context, either because an "attack on the home [is] synonymous with an attack on the occupants," Model Penal Code §3.06 Comment at 92, or because "Anglo-American culture attaches such great meaning to the home" that "the integrity of the home" ought to be "protected . . . wholly separate and independent from the life of the homeowner"? Elaine M. Chiu, *Culture in Our Midst*, 17 U. Fla. J.L. & Pub. Pol'y 231, 256 (2006). Or is there "a seemingly intractable conflict" between these rules and the law of self-defense? Stuart P. Green, *Castles and Carjackers: Proportionality and the Use of Deadly Force in Defense of Dwellings and Vehicles*, 1999 U. Ill. L. Rev. 1, 2. For an analysis tying the Colorado and Florida statutes to a "popular revolt against certain notions of proportionality" in self-defense law, to "deep distrust of governmental authority" and "legal and other elites generally," and to the perception that "the state is unable to defend law-abiding citizens against crime," see Renee Lettow Lerner, *The Worldwide Popular Revolt Against Proportionality in Self-Defense Law*, 2 J.L. Econ. & Pol'y 331, 333 (2006).

Even if the occupants of a home are given substantial leeway in using deadly force to protect their place of residence, did the *Anderson* court properly extend that right to visitors? Or should the babysitter and houseguest referred to in the court's hypotheticals be allowed to use deadly force only if they are acting in self-defense?

3. Using "Spring" or "Trap" Guns. Given the right to use deadly force to protect the home at least in some circumstances, may a homeowner set up a spring or trap gun that is rigged to go off, for example, when someone opens the door? The common-law rule permitted defendants to use such a device if they would have been justified in using deadly force (under any of the defenses described in this Chapter) had they been present when the intruder entered their home. But some courts have departed from the common-law approach and prohibit the use of spring guns under any circumstances. *See, e.g., People v. Ceballos*, 526 P.2d 241 (Cal. 1974); *Bishop v. State*, 356 S.E.2d 503 (Ga. 1987).

Are these courts right to reject the common-law view because "it turns liability upon the fortuity of who happens to be injured by the device"? Model Penal Code § 3.06 Comment at 101. Or is the common-law rule sensible because "as long as the law permits use of deadly force to protect a dweller of a home, the means used to inflict it—personally or by his 'agent,' the spring gun—should not matter"? Joshua Dressler, Understanding Criminal Law § 20.04[A], at 269 (7th ed. 2015). In addition, is the common-law approach preferable because it better protects "elderly or infirm resident[s]" and those who are "untrained in firearm use," and also guards against the dangers that might befall those who come home unexpectedly and surprise a burglar? *Id.*

If spring guns are permitted under some circumstances, does the common law properly focus on the moment when the gun goes off? Or should a defense be available if, "at the time that he sets the spring gun," the defendant "possessed a reasonable expectation that someone would be breaking into his home to commit a felony" and the intruder was in fact doing so? *Bishop*, 356 S.E.2d at 507 (Smith, J., dissenting).

4. The Model Penal Code Approach. Section 3.06 of the Model Penal Code contains provisions relating to defense of home and property. In general, the Code permits defendants to use nondeadly force if they believe it is immediately necessary to protect their home or property, so long as (1) they first ask the other person to stop interfering with the property in cases where it is reasonable to do so and (2) they do

not use force that they know will "expose [the other person] to substantial danger of
serious bodily harm." Model Penal Code §§ 3.06(1), 3.06(3). Although the Code thus
requires only an honest belief in the need for force, this defense is subject to the limitations regarding reckless and negligent mistakes contained in § 3.09(2) and
described above in connection with the law of self-defense. *See* Note 6 following
People v. Goetz in Section B.

The Code authorizes the use of deadly force to protect the home or property in
two circumstances. First, the Code permits defendants to use deadly force if they
believe that an intruder is not merely attempting to enter their home unlawfully, but
is doing so in order to "dispossess" them of the home and has no "claim of right to
its possession." Model Penal Code § 3.06(3)(d)(i). In authorizing deadly force in such
cases, the Comments explain:

> To kill a man is, on a dispassionate view, an evil both more serious and more
> irrevocable than the loss of possession of a dwelling for a period during which
> a court order is being obtained to recover it. . . . On the other hand, to be
> illegally ousted from one's dwelling is a provocation that is not to be depre-
> ciated. . . . Moreover, any persistent effort to break into a home is likely to
> arouse in the householder a reasonable fear for his own safety, unless he
> knows that the assailant is breaking in under a claim of right.

Id. § 3.06 Comment at 93.

Second, the Code provides that defendants may use deadly force if they believe
that someone is attempting to commit arson, burglary, robbery, or some other felony involving the theft or destruction of property, so long as (1) that person has used
or threatened deadly force against them or in their presence, or (2) using nondeadly
force under the circumstances would "expose [them] to substantial danger of serious bodily injury." *Id.* § 3.06(3)(d)(ii). As the drafters acknowledged, the first sub-
part of this provision breaches "the basic value judgment . . . that the protection of
property interests should not justify the taking of life" because it "permits the use of
deadly force in a number of . . . situations where any danger to life or well-being . . . ,
though once existing, has passed"—for example, where a thief "has once manifested
or threatened deadly force in the attempt to commit . . . one of the enumerated
property crimes" and deadly force is used "to prevent him from capitalizing upon
his offense." *Id.* § 3.06 Comment at 96. Nevertheless, the drafters reasoned that
"resort to deadly force in this context is a predictable response of reasonable people,"
and the aggressor's "willingness to resort to [deadly] force on one occasion may be
thought to indicate a willingness to do so again, [so that] the privilege afforded here
may be thought to protect the bodily safety of potential future victims." *Id.* However, the Code prohibits the use of deadly mechanical devices like spring or trap guns
under any circumstances. *See id.* § 3.06(5).

[2] Law Enforcement

Plumhoff v. Rickard

134 S. Ct. 2012 (2014)

JUSTICE ALITO delivered the opinion of the Court.[8]

The courts below denied qualified immunity for police officers who shot the driver of a fleeing vehicle to put an end to a dangerous car chase. We reverse and hold that the officers did not violate the Fourth Amendment. . . .

I

Because this case arises from the denial of the officers' motion for summary judgment, we view the facts in the light most favorable to the nonmoving party, the daughter of the driver who attempted to flee. Near midnight on July 18, 2004, Lieutenant Joseph Forthman of the West Memphis, Arkansas, Police Department pulled over a white Honda Accord because the car had only one operating headlight. Donald Rickard was the driver of the Accord, and Kelly Allen was in the passenger seat. Forthman noticed an indentation, "roughly the size of a head or a basketball" in the windshield of the car. He asked Rickard if he had been drinking, and Rickard responded that he had not. Because Rickard failed to produce his driver's license upon request and appeared nervous, Forthman asked him to step out of the car. Rather than comply with Forthman's request, Rickard sped away.

Forthman gave chase and was soon joined by five other police cruisers driven by Sergeant Vance Plumhoff and Officers Jimmy Evans, Lance Ellis, Troy Galtelli, and John Gardner. The officers pursued Rickard east on Interstate 40 toward Memphis, Tennessee. While on I-40, they attempted to stop Rickard using a "rolling roadblock," but they were unsuccessful. The District Court described the vehicles as "swerving through traffic at high speeds," and respondent does not dispute that the cars attained speeds over 100 miles per hour.[9] During the chase, Rickard and the officers passed more than two dozen vehicles.

Rickard eventually exited I-40 in Memphis, and shortly afterward he made "a quick right turn," causing "contact [to] occu[r]" between his car and Evans' cruiser. As a result of that contact, Rickard's car spun out into a parking lot and collided with Plumhoff's cruiser. Now in danger of being cornered, Rickard put his car into reverse "in an attempt to escape." As he did so, Evans and Plumhoff got out of their cruisers

8. Justice Ginsburg joined the judgment and Parts I and II of the majority opinion, as well as Part III(C) (which is omitted here and concluded that, even if Rickard's Fourth Amendment rights were violated, the officers were entitled to qualified immunity from the §1983 suit because his constitutional rights were not clearly established at the time they acted). Justice Breyer joined the majority opinion except for Part III(B)(2).

9. [n.1] It is also undisputed that Forthman saw glass shavings on the dashboard of Rickard's car, a sign that the windshield had been broken recently; that another officer testified that the windshield indentation and glass shavings would have justified a suspicion "that someone had possibly been struck by that vehicle, like a pedestrian"; and that Forthman saw beer in Rickard's car.

and approached Rickard's car, and Evans, gun in hand, pounded on the passenger-side window. At that point, Rickard's car "made contact with" yet another police cruiser. Rickard's tires started spinning, and his car "was rocking back and forth," indicating that Rickard was using the accelerator even though his bumper was flush against a police cruiser. At that point, Plumhoff fired three shots into Rickard's car. Rickard then "reversed in a 180 degree arc" and "maneuvered onto" another street, forcing Ellis to "step to his right to avoid the vehicle." As Rickard continued "fleeing down" that street, Gardner and Galtelli fired 12 shots toward Rickard's car, bringing the total number of shots fired during this incident to 15. Rickard then lost control of the car and crashed into a building. Rickard and Allen both died from some combination of gunshot wounds and injuries suffered in the crash that ended the chase.

Respondent, Rickard's surviving daughter, filed this action under . . . 42 U.S.C. § 1983, against the six individual police officers and the mayor and chief of police of West Memphis. She alleged that the officers used excessive force in violation of the Fourth . . . Amendment['s prohibition of "unreasonable searches and seizures"].

. . . .

III

A

Petitioners contend . . . that they did not violate Rickard's Fourth Amendment rights . . . .

B

A claim that law-enforcement officers used excessive force to effect a seizure is governed by the Fourth Amendment's "reasonableness" standard. *See Graham v. Connor*, 490 U.S. 386 (1989); *Tennessee v. Garner*, 471 U.S. 1 (1985). In *Graham*, we held that determining the objective reasonableness of a particular seizure under the Fourth Amendment "requires a careful balancing of the nature and quality of the intrusion on the individual's Fourth Amendment interests against the countervailing governmental interests at stake." The inquiry requires analyzing the totality of the circumstances.

We analyze this question from the perspective "of a reasonable officer on the scene, rather than with the 20/20 vision of hindsight." We thus "allo[w] for the fact that police officers are often forced to make split-second judgments—in circumstances that are tense, uncertain, and rapidly evolving—about the amount of force that is necessary in a particular situation."

In this case, respondent advances two main Fourth Amendment arguments. First, she contends that the Fourth Amendment did not allow petitioners to use deadly force to terminate the chase. Second, she argues that the "degree of force was excessive," that is, that even if the officers were permitted to fire their weapons, they went too far when they fired as many rounds as they did. We address each issue in turn.

1

In *Scott* [*v. Harris*, 550 U.S. 372 (2007)], we considered a claim that a police officer violated the Fourth Amendment when he terminated a high-speed car chase by using a technique that placed a "fleeing motorist at risk of serious injury or death." The record in that case contained a videotape of the chase, [which began when the police tried to stop the nineteen-year-old respondent for driving 73 m.p.h. in a 55 m.p.h. zone,] and we found that the events recorded on the tape justified the officer's conduct [of ramming his car into the back of the respondent's vehicle, causing the respondent to lose control of the car, run down an embankment, and turn over, leaving him a quadriplegic]. We wrote as follows: "Although there is no obvious way to quantify the risks on either side, it is clear from the videotape that respondent posed an actual and imminent threat to the lives of any pedestrians who might have been present, to other civilian motorists, and to the officers involved in the chase." We also wrote:

> "[R]espondent's vehicle rac[ed] down narrow, two-lane roads in the dead of night at speeds that are shockingly fast. We see it swerve around more than a dozen other cars, cross the double-yellow line, and force cars traveling in both directions to their respective shoulders to avoid being hit. We see it run multiple red lights and travel for considerable periods of time in the occasional center left-turn-only lane, chased by numerous police cars forced to engage in the same hazardous maneuvers just to keep up."

In light of those facts, "we [thought] it [was] quite clear that [the police officer] did not violate the Fourth Amendment." We held that a "police officer's attempt to terminate a dangerous high-speed car chase that threatens the lives of innocent bystanders does not violate the Fourth Amendment, even when it places the fleeing motorist at risk of serious injury or death."[10]

We see no basis for reaching a different conclusion here. As we have explained . . . , the chase in this case exceeded 100 miles per hour and lasted over five minutes. During that chase, Rickard passed more than two dozen other vehicles, several of which were forced to alter course. Rickard's outrageously reckless driving posed a grave

---

10. [n.3] In holding that petitioners' conduct violated the Fourth Amendment, the District Court relied on reasoning that is irreconcilable with our decision in *Scott.* The District Court held that the danger presented by a high-speed chase cannot justify the use of deadly force because that danger was caused by the officers' decision to continue the chase. In *Scott*, however, we declined to "lay down a rule requiring the police to allow fleeing suspects to get away whenever they drive so recklessly that they put other people's lives in danger," concluding that the Constitution "assuredly does not impose this invitation to impunity-earned-by-recklessness." [*But cf. Scott*, 550 U.S. at 394 (Stevens, J., dissenting) (questioning the "assumption that dangers caused by flight . . . will continue after the pursuit ends," and citing "rules adopted by countless police departments" advising officers to end a chase if, for example, "the immediate danger to the public created by the pursuit is greater than the immediate or potential danger to the public should the suspect remain at large" or "the violator's identity has been established to the point that later apprehension can be accomplished without danger to the public").]

public safety risk. And while it is true that Rickard's car eventually collided with a police car and came temporarily to a near standstill, that did not end the chase. Less than three seconds later, Rickard resumed maneuvering his car. Just before the shots were fired, when the front bumper of his car was flush with that of one of the police cruisers, Rickard was obviously pushing down on the accelerator because the car's wheels were spinning, and then Rickard threw the car into reverse "in an attempt to escape." Thus, the record conclusively disproves respondent's claim that the chase in the present case was already over when petitioners began shooting. Under the circumstances at the moment when the shots were fired, all that a reasonable police officer could have concluded was that Rickard was intent on resuming his flight and that, if he was allowed to do so, he would once again pose a deadly threat for others on the road. Rickard's conduct even after the shots were fired—as noted, he managed to drive away despite the efforts of the police to block his path—underscores the point.

In light of the circumstances we have discussed, it is beyond serious dispute that Rickard's flight posed a grave public safety risk, and here, as in *Scott*, the police acted reasonably in using deadly force to end that risk.

2

We now consider respondent's contention that, even if the use of deadly force was permissible, petitioners acted unreasonably in firing a total of 15 shots. We reject that argument. It stands to reason that, if police officers are justified in firing at a suspect in order to end a severe threat to public safety, the officers need not stop shooting until the threat has ended. As petitioners noted below, "if lethal force is justified, officers are taught to keep shooting until the threat is over."

Here, during the 10-second span when all the shots were fired, Rickard never abandoned his attempt to flee. Indeed, even after all the shots had been fired, he managed to drive away and to continue driving until he crashed. This would be a different case if petitioners had initiated a second round of shots after an initial round had clearly incapacitated Rickard and had ended any threat of continued flight, or if Rickard had clearly given himself up. But that is not what happened.

In arguing that too many shots were fired, respondent relies in part on the presence of Kelly Allen in the front seat of the car, but we do not think that this factor changes the calculus. Our cases make it clear that "Fourth Amendment rights are personal rights which . . . may not be vicariously asserted." Thus, the question before us is whether petitioners violated Rickard's Fourth Amendment rights, not Allen's. If a suit were brought on behalf of Allen under either § 1983 or state tort law, the risk to Allen would be of central concern. But Allen's presence in the car cannot enhance Rickard's Fourth Amendment rights. After all, it was Rickard who put Allen in danger by fleeing and refusing to end the chase, and it would be perverse if his disregard for Allen's safety worked to his benefit.

Notes and Questions

1. Constitutional Limits on Police Use of Force. *Plumhoff v. Rickard*, like its predecessors, *Tennessee v. Garner*, 471 U.S. 1 (1985), and *Scott v. Harris*, 550 U.S. 372 (2007), addresses the federal constitutional limits on a law enforcement official's use of deadly force, rather than the question discussed in the other cases in this chapter—whether a criminal defendant charged with homicide or assault in connection with the use of force has a defense under state law. In finding unconstitutional the common-law rule that allowed law enforcement officials to use any amount of force in order to apprehend a fleeing felon, the majority in *Garner*, 471 U.S. at 11–12, explained:

> It is not better that all felony suspects die than that they escape. Where the suspect poses no immediate threat to the officer and no threat to others, the harm resulting from failing to apprehend him does not justify the use of deadly force to do so. It is no doubt unfortunate when a suspect who is in sight escapes, but the fact that the police arrive a little late or are a little slower afoot does not always justify killing the suspect. A police officer may not seize an unarmed, nondangerous suspect by shooting him dead. . . .
>
> . . . Where the officer has probable cause to believe that the suspect poses a threat of serious physical harm, either to the officer or to others, it is not constitutionally unreasonable to prevent escape by using deadly force. Thus, if the suspect threatens the officer with a weapon or there is probable cause to believe that he has committed a crime involving the infliction or threatened infliction of serious physical harm, deadly force may be used if necessary to prevent escape, and if, where feasible, some warning has been given.

Applying that standard to the facts before it, the *Garner* majority found the use of deadly force excessive in that case:

> Officer Hymon could not reasonably have believed that Garner—young, slight, and unarmed—posed any threat. Indeed, Hymon never attempted to justify his actions on any basis other than the need to prevent an escape. . . . Hymon did not have probable cause to believe that Garner, whom he correctly believed to be unarmed, posed any physical danger to himself or others.
>
> The dissent argues that the shooting was justified by the fact that Officer Hymon had probable cause to believe that Garner had committed a nighttime burglary. While we agree that burglary is a serious crime, we cannot agree that it is so dangerous as automatically to justify the use of deadly force. The FBI classifies burglary as a "property" rather than a "violent" crime. Although the armed burglar would present a different situation, the fact that an unarmed suspect has broken into a dwelling at night does not automatically mean he is physically dangerous.

Id. at 21. The three dissenting Justices responded that "burglary is a serious and dangerous felony," and "[w]here a police officer has probable cause to arrest a suspected burglar, the use of deadly force as a last resort might well be the only means of apprehending the suspect." *Id.* at 27 (O'Connor, J., dissenting).

Given the Court's conclusion that the use of force was reasonable on the facts of *Plumhoff v. Rickard* and *Scott v. Harris*, would the *Garner* dissenters prevail today if the police used deadly force to apprehend a fleeing burglar? *Cf. Mullenix v. Luna*, 136 S. Ct. 305, 310 (2015) (per curiam) (granting an officer qualified immunity on the grounds that he did not violate clearly established Fourth Amendment rights by firing six shots at a fleeing vehicle without waiting to see whether spike strips that other officers had set up would succeed in stopping the car, noting that the Court had never "den[ied] qualified immunity because officers entitled to terminate a high-speed chase selected one dangerous alternative over another"). For the argument that the Court's rulings in this area are "notoriously opaque and fact-dependent," and therefore "not only poorly suited for police training, but actually counterproductive, confounding efforts to draft clear use of force policies," see Brandon L. Garrett & Seth W. Stoughton, *A Tactical Fourth Amendment*, 103 Va. L. Rev. 211 (2017).

2. Other Federal Limits on Police Use of Force. In 1995, the U.S. Department of Justice adopted its first uniform policy on the use of deadly force by federal law enforcement officials. The policy was prompted by the 11-day standoff at Ruby Ridge, Idaho, between FBI agents and Randall Weaver, a white separatist. The 1992 siege led to the deaths of Weaver's wife and 14-year-old son, as well as a federal marshal, in what FBI Director Louis Freeh would later call a "terribly flawed law-enforcement operation . . . with tragic consequences." David Johnston, *F.B.I. Director Says Agency Blundered in Idaho Standoff*, N.Y. Times, Oct. 20, 1995, at A28. After Weaver's trial in connection with the death of the marshal led to an acquittal on the most serious charges, Weaver filed a civil suit against federal agents that was eventually settled for $3.1 million. *See* Stephen LaBaton, *Separatist Family Given $3.1 Million from Government*, N.Y. Times, Aug. 16, 1995, at A1. The Ninth Circuit held that the FBI agent who shot Weaver's wife could be tried on state manslaughter charges, *see Idaho v. Horiuchi*, 253 F.3d 359 (9th Cir.) (en banc), *vacated as moot*, 266 F.3d 979 (9th Cir. 2001), but prosecutors ultimately elected not to proceed with the charges. *See* Sam Howe Verhovek, *F.B.I. Agent to Be Spared Prosecution in Shooting*, N.Y. Times, June 15, 2001, at A16.

The Justice Department policy that resulted from Ruby Ridge authorizes the use of deadly force to prevent fleeing felons from escaping only if a verbal warning has been given, where feasible, and only if there is "probable cause to believe: (1) the subject has committed a felony involving the infliction or threatened infliction of serious physical injury or death, and (2) the escape of the subject would pose an imminent danger of death or serious physical injury to the officer or to another person." U.S. Dep't of Justice Policy Statement on Use of Deadly Force (Oct. 17, 1995), *available at* http://www.usdoj.gov/ag/readingroom/resolution14b.htm. How does this policy compare with the constitutional standards set out in *Plumhoff v. Rickard* and the other Supreme Court precedents discussed above?

3. Criminal Law Limits: Using Force to Apprehend a Suspect. The criminal laws of most states allow the use of nondeadly force to apprehend a fleeing suspect or otherwise effect an arrest if a police officer reasonably believes force is necessary to prevent the suspect's escape. *Cf.* Model Penal Code § 3.07(2)(a)(i) (requiring in addition that, where feasible, the police first notify the suspect of the purpose of the arrest).

The common-law rule struck down in *Tennessee v. Garner*, 475 U.S. 1 (1985), broadly permitted the use of deadly force if necessary to prevent the escape of any fleeing felon. Today, most statutes limit the use of deadly force to certain felonies — for example, "forcible" felonies or felonies "believed to involve the use or threat of deadly force." 2 Wayne R. LaFave, Substantive Criminal Law § 10.7(a), at 177–78 (2d ed. 2003). *Cf.* Model Penal Code § 3.07(2)(b) (requiring in addition that the officer believe the use of deadly force "creates no substantial risk of injury to innocent persons," but also permitting the use of deadly force to arrest if a delay in apprehending the suspect is believed to pose a substantial risk of death or serious bodily harm).

Does the prevailing view repudiating the common-law approach make sense? Would it be anomalous to permit deadly force in cases where a suspect threatened only property damage or nonserious bodily injury, and where deadly force therefore would not be authorized under the principles governing self-defense and defense of property?

Even if the common-law rule is too broad, should the police be permitted to use deadly force to apprehend any suspect who they have reason to believe committed a dangerous crime in the past, even if the suspect currently poses no significant threat of death or serious physical injury? What about, for example, a suspect who killed a relative in the heat of passion or who committed a violent felony years earlier? *See* H. Richard Uviller, *Seizure by Gunshot: The Riddle of the Fleeing Felon*, 14 N.Y.U. Rev. L. & Soc. Change 705, 712 (1986).

4. Criminal Law Limits: Using Force to Prevent Commission of a Crime. Cases like *Plumhoff v. Rickard*, where force is used to apprehend a fleeing suspect, must be distinguished from cases where force is used to serve the similar law enforcement interest of preventing commission of a crime. In general, nondeadly force is justified by a reasonable belief that it is necessary to prevent the commission of a felony or a misdemeanor serious enough to be considered a breach of the peace. *See* 2 Wayne R. LaFave, Substantive Criminal Law § 10.7(c), at 183 (2d ed. 2003). *Cf.* Model Penal Code § 3.07(5)(a) (allowing nondeadly force to prevent the commission of a crime "involving or threatening bodily injury, damage to or loss of property or a breach of the peace").

Although some jurisdictions permit the use of deadly force to prevent the commission of any felony, the majority approach is to limit the use of deadly force to avert "forcible" or "atrocious" felonies. *See* Joshua Dressler, Understanding Criminal Law § 21.03[B][1], at 278 (7th ed. 2015). *Cf.* Model Penal Code § 3.07(5)(a)(ii)(A) (prohibiting deadly force unless the officer believes both (1) that there is a substantial risk the suspect will cause death or serious bodily injury unless the crime is prevented, and (2) that the use of deadly force does not create a substantial risk of injury to innocent people).

Should the right to use deadly force to prevent crime extend only to cases where deadly force could be used to apprehend the suspect because "the same concern for the protection of life and limb that underlies the provision on arrest applies also to the prevention of crime"? *Id.* § 3.07 Comment at 132. Or is deadly force "more justifiable to prevent a crime than to arrest a criminal when the crime has become an accomplished fact"? *Id.*

5. Racial Disparities in Law Enforcement's Use of Force. In thinking about the appropriate limits on law enforcement officials' use of force, note that researchers have found that the use of deadly force by the police is directed disproportionately at people of color. In 2015, 1,146 individuals were killed by the police in this country, and the 2016 figure was 1092. During both years, the fatality rate for African-Americans was more than twice that for whites. *See The Counted: Tracking People Killed by Police in the United States*, The Guardian, https://www.theguardian.com/us-news/series/counted-us-police-killings. Moreover, the African-Americans killed by the police were more than twice as likely as whites to be unarmed. *See* Jon Swaine et al., *Black Americans Killed by Police Twice as Likely to Be Unarmed as White People*, The Guardian (June 1, 2015), https://www.theguardian.com/us-news/2015/jun/01/black-americans-killed-by-police-analysis (reporting that almost two-thirds of those killed by police in the first five months of 2015 were people of color). *See also, e.g.*, Samuel Walker et al., The Color of Justice: Race, Ethnicity, and Crime in America 131 (5th ed. 2012) (finding a four-to-one disparity between African-Americans and whites who were shot and killed by the police, a figure that was twice as high in the early 1970s); James J. Frye, Tennessee v. Garner*: The Issue Not Addressed*, 14 N.Y.U. Rev. L. & Soc. Change 721, 727–30 (1986) (reporting the results of a study conducted between 1969 and 1974 in Memphis, where Edward Garner was shot, which showed that the police were more than twice as likely to shoot at African-Americans suspected of committing property crimes (burglary, larceny, auto larceny) than at whites). For an article setting out a six-part theoretical model designed to explain "blue-on-black violence," which concludes that "police violence against African-Americans [is] a structural phenomenon and not simply . . . a product of rogue police officers who harbor racial animus against black people," see Devon W. Carbado, *Blue-on-Black Violence: A Provisional Model of Some of the Causes*, 104 Geo. L.J. 1479, 1481 (2016).

As the result of widely publicized incidents in 2014 and 2015 where police officers killed unarmed African-American men, the Black Lives Matter movement and the racial disparities in law enforcement's use of deadly force against people of color received international attention. In some of these cases, no criminal charges were filed: grand jurors refused to indict Officer Darren Wilson in connection with the shooting of Michael Brown in Ferguson, Missouri; Officer Daniel Pantaleo, who was videotaped seemingly choking Eric Garner while trying to arrest him for illegally selling cigarettes in Staten Island, New York; and Officer Timothy Loehmann, who shot Tamir Rice as the 12-year-old was playing with a fake plastic pistol. For discussion of the "preferential procedures" prosecutors often use when deciding whether to bring charges against police officers, see Kate Levine, *How We Prosecute the Police*, 104 Geo. L.J. 745, 745 (2016) (explaining that prosecutors tend to "conduct a thorough precharge investigation" in these cases and "present a full account of an accusation, including exculpatory evidence, to grand juries").

On the other hand, some of the police involved in these high-profile killings are facing murder charges. First-degree murder charges have been filed against Officer Jason Van Dyke, who shot Laquan McDonald 16 times in Chicago as videos showed the 17-year-old walking away. Officer Michael Slager, who was caught on video shooting Walter Scott in the back as Scott ran away following a traffic stop in North Charleston, South Carolina, was tried on murder charges. The jury was unable to reach a verdict when one juror refused to convict. Facing a retrial on the state murder charge as well as federal charges, Slager pled guilty to willfully using excessive force to deprive Scott of his civil rights and will be sentenced in federal court on that charge. *See* Alan Blinder, *Ex-Officer Who Fatally Shot Unarmed Black Motorist Pleads Guilty in Charleston*, N.Y. Times, May 3, 2017, at A10. Charges ranging from second-degree murder to reckless endangerment were also filed against six officers in connection with the death of Freddie Gray in a police van in Baltimore, Maryland, although all remaining charges were dropped after the first four trials ended with three acquittals and a hung jury. *See* Sheryl Gay Stolberg & Jess Bidgood, *Baltimore Case Closed, with No Guilty Verdicts*, N.Y. Times, July 28, 2016, at A1. A civil suit filed by Michael Brown's family is still pending, but the five other families in these cases have each received settlements of their civil claims ranging between five and six and a half million dollars. *See* Mitch Smith, *Cleveland Will Pay $6 Million to Family of Boy Killed by Police*, N.Y. Times, Apr. 26, 2016, at A2. *See generally Developments in the Law — Policing*, 128 Harv. L. Rev. 1706 (2015).

6. A Private Citizen's Use of Force for Law Enforcement Purposes. Because the Fourth Amendment governs only the conduct of government officials, Supreme Court opinions like *Plumhoff v. Rickard* do not speak directly to the question whether private persons may use force in order to serve any of the law enforcement purposes described above. The criminal laws of most states, however, give a citizen who acts in response to a police officer's request for help the same right to use force that the officer has — or an even broader right given the unreasonableness of requiring the citizen to second-guess the officer's authority. *See* 2 Wayne R. LaFave, Substantive Criminal Law § 10.7(a), at 180 (2d ed. 2003). *Cf.* Model Penal Code § 3.07(2)(b)(ii) (allowing private citizens to use deadly force to effect an arrest if they are assisting someone they believe is a police officer).

What if private citizens are acting on their own? For example, could the owner of the home that was burglarized in *Tennessee v. Garner* have used deadly force to prevent the burglary, effect a citizen's arrest, or prevent Edward Garner's escape? (Although private persons are permitted to make arrests, their authority is often limited to cases where the crime in fact occurred or took place in their presence. *See* LaFave, *supra*, at 181 & n.38.) A private person may generally use nondeadly force if a police officer would be justified in doing so under similar circumstances. *See, e.g.,* Model Penal Code § 3.07(1)–(2). Likewise, a private citizen's right to use deadly force in order to prevent commission of a crime is equivalent to the police officer's right. *See, e.g., id.* § 3.07(5).

But a citizen's right to use deadly force in order to effect an arrest is often more limited in some respect than the comparable right of the police officer. For example, the citizen's right to use deadly force for this purpose may be restricted to cases where the suspect actually committed the felony, where the felony was forcible, or where the citizen first gave notice of the intent to arrest the suspect. Moreover, a substantial number of states, as well as MPC § 3.07(2)(b)(ii), prohibit any private use of deadly force to apprehend a suspect. *See* Joshua Dressler, Understanding Criminal Law § 21.03[B][2][b], at 279–80 (7th ed. 2015); 2 Paul H. Robinson, Criminal Law Defenses § 142(f), at 143 (1984).

Should private persons be barred altogether from using deadly force to arrest or apprehend a suspect given "the dangers of uncontrolled vigilantism and anarchistic actions" and the risk that innocent people might be injured "at the hands of untrained volunteers using firearms"? *Commonwealth v. Klein*, 363 N.E.2d 1313, 1317–18 (Mass. 1977). Is it reasonable to distinguish between deadly force aimed at preventing crime from that used to effect arrests because "[i]n modern conditions, the arrest of suspected criminals is peculiarly the concern of the police," whereas preventing crime "is properly the concern of everybody"? Model Penal Code § 3.07 Comment at 132. Or should citizens be allowed to use deadly force even to apprehend suspects because "the police cannot be everywhere they are needed at once"? *People v. Couch*, 439 N.W.2d 354, 355 (Mich. Ct. App. 1989), *rev'd in part on other grounds*, 461 N.W.2d 683 (Mich. 1990).

If private persons are permitted to use deadly force in order to arrest or apprehend a suspect at least under some circumstances, should the same constitutional limitations that restrict the use of force by police officers be applied here as well? On the one hand, the Supreme Court's constitutional rulings in cases like *Plumhoff v. Rickard* do not govern the use of force by nongovernmental actors and therefore perhaps ought to be deemed irrelevant in this context. *See State v. Clothier*, 753 P.2d 1267, 1270 (Kan. 1988); *People v. Couch*, 461 N.W.2d 683, 684 (Mich. 1990); *State v. Cooney*, 463 S.E.2d 597, 599 (S.C. 1995). On the other hand, perhaps those constitutional decisions, though not controlling, should be followed by analogy because "the public policy informing the reasoning of the Supreme Court [is] highly relevant . . . [w]hether the individual pursuing an unarmed felon is a police officer or a person attempting to make a citizen's arrest." *State v. Johnson*, 954 P.2d 79, 86 (N.M. Ct. App. 1997). *Cf. State v. Weddell*, 43 P.3d 987, 991 (Nev. 2002) (concluding that the state legislature "could not have meant to repose what might easily amount to vigilante justice in the hands of private persons while restricting the use of force in making an arrest by those who are charged by law with duties of public safety and protection").

7. The Model Penal Code Approach. Section 3.07 of the Model Penal Code, the specific contours of which are described in the preceding Notes, authorizes the use of force if one believes it is immediately necessary for any of the law enforcement purposes discussed above. Thus, an honest belief in the need for force is sufficient to make out a defense here just as it is under the Code's self-defense provision.

The right to use force under §3.07 is, however, subject to the limitations set out in §3.09 of the Code. As explained above in the context of self-defense, §3.09(2) provides that those who make a negligent or reckless mistake about the need for force have no defense to a crime requiring a mens rea of only negligence or recklessness. *See* Note 6 following *People v. Goetz* in Section B.

In addition, §3.09(1) denies a defense to those who erroneously think their use of force is justified because they are mistaken about some aspect of the criminal law or the law governing the legality of searches and arrests. Thus, for example, police officers who mistakenly believe that they may arrest a suspect without first obtaining an arrest warrant have no defense under §3.07 if they use force to effect that arrest. But if they erroneously think they have probable cause to arrest the suspect, the mistake involves an issue of fact, or a mixed question of law and fact, and therefore the defense is not lost by virtue of §3.09(1) (although it might be unavailable under §3.09(2)). *See* Model Penal Code §3.07 Comment at 108 n.3; *id.* §3.09 Comment at 148.

The Code creates two exceptions to §3.09(1), however. First, those who have what they believe to be a proper arrest warrant do not forfeit their right to use force under §3.07 if the warrant turns out to be invalid. *See id.* §3.07(2)(a)(ii); *id.* §3.07 Comment at 110. Second, a private citizen who responds to a police officer's request for assistance in making an unlawful arrest "is justified in using any force that he would be justified in using if the arrest were lawful, provided that he does not believe the arrest is unlawful." If the private person using force in this situation is not answering an official call for help, the Code also requires a finding that the arrest would have been lawful "if the facts were as he believe[d] them to be." *Id.* §3.07(4).

8. Using Force to Resist an Unlawful Arrest. The common law permitted the use of reasonable nondeadly force to resist an unlawful arrest—for example, an arrest without probable cause, an arrest for a nonexistent crime, or a warrantless arrest under circumstances calling for an arrest warrant. Deadly force was not permitted under the common law, although one who killed a police officer while resisting an unlawful arrest might be considered reasonably provoked and therefore guilty of voluntary manslaughter rather than murder. The modern trend is to reject the common-law approach and prohibit any use of force to resist a police officer's illegal arrest—unless the arresting officer is using excessive force, in which case even deadly force may generally be used if the arrestee reasonably fears death or serious bodily harm.

See Joshua Dressler, Understanding Criminal Law § 18.05[D], at 250–51 (7th ed. 2015). *Cf.* Model Penal Code § 3.04(2)(a)(i) (forbidding the use of force to resist an illegal arrest that a suspect knows is being made by a police officer).

Is the modern view preferable because "the legality of a peaceful arrest should be determined by courts of law and not through a trial by battle in the streets"? *State v. Hobson*, 577 N.W.2d 825, 837 (Wis. 1998). Should one who is illegally arrested therefore be required to "submit peacefully to the inevitable and to pursue his available remedies through the orderly judicial process"—that is, whatever criminal process is triggered by the arrest and any additional civil and administrative remedies? *People v. Curtis*, 450 P.2d 33, 36–37 (Cal. 1969). Likewise, is the modern trend sensible because "[s]elf-help measures . . . can lead to violence and serious physical injury," *State v. Trane*, 57 P.3d 1052, 1061 (Utah 2002) (quoting *State v. Doe*, 583 P.2d 464, 466–67 (N.M. 1978)), and it is "highly unlikely that a suspect, using *reasonable* force, can escape from or effectively deter an arrest, whether lawful or unlawful"? *Curtis*, 450 P.2d at 36.

On the other hand, is the common-law approach sounder because denying the right to resist unlawful arrests "encourage[s] abuses of authority, eliminating one restraint on illegal police behavior"? Model Penal Code § 3.04 Comment at 43. *Cf.* Samuel Walker et al., The Color of Justice: Race, Ethnicity, and Crime in America 150–51 (5th ed. 2012) (describing racial disparities in arrest rates). Does the common-law rule also make sense because, if the "impulse to resist is provoked by arbitrary police behavior, it is fundamentally unfair to punish [the arrestee] for giving in to that impulse with measured resistance"? Paul G. Chevigny, *The Right to Resist an Unlawful Arrest*, 78 Yale L.J. 1128, 1334 (1969). *See also State v. Weigmann*, 714 A.2d 841, 851 (Md. 1998) (refusing to conclude that "the right to resist [arrest] is unsound or unsuitable to a modern society," and instead leaving that issue to the legislature, noting that the alternative remedies available to those who are arrested illegally "often may not be adequate"); *People v. Moreno*, 814 N.W.2d 624 (Mich. 2012) (finding that the legislature did not intend to abrogate the common-law right to resist unlawful arrests).

Assuming it is reasonable to prohibit suspects from resisting an unlawful arrest, why create an exception for cases where the arresting officer uses an unreasonable amount of force? Consider the California Supreme Court's explanation:

> There are . . . two distinct and separate rights at stake. The common law rule allowing resistance to technically unlawful arrests protects a person's freedom from unreasonable seizure and confinement; the rule allowing resistance to excessive force, which applies during a technically lawful *or* unlawful arrest, protects a person's right to bodily integrity and permits resort to self-defense. Liberty can be restored through legal processes, but life and limb cannot be repaired in a courtroom.

Curtis, 450 P.2d at 38–39.

Does this distinction make sense, or does the modern rule's "concern[] with decreasing the physical risks associated with unlawful arrests" militate against creating an exception for excessive force cases because "those situations present[] the greatest risk of danger"? *Hobson*, 577 N.W.2d at 841 (Abrahamson, C.J., concurring).

[D] Necessity

The pressure of natural physical forces sometimes confronts a person in an emergency with a choice of two evils: either he may violate the literal terms of the criminal law and thus produce a harmful result, or he may comply with those terms and thus produce a greater or equal or lesser amount of harm. For reasons of social policy, if the harm which will result from compliance with the law is greater than that which will result from violation of it, he is by virtue of the defense of necessity justified in violating it.

2 Wayne R. LaFave, Substantive Criminal Law § 10.1, at 116 (2d ed. 2003).

One commentator offered the following illustrations of conduct justified by the necessity defense:

The necessity defense essentially permits an accused to admit the elements of an offense but avoid punishment if her illegal acts were designed to obtain a greater good. A driver may exceed the speed limit to rush an injured person to the hospital. An onlooker is permitted to destroy a home to prevent a fire from spreading. A prisoner may leave a burning jail. A captain may enter an embargoed port in a storm.

Shaun P. Martin, *The Radical Necessity Defense*, 73 U. Cin. L. Rev. 1527, 1527–28 (2005).

State v. Reese

272 N.W.2d 863 (Iowa 1978)

McGiverin, Justice.

. . . .

Defendant was charged by county attorney's information with escape from the Iowa State Penitentiary, Ft. Madison. He organized the escape and departed with other inmates from inside the penitentiary without permission on March 29, 1977.

At trial defendant testified in his own behalf and admitted leaving the penitentiary without authorization, but claimed his departure was due to a fear of further homosexual attack and possible death. Defendant described difficulties he experienced with another inmate who defendant would identify only as "the lifer." According to defendant, the lifer had established a scheme whereby he offered new inmates protection from homosexual attack by others in exchange for voluntary homosexual liaisons with the lifer. When defendant attempted to disrupt the lifer's scheme, the lifer threatened to kill Reese. Defendant is five feet, nine inches tall and weighs 150 pounds. The lifer was six feet, two inches and weighed 225 pounds.

Defendant further testified that after the lifer's initial threats, defendant twice contacted his counselor by note, but received no response. He also informed the penitentiary psychiatrist of the problem. This too failed to obtain any results. On March 26, the lifer renewed his threats against defendant and carried out a homosexual attack. Defendant made no further attempts to contact prison officials but accomplished an escape on March 29.

Defendant was apprehended over 24 hours later hiding in a shed on a private farm about eight miles from the penitentiary. . . . [H]e was unarmed and offered no resistance to the arresting officers. He testified he had considered contacting an attorney after his escape but had no opportunity to do so. He had not turned himself in to police authorities after his departure from the prison.

At the time in question the penitentiary was being operated with eighteen employees less than its full complement. The approximately 300 prisoners in defendant's cellhouse were supervised by five guards.

Defendant requested the court to instruct the jury on defenses of necessity and compulsion. . . . Defendant also objected to the failure of the court to so instruct the jury. The request and objection were overruled by the trial court. Defendant was convicted and sentenced.

. . . .

The defense of necessity. Defendant contends that this court should recognize the defense of necessity in an escape prosecution. . . .

The State's response to defendant's contention is that recognition of a defense of necessity would require that *State v. Cahill*, 196 Iowa 486, 194 N.W. 191 (1923), be overruled. The State also argues that such a defense would be disruptive of prison discipline and that the facts of this case do not allow Reese to avail himself of the necessity defense in any event.

We agree that *State v. Cahill* does not control the disposition of this case. In *Cahill* the defendant prisoner in an escape case complained of being placed in solitary confinement with an inadequate amount of food and in unsanitary conditions. The prisoner was on bread and water as punishment for unruly behavior. We held those conditions could not justify an escape. A specific threat of death, attack, or substantial bodily injury, however, was not involved. Because the evil Reese claimed to avoid was substantially greater than that involved in *Cahill*, *Cahill* can be readily distinguished on the facts.

The precise question of existence of a necessity defense to an escape charge based on fear of injury or death from physical attack has never previously been decided by us. . . . In [*State v. Ward*, 170 Iowa 185, 152 N.W. 501 (1915)], the defendant was permitted to raise, and ultimately prevailed on, a necessity defense to a charge of unlawfully killing a deer. . . . The defendant in *Ward* killed the deer because several deer had regularly eaten his crops. He promptly reported the killing to the authorities and turned the carcass over to them to establish a test case of the right to protect his property from the forces of nature. He contended the killing was wholly defensive and preventive. We there said: "The right of defense of person and property is a constitutional right (Art. 1, Sec. 1, Constitution of Iowa), and is recognized in the construction of all statutes." We further said, "We think, therefore, that the defendant was entitled to make an issue of fact on the question of justification . . . ."

Therefore, it appears the defense of necessity exists in Iowa. . . . What should be the conditions attendant to a defense of necessity as it applies to an escape charge . . . ?

Two approaches to the definition of the defense are found in other jurisdictions. The first approach is that of the leading case, *People v. Lovercamp*, 43 Cal. App. 3d 823, 831–32, 118 Cal. Rptr. 110, 115 (1974). There the court held that "a limited defense of necessity is available if the following conditions exist:

(1) The prisoner is faced with a specific threat of death, forcible sexual attack or substantial bodily injury in the immediate future;

(2) There is no time for a complaint to the authorities or there exists a history of futile complaints which make any result from such complaints illusory;

(3) There is no time or opportunity to resort to the courts;

(4) There is no evidence of force or violence used towards prison personnel or other innocent persons in the escape; and

(5) The prisoner immediately reports to the proper authorities when he has attained a position of safety from the immediate threat."

The approach of adopting specific and carefully defined limitations has been rejected by other courts. However, those courts have held that the *Lovercamp* conditions go to the weight and credibility of defendant's testimony. [Here the court cites, *inter alia*, *People v. Unger*, 362 N.E.2d 319, 323 (Ill. 1977).]

. . . .

We are inclined to follow the first approach and hereby adopt the *Lovercamp* conditions for any defense of necessity to an escape charge. . . . We also approve this language from *Lovercamp*:

However, before *Lovercamp* becomes a household word in prison circles and we are exposed to the spectacle of hordes of prisoners leaping over the walls screaming "rape," we hasten to add that the defense of necessity to an escape charge is extremely limited in its application. . . .

The *Lovercamp* conditions for submission of a defense of necessity to an escape charge would allow a defendant to remove himself from an intolerable immediate situation, and yet place responsibility on him to immediately turn himself in or report to proper authorities when he had reached a position of safety. This condition would at least in part answer the State's contention that the necessity defense would disrupt prison conditions.

At the same time our prison authorities should take all reasonable precautions for the safety of their inmates. We approve this statement from the Michigan Court of Appeals in *People v. Harmon*, 53 Mich. App. 482, 220 N.W.2d 212, 213 (1974), *affirmed*, 394 Mich. 625, 232 N.W.2d 187 (1975):

> The persons in charge of our prisons and jails are obligated to take reasonable precautions in order to provide a safe place of confinement where a prisoner is safe from gang rapes and beatings by fellow inmates, safe from guard ignorance of pleas for help, and safe from intentional placement into situations where an assault of one type or another is likely to result. If our prison system fails to live up to its responsibilities in this regard we should not, indirectly, countenance such a failure by precluding the presentation of a defense based upon those facts.

. . . .

Was a necessity defense submissible here? Under the conditions for a necessity defense set forth above, we must decide whether defendant generated a fact question sufficient that the defense should have been submitted to the jury. We believe he did not.

Defendant did not immediately report to the proper authorities when he had attained a position of safety from the immediate threat of attack by the lifer. Instead, defendant traveled several miles from the penitentiary and hid on private property until found by the authorities over 24 hours after the escape. We hold the trial court was right in refusing to instruct the jury on a defense of necessity under this record. . . .

McCormick, Justice, dissenting.

. . . .

. . . The necessity defense is available to a farmer who kills a deer foraging in his corn, and it is available to a prisoner who flees prison to save his life. However, under the court's holding today the prisoner does not have the defense unless he turns himself in immediately after his escape, so far as he knows to be returned to the very danger from which he was presumably justified in fleeing. Requiring the prisoner to turn himself in once he is over the wall, on the possibility that conditions in the prison will be different when he is back inside, demands a measure of faith and sophistication of reasoning on his part which are neither realistic nor warranted.

If the jury believed defendant, as it would have a right to do, it could find he escaped three days after having his life threatened and being assaulted and sodomized at knifepoint by an imprisoned murderer. Defendant testified as follows:

Q. Can you tell the jury why you left, Michael?

A. I was afraid it was going to happen again. I didn't want it to happen again so I left.

Q. Did you make any efforts after you had left to contact institutional officials?

A. I thought about getting an attorney and seeing what I could work out so that I wouldn't have to be on escape, but I wasn't out long enough to contact anyone before I was recaptured.

Q. Can you tell the jury, Michael, a little bit about what you did and what you observed . . . having left the penitentiary? . . .

A. Ran and hid. I just hid. Didn't do anything else. I hid in a barn for about twenty-four hours trying to stay warm and get dry.

From the testimony of prison officials the jury could find the prison was understaffed, many prisoners possessed deadly weapons, and violence among inmates could be prevented only by locking them in isolation. From defendant's testimony the jury could also find he had informed staff members of his problem on three occasions but received no help.

I believe the jury should have had the right to acquit defendant of escape if it found this evidence to be true.

. . . .

I believe we should define the necessity defense in traditional terms in prison escape cases and recognize the *Lovercamp* conditions as factors affecting the defendant's credibility but not as conditions precedent. We should do so upon the reasoning employed by the Illinois court in *Unger* in facts analogous to those in the present case. There the defendant was apprehended in a motel room two days after his escape. The court said:

> The preconditions set forth in *Lovercamp* are, in our view, matters which go to the weight and credibility of the defendant's testimony. . . . The absence of one or more of the elements listed in *Lovercamp* would not necessarily mandate a finding that the defendant could not assert the defense of necessity.
>
> By way of example, in the present case defendant did not report to the authorities immediately after securing his safety. In fact, defendant never voluntarily turned himself in to the proper officials. However, defendant testified that he intended to return to the prison upon obtaining legal advice from an attorney and claimed that he was attempting to get money from friends to pay for such counsel. Regardless of our opinion as to the believability of defendant's tale, this testimony, if accepted by the jury, would have negated any negative inference which would arise from defendant's failure to report to proper authorities after the escape. The absence of one of the *Lovercamp* preconditions does not alone disprove the claim of necessity and should not, therefore, automatically preclude an instruction on the defense. We therefore reject the contention that the availability of the necessity defense be expressly conditioned upon the elements set forth in *Lovercamp*.

[*Unger*, 362 N.E.2d at 323.]

. . . .

Notes and Questions

1. The Policies Underlying the Necessity Defense. Although there is "no single accepted definition" of the necessity defense and it is not expressly included in many state criminal codes, including the Iowa statutes at issue in *Reese*, the defense is "part of the common-law tradition of the United States." Joshua Dressler, Understanding Criminal Law § 22.02, at 289 (7th ed. 2015). Under a standard common-law formulation of the defense, it is available if the defendant "reasonably believed that criminal action 'was necessary to avoid a harm more serious than that sought to be prevented by the statute defining the offense.'" *United States v. Bailey*, 444 U.S. 394, 410 (1980) (quoting the lower court).

Is the theory underlying the necessity defense one of statutory interpretation—that "the legislature [has] delegate[d] . . . authority to the courts to carve out exceptions from the blanket prohibition" contained in a criminal statute? George P. Fletcher, A Crime of Self-Defense 163 (1988). Does the availability of the necessity defense therefore turn on whether the legislature "would have created an exception" if it "had foreseen the circumstances faced by the defendant"? *State v. Tate*, 505 A.2d 941, 946 (N.J. 1986). On the other hand, is the necessity defense based on "a 'higher law' of right and wrong"—the notion that "regardless of the legislative purpose, conduct that is socially beneficial is by its nature not criminal and therefore ought not to be punished"? Fletcher, *supra*, at 163–64. Or is that reasoning inconsistent with the traditional refusal in this country to impose a "duty to help others even when that help would cause only a minor inconvenience"? Vera Bergelson, *Choice of Evils: In Search of a Viable Rationale*, 6 Crim. L. & Phil. 289, 301 (2012) (emphasis omitted). (For a discussion of the duty to rescue, see Chapter 3, Section B.)

Whatever the underlying theory, is the necessity defense so vague that it leads to arbitrary decisions and uncertainty about the scope of the criminal laws? Should the necessity defense be abolished on the theory that the prosecutor can elect not to bring charges, the jury can nullify the law and acquit, or the executive can grant a pardon in cases where a defendant reasonably thought it was necessary to commit a crime in order to avoid a greater evil? *See* Model Penal Code § 3.02 Comment at 11 n.3 (citing several law reform reports recommending this approach). Or is it "better to be allowed a defense of uncertain ambit than none at all," especially because any uncertainty in this context is "less objectionable than it would be in defining an offense"? *Id.* at 17. For discussion of state legislatures' "traditional legal hostility" to the necessity defense and a description of the necessity statutes in effect in this country, see Michael H. Hoffheimer, *Codifying Necessity: Legislative Resistance to Enacting Choice-of-Evils Defenses to Criminal Liability*, 82 Tul. L. Rev. 191, 243 (2007).

2. Necessity Versus Duress as a Defense in Prison Escape Cases. Reese requested jury instructions on two defenses—compulsion (i.e., duress) and necessity—but apparently he did not press the duress argument before the Iowa Supreme Court. In prison escape cases like *Reese*, "the distinction between duress/coercion and necessity has been hopelessly blurred," and "courts seem to use the two terms interchangeably." *United States v. Lopez*, 662 F. Supp. 1083, 1086 (N.D. Cal. 1987), *aff'd*, 885 F.2d 1428 (9th Cir. 1989). Thus, while *Reese* focused on the necessity defense, other courts have analyzed these cases under the duress doctrine — even though the duress defense "does not precisely apply because no one has commanded the prisoner to escape." *Id.* For illustrations of prison escape cases using a duress analysis, see *United States v. Haney*, 287 F.3d 1266 (10th Cir. 2002), *vacated & remanded*, 318 F.3d 1161 (10th Cir. 2003) (en banc); *State v. Irons*, 827 P.2d 722 (Kan. 1992); *People v. Harmon*, 220 N.W.2d 212 (Mich. Ct. App. 1974), *aff'd*, 232 N.W.2d 187 (Mich. 1975). For a detailed discussion of duress, see Chapter 15, Section A.

3. The Scope of the Necessity Defense in Prison Escape Cases. Was the *Reese* court right to allow escaped prisoners to raise a necessity defense, given "[t]he atrocities and inhuman conditions of prison life in America"? *United States v. Bailey*, 444 U.S. 394, 421 (1980) (Blackmun, J., dissenting). Justice Blackmun explained:

> A youthful inmate can be expected to be subjected to homosexual gang rape his first night in jail, or, it has been said, even in the van on the way to jail. Weaker inmates become the property of stronger prisoners or gangs, who sell the sexual services of the victim. Prison officials either are disinterested in stopping abuse of prisoners by other prisoners or are incapable of doing so, given the limited resources society allocates to the prison system. Prison officials often are merely indifferent to serious health and safety needs of prisoners as well.

> Even more appalling is the fact that guards frequently participate in the brutalization of inmates. The classic example is the beating or other punishment in retaliation for prisoner complaints or court actions.

Id. at 421–22. (For further discussion of the problem of prison rape, see the Capers excerpt in Chapter 7, Section B.1.)

Despite the harsh realities of prison conditions, should the necessity defense be unavailable because "the crime of escape [is] a greater harm than the threat of sexual assault"? *People v. Lovercamp*, 118 Cal. Rptr. 110, 113 (Cal. Ct. App. 1974) (summarizing the court's reasoning in *People v. Richards*, 75 Cal. Rptr. 597 (Cal. Ct. App. 1969)). Does the answer to that question depend on the type of crime for which the inmate was originally imprisoned?

If necessity is recognized as a defense in prison escape cases, did the *Reese* court wisely limit the defense along the lines suggested in *Lovercamp*? Are the five prerequisites set out in *Lovercamp* crucial in order to ensure that "the act of escape was the only viable and reasonable choice available" and thus truly necessary? *Id.* at 112. Should "a more stringent standard" be required to support a defense to the crime of escape "[b]ecause of the difficulties inherent in long-term housing and containment of criminals"? *State v. Wolf*, 689 P.2d 188, 191 (Ariz. Ct. App. 1984). Or was the *Reese* dissent right in thinking that the general contours of the necessity defense should "apply to all offenses" equally, absent some contrary suggestion from the legislature, *Spakes v. State*, 913 S.W.2d 597, 598 (Tex. Crim. App. 1996) (per curiam), with the five *Lovercamp* factors relevant considerations for the jury to take into account?

For example, should Reese automatically lose his necessity defense because he hid instead of turning himself in? Even though his initial departure from the prison might have been necessary to protect himself, is escape "a continuing offense" such that his continued absence cannot be justified unless he made "a bona fide effort to surrender or return to custody as soon as the claimed . . . necessity had lost its coercive force"? *United States v. Bailey*, 444 U.S. at 413. Or is "the offense . . . complete at the time the escape from prison is made"? *People v. Mendoza*, 310 N.W.2d 860, 864 (Mich. Ct. App. 1981).

What about the other *Lovercamp* factors? Should the necessity defense be unavailable to Reese because he faced no "immediate" danger at the time he escaped, three days after he had been attacked? *Cf. United States v. Sahakian*, 453 F.3d 905, 909–10 (7th Cir. 2006) (denying necessity defense to an inmate charged with possessing a weapon in prison, noting that "the word 'imminent' should be construed narrowly in the prison context" and concluding that "[t]he rumor that there was a contract out on [the defendant's] life presents, at best, a threat of *future* violence against him at some unspecified time, as opposed to a threat which was immediate or imminent in nature"). (For discussion of the appropriateness of including imminence as an element of the necessity defense, see Note 1 following *United States v. Maxwell* below.)

Should Reese forfeit his defense because he made no effort to report the assault to the prison authorities before escaping? Could he reasonably have considered complaining "futile" based on prior experience even though his previous complaints involved only threats and not an actual attack? *Cf. United States v. Capozzi*, 723 F.3d 720, 726 (6th Cir. 2013) (rejecting necessity defense raised by a prisoner who alleged that he escaped to obtain medical treatment for his heart condition, dismissing his claim that, in response to "many requests and grievances [filed] with prison officials," he was "continually told that he was going to be treated" but "never received the proper care," on the grounds that the "promise of treatment . . . could have been the basis for a further grievance, an expedited administrative action, or a petition for a writ of mandamus").

4. **The "At Fault" Exception.** The necessity defense is generally unavailable if the defendant was at fault in bringing about the situation that required the choice of evils. *See* 2 Wayne R. LaFave, Substantive Criminal Law § 10.1(d)(6), at 132 (2d ed. 2003).

In *United States v. Luker*, 395 F.3d 830 (8th Cir. 2005), for example, the defendant raised a necessity defense to charges of unlawful possession of a weapon, claiming that he carried the gun because he had received death threats from another man. The court rejected his defense, observing that "it almost goes without saying that when the man making the threats is Luker's girlfriend's *husband*, no reasonable juror could surmise that Luker had not recklessly or negligently placed himself in a situation 'in which it was probable that he would be [forced to choose the criminal conduct].'" *Id.* at 833.

Should the "at fault" exception likewise apply to Reese, either because he chose to commit the crime that led to his imprisonment in the first place or because he foolishly tried to take on "the lifer"?

5. The Murder Exception. Is there any limit to the type of crime that can be justified by necessity? Should a necessity defense be available in murder cases? Some states say no, *see* 2 Wayne R. LaFave, Substantive Criminal Law § 10.1(d)(2), at 125 n.47 (2d ed. 2003), as did the court in the most famous case to raise the issue, *The Queen v. Dudley & Stephens*, 14 Q.B.D. 273 (1884). The defendants in that case were convicted of murder when they killed the weakest of the four surviving crew members on a shipwrecked yacht and ate his remains. Review the court's opinion in *Dudley & Stephens*, which is excerpted above in Chapter 1, Section A.2. *See also United States v. Holmes*, 26 F. Cas. 360 (C.C.E.D. Pa. 1842) (concluding that sailors who threw a number of passengers overboard in order to save the others stranded on a leaking, overcrowded lifeboat had no necessity defense because they did not use lots to select the victims and, as members of the crew, they had a duty to sacrifice themselves to save the passengers).

Is it sensible to preclude defendants from raising a necessity defense in murder cases? Are the objections raised by the court in *Dudley & Stephens* persuasive? Is it simply never "acceptable for a defendant to decide that it is necessary to kill an innocent person in order that he [or she] may live"? *People v. Coffman*, 96 P.3d 30, 106 (Cal. 2004) (quoting the State's argument). Or should the defense be available to murder defendants because "the sanctity of life [may have] a supreme place in the hierarchy of values, [but] it is nonetheless true that conduct that results in taking life may promote the very value sought to be protected by the law of homicide"? Model Penal Code § 3.02 Comment at 14. For example, did Dudley and Stephens choose the lesser evil by killing one to save three? And even though they could not know for sure that it was necessary to kill in order to save themselves, weren't they reasonable in so thinking?

Alternatively, can it be said that Dudley and Stephens did not choose the lesser evil because "the inherent wrongness of the actor's conduct counts in the balance of harms, so that the intentional killing of an innocent person might be viewed as a greater harm than the loss of two innocent lives"? Kent Greenawalt, *Natural Law and Political Choice: The General Justification Defense — Criteria for Political Action and the Duty to Obey the Law*, 36 Cath. U. L. Rev. 1, 5 (1986). Moreover, would recognizing a necessity defense in *Dudley & Stephens* also lead to the acquittal of a doctor who "thinks that by killing one healthy person and using his body parts, she could save five others desperately in need of organ transplants"? *Id.* at 13. Perhaps, then, the court was right to reject the necessity defense in *Dudley & Stephens* and leave the case in the hands of the executive branch. Consider Professor Greenawalt's views:

> The situations in which anyone thinks the intentional killing of innocent people is morally acceptable are extremely rare. If such situations exist, legal institutions will have a very difficult time sorting them out, and should not attempt to do so. The law should adopt a straightforward principle that will coincide with what is morally right in the vast majority of instances, sending a strong message that the intentional killing of innocents is wrong. Appropriate leniency can be introduced at the sentencing stage or by executive clemency.

Id. at 25. *See also* Lon L. Fuller, *The Case of the Speluncean Explorers*, 62 Harv. L. Rev. 616 (1949) (describing a fictional murder case raising these issues); *The Case of the Speluncean Explorers: A Fiftieth Anniversary Symposium*, 112 Harv. L. Rev. 1834 (1999). For a discussion of whether criminal law should go even further and "*require* necessity killing in cases where the actor [has] legal responsibility for all of the available choices," see Tom Stacy, *Acts, Omissions, and the Necessity of Killing Innocents*, 29 Am. J. Crim. L. 481, 483 (2002) (emphasis added) (citing the 2000 case of the British conjoined twins, Jodie and Mary Attard, as an example).

6. The Model Penal Code Approach. Section 3.02(1)(a) of the Model Penal Code recognizes a necessity defense when the defendant honestly believes that committing a crime is necessary to avoid a greater evil. The necessity defense is unavailable, however, to a defendant charged with a crime requiring a mens rea of only recklessness or negligence if the defendant was reckless or negligent either "in bringing about the situation requiring a choice of . . . evils or in appraising the necessity for his conduct." Model Penal Code § 3.02(2). (For a description of the analogous rule applied to self-defense claims by MPC § 3.09, see Note 6 following *People v. Goetz* in Section B above.)

The MPC also denies a necessity defense if "the issue of competing values has been previously foreclosed by a deliberate legislative choice, as when some provision of the law deals explicitly with the specific situation that presents the choice of evils or a legislative purpose to exclude the claimed justification otherwise appears." Model Penal Code § 3.02 Comment at 13. (For discussion of this legislative foreclosure exception, see Note 5 following *United States v. Maxwell* below.)

The MPC does not preclude murder defendants from raising a necessity defense, but provides that each life must be valued equally in determining whether the defendant avoided the greater evil. *See* Model Penal Code § 3.02 Comment at 15.

7. Applying the Necessity Defense in Other Contexts.

(a) Suppose a group of AIDS or cancer patients finds that marijuana alleviates their pain or otherwise eases their symptoms by making it easier to eat, sleep, and relax. Should necessity constitute a defense to drug possession charges in these circumstances because the law "should allow an individual to seek relief from the agonizing symptoms caused by an incurable disease that will eventually lead to death"? *State v. Bonjour*, 694 N.W.2d 511, 517 (Iowa 2005) (Wiggins, J., dissenting). *See also Jenks v. State*, 582 So. 2d 676 (Fla. Dist. Ct. App. 1991) (reversing conviction and entering judgment of acquittal in a case where AIDS patients used marijuana because it was the only drug that controlled their nausea and enabled them to eat), *review denied*, 589 So. 2d 292 (Fla. 1991); *State v. Hastings*, 801 P.2d 563 (Idaho 1990) (holding that arthritis patient charged with possession of marijuana should be allowed to present evidence of necessity).

On the other hand, is "[u]se of marijuana . . . a public-policy issue best suited for the legislature because it is driven by legal, moral, philosophical, and medical concerns that are ill-suited for resolution" by courts and juries? *Bonjour*, 694 N.W.2d at 514. Likewise, should the defense be unavailable because it is not necessary for these patients to violate the drug laws given that they can try to obtain a prescription for other, legal "medications for [their] condition, including Marinol, the legal form of THC," which is the active ingredient in marijuana? *State v. Ducheneaux*, 671 N.W.2d 841, 845 (S.D. 2003). *Compare* Jessica Winter, *Weed Control*, Bos. GLOBE, May 28, 2006, at E1 (pointing out that Marinol is not as effective as marijuana for some patients), *with Emry v. United States*, 829 A.2d 970, 973 (D.C. 2003) (observing that "there is no drug [that is] without side effects," including marijuana, and rejecting necessity defense because the defendant had not tried "any of the dozens of other drugs used to alleviate her condition").

Beginning with California in 1996, 29 states and the District of Columbia have authorized the use of marijuana for medical purposes either through voter-passed initiatives or legislation. The specific provisions in effect in these jurisdictions vary. For example, in response to concerns that medical marijuana is "so loosely regulated" in some states that the drug "has essentially been decriminalized," New Jersey only permits patients to use a maximum of two ounces of marijuana per month if they suffer from "a set list of serious, chronic illnesses." *See* David Kocieniewski, *New Jersey Vote Backs Marijuana for Severely Ill*, N.Y. TIMES, Jan. 12, 2010, at A1. By contrast, California has the most liberal policy, requiring only a physician's "written or oral recommendation" that a patient "would benefit from medical marijuana." For details about the policies followed in each of the states that authorizes the medical use of marijuana, see *29 Legal Medical Marijuana States and DC: Laws, Fees, and Possession Limits*, PROCON.ORG, http://medicalmarijuana.procon.org/view.resource.php?resourceID=000881.

Despite this activity in the states, the United States Supreme Court has dealt several blows to the medical marijuana movement. In *United States v. Oakland Cannabis Buyers' Cooperative*, 532 U.S. 483 (2001), the Court refused to read a medical necessity defense into the provisions of the Controlled Substances Act that prohibit the manufacture and distribution of marijuana. Noting that "it is an open question whether federal courts *ever* have authority to recognize a necessity defense not provided by statute," the Court concluded that a medical necessity defense, though "not explicitly abrogated" by the Controlled Substances Act, would be "at odds" with it. *Id.* at 490, 491 (emphasis added). The Court explained that "the statute reflects a determination that marijuana has . . . 'no currently accepted medical use.'" *Id.* at 491. Three of the Justices, however, expressly reserved judgment whether a necessity defense might be available to "a seriously ill patient for whom there is no alternative means of avoiding starvation or extraordinary suffering." *Id.* at 501 (Stevens, J., concurring in the judgment).

Then, in a later civil case, the Supreme Court held that the Commerce Clause gives Congress the power to use the federal drug laws to prosecute patients who use locally grown marijuana under a doctor's orders even in one of the states permitting the medical use of marijuana. *See Gonzales v. Raich*, 545 U.S. 1 (2005). In light of "the enforcement difficulties" involved in "distinguishing between marijuana cultivated locally and marijuana grown elsewhere," the Court explained, "Congress had a rational basis for believing that failure to regulate the intrastate manufacture and possession of marijuana would leave a gaping hole" in the federal drug laws' efforts to create "a comprehensive regime to combat the international and interstate traffic in illicit drugs." *Id.* at 22, 12. Writing for the three dissenters, Justice O'Connor criticized the majority for interfering with "[t]he States' core police powers . . . to define criminal law and to protect the health, safety, and welfare of their citizens." *Id.* at 42 (O'Connor, J., dissenting).

On remand, the Ninth Circuit concluded that although Raich "appears to satisfy the factual predicate for a necessity defense," her "necessity claim is best resolved within the context of a specific prosecution." The court of appeals noted, however, that the Supreme Court's decision in *Oakland Cannabis* might "foreclose a necessity defense to a prosecution of a seriously ill defendant under the Controlled Substances Act" and the federal statute might "encompass a legislative 'determination of values' that would preclude a necessity defense." *Raich v. Gonzales*, 500 F.3d 850, 860 (9th Cir. 2007) (quoting *Oakland Cannabis*, 532 U.S. at 491).

For the moment, the potential conflict between federal and state law seems to be moot, because the Obama Department of Justice announced in 2013 that it would refrain from prosecuting marijuana use that was permissible under state law, instead relying on the states as "the primary means of addressing marijuana-related activity." *See* U.S. Dep't of Justice, Office of the Deputy Attorney General, Memorandum for All United States Attorneys: Guidance Regarding Marijuana Enforcement 3 (2013), *available at* http://www.justice.gov/iso/opa/resources/3052013829132756857467.pdf. For discussion of the federalism issues arising from the discrepancies between federal and state marijuana laws, see Erwin Chemerinsky et al., *Cooperative Federalism and Marijuana Regulation*, 62 UCLA L. Rev. 74 (2015); Symposium, *Marijuana, Federal Power, and the States*, 65 Case W. Res. L. Rev. 505 (2015).

(b) Suppose Bernhard Goetz had raised a necessity defense to the weapons possession charges brought against him, arguing that he "had been once victimized and was fearful of walking the streets" unarmed and that he had been denied a permit for a gun even though he was "well trained in handling weapons"? George P. Fletcher, A Crime of Self-Defense 165 (1988). Would the defense have been unavailing because Goetz was not "confronted with an immediate, compelling, and direct threat," as opposed to a "more attenuated and speculative" one, during the entire three years he was carrying the gun? *United States v. White*, 552 F.3d 240, 248 (2d Cir. 2009). Likewise, would affording Goetz a necessity defense tend to "exonerate every unlicensed person who wants to carry a gun," given that "[s]uch a person wants to carry a gun precisely because he fears that at some time he might be threatened with serious bodily injury"? *Commonwealth v. Lindsey*, 489 N.E.2d 666, 669 (Mass. 1986) (denying defense to a defendant who had been assaulted two days earlier and had been threatened the prior day). *But cf. United States v. Gomez*, 92 F.3d 770 (9th Cir. 1996) (finding that a confidential government informant charged with illegal possession of a weapon was entitled to a jury instruction on the necessity defense when he procured a gun to protect himself from death threats he began receiving after the prosecutor disclosed his identity to a drug dealer who had solicited the murder of several other witnesses). Is *Gomez* distinguishable from *Lindsey* and *Goetz*, either because the defendant in *Gomez* was a government informant or because the government that enacted the weapons laws was responsible for putting him at risk? Or simply because *Gomez* involves "extraordinary" facts? *United States v. Beasley*, 346 F.3d 930, 935 (9th Cir. 2003).

(c) Suppose that a parent has three young children who have serious health problems and have not eaten in more than a day. After being turned down by several food banks, the parent tries to cash a forged check in order to buy groceries, "fear[ing] that a lack of food [will] exacerbate his children's health problems and lead to malnutrition and death." *People v. Fontes*, 89 P.3d 484, 486 (Colo. App. 2003). Should a necessity defense be available to parents who steal or commit some other crime in order to feed their starving children? Or, despite our "sympathy for the downtrodden," should the law take the view that "economic necessity alone cannot support a choice of crime"? *Id.* Is stealing never really "necessary" given the availability of public assistance, and would recognizing a necessity defense in this context "leave to the individual the right to take the law into his own hands"? *State v. Moe*, 24 P.2d 638, 640 (Wash. 1933).

Does the calculus change when the theft occurs in the midst of a natural disaster? For example, was the looting in 2005 that occurred in the wake of Hurricane Katrina justified by necessity because the looters were protecting their families "at a relatively low cost to the [store] owner (namely, the loss of food and whatever minimal damage [was] caused to the window or door through which the looter entered)"? Stuart P. Green, *Looting, Law, and Lawlessness*, 81 Tul. L. Rev. 1129, 1152 (2007). Or is "the calculation of evils . . . more complicated," both because looting creates "less direct harms . . . to the community generally, including the loss of civil order and the sense of fear that [it] is likely to cause," and because looting might be "contagious" and might lead others to "engage in similar, perhaps less clearly justified, conduct"? *Id.* However the evils are weighed, should the necessity defense be denied to the looters on the grounds that "relief might have been on the way" or they might have "contributed to [their] own plight — for example, by failing to abide by a mandatory, pre-storm evacuation order"? *Id.* at 1152–53. *See also* Stephanie J. Hamrick, Note, *Is Looting Ever Justified?: An Analysis of Looting Laws and the Applicability of the Necessity Defense During Natural Disasters and States of Emergency*, 7 Nev. L.J. 182 (2006).

(d) Suppose a mother unlawfully takes her child to another state because she believes her former spouse is abusing the child. Should a necessity defense be available, particularly if there is a history of unheeded complaints? *See State v. Boettcher*, 443 N.W.2d 1, 4 n.1 (S.D. 1989) (finding that the trial court erred in denying the defendant an opportunity to present this defense); *State v. Rome*, 426 N.W.2d 19 (S.D. 1988) (same). Or should a necessity defense be unavailable because "totally eliminat[ing]" the father's contact with the child is not the lesser evil, given that he "would at least have had an opportunity for controlled visitation" even if the allegations of abuse were proven and the mother were awarded custody? *Gerlach v. State*, 699 P.2d 358, 361 (Alaska Ct. App. 1985). Should the defense likewise be denied if the defendant had "time . . . to complain to authorities about her concerns before she acted on her own" and if she "did not immediately report to the proper authorities when she attained a position of safety from the perceived immediate threat"? *State v. W.M.S.*, 465 S.E.2d 580, 583 (S.C. Ct. App. 1995). Finally, does recognizing a necessity defense in this context risk giving "every noncustodial parent a means of relitigating a custody determination before a jury"? *Boettcher*, 443 N.W.2d at 4 n.1 (Wuest, C.J., dissenting).

(e) Suppose an undocumented immigrant illegally enters the United States because he has a gang tattoo that cannot be removed due to a skin condition and he fears reprisals from the police and rival gangs in his home country. Should his necessity defense be denied because he cannot prove he "lacked a reasonable, legal alternative . . . because he did not exclude the option of going to a country other than the United States"? *United States v. Bonilla-Siciliano*, 643 F.3d 589, 591 (8th Cir. 2011) (also reasoning that the defendant "failed to identify any specific threat to his safety, and relied only on a generalized fear of harm from the government and gang members"). *See also United States v. Cervantes-Flores*, 421 F.3d 825, 829 (9th Cir. 2005) (likewise rejecting necessity defense where a father entered the country illegally, hoping to see his children before he died, because "testing positive for HIV did not constitute imminent harm" and therefore he did not establish that he was "in imminent danger of losing his final opportunity to speak to his children"), *overruled on other grounds by Melendez-Diaz v. Massachusetts*, 557 U.S. 305 (2009).

(f) Suppose that law enforcement officials arrest a terrorist who they believe knows the location of a ticking time bomb hidden in a major metropolitan area. Should the officers have a necessity defense if they torture the suspected terrorist in hopes of finding the bomb before it explodes, as President George W. Bush's Justice Department suggested in a 2002 memorandum (that was later withdrawn)? *See* Memorandum from Jay S. Bybee, Assistant Attorney General, Office of Legal Counsel, Dep't of Justice, to Alberto R. Gonzales, Counsel to the President 39–41 (Aug. 1, 2002), *available at* http://www.washingtonpost.com/wp-srv/nation/documents/dojinterrogationmemo20020801.pdf. Is torture the "least worst choice" when "it provides the last remaining chance to save lives that are in imminent peril"? John T. Parry & Welsh S. White, *Interrogating Suspected Terrorists: Should Torture Be an Option?*, 63 U. Pitt. L. Rev. 743, 761, 763 (2002). Or should the necessity defense be rejected given that torture may well be "ineffective as a means of obtaining truthful information" and other more productive, nonviolent interrogation techniques are available? Marcy Strauss, *Torture*, 48 N.Y.L. Sch. L. Rev. 201, 262 (2003). Is recognizing a necessity defense in the ticking bomb scenario also inadvisable because it inevitably creates slippery slope problems, potentially allowing government officials to torture the children of a suspected terrorist who has "an unusually high tolerance for pain" but is "particularly fond of his two daughters," or, in a "more realistic" version of the ticking bomb hypothetical, to torture "large numbers of individuals to find the one person who can provide the necessary information" about the bomb's location? Thomas B. Crocker, *Overcoming Necessity: Torture and the State of Constitutional Culture*, 61 SMU L. Rev. 221, 256, 258–59 (2008).

United States v. Maxwell
254 F.3d 21 (1st Cir. 2001)

Selya, Circuit Judge.

. . . .

I. BACKGROUND

The United States Navy maintains a naval installation known as Camp Garcia on the island of Vieques, Puerto Rico, and periodically conducts military training operations there. Pursuant to regulations promulgated by the Department of the Navy, Camp Garcia is a "closed" base, meaning that entry by members of the general public requires permission from the commanding officer. Camp Garcia contains a "live impact area," historically used by the Navy for live-fire artillery and bombardment exercises. The Navy's presence on Vieques spans some sixty years, and these exercises have sparked numerous protests.

The political controversy attendant to the Navy's use of Vieques recently reached a fever pitch. In the calendar year 2000, approximately 400 persons were prosecuted for protest-related trespasses. Maxwell joined this effort: the authorities arrested him three times in quick succession (June 1, June 13, and June 21, 2000) for entering Camp Garcia without the permission of its commanding officer.

The June 13 arrest which underlies this appeal came about after Maxwell peacefully approached a naval security officer inside the north fence line of the base, identified himself as a protester, and asked for a bottle of water. In the wake of this arrest, the government charged Maxwell, by means of a one-count information, with violating a statute which reads in pertinent part:

> Whoever, within the jurisdiction of the United States, goes upon any military, naval, or Coast Guard reservation, post, fort, arsenal, yard, station, or installation, for any purpose prohibited by law or lawful regulation . . . shall be fined under this title or imprisoned not more than six months, or both.

18 U.S.C. § 1382. Insofar as relevant here, the "purpose prohibited by . . . lawful regulation" is the one set out in 32 C.F.R. § 770.38, namely, "entry . . . for any purpose whatsoever without the advance consent of the Commanding Officer."

Maxwell filed a pretrial motion, accompanied by an exegetic offer of proof, reflecting his desire to present affirmative defenses based upon necessity and international law. The government objected and the district court ruled, as a matter of law, that the proposed defenses could not be maintained because of the lack of a proper predicate. For the same reason, the court excluded the tendered evidence as irrelevant.

The trial itself was anticlimactic: the court, sitting without a jury, found that Maxwell had knowingly entered Camp Garcia without leave and in so doing had violated 18 U.S.C. § 1382. The court thereupon imposed a thirty-day incarcerative sentence. . . .

II. ANALYSIS

. . . .

A. The Statute of Conviction

Maxwell asserts that because section 1382 criminalizes entry onto the grounds of a military or naval installation "for any purpose prohibited," the government must show that a defendant had an improper purpose in entering such a facility. . . . But . . . all that is presently needed to satisfy section 1382's "purpose" requirement is proof that Maxwell's entry was deliberate.

The government unquestionably carried that modest burden in this case. The trial judge specifically found that Maxwell intentionally entered Camp Garcia, and the record fully supports that finding. . . . Since Maxwell does not dispute that he had such a purpose — nor could he, on this record — his specific reason for trespassing is irrelevant. . . .

B. The Necessity Defense

. . . The district court determined that the [necessity] defense was unavailable and ordered that Maxwell forgo it at trial. Maxwell protests both that ruling and the court's exclusion of expert testimony related to his proposed necessity defense.

. . . .

. . . The necessity defense requires the defendant to show that he (1) was faced with a choice of evils and chose the lesser evil, (2) acted to prevent imminent harm, (3) reasonably anticipated a direct causal relationship between his acts and the harm to be averted, and (4) had no legal alternative but to violate the law.

[Maxwell's argument] runs roughly as follows: the grave risks triggered by the deployment of Trident nuclear submarines are a far greater evil than the commission of a criminal trespass designed to stop their deployment; harm was imminent in that Maxwell suspected that at least one Trident submarine already was present in the waters off Puerto Rico to participate in the training exercises; he reasonably believed that his disruption of the exercises would lead to dispersion of the Trident submarine(s); and, having previously taken a wide variety of political actions to no avail, he had no practical alternative but to break the law. . . . We assume, for argument's sake, that Maxwell carried the entry-level burden of production on the first component ("lesser of two evils").[11] We specifically address Maxwell's proffer on the remaining three components.

1. *Imminent Harm.*   Assuming, favorably to Maxwell, that the deployment of Trident submarines in waters near Puerto Rico constitutes a harm, Maxwell had the burden of showing its immediacy. After all, the term "imminent harm" connotes a real emergency, a crisis involving immediate danger to oneself or to a third party. The record contains no evidence to support Maxwell's naked averment that the harm he feared was imminent. Moreover, even if Maxwell could have shown that a nuclear submarine was close at hand, it is doubtful that the mere presence of such a vessel, without some kind of realistic threat of detonation, would suffice to pose an imminent harm. *E.g., United States v. May*, 622 F.2d 1000, 1008–09 (9th Cir. 1980) (finding that the existence of Trident missile system failed to satisfy the imminent harm prong of the necessity defense).

. . . .

2. *Reasonable Anticipation of Averting Harm.*   Maxwell argues that he reasonably believed that his disruption of the naval exercises at Camp Garcia would effect the exodus of any Trident submarines that were in the vicinity. A reasonable anticipation of averting harm, however, requires more than seeing ghosts under every bed. In this case, Maxwell's anticipation is pure conjecture, not reasonable belief.

A defendant must demonstrate cause and effect between an act of protest and the achievement of the goal of the protest by competent evidence. He cannot will a causal relationship into being simply by the fervor of his convictions (no matter how sincerely held). *E.g., United States v. Montgomery*, 772 F.2d 733, 736 (11th Cir. 1985) (holding that defendants could not reasonably have believed that their entry into a defense plant would bring about nuclear disarmament); *United States v. Cassidy*, 616 F.2d 101, 102 (4th Cir. 1979) (per curiam) (finding it unlikely that splashing blood on Pentagon walls would impel the United States to divest itself of nuclear weapons).

We have combed the record in this case and find nothing to indicate any linkage between the Navy's exercises at Camp Garcia and the presence of Trident submarines in Puerto Rican waters. Equally as important, we find nothing to indicate that the

---

11. In other cases, defendants prosecuted under similar circumstances argued that "the Navy's activities, including live-fire artillery and bombardment exercises, were causing civilian deaths, serious health threats to Vieques' residents, and environmental damage," *United States v. Sued-Jimenez*, 275 F.3d 1, 5 (1st Cir. 2001), and, more specifically, that "they reasonably believed that entering the Camp Garcia installation was necessary to avert a greater evil, which they characterize as 'the Navy's violation of the procedural and substantive requirements of the Endangered Species Act by continuously bombing Vieques without completing or submitting to the United States Fish and Wildlife Service . . . a proper biological assessment, detailing the [likely] impact of the bombing on 13 separate species of endangered or threatened animals and [plants] in the Vieques area.'" *United States v. Ayala*, 289 F.3d 16, 26 (1st Cir. 2002).

movement of such vessels likely would be influenced by the temporary disruption of the exercises. On this record, then, Maxwell could not reasonably have anticipated that his act of trespass would avert the harm that he professed to fear.

3. *Legal Alternatives.*   To succeed on a necessity defense, a defendant must show that he had no legal alternative to violating the law. This makes perfect sense: the necessity defense does not arise from a defendant's choice of a preferred course of action from among a universe of possible courses of action (some legal, some not), but from an emergent crisis that, as a practical matter, precludes all principled options but one. In other words, the defendant's act must be necessary, not merely desirable.

In the case at hand, Maxwell testified at trial to the many avenues he has explored to further nuclear disarmament (e.g., participating in letter-writing campaigns, attending a nonproliferation treaty conference, and taking part in demonstrations). His level of commitment is laudable, but the panoramic range of his activities clearly demonstrates that he has many legal options for advancing his political goals. *Cf. United States v. Quilty*, 741 F.2d 1031, 1033 (7th Cir. 1984) (per curiam) ("There are thousands of opportunities for the propagation of the anti-nuclear message: in the nation's electoral process; by speech on public streets, in parks, in auditoriums, in churches and lecture halls; and by the release of information to the media, to name only a few."). The fact that Maxwell is unlikely to effect the changes he desires through legal alternatives does not mean, ipso facto, that those alternatives are nonexistent. Accepting such an argument would be tantamount to giving an individual carte blanche to interpose a necessity defense whenever he becomes disaffected by the workings of the political process.

. . . .

C. The International Law Defense

Maxwell's final plaint concerns the district court's rejection of his international law defense. This affirmative defense hinges on Maxwell's claim that the deployment of Trident submarines is a "war crime," giving him the privilege of breaking domestic law to stop it. When asked to identify the source of this privilege, he points to decisions by the international tribunal that presided over the trials of Nazi war criminals in Nuremberg after World War II.

. . . .

Maxwell is not the first to attempt to import the Nuremberg defense into our criminal law. . . . [T]he Nuremberg defendants undertook acts that were required by domestic law but violated international law. The Nuremberg tribunal held that the defendants could not escape responsibility for these acts by pointing to their domestic law obligations; they had a privilege under international law to violate domestic law in order to prevent the ongoing crimes against humanity that their country was perpetrating through them. . . .

Because Maxwell was under no compulsion to violate international law, his attempt to cloak himself in the Nuremberg mantle fails. Under his formulation, an individual gains the privilege to violate domestic law simply by being a citizen of a nation that possesses nuclear weapons. This is a quantum leap beyond the frontier of the classic Nuremberg defense — and one that we refuse to undertake.

. . . .

This holding also disposes of Maxwell's lament anent the lower court's exclusion of the expert testimony that he proffered on the illegality of nuclear weapons under international law. Since the Nuremberg defense is unavailable to him, the status of nuclear weapons under international law is irrelevant in his case. The district court's evidentiary ruling was, therefore, unimpugnable. . . .

Notes and Questions

1. The Imminence Requirement. The First Circuit rejected Maxwell's necessity defense in part because the evil he sought to avoid was not an imminent one. Is it appropriate to include imminence as an element of the necessity defense, or should it suffice that a defendant reasonably believed the criminal act was necessary to prevent a greater evil?

The drafters of the Model Penal Code elected not to require imminence, reasoning that "[s]uch a requirement unduly emphasizes one ingredient in the judgment that is called for at the expense of others just as important":

> It is true that genuine necessity rests on the unavailability of alternatives that would avoid both evils, and that typically when the evil is not imminent some such alternative will be available; but it is a mistake to erect imminence as an absolute requirement, since there may be situations in which an otherwise illegal act is necessary to avoid an evil that may occur in the future. If, for example, *A* and *B* have driven in *A*'s car to a remote mountain location for a month's stay and *B* learns that *A* plans to kill him near the end of the stay, *B* would be justified in escaping with *A*'s car although the threatened harm will not occur for three weeks.

Model Penal Code § 3.02 Comment at 17. *See also* Shaun P. Martin, *The Radical Necessity Defense*, 73 U. Cin. L. Rev. 1527, 1569 (2005) (arguing that "the necessity doctrine does not require that harm be imminent, but rather requires only that the damage caused by the illegality be less than the presently discounted probability of future social loss"). Nevertheless, the overwhelming majority of jurisdictions require proof of imminence in order to make out a claim of necessity. *See id.* at 1567 n.169 (listing 44 states).

Even if imminence is properly considered a prerequisite of the necessity defense, does the *Maxwell* court's rejection of "the possibility that even nuclear weapons might constitute a crisis or a real emergency . . . suggest[] that no set of circumstances will likely meet the definition of imminent harm and that no jury will likely get to hear any evidence of the necessity defense in any civil disobedience case"? William P. Quigley, *The Necessity Defense in Civil Disobedience Cases: Bring in the Jury*, 38 New Engl. L. Rev. 3, 58–59 (2003) (also noting that "[a] single U.S. nuclear submarine carries up to 192 warheads and could kill or maim . . . some 50 million people [and] our nuclear war plan keeps many of these weapons on hair-trigger alert") (quoting the National Resources Defense Council).

2. The Existence of Legal Alternatives. Linked to the finding that no imminent danger was present in *Maxwell* was the First Circuit's conclusion that the defendant's crime was not necessary because alternative, legal courses of action were available to him—for example, the right of free speech and the opportunity to participate in the political process.

Does this argument reflect a naive view of the political process? Is interest group politics "skewed dramatically toward narrow economic interests" because it is "nearly impossible to organize large groups of individuals to seek broadly dispersed public goods" (like the ones motivating Maxwell)? Daniel A. Farber & Philip P. Frickey, Law and Public Choice: A Critical Introduction 19, 36 (1991) (summarizing the work of others). As a result, is politics "dominated by small groups of individuals or firms [like weapons producers] seeking government benefits for themselves, usually at the public expense"? *Id.* at 23. *See* Reid Wilson, *Lobbyists Turn Attention to State Level*, Wash. Post, May 11, 2015, at A15 (reporting that $3.24 billion was spent on federal lobbying activities in 2014, and at least $2.2 billion on lobbying in 28 states during 2013 and 2014). *See also* Martin Gilens, Affluence and Influence: Economic Inequality and Political Power in America 1, 10 (2012) (describing empirical research which concluded that the "responsiveness [of decision makers in Washington] is strongly tilted toward the most affluent citizens," "[m]oney . . . is the root of representational inequality, and as political campaigns have become more expensive . . . , the responsiveness to those who supply the necessary resources has grown"); Lawrence Lessig, Republic Lost: How Money Corrupts Congress and a Plan to Stop It 95, 103–04 (2011) (detailing how fundraising has become "the central activity of congressmen," making lobbyists "'indispensable' to politicians" and their "effect on our democracy . . . more systemic"). (For a general discussion of critical theorists' analysis of criminal law, see Chapter 16, Section C.)

Note that the First Circuit was unimpressed by the defendant's contention that other, legal protests and political efforts had failed. *See also United States v. Schoon*, 971 F.2d 193, 199 (9th Cir. 1992) (observing that "petitioning Congress to change a policy is *always* a legal alternative . . . , regardless of the plea's success"). But if these alternative methods are "illusionary," does it follow that "there may well be no legal alternative"? *United States v. Hill*, 893 F. Supp. 1044, 1047 (N.D. Fla. 1994). Moreover, if Maxwell reasonably believed that committing a crime was his only real hope of achieving his goal, can his case be analogized to a prison escape where "a history of futile complaints" justifies a prisoner's failure to complain to the authorities before escaping to avoid harm? *People v. Lovercamp*, 118 Cal. Rptr. 110, 115 (Cal. Ct. App. 1974). *Cf.* Shaun P. Martin, *The Radical Necessity Defense*, 73 U. Cin. L. Rev. 1527, 1587–88 (2005) (pointing out that courts "do not apply this requirement with the same doctrinal rigor in nonactivist cases," and noting by way of example that a "bystander who spots a child about to drown in a pool . . . may permissibly use a direct but trespassing path to the child even if there exists a circuitous but legal route that may be only slightly less effective"); *State v. L'Heureux*, 846 A.2d 1193, 1197 (N.H. 2004) (reversing conviction in one such nonpolitical case because the trial judge applied a standard that was "too high" in requiring that "'no lawful alternative' [be] available, no matter how unreasonable any such alternative might be").

3. The Causal Link Between the Criminal Conduct and the Avoidance of Harm. The First Circuit concluded that Maxwell's criminal act was unnecessary not only because he had other legal alternatives, but also because the requisite causal relationship between the crime and his goal was missing—he could not realistically have thought that entering the naval base would have any greater impact than the "temporary disruption of the [naval] exercises." Is the First Circuit's causality requirement inherently inconsistent with its strict imminence standard because "the longer the actor waits in order to satisfy the immediacy requirement, the less likely her action reasonably can be expected effectively to avert the harm"? Laura J. Schulkind, Note, *Applying the Necessity Defense to Civil Disobedience Cases*, 64 N.Y.U. L. Rev. 79, 97 (1989).

Even if causality is properly included as an element of the necessity defense, does the court's characterization of Maxwell's claim "belittle" him, "twisting [his] beliefs into incredible absolutes that portray [him as a] moron or worse"? William P. Quigley, *The Necessity Defense in Civil Disobedience Cases: Bring in the Jury*, 38 New Engl. L. Rev. 3, 51 (2003). Was Maxwell really arguing that he reasonably thought his criminal trespass, though unlikely to stop the Navy's activities at Camp Garcia by itself, might "in combination with the actions of others," serve to increase public awareness and thereby "accelerate a political process ultimately leading" to the end he desired? *Commonwealth v. Berrigan*, 472 A.2d 1099, 1115 (Pa. Super. Ct. 1984) (Spaeth, J., concurring), *rev'd*, 501 A.2d 226 (Pa. 1985).

Is the First Circuit's causality analysis also open to criticism because the court "equate[s] 'reasonableness' with 'success,'" whereas the necessity defense requires only that defendants reasonably believe their acts are necessary to avoid a greater evil? *Id.* If the evil Maxwell sought to avoid is truly serious, shouldn't he be justified in committing a crime designed to avert that evil even if his efforts ultimately fail?

4. The Necessity Defense in the Abortion Context. A necessity defense along the lines raised in *Maxwell* has been asserted in a number of criminal cases involving anti-abortion protestors who blocked access to abortion clinics or otherwise tried to interfere with their operation. If the defendants in these cases do not claim that their criminal acts were intended to put an end to the practice of abortion altogether, but merely to save the fetuses that were to be aborted in that particular clinic on that particular day, can they overcome the obstacles described in the three preceding Notes? Consider *United States v. Hill*, 893 F. Supp. 1044, 1046–47 (N.D. Fla. 1994):

> Protestors seeking nuclear disarmament are in a different position from that of defendant Hill, who protests the performing of abortions. . . . [I]t is possible to hold a reasonable belief that injuring or interfering with abortion

providers will prevent at least one or some abortions from occurring. The fact that the number of medical doctors willing to perform abortions continues to decline makes the causal connection stronger. One doctor may provide services for many clinics in several states: injuring or interfering with such a doctor could effectively eliminate services for a large number of patients for a period of weeks or months. Therefore, for purposes of the necessity defense analysis, a causal connection may exist here that is lacking in the case of nuclear protestors.

. . . [Moreover,] a defendant in Hill's position could potentially produce evidence that abortions were about to be performed by an abortion provider, and that injuring or interfering with the provider would avert the imminent peril of the abortion being performed. Such a situation may be distinguished from the anti-nuclear cases, in which the defendant protestors could present no evidence of any imminent peril.

Compare Commonwealth v. Markum, 541 A.2d 347, 353 (Pa. Super. Ct. 1988) (McEwen, J., concurring and dissenting) (concluding that anti-abortion protestors had "no legal alternative available" given that "[t]he disaster which [they] sought to prevent was the abortions that would be completed in a very brief time after the women entered the building"), *with McMillan v. City of Jackson*, 701 So. 2d 1105, 1108 (Miss. 1997) (rejecting this reasoning, and suggesting that seeking "an injunction to prevent any unlawful action at the clinic in advance of the date McMillan was compelled to trespass . . . would have been a better alternative than violating the law"). *See also* Patrick G. Senftle, Comment, *The Necessity Defense in Abortion Clinic Trespass Cases*, 32 St. Louis U. L.J. 523, 535 (1987) (observing that anti-abortion trespassers have successfully convinced some women not to obtain abortions).

5. Legislative Foreclosure of the Necessity Defense. Even if anti-abortion protestors clear the hurdles described above, many courts have concluded that their necessity defense ultimately fails because the state legislature, or the Supreme Court's decision in *Roe v. Wade*, 410 U.S. 113 (1973), has foreclosed the defense. If abortion is legal—in fact, constitutionally protected—the defendant cannot deem it an "evil" that ought to be avoided. *See, e.g., United States v. Turner*, 44 F.3d 900, 903 (10th Cir. 1995); *Hill v. State*, 688 So. 2d 901, 905–06 (Fla. 1996); *State v. Roeder*, 336 P.3d 831, 844 (Kan. 2014); *McMillan v. City of Jackson*, 701 So. 2d 1105, 1107 (Miss. 1997); *Commonwealth v. Markum*, 541 A.2d 347, 350–51 (Pa. Super. Ct. 1988).

As the drafters of the Model Penal Code observed, "the balancing of evils is not committed to the private judgment of the actor" by virtue of the necessity defense. Model Penal Code § 3.02 Comment at 12. Even under the Code's subjective definition of the defense—which requires only that the defendant believe the crime is necessary to avoid a greater evil, and not that the belief be a reasonable one (subject to § 3.02(2))—the defendant who "genuinely believes that the life of another is less valuable than his own financial security" has no justification. Rather, the necessity defense requires that the evil the defendant seeks to avoid must actually be "greater than that which would be caused by the commission of the offense, not that the defendant believe it to be so." *Id.*

Thus, once the legislature—or, in the abortion context, the Supreme Court—has balanced the evils and determined that a pregnant woman's privacy interests override a fetus' interest in potential life, the defendant cannot reweigh the evils and reach a different conclusion. Entertaining a necessity defense in such cases would involve the judicial process in difficult policy issues, "oftentimes requir[ing] the courts to tread into areas constitutionally committed to other branches of government." *United States v. Schoon*, 971 F.2d 193, 199 (9th Cir. 1992). As one commentator explained, "as long as the laws or policies being protested have been lawfully adopted, they are conclusive evidence of the community's view on the issue." 2 Paul H. Robinson, Criminal Law Defenses § 124(d)(1), at 52 (1984). *See also Roeder*, 336 P.3d at 844 ("[t]o allow the personal, ethical, moral, or religious beliefs of a person, no matter how sincere or well-intended, as a justification for criminal activity ... would not only lead to chaos but would be tantamount to sanctioning anarchy") (quoting *City of Wichita v. Tilson*, 855 P.2d 911, 918 (Kan. 1993)). *But cf. United States v. Lynch*, 952 F. Supp. 167, 170 n.3 (S.D.N.Y. 1997) (observing in dictum that the court was "not persuaded" by the prosecution's argument that a necessity defense is foreclosed "merely because the conduct at issue i.e. abortion, is legal as a matter of positive law," posing the question "[w]ere a person to have violated a court order directing the return of a runaway slave when Dred Scott was the law, would a genuinely held belief that a slave was a human person and not an article of property be a matter the Court could not consider in deciding whether that person was guilty of a criminal contempt charge"?), *appeal dismissed*, 181 F.3d 330 (2d Cir. 1998).

A few courts have drawn a distinction between legal and illegal abortions, observing that "[a]bortions, if performed illegally, would be an 'evil' or 'harm' in the eyes of the law." *United States v. Hill*, 893 F. Supp. 1044, 1046 (N.D. Fla. 1994). Thus, in *People v. Archer*, 537 N.Y.S.2d 726, 734–35 (N.Y. City Ct. 1988), the court acknowledged that "*Roe* prohibits the State statutory necessity defense whenever there are intentional interruptions which interfere with the performance of first trimester abortions," but instructed the jurors that they could consider the defendants' necessity defense if they found that the abortion provider "was about to perform other than first trimester abortions" on the date of the defendants' criminal trespass. *See also United States v. Lynch*, 952 F. Supp. at 170 n.3 (endorsing this distinction in dictum). *Cf. McMillan*, 701 So. 2d at 1107 (rejecting a similar claim on the grounds that "[b]esides McMillan's own suspicions, the offer of proof includes nothing which proves that any illegal harm was afoot at the clinic [and] [e]ven if illegal abortions were routinely taking place at the clinic, there is nothing which establishes that an illegal abortion was underway at the time of McMillan's trespass"); *Roeder*, 336 P.3d at 845 (barring a defendant, who was charged with killing one of the country's few providers of late-term abortions while the doctor was attending church, from raising a necessity defense based on the doctor's alleged failure to follow certain administrative and procedural requirements governing abortions).

6. The History of Civil Disobedience. Civil disobedience has long played an important role in this country's history. As one judge explained in a political protest case:

> We must recognize that civil disobedience in various forms, used without violent acts against others, is ingrained in our society and the moral correctness of political protestors' views has on occasion served to change and better our society. Civil disobedience has been prevalent throughout this nation's history extending from the Boston Tea Party and the signing of the Declaration of Independence, to the freeing of the slaves by operation of the underground railroad in the mid-1800's. More recently, disobedience of "Jim Crow" laws served, among other things, as a catalyst to end segregation by law in this country, and violation of selective service laws contributed to our eventual withdrawal from the Vietnam War.

United State v. Kabat, 797 F.2d 580, 601 (8th Cir. 1986) (Bright, J., dissenting).

Does this history support Maxwell's necessity defense by suggesting that civil disobedience can "stir[] our nation's collective conscience and spur[] us to change or repeal unjust laws"? John Alan Cohan, *Civil Disobedience and the Necessity Defense*, 6 Pierce L. Rev. 111, 135 (2007). Or is history unhelpful to Maxwell because while it indicates that "in restricted circumstances a morally motivated act contrary to law may be ethically justified," it also assumes that "the actor must accept the penalty for his action"? *United States v. Kroncke*, 459 F.2d 697, 703 (8th Cir. 1972).

Some political protestors who have been allowed to present necessity defenses have been acquitted. *See, e.g., People v. Gray*, 571 N.Y.S.2d 851 (N.Y. Crim. Ct. 1991) (trial judge acquitted defendants who where charged with disorderly conduct when they participated in a demonstration protesting the decision to allow cars to travel in lanes previously reserved for bicycles and pedestrians); Rick DelVecchio, *Needle Exchange Workers Acquitted*, S.F. Chron., Mar. 10, 1995, at A14 (reporting that defendants who exchanged dirty needles for clean ones in an effort to prevent the spread of AIDS were acquitted of distributing drug paraphernalia); Matthew L. Wald, *Amy Carter Is Acquitted over Protest*, N.Y. Times, Apr. 16, 1987, at A17 (describing the acquittal of the daughter of former President Jimmy Carter, who raised a necessity defense to disorderly conduct charges stemming from her participation in a demonstration protesting the presence of a C.I.A. recruiter on campus). *See generally* William P. Quigley, *The Necessity Defense in Civil Disobedience Cases: Bring in the Jury*, 38 New Engl. L. Rev. 3, 26–37 (2003) (citing numerous decisions and concluding that state courts are more sympathetic to necessity defenses in this context than federal courts).

But defendants like Maxwell who have not prevailed at trial have almost always lost on appeal. In fact, the Ninth Circuit went even further in *United States v. Schoon*, 971 F.2d 193 (9th Cir. 1992), barring the necessity defense in all cases like *Maxwell* where defendants engage in indirect civil disobedience—where the criminal law they violate is not the same one they are protesting. Noting that the elements of the necessity defense can never be met under such circumstances, the court reasoned that the case-by-case approach currently used to resolve these cases wastes judicial resources and encourages judges to "sabotage the usually low threshold for getting a defense theory before the jury." *Id.* at 199. *But cf.* Quigley, *supra*, at 41 (arguing that "it makes little sense to draw an arbitrary legal line between direct and indirect civil disobedience").

Chapter 15

Excuse

[A] Duress

State v. Scott

827 P.2d 733 (Kan. 1992)

Abbott, Justice.

This is a direct appeal by Sedrick Scott from his convictions of two counts of aggravated battery, one count of aggravated assault, and one count of aggravated kidnapping. [He was sentenced to life in prison.]

. . . Scott contends the trial court erred in refusing to give a requested instruction on compulsion. . . .

On September 7, 1989, the victim, 14-year-old Charles Green, discussed selling drugs with LaMacey Woods. . . . Woods gave Green $80 worth of crack cocaine, which Green agreed to sell and then to give the proceeds from the sale to Woods. Green sold the cocaine and brought the money back to Woods. Woods then gave Green $40 worth of cocaine to sell. Green returned to his sister's house.

About one hour later, someone came over to Green's sister's home and told Green that Woods wanted to see him. Green voluntarily returned to Woods' house across the street. Woods and a man named Phil were outside working on Phil's car. Green voluntarily went into Woods' house with Woods and Phil. Woods directed Green to take a seat in the living room. There were several other people in the house, including Scott.

Woods inquired about the money from the cocaine Green was supposed to sell. Green explained he had not yet sold the cocaine and gave it to Woods. Woods told Green that this cocaine was not the cocaine he had given Green and that Green had "messed up his money." Scott did not say anything while this was transpiring.

Green complied with Woods' order for Green to follow Woods into a back room. Scott, Phil, and another man followed Green into the room. In the back room, Woods began loading and unloading a gun. Scott, Phil, and the other man started hitting Green. Everyone in the room said he was going to kill Green. Green testified that Woods and Phil told Scott to hit Green and that this was the only occasion Scott hit him. At Woods' direction, Scott tied Green's hands behind his back with a bathrobe belt, and the men continued beating and kicking Green. Although no one directed him to do so, Scott took off Green's shirt. Scott told Green to lie on his back, and then, upon Woods' direction, told Green to turn over. After Woods burned Green's back with a clothes iron, someone poured salt on the wound. Scott cut Green's arm with a razor blade; Phil then took the razor from Scott and said he would show Scott how to do it. Again, someone poured salt on the wound. Scott and the others continued hitting Green.

After someone put a gun to Green's head to get him to stand up, Woods took Green into the bathroom and made him stand in a bathtub filled with water. Woods attempted to electrocute Green by dropping a curling iron into the water, but the cord was not long enough. Scott did not have anything to do with the attempted electrocution.

Woods then took Green back to the back room and shocked his feet with an extension cord. The extension cord was plugged into a wall outlet, and pieces of clothes hangers were plugged into the outlets on the cord. Scott did not participate. Green testified that Scott stood in the doorway and looked surprised.

Green again was beaten and then taken to the living room. Woods told Green he was now part of their "family" and could not go back home. Woods told Scott that Green was now Scott's "man" or "shadow." Green was directed to do whatever Scott told him to do. Woods told Scott to take Green with him to sell drugs.

Scott allowed Green to run across the street to his sister's house for a few minutes. Green's sister wanted to call the police, but Green told her not to because Woods and others present had stated that if Green told the police, they would kill him. Green was not sure whether Scott had participated in his verbal terrorizing.

Scott then took Green to a club where he bought Green a sandwich and a drink. When Green finished eating, Scott was gone. Green went home and the next day went to the hospital. He did not tell the police the truth about how he received his injuries.

On cross-examination, Green admitted that on the evening of September 7, he voluntarily returned to Woods' house to see if Scott was there. Scott was not. Woods gave Green $200 worth of cocaine and said he would see Green in the morning.

On September 11, 1989, Green was at a club with friends. Around 6:30 or 7:00 p.m., Scott came into the club, put a .25 automatic into Green's side, and told him that Woods was waiting for him outside. Green testified that Woods had sent Scott into the club to summon him.

Woods, who was standing by the door, put his arm around Green and said, "Let's go." Woods walked Green to Woods' car. Woods drove the car. A man Green did not know was also in the front seat. Green, Scott, and another man with whom Green was not acquainted sat in the back seat. . . .

Woods drove back to his house, parked the car in the back yard, and told the others to wait in the car. Green testified there was nothing that stopped Scott from getting out of the car and leaving. Green did not get out of the car and leave because Scott was sitting next to him with the gun.

Woods returned to the car and ordered everyone out. They walked to the front of the house, with Woods leading the way. . . .

Once inside the house, Woods, Scott, and another man took Green to the back room. Woods and possibly others told Green they were going to kill him this time. Green testified that Scott did not make such a statement.

On direct examination, Green testified that Woods was not in the room when Scott tied Green's hands behind his back and ripped off Green's shirt. Woods returned with a clothes iron and burned Green on his chest and stomach. The other man stabbed Green with a knife. Woods shocked Green with the extension cord device. Scott was "[j]ust standing around watching." Woods then started beating Green's legs with a sawed-off .12 gauge shotgun. People were yelling, "Break his legs."

On cross-examination, Green testified that upon going to the back room, a man called Val started punching him. Woods returned with a .38 revolver and played Russian roulette with Green. . . . Green testified that Scott appeared to be frightened of Woods while this was happening. Woods then unloaded a sawed-off shotgun and started hitting Green with the butt of the gun. The record is not clear, but it appears Scott was not present all the time, having left the room during part of the torture.

Woods then took Green outside. Scott and others were present. They made Green take off all of his clothing. . . . They locked Green in the car trunk. Later, Scott checked on Green to see if he was okay. Green told Scott he was cold. About an hour later, Scott returned with clothing and food. Green testified that Scott appeared to be concerned and was the only one trying to help him.

Woods finally came out and released Green from the trunk about 2:30 a.m. Woods drove Green to a hospital, but did not stop because police were in the vicinity. Woods took Green to a motel and told him someone would pick him up in the morning. When no one came to pick him up, Green called his uncle, who took him to the hospital. Green spent six days in the hospital.

. . . .

Scott argues that all acts in which he participated on September 7 and 11, 1989, were because he was terrorized by and in fear of Woods. Scott did not testify, but based upon Green's testimony, Scott maintains the trial court should have instructed the jury on the defense of compulsion. . . .

The defense of compulsion is governed by K.S.A. 21-3209, which provides:

> (1) A person is not guilty of a crime other than murder or voluntary manslaughter by reason of conduct which he performs under the compulsion or threat of the imminent infliction of death or great bodily harm, if he reasonably believes that death or great bodily harm will be inflicted upon him or upon his spouse, parent, child, brother or sister if he does not perform such conduct.

(2) The defense provided by this section is not available to one who willfully or wantonly places himself in a situation in which it is probable that he will be subjected to compulsion or threat.[1]

The Judicial Council's comment to K.S.A. 21-3209(2) specifies that "[s]ubsection (2) creates an exception for the person who connects himself with criminal activities or is otherwise indifferent to known risk."

In *State v. Hunter*, 241 Kan. 629, 740 P.2d 559 (1987), this court discussed application of the compulsion defense:

> In order to constitute the defense of compulsion, the coercion or duress must be present, imminent, and impending, and of such a nature as to induce a well-grounded apprehension of death or serious bodily injury if the act is not done. The doctrine of coercion or duress cannot be invoked as an excuse by one who had a reasonable opportunity to avoid doing the act without undue exposure to death or serious bodily harm. In addition, the compulsion must be continuous and there must be no reasonable opportunity to escape the compulsion without committing the crime.

In his brief, Scott claims Green and he held essentially the same position in the Insanes or Crips organization. Scott suggests the only difference is that he was already a member of the group, whereas Green was still in the recruitment state. Scott argues Woods

> ruled his underlings in a way that made them totally dependent upon him for their needs. [Woods] required his recruits to hand over to him all proceeds from the cocaine they sold so they could in Woods' words, "work up enough money." [Woods] provided motel rooms where they spent most of their nights. They [were not] allowed to see their own families once they became a member of [Woods'] "family." [Woods] punished those who did not follow his orders.... [Y]oung men like [Scott] and [Green] were induced, through financial and emotional dependence, and most importantly, through fear, to do exactly what [Woods] ordered them to do.... This financial and emotional dependency upon and fear of Macey Woods, once established, rendered any conceivable opportunity to escape from his grasp quite unlikely.

. . . .

Regardless of the veracity of Scott's argument that he and others were emotionally and financially dependent upon Woods, Green's testimony does not support the argument. Green's testimony does not support the contentions that Scott was suffering present, imminent, or impending coercion or duress, that Woods' intimidation of Scott was continual, or that Scott had a reasonable apprehension of death or

---

1. The current version of the Kansas statute denies a compulsion defense to those who "intentionally or recklessly place[] [themselves] in a situation in which [they] will be subjected to compulsion or threat." Kan. Stat. Ann. § 21-5206(b).

serious bodily injury if he did not participate in the attacks upon Green. There is evidence that Scott had a reasonable opportunity to escape. After the September 7 attack, Scott took Green to a club; Woods remained at his house. Scott did not live at Woods' house. Scott had his own car. Nonetheless, Scott returned with Woods to the club on September 11. Although Green testified Woods told Scott to summon Green, there is no evidence that Woods told or forced Scott to pull the gun on Green.

It appears Scott and Woods often went their separate ways. In *State v. Dunn*, 243 Kan. 414, 422, 758 P.2d 718 (1988), this court ruled that if the intimidation is not continuous and if there is a reasonable opportunity to escape, the defendant cannot claim he "was compelled to be present when the crimes were committed."

. . . .

Scott also claims the need for a compulsion instruction was evidenced by the jury's request for a read-back of "the testimonial evidence by Charles Green pertaining to the fear of [Woods] possessed by Sedrick Scott." Mere fear will not support a compulsion defense instruction.

Additionally, Scott knowingly associated himself with the selling of drugs, a criminal activity, and with a gang noted for violence. The trial court did not err in refusing to give an instruction on the defense of compulsion.[2]

Notes and Questions

1. The Policies Underlying the Duress Defense. The rationale for the duress defense has been a matter of some controversy. Although some authorities have taken the position that an act committed under duress is "no longer the voluntary act of the accused," *The Queen v. Hudson*, [1971] 2 Q.B. 202, 206 (C.A.), or that duress "overcomes the defendant's free will [so that] his actions lack the required mens rea," *People v. Luther*, 232 N.W.2d 184, 186 (Mich. 1975), those views have now largely been discredited. Thus, courts reason that a crime committed under duress is a voluntary act because the defendant " 'makes a choice' to violate the law, even though that choice is compelled." *State v. Daoud*, 679 A.2d 577, 581 (N.H. 1996). Moreover, the defendant generally has the requisite mens rea to commit the crime because "the defense of duress does not negate a defendant's criminal state of mind . . . ; instead, it allows the defendant to 'avoid liability . . . because coercive conditions . . . negate a conclusion of guilt even though the necessary mens rea was present.' " *Dixon v. United States*, 548 U.S. 1, 6 (2006). Even if the crime in question requires a mens rea of purpose or knowledge, "a defendant can [act] with the intent to inflict injury, in the sense that he knows that his actions will lead to injury or that his purpose is to cause injury, but act in this manner in order to comply with the demands of another." *United States v. Xue Fei Lin*, 139 F.3d 1303, 1307 (9th Cir. 1998).

---

2. Woods was also charged in connection with the torture of Green. He was convicted of two counts of aggravated kidnapping, two counts of aggravated battery, one count of aggravated assault, and one count of selling cocaine. Like Scott, Woods was sentenced to life in prison. *See State v. Woods*, 825 P.2d 514 (Kan. 1992).

Some jurisdictions treat duress as a variation of the necessity defense, where the source of the pressure is another person as opposed to a force of nature. Duress is not a defense according to this view unless the crime the defendants committed was a lesser evil than the threat they faced. *See, e.g., People v. Lemons*, 562 N.W.2d 447, 453 (Mich. 1997). But most states have not limited the duress defense in this fashion. Even though defendants who act under duress made the wrong choice, their crimes are excused because they are considered less culpable than those who were not coerced to commit a crime, and because society understands and sympathizes with their predicament even though it does not condone their conduct. *See* Joshua Dressler, Understanding Criminal Law § 23.01[C] (7th ed. 2015).

Does it make sense to give a defendant who acted under duress a complete defense to criminal charges? Scott, for example, would have had a classic duress defense if Woods had held a gun to his head and threatened to shoot him unless he assaulted Green. Under such circumstances, should a criminal act be excused because "[c]ondemnation . . . is bound to be an ineffective threat" and, even "more significant," is "unjust" and "divorced from any moral base"? Model Penal Code § 2.09 Comment at 375. Or should the pressures under which the defendant acted be considered only at the sentencing stage to mitigate punishment because "it is at the moment when temptation to crime is strongest that the law should speak most clearly and emphatically to the contrary"? 2 James F. Stephen, A History of the Criminal Law of England 107 (1883). *See also* Joshua Dressler, *Exegesis of the Law of Duress: Justifying the Excuse and Searching for Its Proper Limits*, 62 S. Cal. L. Rev. 1331, 1360 (1989) (noting that "[i]n no other circumstance does the law excuse a person for his rational and intentionally chosen harmful acts"). At the other extreme, if "the 'reasonableness' of the agent's yielding under the circumstances" is at the heart of a duress claim, does the defense not only clearly deserve recognition but in fact begin to "sound suspiciously like a justification rather than an excuse"? Stephen J. Morse, *Culpability and Control*, 142 U. Pa. L. Rev. 1587, 1618 (1994).

2. The Imminence and Inescapability Requirements. The Kansas Supreme Court rejected Scott's duress claim in large part because any threat posed by Woods was not imminent and Scott therefore had an opportunity to escape. Most duress statutes, like the one at issue in *Scott*, require proof of an imminent threat. *See* 2 Wayne R. LaFave, Substantive Criminal Law § 9.7(b), at 80 (2d ed. 2003).

Do the imminence and inescapability requirements make sense because a crime is not actually coerced if the defendant faced only "a 'vague threat of future harm'" and had an opportunity to avoid committing the crime by escaping or reporting the threat to the authorities? *United States v. Vazquez*, 724 F.3d 15, 28 (1st Cir. 2013). Or does "say[ing] that a threat of future harm is not sufficient . . . ignore the fact that the nature of a threat is to hold out a future harm" and thus "[a]ll danger to the 'duressed' is in the future"? Lawrence Newman & Lawrence Weitzer, *Duress, Free Will, and the Criminal Law*, 30 S. Cal. L. Rev. 313, 328 (1957). Moreover, is it possible that "long and wasting pressure may break down resistance more effectively than a threat of immediate destruction"? Model Penal Code § 2.09 Comment at 376.

Was the Kansas Supreme Court right to find that Scott did not present sufficient evidence of imminence and inescapability to make out a duress defense? Would Scott have had a defense if he had testified that he joined the gang only after being subjected to the same torture that Green experienced? Should the trial judge have decided as a matter of law to take the issue of duress away from the jury, or should the jury have been allowed to determine whether the imminence and inescapability requirements were met in Scott's case?

3. *United States v. Contento-Pachon.* Compare *Scott* with *United States v. Contento-Pachon*, 723 F.2d 691 (9th Cir. 1984). The defendant in that case, a taxicab driver in Bogota, Colombia, was asked by a passenger named Jorge whether he was interested in a job driving a private car. When Contento-Pachon met with Jorge the following day, it turned out that Jorge was a drug dealer who really wanted Contento-Pachon to swallow cocaine-filled balloons and transport them to the United States. The court described the facts of the case as follows:

> Contento-Pachon agreed to consider the proposition. He was told not to mention the proposition to anyone, otherwise he would "get into serious trouble." Contento-Pachon testified that he did not contact the police because he believes that the Bogota police are corrupt and that they are paid off by drug traffickers.
>
> Approximately one week later, Contento-Pachon told Jorge that he would not carry the cocaine. In response, Jorge mentioned facts about Contento-Pachon's personal life, including private details that Contento-Pachon had never mentioned to Jorge. Jorge told Contento-Pachon that his failure to cooperate would result in the death of his wife and three-year-old child.
>
> The following day the pair met again. Contento-Pachon's life and the lives of his family were again threatened. At this point, Contento-Pachon agreed to take the cocaine into the United States.
>
> The pair met two more times. At the last meeting, Contento-Pachon swallowed 129 balloons of cocaine. He was informed that he would be watched at all times during the trip, and that if he failed to follow Jorge's instruction he and his family would be killed.
>
> After leaving Bogota, Contento-Pachon's plane landed in Panama. Contento-Pachon asserts that he did not notify the authorities there because he felt that the Panamanian police were as corrupt as those in Bogota. Also, he felt that any such action on his part would place his family in jeopardy.
>
> When he arrived at the customs inspection point in Los Angeles, Contento-Pachon consented to have his stomach x-rayed. The x-rays revealed a foreign substance which was later determined to be cocaine.

Id. at 693.

The district judge refused to permit Contento-Pachon to present this evidence to the jury, believing that it was insufficient to make out a duress defense as a matter of law. Specifically, the district court found inadequate evidence of imminence and inescapability:

> The first threat made to defendant and his family about three weeks before the flight was not immediate; the threat was conditioned upon defendant's failure to cooperate in the future and did not place the defendant and his family in immediate danger or harm. Moreover, after the initial threat and until he went to the house where he ingested the balloons containing cocaine, defendant and his family were not physically restrained and could have sought help from the police or fled.

Id. at 696 (Coyle, J., dissenting in part and concurring in part) (quoting district court's order).

The Ninth Circuit reversed, reasoning as follows:

> [T]he defendant was dealing with a man who was deeply involved in the exportation of illegal substances. Large sums of money were at stake and, consequently, Contento-Pachon had reason to believe that Jorge would carry out his threats. Jorge had gone to the trouble to discover that Contento-Pachon was married, that he had a child, the names of his wife and child, and the location of his residence. These were not vague threats of possible future harm. According to the defendant, if he had refused to cooperate, the consequences would have been immediate and harsh.
>
> Contento-Pachon contends that he was being watched by one of Jorge's accomplices at all times during the airplane trip. As a consequence, the force of the threats continued to restrain him. . . .
>
> . . . Contento-Pachon explained that he did not report the threats because he feared that the police were corrupt. The trier of fact should decide whether one in Contento-Pachon's position might believe that some of the Bogota police were paid informants for drug traffickers and that reporting the matter to the police did not represent a reasonable opportunity of escape.
>
> If he chose not to go to the police, Contento-Pachon's alternative was to flee. We reiterate that the opportunity to escape must be reasonable. To flee, Contento-Pachon, along with his wife and three-year-old child, would have been forced to pack his possessions, leave his job, and travel to a place beyond the reaches of the drug traffickers. A juror might find that this was not a reasonable avenue of escape.

Id. at 694 (majority opinion).

Are the Kansas Supreme Court and the Ninth Circuit applying different standards of imminence and inescapability? If so, which approach makes more sense? Would Scott have had a valid duress defense under the Ninth Circuit's reasoning in *Contento-Pachon*? Note that the Ninth Circuit concluded only that the jurors "might" have found Contento-Pachon's duress claim to be valid and that the trial judge should have let them make the ultimate decision.

4. The Requisite Nature of the Coercive Threats. Kansas, like a number of other states, follows the common-law approach and restricts the duress defense to cases where a defendant was threatened with death or serious bodily harm. *See* Joshua Dressler, Understanding Criminal Law § 23.01[B], at 300 (7th ed. 2015). Although the common law likewise required a threat directed at either the defendant or a family member, many states (unlike Kansas) no longer adhere to that rule. *See id.* at 301 & n.13.

Is it sensible to limit the type of threats that will support a duress defense? Or should the gravity of the threat be only one factor to be weighed in evaluating a claim of duress because "[u]nder some circumstances, the commission of a minor criminal offense should be excusable even if the coercive agent does not use or threaten" death or serious bodily harm? *State v. Toscano*, 378 A.2d 755, 762 (N.J. 1977).

Even if the restrictions imposed by the Kansas statute are too strict, should the defense be confined to cases where the defendant was threatened with some type of physical injury? Is it fair to say that "threats to property or even reputation cannot exercise sufficient power over persons of 'reasonable firmness'" to make a crime "irresistible"? Model Penal Code § 2.09 Comment at 375. Or should the law of duress recognize that threats to property—for example, threats to fire defendants from their jobs or evict them from their homes—can be "as potent in overbearing the actor's wish not to perform the prohibited act as a threat of physical harm"? *Director of Public Prosecutions v. Lynch*, [1975] App. Cas. 653, 686 (H.L.) (Lord Simon).

5. The "At Fault" Exception. In most jurisdictions, a duress defense is unavailable to defendants who were at fault in bringing about the situation that led to their commission of the crime—that is, those who recklessly put themselves in a situation where coercion was likely. *See* 2 Wayne R. LaFave, Substantive Criminal Law § 9.7(b), at 82 (2d ed. 2003). This exception is applied most frequently in cases like *Scott*, where the court concluded that the defendant voluntarily exposed himself to the risk of coercion by "knowingly associat[ing] himself with the selling of drugs, a criminal activity, and with a gang noted for violence." Duress is no defense in such circumstances because "it would be only too easy for every member of an unlawful conspiracy and for every member of a gang except the leader to obtain an immunity denied to ordinary citizens"; in fact, "the better organised the conspiracy and the more brutal its internal discipline, the surer would be the defense for its members." *The Queen v. Fitzpatrick*, [1977] N. Ir. 20, 31 (Crim. App.).

Was the Kansas Supreme Court right to find the "at fault" exception applicable in *Scott*, or was it unfair to blame Scott for joining Woods' gang if he did so only after being subjected to the type of torture that Green experienced? What if Scott had argued that he lived in a neighborhood where young men realistically have to join a gang in order to survive? *See* Martín S. Jankowski, Islands in the Street: Gangs and American Urban Society 44–45, 55–59 (1991) (noting that some young people join gangs to obtain "personal protection from the predatory elements" in their neighborhoods, and describing the coercive forms of recruitment used by certain gangs);

Sudir Venkatesh, Gang Leader for a Day: A Rogue Sociologist Takes to the Streets 84, 250, 180, 130, 255 (2008) (reporting that gang membership "represented security" in a neighborhood where "there was no such thing as neutral" and where calls to the police went unheeded, and observing that gang leaders employed a "leadership style" of "[f]ear" and some members believed they would be killed if they tried to leave the gang).

6. **The Murder Exception.** Most states preclude defendants who intentionally kill from raising a duress defense, *see* 2 Wayne R. LaFave, Substantive Criminal Law § 9.7(b), at 81 (2d ed. 2003), and some courts have likewise extended the ban to second-degree murder. *See People v. Anderson*, 50 P.3d 368, 376 (Cal. 2002); *Commonwealth v. Vasquez*, 971 N.E.2d 783, 792 (Mass. 2012). There is a split of authority as to whether this exception also applies to felony murder cases where defendants claim they were forced to participate in the underlying felony that led to death. *See* Joshua Dressler, Understanding Criminal Law § 23.04[A], at 305 (7th ed. 2015).

Is it sensible to foreclose a duress defense in murder cases because one who is threatened even with death "ought rather to die himself than escape by the murder of an innocent"? 4 William Blackstone, Commentaries on the Laws of England *30. Should the criminal law "encourage . . . everyone to seek an alternative to killing" because a person subjected to coercion can "always choose to resist rather than kill an innocent person"? *Anderson*, 50 P.3d at 374. Consider the views expressed by Lord Salmon in *Abbott v. The Queen*, [1976] 3 W.L.R. 462, 469 (P.C.):

> A terrorist of notorious violence might . . . threaten death to "A" and his family unless "A" obeys his instructions to put a bomb with a time fuse set by "A" in a certain passenger aircraft, and/or in a thronged market, railway station or the like. "A", under duress, obeys his instructions and as a result, hundreds of men, women and children are killed or mangled. . . . Having now gained some real experience and expertise, he might again be approached by the terrorist who would make the same threats and exercise the same duress under which "A" would then give a repeat performance. . . . Is there any limit to the number of people you may kill to save your own life and that of your family?

On the other hand, is the law being "woefully unrealistic about human nature" in blaming those who decide to protect themselves and their families rather than act as martyrs? Steven J. Mulroy, *The Duress Defense's Uncharted Terrain: Applying It to Murder, Felony Murder, and the Mentally Retarded Defendant*, 43 San Diego L. Rev. 159, 175 (2006). Can even murder "sometimes be the product of coercion that is truly irresistible"? Model Penal Code § 2.09 Comment at 376. Rather than automatically foreclosing a duress defense in murder cases, is it more sensible to include the severity of the crime among the factors to be weighed in determining whether the defendant acted under duress, with the understanding that "the greater the degree of heinousness of the crime, the greater and less irresistible must be the degree of pressure"? *Director of Public Prosecutions v. Lynch*, [1975] App. Cas. 653, 681 (H.L.) (Lord Wilberforce).

Finally, is precluding murder defendants from raising a duress defense inconsistent with the heat of passion doctrine? "Why should a person who kills in sudden *anger* as the result of adequate provocation be permitted to mitigate her offense to manslaughter, while one who kills out of *fear* for her own or another person's safety receives no formal mitigation?" DRESSLER, *supra*, § 23.04[B], at 307. A few jurisdictions have been troubled by this discrepancy and therefore find defendants who killed under duress guilty of manslaughter rather than murder. *See, e.g.*, Minn. Stat. § 609.20(3). *But see United States v. LaFleur*, 971 F.2d 200, 206 (9th Cir. 1992) (rejecting this view on the grounds that "[t]he same rationale which dictates that duress is not a complete defense to murder demands that duress not be used . . . to mitigate the intentional killing of an innocent third person").

7. Burden of Proof. In *Dixon v. United States*, 548 U.S. 1 (2006), the U.S. Supreme Court upheld a jury instruction imposing the burden of proving the duress defense on the defendant. In concluding that the Constitution did not require the prosecution to shoulder the burden of proof on duress, the Court observed that, "even if we assume that [the defendant's] will was overborne by the threats [her boyfriend] made against her and her daughters," she knew what she was doing and therefore had the mens rea necessary to commit the crime. *Id.* at 6. "The duress defense, like the defense of necessity," the Court continued, "may excuse conduct that would otherwise be punishable, but the existence of duress normally does not controvert any of the elements of the offense itself" and therefore need not be disproved by the prosecutor. *Id.* Given the absence of a federal duress statute, and finding no evidence of Congress' intent in the legislative history of the federal firearms statute Dixon was charged with violating, the Court assumed that Congress was aware of and intended to endorse the "long-established common-law rule" placing the burden of proving duress on the defense. *Id.* at 17.

Despite the Court's holding in *Dixon*, most states impose the burden of disproving duress on the prosecution, once the defendant has satisfied the burden of production. *See id.* at 26 (Breyer, J., dissenting). For additional background on the constitutional principles governing burden of proof questions and a description of the Model Penal Code's position on these issues, see Note 4 following *People v. Tomlins* in Chapter 14, Section B.

8. The Model Penal Code Approach. The Model Penal Code provision on duress, which has influenced a substantial number of state criminal codes, affords a defense in cases where a defendant was coerced to commit a crime by the use or threat of "unlawful force against his person or the person of another, that a person of reasonable firmness in his situation would have been unable to resist." Model Penal Code § 2.09(1). The Code thus requires a threat of physical injury (although one who acts to protect property may have a necessity defense under § 3.02 if committing the crime was the lesser evil), but it does not limit the duress defense to cases involving an imminent threat of death or serious bodily harm. Likewise, it does not foreclose the defense in murder cases. Instead, the Code envisions that the gravity and imminence of the threat and the seriousness of the crime will be "given evidential weight, along with other circumstances," in evaluating whether "a person of 'reasonable firmness' would have succumbed to the pressure." *Id.* § 2.09 Comment at 375–76.

The Code does provide, however, that the duress defense is unavailable if a defendant "recklessly placed himself in a situation in which it was probable that he would be subjected to duress." A defendant who was merely negligent in so doing loses the defense only with respect to those crimes requiring a mens rea of negligence. *Id.* § 2.09(2). The drafters acknowledged that "this provision may have the effect of sanctioning conviction of a crime of purpose when the actor's culpability was limited to recklessness" and therefore constitutes "a deliberate departure . . . from the general approach of the Code." *Id.* § 2.09 Comment at 379 & n.48. *Cf. id.* § 3.02(2) (providing that defendants who were reckless in placing themselves in a situation calling for a choice of evils may not be convicted of crimes requiring a mens rea more culpable than recklessness). Nevertheless, the drafters felt that this departure was justified by "the exceptional nature" of the duress defense. *Id.* § 2.09 Comment at 379. The Code adheres to the "normal pattern" for defendants who were merely negligent in exposing themselves to duress because "[t]he difference between inadvertence and the conscious creation involved in recklessness appears to justify discriminating in this way." *Id.* at 379–80.

Although § 2.09 does not explicitly say so, the Comments indicate that the drafters intended to create a second exception to the duress defense. Under this exception, defendants who erroneously believed they had received the type of threat "that a person of reasonable firmness . . . would have been unable to resist" lose the duress defense—but only if their mistake was reckless (or negligent) and they are charged with a crime requiring a mens rea of recklessness (or negligence). *See id.* at 380. Comparable provisions governing self-defense (§ 3.09(2)) and necessity (§ 3.02(2)) are discussed in Note 6 following *People v. Goetz* in Chapter 14, Section B, and in Note 6 following *State v. Reese* in Chapter 14, Section D.

Finally, the Code specifies that § 2.09 does not preclude defendants who acted under duress from raising a necessity defense if they can satisfy the requirements of § 3.02. *See* Model Penal Code § 2.09(4). The Code thus rejects the view that duress and necessity are simply variations of the same defense, depending on the source of the pressure confronting the defendant, so that one must choose the lesser evil in order to take advantage of either defense. If the defendant does choose the lesser evil, the Model Penal Code considers the act justified regardless of the source of the pressure because, the drafters explained, there is "no reason why [the necessity defense] should be denied full application when the evil apprehended has its source in the action or the threatened action of another person, rather than the forces and perils of the physical world." *Id.* § 2.09 Comment at 373.

If, on the other hand, the defendant does not choose the lesser evil, the act may be excused by virtue of the duress defense—but only if the source of the pressure was another person's coercion. The Model Penal Code's duress defense applies only in cases involving threats of "unlawful force" and therefore does not include cases where "the danger . . . arises from the effect of natural causes and an otherwise criminal act is performed to meet the danger." *Id.* at 378. By way of example, the drafters pointed out that the duress defense would not protect a defendant whose brakes suddenly failed on a narrow mountain road and who then chose to run over two intoxicated individuals passed out in the middle of the road in order to avoid being killed. The Comments explain:

> It will be an extraordinarily rare case in which a person will not be able to claim successfully that a response to natural causes was a choice of a lesser evil but could successfully claim that the choice was one a person of reasonable firmness would make. And there is a significant difference between the situations in which the actor makes the choice of an equal or greater evil under the threat of unlawful human force and when he does so because of a natural event. In the former situation, the basic interests of the law may be satisfied by prosecution of the agent of unlawful force; in the latter circumstance, if the actor is excused, no one is subject to the law's application.

Id. at 379. Does this reasoning make sense, or should the unfortunate driver have a defense if a person of "reasonable firmness" would have acted in precisely the same way?

9. Analogous Defenses. Given the rationale underlying the duress defense, should a defense be recognized in any of the following cases?

(a) Under the common-law doctrine of coverture, any crime committed by a married woman in her husband's presence was presumed to have been coerced by him. Even when the husband was not present at the time of the crime, the woman was excused if she was in fact coerced by him, with coercion found to exist in some cases simply because the husband commanded her to commit the crime, and in any event on less evidence than was generally required to make out a case of duress. *See* Model Penal Code § 2.09 Comment at 385. The rationale for the common-law approach has been explained as follows:

> The so-called "doctrine of coercion" has been attributed to the "legal identity of husband and wife"; to the "duty of obedience to her husband"; to the original status of the wife as only "the servant of the husband," or a "marionette, moved at will by the husband"; to the power of the husband to chastise the wife; to the "matrimonial subjection of the wife to her husband"; to the "power and authority which her husband has over her"; and even to a "relic of a belief in the ignorance and pusillanimity of women which is not, and perhaps never was, well founded."

Rollin M. Perkins & Ronald N. Boyce, Criminal Law 1019 (3d ed. 1982) (quoting a number of sources published between 1788 and 1932). *See also Commonwealth v. Jones*, 1 Pa. D. & C.2d 269, 275 (Pa. C.P. Ct. 1954) (noting that this doctrine is based upon "human experience"—specifically, "the wife's tendency to follow her husband's bidding"—and "therefore its continuing validity is not affected by any change in a wife's property or personal rights").

Section 2.09(3) of the Model Penal Code endorses the abolition of these rules, and today cases in this country involving married women are resolved according to the general principles governing duress. *See* Anne M. Coughlin, *Excusing Women*, 82 CAL. L. REV. 1, 33 n.162 (1994) (reporting that the most recent judicial opinion she found subscribing to the common-law doctrines was decided in 1977).

In recent years, victims of domestic violence charged with a variety of offenses have alleged that their abusive partners threatened to harm them if they did not commit the crime. Faced with such claims, some courts have allowed these defendants to introduce evidence to support a duress defense. In *United States v. Marenghi*, 893 F. Supp. 85, 94–95 (D. Me. 1995), for example, the court refused to create a per se rule barring expert testimony on the battered woman syndrome in such cases, noting that "if the defendant is permitted to pull the camera back to provide the broader picture, so to speak, of her circumstances, the jury could learn of a pattern of violence, control, and coercion leading up to the criminal act." The court concluded that expert testimony can help "explain[] how a reasonable person can . . . be trapped and controlled by another at all times even if there is no overt threat of violence at any given moment." *See also, e.g., United States v. Nwoye*, 824 F.3d 1129, 1139 (D.C. Cir. 2016) (finding that expert testimony on the battered woman syndrome was admissible and "would have entitled [the defendant] to a jury instruction on duress"); *Dando v. Yukins*, 461 F.3d 791, 801 (6th Cir. 2006) (concluding that such testimony was admissible by analogizing to "the related affirmative defense of self-defense"); *Miller v. State*, 36 S.W.3d 503, 508–09 (Tex. Crim. App. 2001) (holding that the defendant was entitled to introduce evidence of assaults occurring both before and even shortly after she committed the crime to support her claim of duress); *State v. Williams*, 937 P.2d 1052, 1058 (Wash. 1997) (ruling that the defendant was entitled to a jury instruction on the duress defense, and directing that "the reasonableness of the defendant's perception of immediacy [of the threat posed by her abusive boyfriend] should be evaluated in light of the defendant's experience of abuse").

Other courts have disagreed. In *United States v. Dixon*, 413 F.3d 520, 523–24 (5th Cir. 2005), *aff'd on other grounds*, 548 U.S. 1 (2006), for example, the court ruled that expert testimony on the effects of battering is "not relevant" to the issue of duress because it is "inherently subjective," whereas duress turns on an "objective inquiry into whether a defendant's conduct, although illegal, represented her only reasonable alternative to serious bodily injury or death." *Cf. State v. B.H.*, 870 A.2d 273, 288, 291, 290 (N.J. 2005) (allowing expert testimony on the battered woman syndrome to dispel "any lay misperception that a defendant is reckless [in putting herself in a situation where she will likely be subjected to duress] simply because she remained in the abusive relationship," and also to "assess the sincerity of defendant's perception of a threat from her alleged abuser," but holding that "the idiosyncratic fact that the defendant may be susceptible to the demands of her abuser because she suffers from battered woman syndrome" is "irrelevant" in making the objective determination whether "the defendant experienced a coercion that a person of reasonable firmness in that situation would have been unable to withstand").

Ultimately, even though evidence describing the effects of intimate partner violence is arguably "a better 'fit'" with the duress defense than with self-defense, victims of domestic violence have had much less success with the duress defense. Alafair S. Burke, *Rational Actors, Self-Defense, and Duress: Making Sense, Not Syndromes, Out of the Battered Woman*, 81 N.C. L. Rev. 211, 308 (2002). In *United States v. Sixty Acres*, 930 F.2d 857, 860–61 (11th Cir. 1991), for example, the court rejected a duress defense raised by a battered woman whose husband had threatened to "have her done away with" if she ever left him, who had beaten his prior wife to death, and who was described by a government witness as a "madman." Although the court acknowledged that the husband's "presence induced fear, anxiety and fierce discomfort in the members of his household," it concluded that the defendant's "*generalized* fear of persecution from her husband . . . , although genuine and profound, did not excuse her conduct on the grounds of duress" because "[n]othing in the record . . . suggests that [he] threatened immediate retaliation . . . if she refused to cooperate in the drug scheme [and] [e]verything in the record . . . suggests that [she] had ample opportunity to flee or to contact law enforcement agents regarding her husband's activities." *See also Neelley v. State*, 642 So. 2d 494, 508 (Ala. Crim. App. 1993) (quoting trial court's comments in a capital case that a "major distinguishing fact" between self-defense and duress claims raised by domestic violence victims is that "[t]he battered woman syndrome offers no plausible explanation" for the decision to "kill an innocent third party, a choice which falls outside any acceptable notion of self-protection," and therefore the judge was "unconvinced that the battered woman syndrome provides any reason for mitigating petitioner's [death] sentence").[3] (For a description of the battered woman syndrome and a discussion of self-defense claims raised by victims of domestic violence, see *State v. Norman* and the accompanying Notes in Chapter 14, Section B.)

(b) In *United States v. North*, 910 F.2d 843 (per curiam), *modified on other grounds*, 920 F.2d 940 (D.C. Cir. 1990) (per curiam), Lieutenant Colonel Oliver North, a former member of the National Security Council staff, was convicted of several charges, including destroying government documents, in connection with his role in the so-called "Iran/Contra Affair." His primary defense was that his superiors, including President Ronald Reagan, had authorized his actions and that he had reasonably relied on their orders.

Although the Court of Appeals reversed the conviction on other grounds, and all charges were ultimately dropped, the court rejected North's claim that "following orders, without more, can transform an illegal act into a legal one." The court

---

3. In 1999, the outgoing Governor of Alabama commuted Neelley's sentence to life in prison. *See Neelley v. Walker,* 67 F. Supp. 3d 1319, 1322 (M.D. Ala. 2014).

observed that the defendant's argument "conjure[s] up the notion of a 'Nuremberg' defense, a notion from which our criminal justice system, one based on individual accountability and responsibility, has historically recoiled." *Id.* at 881.[4] *See also Calley v. Callaway*, 519 F.2d 184, 193 (5th Cir. 1975) (finding no error in murder conviction of U.S. Army lieutenant who ordered the soldiers in his platoon to kill more than 100 unarmed, unresisting Vietnamese civilians at the My Lai Massacre, and noting that he could not rely on the defense that he was obeying military orders if he knew or should have known the order was illegal). *Cf.* Model Penal Code § 2.10 (recognizing a defense when a defendant "does no more than execute an order of his superior in the armed forces which he does not know to be unlawful"); *id.* § 3.03 (creating a defense for conduct "required or authorized" by the law prescribing a public official's responsibilities or "any other provision of law imposing a public duty").

Issues surrounding the superior orders defense have recently resurfaced in connection with the military efforts in Iraq and Afghanistan. *See, e.g.,* Harold Hongju Koh, *Can the President Be Torturer in Chief?*, 81 IND. L.J. 1145, 1149, 1153 (2005) (describing a Justice Department memo, written in 2002 and withdrawn two years later, which concluded that "U.S. officials can use tactics tantamount to torture against suspected terrorists, without being held liable under a federal statute that criminalizes torture," and criticizing the memo for "revers[ing] half a century of history by declaring the 'superior orders' defense presumptively legal"); Martha Minow, *Living Up to Rules: Holding Soldiers Responsible for Abusive Conduct and the Dilemma of the Superior Orders Defence*, 52 McGILL L.J. 1, 6 (2007) (analyzing the extent to which U.S. and international laws recognize a superior orders defense, and discussing social science literature that explains "why people participate in atrocities" and "how difficult it would be for individuals to understand and comply with a rule expecting compliance with superior orders except those that are illegal"). *Cf.* Monu Bedi, *Entrapped: A Reconceptualization of the Obedience to Orders Defense*, 98 MINN. L. REV. 2103, 2106 (2014) (suggesting that "the presence of government coercion" links the superior orders defense more closely to entrapment, discussed below in Section B, than to duress).

(c) In 1974, Patty Hearst, the daughter of a wealthy newspaper publisher, was kidnapped by members of a revolutionary group known as the Symbionese Liberation Army (SLA). Two months later, she walked into a San Francisco bank armed with a semiautomatic weapon and helped members of the SLA rob the bank. At her trial on charges of armed robbery, Hearst claimed that the SLA had in effect brainwashed her to join their cause by using a number of techniques similar to those used against prisoners of war, including keeping her blindfolded in a closet for two weeks and subjecting her to physical and sexual assault. Hearst was convicted and sentenced to

---

4. The court did say, however, that North could introduce evidence suggesting he was simply following orders in support of his argument that he did not have the mens rea to willfully and unlawfully destroy government documents. *See North*, 910 F.2d at 884–88. For further discussion of this type of mistake defense, see *United States v. Barker* and the accompanying Notes in Chapter 4, Section C.2.

seven years in jail. *See United States v. Hearst*, 563 F.2d 1331 (9th Cir. 1977); Jeffrey Toobin, American Heiress: The Wild Saga of the Kidnapping, Crimes and Trial of Patty Hearst (2016); Tom Mathews & William J. Cook, *Patty's Defense*, Newsweek, Mar. 1, 1976, at 20. (For discussion of this case in the context of the voluntary act requirement, see Chapter 3, Section A, Note 5.) (Patty Hearst's story has also been the subject of several critically acclaimed fictionalized accounts. *See* Susan Choi, American Woman (2003); Christopher Sorrentino, Trance (2005).)

Lee Malvo, the 17-year-old convicted in connection with the highly publicized 2002 Washington-area sniper shootings that left 10 people dead, also raised a type of brainwashing defense. His insanity claim was premised on the theory that John A. Muhammad, the man who orchestrated the attacks, had "effectively brainwashed [Malvo] into participating in the shootings," so that he "'lost his sense of identity as a result of . . . prolonged and coercive persuasion or indoctrination.'" James Dao, *Mental Health Experts Call Sniper Defendant Brainwashed*, N.Y. Times, Dec. 11, 2003, at A38 (quoting defense expert). A Virginia jury rejected this defense and convicted Malvo of murder and terrorism, but spared his life and sentenced him to life in prison.

In 2015, a federal jury in Boston likewise convicted Dzhokhar Tsarnaev on each of the 30 charges brought against him in connection with the 2013 Boston Marathon bombings that killed three people and injured more than 260 others. Defense counsel's principal argument was that Tsarnaev, who was 19 years old at the time of the bombings, was manipulated by his 26-year-old brother Tamerlan, who masterminded the attacks and died while the two brothers were trying to avoid apprehension. The jury verdict forms indicated that only three jurors thought the defendant was acting under his brother's influence. Despite public opinion polls showing that Massachusetts residents overwhelmingly favored sentencing Tsarnaev to life in prison, the jury sentenced him to die. Tsarnaev's appeal of his sentence is pending. *See* Katharine Q. Seelye, *Tsarnaev Given Death Sentence in Boston Attack*, N.Y. Times, May 16, 2015, at A1.

Defendants like these three typically cannot take advantage of a traditional duress defense because "[t]he coercive aspects of the indoctrination process may occur long before the commission of the crime," such that by the time the crime takes place, the defendant may be "under no immediate duress." Donald T. Lunde & Thomas E. Wilson, *Brainwashing as a Defense to Criminal Liability: Patty Hearst Revisited*, 13 Crim. L. Bull. 341, 358 (1977). Despite the differences between the brainwashed defendant and one who acted under duress, should a defense be available to both? Consider the views of Richard Delgado:

> Many authorities, including the drafters of a Department of Defense report prepared in response to evidence of widespread collaboration by American prisoners of war (POWs) during the Korean conflict, have concluded that a determined captor, possessing total control over the life and environment of a captive, can produce behavioral and attitudinal change in even the most strongly resistant individual.

Richard Delgado, *Ascription of Criminal States of Mind: Toward a Defense Theory for the Coercively Persuaded ("Brainwashed") Defendant*, 63 MINN. L. REV. 1, 3 (1978). Should the brainwashed defendant's crime therefore be excused because "[t]he breakdown of [his] identity and will in the latter stages of the coercive persuasion process destroys the very mechanisms by which he might have offered resistance," and thus the "choice to act criminally was not freely made and, indeed, appears to be not his choice at all"? *Id.* at 8, 10. *Cf.* Model Penal Code § 2.09 Comment at 377 (suggesting that brainwashed defendants would have a duress defense if they committed a crime because of "subconscious fears [that earlier threats would] be carried out," such that their conduct was "truly the product of unlawful force and would have been performed by a person of reasonable firmness subjected to similar conditions").

On the other hand, should brainwashed defendants be punished because they had the mens rea to commit their crimes and are not as sympathetic as those who acted under duress? Consider Joshua Dressler, *Professor Delgado's "Brainwashing" Defense: Courting a Determinist Legal System*, 63 MINN. L. REV. 335, 347–49, 354 (1979):

> [T]he captive comes to share the captor's view, and later commits supportive crimes, because he wants—that is, intends—to commit the acts. The intent itself may derive from any one of various psychological sources but the mens rea is clearly present. . . .
>
>   . . . .
>
> The case for the coercively persuaded defendant is . . . weaker than that of one acting under duress. A loaded and cocked gun pressed to one's head presents more substantial loss of choice, and a clearer example of blamelessness, than do the conditions undergone by . . . Patricia Hearst. In the latter type of case, the person may experience a harsh environment, and thus have limited choice, but the residual options cannot be equated to the alternatives available to an actor under threat of immediate death.

[B] Entrapment

United States v. Russell

411 U.S. 423 (1973)

MR. JUSTICE REHNQUIST delivered the opinion of the Court.

[Russell was charged with manufacturing and selling methamphetamine. At trial, he argued that he had been entrapped when an undercover federal agent named Joe Shapiro offered to supply a necessary chemical ingredient of methamphetamine, which was difficult to obtain, in return for half of the drugs Russell produced. Russell agreed to the plan, telling Shapiro that he had been manufacturing the drug for a number of months and giving the agent a sample from his most recent batch. Approximately one month after Russell produced methamphetamine with the chemicals supplied by Shapiro, he gave Shapiro additional methamphetamine that he had subsequently made after finding another supply of the chemical. Russell was convicted and sentenced to six months in prison and three years' probation.]

. . . .

This Court first recognized and applied the entrapment defense in *Sorrells v. United States*, 287 U.S. 435 (1932). In *Sorrells*, a federal prohibition agent visited the defendant while posing as a tourist and engaged him in conversation about their common war experiences. After gaining the defendant's confidence, the agent asked for some liquor, was twice refused, but upon asking a third time the defendant finally capitulated, and was subsequently prosecuted for violating the National Prohibition Act.

Mr. Chief Justice Hughes, speaking for the Court, held that as a matter of statutory construction the defense of entrapment should have been available to the defendant. Under the theory propounded by the Chief Justice, the entrapment defense prohibits law enforcement officers from instigating a criminal act by persons "otherwise innocent in order to lure them to its commission and to punish them." Thus, the thrust of the entrapment defense was held to focus on the intent or predisposition of the defendant to commit the crime. . . .

In 1958 the Court again considered the theory underlying the entrapment defense and expressly reaffirmed the view expressed by the *Sorrells* majority. *Sherman v. United States*, [356 U.S. 369 (1958)]. In *Sherman* the defendant was convicted of selling narcotics to a Government informer. As in *Sorrells*, it appears that the Government agent gained the confidence of the defendant and, despite initial reluctance, the defendant finally acceded to the repeated importunings of the agent to commit the criminal act. On the basis of *Sorrells*, this Court reversed the affirmance of the defendant's conviction.

In affirming the theory underlying *Sorrells*, Mr. Chief Justice Warren for the Court, held that "[t]o determine whether entrapment has been established, a line must be drawn between the trap for the unwary innocent and the trap for the unwary criminal." . . .

Those cases establish that entrapment is a relatively limited defense. It is rooted, not in any authority of the Judicial Branch to dismiss prosecutions for what it feels to have been "overzealous law enforcement," but instead in the notion that Congress could not have intended criminal punishment for a defendant who has committed all the elements of a proscribed offense, but was induced to commit them by the Government.

Sorrells and *Sherman* both recognize "that the fact that officers or employees of the Government merely afford opportunities or facilities for the commission of the offense does not defeat the prosecution." Nor will the mere fact of deceit defeat a prosecution, for there are circumstances when the use of deceit is the only practicable law enforcement technique available. It is only when the Government's deception actually implants the criminal design in the mind of the defendant that the defense of entrapment comes into play.

. . . .

Mr. Justice Stewart, with whom Mr. Justice Brennan and Mr. Justice Marshall join, dissenting.

It is common ground that "[t]he conduct with which the defense of entrapment is concerned is the *manufacturing* of crime by law enforcement officials and their agents." For the Government cannot be permitted to instigate the commission of a criminal offense in order to prosecute someone for committing it. . . .

In *Sorrells v. United States* and *Sherman v. United States*, the Court took what might be called a "subjective" approach to the defense of entrapment. In that view, the defense is predicated on an unexpressed intent of Congress to exclude from its criminal statutes the prosecution and conviction of persons, "otherwise innocent," who have been lured to the commission of the prohibited act through the Government's instigation. The key phrase in this formulation is "otherwise innocent," for the entrapment defense is available under this approach only to those who would not have committed the crime but for the Government's inducements. Thus, the subjective approach focuses on the conduct and propensities of the particular defendant in each individual case: if he is "otherwise innocent," he may avail himself of the defense; but if he had the "predisposition" to commit the crime, or if the "criminal design" originated with him, then—regardless of the nature and extent of the Government's participation—there has been no entrapment. And, in the absence of a conclusive showing one way or the other, the question of the defendant's "predisposition" to the crime is a question of fact for the jury. The Court today adheres to this approach.

The concurring opinion of Mr. Justice Roberts, joined by Justices Brandeis and Stone, in the *Sorrells* case, and that of Mr. Justice Frankfurter, joined by Justices Douglas, Harlan, and Brennan, in the *Sherman* case, took a different view of the entrapment defense. In their concept, the defense is not grounded on some unexpressed intent of Congress . . . , but rather on the belief that "the methods employed on behalf of the Government to bring about conviction cannot be countenanced." . . . Phrased another way, the question is whether—regardless of the predisposition to crime of the particular defendant involved—the governmental agents have acted in such a way as is likely to instigate or create a criminal offense. Under this approach, the determination of the lawfulness of the Government's conduct must be made—as it is on all questions involving the legality of law enforcement methods—by the trial judge, not the jury.

In my view, this objective approach to entrapment advanced by the Roberts opinion in *Sorrells* and the Frankfurter opinion in *Sherman* is the only one truly consistent with the underlying rationale of the defense. . . . I find it impossible to believe that the purpose of the defense is to effectuate some unexpressed congressional intent to exclude from its criminal statutes persons who committed a prohibited act, but would not have done so except for the Government's inducements. For, as Mr. Justice Frankfurter put it, "the only legislative intention that can with any show of reason be extracted from the statute is the intention to make criminal precisely the conduct in which the defendant engaged."

. . . .

Moreover, a test that makes the entrapment defense depend on whether the defendant had the requisite predisposition permits the introduction into evidence of all kinds of hearsay, suspicion, and rumor—all of which would be inadmissible in any other context—in order to prove the defendant's predisposition. It allows the prosecution, in offering such proof, to rely on the defendant's bad reputation or past criminal activities, including even rumored activities of which the prosecution may have insufficient evidence to obtain an indictment. . . . This sort of evidence is not only unreliable, as the hearsay rule recognizes; but it is also highly prejudicial, especially if the matter is submitted to the jury, for, despite instructions to the contrary, the jury may well consider such evidence as probative not simply of the defendant's predisposition, but of his guilt of the offense with which he stands charged.

More fundamentally, focusing on the defendant's innocence or predisposition has the direct effect of making what is permissible or impermissible police conduct depend upon the past record and propensities of the particular defendant involved. Stated another way, this subjective test means that the Government is permitted to entrap a person with a criminal record or bad reputation, and then to prosecute him for the manufactured crime, confident that his record or reputation itself will be enough to show that he was predisposed to commit the offense anyway.

. . . .

. . . [A]s Mr. Justice Frankfurter pointed out:

Permissible police activity does not vary according to the particular defendant concerned; surely if two suspects have been solicited at the same time in the same manner, one should not go to jail simply because he has been convicted before and is said to have a criminal disposition. . . .

. . . .

This does not mean, of course, that the Government's use of undercover activity, strategy, or deception is necessarily unlawful. Indeed, many crimes, especially so-called victimless crimes, could not otherwise be detected. Thus, government agents may engage in conduct that is likely, when objectively considered, to afford a person ready and willing to commit the crime an opportunity to do so.

But when the agents' involvement in criminal activities goes beyond the mere offering of such an opportunity, and when their conduct is of a kind that could induce or instigate the commission of a crime by one not ready and willing to commit it, then—regardless of the character or propensities of the particular person induced—the Government has engaged in the impermissible manufacturing of crime, and the federal courts should bar the prosecution in order to preserve the institutional integrity of the system of federal criminal justice.

Notes and Questions

1. The Subjective and Objective Approaches to Entrapment. Although the entrapment defense is "virtually unique to the criminal jurisprudence of the United States," GEORGE FLETCHER, RETHINKING CRIMINAL LAW 541 (1978), it continues to be followed in this country despite the fact that the only "consensus on entrapment" seems to be that "we are better off with it than without it." Joseph A. Colquitt, *Rethinking Entrapment*, 41 AM. CRIM. L. REV. 1389, 1390 (2004). The federal courts and a majority of states follow the subjective approach to entrapment, while approximately a dozen states have adopted the objective test. *See* PAUL MARCUS, THE ENTRAPMENT DEFENSE § 1.05A (4th ed. 2009). Section 2.13(1) of the Model Penal Code likewise endorses the objective approach, providing that entrapment is a defense whenever a government agent "induces or encourages another person to engage in conduct constituting [an] offense by either: (a) making knowingly false representations designed to induce the belief that such conduct is not prohibited; or (b) employing methods of persuasion or inducement that create a substantial risk that such an offense will be committed by persons other than those who are ready to commit it." (Section 2.13(3) provides, however, that the defense is unavailable to defendants charged with crimes involving bodily injury or the threat of such injury.)

Does the *Russell* dissent make a persuasive case for the objective test? That approach has been defended on the grounds that "[n]o matter what the defendant's past record and present inclinations to criminality," it is still possible that "[he] might not have committed the particular crime unless confronted with inordinate inducements" and, in any event, "certain police conduct to ensnare him into further crime is not to be tolerated by an advanced society." *Sherman v. United States*, 356 U.S. 369, 382–83 (1958) (Frankfurter, J., concurring in the result). Likewise, the drafters of the MPC thought that allowing "the use against a previously convicted person of police measures not permitted against the rest of society is to fix a permanent status of criminality on that person against the hopes of enlightened penology." Model Penal Code § 2.13 Comment at 412.

On the other hand, the subjective approach has been commended for "attempt[ing] to distinguish between persons who are blameworthy and persons who are not," which, "[i]n the absence of extraordinary circumstances, . . . should be the goal of our law of crimes." Roger Park, *The Entrapment Controversy*, 60 MINN. L. REV. 163, 217 (1976). Some of the MPC's drafters likewise favored the subjective approach because it recognizes that "the greatest vice in entrapment cases inheres in police behavior that leads the previously innocent to crime." Model Penal Code § 2.13 Comment at 413. In a more instrumental vein, others have argued that the subjective approach allows the criminal justice system to incarcerate those who are likely to commit crimes in the future under "circumstances that would [make] it harder for the police to catch [them]." RICHARD A. POSNER, ECONOMIC ANALYSIS OF LAW § 7.3, at 273 (9th ed. 2014). Are these arguments persuasive, or does the subjective approach simply serve to protect more privileged defendants by providing a defense to "those with ordinary, rather than disfavored, life-styles"? Louis M. Seidman, *The Supreme*

Court, Entrapment, and Our Criminal Justice Dilemma, 1981 Sᴜᴘ. Cᴛ. Rᴇᴠ. 111, 147 (1981). *See also* Ronald J. Allen et al., *Clarifying Entrapment*, 89 J. Cʀɪᴍ. L. & Cʀɪᴍɪɴᴏʟᴏɢʏ 407, 413 (1999) (arguing that the concept of predisposition "cannot usefully distinguish" among different defendants because "[e]veryone except saints" "has a price" and is thus "predisposed to commit crimes," and "[t]he only salient question is whether a person's price has been met").

Supporters of the subjective test have also leveled several criticisms at the objective approach. First, they consider the objective test's refusal to place any weight on a defendant's predisposition "inherently defective" because "predisposition, at least if known by the police when the investigation in question was conducted, has an important bearing upon the question of whether the conduct of the police and their agents was proper." 2 Wᴀʏɴᴇ R. LᴀFᴀᴠᴇ, Sᴜʙsᴛᴀɴᴛɪᴠᴇ Cʀɪᴍɪɴᴀʟ Lᴀᴡ §9.8(e), at 103 (2d ed. 2003). As one commentator explained:

> An appeal to friendship that causes an obviously reluctant person to sell a small amount of drugs is reprehensible; a similar appeal to a corrupt public official by an informer may be justifiable, particularly if the target's reluctance is expressly based upon considerations of expediency, and his methods of operation preclude approach except through friends. Similarly, an offer above the black market price for drugs would be inexcusable when used to induce an addict to sell a small amount, but might be justifiable if agents were negotiating a $100,000 purchase.

Park, *supra*, at 227–28. *See also* Model Penal Code §2.13 Comment at 413 (describing the view of a minority of the MPC's drafters that "[w]hen officers deal with the criminally disposed, they may find it necessary to employ methods that would be quite out of place if directed to the 'innocent'").

Second, the objective approach has been criticized for "creat[ing] a risk of acquitting dangerous chronic offenders," *People v. Barraza*, 591 P.2d 947, 958 (Cal. 1979), by giving them "complete immunity from prosecution . . . simply because government undercover agents subjected [them] to inducements which might have seduced a hypothetical individual who was not so predisposed." *Russell*, 411 U.S. at 434. *See also* Model Penal Code §2.13 Comment at 413 (describing the minority view that "defendants who are predisposed to commit crime are largely the professionals, who constitute the greatest crime problem," and "[f]reeing them in order to discipline the police [is] too great a price").

Finally, critics of the objective approach have observed that courts face an intractable dilemma in trying to establish rules of conduct for the police:

> Very frequently, an agent will need to make more than one solicitation. The target may initially disclaim any connection with illegal activity, or tell the agent that he lacks present ability to fulfill the request. The agent will persist, but without exerting any overwhelming pressure. . . .

A tribunal that must decide whether to convict on the basis of the evidence just described faces a hard choice. If it holds that such inducements are permissible, then some defendants will be convicted who might never have [committed the crime] but for the friendly overtures of an agent. On the other hand, if it deems the agent's conduct to be an entrapment, then apparently any bootlegger (or drug dealer . . .) can do business freely if he screens his new customers by engaging them in friendly conversation for an hour or two and refusing to sell until the third request. . . . Because of the restrictions such a result would place on law enforcement, it seems probable that many courts applying the hypothetical-person approach would hold conduct like that . . . to be permissible. . . .

Park, *supra*, at 217–18.

2. The Hybrid Approach. A few states, persuaded by both sides of this debate, have adopted a hybrid approach to entrapment that borrows elements from both the subjective and the objective tests. In most of these jurisdictions, the entrapment defense is unavailable unless *both* tests are met — that is, the defendant must have actually been induced to commit the crime (i.e., not predisposed) by governmental tactics that create a substantial risk of inducing a law-abiding person to commit the crime. *See State v. Little*, 435 A.2d 517, 520–21 (N.H. 1981); *State v. Rockholt*, 476 A.2d 1236, 1239–40 (N.J. 1984); *England v. State*, 887 S.W.2d 902, 913 (Tex. Crim. App. 1994).

In New Mexico, however, defendants are entitled to an entrapment defense if *either* test is met — that is, if they were induced to commit a crime they were not otherwise predisposed to commit, *or*, regardless of their predisposition, if the government agent's tactics were likely to induce those who were not ready and willing to commit the crime. *See State v. Vallejos*, 945 P.2d 957, 959 (N.M. 1997). *See generally* Paul Marcus, The Entrapment Defense § 1.05C (4th ed. 2009).

3. Questioning the Distinction Between the Subjective and Objective Approaches. Is there really much difference between the subjective and objective approaches to entrapment? Consider Louis M. Seidman, *The Supreme Court, Entrapment, and Our Criminal Justice Dilemma*, 1981 Sup. Ct. Rev. 111, 118–20:

The [subjective] test is premised on the notion that it is possible to isolate . . . "unwary criminals" who are "ready and willing" to engage in crime apart from the inducements offered by the government. But whether a person is "ready and willing" to break the law depends on what the person expects to get in return — that is, on the level of inducement. Like the rest of us, criminals do not generally work for free. . . .

Consequently, so long as one equates "predisposition" with a readiness to commit crime, no definition of "predisposition" can be complete without an articulation of the level of inducement to which a "predisposed" defendant would respond. Furthermore, the "predisposed" cannot be distinguished from the "nondisposed" without focusing on the propriety of the government's conduct — the very factor that the subjective approach professes to ignore. This is true because a defendant who responds favorably to a "proper" inducement has thereby conclusively demonstrated that he is predisposed to crime . . . . The entrapment test is "subjective" only in the sense that even if the government offers an "excessive" inducement, the defendant may nonetheless be convicted . . . if he would have responded favorably to a proper one.

. . . .

. . . [T]he objective test in theory avoids analysis of the defendant's predisposition and focuses, instead, exclusively on the propriety of the inducement[,] . . . "the likelihood, objectively considered, that it would entrap only those ready and willing to commit the crime." But plainly that likelihood depends in large measure on the group to whom the inducement is targeted. So long as the police direct their attention toward only those likely to be predisposed, the risk of entrapment, objectively considered, is small . . . . Thus, in most cases, both the objective and subjective approaches would permit an inducement, so long as the defendant is predisposed. The two approaches would reach different results only in the rare case where the police reasonably, but incorrectly, believe the defendant to be predisposed . . . .

4. Procedural Issues. As indicated in Justice Stewart's dissenting opinion in *Russell*, entrapment questions are usually resolved by the jury in jurisdictions that follow the subjective approach, whereas the judge typically makes the decision in jurisdictions that subscribe to the objective approach. *See, e.g.,* Model Penal Code § 2.13(2). *See generally* PAUL MARCUS, THE ENTRAPMENT DEFENSE §§ 6.05, 6.09 (4th ed. 2009). For the view that, even under the subjective test, the trial judge should make an initial pretrial ruling on entrapment claims because entrapment "feels like a question of procedure rather than substance, analogous to whether government agents abided by the [constitutional] rules in conducting a search or interrogation," see Jessica A. Roth, *The Anomaly of Entrapment*, 91 WASH. U. L. REV. 979, 1033 (2014) (concluding that entrapment "wound up in the substantive criminal law category largely by historical happenstance," because the first Supreme Court opinions to discuss the defense arose before the Court created the exclusionary rule).

In most jurisdictions that follow the subjective approach, defendants are required to prove that a government agent induced them to commit the crime, typically by a preponderance of the evidence. Once defendants satisfy that burden, however, the prosecution must prove beyond a reasonable doubt that they were predisposed. Jurisdictions that have adopted the objective approach usually impose the burden of proof on defendants by a preponderance of the evidence. *See, e.g.,* Model Penal Code § 2.13(2). *See generally* MARCUS, *supra*, §§ 6.01–6.03.

In *Mathews v. United States*, 485 U.S. 58 (1988), the Court held that defendants may raise an entrapment defense in federal court even if they deny committing the crime. In some states, however, defendants are prohibited from relying on such inconsistent defenses and therefore must admit they committed the crime if they wish to claim entrapment. *See generally* Paul Marcus, The Entrapment Defense §§ 6.10–6.14 (4th ed. 2009).

5. Inducement by Private Persons; Derivative Entrapment. Entrapment is somewhat reminiscent of duress in that both defenses involve a claim that the defendant was pressured to commit the crime — in the case of duress, by a coercive threat and in the case of entrapment, by an enticing inducement or offer. *See* Louis M. Seidman, *The Supreme Court, Entrapment, and Our Criminal Justice Dilemma*, 1981 Sup. Ct. Rev. 111, 133 & n.39 (drawing the distinction between threats and offers). Unlike duress, however, entrapment is no defense when the inducement came from private individuals rather than law enforcement officials or their agents.

Is it sensible to limit the entrapment defense in this fashion, or is it more appropriate to recognize that a defendant who "was induced, provoked, or tempted . . . by government agents [is not] any more innocent or any less predisposed than he would be if he had been induced, provoked, or tempted by a private person"? *Russell*, 411 U.S. at 443 (Stewart, J., dissenting). On the other hand, would extending the entrapment defense to those induced by private persons "work a revolutionary change in our law of excuse" because "[f]rom a culpability perspective," there is no principled distinction between enticing inducements and "circumstances of any kind [which make] the lure of crime difficult to resist"? Seidman, *supra*, at 132. *Cf. United States v. Morris*, 549 F.3d 548, 550–51 (7th Cir. 2008) (applying the traditional rule, though acknowledging that the Internet has facilitated private sting operations, creating "legitimate concern[s]" that vigilantes will conduct online stings in an effort to blackmail rather than apprehend their target or will "botch their investigation, alerting the offender in time for him to elude justice").

Even if it makes sense to require the participation of a government agent in order to trigger an entrapment defense, what about cases of "derivative entrapment," where a private person unknowingly acted at the behest of a government agent to induce the defendant to commit a crime? Should a defense be afforded in such cases in order "to prevent the government from circumventing rules against entrapment merely by deploying intermediaries, only one degree removed from the officials themselves"? *United States v. Washington*, 106 F.3d 983, 994 (D.C. Cir. 1997) (per curiam).

Some courts have rejected the possibility of "entrapment by an unwitting agent." *United States v. Thickstun*, 110 F.3d 1394, 1399 (9th Cir. 1997); *see also United States v. Hsu*, 364 F.3d 192, 202 (4th Cir. 2004). Others, however, have accepted the theory of derivative entrapment, though generally with some limits. *See United States v. Luisi*, 482 F.3d 43, 55 (1st Cir. 2007) (restricting the defense to cases where a government agent "specifically targeted" the defendant, instructing an intermediary to offer the defendant a specific inducement "after other government attempts at inducing the defendant . . . failed"); *United States v. Hollingsworth*, 27 F.3d 1196, 1204 (7th Cir. 1994) (en banc) (recognizing a defense only where "a private individual, *himself entrapped*, act[ed] as agent or conduit for governmental efforts" to entrap the defendant) (emphasis added).

6. Applying the Subjective Approach: Proving Inducement. Does "government inducement occur[] when an agent merely solicits the commission of an offense," or is "something more . . . required, such as use of persuasion, badgering, or pressure"? Roger Park, *The Entrapment Controversy*, 60 MINN. L. REV. 163, 179 (1976). Some federal cases have suggested that "the element of 'inducement' can be established without any showing that an agent 'engaged in activities beyond the reasonable limits of those artifices or stratagems necessary to produce evidence of criminality.' " *Id.* at 180. Thus, for example, Judge Learned Hand defined inducement as "soliciting, proposing, initiating, broaching or suggesting the commission of the offense charged." *United States v. Sherman*, 200 F.2d 880, 883 (2d Cir. 1952).

Today, however, most courts take a narrower view, requiring some evidence of inducement or persuasion beyond simply affording an opportunity to commit the crime. *See, e.g., United States v. Mayfield*, 771 F.3d 417, 434–35 (7th Cir. 2014) (en banc) (calling for "government solicitation . . . *plus* some other government conduct that creates a risk that a person who would not commit the crime if left to his own devices will do so in response to the government's efforts," such as "repeated attempts at persuasion, fraudulent representations, threats, coercive tactics, harassment, promises of reward beyond that inherent in the customary execution of the crime, [or] pleas based on need, sympathy, or friendship"); *United States v. Vasco*, 564 F.3d 12, 18 (1st Cir. 2009) (requiring "the existence of a 'plus' factor that raises concerns of 'government overreaching' "); *Commonwealth v. Madigan*, 871 N.E.2d 478, 483 (Mass. 2007) ("The types of conduct that possess the indicia of inducement include 'aggressive persuasion, coercive encouragement, lengthy negotiations, pleading or arguing with the defendant, *repeated or persistent solicitation*, persuasion, importuning, and playing on sympathy or other emotion . . . .' "). *See generally* PAUL MARCUS, THE ENTRAPMENT DEFENSE §§ 4.04A–C (4th ed. 2009).

7. Applying the Subjective Approach: Proving Predisposition. Defendants are considered predisposed if they were "ready and willing to commit the type of crime charged whenever presented with a favorable opportunity." Roger Park, *The Entrapment Controversy*, 60 MINN. L. REV. 163, 176 (1976). Courts adhering to the subjective approach have suggested several considerations to be weighed in evaluating predisposition. A number of courts, for example, rely on the following five factors:

> (1) the character and reputation of the defendant; (2) whether the government made the initial suggestion of criminal activity; (3) whether the defendant engaged in the activity for profit; (4) whether the defendant showed any reluctance; and (5) the nature of the government's inducement.

United States v. Temkin, 797 F.3d 682, 691 (9th Cir. 2015) (quoting *United States v. Jones*, 231 F.3d 508, 518 (9th Cir. 2000)). Of these, the Ninth Circuit indicated, the "most important" is whether the defendant was reluctant to commit the crime. *Id.* Likewise, in *State v. Wheeler*, 468 So. 2d 978, 981 (Fla. 1985), the court held that the prosecution can establish predisposition "by showing that the defendant had prior convictions or a reputation for engaging in similar illicit acts, by showing that the investigating officers had a reasonable suspicion that the defendant was engaging in such acts, or by showing the defendant's 'ready acquiescence.'"

Does focusing so heavily on the defendant's "ready acquiescence" or absence of "reluctance" in essence make the circular argument that a defendant "is predisposed because he committed the act, and then is . . . responsible for the act because he was predisposed"? Bennett L. Gershman, *Abscam, the Judiciary, and the Ethics of Entrapment*, 91 YALE L.J. 1565, 1581 (1982).

For discussion of how similar the defendant's prior misdeeds must be to the charged crime in order to be considered relevant to predisposition, see PAUL MARCUS, THE ENTRAPMENT DEFENSE § 4.05I (4th ed. 2009). For a study finding that jurors are significantly more likely to reject an entrapment defense when the defendant's prior record is introduced to show predisposition, see Eugene Borgida & Roger Park, *The Entrapment Defense: Juror Comprehension and Decision Making*, 12 LAW & HUM. BEHAV. 19 (1988).

8. Applying the Objective Approach: Determining What Tactics Are Likely to Induce a Normally Law-Abiding Person to Commit a Crime. Although acknowledging that implementation of the objective test "must to some extent proceed on an ad hoc basis," the California Supreme Court suggested in *People v. Barraza*, 591 P.2d 947, 955 (Cal. 1979), that "guidance will generally be found in the application of one or both of two principles":

> First, if the actions of the law enforcement agent would generate in a normally law-abiding person a motive for the crime other than ordinary criminal intent, entrapment will be satisfied. An example of such conduct would be an appeal by the police that would induce such a person to commit the act because of friendship or sympathy, instead of a desire for personal gain or other typical criminal purpose. Second, affirmative police conduct that would make commission of the crime unusually attractive to a normally law-abiding person will likewise constitute entrapment. Such conduct would include, for example, a guarantee that the act is not illegal or the offense will go undetected, an offer of exorbitant consideration, or any similar enticement.

As made clear in the *Russell* dissent, the objective approach focuses on the effect the government's inducements would have had on a hypothetical person—one who was not ready and willing to commit the crime—and not on the effect they had on the particular defendant. But are the defendant's characteristics and/or the circumstances confronting the defendant relevant considerations in constructing this hypothetical person? That is, do the issues that arise in defining the hypothetical reasonable person in other contexts come up here as well? *See* Notes 11–12 following *State v. Thornton* in Chapter 6, Section B.2 (voluntary manslaughter); Note 5 following *State v. Norman* in Chapter 14, Section B (self-defense).

In *People v. Juillet*, 475 N.W.2d 786, 793 (Mich. 1991), the four justices in the majority concluded that the objective definition of entrapment ought to analyze "whether the police conduct would induce a similarly situated person, with an otherwise law-abiding disposition, to commit the charged crime." For example, the court noted, the defendant's "potential vulnerability" and "weakness," as well as her age and education level, were relevant factors, though her "predisposition, such as prior convictions or activities not related to the circumstances involved in the current case," were not. *Id.* at 794, 799. Although the remaining three justices disagreed, they thought that the relevant inquiry was what effect the government's inducement would have had on "the average hypothetical drug user." *Id.* at 802 (opinion of Cavanagh, C.J.). In *Oliver v. State*, 703 P.2d 869, 870 (Nev. 1985), the court did not specifically address this question, but it found the defendant was entrapped because law enforcement officials used methods "calculated to tempt any needy person in the area, whether immediately disposed to crime or not."[5] And in deciding that the defendant in *Commonwealth v. Lucci*, 662 A.2d 1, 6 (Pa. Super. Ct. 1995), was entrapped into selling cocaine to a paid police informant, the court thought it relevant—again with no analysis of this issue—that the defendant had recently been released from a drug rehabilitation program when he was contacted by the informant.

Are these courts right to incorporate some subjectivity into the objective test because "[t]he normally law-abiding or average person probably cannot be induced or tempted into criminal conduct absent duress or coercion"? *Juillet*, 475 N.W.2d at 812 (Boyle, J., concurring in part and dissenting in part). Would "construing the objective test so that it required an inducement that would seduce the average person . . . rob it of significance in cases involving crimes that average people rarely commit"? Eugene Borgida & Roger Park, *The Entrapment Defense: Juror Comprehension and Decision Making*, 12 Law & Hum. Behav. 19, 21 (1988).

On the other hand, are these courts ignoring the very essence of the objective test because it is not meant to turn on whether a particular defendant "was exceptionally vulnerable to entrapment or to the temptations of crime . . . , but on whether the police conduct was so reprehensible that . . . it posed the objective threat of causing the average hypothetical person . . . to commit crimes"? *Juillet*, 475 N.W.2d at 802 (opinion of Cavanagh, C.J.). *See also State v. Zaccaro*, 574 A.2d 1256, 1263 & n.4 (Vt. 1990) (rejecting defendant's request that the jury be instructed to focus on the reasonable 22-year-old male college student who used cocaine, because such a standard "would lead to different results depending on the identity of the defendant"). In addition, does subjectifying the objective approach send us down "the most famous and well-traveled slippery slope in criminal law," leading to acquittals simply because "[t]he average person . . . placed in precisely the defendant's situation . . . would then become the defendant and, by definition, would respond as the defendant responded"? Louis M. Seidman, *The Supreme Court, Entrapment, and Our Criminal Justice Dilemma*, 1981 Sup. Ct. Rev. 111, 123.

---

5. Note that Nevada now follows the subjective approach to entrapment. *See Miller v. State*, 110 P.3d 53, 56 (Nev. 2005).

Jacobson v. United States

503 U.S. 540 (1992)

JUSTICE WHITE delivered the opinion of the Court.

On September 24, 1987, petitioner Keith Jacobson was indicted for violating a provision of the Child Protection Act of 1984, which criminalizes the knowing receipt through the mails of a "visual depiction [that] involves the use of a minor engaging in sexually explicit conduct . . . ." Petitioner defended on the ground that the Government entrapped him into committing the crime through a series of communications from undercover agents that spanned the 26 months preceding his arrest. . . . [He was convicted and sentenced to two years' probation and 250 hours of community service.]

Because the Government overstepped the line between setting a trap for the "unwary innocent" and the "unwary criminal," and as a matter of law failed to establish that petitioner was independently predisposed to commit the crime for which he was arrested, we reverse the Court of Appeals' judgment affirming his conviction.

I

In February 1984, petitioner, a 56-year-old veteran-turned-farmer who supported his elderly father in Nebraska, ordered two magazines and a brochure from a California adult bookstore. The magazines, entitled Bare Boys I and Bare Boys II, contained photographs of nude preteen and teenage boys. The contents of the magazines startled petitioner, who testified that he had expected to receive photographs of "young men 18 years or older." . . . The young men depicted in the magazines were not engaged in sexual activity, and petitioner's receipt of the magazines was legal under both federal and Nebraska law. Within three months, the law with respect to child pornography changed; Congress passed the Act illegalizing the receipt through the mails of sexually explicit depictions of children. In the very month that the new provision became law, postal inspectors found petitioner's name on the mailing list of the California bookstore that had mailed him Bare Boys I and II. There followed over the next 2½ years repeated efforts by two Government agencies, through five fictitious organizations and a bogus pen pal, to explore petitioner's willingness to break the new law by ordering sexually explicit photographs of children through the mail.

[At this point, the Court's opinion contains a lengthy description of the U.S. Postal Service's initial communications with Jacobson, which consisted of questionnaires and surveys sent under the name of three fictitious organizations, two of which claimed to be committed to the "right to read what we desire [and] to seek pleasure without restrictions being placed on us by outdated puritan morality" and to the belief that "arbitrarily imposed legislative sanctions restricting your sexual freedom should be rescinded through the legislative process." Jacobson's responses to these questionnaires indicated that he was "interested in teenage sexuality," that "his interest in 'preteen sex-homosexual' material was above average, but not high," and that he liked "good looking young guys (in their late teens and early 20's) doing their thing together." In response to one survey question, Jacobson wrote: "Not only sexual expression but freedom of the press is under attack. We must be ever vigilant to counter attack right wing fundamentalists who are determined to curtail our freedoms."]

By March 1987, 34 months had passed since the Government obtained petitioner's name from the mailing list of the California bookstore, and 26 months had passed since the Postal Service had commenced its mailings to petitioner. Although petitioner had responded to surveys and letters, the Government had no evidence that petitioner had ever intentionally possessed or been exposed to child pornography. The Postal Service had not checked petitioner's mail to determine whether he was receiving questionable mailings from persons—other than the Government— involved in the child pornography industry.

At this point, a second Government agency, the Customs Service, included petitioner in its own child pornography sting, "Operation Borderline," after receiving his name on lists submitted by the Postal Service. Using the name of a fictitious Canadian company called "Produit Outaouais," the Customs Service mailed petitioner a brochure advertising photographs of young boys engaging in sex. Petitioner placed an order that was never filled.

The Postal Service also continued its efforts in the Jacobson case, writing to petitioner as the "Far Eastern Trading Company Ltd." The letter began:

> As many of you know, much hysterical nonsense has appeared in the American media concerning "pornography" and what must be done to stop it from coming across your borders. This brief letter does not allow us to give much comments; however, why is your government spending millions of dollars to exercise international censorship while tons of drugs, which makes yours the world's most crime ridden country are passed through easily.

The letter went on to say:

> [W]e have devised a method of getting these to you without prying eyes of U.S. Customs seizing your mail. . . . After consultations with American solicitors, we have been advised that once we have posted our material through your system, it cannot be opened for any inspection without authorization of a judge.

The letter invited petitioner to send for more information. . . . Petitioner responded. A catalogue was sent, and petitioner ordered Boys Who Love Boys, a pornographic magazine depicting young boys engaged in various sexual activities. Petitioner was arrested after a controlled delivery of a photocopy of the magazine.

When petitioner was asked at trial why he placed such an order, he explained that the Government had succeeded in piquing his curiosity:

> Well, the statement was made of all the trouble and the hysteria over pornography and I wanted to see what the material was. It didn't describe the—I

didn't know for sure what kind of sexual action they were referring to in the Canadian letter. . . .

In petitioner's home, the Government found the Bare Boys magazines and materials that the Government had sent to him in the course of its protracted investigation, but no other materials that would indicate that petitioner collected or was actively interested in child pornography.

. . . .

II

. . . .

In their zeal to enforce the law, Government agents may not originate a criminal design, implant in an innocent person's mind the disposition to commit a criminal act, and then induce commission of the crime so that the Government may prosecute. Where the Government has induced an individual to break the law and the defense of entrapment is at issue, as it was in this case, the prosecution must prove beyond reasonable doubt that the defendant was disposed to commit the criminal act prior to first being approached by Government agents.[6]

Thus, an agent deployed to stop the traffic in illegal drugs may offer the opportunity to buy or sell drugs, and, if the offer is accepted, make an arrest on the spot or later. In such a typical case, or in a more elaborate "sting" operation involving government-sponsored fencing where the defendant is simply provided with the opportunity to commit a crime, the entrapment defense is of little use because the ready commission of the criminal act amply demonstrates the defendant's predisposition. Had the agents in this case simply offered petitioner the opportunity to order child pornography through the mails, and petitioner—who must be presumed

---

6. [n.2] Inducement is not at issue in this case. The Government does not dispute that it induced petitioner to commit the crime. The sole issue is whether the Government carried its burden of proving that petitioner was predisposed to violate the law *before* the Government intervened. The dissent is mistaken in claiming that this is an innovation in entrapment law and in suggesting that the Government's conduct prior to the moment of solicitation is irrelevant. . . . Indeed, the proposition that the accused must be predisposed prior to contact with law enforcement officers is so firmly established that the Government conceded the point at oral argument, submitting that the evidence it developed during the course of its investigation was probative because it indicated petitioner's state of mind prior to the commencement of the Government's investigation.

This long established standard in no way encroaches upon Government investigatory activities. Indeed, the Government's internal guidelines for undercover operations provide that an inducement to commit a crime should not be offered unless:

"(a) [T]here is a reasonable indication, based on information developed through informants or other means, that the subject is engaging, has engaged, or is likely to engage in illegal activity of a similar type; *or*

"(b) The opportunity for illegal activity has been structured so that there is reason for believing that persons drawn to the opportunity, or brought to it, are predisposed to engage in the contemplated illegal activity." Attorney General's Guidelines on FBI Undercover Operations (Dec. 31, 1980), *reprinted in* S. Rep. No. 97-682, p. 551 (1982).

to know the law — had promptly availed himself of this criminal opportunity, it is unlikely that his entrapment defense would have warranted a jury instruction.

But that is not what happened here. By the time petitioner finally placed his order, he had already been the target of 26 months of repeated mailings and communications from Government agents and fictitious organizations. Therefore, although he had become predisposed to break the law by May 1987, it is our view that the Government did not prove that this predisposition was independent and not the product of the attention that the Government had directed at petitioner since January 1985.

The prosecution's evidence of predisposition falls into two categories: evidence developed prior to the Postal Service's mail campaign, and that developed during the course of the investigation. The sole piece of preinvestigation evidence is petitioner's 1984 order and receipt of the Bare Boys magazines. But this is scant if any proof of petitioner's predisposition to commit an illegal act, the criminal character of which a defendant is presumed to know. It may indicate a predisposition to view sexually-oriented photographs that are responsive to his sexual tastes; but evidence that merely indicates a generic inclination to act within a broad range, not all of which is criminal, is of little probative value in establishing predisposition.

Furthermore, petitioner was acting within the law at the time he received these magazines. . . . Evidence of predisposition to do what once was lawful is not, by itself, sufficient to show predisposition to do what is now illegal, for there is a common understanding that most people obey the law even when they disapprove of it. . . . This is particularly true given petitioner's unchallenged testimony that he did not know until they arrived that the magazines would depict minors.

The prosecution's evidence gathered during the investigation also fails to carry the Government's burden. Petitioner's responses to the many communications prior to the ultimate criminal act were at most indicative of certain personal inclinations, including a predisposition to view photographs of preteen sex and a willingness to promote a given agenda by supporting lobbying organizations. Even so, petitioner's responses hardly support an inference that he would commit the crime of receiving child pornography through the mails.[7] Furthermore, a person's inclinations and "fantasies . . . are his own and beyond the reach of government . . . ."

On the other hand, the strong arguable inference is that, by waving the banner of individual rights and disparaging the legitimacy and constitutionality of efforts to restrict the availability of sexually explicit materials, the Government not only excited petitioner's interest in sexually explicit materials banned by law but also exerted substantial pressure on petitioner to obtain and read such material as part of a fight against censorship and the infringement of individual rights. . . .

---

7. [n.3] We do not hold, as the dissent suggests, that the Government was required to prove that petitioner knowingly violated the law. We simply conclude that proof that petitioner engaged in legal conduct and possessed certain generalized personal inclinations is not sufficient evidence to prove beyond a reasonable doubt that he would have been predisposed to commit the crime charged independent of the Government's coaxing.

Petitioner's ready response to these solicitations cannot be enough to establish beyond reasonable doubt that he was predisposed, prior to the Government acts intended to create predisposition, to commit the crime of receiving child pornography through the mails. The evidence that petitioner was ready and willing to commit the offense came only after the Government had devoted 2½ years to convincing him that he had or should have the right to engage in the very behavior proscribed by law. Rational jurors could not say beyond a reasonable doubt that petitioner possessed the requisite predisposition prior to the Government's investigation and that it existed independent of the Government's many and varied approaches to petitioner. . . .

. . . When the Government's quest for convictions leads to the apprehension of an otherwise law-abiding citizen who, if left to his own devices, likely would have never run afoul of the law, the courts should intervene.

JUSTICE O'CONNOR, with whom THE CHIEF JUSTICE and JUSTICE KENNEDY join, and with whom JUSTICE SCALIA joins except as to Part II, dissenting.

Keith Jacobson was offered only two opportunities to buy child pornography through the mail. Both times, he ordered. Both times, he asked for opportunities to buy more. He needed no Government agent to coax, threaten, or persuade him; no one played on his sympathies, friendship, or suggested that his committing the crime would further a greater good. In fact, no Government agent even contacted him face-to-face. The Government contends that from the enthusiasm with which Mr. Jacobson responded to the chance to commit a crime, a reasonable jury could permissibly infer beyond a reasonable doubt that he was predisposed to commit the crime. I agree.

The first time the Government sent Mr. Jacobson a catalog of illegal materials, he ordered a set of photographs advertised as picturing "young boys in sex action fun." He enclosed the following note with his order: "I received your brochure and decided to place an order. If I like your product, I will order more later." For reasons undisclosed in the record, Mr. Jacobson's order was never delivered.

The second time the Government sent a catalog of illegal materials, Mr. Jacobson ordered a magazine called "Boys Who Love Boys," described as: "11 year old and 14 year old boys get it on in every way possible. Oral, anal sex and heavy masturbation. If you love boys, you will be delighted with this." Along with his order, Mr. Jacobson sent the following note: "Will order other items later. I want to be discreet in order to protect you and me."

Government agents admittedly did not offer Mr. Jacobson the chance to buy child pornography right away. Instead, they first sent questionnaires in order to make sure that he was generally interested in the subject matter. Indeed, a "cold call" in such a business would not only risk rebuff and suspicion, but might also shock and offend the uninitiated, or expose minors to suggestive materials. Mr. Jacobson's responses to the questionnaires gave the investigators reason to think he would be interested in photographs depicting preteen sex.

The Court, however, concludes that a reasonable jury could not have found Mr. Jacobson to be predisposed beyond a reasonable doubt on the basis of his responses to the Government's catalogs, even though it admits that, by that time, he was predisposed to commit the crime. . . .

I

. . . .

Today, the Court holds that Government conduct may be considered to create a predisposition to commit a crime, even before any Government action to induce the commission of the crime. In my view, this holding changes entrapment doctrine. Generally, the inquiry is whether a suspect is predisposed before the Government induces the commission of the crime, not before the Government makes initial contact with him. There is no dispute here that the Government's questionnaires and letters were not sufficient to establish inducement; they did not even suggest that Mr. Jacobson should engage in any illegal activity. If all the Government had done was to send these materials, Mr. Jacobson's entrapment defense would fail. Yet the Court holds that the Government must prove not only that a suspect was predisposed to commit the crime before the opportunity to commit it arose, but also before the Government came on the scene.

The rule that preliminary Government contact can create a predisposition has the potential to be misread by lower courts as well as criminal investigators as requiring that the Government must have sufficient evidence of a defendant's predisposition *before it ever seeks to contact him.* Surely the Court cannot intend to impose such a requirement, for it would mean that the Government must have a reasonable suspicion of criminal activity before it begins an investigation, a condition that we have never before imposed. The Court denies that its new rule will affect run-of-the-mill sting operations, and one hopes that it means what it says. Nonetheless, after this case, every defendant will claim that something the Government agent did before soliciting the crime "created" a predisposition that was not there before. For example, a bribe taker will claim that the description of the amount of money available was so enticing that it implanted a disposition to accept the bribe later offered. A drug buyer will claim that the description of the drug's purity and effects was so tempting that it created the urge to try it for the first time. In short, the Court's opinion could be read to prohibit the Government from advertising the seductions of criminal activity as part of its sting operation, for fear of creating a predisposition in its suspects. That limitation would be especially likely to hamper sting operations such as this one, which mimic the advertising done by genuine purveyors of pornography. No doubt the Court would protest that its opinion does not stand for so broad a proposition, but the apparent lack of a principled basis for distinguishing these scenarios exposes a flaw in the more limited rule the Court today adopts.

The Court's rule is all the more troubling because it does not distinguish between Government conduct that merely highlights the temptation of the crime itself, and Government conduct that threatens, coerces, or leads a suspect to commit a crime in order to fulfill some other obligation. For example, in *Sorrells*, the Government agent repeatedly asked for illegal liquor, coaxing the defendant to accede on the ground that "one former war buddy would get liquor for another." In *Sherman*, the Government agent played on the defendant's sympathies, pretending to be going through drug withdrawal and begging the defendant to relieve his distress by helping him buy drugs.

The Government conduct in this case is not comparable. While the Court states that the Government "exerted substantial pressure on petitioner to obtain and read such material as part of a fight against censorship and the infringement of individual rights," one looks at the record in vain for evidence of such "substantial pressure." The most one finds is letters advocating legislative action to liberalize obscenity laws, letters which could easily be ignored or thrown away. Much later, the Government sent separate mailings of catalogs of illegal materials. Nowhere did the Government suggest that the proceeds of the sale of the illegal materials would be used to support legislative reforms. While one of the [early] letters suggested that lobbying efforts would be funded by sales from a catalog, the catalogs actually sent, nearly a year later, were from different fictitious entities (Produit Outaouais and Far Eastern Trading Company), and gave no suggestion that money would be used for any political purposes. . . . In sum, the Court fails to construe the evidence in the light most favorable to the Government, and fails to draw all reasonable inferences in the Government's favor. It was surely reasonable for the jury to infer that Mr. Jacobson was predisposed beyond a reasonable doubt, even if other inferences from the evidence were also possible.

II

The second puzzling thing about the Court's opinion is its redefinition of predisposition. The Court acknowledges that "petitioner's responses to the many communications prior to the ultimate criminal act were . . . indicative of certain personal inclinations, including a predisposition to view photographs of preteen sex . . . ." If true, this should have settled the matter; Mr. Jacobson was predisposed to engage in the illegal conduct. Yet, the Court concludes, "petitioner's responses hardly support an inference that he would commit the crime of receiving child pornography through the mails."

The Court seems to add something new to the burden of proving predisposition. Not only must the Government show that a defendant was predisposed to engage in the illegal conduct, here, receiving photographs of minors engaged in sex, but also that the defendant was predisposed to break the law knowingly in order to do so. The statute violated here, however, does not require proof of specific intent to break the law; it requires only knowing receipt of visual depictions produced by using minors engaged in sexually explicit conduct. Under the Court's analysis, however, the Government must prove more to show predisposition than it need prove in order to convict.

The Court ignores the judgment of Congress that specific intent is not an element of the crime of receiving sexually explicit photographs of minors. The elements of predisposition should track the elements of the crime. . . . In sum, although the fact that Mr. Jacobson's purchases of Bare Boys I and Bare Boys II were legal at the time may have some relevance to the question of predisposition, it is not, as the Court suggests, dispositive.

Notes and Questions

1. The Timing of the Defendant's Predisposition. The *Jacobson* majority focused on the defendant's predisposition prior to the time he was first "approached" by government agents. Does this view make sense because "the underlying rationale of the entrapment defense is that a person should not be prosecuted for criminal activity instigated by the government," and therefore "it should not matter whether the activity of the government which caused the disposition came before or after the solicitation"? Eulis Simien, Jr., *Criminal Law and Procedure: 1991–92 in Review*, 53 La. L. Rev. 771, 773 (1993). Or is it more appropriate to focus, as the *Jacobson* dissent did, on the defendant's predisposition at the time government agents first suggested the crime because "the target's actions during negotiations leading to the offense" may indicate predisposition? Roger Park, *The Entrapment Controversy*, 60 Minn. L. Rev. 163, 200 (1976).

Note that a number of courts have concluded that *Jacobson* does not foreclose the prosecution from using evidence of actions defendants took *after* the government contacted them to show they were predisposed *before* they were approached by the government. *See, e.g., United States v. Nguyen*, 413 F.3d 1170, 1178 (10th Cir. 2005) (citing cases). *But cf. United States v. Mayfield*, 771 F.3d 417, 442 (7th Cir. 2014) (en banc) (warning that a defendant's "active engagement in the scheme *after* the government's extended efforts to procure his participation has limited bearing on his predisposition when the government first proposed it" because, if "the government's conduct might have ensnared a person who otherwise would not have committed the crime, . . . 'it is irrelevant that the entrapment was so effective as to make him not only a willing but an eager participant'").

2. Requiring Reasonable Suspicion to Approach a Target. Does the *Jacobson* majority's ruling on the timing question in essence imply that law enforcement officials need reasonable suspicion of predisposition before they approach a particular target? Even if *Jacobson* did not expressly require reasonable suspicion, will the "practical effect" of the Court's decision be to "strongly discourage lengthy sting operations unless evidence of predisposition is available before the onset of undercover activities"? Elena L. Garella, *Reshaping the Federal Entrapment Defense:* Jacobson v. United States, 68 Wash. L. Rev. 185, 202 (1993). *But cf. United States v. Kussmaul*, 987 F.2d 345, 348–49 (6th Cir. 1993) (rejecting the defendant's argument that *Jacobson* obligates the government to have reasonable suspicion before instituting sting operations); *Commonwealth v. Mance*, 652 A.2d 299, 301–02 (Pa. 1995) (same).

Would it have been preferable for the Court to explicitly mandate that government agents have reasonable suspicion of predisposition before attempting to persuade a target to commit a crime? The reasonable suspicion requirement has been defended on the grounds that it would limit law enforcement's otherwise "'untrammelled discretion to test the criminal propensities of any citizen,'" thereby helping to ensure that "the police detect but not create crime." 2 Wayne R. LaFave et al., Criminal Procedure §5.4(b), at 660–61 (4th ed. 2012) (quoting Richard D. Cleary, Case Comment, *Due Process Defense When Government Agents Instigate and Abet Crime*, 67 Geo. L.J. 1455, 1471 (1979)). Critics of the reasonable suspicion requirement respond, however, that it "unduly restricts reasonably designed police undercover operations implemented to ferret out crime" and that "the well-settled law of entrapment . . . is sufficient protection against the possibility of police excess." *Foster v. State*, 13 P.3d 61, 64 (Nev. 2000) (overturning state court precedent requiring reasonable suspicion, noting that Nevada was "in the minority if not the only remaining jurisdiction" to impose such a restriction on undercover police activities). Likewise, one commentator has pointed out the "inherent inconsistency between recognizing the need for undercover investigations in order to detect crimes that, because they are covert, are difficult to detect by other means, and requiring that evidence of these crimes be obtained by other means before an undercover investigation may be used." Katherine Goldwasser, *After Abscam: An Examination of Congressional Proposals to Limit Targeting Discretion in Federal Undercover Investigations*, 36 Emory L.J. 75, 105 (1987). But are "[o]perations directed at targets whom the police have no reason to suspect . . . an inefficient as well as arbitrary means of law enforcement"? *United States v. Luttrell*, 889 F.2d 806, 813 (9th Cir. 1989), *vacated*, 923 F.2d 764 (9th Cir. 1991) (en banc). (For further discussion of proposals to require reasonable suspicion, see Note 5(d) below.)

3. The Nature of the Defendant's Predisposition; "Positional" Predisposition. Was the *Jacobson* majority right to require proof that the defendant was predisposed to commit the crime of receiving child pornography through the mails? Why wasn't it sufficient that Jacobson was predisposed to view or receive child pornography?

In *United States v. Hollingsworth*, 27 F.3d 1196, 1198 (7th Cir. 1994) (en banc), a closely divided court concluded that the *Jacobson* decision redefined "predisposition" such that it is no longer enough that the defendant was "'willing,' in the sense of psychologically prepared, to commit the crime"—a definition the court of appeals majority thought would have applied to Jacobson. Instead, the Seventh Circuit read language appearing at the end of the majority opinion in *Jacobson* (the reference to the "otherwise law-abiding citizen who, if left to his own devices, likely would have never run afoul of the law") to add a "positional" element to the concept of predisposition—to require that the defendant be "so situated by reason of previous training or experience or occupation or acquaintances that it is likely that if the government had not induced him to commit the crime some criminal would have done so." *Id.* at 1200, 1199. Applying this standard, the Seventh Circuit found insufficient evidence of predisposition on the part of the "objectively harmless" defendants in that case, who did not have "underworld contacts, financial acumen or assets, access to foreign banks or bankers, or other assets" and therefore had "no prayer of becoming money launderers without the government's aid." *Id.* at 1202.

The dissenting judges in *Hollingsworth* accused the majority of "chang[ing] the 'ready' defendant from one who is inclined, feeling or exhibiting no reluctance, to one on the point of acting," thereby affording a defense to "a very willing but also not very well organized or inept first offender." *Id.* at 1215, 1217 (Ripple, J., dissenting). The Ninth Circuit has rejected the Seventh Circuit's requirement of "positional" predisposition, interpreting *Jacobson* as merely applying "settled entrapment law" and therefore not intending to make "[a] person's ability to commit a crime . . . a separate element" of the entrapment defense. *United States v. Thickstun*, 110 F.3d 1394, 1398 (9th Cir. 1997). *See also United States v. Cromitie*, 727 F.3d 194, 216–17 (2d Cir. 2013) (likewise refusing to follow *Hollingsworth*). *But cf.* Richard A. McAdams, *Reforming Entrapment Doctrine in* United States v Hollingsworth, 74 U. Chi. L. Rev. 1795, 1809, 1805 (2007) (arguing that *Hollingsworth*'s approach makes the law of entrapment "more rational" by exculpating one who "poses no threat to society because, if the police leave him alone, he will not offend").

4. Revisiting the Debate Between the Subjective and Objective Approaches to Entrapment. Does the Court's reasoning in *Jacobson* more closely resemble the objective approach than the subjective approach the Court purported to be applying? Does the outcome of the case essentially reflect the majority's "tacit disapproval" of the "misallocation of police resources" used to apprehend Jacobson, rather than its view that Jacobson lacked predisposition? Elena L. Garella, *Reshaping the Federal Entrapment Defense:* Jacobson v. United States, 68 Wash. L. Rev. 185, 203 (1993). Consider Douglas O. Linder, *Journeying Through the Valley of Evil*, 71 N.C. L. Rev. 1111, 1133–37 (1993):

> Child pornography had been all but eradicated in the United States when the Federal Government began sending advertisements and letters to people like [Jacobson]. The Attorney General's Commission on Pornography reported in 1986 that federal statutes enacted in the 1970s aimed at child pornography distributors had "effectively halted the bulk of the commercial child pornography industry." The report also suggested that 1984 federal statutes criminalizing the receipt of child pornography had largely eliminated the market for noncommercial child pornography. . . .

> By far the largest advertiser, manufacturer, and distributor of child pornography is the United States Government. In its zeal to promote itself as the protector of family values, the government has implemented elaborate sting operations to identify and capture individuals . . . , many of whom had never before purchased child pornography. . . .

> The stigma and shame associated with an interest in child pornography led planners of the sting to "expect" suicides, and, predictably, four happened. [Two of the sting's targets] shot [themselves] just prior to

arraignment. [A third] committed suicide hours before his indictment was to be announced publicly. [The fourth] left a suicide note stating that he had been "cursed with a demon for a sexual preference."

5. The Entrapment Defense in Other Contexts. Should any of the defendants in the following cases have an entrapment defense?

(a) An undercover police officer, posing as a homeless alcoholic, is lying on a corner with a $100 bill protruding from his back pocket. Should an entrapment defense be unavailable to one who walks by and takes the money from the seemingly unconscious alcoholic because "there was no importuning, cajoling, badgering or affirmative measures taken to induce [the defendant] to commit the crime"? *Sheriff, Washoe County v. Hawkins*, 752 P.2d 769, 779 (Nev. 1988) (Steffen, J., dissenting).

The *Hawkins* majority concluded that the defendant had been entrapped on similar facts because there had been no reports of comparable crimes against helpless street people in the area. Therefore, the court reasoned, the decoy operation did "not address any actual crime problem," but instead "planted the idea of crime in the mind[]" of the defendant, "creat[ing]" crime rather than "uncover[ing]" it. *Id.* at 771 (majority opinion). The majority also noted that "when the defendant ultimately succumbed to temptation, he did no more than slip the exposed money from the decoy's pocket and walk away," and "neither engaged in acts of violence, nor in attempts to find other valuables on the decoy's person." *Id. See also Cruz v. State*, 465 So. 2d 516, 522 (Fla. 1985) ("the criminal scenario here, with $150 . . . enticingly protruding from the back pocket of a person seemingly incapable of noticing its removal, carries with it the 'substantial risk that [the] offense will be committed by persons other than those who are ready to commit it' "); *Oliver v. State*, 703 P.2d 869, 870 (Nev. 1985) ("the decoy displayed his ten-dollar-bill in a manner calculated to tempt any needy person in the area, whether immediately disposed to crime or not").[8]

The *Hawkins* majority criticized this type of decoy operation as having little "social utility." Specifically, the court noted that these operations prevent the police from "utiliz[ing] their energies discerning real crime elsewhere" and create "the probable social cost of making criminals and convicts out of productive persons, who may upon release never return to the ranks of the gainfully employed." *Hawkins*, 752 P.2d at 774, 775. Are these arguments persuasive, or is it "a sad commentary on our society if the mere presence of a vulnerable individual [is deemed] capable of inducing an ordinary person to succumb to crime"? *State v. Long*, 523 A.2d 672, 677 (N.J. Super. Ct. App. Div. 1987). Whatever the better answer to these questions, should "judges shielded from political responsibility" be given "the power to make [such] value choice[s]"? Louis M. Seidman, *The Supreme Court, Entrapment, and Our Criminal Justice Dilemma*, 1981 SUP. CT. REV. 111, 144.

---

8. Both Florida and Nevada now adhere to the subjective definition of the entrapment defense, and the standards applied in *Cruz* and *Oliver* have thus been superseded. *See Munoz v. State*, 629 So. 2d 90, 99 (Fla. 1993); *Miller v. State*, 110 P.3d 53, 56 (Nev. 2005).

If an entrapment claim is available in at least some of these decoy cases, should the success of the defense depend on how well-dressed the unconscious decoy was? If so, which way does that factor cut? *Compare Hawkins*, 752 P.2d at 776 (rejecting any such distinction), *with id.* at 778 (Steffen, J., dissenting) ("[t]hose who pass [a well-dressed decoy can] only speculate as to the cause of his plight," and "[t]he currency observably protruding from an envelope in his rear pocket [is] not hanging as an invitation to removal"). Should it matter whether the defendant took money that was sticking out of the decoy's pocket or instead reached into the pocket and retrieved a wallet that was previously hidden from view? *See State v. Dawson*, 681 So. 2d 1206, 1209 (Fla. Dist. Ct. App. 1996) (distinguishing cases involving unconscious decoys in rejecting entrapment claim made by a defendant who took a "closed [camera] bag bearing identification, the contents of which could not be known without opening" it, from an airport telephone booth); *Miller v. State*, 110 P.3d 53, 56–57 (Nev. 2005) (contrasting a "decoy officer [who] poses as an unconscious vagrant with exposed money hanging from his pockets" from "a realistic decoy" walking down the street with the edges of some bills visible in a shirt pocket). *See also People v. Watson*, 990 P.2d 1031 (Cal. 2000) (upholding trial court's refusal to instruct the jury on entrapment where the defendant stole an unlocked car left in a parking lot with the keys in the ignition).

(b) In a "reverse sting" operation, the defendant agrees to purchase a controlled substance or other prohibited item from an undercover police officer. Should a defendant caught in a reverse sting have a valid entrapment claim because "[t]here is a decided difference between . . . furnishing contraband with which to commit [a crime], and [simply] setting the stage to catch an accused in the execution of criminal designs of his own conception"? *Barnes v. State*, 493 So. 2d 313, 315 (Miss. 1986). In a reverse sting, is "the criminal design . . . that of the [government agent] rather than the defendant" because the agent is the one supplying the controlled substance? *Id. See also Pezzella v. State*, 513 So. 2d 1328, 1330 (Fla. Dist. Ct. App. 1987) ("by supplying the drugs involved in the transaction, the police did not 'facilitate discovery or suppression of ongoing illicit traffic in drugs'"); *State v. Kummer*, 481 N.W.2d 437, 441–44 (N.D. 1992) (applying objective standard and finding entrapment as a matter of law). Moreover, is the reverse buy "a dangerous and unnecessary law enforcement technique" because "[i]f an agent suspects that a target is dealing in contraband, the agent can attempt to make a decoy purchase from him"? Roger Park, *The Entrapment Controversy*, 60 Minn. L. Rev. 163, 191 (1976).

On the other hand, should the entrapment defense fail in cases involving reverse stings because there is no difference between an undercover sale and an undercover purchase of contraband, and because the government is merely providing an opportunity to commit crime to one who is ready and willing to do so? A number of courts have taken this position, rejecting defenses raised in reverse-sting cases. *See, e.g., State v. Agrabante*, 830 P.2d 492, 500 (Haw. 1992); *People v. Butler*, 512 N.W.2d 583, 583 (Mich. 1994); *Moore v. State*, 534 So. 2d 557, 559–60 (Miss. 1988).

Assuming the permissibility of the reverse sting, what about "supply-and-buy" cases, where "the Government . . . is on all sides of a transaction—both buyer and seller"? *United States v. Lakhani*, 480 F.3d 171, 182 (3d Cir. 2007). Is the supply-and-buy technique sufficiently different from the reverse sting to justify a different outcome when the defendant claims entrapment? In *Baca v. State*, 742 P.2d 1043 (N.M. 1987), for example, a government informant asked Baca to sell cocaine to the informant's "friend" (an undercover police officer) on the pretense that the informant owed the "friend" money and was therefore afraid of him. When Baca agreed, the informant bought the cocaine and gave it to Baca, who then sold it to the undercover officer. In reversing Baca's drug distribution conviction on the grounds that he was entrapped, the court reasoned as follows:

> It was the police informant . . . who procured the cocaine, and it was he who arranged for the purported sale between Baca and [the undercover officer]. Baca acted as nothing more than a conduit, conveying cocaine from a police informant to a policeman. Such detailed involvement on the part of the police in the cocaine transaction exceeds proper investigative procedure, and puts the police into the category of "instigators" of the criminal conduct . . . .

Id. at 1045; *see also Tanner v. State*, 566 So. 2d 1246, 1249 (Miss. 1990) (criticizing the supply-and-buy technique because it "vests in the Bureau of Narcotics great power to decide who is guilty"). *Cf. United States v. Brooks*, 215 F.3d 842, 846, 844 (8th Cir. 2000) (finding "an improper level of governmental involvement and inducement," and thus "entrapment as a matter of law," in drug distribution case where a government agent sold Brooks (a heroin addict) six packets of heroin and then, later the same day, repeatedly asked Brooks to return some of the heroin, claiming that the agent's "supply . . . had run out, and . . . he had a customer who needed heroin badly as she was suffering from withdrawal"; the agent ultimately convinced Brooks to return two of the packets after threatening to "cut off Brooks' own heroin supply").

In *United States v. Lakhani*, by contrast, the defendant—an international arms dealer whose previous sales were, however, apparently legal—was approached by an informant who claimed to be associated with a terrorist group that wanted to buy missiles to use against American airplanes. When Lakhani was unable to produce any missiles, Russian and American law enforcement officials created a mock missile, which Lakhani bought from undercover Russian officials and then sold to the informant. In upholding the jury's rejection of Lakhani's entrapment defense, the Third Circuit found sufficient evidence of predisposition. The court relied on Lakhani's enthusiasm about the transaction and noted in addition that "other than the missile's actual transportation and border crossing, Lakhani accomplished many technical aspects of the deal himself, without the suggestion or aid of the Government, . . . includ[ing], not insignificantly, the entire money laundering scheme and fraudulent bill of lading." *Lakhani*, 480 F.3d at 180.

For examples of other supply-and-buy cases in which entrapment claims have been rejected, see *People v. Marshall*, 427 N.E.2d 1333, 1335 (Ill. App. Ct. 1981) (applying the subjective test); *People v. Jamieson*, 461 N.W.2d 884, 891–97 (Mich. 1990) (applying the objective test). For discussion of the Supreme Court's treatment of a supply-and-buy case, see the description of *Hampton v. United States* in Note 6 below.

(c) In thinking about the supply-and-buy scenarios discussed in the prior Note, is *United States v. Lakhani*, 480 F.3d 171, 183 (3d Cir. 2007), distinguishable from the drug cases like *Baca* on any ground other than the fact that, as the Third Circuit noted, "[w]e have here a Government investigation of international terrorism"? In another terrorism prosecution, *United States v. Cromitie*, 727 F.3d 194, 217 (2d Cir. 2013), the Second Circuit rejected the concept of "positional" disposition described above in Note 3 on the grounds that "[a] person who has a pre-existing design to commit terrorist acts against United States interests or who promptly agrees to play a part in such activity should not escape punishment just because he was not in a position to obtain . . . missiles and launch them at United States airplanes." Does that view allow the government to make "naked attempt[s] to manufacture predisposition evidence for a vulnerable group that perhaps share[s] violent aspirations but likely [does] not have the capability or initiative to commit an act of terrorism"? Jon Sherman, *"A Person Otherwise Innocent": Policing Entrapment in Preventative, Undercover Counterterrorism Investigations*, 11 U. Pa. J. Const. L. 1475, 1500 (2009). Or was the Second Circuit right to believe that the government "need not leave [such individuals] at large until a real terrorist" comes along and "supplies real missiles"? *Cromitie*, 727 F.3d at 217.

More generally, should different entrapment rules apply in terrorism investigations, where undercover operations have become "a mainstay" and "have changed in response to the post-9/11 focus on prevention"? David K. Shipler, *Terrorist Plots, Hatched by the F.B.I.*, N.Y. Times, Apr. 29, 2012, at SR4 (quoting an ACLU lawyer and former FBI agent as saying that "[p]rior to 9/11 it would be very unusual for the F.B.I. to present a crime opportunity that wasn't in the scope of the activities that a person was already involved in"). *See also* Jesse J. Norris & Hanna Grol-Prokopczyk, *Estimating the Prevalence of Entrapment in Post-9/11 Terrorism Cases*, 105 J. Crim. L. & Criminology 609, 673 (2015) (finding, in empirical study of all 580 post-9/11 terrorism prosecutions, a "widespread" use of the core indicators of entrapment in the 317 cases involving an informant or undercover agent, especially in those with "jihadi and left-wing defendants," and concluding that about nine percent of all jihadi cases and five percent of those involving undercover operations represented "genuine threats" to national security).

Should the internal Justice Department guidelines quoted in footnote 2 of the Supreme Court's opinion in *Jacobson*, which bar an undercover operation absent some reason to believe the target was predisposed to commit the crime, be extended to terrorism investigations? *See* Wadie E. Said, *The Terrorist Informant*, 85 Wash. L. Rev. 687 (2010) (endorsing this approach). *But cf.* U.S. Dep't of Justice, The Attorney General's Guidelines for Domestic FBI Operations 31 (Sept. 29, 2008), *available at* www.justice.gov/ag/readingroom/guidelines.pdf (exempting national security and foreign intelligence cases from this requirement). Should a "more robust" entrapment standard apply at least in those terrorism cases where defendants are charged with extremely inchoate crimes like conspiracy, as opposed to "attempted or completed offenses," in order to "protect defendants from impermissible implantation of criminal intent"? Sherman, *supra*, at 1500. Alternatively, should entrapment be a more difficult defense to mount in terrorism prosecutions given the severity of the crime? Should "the rare person who actually succumbs" and "agree[s] to engage in such a horrible act" be presumed to be predisposed because "most citizens would find this crime so offensive that it outweighs almost any inducement"? Dru Stevenson, *Entrapment and Terrorism*, 49 B.C. L. Rev. 125, 138, 144 (2008); *see also id.* at 215 (noting that "[s]ting operations are discreet, narrowly targeted, and pragmatic, avoiding the extensive privacy invasions that [dragnet] surveillance brings").

(d) When the 2013 film *American Hustle* opens with the words "[s]ome of this actually happened," it is referring to the FBI undercover operation known as Abscam, which began in 1978 to investigate political corruption, initially in New Jersey and then in the United States Congress. Aided by Melvin Weinberg, a convicted con artist who assisted with the investigation in exchange for a sentence of three years' probation on a mail and wire fraud conviction (as well as a monthly fee that started at $1,000 and eventually grew to $3,000), FBI agents approached a number of politicians, claiming to represent two wealthy Arab sheiks who wanted to immigrate to this country and invest in American business and real estate. The agents offered to pay generous sums of money ($50,000 for Senators and $25,000 for Representatives) in return for assistance with government contracts and immigration matters. The Abscam investigation culminated in the conviction of one U.S. Senator and six members of the House of Representatives, as well as a number of lawyers and local public officials, on charges of conspiracy, racketeering, extortion, and bribery. *See generally* Bennett L. Gershman, *Abscam, the Judiciary, and the Ethics of Entrapment*, 91 Yale L.J. 1565, 1571–75 (1982); Maura F.J. Whelan, *Lead Us Not into (Unwarranted) Temptation: A Proposal to Replace the Entrapment Defense with a Reasonable-Suspicion Requirement*, 133 U. Pa. L. Rev. 1193, 1200–03 (1985); Matthew W. Kinskey, Note, *American Hustle: Reflections on Abscam and the Entrapment Defense*, 41 Am. J. Crim. L. 233 (2014).

Did the Abscam investigation "stretch the concept of inducement . . . to its limit" because "[h]uge amounts of money were dangled as bait"? Gershman, *supra*, at 1583–84. Or were the defendants' entrapment claims properly rejected because "$50,000 is simply not an overpowering sum of money" and, in any event, "[n]o matter how much money is offered to a government official as a bribe or gratuity, he should be punished if he accepts"? *United States v. Myers*, 527 F. Supp. 1206, 1228 (E.D.N.Y. 1981), *aff'd*, 692 F.2d 823 (2d Cir. 1982).

Representative Richard Kelly was one of the politicians implicated in the scheme. Although he initially rejected the agents' offers, he was ultimately videotaped stuffing $25,000 into his pockets after promising that he would introduce private legislation if necessary to permit the sheiks to immigrate. Like the other Abscam defendants, he was convicted despite his claim of entrapment. *See United States v. Kelly*, 707 F.2d 1460 (D.C. Cir. 1983). Is it relevant that Kelly and the other Abscam defendants did nothing to solicit the agents' offers, and "there was not even a scent of suspicion of criminal conduct . . . by Kelly or any other individual," so that "the sole objective of the operation" was to "test the virtue of members of Congress"? *United States v. Kelly*, 539 F. Supp. 363, 373 (D.D.C. 1982), *rev'd*, 707 F.2d 1460 (D.C. Cir. 1983). Does the entrapment defense's lack of success in the Abscam cases leave "the police . . . free to utilize unlimited government resources and irresistible temptations to seduce unsuspecting persons who might not otherwise commit crimes"? Gershman, *supra*, at 1580.

In the wake of the Abscam investigation, the Attorney General issued the Guidelines on FBI Undercover Operations cited in footnote 2 of the Supreme Court's opinion in *Jacobson*. In addition, committees in both the House and Senate held hearings on undercover investigations. Both committees ultimately recommended legislation that would have required probable cause or reasonable suspicion before federal law enforcement officials could begin an undercover investigation or offer an inducement to the target of an ongoing investigation, and the House Committee even proposed a warrant requirement. A bill incorporating the Senate Committee's recommendations was introduced in the Senate but died when Congress adjourned, and no legislation was ever introduced in the House. *See* Katherine Goldwasser, *After Abscam: An Examination of Congressional Proposals to Limit Targeting Discretion in Federal Undercover Investigations*, 36 EMORY L.J. 75, 80 n.19, 90–97 (1987).

Are the safeguards endorsed by the congressional committees particularly important for political corruption investigations because "[t]he potential for hidden discrimination and arbitrariness is greatest with respect to federal undercover investigations of public officials," who are "especially likely to make political enemies, and to be targeted for investigation for that reason"? *Id.* at 102. *See also* Gershman, *supra*, at 1585 (warning that "integrity testing could easily become a tool of political oppression" used to "silence enemies, opponents, and political dissidents"). On the other hand, is it unwise to impose restrictions on undercover operations like Abscam because political corruption is the "type of elusive, difficult to detect, covert crime which may justify Government infiltration and undercover activities"? *United States v. Alexandro*, 675 F.2d 34, 42 (2d Cir. 1982). Do the congressional efforts to restrict undercover operations in the aftermath of Abscam simply reflect the fact that Congress gets "serious about [the dangers of undercover operations] only when [its] own ox is being gored"? *FBI Undercover Operations: Hearings Before the Subcomm. on Civil and Constitutional Rights of the House Comm. on the Judiciary*, 97th Cong., 2d Sess. 344 (1982) (statement of Rep. Hyde).

6. The Due Process Defense for Outrageous Police Conduct. The Supreme Court's entrapment decisions are not based on the Constitution, and thus are not binding on the states. As a result, the states remain free to determine the contours of the entrapment defense, just as they have substantial leeway generally in defining crimes and defenses. In *Russell*, however, the Court left open the possibility that it might "some day be presented with a situation in which the conduct of law enforcement agents is so outrageous that due process principles would absolutely bar the government from invoking judicial processes to obtain a conviction." *Russell*, 411 U.S. at 431–32 (citing *Rochin v. California*, 342 U.S. 165 (1952)). But the Court implied that

that standard would not be met absent "law enforcement conduct . . . violating that 'fundamental fairness, shocking to the universal sense of justice,' mandated by the Due Process Clause." *Id.* at 432.

Subsequently, in *Hampton v. United States*, 425 U.S. 484 (1976), a deeply divided Supreme Court found no due process violation in a supply-and-buy case where a government informant supplied drugs to the defendant, who then sold them to other government agents. The three Justices in the plurality concluded that the defendant's "remedy . . . lies solely in the defense of entrapment"—a defense that was unavailable because the defendant conceded predisposition. *Id.* at 490 (opinion of Rehnquist, J.). Two Justices concurred only in the judgment, preferring to leave open the possibility that in a "rare" case, "[p]olice over-involvement in crime [may] reach a demonstrable level of outrageousness" sufficient to "bar conviction" of even a predisposed defendant. *Id.* at 495 n.7 (Powell, J., concurring in the judgment). For example, these Justices suggested, "[i]t would be unthinkable . . . to permit government agents to instigate robberies and beatings merely to gather evidence to convict other members of a gang of hoodlums." *Id.* at 493 n.4. The three Justices in dissent would have reversed the defendant's conviction because "the Government's role has passed the point of toleration" where it "buy[s] contraband from itself through an intermediary and jail[s] the intermediary." *Id.* at 498 (Brennan, J., dissenting).

The due process defense has not fared particularly well in the lower courts, and few convictions have been overturned because of outrageous police conduct. The most recent federal appellate decision to do so was *United States v. Twigg*, 588 F.2d 373 (3d Cir. 1978). In *Twigg*, a government informant approached one of the two defendants and suggested setting up a laboratory to manufacture speed. The government supplied most of the necessary ingredients as well as the farmhouse where the lab was located; the informant provided all the technical expertise and was completely in charge of the production process. The defendants, on the other hand, did not have the chemical expertise needed to manufacture speed, may not have had the funds necessary to purchase the raw materials, and provided only minimal assistance. In reversing their convictions, the court of appeals reasoned that "the nature and extent of police involvement in this crime was so overreaching as to bar prosecution of the defendants as a matter of due process of law." *Id.* at 377. *Cf. United States v. Black*, 733 F.3d 294, 310 (9th Cir. 2013) (noting that this defense requires that "government agents engineer and direct the criminal enterprise *from start to finish*"). *But cf. United States v. Cromitie*, 727 F.3d 194, 219 (2d Cir. 2013) (rejecting due process claim despite acknowledging that "[t]he Government invented all of the details of the scheme," including "planning the entire operation with respect to launching missiles to destroy airplanes" at an airport, providing "fake bombs" to be used on synagogues, and "instruct[ing] the defendants how to detonate them," reasoning that "[t]he idea of bombing synagogues appears to have originated with Cromitie" and when the FBI discovered that he "had expressed a desire to 'do something to America'" and had said "he wanted to die like a martyr, the FBI agents would have been derelict in their duties if they did not test how far [he] would go to carry out his desires").

One of the few state court opinions to reverse a conviction on due process grounds is *State v. Williams*, 623 So. 2d 462 (Fla. 1993), where the Florida Supreme Court concluded that the defendant's due process rights under the state constitution were violated when he was convicted for purchasing crack cocaine that had been manufactured by a law enforcement chemist using powder cocaine the police had found in a bus station locker. The court acknowledged that "[u]ndercover tactics and limited participation in drug rings are often the only methods law enforcement officials have to gather evidence of drug-related offenses" and that reverse-buy operations involving the simple sale of narcotics by police officers do not violate due process. *Id.* at 465. Nevertheless, the court noted that while law enforcement officials were expressly immune from state criminal laws prohibiting the possession and sale of narcotics, there was no such exemption for the manufacture of narcotics. "The delivery of a controlled substance in a reverse-sting operation is worlds apart from the manufacture of a dangerous controlled substance," the court concluded. *Id.* at 466. *But cf. Gober v. State*, 566 S.E.2d 317, 318 (Ga. 2002) (rejecting a due process claim where the undercover officer in a reverse-sting case sold the defendant narcotics that should have been destroyed under the terms of a state statute, reasoning that the statute did not "create any right in the defendant" protected by the Due Process Clause but merely "impose[d] a separate, unrelated obligation on the police") (citing *Hampton*, 425 U.S. at 490); *State v. Fitzpatrick*, 291 P.3d 1106, 1114 (Mont. 2012) (finding no due process violation even though an undercover agent violated state law by obtaining a phony driver's license and using it for a prescription for medical marijuana, explaining that "[t]his type of law enforcement subterfuge" consisted only of "*malum prohibitum* offenses" and not "'inherently immoral' crimes such as rape or murder").

State v. Lively, 921 P.2d 1035 (Wash. 1996), is another of the few cases in which a government agent's conduct was deemed sufficiently outrageous to violate the defendant's federal due process rights. The defendant in that case was "[a] recovering drug addict recently released from treatment, with no prior connection to the sale of narcotics nor any known predisposition to commit such an offense." *Id.* at 1048. She met an informant at an Alcoholics/Narcotics Anonymous meeting, where he had gone "'trolling for targets' for [a] police undercover operation." *Id.* at 1046. Within a few weeks, the defendant and informant were living together, and at one point the informant asked the defendant to marry him. At his request, the defendant agreed to purchase narcotics for one of his "friends." In reversing her conviction on two counts of delivering a controlled substance, the court observed that "attending AA/NA meetings to lure recovering drug addicts to commit illegal acts is contrary to proper police objectives and counterproductive to the public policy of reducing the illegal drug trade." *Id. Cf. United States v. Nolan-Cooper*, 155 F.3d 221, 233, 234 (3d Cir. 1998) (suggesting that due process would be violated if "the government consciously set out to use sex as a weapon in its investigatory arsenal, or acquiesced in such conduct for its own purposes once it knew or should have known that such a relationship existed," but finding no constitutional impediment to "a one-time sexual encounter that served no investigatory purpose occurring near the end of an investigation"); *United States v. Cuervelo*, 949 F.2d 559, 567–69 (2d Cir. 1991) (endorsing a similar standard, and holding that the defendant was entitled to a hearing on her due process claim where she alleged that a federal narcotics agent initiated a sexual relationship with her and gave her gifts (including a visa enabling her to enter the country) in order to convince her to assist in his alleged drug dealings). *But cf. United States v. Simpson*, 813 F.2d 1462, 1465, 1467, 1468 n.4 (9th Cir. 1987) (rejecting the defendant's due process challenge to a government informant's "use of sex to deceive him into believing she was an intimate friend just so she could lure him into selling heroin to undercover FBI agents," and explaining that "[e]xploiting an emotionally intimate relationship between lovers [is] no more egregious than exploiting an emotionally intimate relationship between family members," though leaving open the constitutional implications of a sexual relationship involving a government agent rather than an informant).

Notwithstanding the handful of cases where convictions have been reversed on due process grounds, most claims of outrageous government conduct have been rejected. Some courts have indicated, for example, that the Due Process Clause does not bar "morally offensive" practices, *id.* at 1468, "obnoxious behavior or even flagrant misconduct on the part of the police." *United States v. Walls*, 70 F.3d 1323, 1330 n.3 (D.C. Cir. 1995), *overruled on other grounds by United States v. Booker*, 543 U.S. 220 (2005). Others have taken the position that the due process defense is not implicated absent evidence of "coercion, violence or brutality to the person." *Id.*; *see also Cromitie*, 727 F.3d at 218; *Simpson*, 813 F.2d at 1465–66.

Several federal appellate courts have gone even further, rejecting the due process defense for outrageous conduct altogether and thereby limiting defendants in those jurisdictions to the entrapment defense. *See United States v. Amawi*, 695 F.3d 457, 483–84 (6th Cir. 2012); *United States v. Skoczen*, 405 F.3d 537, 543 (7th Cir. 2005). Are these narrow interpretations of the Due Process Clause necessary to ensure that the Supreme Court's "consistent rejection of the objective test of entrapment" is not circumvented "by permitting it to reemerge cloaked as a due process defense"? *United States v. Lakhani*, 480 F.3d 171, 180 (3d Cir. 2007). *See also United States v. Santana*, 6 F.3d 1, 3 (1st Cir. 1993) (referring to the due process defense as "the deathbed child of objective entrapment").

Should the Due Process Clause at least be read, as the *Williams* court interpreted its state constitution, to prohibit government agents from engaging in criminal conduct? Or is it unreasonable to expect legislatures to create a specific exemption for each criminal statute the police are authorized to violate? In *Olmstead v. United States*, 277 U.S. 438, 485 (1928), Justice Brandeis' dissenting opinion issued the following warning: "[i]n a government of laws, existence of the government will be imperilled if it fails to observe the law scrupulously"; "[i]f the Government becomes a lawbreaker, it breeds contempt for law." Are Brandeis' views outdated because law enforcement needs have changed since 1928? If so, does the Due Process Clause nevertheless impose some limit on the types of criminal acts undercover agents may commit?

For example, should an informant who has infiltrated a terrorist organization be permitted to teach the organization's members how to make a bomb? *Cf.* Joseph B. Treaster, *Secret Tapes Are Disclosed in Bomb Plot*, N.Y. Times, Aug. 3, 1993, at B1 (taped conversations between a government informant and the suspected leader of a plot to bomb the United Nations suggested that at times the informant was "instructing [the suspect] in the intricacies of bomb-building"). Should officers working undercover in a white supremacist organization be allowed to participate in firebombing an African-American church in order to protect their cover? Should gang leaders who are acting as government informants be permitted to kill rival gang members in order to alleviate suspicions that they are cooperating with the police? Should the courts be the ones to decide when law enforcement interests are sufficiently weighty to justify criminal conduct on the part of government agents?

7. **Sentencing Entrapment.** A number of defendants have tried to raise the defense of "sentencing entrapment" — that government agents induced them to commit a more serious crime, carrying a heavier sentence, than they were otherwise predisposed to commit. In *United States v. Staufer*, 38 F.3d 1103, 1107 (9th Cir. 1994), the court accepted a sentencing entrapment defense, commenting on "the unfairness and arbitrariness of allowing drug enforcement agents to put unwarranted pressure on a defendant in order to increase his or her sentence [under the Federal Sentencing Guidelines] without regard for his predisposition, his capacity to commit the crime on his own, and the extent of his culpability." The court acknowledged that the defendant may have been predisposed to sell drugs " 'on a very small level for his friends,' [but] he was not predisposed 'to involve himself in what turned out to be, from the standpoint of the Sentencing Guidelines, an immense amount of drugs.' " *Id.* at 1108. *Cf. United States v. Yuman-Hernandez*, 712 F.3d 471, 474 (9th Cir. 2013) (expressing concern that stings involving "[f]ictitious stash house robberies" give government agents "virtually unfettered ability" to "easily manipulate" the inquiry into the defendant's "capability" to commit the theft by "inflat[ing] the amount of drugs supposedly in the house" and "minimiz[ing] the obstacles that a defendant must overcome to obtain the drugs," and therefore allowing a sentencing entrapment defense in such cases if the defendant can establish either "a lack of intent or lack of capability to deal in the quantity of drugs charged"). (For a description of the Federal Sentencing Guidelines, see Chapter 2, Section D.2.b.)

Although a number of federal courts have accepted the notion of sentencing entrapment on a theoretical level, they have generally rejected the defense on the merits, *see, e.g., United States v. Turner*, 569 F.3d 637, 641–42 (7th Cir. 2009); *United States v. Searcy*, 284 F.3d 938, 942–43 (8th Cir. 2002), and other courts have expressly refused to recognize sentencing entrapment as a defense at all. *See United States v. Williams*, 954 F.2d 668, 673 (11th Cir. 1992). Is this latter group of judges right to be skeptical because sentencing entrapment claims in essence ask the courts to "fundamentally alter[] the sentencing scheme duly established by Congress"? Joan Malmud, Comment, *Defending a Sentence: The Judicial Establishment of Sentencing*

Entrapment and Sentencing Manipulation Defenses, 145 U. Pa. L. Rev. 1359, 1399 (1997). *Cf. People v. Smith*, 80 P.3d 662, 667 (Cal. 2003) (rejecting the doctrine of sentencing entrapment on the grounds that it "focuses on the intent of the defendant" and therefore "does not fit" with the objective approach to entrapment followed in California).

[C] Insanity

The material that follows paints a picture of a defense that has been controversial since its inception and has produced little consensus on when mental illness constitutes an excuse to criminal charges. Historically, several concerns have emerged when insanity is raised as a defense: dangerous people may be acquitted for egregious crimes, including homicide and attempted homicide; devious defendants may successfully feign mental illness; doctors may usurp the role of juries; and judges and juries may have difficulty assessing the validity of psychiatric and psychological evidence. Born in controversy, the defense continues to generate debate and disagreement.

[1] The Scope of the Insanity Defense

Daniel M'Naghten's Case
8 Eng. Rep. 718 (1843)

Lord Chief Justice Tindal.

. . . .

Your Lordships are pleased to inquire of us . . . , "What are the proper questions to be submitted to the jury, where a person alleged to be afflicted with insane delusion respecting one or more particular subjects or persons, is charged with the commission of a crime (murder, for example), and insanity is set up as a defence?" . . . [We] submit our opinion to be, that the jurors ought to be told in all cases that every man is to be presumed to be sane, and to possess a sufficient degree of reason to be responsible for his crimes, until the contrary be proved to their satisfaction; and that to establish a defence on the ground of insanity, it must be clearly proved that, at the time of the committing of the act, the party accused was labouring under such a defect of reason, from disease of the mind, as not to know the nature and quality of the act he was doing; or, if he did know it, that he did not know he was doing what was wrong. The mode of putting the latter part of the question to the jury on these occasions has generally been, whether the accused at the time of doing the act knew the difference between right and wrong: which mode, though rarely, if ever, leading to any mistake with the jury, is not, as we conceive, so accurate when put generally and in the abstract, as when put with reference to the party's knowledge of right and wrong in respect to the very act with which he is charged. If the question were to be put as to the knowledge of the accused solely and exclusively with reference to the law of the land, it might tend to confound the jury, by inducing them to believe that an actual knowledge of the law of the land was essential in order to lead to a conviction; whereas the law is administered upon the principle that every one must be taken conclusively to know it, without proof that he does know it. If the accused was conscious that the act was one which he ought not to do, and if that act was at the same time contrary to the law of the land, he is punishable. . . .

Notes and Questions

1. **The Background of *M'Naghten*.** The events leading up to the *M'Naghten* decision are described in *United States v. Freeman*, 357 F.2d 606, 616–18 (2d Cir. 1966):

> Daniel M'Naghten suffered from what now would be described as delusions of persecution. Apparently, he considered his major persecutor to be Robert Peel, then Prime Minister of England, for M'Naghten came to London with the intention of assassinating the chief of the Queen's government. His plan would have succeeded but for the fact that Peel chose to ride in Queen Victoria's carriage because of her absence from the city, while Drummond, his secretary, rode in the vehicle which normally would have been occupied by Peel. M'Naghten, believing that the Prime Minister was riding in his own carriage, shot and killed Drummond in error.
>
> After a lengthy trial in 1843, M'Naghten was found "not guilty by reason of insanity." M'Naghten's exculpation from criminal responsibility was most significant for several reasons. His defense counsel had relied in part upon Dr. Isaac Ray's historic work, Medical Jurisprudence of Insanity which had been published in 1838. This book, which was used and referred to extensively at the trial, contained many enlightened views on the subject of criminal responsibility in general and on the weaknesses of the right and wrong test in particular. Thus, for example, the jury was told that the human mind is not compartmentalized and that a defect in one aspect of the personality could spill over and affect other areas. . . . [T]he court was so impressed with this and other medical evidence of M'Naghten's incompetency that Lord Chief Justice Tindal practically directed a verdict for the accused.
>
> For these reasons, M'Naghten's case could have been the turning point for a new approach to more modern methods of determining criminal responsibility. But the Queen's ire was raised by the acquittal and she was prompted to intervene. Mid-19th Century England was in a state of social upheaval and there had been three attempts on the life of the Queen and one on the Prince Consort. Indeed, Queen Victoria was so concerned about M'Naghten's acquittal that she summoned the House of Lords to "take the opinion of the Judges on the law governing such cases." Consequently, the fifteen judges of the common law courts were called in a somewhat extraordinary session under a not too subtle atmosphere of pressure to answer five prolix and obtuse questions on the status of criminal responsibility in England. Significantly, it was Lord Chief Justice Tindal who responded for fourteen of the fifteen judges, and thus articulated what has

come to be known as the M'Naghten Rules or M'Naghten test. Rather than relying on Dr. Ray's monumental work which had apparently impressed him at M'Naghten's trial, Tindal, with the Queen's breath upon him, reaffirmed the old restricted right-wrong test despite its 16th Century roots and the fact that it, in effect, echoed such uninformed concepts as phrenology and monomania. In this manner, Dr. Ray's insights were to be lost to the common law for over one hundred years except in the small state of New Hampshire.

2. **Criticisms of *M'Naghten* and Proposed Alternatives.** The Second Circuit's opinion in *Freeman* went on to summarize criticisms that have been directed at the *M'Naghten* rule and alternatives that have been considered:

> [T]he principal objection to M'Naghten is not that it was arrived at by this extraordinary process. Rather, the rule is faulted because it has several serious deficiencies which stem in the main from its narrow scope. Because M'Naghten focuses only on the cognitive aspect of the personality, i.e., the ability to know right from wrong, we are told by eminent medical scholars that it does not permit the jury to identify those who can distinguish between good and evil but who cannot control their behavior. The result is that instead of being treated at appropriate mental institutions for a sufficiently long period to bring about a cure or sufficient improvement so that the accused may return with relative safety to himself and the community, he is ordinarily sentenced to a prison term as if criminally responsible and then released as a potential recidivist with society at his mercy. To the extent that these individuals continue to be released from prison because of the narrow scope of M'Naghten, that test poses a serious danger to society's welfare.
>
>   . . . .
>
> The tremendous growth of psychiatric knowledge since the Victorian origins of M'Naghten and even the near-universal disdain in which it is held by present-day psychiatrists are not by themselves sufficient reasons for abandoning the test. At bottom, the determination whether a man is or is not held responsible for his conduct is not a medical but a legal, social or moral judgment. . . .
>
>   . . . .
>
> Efforts to supplement or replace the M'Naghten Rules with a more meaningful and workable test have persisted for generations, with varying degrees of success. Perhaps the first to receive judicial approval, however, was more an added fillip to M'Naghten than a true substitute: the doctrine which permits acquittal on grounds of lack of responsibility when a defendant is found to have been driven by an "irresistible impulse" to commit his offense. . . .
>
>   . . . Psychiatrists have long questioned whether "irresistible impulses" actually exist; the more basic legal objection to the term "irresistible impulse" is that it is too narrow and carries the misleading implication that a crime

impulsively committed must have been perpetrated in a sudden and explosive fit. Thus, the "irresistible impulse" test is unduly restrictive because it excludes the far more numerous instances of crimes committed after excessive brooding and melancholy by one who is unable to resist sustained psychic compulsion or to make any real attempt to control his conduct. . . .

. . . .

In 1953, the American Law Institute commenced an exhaustive study of criminal conduct including the problem of criminal responsibility. . . . Nine long years of research, exploration and consideration culminated in the definitive version of Section 4.01, which was finally adopted by the Institute in 1962.

Section 4.01 [of the Model Penal Code] provides that "A person is not responsible for criminal conduct if at the time of such conduct as a result of mental disease or defect he lacks substantial capacity either to appreciate the [criminality/]wrongfulness of his conduct or to conform his conduct to the requirements of law."

United States v. Freeman, 357 F.2d 606, 618–22 (2d Cir. 1966).

3. The Policies Underlying the Insanity Defense. As the controversy surrounding the M'Naghten verdict reflects, the insanity defense has always received a good deal of attention. One commentator colorfully noted that "[r]ivers of ink, mountains of printer's lead, forests of paper have been expended on this issue." Norval Morris, *Psychiatry and the Dangerous Criminal*, 41 S. Cal. L. Rev. 514, 516 (1968). Critics of the defense have raised a number of objections. First, as the Michigan Supreme Court observed, "there seems to be a tendency for people to assume that someone who commits a particularly offensive crime 'must be insane.'" *People v. Ramsey*, 375 N.W.2d 297, 301 (Mich. 1985). Second, the cost of obtaining the expert testimony typically required to establish an insanity claim may make insanity primarily "a rich man's defense." *See* Steven V. Roberts, *High U.S. Officials Express Outrage, Asking for New Laws on Insanity Plea*, N.Y. Times, June 23, 1982, at B6 (quoting U.S. Senator Larry Pressler's reaction to the verdict in the Hinckley case, which is described below in Note 10).[9] Third, some critics have suggested that the goals of educating and protecting society are better served by "hold[ing] individuals who act with a proven criminal state of mind accountable for their acts, regardless of motivation or mental condition." *State v. Korell*, 690 P.2d 992, 1002 (Mont. 1984).

---

9. One author estimated, for example, that defense counsel's fees in John Hinckley's case "would have easily topped half a million dollars" if the attorneys billed even half the time they spent on the case. Lincoln Caplan, The Insanity Defense and the Trial of John W. Hinckley, Jr. 59–60 (1984). Another commented that M'Naghten "probably had the best-financed defense in the history of the Old Bailey." Richard Moran, Knowing Right from Wrong 90 (1981). *But cf. Ake v. Oklahoma*, 470 U.S. 68 (1985) (holding that indigent defendants who show that their sanity is likely to be a significant issue at trial have a constitutional right to the assistance of a court-appointed psychiatrist in presenting an insanity defense).

Finally, some researchers have questioned the accuracy of psychiatric assessments of mental condition. For example, the dissenting opinion in *People v. Drew*, 583 P.2d 1318, 1334 (Cal. 1978) (Richardson, J., dissenting), raised this concern, citing the results of two experiments. In the first, researchers sent to psychiatric hospitals pretending to be patients claimed that they heard voices but otherwise responded truthfully to every question they were asked. Almost all of them were diagnosed as schizophrenic or manic depressive. In the second, a psychiatric hospital was told that it would be receiving some fake patients; thereafter, more than one-fifth of its actual patients were thought to be feigning illness by at least one staff member. Others have likewise criticized the psychiatric profession for assuming that any "behavior . . . society considers strange, frightening, or disagreeable" is symptomatic of mental disease. JOSHUA DRESSLER, UNDERSTANDING CRIMINAL LAW § 25.06[A][4], at 358 (7th ed. 2015) (citing the views of others). For example, African-Americans who tried to escape slavery were considered mentally ill, some Freudian psychologists historically associated feminism with neurosis, and the American Psychiatric Association treated homosexuality as a mental disease until 1973. *See id.* at 358–59. Persuaded by these arguments, a few state legislatures have abolished insanity as a separate defense (as discussed in Note 5 in Part 2 below). Is there a convincing case in support of the insanity defense?

4. The "Product" and "Blameworthiness" Tests. Arguably, both *M'Naghten* and the Model Penal Code's formulation are too narrow because they do not apply to some defendants who are indisputably mentally ill, but whose mental disease does not happen to have one of the specific consequences required to make out a defense. In *Commonwealth v. Tempest*, 437 A.2d 952 (Pa. 1981), for example, the defendant, a chronic schizophrenic, was convicted of first-degree murder and sentenced to life in prison after she drowned her six-year-old son in the bathtub. The defendant had a history of emotional disturbance dating back to adolescence, had been hospitalized on seven or eight occasions, and had twice tried to commit suicide. In explaining her reasons for killing the boy, the defendant said:

> My husband made friends down the street. Greg [the son] played with Joey, the little boy down the street. I didn't have any friends. I'm afraid of everybody. I don't really know why I did it. I just did — I didn't want Ronnie [her husband] and Greg in my life anymore.
>
> . . . .
>
> Greg was too demanding. He got on my nerves. Just having to do things for him. I didn't want the responsibility. I didn't want him to go into the 1st grade because I would have to talk to other people. I didn't want to be a housekeeper and have people come to my house. My husband did most of the work.

Id. at 953–54. The Pennsylvania Supreme Court acknowledged that the killing "was not the product of a sound mind," but noted that "mental illness alone cannot absolve appellant from criminal responsibility." *Id.* at 954. The court ultimately concluded that the evidence was sufficient to prove the defendant's sanity under the *M'Naghten* standard because she was "coherent" and "lucid" when interviewed by the police and she admitted in her confession that she knew killing her son was wrong. *Id.*

Does the ruling in *Tempest* suggest that the insanity defense should excuse any defendant whose "unlawful act was the product of mental disease or defect"? *Durham v. United States*, 214 F.2d 862, 875 (D.C. Cir. 1954), *overruled by United States v. Brawner*, 471 F.2d 969 (D.C. Cir. 1972) (en banc). Or is the *Durham* standard "too broad" if it encompasses any defendants whose "crime would not have been committed but for the presence of the mental disease or defect," because many such individuals "clearly should be held responsible"? Model Penal Code §4.01 Comment at 173. *See also State v. Johnson*, 399 A.2d 469, 474 (R.I. 1979) (criticizing the *Durham* test because "[t]he elusive, undefined concept of productivity pose[s] serious problems of causation and [gives] the jury inadequate guidance," thereby allowing expert witnesses to "usurp the jury function"). *Cf. State v. Fichera*, 903 A.2d 1030, 1034 (N.H. 2006) (applying a *Durham*-type definition of insanity). *But cf. State v. Gribble*, 66 A.3d 1194, 1216 (N.H. 2013) (upholding an instruction allowing jurors to "consider any evidence of insanity," including the prongs of the *M'Naghten* test and the defendant's volitional capacity).

Alternatively, can all of these tests — *M'Naghten*, the Model Penal Code, and *Durham* — be faulted for failing to "focus attention on the right question," that is, "the blameworthiness of the defendant's action measured by prevailing community standards"? *Brawner*, 471 F.2d at 1031 (Bazelon, C.J., concurring in part and dissenting in part). Would it therefore be preferable to simply instruct the jury that "a defendant is not responsible if . . . his mental or emotional processes or behavior controls were impaired to such an extent that he cannot justly be held responsible for his act"? *Id.* at 1032. *See also* Model Penal Code §4.01 Comment at 172 n.19 (noting that a minority of the MPC's drafters endorsed a similar approach). Is this standard superior to any of the others described above because "it clearly delegates the issue of criminal responsibility to the jury" and focuses "the jury's attention . . . upon the legal and moral aspects of responsibility"? *Johnson*, 399 A.2d at 476 (adopting the minority MPC position); *see also* Stephen J. Morse, *Excusing the Crazy: The Insanity Defense Reconsidered*, 58 S. CAL. L. REV. 777, 820–21 (1985) (proposing a similar standard because it "tracks the moral issues with greater honesty and precision . . . and without pseudomedicalization"). *Cf. State v. Carpio*, 43 A.3d 1, 10 (R.I. 2012) (approving an instruction under this approach that advised the jurors to vote for an insanity acquittal only if "the degree of [the defendant's] mental impairment . . . satisf[ied] the community's sense of justice").

If the proper focus of the insanity defense is on an individual's overall blameworthiness or responsibility, should a defendant's refusal to take antipsychotic medications be a relevant factor in evaluating an insanity claim? *See* Zachary D. Torry & Kenneth J. Weiss, *Medication Noncompliance and Criminal Responsibility:*

Is the Insanity Defense Legitimate?, 40 J. Psychiatry & L. 219, 231, 222 (2012) (noting that only one-third of mentally ill patients "reliably take medications as prescribed," even though advances in medicine have led to "an increasing capacity to control even severe psychotic states").

5. Applying *M'Naghten*: Knowing the Nature and Quality of One's Act. The first prong of *M'Naghten*'s two-part test may seem relatively straightforward, but some ambiguity surrounds both the word "know" and the concept of "the nature and quality" of an act. First, although juries typically receive no instruction concerning the meaning of the word "know," some courts have interpreted it to refer not simply to knowledge in a sterile, intellectual sense, but to an emotional understanding and appreciation. *See, e.g., People v. Skinner*, 704 P.2d 752, 761 (Cal. 1985); *State v. Rawland*, 199 N.W.2d 774, 790 (Minn. 1972). *But cf. State v. Worlock*, 569 A.2d 1314, 1319 (N.J. 1990) (noting that "[t]he difference between 'know' and 'appreciate' may be more apparent than real"); *State v. Thompson*, 402 S.E.2d 386, 390–91 (N.C. 1991) (upholding the trial court's refusal to instruct the jury that "know" means "appreciate" on the grounds that such an instruction would likely confuse the jurors).

Second, one court described *M'Naghten*'s reference to "the nature and quality" of an act as "one of the most ambiguous phrases in the history of the English common law." *Hart v. State*, 702 P.2d 651, 654 (Alaska Ct. App. 1985). The court explained: "Knowing the nature and quality of an act can refer to the physical aspects of an act—for example, whether the defendant knows he is firing a gun—or it can refer to all aspects of an act including its likely consequences to the actor and others." *Id.* at 654 n.2. Is awareness of the nature and quality of a criminal act absent only in cases where the defendant does not "realize that he is shooting someone with a gun when he pulls the trigger on what he believes to be a water pistol" or "believes he is attacking the ghost of his mother rather than a living human being"? *State v. Patterson*, 740 P.2d 944, 946 n.8 (Alaska 1987). Or should a defense also be available under *M'Naghten*'s first prong if the defendant did not understand "the social implications [of his crime] or the nature or meaning of what [it] meant to him at that moment"? *United States v. Freeman*, 357 F.2d 606, 610 (2d Cir. 1966) (quoting defense expert).

6. Applying *M'Naghten*: Knowing that One's Act Is Wrong. Ambiguity surrounds *M'Naghten*'s second prong as well: do defendants know that their act is wrong so long as they realize that it is illegal, or must they also know that it is immoral? Given that the criminal laws reflect societal mores, this distinction will be of little consequence in most cases because defendants who are aware that their conduct is illegal will probably realize that it is immoral as well. But what about deluded defendants who are convinced that God has ordered them to kill? Should an insanity defense be available under *M'Naghten*'s second prong even if these defendants know that the law prohibits homicide? (Note that § 4.01 of the Model Penal Code does not resolve this issue, but instead lets legislatures choose between a cognitive test that focuses on "criminality" (illegality) and one that focuses on "wrongfulness" (immorality).)

Many of the states that follow *M'Naghten* do not define the term "wrong" for the jury, *see State v. Morgan*, 863 So. 2d 520, 524 n.5 (La. 2004), and there is a split in the states that have taken a position, both in the jurisdictions that follow *M'Naghten* and those that have adopted the Model Penal Code. *See State v. Singleton*, 48 A.3d 285, 295–96 (N.J. 2012). The Washington Supreme Court, for example, defined "wrong" as "illegal," reasoning that defendants who know their act is prohibited by the criminal laws "might possibly be deterred" and thus are not completely "beyond any of the influences of the criminal law." *State v. Crenshaw*, 659 P.2d 488, 493 (Wash. 1983). *But cf. State v. Cameron*, 674 P.2d 650, 654 (Wash. 1983) (applying the "deific decree" exception recognized in *Crenshaw* and finding that jury instructions defining "wrong" as "illegal" erroneously precluded the jury from considering the defendant's evidence that he thought the victim was an agent of Satan whom God wanted him to kill). The Iowa Supreme Court likewise concluded that legality is a "more workable" standard because "it is futile to pretend that our society maintains a consensus on moral questions beyond what it writes into its laws," and reliance on the "amorphous and shifting standard" of morality "invites the functional equivalent of jury nullification." *State v. Hamann*, 285 N.W.2d 180, 184, 183 (Iowa 1979). *See also The Queen v. Windle*, [1952] 2 Q.B. 826, 832 (Crim. App.) (defining "wrong" as "contrary to law").

But other states have taken the opposite tack and have defined "wrong" as "immoral." For example, then-Judge Cardozo considered it "a mockery" to say that defendants who believe they are following the dictates of God realize that their act is wrong. *People v. Schmidt*, 110 N.E. 945, 949 (N.Y. 1915). Likewise, the Colorado Supreme Court noted that mental illness can "impair a person's cognitive ability to distinguish moral right from wrong and yet have no effect whatever on the person's rather sterile awareness that a certain act is contrary to law." *People v. Serravo*, 823 P.2d 128, 136–37 (Colo. 1992). The court therefore thought that focusing on legality "injects a formalistic legalism into the insanity equation [and] disregard[s] the psychological underpinnings" of the defense. *Id.* at 135. *See also The Queen v. Chaulk*, [1990] 3 S.C.R. 1303, 1354 (Can.) (overruling precedent and holding that defendants must know their act was something they "ought not have done" in a moral sense). *Cf. People v. Houston*, 281 P.3d 799, 831(Cal. 2012) (approving a jury instruction that allowed an insanity acquittal based on the defendant's lack of understanding of either legal or moral wrong).

The courts that have chosen to define "wrong" as immoral make clear that an insanity defense is available only if defendants believed that society would consider their act to be moral. Defendants who knew that their act would be deemed illegal as well as immoral "under prevailing social norms" have no defense merely because they were acting according to their own "personal moral code." *Singleton*, 48 A.3d at 297. As one court explained: "If wrong meant moral wrong judged by the individual's own conscience, this would seriously undermine the criminal law, for it would allow one who violated the law to be excused from criminal responsibility solely because, in his own conscience, his act was not morally wrong." *Crenshaw*, 659 P.2d at 493. *See also United States v. Ewing*, 494 F.3d 607, 622 (7th Cir. 2007) (holding that "wrongfulness for purposes of the federal insanity defense statute is defined by reference to objective societal or public standards of moral wrongfulness, not the defendant's subjective personal standards of moral wrongfulness"). *Cf. State v. Wilson*, 700 A.2d 633, 643 (Conn. 1997) (adopting the moral wrong standard, though concluding that it suffices that the defendant "sincere[ly]" thought "society would condone his actions under the circumstances as [he] honestly perceived them").

It is vital that a defendant's mental disease or defect (a concept discussed below in Notes 6–7 in Part 2) is what caused the defendant to believe the act was moral or legal. Jihadists may commit murder because they think a Divine Being ordered or blessed their acts, but the law does not excuse them from responsibility. The law does not permit actors to substitute their religious or moral views for those that underlie the criminal statutes. *Cf.* Grant H. Morris & Ansar Haroun, *"God Told Me to Kill": Religion or Delusion?*, 38 San Diego L. Rev. 973, 978 (2001) (arguing that insanity is not an appropriate verdict in deific decree cases because a defendant's "sincerely held belief that God ordered him or her to kill qualifies as a religious belief, . . . not . . . a delusion").

7. **Irresistible Impulse.** Although a few jurisdictions have broadened *M'Naghten* by extending an insanity defense to those whose crimes were the result of an "irresistible impulse," *see Clark v. Arizona*, 548 U.S. 735, 751 & n.17 (2006) (citing three states), that approach has been characterized as "a somewhat haphazard modification of *M'Naghten*." *State v. White*, 456 P.2d 797, 803 (Idaho 1969). As described above in Note 2, the Second Circuit criticized the narrow scope of this doctrine in *United States v. Freeman*, and others have objected that it, like *M'Naghten*, unrealistically requires "a complete destruction of the governing power of the mind." *State v. Johnson*, 399 A.2d 469, 474 (R.I. 1979).

As a practical matter, however, most judges do not seem to require that a crime be either totally irresistible or completely unplanned in order to fall within the irresistible impulse doctrine. *See* Joshua Dressler, Understanding Criminal Law § 25.04[C][2][b], at 349 (7th ed. 2015). Whatever its scope, the concept of an irresistible impulse clearly adds a volitional component to *M'Naghten*'s purely cognitive test — as does the two-part Model Penal Code definition of insanity, which appears in § 4.01 of the Code and is quoted above in Note 2. The advisability of incorporating a volitional element in defining insanity is addressed in the following Note.

8. **Evaluating the Need for a Volitional Prong.** As discussed above in Note 2, the Second Circuit took the position in *United States v. Freeman* that a volitional element is an indispensable component of the insanity defense. As a result, the *Freeman* court chose to adopt the Model Penal Code's definition of insanity.

In *United States v. Lyons*, 731 F.2d 243 (5th Cir. 1984) (en banc), by contrast, the Fifth Circuit decided to abandon the MPC standard, in part because of its dissatisfaction with the volitional prong. The *Lyons* court offered the following reasons for its decision: "a majority of psychiatrists now believe that they do not possess sufficient accurate scientific bases for measuring a person's capacity for self-control or for calibrating the impairment of that capacity," i.e., for "distinguishing between offenders who were undeterrable and those who were merely undeterred"; "the risks of fabrication and 'moral mistakes' in administering the insanity defense are greatest 'when the experts and the jury are asked to speculate whether the defendant had the capacity to "control" himself or whether he could have "resisted" the criminal impulse'"; "psychiatric testimony about volition is more likely to produce confusion for jurors than is psychiatric testimony concerning a defendant's appreciation of the wrongfulness of his act"; the volitional test is "superfluous" because there is "considerable overlap between a psychotic person's inability to understand and his ability to control his behavior" and "[m]ost psychotic persons who fail a volitional test would also fail a cognitive test."[10] Finally, the court feared that "the present murky state of medical knowledge" makes it "an all but impossible task" for prosecutors to convince juries that a defendant is sane. *Id.* at 248–49. *See also* Christopher Slobogin, *The Integrationist Alternative to the Insanity Defense: Reflections on the Exculpatory Scope of Mental Illness in the Wake of the Andrea Yates Trial*, 30 Am. J. Crim. L. 315, 322 (2003) (criticizing the volitional prong on the ground that "[t]he subjectively experienced urges of a person with mental illness are not provably greater than the urges of people we would never think of excusing," such as "pedophiles, repeat rapists, . . . serial murderers . . . , and thieves who steal to feed an addiction").

By contrast, the two dissenting judges in *United States v. Lyons* defended the volitional prong, observing that the criminal law's notion of blameworthiness "postulates a free agent confronted with a choice between doing right and wrong, and choosing freely to do wrong." In addition, these judges noted that the majority, "[w]ithout citing any data that verdicts in insanity cases decided under a control test are frequently inaccurate, . . . embraces a rule certain to result in the conviction of at least some who are not morally responsible and the punishment of those for whom retributive, deterrent, and rehabilitative penal goals are inappropriate. A decision that virtually ensures undeserved, and therefore unjust, punishment in the name of avoiding moral mistakes rests on a peculiar notion of morality." *United States v. Lyons*, 739 F.2d 994, 995, 999 (5th Cir. 1984) (Rubin, J., dissenting). *See also* Melinda Carrido, Comment, *Revisiting the Insanity Defense: A Case for Resurrecting the Volitional Prong of the Insanity Defense in Light of Neuroscientific Advances*, 41 Sw. L. Rev. 309, 311 (2012) (discussing the brain damage caused by repetitive head trauma and defending the volitional prong because "neuroscience can presently identify particular sections of the brain (specifically, those that control behavior) that, if

---

10. Compare the following list of cases which, according to the California Supreme Court, would result in an insanity acquittal only under a volitional test: "the deluded defendant in *People v. Gorshen* [(1959)] 336 P.2d 492, who believed he would be possessed by devilish visions unless he killed his foreman; the schizophrenic boy in *People v. Wolff* [(1964)] 394 P.2d 959, who knew that killing his mother was murder but was unable emotionally to control his conduct despite that knowledge; the defendant in *People v. Robles* (1970) 466 P.2d 710, suffering from organic brain damage, who mutilated himself and killed others in sudden rages." *People v. Drew*, 583 P.2d 1318, 1322 (Cal. 1978).

damaged, could be a possible source of criminal behavior"). *Cf.* Michael Corrado, *The Case for a Purely Volitional Insanity Defense*, 42 Tex. Tech L. Rev. 481, 509, 484 (2014) (proposing a definition of insanity consisting only of a volitional prong on the grounds that any mental condition that "depriv[es] [one] of the ability to reason" also "deprives her of the ability to choose to conform her behavior to the law," and therefore "all exculpatory mental defects are, in the end, defects of control or . . . volition").

The *Lyons* dissenters also pointed out that juries tend to be "skeptical" of the insanity defense and that "the frequency and the success rate of insanity pleas are grossly overestimated by professionals and lay persons alike." In fact, the dissenters noted, "the plea is rarely made, and even more rarely successful. The number of insanity pleas based on control defects, as compared to those based on lack of cognition, must have been almost negligible":

> For example, one extensive study examined the opinions held by college students, the general public, state legislators, law enforcement officers, and mental health personnel in Wyoming. Estimates of the frequency with which criminal defendants entered the plea ranged from 13% to 57%. During the time period considered, however, the actual frequency was only 0.47%: one case in 200. Similarly, although estimates of its success rate varied from 19% to 44%, during the relevant period only one of the 102 defendants who entered the plea was acquitted by reason of insanity.

Lyons, 739 F.2d at 998, 995–96 & n.8 (Rubin, J., dissenting). Other researchers have reported similar findings. *See* Randy Borum & Solomon M. Fulero, *Empirical Research on the Insanity Defense and Attempted Reforms: Evidence Toward Informed Policy*, 23 Law & Hum. Behav. 117, 120 (1999) (describing the results of studies which found that an insanity defense is raised by fewer than one percent of felony defendants and is successful in only 15 percent to 25 percent of those cases); Carmen Cirincione & Charles Jacobs, *Identifying Insanity Acquittals: Is It Any Easier?*, 23 Law & Hum. Behav. 487, 490 (1999) (reporting that a survey conducted in 36 states found an average of 33.4 insanity acquittals per jurisdiction in each year during the period 1970 to 1995).

9. The "Severe Environmental Deprivation" (or "Rotten Social Background") Defense. Does the argument in favor of adding a volitional component to the insanity defense — that defendants cannot fairly be blamed if mental illness impaired their ability to conform to the law — also support recognition of the so-called "rotten social background" defense? *United States v. Alexander*, 471 F.2d 923, 959 (D.C. Cir. 1972) (Bazelon, C.J., dissenting). That is, if "blame is inappropriate when a defendant's criminal behavior is caused by extrinsic factors beyond his or her control," should a defense exist in cases where "[a]n environment of extreme poverty and deprivation creates in individuals a propensity to commit crime"? Richard Delgado, *"Rotten Social Background": Should the Criminal Law Recognize a Defense of Severe Environmental Deprivation?*, 3 Law & Ineq. J. 9, 54, 55 (1985). Can growing up in an environment that "normalize[s] . . . violence and deceit as acceptable . . . methods of negotiating the challenges of daily life" be analogized to "a process of coercive indoctrination"? Paul H. Robinson, *Are We Responsible for Who We Are? The Challenge for Criminal Law Theory in the Defenses of Coercive Indoctrination and "Rotten Social Background"*, 2 Ala. C.R. & C.L. L. Rev. 53, 54 (2011). Consider Norval Morris, *Psychiatry and the Dangerous Criminal*, 41 S. Cal. L. Rev. 514, 520 (1968):

> Adverse social and subcultural background is statistically *more* criminogenic than is psychosis; like insanity, it also severely circumscribes the freedom of choice which [the] criminal law . . . attributes to accused persons. . . . [I]nsanity destroys, undermines, diminishes man's capacity to reject what is wrong and to adhere to what is right. So does the ghetto—more so.

See also Richard Delgado, *The Wretched of the Earth*, 2 Ala. C.R. & C.L. L. Rev. 1, 7 (2011) (asking, in light of mass incarceration rates and increasing wealth disparities, "[i]f [our] society . . . contains a large number of people who live under sufficiently poor conditions that they predictably turn to crime—yet, we continue to incarcerate them—what does this say about us?").

Others have found this reasoning unpersuasive given that "the majority of poor people are not violent criminals," and therefore "[p]overty is neither a sufficient nor a necessary cause of crime." Stephen J. Morse, *The Twilight of Welfare Criminology: A Reply to Judge Bazelon*, 49 S. Cal. L. Rev. 1247, 1259 (1976). Even if "obeying the law is harder for some persons than for others," Morse argued, the indigent defendant's "decision to offend is still a result of . . . choice" and thus subject to punishment "on retributive as well as deterrent grounds." *Id.* at 1253. More recently, Morse criticized the rotten social background defense as "demeaning and patronizing" because it implies that all those with "severe environmental deprivation" are "impaired in [a] way that diminishes their responsibility and autonomy." Stephen J. Morse, *Severe Environmental Deprivation (AKA RSB): A Tragedy, Not a Defense*, 2 Ala. C.R. & C.L. L. Rev. 147, 151 (2011). Is the whole notion of this defense therefore "an insult" to "the downtrodden"? Sanford H. Kadish, *Excusing Crime*, 75 Cal. L. Rev. 257, 284–85 (1987). Consider Mark Kelman, *Interpretive Construction in the Substantive Criminal Law*, 33 Stan. L. Rev. 591, 646 (1981):

> [The assumptions that] people are generally accountable for what they do . . . are particularly suspect when the people administering our criminal justice systems, who know they will never . . . face the pressures of a truly bleak social background, but who are as likely as anyone to encounter short-run incidental pressures that are legally recognized as excuses, blame those who have faced long-term background pressures.

10. John Hinckley. In support of its concern that adding a volitional component to the insanity defense would have the practical effect of precluding prosecutors from proving a defendant's sanity, the Fifth Circuit's en banc opinion in *United*

States v. Lyons, cited above in Note 8, referred to the 1982 trial of John Hinckley, which it described as follows:

> John Hinckley is the young man who attempted to assassinate President Reagan in order to attract attention to himself and to impress a movie actress [Jodie Foster] whom he admired from a distance. The subsequent proceedings called into question not only the insanity defense but the rationality of our adversarial jury-trial system. After more than a year of expensive pretrial maneuvering and psychiatric examinations, the lawyers jousted for eight weeks of trial, examining and cross-examining expert witnesses who naturally gave conflicting and confusing testimony on whether Hinckley's obviously warped mentality amounted to legal insanity. The judge instructed the jury to return a verdict of not guilty unless they could agree "beyond a reasonable doubt" that Hinckley was sane. If taken literally, the instruction amounted to a directed verdict of not guilty, considering the deadlock of expert opinion and the difficulty of certifying the sanity of a young man who shot the President to impress a movie star. Juries usually ignore such unpopular legal standards, but the Hinckley jury surprised everybody by taking the law seriously and finding him not guilty. Hinckley will now be confined to a mental hospital indefinitely because he is "dangerous," although there is no reliable way to predict what he would do if released and no reliable test to determine if he has been "cured."

United States v. Lyons, 731 F.2d 243, 249 n.13 (5th Cir. 1984) (en banc) (quoting Phillip E. Johnson, *Book Review*, 50 U. Chi. L. Rev. 1534, 1536 (1983)).

John Hinckley was committed to St. Elizabeths Hospital in Washington, D.C., when his trial ended in June 1982. His mental condition eventually improved such that he was allowed to take periodic day trips supervised by hospital staff as part of his treatment. *See Hinckley v. United States*, 163 F.3d 647 (D.C. Cir. 1999) (holding that such supervised outings did not require court approval). Beginning in 2003, Hinckley was also permitted to take unsupervised outings in the custody of his parents and then several overnight trips within a 50-mile radius of Washington, D.C. *See United States v. Hinckley*, 292 F. Supp. 2d 125 (D.D.C. 2003).

Two years later, the court agreed to let Hinckley take a number of unsupervised multiple-day visits to his parents' home in Williamsburg, Virginia, outside the 50-mile radius, after finding that the previous outings had been "entirely successful" and "very therapeutic." *United States v. Hinckley*, 407 F. Supp. 2d 248, 252 (D.D.C. 2005). In 2009, the court allowed Hinckley to obtain a driver's license and extended the length of his visits to his mother's home to a maximum of 10 days. Under the terms of the order, Hinckley was permitted to do volunteer work while visiting his mother, but he was not allowed to leave her subdivision unless accompanied by a family member and was required to use a cellphone equipped with GPS technology so that the Secret Service could track his location. *See United States v. Hinckley*, 625 F. Supp. 2d 3 (D.D.C. 2009). In 2013, the court increased the length of Hinckley's unsupervised visits to his mother's home to 17 days a month and also allowed Hinckley to drive to certain specified places on his own, but still required him to carry the cellphone when he was unsupervised. *See United States v. Hinckley*, 40 F. Supp. 3d 8 (D.D.C. 2013).

The case returned to court in May 2015, as the district judge held six days of hearings on Hinckley's request to be released from the hospital and permitted to live with his mother on a full-time basis. In July 2016, four months after Nancy Reagan's death, the court granted Hinckley's request, reasoning as follows:

> Mr. Hinckley is 61 years old and suffering from arthritis, high blood pressure, and various other physical ailments like many men his age. He has been under the care of St. Elizabeths Hospital for over three decades. Since 1983, when he last attempted suicide, he has displayed no symptoms of active mental illness, exhibited no violent behavior, shown no interest in weapons, and demonstrated no suicidal ideation. The government and the Hospital both agree that Mr. Hinckley's primary diagnoses of psychotic disorder not otherwise specified and major depression have been in full and sustained remission for well over twenty years, perhaps more than 27 years. In addition, since 2006, Mr. Hinckley has successfully completed over 80 unsupervised visits with his family in Williamsburg, Virginia, fully complying with the Court's strict conditions, with two minor exceptions. The government and its expert, . . . [another] independent expert who conducted a comprehensive risk assessment in this case, . . . and all of Mr. Hinckley's treatment providers both at St. Elizabeths Hospital and in Williamsburg now agree — unanimously — that Mr. Hinckley is clinically ready for full-time convalescent leave and that, with certain conditions, he will not be a danger to himself or others. In the view of most of the experts who testified before this Court, Mr. Hinckley has by now received the maximum benefits possible in an in-patient setting.

United States v. Hinckley, 200 F. Supp. 3d 1, 3–4 (D.D.C. 2016).

The court's order included 34 conditions, requiring, for example, that Hinckley continue to meet with his therapists, share with them a daily log of his unsupervised activities, obtain permission to travel more than 50 miles from his mother's home, spend at least three days a week doing paid or volunteer work, carry a cellphone whenever he leaves his mother's house to enable the Secret Service to track his movements, and live with his mother for at least one year. The court order prohibits Hinckley from creating accounts on any social media website, speaking to the media, using alcohol, obtaining a weapon, and having any contact with the Reagan family, Jodie Foster, or anyone protected by the Secret Service. But the court denied the government's request to require Hinckley to wear some sort of tracking device. The judge ordered an updated risk assessment in 12 to 18 months, with the parties to return to court only if they could not agree on any proposed changes in these conditions. *See id.* at 56–62. Hinckley left St. Elizabeths in August 2016. *See* Lisa Miller, *John Hinckley Left the Mental Hospital Seven Months Ago*, N.Y. Magazine, Mar. 20, 2017.

11. **The Aftermath of the Hinckley Verdict.** The scope of the insanity defense appears to be heavily influenced by the public reaction to insanity acquittals in celebrated cases. In the two decades after the Model Penal Code was officially promulgated in 1962, its definition of insanity was adopted by 10 of the then-11 federal courts of appeals and more than half of the states, and "[t]he trend in favor of [that] test seemed unstoppable until [John Hinckley's] attempted assassination of President Ronald Reagan" in 1981. Joshua Dressler, Understanding Criminal Law § 25.04[A], at 344 (7th ed. 2015). The verdict in the Hinckley case, described above in the prior Note, generated considerable controversy, with one national poll showing that 83 percent of those surveyed believed that justice had not been done. *See* Lincoln Caplan, The Insanity Defense and the Trial of John W. Hinckley, Jr. 116 (1984).

The public outrage evoked a reaction similar to that which followed the jury's acquittal of M'Naghten. In the wake of the Hinckley verdict, the Fifth Circuit issued its opinion in *Lyons*, abandoning the volitional prong of the insanity defense — even though Hinckley's defense was premised on both cognitive and volitional defects. *See* Peter W. Low et al., The Trial of John W. Hinckley, Jr. 96–107 (3d ed. 2008) (reprinting defense counsel's closing argument). Given that the medical experts who testified at Hinckley's trial disagreed on the fundamental question whether he suffered from schizophrenia or a mere personality disorder, one commentator noted that "the only way" controversy could have been avoided in that case would have been "to eliminate psychiatric testimony" altogether. Alan A. Stone, Law, Psychiatry, and Morality 90–91, 94–95 (1984).

In addition to the Fifth Circuit, two-thirds of the states took steps to limit the insanity defense in the three years following the Hinckley verdict. Some of them narrowed the definition of insanity, and others abolished the defense altogether. *See* Henry J. Steadman et al., Before and After Hinckley: Evaluating Insanity Defense Reform 3, 40 (1993). As a result of this flurry of legislative activity, *M'Naghten* became the prevailing standard in the majority of states. *See* 2 Paul H. Robinson, Criminal Law Defenses § 173(a), at 280–83 & nn.2–5 (1984). *But see* Steadman, *supra*, at 45–62 (concluding that California's adoption of the *M'Naghten* standard in place of the MPC formulation did not have a significant impact on the number of insanity pleas or their success rate). *See generally* Jennifer L. Skeem et al., *Venirepersons's Attitudes Toward the Insanity Defense: Developing, Refining, and Validating a Scale*, 28 Law & Hum. Behav. 623, 625 (2004) (citing studies finding that mock jurors often failed to follow their instructions on the definition of insanity and reached the same verdict even when given no such instruction, but merely told to "use their own 'best lights' to decide the case").

Congress got into the act as well. It convened hearings on the insanity defense three days after the Hinckley verdict and ultimately passed the Insanity Defense Reform Act of 1984, the first federal legislation to define the insanity defense. That statute, which superseded *Freeman*, *Lyons*, and every other previous federal court ruling on insanity, opted for a *M'Naghten*-type formulation, authorizing an insanity acquittal only if the defendant, "as a result of a severe mental disease or defect, was unable to appreciate the nature and quality or the wrongfulness of his acts." 18 U.S.C. § 17.

12. "Guilty but Mentally Ill." Another innovation that gained momentum after the Hinckley trial was the "guilty but mentally ill" (GBMI) verdict. In jurisdictions that give juries the alternative option of returning this verdict, defendants are typically considered guilty but mentally ill if they suffered from mental illness, but were not legally insane, at the time they committed their crimes. A GBMI finding leads to a conviction and sentence just like a guilty verdict, but the defendant may then receive psychiatric treatment if appropriate. These defendants serve their sentence just like any other prisoner, and they are released at the expiration of the sentence whether or not their mental illness has been cured.

In 1975, the Michigan legislature became the first to create a GBMI verdict. It did so in response to the public outcry that arose when a state supreme court opinion prohibiting the automatic commitment of insanity acquittees led to the release of 64 individuals who were no longer considered insane, one of whom murdered his wife and another of whom committed two rapes. Between 1975 and 1982, only Indiana joined Michigan—likewise after a well-publicized case in that state involving an insanity acquittee who committed a violent crime after being released. Following the Hinckley verdict, however, other states followed suit, *see Commonwealth v. Trill*, 543 A.2d 1106, 1116–17 (Pa. Super. Ct. 1988), and more than 20 states have now jumped on the GBMI bandwagon. *See* Bradford H. Charles, *Pennsylvania's Definitions of Insanity and Mental Illness: A Distinction with a Difference?*, 12 Temp. Pol. & Civ. Rts. L. Rev. 265, 268 & n.22 (2003).

The states that have adopted this approach define "guilty but mentally ill" in various ways. On the one hand, those that follow *M'Naghten*'s definition of insanity may use the Model Penal Code formulation to define "guilty but mentally ill." *See, e.g.*, 18 Pa. Cons. Stat. Ann. § 314(c). On the other hand, those that have adopted the Model Penal Code's definition of insanity may consider a defendant guilty but mentally ill who suffers from "a substantial disorder of thought, mood, or behavior which afflicted [the] person at the time of the commission of the offense and which impaired that person's judgment, but not to the extent that he is unable to appreciate the wrongfulness of his behavior." 720 Ill. Comp. Stat. 5/6-2(d).

Supporters of the GBMI verdict argue that it "alleviate[s] the incidence of insanity acquittals" and "allow[s] the finder of fact to hold responsible those mentally ill defendants who deviate from the laws . . . , while at the same time providing them with the humane psychiatric treatment for their mental infirmities." *Trill*, 543 A.2d at 1119, 1120. In addition, the GBMI verdict has been defended on the grounds that it helps "insure that the jury applies the *legal* definition of insanity, by underscoring that a person might be 'mentally ill' in clinical terms, 'crazy' in common sense terms, yet not legally insane." *People v. Lantz*, 712 N.E.2d 314, 322 (Ill. 1999).

On the other hand, critics of GBMI "question why the fact-finder in a criminal trial is an appropriate body to determine whether an offender may be mentally ill and in need of treatment." 2 PAUL H. ROBINSON, CRIMINAL LAW DEFENSES § 173(h), at 311 (1984). Moreover, they consider this option unnecessary because "[e]ven without a special verdict, simple humanity and the federal Constitution require that all prisoners who are ill—whether physically or mentally—must receive minimally adequate treatment." Stephen J. Morse, *Excusing the Crazy: The Insanity Defense Reconsidered*, 58 S. CAL. L. REV. 777, 804 (1985); *see also* PETER W. LOW ET AL., THE TRIAL OF JOHN W. HINCKLEY, JR. 132 (3d ed. 2008) (noting that "all states either operate psychiatric hospitals within the correctional system or have well-established procedures for transferring prisoners to secure mental health facilities"). The GBMI verdict has also been attacked on the grounds that it does not guarantee a defendant will receive mental health services and, in fact, has done "little or nothing to ensure effective treatment for mentally disabled offenders." MICHAEL L. PERLIN, THE JURISPRUDENCE OF THE INSANITY DEFENSE 93 (1994) (citing, inter alia, a study which found that only three of 150 GBMI prisoners in Georgia were being treated in a hospital). *See also Wilson v. Gaetz*, 608 F.3d 347, 352–53 (7th Cir. 2010) (describing studies that found no difference in treatment of prisoners found guilty but mentally ill); *Brown v. Commonwealth*, 934 S.W.2d 242, 245 (Ky. 1996) (expressing concern that the state legislature seemingly "put in place a system lacking in adequate funding, and [took] no positive measures to correct this deficiency, thus falling clearly in contravention of its own mandate for treatment").

Finally, critics fear that the GBMI option creates a risk of compromise verdicts in violation of the reasonable doubt requirement because the jury may, "in lieu of reaching a considered and deliberate decision on whether the defendant was legally insane under the statutory definition, 'settle' on a perceived intermediate verdict that appears to designate the defendant as criminally responsible and yet deserving of psychiatric care and treatment." *People v. Ramsey*, 375 N.W.2d 297, 320 (Mich. 1985) (Levin, J., dissenting); *see also Lantz*, 712 N.E.2d at 324 (Heiple, J., dissenting) (calling GBMI "a meaningless verdict which dupes the jury into believing that there is a middle ground between guilty and not guilty by reason of insanity"). The verdict's supporters respond that "[t]he risk of a compromise is neither greater than nor different from that presented when a jury is instructed on lesser included offenses." *State v. Hornsby*, 484 S.E.2d 869, 874 (S.C. 1997).

Despite these concerns, the GBMI verdict has survived constitutional challenge in a number of jurisdictions. *See, e.g., Lantz*, 712 N.E.2d at 318–22; *Ramsey*, 375 N.W.2d at 300–03; *Trill*, 543 A.2d at 1115–30; *Hornsby*, 484 S.E.2d at 871–74. *But cf. Brown*, 934 S.W.2d at 245 (expressing reservations about the constitutionality of the verdict, but ultimately declining to decide given the inadequate state of the record before the court). Nevertheless, it is not evident that the reform is having its intended effect. *See Wilson v. Gaetz*, 608 F.3d at 352 (citing studies pointing out that the GBMI verdict has not significantly decreased the number of insanity acquittals).

[2] The Current State of the Law

Clark v. Arizona

548 U.S. 735 (2006)

JUSTICE SOUTER delivered the opinion of the Court.

. . . .

I

In the early hours of June 21, 2000, Officer Jeffrey Moritz of the Flagstaff Police responded in uniform to complaints that a pickup truck with loud music blaring was circling a residential block. When he located the truck, the officer turned on the emergency lights and siren of his marked patrol car, which prompted petitioner Eric Clark, the truck's driver (then 17), to pull over. Officer Moritz got out of the patrol car and told Clark to stay where he was. Less than a minute later, Clark shot the officer, who died soon after but not before calling the police dispatcher for help. Clark ran away on foot but was arrested later that day with gunpowder residue on his hands; the gun that killed the officer was found nearby, stuffed into a knit cap.

Clark was charged with first-degree murder under Ariz. Rev. Stat. Ann. § 13-1105(A)(3) for intentionally or knowingly killing a law enforcement officer in the line of duty.[11] In March 2001, Clark was found incompetent to stand trial and was committed to a state hospital for treatment, but two years later the same trial court found his competence restored and ordered him to be tried.[12] Clark waived his right to a jury, and the case was heard by the court.

---

11. [n.1] Section 13-1105(A)(3) provides that "[a] person commits first degree murder if . . . [i]ntending or knowing that the person's conduct will cause death to a law enforcement officer, the person causes the death of a law enforcement officer who is in the line of duty."

12. Unlike the insanity defense, which examines a defendant's mental condition at the time of the crime, evaluation of a defendant's competence to stand trial focuses on the defendant's mental capacity at the time of trial. The inquiry in competency hearings is whether the defendant "has sufficient present ability to consult with his lawyer with a reasonable degree of rational understanding—and whether he has a rational as well as factual understanding of the proceedings against him." *Dusky v. United States*, 362 U.S. 402, 402 (1960) (per curiam). For the Model Penal Code's similar definition and its description of the procedures to be followed in evaluating competence, see Model Penal Code §§ 4.04, 4.06. *See also Jackson v. Indiana*, 406 U.S. 715, 733 (1972) (concluding that a defendant who is not competent to stand trial may be "held only for a 'reasonable period of time' necessary to determine whether there is a substantial chance of his attaining the capacity to stand trial in the foreseeable future"). *Cf. Sell v. United States*, 539 U.S. 166, 179 (2003) (holding that the Due Process Clause permits the government to forcibly administer antipsychotic drugs in order to render a defendant competent to stand trial if "the treatment is medically appropriate" and "necessary significantly to further important governmental trial-related interests"). *But cf.* Susan A. McMahon, *It Doesn't Pass the* Sell *Test: Focusing on "the Facts of the Individual Case" in Involuntary Medication Inquiries*, 50 AM. CRIM. L. REV. 387, 388 (2013) (criticizing *Sell*'s "tilt in favor of the government" and finding that, despite the Supreme Court's prediction that involuntary medication of incompetent defendants "'may be rare,'" it has in fact "become routine" even in cases involving "non-dangerous defendants") (quoting *Sell*, 539 U.S. at 180).

At trial, Clark did not contest the shooting and death, but relied on his undisputed paranoid schizophrenia at the time of the incident in denying that he had the specific intent to shoot a law enforcement officer or knowledge that he was doing so, as required by the statute. Accordingly, the prosecutor offered circumstantial evidence that Clark knew Officer Moritz was a law enforcement officer. The evidence showed that the officer was in uniform at the time, that he caught up with Clark in a marked police car with emergency lights and siren going, and that Clark acknowledged the symbols of police authority and stopped. The testimony for the prosecution indicated that Clark had intentionally lured an officer to the scene to kill him, having told some people a few weeks before the incident that he wanted to shoot police officers. . . .

In presenting the defense case, Clark claimed mental illness, which he sought to introduce for two purposes. First, he raised the affirmative defense of insanity, putting the burden on himself to prove by clear and convincing evidence, § 13-502(C), that "at the time of the commission of the criminal act [he] was afflicted with a mental disease or defect of such severity that [he] did not know the criminal act was wrong," § 13-502(A).[13] Second, he aimed to rebut the prosecution's evidence of the requisite mens rea, that he had acted intentionally or knowingly to kill a law enforcement officer.

The trial court ruled that Clark could not rely on evidence bearing on insanity to dispute the mens rea. The court cited *State v. Mott*, 187 Ariz. 536, 931 P.2d 1046 (en banc), *cert. denied*, 520 U.S. 1234 (1997), which "refused to allow psychiatric testimony to negate specific intent," and held that "Arizona does not allow evidence of a defendant's mental disorder short of insanity . . . to negate the mens rea element of a crime."

As to his insanity, then, Clark presented testimony from classmates, school officials, and his family describing his increasingly bizarre behavior over the year before the shooting. Witnesses testified, for example, that paranoid delusions led Clark to rig a fishing line with beads and wind chimes at home to alert him to intrusion by invaders, and to keep a bird in his automobile to warn of airborne poison. There was lay and expert testimony that Clark thought Flagstaff was populated with "aliens" (some impersonating government agents), the "aliens" were trying to kill him, and

---

13. [n.2] Section 13-502(A) provides in full that "A person may be found guilty except insane if at the time of the commission of the criminal act the person was afflicted with a mental disease or defect of such severity that the person did not know the criminal act was wrong. A mental disease or defect constituting legal insanity is an affirmative defense. Mental disease or defect does not include disorders that result from acute voluntary intoxication or withdrawal from alcohol or drugs, character defects, psychosexual disorders or impulse control disorders. Conditions that do not constitute legal insanity include but are not limited to momentary, temporary conditions arising from the pressure of the circumstances, moral decadence, depravity or passion growing out of anger, jealousy, revenge, hatred or other motives in a person who does not suffer from a mental disease or defect or an abnormality that is manifested only by criminal conduct." A defendant found "guilty except insane" is committed to a state mental health facility for treatment.

bullets were the only way to stop them. A psychiatrist testified that Clark was suffering from paranoid schizophrenia with delusions about "aliens" when he killed Officer Moritz, and he concluded that Clark was incapable of luring the officer or understanding right from wrong and that he was thus insane at the time of the killing. In rebuttal, a psychiatrist for the State gave his opinion that Clark's paranoid schizophrenia did not keep him from appreciating the wrongfulness of his conduct, as shown by his actions before and after the shooting (such as circling the residential block with music blaring as if to lure the police to intervene, evading the police after the shooting, and hiding the gun).

. . . The judge . . . issued a special verdict of first-degree murder. . . . The judge noted that though Clark was indisputably afflicted with paranoid schizophrenia at the time of the shooting, the mental illness "did not . . . distort his perception of reality so severely that he did not know his actions were wrong." . . . The sentence was life imprisonment without the possibility of release for 25 years.

. . . .

II

Clark first says that Arizona's definition of insanity, being only a fragment of the Victorian [*M'Naghten*] standard from which it derives, violates due process. . . .

The first part [of the *M'Naghten* test] asks about cognitive capacity: whether a mental defect leaves a defendant unable to understand what he is doing. The second part presents an ostensibly alternative basis for recognizing a defense of insanity understood as a lack of moral capacity: whether a mental disease or defect leaves a defendant unable to understand that his action is wrong.[14]

When the Arizona Legislature first codified an insanity rule, it adopted the full *M'Naghten* statement. . . .

In 1993, the legislature dropped the cognitive incapacity part, leaving only moral incapacity as the nub of the stated definition.[15] Under current Arizona law, a defendant will not be adjudged insane unless he demonstrates that "at the time of the commission of the criminal act [he] was afflicted with a mental disease or defect of such severity that [he] did not know the criminal act was wrong."

---

14. *But cf.* Stephen J. Morse & Morris B. Hoffman, *The Uneasy Entente Between Legal Insanity and Mens Rea: Beyond Clark v. Arizona*, 97 J. Crim. L. & Criminology 1071, 1100 (2007) (pointing out that what the Court referred to as "cognitive capacity" and "moral capacity" are, "[i]n fact, both . . . cognitive questions" that "differ only in the object of the knowledge required").

15. [n.6] This change was accompanied by others, principally an enumeration of mental states excluded from the category of "mental disease or defect," such as voluntary intoxication and other conditions, and a change of the insanity verdict from "not responsible for criminal conduct" by reason of insanity to "guilty except insane." The 1993 amendments were prompted, at least in part, by an acquittal by reason of insanity in a murder case. *See* Note, *Arizona's Insane Response to Insanity*, 40 Ariz. L. Rev. 287, 290 (1998).

A

Clark . . . insists that the side-by-side *M'Naghten* test represents the minimum that a government must provide . . . , and he argues that elimination of the *M'Naghten* reference to nature and quality " 'offends [a] principle of justice so rooted in the traditions and conscience of our people as to be ranked as fundamental,' " *Patterson v. New York*, 432 U.S. 197, 202 (1977) (quoting *Speiser v. Randall*, 357 U.S. 513, 523 (1958)); *see also Leland v. Oregon*, 343 U.S. 790, 798 (1952).

The claim entails no light burden, *see Montana v. Egelhoff*, 518 U.S. 37, 43 (1996) (plurality opinion), and Clark does not carry it. History shows no deference to *M'Naghten* that could elevate its formula to the level of fundamental principle, so as to limit the traditional recognition of a State's capacity to define crimes and defenses.

Even a cursory examination of the traditional Anglo-American approaches to insanity reveals significant differences among them, with four traditional strains variously combined to yield a diversity of American standards. The main variants are the cognitive incapacity, the moral incapacity, the volitional incapacity, and the product-of-mental-illness tests.[16] The first two emanate from the alternatives stated in the *M'Naghten* rule. The volitional incapacity or irresistible-impulse test, which surfaced over two centuries ago (first in England, then in this country), asks whether a person was so lacking in volition due to a mental defect or illness that he could not have controlled his actions. And the product-of-mental-illness test was used as early as 1870, and simply asks whether a person's action was a product of a mental disease or defect.[17] Seventeen States and the Federal Government have adopted a recognizable version of the *M'Naghten* test with both its cognitive incapacity and moral incapacity components.[18] One State has adopted only *M'Naghten*'s cognitive incapacity test,[19] and 10 (including Arizona) have adopted the moral incapacity test alone.[20] Fourteen jurisdictions, inspired by the Model Penal Code, have in place an

16. [n.7] "Capacity" is understood to mean the ability to form a certain state of mind or motive, understand or evaluate one's actions, or control them.

17. [n.11] This distillation of the Anglo-American insanity standards into combinations of four building blocks should not be read to signify that no other components contribute to these insanity standards or that there are no material distinctions between jurisdictions testing insanity with the same building blocks. For example, the jurisdictions limit, in varying degrees, which sorts of mental illness or defect can give rise to a successful insanity defense. We need not compare the standards under a finer lens because our coarser analysis shows that the standards vary significantly.

18. [n.12] [The 17 states cited here are Alabama, California, Colorado, Florida, Iowa, Minnesota, Mississippi, Missouri, Nebraska, Nevada, New Jersey, New York, North Carolina, Oklahoma, Pennsylvania, Tennessee, and Washington.] North Dakota has a unique test, which appears to be a modified version of *M'Naghten*, asking whether a defendant "lacks substantial capacity to comprehend the harmful nature or consequences of the conduct, or the conduct is the result of a loss or serious distortion of the individual's capacity to recognize reality," when "it is an essential element of the crime charged that the individual act willfully."

19. [n.13] [Here the Court cited Alaska.]

20. [n.14] [The 10 states cited here are Arizona, Delaware, Illinois, Indiana, Louisiana, Maine, Ohio, South Carolina, South Dakota, and Texas.]

amalgam of the volitional incapacity test and some variant of the moral incapacity test, satisfaction of either (generally by showing a defendant's substantial lack of capacity) being enough to excuse.[21] Three States combine a full *M'Naghten* test with a volitional incapacity formula.[22] And New Hampshire alone stands by the product-of-mental-illness test. The alternatives are multiplied further by variations in the prescribed insanity verdict: a significant number of these jurisdictions supplement the traditional "not guilty by reason of insanity" verdict with an alternative of "guilty but mentally ill."[23] Finally, four States have no affirmative insanity defense,[24] though one provides for a "guilty and mentally ill" verdict.[25] These four, like a number of others that recognize an affirmative insanity defense, allow consideration of evidence of mental illness directly on the element of mens rea defining the offense.

With this varied background, it is clear that no particular formulation has evolved into a baseline for due process, and that the insanity rule, like the conceptualization of criminal offenses, is substantially open to state choice. . . . [M]edical definitions devised to justify treatment, like legal ones devised to excuse from conventional criminal responsibility, are subject to flux and disagreement. There being such fodder for reasonable debate about what the cognate legal and medical tests should be, due process imposes no single canonical formulation of legal insanity.

B

Nor does Arizona's abbreviation of the *M'Naghten* statement raise a proper claim that some constitutional minimum has been shortchanged. Clark's argument of course assumes that Arizona's former statement of the *M'Naghten* rule, with its express alternative of cognitive incapacity, was constitutionally adequate (as we agree). That being so, the abbreviated rule is no less so, for cognitive incapacity is relevant under that statement, just as it was under the more extended formulation, and evidence going to cognitive incapacity has the same significance under the short form as it had under the long.

Though Clark is correct that the application of the moral incapacity test (telling right from wrong) does not necessarily require evaluation of a defendant's cognitive capacity to appreciate the nature and quality of the acts charged against him, his argument fails to recognize that cognitive incapacity is itself enough to demonstrate moral incapacity. . . . In practical terms, if a defendant did not know what he was

---

21. [n.16] [The 14 jurisdictions cited here are Arkansas, Connecticut, District of Columbia, Georgia, Hawaii, Kentucky, Maryland, Massachusetts, Oregon, Rhode Island, Vermont, West Virginia, Wisconsin, and Wyoming.]

22. [n.17] [Here the Court cited Michigan, New Mexico, and Virginia.]

23. [n.19] [Here the Court cited 11 states: Alaska, Delaware, Georgia, Illinois, Indiana, Kentucky, Michigan, New Mexico, Pennsylvania, South Carolina, and South Dakota.] . . .

24. [n.20] [The four states cited here are Idaho, Kansas, Montana, and Utah.] We have never held that the Constitution mandates an insanity defense, nor have we held that the Constitution does not so require. This case does not call upon us to decide the matter.

25. [n.21] [Here the Court cited Utah.]

doing when he acted, he could not have known that he was performing the wrong-ful act charged as a crime. . . .

. . . .

Clark, indeed, adopted this very analysis himself in the trial court: "If [Clark] did not know he was shooting at a police officer, or believed he had to shoot or be shot, even though his belief was not based in reality, this would establish that he did not know what he was doing was wrong." The trial court apparently agreed, for the judge admitted Clark's evidence of cognitive incapacity for consideration under the State's moral incapacity formulation. And Clark can point to no evidence bearing on insan-ity that was excluded. . . .

We are satisfied that neither in theory nor in practice did Arizona's 1993 abridg-ment of the insanity formulation deprive Clark of due process.

III

Clark's second claim of a due process violation challenges the rule adopted by the Supreme Court of Arizona in *Mott*. . . . The state court held that testimony of a pro-fessional psychologist or psychiatrist about a defendant's mental incapacity owing to mental disease or defect was admissible, and could be considered, only for its bear-ing on an insanity defense; such evidence could not be considered on the element of mens rea. . . .

A

Understanding Clark's claim requires attention to the categories of evidence with a potential bearing on mens rea. First, there is "observation evidence" in the every-day sense, testimony from those who observed what Clark did and heard what he said; this category would also include testimony that an expert witness might give about Clark's tendency to think in a certain way and his behavioral characteristics. This evidence may support a professional diagnosis of mental disease and in any event is the kind of evidence that can be relevant to show what in fact was on Clark's mind when he fired the gun. Observation evidence in the record covers Clark's behavior at home and with friends, his expressions of belief around the time of the killing that "aliens" were inhabiting the bodies of local people (including government agents), his driving around the neighborhood before the police arrived, and so on. Contrary to the dissent's characterization, observation evidence can be presented by either lay or expert witnesses.

Second, there is "mental-disease evidence" in the form of opinion testimony that Clark suffered from a mental disease with features described by the witness. As was true here, this evidence characteristically but not always comes from professional psy-chologists or psychiatrists who testify as expert witnesses and base their opinions in part on examination of a defendant, usually conducted after the events in question. The thrust of this evidence was that, based on factual reports, professional observa-tions, and tests, Clark was psychotic at the time in question, with a condition that fell within the category of schizophrenia.

Third, there is evidence we will refer to as "capacity evidence" about a defendant's capacity for cognition and moral judgment (and ultimately also his capacity to form mens rea). This, too, is opinion evidence. Here, as it usually does, this testimony came from the same experts and concentrated on those specific details of the mental condition that make the difference between sanity and insanity under the Arizona definition. In their respective testimony on these details the experts disagreed: the defense expert gave his opinion that the symptoms or effects of the disease in Clark's case included inability to appreciate the nature of his action and to tell that it was wrong, whereas the State's psychiatrist was of the view that Clark was a schizophrenic who was still sufficiently able to appreciate the reality of shooting the officer and to know that it was wrong to do that.

A caveat about these [three] categories is in order. . . . What we can say about these categories goes to their cores, . . . not their margins. . . . Necessarily, then, our own decision can address only core issues, leaving for other cases any due process claims that may be raised about the treatment of evidence whose categorization is subject to dispute.

B

It is clear that *Mott* itself imposed no restriction on considering evidence of the first sort, the observation evidence. We read the *Mott* restriction to apply, rather, to evidence addressing the two issues in testimony that characteristically comes only from . . . expert witnesses: mental-disease evidence (whether at the time of the crime a defendant suffered from a mental disease or defect, such as schizophrenia) and capacity evidence (whether the disease or defect left him incapable of performing or experiencing a mental process defined as necessary for sanity such as appreciating the nature and quality of his act and knowing that it was wrong). . . .[26]

. . . .

D

Clark's argument that the *Mott* rule violates the Fourteenth Amendment guarantee of due process turns on the application of the presumption of innocence in criminal cases, the presumption of sanity, and the principle that a criminal defendant is entitled to present relevant and favorable evidence on an element of the offense charged against him.

The first presumption is that a defendant is innocent unless and until the government proves beyond a reasonable doubt each element of the offense charged. . . .

The presumption of sanity is equally universal in some variety or other, being (at least) a presumption that a defendant has the capacity to form the mens rea necessary for a verdict of guilt and the consequent criminal responsibility. This

---

26. [n.34] . . . Nothing that we hold here is authority for restricting a factfinder's consideration of observation evidence indicating state of mind at the time of a criminal offense (conventional mens rea evidence) as distinct from professional mental-disease or capacity evidence . . . .

presumption dispenses with a requirement on the government's part to include as an element of every criminal charge an allegation that the defendant had such a capacity. . . .

There are two points where the sanity or capacity presumption may be placed in issue. First, a State may allow a defendant to introduce (and a factfinder to consider) evidence of mental disease or incapacity for the bearing it can have on the government's burden to show mens rea. . . . If it is shown that a defendant with mental disease thinks all blond people are robots, he could not have intended to kill a person when he shot a man with blond hair, even though he seemed to act like a man shooting another man.[27] . . .

The second point where the force of the presumption of sanity may be tested is in the consideration of a defense of insanity raised by a defendant. . . .

The third principle implicated by Clark's argument is a defendant's right as a matter of simple due process to present evidence favorable to himself on an element that must be proven to convict him. As already noted, evidence tending to show that a defendant suffers from mental disease and lacks capacity to form mens rea is relevant to rebut evidence that he did in fact form the required mens rea at the time in question. . . .

As Clark recognizes, however, the right to introduce relevant evidence can be curtailed if there is a good reason for doing that. . . . And if evidence may be kept out entirely, its consideration may be subject to limitation . . . [if the] reasons for requiring it to be channeled and restricted are good enough to satisfy the standard of fundamental fairness that due process requires. We think they are.

E

The first reason supporting the *Mott* rule is Arizona's authority to define its presumption of sanity (or capacity or responsibility) by choosing an insanity definition, . . . and by placing the burden of persuasion on defendants who claim incapacity as an excuse from customary criminal responsibility. . . .

. . . [I]f a State is to have this authority in practice as well as in theory, it must be able to deny a defendant the opportunity to displace the presumption of sanity more easily when addressing a different issue in the course of the criminal trial. Yet, . . . just such an opportunity would be available if expert testimony of mental disease and incapacity could be considered for whatever a factfinder might think it was worth on the issue of mens rea. . . . [O]nce reasonable doubt was found, acquittal would be

---

27. [n.38] We reject the State's argument that mens rea and insanity, as currently understood, are entirely distinguishable, so that mental-disease and capacity evidence relevant to insanity is simply irrelevant to mens rea. Not only does evidence accepted as showing insanity trump mens rea, but evidence of behavior close to the time of the act charged may indicate both the actual state of mind at that time and also an enduring incapacity to form the criminal state of mind necessary to the offense charged.

required, and the standards established for the defense of insanity would go by the boards.

. . . .

A State's insistence on preserving its chosen standard of legal insanity cannot be the sole reason for a rule like *Mott*, however, for it fails to answer an objection the dissent makes in this case. An insanity rule gives a defendant already found guilty the opportunity to excuse his conduct by showing he was insane when he acted, that is, that he did not have the mental capacity for conventional guilt and criminal responsibility. But, as the dissent argues, if the same evidence that affirmatively shows he was not guilty by reason of insanity . . . also shows it was at least doubtful that he could form mens rea, then he should not be found guilty in the first place; it thus violates due process when the State impedes him from using mental-disease and capacity evidence directly to rebut the prosecution's evidence that he did form mens rea.

Are there, then, characteristics of mental-disease and capacity evidence giving rise to risks that may reasonably be hedged by channeling the consideration of such evidence to the insanity issue on which, in States like Arizona, a defendant has the burden of persuasion? We think there are: in the controversial character of some categories of mental disease, in the potential of mental-disease evidence to mislead, and in the danger of according greater certainty to capacity evidence than experts claim for it.

To begin with, the diagnosis may mask vigorous debate within the profession about the very contours of the mental disease itself. *See*, *e.g.*, American Psychiatric Association, Diagnostic and Statistical Manual of Mental Disorders xxxiii (4th ed. text rev. 2000) (hereinafter DSM-IV-TR) ("DSM-IV reflects a consensus about the classification and diagnosis of mental disorders derived at the time of its initial publication. New knowledge . . . will undoubtedly lead to an increased understanding of the disorders included in DSM-IV, to the identification of new disorders, and to the removal of some disorders in future classifications. . . ."). . . .

Next, there is the potential of mental-disease evidence to mislead jurors. . . . Even when a category of mental disease is broadly accepted and the assignment of a defendant's behavior to that category is uncontroversial, the classification may suggest something very significant about a defendant's capacity, when in fact the classification tells us little or nothing about the ability of the defendant to form mens rea or to exercise the cognitive, moral, or volitional capacities that define legal sanity. The limits of the utility of a professional disease diagnosis are evident in the dispute between the two testifying experts in this case; they agree that Clark was schizophrenic, but they come to opposite conclusions on whether the mental disease in his particular case left him bereft of cognitive or moral capacity. . . . [I]t is very easy to slide from evidence that an individual with a professionally recognized mental disease is very different, into doubting that he has the capacity to form mens rea, whereas that doubt may not be justified. . . . Because allowing mental-disease evidence on mens rea can thus easily mislead, it is not unreasonable to address that tendency by confining consideration of this kind of evidence to insanity, on which a defendant may be assigned the burden of persuasion.

There are, finally, particular risks inherent in the opinions of the experts who supplement the mental-disease classifications with opinions on incapacity. . . . Unlike observational evidence bearing on mens rea, capacity evidence consists of judgment, and judgment fraught with multiple perils. . . . Although such capacity judgments may be given in the utmost good faith, their potentially tenuous character is indicated by the candor of the defense expert in this very case. Contrary to the State's expert, he testified that Clark lacked the capacity to appreciate the circumstances realistically and to understand the wrongfulness of what he was doing, but he said that "no one knows exactly what was on [Clark's] mind" at the time of the shooting. And even when an expert is confident that his understanding of the mind is reliable, judgment addressing the basic categories of capacity requires a leap from the concepts of psychology, which are devised for thinking about treatment, to the concepts of legal sanity, which are devised for thinking about criminal responsibility. . . . [T]hese empirical and conceptual problems add up to a real risk that an expert's judgment in giving capacity evidence will come with an apparent authority that psychologists and psychiatrists do not claim to have. We think that this risk, like the difficulty in assessing the significance of mental-disease evidence, supports the State's decision to channel such expert testimony to consideration on the insanity defense, on which the party seeking the benefit of this evidence has the burden of persuasion.

It bears repeating that not every State will find it worthwhile to make the judgment Arizona has made, and the choices the States do make about dealing with the risks posed by mental-disease and capacity evidence will reflect their varying assessments about the presumption of sanity as expressed in choices of insanity rules.[28] The point here simply is that Arizona has sensible reasons to assign the risks as it has done by channeling the evidence.[29]

. . . .

JUSTICE BREYER, concurring in part and dissenting in part.

. . . .

---

28. [n.44] A State in which the burden of persuasion as to a defendant's sanity lies with the prosecution might also be justified in restricting mental-disease and capacity evidence to insanity determinations owing to the potential of mental-disease evidence to mislead and the risk of misjudgment inherent in capacity evidence. We need not, in the context of this case, address that issue.

29. [n.45] Arizona's rule is supported by a further practical reason, though not as weighty as those just considered. As mentioned before, if substantial mental-disease and capacity evidence is accepted as rebutting mens rea in a given case, the affirmative defense of insanity will probably not be reached or ruled upon; the defendant will simply be acquitted (or perhaps convicted of a lesser included offense). If an acquitted defendant suffers from a mental disease or defect that makes him dangerous, he will neither be confined nor treated psychiatrically unless a judge so orders after some independent commitment proceeding. . . .

I agree with the Court's basic categorization [of the three categories of evidence related to mens rea and insanity]. I also agree that the Constitution permits a State to provide for consideration of the second and third types of evidence solely in conjunction with the insanity defense.

Nonetheless, I believe the distinction among these kinds of evidence will be unclear in some cases. . . .

Consequently, I would remand this case so that Arizona's courts can determine whether Arizona law, as set forth in *Mott* and other cases, is consistent with the distinction the Court draws and whether the trial court so applied Arizona law here. I would also reserve the question (as I believe the Court has done) as to the burden of persuasion in a case where the defendant produces sufficient [expert opinion evidence on the defendant's capacity to form the requisite mens rea] as to raise a reasonable doubt that he suffered from a mental illness so severe as to prevent him from forming any relevant intent at all.

. . . .

JUSTICE KENNEDY, with whom JUSTICE STEVENS and JUSTICE GINSBURG join, dissenting.

In my submission the Court is incorrect in holding that Arizona may convict petitioner Eric Clark of first-degree murder for the intentional or knowing killing of a police officer when Clark was not permitted to introduce critical and reliable evidence showing he did not have that intent or knowledge. . . .

Since I would reverse the judgment of the Arizona Court of Appeals on this ground, . . . it is unnecessary for me to address the argument that Arizona's definition of insanity violates due process.

I

. . . .

The Court . . . adopts an evidentiary framework that, in my view, will be unworkable in many cases. . . . The most common type of schizophrenia, and the one Clark suffered from, is paranoid schizophrenia. . . . Common symptoms of the condition are delusions accompanied by hallucinations, often of the auditory type, which can cause disturbances of perception. Clark's expert testified that people with schizophrenia often play radios loudly to drown out the voices in their heads. Clark's attorney argued to the trial court that this, rather than a desire to lure a policeman to the scene, explained Clark's behavior just before the killing. The observation that schizophrenics play radios loudly is a fact regarding behavior, but it is only a relevant fact if Clark has schizophrenia.

. . . More generally, the opinion that Clark had paranoid schizophrenia—an opinion shared by experts for both the prosecution and defense—bears on efforts to determine, as a factual matter, whether he knew he was killing a police officer. . . . Simply put, knowledge relies on cognition, and cognition can be affected by schizophrenia.

The mental-disease evidence at trial was also intertwined with the observation evidence because it lent needed credibility. Clark's parents and friends testified Clark thought the people in his town were aliens trying to kill him. These claims might not be believable without a psychiatrist confirming the story based on his experience with people who have exhibited similar behaviors. It makes little sense to divorce the observation evidence from the explanation that makes it comprehensible.

. . . .

The razor-thin distinction the Court draws between evidence being used to show incapacity and evidence being used to show lack of mens rea directly does not identify two different claims. Clark's single claim, however characterized, involves the use of the same mental-illness evidence to decide whether he had the requisite knowledge or intent. The various ways in which the evidence is relevant in disproving mens rea hardly qualify as separate claims. . . .

. . . .

II

. . . .

. . . "Whether rooted directly in the Due Process Clause of the Fourteenth Amendment or in the Compulsory Process or Confrontation Clauses of the Sixth Amendment, the Constitution guarantees criminal defendants 'a meaningful opportunity to present a complete defense.'" *Holmes v. South Carolina*, 547 U.S. 319, 324 (2006). "This right is abridged by evidence rules that 'infringe upon a weighty interest of the accused' and are 'arbitrary' or 'disproportionate to the purposes they are designed to serve.'" *Holmes, supra*, at 324.

. . . .

The issue is not, as the Court insists, whether Clark's mental illness acts as an "excuse from customary criminal responsibility," but whether his mental illness, as a factual matter, made him unaware that he was shooting a police officer. If it did, Clark needs no excuse, as then he did not commit the crime as Arizona defines it. . . .

. . . .

Arizona's rule is problematic because it excludes evidence no matter how credible and material it may be in disproving an element of the offense. . . .

. . . .

In the instant case Arizona's proposed reasons are insufficient to support its categorical exclusion. While the State contends that testimony regarding mental illness may be too incredible or speculative for the jury to consider, this does not explain why the exclusion applies in all cases to all evidence of mental illness. . . .

The risk of jury confusion also fails to justify the rule. . . . Considered on its own terms, the issue of intent and knowledge is a straightforward factual question. A trier of fact is quite capable of weighing defense testimony and then determining whether the accused did or did not intend to kill or knowingly kill a human being who was a police officer. True, the issue can be difficult to decide in particular instances, but no more so than many matters juries must confront.

. . . It is striking that while the Court discusses at length the likelihood of misjudgment from placing too much emphasis on evidence of mental illness, it ignores the risk of misjudging an innocent man guilty from refusing to consider this highly relevant evidence at all. . . .

. . . .

Contrary to the Court's suggestion, the fact that the state and defense experts drew different conclusions about the effect of Clark's mental illness on his mental state only made Clark's evidence contested; it did not make the evidence irrelevant or misleading. . . . In fact, the potential to mislead will be far greater under the Court's new evidentiary system, where jurors will receive observation evidence without the necessary explanation from experts.

The fact that mental-illness evidence may be considered in deciding criminal responsibility does not compensate for its exclusion from consideration on the mens rea elements of the crime. . . . Criminal responsibility involves an inquiry into whether the defendant knew right from wrong, not whether he had the mens rea elements of the offense. . . .

Even if the analyses were equivalent, there is a different burden of proof for insanity than there is for mens rea. . . . While evidentiary rules do not generally shift the burden impermissibly, where there is a right to have evidence considered on an element of the offense, the right is not respected by allowing the evidence to come in only on an issue for which the defendant bears the burden of proof. . . .

. . . .

. . . While defining mental illness is a difficult matter, the State seems to exclude the evidence one would think most reliable by . . . excluding relatively well-understood psychiatric testimony regarding well-documented mental illnesses. It is unclear, moreover, what would have happened in this case had the defendant wanted to testify that he thought Officer Moritz was an alien. If disallowed, it would be tantamount to barring Clark from testifying on his behalf to explain his own actions. If allowed, then Arizona's rule would simply prohibit the corroboration necessary to make sense of Clark's explanation. In sum, the rule forces the jury to decide guilt in a fictional world with undefined and unexplained behaviors but without mental illness. This rule has no rational justification. . . .

. . . .

Notes and Questions

1. Is the First Prong of *M'Naghten* Irrelevant? In Part II of the majority opinion in *Clark*, the Court upheld Arizona's decision to adopt only one prong of the *M'Naghten* definition of insanity, reasoning that "cognitive incapacity is itself enough to demonstrate moral incapacity." Is this right? If Clark knew it was wrong to kill a police officer and killed the officer because he could not distinguish between "alien" police officers and human officers, would he have a defense in Arizona? Is it possible to have moral capacity and lack cognitive capacity? *Compare* Stephen J. Morse & Morris B. Hoffman, *The Uneasy Entente Between Legal Insanity and Mens Rea: Beyond* Clark v. Arizona, 97 J. Crim. L. & Criminology 1071, 1101 (2007) (agreeing with the Court that "if the agent does not know what he is doing, he cannot rationally know that it is right or wrong"), *with* Susan D. Rozelle, *Fear and Loathing in Insanity Law: Explaining the Otherwise Inexplicable* Clark v. Arizona, 58 Case W. Res. L. Rev. 19, 38–39 (2007) (arguing that *M'Naghten*'s "two separate prongs [are] not collapsible into . . . one" because "[o]ne can know very well that x is wrong without realizing that what one is doing is x").

2. The Relationship Between Mens Rea and Insanity. Clark claimed that he lacked the mens rea required under Arizona law. Section 13-1105(A)(3) defines first-degree murder to encompass cases where a person, "[i]ntending or knowing that the person's conduct will cause death to a law enforcement officer, . . . causes the death of a law enforcement officer who is in the line of duty." If Clark believed that the victim was an "alien" law enforcement officer, did he have the requisite intent? If he thought that the victim was an "alien" posing as a law enforcement officer, did he have the requisite intent?

The relationship between mens rea and insanity has been murky since *M'Naghten*. Consider, for example, a defendant who shot and killed another person. As a result of a mental illness, the defendant believed the victim was actually a rampaging bull. Did this defendant have the requisite intent to commit murder? Did the defendant intend to kill? The answer is clearly yes. Did the defendant intend to kill a human being? The answer is clearly no. Is this mistake one that a person without mental illness would make? Again, the answer is no. So, should a court focus on insanity or mens rea, or both? *See* Stephen J. Morse & Morris B. Hoffman, *The Uneasy Entente Between Legal Insanity and Mens Rea: Beyond* Clark v. Arizona, 97 J. Crim. L. & Criminology 1071, 1096–97 (2007) (noting that, although "it is very uncommon for mental disorder to negate all mens rea, even if the defendant is profoundly delusional," "the mens rea issue is entirely distinct from the legal insanity issue, even if precisely the same evidence would be relevant to adjudicating both claims").

The confusion surrounding mens rea and insanity has led some jurisdictions to bifurcate the issue of insanity from the rest of the trial, holding a second, separate trial on the insanity defense only after the jury finds the defendant guilty of the crime. A few states require this bifurcated approach, *see, e.g., People v. Mills*, 286 P.3d 754 (Cal. 2012) (applying Cal. Penal Code § 1026(a)), and others permit trial judges to bifurcate the trial at the defendant's request or to avoid prejudice. *See* 1 Wayne R. LaFave, Substantive Criminal Law § 8.3, at 136 (2d ed. Supp. 2015). But other jurisdictions refuse to follow this procedure. *See, e.g., State v. Handy*, 73 A.3d 421 (N.J. 2013) (reversing prior practice and requiring a unitary trial). *See generally* Debra T. Landis, Annotation, *Necessity or Propriety of Bifurcated Criminal Trial on Issue of Insanity Defense*, 1 A.L.R.4th 884 (1980).

3. Limiting the Use of Evidence. Arizona permits a defendant to use evidence of mental disease or defect to negate mens rea and to support an insanity defense, but the state restricts psychiatric/psychological opinion evidence to the insanity defense.[30] Part III of the Supreme Court's opinion in *Clark*, upholding the constitutionality of this approach, has come under attack. *See, e.g.,* Arnold H. Loewy, *The Two Faces of Insanity*, 42 Tex. Tech L. Rev. 513, 520 (2009) (pointing out that a defendant with poor eyesight could introduce expert testimony to prove lack of intent to kill a police officer even though "schizophrenia . . . plays precisely the same role as poor vision"); Peter Westen, *The Supreme Court's Bout with Insanity:* Clark v. Arizona, 4 Ohio St. J. Crim. L. 143, 160 (2006) (charging that the *Clark* majority "implicitly allowed the states to shift the burden of persuasion to defendants in insanity cases to disprove an issue of mens rea that the prosecution must otherwise prove beyond a reasonable doubt").

Unlike Arizona, however, most states permit a defendant to offer relevant expert testimony to rebut mens rea. In his dissenting opinion in *Clark*, 548 U.S. at 800, Justice Kennedy cited a Justice Department brief for the proposition that 13 states restrict the admission of mental health evidence on mens rea issues. *See, e.g., Thompson v. State*, 757 S.E.2d 846, 849 (Ga. 2014) (noting that "evidence of a defendant's diminished mental condition" may not be introduced "to negate the intent element of a crime," and therefore upholding the refusal to permit an expert to testify that a murder defendant had an IQ of 67, offered to support his claim that the death was an accident because "his mental disability prevented him from understanding how to use the crossbow properly"). Some states ban mental health evidence when offered to establish the defendant's lack of capacity to form a particular mental state, but permit the testimony on the question whether the defendant actually had the required mental state. California is an example, although it permits mental health evidence to disprove mens rea only for specific intent crimes. *See* Cal. Penal Code § 28(a).[31]

---

30. Interestingly, the argument that mental illness negated mens rea, and not the insanity defense, was the theory that Theodore Kaczynski, the infamous "Unabomber," was apparently going to use at his trial on federal charges stemming from a 17-year bombing spree that killed three people, injured 23 others, and led to "[t]he longest, most expensive manhunt in American history." William Finnegan, *Defending the Unabomber*, The New Yorker, Mar. 16, 1998, at 52. The brilliant math-professor-turned-hermit, who lived for 25 years in a remote Montana cabin without electricity or indoor plumbing, refused to permit his attorneys to raise an insanity defense, purportedly because he did not want his anti-technology views portrayed as crazy. When the trial judge denied as untimely Kaczynski's last-minute requests to replace his attorneys and then to represent himself (after he discovered the extent to which the lawyers were planning on introducing evidence of mental illness), Kaczynski pled guilty to all charges in return for a life sentence. *Id.*; *see also* Michael Mello, *The Non-Trial of the Century: Representations of the Unabomber*, 24 Vt. L. Rev. 417 (2000). *Cf.* Kevin Sack & Alan Blinder, *With His Life Now at Stake, Killer Rejects Best Defense*, N.Y. Times, Jan. 2, 2017, at A8 (describing Dylann Roof's similarly motivated decision to represent himself at his capital sentencing hearing and not to introduce any mental health evidence, despite his trial attorney's use of words like "abnormal," "irrational[]," and "delusional" in describing Roof's shooting of nine African-American members of the Emanuel A.M.E. Church in Charleston, South Carolina); Kevin Sack, *Evidence Not Seen by Jury Raises Questions About Gunman's Death Sentence*, N.Y. Times, June 1, 2017, at A17.

31. Some courts refer to mental health evidence offered to disprove mens rea as "diminished responsibility" or "diminished capacity" evidence, while other courts prefer to avoid that terminology.

The weight of authority in the federal courts is that Congress did not intend to prohibit a defendant from challenging mens rea with mental health evidence when it enacted 18 U.S.C. § 17 (adopting a *M'Naghten*-type insanity test and providing that "mental disease or defect does not otherwise constitute a defense"). *See, e.g., United States v. Veach*, 455 F.3d 628 (6th Cir. 2006). (For a description of the federal insanity statute, see Note 11 in Part 1 above.)

4. James Holmes. Colorado, like Arizona, omits *M'Naghten*'s first prong in its insanity statute, requiring an insanity acquittal when a defendant was "so diseased or defective in mind at the time of the commission of the act as to be incapable of distinguishing right from wrong with respect to that act." But Colorado's definition of insanity also includes a person whose "mental disease or defect . . . prevented the person from forming a culpable mental state that is an essential element" of the crime. Colo. Rev. Stat. § 16-8-101.5(1). Colorado was the site of the trial of James Holmes, who was convicted of killing 12 people and wounding 70 others at an Aurora, Colorado, movie theatre during a midnight screening of *The Dark Knight Rises* in 2012.

At Holmes' trial on more than 160 counts of murder, attempted murder, and other charges, the prosecution argued that Holmes carefully planned the attack in order to bolster his sense of self-worth after he dropped out of graduate school and his girlfriend broke up with him. The prosecution introduced a notebook in which Holmes wrote about a "mass murder spree" and considered what location would lead to "maximum casualties." Two psychiatric experts testified for the prosecution that, while Holmes suffered from a severe mental illness on a spectrum with schizophrenia, he knew what he was doing and realized that it was wrong. During a 22-hour recorded interview with one of the State's psychiatric witnesses, much of which was played for the jury at trial, Holmes spoke without affect and explained that, although he knew he was likely to be caught, "[t]hat's just the price you have to pay for completing the mission."

Lawyers for Holmes, who was prescribed antidepressants and antipsychotic medication after his arrest, also called two expert psychiatrists, who testified that the defendant was unable to distinguish right from wrong and therefore was legally insane. One concluded that Holmes suffered from "a 'psychotic mental illness' that revealed itself through delusions, severe anxiety and a stark emotional disconnect from the world." The second testified that Holmes was schizophrenic and "began to believe he could replenish his own worth only by killing others."

Although the jurors rejected Holmes' insanity defense and convicted him on every count, they did not sentence him to death. Nine members of the jury were in favor of the death penalty and two were on the fence, but one was unalterably opposed and Colorado law requires a unanimous jury vote in favor of a capital sentence. The

---

See, e.g., United States v. Brawner, 471 F.2d 969, 998 (D.C. Cir. 1972). For discussion of the diminished capacity defense recognized in a few jurisdictions, which provides a partial excuse in homicide cases, mitigating the defendant's killing to a less culpable form of homicide, see Note 7 following *People v. Anderson* in Chapter 6, Section B.1, and Note 15 following *State v. Thornton* in Chapter 6, Section B.2.

trial judge then sentenced Holmes to 12 life sentences, one for each murder victim, and an additional 3,318 years on the nonhomicide charges. Holmes' attorneys said they were not planning to file an appeal. *See* Julie Turkewitz, *Aurora Gunman Receives 12 Life Terms in Prison*, N.Y. Times, Aug. 27, 2015, at A15; Jack Healy, *Theater Gunman Is Spared Death in Aurora Case*, N.Y. Times, Aug. 8, 2015, at A1; Julie Turkewitz, *Aurora Gunman Legally Insane, Psychiatrist Says*, N.Y. Times, July 9, 2015, at A19; Jack Healy, *Defense Tries to Put Focus on Sanity of Gunman*, N.Y. Times, June 26, 2015, at A12; Jack Healy, *Ex-Girlfriend of Aurora Gunman Recalls Awkwardness and Ghoulish Remarks*, N.Y. Times, June 12, 2015, at A16; Jack Healy, *Gunman Calmly Recalls Theater Rampage in Video*, N.Y. Times, June 3, 2015, at A12; Jack Healy, *Colorado Killer's Notes: Detailed Plans vs. 'a Whole Lot of Crazy'*, N.Y. Times, May 29, 2015, at A1.

5. Abolishing the Insanity Defense. Do cases like *Clark* and *Holmes* suggest that, notwithstanding the Supreme Court majority's views, it makes more sense to consider mental illness only in determining whether the defendant had the mens rea necessary to commit the crime? That is the approach taken by the four state legislatures—Idaho, Kansas, Montana, and Utah—which have abolished insanity as a separate defense. The Utah Supreme Court explained the practical consequences of these statutes as follows:

> If A kills B, thinking that he is merely squeezing a grapefruit, A does not have the requisite mens rea for murder and would be acquitted under both the prior and the new law. However, if A kills B, thinking that B is an enemy soldier and that the killing is justified as self-defense, then A has the requisite mens rea for murder and could be convicted under the new law but not under the prior law, because he knowingly and intentionally took another's life.

State v. Herrera, 895 P.2d 359, 362 (Utah 1995).

The court's hypotheticals raise another question: if *A* genuinely thinks *B* is an enemy soldier, is *A* entitled to claim self-defense? Or, can *A* argue mistake of fact? The problem for *A* is that the belief is likely to be regarded as unreasonable, because ordinary people would not have made the same mistake. *A*'s mistake is attributable to mental illness, and if no insanity defense is available, the courts will presumably regard *A*'s mental illness as irrelevant to other defenses that require a reasonable belief and use an objective standard to assess reasonableness. *But cf.* Christopher Slobogin, *A Defense of the Integrationist Test as a Replacement for the Special Defense of Insanity*, 42 Tex. Tech L. Rev. 523, 528 (2014) (taking the position that insanity should be abolished as a separate defense, and that instead mental disorder should afford a defense if it would do so under the "relatively subjectivized framework that the MPC applies to people who are not mentally ill"—e.g., where the mental disorder led to a lack of mens rea or a mistaken belief that one's act was justified or committed under duress).

The Supreme Court, in footnote 20 of its opinion in *Clark*, specifically refused to take a position on the constitutionality of abolishing the insanity defense, and in 2012, the Court came one vote short of granting certiorari on that question. *See*

Delling v. Idaho, 133 S. Ct. 504 (2012) (Breyer, J., dissenting from denial of certiorari). Nevertheless, the statutes eliminating the insanity defense have for the most part survived constitutional challenges in the state courts. *See State v. Searcy*, 798 P.2d 914, 916–19 (Idaho 1990); *State v. Korell*, 690 P.2d 992, 996–1002 (Mont. 1984); *Herrera*, 895 P.2d at 363–71.

But when the Nevada legislature abolished insanity as a separate defense, the state supreme court struck the statute down on the grounds that "legal insanity is a well-established and fundamental principle of the law of the United States . . . protected by the Due Process Clauses of both the United States and Nevada Constitutions." *Finger v. State*, 27 P.3d 66, 84 (Nev. 2001), *cert. denied*, 534 U.S. 1127 (2002). The court explained:

> Historically, the mens rea of most crimes, particularly specific intent crimes, incorporates some element of wrongfulness as that term is used in . . . *M'Naghten*. The Legislature can only eliminate this concept of wrongfulness if it redefines the crime itself, in other words, if it chooses to make the act, regardless of the mental state, the crime. Thus murder could simply be defined as the killing of a human being. But so long as a crime requires some additional mental intent, then legal insanity must be a complete defense to that crime.

Id.

The Kansas Supreme Court, however, came to the opposite conclusion in *State v. Bethel*, 66 P.3d 840 (Kan.), *cert. denied*, 540 U.S. 1006 (2003), agreeing with the other state courts that had previously upheld the constitutionality of statutes abolishing insanity as a separate defense. The Kansas court distinguished the Nevada Supreme Court's decision in *Finger* on the grounds that "malice is not a requisite element of murder" in Kansas, and "the only intent required is the intent to kill a human being." *Id.* at 850. The court also reasoned that "the affirmative insanity defense is a creature of the 19th century and is not so ingrained in our legal system to constitute a fundamental principle of law." *Id.* at 851. *But see* Stephen Morse & Richard J. Bonnie, *Abolition of the Insanity Defense Violates Due Process*, 41 J. Am. Acad. Psychiatry & L. 488, 489–90 (2013) (taking the position that the insanity defense is constitutionally required, given its historical pedigree as "a feature of ancient law and of English law since the fourteenth century," the "near consensus among state and federal lawmakers that the defense must be retained," and "the fundamental unfairness of blaming and punishing legally insane offenders").[32]

Note that abolishing the insanity defense does not necessarily decrease the number of defendants who avoid criminal punishment. A study of the Montana statute, for

---

32. Following the prevailing sentiment in the jurisdictions that have addressed the abolition question, some courts have held that insanity may not be raised as a defense in juvenile delinquency proceedings. *See Golden v. State*, 21 S.W.3d 801 (Ark.), *cert. denied*, 531 U.S. 1022 (2000); *Commonwealth v. Chatman*, 538 S.E.2d 304 (Va. 2000). *But see In re Winburn*, 145 N.W.2d 178, 183 (Wis. 1966).

example, found that defendants who probably would have been acquitted by reason of insanity before the insanity defense was abolished are now being found incompetent to stand trial and are confined in the same hospitals as the insanity acquittees. *See* Henry J. Steadman et al., Before and After Hinckley: Evaluating Insanity Defense Reform 121–37 (1993).

6. Defining "Mental Disease or Defect." Neither *M'Naghten* nor the Model Penal Code expressly defines the term "mental disease or defect"; instead, they focus on what effect a mental illness must have in order to render a defendant legally insane. The question whether a defendant was mentally ill at the time of the crime is a legal and moral one, however, rather than a medical one.

The difficulties that would arise if the criminal justice system were to cede the task of defining mental illness to psychiatrists were graphically illustrated by the so-called "weekend flip flop case," *In re Rosenfield*, 157 F. Supp. 18 (D.D.C. 1957), *remanded*, 262 F.2d 34 (D.C. Cir. 1958) (per curiam). On Friday afternoon, a psychiatrist from St. Elizabeths Hospital in Washington, D.C. testified that the defendant in that case, who had a sociopathic personality, did not have a mental disease. At a weekend staff meeting, the doctors at St. Elizabeths decided that sociopathy was in fact a mental disease, and the expert changed his testimony on Monday morning. *See United States v. Brawner*, 471 F.2d 969, 978 (D.C. Cir. 1972) (en banc).

Traditionally, juries have not been instructed on the meaning of the phrase "mental disease or defect." *See* Joshua Dressler, Understanding Criminal Law § 25.04[B][3], at 345 (7th ed. 2015). However, the District of Columbia Circuit suggested that juries be told the term "includes any abnormal condition of the mind which substantially affects mental or emotional processes and substantially impairs behavior controls." *McDonald v. United States*, 312 F.2d 847, 851 (D.C. Cir. 1962) (en banc). Although the court later acknowledged that this definition is "not without an attribute of circularity," it defended the *McDonald* formulation as "useful in . . . [making] plain that clinical and legal definitions of mental disease [are] distinct." *Brawner*, 471 F.2d at 978.

In thinking about how "mental disease or defect" ought to be defined in a legal setting, consider whether an insanity defense should be available in the following circumstances.

(a) Gambling Disorder — defined as "[p]ersistent and recurrent problematic gambling behavior leading to clinically significant impairment or distress" — is recognized as an addictive disorder in the American Psychiatric Association's Diagnostic and Statistical Manual of Mental Disorders 585 (5th ed. 2013) (DSM-5). The indicators of this disorder include being "preoccupied with gambling," "[n]eed[ing] to gamble with increasing amounts of money in order to achieve the desired excitement," making "repeated unsuccessful efforts to . . . stop," "jeopardiz[ing] or los[ing] a significant relationship, job, [or other] opportunity because of gambling," and "[r]el[ying] on others to provide money to relieve desperate financial situations caused by gambling." *Id.*

Edward Lowitzki served as treasurer for his son's high school club. He stole about $100,000 from the club in order to finance his gambling habit. Should he have a valid insanity defense because he needed money in order to satisfy his craving for gambling and, "once a person has reached the desperation phase of [the] illness, that person is unable to conform his or her conduct to the law"? *People v. Lowitzki*, 674 N.E.2d 859, 861 (Ill. App. Ct. 1996) (summarizing defense expert's testimony). Or should his insanity defense be rejected because although theft may be "a common crime" among compulsive gamblers, some people "reach desperate financial conditions due to pathological gambling and seek help without breaking the law"? *Id.* at 864, 861.

The court rejected Lowitzki's defense, concluding that compulsive gamblers are precluded from raising an insanity defense, at least for nongambling offenses. *See id.* at 863; *see also United States v. Carmel*, 801 F.2d 997, 999 (7th Cir. 1986) (citing a number of federal decisions that took the same position). *But cf.* Alan J. Cunnien, *Pathological Gambling as an Insanity Defense*, 3 Behav. Sci. & L. 85, 90 (1985) (describing two cases where compulsive gamblers charged with writing bad checks and larceny were found not guilty by reason of insanity).

(b) Post-traumatic stress disorder (PTSD) occurs when "clinically significant distress or impairment in social, occupational, or other important areas of functioning" is caused by "[e]xposure to actual or threatened death, serious injury, or sexual violence" — by, for example, "[d]irectly experiencing the traumatic event[]" or "[w]itnessing, in person, the event[] as it occurred to others." DSM-5, *supra*, at 271. The traumatic events that can lead to PTSD include military combat, violent assaults (like those experienced by victims of domestic violence), natural disasters, terrorist attacks, serious automobile accidents, and torture. PTSD is characterized by the following symptoms: "intrusion symptoms" (e.g., flashbacks, recurring memories or dreams, or "intense . . . psychological distress at exposure to . . . cues that . . . resemble . . . the traumatic event[]"); "[p]ersistent avoidance of stimuli associated with the traumatic event[]"; "negative alterations in cognitions and mood associated with the traumatic event[]" (e.g., blaming oneself for the event, decreased interest in other activities, or "estrangement from others"); and "[m]arked alterations in arousal and reactivity" (e.g., hypervigilance, self-destructive behavior, or problems sleeping or concentrating). *Id.* at 271–72. About 30 percent of Vietnam veterans reportedly suffer from PTSD, and at one time one of seven federal prisoners and one of 10 state prisoners were Vietnam veterans. *See* Thomas L. Hafemeister & Nicole A. Stockey, *Last Stand? The Criminal Responsibility of War Veterans Returning from Iraq and Afghanistan with Posttraumatic Stress Disorder*, 85 Ind. L.J. 87, 100–02 (2010). Although the impact of the wars in Iraq and Afghanistan is not yet known, researchers estimate that 10 percent to 20 percent of veterans returning from those wars show signs of PTSD, and that figure may eventually increase to 35 percent. In addition, suicide rates among veterans are increasing. *See id.* at 88–92.

Jearl Wood, a Vietnam veteran, suffered from PTSD. He worked in a plant where the loud noises and physical conditions were somewhat reminiscent of combat. One day, his supervisor accused him of drinking on the job and sent him home. Wood walked to the parking lot, retrieved a gun from his car, and returned to the plant, firing two shots that seriously injured the supervisor. At trial, a defense expert testified that, when threatened with the loss of his job, Wood began to act in the same "survivor mode" of behavior that he had relied on while in Vietnam. At the time of the shooting, therefore, he "was once again the frightened 18-year-old Marine who carried his .45 caliber automatic pistol everywhere and who survived his traumatic Vietnam experiences by learning to react without thinking." The jury voted to acquit by reason of insanity. *See* C. Peter Erlinder, *Paying the Price for Vietnam: Post-Traumatic Stress Disorder and Criminal Behavior*, 25 B.C. L. Rev. 305, 323 (1984) (describing the facts of *People v. Wood*, No. 80-7410 (Ill. Cir. Ct. May 1982)). *See also Porter v. McCollum*, 558 U.S. 30, 30, 35 (2009) (per curiam) (reversing death sentence imposed on George Porter, a decorated Korean War veteran who returned from combat "a traumatized, changed man" and later killed his former girlfriend and her boyfriend, on the grounds that Porter was denied effective assistance of counsel when his lawyer failed to present evidence suggesting Porter suffered from PTSD, including evidence that he had "dreadful nightmares and would attempt to climb his bedroom walls with knives at night"); *United States v. Rezaq*, 918 F. Supp. 463, 467–68 (D.D.C. 1996) (concluding that evidence of severe PTSD and depression can satisfy the federal insanity statute's requirement of a "severe" mental disease).

By contrast, a Texas jury rejected the insanity defense raised by Eddie Ray Routh, a veteran who was convicted of murder in 2015 and sentenced to life in prison without parole after he shot former Navy SEAL Chris Kyle and his friend Chad Littlefield at a gun range. The Veterans Administration had diagnosed Routh with PTSD as well as various other mental illnesses, and he had been hospitalized after threatening to kill himself and his family. At his trial, the defense introduced expert testimony that Routh was schizophrenic and believed the victims were "pig assassins ... sent here to kill people." The jury also learned that Kyle, whose autobiography was the basis of the film *American Sniper*, sent Littlefield a text message on the way to the gun range asking Littlefield to "[w]atch [his] back" and calling Routh "straight-up nuts." On the other hand, one of the government's experts testified that Routh suffered from cannabis-induced psychosis, and the other testified that he was intoxicated and not insane at the time of the killings. The prosecution argued that Routh did not suffer from PTSD, feigned the symptoms of his illness, and knew that his actions were wrong. The Texas Court of Appeals affirmed his conviction, finding sufficient evidence to support the jury's rejection of his insanity defense. *See Routh v. State*, 2017 Tex. App. Lexis 2833 (Tex. App. Mar. 31, 2017). *See also* Mike Spies, *Inside the Tortured Mind of Eddie Ray Routh, the Man Who Killed American Sniper Chris Kyle*, Newsweek, Jan. 8, 2016 (describing medical records suggesting Routh may suffer from schizophrenia). *Cf.* Hafemeister & Starkey, *supra*, at 119–28, 134–40 (discussing the obstacles veterans have faced in trying to use PTSD to support insanity and other defenses); Michael L. Perlin, *"I Expected It to Happen/I Knew He'd Lost Control": The Impact of PTSD on Criminal Sentencing After the Promulgation of DSM-5*, 2015 Utah L. Rev. 881, 914 (noting that skepticism surrounds the PTSD diagnosis, despite recent advances in testing, because it is "so dependent upon the defendant's self-reporting of symptoms").

For discussion of somewhat similar defenses—that exposure to the violence prevalent in inner-city neighborhoods can lead to "urban psychosis" and that the stress caused by experiencing the effects of racism can trigger "black rage"—compare Patricia J. Falk, *Novel Theories of Criminal Defense Based upon the Toxicity of the Social Environment: Urban Psychosis, Television Intoxication, and Black Rage*, 74 N.C. L. Rev. 731, 801 (1996) (arguing that these theories "simply provide new causal explanations for mental illness" and thus require "little substantive innovation or expansion" of the insanity defense), with Alan M. Dershowitz, The Abuse Excuse 90 (1994) (describing these defenses as "an insult to millions of law-abiding black Americans").

(c) Some 50 to 80 percent of new mothers experience a mild form of postpartum depression, or "baby blues." Between 10 and 15 percent suffer from a more serious postpartum depression, which resembles clinical depression and can last anywhere from a few weeks to a year or more. Postpartum psychosis, an even more severe disorder, occurs after 0.1 percent to 0.2 percent of all births. A woman suffering from postpartum psychosis may have hallucinations and delusions about her baby's well-being and her ability to care for the child. For example, she may hear voices saying that her baby is a demon or that she should kill the child. *See* DSM-5, *supra*, at 186–87; Michelle Oberman, *Mothers Who Kill: Coming to Terms with Modern American Infanticide*, 34 Am. Crim. L. Rev. 1, 33–34 (1996); Anne D. Brusca, Note, *Postpartum Psychosis: A Way Out for Murderous Moms?*, 18 Hofstra L. Rev. 1133, 1141–44 (1990).

Psychiatrists disagree about the causes of postpartum depression and psychosis. Some attribute the disorders to physiological factors—hormonal and chemical imbalances—whereas others associate them with a prior history of mental illness or cultural factors such as lack of social and economic support. *See* Oberman, *Mothers Who Kill, supra*, at 34; Michelle Oberman, *"Lady Madonna, Children at Your Feet": Tragedies at the Intersection of Motherhood, Mental Illness and the Law*, 10 Wm. & Mary J. Women & L. 33, 33–35 (2003). Whatever the cause, women who have previously experienced postpartum psychosis have a 30 to 50 percent risk of recurrence with subsequent births. *See* DSM-5, *supra*, at 187. Although the American Psychiatric Association does not categorize any of these postpartum conditions as a separate mental disorder, it considers the postpartum period one of the factors that can lead to the onset of a depressive or other disorder. *See id.* at 186 (specifying that "major depressive disorder" has a "peripartum onset" if the symptoms appeared during pregnancy or within four weeks after giving birth).

The issue of postpartum psychosis was the focus of national attention during the 2001 trial of Andrea Yates, a Texas woman who took her five children, ranging in age from six months to seven years, into the bathroom, one by one, and drowned them in the bathtub. She immediately telephoned the police and then her husband, telling him, "It's time. I finally did it." Yates had a history of mental illness: she experienced hallucinations, starting with visions of stabbing someone shortly after her first child was born; she attempted suicide and was hospitalized two years before killing her children; and she was hospitalized again two months prior to the children's death. Yates feared that her children would be "'tormented by Satan' as she was," that "'Satan would lure [her] children to himself,'" and she felt that drowning them would be "'a way out' because the children 'would go up to heaven and be with God, be safe.'" Deborah W. Denno, *Who Is Andrea Yates? A Short Story About Insanity*, 10 Duke J. Gender L. & Pol'y 1, 35, 37 (2003) (quoting Yates' interview with psychiatrist Park Dietz).

At her first trial, the jury rejected Yates' insanity claim under the Texas statute, which required proof that a "severe" mental disease or defect led her not to know that her conduct was wrong. Tex. Penal Code § 8.01. Yate was convicted of capital murder and sentenced to life in prison. On appeal, however, the appellate court granted her a new trial, finding "a reasonable likelihood" that "false testimony" given by Park Dietz, a well-known psychiatrist who testified for the prosecution, "could have affected the judgment of the jury." *Yates v. State*, 171 S.W.3d 215, 222 (Tex. App. 2005). Specifically, Dietz—who agreed Yates was psychotic but was the only one of six experts appearing at her trial who concluded that she knew right from wrong—incorrectly testified that "there was a [Law & Order television] show of a woman with postpartum depression who drowned her children in the bathtub and was found insane and it was aired shortly before [this] crime occurred." *Id.* at 218. After a second trial, the jury found that Yates was in fact insane, and acquitted her of murder charges. *See* Peggy O'Hare et al., *The Andrea Yates Case*, Hous. Chron., July 27, 2006, at A1.[33]

Was the second jury wrong to accept Yates' insanity defense because postpartum disorders are not recognized by the psychiatric profession as a separate category of mental illness, and because "[t]he fact that the epidemiology of the disorder is unclear could lead to abuse of the defense, since there is no typical profile of the woman likely to develop postpartum psychosis"? Brusca, *supra*, at 1168. Or was an insanity acquittal appropriate because a history of hallucinations "clearly indicate[s] an impaired concept of reality"? Laura E. Reece, Comment, *Mothers Who Kill: Postpartum Disorders and Criminal Infanticide*, 38 UCLA L. Rev. 699, 700, 741 (1991).

Although Yates' insanity plea was ultimately successful, the results in other cases involving women with postpartum disorders have been mixed. Approximately half of these defendants are acquitted by reason of insanity, about one-quarter are convicted and sentenced leniently, and the remaining quarter receive heavy sentences. *See id.* at 701–02. *See also* Oberman, *Mothers Who Kill*, *supra*, at 99–100, 109–10 (cataloguing the outcomes of almost 100 cases of neonaticide and infanticide occurring between 1988 and 1995). *Cf. id.* at 14–19 (describing statutes passed in numerous other

---

33. Yates, who is now in her fifties, is hospitalized in Texas. In 2012, a judge rejected her doctors' request that she be allowed to leave the hospital to attend church services. Two years later, the doctors asked the court to permit Yates to attend supervised events like picnics with other patients, but they withdrew the request because of the public controversy it generated. *See* Craig Hlavaty, *13 Years Later, the Andrea Yates Drownings Still Haunt*, Hous. Chronicle (June 20, 2014).

countries that make infanticide a separate crime, almost all of which prescribe a maximum sentence less than the typical penalty for murder and manslaughter); Eric Vallillee, *Deconstructing Infanticide*, 5 W. J. Leg. Stud., no. 4, 2015, at 1, http://ir.lib .uwo.ca/uwojls/vol5/iss4/1 (discussing similar laws in England and Canada).

(d) Although most people have two sex-determining chromosomes—XX in women and XY in men—approximately 0.1 to 0.2 percent of the male population has an extra chromosome (XYY). Studies suggest that XYY syndrome, which is found in substantially higher rates among male prisoners than in the general population, is associated with increased levels of antisocial and criminal behavior, in addition to above-average height and subnormal intelligence. *See* Andrew Saulitis, *Chromosomes and Criminality: The Legal Implications of the XYY Syndrome*, 1 J. Leg. Med. 269, 273, 277–78 (1979); Susan Horan, Note, *The XYY Supermale and the Criminal Justice System: A Square Peg in a Round Hole*, 25 Loy. L.A. L. Rev. 1343, 1350–53 (1992) (reporting similar findings in later studies). In addition, some researchers have found a link between XYY syndrome and violent, aggressive behavior. *See State v. Roberts*, 544 P.2d 754, 758 (Wash. Ct. App. 1976). *But cf.* Saulitis, *supra*, at 281–82 (describing research concluding that XYY defendants were more likely to commit crimes against property than against other people).

Should an XYY defendant be foreclosed from raising an insanity defense to assault or homicide charges because XYY syndrome is a "physical abnormality" rather than a mental defect? Roger Housley, Note, *Criminal Law: The XYY Chromosome Complement and Criminal Conduct*, 22 Okla. L. Rev. 287, 299 (1969). Or is XYY syndrome indistinguishable from many mental disorders that can be traced to chemical, genetic, or other physiological factors? *See, e.g.*, Deborah W. Denno, *Courts' Increasing Consideration of Behavioral Genetics Evidence in Criminal Cases: Results of a Longitudinal Study*, 2011 Mich. St. L. Rev. 967, 976 (citing research establishing a link between genetics and mental illness); Thomas Insel, *Director's Blog: Transforming Diagnosis*, National Institute of Mental Health (Apr. 29, 2013), http://www. nimh.nih.gov/about/directors/thomas-insel/blog/2013/transforming-diagnosis. shtml (criticizing the DSM-5 for its "lack of validity" and emphasizing the need for "a more precise diagnostic system" which recognizes that "[m]ental disorders are biological disorders involving brain circuits that implicate specific domains of cognition, emotion, or behavior").

Regardless of its origins, should XYY syndrome qualify as a mental disease because "the purported consequences of the chromosomal defect are incident upon one's intellect and affect"? Saulitis, *supra*, at 286. Even if XYY syndrome is properly characterized as a mental disease, however, is it an inadequate basis for an insanity acquittal because the research does not suggest that "all XYY individuals are by nature involuntarily aggressive," *People v. Tanner*, 91 Cal. Rptr. 656, 659 (Cal. Ct. App. 1970), and therefore "presently available medical evidence is unable to establish a reasonably certain causal connection between the XYY defect and criminal conduct"? 2 Wayne R. LaFave, Substantive Criminal Law § 9.3(b), at 28–29 (2d ed. 2003); *see also Tanzi v. Secretary, Florida Dep't of Corrections*, 772 F.3d 644, 655 (11th Cir. 2014) (relying on similar reasoning in rejecting ineffective assistance of counsel claim based on defense attorney's failure to present XYY evidence at the defendant's capital sentencing hearing). *Cf.* Saulitis, *supra*, at 273–74, 284 (describing a few trials in the late 1960s where evidence of XYY syndrome was admitted, although only one led to an insanity acquittal).

(e) In *United States v. Lyons*, 731 F.2d 243, 245 (5th Cir. 1984) (en banc), the Fifth Circuit adopted the traditional view that "narcotics addiction, standing alone . . . , raises no issue of such a mental defect or disease as can serve as a basis for the insanity defense." Likewise in *United States v. Freeman*, 357 F.2d 606, 625 (2d Cir. 1966), the Second Circuit acknowledged that "narcotics addiction without more" cannot be "the sole evidence of abnormality" under the Model Penal Code's definition of insanity.

The Fifth Circuit explained that "there is an element of reasoned choice when an addict knowingly acquires and uses drugs [because] he could instead have participated in an addiction treatment program." *Lyons*, 731 F.2d at 245. Moreover, the court noted, it "seems anomalous" to excuse addicts and "immunize [them] from other criminal sanctions when Congress has decreed severe penalties for mere possession and sale of narcotics." *Id.*

Nevertheless, observing that "[a]n actual drug-induced or drug-aggravated psychosis, or physical damage to the brain or nervous system would . . . be another matter," the *Lyons* court thought that the defendant in that case should be allowed to argue that "his drug addiction caused physiological damage to his brain," thus triggering a mental disease that could form the basis for an insanity plea. *Id.* at 246–47. *See also* DSM-5, *supra*, at 112 (describing "substance/medication-induced psychotic disorder," which is characterized by "delusions and/or hallucinations . . . due to the physiological effects of a substance" like drugs or alcohol).

In thinking about how the law of insanity should treat these issues, consider the case of Charles Freeman. Freeman, who was charged with selling heroin to an undercover police officer on two occasions, was 35 years old and had been a heroin addict for 14 years. His prior efforts to seek treatment for his addiction had been unsuccessful, and, at the time of his arrest, he was consuming as much as three bags of heroin a day as well as one or two bottles of wine and six to nine shots of whiskey. A defense psychiatric expert testified that Freeman "spoke in a flat monotone and paused for excessively long periods before responding to questions," suffered from amnesia at times, and was "general[ly] vague[] about details." *Freeman*, 357 F.2d at 609–10. In addition, Freeman would pass out stone cold on the street and, approximately 12 times a year, "experienced auditory and visual hallucinations," for example, seeing "people in miniature and hear[ing] them call his name from under his bed." *Id.* at 610 n.8. Freeman told the government's expert that he "felt very 'leery and scared and suspicious of everything.' 'I worry about myself mentally. People feel there is something wrong with me mentally. I don't talk too much. I can't read a book. I can't concentrate.'" *Id.* at 611. The defense expert concluded that Freeman suffered from "toxic psychosis" and had "organic and structural changes" in his brain. *Id.* at 610. The prosecution's expert, on the other hand, found "a dulling of [Freeman's] thinking process" but no indication of "brain disease" or "overly severe damage to the higher thinking areas of the brain." *Id.* at 611–12. Did Charles Freeman have a mental disease or defect for purposes of the insanity defense?

If so, does even the limited use of substance abuse to support an insanity defense acknowledged by the *Lyons* court go too far because it "excuse[s] a defendant's actions . . . based upon a mental disturbance or illness that he or she actively and voluntarily contracted"? *Bieber v. People*, 856 P.2d 811, 817 (Colo. 1993). The Arizona legislature thought so, *see* footnote 2 of the U.S. Supreme Court's opinion in *Clark*, as did the Colorado Supreme Court. In *Bieber*, the Colorado court rejected the notion that an insanity defense can be based on a mental disease resulting from addiction, reasoning that "[t]here is no principled basis to distinguish between the short-term and long-term effects of voluntary intoxication by punishing the first and excusing the second. If anything, the moral blameworthiness would seem to be even greater with respect to the long-term effects of many, repeated instances of voluntary intoxication occurring over an extended period of time." *Bieber*, 856 P.2d at 817. (For a discussion of voluntary intoxication as a defense, see Chapter 4, Section C.3.)

Does the Colorado Supreme Court's argument make sense, or "at some point" do an addict's "earlier voluntary decisions become morally remote"? Joshua Dressler, Understanding Criminal Law § 24.05[B], at 329–30 (7th ed. 2015). Even if the Colorado court is right, should an exception be recognized where a defendant became addicted to pain medication that was legally prescribed to treat a medical condition? *See, e.g., Lyons*, 731 F.2d at 244 (noting that Lyons, who was charged with multiple counts of fraudulently obtaining a controlled substance, argued that he had become addicted to medications that were initially prescribed for "several painful ailments").

Cases like these, where addicts and alcoholics present an insanity defense, must be distinguished from cases raising an *involuntary* intoxication defense. *See, e.g., State v. Anderson*, 851 N.W.2d 760, 765 (Wis. 2014) (differentiating between the two). Involuntary intoxication occurs when defendants are unaware they are consuming an intoxicating substance, when they consume it under force or duress, or when they do so in accord with medical advice. The involuntary consumption of drugs or alcohol is a defense when it renders the defendant unable to form the necessary mens rea or, in some jurisdictions, when it has an effect similar to that required to satisfy the state's definition of insanity—even though an insanity defense would be unavailable because the effect is temporary and is not the result of a mental disease or defect. *But cf.* Russell D. Covey, *Temporary Insanity: The Strange Life and Times of the Perfect Defense*, 91 B.U. L. Rev. 1597, 1602, 1599 (2011) (noting that while the notion of "temporary insanity" "lacks any settled definition" and has "lost its standing as a distinct—or even a coherent—legal claim," some defendants have nevertheless successfully raised the defense). For further discussion of involuntary intoxication, see Chapter 4, Section C.3, Note 5. For discussion of the constitutional limits on punishing drug addicts and alcoholics for status crimes, see Chapter 3, Section D.

7. The Model Penal Code's Caveat Paragraph. Although the Model Penal Code does not affirmatively define "mental disease or defect," it specifies that the term excludes "an abnormality manifested only by repeated criminal or otherwise anti-social conduct." Model Penal Code § 4.01(2). The majority of jurisdictions that follow the MPC's definition of insanity have also adopted this caveat paragraph, *see* 2 Paul H. Robinson, Criminal Law Defenses § 173(b), at 288 & n.15 (1984), and some jurisdictions that derive their insanity defense from *M'Naghten*—like Arizona—do so as well. *See* S. Rep. No. 225, 98th Cong., 2d Sess. 229 (1983) (indicating that the language in the federal insanity statute requiring a "severe" mental disease or defect was intended "to emphasize that nonpsychotic behavior disorders or neuroses such as . . . a pattern of antisocial tendencies do not constitute the defense").

The Model Penal Code's caveat is typically justified on several grounds. First, "[i]f a pattern of antisocial behavior is sufficient basis for an insanity defense, then a substantial proportion of serious criminal offenders would be able to assert this defense." *People v. Fields*, 673 P.2d 680, 707 (Cal. 1983); *see also* Christopher Slobogin, *A Defense of the Integrationist Test as a Replacement for the Special Defense of Insanity*, 42 Tex. Tech L. Rev. 523, 525–26 & n.22 (2009) (estimating that 20 to 30 percent of prisoners are psychopaths and more than half show signs of antisocial personality disorder). Second, recognizing an insanity defense in such cases "would put in the mental institutions persons for whom there is currently no suitable treatment, and who would be a constant danger to the staff and other inmates." *Fields*, 673 P.2d at 707–08. Third, "this condition is exclusively behavioral in nature" and "does not seem to be biochemical in etiology." Bruce J. Winick, *Ambiguities in the Legal Meaning and Significance of Mental Illness*, 1 Psychol. Pub. Pol'y & L. 534, 560 (1995). Do these arguments make sense?

Or is "defin[ing] by legislative fiat what is and what is not a psychiatric condition" as "arbitrary and capricious" as prohibiting defendants with "red hair or blue eyes" from raising an insanity defense? Bernard L. Diamond, *From M'Naghten to Currens, and Beyond*, 50 Calif. L. Rev. 189, 194 (1962). Is the focus on "treatability" inappropriate in light of the fact that prior to the discovery of "psychotropic drugs in the 1950s, schizophrenia may have been essentially untreatable"? Winick, *supra*, at 558. In addition, does the caveat discriminate against indigent defendants? Consider Diamond's observations:

> In practically any case where the crime itself, or alcoholism or drug addiction, is supposedly the only evidence of mental disease, a skilled, competent, and interested psychiatrist who spends sufficient time could discover other manifestations of mental abnormality sufficient to exculpate under [the Model Penal Code]. But the routine case, superficially examined by court-appointed psychiatrists devoting a wholly inadequate time to the study of the defendant, would seldom end in acquittal.

Diamond, *supra*, at 194.

Antisocial personality disorder—the current counterpart to what was once called psychopathy or sociopathy—is recognized as a personality disorder by the American Psychiatric Association. *See* AMERICAN PSYCHIATRIC ASSOCIATION, DIAGNOSTIC AND STATISTICAL MANUAL OF MENTAL DISORDERS 659 (5th ed. 2013). The "essential feature" of antisocial personality disorder is "a pervasive pattern of disregard for, and violation of, the rights of others" beginning before the age of 15 and "continu[ing] into adulthood." *Id.* "[D]eceit and manipulation are central features of antisocial personality disorder," and the "specific behaviors" that characterize the disorder "fall into one of four categories: aggression to people and animals, destruction of property, deceitfulness or theft, or serious violation of rules." *Id.* At least three of the following seven types of behavior must be present: "[f]ailure to conform to social norms with respect to lawful behaviors, as indicated by repeatedly performing acts that are grounds for arrest"; "[d]eceitfulness, as indicated by repeated lying, use of aliases, or conning others for personal profit or pleasure"; "[i]mpulsivity or failure to plan ahead"; "[i]rritability and aggressiveness, as indicated by repeated physical fights or assaults"; "[r]eckless disregard for safety of self or others"; "[c]onsistent irresponsibility, as indicated by repeated failure to sustain consistent work behavior or honor financial obligations"; and "[l]ack of remorse, as indicated by being indifferent to or rationalizing having hurt, mistreated, or stolen from another." *Id. But cf.* Kathleen Wayland & Sean D. O'Brien, *Deconstructing Antisocial Personality Disorder and Psychopathy: A Guidelines-Based Approach to Prejudicial Psychiatric Labels*, 42 HOFSTRA L. REV. 519, 539–42 (2013) (describing the controversies engendered by antisocial personality disorder and the "potential for misdiagnosis," given its "[i]mprecise criteria" and "general insensitivity to social class differences," as well as "the seemingly innumerable possibilities for reaching [the] threshold for a diagnosis" of the disorder).[34]

Does the Model Penal Code's caveat paragraph preclude defendants with antisocial personality disorder from successfully raising an insanity defense? Or, although "designed to deny an insanity defense to psychopaths and sociopaths," does the MPC fail to do so because the caveat's reference to diseases "manifested *only* by repeated criminal or otherwise antisocial conduct" means that an illness with other symptoms can qualify as a mental disease and "instances of criminal or antisocial conduct can be ascribed to that disease or cited as evidence of its severity"? *Fields*, 673 P.2d at 706. *See also Wade v. United States*, 426 F.2d 64, 73 (9th Cir. 1970) (en banc)

---

34. Recognizing the "numerous shortcomings of the current approach," the DSM-5 also includes an alternative model for personality disorders that focuses on "impairments in personality *functioning* and pathological personality *traits*." DSM-5, *supra*, at 761. Under this approach, antisocial personality disorder requires impairment in at least two of four areas: "[i]dentity" (i.e., "[e]gocentrism"); "[s]elf-direction" (i.e., "[g]oal setting based on personal gratification, . . . associated with failure to conform to lawful or culturally normative ethical behavior"); "[e]mpathy" or "lack of remorse"; and "[i]ncapacity for mutually intimate relationships." *Id.* at 764. In addition, at least six of the following seven personality traits must be present: "[m]anipulativeness," "[c]allousness," "[d]eceitfulness," "[h]ostility," "[r]isk taking," "[i]mpulsivity," and "[i]rresponsibility." *Id.* at 764–65.

(finding it "practically inconceivable" that a mental disease or defect would be manifested only by repeated criminal or antisocial conduct); Paul Litton, *Responsibility Status of the Psychopath: On Moral Reasoning and Rational Self-Governance*, 39 RUTGERS L.J. 349, 386 (2008) (agreeing that "psychopathy involves more than repetitive antisocial behavior"). *But cf.* Gerald F. Uelmen, *The Psychiatrist, the Sociopath and the Courts: New Lines for an Old Battle*, 14 LOY. L.A. L. REV. 1 (1980) (arguing that antisocial personality disorder is excluded by the caveat paragraph).

8. Burden of Proof. In federal cases, the prosecution historically had the burden of proving beyond a reasonable doubt that the defendant was not insane. *See Davis v. United States*, 160 U.S. 469 (1895). Likewise, the Model Penal Code imposes the burden of persuasion on the government once the defendant has satisfied the burden of production. *See* Model Penal Code §§ 1.12(1)–(2), 4.03(1). In *Leland v. Oregon*, 343 U.S. 790 (1952), however, the Supreme Court ruled that a state may constitutionally require defendants to shoulder the burden of proving the insanity defense — even by a reasonable doubt standard. *See also Patterson v. New York*, 432 U.S. 197, 207 (1977) (reaffirming *Leland*'s validity). *But cf. Cooper v. Oklahoma*, 517 U.S. 348, 367 (1996) (concluding that the "fundamental" due process "right to be tried only while competent" prohibits states from requiring defendants to prove incompetence to stand trial by clear and convincing evidence, rather than by the usual preponderance of the evidence standard).

As part of the Insanity Defense Reform Act of 1984, Congress changed the federal practice and required defendants to prove insanity by a standard of clear and convincing evidence. *See* 18 U.S.C. § 17(b). Prior to the Hinckley trial, a slight majority of states imposed the burden of proof on the prosecution. In the wake of the Hinckley verdict, however, a substantial number of states shifted the burden, and now about four-fifths of the states that recognize an insanity defense place the burden of proof on the defendant, typically by a preponderance of the evidence. *See* 1 WAYNE R. LAFAVE, SUBSTANTIVE CRIMINAL LAW § 8.3(a), at 600–01 (2d ed. 2003). For a discussion of the burden of proof issues that arise with other defenses, see Note 7 in Section A above and Note 4 following *People v. Tomlins* in Chapter 14, Section B.

[3] The Effect of an Insanity Acquittal

Jones v. United States
463 U.S. 354 (1983)

JUSTICE POWELL delivered the opinion of the Court.

The question presented is whether petitioner, who was committed to a mental hospital upon being acquitted of a criminal offense by reason of insanity, must be released because he has been hospitalized for a period longer than he might have served in prison had he been convicted.

I

In the District of Columbia a criminal defendant may be acquitted by reason of insanity if his insanity is "affirmatively established by a preponderance of the evidence." D.C. Code § 24-301(j) (1981). If he successfully invokes the insanity defense, he is committed to a mental hospital. § 24-301(d)(1). The statute provides several ways of obtaining release. Within 50 days of commitment the acquittee is entitled to a judicial hearing to determine his eligibility for release, at which he has the burden of proving by a preponderance of the evidence that he is no longer mentally ill or dangerous. § 24-301(d)(2). If he fails to meet this burden at the 50-day hearing, the committed acquittee subsequently may be released, with court approval, upon certification of his recovery by the hospital chief of service. Alternatively, the acquittee is entitled to a judicial hearing every six months at which he may establish by a preponderance of the evidence that he is entitled to release.

Independent of its provision for the commitment of insanity acquittees, the District of Columbia also has adopted a civil-commitment procedure, under which an individual may be committed upon clear and convincing proof by the Government that he is mentally ill and likely to injure himself or others. The individual may demand a jury in the civil-commitment proceeding. Once committed, a patient may be released at any time upon certification of recovery by the hospital chief of service. Alternatively, the patient is entitled after the first 90 days, and subsequently at 6-month intervals, to request a judicial hearing at which he may gain his release by proving by a preponderance of the evidence that he is no longer mentally ill or dangerous.

II

On September 19, 1975, petitioner was arrested for attempting to steal a jacket from a department store. The next day he was arraigned in the District of Columbia Superior Court on a charge of attempted petit larceny, a misdemeanor punishable by a maximum prison sentence of one year. The court ordered petitioner committed to St. Elizabeths, a public hospital for the mentally ill, for a determination of his competency to stand trial. On March 1, 1976, a hospital psychologist submitted a report to the court stating that petitioner was competent to stand trial, that petitioner suffered from "Schizophrenia, paranoid type," and that petitioner's alleged offense was "the product of his mental disease." The court ruled that petitioner was competent to stand trial. Petitioner subsequently decided to plead not guilty by reason of insanity. The Government did not contest the plea, and it entered into a stipulation of facts with petitioner. On March 12, 1976, the Superior Court found petitioner not guilty by reason of insanity and committed him to St. Elizabeths pursuant to § 24-301(d)(1).

On May 25, 1976, the court held the 50-day hearing required by § 24-301(d)(2)(A). A psychologist from St. Elizabeths testified on behalf of the Government that, in the opinion of the staff, petitioner continued to suffer from paranoid schizophrenia and that "because his illness is still quite active, he is still a danger to himself and to others." Petitioner's counsel conducted a brief cross-examination, and presented no evidence. . . . Petitioner was returned to St. Elizabeths. Petitioner obtained new counsel and, following some procedural confusion, a second release hearing was held on February 22, 1977. . . . The Superior Court . . . reaffirmed the findings made at the May 25, 1976, hearing, and continued petitioner's commitment to St. Elizabeths.

. . . .

III

It is clear that "commitment for any purpose constitutes a significant deprivation of liberty that requires due process protection." *Addington v. Texas,* 441 U.S. 418, 425 (1979). Therefore, a State must have "a constitutionally adequate purpose for the confinement." *O'Connor v. Donaldson,* 422 U.S. 563, 574 (1975). Congress has determined that a criminal defendant found not guilty by reason of insanity in the District of Columbia should be committed indefinitely to a mental institution for treatment and the protection of society. . . .

A

We turn first to the question whether the finding of insanity at the criminal trial is sufficiently probative of mental illness and dangerousness to justify commitment. A verdict of not guilty by reason of insanity establishes two facts: (i) the defendant committed an act that constitutes a criminal offense, and (ii) he committed the act because of mental illness. Congress has determined that these findings constitute an adequate basis for hospitalizing the acquittee as a dangerous and mentally ill person. *See* H.R. Rep. No. 91-907, at 74 (expressing fear that "dangerous criminals, particularly psychopaths, [may] win acquittals of serious criminal charges on grounds of insanity" and yet "escape hospital commitment"). We cannot say that it was unreasonable and therefore unconstitutional for Congress to make this determination.

The fact that a person has been found, beyond a reasonable doubt, to have committed a criminal act certainly indicates dangerousness.[35] . . . We do not agree with petitioner's suggestion that the requisite dangerousness is not established by proof that a person committed a nonviolent crime against property. This Court never has held that "violence," however that term might be defined, is a prerequisite for a constitutional commitment.[36]

---

35. [n.12] The proof beyond a reasonable doubt that the acquittee committed a criminal act distinguishes this case from *Jackson v. Indiana,* 406 U.S. 715 (1972), in which the Court held that a person found incompetent to stand trial could not be committed indefinitely solely on the basis of the finding of incompetency. In *Jackson* there never was any affirmative proof that the accused had committed criminal acts or otherwise was dangerous. [Competence to stand trial is discussed above in n.12.]

36. [n.14] *See Overholser v. O'Beirne,* 112 U.S. App. D.C. 267, 276, 302 F.2d 852, 861 (1961) (Burger, J.) ("[To] describe the theft of watches and jewelry as 'nondangerous' is to confuse danger with violence. Larceny is usually less violent than murder or assault, but in terms of public policy the purpose of the statute is the same as to both"). Thus, the "danger" may be to property rights as well as to persons. It also may be noted that crimes of theft frequently may result in violence from

Nor can we say that it was unreasonable for Congress to determine that the insanity acquittal supports an inference of continuing mental illness. It comports with common sense to conclude that someone whose mental illness was sufficient to lead him to commit a criminal act is likely to remain ill and in need of treatment. . . . Because a hearing is provided within 50 days of the commitment, there is assurance that every acquittee has prompt opportunity to obtain release if he has recovered.

Petitioner also argues that, whatever the evidentiary value of the insanity acquittal, the Government lacks a legitimate reason for committing insanity acquittees automatically because it can introduce the insanity acquittal as evidence in a subsequent civil [commitment] proceeding. This argument fails to consider the Government's strong interest in avoiding the need to conduct a *de novo* commitment hearing following every insanity acquittal—a hearing at which a jury trial may be demanded, and at which the Government bears the burden of proof by clear and convincing evidence. Instead of focusing on the critical question whether the acquittee has recovered, the new proceeding likely would have to relitigate much of the criminal trial. These problems accent the Government's important interest in automatic commitment. We therefore conclude that a finding of not guilty by reason of insanity is a sufficient foundation for commitment of an insanity acquittee for the purposes of treatment and the protection of society.

B

Petitioner next contends that his indefinite commitment is unconstitutional because the proof of his insanity was based only on a preponderance of the evidence, as compared to *Addington*'s civil-commitment requirement of proof by clear and convincing evidence. In equating these situations, petitioner ignores important differences between the class of potential civil-commitment candidates and the class of insanity acquittees that justify differing standards of proof. The *Addington* Court expressed particular concern that members of the public could be confined on the basis of "some abnormal behavior which might be perceived by some as symptomatic of a mental or emotional disorder, but which is in fact within a range of conduct that is generally acceptable." In view of this concern, the Court deemed it inappropriate to ask the individual "to share equally with society the risk of error." But since automatic commitment under § 24-301(d)(1) follows only if the *acquittee himself* advances insanity as a defense and proves that his criminal act was a product of his mental illness,[37] there is good reason for diminished concern as to the risk of error. More important, the proof that he committed a criminal act as a

---

the efforts of the criminal to escape or the victim to protect property or the police to apprehend the fleeing criminal. The relative "dangerousness" of a particular individual, of course, should be a consideration at the release hearings. . . .

37. Note that the states conflict on the question whether an insanity defense may be raised over the defendant's objection. *Compare State v. Handy*, 73 A.3d 421 (N.J. 2013) (allowing a competent defendant to waive the right to pursue an insanity defense), *with Hendricks v. People*, 10 P.3d 1231 (Colo. 2000) (upholding a statute following the minority view and allowing insanity to be asserted over the defendant's objection).

result of mental illness eliminates the risk that he is being committed for mere "idiosyncratic behavior." A criminal act by definition is not "within a range of conduct that is generally acceptable."

We therefore conclude that concerns critical to our decision in *Addington* are diminished or absent in the case of insanity acquittees. Accordingly, there is no reason for adopting the same standard of proof in both cases. The preponderance of the evidence standard comports with due process for commitment of insanity acquittees.

C

The remaining question is whether petitioner nonetheless is entitled to his release because he has been hospitalized for a period longer than he could have been incarcerated if convicted. The Due Process Clause "requires that the nature and duration of commitment bear some reasonable relation to the purpose for which the individual is committed." The purpose of commitment following an insanity acquittal, like that of civil commitment, is to treat the individual's mental illness and protect him and society from his potential dangerousness. The committed acquittee is entitled to release when he has recovered his sanity or is no longer dangerous. And because it is impossible to predict how long it will take for any given individual to recover — or indeed whether he ever will recover — Congress has chosen, as it has with respect to civil commitment, to leave the length of commitment indeterminate, subject to periodic review of the patient's suitability for release.

In light of the congressional purposes underlying commitment of insanity acquittees, we think petitioner clearly errs in contending that an acquittee's hypothetical maximum sentence provides the constitutional limit for his commitment. A particular sentence of incarceration is chosen to reflect society's view of the proper response to commission of a particular criminal offense, based on a variety of considerations such as retribution, deterrence, and rehabilitation. The State may punish a person convicted of a crime even if satisfied that he is unlikely to commit further crimes.

Different considerations underlie commitment of an insanity acquittee. As he was not convicted, he may not be punished. His confinement rests on his continuing illness and dangerousness. Thus, under the District of Columbia statute, no matter how serious the act committed by the acquittee, he may be released within 50 days of his acquittal if he has recovered. In contrast, one who committed a less serious act may be confined for a longer period if he remains ill and dangerous. There simply is no necessary correlation between severity of the offense and length of time necessary for recovery. The length of the acquittee's hypothetical criminal sentence therefore is irrelevant to the purposes of his commitment.

JUSTICE BRENNAN, with whom JUSTICE MARSHALL and JUSTICE BLACKMUN join, dissenting.

. . . .

. . . Petitioner's argument rests primarily on two cases dealing with civil commitments: *O'Connor v. Donaldson*, 422 U.S. 563 (1975), and *Addington v. Texas*, 441 U.S. 418 (1979). *O'Connor* held that a mentally ill individual has a "right to liberty" that a State may not abridge by confining him to a mental institution, even for the purpose of treating his illness, unless in addition to being mentally ill he is likely to harm himself or others if released. Then, in *Addington,* we carefully evaluated the standard of proof in civil commitment proceedings. Applying the due process analysis of *Mathews v. Eldridge*, 424 U.S. 319, 335 (1976), we held that "due process requires the state to justify confinement by proof more substantial than a mere preponderance of the evidence," specifically "clear and convincing evidence."

. . . .

The obvious difference between insanity acquittees and other candidates for civil commitment is that, at least in the District of Columbia, an acquittal by reason of insanity implies a determination beyond a reasonable doubt that the defendant in fact committed the criminal act with which he was charged. Conceivably, the Government may have an interest in confining insanity acquittees to punish them for their criminal acts, but the Government disclaims any such interest, and the Court does not rely on it. In any event, we have held that the Government may not impose psychiatric commitment as an alternative to penal sentencing for longer than the maximum period of incarceration the legislature has authorized as punishment for the crime committed. . . .

Instead of relying on a punishment rationale, the Court holds that a finding of insanity at a criminal trial "is sufficiently probative of mental illness and dangerousness to justify commitment." . . .

The Government's interests in committing petitioner are the same interests involved in *Addington* [and] *O'Connor*—isolation, protection, and treatment of a person who may, through no fault of his own, cause harm to others or to himself. Whenever involuntary commitment is a possibility, the Government has a strong interest in accurate, efficient commitment decisions. Nevertheless, *Addington* held both that the government's interest in accuracy was not impaired by a requirement that it bear the burden of persuasion by clear and convincing evidence, and that the individual's interests in liberty and autonomy required the government to bear at least that burden. An acquittal by reason of insanity of a single, nonviolent misdemeanor is not a constitutionally adequate substitute for the due process protections of *Addington* and *O'Connor,* i.e., proof by clear and convincing evidence of present mental illness or dangerousness, with the government bearing the burden of persuasion.

A "not guilty by reason of insanity" verdict is backward looking, focusing on one moment in the past, while commitment requires a judgment as to the present and future. In some jurisdictions, most notably in federal criminal trials, an acquittal by reason of insanity may mean only that a jury found a reasonable doubt as to a defendant's sanity and as to the causal relationship between his mental condition and his crime. *See Davis v. United States,* 160 U.S. 469 (1895) . . . .

It is worth examining what is known about the possibility of predicting danger-ousness from *any* set of facts. . . . Commentators and researchers have long acknowl-edged that even the best attempts to identify dangerous individuals on the basis of specified facts have been inaccurate roughly two-thirds of the time, almost always on the side of overprediction. On a clinical basis, mental health professionals can diagnose past or present mental condition with some confidence, but strong institu-tional biases lead them to err when they attempt to determine an individual's dan-gerousness, especially when the consequence of a finding of dangerousness is that an obviously mentally ill patient will remain within their control. Research is prac-tically nonexistent on the relationship of *nonviolent* criminal behavior, such as peti-tioner's attempt to shoplift, to future dangerousness. We do not even know whether it is even statistically valid as a predictor of similar nonviolent behavior, much less of behavior posing more serious risks to self and others.

. . . Finally, it cannot be gainsaid that some crimes are more indicative of danger-ousness than others. Subject to the limits of *O'Connor,* a State may consider nonvio-lent misdemeanors "dangerous," but there is room for doubt whether a single attempt to shoplift and a string of brutal murders are equally accurate and equally permanent predictors of dangerousness.[38]

. . . .

Given the close similarity of the governmental interests at issue in this case and those at issue in *Addington,* and the highly imperfect "fit" between the findings required for an insanity acquittal and those required under *O'Connor* to support an indefinite commitment, I cannot agree that the Government should be excused from the burden that *Addington* held was required by due process.[39]

. . . .

---

38. [n.13] The Court responds that "crimes of theft frequently may result in violence." When they do, that fact may well be relevant to, or even dispositive of, the dangerousness issue at a proper commitment hearing. In this case, however, petitioner's attempt to shoplift involved neither actual violence nor any attempt to resist or evade arrest. It is difficult to see how the Court's generaliza-tion justifies relieving the Government of its *Addington-O'Connor* burden of proving present dan-gerousness by clear and convincing evidence.

39. [n.16] Note that extended institutionalization may effectively make it impossible for an individual to prove that he is no longer mentally ill and dangerous, both because it deprives him of the economic wherewithal to obtain independent medical judgments and because the treatment he receives may make it difficult to demonstrate recovery. The current emphasis on using psychotro-pic drugs to eliminate the characteristic signs and symptoms of mental illness, especially schizo-phrenia, may render mental patients docile and unlikely to engage in violent or bizarre behaviors while they are institutionalized, but it does not "cure" them or allow them to demonstrate that they would remain nonviolent if they were not drugged. At petitioner's May 1976 hearing, the Govern-ment relied on testimony that petitioner was "not always responsive in a positive way to what goes on" and was "not a very active participant in the informal activities on the Ward" to support its contention that he had not recovered. The amount of medication he was receiving, however, made it unlikely he could be an active participant in anything.

If the Government's interests were the only ones at stake, an insanity acquittal would furnish a reasonable basis for indefinite commitment. Under the Constitution, however, the Government's interests must be considered in light of the liberty interests of the individual who is subject to commitment. . . .

In many respects, confinement in a mental institution is even more intrusive than incarceration in a prison. Inmates of mental institutions, like prisoners, are deprived of unrestricted association with friends, family, and community; they must contend with locks, guards, and detailed regulation of their daily activities. In addition, a person who has been hospitalized involuntarily may to a significant extent lose the right enjoyed by others to withhold consent to medical treatment. The treatments to which he may be subjected include physical restraints such as straightjacketing, as well as electroshock therapy, aversive conditioning, and even in some cases psychosurgery. Administration of psychotropic medication to control behavior is common. . . .

Indefinite commitment without the due process protections adopted in *Addington* and *O'Connor* is not reasonably related to any of the Government's purported interests in confining insanity acquittees for psychiatric treatment. The rationales on which the Court justifies § 24-301's departures from *Addington* at most support deferring *Addington*'s due process protections—specifically, its requirement that the Government carry the burden of proof by clear and convincing evidence—for a limited period only, not indefinitely.

The maximum sentence for attempted petit larceny in the District of Columbia is one year. Beyond that period, petitioner should not have been kept in involuntary confinement unless he had been committed under the standards of *Addington* and *O'Connor*. . . .

Notes and Questions

1. Committing Insanity Acquittees. Some jurisdictions automatically hospitalize defendants who have been found not guilty by reason of insanity. *See, e.g.,* Model Penal Code § 4.08. But in most states, the commitment of insanity acquittees is discretionary. *See* 1 Wayne R. LaFave, Substantive Criminal Law § 8.4(a), at 610–11 (2d ed. 2003).

In the federal system, a hearing must be held within 40 days of an insanity acquittal to determine the defendant's dangerousness. If the charge that led to the acquittal involved "bodily injury" or "serious damage to the property" of another person, or "a substantial risk of such injury or damage," the acquittee has the burden of proving by clear and convincing evidence that "release would not create a substantial risk of bodily injury to another person or serious damage of property of another due to a present mental disease or defect." For other charges, the acquittee must meet the same standard by a preponderance of the evidence. 18 U.S.C. § 4243.

2. The Length of Commitment. Numerous studies indicate that most insanity acquittees are hospitalized for a significant length of time—often for a similar or longer term than they would have served in jail had they been convicted of the crime. *See* Michael L. Perlin, The Jurisprudence of the Insanity Defense 110–11 (1994); Randy Borum & Solomon M. Fulero, *Empirical Research on the Insanity Defense and Attempted Reforms: Evidence Toward Informed Policy*, 23 Law & Hum. Behav. 117, 120–21 (1999). Did the *Jones* majority make a persuasive case for allowing the government to hospitalize insanity acquittees for a period longer than the maximum potential sentence for their crimes? *Cf.* Cal. Penal Code § 1026.5 (providing that insanity acquittees may not be confined beyond the maximum sentence for their crimes, unless they were charged with a felony and "by reason of a mental disease, defect, or disorder represent[] a substantial danger of physical harm to others").

3. Releasing Insanity Acquittees. Although the District of Columbia's release procedures were not directly at issue in *Jones*, the Court noted that "[t]he committed acquittee is entitled to release when he has recovered his sanity or is no longer dangerous." In *Foucha v. Louisiana*, 504 U.S. 71 (1992), the Court made clear that this standard is constitutionally required. Thus, the Court ruled in that case, "the basis for holding" insanity acquittees "has disappeared" if they are no longer mentally ill— even if they might still pose a danger to themselves or others. *Id.* at 78.

This holding was somewhat precarious, however, because Justice O'Connor, who represented the critical fifth vote for the majority, suggested that "[i]t might . . . be permissible for Louisiana to confine an insanity acquittee who has regained sanity, if, unlike the situation in this case, the nature and duration of detention were tailored to reflect pressing public safety concerns related to the acquittee's continuing dangerousness." *Id.* at 87–88 (O'Connor, J., concurring in part and concurring in the judgment). Justice O'Connor did not explain precisely what she meant—or how her view was consistent with the majority's seemingly flat prohibition on confining insanity acquittees who are no longer mentally ill. But she did indicate that she did not read the majority opinion to "necessarily invalid[ate]" laws that "limit the maximum duration of criminal commitment to reflect the acquittee's specific crimes." *Id.* at 89. Picking up on that suggestion, the Wisconsin Supreme Court distinguished the Louisiana statute at issue in *Foucha* and upheld a Wisconsin provision that allowed the continued detention of insanity acquittees who were dangerous, but no longer ill, so long as they were not held longer than the maximum sentence for their crimes and the state shouldered the burden of proof at their release hearings. *See State v. Randall*, 532 N.W.2d 94, 105–06 & n.19 (Wis. 1995).

4. Informing Juries About the Effect of an Insanity Acquittal. There is substantial disagreement concerning the advisability of informing juries about the practical impact of an insanity acquittal. *See State v. Becker*, 818 N.W.2d 135, 156–57 (Iowa 2012) (noting that the states are about evenly split on this issue), *overruled on other grounds by Alcala v. Marriott International, Inc.*, 880 N.W.2d 699 (Iowa 2016). In *Shannon v. United States*, 512 U.S. 573 (1994), the Supreme Court held that federal juries generally need not be told about the consequences of an insanity acquittal.

Is the Supreme Court's decision unwise given that "jurors who are not informed about dispositional consequences will speculate about the practical results of a non-responsibility verdict"? *Erdman v. State*, 553 A.2d 244, 249–50 (Md. 1989). Does the jury therefore have "a right to know the meaning of this . . . verdict as accurately as it knows by common knowledge the meaning of the . . . verdicts" guilty and not guilty? *Lyles v. United States*, 254 F.2d 725, 728 (D.C. Cir. 1957) (en banc) (per curiam). Is such information necessary to shield defendants from "an obvious risk of injustice," *Shannon*, 512 U.S. at 590 (Stevens, J., dissenting), i.e., to "overcome the [jurors'] fear" that an insanity acquittal will "result in the release of a dangerous person back into society"? *State v. Amini*, 28 P.3d 1204, 1212 (Or. Ct. App. 2001). *See also* Shannon R. Wheatman & David R. Shaffer, *On Finding for Defendants Who Plead Insanity: The Crucial Impact of Dispositional Instructions and Opportunity to Deliberate*, 25 Law & Hum. Behav. 167 (2001) (finding that mock jurors who received a jury instruction on the effect of an insanity acquittal were significantly more likely to find the defendant not guilty by reason of insanity after jury deliberations, even though it had no impact on the mock jurors prior to deliberation).

On the other hand, is the Supreme Court's decision in *Shannon* simply "a reflection of the basic division of labor in our legal system between judge and jury," and thus an illustration of the traditional view that "[i]nformation regarding the consequences of a verdict is . . . irrelevant to the jury's task"? *Shannon*, 512 U.S. at 579. Does such information "raise questions foreign to the jury's primary duty," *Burns v. State*, 913 S.W.2d 789, 791 (Ark. 1996), because "the disposition of a criminal defendant acquitted on a defense of insanity is a matter for the court, not the jury"? *Becker*, 818 N.W.2d at 154. In addition, would instructing juries on the effect of an insanity acquittal "invite them to ponder matters that are not within their province, distract them from their factfinding responsibilities, and create a strong possibility of confusion"? *Shannon*, 512 U.S. at 579. Should trial judges compensate for the possibility that jurors may not understand the practical consequences of an insanity acquittal by instructing them not to consider those issues in reaching their verdict and then relying on "the almost invariable assumption of the law that jurors follow their instructions"? *Id.* at 585.

Comparable questions have arisen in those jurisdictions that have created a guilty but mentally ill verdict, and have led to a similar divergence of views as to whether juries should be educated about the different ramifications of an insanity acquittal and a verdict of guilty but mentally ill. *Compare Neely v. Newton*, 149 F.3d 1074, 1081 (10th Cir. 1998) (upholding New Mexico statute barring such instructions), *and People v. Lantz*, 712 N.E.2d 314, 322 (Ill. 1999) (same), *with Minter v. State*, 463 S.E.2d 119, 120–21 (Ga. 1995) (taking the contrary position, though finding any error harmless on the facts of that case), *and Georgopolus v. State*, 735 N.E.2d 1138, 1143 (Ind. 2000) (requiring an instruction if the defendant so requests). (For a general description of the guilty but mentally ill verdict, see Note 12 in Part 1 above.)

5. Committing Sexual Predators. In recent years, a substantial number of states have passed sexual predator laws that permit the involuntary civil commitment of sexually violent individuals even if they do not have a mental disease or defect normally required for civil commitment. *See* Jeslyn A. Miller, Comment, *Sex Offender Civil Commitment: The Treatment Paradox*, 98 Calif. L. Rev. 2093, 2096–99 (2010) (discussing the history and criticisms of these statutes). In *Kansas v. Hendricks*, 521 U.S. 346, 357 (1997), the Court upheld Kansas' Sexually Violent Predator Act, which provides for the commitment of individuals who have been "convicted of or charged with a sexually violent offense" and who "suffer from a mental abnormality or personality disorder which makes [them] likely to engage in the predatory acts of sexual violence." Defendants acquitted by reason of insanity of sexually violent crimes are included within the coverage of the statute, *see id.* at 352, and can therefore be committed under this legislation following their release from a hospital. The statute likewise authorizes the commitment of defendants who have already served their prison time, as well as those who were charged but never convicted.

In a subsequent opinion addressing the same statute, the Supreme Court held that, in order to distinguish "the dangerous sexual offender whose serious mental illness, abnormality, or disorder subjects him to civil commitment" from "the dangerous but typical recidivist convicted in an ordinary criminal case," who is "'more properly dealt with exclusively through criminal proceedings,'" civil commitment under the Kansas sexual predator statute requires "proof of serious difficulty in controlling behavior." *Kansas v. Crane*, 534 U.S. 407, 412–13 (2002) (quoting *Kansas v. Hendricks*, 521 U.S. at 360).

The constitutionality of the federal statute authorizing the civil commitment of mentally ill, "sexually dangerous" offenders after the expiration of their prison sentence, 18 U.S.C. § 4248, reached the Court in *United States v. Comstock*, 560 U.S. 126 (2010). The majority upheld the statute, concluding that it was a proper exercise of Congress' power under the Necessary and Proper Clause, Art. 1, § 8, cl. 18, and did not violate the Tenth Amendment. Writing in dissent for himself and Justice Scalia, Justice Thomas thought that the statute exceeded Congress' Article I power because it was not "'necessary and proper for carrying into Execution' one or more of those federal powers actually enumerated in the Constitution." *Comstock*, 560 U.S. at 163 (Thomas, J., dissenting). *See also People v. McKee*, 144 Cal. Rptr. 3d 308 (Cal. Ct. App. 2012) (reasoning that sexually violent predators pose a greater danger to society than either insanity acquittees or mentally disordered prisoners convicted of violent crimes, and thus rejecting an equal protection challenge to a proposition passed by the California electorate in 2006 that imposed harsher requirements on sexually violent predators, authorizing their commitment for an indeterminate period unless they can prove they have the right to be released).

Chapter 16

Philosophical Foundations of Criminal Law

[A] Explaining Prohibitory Rules and Responsibility

We saw in Chapter 1 that John Stuart Mill's formulation of the "harm to others" principle is a persuasive starting point for explaining and justifying criminal law, justifying public interventions in private lives and public condemnation of private choices. Mill's principle is just the start of a philosophical conversation. He took for granted that, within a society, there would be general agreement about what constitutes serious harm and about the kinds of harm that should concern legislators.

Mill himself was aware of a paradox underlying these ideas about freedom and social order. More recent philosophers have refined our understanding of this paradox. The paradox is that infringing on freedom is itself a kind of second-order harm. The first level is simply the level at which we pursue the things we value or enjoy and avoid those that we don't. At the second level is the freedom to define for ourselves, perhaps in sharp contrast to those around us, the sorts of things that we value and enjoy. Whenever the legislature creates a criminal prohibition, it not only puts certain enjoyments out of reach, but it also homogenizes society to the extent that it enforces shared values and shared moral views.

In Chapter 1 we considered several kinds of acts that raise questions about the purpose and scope of criminal law, its nature and its aims. In several instances, we saw disagreement about (a) whether certain conduct should be criminalized and (b) why it should or should not be criminalized.

Even when there is no disagreement about the first question (no disagreement, for example, about whether to prohibit homicide or arson), there may be significant debate about the second. In fact, the social and political consensus about criminalizing homicide may *mask* the diverse ways in which we would explain and justify the rule. Consider the following alternatives:

(a) Some may say that we share moral values and that taking another's life violates our shared morality.

(b) A second justification challenges the first premise and claims that we have sharply divergent moral views. To preserve a community in which each person has the autonomy to pursue his or her own conception of moral value, we need ground rules such as the prohibition of taking lives.

(c) A third position is a variant of the second. Under this view, persons differ not merely in moral belief but generally in their preferences about what is worth doing. The purpose of law is to provide an efficient society in which individuals can carry out transactions to achieve their particular goals. Homicide interferes, in a decisive way, with participation by some in such a "market."

(d) Yet another approach argues that legislative and judicial decisions to prohibit conduct reflect the assumptions and biases of those who have power, those whose views and interests dominate the legal culture. Such issues as whether to criminalize prostitution, drug use, and pornography, whether to recognize intoxication as a defense, how to set the boundaries of self-defense, and whether and how to use capital punishment are all obviously politically colored issues. This approach, called "critical theory," argues that all legal determinations are, in analogous ways, political.

The following materials illustrate various approaches to explaining and/or justifying criminal law. In particular, each theory sees the *margins* of criminal law differently and therefore sees different kinds of cases as controversial.

[B] Moral Consensus Theories and Classical Liberalism

[1] Criminal Law and the Enforcement of Morality

Patrick Devlin, The Enforcement of Morals 6–7, 12–15 (1958)[1]

The criminal law of England has from the very first concerned itself with moral principles. . . .

There is only one explanation of what has hitherto been accepted as the basis of the criminal law and that is that there are certain standards of behaviour or moral principles which society requires to be observed; and the breach of them is an offence not merely against the person who is injured but against society as a whole. . . .

I think, therefore, that it is not possible to set theoretical limits to the power of the State to legislate against immorality. It is not possible to settle in advance exceptions to the general rule or to define inflexibly areas of morality into which the law is in no circumstances to be allowed to enter. Society is entitled by means of its laws to protect itself from dangers, whether from within or without. Here again I think that the political parallel is legitimate. The law of treason is directed against aiding the king's enemies and against sedition from within. The justification for this is that established government is necessary for the existence of society and therefore its safety against violent overthrow must be secured. But an established morality is as necessary as good government to the welfare of society. Societies disintegrate from within

---

more frequently than they are broken up by external pressures. There is disintegration when no common morality is observed and history shows that the loosening of moral bonds is often the first stage of disintegration, so that society is justified in taking the same steps to preserve its moral code as it does to preserve its government and other essential institutions. The suppression of vice is as much the law's business as the suppression of subversive activities; it is no more possible to define a sphere of private morality than it is to define one of private subversive activity. It is wrong to talk of private morality or of the law not being concerned with immorality as such or to try to set rigid bounds to the part which the law may play in the suppression of vice. There are no theoretical limits to the power of the State to legislate against treason and sedition, and likewise I think there can be no theoretical limits to legislation against immorality. You may argue that if a man's sins affect only himself it cannot be the concern of society. If he chooses to get drunk every night in the privacy of his own home, is any one except himself the worse for it? But suppose a quarter or a half of the population got drunk every night, what sort of society would it be? You cannot set a theoretical limit to the number of people who can get drunk before society is entitled to legislate against drunkenness. . . .

How are the moral judgements of society to be ascertained? By leaving it until now, I can ask it in the more limited form that is now sufficient for my purpose. How is the law-maker to ascertain the moral judgements of society? It is surely not enough that they should be reached by the opinion of the majority; it would be too much to require the individual assent of every citizen. English law has evolved and regularly uses a standard which does not depend on the counting of heads. It is that of the reasonable man. He is not to be confused with the rational man. He is not expected to reason about anything and his judgement may be largely a matter of feeling. It is the viewpoint of the man in the street — or to use an archaism familiar to all lawyers — the man in the Clapham omnibus. He might also be called the right-minded man. For my purpose I should like to call him the man in the jury box, for the moral judgement of society must be something about which any twelve men or women drawn at random might after discussion be expected to be unanimous. This was the standard the judges applied in the days before Parliament was as active as it is now and when they laid down rules of public policy. They did not think of themselves as making law but simply as stating principles which every right-minded person would accept as valid. It is what Pollock called "practical morality," which is based not on theological or philosophical foundations but "in the mass of continuous experience half-consciously or unconsciously accumulated and embodied in the morality of common sense." He called it also "a certain way of thinking on questions of morality which we expect to find in a reasonable civilized man or a reasonable Englishman, taken at random."

Immorality then, for the purpose of the law, is what every right-minded person is presumed to consider to be immoral.

Notes and Questions

1. **What Is a Moral Consensus?** Devlin relies heavily on the idea of a moral consensus. What is the criterion of a moral consensus? Does it require that all persons in the society share the same moral beliefs? Or that almost all persons share such beliefs? Or that a majority shares moral beliefs? Or, as Devlin says, that "right-thinking" persons share such beliefs?

2. **Problems of Eliciting a Moral Consensus.** When one considers the universal moral condemnation of homicide or rape or theft, it seems easy to argue that these criminal prohibitions reflect moral consensus. On the other hand, when one considers such moral issues as abortion, euthanasia, sodomy, and pornography, it seems equally clear that the search for a moral consensus is perilous.

Writing in England in the late 1950s, Devlin seems to presuppose a more homogeneous society than our own, one in which harmony about moral views is the norm. But consider whether such harmony may be an illusion. The fact that the media, political leaders, and cultural spokespersons all echo the same moral opinions may not show that there is a consensus. It may merely reflect the fact that one group among many in the society has hegemony over the public media.

Even if a public opinion poll says that an overwhelming majority claims to have one view, this *may* merely reflect widespread hypocrisy, especially when dissent is not easily tolerated. People may say what they are expected to believe rather than what they really believe. Thus, the existence of a true consensus is very hard to determine.

3. **Should Law Reflect a Moral Consensus?** Even when a moral consensus really does exist, the proposition that laws should reflect that moral consensus is questionable. Consider two objections.

First, there are obviously many practices that are almost universally disapproved but that are not appropriate subjects for criminal prohibition. Habitual promise-breaking has little to be said for it on moral grounds. But how would we enforce a law against it? And how could we justify the invasions of privacy that such a law would entail?

On the other hand, lots of criminal prohibitions involve regulatory matters with no moral content. Parking and driving regulations, tax laws, etc., are all based on legislative decisions about matters that, for the most part, are morally arbitrary. Thus, it is not the case that driving on the wrong side of the road is forbidden because it is immoral. The opposite is true: doing it deliberately takes on moral connotations only because it is forbidden.

4. **Legal Moralism and American Countermajoritarianism.** Keep in mind that Devlin, as a British jurist, is writing in the context of a system of law that differs significantly from our own. Our constitutional system, with its tradition of judicial review and a robust Bill of Rights, is generally explained and justified as representing a countermajoritarian ideal. The philosophical idea is that this system serves the purpose of protecting individuals and minorities from the will of the majority. Thus

it insures autonomy and diversity. There is general agreement among writers on constitutional theory that these constitutional guarantees preclude automatic transformation of the will of the majority into law.

5. Countermajoritarianism and Classical Liberalism. Even writers in the English tradition endorse some of these countermajoritarian values, values that (as the following selection by Hart indicates) are part of the so-called liberal tradition in politics. Liberalism in this sense draws its essence from such early nineteenth-century writers as John Stuart Mill. It "supposes that government must be neutral on what might be called the question of the good life. . . . Each person follows a more-or-less articulate conception of what gives value to life. . . . [The liberal theory] supposes that political decisions must be, so far as is possible, independent of any particular conception of the good life, or of what gives value to life. Since the citizens of a society differ in their conceptions, the government does not treat them as equals if it prefers one conception to another, either because the officials believe that one is intrinsically superior, or because one is held by the more numerous or more powerful group." Ronald Dworkin, *Liberalism, in* PUBLIC AND PRIVATE MORALITY 113, 127 (Stuart Hampshire ed., 1978).

6. Defining Liberalism. Liberalism in this sense must be distinguished from liberalism in the sense of a particular political agenda that relies on beliefs about the particular rights of individuals and about the scope and role of government. Of course, liberalism in Mill's sense *implies* that individuals have the right to be treated as equals and that government must justify its interventions by reference to equality. But many different political programs can fit these constraints.

[2] Criticizing Legal Moralism

H.L.A. Hart, *Immorality and Treason,* THE LISTENER, July 30, 1959, at 162, 162–63[2]

The most remarkable feature of Sir Patrick [Devlin]'s lecture is his view of the nature of morality—the morality which the criminal law may enforce. Most previous thinkers who have repudiated the liberal point of view have done so because they thought that morality consisted either of divine commands or of rational principles of human conduct discoverable by human reason. Since morality for them had this elevated divine or rational status as the law of God or reason, it seemed obvious that the state should enforce it, and that the function of human law should not be merely to provide men with the opportunity for leading a good life, but actually to see that they lead it. Sir Patrick does not rest his repudiation of the liberal point of view on these religious or rationalist conceptions. Indeed much that he writes reads like an abjuration of the notion that reasoning or thinking has much to do with morality. English popular morality has no doubt its historical connexion

---

2. Reprinted with permission, all rights reserved.

with the Christian religion: "That," says Sir Patrick, "is how it got there." But it does not owe its present status or social significance to religion any more than to reason.

What, then, is it? According to Sir Patrick it is primarily a matter of feeling. "Every moral judgment," he says, "is a feeling that no right-minded man could act in any other way without admitting that he was doing wrong."

Intolerance, Indignation, and Disgust

But what precisely are the relevant feelings, the feelings which may justify use of the criminal law? Here the argument becomes a little complex. Widespread dislike of a practice is not enough. There must, says Sir Patrick, be "a real feeling of reprobation." Disgust is not enough either. What is crucial is a combination of intolerance, indignation, and disgust. These three are the forces behind the moral law, without which it is not "weighty enough to deprive the individual of freedom of choice." Hence there is, in Sir Patrick's outlook, a crucial difference between the mere adverse moral judgment of society and one which is inspired by feeling raised to the concert pitch of intolerance, indignation, and disgust. . . .

A Shared Morality

If this is what morality is—a compound of indignation, intolerance, and disgust— we may well ask what justification there is for taking it, and turning it as such, into criminal law with all the misery which criminal punishment entails. . . .

Society and Moral Opinion

No doubt we would all agree that a consensus of moral opinion on certain matters is essential if society is to be worth living in. . . . But it does not follow that everything to which the moral vetoes of accepted morality attach is of equal importance to society; nor is there the slightest reason for thinking of morality as a seamless web: one which will fall to pieces carrying society with it, unless all its emphatic vetoes are enforced by law. Surely even in the face of the moral feeling that is up to concert pitch—the trio of intolerance, indignation, and disgust—we must pause to think. We must ask a question at two different levels which Sir Patrick never clearly enough identifies or separates. First, we must ask whether a practice which offends moral feeling is harmful, independently of its repercussion on the general moral code. Secondly, what about repercussion on the moral code? Is it really true that failure to translate this item of general morality into criminal law will jeopardize the whole fabric of morality and so of society? . . .

Nothing perhaps shows more clearly the inadequacy of Sir Patrick's approach to his problem than his comparison between the suppression of sexual immorality and the suppression of treason or subversive activity. Private subversive activity is, of course, a contradiction in terms because "subversion" means overthrowing government, which is a public thing. But it is grotesque, even where moral feeling against homosexuality is up to concert pitch, to think of the homosexual behaviour of two adults in private as in any way like treason or sedition either in intention or effect. We can make it *seem* like treason only if we assume that deviation from a general moral code is bound to affect that code, and to lead not merely to its modification but to its destruction. The analogy could begin to be plausible only if it was clear that offending against this item of morality was likely to jeopardize the whole structure. But we have ample evidence for believing that people will not abandon morality, will not think any better of murder, cruelty, and dishonesty, merely because some private sexual practice which they abominate is not punished by the law.

Because this is so the analogy with treason is absurd. Of course "No man is an island": what one man does in private, if it is known, may affect others in many different ways. Indeed it may be that deviation from general sexual morality by those whose lives, like the lives of many homosexuals, are noble ones and in all other ways exemplary will lead to what Sir Patrick calls the shifting of the limits of tolerance. But if this has any analogy in the sphere of government it is not the overthrow of ordered government, but a peaceful change in its form. So we may listen to the promptings of common sense and of logic, and say that though there could not logically be a sphere of private treason there is a sphere of private morality and immorality. . . .

Curious Logic

It is impossible to see what curious logic has led Sir Patrick to this result. For him a practice is immoral if the thought of it makes the man on the Clapham omnibus sick. So be it. Still, why should we not summon all the resources of our reason, sympathetic understanding, as well as critical intelligence, and insist that before general moral feeling is turned into criminal law it is submitted to scrutiny of a different kind from Sir Patrick's? Surely, the legislator should ask whether the general morality is based on ignorance, superstition, or misunderstanding; whether there is a false conception that those who practice what it condemns are in other ways dangerous or hostile to society; and whether the misery to many parties, the blackmail and the other evil consequences of criminal punishment, especially for sexual offences, are well understood. It is surely extraordinary that among the things which Sir Patrick says are to be considered before we legislate against immorality these appear nowhere; not even as "practical considerations," let alone "theoretical limits." To any theory which, like this one, asserts that the criminal law may be used on the vague ground that the preservation of morality is essential to society and yet omits to stress the need for critical scrutiny, our reply should be: "Morality, what crimes may be committed in thy name!"

Notes and Questions

1. Distinguishing Positive Morality and Political Morality. The idea of countermajoritarian values is implicit in Hart's analysis. Government, according to the liberal view, exists to protect the values of the majority and the minority, of all individuals, equally. We can distinguish two senses of morality, the so-called "positive" morality of individuals and the political or critical morality that should guide the decisions of government. Equality and justice play their significant role in political morality.

Positive morality is defined by the moral preferences of the majority. But, as Hart suggests, to incorporate these preferences into law is to ignore the conflicting preferences of a minority and the rights of all individuals to autonomy in pursuing their preferences. Thus, the task of political/critical morality is to sort out the public and the private dimensions of positive morality, to decide what moral matters must be enforced by law and what concerns are best left to the individual.

2. Rationality and Political Morality. Even the idea of *positive* morality needs further examination. Is such morality *merely* a matter of one's preferences about the behavior of others—or is the notion of morality more complex and limited? In other words, do we not need to look beyond the mere fact that persons have preferences to see whether the preferences are based on *reason* or on mere *feeling*, to see whether or not they are rooted in bias and prejudice? *See* RONALD DWORKIN, TAKING RIGHTS SERIOUSLY 248–53 (1977).

3. Classical Liberalism and Political/Critical Morality. According to such liberals as Mill, critical morality allows us to identify a limited set of behaviors that are generally threatening to community harmony and individual freedom. These are the proper subjects for criminal law.

4. The Subtext of the Debate. Devlin's covert agenda was to oppose any revision of British law that would decriminalize homosexual activity. In the American context, *Lawrence v. Texas*, 539 U.S. 558 (2003), is the landmark case declaring Texas' same-sex anti-sodomy law unconstitutional and concluding that intimate consensual sexual activity is a liberty protected by the Due Process Clause of the Fourteenth Amendment.

[3] Liberal Justifications of Criminal Law

As we saw earlier in this Chapter, the liberal commitment to neutrality and equality has two dimensions. It assumes that we can distinguish public (political) and private (positive) morality, that we can agree about what kind of conduct is generally dangerous and about how dangerous it is while disagreeing in our judgments about private morality. It also assumes that morality is an arena of conflicting reasons rather than just feelings or impulses, and that a genuine moral position is one for which a person can give reasons that will be understood and debated in the community.

The attempt to explicate this shared notion of dangerous conduct is one of the main preoccupations of many writers on substantive criminal law. One of the most influential of these, Joel Feinberg, divides the project into four parts and looks at criminal prohibitions based on: (1) harm to others, (2) harm to self, (3) offense to others, and (4) harmless wrongdoing.

The first category, harm to others, obviously forms the core of criminal law. While it raises difficult conceptual questions about what constitutes harm and about how serious various kinds of harm are, many writers take for granted that rational arguments can be given to explain the consensus surrounding this core.

The three other categories, from the liberal point of view, all need special attention. Some writers assume that respect for individual autonomy should prevent the government from using criminal sanctions to forbid self-regarding conduct. Thus, there is a presumption against paternalistic uses of criminal law. Similarly, writers often assume that offense, unlike harm, is not a serious enough consequence to justify prohibiting choice and circumscribing autonomy. And the notion that criminal law should concern itself with harmless wrongdoing is suspect. None of this implies that these liberal writers reject the three categories out of hand. It does however mean that special arguments are needed to show why preventing self-harm or offensive conduct or harmless wrongs is a justifiable basis for using criminal law to limit freedom.

In his highly influential book, HARM TO OTHERS, the philosopher Joel Feinberg states the basic assumptions and premises of the liberal approach to criminal law.

> While it is easy to overemphasize the value of liberty, there is no denying its necessity, and for that reason most writers on our subject have endorsed a kind of "presumption in favor of liberty" requiring that whenever a legislator is faced with a choice between imposing a legal duty on citizens or leaving them at liberty, other things being equal, he should leave individuals free to make their own choices. Liberty should be the norm; coercion always needs some special justification. That "presumption" together with its justifying reasons we can call the "presumptive case for liberty." . . .
>
> [W]e can assert tentatively that it is legitimate for the state to prohibit conduct that causes serious private harm, or the unreasonable risk of such harm, or harm to important public institutions and practices. In short, state interference with a citizen's behavior tends to be morally justified when it is reasonably necessary (that is, when there are reasonable grounds for taking it to be necessary as well as effective) to prevent harm or the unreasonable risk of harm to parties other than the person interfered with.

JOEL FEINBERG, HARM TO OTHERS: MORAL LIMITS OF THE CRIMINAL LAW 9, 11 (1984).

Feinberg concedes that the harm principle is vague, that we may disagree about the nature and seriousness of certain harms, that some harmful acts cannot be prohibited, and that some acts appropriately criminalized may not obviously involve harm. He elaborates this view that there are other identifiable bases for criminal prohibition that have a long history and that, from a theoretical standpoint, may be highly controversial.

> It has been held (but not always by the same person) that it is always a good and relevant reason in support of penal legislation that: (1) it is reasonably necessary to prevent hurt or offense (as opposed to injury or harm) to others (the *offense principle*); (2) it is reasonably necessary to prevent harm to the very person it prohibits from acting, as opposed to "others" (*legal paternalism*); (3) it is reasonably necessary to prevent inherently immoral conduct whether or not such conduct is harmful or offensive to

anyone (*legal moralism*). An especially interesting position, and one which deserves separate discussion, is that formed by the intersection of moralism and paternalism which holds that a good reason for restricting a person's liberty is that it is reasonably necessary to prevent moral (as opposed to physical or economic) harm to that person himself.

Id. at 12.

———————

Many contemporary theorists of law—and of criminal law in particular—disagree with liberalism. They challenge the ideas of consensus, neutrality, and reason that are the heart of the liberal point of view. They claim that consensus is unattainable, that neutrality is a myth, and that appeals to reason merely conceal uses of power and coercion. In the next Section we will get acquainted with these alternative conceptions of criminal law.

[C] Critical Jurisprudence

[1] Critical Legal Studies

The critical legal studies movement attacks liberalism at its root. It challenges the claim that law aspires to be, and is, neutral, objective, and rational. In the context of criminal law, this means that critical legal theorists raise doubts about whether we have shared and "objective" notions of harm, dangerousness, and responsibility and about how these concepts are used politically.

Robert Gordon's article, *Critical Legal Histories*, is one of the best summaries of ways in which the critical approach seeks to undermine liberal optimism.

Robert W. Gordon, *Critical Legal Histories*, 36 Stan. L. Rev. 57, 93–95, 96 (1984)[3]

[T]he dominant vision of the meaning of modern history is an optimistic liberal vision. Its principal story-line is one of the gradual recession of error before the advance of commerce, liberty, and science—an advance modestly but invaluably assisted by ever more efficiently adaptive technologies of law. There have been failures and setbacks, and work remains to be done; but we have triumphed over the major obstacles, and the remaining work is remedial reform of the details. . . .

Let me, for convenience's sake, try to arrange some theories [that are critical of the dominant vision] on a spectrum, starting with those closest to straight instrumental theories, and ending with those emphasizing the most diffuse and indirect ways in which law makes up the elements of a culture:

———————

3. Copyright © 1984 by the Board of Trustees of the Leland Stanford Junior University. Reprinted with permission.

(1) "All law is pig law dressed up in judges' robes." That is, law is a means for organizing the ruling class and for coercing, cheating, and disorganizing the working class. Thus, law allows capital freely to collectivize but sets limits on labor combinations; it allows "capital strikes" (disinvestment) but restricts labor strikes; it confirms capitalist control over the organization of work; it criminalizes "vagrancy" as a means of keeping docile the urban unemployed; and it provides that employment is "at will" so that the unorganized work force has no job security.

(2) "The ruling class induces consent and demobilizes opposition by masking its rule in widely shared utopian norms and fair procedures, which it then distorts to its own purposes." For example, the classical bourgeois legal norms of "private property," "free contract," "free speech," and "due process" express universal longings for security, privacy, autonomy, free choice about what to buy and sell and whom to work for, the right to speak one's mind freely, and the universal desire for protection against arbitrary coercion. But in a class society these supposedly universal norms are deployed for the benefit of a particular class. Private property, free contract, (complex and expensive) due process, (well-heeled-and-organized-interest-group-responsive) democratic procedures, and even (expensive-and-technology-dependent) free speech operate de facto to reinforce the advantages of wealth and power. The victims of these outcomes feel powerless to complain because the outcomes seem to have been produced by legitimate rules and procedures.

(3) "The ruling class confirms its rule by actually making good on enough of its utopian promises to convince potential opposition that the system is tolerably fair and capable of improvement, even with all its faults." This proposition is essentially Machiavellian. The ruling class periodically sets up demonstrations to convince people that it really does rule in the universal interest.

(4) "The ruling class itself is taken in by legal ideology; it believes that it's acting justly when it acts according to law, that everyone is getting approximately the best possible deal, and that change would make everyone worse off." This formulation is getting closer to the meaning of ideology in classical social theory: a partial vision of the world that appears to its proponents as well as to its victims as a universal vision. (In fact, in the case of the ideology of the "rule of law," middle-class people are rather more sold on it than working or lower-class people.)

(5) "Law isn't just an instrument of class domination, it's an arena of class struggle." The content of legal rules and practices is ideologically tilted in favor of class rule (or, more generally, the reproduction of current modes of hierarchical domination, class-based or otherwise), but ruling classes don't have everything their own way when it comes to specifying that content. The concessions that cause legal systems to respond to the interests and ideal aspirations of the dominated result from bargains struck after hard struggle. The norms embodied in legal rules therefore are always double-edged: The underdogs who have won them can also be co-opted by them; the overdogs who concede them in order to co-opt are always vulnerable to being undermined by their radical potential.

(6) "The discourse of law — its categories, arguments, reasoning modes, rhetorical tropes, and procedural rituals — fits into a complex of discursive practices that together structure how people perceive and that therefore act to reproduce or to try to change people's social reality."

Notes and Questions

1. **Challenging the Political Neutrality of Law.** For critical thinkers, there is a necessary connection between the idea that law evolves, progresses, and serves the interests of all segments of the community (functionalism) and the idea of an objective, intelligible moral order. Their argument is that we can validate the liberal suggestion that law transcends politics and ideology, that law moves toward embodying a shared ideal of community interest and community harmony, only if we can identify values that are not *merely* the particular preferences of one or another group of individuals. Critical theorists tend to criticize and reject the notion that there are any such transcendent values (values on which we can all agree) and, if they exist, that law is determined by them.

2. **The Relative Objectivity of Values.** Is the question of the objectivity of value an all-or-nothing question? Can we say that *some* values are objectively justifiable — personal security and personal freedom for example — even if other values are matters of endless dispute? Liberal theory assumes that some values have this "objective" status; liberal criminal theory assumes that dangerousness and harm can be explained in objective terms. Critical theory, on the other hand, counterattacks by saying that such ideas as security, freedom, and harm are indefinitely malleable. In the interest of security from harm, one group will invariably demand constraints on the kinds of behavior that another group will see as essential to freedom.

Given what you have learned about various aspects of criminal law, consider whether the underlying choices and values can be defended objectively. Critical theory is committed to seeing all law, including criminal law, as the product of class conflict, if not class warfare. Is this a useful and accurate perspective from which to understand legal doctrine and legal change?

3. **On Self-Deception.** Note that, according to Gordon, an important possibility to consider is that "the ruling class itself is taken in by legal ideology," that those whose subjective agendas become law *genuinely* believe in the objectivity and universality of their values. If this is true, how can anyone distinguish reality from illusion?

Critical theorists, looking at criminal law, stress the indeterminate character of so many of the choices at the heart of criminal law. When do we say that certain conduct is so harmful that it must be prohibited, as opposed to saying that its benefits outweigh its harms? When do we decide that security outweighs freedom, and when do we decide the opposite? When do we hold persons responsible for their conduct, and when do we exculpate them? From the critical point of view, the answers to these questions depend neither on facts nor on an "objective moral realm" but rather on subjective values that are political and endlessly controversial.

4. Description and Prescription. In what ways is critical legal theory descriptive and in what ways is it prescriptive? Gordon implies that the descriptive aspect is largely historical and sociological, telling the story of the origins and development of criminal law from various perspectives. These perspectives will reflect the points of view of different classes, for example the points of view of the "losers" (those groups whose agendas did not prevail politically and become law) as well as the "winners." To deconstruct the law is to see it in terms of these several conflicting accounts.

On the other hand, some writers use the methods and presuppositions of critical theory to put forth a concrete and well-focused prescriptive agenda for reform of the law. This tends to be true of feminist and critical race theorists, as the next sections reflect.

[2] Feminist Theory

Some feminist writers take their methodology from critical legal studies. Their message is twofold. On one hand, they attack the idea that law reflects a point of view that is neutral, objective, and universally fair rather than the assumptions of the social class that has had political and economic power, a class comprised of privileged white men. Also, they offer an assessment of law from the standpoint of women—their perceptions, their interests, and their goals.

Much of the critical feminist literature is concerned with substantive goals and policies, as well as with methodology. Some crimes, of course, directly involve sex-based stereotypes and social values. These crimes, it is said, perpetuate men's fantasies and expectations about women's nature and roles. The laws involving harassment, rape, pornography, battery, and prostitution are among the most controversial.

In her book, FEMINIST JURISPRUDENCE, Patricia Smith argues that our conception of harm is crucially related to our conception of the gender roles and that this has led to long-term biases in the law.

> Harm has been analyzed as the impairment of an interest. If you are harmed, it means that something that is a concern of yours, something in which you have a stake, something that matters to you or to your life has been impaired. But what your legitimate interests are or what is in your interest varies with time and place. A slave had no legitimate interest in freedom, nor for many centuries did a woman. In fact, for most of history, slaves and women did not have any interests of their own, especially not interests that conflicted with the interests of their masters, the men who owned them. Even today the freedom of many women is highly restricted, but it is not seen as an impairment of their interests, although other women would certainly find it so. In many Arab countries, for example, women are not allowed to vote, to drive, or to show themselves in public without covering their faces or heads. American and European women would find such restrictions offensive and harmful, but Arabs do not believe that they are offending or harming their women. They believe that their way of life is

natural, ordinary, normal, perhaps inevitable, and, in many cases, ordained by God. In other words, they believe very much the same thing that we believe about the way we live. What happens all the time feels like what is normal, and so it requires imagination and judgment to decide that what feels normal may not be what is right.

The point is that what counts as a harm depends crucially on social attitudes toward what counts as an interest, and these various social attitudes can put certain members of any given society at a great disadvantage without even the possibility of recognizing that disadvantage as a harm. We thus have good reason to examine carefully what we recognize or, even more importantly, what we do not recognize as harmful and whether we have good and legitimate reasons to support our views.

PATRICIA SMITH, FEMINIST JURISPRUDENCE 139 (1993).

Smith concludes that when we look at what should be criminalized and determine accordingly what weight should be given to different kinds of violence, the underlying gender assumptions can be decisive, unarticulated, and unquestioned premises.

In sum, not all harms are addressed; not all rights are protected; and not all violence is prevented. All state interference is limited by a commitment to individual freedom. This leaves private parties vulnerable to one another, which is sometimes fair and sometimes not. It takes a decision to determine when the state should intervene and when it should permit individuals to settle their differences by themselves. There is no magic formula for making this decision. It requires a judgment based on many factors and a thoughtful consideration of diverse individual circumstances.

Id. at 139.

Victoria Nourse, *Law's Constitution: A Relational Critique,* 17 WIS. WOMEN'S L.J. 23, 35–37 (2002)[4]

Let us look at a single case that makes the point rather clearly [*Commonwealth v. Watson*, 431 A.2d 949 (Pa. 1981)]: Mrs. Watson was down on the ground, fighting for her life. The state's own witness said so. They said that, when she shot, her attacker had her around the neck; the witness said that she was struggling when the gun fired. All of the elements of self-defense appeared to be met: there was an unlawful threat, the threat was grave, and it was imminent. The trial judge had a different idea; he denied Mrs. Watson's claim of self-defense. Why? This woman was not asking for a special favor, a subjective standard. . . . This was real self-defense, by the book. But the trial judge found that the threat was not "imminent," that there was too much time.

Now, even the most untutored student of the law of self-defense must ask how any trial judge can come to the conclusion that a woman who is down on the ground struggling has no claim of self-defense. To speak of imminence in the context of such a case is the equivalent of legal irrationality. Imminence could not have been an issue in Mrs. Watson's case—the hands were around her neck; there was no time to call the police or to run away. The actual threat was "now"; it was "immediate." Well, the sad, but true answer to this quandary is that the threat was not imminent, according to the trial judge, because "of the parties' relationship involving a 'long course of physical abuse.'" Put another way, the threat was not imminent because Mrs. Watson was a battered woman.

. . . Long ago, realism taught us that legal concepts are not autonomous, created out of nowhere, and that law absorbs social norms and vice-versa. We also know that, by masking these norms, within a purportedly objective, natural guise, the guise of "time," the law tends to legitimate the existing order. We know that from critical legal studies. But what we don't know, or if we know we have not paid sufficient attention to, is the mechanics of law's constitution (the "how" it happens as opposed to "that" it happens). The kind of thing we have failed to note are the ways in which relations constitute the natural and, in turn, naturalize relations.

It is one thing for members of society to tacitly share a social norm that women should leave violent relationships. But transformed into law, and in particular self-defense law, the institution changes the legal relations implicit in the norm. The neighbor who says over the fence "she really should leave him," is not the judge or jury who appropriates that norm within the institution we know as law. When we move from time as brute fact to institutional norm, we move from a natural context to an institutional context, a context that is quite complex, subject to its own internal norms and bound by a set of self-regarding institutional imperatives. Once a judge takes that leaving-norm and places it within the legal institution, the norm gains hard edges; it becomes a category of up or down, in or out; it gains power—it takes on the characteristics of the institution in which it is placed. A perceived social obligation imposed on a defendant becomes a measure of legal right and wrong, it becomes a measure of hard and fast exclusion. It thus becomes the way in which a battered woman can be refused a defense because she was battered, but more importantly, it becomes a way to naturalize discrimination, to give it the legitimacy of law.

Notes and Questions

1. **Feminist Methodology.** Many feminist writers raise broad methodological questions. Consider the extent to which gender hierarchy has affected the development of the law. With regard to such notions as harm, autonomy, and privacy, are you persuaded that there is: (1) a characteristic men's point of view, (2) a characteristic women's point of view, and (3) a history of domination by the first of these? If so, how should society and legal institutions address this predicament?

2. Essentialism. Note that the claim that there is a distinctive women's point of view and way of experiencing is criticized as "essentialism," the notion that women have an identifiable *essence*. Many feminists reject essentialism and emphasize the diversity of women's modes of experiencing and understanding. For these writers, the attempt to ascribe an essence to women is symptomatic of the way in which men have treated and dominated women. *See, e.g.*, Angela Harris, *Race and Essentialism in Feminist Legal Theory*, 42 Stan. L. Rev. 581 (1990).

3. On the Pervasiveness of Sexism. Feminist writers typically try to show that disregard for women's points of view and interests permeates all aspects of criminal law, not merely such sex-based crimes as rape and prostitution. For example, they assert that the way in which we characterize the reasonableness of self-defensive acts or acts committed under duress carries a bias toward what is a reasonable response for a *man*. They argue that when we mitigate responsibility because of "extreme emotional distress," our way of assessing distress also conveys a male bias. Now that you have examined various distinctions made in determining criminal liability, consider their objectivity and their relation to questions of gender.

[3] Critical Race Theory

Like feminism, critical race theory inherits and expands the critique of liberalism that is basic to critical legal studies. It claims that, in arguing for the neutrality, objectivity, and rationality of law, many liberal theorists have practiced obfuscation and self-delusion. Again, the criticism is at two levels. On the first level, critics say that the substantive law perpetuates discrimination against racial and ethnic minorities. On a deeper level, they claim that the law disregards the ways in which members of minority groups understand their interests, human nature, and the role of government. Thus, law perpetuates domination at both levels.

Mari Matsuda, Charles Lawrence, Richard Delgado & Kimberle Crenshaw, Words That Wound 3, 6–7 (1993)

Critical race theory is grounded in the particulars of a social reality that is defined by our experiences and the collective historical experience of our communities of origin. Critical race theorists embrace subjectivity of perspective and are avowedly political. Our work is both pragmatic and utopian, as we seek to respond to the immediate needs of the subordinated and oppressed even as we imagine a different world and offer different values. It is work that involves both action and reflection. It is informed by active struggle and in turn informs that struggle.

Critical race theory cannot be understood as an abstract set of ideas or principles. Among its basic theoretical themes is that of privileging contextual and historical descriptions over transhistorical or purely abstract ones. . . .

In a search for a tentative expository answer to the question "What is critical race theory?" critical race scholars have identified the following defining elements:

1. Critical race theory recognizes that racism is endemic to American life. Thus, the question for us is not so much whether or how racial discrimination can be eliminated while maintaining the integrity of other interests implicated in the status quo such as federalism, privacy, traditional values, or established property interests. Instead we ask how these traditional interests and values serve as vessels of racial subordination.

2. Critical race theory expresses skepticism toward dominant legal claims of neutrality, objectivity, color blindness, and meritocracy. These claims are central to an ideology of equal opportunity that presents race as an immutable characteristic devoid of social meaning and tells an ahistorical, abstracted story of racial inequality as a series of randomly occurring, intentional, and individualized acts.

3. Critical race theory challenges ahistoricism and insists on a contextual/historical analysis of the law. Current inequalities and social/institutional practices are linked to earlier periods in which the intent and cultural meaning of such practices were clear. More important, as critical race theorists we adopt a stance that presumes that racism has contributed to all contemporary manifestations of group advantage and disadvantage along racial lines, including differences in income, imprisonment, health, housing, education, political representation, and military service. Our history calls for this presumption.

4. Critical race theory insists on recognition of the experiential knowledge of people of color and our communities of origin in analyzing law and society. This knowledge is gained from critical reflection on the lived experience of racism and from critical reflection upon active political practice toward the elimination of racism.

5. Critical race theory is interdisciplinary and eclectic. It borrows from several traditions, including liberalism, law and society, feminism, Marxism, poststructuralism, critical legal theory, pragmatism, and nationalism. This eclecticism allows critical race theory to examine and incorporate those aspects of a methodology or theory that effectively enable our voice and advance the cause of racial justice even as we maintain a critical posture.

Notes

Methodological Issues. For a variety of articles exploring the perspectives of critical race theory, see several wide-ranging collections of essays: KIMBERLE CRENSHAW ET AL., CRITICAL RACE THEORY: THE KEY WRITINGS THAT FORMED THE MOVEMENT (1995); RICHARD DELGADO, CRITICAL RACE THEORY: THE CUTTING EDGE (1995); LAURA LEDERER & RICHARD DELGADO, THE PRICE WE PAY: THE CASE AGAINST RACIST SPEECH, HATE PROPAGANDA, AND PORNOGRAPHY (1995).

Two overlapping methodological issues concern many writers. The first issue is the significance of what has come to be called the "narrative method." A concern shared by feminist and critical race theorists is that many groups, in particular women and persons of color, have not had a representative voice in the creation and application of law, as well as in the prevailing accounts of political, social, and legal history. The claim is that social and institutional arrangements tend to "silence" such groups. The dominant groups thus claim to speak objectively and for all. Feminist and critical race writers suggest that it is appropriate for them *not* to offer conflicting claims to objectivity but to speak narratively about the impact of law and politics on their lives. Some claim to speak neither objectively nor for their group, gender, or race, but only for themselves.

The challenge for practitioners of the narrative method is to show how autobiography can lead to legal reform or at least legal change. Legislators and judges need to address not only individual lives but general circumstances. It is an open question how much guidance they can draw from particular and conflicting narratives, however insightful they may be.

A second methodological issue is closely related to the first. Many critical writers, for example Kimberle Crenshaw, discuss "intersectionality," the issue that individuals face when they have different affiliations that reflect differing points of view on a given political and legal issue. For example, black women may see the work of black rap musicians from a feminist perspective, regarding it as pornographic and discriminatory, undeserving of legal protection. Or they may see the prosecution of rap musicians as racially discriminatory and as a manifestation of cultural suppression.

[D] Summary

In the eyes of almost all legislators, certainly in the eyes of the drafters of the Model Penal Code, the content of criminal law is explained by reference to the shared values of the community — security, autonomy, cooperation — and to the goal of identifying and punishing those persons ("outlaws") who culpably infringe upon these interests. This explanation fits the classical liberal ideal whereby government exists to enforce neutral and objective rules that allow individuals to carry out their private conceptions of the good life. By contrast, critical theory questions whether there are shared values and whether it is possible, in practice, for social and legal institutions to realize them.

As you reflect on the content and structure of criminal law described in the previous Chapters, ask yourself what is the best explanation of each detail. Does it express an objective sense of what threatens the common interest? Or does it represent the interests of a particular sub-community — class, gender, or race?

Appendix A

Model Penal Code[1]

Synopsis

---

[1]. Model Penal Code, copyright © 1985 by the American Law Institute. Reproduced with permission. All rights reserved.

[PART I.] GENERAL PROVISIONS
[ARTICLE 1.] PRELIMINARY

Section 1.01. Title and Effective Date.

(1)   This Act is called the Penal and Correctional Code and may be cited as P.C.C. It shall become effective on _____.

(2)   Except as provided in Subsections (3) and (4) of this Section, the Code does not apply to offenses committed prior to its effective date and prosecutions for such offenses shall be governed by the prior law, which is continued in effect for that purpose, as if this Code were not in force. For the purposes of this Section, an offense was committed prior to the effective date of the Code if any of the elements of the offense occurred prior thereto.

(3)   In any case pending on or after the effective date of the Code, involving an offense committed prior to such date:

   (a)   procedural provisions of the Code shall govern, insofar as they are justly applicable and their application does not introduce confusion or delay;

   (b)   provisions of the Code according a defense or mitigation shall apply, with the consent of the defendant;

   (c)   the Court, with the consent of the defendant, may impose sentence under the provisions of the Code applicable to the offense and the offender.

(4)   Provisions of the Code governing the treatment and the release or discharge of prisoners, probationers and parolees shall apply to persons under sentence for offenses committed prior to the effective date of the Code, except that the minimum or maximum period of their detention or supervision shall in no case be increased.

Section 1.02. Purposes; Principles of Construction.

(1)   The general purposes of the provisions governing the definition of offenses are:

   (a)   to forbid and prevent conduct that unjustifiably and inexcusably inflicts or threatens substantial harm to individual or public interests;

   (b)   to subject to public control persons whose conduct indicates that they are disposed to commit crimes;

   (c)   to safeguard conduct that is without fault from condemnation as criminal;

   (d)   to give fair warning of the nature of the conduct declared to constitute an offense;

(e)   to differentiate on reasonable grounds between serious and minor offenses.

(2)   The general purposes of the provisions governing the sentencing and treatment of offenders are:

(a)   to prevent the commission of offenses;

(b)   to promote the correction and rehabilitation of offenders;

(c)   to safeguard offenders against excessive, disproportionate or arbitrary punishment;

(d)   to give fair warning of the nature of the sentences that may be imposed on conviction of an offense;

(e)   to differentiate among offenders with a view to a just individualization in their treatment;

(f)   to define, coordinate and harmonize the powers, duties and functions of the courts and of administrative officers and agencies responsible for dealing with offenders;

(g)   to advance the use of generally accepted scientific methods and knowledge in the sentencing and treatment of offenders;

(h)   to integrate responsibility for the administration of the correctional system in a State Department of Correction [or other single department or agency].

(3)   The provisions of the Code shall be construed according to the fair import of their terms but when the language is susceptible of differing constructions it shall be interpreted to further the general purposes stated in this Section and the special purposes of the particular provision involved. The discretionary powers conferred by the Code shall be exercised in accordance with the criteria stated in the Code and, insofar as such criteria are not decisive, to further the general purposes stated in this Section.

Section 1.03. Territorial Applicability.

(1)   Except as otherwise provided in this Section, a person may be convicted under the law of this State of an offense committed by his own conduct or the conduct of another for which he is legally accountable if:

(a)   either the conduct which is an element of the offense or the result which is such an element occurs within this State; or

(b)   conduct occurring outside the State is sufficient under the law of this State to constitute an attempt to commit an offense within the State; or

(c)   conduct occurring outside the State is sufficient under the law of this State to constitute a conspiracy to commit an offense within the State and an overt act in furtherance of such conspiracy occurs within the State; or

(d)   conduct occurring within the State establishes complicity in the commission of, or an attempt, solicitation or conspiracy to commit, an offense in another jurisdiction which also is an offense under the law of this State; or

(e)   the offense consists of the omission to perform a legal duty imposed by the law of this State with respect to domicile, residence or a relationship to a person, thing or transaction in the State; or

(f)   the offense is based on a statute of this State which expressly prohibits conduct outside the State, when the conduct bears a reasonable relation to a legitimate interest of this State and the actor knows or should know that his conduct is likely to affect that interest.

(2)   Subsection (1)(a) does not apply when either causing a specified result or a purpose to cause or danger of causing such a result is an element of an offense and the result occurs or is designed or likely to occur only in another jurisdiction where the conduct charged would not constitute an offense, unless a legislative purpose plainly appears to declare the conduct criminal regardless of the place of the result.

(3)   Subsection (1)(a) does not apply when causing a particular result is an element of an offense and the result is caused by conduct occurring outside the State which would not constitute an offense if the result had occurred there, unless the actor purposely or knowingly caused the result within the State.

(4)   When the offense is homicide, either the death of the victim or the bodily impact causing death constitutes a "result," within the meaning of Subsection (1)(a) and if the body of a homicide victim is found within the State, it is presumed that such result occurred within the State.

(5)   This State includes the land and water and the air space above such land and water with respect to which the State has legislative jurisdiction.

Section 1.04. Classes of Crimes; Violations.

(1)   An offense defined by this Code or by any other statute of this State, for which a sentence of [death or of] imprisonment is authorized, constitutes a crime. Crimes are classified as felonies, misdemeanors or petty misdemeanors.

(2)   A crime is a felony if it is so designated in this Code or if persons convicted thereof may be sentenced [to death or] to imprisonment for a term which, apart from an extended term, is in excess of one year.

(3)   A crime is a misdemeanor if it is so designated in this Code or in a statute other than this Code enacted subsequent thereto.

(4)   A crime is a petty misdemeanor if it is so designated in this Code or in a statute other than this Code enacted subsequent thereto or if it is defined by a statute other than this Code which now provides that persons convicted thereof may be sentenced to imprisonment for a term of which the maximum is less than one year.

(5)   An offense defined by this Code or by any other statute of this State constitutes a violation if it is so designated in this Code or in the law defining the offense or if no other sentence than a fine, or fine and forfeiture or other civil penalty is authorized upon conviction or if it is defined by a statute other than this Code which now provides that the offense shall not constitute a crime. A violation does not constitute a crime and conviction of a violation shall not give rise to any disability or legal disadvantage based on conviction of a criminal offense.

(6)   Any offense declared by law to constitute a crime, without specification of the grade thereof or of the sentence authorized upon conviction, is a misdemeanor.

(7)   An offense defined by any statute of this State other than this Code shall be classified as provided in this Section and the sentence that may be imposed upon conviction thereof shall hereafter be governed by this Code.

Section 1.05. All Offenses Defined by Statute; Application of General Provisions of the Code.

(1)   No conduct constitutes an offense unless it is a crime or violation under this Code or another statute of this State.

(2)   The provisions of Part I of the Code are applicable to offenses defined by other statutes, unless the Code otherwise provides.

(3)   This Section does not affect the power of a court to punish for contempt or to employ any sanction authorized by law for the enforcement of an order or a civil judgment or decree.

Section 1.06. Time Limitations.

(1)   A prosecution for murder may be commenced at any time.

(2)   Except as otherwise provided in this Section, prosecutions for other offenses are subject to the following periods of limitation:

    (a)   a prosecution for a felony of the first degree must be commenced within six years after it is committed;

    (b)   a prosecution for any other felony must be commenced within three years after it is committed;

    (c)   a prosecution for a misdemeanor must be commenced within two years after it is committed;

    (d)   a prosecution for a petty misdemeanor or a violation must be commenced within six months after it is committed.

(3)   If the period prescribed in Subsection (2) has expired, a prosecution may nevertheless be commenced for:

(a)   any offense a material element of which is either fraud or a breach of fiduciary obligation within one year after discovery of the offense by an aggrieved party or by a person who has legal duty to represent an aggrieved party and who is himself not a party to the offense, but in no case shall this provision extend the period of limitation otherwise applicable by more than three years; and

(b)   any offense based upon misconduct in office by a public officer or employee at any time when the defendant is in public office or employment or within two years thereafter, but in no case shall this provision extend the period of limitation otherwise applicable by more than three years.

(4)   An offense is committed either when every element occurs, or, if a legislative purpose to prohibit a continuing course of conduct plainly appears, at the time when the course of conduct or the defendant's complicity therein is terminated. Time starts to run on the day after the offense is committed.

(5)   A prosecution is commenced either when an indictment is found [or an information filed] or when a warrant or other process is issued, provided that such warrant or process is executed without unreasonable delay.

(6)   The period of limitation does not run:

(a)   during any time when the accused is continuously absent from the State or has no reasonably ascertainable place of abode or work within the State, but in no case shall this provision extend the period of limitation otherwise applicable by more than three years; or

(b)   during any time when a prosecution against the accused for the same conduct is pending in this State.

Section 1.07. Method of Prosecution When Conduct Constitutes More Than One Offense.

(1)   *Prosecution for Multiple Offenses; Limitation on Convictions.* When the same conduct of a defendant may establish the commission of more than one offense, the defendant may be prosecuted for each such offense. He may not, however, be convicted of more than one offense if:

(a)   one offense is included in the other, as defined in Subsection (4) of this Section; or

(b)   one offense consists only of a conspiracy or other form of preparation to commit the other; or

(c)   inconsistent findings of fact are required to establish the commission of the offenses; or

(d) the offenses differ only in that one is defined to prohibit a designated kind of conduct generally and the other to prohibit a specific instance of such conduct; or

(e) the offense is defined as a continuing course of conduct and the defendant's course of conduct was uninterrupted, unless the law provides that specific periods of such conduct constitute separate offenses.

(2) *Limitation on Separate Trials for Multiple Offenses.* Except as provided in Subsection (3) of this Section, a defendant shall not be subject to separate trials for multiple offenses based on the same conduct or arising from the same criminal episode, if such offenses are known to the appropriate prosecuting officer at the time of the commencement of the first trial and are within the jurisdiction of a single court.

(3) *Authority of Court to Order Separate Trials.* When a defendant is charged with two or more offenses based on the same conduct or arising from the same criminal episode, the Court, on application of the prosecuting attorney or of the defendant, may order any such charge to be tried separately, if it is satisfied that justice so requires.

(4) *Conviction of Included Offense Permitted.* A defendant may be convicted of an offense included in an offense charged in the indictment [or the information]. An offense is so included when:

(a) it is established by proof of the same or less than all the facts required to establish the commission of the offense charged; or

(b) it consists of an attempt or solicitation to commit the offense charged or to commit an offense otherwise included therein; or

(c) it differs from the offense charged only in the respect that a less serious injury or risk of injury to the same person, property or public interest or a lesser kind of culpability suffices to establish its commission.

(5) *Submission of Included Offense to Jury.* The Court shall not be obligated to charge the jury with respect to an included offense unless there is a rational basis for a verdict acquitting the defendant of the offense charged and convicting him of the included offense.

Section 1.08. When Prosecution Barred by Former Prosecution for the Same Offense.

When a prosecution is for a violation of the same provision of the statutes and is based upon the same facts as a former prosecution, it is barred by such former prosecution under the following circumstances:

(1) The former prosecution resulted in an acquittal. There is an acquittal if the prosecution resulted in a finding of not guilty by the trier of fact or in a

determination that there was insufficient evidence to warrant a conviction. A finding of guilty of a lesser included offense is an acquittal of the greater inclusive offense, although the conviction is subsequently set aside.

(2)   The former prosecution was terminated, after the information had been filed or the indictment found, by a final order or judgment for the defendant, which has not been set aside, reversed, or vacated and which necessarily required a determination inconsistent with a fact or a legal proposition that must be established for conviction of the offense.

(3)   The former prosecution resulted in a conviction. There is a conviction if the prosecution resulted in a judgment of conviction which has not been reversed or vacated, a verdict of guilty which has not been set aside and which is capable of supporting a judgment, or a plea of guilty accepted by the Court. In the latter two cases failure to enter judgment must be for a reason other than a motion of the defendant.

(4)   The former prosecution was improperly terminated. Except as provided in this Subsection, there is an improper termination of a prosecution if the termination is for reasons not amounting to an acquittal, and it takes place after the first witness is sworn but before verdict. Termination under any of the following circumstances is not improper:

(a)   The defendant consents to the termination or waives, by motion to dismiss or otherwise, his right to object to the termination.

(b)   The trial court finds that the termination is necessary because:

(i)   it is physically impossible to proceed with the trial in conformity with law; or

(ii)   there is a legal defect in the proceedings which would make any judgment entered upon a verdict reversible as a matter of law; or

(iii)   prejudicial conduct, in or outside the courtroom, makes it impossible to proceed with the trial without injustice to either the defendant or the State; or

(iv)   the jury is unable to agree upon a verdict; or

(v)   false statements of a juror on voir dire prevent a fair trial.

Section. 1.09. When Prosecution Barred by Former Prosecution for Different Offense.

Although a prosecution is for a violation of a different provision of the statutes than a former prosecution or is based on different facts, it is barred by such former prosecution under the following circumstances:

(1)   The former prosecution resulted in an acquittal or in a conviction as defined in Section 1.08 and the subsequent prosecution is for:

(a) any offense of which the defendant could have been convicted on the first prosecution; or

(b) any offense for which the defendant should have been tried on the first prosecution under Section 1.07, unless the Court ordered a separate trial of the charge of such offense; or

(c) the same conduct, unless (i) the offense of which the defendant was formerly convicted or acquitted and the offense for which he is subsequently prosecuted each requires proof of a fact not required by the other and the law defining each of such offenses is intended to prevent a substantially different harm or evil, or (ii) the second offense was not consummated when the former trial began.

(2) The former prosecution was terminated, after the information was filed or the indictment found, by an acquittal or by a final order or judgment for the defendant which has not been set aside, reversed or vacated and which acquittal, final order or judgment necessarily required a determination inconsistent with a fact which must be established for conviction of the second offense.

(3) The former prosecution was improperly terminated, as improper termination is defined in Section 1.08, and the subsequent prosecution is for an offense of which the defendant could have been convicted had the former prosecution not been improperly terminated.

Section 1.10. Former Prosecution in Another Jurisdiction: When a Bar.

When conduct constitutes an offense within the concurrent jurisdiction of this State and of the United States or another State, a prosecution in any such other jurisdiction is a bar to a subsequent prosecution in this State under the following circumstances:

(1) The first prosecution resulted in an acquittal or in a conviction as defined in Section 1.08 and the subsequent prosecution is based on the same conduct, unless

(a) the offense of which the defendant was formerly convicted or acquitted and the offense for which he is subsequently prosecuted each requires proof of a fact not required by the other and the law defining each of such offenses is intended to prevent a substantially different harm or evil or

(b) the second offense was not consummated when the former trial began; or

(2) The former prosecution was terminated, after the information was filed or the indictment found, by an acquittal or by a final order or judgment for the defendant which has not been set aside, reversed or vacated and which acquittal, final order or judgment necessarily required a determination inconsistent with a fact which must be established for conviction of the offense of which the defendant is subsequently prosecuted.

Section 1.11. Former Prosecution Before Court Lacking Jurisdiction or When Fraudulently Procured by the Defendant.

A prosecution is not a bar within the meaning of Sections 1.08, 1.09 and 1.10 under any of the following circumstances:

(1)   The former prosecution was before a court which lacked jurisdiction over the defendant or the offense; or

(2)   The former prosecution was procured by the defendant without the knowledge of the appropriate prosecuting officer and with the purpose of avoiding the sentence which might otherwise be imposed; or

(3)   The former prosecution resulted in a judgment of conviction which was held invalid in a subsequent proceeding on a writ of habeas corpus, coram nobis or similar process.

Section 1.12. Proof Beyond a Reasonable Doubt; Affirmative Defenses; Burden of Proving Fact When Not an Element of an Offense; Presumptions.

(1)   No person may be convicted of an offense unless each element of such offense is proved beyond a reasonable doubt. In the absence of such proof, the innocence of the defendant is assumed.

(2)   Subsection (1) of this Section does not:

    (a)   require the disproof of an affirmative defense unless and until there is evidence supporting such defense; or

    (b)   apply to any defense which the Code or another statute plainly requires the defendant to prove by a preponderance of evidence.

(3)   A ground of defense is affirmative, within the meaning of Subsection (2)(a) of this Section, when:

    (a)   it arises under a section of the Code which so provides; or

    (b)   it relates to an offense defined by a statute other than the Code and such statute so provides; or

    (c)   it involves a matter of excuse or justification peculiarly within the knowledge of the defendant on which he can fairly be required to adduce supporting evidence.

(4)   When the application of the Code depends upon the finding of a fact which is not an element of an offense, unless the Code otherwise provides:

    (a)   the burden of proving the fact is on the prosecution or defendant, depending on whose interest or contention will be furthered if the finding should be made; and

    (b)   the fact must be proved to the satisfaction of the Court or jury, as the case may be.

(5)   When the Code establishes a presumption with respect to any fact which is an element of an offense, it has the following consequences:

(a)   when there is evidence of the facts which give rise to the presumption, the issue of the existence of the presumed fact must be submitted to the jury, unless the Court is satisfied that the evidence as a whole clearly negatives the presumed fact; and

(b)   when the issue of the existence of the presumed fact is submitted to the jury, the Court shall charge that while the presumed fact must, on all the evidence, be proved beyond a reasonable doubt, the law declares that the jury may regard the facts giving rise to the presumption as sufficient evidence of the presumed fact.

(6)   A presumption not established by the Code or inconsistent with it has the consequences otherwise accorded it by law.

Section 1.13. General Definitions.

In this Code, unless a different meaning plainly is required:

(1)   "statute" includes the Constitution and a local law or ordinance of a political subdivision of the State;

(2)   "act" or "action" means a bodily movement whether voluntary or involuntary;

(3)   "voluntary" has the meaning specified in Section 2.01;

(4)   "omission" means a failure to act;

(5)   "conduct" means an action or omission and its accompanying state of mind, or, where relevant, a series of acts and omissions;

(6)   "actor" includes, where relevant, a person guilty of an omission;

(7)   "acted" includes, where relevant, "omitted to act";

(8)   "person," "he" and "actor" include any natural person and, where relevant, a corporation or an unincorporated association;

(9)   "element of an offense" means (i) such conduct or (ii) such attendant circumstances or (iii) such a result of conduct as

(a)   is included in the description of the forbidden conduct in the definition of the offense; or

(b)   establishes the required kind of culpability; or

(c)   negatives an excuse or justification for such conduct; or

(d)   negatives a defense under the statute of limitations; or

(e)   establishes jurisdiction or venue;

(10) "material element of an offense" means an element that does not relate exclusively to the statute of limitations, jurisdiction, venue or to any other matter

similarly unconnected with (i) the harm or evil, incident to conduct, sought to be prevented by the law defining the offense, or (ii) the existence of a justification or excuse for such conduct;

(11) "purposely" has the meaning specified in Section 2.02 and equivalent terms such as "with purpose," "designed" or "with design" have the same meaning;

(12) "intentionally" or "with intent" means purposely;

(13) "knowingly" has the meaning specified in Section 2.02 and equivalent terms such as "knowing" or "with knowledge" have the same meaning;

(14) "recklessly" has the meaning specified in Section 2.02 and equivalent terms such as "recklessness" or "with recklessness" have the same meaning;

(15) "negligently" has the meaning specified in Section 2.02 and equivalent terms such as "negligence" or "with negligence" have the same meaning;

(16) "reasonably believes" or "reasonable belief" designates a belief which the actor is not reckless or negligent in holding.

[ARTICLE 2.]   GENERAL PRINCIPLES OF LIABILITY

Section 2.01. Requirement of Voluntary Act; Omission as Basis of Liability; Possession as an Act.

(1)   A person is not guilty of an offense unless his liability is based on conduct which includes a voluntary act or the omission to perform an act of which he is physically capable.

(2)   The following are not voluntary acts within the meaning of this Section:

(a)   a reflex or convulsion;

(b)   a bodily movement during unconsciousness or sleep;

(c)   conduct during hypnosis or resulting from hypnotic suggestion;

(d)   a bodily movement that otherwise is not a product of the effort or determination of the actor, either conscious or habitual.

(3)   Liability for the commission of an offense may not be based on an omission unaccompanied by action unless:

(a)   the omission is expressly made sufficient by the law defining the offense; or

(b)   a duty to perform the omitted act is otherwise imposed by law.

(4)   Possession is an act, within the meaning of this Section, if the possessor knowingly procured or received the thing possessed or was aware of his control thereof for a sufficient period to have been able to terminate his possession.

Section 2.02. General Requirements of Culpability.

(1)   *Minimum Requirements of Culpability.* Except as provided in Section 2.05, a person is not guilty of an offense unless he acted purposely, knowingly, recklessly or negligently, as the law may require, with respect to each material element of the offense.

(2)   *Kinds of Culpability Defined.*

   (a)   *Purposely.*

   A person acts purposely with respect to a material element of an offense when:

   (i)   if the element involves the nature of his conduct or a result thereof, it is his conscious object to engage in conduct of that nature or to cause such a result; and

   (ii)   if the element involves the attendant circumstances, he is aware of the existence of such circumstances or he believes or hopes that they exist.

   (b)   *Knowingly.*

   A person acts knowingly with respect to a material element of an offense when:

   (i)   if the element involves the nature of his conduct or the attendant circumstances, he is aware that his conduct is of that nature or that such circumstances exist; and

   (ii)   if the element involves a result of his conduct, he is aware that it is practically certain that his conduct will cause such a result.

   (c)   *Recklessly.*

   A person acts recklessly with respect to a material element of an offense when he consciously disregards a substantial and unjustifiable risk that the material element exists or will result from his conduct. The risk must be of such a nature and degree that, considering the nature and purpose of the actor's conduct and the circumstances known to him, its disregard involves a gross deviation from the standard of conduct that a law-abiding person would observe in the actor's situation.

   (d)   *Negligently.*

   A person acts negligently with respect to a material element of an offense when he should be aware of a substantial and unjustifiable risk that the material element exists or will result from his conduct. The risk must be of such a nature and degree that the actor's failure to perceive it, considering the nature and purpose of his conduct and the circumstances known to him, involves a gross deviation from the standard of care that a reasonable person would observe in the actor's situation.

(3)   *Culpability Required Unless Otherwise Provided.* When the culpability sufficient to establish a material element of an offense is not prescribed by law, such element is established if a person acts purposely, knowingly or recklessly with respect thereto.

(4)   *Prescribed Culpability Requirements Applies to All Material Elements.* When the law defining an offense prescribes the kind of culpability that is sufficient for the commission of an offense, without distinguishing among the material elements thereof, such provision shall apply to all the material elements of the offense, unless a contrary purpose plainly appears.

(5)   *Substitutes for Negligence, Recklessness and Knowledge.* When the law provides that negligence suffices to establish an element of an offense, such element also is established if a person acts purposely, knowingly or recklessly. When recklessness suffices to establish an element, such element also is established if a person acts purposely or knowingly. When acting knowingly suffices to establish an element, such element also is established if a person acts purposely.

(6)   *Requirements of Purpose Satisfied if Purpose Is Conditional.* When a particular purpose is an element of an offense, the element is established although such purpose is conditional, unless the condition negatives the harm or evil sought to be prevented by the law defining the offense.

(7)   *Requirement of Knowledge Satisfied by Knowledge of High Probability.* When knowledge of the existence of a particular fact is an element of an offense, such knowledge is established if a person is aware of a high probability of its existence, unless he actually believes that it does not exist.

(8)   *Requirement of Wilfulness Satisfied by Acting Knowingly.* A requirement that an offense be committed wilfully is satisfied if a person acts knowingly with respect to the material elements of the offense, unless a purpose to impose further requirements appears.

(9)   *Culpability as to Illegality of Conduct.* Neither knowledge nor recklessness or negligence as to whether conduct constitutes an offense or as to the existence, meaning or application of the law determining the elements of an offense is an element of such offense, unless the definition of the offense or the Code so provides.

(10) *Culpability as Determinant to Grade of Offense.* When the grade or degree of an offense depends on whether the offense is committed purposely, knowingly, recklessly or negligently, its grade or degree shall be the lowest for which the determinative kind of culpability is established with respect to any material element of the offense.

Section 2.03. Causal Relationship Between Conduct and Result; Divergence Between Result Designed or Contemplated and Actual Result or Between Probable and Actual Result.

(1)   Conduct is the cause of a result when:

(a)   it is an antecedent but for which the result in question would not have occurred; and

(b)   the relationship between the conduct and result satisfies any additional causal requirements imposed by the Code or by the law defining the offense.

(2)   When purposely or knowingly causing a particular result is an element of an offense, the element is not established if the actual result is not within the purpose or the contemplation of the actor unless:

(a)   the actual result differs from that designed or contemplated, as the case may be, only in the respect that a different person or different property is injured or affected or that the injury or harm designed or contemplated would have been more serious or more extensive than that caused; or

(b)   the actual result involves the same kind of injury or harm as that designed or contemplated and is not too remote or accidental in its occurrence to have a [just] bearing on the actor's liability or on the gravity of his offense.

(3)   When recklessly or negligently causing a particular result is an element of an offense, the element is not established if the actual result is not within the risk of which the actor is aware or, in the case of negligence, of which he should be aware unless:

(a)   the actual result differs from the probable result only in the respect that a different person or different property is injured or affected or that the probable injury or harm would have been more serious or more extensive than that caused; or

(b)   the actual result involves the same kind of injury or harm as the probable result and is not too remote or accidental in its occurrence to have a [just] bearing on the actor's liability or on the gravity of his offense.

(4)   When causing a particular result is a material element of an offense for which absolute liability is imposed by law, the element is not established unless the actual result is a probable consequence of the actor's conduct.

Section 2.04. Ignorance or Mistake.

(1)   Ignorance or mistake as to a matter of fact or law is a defense if:

(a)   the ignorance or mistake negatives the purpose, knowledge, belief, recklessness or negligence required to establish a material element of the offense; or

(b)   the law provides that the state of mind established by such ignorance or mistake constitutes a defense.

(2)   Although ignorance or mistake would otherwise afford a defense to the offense charged, the defense is not available if the defendant would be guilty of another offense had the situation been as he supposed. In such case, however, the ignorance or mistake of the defendant shall reduce the grade and degree of the offense of which he may be convicted to those of the offense of which he would be guilty had the situation been as he supposed.

(3)   A belief that conduct does not legally constitute an offense is a defense to a prosecution for that offense based upon such conduct when:

> (a)   the statute or other enactment defining the offense is not known to the actor and has not been published or otherwise reasonably made available prior to the conduct alleged; or

> (b)   he acts in reasonable reliance upon an official statement of the law, afterward determined to be invalid or erroneous, contained in (i) a statute or other enactment; (ii) a judicial decision, opinion or judgment; (iii) an administrative order or grant of permission; or (iv) an official interpretation of the public officer or body charged by law with responsibility for the interpretation, administration or enforcement of the law defining the offense.

(4)   The defendant must prove a defense arising under Subsection (3) of this Section by a preponderance of evidence.

Section 2.05. When Culpability Requirements Are Inapplicable to Violations and to Offenses Defined by Other Statutes; Effect of Absolute Liability in Reducing Grade of Offense to Violation.

(1)   The requirements of culpability prescribed by Sections 2.01 and 2.02 do not apply to:

> (a)   offenses which constitute violations, unless the requirement involved is included in the definition of the offense or the Court determines that its application is consistent with effective enforcement of the law defining the offense; or

> (b)   offenses defined by statutes other than the Code, insofar as a legislative purpose to impose absolute liability for such offenses or with respect to any material element thereof plainly appears.

(2)   Notwithstanding any other provision of existing law and unless a subsequent statute otherwise provides:

> (a)   when absolute liability is imposed with respect to any material element of an offense defined by a statute other than the Code and a conviction is based upon such liability, the offense constitutes a violation; and

> (b)   although absolute liability is imposed by law with respect to one or more of the material elements of an offense defined by a statute other

than the Code, the culpable commission of the offense may be charged and proved, in which event negligence with respect to such elements constitutes sufficient culpability and the classification of the offense and the sentence that may be imposed therefore upon conviction are determined by Section 1.04 and Article 6 of the Code.

Section 2.06. Liability for Conduct of Another; Complicity.

(1)   A person is guilty of an offense if it is committed by his own conduct or by the conduct of another person for which he is legally accountable, or both.

(2)   A person is legally accountable for the conduct of another person when:

(a)   acting with the kind of culpability that is sufficient for the commission of the offense, he causes an innocent or irresponsible person to engage in such conduct; or

(b)   he is made accountable for the conduct of such other person by the Code or by the law defining the offense; or

(c)   he is an accomplice of such other person in the commission of the offense.

(3)   A person is an accomplice of another person in the commission of an offense if:

(a)   with the purpose of promoting or facilitating the commission of the offense, he

(i)   solicits such other person to commit it; or

(ii)   aids or agrees or attempts to aid such other person in planning or committing it; or

(iii)   having a legal duty to prevent the commission of the offense, fails to make proper effort so to do; or

(b)   his conduct is expressly declared by law to establish his complicity.

(4)   When causing a particular result is an element of an offense, an accomplice in the conduct causing such result is an accomplice in the commission of that offense, if he acts with the kind of culpability, if any, with respect to that result that is sufficient for the commission of the offense.

(5)   A person who is legally incapable of committing a particular offense himself may be guilty thereof if it is committed by the conduct of another person for which he is legally accountable, unless such liability is inconsistent with the purpose of the provision establishing his incapacity.

(6)   Unless otherwise provided by the Code or by the law defining the offense, a person is not an accomplice in an offense committed by another person if:

(a)   he is a victim of that offense; or

(b)   the offense is so defined that his conduct is inevitably incident to its commission; or

(c)   he terminates his complicity prior to the commission of the offense and

    (i)   wholly deprives it of effectiveness in the commission of the offense; or

    (ii)   gives timely warning to the law enforcement authorities or otherwise makes proper effort to prevent the commission of the offense.

(7)   An accomplice may be convicted on proof of the commission of the offense and of his complicity therein, though the person claimed to have committed the offense has not been prosecuted or convicted or has been convicted of a different offense or degree of offense or has an immunity to prosecution or conviction or has been acquitted.

Section 2.07. Liability of Corporations, Unincorporated Associations and Persons Acting, or Under a Duty to Act, in Their Behalf.

(1)   A corporation may be convicted of the commission of an offense if:

(a)   the offense is a violation or the offense is defined by a statute other than the Code in which a legislative purpose to impose liability on corporations plainly appears and the conduct is performed by an agent of the corporation acting in behalf of the corporation within the scope of his office or employment, except that if the law defining the offense designates the agents for whose conduct the corporation is accountable or the circumstances under which it is accountable, such provisions shall apply; or

(b)   the offense consists of an omission to discharge a specific duty of affirmative performance imposed on corporations by law; or

(c)   the commission of the offense was authorized, requested, commanded, performed or recklessly tolerated by the board of directors or by a high managerial agent acting in behalf of the corporation within the scope of his office or employment.

(2)   When absolute liability is imposed for the commission of an offense, a legislative purpose to impose liability on a corporation shall be assumed, unless the contrary plainly appears.

(3)   An unincorporated association may be convicted of the commission of an offense if:

(a)   the offense is defined by a statute other than the Code which expressly provides for the liability of such an association and the conduct is performed by an agent of the association acting in behalf of the association within the scope of his office or employment, except that if the law defining the offense designates the agents for whose conduct the association is accountable or the circumstances under which it is accountable, such provisions shall apply; or

(b)　the offense consists of an omission to discharge a specific duty of affirmative performance imposed on associations by law.

(4)　As used in this Section:

(a)　"corporation" does not include an entity organized as or by a governmental agency for the execution of a governmental program;

(b)　"agent" means any director, officer, servant, employee or other person authorized to act in behalf of the corporation or association and, in the case of an unincorporated association, a member of such association;

(c)　"high managerial agent" means an officer of a corporation or an unincorporated association, or, in the case of a partnership, a partner, or any other agent of a corporation or association having duties of such responsibility that his conduct may fairly be assumed to represent the policy of the corporation or association.

(5)　In any prosecution of a corporation or an unincorporated association for the commission of an offense included within the terms of Subsection (1)(a) or Subsection (3)(a) of this Section, other than an offense for which absolute liability has been imposed, it shall be a defense if the defendant proves by a preponderance of evidence that the high managerial agent having supervisory responsibility over the subject matter of the offense employed due diligence to prevent its commission. This paragraph shall not apply if it is plainly inconsistent with the legislative purpose in defining the particular offense.

(6)　(a)　A person is legally accountable for any conduct he performs or causes to be performed in the name of the corporation or an unincorporated association or in its behalf to the same extent as if it were performed in his own name or behalf.

(b)　Whenever a duty to act is imposed by law upon a corporation or an unincorporated association, any agent of the corporation or association having primary responsibility for the discharge of the duty is legally accountable for a reckless omission to perform the required act to the same extent as if the duty were imposed by law directly upon himself.

(c)　When a person is convicted of an offense by reason of his legal accountability for the conduct of a corporation or an unincorporated association, he is subject to the sentence authorized by law when a natural person is convicted of an offense of the grade and the degree involved.

Section 2.08. Intoxication.

(1)   Except as provided in Subsection (4) of this Section, intoxication of the actor is not a defense unless it negatives an element of the offense.

(2)   When recklessness establishes an element of the offense, if the actor, due to self-induced intoxication, is unaware of a risk of which he would have been aware had he been sober, such unawareness is immaterial.

(3)   Intoxication does not, in itself, constitute mental disease within the meaning of Section 4.01.

(4)   Intoxication which (a) is not self-induced or (b) is pathological is an affirmative defense if by reason of such intoxication the actor at the time of his conduct lacks substantial capacity either to appreciate its criminality [wrongfulness] or to conform his conduct to the requirements of law.

(5)   *Definitions.* In this Section unless a different meaning plainly is required:

(a)   "intoxication" means a disturbance of mental or physical capacities resulting from the introduction of substances into the body;

(b)   "self-induced intoxication" means intoxication caused by substances which the actor knowingly introduces into his body, the tendency of which to cause intoxication he knows or ought to know, unless he introduces them pursuant to medical advice or under such circumstances as would afford a defense to a charge of crime;

(c)   "pathological intoxication" means intoxication grossly excessive in degree, given the amount of the intoxicant, to which the actor does not know he is susceptible.

Section 2.09. Duress.

(1)   It is an affirmative defense that the actor engaged in the conduct charged to constitute an offense because he was coerced to do so by the use of, or a threat to use, unlawful force against his person or the person of another, which a person of reasonable firmness in his situation would have been unable to resist.

(2)   The defense provided by this Section is unavailable if the actor recklessly placed himself in a situation in which it was probable that he would be subjected to duress. The defense is also unavailable if he was negligent in placing himself in such a situation, whenever negligence suffices to establish culpability for the offense charged.

(3)   It is not a defense that a woman acted on the command of her husband, unless she acted under such coercion as would establish a defense under this Section. [The presumption that a woman, acting in the presence of her husband, is coerced is abolished.]

(4)   When the conduct of the actor would otherwise be justifiable under Section 3.02, this Section does not preclude such defense.

Section 2.10. Military Orders.

It is an affirmative defense that the actor, in engaging in the conduct charged to constitute an offense, does no more than execute an order of his superior in the armed services which he does not know to be unlawful.

Section 2.11. Consent.

(1)   *In General.* The consent of the victim to conduct charged to constitute an offense or to the result thereof is a defense if such consent negatives an element of the offense or precludes the infliction of the harm or evil sought to be prevented by the law defining the offense.

(2)   *Consent to Bodily Harm.* When conduct is charged to constitute an offense because it causes or threatens bodily harm, consent to such conduct or to the infliction of such harm is a defense if:

    (a)   the bodily harm consented to or threatened by the conduct consented to is not serious; or

    (b)   The conduct and the harm are reasonably foreseeable hazards of joint participation in a lawful athletic contest or competitive sport; or

    (c)   the consent establishes a justification for the conduct under Article 3 of the Code.

(3)   *Ineffective Consent.* Unless otherwise provided by the Code or by the law defining the offense, assent does not constitute consent if:

    (a)   it is given by a person who is legally incompetent to authorize the conduct charged to constitute the offense; or

    (b)   it is given by a person who by reason of youth, mental disease or defect or intoxication is manifestly unable or known by the actor to be unable to make a reasonable judgment as to the nature or harmfulness of the conduct charged to constitute the offense; or

    (c)   it is given by a person whose improvident consent is sought to be prevented by the law defining the offense; or

    (d)   it is induced by force, duress or deception of a kind sought to be prevented by the law defining the offense.

Section 2.12. De Minimis Infractions.

The Court shall dismiss a prosecution if, having regard to the nature of the conduct charged to constitute an offense and the nature of the attendant circumstances, it finds that the defendant's conduct:

(1)   was within a customary license or tolerance, neither expressly negatived by the person whose interest was infringed or inconsistent with the purpose of the law defining the offense; or

(2)   did not actually cause or threaten the harm or evil sought to be prevented by the law defining the offense or did so only to an extent too trivial to warrant the condemnation of conviction; or

(3)   presents such other extenuations that it cannot reasonably be regarded as envisaged by the legislature in forbidding the offense.

The Court shall not dismiss a prosecution under Subsection (3) of this Section without filing a written statement of its reasons.

Section 2.13. Entrapment.

(1)   A public law enforcement official or a person acting in cooperation with such an official perpetrates an entrapment if for the purpose of obtaining evidence of the commission of an offense, he induces or encourages another person to engage in conduct constituting such offense by either:

> (a)   making knowingly false representations designed to induce the belief that such conduct is not prohibited; or
>
> (b)   employing methods of persuasion or inducement which create a substantial risk that such an offense will be committed by persons other than those who are ready to commit it.

(2)   Except as provided in Subsection (3) of this Section, a person prosecuted for an offense shall be acquitted if he proves by a preponderance of evidence that his conduct occurred in response to an entrapment. The issue of entrapment shall be tried by the Court in the absence of the jury.

(3)   The defense afforded by this Section is unavailable when causing or threatening bodily injury is an element of the offense charged and the prosecution is based on conduct causing or threatening such injury to a person other than the person perpetrating the entrapment.

[ARTICLE 3.]   GENERAL PRINCIPLES OF JUSTIFICATION

Section 3.01. Justification an Affirmative Defense; Civil Remedies Unaffected.

(1)   In any prosecution based on conduct which is justifiable under this Article, justification is an affirmative defense.

(2)   The fact that conduct is justifiable under this Article does not abolish or impair any remedy for such conduct which is available in any civil action.

Section 3.02. Justification Generally: Choice of Evils.

(1)   Conduct which the actor believes to be necessary to avoid a harm or evil to himself or to another is justifiable, provided that:

> (a)   the harm or evil sought to be avoided by such conduct is greater than that sought to be prevented by the law defining the offense charged; and

(b) neither the Code nor other law defining the offense provides exceptions or defenses dealing with the specific situation involved; and

(c) a legislative purpose to exclude the justification claimed does not otherwise plainly appear.

(2) When the actor was reckless or negligent in bringing about the situation requiring a choice of harms or evils or in appraising the necessity for his conduct, the justification afforded by this Section is unavailable in a prosecution for any offense for which recklessness or negligence, as the case may be, suffices to establish culpability.

Section 3.03. Execution of Public Duty.

(1) Except as provided in Subsection (2) of this Section, conduct is justifiable when it is required or authorized by:

(a) the law defining the duties or functions of a public officer or the assistance to be rendered to such officer in the performance of his duties; or

(b) the law governing the execution of legal process; or

(c) the judgment or order of a competent court or tribunal; or

(d) the law governing the armed services or the lawful conduct of war; or

(e) any other provision of law imposing a public duty.

(2) The other sections of this Article apply to:

(a) the use of force upon or toward the person of another for any of the purposes dealt with in such sections; and

(b) the use of deadly force for any purpose, unless the use of such force is otherwise expressly authorized by law or occurs in the lawful conduct of war.

(3) The justification afforded by Subsection (1) of this Section applies:

(a) when the actor believes his conduct to be required or authorized by the judgment or direction of a competent court or tribunal or in the lawful execution of legal process, notwithstanding lack of jurisdiction of the court or defect in the legal process; and

(b) when the actor believes his conduct to be required or authorized to assist a public officer in the performance of his duties, notwithstanding that the officer exceeded his legal authority.

Section 3.04. Use of Force in Self-Protection.

(1) *Use of Force Justifiable for Protection of the Person.* Subject to the provisions of this Section and of Section 3.09, the use of force upon or toward another person is

justifiable when the actor believes that such force is immediately necessary for the purpose of protecting himself against the use of unlawful force by such other person on the present occasion.

(2) *Limitations on Justifying Necessity for Use of Force.*

    (a) The use of force is not justifiable under this Section:

        (i) to resist an arrest which the actor knows is being made by a peace officer, although the arrest is unlawful; or

        (ii) to resist force used by the occupier or possessor of property or by another person on his behalf, where the actor knows that the person using the force is doing so under a claim of right to protect the property, except that this limitation shall not apply if:

            (A) the actor is a public officer acting in the performance of his duties or a person lawfully assisting him therein or a person making or assisting in a lawful arrest; or

            (B) the actor has been unlawfully dispossessed of the property and is making a re-entry or recaption justified by Section 3.06; or

            (C) the actor believes that such force is necessary to protect himself against death or serious bodily harm.

    (b) The use of deadly force is not justifiable under this Section unless the actor believes that such force is necessary to protect himself against death, serious bodily harm, kidnapping or sexual intercourse compelled by force or threat; nor is it justifiable if:

        (i) the actor, with the purpose of causing death or serious bodily harm, provoked the use of force against himself in the same encounter; or

        (ii) the actor knows that he can avoid the necessity of using such force with complete safety by retreating or by surrendering possession of a thing to a person asserting a claim of right thereto or by complying with a demand that he abstain from any action which he has no duty to take, except that:

            (A) the actor is not obliged to retreat from his dwelling or place of work, unless he was the initial aggressor or is assailed in his place of work by another person whose place of work the actor knows it to be; and

            (B) a public officer justified in using force in the performance of his duties or a person justified in using force in his assistance or a person justified in using force in making an arrest or preventing an escape is not obliged to desist from efforts to perform such duty, effect such arrest or prevent such escape because of resistance or threatened resistance by or on behalf of the person against whom such action is directed.

    (C)   Except as required by paragraphs (a) and (b) of this Subsection, a person employing protective force may estimate the necessity thereof under the circumstances as he believes them to be when the force is used, without retreating, surrendering possession, doing any other act which he has no legal duty to do or abstaining from any lawful action.

(3) *Use of Confinement as Protective Force.* The justification afforded by this Section extends to the use of confinement as protective force only if the actor takes all reasonable measures to terminate the confinement as soon as he knows that he safely can, unless the person confined has been arrested on a charge of crime.

Section 3.05. Use of Force for the Protection of Other Persons.

(1)   Subject to the provisions of this Section and of Section 3.09, the use of force upon or toward the person of another is justifiable to protect a third person when:

    (a)   the actor would be justified under Section 3.04 in using such force to protect himself against the injury he believes to be threatened to the person whom he seeks to protect; and

    (b)   under the circumstances as the actor believes them to be, the person whom he seeks to protect would be justified in using such protective force; and

    (c)   the actor believes that his intervention is necessary for the protection of such other person.

(2)   Notwithstanding Subsection (1) of this Section:

    (a)   when the actor would be obliged under Section 3.04 to retreat, to surrender the possession of a thing or to comply with a demand before using force in self-protection, he is not obliged to do so before using force for the protection of another person, unless he knows that he can thereby secure the complete safety of such other person; and

    (b)   when the person whom the actor seeks to protect would be obliged under Section 3.04 to retreat, to surrender the possession of a thing or to comply with a demand if he knew that he could obtain complete safety by so doing, the actor is obliged to try to cause him to do so before using force in his protection if the actor knows that he can obtain complete safety in that way; and

    (c)   neither the actor nor the person whom he seeks to protect is obliged to retreat when in the other's dwelling or place of work to any greater extent than in his own.

Section 3.06. Use of Force for the Protection of Property.

(1)   *Use of Force Justifiable for Protection of Property.* Subject to the provisions of this Section and of Section 3.09, the use of force upon or toward the person of another is justifiable when the actor believes that such force is immediately necessary:

(a)   to prevent or terminate an unlawful entry or other trespass upon land or a trespass against or the unlawful carrying away of tangible, movable property, provided that such land or movable property is, or is believed by the actor to be, in his possession or in the possession of another person for whose protection he acts; or

(b)   to effect an entry or re-entry upon land or to retake tangible movable property, provided that the actor believes that he or the person by whose authority he acts or a person from whom he or such other person derives title was unlawfully dispossessed of such land or movable property and is entitled to possession, and provided, further, that:

(i)   the force is used immediately or on fresh pursuit after such dispossession; or

(ii)   the actor believes that the person against whom he uses force has no claim of right to the possession of the property and, in the case of land, the circumstances, as the actor believes them to be, are of such urgency that it would be an exceptional hardship to postpone the entry or re-entry until a court order is obtained.

(2)   *Meaning of Possession.* For the purposes of Subsection (1) of this Section:

(a)   a person who has parted with the custody of property to another who refuses to restore it to him is no longer in possession, unless the property is movable and was and still is located on land in his possession;

(b)   a person who has been dispossessed of land does not regain possession thereof merely by setting foot thereon;

(c)   a person who has a license to use or occupy real property is deemed to be in possession thereof except against the licensor acting under claim of right.

(3)   *Limitations on Justifiable Use of Force.*

(a)   *Request to Desist.* The use of force is justifiable under this Section only if the actor first requests the person against whom such force is used to desist from his interference with the property, unless the actor believes that:

(i)   such request would be useless; or

    (ii) it would be dangerous to himself or another person to make the request; or

    (iii) substantial harm will be done to the physical condition of the property which is sought to be protected before the request can effectively be made.

(b) *Exclusion of Trespasser.* The use of force to prevent or terminate a trespass is not justifiable under this Section if the actor knows that the exclusion of the trespasser will expose him to substantial danger of serious bodily harm.

(c) *Resistance of Lawful Re-entry or Recaption.* The use of force to prevent an entry or re-entry upon land or the recaption of movable property is not justifiable under this Section, although the actor believes that such re-entry or recaption is unlawful, if:

    (i) the re-entry or recaption is made by or on behalf of a person who was actually dispossessed of the property; and

    (ii) it is otherwise justifiable under paragraph (1)(b) of this Section.

(d) *Use of Deadly Force.* The use of deadly force is not justifiable under this Section unless the actor believes that:

    (i) the person against whom the force is used is attempting to dispossess him of his dwelling otherwise than under a claim of right to its possession; or

    (ii) the person against whom the force is used is attempting to commit or consummate arson, burglary, robbery or other felonious theft or property destruction and either:

        (A) has employed or threatened deadly force against or in the presence of the actor; or

        (B) the use of force other than deadly force to prevent the commission or the consummation of the crime would expose the actor or another in his presence to substantial danger of serious bodily injury.

(4) *Use of Confinement as Protective Force.* The justification afforded by this Section extends to the use of confinement as protective force only if the actor takes all reasonable measures to terminate the confinement as soon as he knows that he can do so with safety to the property, unless the person confined has been arrested on a charge of crime.

(5) *Use of Device to Protect Property.* The justification afforded by this Section extends to the use of a device for the purpose of protecting property only if:

(a) the device is not designed to cause or known to create a substantial risk of causing death or serious bodily harm; and

(b)   the use of the particular device to protect the property from entry or trespass is reasonable under the circumstances, as the actor believes them to be; and

(c)   the device is one customarily used for such a purpose or reasonable care is taken to make known to probable intruders the fact that it is used.

(6)   *Use of Force to Pass Wrongful Obstructor.* The use of force to pass a person whom the actor believes to be purposely or knowingly and unjustifiably obstructing the actor from going to a place to which he may lawfully go is justifiable, provided that:

(a)   the actor believes that the person against whom he uses force has no claim of right to obstruct the actor; and

(b)   the actor is not being obstructed from entry or movement on land which he knows to be in the possession or custody of the person obstructing him, or in the possession or custody of another person by whose authority the obstructor acts, unless the circumstances, as the actor believes them to be, are of such urgency that it would not be reasonable to postpone the entry or movement on such land until a court order is obtained; and

(c)   the force used is not greater than would be justifiable if the person obstructing the actor were using force against him to prevent his passage.

Section 3.07. Use of Force in Law Enforcement.

(1)   *Use of Force Justifiable to Effect an Arrest.* Subject to the provisions of this Section and of Section 3.09, the use of force upon or toward the person of another is justifiable when the actor is making or assisting in making an arrest and the actor believes that such force is immediately necessary to effect a lawful arrest.

(2)   *Limitations on the Use of Force.*

(a)   The use of force is not justifiable under this Section unless:

(i)   the actor makes known the purpose of the arrest or believes that it is otherwise known by or cannot reasonably be made known to the person to be arrested; and

(ii)   when the arrest is made under a warrant, the warrant is valid or believed by the actor to be valid.

(b)   The use of deadly force is not justifiable under this Section unless:

(i)   the arrest is for a felony; and

(ii)   the person effecting the arrest is authorized to act as a peace officer or is assisting a person whom he believes to be authorized to act as a peace officer; and

    (iii) the actor believes that the force employed creates no substantial risk of injury to innocent persons; and

    (iv) the actor believes that:

        (A) the crime for which the arrest is made involved conduct including the use or threatened use of deadly force; or

        (B) there is a substantial risk that the person to be arrested will cause death or serious bodily harm if his apprehension is delayed.

(3)   *Use of Force to Prevent Escape from Custody.* The use of force to prevent the escape of an arrested person from custody is justifiable when the force could justifiably have been employed to effect the arrest under which the person is in custody, except that a guard or other person authorized to act as a peace officer is justified in using any force, including deadly force, which he believes to be immediately necessary to prevent the escape of a person from a jail, prison, or other institution for the detention of persons charged with or convicted of a crime.

(4)   *Use of Force by Private Person Assisting an Unlawful Arrest.*

    (a) A private person who is summoned by a peace officer to assist in effecting an unlawful arrest, is justified in using any force which he would be justified in using if the arrest were lawful, provided that he does not believe the arrest is unlawful.

    (b) A private person who assists another private person in effecting an unlawful arrest, or who, not being summoned, assists a peace officer in effecting an unlawful arrest, is justified in using any force which he would be justified in using if the arrest were lawful, provided that (i) he believes the arrest is lawful, and (ii) the arrest would be lawful if the facts were as he believes them to be.

(5)   *Use of Force to Prevent Suicide or the Commission of a Crime.*

    (a) The use of force upon or toward the person of another is justifiable when the actor believes that such force is immediately necessary to prevent such other person from committing suicide, inflicting serious bodily harm upon himself, committing or consummating the commission of a crime involving or threatening bodily harm, damage to or loss of property or a breach of the peace, except that:

        (i) any limitations imposed by the other provisions of this Article on the justifiable use of force in self-protection, for the protection of others, the protection of property, the effectuation of an arrest or the prevention of an escape from custody shall apply notwithstanding the criminality of the conduct against which such force is used; and

        (ii) the use of deadly force is not in any event justifiable under this Subsection unless:

(A)   the actor believes that there is a substantial risk that the person whom he seeks to prevent from committing a crime will cause death or serious bodily harm to another unless the commission or the consummation of the crime is prevented and that the use of such force presents no substantial risk of injury to innocent persons; or

(B)   the actor believes that the use of such force is necessary to suppress a riot or mutiny after the rioters or mutineers have been ordered to disperse and warned, in any particular manner that the law may require, that such force will be used if they do not obey.

(b)   The justification afforded by this Subsection extends to the use of confinement as preventive force only if the actor takes all reasonable measures to terminate the confinement as soon as he knows that he safely can, unless the person confined has been arrested on a charge of crime.

Section 3.08. Use of Force by Persons with Special Responsibility for Care, Discipline or Safety of Others.

The use of force upon or toward the person of another is justifiable if:

(1)   the actor is the parent or guardian or other person similarly responsible for the general care and supervision of a minor or a person acting at the request of such parent, guardian or other responsible person and:

(a)   the force is used for the purpose of safeguarding or promoting the welfare of the minor, including the prevention or punishment of his misconduct; and

(b)   the force used is not designed to cause or known to create a substantial risk of causing death, serious bodily harm, disfigurement, extreme pain or mental distress or gross degradation; or

(2)   the actor is a teacher or a person otherwise entrusted with the care or supervision for a special purpose of a minor and:

(a)   the actor believes that the force used is necessary to further such special purpose, including the maintenance of reasonable discipline in a school, class or other group, and that the use of such force is consistent with the welfare of the minor; and

(b)   the degree of force, if it had been used by the parent or guardian of the minor, would not be unjustifiable under Subsection (1)(b) of this Section; or

(3)   the actor is the guardian or other person similarly responsible for the general care and supervision of an incompetent person; and:

(a) the force is used for the purpose of safeguarding or promoting the welfare of the incompetent person, including the prevention of his misconduct, or, when such incompetent person is in a hospital or other institution for his care and custody, for the maintenance of reasonable discipline in such institution; and

(b) the force used is not designed to cause or known to create a substantial risk of causing death, serious bodily harm, disfigurement, extreme or unnecessary pain, mental distress, or humiliation; or

(4) the actor is a doctor or other therapist or a person assisting him at his direction, and:

(a) the force is used for the purpose of administering a recognized form of treatment which the actor believes to be adapted to promoting the physical or mental health of the patient; and

(b) the treatment is administered with the consent of the patient or, if the patient is a minor or an incompetent person, with the consent of his parent or guardian or other person legally competent to consent in his behalf, or the treatment is administered in an emergency when the actor believes that no one competent to consent can be consulted and that a reasonable person, wishing to safeguard the welfare of the patient, would consent; or

(5) the actor is a warden or other authorized official of a correctional institution, and:

(a) he believes that the force used is necessary for the purpose of enforcing the lawful rules or procedures of the institution, unless his belief in the lawfulness of the rule or procedure sought to be enforced is erroneous and his error is due to ignorance or mistake as to the provisions of the Code, any other provision of the criminal law or the law governing the administration of the institution; and

(b) the nature or degree of force used is not forbidden by Article 303 or 304 of the Code; and

(c) if deadly force is used, its use is otherwise justifiable under this Article; or

(6) the actor is a person responsible for the safety of a vessel or an aircraft or a person acting at his direction, and

(a) he believes that the force used is necessary to prevent interference with the operation of the vessel or aircraft or obstruction of the execution of a lawful order, unless his belief in the lawfulness of the order is erroneous and his error is due to ignorance or mistake as to the law defining his authority; and

(b) if deadly force is used, its use is otherwise justifiable under this Article; or

(7)   the actor is a person who is authorized or required by law to maintain order or decorum in a vehicle, train or other carrier or in a place where others are assembled, and:

>   (a)   he believes that the force used is necessary for such purpose; and
>
>   (b)   the force used is not designed to cause or known to create a substantial risk of causing death, bodily harm, or extreme mental distress.

Section 3.09. Mistake of Law as to Unlawfulness of Force or Legality of Arrest; Reckless or Negligent Use of Otherwise Justifiable Force; Reckless or Negligent Injury or Risk of Injury to Innocent Persons.

(1)   The justification afforded by Sections 3.04 to 3.07, inclusive, is unavailable when:

>   (a)   the actor's belief in the unlawfulness of the force or conduct against which he employs protective force or his belief in the lawfulness of an arrest which he endeavors to effect by force is erroneous; and
>
>   (b)   his error is due to ignorance or mistake as to the provisions of the Code, any other provision of the criminal law or the law governing the legality of an arrest or search.

(2)   When the actor believes that the use of force upon or toward the person of another is necessary for any of the purposes for which such belief would establish a justification under Sections 3.03 to 3.08 but the actor is reckless or negligent in having such belief or in acquiring or failing to acquire any knowledge or belief which is material to the justifiability of his use of force, the justification afforded by those Sections is unavailable in a prosecution for an offense for which recklessness or negligence, as the case may be, suffices to establish culpability.

(3)   When the actor is justified under Sections 3.03 to 3.08 in using force upon or toward the person of another but he recklessly or negligently injures or creates a risk of injury to innocent persons, the justification afforded by those Sections is unavailable in a prosecution for such recklessness or negligence towards innocent persons.

Section 3.10. Justification in Property Crimes.

Conduct involving the appropriation, seizure or destruction of, damage to, intrusion on or interference with property is justifiable under circumstances which would establish a defense of privilege in a civil action based thereon, unless:

(1)   the Code or the law defining the offense deals with the specific situation involved; or

(2)   a legislative purpose to exclude the justification claimed otherwise plainly appears.

Section 3.11. Definitions.

In this Article, unless a different meaning plainly is required:

(1)   "unlawful force" means force, including confinement, which is employed without the consent of the person against whom it is directed and the employment of which constitutes an offense or actionable tort or would constitute such offense or tort except for a defense (such as the absence of intent, negligence, or mental capacity; duress; youth; or diplomatic status) not amounting to a privilege to use the force. Assent constitutes consent, within the meaning of this Section, whether or not it otherwise is legally effective, except assent to the infliction of death or serious bodily harm;

(2)   "deadly force" means force which the actor uses with the purpose of causing or which he knows to create a substantial risk of causing death or serious bodily harm. Purposely firing a firearm in the direction of another person or at a vehicle in which another person is believed to be constitutes deadly force. A threat to cause death or seriously bodily harm, by the production of a weapon or otherwise, so long as the actor's purpose is limited to creating an apprehension that he will use deadly force if necessary, does not constitute deadly force;

(3)   "dwelling" means any building or structure, though movable or temporary, or a portion thereof, which is for the time being the actor's home or place of lodging.

[ARTICLE 4.]   RESPONSIBILITY

Section 4.01. Mental Disease or Defect Excluding Responsibility.

(1)   A person is not responsible for criminal conduct if at the time of such conduct as a result of mental disease or defect he lacks substantial capacity either to appreciate the criminality [wrongfulness] of his conduct or to conform his conduct to the requirements of law.

(2)   As used in this Article, the terms "mental disease or defect" do not include an abnormality manifested only by repeated criminal or otherwise anti-social conduct.

Section 4.02. Evidence of Mental Disease or Defect Admissible When Relevant to Element of the Offense; [Mental Disease or Defect Impairing Capacity as Ground for Mitigation of Punishment in Capital Cases].

(1)   Evidence that the defendant suffered from a mental disease or defect is admissible whenever it is relevant to prove that the defendant did or did not have a state of mind which is an element of the offense.

(2)   [Whenever the jury or the Court is authorized to determine or to recommend whether or not the defendant shall be sentenced to death or imprisonment upon conviction, evidence that the capacity of the defendant to appreciate the

criminality [wrongfulness] of his conduct or to conform his conduct to the requirements of law was impaired as a result of mental disease or defect is admissible in
favor of sentence of imprisonment.]

Section 4.03. Mental Disease or Defect Excluding Responsibility Is Affirmative Defense; Requirement of Notice; Form of Verdict and Judgment When Finding of Irresponsibility Is Made.

(1)   Mental disease or defect excluding responsibility is an affirmative defense.

(2)   Evidence of mental disease or defect excluding responsibility is not admissible unless the defendant, at the time of entering his plea of not guilty or within ten
days thereafter or at such later time as the Court may for good cause permit, files a
written notice of his purpose to rely on such defense.

(3)   When the defendant is acquitted on the ground of mental disease or defect
excluding responsibility, the verdict and the judgment shall so state.

Section 4.04. Mental Disease or Defect Excluding Fitness to Proceed.

No person who as a result of mental disease or defect lacks capacity to understand
the proceedings against him or to assist in his own defense shall be tried, convicted
or sentenced for the commission of an offense so long as such incapacity endures.

Section 4.05. Psychiatric Examination of Defendant with Respect to Mental Disease or Defect.

(1)   Whenever the defendant has filed a notice of intention to rely on the defense
of mental disease or defect excluding responsibility, or there is reason to doubt his
fitness to proceed, or reason to believe that mental disease or defect of the defendant
will otherwise become an issue in the cause, the Court shall appoint at least one qualified psychiatrist or shall request the Superintendent of the Hospital to designate at
least one qualified psychiatrist, which designation may be or include himself, to
examine and report upon the mental condition of the defendant. The Court may
order the defendant to be committed to a hospital or other suitable facility for the
purpose of the examination for a period of not exceeding sixty days or such longer
period as the Court determines to be necessary for the purpose and may direct
that a qualified psychiatrist retained by the defendant be permitted to witness and
participate in the examination.

(2)   In such examination any method may be employed which is accepted by
the medical profession for the examination of those alleged to be suffering from
mental disease or defect.

(3)   The report of the examination shall include the following: (a) a description
of the nature of the examination; (b) a diagnosis of the mental condition of the
defendant; (c) if the defendant suffers from a mental disease or defect, an opinion as
to his capacity to understand the proceedings against him and to assist in his own
defense; (d) when a notice of intention to rely on the defense of irresponsibility has

been filed, an opinion as to the extent, if any, to which the capacity of the defendant to appreciate the criminality [wrongfulness] of his conduct or to conform his conduct to the requirements of law was impaired at the time of the criminal conduct charged; and (e) when directed by the Court, an opinion as to the capacity of the defendant to have a particular state of mind which is an element of the offense charged.

If the examination cannot be conducted by reason of the unwillingness of the defendant to participate therein, the report shall so state and shall include, if possible, an opinion as to whether such unwillingness of the defendant was the result of mental disease or defect.

The report of the examination shall be filed [in triplicate] with the clerk of the Court, who shall cause copies to be delivered to the district attorney and to counsel for the defendant.

Section 4.06. Determination of Fitness to Proceed; Effect of Finding of Unfitness; Proceeding if Fitness Is Regained [; Post-Commitment Hearing].

(1) When the defendant's fitness to proceed is drawn in question, the issue shall be determined by the Court. If neither the prosecuting attorney nor counsel for the defendant contests the finding of the report filed pursuant to Section 4.05, the Court may make the determination on the basis of such report. If the finding is contested, the Court shall hold a hearing on the issue. If the report is received in evidence upon such hearing, the party who contests the finding thereof shall have the right to summon and to cross-examine the psychiatrists who joined in the report and to offer evidence upon the issue.

(2) If the Court determines that the defendant lacks fitness to proceed, the proceeding against him shall be suspended, except as provided in Subsection (3)[Subsections (3) and (4)] of this Section, and the Court shall commit him to the custody of the Commissioner of Mental Hygiene [Public Health or Correction] to be placed in an appropriate institution of the Department of Mental Hygiene [Public Health or Correction] for so long as such unfitness shall endure. When the Court, on its own motion or upon the application of the Commissioner of Mental Hygiene [Public Health or Correction] or the prosecuting attorney, determines, after a hearing if a hearing is requested, that the defendant has regained fitness to proceed, the proceeding shall be resumed. If, however, the Court is of the view that so much time has elapsed since the commitment of the defendant that it would be unjust to resume the criminal proceeding, the Court may dismiss the charge and may order the defendant to be discharged or, subject to the law governing the civil commitment of persons suffering from mental disease or defect, order the defendant to be committed to an appropriate institution of the Department of Mental Hygiene [Public Health].

(3) The fact that the defendant is unfit to proceed does not preclude any legal objection to the prosecution which is susceptible of fair determination prior to trial and without the personal participation of the defendant.

[Alternative: (3) At any time within ninety days after commitment as provided in Subsection (2) of this Section, or at any later time with permission of the Court granted for good cause, the defendant or his counsel or the Commissioner of Mental Hygiene [Public Health or Correction] may apply for a special post-commitment hearing. If the application is made by or on behalf of a defendant not represented by counsel, he shall be afforded a reasonable opportunity to obtain counsel, and if he lacks funds to do so, counsel shall be assigned by the Court. The application shall be granted only if the counsel for the defendant satisfies the Court by affidavit or otherwise that as an attorney he has reasonable grounds for a good faith belief that his client has, on the facts and the law, a defense to the charge other than mental disease or defect excluding responsibility.

[(4) [If the motion for a special post-commitment hearing is granted, the hearing shall be by the Court without a jury. No evidence shall be offered at the hearing by either party on the issue of mental disease or defect as a defense to, or in mitigation of, the crime charged. After hearing, the Court may in an appropriate case quash the indictment or other charge, or find it to be defective or insufficient, or determine that it is not proved beyond a reasonable doubt by the evidence, or otherwise terminate the proceedings on the evidence or the law. In any such case, unless all defects in the proceedings are promptly cured, the Court shall terminate the commitment ordered under Subsection (2) of this Section and order the defendant to be discharged or, subject to the law governing the civil commitment of persons suffering from mental disease or defect, order the defendant to be committed to an appropriate institution of the Department of Mental Hygiene [Public Health].]

Section 4.07. Determination of Irresponsibility on Basis of Report; Access to Defendant by Psychiatrist of His Own Choice; Form of Expert Testimony When Issue of Responsibility Is Tried.

(1)   If the report filed pursuant to Section 4.05 finds that the defendant at the time of the criminal conduct charged suffered from a mental disease or defect which substantially impaired his capacity to appreciate the criminality [wrongfulness] of his conduct or to conform his conduct to the requirements of law, and the Court, after a hearing if a hearing is requested by the prosecuting attorney or the defendant, is satisfied that such impairment was sufficient to exclude responsibility, the Court on motion of the defendant shall enter judgment of acquittal on the ground of mental disease or defect excluding responsibility.

(2)   When, notwithstanding the report filed pursuant to Section 4.05, the defendant wishes to be examined by a qualified psychiatrist or other expert of his own choice, such examiner shall be permitted to have reasonable access to the defendant for the purposes of such examination.

(3)   Upon the trial, the psychiatrists who reported pursuant to Section 4.05 may be called as witnesses by the prosecution, the defendant or the Court. If the issue is being tried before a jury, the jury may be informed that the psychiatrists were designated by the Court or by the Superintendent of the Hospital at the request of the

Court, as the case may be. If called by the Court, the witness shall be subject to cross-examination by the prosecution and by the defendant. Both the prosecution and the defendant may summon any other qualified psychiatrist or other expert to testify, but no one who has not examined the defendant shall be competent to testify to an expert opinion with respect to the mental condition or responsibility of the defendant, as distinguished from the validity of the procedure followed by, or the general scientific propositions stated by, another witness.

(4)   When a psychiatrist or other expert who has examined the defendant testifies concerning his mental condition, he shall be permitted to make a statement as to the nature of his examination, his diagnosis of the mental condition of the defendant at the time of the commission of the offense charged and his opinion as to the extent, if any, to which the capacity of the defendant to appreciate the criminality [wrongfulness] of his conduct or to conform his conduct to the requirements of law or to have a particular state of mind which is an element of the offense charged was impaired as a result of mental disease or defect at that time. He shall be permitted to make any explanation reasonably serving to clarify his diagnosis and opinion and may be cross-examined as to any matter bearing on his competency or credibility or the validity of his diagnosis or opinion.

Section 4.08. Legal Effect of Acquittal on the Ground of Mental Disease or Defect Excluding Responsibility; Commitment; Release or Discharge.

(1)   When a defendant is acquitted on the ground of mental disease or defect excluding responsibility, the Court shall order him to be committed to the custody of the Commissioner of Mental Hygiene [Public Health] to be placed in an appropriate institution for custody, care and treatment.

(2)   If the Commissioner of Mental Hygiene [Public Health] is of the view that a person committed to his custody, pursuant to paragraph (1) of this Section, may be discharged or released on condition without danger to himself or to others, he shall make application for the discharge or release of such person in a report to the Court by which such person was committed and shall transmit a copy of such application and report to the prosecuting attorney of the county [parish] from which the defendant was committed. The Court shall thereupon appoint at least two qualified psychiatrists to examine such person and to report within sixty days, or such longer period as the Court determines to be necessary for the purpose, their opinion as to his mental condition. To facilitate such examination and the proceedings thereon, the Court may cause such person to be confined in any institution located near the place where the Court sits, which may hereafter be designated by the Commissioner of Mental Hygiene [Public Health] as suitable for the temporary detention of irresponsible persons.

(3)   If the Court is satisfied by the report filed pursuant to paragraph (2) of this Section and such testimony of the reporting psychiatrists as the Court deems necessary that the committed person may be discharged or released on condition without danger to himself or others, the Court shall order his discharge or his release on such

conditions as the Court determines to be necessary. If the Court is not so satisfied, it shall promptly order a hearing to determine whether such person may safely be discharged or released. Any such hearing shall be deemed a civil proceeding and the burden shall be upon the committed person to prove that he may safely be discharged or released. According to the determination of the Court upon the hearing, the committed person shall thereupon be discharged or released on such conditions as the Court determines to be necessary, or shall be recommitted to the custody of the Commissioner of Mental Hygiene [Public Health], subject to discharge or release only in accordance with the procedure prescribed above for a first hearing.

(4)   If, within [five] years after the conditional release of a committed person, the Court shall determine, after hearing evidence, that the conditions of release have not been fulfilled and that for the safety of such person or for the safety of others his conditional release should be revoked, the Court shall forthwith order him to be recommitted to the Commissioner of Mental Hygiene [Public Health], subject to discharge or release only in accordance with the procedure prescribed above for a first hearing.

(5)   A committed person may make application for his discharge or release to the Court by which he was committed, and the procedure to be followed upon such application shall be the same as that prescribed above in the case of an application by the Commissioner of Mental Hygiene [Public Health]. However, no such application by a committed person need be considered until he has been confined for a period of not less than [six months] from the date of the order of commitment, and if the determination of the Court be adverse to the application, such person shall not be permitted to file a further application until [one year] has elapsed from the date of any preceding hearing on an application for his release or discharge.

Section 4.09. Statements for Purposes of Examination or Treatment Inadmissible Except on Issue of Mental Condition.

A statement made by a person subjected to psychiatric examination or treatment pursuant to Sections 4.05, 4.06 or 4.08 for the purposes of such examination or treatment shall not be admissible in evidence against him in any criminal proceeding on any issue other than that of his mental condition but it shall be admissible upon that issue, whether or not it would otherwise be deemed a privileged communication [, unless such statement constitutes an admission of guilt of the crime charged].

Section 4.10. Immaturity Excluding Criminal Conviction; Transfer of Proceedings to Juvenile Court.

(1)   A person shall not be tried for or convicted of an offense if:

(a)   at the time of the conduct charged to constitute the offense he was less than sixteen years of age [, in which case the Juvenile Court shall have exclusive jurisdiction]; or

(b) at the time of the conduct charged to constitute the offense he was sixteen or seventeen years of age, unless:

(i) the Juvenile Court has no jurisdiction over him, or,

(ii) the Juvenile Court has entered an order waiving jurisdiction and consenting to the institution of criminal proceedings against him.

(2) No court shall have jurisdiction to try or convict a person of an offense if criminal proceedings against him are barred by Subsection (1) of this Section. When it appears that a person charged with the commission of an offense may be of such an age that criminal proceedings may be barred under Subsection (1) of this Section, the Court shall hold a hearing thereon, and the burden shall be on the prosecution to establish to the satisfaction of the Court that the criminal proceeding is not barred upon such grounds. If the Court determines that the proceeding is barred, custody of the person charged shall be surrendered to the Juvenile Court, and the case, including all papers and processes relating thereto, shall be transferred.

[ARTICLE 5.]   INCHOATE CRIMES

Section 5.01. Criminal Attempt.

(1) *Definition of Attempt.* A person is guilty of an attempt to commit a crime if, acting with the kind of culpability otherwise required for commission of the crime, he:

(a) purposely engages in conduct which would constitute the crime if the attendant circumstances were as he believes them to be; or

(b) when causing a particular result is an element of the crime, does or omits to do anything with the purpose of causing or with the belief that it will cause such result without further conduct on his part; or

(c) purposely does or omits to do anything which, under the circumstances as he believes them to be, is an act or omission constituting a substantial step in a course of conduct planned to culminate in his commission of the crime.

(2) *Conduct Which May Be Held Substantial Step Under Subsection (1)(c).* Conduct shall not be held to constitute a substantial step under Subsection (1)(c) of this Section unless it is strongly corroborative of the actor's criminal purpose. Without negativing the sufficiency of other conduct, the following, if strongly corroborative of the actor's criminal purpose, shall not be held insufficient as a matter of law:

(a) lying in wait, searching for or following the contemplated victim of the crime;

(b) enticing or seeking to entice the contemplated victim of the crime to go to the place contemplated for its commission;

(c) reconnoitering the place contemplated for the commission of the crime;

(d)   unlawful entry of a structure, vehicle or enclosure in which it is contemplated that the crime will be committed;

(e)   possession of materials to be employed in the commission of the crime, which are specially designed for such unlawful use or which can serve no lawful purpose of the actor under the circumstances;

(f)   possession, collection or fabrication of materials to be employed in the commission of the crime, at or near the place contemplated for its commission, where such possession, collection or fabrication serves no lawful purpose of the actor under the circumstances;

(g)   soliciting an innocent agent to engage in conduct constituting an element of the crime.

(3)   *Conduct Designed to Aid Another in Commission of a Crime.* A person who engages in conduct designed to aid another to commit a crime which would establish his complicity under Section 2.06 if the crime were committed by such other person, is guilty of an attempt to commit the crime, although the crime is not committed or attempted by such other person.

(4)   *Renunciation of Criminal Purpose.* When the actor's conduct would otherwise constitute an attempt under Subsection (1)(b) or (1)(c) of this Section, it is an affirmative defense that he abandoned his effort to commit the crime or otherwise prevented its commission, under circumstances manifesting a complete and voluntary renunciation of his criminal purpose. The establishment of such defense does not, however, affect the liability of an accomplice who did not join in such abandonment or prevention.

Within the meaning of this Article, renunciation of criminal purpose is not voluntary if it is motivated, in whole or in part, by circumstances, not present or apparent at the inception of the actor's course of conduct, which increase the probability of detection or apprehension or which make more difficult the accomplishment of the criminal purpose. Renunciation is not complete if it is motivated by a decision to postpone the criminal conduct until a more advantageous time or to transfer the criminal effort to another but similar objective or victim.

Section 5.02. Criminal Solicitation.

(1)   *Definition of Solicitation.* A person is guilty of solicitation to commit a crime if with the purpose of promoting or facilitating its commission he commands, encourages or requests another person to engage in specific conduct which would constitute such crime or an attempt to commit such crime or which would establish his complicity in its commission or attempted commission.

(2)   *Uncommunicated Solicitation.* It is immaterial under Subsection (1) of this Section that the actor fails to communicate with the person he solicits to commit a crime if his conduct was designed to effect such communication.

(3) *Renunciation of Criminal Purpose.* It is an affirmative defense that the actor, after soliciting another person to commit a crime, persuaded him not to do so or otherwise prevented the commission of the crime, under circumstances manifesting a complete and voluntary renunciation of his criminal purpose.

Section 5.03. Criminal Conspiracy.

(1) *Definition of Conspiracy.* A person is guilty of conspiracy with another person or persons to commit a crime if with the purpose of promoting or facilitating its commission he:

> (a) agrees with such other person or persons that they or one or more of them will engage in conduct which constitutes such crime or an attempt or solicitation to commit such crime; or

> (b) agrees to aid such other person or persons in the planning or commission of such crime or of an attempt or solicitation to commit such crime.

(2) *Scope of Conspiratorial Relationship.* If a person guilty of conspiracy, as defined by Subsection (1) of this Section, knows that a person with whom he conspires to commit a crime has conspired with another person or persons to commit the same crime, he is guilty of conspiring with such other person or persons, whether or not he knows their identity, to commit such crime.

(3) *Conspiracy With Multiple Criminal Objectives.* If a person conspires to commit a number of crimes, he is guilty of only one conspiracy so long as such multiple crimes are the object of the same agreement or continuous conspiratorial relationship.

(4) *Joinder and Venue in Conspiracy Prosecutions.*

> (a) Subject to the provisions of paragraph (b) of this Subsection, two or more persons charged with criminal conspiracy may be prosecuted jointly if:

>> (i) they are charged with conspiring with one another; or

>> (ii) the conspiracies alleged, whether they have the same or different parties, are so related that they constitute different aspects of a scheme of organized criminal conduct.

> (b) In any joint prosecution under paragraph (a) of this Subsection:

>> (i) no defendant shall be charged with a conspiracy in any county [parish or district] other than one in which he entered into such conspiracy or in which an overt act pursuant to such conspiracy was done by him or by a person with whom he conspired; and

>> (ii) neither the liability of any defendant nor the admissibility against him of evidence of acts or declarations of another shall be enlarged by such joinder; and

(iii) the Court shall order a severance or take a special verdict as to any defendant who so requests, if it deems it necessary or appropriate to promote the fair determination of his guilt or innocence, and shall take any other proper measures to protect the fairness of the trial.

(5) *Overt Act.* No person may be convicted of conspiracy to commit a crime, other than a felony of the first or second degree, unless an overt act in pursuance of such conspiracy is alleged and proved to have been done by him or by a person with whom he conspired.

(6) *Renunciation of Criminal Purpose.* It is an affirmative defense that the actor, after conspiring to commit a crime, thwarted the success of the conspiracy, under circumstances manifesting a complete and voluntary renunciation of his criminal purpose.

(7) *Duration of Conspiracy.* For purposes of Section 1.06(4):

(a) conspiracy is a continuing course of conduct which terminates when the crime or crimes which are its object are committed or the agreement that they be committed is abandoned by the defendant and by those with whom he conspired; and

(b) such abandonment is presumed if neither the defendant nor anyone with whom he conspired does any overt act in pursuance of the conspiracy during the applicable period of limitation; and

(c) if an individual abandons the agreement, the conspiracy is terminated as to him only if and when he advises those with whom he conspired of his abandonment or he informs the law enforcement authorities of the existence of the conspiracy and of his participation therein.

Section 5.04. Incapacity, Irresponsibility or Immunity of Party to Solicitation or Conspiracy.

(1) Except as provided in Subsection (2) of this Section, it is immaterial to the liability of a person who solicits or conspires with another to commit a crime that:

(a) he or the person whom he solicits or with whom he conspires does not occupy a particular position or have a particular characteristic which is an element of such crime, if he believes that one of them does; or

(b) the person whom he solicits or with whom he conspires is irresponsible or has an immunity to prosecution or conviction for the commission of the crime.

(2) It is a defense to a charge of solicitation or conspiracy to commit a crime that if the criminal object were achieved, the actor would not be guilty of a crime under the law defining the offense or as an accomplice under Section 2.06(5) or 2.06(6)(a) or (b).

Section 5.05. Grading of Criminal Attempt, Solicitation and Conspiracy; Mitigation in Cases of Lesser Danger; Multiple Convictions Barred.

(1)   *Grading.* Except as otherwise provided in this Section, attempt, solicitation and conspiracy are crimes of the same grade and degree as the most serious offense which is attempted or solicited or is an object of the conspiracy. An attempt, solicitation or conspiracy to commit a [capital crime or a] felony of the first degree is a felony of the second degree.

(2)   *Mitigation.* If the particular conduct charged to constitute a criminal attempt, solicitation or conspiracy is so inherently unlikely to result or culminate in the commission of a crime that neither such conduct nor the actor presents a public danger warranting the grading of such offense under this Section, the Court shall exercise its power under Section 6.12 to enter judgment and impose sentence for a crime of lower grade or degree or, in extreme cases, may dismiss the prosecution.

(3)   *Multiple Convictions.* A person may not be convicted of more than one offense defined by this Article for conduct designed to commit or to culminate in the commission of the same crime.

Section 5.06. Possessing Instruments of Crime; Weapons.

(1)   *Criminal Instruments Generally.* A person commits a misdemeanor if he possesses any instrument of crime with purpose to employ it criminally. "Instrument of crime" means:

>   (a)   anything specially made or specially adapted for criminal use; or

>   (b)   anything commonly used for criminal purposes and possessed by the actor under circumstances which do not negative unlawful purpose.

(2)   *Presumption of Criminal Purpose from Possession of Weapon.* If a person possesses a firearm or other weapon on or about his person, in a vehicle occupied by him, or otherwise readily available for use, it shall be presumed that he had the purpose to employ it criminally, unless:

>   (a)   the weapon is possessed in the actor's home or place of business;

>   (b)   the actor is licensed or otherwise authorized by law to possess such weapon; or

>   (c)   the weapon is of a type commonly used in lawful sport. "Weapon" means anything readily capable of lethal use and possessed under circumstances not manifestly appropriate for lawful uses which it may have; the term includes a firearm which is not loaded or lacks a clip or other component to render it immediately operable, and components which can readily be assembled into a weapon.

(3)   *Presumptions as to Possession of Criminal Instruments in Automobiles.* Where a weapon or other instrument of crime is found in an automobile, it shall

be presumed to be in the possession of the occupant if there is but one. If there is more than one occupant, it is presumed to be in the possession of all, except under the following circumstances:

(a) where it is found upon the person of one of the occupants;

(b) where the automobile is not a stolen one and the weapon or instrument is found out of view in a glove compartment, car trunk, or other enclosed customary depository, in which case it shall be presumed to be in the possession of the occupant or occupants who own or have authority to operate the automobile;

(c) in the case of a taxicab, a weapon or instrument found in the passengers' portion of the vehicle shall be presumed to be in the possession of all the passengers, if there are any, and, if not, in the possession of the driver.

Section 5.07. Prohibited Offensive Weapons.

A person commits a misdemeanor if, except as authorized by law, he makes, repairs, sells, or otherwise deals in, uses, or possesses any offensive weapon. "Offensive weapon" means any bomb, machine gun, sawed-off shotgun, firearm specially made or specially adapted for concealment or silent discharge, any blackjack, sandbag, metal knuckles, dagger, or other implement for the infliction of serious bodily injury which serves no common lawful purpose. It is a defense under this Section for the defendant to prove by a preponderance of evidence that he possessed or dealt with the weapon solely as a curio or in a dramatic performance, or that he possessed it briefly in consequence of having found it or taken it from an aggressor, or under circumstances similarly negativing any purpose or likelihood that the weapon would be used unlawfully. The presumptions provided in Section 5.06(3) are applicable to prosecutions under this Section.

[ARTICLE 6.]   AUTHORIZED DISPOSITION OF OFFENDERS

Section 6.01. Degrees of Felonies.

(1) Felonies defined by this Code are classified, for the purpose of sentence, into three degrees, as follows:

(a) felonies of the first degree;

(b) felonies of the second degree;

(c) felonies of the third degree.

A felony is of the first or second degree when it is so designated by the Code. A crime declared to be a felony, without specification of degree, is of the third degree.

(2) Notwithstanding any other provision of law, a felony defined by any statute of this State other than this Code shall constitute for the purpose of sentence a felony of the third degree.

Section 6.02. Sentence in Accordance with Code; Authorized Dispositions.

(1)   No person convicted of an offense shall be sentenced otherwise than in accordance with this Article.

(2)   [The Court shall sentence a person who has been convicted of murder to death or imprisonment, in accordance with Section 210.6.]

(3)   Except as provided in Subsection (2) of this Section and subject to the applicable provisions of the Code, the Court may suspend the imposition of sentence on a person who has been convicted of a crime, may order him to be committed in lieu of sentence, in accordance with Section 6.13, or may sentence him as follows:

> (a)   to pay a fine authorized by Section 6.03; or
>
> (b)   to be placed on probation [, and, in the case of a person convicted of a felony or misdemeanor to imprisonment for a term fixed by the Court not exceeding thirty days to be served as a condition of probation]; or
>
> (c)   to imprisonment for a term authorized by Sections 6.05, 6.06, 6.07, 6.08, 6.09, or 7.06; or
>
> (d)   to fine and probation or fine and imprisonment, but not to probation and imprisonment [, except as authorized in paragraph (b) of this Subsection].

(4)   The Court may suspend the imposition of sentence on a person who has been convicted of a violation or may sentence him to pay a fine authorized by Section 6.03.

(5)   This Article does not deprive the Court of any authority conferred by law to decree a forfeiture of property, suspend or cancel a license, remove a person from office, or impose any other civil penalty. Such a judgment or order may be included in the sentence.

Section 6.03. Fines.

A person who has been convicted of an offense may be sentenced to pay a fine not exceeding:

(1) $10,000, when the conviction is of a felony of the first or second degree;

(2) $5,000, when the conviction is of a felony of the third degree;

(3) $1,000, when the conviction is of a misdemeanor;

(4) $500, when the conviction is of a petty misdemeanor or a violation;

(5)   any higher amount equal to double the pecuniary gain derived from the offense by the offender;

(6)   any higher amount specifically authorized by statute.

Section 6.04. Penalties Against Corporations and Unincorporated Associations; Forfeiture of Corporate Charter or Revocation of Certificate Authorizing Foreign Corporation to Do Business in the State.

(1)   The Court may suspend the sentence of a corporation or an unincorporated association which has been convicted of an offense or may sentence it to pay a fine authorized by Section 6.03.

(2)   (a)   The [prosecuting attorney] is authorized to institute civil proceedings in the appropriate court of general jurisdiction to forfeit the charter of a corporation organized under the laws of this State or to revoke the certificate authorizing a foreign corporation to conduct business in this State. The Court may order the charter forfeited or the certificate revoked upon finding

(i)   that the board of directors or a high managerial agent acting in behalf of the corporation has, in conducting the corporation's affairs, purposely engaged in a persistent course of criminal conduct and

(ii)   that for the prevention of future criminal conduct of the same character, the public interest requires the charter of the corporation to be forfeited and the corporation to be dissolved or the certificate to be revoked.

(b)   When a corporation is convicted of a crime or a high managerial agent of a corporation, as defined in Section 2.07, is convicted of a crime committed in the conduct of the affairs of the corporation, the Court, in sentencing the corporation or the agent, may direct the [prosecuting attorney] to institute proceedings authorized by paragraph (a) of this Subsection.

(c)   The proceedings authorized by paragraph (a) of this Subsection shall be conducted in accordance with the procedures authorized by law for the involuntary dissolution of a corporation or the revocation of the certificate authorizing a foreign corporation to conduct business in this State. Such proceedings shall be deemed additional to any other proceedings authorized by law for the purpose of forfeiting the charter of a corporation or revoking the certificate of a foreign corporation.

Section 6.05. Young Adult Offenders.

(1)   *Specialized Correctional Treatment.* A young adult offender is a person convicted of a crime who, at the time of sentencing, is sixteen but less than twenty-two years of age. A young adult offender who is sentenced to a term of imprisonment which may exceed thirty days [alternatives: (1) ninety days; (2) one year] shall be committed to the custody of the Division of Young Adult Correction of the Department of

Correction, and shall receive, as far as practicable, such special and individualized correctional and rehabilitative treatment as may be appropriate to his needs.

(2) *Special Term.* A young adult offender convicted of a felony may, in lieu of any other sentence of imprisonment authorized by this Article, be sentenced to a special term of imprisonment without a minimum and with a maximum of four years, regardless of the degree of the felony involved, if the Court is of the opinion that such special term is adequate for his correction and rehabilitation and will not jeopardize the protection of the public.

(3) *[Removal of Disabilities; Vacation of Conviction.*

    (a) In sentencing a young adult offender to the special term provided by this Section or to any sentence other than one of imprisonment, the Court may order that so long as he is not convicted of another felony, the judgment shall not constitute a conviction for the purposes of any disqualification or disability imposed by law upon conviction of a crime.

    (b) When any young adult offender is unconditionally discharged from probation or parole before the expiration of the maximum term thereof, the Court may enter an order vacating the judgment of conviction.]

(4) *[Commitment for Observation.* If, after pre-sentence investigation, the Court desires additional information concerning a young adult offender before imposing sentence, it may order that he be committed, for a period not exceeding ninety days, to the custody of the Division of Young Adult Correction of the Department of Correction for observation and study at an appropriate reception or classification center. Such Division of the Department of Correction and the [Young Adult Division of the] Board of Parole shall advise the Court of their findings and recommendations on or before the expiration of such ninety-day period.]

Section 6.06. Sentence of Imprisonment for Felony; Ordinary Terms.

A person who has been convicted of a felony may be sentenced to imprisonment, as follows:

(1) in the case of a felony of the first degree, for a term the minimum of which shall be fixed by the Court at not less than one year nor more than ten years, and the maximum of which shall be life imprisonment;

(2) in the case of a felony of the second degree, for a term the minimum of which shall be fixed by the Court at not less than one year nor more than three years, and the maximum of which shall be ten years;

(3) in the case of a felony of the third degree, for a term the minimum of which shall be fixed by the Court at not less than one year nor more than two years, and the maximum of which shall be five years.

Alternate Section 6.06. Sentence of Imprisonment for Felony; Ordinary Terms.

A person who has been convicted of a felony may be sentenced to imprisonment, as follows:

(1)   in the case of a felony of the first degree, for a term the minimum of which shall be fixed by the Court at not less than one year nor more than ten years, and the maximum at not more than twenty years or at life imprisonment;

(2)   in the case of a felony of the second degree, for a term the minimum of which shall be fixed by the Court at not less than one year nor more than three years, and the maximum at not more than ten years;

(3)   in the case of a felony of the third degree, for a term the minimum of which shall be fixed by the Court at not less than one year nor more than two years, and the maximum at not more than five years.

No sentence shall be imposed under this Section of which the minimum is longer than one-half the maximum, or, when the maximum is life imprisonment, longer than ten years.

Section 6.07. Sentence of Imprisonment for Felony; Extended Terms.

In the cases designated in Section 7.03, a person who has been convicted of a felony may be sentenced to an extended term of imprisonment, as follows:

(1)   in the case of a felony of the first degree, for a term the minimum of which shall be fixed by the Court at not less than five years nor more than ten years, and the maximum of which shall be life imprisonment;

(2)   in the case of a felony of the second degree, for a term the minimum of which shall be fixed by the Court at not less than one year nor more than five years, and the maximum of which shall be fixed by the Court at not less than ten nor more than twenty years;

(3)   in the case of a felony of the third degree, for a term the minimum of which shall be fixed by the Court at not less than one year nor more than three years, and the maximum of which shall be fixed by the Court at not less than five nor more than ten years.

Section 6.08. Sentence of Imprisonment for Misdemeanors and Petty Misdemeanors; Ordinary Terms.

A person who has been convicted of a misdemeanor or a petty misdemeanor may be sentenced to imprisonment for a definite term which shall be fixed by the Court and shall not exceed one year in the case of a misdemeanor or thirty days in the case of a petty misdemeanor.

Section 6.09. Sentence of Imprisonment for Misdemeanors and Petty Misdemeanors; Extended Terms.

(1)   In the cases designated in Section 7.04, a person who has been convicted of a misdemeanor or a petty misdemeanor may be sentenced to an extended term of imprisonment, as follows:

>   (a)   in the case of a misdemeanor, for a term the minimum of which shall be fixed by the Court at not more than one year and the maximum of which shall be three years;

>   (b)   in the case of a petty misdemeanor, for a term the minimum of which shall be fixed by the Court at not more than six months and the maximum of which shall be two years.

(2)   No such sentence for an extended term shall be imposed unless:

>   (a)   the Director of Correction has certified that there is an institution in the Department of Correction, or in a county, city [or other appropriate political subdivision of the State] which is appropriate for the detention and correctional treatment of such misdemeanants or petty misdemeanants, and that such institution is available to receive such commitments; and

>   (b)   the [Board of Parole] [Parole Administrator] has certified that the Board of Parole is able to visit such institution and to assume responsibility for the release of such prisoners on parole and for their parole supervision.

Section 6.10. First Release of All Offenders on Parole; Sentence of Imprisonment Includes Separate Parole Term; Length of Parole Term; Length of Recommitment and Reparole After Revocation of Parole; Final Unconditional Release.

(1)   *First Release of All Offenders on Parole.* An offender sentenced to an indefinite term of imprisonment in excess of one year under Section 6.05, 6.06, 6.07, 6.09 or 7.06 shall be released conditionally on parole at or before the expiration of the maximum of such term, in accordance with Article 305.

(2)   *Sentence of Imprisonment Includes Separate Parole Term; Length of Parole Term.* A sentence to an indefinite term of imprisonment in excess of one year under Section 6.05, 6.06, 6.07, 6.09 or 7.06 includes as a separate portion of the sentence a term of parole or of recommitment for violation of the conditions of parole which governs the duration of parole or recommitment after the offender's first conditional release on parole. The minimum of such term is one year and the maximum is five years, unless the sentence was imposed under Section 6.05(2) or Section 6.09, in which case the maximum is two years.

(3)   *Length of Recommitment and Reparole After Revocation of Parole.* If an offender is recommitted upon revocation of his parole, the term of further

imprisonment upon such recommitment and of any subsequent reparole or recommitment under the same sentence shall be fixed by the Board of Parole but shall not exceed in aggregate length the unserved balance of the maximum parole term provided by Subsection (2) of this Section.

(4)   *Final Unconditional Release.* When the maximum of his parole term has expired or he has been sooner discharged from parole under Section 305.12, an offender shall be deemed to have served his sentence and shall be released unconditionally.

Section 6.11. Place of Imprisonment.

(1)   When a person is sentenced to imprisonment for an indefinite term with a maximum in excess of one year, the Court shall commit him to the custody of the Department of Correction [or other single department or agency] for the term of his sentence and until released in accordance with law.

(2)   When a person is sentenced to imprisonment for a definite term, the Court shall designate the institution or agency to which he is committed for the term of his sentence and until released in accordance with law.

Section 6.12. Reduction of Conviction by Court to Lesser Degree of Felony or to Misdemeanor.

If, when a person has been convicted of a felony, the Court, having regard to the nature and circumstances of the crime and to the history and character of the defendant, is of the view that it would be unduly harsh to sentence the offender in accordance with the Code, the Court may enter judgment of conviction for a lesser degree of felony or for a misdemeanor and impose sentence accordingly.

Section 6.13. Civil Commitment in Lieu of Prosecution or of Sentence.

(1)   When a person prosecuted for a [felony of the third degree,] misdemeanor or petty misdemeanor is a chronic alcoholic, narcotic addict [or prostitute] or person suffering from mental abnormality and the Court is authorized by law to order the civil commitment of such person to a hospital or other institution for medical, psychiatric or other rehabilitative treatment, the Court may order such commitment and dismiss the prosecution. The order of commitment may be made after conviction, in which event the Court may set aside the verdict or judgment of conviction and dismiss the prosecution.

(2)   The Court shall not make an order under Subsection (1) of this Section unless it is of the view that it will substantially further the rehabilitation of the defendant and will not jeopardize the protection of the public.

[ARTICLE 7.]   AUTHORITY OF COURT IN SENTENCING

Section 7.01. Criteria for Withholding Sentence of Imprisonment and for Placing Defendant on Probation.

(1)   The Court shall deal with a person who has been convicted of a crime without imposing sentence of imprisonment unless, having regard to the nature and circumstances of the crime and the history, character and condition of the defendant, it is of the opinion that his imprisonment is necessary for protection of the public because:

(a)   there is undue risk that during the period of a suspended sentence or probation the defendant will commit another crime; or

(b)   the defendant is in need of correctional treatment that can be provided most effectively by his commitment to an institution; or

(c)   a lesser sentence will depreciate the seriousness of the defendant's crime.

(2)   The following grounds, while not controlling the discretion of the Court, shall be accorded weight in favor of withholding sentence of imprisonment:

(a)   the defendant's criminal conduct neither caused nor threatened serious harm;

(b)   the defendant did not contemplate that his criminal conduct would cause or threaten serious harm;

(c)   the defendant acted under a strong provocation;

(d)   there were substantial grounds tending to excuse or justify the defendant's criminal conduct, though failing to establish a defense;

(e)   the victim of the defendant's criminal conduct induced or facilitated its commission;

(f)   the defendant has compensated or will compensate the victim of his criminal conduct for the damage or injury that he sustained;

(g)   the defendant has no history of prior delinquency or criminal activity or has led a law-abiding life for a substantial period of time before the commission of the present crime;

(h)   the defendant's criminal conduct was the result of circumstances unlikely to recur;

(i)   the character and attitudes of the defendant indicate that he is unlikely to commit another crime;

(j)   the defendant is particularly likely to respond affirmatively to probationary treatment;

(k)   the imprisonment of the defendant would entail excessive hardship to himself or his dependents.

(3)   When a person who has been convicted of a crime is not sentenced to imprisonment, the Court shall place him on probation if he is in need of the super-vision, guidance, assistance or direction that the probation service can provide.

Section 7.02. Criteria for Imposing Fines.

(1)   The Court shall not sentence a defendant only to pay a fine, when any other disposition is authorized by law, unless having regard to the nature and circum-stances of the crime and to the history and character of the defendant, it is of the opinion that the fine alone suffices for protection of the public.

(2)   The Court shall not sentence a defendant to pay a fine in addition to a sen-tence of imprisonment or probation unless:

(a)   the defendant has derived a pecuniary gain from the crime; or

(b)   the Court is of opinion that a fine is specially adapted to deterrence of the crime involved or to the correction of the offender.

(3)   The Court shall not sentence a defendant to pay a fine unless:

(a)   the defendant is or will be able to pay the fine; and

(b)   the fine will not prevent the defendant from making restitution or reparation to the victim of the crime.

(4)   In determining the amount and method of payment of a fine, the Court shall take into account the financial resources of the defendant and the nature of the burden that its payment will impose.

Section 7.03. Criteria for Sentence of Extended Term of Imprisonment; Felonies.

The Court may sentence a person who has been convicted of a felony to an extended term of imprisonment if it finds one or more of the grounds specified in this Section. The finding of the Court shall be incorporated in the record.

(1)   The defendant is a persistent offender whose commitment for an extended term is necessary for protection of the public.

The Court shall not make such a finding unless the defendant is over twenty-one years of age and has previously been convicted of two felonies or of one felony and two misdemeanors, committed at different times when he was over [insert Juvenile Court age] years of age.

(2)   The defendant is a professional criminal whose commitment for an extended term is necessary for protection of the public.

The Court shall not make such a finding unless the defendant is over twenty-one years of age and:

(a)   the circumstances of the crime show that the defendant has know-ingly devoted himself to criminal activity as a major source of liveli-hood; or

    (b)   the defendant has substantial income or resources not explained to be derived from a source other than criminal activity.

(3)   The defendant is a dangerous, mentally abnormal person whose commitment for an extended term is necessary for protection of the public.

The Court shall not make such a finding unless the defendant has been subjected to a psychiatric examination resulting in the conclusions that his mental condition is gravely abnormal; that his criminal conduct has been characterized by a pattern of repetitive or compulsive behavior or by persistent aggressive behavior with heedless indifference to consequences; and that such condition makes him a serious danger to others.

(4)   The defendant is a multiple offender whose criminality was so extensive that a sentence of imprisonment for an extended term is warranted.

The Court shall not make such a finding unless:

    (a)   the defendant is being sentenced for two or more felonies, or is already under sentence of imprisonment for felony, and the sentences of imprisonment involved will run concurrently under Section 7.06; or

    (b)   the defendant admits in open court the commission of one or more other felonies and asks that they be taken into account when he is sentenced; and

    (c)   the longest sentences of imprisonment authorized for each of the defendant's crimes, including admitted crimes taken into account, if made to run consecutively would exceed in length the minimum and maximum of the extended term imposed.

Section 7.04. Criteria for Sentence of Extended Term of Imprisonment; Misdemeanors and Petty Misdemeanors.

The Court may sentence a person who has been convicted of a misdemeanor or petty misdemeanor to an extended term of imprisonment if it finds one or more of the grounds specified in this Section. The finding of the Court shall be incorporated in the record.

(1)   The defendant is a persistent offender whose commitment for an extended term is necessary for protection of the public.

The Court shall not make such a finding unless the defendant has previously been convicted of two crimes, committed at different times when he was over [insert Juvenile Court age] years of age.

(2)   The defendant is a professional criminal whose commitment for an extended term is necessary for protection of the public.

The Court shall not make such a finding unless:

(a)   the circumstances of the crime show that the defendant has knowingly devoted himself to criminal activity as a major source of livelihood; or

(b)   the defendant has substantial income or resources not explained to be derived from a source other than criminal activity.

(3)   The defendant is a chronic alcoholic, narcotic addict, prostitute or person of abnormal mental condition who requires rehabilitative treatment for a substantial period of time.

The Court shall not make such a finding unless, with respect to the particular category to which the defendant belongs, the Director of Correction has certified that there is a specialized institution or facility which is satisfactory for the rehabilitative treatment of such persons and which otherwise meets the requirements of Section 6.09, Subsection (2).

(4)   The defendant is a multiple offender whose criminality was so extensive that a sentence of imprisonment for an extended term is warranted.

The Court shall not make such a finding unless:

(a)   the defendant is being sentenced for a number of misdemeanors or petty misdemeanors or is already under sentence of imprisonment for crimes of such grades, or admits in open court the commission of one or more such crimes and asks that they be taken into account when he is sentenced; and

(b)   maximum fixed sentences of imprisonment for each of the defendant's crimes, including admitted crimes taken into account, if made to run consecutively, would exceed in length the maximum period of the extended term imposed.

Section 7.05. Former Conviction in Another Jurisdiction; Definition and Proof of Conviction; Sentence Taking into Account Admitted Crimes Bars Subsequent Conviction for Such Crimes.

(1)   For purposes of paragraph (1) of Section 7.03 or 7.04, a conviction of the commission of a crime in another jurisdiction shall constitute a previous conviction. Such conviction shall be deemed to have been of a felony if sentence of death or of imprisonment in excess of one year was authorized under the law of such other jurisdiction, of a misdemeanor if sentence of imprisonment in excess of thirty days but not in excess of a year was authorized and of a petty misdemeanor if sentence of imprisonment for not more than thirty days was authorized.

(2)   An adjudication by a court of competent jurisdiction that the defendant committed a crime constitutes a conviction for purposes of Sections 7.03 to 7.05 inclusive, although sentence or the execution thereof was suspended, provided that the time to appeal has expired and that the defendant was not pardoned on the ground of innocence.

(3)   Prior conviction may be proved by any evidence, including fingerprint records made in connection with arrest, conviction or imprisonment, that reasonably satisfies the Court that the defendant was convicted.

(4)   When the defendant has asked that other crimes admitted in open court be taken into account when he is sentenced and the Court has not rejected such request, the sentence shall bar the prosecution or conviction of the defendant in this State for any such admitted crime.

Section 7.06. Multiple Sentences; Concurrent and Consecutive Terms.

(1)   *Sentences of Imprisonment for More Than One Crime.* When multiple sentences of imprisonment are imposed on a defendant for more than one crime, including a crime for which a previous suspended sentence or sentence of probation has been revoked, such multiple sentences shall run concurrently or consecutively as the Court determines at the time of sentence, except that:

  (a)   a definite and an indefinite term shall run concurrently and both sentences shall be satisfied by service of the indefinite term; and

  (b)   the aggregate of consecutive definite terms shall not exceed one year; and

  (c)   the aggregate of consecutive indefinite terms shall not exceed in minimum or maximum length the longest extended term authorized for the highest grade and degree of crime for which any of the sentences was imposed; and

  (d)   not more than one sentence for an extended term shall be imposed.

(2)   *Sentences of Imprisonment Imposed at Different Times.* When a defendant who has previously been sentenced to imprisonment is subsequently sentenced to another term for a crime committed prior to the former sentence, other than a crime committed while in custody:

  (a)   the multiple sentences imposed shall so far as possible conform to Subsection (1) of this Section; and

  (b)   whether the Court determines that the terms shall run concurrently or consecutively, the defendant shall be credited with time served in imprisonment on the prior sentence in determining the permissible aggregate length of the term or terms remaining to be served; and

  (c)   when a new sentence is imposed on a prisoner who is on parole, the balance of the parole term on the former sentence shall be deemed to run during the period of the new imprisonment.

(3)   *Sentence of Imprisonment for Crime Committed While on Parole.* When a defendant is sentenced to imprisonment for a crime committed while on parole in this State, such term of imprisonment and any period of reimprisonment that the

Board of Parole may require the defendant to serve upon the revocation of his parole shall run concurrently, unless the Court orders them to run consecutively.

(4)   *Multiple Sentences of Imprisonment in Other Cases.* Except as otherwise provided in this Section, multiple terms of imprisonment shall run concurrently or consecutively as the Court determines when the second or subsequent sentence is imposed.

(5)   *Calculation of Concurrent and Consecutive Terms of Imprisonment.*

(a)   When indefinite terms run concurrently, the shorter minimum terms merge in and are satisfied by serving the longest minimum term and the shorter maximum terms merge in and are satisfied by discharge of the longest maximum term.

(b)   When indefinite terms run consecutively, the minimum terms are added to arrive at an aggregate minimum to be served equal to the sum of all minimum terms and the maximum terms are added to arrive at an aggregate maximum equal to the sum of all maximum terms.

(c)   When a definite and an indefinite term run consecutively, the period of the definite term is added to both the minimum and maximum of the indefinite term and both sentences are satisfied by serving the indefinite term.

(6)   *Suspension of Sentence or Probation and Imprisonment; Multiple Terms of Suspension and Probation.* When a defendant is sentenced for more than one offense or a defendant already under sentence is sentenced for another offense committed prior to the former sentence:

(a)   the Court shall not sentence to probation a defendant who is under sentence of imprisonment [with more than thirty days to run] or impose a sentence of probation and a sentence of imprisonment [, except as authorized by Section 6.02(3)(b)]; and

(b)   multiple periods of suspension or probation shall run concurrently from the date of the first such disposition; and

(c)   when a sentence of imprisonment is imposed for an indefinite term, the service of such sentence shall satisfy a suspended sentence on another count or a prior suspended sentence or sentence to probation; and

(d)   when a sentence of imprisonment is imposed for a definite term, the period of a suspended sentence on another count or a prior suspended sentence or sentence to probation shall run during the period of such imprisonment.

(7)   *Offense Committed While Under Suspension of Sentence or Probation.* When a defendant is convicted of an offense committed while under suspension of sentence or on probation and such suspension or probation is not revoked:

(a) if the defendant is sentenced to imprisonment for an indefinite term, the service of such sentence shall satisfy the prior suspended sentence or sentence to probation; and

(b) if the defendant is sentenced to imprisonment for a definite term, the period of the suspension or probation shall not run during the period of such imprisonment; and

(c) if sentence is suspended or the defendant is sentenced to probation, the period of such suspension or probation shall run concurrently with or consecutively to the remainder of the prior periods, as the Court determines at the time of sentence.

Section 7.07. Procedure on Sentence; Pre-sentence Investigation and Report; Remand for Psychiatric Examination; Transmission of Records to Department of Correction.

(1) The Court shall not impose sentence without first ordering a pre-sentence investigation of the defendant and according due consideration to a written report of such investigation where:

(a) the defendant has been convicted of a felony; or

(b) the defendant is less than twenty-two years of age and has been convicted of a crime; or

(c) the defendant will be [placed on probation or] sentenced to imprisonment for an extended term.

(2) The Court may order a pre-sentence investigation in any other case.

(3) The pre-sentence investigation shall include an analysis of the circumstances attending the commission of the crime, the defendant's history of delinquency or criminality, physical and mental condition, family situation and background, economic status, education, occupation and personal habits and any other matters that the probation officer deems relevant or the Court directs to be included.

(4) Before imposing sentence, the Court may order the defendant to submit to psychiatric observation and examination for a period of not exceeding sixty days or such longer period as the Court determines to be necessary for the purpose. The defendant may be remanded for this purpose to any available clinic or mental hospital or the Court may appoint a qualified psychiatrist to make the examination. The report of the examination shall be submitted to the Court.

(5) Before imposing sentence, the Court shall advise the defendant or his counsel of the factual contents and the conclusions of any pre-sentence investigation or psychiatric examination and afford fair opportunity, if the defendant so requests, to controvert them. The sources of confidential information need not, however, be disclosed.

(6) The Court shall not impose a sentence of imprisonment for an extended term unless the ground therefor has been established at a hearing after the

conviction of the defendant and on written notice to him of the ground proposed. Subject to the limitation of Subsection (5) of this Section, the defendant shall have the right to hear and controvert the evidence against him and to offer evidence upon the issue.

(7)   If the defendant is sentenced to imprisonment, a copy of the report of any pre-sentence investigation or psychiatric examination shall be transmitted forthwith to the Department of Correction [or other state department or agency] or, when the defendant is committed to the custody of a specific institution, to such institution.

Section 7.08. Commitment for Observation; Sentence of Imprisonment for Felony Deemed Tentative for Period of One Year; Re-sentence on Petition of Commissioner of Correction.

(1)   If, after pre-sentence investigation, the Court desires additional information concerning an offender convicted of a felony or misdemeanor before imposing sentence, it may order that he be committed, for a period not exceeding ninety days, to the custody of the Department of Correction, or, in the case of a young adult offender, to the custody of the Division of Young Adult Correction, for observation and study at an appropriate reception or classification center. The Department and the Board of Parole, or the Young Adult Divisions thereof, shall advise the Court of their findings and recommendations on or before the expiration of such ninety-day period. If the offender is thereafter sentenced to imprisonment, the period of such commitment for observation shall be deducted from the maximum term and from the minimum, if any, of such sentence.

(2)   When a person has been sentenced to imprisonment upon conviction of a felony, whether for an ordinary or extended term, the sentence shall be deemed tentative, to the extent provided in this Section, for the period of one year following the date when the offender is received in custody by the Department of Correction [or other state department or agency].

(3)   If, as a result of the examination and classification by the Department of Correction [or other state department or agency] of a person under sentence of imprisonment upon conviction of a felony, the Commissioner of Correction [or other department head] is satisfied that the sentence of the Court may have been based upon a misapprehension as to the history, character or physical or mental condition of the offender, the Commissioner, during the period when the offender's sentence is deemed tentative under Subsection (2) of this Section shall file in the sentencing Court a petition to re-sentence the offender. The petition shall set forth the information as to the offender that is deemed to warrant his re-sentence and may include a recommendation as to the sentence to be imposed.

(4)   The Court may dismiss a petition filed under Subsection (3) of this Section without a hearing if it deems the information set forth insufficient to warrant reconsideration of the sentence. If the Court is of the view that the petition warrants such

reconsideration, a copy of the petition shall be served on the offender, who shall have the right to be heard on the issue and to be represented by counsel.

(5)   When the Court grants a petition filed under Subsection (3) of this Section, it shall re-sentence the offender and may impose any sentence that might have been imposed originally for the felony of which the defendant was convicted. The period of his imprisonment prior to re-sentence and any reduction for good behavior to which he is entitled shall be applied in satisfaction of the final sentence.

(6)   For all purposes other than this Section, a sentence of imprisonment has the same finality when it is imposed that it would have if this Section were not in force.

(7)   Nothing in this Section shall alter the remedies provided by law for vacating or correcting an illegal sentence.

Section 7.09. Credit for Time of Detention Prior to Sentence; Credit for Imprisonment Under Earlier Sentence for the Same Crime.

(1)   When a defendant who is sentenced to imprisonment has previously been detained in any state or local correctional or other institution following his [conviction of] [arrest for] the crime for which such sentence is imposed, such period of detention following his [conviction] [arrest] shall be deducted from the maximum term, and from the minimum, if any, of such sentence. The officer having custody of the defendant shall furnish a certificate to the Court at the time of sentence, showing the length of such detention of the defendant prior to sentence in any state or local correctional or other institution, and the certificate shall be annexed to the official records of the defendant's commitment.

(2)   When a judgment of conviction is vacated and a new sentence is thereafter imposed upon the defendant for the same crime, the period of detention and imprisonment theretofore served shall be deducted from the maximum term, and from the minimum, if any, of the new sentence. The officer having custody of the defendant shall furnish a certificate to the Court at the time of sentence, showing the period of imprisonment served under the original sentence, and the certificate shall be annexed to the official records of the defendant's new commitment.

[PART II.]   DEFINITION OF SPECIFIC CRIMES
OFFENSES AGAINST EXISTENCE OR STABILITY OF THE STATE

[This category of offenses, including treason, sedition, espionage and like crimes, was excluded from the scope of the Model Penal Code. These offenses are peculiarly the concern of the federal government. The Constitution itself defines treason: "Treason against the United States shall consist only in levying War against them, or in adhering to their Enemies, giving them Aid and Comfort . . . ." Article III, Section 3; cf. Pennsylvania v. Nelson, 350 U.S. 497 (supersession of state sedition legislation by federal law). Also, the definition of offenses against the stability of the state is inevitably affected by special political considerations. These factors militated against the use of the Institute's limited resources to attempt to draft "model" provisions in this area. However we provide at this point in the Plan of the Model Penal Code for an Article 200, where definitions of offenses against the existence or stability of the state may be incorporated.]

OFFENSES INVOLVING DANGER TO THE PERSON

[ARTICLE 210.]   CRIMINAL HOMICIDE

Section 210.0. Definitions.

In Articles 210–213, unless a different meaning plainly is required:

(1)   "human being" means a person who has been born and is alive;

(2)   "bodily injury" means physical pain, illness or any impairment of physical condition;

(3)   "serious bodily injury" means bodily injury which creates a substantial risk of death or which causes serious, permanent disfigurement, or protracted loss or impairment of the function of any bodily member or organ;

(4)   "deadly weapon" means any firearm, or other weapon, device, instrument, material or substance, whether animate or inanimate, which in the manner it is used or is intended to be used is known to be capable of producing death or serious bodily injury.

Section 210.1. Criminal Homicide.

(1)   A person is guilty of criminal homicide if he purposely, knowingly, recklessly or negligently causes the death of another human being.

(2)   Criminal homicide is murder, manslaughter or negligent homicide.

Section 210.2. Murder.

(1)   Except as provided in Section 210.3(1)(b), criminal homicide constitutes murder when:

(a)   it is committed purposely or knowingly; or

(b)   it is committed recklessly under circumstances manifesting extreme indifference to the value of human life. Such recklessness and indifference are presumed if the actor is engaged or is an accomplice in the commission of, or an attempt to commit, or flight after committing or attempting to commit robbery, rape or deviate sexual intercourse by force or threat of force, arson, burglary, kidnapping or felonious escape.

(2)   Murder is a felony of the first degree [but a person convicted of murder may be sentenced to death, as provided in Section 210.6].

Section 210.3. Manslaughter.

(1)   Criminal homicide constitutes manslaughter when:

    (a)   it is committed recklessly; or

    (b)   a homicide which would otherwise be murder is committed under the influence of extreme mental or emotional disturbance for which there is reasonable explanation or excuse. The reasonableness of such explanation or excuse shall be determined from the viewpoint of a person in the actor's situation under the circumstances as he believes them to be.

(2)   Manslaughter is a felony of the second degree.

Section 210.4. Negligent Homicide.

(1)   Criminal homicide constitutes negligent homicide when it is committed negligently.

(2)   Negligent homicide is a felony of the third degree.

Section 210.5. Causing or Aiding Suicide.

(1)   *Causing Suicide as Criminal Homicide.* A person may be convicted of criminal homicide for causing another to commit suicide only if he purposely causes such suicide by force, duress or deception.

(2)   *Aiding or Soliciting Suicide as an Independent Offense.* A person who purposely aids or solicits another to commit suicide is guilty of a felony of the second degree if his conduct causes such suicide or an attempted suicide, and otherwise of a misdemeanor.

[Section 210.6. Sentence of Death for Murder; Further Proceedings to Determine Sentence.[2]

(1)   *Death Sentence Excluded.* When a defendant is found guilty of murder, the Court shall impose sentence for a felony of the first degree if it is satisfied that:

    (a)   none of the aggravating circumstances enumerated in Subsection (3) of this Section was established by the evidence at the trial or will be established if further proceedings are initiated under Subsection (2) of this Section; or

    (b)   substantial mitigating circumstances, established by the evidence at the trial, call for leniency; or

---

2. The brackets signified that the American Law Institute did not take a position on the abolition or retention of capital punishment. In 2009, the American Law Institute voted to withdraw § 210.6 of the Model Penal Code.

(c)   the defendant, with the consent of the prosecuting attorney and the approval of the Court, pleaded guilty to murder as a felony of the first degree; or

(d)   the defendant was under 18 years of age at the time of the commission of the crime; or

(e)   the defendant's physical or mental condition calls for leniency; or

(f)   although the evidence suffices to sustain the verdict, it does not foreclose all doubt respecting the defendant's guilt.

(2)   *Determination by Court or by Court and Jury.* Unless the Court imposes sentence under Subsection (1) of this Section, it shall conduct a separate proceeding to determine whether the defendant should be sentenced for a felony of the first degree or sentenced to death. The proceeding shall be conducted before the Court alone if the defendant was convicted by a Court sitting without a jury or upon his plea of guilty or if the prosecuting attorney and the defendant waive a jury with respect to sentence. In other cases it shall be conducted before the Court sitting with the jury which determined the defendant's guilt or, if the Court for good cause shown discharges that jury, with a new jury empaneled for the purpose.

In the proceeding, evidence may be presented as to any matter that the Court deems relevant to sentence, including but not limited to the nature and circumstances of the crime, the defendant's character, background, history, mental and physical condition and any of the aggravating or mitigating circumstances enumerated in Subsections (3) and (4) of this Section. Any such evidence, not legally privileged, which the Court deems to have probative force, may be received, regardless of its admissibility under the exclusionary rules of evidence, provided that the defendant's counsel is accorded a fair opportunity to rebut such evidence. The prosecuting attorney and the defendant or his counsel shall be permitted to present argument for or against sentence of death.

The determination whether sentence of death shall be imposed shall be in the discretion of the Court, except that when the proceeding is conducted before the Court sitting with a jury, the Court shall not impose sentence of death unless it submits to the jury the issue whether the defendant should be sentenced to death or to imprisonment and the jury returns a verdict that the sentence should be death. If the jury is unable to reach a unanimous verdict, the Court shall dismiss the jury and impose sentence for a felony of the first degree.

The Court, in exercising its discretion as to sentence, and the jury, in determining upon its verdict, shall take into account the aggravating and mitigating circumstances enumerated in Subsections (3) and (4) and any other facts that it deems relevant, but it shall not impose or recommend sentence of death unless it finds one of the aggravating circumstances enumerated in Subsection (3) and further finds that there are no mitigating circumstances sufficiently substantial to call for leniency. When the issue is submitted to the jury, the Court shall so instruct and also shall inform the jury of the nature of the sentence of imprisonment that may be imposed, including its implication with respect to possible release upon parole, if the jury verdict is against sentence of death.

Alternative formulation of Subsection (2):

(2)   *Determination by Court.* Unless the Court imposes sentence under Subsection (1) of this Section, it shall conduct a separate proceeding to determine whether the defendant should be sentenced for a felony of the first degree or sentenced to death. In the proceeding, the Court, in accordance with Section 7.07, shall consider the report of the pre-sentence investigation and, if a psychiatric examination has been ordered, the report of such examination. In addition, evidence may be presented as to any matter that the Court deems relevant to sentence, including but not limited to the nature and circumstances of the crime, the defendant's character, background, history, mental and physical condition and any of the aggravating or mitigating circumstances enumerated in Subsections (3) and (4) of this Section. Any such evidence, not legally privileged which the Court deems to have probative force, may be received, regardless of its admissibility under the exclusionary rules of evidence, provided that the defendant's counsel is accorded a fair opportunity to rebut such evidence. The prosecuting attorney and the defendant or his counsel shall be permitted to present argument for or against sentence of death.

The determination whether sentence of death shall be imposed shall be in the discretion of the Court. In exercising such discretion, the Court shall take into account the aggravating and mitigating circumstances enumerated in Subsections (3) and (4) and any other facts that it deems relevant but shall not impose sentence of death unless it finds one of the aggravating circumstances enumerated in Subsection (3) and further finds that there are no mitigating circumstances sufficiently substantial to call for leniency.

(3)   *Aggravating Circumstances.*

(a)   The murder was committed by a convict under sentence of imprisonment.

(b)   The defendant was previously convicted of another murder or of a felony involving the use or threat of violence to the person.

(c)   At the time the murder was committed the defendant also committed another murder.

(d)   The defendant knowingly created a great risk of death to many persons.

(e)   The murder was committed while the defendant was engaged or was an accomplice in the commission of, or an attempt to commit, or flight after committing or attempting to commit robbery, rape or deviate sexual intercourse by force or threat of force, arson, burglary or kidnapping.

(f)   The murder was committed for the purpose of avoiding or preventing a lawful arrest or effecting an escape from lawful custody.

(g)   The murder was committed for pecuniary gain.

(h)   The murder was especially heinous, atrocious or cruel, manifesting exceptional depravity.

(4)   *Mitigating Circumstances.*

(a)   The defendant has no significant history of prior criminal activity.

(b)   The murder was committed while the defendant was under the influence of extreme mental or emotional disturbance.

(c)   The victim was a participant in the defendant's homicidal conduct or consented to the homicidal act.

(d)   The murder was committed under circumstances which the defendant believed to provide a moral justification or extenuation for his conduct.

(e)   The defendant was an accomplice in a murder committed by another person and his participation in the homicidal act was relatively minor.

(f)   The defendant acted under duress or under the domination of another person.

(g)   At the time of the murder, the capacity of the defendant to appreciate the criminality [wrongfulness] of his conduct or to conform his conduct to the requirements of law was impaired as a result of a mental disease or defect or intoxication.

(h)   The youth of the defendant at the time of the crime.]

[ARTICLE 211.]   ASSAULT; RECKLESS ENDANGERING; THREATS

Section 211.0. Definitions.

In this Article, the definitions given in Section 210.0 apply unless a different meaning plainly is required.

Section 211.1. Assault.

(1)   *Simple Assault.* A person is guilty of assault if he:

(a)   attempts to cause or purposely, knowingly, or recklessly causes bodily injury to another; or

(b)   negligently causes bodily injury to another with a deadly weapon; or

(c)   attempts by physical menace to put another in fear of imminent serious bodily injury.

Simple assault is a misdemeanor unless committed in a fight or scuffle entered into by mutual consent, in which case it is a petty misdemeanor.

(2)   *Aggravated Assault.* A person is guilty of aggravated assault if he:

   (a)   attempts to cause serious bodily injury to another, or causes such injury purposely, knowingly or recklessly under circumstances manifesting extreme indifference to the value of human life; or

   (b)   attempts to cause or purposely or knowingly causes bodily injury to another with a deadly weapon.

Aggravated assault under paragraph (a) is a felony of the second degree; aggravated assault under paragraph (b) is a felony of the third degree.

Section 211.2. Recklessly Endangering Another Person.

A person commits a misdemeanor if he recklessly engages in conduct which places or may place another person in danger of death or serious bodily injury. Recklessness and danger shall be presumed where a person knowingly points a firearm at or in the direction of another, whether or not the actor believed the firearm to be loaded.

Section 211.3. Terroristic Threats.

A person is guilty of a felony of the third degree if he threatens to commit any crime of violence with purpose to terrorize another or to cause evacuation of a building, place of assembly, or facility of public transportation, or otherwise to cause serious public inconvenience, or in reckless disregard of the risk of causing such terror or inconvenience.

[ARTICLE 212.]   KIDNAPPING AND RELATED OFFENSES; COERCION

Section 212.0. Definitions.

In this Article, the definitions given in Section 210.0 apply unless a different meaning plainly is required.

Section 212.1. Kidnapping.

A person is guilty of kidnapping if he unlawfully removes another from his place of residence or business, or a substantial distance from the vicinity where he is found, or if he unlawfully confines another for a substantial period in a place of isolation, with any of the following purposes:

   (a) to hold for ransom or reward, or as a shield or hostage; or

   (b) to facilitate commission of any felony or flight thereafter; or

   (c) to inflict bodily injury on or to terrorize the victim or another; or

   (d) to interfere with the performance of any governmental or political function.

Kidnapping is a felony of the first degree unless the actor voluntarily releases the victim alive and in a safe place prior to trial, in which case it is a felony of the second degree. A removal or confinement is unlawful within the meaning of this Section if it is accomplished by force, threat or deception, or, in the case of a person who is under the age of 14 or incompetent, if it is accomplished without the consent of a parent, guardian or other person responsible for general supervision of his welfare.

Section 212.2. Felonious Restraint.

A person commits a felony of the third degree if he knowingly:

(a) restrains another unlawfully in circumstances exposing him to risk of serious bodily injury; or

(b) holds another in a condition of involuntary servitude.

Section 212.3. False Imprisonment.

A person commits a misdemeanor if he knowingly restrains another unlawfully so as to interfere substantially with his liberty.

Section 212.4. Interference with Custody.

(1) *Custody of Children.* A person commits an offense if he knowingly or recklessly takes or entices any child under the age of 18 from the custody of its parent, guardian or other lawful custodian, when he has no privilege to do so. It is an affirmative defense that:

> (a) the actor believed that his action was necessary to preserve the child from danger to its welfare; or
>
> (b) the child, being at the time not less than 14 years old, was taken away at its own instigation without enticement and without purpose to commit a criminal offense with or against the child.

Proof that the child was below the critical age gives rise to a presumption that the actor knew the child's age or acted in reckless disregard thereof. The offense is a misdemeanor unless the actor, not being a parent or person in equivalent relation to the child, acted with knowledge that his conduct would cause serious alarm for the child's safety, or in reckless disregard of a likelihood of causing such alarm, in which case the offense is a felony of the third degree.

(2) *Custody of Committed Persons.* A person is guilty of a misdemeanor if he knowingly or recklessly takes or entices any committed person away from lawful custody when he is not privileged to do so. "Committed person" means, in addition to anyone committed under judicial warrant, any orphan, neglected or delinquent child, mentally defective or insane person, or other dependent or incompetent person entrusted to another's custody by or through a recognized social agency or otherwise by authority of law.

Section 212.5. Criminal Coercion.

(1) *Offense Defined.* A person is guilty of criminal coercion if, with purpose unlawfully to restrict another's freedom of action to his detriment, he threatens to:

(a)   commit any criminal offense; or

(b)   accuse anyone of a criminal offense; or

(c)   expose any secret tending to subject any person to hatred, contempt or ridicule, or to impair his credit or business repute; or

(d)   take or withhold action as an official, or cause an official to take or withhold action.

It is an affirmative defense to prosecution based on paragraphs (b), (c) or (d) that the actor believed the accusation or secret to be true or the proposed official action justified and that his purpose was limited to compelling the other to behave in a way reasonably related to the circumstances which were the subject of the accusation, exposure or proposed official action, as by desisting from further misbehavior, making good a wrong done, refraining from taking any action or responsibility for which the actor believes the other disqualified.

(2)   *Grading.* Criminal coercion is a misdemeanor unless the threat is to commit a felony or the actor's purpose is felonious, in which cases the offense is a felony of the third degree.

[ARTICLE 213.]   SEXUAL OFFENSES

Section 213.0. Definitions.

In this Article, unless a different meaning plainly is required:

(1)   the definitions given in Section 210.0 apply;

(2)   "Sexual intercourse" includes intercourse per os or per anum, with some penetration however slight; emission is not required;

(3)   "Deviate sexual intercourse" means sexual intercourse per os or per anum between human beings who are not husband and wife, and any form of sexual intercourse with an animal.

Section 213.1. Rape and Related Offenses.

(1)   *Rape.* A male who has sexual intercourse with a female not his wife is guilty of rape if:

(a)   he compels her to submit by force or by threat of imminent death, serious bodily injury, extreme pain or kidnapping, to be inflicted on anyone; or

(b)   he has substantially impaired her power to appraise or control her conduct by administering or employing without her knowledge drugs, intoxicants or other means for the purpose of preventing resistance; or

(c)   the female is unconscious; or

(d)   the female is less than 10 years old.

Rape is a felony of the second degree unless (i) in the course thereof the actor inflicts serious bodily injury upon anyone, or (ii) the victim was not a voluntary social companion of the actor upon the occasion of the crime and had not previously permitted him sexual liberties, in which cases the offense is a felony of the first degree.

(2) *Gross Sexual Imposition.* A male who has sexual intercourse with a female not his wife commits a felony of the third degree if:

> (a) he compels her to submit by any threat that would prevent resistance by a woman of ordinary resolution; or
>
> (b) he knows that she suffers from a mental disease or defect which renders her incapable of appraising the nature of her conduct; or
>
> (c) he knows that she is unaware that a sexual act is being committed upon her or that she submits because she mistakenly supposes that he is her husband.

Section 213.2. Deviate Sexual Intercourse by Force or Imposition.

(1) *By Force or Its Equivalent.* A person who engages in deviate sexual intercourse with another person, or who causes another to engage in deviate sexual intercourse, commits a felony of the second degree if:

> (a) he compels the other person to participate by force or by threat of imminent death, serious bodily injury, extreme pain or kidnapping, to be inflicted on anyone; or
>
> (b) he has substantially impaired the other person's power to appraise or control his conduct, by administering or employing without the knowledge of the other person drugs, intoxicants or other means for the purpose of preventing resistance; or
>
> (c) the other person is unconscious; or
>
> (d) the other person is less than 10 years old.

(2) *By Other Imposition.* A person who engages in deviate sexual intercourse with another person, or who causes another to engage in deviate sexual intercourse, commits a felony of the third degree if:

> (a) he compels the other person to participate by any threat that would prevent resistance by a person of ordinary resolution; or
>
> (b) he knows that the other person suffers from a mental disease or defect which renders him incapable of appraising the nature of his conduct; or
>
> (c) he knows that the other person submits because he is unaware that a sexual act is being committed upon him.

Section 213.3. Corruption of Minors and Seduction.

(1) *Offense Defined.* A male who has sexual intercourse with a female not his wife, or any person who engages in deviate sexual intercourse or causes another to engage in deviate sexual intercourse, is guilty of an offense if:

(a) the other person is less than [16] years old and the actor is at least [4] years older than the other person; or

(b) the other person is less than 21 years old and the actor is his guardian or otherwise responsible for general supervision of his welfare; or

(c) the other person is in custody of law or detained in a hospital or other institution and the actor has supervisory or disciplinary authority over him; or

(d) the other person is a female who is induced to participate by a promise of marriage which the actor does not mean to perform.

(2) *Grading.* An offense under paragraph (a) of Subsection (1) is a felony of the third degree. Otherwise an offense under this section is a misdemeanor.

Section 213.4. Sexual Assault.

A person who has sexual contact with another not his spouse, or causes such other to have sexual conduct with him, is guilty of sexual assault, a misdemeanor, if:

(1) he knows that the contact is offensive to the other person; or

(2) he knows that the other person suffers from a mental disease or defect which renders him or her incapable of appraising the nature of his or her conduct; or

(3) he knows that the other person is unaware that a sexual act is being committed; or

(4) the other person is less than 10 years old; or

(5) he has substantially impaired the other person's power to appraise or control his or her conduct, by administering or employing without the other's knowledge drugs, intoxicants or other means for the purpose of preventing resistance; or

(6) the other person is less than [16] years old and the actor is at least [four] years older than the other person; or

(7) the other person is less than 21 years old and the actor is his guardian or otherwise responsible for general supervision of his welfare; or

(8) the other person is in custody of law or detained in a hospital or other institution and the actor has supervisory or disciplinary authority over him.

Sexual contact is any touching of the sexual or other intimate parts of the person for the purpose of arousing or gratifying sexual desire.

Section 213.5. Indecent Exposure.

A person commits a misdemeanor if, for the purpose of arousing or gratifying sexual desire of himself or of any person other than his spouse, he exposes his genitals under circumstances in which he knows his conduct is likely to cause affront or alarm.

Section 213.6. Provisions Generally Applicable to Article 213.

(1) *Mistake as to Age.* Whenever in this Article the criminality of conduct depends on a child's being below the age of 10, it is no defense that the actor did not know the child's age, or reasonably believed the child to be older than 10. When criminality depends on the child's being below a critical age other than 10, it is a defense for the actor to prove by a preponderance of the evidence that he reasonably believed the child to be above the critical age.

(2) *Spouse Relationships.* Whenever in this Article the definition of an offense excludes conduct with a spouse, the exclusion shall be deemed to extend to persons living as man and wife, regardless of the legal status of their relationship. The exclusion shall be inoperative as respects spouses living apart under a decree of judicial separation. Where the definition of an offense excludes conduct with a spouse or conduct by a woman, this shall not preclude conviction of a spouse or woman as accomplice in a sexual act which he or she causes another person, not within the exclusion, to perform.

(3) *Sexually Promiscuous Complainants.* It is a defense to prosecution under Section 213.3 and paragraphs (6), (7) and (8) of Section 213.4 for the actor to prove by a preponderance of the evidence that the alleged victim had, prior to the time of the offense charged, engaged promiscuously in sexual relations with others.

(4) *Prompt Complaint.* No prosecution may be instituted or maintained under this Article unless the alleged offense was brought to the notice of public authority within [3] months of its occurrence or, where the alleged victim was less than [16] years old or otherwise incompetent to make complaint, within [3] months after a parent, guardian or other competent person specially interested in the victim learns of the offense.

(5) *Testimony of Complainants.* No person shall be convicted of any felony under this Article upon the uncorroborated testimony of the alleged victim. Corroboration may be circumstantial. In any prosecution before a jury for an offense under this Article, the jury shall be instructed to evaluate the testimony of a victim or complaining witness with special care in view of the emotional involvement of the witness and the difficulty of determining the truth with respect to alleged sexual activities carried out in private.

OFFENSES AGAINST PROPERTY

[ARTICLE 220.]   ARSON, CRIMINAL MISCHIEF, AND OTHER PROPERTY
DESTRUCTION

Section 220.1. Arson and Related Offenses.

(1)   *Arson.* A person is guilty of arson, a felony of the second degree, if he starts a fire or causes an explosion with the purpose of:

    (a)   destroying a building or occupied structure of another; or

    (b)   destroying or damaging any property, whether his own or another's, to collect insurance for such loss. It shall be an affirmative defense to prosecution under this paragraph that the actor's conduct did not recklessly endanger any building or occupied structure of another or place any other person in danger of death or bodily injury.

(2)   *Reckless Burning or Exploding.* A person commits a felony of the third degree if he purposely starts a fire or causes an explosion, whether on his own property or another's and thereby recklessly:

    (a)   places another person in danger of death or bodily injury; or

    (b)   places a building or occupied structure of another in danger of damage or destruction.

(3)   *Failure to Control or Report Dangerous Fire.* A person who knows that a fire is endangering life or a substantial amount of property of another and fails to take reasonable measures to put out or control the fire, when he can do so without substantial risk to himself, or to give a prompt fire alarm, commits a misdemeanor if:

    (a)   he knows that he is under an official, contractual, or other legal duty to prevent or combat the fire; or

    (b)   the fire was started, albeit lawfully, by him or with his assent, or on property in his custody or control.

(4)   *Definitions.* "Occupied structure" means any structure, vehicle or place adapted for overnight accommodation of persons, or for carrying on business therein, whether or not a person is actually present. Property is that of another, for the purposes of this section, if anyone other than the actor has a possessory or proprietary interest therein. If a building or structure is divided into separately occupied units, any unit not occupied by the actor is an occupied structure of another.

Section 220.2. Causing or Risking Catastrophe.

(1)   *Causing Catastrophe.* A person who causes a catastrophe by explosion, fire, flood, avalanche, collapse of building, release of poison gas, radioactive material or other harmful or destructive force or substance, or by any other means of causing potentially widespread injury or damage, commits a felony of the second degree if he does so purposely or knowingly, or a felony of the third degree if he does so recklessly.

(2) *Risking Catastrophe.* A person is guilty of a misdemeanor if he recklessly creates a risk of catastrophe in the employment of fire, explosives or other dangerous means listed in Subsection (1).

(3) *Failure to Prevent Catastrophe.* A person who knowingly or recklessly fails to take reasonable measures to prevent or mitigate a catastrophe commits a misdemeanor if:

(a) he knows that he is under an official, contractual or other legal duty to take such measures; or

(b) he did or assented to the act causing or threatening the catastrophe.

Section 220.3. Criminal Mischief.

(1) *Offense Defined.* A person is guilty of criminal mischief if he:

(a) damages tangible property of another purposely, recklessly, or by negligence in the employment of fire, explosives, or other dangerous means listed in Section 220.2(1); or

(b) purposely or recklessly tampers with tangible property of another so as to endanger person or property; or

(c) purposely or recklessly causes another to suffer pecuniary loss by deception or threat.

(2) *Grading.* Criminal mischief is a felony of the third degree if the actor purposely causes pecuniary loss in excess of $5,000, or a substantial interruption or impairment of public communication, transportation, supply of water, gas or power, or other public service. It is a misdemeanor if the actor purposely causes pecuniary loss in excess of $100, or a petty misdemeanor if he purposely or recklessly causes pecuniary loss in excess of $25. Otherwise criminal mischief is a violation.

[ARTICLE 221.]   BURGLARY AND OTHER CRIMINAL INTRUSION

Section 221.0. Definitions.

In this Article, unless a different meaning plainly is required:

(1) "occupied structure" means any structure, vehicle or place adapted for overnight accommodation of persons, or for carrying on business therein, whether or not a person is actually present.

(2) "night" means the period between thirty minutes past sunset and thirty minutes before sunrise.

Section 221.1. Burglary.

(1) *Burglary Defined.* A person is guilty of burglary if he enters a building or occupied structure, or separately secured or occupied portion thereof, with purpose to commit a crime therein, unless the premises are at the time open to the public or

the actor is licensed or privileged to enter. It is an affirmative defense to prosecution for burglary that the building or structure was abandoned.

(2)   *Grading.* Burglary is a felony of the second degree if it is perpetrated in the dwelling of another at night, or if, in the course of committing the offense, the actor:

(a)   purposely, knowingly or recklessly inflicts or attempts to inflict bodily injury on anyone; or

(b)   is armed with explosives or a deadly weapon.

Otherwise, burglary is a felony of the third degree. An act shall be deemed "in the course of committing" an offense if it occurs in an attempt to commit the offense or in flight after the attempt or commission.

(3)   *Multiple Convictions.* A person may not be convicted both for burglary and for the offense which it was his purpose to commit after the burglarious entry or for an attempt to commit that offense, unless the additional offense constitutes a felony of the first or second degree.

Section 221.2. Criminal Trespass.

(1)   *Buildings and Occupied Structures.* A person commits an offense if, knowing that he is not licensed or privileged to do so, he enters or surreptitiously remains in any building or occupied structure, or separately secured or occupied portion thereof. An offense under this Subsection is a misdemeanor if it is committed in a dwelling at night. Otherwise it is a petty misdemeanor.

(2)   *Defiant Trespasser.* A person commits an offense if, knowing that he is not licensed or privileged to do so, he enters or remains in any place as to which notice against trespass is given by:

(a)   actual communication to the actor; or

(b)   posting in a manner prescribed by law or reasonably likely to come to the attention of intruders; or

(c)   fencing or other enclosure manifestly designed to exclude intruders.

An offense under this Subsection constitutes a petty misdemeanor if the offender defies an order to leave personally communicated to him by the owner of the premises or other authorized person. Otherwise it is a violation.

(3)   *Defenses.* It is an affirmative defense to prosecution under this Section that:

(a)   a building or occupied structure involved in an offense under Subsection (1) was abandoned; or

(b)   the premises were at the time open to members of the public and the actor complied with all lawful conditions imposed on access to or remaining in the premises; or

(c)   the actor reasonably believed that the owner of the premises, or other person empowered to license access thereto, would have licensed him to enter or remain.

[ARTICLE 222.]   ROBBERY

Section 222.1. Robbery.

(1)   *Robbery Defined.* A person is guilty of robbery if, in the course of committing a theft, he:

(a)   inflicts serious bodily injury upon another; or

(b)   threatens another with or purposely puts him in fear of immediate serious bodily injury; or

(c)   commits or threatens immediately to commit any felony of the first or second degree.

An act shall be deemed "in the course of committing a theft" if it occurs in an attempt to commit theft or in flight after the attempt or commission.

(2)   *Grading.* Robbery is a felony of the second degree, except that it is a felony of the first degree if in the course of committing the theft the actor attempts to kill anyone, or purposely inflicts or attempts to inflict serious bodily injury.

[ARTICLE 223.]   THEFT AND RELATED OFFENSES

Section 223.0. Definitions.

In this Article, unless a different meaning plainly is required:

(1)   "deprive" means: (a) to withhold property of another permanently or for so extended a period as to appropriate a major portion of its economic value, or with intent to restore only upon payment of reward or other compensation; or (b) to dispose of the property so as to make it unlikely that the owner will recover it.

(2)   "financial institution" means a bank, insurance company, credit union, building ad loan association, investment trust or other organization held out to the public as a place of deposit of funds or medium of savings or collective investment.

(3)   "government" means the United States, any State, county, municipality, or other political unit, or any department, agency or subdivision of any of the foregoing, or any corporation or other association carrying out the functions of government.

(4)   "movable property" means property the location of which can be changed, including things growing on, affixed to, or found in land, and documents although the rights represented thereby have no physical location. "Immovable property" is all other property.

(5)   "obtain" means: (a) in relation to property, to bring about a transfer or purported transfer of a legal interest in the property, whether to the obtainer or another; or (b) in relation to labor or service, to secure performance thereof.

(6)   "property" means anything of value, including real estate, tangible and intangible personal property, contract rights, choses-in-action and other interests in or claims to wealth, admission or transportation tickets, captured or domestic animals, food and drink, electric or other power.

(7)   "property of another" includes property in which any person other than the actor has an interest which the actor is not privileged to infringe, regardless of the fact that the actor also has an interest in the property and regardless of the fact that the other person might be precluded from civil recovery because the property was used in an unlawful transaction or was subject to forfeiture as contraband. Property in possession of the actor shall not be deemed property of another who has only a security interest therein, even if legal title is in the creditor pursuant to a conditional sales contract or other security agreement.

Section 223.1. Consolidation of Theft Offenses; Grading; Provisions Applicable to Theft Generally.

(1)   *Consolidation of Theft Offenses.* Conduct denominated theft in this Article constitutes a single offense. An accusation of theft may be supported by evidence that it was committed in any manner that would be theft under this Article, notwithstanding the specification of a different manner in the indictment or information, subject only to the power of the Court to ensure fair trial by granting a continuance or other appropriate relief where the conduct of the defense would be prejudiced by lack of fair notice or by surprise.

(2)   *Grading of Theft Offenses.*

    (a)   Theft constitutes a felony of the third degree if the amount involved exceeds $500, or if the property stolen is a firearm, automobile, airplane, motorcycle, motorboat, or other motor-propelled vehicle, or in the case of theft by receiving stolen property, if the receiver is in the business of buying or selling stolen property.

    (b)   Theft not within the preceding paragraph constitutes a misdemeanor, except that if the property was not taken from the person or by threat, or in breach of a fiduciary obligation, and the actor proves by a preponderance of the evidence that the amount involved was less than $50, the offense constitutes a petty misdemeanor.

    (c)   The amount involved in a theft shall be deemed to be the highest value, by any reasonable standard, of the property or services which the actor stole or attempted to steal. Amounts involved in thefts committed pursuant to one scheme or course of conduct, whether from the same person or several persons, may be aggregated in determining the grade of the offense.

(3) *Claim of Right.* It is an affirmative defense to prosecution for theft that the actor:

    (a) was unaware that the property or service was that of another; or

    (b) acted under an honest claim of right to the property or service involved or that he had a right to acquire or dispose of it as he did; or

    (c) took property exposed for sale, intending to purchase and pay for it promptly, or reasonably believing that the owner, if present, would have consented.

(4) *Theft from Spouse.* It is no defense that theft was from the actor's spouse, except that misappropriation of household and personal effects, or other property normally accessible to both spouses, is theft only if it occurs after the parties have ceased living together.

Section 223.2. Theft by Unlawful Taking or Disposition.

(1) *Movable Property.* A person is guilty of theft if he unlawfully takes, or exercises unlawful control over, movable property of another with purpose to deprive him thereof.

(2) *Immovable Property.* A person is guilty of theft if he unlawfully transfers immovable property of another or any interest therein with purpose to benefit himself or another not entitled thereto.

Section 223.3. Theft by Deception.

A person is guilty of theft if he purposely obtains property of another by deception. A person deceives if he purposely:

(1) creates or reinforces a false impression, including false impressions as to law, value, intention or other state of mind; but deception as to a person's intention to perform a promise shall not be inferred from the fact alone that he did not subsequently perform the promise; or

(2) prevents another from acquiring information which would affect his judgment of a transaction; or

(3) fails to correct a false impression which the deceiver previously created or reinforced, or which the deceiver knows to be influencing another to whom he stands in a fiduciary or confidential relationship; or

(4) fails to disclose a known lien, adverse claim or other legal impediment to the enjoyment of property which he transfers or encumbers in consideration for the property obtained, whether such impediment is or is not valid, or is or is not a matter of official record.

The term "deceive" does not, however, include falsity as to matters having no pecuniary significance, or puffing by statements unlikely to deceive ordinary persons in the group addressed.

Section 223.4. Theft by Extortion.

A person is guilty of theft if he purposely obtains property of another by threatening to:

(1)   inflict bodily injury on anyone or commit any other criminal offense; or

(2)   accuse anyone of a criminal offense; or

(3)   expose any secret tending to subject any person to hatred, contempt or ridicule, or to impair his credit or business repute; or

(4)   take or withhold action as an official, or cause an official to take or withhold action; or

(5)   bring about or continue a strike, boycott or other collective unofficial action, if the property is not demanded or received for the benefit of the group in whose interest the actor purports to act; or

(6)   testify or provide information or withhold testimony or information with respect to another's legal claim or defense; or

(7) inflict any other harm which would not benefit the actor.

It is an affirmative defense to prosecution based on paragraphs (2), (3) or (4) that the property obtained by threat of accusation, exposure, lawsuit or other invocation of official action was honestly claimed as restitution or indemnification for harm done in the circumstances to which such accusation, exposure, lawsuit or other official action relates, or as compensation for property or lawful services.

Section 223.5. Theft of Property Lost, Mislaid, or Delivered by Mistake.

A person who comes into control of property of another that he knows to have been lost, mislaid, or delivered under a mistake as to the nature or amount of the property or the identity of the recipient is guilty of theft if, with purpose to deprive the owner thereof, he fails to take reasonable measures to restore the property to a person entitled to have it.

Section 223.6. Receiving Stolen Property.

(1)   *Receiving.* A person is guilty of theft if he purposely receives, retains, or disposes of movable property of another knowing that it has been stolen, or believing that it has probably been stolen, unless the property is received, retained, or disposed with purpose to restore it to the owner. "Receiving" means acquiring possession, control or title, or lending on the security of the property.

(2)   *Presumption of Knowledge.* The requisite knowledge or belief is presumed in the case of a dealer who:

    (a)   is found in possession or control of property stolen from two or more persons on separate occasions; or

    (b)   has received stolen property in another transaction within the year preceding the transaction charged; or

    (c)   being a dealer in property of the sort received, acquires it for a consideration which he knows is far below its reasonable value.

"Dealer" means a person in the business of buying or selling goods including a pawnbroker.

Section 223.7. Theft of Services.

(1)   A person is guilty of theft if he purposely obtains services which he knows are available only for compensation, by deception or threat, or by false token or other means to avoid payment for the service. "Services" includes labor, professional service, transportation, telephone or other public service, accommodation in hotels, restaurants or elsewhere, admission to exhibitions, use of vehicles or other movable property. Where compensation for service is ordinarily paid immediately upon the rendering of such service, as in the case of hotels and restaurants, refusal to pay or absconding without payment or offer to pay gives rise to a presumption that the service was obtained by deception as to intention to pay.

(2)   A person commits theft if, having control over the disposition of services of others, to which he is not entitled, he knowingly diverts such services to his own benefit or to the benefit of another not entitled thereto.

Section 223.8. Theft by Failure to Make Required Disposition of Funds Received.

A person who purposely obtains property upon agreement, or subject to a known legal obligation, to make specified payment or other disposition, whether from such property or its proceeds or from his own property to be reserved in equivalent amount, is guilty of theft if he deals with the property obtained as his own and fails to make the required payment or disposition. The foregoing applies notwithstanding that it may be impossible to identify particular property as belonging to the victim at the time of the actor's failure to make the required payment or disposition. An officer or employee of the government or of a financial institution is presumed: (i) to know any legal obligation relevant to his criminal liability under this Section, and (ii) to have dealt with the property as his own if he fails to pay or account upon lawful demand, or if an audit reveals a shortage or falsification of accounts.

Section 223.9. Unauthorized Use of Automobiles and Other Vehicles.

A person commits a misdemeanor if he operates another's automobile, airplane, motorcycle, motorboat, or other motor-propelled vehicle without consent of the owner. It is an affirmative defense to prosecution under this Section that the actor reasonably believed that the owner would have consented to the operation had he known of it.

[ARTICLE 224.]   FORGERY AND FRAUDULENT PRACTICE

Section 224.0. Definitions.

In this Article, the definitions given in Section 223.0 apply unless a different meaning plainly is required.

Section 224.1. Forgery.

(1)   *Definition.* A person is guilty of forgery if, with purpose to defraud or injure anyone, or with knowledge that he is facilitating a fraud or injury to be perpetrated by anyone, the actor:

> (a)   alters any writing of another without his authority; or
>
> (b)   makes, completes, executes, authenticates, issues or transfers any writing so that it purports to be the act of another who did not authorize that act, or to have been executed at a time or place or in a numbered sequence other than was in fact the case, or to be a copy of an original when no such original existed; or
>
> (c)   utters any writing which he knows to be forged in a manner specified in paragraphs (a) or (b).

"Writing" includes printing or any other method of recording information, money, coins, tokens, stamps, seals, credit cards, badges, trademarks, and other symbols of value, right, privilege, or identification.

(2)   *Grading.* Forgery is a felony of the second degree if the writing is or purports to be part of an issue of money, securities, postage or revenue stamps, or other instruments issued by the government, or part of an issue of stock, bonds or other instruments representing interests in or claims against any property or enterprise. Forgery is a felony of the third degree if the writing is or purports to be a will, deed, contract, release, commercial instrument, or other document evidencing, creating, transferring, altering, terminating, or otherwise affecting legal relations. Otherwise forgery is a misdemeanor.

Section 224.2. Simulating Objects of Antiquity, Rarity, Etc.

A person commits a misdemeanor if, with purpose to defraud anyone or with knowledge that he is facilitating a fraud to be perpetrated by anyone, he makes, alters or utters any object so that it appears to have value because of antiquity, rarity, source, or authorship which it does not possess.

Section 224.3. Fraudulent Destruction, Removal or Concealment of Recordable Instruments.

A person commits a felony of the third degree if, with purpose to deceive or injure anyone, he destroys, removes or conceals any will, deed, mortgage, security instrument or other writing for which the law provides public recording.

Section 224.4. Tampering with Records.

A person commits a misdemeanor if, knowing that he has no privilege to do so, he falsifies, destroys, removes or conceals any writing or record, with purpose to deceive or injure anyone or to conceal any wrongdoing.

Section 224.5. Bad Checks.

A person who issues or passes a check or similar sight order for the payment of money, knowing that it will not be honored by the drawee, commits a misdemeanor.

For the purposes of this Section as well as in any prosecution for theft committed by means of a bad check, an issuer is presumed to know that the check or order (other than a postdated check or order) would not be paid, if:

(1)   the issuer had no account with the drawee at the time the check or order was issued; or

(2)   payment was refused by the drawee for lack of funds, upon presentation within 30 days after issue, and the issuer failed to make good within 10 days after receiving notice of that refusal.

Section 224.6. Credit Cards.

A person commits an offense if he uses a credit card for the purpose of obtaining property or services with knowledge that:

(1)   the card is stolen or forged; or

(2)   the card has been revoked or canceled; or

(3)   for any other reason his use of the card is unauthorized by the issuer.

It is an affirmative defense to prosecution under paragraph (3) if the actor proves by a preponderance of the evidence that he had the purpose and ability to meet all obligations to the issuer arising out of his use of the card. "Credit card" means a writing or other evidence of an undertaking to pay for property or services delivered or rendered to or upon the order of a designated person or bearer. An offense under this Section is a felony of the third degree if the value of the property or services secured or sought to be secured by means of the credit card exceeds $500; otherwise it is a misdemeanor.

Section 224.7. Deceptive Business Practices.

A person commits a misdemeanor if in the course of business he:

(1)   uses or possesses for use a false weight or measure, or any other device for falsely determining or recording any quality or quantity; or

(2)   sells, offers or exposes for sale, or delivers less than the represented quantity of any commodity or service; or

(3)   takes or attempts to take more than the represented quantity of any commodity or service when as buyer he furnishes the weight or measure; or

(4)   sells, offers or exposes for sale adulterated or mislabeled commodities. "Adulterated" means varying from the standard of composition or quality prescribed by or pursuant to any statute providing criminal penalties for such variance, or set by established commercial usage. "Mislabeled" means varying from the standard of truth or disclosure in labeling prescribed by or pursuant to any statute providing criminal penalties for such variance, or set by established commercial usage; or

(5)   makes a false or misleading statement in any advertisement addressed to the public or to a substantial segment thereof for the purpose of promoting the purchase or sale of property or services; or

(6)   makes a false or misleading written statement for the purpose of obtaining property or credit; or

(7)   makes a false or misleading written statement for the purpose of promoting the sale of securities, or omits information required by law to be disclosed in written documents relating to securities.

It is an affirmative defense to prosecution under this Section if the defendant proves by a preponderance of the evidence that his conduct was not knowingly or recklessly deceptive.

Section 224.8. Commercial Bribery and Breach of Duty to Act Disinterestedly.

(1)   A person commits a misdemeanor if he solicits, accepts or agrees to accept any benefit as consideration for knowingly violating or agreeing to violate a duty of fidelity to which he is subject as:

    (a)   partner, agent, or employee of another;

    (b)   trustee, guardian, or other fiduciary;

    (c)   lawyer, physician, accountant, appraiser, or other professional adviser or informant;

    (d)   officer, director, manager or other participant in the direction of the affairs of an incorporated or unincorporated association; or

    (e)   arbitrator or other purportedly disinterested adjudicator or referee.

(2)   A person who holds himself out to the public as being engaged in the business of making disinterested selection, appraisal, or criticism of commodities or services commits a misdemeanor if he solicits, accepts or agrees to accept any benefit to influence his selection, appraisal or criticism.

(3)   A person commits a misdemeanor if he confers, or offers or agrees to confer, any benefit the acceptance of which would be criminal under this Section.

Section 224.9. Rigging Publicly Exhibited Contest.

(1)   A person commits a misdemeanor if, with purpose to prevent a publicly exhibited contest from being conducted in accordance with the rules and usages purporting to govern it, he:

> (a)   confers or offers or agrees to confer any benefit upon, or threatens any injury to a participant, official or other person associated with the contest or exhibition; or
>
> (b)   tampers with any person, animal or thing.

(2)   Soliciting or Accepting Benefit for Rigging. A person commits a misdemeanor if he knowingly solicits, accepts or agrees to accept any benefit the giving of which would be criminal under Subsection (1).

(3)   Participation in Rigged Contest. A person commits a misdemeanor if he knowingly engages in, sponsors, produces, judges, or otherwise participates in a publicly exhibited contest knowing that the contest is not being conducted in compliance with the rules and usages purporting to govern it, by reason of conduct which would be criminal under this Section.

Section 224.10. Defrauding Secured Creditors.

A person commits a misdemeanor if he destroys, removes, conceals, encumbers, transfers or otherwise deals with property subject to a security interest with purpose to hinder enforcement of that interest.

Section 224.11. Fraud in Insolvency.

A person commits a misdemeanor if, knowing that proceedings have been or are about to be instituted for the appointment of a receiver or other person entitled to administer property for the benefit of creditors, or that any other composition or liquidation for the benefit of creditors has been or is about to be made, he:

(1)   destroys, removes, conceals, encumbers, transfers, or otherwise deals with any property with purpose to defeat or obstruct the claim of any creditor, or otherwise to obstruct the operation of any law relating to administration of property for the benefit of creditors; or

(2)   knowingly falsifies any writing or record relating to the property; or

(3)   knowingly misrepresents or refuses to disclose to a receiver or other person entitled to administer property for the benefit of creditors, the existence, amount or location of the property, or any other information which the actor could be legally required to furnish in relation to such administration.

Section 224.12. Receiving Deposits in a Failing Financial Institution.

An officer, manager or other person directing or participating in the direction of a financial institution commits a misdemeanor if he receives or permits the receipt of a deposit, premium payment or other investment in the institution knowing that:

(1)   due to financial difficulties the institution is about to suspend operations or go into receivership or reorganization; and

(2)   the person making the deposit or other payment is unaware of the precarious situation of the institution.

Section 224.13. Misapplication of Entrusted Property and Property of Government or Financial Institution.

A person commits an offense if he applies or disposes of property that has been entrusted to him as a fiduciary, or property of the government or of a financial institution, in a manner which he knows is unlawful and involves substantial risk of loss or detriment to the owner of the property or to a person for whose benefit the property was entrusted. The offense is a misdemeanor if the amount involved exceeds $50; otherwise it is a petty misdemeanor. "Fiduciary" includes trustee, guardian, executor, administrator, receiver and any person carrying on fiduciary functions on behalf of a corporation or other organization which is a fiduciary.

Section 224.14. Securing Execution of Documents by Deception.

A person commits a misdemeanor if by deception he causes another to execute any instrument affecting, purporting to affect, or likely to affect the pecuniary interest of any person.

OFFENSES AGAINST THE FAMILY

[ARTICLE 230.]   OFFENSES AGAINST THE FAMILY

Section 230.1. Bigamy and Polygamy.

(1)   *Bigamy.* A married person is guilty of bigamy, a misdemeanor, if he contracts or purports to contract another marriage, unless at the time of the subsequent marriage:

      (a)   the actor believes that the prior spouse is dead; or

      (b)   the actor and the prior spouse have been living apart for five consecutive years throughout which the prior spouse was not known by the actor to be alive; or

      (c)   a Court has entered a judgment purporting to terminate or annul any prior disqualifying marriage, and the actor does not know that judgment to be invalid; or

      (d)   the actor reasonably believes that he is legally eligible to remarry.

(2)   *Polygamy.* A person is guilty of polygamy, a felony of the third degree, if he marries or cohabits with more than one spouse at a time in purported exercise of the right of plural marriage. The offense is a continuing one until all cohabitation and claim of marriage with more than one spouse terminates. This section does not apply to parties to a polygamous marriage, lawful in the country of which they are residents or nationals, while they are in transit through or temporarily visiting this State.

(3)   *Other Party to Bigamous or Polygamous Marriage.* A person is guilty of bigamy or polygamy, as the case may be, if he contracts or purports to contract marriage with another knowing that the other is thereby committing bigamy or polygamy.

Section 230.2. Incest.

A person is guilty of incest, a felony of the third degree, if he knowingly marries or cohabits or has sexual intercourse with an ancestor or descendant, a brother or sister of the whole or half blood [or an uncle, aunt, nephew or niece of the whole blood]. "Cohabit" means to live together under the representation or appearance of being married. The relationships referred to herein include blood relationships without regard to legitimacy, and relationship of parent and child by adoption.

Section 230.3. Abortion.

(1)   *Unjustified Abortion.* A person who purposely and unjustifiably terminates the pregnancy of another otherwise than by a live birth commits a felony of the third degree or, where the pregnancy has continued beyond the twenty-sixth week, a felony of the second degree.

(2)   *Justifiable Abortion.* A licensed physician is justified in terminating a pregnancy if he believes there is substantial risk that continuance of the pregnancy would gravely impair the physical or mental health of the mother or that the child would be born with grave physical or mental defect, or that the pregnancy resulted from rape, incest, or other felonious intercourse. All illicit intercourse with a girl below the age of 16 shall be deemed felonious for purposes of this subsection. Justifiable abortions shall be performed only in a licensed hospital except in case of emergency when hospital facilities are unavailable. [Additional exceptions from the requirement of hospitalization may be incorporated here to take account of situations in sparsely settled areas where hospitals are not generally accessible.]

(3)   *Physicians' Certificates; Presumption from Non-Compliance.* No abortion shall be performed unless two physicians, one of whom may be the person performing the abortion, shall have certified in writing the circumstances which they believe to justify the abortion. Such certificate shall be submitted before the abortion to the hospital where it is to be performed and, in the case of abortion following felonious intercourse, to the prosecuting attorney or the police. Failure to comply

with any of the requirements of this Subsection gives rise to a presumption that the abortion was unjustified.

(4)   *Self-Abortion.* A woman whose pregnancy has continued beyond the twenty-sixth week commits a felony of the third degree if she purposely terminates her own pregnancy otherwise than by a live birth, or if she uses instruments, drugs or violence upon herself for that purpose. Except as justified under Subsection (2), a person who induces or knowingly aids a woman to use instruments, drugs or violence upon herself for the purpose of terminating her pregnancy otherwise than by a live birth commits a felony of the third degree whether or not the pregnancy has continued beyond the twenty-sixth week.

(5)   *Pretended Abortion.* A person commits a felony of the third degree if, representing that it is his purpose to perform an abortion, he does an act adapted to cause abortion in a pregnant woman although the woman is in fact not pregnant, or the actor does not believe she is. A person charged with unjustified abortion under Subsection (1) or an attempt to commit that offense may be convicted thereof upon proof of conduct prohibited by this Subsection.

(6)   *Distribution of Abortifacients.* A person who sells, offers to sell, possesses with intent to sell, advertises, or displays for sale anything specially designed to terminate a pregnancy, or held out by the actor as useful for that purpose, commits a misdemeanor, unless:

  (a)   the sale, offer or display is to a physician or druggist or to an intermediary in a chain of distribution to physicians or druggists; or

  (b)   the sale is made upon prescription or order of a physician; or

  (c)   the possession is with intent to sell as authorized in paragraphs (a) and (b); or

  (d)   the advertising is addressed to persons named in paragraph (a) and confined to trade or professional channels not likely to reach the general public.

(7)   *Section Inapplicable to Prevention of Pregnancy.* Nothing in this Section shall be deemed applicable to the prescription, administration or distribution of drugs or other substances for avoiding pregnancy, whether by preventing implantation of a fertilized ovum or by any other method that operates before, at or immediately after fertilization.

Section 230.4. Endangering Welfare of Children.

A parent, guardian, or other person supervising the welfare of a child under 18 commits a misdemeanor if he knowingly endangers the child's welfare by violating a duty of care, protection or support.

Section 230.5. Persistent Non-Support.

A person commits a misdemeanor if he persistently fails to provide support which he can provide and which he knows he is legally obliged to provide to a spouse, child or other dependent.

OFFENSES AGAINST PUBLIC ADMINISTRATION

[ARTICLE 240.] BRIBERY AND CORRUPT INFLUENCE

Section 240.0. Definitions.

In Articles 240–243, unless a different meaning plainly is required:

(1) "benefit" means gain or advantage, or anything regarded by the beneficiary as gain or advantage, including benefit to any other person or entity in whose welfare he is interested, but not an advantage promised generally to a group or class of voters as a consequence of public measures which a candidate engages to support or oppose;

(2) "government" includes any branch, subdivision or agency of the government of the State or any locality within it;

(3) "harm" means loss, disadvantage or injury, or anything so regarded by the person affected, including loss, disadvantage or injury to any other person or entity in whose welfare he is interested;

(4) "official proceeding" means a proceeding heard or which may be heard before any legislative, judicial, administrative or other governmental agency or official authorized to take evidence under oath, including any referee, hearing examiner, commissioner, notary or other person taking testimony or deposition in connection with any such proceeding;

(5) "party official" means a person who holds an elective or appointive post in a political party in the United States by virtue of which he directs or conducts, or participates in directing or conducting party affairs at any level of responsibility;

(6) "pecuniary benefit" is benefit in the form of money, property, commercial interests or anything else the primary significance of which is economic gain;

(7) "public servant" means any officer or employee of government, including legislators and judges, and any person participating as juror, advisor, consultant or otherwise, in performing a governmental function; but the term does not include witnesses;

(8) "administrative proceeding" means any proceeding, other than a judicial proceeding, the outcome of which is required to be based on a record or documentation prescribed by law, or in which law or regulation is particularized in application to individuals.

Section 240.1. Bribery in Official and Political Matters.

A person is guilty of bribery, a felony of the third degree, if he offers, confers or agrees to confer upon another, or solicits, accepts or agrees to accept from another:

(1)   any pecuniary benefit as consideration for the recipient's decision, opinion, recommendation, vote or other exercise of discretion as a public servant, party official or voter; or

(2)   any benefit as consideration for the recipient's decision, vote, recommendation or other exercise of official discretion in a judicial or administrative proceeding; or

(3)   any benefit as consideration for a violation of a known legal duty as public servant or party official.

It is no defense to prosecution under this section that a person whom the actor sought to influence was not qualified to act in the desired way whether because he had not yet assumed office, or lacked jurisdiction, or for any other reason.

Section 240.2. Threats and Other Improper Influence in Official and Political Matters.

(1)   *Offenses Defined.* A person commits an offense if he:

    (a)   threatens unlawful harm to any person with purpose to influence his decision, opinion, recommendation, vote or other exercise of discretion as a public servant, party official or voter; or

    (b)   threatens harm to any public servant with purpose to influence his decision, opinion, recommendation, vote or other exercise of discretion in a judicial or administrative proceeding; or

    (c)   threatens harm to any public servant or party official with purpose to influence him to violate his known legal duty; or

    (d)   privately addresses to any public servant who has or will have an official discretion in a judicial or administrative proceeding any representation, entreaty, argument or other communication with purpose to influence the outcome on the basis of considerations other than those authorized by law.

It is no defense to prosecution under this Section that a person whom the actor sought to influence was not qualified to act in the desired way, whether because he had not yet assumed office, or lacked jurisdiction, or for any other reason.

(2)   *Grading.* An offense under this Section is a misdemeanor unless the actor threatened to commit a crime or made a threat with purpose to influence a judicial or administrative proceeding, in which cases the offense is a felony of the third degree.

Section 240.3. Compensation for Past Official Action.

A person commits a misdemeanor if he solicits, accepts or agrees to accept any pecuniary benefit as compensation for having, as public servant, given a decision, opinion, recommendation or vote favorable to another, or for having otherwise exercised a discretion in his favor, or for having violated his duty. A person commits a misdemeanor if he offers, confers or agrees to confer compensation acceptance of which is prohibited by this Section.

Section 240.4. Retaliation for Past Official Action.

A person commits a misdemeanor if he harms another by any unlawful act in retaliation for anything lawfully done by the latter in the capacity of public servant.

Section 240.5. Gifts to Public Servants by Persons Subject to Their Jurisdiction.

(1) *Regulatory and Law Enforcement Officials.* No public servant in any department or agency exercising regulatory functions, or conducting inspections or investigations, or carrying on civil or criminal litigation on behalf of the government, or having custody of prisoners, shall solicit, accept or agree to accept any pecuniary benefit from a person known to be subject to such regulation, inspection, investigation or custody, or against whom such litigation is known to be pending or contemplated.

(2) *Officials Concerned with Government Contracts and Pecuniary Transactions.* No public servant having any discretionary function to perform in connection with contracts, purchases, payments, claims or other pecuniary transactions of the government shall solicit, accept or agree to accept any pecuniary benefit from any person known to be interested in or likely to become interested in any such contract, purchase, payment, claim or transaction.

(3) *Judicial and Administrative Officials.* No public servant having judicial or administrative authority and no public servant employed by or in a court or other tribunal having such authority, or participating in the enforcement of its decisions, shall solicit, accept or agree to accept any pecuniary benefit from a person known to be interested in or likely to become interested in any matter before such public servant or a tribunal with which he is associated.

(4) *Legislative Officials.* No legislator or public servant employed by the legislature or by any committee or agency thereof shall solicit, accept or agree to accept any pecuniary benefit from any person known to be interested in a bill, transaction or proceeding, pending or contemplated, before the legislature or any committee or agency thereof.

(5) *Exceptions.* This Section shall not apply to:

    (a) fees prescribed by law to be received by a public servant, or any other benefit for which the recipient gives legitimate consideration or to which he is otherwise legally entitled; or

(b)   gifts or other benefits conferred on account of kinship or other personal, professional or business relationship independent of the official status of the receiver; or

(c)   trivial benefits incidental to personal, professional or business contacts and involving no substantial risk of undermining official impartiality.

(6)   *Offering Benefits Prohibited.* No person shall knowingly confer, or offer or agree to confer, any benefit prohibited by the foregoing Subsections.

(7)   *Grade of Offense.* An offense under this Section is a misdemeanor.

Section 240.6. Compensating Public Servant for Assisting Private Interests in Relation to Matters Before Him.

(1)   *Receiving Compensation.* A public servant commits a misdemeanor if he solicits, accepts or agrees to accept compensation for advice or other assistance in preparing or promoting a bill, contract, claim, or other transaction or proposal as to which he knows that he has or is likely to have an official discretion to exercise.

(2)   *Paying Compensation.* A person commits a misdemeanor if he pays or offers or agrees to pay compensation to a public servant with knowledge that acceptance by the public servant is unlawful.

Section 240.7. Selling Political Endorsement; Special Influence.

(1)   *Selling Political Endorsement.* A person commits a misdemeanor if he solicits, receives, agrees to receive, or agrees that any political party or other person shall receive, any pecuniary benefit as consideration for approval or disapproval of an appointment or advancement in public service, or for approval or disapproval of any person or transaction for any benefit conferred by an official or agency of government. "Approval" includes recommendation, failure to disapprove, or any other manifestation of favor or acquiescence. "Disapproval" includes failure to approve, or any other manifestation of disfavor or nonacquiescence.

(2)   *Other Trading in Special Influence.* A person commits a misdemeanor if he solicits, receives or agrees to receive any pecuniary benefit as consideration for exerting special influence upon a public servant or procuring another to do so. "Special influence" means power to influence through kinship, friendship or other relationship, apart from the merits of the transaction.

(3)   *Paying for Endorsement or Special Influence.* A person commits a misdemeanor if he offers, confers or agrees to confer any pecuniary benefit receipt of which is prohibited by this Section.

[ARTICLE 241.]   PERJURY AND OTHER FALSIFICATION IN OFFICIAL MATTERS

Section 241.0. Definitions.

In this Article, unless a different meaning plainly is required:

(1)   the definitions given in Section 240.0 apply; and

(2)   "statement" means any representation, but includes a representation of opinion, belief or other state of mind only if the representation clearly relates to state of mind apart from or in addition to any facts which are the subject of the representation.

Section 241.1. Perjury.

(1)   *Offense Defined.* A person is guilty of perjury, a felony of the third degree, if in any official proceeding he makes a false statement under oath or equivalent affirmation, or swears or affirms the truth of a statement previously made, when the statement is material and he does not believe it to be true.

(2)   *Materiality.* Falsification is material, regardless of the admissibility of the statement under rules of evidence, if it could have affected the course or outcome of the proceeding. It is no defense that the declarant mistakenly believed the falsification to be immaterial. Whether a falsification is material in a given factual situation is a question of law.

(3)   *Irregularities No Defense.* It is not a defense to prosecution under this Section that the oath or affirmation was administered or taken in an irregular manner or that the declarant was not competent to make the statement. A document purporting to be made upon oath or affirmation at any time when the actor presents it as being so verified shall be deemed to have been duly sworn or affirmed.

(4)   *Retraction.* No person shall be guilty of an offense under this Section if he retracted the falsification in the course of the proceeding in which it was made before it became manifest that the falsification was or would be exposed and before the falsification substantially affected the proceeding.

(5)   *Inconsistent Statements.* Where the defendant made inconsistent statements under oath or equivalent affirmation, both having been made within the period of the statute of limitations, the prosecution may proceed by setting forth the inconsistent statements in a single count alleging in the alternative that one or the other was false and not believed by the defendant. In such case it shall not be necessary for the prosecution to prove which statement was false but only that one or the other was false and not believed by the defendant to be true.

(6)   *Corroboration.* No person shall be convicted of an offense under this Section where proof of falsity rests solely upon contradiction by testimony of a single person other than the defendant.

Section 241.2. False Swearing.

(1)   *False Swearing in Official Matters.* A person who makes a false statement under oath or equivalent affirmation, or swears or affirms the truth of such a statement previously made, when he does not believe the statement to be true, is guilty of a misdemeanor if:

(a)   the falsification occurs in an official proceeding; or

(b)   the falsification is intended to mislead a public servant in performing his official function.

(2)   *Other False Swearing.* A person who makes a false statement under oath or equivalent affirmation, or swears or affirms the truth of such a statement previously made, when he does not believe the statement to be true, is guilty of a petty misdemeanor, if the statement is one which is required by law to be sworn or affirmed before a notary or other person authorized to administer oaths.

(3)   *Perjury Provisions Applicable.* Subsections (3) to (6) of Section 241.1 apply to the present Section.

Section 241.3. Unsworn Falsification to Authorities.

(1)   *In General.* A person commits a misdemeanor if, with purpose to mislead a public servant in performing his official function, he:

(a)   makes any written false statement which he does not believe to be true; or

(b)   purposely creates a false impression in a written application for any pecuniary or other benefit, by omitting information necessary to prevent statements therein from being misleading; or

(c)   submits or invites reliance on any writing which he knows to be forged, altered or otherwise lacking in authenticity; or

(d)   submits or invites reliance on any sample, specimen, map, boundary mark, or other object which he knows to be false.

(2)   *Statements "Under Penalty."* A person commits a petty misdemeanor if he makes a written false statement which he does not believe to be true, on or pursuant to a form bearing notice, authorized by law, to the effect that false statements made therein are punishable.

(3)   *Perjury Provisions Applicable.* Subsections (3) to (6) of Section 241.1 apply to the present section.

Section 241.4. False Alarms to Agencies of Public Safety.

A person who knowingly causes a false alarm of fire or other emergency to be transmitted to or within any organization, official or volunteer, for dealing with emergencies involving danger to life or property commits a misdemeanor.

Section 241.5. False Reports to Law Enforcement Authorities.

(1)   *Falsely Incriminating Another.* A person who knowingly gives false information to any law enforcement officer with purpose to implicate another commits a misdemeanor.

(2)   *Fictitious Reports.* A person commits a petty misdemeanor if he:

(a)   reports to law enforcement authorities an offense or other incident within their concern knowing that it did not occur; or

(b)   pretends to furnish such authorities with information relating to an offense or incident when he knows he has no information relating to such offense or incident.

Section 241.6. Tampering with Witnesses and Informants; Retaliation Against Them.

(1)   *Tampering.* A person commits an offense if, believing that an official proceeding or investigation is pending or about to be instituted, he attempts to induce or otherwise cause a witness or informant to:

(a)   testify or inform falsely; or

(b)   withhold any testimony, information, document or thing; or

(c)   elude legal process summoning him to testify or supply evidence; or

(d)   absent himself from any proceeding or investigation to which he has been legally summoned.

The offense is a felony of the third degree if the actor employs force, deception, threat or offer of pecuniary benefit. Otherwise it is a misdemeanor.

(2)   *Retaliation Against Witness or Informant.* A person commits a misdemeanor if he harms another by any unlawful act in retaliation for anything lawfully done in the capacity of witness or informant.

(3)   *Witness or Informant Taking Bribe.* A person commits a felony of the third degree if he solicits, accepts or agrees to accept any benefit in consideration of his doing any of the things specified in clauses (a) to (d) of Subsection (1).

Section 241.7. Tampering with or Fabricating Physical Evidence.

A person commits a misdemeanor if, believing that an official proceeding or investigation is pending or about to be instituted, he:

(1)   alters, destroys, conceals or removes any record, document or thing with purpose to impair its verity or availability in such proceeding or investigation; or

(2)   makes, presents or uses any record, document or thing knowing it to be false and with purpose to mislead a public servant who is or may be engaged in such proceeding or investigation.

Section 241.8. Tampering with Public Records or Information.

(1)   *Offense Defined.* A person commits an offense if he:

(a)   knowingly makes a false entry in, or false alteration of, any record, document or thing belonging to, or received or kept by, the government for information or record, or required by law to be kept by others for information of the government; or

    (b)   makes, presents or uses any record, document or thing knowing it to be false, and with purpose that it be taken as a genuine part of information or records referred to in paragraph (a); or

    (c)   purposely and unlawfully destroys, conceals, removes or otherwise impairs the verity or availability of any such record, document or thing.

(2)   *Grading.* An offense under this Section is a misdemeanor unless the actor's purpose is to defraud or injure anyone, in which case the offense is a felony of the third degree.

Section 241.9. Impersonating a Public Servant.

A person commits a misdemeanor if he falsely pretends to hold a position in the public service with purpose to induce another to submit to such pretended official authority or otherwise to act in reliance upon that pretense to his prejudice.

[ARTICLE 242.]   OBSTRUCTING GOVERNMENTAL OPERATIONS; ESCAPES

Section 242.0. Definitions.

In this Article, unless another meaning plainly is required, the definitions given in Section 240.0 apply.

Section 242.1. Obstructing Administration of Law or Other Governmental Function.

A person commits a misdemeanor if he purposely obstructs, impairs or perverts the administration of law or other governmental function by force, violence, physical interference or obstacle, breach of official duty, or any other unlawful act, except that this Section does not apply to flight by a person charged with crime, refusal to submit to arrest, failure to perform a legal duty other than an official duty, or any other means of avoiding compliance with law without affirmative interference with governmental functions.

Section 242.2. Resisting Arrest or Other Law Enforcement.

A person commits a misdemeanor if, for the purpose of preventing a public servant from effecting a lawful arrest or discharging any other duty, the person creates a substantial risk of bodily injury to the public servant or anyone else, or employs means justifying or requiring substantial force to overcome the resistance.

Section 242.3. Hindering Apprehension or Prosecution.

A person commits an offense if, with purpose to hinder the apprehension, prosecution, conviction or punishment of another for crime, he:

(1)   harbors or conceals the other; or

(2)   provides or aids in providing a weapon, transportation, disguise or other means of avoiding apprehension or effecting escape; or

(3)   conceals or destroys evidence of the crime, or tampers with a witness, informant, document or other source of information, regardless of its admissibility in evidence; or

(4)   warns the other of impending discovery or apprehension, except that this paragraph does not apply to a warning given in connection with an effort to bring another into compliance with law; or

(5)   volunteers false information to a law enforcement officer.

The offense is a felony of the third degree if the conduct which the actor knows has been charged or is liable to be charged against the person aided would constitute a felony of the first or second degree. Otherwise it is a misdemeanor.

Section 242.4. Aiding Consummation of Crime.

A person commits an offense if he purposely aids another to accomplish an unlawful object of a crime, as by safeguarding the proceeds thereof or converting the proceeds into negotiable funds. The offense is a felony of the third degree if the principal offense was a felony of the first or second degree. Otherwise it is a misdemeanor.

Section 242.5. Compounding.

A person commits a misdemeanor if he accepts or agrees to accept any pecuniary benefit in consideration of refraining from reporting to law enforcement authorities the commission or suspected commission of any offense or information relating to an offense. It is an affirmative defense to prosecution under this Section that the pecuniary benefit did not exceed an amount which the actor believed to be due as restitution or indemnification for harm caused by the offense.

Section 242.6. Escape.

(1)   *Escape.* A person commits an offense if he unlawfully removes himself from official detention or fails to return to official detention following temporary leave granted for a specific purpose or limited period. "Official detention" means arrest, detention in any facility for custody of persons under charge or conviction of crime or alleged or found to be delinquent, detention for extradition or deportation, or any other detention for law enforcement purposes; but "official detention" does not include supervision of probation or parole, or constraint incidental to release on bail.

(2)   *Permitting or Facilitating Escape.* A public servant concerned in detention commits an offense if he knowingly or recklessly permits an escape. Any person who knowingly causes or facilitates an escape commits an offense.

(3)   *Effect of Legal Irregularity in Detention.* Irregularity in bringing about or maintaining detention, or lack of jurisdiction of the committing or detaining

authority, shall not be a defense to prosecution under this Section if the escape is from a prison or other custodial facility or from detention pursuant to commitment by official proceedings. In the case of other detentions, irregularity or lack of jurisdiction shall be a defense only if:

    (a)   the escape involved no substantial risk of harm to the person or property of anyone other than the detainee; or

    (b)   the detaining authority did not act in good faith under color of law.

(4)   *Grading of Offenses.* An offense under this Section is a felony of the third degree where:

    (a)   the actor was under arrest for or detained on a charge of felony or following conviction of crime; or

    (b)   the actor employs force, threat, deadly weapon or other dangerous instrumentality to effect the escape; or

    (c)   a public servant concerned in detention of persons convicted of crime purposely facilitates or permits an escape from a detention facility.

Otherwise an offense under this section is a misdemeanor.

Section 242.7. Implements for Escape; Other Contraband.

(1)   *Escape Implements.* A person commits a misdemeanor if he unlawfully introduces within a detention facility, or unlawfully provides an inmate with, any weapon, tool or other thing which may be useful for escape. An inmate commits a misdemeanor if he unlawfully procures, makes, or otherwise provides himself with, or has in his possession, any such implement of escape. "Unlawfully" means surreptitiously or contrary to law, regulation or order of the detaining authority.

(2)   *Other Contraband.* A person commits a petty misdemeanor if he provides an inmate with anything which the actor knows it is unlawful for the inmate to possess.

Section 242.8. Bail Jumping; Default in Required Appearance.

A person set at liberty by court order, with or without bail, upon condition that he will subsequently appear at a specified time and place, commits a misdemeanor if, without lawful excuse, he fails to appear at that time and place. The offense constitutes a felony of the third degree where the required appearance was to answer to a charge of felony, or for disposition of any such charge, and the actor took flight or went into hiding to avoid apprehension, trial or punishment. This Section does not apply to obligations to appear incident to release under suspended sentence or on probation or parole.

[ARTICLE 243.]   ABUSE OF OFFICE

Section 243.0. Definitions.

In this Article, unless a different meaning plainly is required, the definitions given in Section 240.0 apply.

Section 243.1. Official Oppression.

A person acting or purporting to act in an official capacity or taking advantage of such actual or purported capacity commits a misdemeanor if, knowing that his conduct is illegal, he:

(1)   subjects another to arrest, detention, search, seizure, mistreatment, dispossession, assessment, lien or other infringement of personal or property rights; or

(2)   denies or impedes another in the exercise or enjoyment of any right, privilege, power or immunity.

Section 243.2. Speculating or Wagering on Official Action or Information.

A public servant commits a misdemeanor if, in contemplation of official action by himself or by a governmental unit with which he is associated, or in reliance on information to which he has access in his official capacity and which has not been made public, he:

(1)   acquires a pecuniary interest in any property, transaction or enterprise which may be affected by such information or official action; or

(2)   speculates or wagers on the basis of such information or official action; or

(3)   aids another to do any of the foregoing.

OFFENSES AGAINST PUBLIC ORDER AND DECENCY

[ARTICLE 250.]   RIOT, DISORDERLY CONDUCT, AND RELATED OFFENSES

Section 250.1. Riot; Failure to Disperse.

(1)   *Riot.* A person is guilty of riot, a felony of the third degree, if he participates with [two] or more others in a course of disorderly conduct:

    (a)   with purpose to commit or facilitate the commission of a felony or misdemeanor;

    (b)   with purpose to prevent or coerce official action; or

    (c)   when the actor or any other participant to the knowledge of the actor uses or plans to use a firearm or other deadly weapon.

(2)   *Failure of Disorderly Persons to Disperse Upon Official Order.* Where [three] or more persons are participating in a course of disorderly conduct likely to cause substantial harm or serious inconvenience, annoyance or alarm, a peace officer or other public servant engaged in executing or enforcing the law may order the

participants and others in the immediate vicinity to disperse. A person who refuses or knowingly fails to obey such an order commits a misdemeanor.

Section 250.2. Disorderly Conduct.

(1) *Offense Defined.* A person is guilty of disorderly conduct if, with purpose to cause public inconvenience, annoyance or alarm, or recklessly creating a risk thereof, he:

> (a) engages in fighting or threatening, or in violent or tumultuous behavior; or
>
> (b) makes unreasonable noise or offensively coarse utterance, gesture or display, or addresses abusive language to any person present; or
>
> (c) creates a hazardous or physically offensive condition by any act which serves no legitimate purpose of the actor.

"Public" means affecting or likely to affect persons in a place to which the public or a substantial group has access; among the places included are highways, transport facilities, schools, prisons, apartment houses, places of business or amusement, or any neighborhood.

(2) *Grading.* An offense under this section is a petty misdemeanor if the actor's purpose is to cause substantial harm or serious inconvenience, or if he persists in disorderly conduct after reasonable warning or request to desist. Otherwise disorderly conduct is a violation.

Section 250.3. False Public Alarms.

A person is guilty of a misdemeanor if he initiates or circulates a report or warning of an impending bombing or other crime or catastrophe, knowing that the report or warning is false or baseless and that it is likely to cause evacuation of a building, place or assembly, or facility of public transport, or to cause public inconvenience or alarm.

Section 250.4. Harassment.

A person commits a petty misdemeanor if, with purpose to harass another, he:

(1) makes a telephone call without purpose of legitimate communication; or

(2) insults, taunts or challenges another in a manner likely to provoke violent or disorderly response; or

(3) makes repeated communications anonymously or at extremely inconvenient hours, or in offensively coarse language; or

(4) subjects another to an offensive touching; or

(5) engages in any other course of alarming conduct serving no legitimate purpose of the actor.

Section 250.5. Public Drunkenness; Drug Incapacitation.

A person is guilty of an offense if he appears in any public place manifestly under the influence of alcohol, narcotics or other drug, not therapeutically administered, to the degree that he may endanger himself or other persons or property, or annoy persons in his vicinity. An offense under this Section constitutes a petty misdemeanor if the actor has been convicted hereunder twice before within a period of one year. Otherwise the offense constitutes a violation.

Section 250.6. Loitering or Prowling.

A person commits a violation if he loiters or prowls in a place, at a time, or in a manner not usual for law-abiding individuals under circumstances that warrant alarm for the safety of persons or property in the vicinity. Among the circumstances which may be considered in determining whether such alarm is warranted is the fact that the actor takes flight upon appearance of a peace officer, refuses to identify himself, or manifestly endeavors to conceal himself or any object. Unless flight by the actor or other circumstances make it impracticable, a peace officer shall prior to any arrest for an offense under this Section afford the actor an opportunity to dispel any alarm which would otherwise be warranted, by requesting him to identify himself and explain his presence and conduct. No person shall be convicted of an offense under this Section if the peace officer did not comply with the preceding sentence, or if it appears at trial that the explanation given by the actor was true and, if believed by the peace officer at the time, would have dispelled the alarm.

Section 250.7. Obstructing Highways and Other Public Passages.

(1)   A person, who, having no legal privilege to do so, purposely or recklessly obstructs any highway or other public passage, whether alone or with others, commits a violation, or, in case he persists after warning by a law officer, a petty misdemeanor. "Obstructs" means renders impassable without unreasonable inconvenience or hazard. No person shall be deemed guilty of recklessly obstructing in violation of this Subsection solely because of a gathering of persons to hear him speak or otherwise communicate, or solely because of being a member of such a gathering.

(2)   A person in a gathering commits a violation if he refuses to obey a reasonable official request or order to move:

    (a)   to prevent obstruction of a highway or other public passage; or

    (b)   to maintain public safety by dispersing those gathered in dangerous proximity to a fire or other hazard.

An order to move, addressed to a person whose speech or other lawful behavior attracts an obstructing audience, shall not be deemed reasonable if the obstruction can be readily remedied by police control of the size or location of the gathering.

Section 250.8. Disrupting Meetings and Processions.

A person commits a misdemeanor if, with purpose to prevent or disrupt a lawful meeting, procession or gathering, he does any act tending to obstruct or interfere with it physically, or make any utterance, gesture or display designed to outrage the sensibilities of the group.

Section 250.9. Desecration of Venerated Objects.

A person commits a misdemeanor if he purposely desecrates any public monument or structure, or place of worship or burial, or if he purposely desecrates the national flag or any other object of veneration by the public or a substantial segment thereof in any public place. "Desecrate" means defacing, damaging, polluting or otherwise physically mistreating in a way that the actor knows will outrage the sensibilities of persons likely to observe or discover his action.

Section 250.10. Abuse of Corpse.

Except as authorized by law, a person who treats a corpse in a way that he knows would outrage ordinary family sensibilities commits a misdemeanor.

Section 250.11. Cruelty to Animals.

A person commits a misdemeanor if he purposely or recklessly:

(1)   subjects any animal to cruel mistreatment; or

(2)   subjects any animal in his custody to cruel neglect; or

(3)   kills or injures any animal belonging to another without legal privilege or consent of the owner.

Subsections (1) and (2) shall not be deemed applicable to accepted veterinary practices and activities carried on for scientific research.

Section 250.12. Violation of Privacy.

(1)   *Unlawful Eavesdropping or Surveillance.* A person commits a misdemeanor if, except as authorized by law, he:

(a)   trespasses on property with purpose to subject anyone to eavesdropping or other surveillance in a private place; or

(b)   installs in any private place, without the consent of the person or persons entitled to privacy there, any device for observing, photographing, recording, amplifying or broadcasting sounds or events in such place, or uses any such unauthorized installation; or

(c)   installs or uses outside a private place any device for hearing, recording, amplifying or broadcasting sounds originating in such place which would not ordinarily be audible or comprehensible outside, without the consent of the person or persons entitled to privacy there.

"Private place" means a place where one may reasonably expect to be safe from casual or hostile intrusion or surveillance, but does not include a place to which the public or a substantial group thereof has access.

(2)   *Other Breach of Privacy of Messages.* A person commits a misdemeanor if, except as authorized by law, he:

(a)   intercepts without the consent of the sender or receiver a message by telephone, telegraph, letter or other means of communicating privately; but this paragraph does not extend to (i) overhearing of messages through a regularly installed instrument on a telephone party line or on an extension, or (ii) interception by the telephone company or subscriber incident to enforcement of regulations limiting use of the facilities or incident to other normal operation and use; or

(b)   divulges without the consent of the sender or receiver the existence or contents of any such message if the actor knows that the message was illegally intercepted, or if he learned of the message in the course of employment with an agency engaged in transmitting it.

[ARTICLE 251.] PUBLIC INDECENCY

Section 251.1. Open Lewdness.

A person commits a petty misdemeanor if he does any lewd act which he knows is likely to be observed by others who would be affronted or alarmed.

Section 251.2. Prostitution and Related Offenses.

(1)   *Prostitution.* A person is guilty of prostitution, a petty misdemeanor, if he or she:

(a)   is an inmate of a house of prostitution or otherwise engages in sexual activity as a business; or

(b)   loiters in or within view of any public place for the purpose of being hired to engage in sexual activity.

"Sexual activity" includes homosexual and other deviate sexual relations. A "house of prostitution" is any place where prostitution or promotion of prostitution is regularly carried on by one person under the control, management or supervision of another. An "inmate" is a person who engages in prostitution in or through the agency of a house of prostitution. "Public place" means any place to which the public or any substantial group thereof has access.

(2)   *Promoting Prostitution.* A person who knowingly promotes prostitution of another commits a misdemeanor or felony as provided in Subsection (3). The following acts shall, without limitation of the foregoing, constitute promoting prostitution:

    (a)   owning, controlling, managing, supervising or otherwise keeping, alone or in association with others, a house of prostitution or a prostitution business; or

    (b)   procuring an inmate for a house of prostitution or a place in a house of prostitution for one who would be an inmate; or

    (c)   encouraging, inducing, or otherwise purposely causing another to become or remain a prostitute; or

    (d)   soliciting a person to patronize a prostitute; or

    (e)   procuring a prostitute for a patron; or

    (f)   transporting a person into or within this state with purpose to promote that person's engaging in prostitution, or procuring or paying for transportation with that purpose; or

    (g)   leasing or otherwise permitting a place controlled by the actor, alone or in association with others, to be regularly used for prostitution or the promotion of prostitution, or failure to make reasonable effort to abate such use by ejecting the tenant, notifying law enforcement authorities, or other legally available means; or

    (h)   soliciting, receiving, or agreeing to receive any benefit for doing or agreeing to do anything forbidden by this Subsection.

(3) *Grading of Offenses Under Subsection (2).* An offense under Subsection (2) constitutes a felony of the third degree if:

    (a)   the offense falls within paragraph (a), (b) or (c) of Subsection (2); or

    (b)   the actor compels another to engage in or promote prostitution; or

    (c)   the actor promotes prostitution of a child under 16, whether or not he is aware of the child's age; or

    (d)   the actor promotes prostitution of his wife, child, ward or any person for whose care, protection or support he is responsible.

Otherwise the offense is a misdemeanor.

(4) *Presumption from Living off Prostitutes.* A person, other than the prostitute or the prostitute's minor child or other legal dependent incapable of self-support, who is supported in whole or substantial part by the proceeds of prostitution is presumed to be knowingly promoting prostitution in violation of Subsection (2).

(5) *Patronizing Prostitutes.* A person commits a violation if he hires a prostitute to engage in sexual activity with him, or if he enters or remains in a house of prostitution for the purpose of engaging in sexual activity.

(6) *Evidence.* On the issue whether a place is a house of prostitution the following shall be admissible evidence: its general repute; the repute of the persons who reside in or frequent the place; the frequency, timing and duration of visits by non-residents. Testimony of a person against his spouse shall be admissible to prove offenses under this Section.

Section 251.3. Loitering to Solicit Deviate Sexual Relations.

A person is guilty of a petty misdemeanor if he loiters in or near any public place for the purpose of soliciting or being solicited to engage in deviate sexual relations.

Section 251.4. Obscenity.

(1) *Obscene Defined.* Material is obscene if, considered as a whole, its predominant appeal is to prurient interest, that is, a shameful or morbid interest, in nudity, sex or excretion, and if in addition it goes substantially beyond customary limits of candor in describing or representing such matters. Predominant appeal shall be judged with reference to ordinary adults unless it appears from the character of the material or the circumstances of its dissemination to be designed for children or other specially susceptible audience. Undeveloped photographs, molds, printing plates, and the like, shall be deemed obscene notwithstanding that processing or other acts may be required to make the obscenity patent or to disseminate it.

(2) *Offenses.* Subject to the affirmative defense provided in Subsection (3), a person commits a misdemeanor if he knowingly or recklessly:

(a)   sells, delivers or provides, or offers or agrees to sell, deliver or provide, any obscene writing, picture, record or other representation or embodiment of the obscene; or

(b)   presents or directs an obscene play, dance or performance, or participates in that portion thereof which makes it obscene; or

(c)   publishes, exhibits or otherwise makes available any obscene material; or

(d)   possesses any obscene material for purposes of sale or other commercial dissemination; or

(e)   sells, advertises or otherwise commercially disseminates material, whether or not obscene, by representing or suggesting that it is obscene.

A person who disseminates or possesses obscene material in the course of his business is presumed to do so knowingly or recklessly.

(3) *Justifiable and Non-Commercial Private Dissemination.* It is an affirmative defense to prosecution under this Section that dissemination was restricted to:

(a)   institutions or persons having scientific, educational, governmental or other similar justification for possessing obscene material; or

(b)   non-commercial dissemination to personal associates of the actor.

(4) *Evidence; Adjudication of Obscenity.* In any prosecution under this Section evidence shall be admissible to show:

(a)   the character of the audience for which the material was designed or to which it was directed;

(b) what the predominant appeal of the material would be for ordinary adults or any special audience to which it was directed, and what effect, if any, it would probably have on conduct of such people;

(c) artistic, literary, scientific, educational or other merits of the material;

(d) the degree of public acceptance of the material in the United States;

(e) appeal to prurient interest, or absence thereof, in advertising or other promotion of the material; and

(f) the good repute of the author, creator, publisher or other person from whom the material originated.

Expert testimony and testimony of the author, creator, publisher or other person from whom the material originated, relating to factors entering into the determination of the issue of obscenity, shall be admissible. The Court shall dismiss a prosecution for obscenity if it is satisfied that the material is not obscene.

Appendix B

Federal Sentencing Guidelines Tables

SENTENCING TABLE
(in months of imprisonment)

Offense Level	Criminal History Category (Criminal History Points)					
	I (0 or 1)	II (2 or 3)	III (4, 5, 6)	IV (7, 8, 9)	V (10, 11, 12)	VI (13 or more)
1	0-6	0-6	0-6	0-6	0-6	0-6
2	0-6	0-6	0-6	0-6	0-6	1-7
3	0-6	0-6	0-6	0-6	2-8	3-9
4	0-6	0-6	0-6	2-8	4-10	6-12
5	0-6	0-6	1-7	4-10	6-12	9-15
6	0-6	1-7	2-8	6-12	9-15	12-18
7	0-6	2-8	4-10	8-14	12-18	15-21
8	0-6	4-10	6-12	10-16	15-21	18-24
9	4-10	6-12	8-14	12-18	18-24	21-27
10	6-12	8-14	10-16	15-21	21-27	24-30
11	8-14	10-16	12-18	18-24	24-30	27-33
12	10-16	12-18	15-21	21-27	27-33	30-37
13	12-18	15-21	18-24	24-30	30-37	33-41
14	15-21	18-24	21-27	27-33	33-41	37-46
15	18-24	21-27	24-30	30-37	37-46	41-51
16	21-27	24-30	27-33	33-41	41-51	46-57
17	24-30	27-33	30-37	37-46	46-57	51-63
18	27-33	30-37	33-41	41-51	51-63	57-71
19	30-37	33-41	37-46	46-57	57-71	63-78
20	33-41	37-46	41-51	51-63	63-78	70-87
21	37-46	41-51	46-57	57-71	70-87	77-96
22	41-51	46-57	51-63	63-78	77-96	84-105
23	46-57	51-63	57-71	70-87	84-105	92-115
24	51-63	57-71	63-78	77-96	92-115	100-125
25	57-71	63-78	70-87	84-105	100-125	110-137
26	63-78	70-87	78-97	92-115	110-137	120-150
27	70-87	78-97	87-108	100-125	120-150	130-162
28	78-97	87-108	97-121	110-137	130-162	140-175
29	87-108	97-121	108-135	121-151	140-175	151-188
30	97-121	108-135	121-151	135-168	151-188	168-210
31	108-135	121-151	135-168	151-188	168-210	188-235
32	121-151	135-168	151-188	168-210	188-235	210-262
33	135-168	151-188	168-210	188-235	210-262	235-293
34	151-188	168-210	188-235	210-262	235-293	262-327
35	168-210	188-235	210-262	235-293	262-327	292-365
36	188-235	210-262	235-293	262-327	292-365	324-405
37	210-262	235-293	262-327	292-365	324-405	360-life
38	235-293	262-327	292-365	324-405	360-life	360-life
39	262-327	292-365	324-405	360-life	360-life	360-life
40	292-365	324-405	360-life	360-life	360-life	360-life
41	324-405	360-life	360-life	360-life	360-life	360-life
42	360-life	360-life	360-life	360-life	360-life	360-life
43	life	life	life	life	life	life

Zones:
- Zone A
- Zone B
- Zone C
- Zone D

November 1, 2015

Fine Table

Offense Level	A Minimum	B Maximum
3 and below	$200	$9,500
4-5	$500	$9,500
6-7	$1,000	$9,500
8-9	$2,000	$20,000
10-11	$4,000	$40,000
12-13	$5,500	$55,000
14-15	$7,500	$75,000
16-17	$10,000	$95,000
18-19	$10,000	$100,000
20-22	$15,000	$150,000
23-25	$20,000	$200,000
26-28	$25,000	$250,000
29-31	$30,000	$300,000
32-34	$35,000	$350,000
35-37	$40,000	$400,000
38 and above	$50,000	$500,000

Table of Cases

C

M

Index

[References are to pages.]

N

O